New York
New Jersey &
Pennsylvania

Tom Smallman

Michael Clark

David Ellis

LONELY PLANET PUBLICATIONS
Melbourne • Oakland • London • Paris

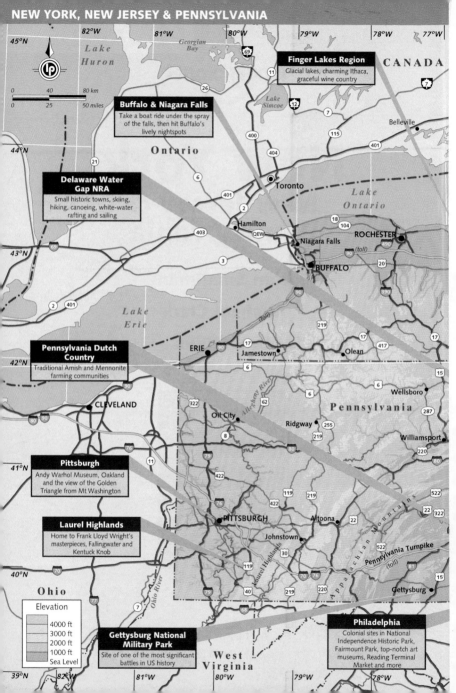

NEW YORK, NEW JERSEY & PENNSYLVANIA

Finger Lakes Region
Glacial lakes, charming Ithaca, graceful wine country

Buffalo & Niagara Falls
Take a boat ride under the spray of the falls, then hit Buffalo's lively nightspots

Delaware Water Gap NRA
Small historic towns, skiing, hiking, canoeing, white-water rafting and sailing

Pennsylvania Dutch Country
Traditional Amish and Mennonite farming communities

Pittsburgh
Andy Warhol Museum, Oakland and the view of the Golden Triangle from Mt Washington

Laurel Highlands
Home to Frank Lloyd Wright's masterpieces, Fallingwater and Kentuck Knob

Gettysburg National Military Park
Site of one of the most significant battles in US history

Philadelphia
Colonial sites in National Independence Historic Park, Fairmount Park, top-notch art museums, Reading Terminal Market and more

CANADA

Lake Huron
Georgian Bay
Ontario
Lake Simcoe
Toronto
Hamilton
Belleville
Lake Ontario
Niagara Falls
ROCHESTER
BUFFALO
Lake Erie
ERIE
Jamestown
Olean
Wellsboro
Williamsport
CLEVELAND
Oil City
Ridgway
Pennsylvania
PITTSBURGH
Altoona
Johnstown
Ohio
West Virginia
Gettysburg

Appalachian Mountains
Pennsylvania Turnpike

Allegheny River
Ohio River

Elevation
4000 ft
3000 ft
2000 ft
1000 ft
Sea Level

0   40   80 km
0   25   50 miles

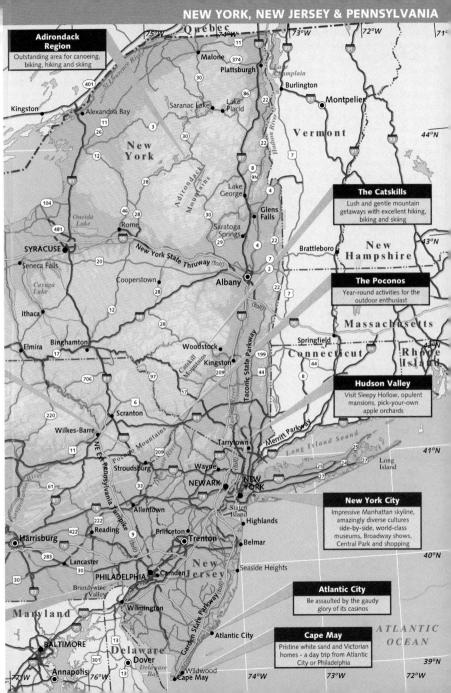

NEW YORK, NEW JERSEY & PENNSYLVANIA

Adirondack Region
Outstanding area for canoeing, biking, hiking and skiing

The Catskills
Lush and gentle mountain getaways with excellent hiking, biking and skiing

The Poconos
Year-round activities for the outdoor enthusiast

Hudson Valley
Visit Sleepy Hollow, opulent mansions, pick-your-own apple orchards

New York City
Impressive Manhattan skyline, amazingly diverse cultures side-by-side, world-class museums, Broadway shows, Central Park and shopping

Atlantic City
Be assaulted by the gaudy glory of its casinos

Cape May
Pristine white sand and Victorian homes – a day trip from Atlantic City or Philadelphia

Quebec

Malone
Plattsburgh
Burlington
Montpelier

Kingston
Alexandria Bay
Saranac Lake
Lake Placid
Vermont

New York
Lake George
Glens Falls

Syracuse
Seneca Falls
Rome
Saratoga Springs
Brattleboro
New Hampshire

Cooperstown
Albany

Ithaca
Elmira
Binghamton

Woodstock
Kingston
Catskill Mountains

Springfield
Connecticut
Rhode Island
Massachusetts

Scranton
Wilkes-Barre

Tarrytown
Long Island Sound
Long Island
Merritt Parkway

Stroudsburg
Wayne
NEWARK
NEW YORK

Harrisburg
Allentown
Reading
Princeton
Trenton
Highlands
Belmar

Lancaster
PHILADELPHIA
Camden
New Jersey
Seaside Heights

Maryland
Brandywine Valley
Wilmington

BALTIMORE
Delaware
Dover
Atlantic City

Annapolis
Wildwood
Cape May

ATLANTIC OCEAN

Oneida Lake
Cayuga Lake
Seneca Falls

Adirondack Mountains
Pocono Mountains
NE EXT Pennsylvania Turnpike
Garden State Parkway (toll)
Taconic State Parkway
New York State Thruway (toll)

St Lawrence River
Lake Champlain
Hudson River
Susquehanna River
Delaware River
Delaware Bay
Brandywine Valley
Staten Island

75°W 74°W 73°W 72°W 71°W
76°W 74°W 73°W 72°W 71°W
44°N
43°N
42°N
41°N
40°N
39°N

New York, New Jersey & Pennsylvania
2nd edition – September 2000
First published – June 1997

Published by
Lonely Planet Publications Pty Ltd ABN 36 005 607 983
90 Maribyrnong St, Footscray, Victoria 3011, Australia

Lonely Planet Offices
Australia Locked Bag 1, Footscray, Victoria 3011
USA 150 Linden St, Oakland, CA 94607
UK 10a Spring Place, London NW5 3BH
France 1 rue du Dahomey, 75011 Paris

Photographs
Most of the images in this guide are available for licensing from
Lonely Planet Images.
email: lpi@lonelyplanet.com.au

Ella and Dizzy photograph courtesy of the Library of Congress

Front cover photograph
Fall foliage in the Adirondacks (Cosmo Condina/Tony Stone Images)

Title page photographs
New York (Michael Clark)
New Jersey (Angus Oborn)
Pennsylvania (Tom Smallman)

ISBN 1 86450 138 3

Printed by SNP SPrint Pte Ltd
Printed in Singapore

Contents

INTRODUCTION

FACTS ABOUT THE REGION

FACTS FOR THE VISITOR

OUTDOOR ACTIVITIES   93

GETTING THERE & AWAY   110

GETTING AROUND   121

FACTS ABOUT NEW YORK   132

ontents

EW YORK CITY 145

LONG ISLAND 267

HUDSON VALLEY 276

CATSKILLS REGION 300

CAPITAL DISTRICT & MOHAWK VALLEY   319

ADIRONDACK REGION   346

THOUSAND ISLANDS & ST LAWRENCE SEAWAY   383

FINGER LAKES REGION   397

WESTERN NEW YORK   433

FACTS ABOUT NEW JERSEY   462

JERSEY SHORE   473

4   Contents

NORTHERN NEW JERSEY   498

CENTRAL NEW JERSEY   513

SOUTHERN NEW JERSEY   523

FACTS ABOUT PENNSYLVANIA   546

PHILADELPHIA   555

PENNSYLVANIA DUTCH COUNTRY   615

SOUTH CENTRAL PENNSYLVANIA 635

SOUTHWESTERN PENNSYLVANIA 651

NORTHERN PENNSYLVANIA 682

ACKNOWLEDGMENTS 706

INDEX 708

MAP LEGEND 720

NEW YORK MAP INDEX

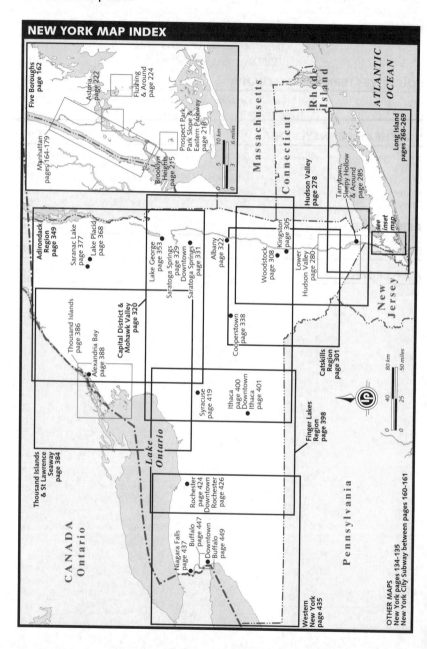

Five Boroughs
page 162

Astoria
page 222

Flushing
& Around
page 224

Manhattan
pages 164-179

Prospect Park
Park Slope &
Eastern Parkway
page 218

Brooklyn
Heights
page 215

0   5   10 km
0   3   6 miles

ATLANTIC
OCEAN

Massachusetts

Rhode Island

Connecticut

Long Island
pages 268-269

Hudson Valley
page 278

Tarrytown,
Sleepy Hollow
& Around
page 285

see
inset
map

Adirondack
Region
page 349

Saranac Lake
page 377

Lake Placid
page 368

Lake George
page 353

Saratoga Springs
page 329

Saratoga Springs
Downtown
page 331

Albany
page 322

Kingston
page 305

Woodstock
page 308

Lower
Hudson Valley
page 280

New
Jersey

Thousand Islands
page 386

Capital District &
Mohawk Valley
page 320

Cooperstown
page 338

Catskills
Region
page 301

Thousand Islands
& St Lawrence
Seaway

Alexandria Bay
page 388

Syracuse
page 419

Ithaca
page 400
Downtown
Ithaca
page 401

Finger Lakes
Region
page 398

Thousand Islands
& St Lawrence
Seaway page 384

Lake
Ontario

0   40   80 km
0   25   50 miles

CANADA
Ontario

Rochester
page 424
Downtown
Rochester
page 426

Niagara Falls
page 437

Buffalo
page 447
Downtown
Buffalo
page 449

Pennsylvania

Western
New York
page 435

OTHER MAPS
New York pages 134-135
New York City Subway between pages 160-161

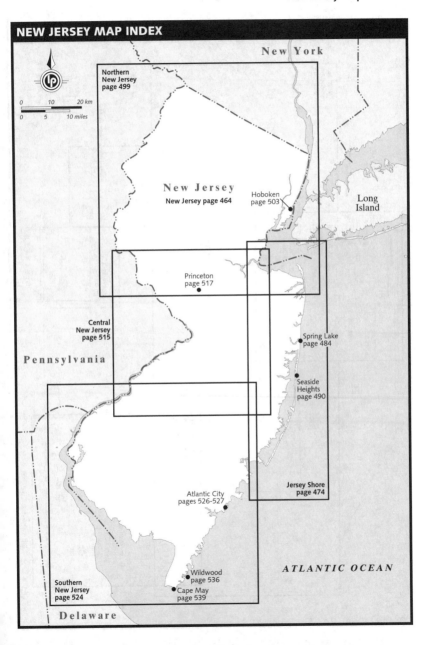

NEW JERSEY MAP INDEX

New York

Northern
New Jersey
page 499

0   10   20 km
0   5   10 miles

New Jersey
New Jersey page 464

Hoboken
page 503

Long
Island

New York

Princeton
page 517

Central
New Jersey
page 515

Pennsylvania

Spring Lake
page 484

Seaside
Heights
page 490

Jersey Shore
page 474

Atlantic City
pages 526-527

ATLANTIC OCEAN

Wildwood
page 536

Cape May
page 539

Southern
New Jersey
page 524

Delaware

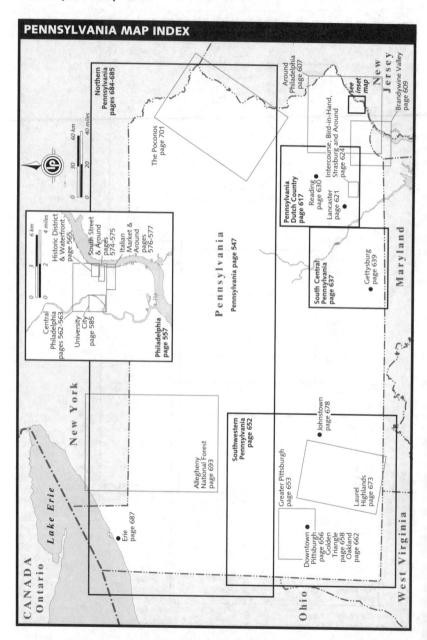

PENNSYLVANIA MAP INDEX

CANADA
Ontario

Lake Erie

New York

Ohio

West Virginia

Maryland

New Jersey

Pennsylvania
Pennsylvania page 547

Northern Pennsylvania
pages 684-685

The Poconos
page 701

Around Philadelphia
page 607

See inset map

Brandywine Valley
page 609

Pennsylvania Dutch Country
page 617

Intercourse, Bird-in-Hand, Strasburg and Around
page 624

Reading
page 630

Lancaster
page 621

South Central Pennsylvania
page 637

Gettysburg
page 639

Historic District & Waterfront
page 565

South Street & Around
pages 574-575

Italian Market & Around
pages 576-577

Central Philadelphia
pages 562-563

University City
page 585

Philadelphia
page 557

Southwestern Pennsylvania
page 652

Allegheny National Forest
page 693

Erie
page 687

Johnstown
page 678

Greater Pittsburgh
page 653

Laurel Highlands
page 673

Downtown Pittsburgh
page 656

Golden Triangle
page 658

Oakland
page 662

0   20   40 miles
0   30   60 km

0   2   4 miles
0   3   6 km

The Authors

Tom Smallman

Tom currently lives in Melbourne, Australia, and had a number of other jobs before joining the staff at Lonely Planet as a guidebook editor. He now works full time as an author and has worked on numerous Lonely Planet titles, including *Britain*, *Scotland*, *Edinburgh*, *Dublin*, *Ireland*, *Australia*, *New South Wales*, *Sydney* and *Canada*, as well as the first edition of this book.

Michael Clark

Michael was born in Ohio, raised in California and has been visiting upstate New York since returning to the US from a two-year stint in Malawi as a Peace Corps volunteer teacher. Long-term stops along the way have included Greece, Hawaii, Malaysia and Japan. When not on the road, Michael teaches English to international students in Berkeley, California, where he lives with his wife Janet and children Melina and Alexander. His work has appeared in the *San Francisco Examiner.* He is a co-author of Lonely Planet's *Myanmar (Burma)* and the first edition of this book; he also updated the Myanmar chapter of *South-East Asia on a shoestring*.

David Ellis

David was born in Greenwich Village and has lived in three of New York City's five boroughs (Manhattan, Brooklyn and the Bronx). Over the last 15 years he has reported on politics, business and culture at *Time* and *People* magazines from a variety of US locations. His work has also appeared in *The New Republic*, *New York* magazine and on the BBC. David is currently an editor at the *The Wall Street Journal*, and he lives in London. He is also the author of Lonely Planet's *New York City* guide and worked on the first edition of this book.

FROM THE AUTHORS

Tom Smallman My thanks go to Sue Graefe for her enduring patience and support, Lindy Mark for her invaluable information, Barbara Pope for her insights into Philly life, Mary Collins in Gettysburg, all those people in the travel industry who patiently answered my questions, my co-researchers David and Michael, the LP staff at Oakland and all those readers who wrote in with comments on the previous edition.

Michael Clark My thanks to New York friends Peter Davis, Bev Lazaar and Ben Davis for endless Saratoga hospitality; Stanley McGaughey for food for thought; North Country friends Art & Donna Herbold, along with Lindsay Pearson, Sam Sherwood, Lisa Davis, Bill Preston, Margi Wald, Kristen Olby and Melissa Erickson for lively support and assistance; Joe Lindsay for sharing his knowledge and respect of baseball mythology; Woodstock's Barry Samuel and James Cox for neighborly insights and graciousness; Nancy Arena, Jeannine Laverty and Kate McGaughey for helping me navigate the byways of the Hudson Valley; Patti Donahue for the best of Rochester's art scene; Nancy Vargo and Mary Summers for the bistro sidestreets of Buffalo; David Gaj in Niagara Falls for all-around appreciation of the falls; Alfred authors Kate Braverman and Alan Littell and photographer Caroline Littell for western New York conviviality.

Among the many people who provided valuable upstate perspectives, Field Horne of the Saratoga Racing Museum, Annamaria Dalton of the Saratoga Chamber of Commerce, Dresden Engle of the Eastman House Museum and Mary Ellen Walsh of the New York State Department of Tourism were always ready with an answer or suggestion. The staff of the Adirondak Loj provided splendid trail and canoe tips, along with Nanette Miranda, Amy and Lucy who added wilderness birthday inspirations.

Special thanks to the LP Oakland staff for their hard work, energy and involvement from beginning to end. Thanks also to New Yorkers-gone-west Donnie Waful and Dave Skibinski.

Last, and not least, love and thanks to Janet, Melina and Alexander for long distance patience and stellar support from home.

David Ellis Many sources were helpful in the collection of information and support, and I would like to specifically thank the staff at the New York City Convention and Visitors Bureau. Most knew me only in a guise as a 'lost tourist' and provided comprehensive help in an unfailingly polite manner. (So much for the gruff reputation of New Yorkers.) Laura Otterbourg's staff at the New Jersey Division of Travel & Tourism also helped guide my update. During the summer months in New Jersey, David and Lisa Furrule provided invaluable support. I would also like to thank Bud Kliment of Columbia University for background help and advice, Daniel Levy for his insights on architecture and Tom Lloyd for his history of contemporary New York music. Journalists Richard Lacayo, Larry Mondi, Barbara Rudolph, Larry Hackett and Mark Solomon provided companionship and, in some instances, spare beds and phone lines to this effort. At Lonely Planet, I'd like to thank Tom Downs for his great work on the first edition, and the whole team in Oakland for their help. Most of all, I thank my grandparents, Ruth and Bernard Wynne, for helping me discover New York City's many hidden glories.

This Book

The core writers from the first edition returned to bring you this update. Tom Smallman served as coordinating author as well as writing the front-matter and Pennsylvania chapters. Michael Clark wrote the New York state chapters, except Long Island and New York City, which were written by David Ellis. David also wrote the New Jersey chapters.

FROM THE PUBLISHERS

Despite a truncated deadline and serious cases of spring fever, the Oakland team of editors, cartographers and designers seamlessly moved this book through production and can proudly say that this edition is new and improved.

Maria Donohoe and China Williams edited the book, with assistance from Valerie Sinzdak, Wendy Taylor-Hall and Erin Corrigan, as well as sage guidance from Brigitte Barta. Proofing was done by Erin, Christine Lee, Elaine Merrill, Kevin Anglin, David Zingarelli, Paige Penland and Rachel Bernstein. Suki Gear and Michele Posner assisted with layout.

Rachel Leising and Kimberly Moses deftly handled the updating of old maps and the making of new maps. Heaps of thanks to Eric Thomsen who tamed the unruly New York City maps. Further assistance was provided by Patrick Bock, Matthew DeMartini, Guphy, Mary Hagemann, Sara Nelson and Kat Smith. Monica Lepe, Kimra McAfee, Amy Dennis and Alex Guilbert oversaw the project.

Margaret Livingston and Josh Schefers handled layout, with guidance from Susan Rimerman. Henia Miedzinski designed the cover, Beca Lafore coordinated illustrations, and Mark Butler, Hugh D'Andrade, Shelley Firth, Hayden Foell, Rini Keagy, Justin Marler, Hannah Reineck, Jennifer Steffey, Jim Swanson and Wendy Yanigahara drew the illustrations. Special thanks to Georgi Shablovsky and Angus Oborn for last-minute photography in New York state and New Jersey.

Foreword

ABOUT LONELY PLANET GUIDEBOOKS

The story begins with a classic travel adventure: Tony and Maureen Wheeler's 1972 journey across Europe and Asia to Australia. Useful information about the overland trail did not exist at that time, so Tony and Maureen published the first Lonely Planet guidebook to meet a growing need.

From a kitchen table, then from a tiny office in Melbourne (Australia), Lonely Planet has become the largest independent travel publisher in the world, an international company with offices in Melbourne, Oakland (USA), London (UK) and Paris (France).

Today Lonely Planet guidebooks cover the globe. There is an ever-growing list of books, and there's information in a variety of forms and media. Some things haven't changed. The main aim is still to help make it possible for adventurous travelers to get out there – to explore and better understand the world.

At Lonely Planet we believe travelers can make a positive contribution to the countries they visit – if they respect their host communities and spend their money wisely. Since 1986 a percentage of the income from each book has been donated to aid projects and human-rights campaigns.

Updates Lonely Planet thoroughly updates each guidebook as often as possible. This usually means there are around two years between editions, although for more unusual or more stable destinations the gap can be longer. Check the imprint page (following the color map at the beginning of the book) for publication dates.

Between editions, up-to-date information is available in two free newsletters – the paper *Planet Talk* and email *Comet* (to subscribe, contact any Lonely Planet office) – and on our website at www.lonelyplanet.com. The *Upgrades* section of the website covers a number of important and volatile destinations and is regularly updated by Lonely Planet authors. *Scoop* covers news and current affairs relevant to travelers. And, lastly, the *Thorn Tree* bulletin board and *Postcards* section of the site carry unverified, but fascinating, reports from travelers.

Correspondence The process of creating new editions begins with the letters, postcards and emails received from travelers. This correspondence often includes suggestions, criticisms and comments about the current editions. Interesting excerpts are immediately passed on via newsletters and the website, and everything goes to our authors to be verified when they're researching on the road. We're keen to get more feedback from organizations or individuals who represent communities visited by travelers.

Lonely Planet gathers information for everyone who's curious about the planet – and especially for those who explore it firsthand. Through guidebooks, phrasebooks, activity guides, maps, literature, newsletters, image library, TV series and website, we act as an information exchange for a worldwide community of travelers.

Research Authors aim to gather sufficient practical information to enable travelers to make informed choices and to make the mechanics of a journey run smoothly. They also research historical and cultural background to help enrich the travel experience and allow travelers to understand and respond appropriately to cultural and environmental issues.

Authors don't stay in every hotel because that would mean spending a couple of months in each medium-size city and, no, they don't eat at every restaurant because that would mean stretching belts beyond capacity. They do visit hotels and restaurants to check standards and prices, but feedback based on readers' direct experiences can be very helpful.

Many of our authors work undercover; others aren't so secretive. None of them accept freebies in exchange for positive write-ups. And none of our guidebooks contain any advertising.

Production Authors submit their raw manuscripts and maps to offices in Australia, the USA, the UK or France. Editors and cartographers – all experienced travelers themselves – then begin the process of assembling the pieces. When the book finally hits the shops, some things are already out of date, we start getting feedback from readers and the process begins again....

WARNING & REQUEST

Things change – prices go up, schedules change, good places go bad and bad places go bankrupt – nothing stays the same. So, if you find things better or worse, recently opened or long since closed, please tell us and help make the next edition even more accurate and useful. We genuinely value all the feedback we receive. Julie Young coordinates a well-traveled team that reads and acknowledges every letter, postcard and email and ensures that every morsel of information finds its way to the appropriate authors, editors and cartographers for verification.

Everyone who writes to us will find their name in the next edition of the appropriate guidebook. They will also receive the latest issue of *Planet Talk*, our quarterly printed newsletter, or *Comet*, our monthly email newsletter. Subscriptions to both newsletters are free. The very best contributions will be rewarded with a free guidebook.

Excerpts from your correspondence may appear in new editions of Lonely Planet guidebooks, the Lonely Planet website, *Planet Talk* or *Comet*, so please let us know if you *don't* want your letter published or your name acknowledged.

Send all correspondence to the Lonely Planet office closest to you:

Australia: Locked Bag 1, Footscray, Victoria 3011
USA: 150 Linden St, Oakland, CA 94607
UK: 10A Spring Place, London NW5 3BH
France: 1 rue du Dahomey, 75011 Paris

Or email us at: talk2us@lonelyplanet.com.au

For news, views and updates, see our website: www.lonelyplanet.com

HOW TO USE A LONELY PLANET GUIDEBOOK

The best way to use a Lonely Planet guidebook is any way you choose. At Lonely Planet, we believe the most memorable travel experiences are often those that are unexpected, and the finest discoveries are those you make yourself. Guidebooks are not intended to be used as if they provided a detailed set of infallible instructions!

Contents All Lonely Planet guidebooks follow the same format. The Facts about the Country chapters or sections give background information ranging from history to weather. Facts for the Visitor gives practical information on issues like visas and health. Getting There & Away gives a brief starting point for researching travel to and from the destination. Getting Around gives an overview of the transport options available when you arrive.

The peculiar demands of each destination determine how subsequent chapters are broken up, but some things remain constant. We always start with background, then proceed to sights, places to stay, places to eat, entertainment, getting there and away, and getting around information – in that order.

Heading Hierarchy Lonely Planet headings are used in a strict hierarchical structure that can be visualized as a set of Russian dolls. Each heading (and its following text) is encompassed by any preceding heading that is higher on the hierarchical ladder.

Entry Points We do not assume guidebooks will be read from beginning to end, but that people will dip into them. The traditional entry points are the list of contents and the index. In addition, however, some books have a complete list of maps and an index map illustrating map coverage.

There may also be a color map that shows highlights. These highlights are dealt with in greater detail later in the book, along with planning questions and suggested itineraries. Each chapter covering a geographical region usually begins with a locator map and another list of highlights. Once you find something of interest in a list of highlights, turn to the index.

Maps Maps play a crucial role in Lonely Planet guidebooks and include a huge amount of information. A legend is printed on the back page. We seek to have complete consistency between maps and text, and to have every important place in the text captured on a map. Map key numbers usually start in the top left corner.

Although inclusion in a guidebook usually implies a recommendation, we cannot list every good place. Exclusion does not necessarily imply criticism. In fact, there are a number of reasons why we might exclude a place – sometimes it is simply inappropriate to encourage an influx of travelers.

Introduction

The states of New York, New Jersey and Pennsylvania – sometimes collectively called the Middle Atlantic states – occupy some of the most urbanized, industrialized and populated sections of the USA. Viewed from the New Jersey Turnpike, Pennsylvania Turnpike or any of the other main routes that traverse the region, this image of industrial sprawl and urban development can be readily reinforced. But it's only part of the picture. The states also encompass vast lakes, many rivers, huge forests, rolling green countryside, beautiful mountains, some expanses of wilderness and long stretches of natural coastline.

The many historical sites in the region reflect the three states' long history, while the major cities, particularly New York City and Philadelphia, are centers for world-class arts, entertainment and dining.

That New York City is one of the most visited cities in the world is no surprise. It has the US's largest collection of museums and galleries, and from thriving Broadway theaters to Greenwich Village jazz clubs it's bustling with entertainment. It has some of the best and most ethnically diverse dining anywhere and the shopping possibilities are almost endless. It does have its urban problems, but this is still the world's most exhilarating city.

When most people think of New York they immediately think of the city, although New York state contains a whole lot more that stands in stark contrast to the skyscraper canyons of Manhattan. Nearby Long Island provides an escape from city life along its sandy beaches while upstate has plenty to offer the outdoor enthusiast. In the far northwest, on the Canadian border between Lake Erie and Lake Ontario, are the spectacular Niagara Falls. The Finger Lakes region south of Lake Ontario has many dairy farms and vineyards producing some of the best wine in the country. The Hudson River takes you north to the forests of the Catskill Mountains and to the Adiron-

dack Mountains. It was the rustic beauty of the upstate section of the Hudson Valley that so caught the imaginations of the Hudson River school of landscape painters.

Small in comparison with its neighbors and often dominated by them, New Jersey nevertheless has much to offer away from the industrialism with which most people associate it. Newark, the state's largest city, has many places of historic and cultural interest, as do Princeton and Trenton, towns closely

associated with events in the Revolutionary War. In the northwest, New Jersey shares the Delaware Water Gap NRA with Pennsylvania while to the south there's the natural beauty of the Pine Barrens. The Jersey Shore not only has the seaside resorts of Atlantic City and Cape May, but also miles of scenic beaches.

Pennsylvania is rich in historical sites and beautiful scenery. Philadelphia and Pittsburgh, the state's two main cities, are both undergoing a revival and offer world-class cultural attractions. West of Philadelphia, Pennsylvania Dutch Country is home to the Amish community, who reject many of the precepts and technologies of the modern world. Gettysburg National Military Park recalls the bloodiest battle in the Civil War. In the southwest the Laurel Highlands is a center for white-water rafting, while in the northwest you'll find the huge expanses of the Allegheny National Forest. In the northeast is the popular resort region and outdoor playground of the Pocono Mountains. The northern part of the state is particularly beautiful during the fall foliage season.

So enjoy the metropolitan centers, but don't forget the region's rural delights.

Facts about the Region

HISTORY
Original Peoples
Around 15,000 to 35,000 years ago, when the accumulated ice of the polar glaciers of the Pleistocene epoch, the last Ice Age, lowered the world's sea levels, the first inhabitants of North America arrived from Asia. They came from Siberia to Alaska via a land bridge across what is now the Bering Strait. Over millennia, subsequent migrations southward and eastward distributed the population throughout the Americas.

These first Americans were nomadic hunter-gatherers who lived in small bands, and this type of society existed on the continent until relatively recently. During the Ice Age they hunted mammoths, cave bears and giant sloths. However, after the Ice Age, these animals became extinct due to changes in the climate and environment. Americans turned to hunting smaller game, fishing, and gathering wild berries, seeds, roots and fruits. The hunter-gatherers' tools and weapons were made from stone, wood and bark, and their houses were made of bark or animal skins. They traveled on foot or by canoe and developed crafts in weaving and pottery.

There were two major groups of Native Americans in this region when Europeans began to arrive – the Algonquians and the Iroquois. Algonquian is a linguistic term commonly applied to tribes that spoke variations of the same family of languages. Algonquian-speaking tribes occupied the Hudson Valley, Long Island, New Jersey, Delaware River Valley and central Pennsylvania including part of the Susquehanna River. They were made up of the Lenni-Lanape (meaning 'Original People' but called the Delaware by the British), Shawnee, Mohegan (or Mohican) and Munsee.

The Iroquois were a military and political confederacy of different Native American tribes that occupied central and western New York and parts of northwestern and central Pennsylvania. They included the Cayuga, Mohawk, Oneida, Onondaga and Seneca peoples who together formed the powerful Iroquois Confederacy in 1570. The Susquehannock people were also Iroquois and were named after the Susquehanna River where they lived.

European Arrival & Colonialism
The first European credited with visiting the region is the Italian navigator Giovanni da Verrazano, who sailed into New York Bay in 1524. In the early 17th century the English and French established trading relations with Native Americans, but Dutch and Swedish settlements initially expanded the European presence. In 1608 John Smith sailed up the Susquehanna River from Virginia into Pennsylvania.

The following year the English explorer Henry Hudson arrived in Delaware Bay and claimed the area for the Dutch East India Company, for whom he was working. (In 1609 it was called the Dutch *East* India Company – formed in 1602. Though Hudson didn't find the fabled Northwest Passage to India, the success of the new fur trading posts led to the formation in 1621 of the Dutch *West* India Company – with the aim of gaining dominance over the Atlantic trade. Why they changed names isn't clear: probably the marketing department's call.) Hudson was followed by Dutch explorers, and in 1624 settlements were established, in what was subsequently named New Netherland, by the Dutch West India Company at Fort Orange (present-day Albany, NY) and Fort Nassau (present-day Gloucester City, NJ). Two years later a settlement was established at New Amsterdam at the southern end of Manhattan Island and in 1630 at Pavonia (in Jersey City, NJ).

Sweden established the permanent settlement of New Sweden at Wilmington (in Delaware), but Governor Johan Printz moved the capital, New Gothenburg, to Tinicum Island in the Delaware River near what would become Philadelphia. The brief Swedish presence in the New World ended in 1655 when the Dutch conquered New Sweden and annexed it to New Netherland. In 1664 the English, in turn, conquered the Dutch settlement (the Dutch were given modern-day Surinam in South America in exchange) and renamed it New York after the Duke of York (who became King James II of England in 1685). Parts of New Jersey were also acquired by the English, but differing proprietorial claims left it divided between East and West Jersey until 1702, at which time it became a royal province. New York and New Jersey shared the same royal governor until 1738.

In the meantime, on March 4, 1681, the Duke of York's brother, King Charles II, had given English Quaker William Penn a charter to own land west of the Delaware River in lieu of a £16,000 payment that was owed William's father, Admiral Penn. Charles II called the colony 'Penn' in honor of the admiral and William Penn added 'sylvania' (meaning 'woodlands'). Pennsylvania would become the richest, most populous and most influential of Britain's colonies in 18th-century North America.

William Penn founded his colony as a 'holy experiment.' Although he only lived there briefly (from 1682 to 1684 and again from 1699 to 1701), as the governor and proprietor he ensured that, to a great degree, the colony respected religious freedom and liberal government. Rather optimistically, he named his capital Philadelphia (Greek for 'Brotherly Love'). He granted several fairly progressive frames of government between himself and the colonists, establishing a code of laws and guaranteeing religious tolerance, trial by jury and protection of property.

These were superseded by the 1701 Charter of Privilege, a constitution giving the Pennsylvania colonial assembly more power than any legislative body in Britain. Christian landholders were the only ones who could vote, but it was a start. The Charter of Privilege remained the colony's constitution until 1776.

Franco-British Rivalry

During the first half of the 18th century there were conflicts in western Pennsylvania

and western New York between the British colonists and their Algonquian allies and the French. These conflicts culminated in the French & Indian War from 1754–63. The Iroquois Confederacy allied itself with the British and this alliance was a significant factor in Britain's eventual defeat of the French.

Much of the earlier stages of the French & Indian War were fought in western Pennsylvania, where France and Britain clashed over trade and access to the Ohio River Valley. The French considered the Ohio River Valley an essential link between their colonies in Canada and Louisiana and were unhappy with merchants from Pennsylvania and Virginia trading with Native Americans in the area.

To protect their interests, the French built a line of forts through western Pennsylvania. The British sent George Washington to warn off the French, but he was first ignored and then beaten at the Battle of Fort Necessity in southwestern Pennsylvania in 1754. The French built Fort Duquesne at the confluence of the Ohio, Allegheny and Monongahela Rivers (the site of present-day Pittsburgh), and in 1755 the British sent General Braddock to dislodge them, but he too was beaten.

In New York the British were able to secure the St Lawrence River in 1758, when Lord Amherst captured Louisburg, and then Lake Champlain in 1759 when he took Fort Carillon (renamed Fort Ticonderoga). General Wolfe's capture of Quebec in the same year meant that Britain's colonies in North America were safe, although peace wasn't signed for another four years.

Despite their alliance with the Iroquois, the British were less conciliatory than the French in their relations with Native Americans. In 1763 an Ottawa Indian, Pontiac, emerged as a prophet and led attacks on British forts throughout western Pennsylvania and western New York in an attempt to drive the British out. Pontiac's fighters at first overwhelmed a number of forts, but by 1764 found that they couldn't succeed. With the defeat of Pontiac, the last impediments to further westward colonial expansion in New York and Pennsylvania were swept away.

Some colonists, such as William Penn, were judicious in dealing with the original inhabitants and purchased land rather than taking it. Eventually, however, all the Native American groups were driven off the land, largely by the encroachment of European settlers.

Break with Britain

The French & Indian War had increased Britain's costs in America tremendously. Britain in turn raised the taxes levied on the colonies and introduced stricter controls of colonial trade partly to protect its home industries. Many in the colonies opposed British policies and some merchants disliked what they saw as excessive British taxation. Philadelphians even turned away a British tea ship in 1773, though they didn't burn it as Bostonians did. A growing number of people began to consider separation from the mother country.

Not everyone was in favor of this course, however. The governor of New Jersey, William Franklin, the son of Benjamin Franklin, supported the British, as did the wealthier merchants in New York. In Pennsylvania there were a good number of pacifist religious groups, like the Quakers, Mennonites and Amish. There was also a Church of England minority that supported Britain and a general disinterest in fighting among many German settlers.

Despite this opposition, and some apathy, most people favored separation, and the New York, New Jersey and Pennsylvania colonial governments voted to support the revolution. The First and Second Continental Congresses met in Philadelphia and the Declaration of Independence was adopted in the State House (now Independence Hall) in July 1776. At the same time the colonial governments of New York, New Jersey and Pennsylvania each approved a state constitution for themselves, but the former royal provinces still had to fight for recognition of their new status.

See the introductory chapter to each state for their individual history from this point.

GEOGRAPHY
Physical Regions

New York, New Jersey and Pennsylvania occupy sections of a number of distinct physical regions. West to east these are classified as: the Central Lowland, Appalachian Plateau, Appalachian Ridge & Valley, Blue Ridge Mountains, Piedmont Plateau, New England Upland and Atlantic Coastal Plain. The Appalachian Plateau, Appalachian Ridge & Valley and Blue Ridge Mountains are part of the geologically ancient, 1500-mile-long Appalachian Mountains, which run from the Canadian border southwest into northern Alabama.

The narrow 30-mile-wide northeastern strip of the Central Lowland follows the southern shores of Lake Erie and Lake Ontario and is known collectively as the Erie-Ontario Lowland. It consists of sedimentary rocks and its fertile clay soils are good for fruit-growing. Also consisting of sedimentary rocks, the Appalachian Plateau covers about half of Pennsylvania and New York and includes the Catskill, Pocono and Allegheny mountains. Its soils, however, are generally poor, except along the major river valleys where there are rich deposits of silt.

Consisting of limestone and sandstone, the Appalachian Ridge & Valley features a series of roughly 1000-foot-high steep ridges separated by wide, largely parallel valleys. The longest of these, including a number of smaller valleys, is the 15-mile-wide Great Valley, which stretches nearly the full length of the Appalachian Mountains. In New Jersey it's known as the Kittatinny Valley. Running northwest from Georgia through Maryland, the Blue Ridge Mountains extend into southern Pennsylvania for about 50 miles. The eastern slopes of these mountains fall away sharply to the Piedmont Plateau, which also meets the Appalachian Ridge & Valley further north. The Piedmont Plateau is an area of low-lying land ranging in elevation from 100 feet to 500 feet and containing fertile limestone soils, underpinned by layers of red sandstone, shale and basalt rock.

North of the Piedmont Plateau the New England Upland stretches from Northern

Pennsylvania and New Jersey through New York into Connecticut and Massachusetts. Largely made up of metamorphic rocks, its southern extension is known as the Reading Prong and includes the Taconic Mountains and Manhattan Island in New York and the New Jersey Highlands.

Stretching from Massachusetts to Mexico, the Atlantic Coastal Plain is a mostly flat, raised, westward extension of the continental shelf. The plain only occupies relatively small sections of New York (Long Island and Staten Island) and Pennsylvania (the Philadelphia region) but covers 60% of New Jersey. Along New Jersey's Atlantic coast and along Delaware Bay are broad expanses of marshland; except in the state's southwest, most of the coastal plain's soil is poor.

Rivers & Lakes

The main river systems are: the Delaware River, which borders eastern Pennsylvania, western New Jersey and southwestern New York and flows into Delaware Bay; the Susquehanna, which drains central Pennsylvania and parts of New York and flows south into Chesapeake Bay; the Ohio River and its tributaries the Allegheny and Monongahela Rivers; and the Hudson River, an important transportation route that forms part of the border between New Jersey and New York.

The area boasts thousands of lakes created by receding glaciers at the end of the last Ice Age. New York has an extensive shoreline along Lake Ontario and Lake Erie, while northwestern Pennsylvania occupies a small section of the Lake Erie shore between New York and Ohio.

CLIMATE

Despite their proximity to the Atlantic Ocean, New York and Pennsylvania have continental climates, characterized by wide temperature differences between winter and summer. This is because the prevailing winds come from the western interior. New Jersey is classified as cool temperate.

Air-flows from the Atlantic Ocean and the Gulf of Mexico affect the climates of all three states, making temperature variations normally less extreme than states further

inland. In New York City, for example, the average January temperature is 14°F, in July 77°F, though much greater extremes have been recorded. The warm moist air from the Gulf of Mexico in summer explains why places like Philadelphia and New York City often get so unbearably humid then. Spring and fall are generally mild with warm days and cool nights, although along the Atlantic coast the shifting wind patterns during these seasons can cause very turbulent weather, including hurricanes.

Inland, the average temperatures for Pittsburgh are 38.9°F in January, 67.7°F in July.

Precipitation is fairly evenly distributed during the year, with annual falls generally between 32 and 48 inches. The highest snowfalls occur along the Erie-Ontario Lowland.

ECOLOGY & ENVIRONMENT

Awareness of ecology and the environment, plus the recognized value in 'green tourism' or 'ecotourism,' means that many natural areas enjoy varying degrees of protection and management from local, state and federal government agencies as well as from private organizations. The modern environmental movement, with broad-based ecological concerns, became important in the 1960s. Marine biologist Rachel Carson (1907–64) from Springdale in rural southwestern Pennsylvania challenged agricultural practices (especially the widespread use of pesticides). Her book, *Silent Spring*, was enormously influential.

Since the 1970s lands have been acquired for important environmental and recreational purposes, and the emission of hazardous wastes and air pollution has come under tighter control.

This is a highly populated, heavily industrialized and intensively farmed part of the country, and the states' broad network of lakes and rivers was traditionally used to dump large, toxic amounts of industrial, agricultural and human waste. Efforts have been made to clean them up, and some places, like Lake Erie and the Hudson River, are much cleaner these days, and marine life has shown regeneration. People actually fish for

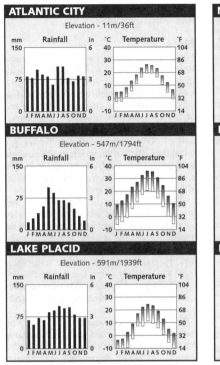

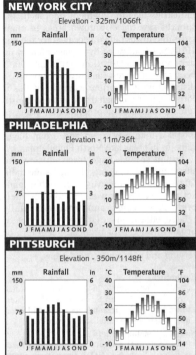

bass in season from New York City's piers, though commercial fishing is banned because the river still contains unsafe levels of industrial pollutants.

New York was one of the first states in the country to adopt acid-rain controls, and air quality across the region has improved significantly since the federal government's 1990 Clean Air Act. One of the biggest ongoing environmental issues in New York is the question of logging in Adirondack Park. See the Ecology & Environment section in the Facts about New York chapter and at the start of the Adirondack Region chapter.

In America's densely populated northeast, garbage-dump sites are becoming scarce, and big cities like New York incur increasing costs to take out the trash. Anyone who spends even a short time in Manhattan can't help but notice the piles of garbage-filled plastic bags on the sidewalk each morning waiting to be picked up. The dump at Fresh Kills on Staten Island is the world's largest but is due to close at the end of 2001, and a solution for dealing with the city's garbage beyond that time has yet to be found. Recycling of glass, aluminum, paper products and some plastics is becoming more widespread through a combination of public support and regulation. New Yorkers can be fined if they don't separate their garbage.

About 20% of US energy comes from nuclear power. The accident at Three Mile Island near Harrisburg in south-central Pennsylvania in 1979 dispelled complacency in the nuclear power industry and led to stricter standards. Compliance with new standards made many new nuclear plants unprofitable.

Following WWII, the decline in traditional industries and the flight of people to the suburbs saw the downtown areas in many cities and towns fall into decay. Since the mid 1970s, partly inspired by the bicentenary independence celebrations, attempts have been made to arrest (and reverse) this urban disintegration. A prime example of this is Pittsburgh: it combated pollution and instituted a regeneration program that has been emulated by other cities. Nevertheless there is still a long way to go and urban blight remains in areas like North Philadelphia.

Urban sprawl, huge tract housing and shopping developments, threatens the habitats of animals. However, many public lands act as preserves for wildlife and offer interpretive activities and environmentally related education programs. A number of organizations, with branches, chapters or clubs in each state, are concerned with preserving and restoring natural areas.

Earthwatch
(☎ 617-926-8200, 800-776-0188, www.earthwatch.org), 680 Mt Auburn St, PO Box 9104, Watertown, MA 02471, organizes national (and international) environmental-science expeditions.

National Audubon Society
(☎ 212-979-3000, www.audubon.org), 700 Broadway, New York, NY 10003, promotes ecology, conservation and the restoration of natural resources, especially wildlife habitats.

Nature Conservancy
(☎ 703-841-5300, www.tnc.org), 4245 N Fairfax Drive, Arlington, VA 22203-1606, is an international, private, nonprofit conservation organization that buys habitats to save them from threatened development or other destruction.

Sierra Club
(☎ 415-977-5500, www.sierraclub.org), 85 2nd St, 2nd Floor 2F, San Francisco, CA 94105, concerns itself with all environmental issues.

FLORA & FAUNA

Following the arrival of Europeans, the pattern of vegetation and animal life altered dramatically. Urbanization, industrialization and the development of agriculture reduced the area in which these occurred naturally. Introduced plants grow alongside indigenous ones and introduced animals compete with native species.

Flora

Much of the region was covered by virgin forest when Europeans first arrived. During the 18th and 19th centuries most of the original forests were cleared for farmland or used for lumber and charcoal. Since the end of the 19th century, however, preservation and reforestation has been successful. Over half of New York and Pennsylvania and more than 40% of New Jersey are covered by forest, the vast bulk of which is new growth intermixed with a number of smaller areas of pristine, old-growth trees.

There are many different species, but most of the region's forests are dominated by northern broad-leaved hardwoods. Beech and sugar maple are the main ones, but others include ash, basswood, birch, cherry, hickory, red maple, walnut and oak. Some forests, especially along the Atlantic coast, are made up chiefly of softwood conifers such as cedar, fir, hemlock, spruce and white and yellow pine.

Wildflowers common to the region include the azalea, black-eyed Susan, daisy, buttercup, honeysuckle, mountain laurel, orchid and violet; dogwood trees are also common. In the Pine Barrens of southern New Jersey are some rare plant species including several insect-eating varieties.

Fauna

Before the arrival of Europeans, the region boasted many species, including black bear, Canada lynx, elk, bison, wolf and panther – some, like the panther, have disappeared and others exist only in small numbers. Commonly seen among the region's smaller mammals are beaver, chipmunk, fox, opossum, rabbit, raccoon, squirrel, skunk and woodchuck. Of the larger mammals the white-tailed deer is widespread, but the black bear is largely restricted to the remote regions of the Appalachian Plateau and the Adirondack Mountains.

Two poisonous snakes are the timber rattlesnake found mostly on mountains and the copperhead common on rocky streambeds; nonpoisonous snakes are far more common.

New York, New Jersey and Pennsylvania are home to many species of year-round birds as well as temporary host to migratory ones. Birds that can be seen all year are the bluebird, bluejay, bobolink, eastern meadowlark, goldfinch, red-tailed hawk, owls and woodpeckers. Migratory birds include the hummingbird, hawk, falcon and bald eagle. Along the shores of lakes and the Atlantic coast are gulls, heron and osprey. Game birds include the wild duck, wild turkey (which Ben Franklin wanted to be the national bird), grouse, partridge, pheasant and quail.

Among the numerous varieties of fish found in the region's fresh waters are black bass, catfish, crappie, walleyed pike, pickerel, salmon, trout, muskellunge and whitefish. Salt waters contain bluefish, marlin, tuna and flounder as well as crabs, clams and oysters.

Endangered Species The reduction in wildlife habitats has meant that animals like the black bear and bobcat are restricted to small, remote woodland areas. The eastern wapiti (elk) became extinct in the 19th century, but a small herd of wapiti, introduced from the west, lives in Northern Pennsylvania.

At one time predatory birds like the hawk, falcon, osprey and bald eagle were threatened with extinction by hunters and the widespread use of chemicals (which become increasingly concentrated the further up the food chain). But their numbers have recovered since they were protected by the federal Migratory Bird Treaty Act of 1972, the Endangered Species Act of 1973 and the 1972 ban on the chemical DDT. The official status of the bald eagle in the US was upgraded from 'endangered' to 'threatened' in 1993, like that of the peregrine falcon in 1999. The bluebird was close to extinction, but its numbers are gradually returning; it can be seen in Northern Pennsylvania.

Nevertheless, some chemicals, though banned, persist in the environment, and natural habitats continue to diminish.

The Massasauga is a rare and poisonous rattlesnake found in the western part of Pennsylvania.

Parks & Forests

The following are state- and federally maintained park and forest lands. For additional federal and national agencies, see the boxed text 'Useful Outdoor Organizations.'

National Parks There are no national parks in this region, but there are two national recreation areas (NRAs), one national reserve and a national seashore all administered by the National Park Service (NPS), an agent of the US Department of the Interior. Unlike national parks, where development is severely restricted, NRAs have usually been substantially altered by human activity but nevertheless retain some exceptional natural features. A national reserve and seashore are undeveloped tracts of land in which natural ecosystems are maintained.

The Gateway NRA, at the entrance to the New York/New Jersey Estuary, is made up of Jamaica Bay (which includes a wildlife refuge), the Rockway Peninsula, Staten Island and Sandy Hook. The Delaware Water Gap NRA straddles the Pennsylvania/New Jersey border along the winding Delaware River through the Kittatinny Ridge.

The Pinelands National Reserve, on the Atlantic Coastal Plain in southern New Jersey, is in a small region known as the Pine Barrens and consists of many bogs, marshes and dwarfed pines. Fire Island National Seashore, off the southern shore of Long Island, is 1400 acres of wilderness.

The NPS also administers a number of national monuments, memorials, historic sites, trails and rivers throughout the region.

For more information contact the NPS, Northeast Region (☎ 215-597-7013), 5th Floor, US Custom House, 200 Chestnut St, Philadelphia, PA 19106. Its website is www.nps.org. The national headquarters (☎ 202-208-6843) is at 1849 C St NW, Washington, DC 20240.

Useful Outdoor Organizations

Bureau of Land Management (BLM) The BLM manages public use of federal lands, primarily concerning mineral and subsurface management. In addition, it offers no-frills camping, often in untouched settings. The eastern US regional office (☎ 703-440-1713) is at 7450 Boston Blvd, Springfield, VA 22153-3121; its website is at www.es.blm.gov.

US Fish & Wildlife Service (USFWS) The USFWS is responsible for conserving, protecting and improving habitats for plants, wildlife and fish. Each state has a few regional offices that provide information about viewing local wildlife. Its phone numbers are in the white pages of the phone directory under 'US Government,' or you can contact the USFWS head office (☎ 800-688-9889), 1849 C St NW, Washington, DC 20240; its website is at www.fws.gov.

US Army Corps of Engineers The northeast has lots of lakes and many of them (and their surrounding land) are operated by the US Army Corps of Engineers. The corps is responsible for flood control, hydropower production, shore protection and restoration, water supply and fish and wildlife management and outdoor recreation. For more information contact the following (there's no office in New Jersey):

New York
　(☎ 212-264-0100) Jacob K Javits Federal Building, 26 Federal Plaza, New York, NY 10278-0090
　(☎ 716-879-4104) 1776 Niagara St, Buffalo, NY 14207

Pennsylvania
　(☎ 215-656-6515) Wanamaker Building, 100 Penn Square East, Philadelphia, PA 19107-3390
　(☎ 412-644-6924) William S Moorhead Federal Building, 1000 Liberty Ave, Pittsburgh, PA 15222

National Forests The country's national forests are operated by the United States Forest Service (USFS), a division of the United States Department of Agriculture (USDA). They are managed under the principle of 'multiple use,' which includes timber cutting, watershed management, wildlife management and privately owned recreational facilities.

In northwestern Pennsylvania, the Allegheny National Forest (see the Northern Pennsylvania chapter) is a huge tract of land (797 sq miles) incorporating reservoirs, lakes, rivers, towns and campgrounds and whose northern extension borders New York's Allegany State Forest. For information, contact the Allegheny National Forest (☎ 814-723-5150), 222 Liberty St, Warren, PA 16365. The much smaller Finger Lakes National Forest in southwest New York is just over 20 sq miles in size. For information contact the Hector Ranger District (☎ 607-546-4470), 5216 State Route 414, Hector, NY 14841.

State Parks & Forests New York, New Jersey and Pennsylvania each maintains its own system of state parks and state forests, many of which contain wildlife and wilderness areas as well as provide recreational activities. State contact addresses are:

New York
　(☎ 518-474-0456, nysparks.state.ny.us) State Office of Parks, Recreation & Historic Preservation, Empire State Plaza, Albany, NY 12238
　(☎ 518-457-2500, www.dec.state.ny.us) Department of Environmental Conservation, Public Lands, 50 Wolf Rd, Room 11 Albany, NY 12233-4255

New Jersey
　(☎ 609-292-2885, www.state.nj.us) Environmental Protection Department, 401 E State St, PO Box 402, Trenton, NJ 08625-0402

Pennsylvania
　(☎ 717-558-2710, 888-727-2757, enved.sp@al-dcnr.state.pa.us, www.dcnr.state.pa.us) Bureau of State Parks, PO Box 8551, Harrisburg, PA 17105-8551

For more information, see the Facts About chapter of each state.

GOVERNMENT & POLITICS

The US is a republic governed federally according to the provisions of the Constitution, which provides for separate executive, legislative and judiciary arms of government, with checks and balances between them. The legislative branch of the government makes the laws, the executive branch carries them out and the judiciary branch studies and interprets them and the Constitution. The Constitution also provides for a balance of power between federal and state governments.

The President

The president is head of state, chief of the executive government and commander-in-chief of the armed forces. A presidential term is for four years and no person can be elected president more than twice. The president isn't elected directly, but by an electoral college in which each state has a number of votes equal to the number of representatives in Congress (which relates to its population) plus the number of its senators. To be elected, the president must obtain a majority of the total 538 electoral votes.

The heads (called secretaries) of the 13 executive departments are political appointments of the president. These secretaries collectively make up the Cabinet.

Congress

The legislative arm of government is the bicameral Congress, consisting of a 100-member Senate and a 435-member House of Representatives. New York, New Jersey and Pennsylvania send 31, 13 and 23 representatives respectively to the US Congress; each elects two senators. All budget, tax and revenue laws originate in the House of Representatives, while the Senate has special powers regarding foreign relations, senior government appointments and impeachment. House members serve two-year terms and senators serve six-year terms. Elections are held every two years for all representatives' seats and approximately one-third of the senators' seats. Every four years, these coincide with presidential elections.

Political Parties

US politics is dominated by two main parties. The Republicans are traditionally more conservative, opposed to big government and for states' rights. The Democrats are generally more progressive and favor a more active role for the federal government. Smaller parties like the Green Party and the Reform Party are insignificant in terms of their elected representation.

The parties aren't as monolithic as in other systems, and there are conservative Democrats and progressive Republicans. Members of Congress don't vote strictly on party lines. It's common for the president to be from one party while both houses of Congress have a majority from the other party.

Judiciary

The highest judicial authority is the US Supreme Court, whose nine justices are appointed for life by the president, with the advice and consent of the Senate. The Supreme Court can overrule federal or state laws or executive action that violates the Constitution. Beneath it are 13 federal courts of appeal, 94 district courts and various special courts.

State & Local Government

Powers not delegated to the federal government by the Constitution are retained by the states. Each state has its own constitution. The governor is the state's chief executive, a state senate and a house delegation enact state laws, and a state police and court system enforce them. The states are further divided into counties, boroughs, parishes, cities, towns, school districts and/or special districts that provide services like police, sanitation, schools etc. Local government units often combine to administer a large urban area as a single unit, as in the five boroughs of New York City.

ECONOMY

The US has a huge, diverse and highly advanced economy with the largest gross domestic product (GDP) in the world. Whether it's the richest country per person depends on currency exchange, the price of oil and which set of figures you believe. The US does have extremes of wealth and poverty, but by most measures it comes up quite well compared to other countries because of the large group of middle income earners. Nevertheless, poverty is a persistent problem and many visitors are shocked at the visible presence of destitute people in affluent cities and at slum-standard housing in some urban areas. Unemployment is historically low, but many poorly paid workers receive income below the poverty line.

New York, New Jersey and Pennsylvania have a number of features in common economically. Pennsylvania and New York have small reserves of oil and larger amounts of natural gas; all three have deposits of salt, clay, sand, limestone and slate and small amounts of mineral ores such as copper, iron, silver, gold and zinc are mined. New York and New Jersey also supply gravel, and Pennsylvania has large amounts of coal (bituminous and anthracite). The timber industry has always been important, though less so in New Jersey and Pennsylvania today. Pennsylvania has a small fishing industry, but commercial fishing is important in New York and New Jersey, particularly the harvesting of saltwater fish and crustaceans.

Although manufacturing has diminished in importance relative to other parts of the US and to other industries, this remains one of the nation's leading industrial regions. The main type of manufactured goods are chemicals, electronic equipment, food products, industrial machinery, paper products, precision instruments and printed materials. Iron and steel production are also significant in New York and Pennsylvania. Tourism, transport, publishing and entertainment are also large industries.

Each state has a diversified agricultural sector, but livestock and dairy farming earn the bulk of farming income for New York and Pennsylvania.

For more information see each state's Facts About chapter.

POPULATION & PEOPLE

The combined population of New York, New Jersey and Pennsylvania is more than 37½ million and is steadily rising. New York has the highest population of the three, and New Jersey is one of the most densely populated states in the country.

Nearly half of New York's population lives in the New York City metropolitan area; in Pennsylvania it is concentrated in the southeast around Philadelphia and in the southwest around Pittsburgh; in New Jersey the highest concentration is in the Newark and Jersey City conurbation. See the introduction to each of these states, especially New York, for more on the racial diversity of the region.

Pennsylvania is the most rural of the states with just over 30% living in country areas. New York and New Jersey are two of the most urbanized states in the nation with respectively 84% and 89% of residents living in urban-designated areas.

Despite a common perception to the contrary, in terms of ethnicity the population of the region is still overwhelmingly white. According to the 1990 census, whites make up 74.4% in New York, 79.3% in New Jersey and 88.5% in Pennsylvania. Blacks make up the second largest ethnic group, comprising 15.9%, 13.1% and 9.2% respectively. These are followed by Asians, Hispanics and Native Americans. In New York and New Jersey many Hispanics are of Puerto Rican or Cuban origin. Native Americans number about 90,000, of whom over two-thirds live in New York.

EDUCATION

School attendance is usually obligatory to the age of 16, and almost everyone graduates from high school. New York has the nation's largest public school system, which each year spends a multibillion dollar budget. In all three states Catholic grammar schools are a prominent private choice.

New York, New Jersey and Pennsylvania have some of the most prestigious universities in the country, including Columbia, New York and Cornell universities in New York, Princeton in New Jersey and the University of Pennsylvania. Other important institutions are the US Military Academy at West Point, the State University system of New

York, Rutgers University in New Jersey and Pennsylvania State University.

Smaller colleges in New York include City College, Hunter, the New School, Parsons and the Fashion Institute of Technology in New York City, Ithaca College, and Skidmore College in Saratoga Springs. Smaller liberal arts colleges in Pennsylvania include Villanova University, the all-female Bryn Mawr College, Haverford College, Carnegie Mellon in Pittsburgh, Beaver College in Glenside (with an excellent exchange program), Swarthmore College, the Catholic Duquesne University in Pittsburgh, York College, Allentown College and Franklin & Marshall College (endowed by Benjamin Franklin).

ARTS

New York City remains the most important center for the arts in the US and, historically, has helped shape much of the country's artistic and cultural life. It is the nation's major training and testing ground for painters, actors, dancers, musicians, writers, filmmakers and so on. That's why so many have spent at least part of their career here and why so many have incorporated aspects of the city into their work.

New York City has been the center of numerous artistic movements, many of which overlapped and influenced later developments. Ragtime musicians, for example, performed in vaudeville theaters and had their music published in Tin Pan Alley. The skills that actors and comics acquired in vaudeville they later used in movies and TV. The Jazz Age, which saw the flourishing of the arts in Harlem and of black music in general, was also reflected in the work of writers like F Scott Fitzgerald.

The country's principle theatrical district is Broadway, while numerous productions also take place in Off Broadway and Off-Off Broadway locations. The major radio and TV networks – ABC, CBS, NBC and FOX – and several cable-TV channels are based in New York City. A number of TV programs are still produced here, and the city is used as the setting for others. Movies also frequently use the city as a backdrop, and many of those working in films honed their skills in theater or TV. New York City is the magazine- and book-publishing center of the US, with a number of important publishing houses based here. It's also an important music publishing and recording center. These different cultural media feed off and into each other.

Helping to make sure that all this endeavor pays off are the Madison Ave advertising companies, the public-relations firms, impresarios, agents and other movers and shakers.

The variety and quantity of artistic pursuits also require financing, and the wealth that exists in New York City allows for both corporate and private sponsorship of the arts. In Philadelphia, sponsorship funds the same variety, but on a smaller scale. The benefit to tourism is recognized and helps ensure that public money is made available to promote the arts, and the whole region gains from the spill-over.

New York City, Philadelphia and the other major cities in the region have some of the foremost artistic institutions in the country. In addition, there are countless smaller theaters, galleries, orchestras, musical venues as well as art museums, and outside the major cities, almost every community of any size has its share of them.

The three states are home to a number of artists' colonies, while numerous arts and craft festivals take place throughout the year.

Popular Music

This region has had an enormous influence on popular music. New York City in particular attracts people from around the country (and abroad), and some of the most popular musical movements of the modern era have either begun or found their strongest expression there. Today, numerous halls, clubs and bars exist where the many forms of music from the past and present can be heard and/or danced to.

Primarily thought of as piano music, ragtime (probably from 'ragged time' referring to its two-four rhythm base and syncopated melody) first became popular at the

WILLIAM P GOTTLIEB

Ella Fitzgerald and Dizzy Gillespie at the Downbeat, New York City, 1947

end of the 19th century, when it was performed in vaudeville theaters. One of its greatest exponents was Jelly Roll Morton, while Scott Joplin was one of its most important composers. A number of dances were identified with ragtime, including the fox trot, turkey trot and tango. Ragtime was popularized nationally through the sheet music published in Tin Pan Alley.

Tin Pan Alley dominated American popular music from the 1890s to the 1960s, when the factory approach to song-writing gave way to rock music's singer-songwriters. Tin Pan Alley originally referred to an area of New York City where music publishers and composers were centered, but it came to refer to popular music in general. Among its most influential composers were Irving Berlin, George and Ira Gershwin, Jerome Kern, Richard Rodgers, Oscar Hammerstein and Cole Porter. They were heavily influenced by the sounds flowing downtown from Harlem.

Strict enforcement of prohibition forced the closure of many clubs in Chicago, putting jazz musicians there out of work. They moved to New York City, which became the center for jazz during the 1920s and '30s. The city's preeminence in radio and recording was a significant factor in attracting musicians who performed in venues like Harlem's Cotton Club. The 1930s saw the emergence of big-band jazz and swing orchestras led by such notables as Cab Calloway, Count Basie, Duke Ellington, Fletcher Henderson, Benny Goodman and Jimmy and Tommy Dorsey. The most enduring was Louis Armstrong, who lived in Queens. Not only did he lead bands and play the trumpet, but he also composed music, performed on stage, radio and TV and in film, and sang jazz, pop, blues and R&B.

The period also produced some brilliant, black, female performers. Arguably the greatest jazz singer of the age was Bessie Smith, who ended her days in Philadelphia, where she is buried. After winning a talent contest at Harlem's famed Apollo Theater in 1934 Ella Fitzgerald went on to become one of the great jazz singers. Born in Philadelphia, Billie Holiday learned her trade in New York's nightclubs before headlining at the Apollo.

In the 1940s Dizzy Gillespie, a celebrated jazz trumpeter, invented the bebop school of jazz improvisation with Charlie Parker and Thelonious Monk.

Although the popularity of jazz declined, the music has survived and can still be heard at the Lincoln Center and numerous small clubs, including the Village Vanguard on Seventh Ave in Greenwich Village.

With R&B in the 1950s, it was again New York City's role as a broadcasting and recording center that attracted performers like Fats Domino and Little Richard from other parts of the US. When white performers added bits of country music to R&B, it became known as rock and roll, a phrase first applied by New York disc jockey Alan Freed and which in black slang was a euphemism for sex. The legacy of Tin Pan Alley meant that many of the great early rock and roll songs were written by songwriters based here. Working from the Brill Building at 50th St and Broadway in midtown Manhattan, these tunesmiths included Jerry Lieber, Mike Stoller, Gerry Goffin, Carole King, Burt Bacharach and Hal David and producer Phil Spector.

In the 1950s black musicians combined rock and roll, R&B and gospel music to produce soul and doo-wop music, the latter so-called because of the meaningless phrases sung in the harmony line. Like other black-music forms these too were copied by white musicians. The most enduring doo-wop band to come out of New York was the Drifters, while Philadelphia produced so many soul musicians (such as the Delfonics, O'Jays and Stylistics) that the phenomenon was called 'Philadelphia Soul.' Jimmy Beaumont and the Skyliners were an all white band from Pittsburgh. The Del Vikings and Johnny Maestro & Brooklyn Bridge were two of the first racially mixed groups. The most successful of the white doo-wop groups

was Frankie Valli and the Four Seasons, from Newark, New Jersey.

Folk music had been around since colonial times, but out of the difficult economic circumstances and political and social upheavals of the 1930s it developed into an important means of popular expression. Many folk musicians came to live in New York. Among the most influential were the leftwing singers Woody Guthrie and Pete Seeger, two of the foremost popularizers of American folk in the middle decades of this century. They inspired the Greenwich Village folk-rock scene of the 1960s, which was led by Minnesota transplant Bob Dylan (who had his first gigs at the club Folk City, now called the Kettle of Fish) and also included Peter, Paul & Mary, the most popular acoustic folk group of that decade. Simon & Garfunkel, from Queens, also had their roots in this music.

The influence of the Beatles led many musicians to develop their own material. One of the most important, creative New York City bands to emerge in the 1960s was The Velvet Underground, led by Lou Reed and John Cale, who also introduced the modern concept of self-promotion through their association with artist Andy Warhol. Their songs of alienation and violence presaged the music of punk rock, which emerged in the 1970s as a reaction to the overly complex, self-important work of some rock bands. Punk artists sought to simplify music and make it more accessible; among them were the Ramones, who had a huge influence on the British punk scene. They performed in CBGB, a club on the Bowery in the Lower East Side and a proving ground for other bands like Talking Heads. CBGB continues the alternative tradition today.

One of the greatest singer-songwriters to surface in this period was Bruce Springsteen, who, in recognition of his talent, was simply called 'The Boss.' He is most closely associated with the Jersey shore, particularly the hardscrabble town of Asbury Park, and his songs often deal with the toughness and disillusionment of working-class life in America.

Around the same time as punk's emergence, there appeared disco music as captured in the film *Saturday Night Fever*. Disco queen Donna Summer dominated the Studio 54 scene.

Rap and hip-hop music and break dancing developed in the discos and streets of New York's black neighborhoods. The two originators were Afrika Bambaataa and Grandmaster Flash and it was spearheaded by Harlem's Sugar Hill Gang. This style of music soon spread to other cities and by the early 1980s it had gone mainstream with white performers either incorporating it into their music or doing straight rap themselves. Later black performers to emerge were the Beastie Boys, Salt 'n' Pepa (a female rap act) and influential but controversial Public Enemy who remain at the forefront of hip-hop. In the late 1990s the Fugees, a New Jersey hip-hop group, combined rap and rock in a commercial hybrid to become the US's top rap group. Its three members have all produced successful solo albums.

Acid jazz is a hybrid of jazz, soul, funk and hip-hop and has been promoted and performed by pioneer Miles Davis and the group Back 2 Basics. Younger jazz artists have embraced more traditional strains in jazz, with trumpeter Wynton Marsalis, sax sensation Joshua Redman and bass player Christian McBride leading the retro way.

Classical Music & Opera

The region has some of the foremost classical music and operatic institutions in the country, most of which undertake nationwide tours. In New York City the Lincoln Center for the Performing Arts is the venue for such prestigious organizations as the New York Philharmonic Orchestra, the Metropolitan Opera Company and the New York City Opera. Carnegie Hall is the venue for performances from solo to orchestral.

Though often overlooked, the New Jersey Symphony Orchestra, based at the New Jersey Performing Arts Center in Newark, travels the state and is worth a special mention.

Founded in 1924, the Curtis Institute of Music in Philadelphia is one of the world's leading centers for the advanced study of music. The Philadelphia Orchestra and the Pittsburgh Symphony Orchestra each have a world-class reputation. The Philadelphia Orchestra, like the New York City Ballet, makes its summer home in Saratoga Springs.

A student of the Curtis Institute of Music, Leonard Bernstein (1918–90) was the first major American-born classical conductor. He achieved fame in 1943 when he stepped in for an ailing conductor to lead the New York Philharmonic Orchestra, an event that wound up on the front page of the next day's *New York Times*. Later, Bernstein became musical director of the philharmonic while making frequent forays into popular music, most notably with the stage works *On The Town*, *Candide* and *West Side Story*.

Philadelphia's Marian Anderson (1902–93) was a noted contralto who broke racial barriers. She was the first permanent black member of the Metropolitan Opera Company, where she debuted in 1955. An earlier member of the company was Polish-born Marcella Sembrich (1858–1931) who settled in Bolton Landing in New York State's Adirondack region.

Theater

The theater is one of New York City's most noteworthy artistic institutions. After surviving periods of decline caused by the advent of talking pictures and then TV, Broadway and the surrounding district now have scores of theaters. They present a whole gamut of shows from experimental drama to big musical productions. At one time Philadelphia competed with New York City as the country's theatrical capital. In 1767, Thomas Godfrey's *The Prince of Parthia*, the first play written by an American colonist, was produced there. Today, however, the city is mainly a testing ground for shows en route to Broadway.

At the end of the 19th century and for more than two decades into the 20th, vaudeville (light or comic theater interspersed with song-and-dance routines or other variety acts) was the most popular form of theater in the country and New York City was its center. The main venue was the

Palace Theater in Times Square, although there were many other vaudeville theaters around town. The most famous vaudeville impresario was Florenz Ziegfeld (1867–1932) best known for his lavish revues, the Ziegfeld Follies, featuring female dancers. Vaudeville attracted performers from other forms of entertainment, including musicians from Tin Pan Alley, and when it finally died out in the 1930s, vaudeville performers like James Cagney and Groucho Marx were able to transfer their skills and experience to films, radio and TV.

Alternative, experimental drama arose in New York City in the 1950s and '60s, partly out of artistic rebellion and partly because of the prohibitive cost of performing on Broadway. New companies were formed, experimentation was encouraged and young actors were urged to explore their skills and take risks. Alternative theater today can be found Off Broadway and Off-Off Broadway, terms which refer as much to the scale and cost of a production as to a theater's location. In the 1990s, Off Broadway attitudes (or perhaps poses) were embraced by the mainstream, as stripped down productions of *Chicago* and *Rent* became Broadway hits.

Broadway and Times Square have experienced a renaissance, with big-dollar investment from companies like Disney inspiring a new generation of plays, which is trickling down to the Off Broadway and Off-Off Broadway scene. Mainstream theater relies mostly on big productions, as well as revivals and some imports from London's West End.

One of the great playwrights of the early 20th century was New York-born Eugene O'Neill (1888–1953), who won three Pulitzer prizes for his plays in the 1920s. In 1936 he also won the Nobel prize for literature. *The Iceman Cometh* (1946) was his last Broadway play before he died, and *Long Day's Journey into Night* (1956) was produced posthumously.

Death of a Salesman (1949), for which he received the Pulitzer prize, is the most powerful play by Arthur Miller. A year later he wrote *The Crucible* about the Salem witch trials, which had contemporary parallels with McCarthyism. His more recent plays,

Broken Glass (1994), about a middle-aged Jewish couple living in Brooklyn, and *The Ride Down Mount Morgan* (1995), about a man confronting his mortality, debuted in London before coming to the US stage. In his '80s, he continues to be a presence in American theater and on film with his screenplay for *The Crucible*.

Alternative theater has produced some of the most prestigious American playwrights, some of whose works have also been shown on Broadway. Sam Shepherd (born 1943) received a Pulitzer prize for *Buried Child* (1979) and later did the screenplay for *Paris, Texas* (1984). Lanford Wilson (born 1937) wrote about the post-Vietnam War world of a Southern family in *Tally's Folly* (1979). In plays like *Speed the Plow* (1987) and *American Buffalo* (1974), David Mamet (born 1947) examined the psychological and ethical issues of modern urban society.

Neil Simon (born 1927), possibly the modern playwright most closely associated with New York, has written many comedies set in the city, most of which have been made into movies. He received a Tony award for *Biloxi Blues* (1985), then again for *Lost in Yonkers* (1990), for which he was also given the Pulitzer prize. He now has a Broadway theater named after him, though his New York production, *London Suite* (1994), actually opened Off Broadway, downtown.

Musicals have always been a mainstay of New York theater, and the Tin Pan Alley composers (see Popular Music earlier) wrote many of the most memorable. George and Ira Gershwin straddled classical and contemporary music in such works as the opera *Porgy & Bess* (1935). Cole Porter wrote the music and lyrics for numerous sophisticated Broadway musicals such as *Kiss Me Kate* (1948) and *Can Can* (1953). Stephen Sondheim (born 1930) wrote varied and experimental popular Broadway fare including the lyrics for *West Side Story*, and music for *A Funny Thing Happened on the way to the Forum* (1962) and the Pulitzer-prize winning *Sunday in the Park with George* (1984).

Many famous performers had their career launched or achieved some of their greatest successes in New York City's theater. After their appearance together in *The Guardsman* (1924) the reputations of Alfred and Lynne Lunt were assured, and they went on to become the US's most successful acting partnership and now have a theater named after them. Carol Channing became a star after her appearance in the musical version of *Gentlemen Prefer Blondes* (1949) and appeared in numerous revivals of her signature role in *Hello Dolly*. Dustin Hoffman first developed his talents in the avant-garde theater of the 1960s and returned in the '90s to play Willy Loman in *Death of a Salesman*. Barbra Streisand's lead role in the Broadway musical *Funny Girl* (1964) brought her immediate stardom.

Dance

Modern Dance Modern dance, which challenged the strictures of classical ballet, was pioneered by Isadora Duncan (1877–1927), who spent four years in New York City before heading for Europe. Basing her ideas on ancient Greek concepts of beauty, she sought to make dance an intense form of self-expression.

In Los Angeles in 1915, Ted Shawn (1891–1972) and Ruth St Denis (1879–1968) formed Denishawn, a modern-dance company and school, which moved to New York in 1920 and remained the nation's leading company into the '30s.

Its most influential student was Pittsburgh's Martha Graham (1894–1991), who founded her Dance Repertory Theater in New York and a modern-dance school at Bennington College in Vermont. In her long career she choreographed over 140 dances and developed a new dance technique, now taught worldwide, aimed at expressing inner emotion and dramatic narrative. Her two most famous works were *Appalachian* (1944), dealing with frontier life, and *Clytemnestra* (1957), based on Greek myths.

Paul Taylor (born 1930) and Twyla Tharp (born 1942), two students of Martha Graham, succeeded her as the leading exponents of modern dance, but differed from her in that they borrowed themes from popular culture. Tharp danced with her own company till 1987, when she became artistic associate of the American Ballet Theater. Another student of Martha Graham, Alvin Ailey (1931–89) set up the Alvin Ailey American Dance Theater in 1958. His most famous work is *Revelations* (1960), a dance suite set to gospel music. Mark Morris (born 1956) is a celebrated dancer and choreographer who formed his own dance group in 1988, which performs at the Brooklyn Academy of Music.

City Center in New York City is the main venue for the dance companies of Martha Graham, Paul Taylor and others, along with the Joyce Theater in Chelsea.

Ballet The School of American Ballet was founded in 1934 by Russian-born choreographer George Balanchine (1904–83). He then became artistic director of the New York City Ballet when it was founded in 1948 and turned it into one of the best ballet companies in the world. He adapted traditional ballet to modern influences and set new standards in performance. The choreographic genius from New Jersey, Jerome Robbins (1918–98) took over from Balanchine in 1983. He had previously collaborated with Leonard Bernstein on several of Broadway's biggest musicals, including *West Side Story* (1957).

The New York City Ballet delights upstate visitors every summer in Saratoga Springs, its summer home. Saratoga Springs is also the home of the fine Museum of Dance.

The Pennsylvania Ballet, founded by Barbara Weisberger in 1964, and the Pittsburgh Ballet are also highly regarded.

Literature

New York City and Philadelphia were important literary centers as far back as colonial times, although the latter declined in relative importance during the 19th century. As New York City developed into the US's publishing capital – a position it retains today – it attracted writers from all over the country. Many of them had their works first published in the city's newspapers and magazines.

18th & 19th Centuries An important early writer was John Woolman (1720–72), a Quaker and abolitionist, whose *Some Considerations upon the Keeping of Negroes* (1756) was influential in the decades prior to the Civil War. Some early writers focused on the American Revolution. *The Federalist*, the country's first literary classic, was a collection of essays by Alexander Hamilton, James Madison and others recommending endorsement of the new constitution. Philip Freneau (1752–1832) was an outstanding, patriotic lyrical poet whose satirical work bridged 18th-century traditionalism and 19th-century romanticism.

An essayist and short-story writer, Washington Irving (1783–1859) was the first American literary figure to receive international recognition. His country estate was called Sunnyside, on the Hudson River near Tarrytown, NY, and the area around it is described by him in the stories 'Sleepy Hollow' and 'The Legend of Sleepy Hollow.' He also wrote a widely praised satire, *History of New York* (1809), under the pen name of Dietrich Knickerbocker.

In tribute to the book a group of writers adopted the term 'Knickerbocker' for their movement to develop a recognizably American literature. Foremost among them was James Fenimore Cooper (1789–1851), who drew images of the landscape and pioneer life on the American frontier in his *Leatherstocking* stories and of Native Americans in such works as *The Last of the Mohicans* (1826).

The Knickerbockers were satirized by literary critic, poet and Gothic horror-story writer Edgar Allan Poe (1809–49), who lived for a time in Philadelphia before settling in New York City. Among his most famous works are 'The Pit and the Pendulum,' 'The Black Cat' and 'The Raven.' An earlier Gothic writer, Charles Brockden Brown (1771–1810) was reputedly the first person in the US to earn a living solely by writing.

Margaret Fuller (1810–50), a contemporary of Poe and a fellow reviewer, wrote *Woman in the Nineteenth Century* (1845) disclosing conditions in prisons and hospitals. It helped inspire the later feminist movement in the US.

Prior to the Civil War a group of writers became known as Pfaff's Cellar because they used to meet at a place by that name on Broadway. Its leading member was Long Island's Walt Whitman (1819–92), whose exuberant poetry celebrated the plurality of American democratic society. His life work is contained in *Leaves of Grass* (originally published in 1855 and enlarged in later editions), which is considered one of the masterpieces of world literature. True to New York fashion, it earned him the distinction of having a mall named after him on Long Island.

As New York City's power in publishing grew during the second half of the century, it attracted more and more writers, some of whom lived in the districts around Gramercy Park and Madison Square. One of the most notable was Henry James (1843–1916), who, though he lived mostly in England, grew up in New York City and returned from time to time in later life. In *Washington Square* (1881) he described upper-class life in that area before the Civil War. The row houses that were occupied by New York society still line the northern edge of Washington Square Park today.

Early 20th Century A close friend of James' was Edith Wharton (1862–1937), who chronicled the gilded-age of New York City in the Pulitzer-prize-winning *Age of Innocence* (1920) and other works. However, most of her old New York – the original Metropolitan Opera house, the Metropolitan Museum of Art and the mansions of Fifth Ave's 'Millionaire's Row' – have disappeared or been altered beyond recognition.

In the 1920s an influential, lively and witty group of literary figures who had gotten to know each other writing for the *New Yorker* magazine met regularly at the Algonquin Hotel. They were known as the Algonquin Round Table and often invited people from the theater and film world to their lunches. Perhaps the most gifted of them was Dorothy Parker (1893–1967), who wrote poetry, plays and short stories as well as reviews for magazines. Others were the essayist Robert Benchley, and commentators

The *New Yorker*

The *New Yorker* was founded in 1925 by Harold Ross and Jane Grant. It began life as a humor magazine directed at a cultured, literate, inquiring audience who were depicted on its first cover by a cartoon of a monocled dandy watching a butterfly. This cover illustration is reused every year on the anniversary of the first edition.

The magazine gradually became more literary and regularly featured poetry and fiction, articles on prominent figures and significant social and political issues, and reviews of art, novels, movies and theater.

By the middle of the century the magazine had become an institution, but declining readership and revenue forced it to make significant changes, including the addition of photographs and more coverage of popular culture. Despite the changes, the *New Yorker* retained its satirical style, sophisticated humor and interest in human foibles.

Over the years the magazine has published and brought to prominence numerous literary figures. Early contributors to the magazine were the members of the Algonquin Round Table, including Dorothy Parker. Other contributors have included JD Salinger, Rebecca West, Ogden Nash, John Cheever, EB White, Marianne Moore, Raymond Carver, Ann Beattie, Rita Dove and John Updike.

Illustrations have always been a signature of the magazine, which has used the work of Rea Irvin (who designed the illustration for the very first cover), Charles Addams and Peter Arno.

When celebrity editor-in-chief Tina Brown took over the magazine she tried to bring its stodgy old ways up to date – to the dismay of old-line New Yorkers. She introduced photographs to the magazine and some writers quit the magazine in protest at her changes. In 1992 she hired as sports writer New Jersey–born David Remnick, who won a Pulitzer prize in 1994 for *Lenin's Tomb*, about the end of the Soviet Union. He subsequently replaced Tina Brown in 1999 as editor-in-chief, only the fifth in the *New Yorker*'s history.

The magazine continues to be an excellent source for local commentary and theater and movie reviews, as well as the site of 'Goings on about Town,' one of the best events calendars.

HL Mencken, Edna Ferber and James Thurber.

From the early 20th century onwards, Greenwich Village rose to prominence as an artistic and literary colony, and many writers achieved fame by contributing to its publications. Among these were the playwright Eugene O'Neill (see Theater earlier) and the poet ee cummings (1894–1962). Some of the early short stories of F Scott Fitzgerald (1896–1940) were published here, too, and with the success of his first novel, *This Side of Paradise* (1920), he became the chronicler and self-styled representative of the Jazz Age. A later collection of his short stories was published under the title *Tales of the Jazz Age* (1922). Many of his works feature upper-crust New York, and Long Island was the site for *The Great Gatsby* (1925), which

has been acknowledged as one of the finest American novels.

By the end of WWI, Harlem had become a vibrant, predominantly black neighborhood with a growing self-assertiveness and authors writing on the black American experience. The publication in 1917 by the short-lived Greenwich Village magazine *Seven Arts* of Claude McKay's story 'Harlem Dancer' is said to mark the start of the Harlem Renaissance, which reached its peak in the 1920s and '30s. As well as McKay, its leading authors included Wallace Thurman, Jean Toomer, Langston Hughes, Countée Cullen and Zora Neale Hurston. McKay's novel, *Home to Harlem* (1928), about a black army deserter, was a best-seller. Hurston's *Their Eyes were Watching God* (1937), whose theme is female independence and male oppression, became an important piece of feminist work.

Beat & Beyond The Beat movement of the 1950s had its origins in the previous decade when Alan Ginsberg and others were still students at Columbia University. Ginsberg moved to the East Village in 1953 and was soon joined by other members of the movement. Aided by drink and drugs, they rejected crass materialism and convention.

One of the early important Beat novels was William S Burroughs' *Junkie* (1953), a stark account of his early life as a drug addict. In 1956, when Ginsberg published a collection of verse called *Howl and Other Poems*, the publisher was tried but acquitted for having put out an obscene work. The media attention made Ginsberg famous. When Jack Kerouac's *On the Road* (written in one sitting, it's said, on a large ream of typewriter paper in the Chelsea Hotel) hit the bookstores in 1957, it became the compulsory reading of a generation. In the same period JD Salinger's *Catcher in the Rye* (1951) spoke to a generation of disaffected young Americans.

By the mid-1960s the Beat era was over, but it did influence the hippie movement (it was Ginsberg who coined the term 'flower power') and today's spoken word performers. Spoken word is an attempt to bring poetry to an audience so it can hear the voice of the poets and the rhythm and music of their poetry.

Though not a beat writer, Thomas Pynchon portrayed the restlessness of younger New Yorkers in *V* (1963). Alternatively, a group of writers including John Cheever and John Updike set out to document northeastern life of the upper-middle class during this time.

Modern Era A newer, more energetic style of writing dominated the 1970s and '80s, with some writers adopting phantasmagoric or gothic styles. Don DeLillo's *Great Jones Street* (1973) and Mark Helprin's *Winter's Tale* (1983) are prime examples of this disturbing view of society. Paul Auster, who lives in Brooklyn, won many followers

abroad for his *New York Trilogy* (1990) and wrote the screenplay for the Brooklyn-based movie *Smoke*.

The works of EL Doctorow (born 1931), including *Ragtime* (1975), *The Book of Daniel* (1971) and *World's Fair* (1985) are loftier ruminations on New York in its various eras, from turn-of-the-century boomtown to cold war ideological battleground.

Jay McInerney was first blessed, then cursed with association to the yuppified early 1980s with his blockbuster first novel *Bright Lights, Big City* (1984). *Bonfire of the Vanities* (1987) by Tom Wolfe (born 1931) followed up with its comic canvass of a city out of control and split along racial lines. Tama Janowitz, author of *Slaves of New York* (1986), covers much of the same ground and enjoys a life of literary celebrity, as has essayist Fran Liebowitz.

In the 1990s, new writers and spoken-word performers emerged in the East Village of New York City, debuting their work at various cafes, but for the most part the generation-X novelists have been based on the West Coast. One literary lion, Jonathan Lethem, has written several novels. His latest, *Motherless Brooklyn* (1999), a detective story whose hero has Tourette's Syndrome, paints a perceptive portrait of the borough.

Film
History Thomas Edison's laboratory in Orange, New Jersey, developed the first practical movie camera in the 1890s, with the sprocket system devised by Edison's employee William Dickson. Another employee, Edwin S Porter, produced the first real US movie and first ever box-office smash, *The Great Train Robbery* (1903). The film's success led to the emergence of the first permanent cinemas, called nickelodeons. Most early production studios were based in New York City, the national center of the movie industry up to WWI. Thereafter, most production moved to Hollywood.

The decade following the war was the heyday of the silent movie era, and the soaring skyscrapers of Manhattan inspired movies such as Fritz Lang's futuristic masterpiece *Metropolis* (1926).

Although the 1920s and '30s were a time when fewer mainstream films were being produced in New York City, the Harlem Renaissance made that neighbourhood a dynamic focal point for black movies. The most prominent black filmmaker was Oscar Micheaux, who fashioned around 40 feature-length films, many of which he wrote, produced, directed and edited himself. Few of his movies have survived, but a notable exception is *Body and Soul* (1924) with Paul Robeson.

In New York City in 1926, *Don Juan*, starring John Barrymore, was the first film with synchronized sound to be shown in a commercial theater. A disc with sound effects and music – but no talking – was played at the same time as the film. The following year, the appearance and success of *The Jazz Singer* with Al Jolson ushered in the talkies. The rise of talking pictures took many Broadway actors to Hollywood. Yet some movies continued to be made in New York City, allowing actors to work on a film while continuing their Broadway commitments.

With the arrival of sound, screen musicals came into favor. A memorable early example, *42nd St* (1933) is about a chorus girl plucked from obscurity to become a star in a Broadway show. *On the Town* (1949), about three sailors on shore leave in New York City, starred Gene Kelly and Frank Sinatra. Sinatra sang 'New York, New York' in the Rockefeller Center.

The greater realism that sound provided also boosted the popularity of gangster movies. One of the first was *Lights of New York* (1928), but the genre only really took off with the success of *Little Caesar* (1931). Three New York actors closely identified with the gangster movies of this period were Humphrey Bogart, James Cagney and Edward G Robinson, who forever created the tough-guy urban image portrayed to the rest of the world.

The search for realism also took filmmakers out onto the streets. Although the city had appeared in numerous films up to the 1940s, these had mostly been studio recreations. *Naked City* (1948), adapted from photographer Weegee's novel about New York police in pursuit of a murderer, was one of the first films to feature a substantial number of city locations.

After WWII, New York City became the center for avant-garde, experimental films typified by Andy Warhol and William Klein. The commercial success of Warhol's *Chelsea Girls* (1966) paved the way for other underground films and inspired later independent filmmakers.

Although TV was seen as a big threat to Hollywood in the 1950s, in New York City the combined presence of the theater, the major TV broadcasters and Madison Ave advertisers promoted the resurgence of the local film industry. Elia Kazan started as an actor and director in theater before making *On the Waterfront* (1954) about corruption on the city's docks. Sidney Lumet got his start in live TV and directed his first film, the courtroom drama *12 Angry Men*, in 1957, and has made many movies in the city since.

In the 1960s and '70s, Woody Allen and Martin Scorsese, born in Brooklyn and Queens, respectively, became strongly associated with the city. Martin Scorsese's films have usually shown the tougher, harder edge to life in the city. In the 1980s and '90s a new generation of filmmakers emerged, among them Spike Lee, whose early films, like *Do the Right Thing* (1989), depicted the black urban experience of the Brooklyn he grew up in. See New York in The Region as a Backdrop section, later in this chapter, for suggested features from these filmmakers.

The Region as a Backdrop Hundreds of feature films have been set in New York in particular, but also in New Jersey and Pennsylvania. The following is a sample of some of the more memorable.

New York One of the most unforgettable films set in New York City is the original *King Kong* (1933), in which a giant ape brought back from Africa terrorizes the city when it escapes. It was produced by Pittsburgh-born David O Selznick (1902–65). The Statue of Liberty features in the dramatic climax to

Woody Allen

Allen Stewart Konigsberg was born in Brooklyn in 1935 and grew up in Flatbush; he changed his name to Woody Allen in 1952. While he was still in high school he began writing gags for newspaper columnists like Earl Wilson and for TV comedians such as Sid Caesar and Art Carney. He also wrote sketches for stage revues. He created an image for himself as an intellectual, sex-obsessed loser – his self-deprecating style of humor became popular, and in 1961 he began performing stand-up comedy using his own material at New York City nightclubs and cafes. He was soon appearing on TV chat shows as well.

During the 1960s he wrote comic essays for the *New Yorker*, several Broadway hits and three books, and he also began his regular Monday-night performances as a jazz clarinetist at Michael's Pub.

His first foray into the world of movies was *What's New Pussycat?* (1965), in which he acted and for which he wrote the screenplay. In the decades since, he has been involved in a succession of films as director, screenwriter, actor or combinations thereof. Most of the films have been set in New York City. Though they feature superb roles for women and lots of comedy, the one constant is Allen's same anxiety-ridden Jewish character.

His most critically and commercially successful film is still *Annie Hall* (1975), which received three Oscars. One of the most autobiographical is *Manhattan* (1979), which dealt with the sex life of a neurotic TV comedy writer obsessed with New York. He also won a best-screenplay Oscar for *Hannah & Her Sisters* (1986) and was nominated again for *Crimes & Misdemeanors* (1989). Allen has never been to Hollywood to receive his awards (it's usually held on a Monday night when he is booked at Michael's).

In 1992–93, the spotlight was turned on him for a less welcome reason during the court battle with Mia Farrow for custody of their three children. He lost the battle when it was revealed that he was having an affair with her daughter Soon-Yi, whom she had adopted during her earlier marriage to André Previn. It was made even worse when Farrow accused him of molesting one of their children, though no evidence of this was ever found. Allen later married Soon-Yi.

He has always had a cult following, and those events don't seem to have had a long-term effect on his audience. He continues to make movies regularly, including *Everyone Says I Love You* (1996), a quirky musical comedy with Allen himself crooning famous love songs in New York, Paris and Venice. Familiar themes of love, sex and the pursuit of happiness reoccur in *Deconstructing Harry* (1997) and *Celebrity* (1998); in the latter, Allen's character, played by Kenneth Branagh, is a travel writer.

Alfred Hitchcock's *Saboteur* (1942), when Norman Lloyd falls to his death.

Breakfast at Tiffany's (1961) stars Audrey Hepburn as Holly Golightly, a somewhat-crazy call girl. Produced in the same year, *West Side Story* is an Oscar-winning musical set in New York's West Side. *Midnight Cowboy* (1969) is the story of a small-town hustler, played by Jon Voight, who teams up with the seedy, streetwise Ratso Rizzo, played by Dustin Hoffman.

In *Saturday Night Fever* (1977), John Travolta and the other boys from North Brooklyn live for their Saturday night disco dancing. Philadelphia-born Sidney Lumet's later films have been mainly set in New York City. *Dog Day Afternoon* (1975), about two inept robbers trapped in a Brooklyn bank and *Serpico* (1974), a true story about police corruption, are two of his better ones.

Most of Neil Simon's stage plays have been set in New York City and subsequently made into movies. These include *Barefoot in the Park* (1967), *The Odd Couple* (1968), *The Goodbye Girl* (1978) and *The Sunshine Boys* (1975). *Lost in Yonkers* (1991) is about growing up in the suburb.

One of Woody Allen's most autobiographical films set in New York was *Manhattan* (1979). About the sex life of a neurotic TV comedy writer obsessed with the city, it's a satirical, romantic, but affectionate ode to the Big Apple. His other New York films include *Annie Hall* (1977), *Bullets over Broadway* (1994), *Mighty Aphrodite* (1995) and *Celebrity* (1998).

Martin Scorsese directed *Taxi Driver* (1975), which starred Robert de Niro as a psychotic ex-Marine who drives a New York City taxi at night. He also directed *New York, New York* (1977), a musical tribute to the city set in the Big-Band era of the late 40s. *Goodfellas* (1990) was a gangster movie about real-life hood Henry Hill.

Starring Michael Douglas and directed by Oliver Stone, *Wall Street* (1987) satirized the 'greed is good' belief of the 1980s' high-rolling money traders. Katz's Deli on the Lower East Side was the setting for Meg Ryan's infamous 'orgasm' scene in *When Harry Met Sally* (1989). Brian de Palma's *Carlito's Way* (1993), starring Al Pacino and Sean Penn, is about an ex-convict from the barrio who tries to go straight. Director Wayne Wang's *Smoke* (1995) and *Blue in the Face* (1996), written by Brooklyn-based author Paul Auster, both starred Harvey Keitel as a cigar-store clerk in that borough.

Other recent films made on location in New York City are *Meet Joe Black*, *Stepmom*, *At First Sight*, *Rounders*, *Random Hearts*, *Thomas Crowne Affair*, *City Hall* and *Die Hard with a Vengeance*.

Spike Lee's chilling *Summer of Sam* (1999) is set in New York during the hot summer of 1977, when serial killer David Birkowitz (dubbed 'Son of Sam') terrorized the city. The film shows a wide range of city settings, from the streets of the Bronx to Studio 54. Other city locations used in box-office hits include Grand Ticino Restaurant, *Moonstruck*; King Cole Bar at the St Regis Hotel and The Oak Room at The Plaza Hotel, *The First Wives Club*; The Unisphere, *Men in Black*; the 21 Club, *One Fine Day*; and Moran's Restaurant, *Wall Street*.

Popular films shot elsewhere in the state have included *The Horse Whisperer* (Saratoga), *Age of Innocence* (Troy), *Ironweed* (Albany), *Nobody's Fool* (lower Hudson River Valley town of Cold Spring) and *Hello Dolly* (Troy). *Niagara*, a steamy 1953 melodrama starring Joseph Cotten and Marilyn Monroe, features fabulous location shots of the famous falls. Independent director Hal Hartley, a Long Island native, returned there for *The Unbelievable Truth* and *Trust*.

New Jersey New Jersey is featured in many films. One of the first films with a distinguishable narrative was Edwin S Porter's *The Great Train Robbery* (1903), filmed in the woods of northern New Jersey.

Hoboken's docks were the setting for Elia Kazan's intense thriller *On the Waterfront* (1954), in which stevedore Terry Malloy gets revenge on the dockland boss responsible for his brother's death. New Jersey often features in the movies of local filmmakers, such as John Sayles, whose films include *Return of the Secaucus Seven* (1979) and *City of Hope* (1992); Kevin Smith, who made *Mallrats* (1995), *Chasing Amy* (1997) and *Dogma* (1998); and Todd Solondz, who wrote and directed *Welcome to the Dollhouse* (1995) and *Happiness* (1998).

Woody Allen's *Stardust Memories* (1980) was filmed largely in Ocean Grove, with the town's auditorium standing in for the Hotel Stardust. In *Atlantic City* (1981), with Burt Lancaster and Susan Sarandon, some small-time crooks try to cash in on the city's new casinos.

Jersey Girl (1992) was a romantic comedy about class differences. *Copland* (1997), which was about cops, corruption, murder and mayhem, starred Robert de Niro and Sylvester Stallone.

Pennsylvania The *Philadelphia Story* (1940) is a romantic comedy about a spoiled, wealthy Philadelphia socialite starring Katherine Hepburn, Cary Grant and Jimmy Stewart (who won an Oscar for his role). The film was later remade as the musical *High Society* (1956), with Bing Crosby, Frank Sinatra and Philadelphia's own Grace Kelly. Adapted from Christopher Morley's popular novel, *Kitty Foyle* (1940) is a film about a working-class woman living in the Philadelphia suburb of Frankford and stars Ginger Rogers.

Cecil B de Mille's *The Unconquered* (1947), about the pioneering days in America, was partly shot in Cook Forest State Park in Northern Pennsylvania.

Steve McQueen met an alien in the 1958 sci-fi movie *The Blob*, set in the western Philadelphia suburb of Phoenixville. The following year Paul Newman played a lawyer in *The Young Philadelphians*. *The Molly Maguires* (1969), with Richard Harris and Sean Connery, tells the story of striking miners in 1870s Pennsylvania.

Sylvester Stallone's five-film Rocky series is about a Philadelphia boxer who makes the big time. Stallone won an Oscar for writing the original *Rocky* (1976). In *The Deer Hunter* (1978), starring Robert de Niro and Meryl Streep, Pittsburgh steel workers experience the horrors of Vietnam.

In *Blow Out* (1981) a presidential candidate dies in a car accident in Wissahickon Creek and a sound technician (John Travolta) suspects murder. Eddie Murphy and Dan Ackroyd swap social positions in Philadelphia in *Trading Places* (1983). In *Witness* (1985) Harrison Ford plays a Philadelphia cop who hides out on an Amish farm in Pennsylvania Dutch Country to protect the young witness to a murder that took place in a restroom in Philadelphia's 30th St Station.

In *Philadelphia* (1993), Tom Hanks is a young AIDS-afflicted lawyer battling the legal, physical and emotional ramifications of the disease and the prejudices surrounding it. *Gettysburg* (1993) is an epic tale of the three-day battle that altered the course of the Civil War.

Terry Gilliam's *12 Monkeys* (1995) is a vision of the future after a virus has wiped out most of the human race; Bruce Willis' character travels back in time to present-day Philadelphia to trace the cause of the virus. Locations include the elaborate John Wanamaker department store (now Lord & Taylor's), City Hall and Eastern State Penitentiary. Willis returned to Philadelphia in the psychological thriller *The Sixth Sense* (1999).

Television

Historically, New York City was the center of the TV industry, and the major networks still have their head offices there, but today many programs set in the city are taped in Los Angeles. Many of these programs are sold around the world and their images of New York City, with their unrealistically large apartments and equally unrealistically dangerous streets, are constantly transmitted into people's homes.

Some notable TV series with a New York City setting include *The Defenders, Kojak, McCloud, The Odd Couple, Cagney & Lacey, Seinfeld, Mad about You* and *Friends*. The TV series *Law & Order* is one of the few network shows shot entirely in New

York, though *NYPD Blue* visits several times a year for extensive location shots. HBO's *Sex and the City* is also filmed in New York. The city is also the backdrop for *Now and Again*, *Third Watch*, *Bellevue*, *Spin City* and the *Cosby Show*.

The NBC's *Today* show broadcasts from the Rockefeller Center and the ABC's *Good Morning America* broadcasts from Times Square as does the chat show *Late Night with David Letterman*. The current affairs program *60 Minutes* is produced in New York City.

In 1999, New Jersey gained a lot of attention (some would say notoriety) by serving as the setting for *The Sopranos*, a hugely popular TV series about a mobster and his family life.

Painting

There are fine examples of American art in the galleries and museums of the main cities, but one of the best places to study its development is the Whitney Museum of American Art in New York City. For an excellent, well-illustrated overview of the subject read Robert Hughes' *American Visions*.

Colonial Art The first colonists on the Atlantic seaboard had few resources and little time for fine arts, but decorated everyday household objects, perhaps as a response to the undomesticated wilderness around them. Religious art was prohibited by Puritans and the first paintings (around 1660) were portraits intended to document the social position of prominent colonists.

Portraitist Benjamin West (1738–1820), a self-taught artist from Pennsylvania, achieved limited success in America, then left for Britain and ultimately became a court painter to George III and president of the Royal Academy of Arts, which he helped found. West's *The Death of General Wolfe* was considered revolutionary because the participants in the Battle of Quebec were dressed in contemporary military uniforms, not Greco-Roman garb.

Neoclassicism West's studio became a center for American painters studying in London and did much to promote the standard of American painting. Portraits and history scenes achieved a high degree of realism and classical formality, sometimes highly romanticized, but, drawing inspiration from the American Revolution, he and others gave them a democratic flavor.

Charles Willson Peale (1741–1827) attended West's studio in 1776 but returned to fight in the revolution and to become a noted painter of history scenes and portraits. His subjects were among the most prominent political and social figures of the day.

American Landscape From about 1825, landscape painting became the strongest current in American art. It reflected the trend of territorial expansion and took a romantic, sometimes allegorical view of a wilderness that was rapidly disappearing in the eastern states. Asher Durand (1796–1886) and Thomas Cole (1801–48) were the leading figures of the Hudson School, which initially concentrated on the Catskill Mountains in New York State. Their 'luminist' emphasis on atmosphere and light was developed in the landscapes of Cole's student Frederic Edwin Church (1820–1900), who extended his subject matter to monumental paintings of New York's Niagara Falls, the Andes and the tropics.

Impressionism Impressionism in the US was best exemplified by the work of Childe Hassam (1859–1935), who explored revised forms of the style in his paintings of cityscapes and interiors. He was also a founding member of The Ten, a group of American impressionists who exhibited together up to WWI. Another impressionist painter, Pittsburgh's Mary Cassatt (1845–1926) was noted for her etchings and oil paintings of domestic scenes, though she spent most of her working life in Europe.

American Realism Thomas Eakins (1844–1916) was the first major artist to draw his inspiration from contemporary American urban life. He studied in Paris but spent his career in Philadelphia, painting surgeons, scientists, oarsmen and sailors in the context of their work or leisure. His paintings emphasized the human figure and perspective. His best known work is the depiction of a surgical operation in *Clinic of Doctor Gross* (1875).

In the early 20th century, a group of artists began to paint with the eye of the muckraking journalist – in New York, of course. Rejecting impressionism, which they saw as too refined, they insisted on a realism that represented urban, working-class life. They were later known as the Ashcan School. The best example is George Bellows (1882–1925), who portrayed the poor of lower Manhattan and the brutality of boxers.

Modernism US artists had followed cubism, fauvism and the early moves toward abstract art, and New York City's 291 Gallery displayed European modernist works from 1908.

In 1913, a young French painter, Marcel Duchamp (1887–1968), caused a sensation at the 1913 'Armory' show (officially called the International Exhibition of Modern Art) with his cubist *Nude Descending a Staircase*, which most critics noted didn't seem to portray a recognizable nude *or* a staircase. Duchamp told the newsman that was exactly the point, and thus the New York school of Dada was begun.

Taking its name from the French slang for hobbyhorse, the Dada movement was led by Duchamp, fellow countryman Francis Picabia and American artist Man Ray (1890–1976), who became known for their anti-war attitudes and deconstructive art that sought to shock and offend. By the '20s, most of the Dadaists had moved on – Ray to photography and Duchamp to full-time celebrity – but the Dada movement remained influential.

Others practised a hybrid form of expression, as in the paintings of Charles Demuth (1883–1935) and Charles Sheeler (1883–1965). Usually using urban and industrial America as their subject matter and identified by straight lines and geometric planes, their work was known as cubist realism or precisionism. The popular Georgia O'Keeffe (1887–1986) did the same with desert flowers and landscapes. In the mid-20th century she spent much of her time at New York's Lake George with her husband Alfred Stieglitz (who had introduced cubism to the US).

Painting thrived in Harlem during the Harlem Renaissance of the 1920s and '30s. One of the most prominent artists was Aaron Douglas (1899–1979), who did illustrations for such publications as Eugene O'Neill's *The Emperor Jones* (1926) as well as murals of black Americans and Africans.

Post WWII American art flourished after WWII with the emergence of a new school of painting called abstract expressionism, which was also called the New York School. Simply defined, it combined spontaneity of expression with abstract forms composed haphazardly. Abstract expressionism dominated world art until the mid-1980s, and two artists who carried it to its ultimate form were Jackson Pollock (1912–56) and William de Kooning (born 1904).

From the 1950s other artists began to borrow images, items and themes from popular culture, enlarging, coloring and combining them in the pop-art style made famous by Roy Lichtenstein (born 1923), Jasper Johns (born 1930) and Andy Warhol (1928–87). Warhol worked in many different media – drawing, painting, sculpture, silk-screening, photography, film, video and music. Accessible, enjoyable and popular, pop art was also identifiably American in its imagery.

During the same period there appeared a school of minimalist art, which uses simple geometric shapes and designs and little color. Frank Stella (born 1936) is among its leading exponents.

In the 1980s Warhol's legacy of artist-as-celebrity spawned a host of well-known painters and illustrators whose talent, to many critics, was somewhat questionable. But several of the artists/hustlers broke out from New York's SoHo gallery scene to become internationally known, among them Julian Schnabel, Kenny Scharf and the late Keith Haring.

The avant-garde art scene is now more international than American, though perhaps the faddishness and commercialism of contemporary art is American in itself. The Next Big Thing, for better or worse, is more likely to appear in the galleries of SoHo and Chelsea than anywhere else.

Photography

Photography developed as an art form at the end of the 19th century, especially under the guidance of Alfred Stieglitz (1864–1946), who produced a number of images of New York City but also did portraits, including many of his wife, Georgia O'Keeffe. Alice Austen (1866–1952) took photographs of the city's middle class as well as of immigrants and street life.

The city's role as a publishing center provided work opportunities for photographers, particularly with the addition of advertising agencies, fashion companies and news-gathering organizations. *Life* magazine was influential in the development of photojournalism and kept a large staff of photographers. Among the staff was Margaret Bourke-White (1904–71), who covered WWII and the Korean War and was one of

Andy Warhol

Andy Warhol (1928–87), one of the most influential US artists of the 20th century, was born in Pittsburgh, PA, in the district of Oakland. His parents were Polish immigrants and it was his mother's encouragement that prompted him to attend art classes at the Carnegie Institute (now Carnegie Mellon University).

When he graduated in 1949 he moved to New York City, where he became one of the country's leading freelance commercial artists. He developed an interest in pop art and by the early 1960s was exhibiting some of his now-famous works, including the innovative, multi-image silkscreen paintings of Marilyn Monroe and the Campbell's soup cans.

At this time he began making experimental 'underground' 16 mm movies; one of his first was the riveting *Sleep* (1963), an eight-hour silent film of a man sleeping. Warhol also managed the rock group The Velvet Underground, which toured the country as part of his multimedia presentation 'The Exploding Plastic Inevitable.' In the early '60s he opened a studio called the Factory (because it produced so many works), which became a center for avant-garde artists.

In 1968 he was near-fatally shot by Valerie Solanas who had been rejected as part of Warhol's artistic circle. (The 1996 film *I Shot Andy Warhol* dramatizes her life, the times and the event.) The following year he began publishing the magazine *Interview*, featuring articles on fashion, movies and glamorous people. During the 1970s and '80s he continued to make celebrity portraits as well as producing some of his greatest paintings.

After Warhol's death it was decided to devote a museum to the man and his work. He had lived most of his life and achieved his fame in New York City, but, despite some controversy, the museum was established in his home town of Pittsburgh.

Other films to portray Warhol were *The Doors* (1991), which gave a glimpse of Warhol and the Factory at work, and *Basquiat* (1996), with Warhol played by his old friend David Bowie, about New York City's art-crazed '80s.

Visitors enjoy the Andy Warhol Museum.

the first woman photographers assigned to cover the US armed forces. Another was Alfred Eisenstaedt (1898–1995), a portraitist and news photographer who took the famous image of a sailor kissing a nurse in Times Square at the end of WWII.

Weegee (1899–1968), whose real name was Arthur H Fellig, was a press photographer noted for his on-the-spot street photography, but who also did portraits of celebrities and world leaders. William Klein and Richard Avedon were fashion photographers who worked for magazines like *Vogue* and *Harper's Bazaar* in the 1950s and '60s. Avedon's work also included portraits and shots of Vietnam War protesters and the civil rights movement.

In more recent years, many photographers have become as famous for their commercial work as their more artistic endeavors. These include Stephen Meisel, Herb Ritts and Annie Liebowitz. Others have forged careers that almost never reach the general public through advertising. Prominent in this latter group are a few who have documented a unique urban scene, including Nan Goldin, who charted the lives (and many deaths) of her transvestite and drug-addicted friends from the '70s to the present day, and Cindy Sherman, who specializes in conceptual series (such as those inspired by movie stills and crime-scene photos).

Museums & Galleries

Important venues where American and international paintings and other artwork can be viewed include New York City's prestigious Metropolitan Museum of Art, the Museum of Modern Art, the Frick, especially for early American works; the Whitney Museum of American Art, especially for modern and contemporary art; the Brooklyn Art Museum and the Guggenheim Museum. The Albany Institute of History and Art has an excellent collection of Hudson River school paintings.

New Jersey is home to the outstanding Art Museum at Princeton University, and the Newark Museum also houses a distinguished art collection.

Pennsylvania boasts the Philadelphia Museum of Art and the Rodin Museum, two of the world's finest art museums, as well as the Barnes Foundation Gallery, which contains one of the world's largest private collections. Also in Philadelphia, the Pennsylvania Academy of the Fine Arts is a noted teaching center and the Second Bank of the United States is home to the National Portrait Gallery. In Pittsburgh, the Carnegie Museum of Art houses many famous paintings and the Andy Warhol Museum is dedicated solely to his work.

Architecture

America's early architectural styles reflect the different origins of the European settlers. These styles, at first distinct, eventually began to merge. The two main early influences in this region were Dutch and British.

Dutch colonial style, which survived to the end of the 18th century, consisted of practical, simple, solid buildings of stone, brick and wood. A distinctive feature of the architecture was Dutch doors – an upper door to let air in and a lower door to keep animals out. It occurred mainly in the Hudson Valley, western Long Island and northern New Jersey. Examples of the style include the Vechte-Cortelyou House in Brooklyn, as well as the Van Riper-Hopper House in Wayne, NJ.

When the British took over, their styles – particularly Georgian, named after the British monarchs – began to dominate. In America this influence lasted roughly from the start of the 18th century until the American Revolution. The red-brick buildings are simple and symmetrical, with delicate glass fanlights over large, elegant doorways. Philadelphia's Independence Hall is a notable example. After the revolution the style was modified slightly and became known as Federal.

From the late 18th century, neoclassical architecture based on Roman and Greek designs became popular, and many state houses and public buildings incorporating these designs were built well into the 20th century. Early exponents of neoclassicism were William Strickland, who designed the

Second Bank of the US (1824) in Philadelphia, and Benjamin Latrobe (1764–1820). During the mid-19th century, architects Richard Morris Hunt (1827–95) and Henry Hobson Richardson (1838–86) studied in Paris and on their return incorporated renaissance and Romanesque styles into their designs.

These architects also designed Gothic Revival buildings, another popular architectural style of the 19th century. It was given expression in many churches, like Trinity Church in New York City (1846), but was also used in colleges and universities (where it was called 'collegiate Gothic'). Examples include City College in upper Manhattan (at 138th St and St Nicholas Ave), and College Hall in the University of Pennsylvania. The most prominent exponent of Gothic Revival toward the end of the 19th century was Frank Furness (1839–1912) who designed numerous buildings in Philadelphia, including the Pennsylvania Academy of the Fine Arts. Gothic Revival was also used in the design of many early skyscrapers, like the Woolworth Building in New York City (1913).

Cass Gilbert (1859–1934) designed the Woolworth Building, but he was also one of the main proponents of the Beaux Arts style, a mixture of classical architecture and elaborate ornamentation, borrowed from Europe. He built New York City's Custom House (1907), now the Museum of the American Indian.

Stanford White (1853–1906), who designed the former Penn Station, was the most influential architect in New York at the turn of the century.

The prolific Frank Lloyd Wright (1869–1959), possibly the greatest architect of the 20th century, was innovative in his use of steel, glass and concrete, creating shapes and structures like nothing in the past. He also pioneered panel heating, indirect lighting, double glazing and air-conditioning. As well as the revolutionary Guggenheim Museum (1959) in New York City, Wright fans should visit Buffalo to see his many creations and southwestern Pennsylvania's Fallingwater (1939) and Kentuck Knob (1953), two famous homes.

It is with the skyscraper that the modern American city is closely identified, and no city more so than New York. The profile of the mid-20th century skyscraper was largely determined by New York 'air rights' ordinances, which required tall buildings to be stepped back from the street frontage as their height increased, allowing some sunlight down to the city streets. The effect was that of a tall, stepped pyramid exemplified in the 1930 Chrysler Building and the 1931 Empire State Building. Decorative details were only important at street level, in the lobby and the office and apartment interiors. Art deco was a feature of the 1932 Rockefeller Center and its Radio City Music Hall and was adopted for other new skyscrapers.

Ludwig Mies van der Rohe (1886–1969), a pioneer of glass skyscrapers, designed the exterior of the Seagram Building (1958), in Manhattan, that signaled the birth of the modern office tower. By using glass 'curtain walls' over a steel frame, the best buildings became abstract shapes – minimalist sculptures on a massive scale.

One response to the starkness of this style was postmodernism which reintroduced decoration, often in whimsical or incongruent ways, like the Chippendale-style pediment atop the AT&T building in New York City.

SOCIETY & CONDUCT

It's difficult to identify specific characteristics of this region that separate it from the wider US culture, largely because as the arts and media capital of the US it has helped to shape so much of that culture. One chief feature is the region's widespread urbanization. Its urban areas are perhaps the most ethnically diverse in the country. However, throughout the region those of Germanic background have always had a strong influence and there is a growing Hispanic influence. Successive waves of immigrants over the centuries have contributed to the broader culture, but many have retained or rediscovered aspects of their original culture. Whole neighborhoods are occupied by specific ethnic groups; statewide, it might be entire towns.

The Amish ('AH-mish') have kept their old customs and dress, and often resist the use of machinery. They still farm with horses and their buggies are a familiar sight in Lancaster County, PA, which has the largest community. Their folk art and cooking are famous. They attract a lot of attention from inquisitive tourists but don't like having photographs taken where their faces can be seen, as these are viewed as graven images.

Upstate New York has a distinctive New England feel – from the self-reliant air of many locals to the occasional Quaker community. Near the Canadian border many of the inhabitants have surnames and traditions tied to French-Canadian life.

The level of patriotism in the US is high and there's a very real sense of national pride. It's well to be aware of this when discussing political and social issues. Critical comments, especially from a foreign visitor, may be interpreted as a slight to national honor and provoke a negative reaction. Don't broadcast your animal rights convictions in a bar full of hunters or denounce clear-cutting in a mill town, for example, without having some idea of your audience. Other sensitive issues are gun control and abortion/right to life.

About the only bastion of fashion politesse are fancy restaurants and a few urban clubs, which still require jackets for men. In any other eatery you'll see everything from black T-shirts to $3000 suits.

RELIGION

The Constitution mandates separation of church and state, and the First Amendment says that Congress 'will make no law respecting an establishment of religion.' Thus prayers aren't allowed in public schools because that promotes religion, though the oath of allegiance refers to 'one nation under God,' and the words 'In God We Trust' are stamped on the currency. The teaching of creationism versus evolution in schools is an ongoing subject of political discourse.

Largely because of the immigrant nature of US society, travelers can find members of just about every religion, faith or sect in the major cities; even smaller towns may have several religious groups. Nominal allegiance is more widespread than church attendance, but many churchgoers are extremely devout.

The oldest religions in North America are Native American religions, greatly modified since contact with Europeans.

Numerically and culturally, the US is predominantly Christian, and Roman Catholics constitute the largest religious group in New York, New Jersey and Pennsylvania. Of the Protestant Christian groups the largest, in descending order, are Baptists, Methodists, Lutherans, Presbyterians and Episcopalians. Some Christian denominations have almost exclusively African American adherents, including the African Methodist Episcopal (AME) Church whose birthplace was the Mother Bethel Church in South Philadelphia. Black churches have been enormously important in promoting the culture and well-being of the black community.

Judaism is the largest non-Christian religion and Islam finds many adherents in the black community. Pennsylvania still has a number of Quakers, whose ancestors, most notably William Penn, founded the state on the principle of religious tolerance. That tolerance attracted religious refugees from Europe, including the Amish and Mennonites, who live mostly in the region known as Pennsylvania Dutch Country.

LANGUAGE

English is spoken throughout the US, though it's not designated as the country's official language. Some believe that it should be, especially those concerned about the increasing use of Spanish, the next most widely spoken language. In Lancaster County west of Philadelphia the Amish speak English when conducting business with outsiders, but at home speak Pennsylvania Dutch, in fact a German dialect ('Dutch' is a corruption of 'Deutsch'). In upstate New York near the Canadian border some French is spoken.

American English is relatively uniform when compared to, say, the varieties of English spoken in Britain, but there are regional differences in accent, idiom and use of vocabulary. Many foreign visitors will be familiar with American English from the mass media, but may have difficulty following, for example, the African American idioms of Harlem or Philadelphia. Conversely, not all Americans are familiar with foreign accents and may have some difficulty understanding English spoken by foreign visitors.

In the 18th century Ben Franklin, by trade a printer, sought to rationalize and standardize the disordered spelling of the English language. Although his plans weren't adopted at the time, he did influence Noah Webster, who published the *American Dictionary of the English Language* in 1828. It was Webster who popularized the change in spellings of such words as 'theatre' to 'theater,' 'colour' to 'color,' for 'centre' to 'center' and 'popularise' to 'popularize.' Today you still see alternative spellings for the same word.

However, what really makes American English so distinctive is the wealth of new words and phrases that it has brought to the language. Several Native American words have come into English including *moccasin*, *moose* and the region's mountains, rivers and other place names. Many more have come from European languages via immigrants (for many of whom New York City or Philadelphia was their first point of arrival). From German there are words like *loafer*, *hoodlum* and *kindergarten*; from Dutch, *boss*, *stoop* (a front step) and *nitwit*; from Yiddish, *schmuck*, *schlock* and *schmaltz*; from Italian, *pasta*, *pizza* and other food words; from Spanish, *canyon*, *ranch*, *rodeo* and food words as well as place names.

The vast majority of Americanisms come from the US itself. American inventiveness produces not only new products, but new words to describe them and a new vocabulary to market them. American business, technology, media, military and especially sports have all contributed words that are so familiar that it's easy to forget they're American.

For more on the American language see Lonely Planet's *USA phrasebook* and Bill Bryson's *Made in America*. For more on 'New York-speak' see Language in the Facts about New York chapter.

Facts for the Visitor

HIGHLIGHTS

Throughout the region, the forests' fall foliage is a huge attraction – even in New York City when the trees in Central Park lighten up. It's hard to believe the trees can produce so many shades of red, yellow and orange. You can easily enjoy the fall spectacle in all three states with a few hours' drive through the countryside, or make an extended tour of it, staying at inns and B&Bs along the way.

New York

The extensive variety of New York's topography and cultures is stimulating, and often startling. Elements of the busy Big Apple, the agricultural Midwest and New England formality exist side by side. Ithaca and Saratoga Springs are two of the most culturally blessed towns in the state, and much more navigable than New York City. Saratoga Springs, in fact, has the best of both worlds in the summer – in addition to horseracing, the city is the summer home to the New York City Ballet and the Philadelphia Philharmonic Orchestra.

New York City The view of Manhattan's skyline from the Staten Island or Statue of Liberty ferries is a familiar yet spectacular sight. You can also visit many different cultures in the space of a single 90-minute walk. For example, walk from Lower Manhattan to Chinatown, then to Little Italy, continuing on to the funky downtown cafes in the East Village, where you'll also find Polish, Middle Eastern, Indian, Korean and Japanese restaurants and antique stores. (Not to mention the astounding number of different cultures found in the boroughs of Brooklyn and Queens.)

That, of course, is in addition to all the architectural and high-culture attractions of the city, including the Metropolitan Museum of Art and the Museum of Modern Art, two world-class institutions on any art-lover's 'must-see' list.

As for shopping in New York City, to paraphrase the song, if you can't buy it here, you can't buy it anywhere. The city offers true bargains (or the best selection at reasonable prices) in clothing, jewelry, electronics, antiquities, food and just plain kitsch. You just need to know where to look and – most importantly – patronize reputable dealers in each category.

Long Island Some of the country's prettiest beaches are accessible by public transportation from New York City. You can reach the family-oriented Robert Moses State Park in about an hour by train from New York City's Penn Station. The more exclusive Hamptons, at the southern fork of Long Island, and the wineries of the north fork, are both about three hours by car or train.

The Catskills Lush, gentle mountain getaways exist alongside excellent hiking, biking and winter skiing, with ridge-top views of the Hudson Valley below. Woodstock, home to a thriving arts and music community, retains a convivial village atmosphere.

Hudson Valley This region, an easy daytrip from New York City, is the site of Washington Irving's *The Legend of Sleepy Hollow*. In summer visit pick-your-own apple orchards, opulent mansions and riverside villages with funky bookstores and sidewalk bistros.

Finger Lakes Visit over 50 wineries between Canandaigua and Seneca lakes to sample the juice of the grape. In this region you'll also find elegant glacial lakes, charming Ithaca and the Cornell University Plantations, river gorges and Taughannock Falls, the highest waterfalls in the state.

Cooperstown Many people make the pilgrimage to this picturesque, franchise-free, lakeside village (covered in the Capital District & Mohawk Valley chapter). It is home to the National Baseball Hall of Fame, always popular with children of all ages.

Adirondack Park This park, a combination of private and public lands, is an outstanding year-round wilderness region – a canoeing, biking and hiking mecca. It's home to Lake Placid, site of the 1932 and 1980 Winter Olympics. Don't miss the excellent collection of Native American lore at the Six Nations Indian Museum, in Onchiota.

Saratoga Springs One of New York's loveliest towns, this is home to old-world mineral baths and to the fastest thoroughbred horses in the country at the Saratoga Race Course, where strolling minstrels delight summer crowds. Saratoga's Caffe Lena is the nation's oldest coffeehouse, and still hosts some of the country's best folk musicians.

Niagara Falls Seeing is believing. Take a boat ride under the spray of the falls or stand next to the roar of the water. In the evening, check out nearby Buffalo's lively theater and cafe scene.

New Jersey
Newark Long overshadowed by New York City, New Jersey's largest city is often ignored by travelers. But if you're in the area for a stay of one-week or more, it's worth considering a quick day-trip to visit the well-regarded Newark Museum, as well as the Ironbound district just east of the train/bus/subway station. There, in the safe and friendly neighborhood of Portuguese immigrants, you'll find a good selection of well-priced establishments offering delicious barbecue fare and wonderful baked goods.

Great Adventure Theme Park Just west of the Jersey Shore is the northeast's largest theme park. It features a drive-through safari park and more than 100 heart-stopping rides.

Princeton This quintessential university town has a beautiful, self-contained campus and an important art collection.

Cape May You can check out many perfectly maintained Victorian homes in this charming town, a short trip from Atlantic City or Philadelphia. You can sun yourself on the town's beach (featuring pristine white sand) or go bird-watching in the nearby observatory. There's also the free Cape May County Park & Zoo, with an impressive collection of animals.

New Jersey State Aquarium Though Camden is one of the most crime-ridden and depressed cities in the state, the aquarium is an admirable and successful attempt to bring life back to the waterfront. It's an easy day trip from Philadelphia's Penn's Landing.

Atlantic City This well-known beachfront community offers three reasons to visit: gambling, gambling and gambling. Be prepared to be assaulted by the gaudy glory of the gaming culture.

Pennsylvania
Philadelphia Many of Philadelphia's historical buildings have been restored, and National Independence Historic Park, with its Independence Hall and Liberty Bell, serves as a reminder of the country's struggle for independence from England.

Take a scenic trip along Kelly Drive beside the Schuylkill River in Fairmount Park, the world's largest city park. At the southern end of the park is the Philadelphia Museum of Art, one of the country's largest and best art museums, and there's a great view of the city from its steps.

Another highlight is Philadelphia's food. It has some of the country's top restaurants, offering the best in haute cuisine, but quality and variety can be found at all budget levels.

Pennsylvania Dutch Country The commercialism notwithstanding, the area of Lancaster County east of the city of Lancaster is worth visiting to see how the Amish retain their traditional way of life in the face of the modern world.

Gettysburg National Military Park The Battle of Gettysburg was one of the most significant in US history. Despite some tacky tourist traps, a visit to the town itself, with its historic buildings, the battlefield and the National Cemetery (where Abraham Lincoln gave his famous address), is well worth it.

Pittsburgh Take the Monongahela or Duquesne Incline up Mt Washington for a terrific view of the city's downtown, known as the Golden Triangle. The Andy Warhol Museum, dedicated entirely to the artist's work, stands as testimony to his importance in modern American and world art. The Cathedral of Learning, in the suburb of Oakland, is an amazing example of Gothic architecture.

Laurel Highlands This popular recreational area in southwestern Pennsylvania is most notable for white-water rafting and canoeing on the Youghiogheny River.

Allegheny National Forest This huge forest in northern Pennsylvania is a great place to get away from it all. It has plenty of wildlife and provides opportunities for outdoor recreation such as hiking, canoeing, cross-country skiing, bird-watching and fishing.

The Poconos The Pocono Mountains in northeastern Pennsylvania form a picturesque part of the state, and include the scenic Delaware Water Gap National Recreation Area. The small town of Jim Thorpe retains its historic character. Skiing, hiking, mountain biking, canoeing and sailing are popular outdoor recreational activities.

Hershey The home of the Hershey chocolate empire contains a heavily promoted but tacky theme park, with its mock chocolate factory, amusement park and nearby zoo. Children love it.

SUGGESTED ITINERARIES

There's no 'right' way to see this region, but it may help to have some sample itineraries. Modify and combine these to suit your interests. In the summer and the fall foliage season try to visit cities on weekends and

Gripes about the Region

- The entire region's seasonal weather extremes
- The high cost of accommodations and car rental in New York City – prohibitively expensive for residents and visitors alike
- The inability to buy liquor or wine from stores anywhere in New York State on Sunday – barbaric
- The hassle of getting to and from New York City's airports
- Getting around, a common gripe among New Yorkers who are annoyed by such facts of life as tolls on the New York State Thruway
- Mud and blackflies in the Adirondacks, enough to drive people to the edge in May and June
- New Jersey's traffic cops
- New Jersey's turnpike tolls and beach fees
- Queuing for gasoline in summer weather in New Jersey, where it's illegal to pump your own gas
- Some of Gettysburg's tacky museums
- Hersheypark

country towns and resorts on weekdays. This will help you find lower prices and avoid the crowds.

One Week or Less

If you only have a week or less, base yourself in New York City. In the first two days you can visit the top attractions – the Statue of Liberty, Empire State Building, South Street Seaport, Rockefeller Center and Wall St, provided you get to the paid-admission spots early in the morning.

Then take another day or two to see the museums, such as the Metropolitan Museum of Art, along Fifth Ave's Museum Mile, and stroll in Central Park. Exploring some well-known neighborhoods – SoHo, Chinatown and Greenwich Village – can be done in one (exhausting) day and might include a trip on the Staten Island Ferry. On any night, take in a famous bar, Broadway show or a club show.

For excursions, you can easily plan a day trip to the lower Hudson Valley, offering an entertaining lesson in history. Tarrytown, on the east bank of the Hudson River, was the home of Washington Irving and his famous Sleepy Hollow stories. Woodstock is in the Catskills, just west of the Hudson Valley and a two-hour drive from Manhattan. This picturesque town has a thriving arts community and offers great views of the Hudson Valley from Overlook Mountain. Further north along the Hudson, between the towns of Hyde Park and Rhinebeck, the Franklin D Roosevelt Library & Museum and Eleanor Roosevelt's comfortable cottage, Val-Kill, are historic landmarks.

Or try to visit New Jersey's major northern cities of Hoboken, Newark or Jersey City. If you're too exhausted to travel to New York City's outer boroughs, all three of these New Jersey cities are readily accessible by public transportation (including ferries from Manhattan to both Jersey City and Hoboken).

It's also possible (though a bit exhausting) to take a bus for a day trip to Atlantic City, NJ. The college towns of Princeton or the state capital of Trenton are also good day trips. The activity-oriented visitor can head by car to the Poconos region of northern Pennsylvania; winter skiing and summer amusements such as hiking and horseback riding are popular in places such as the Delaware Water Gap.

From New York City, a day trip to Philadelphia to see its historic sites and perhaps one or two of its museums is quite feasible by public transportation. If you're driving – and you leave early enough – you might take in some of the sights to the north of Philadelphia such as Washington Crossing Historic Park and the village of New Hope in Bucks County.

Two Weeks

In the second week you can explore further afield to get some taste of the variety of the region. Your itinerary will change depending on the season, but the following may be helpful.

Heading north to upstate New York, continue through the Hudson Valley, past Albany, to Saratoga Springs, a small town with a lot to do and home to culture, horses and bottled water. The town was famous in the 19th century for its European-like spas – the Lincoln and Roosevelt Baths. Take a short drive to view the ornate mansions on N Broadway, just south of Skidmore College. The nearby Saratoga Battlefield, in 1777, was the site of the most pivotal battle of the War of Independence.

Returning to New York City, Cooperstown offers a day or two of touring. In addition to the Baseball Hall of Fame, the James Fenimore Cooper Museum and the Farmers' Museum are both fascinating. Otsego Lake on the edge of town is a must, if only to recover from a busy trip to Cooperstown. The park by the lake is lovely and shaded.

Along the coast south of New York City you can spend a day or so at one or two of the Jersey Shore communities such as Ocean Grove, before heading west to Princeton, then to Camden to visit the New Jersey State Aquarium. From there it's just a short hop across the Delaware River into Philadelphia.

Central Philadelphia is fairly compact, so it's possible to see its major sights – Penn's Landing, Old City, Independence National Historic Park, the Fairmount Parkway museums, South St, Society Hill, Italian Market – before heading to the nearby northwestern picturesque suburbs of Germantown, Manayunk or Chestnut Hill. If you still have time you might consider making a trip out to Valley Forge, Brandywine Valley or Pennsylvania Dutch Country.

Three Weeks or More

With three weeks to spend, you'll have time to see New York City, Philadelphia and other major sights, as well as venturing to some of the more remote areas of the region, many of which are of interest to outdoor enthusiasts. The region is small enough that you can combine many of the routes described below.

Upstate New York With more than seven days to spare, continue north past Saratoga Springs to Lake George and the Adirondack Mountains. Adirondack Park is home to the famous Lake Placid, but many others lakes – including Blue Mountain, Saranac and Long Lakes – adorn this gentle rolling landscape. Hiking trails and canoe trails along chains of lakes and extensive rivers are common.

Exit the Adirondacks to the west through Watertown, then head south through Syracuse to Ithaca, which is on the southern tip of Cayuga Lake in the Finger Lakes region. Ithaca is a cultural gem and a great place to begin a tour of the Finger Lakes. In fact, you can drive west in a zigzag fashion through the lakes, often finding splendid towns at the ends of each lake. Keuka Lake is famous for several wineries, and there's a self-guided winery tour that takes you around the lake. Further west is the beautiful but less-frequented Canandaigua Lake, with the charming town of Naples to the south.

Alternatively, start your upstate New York trip in the Finger Lakes region and continue north from Naples to visit the George Eastman House in Rochester. This is the home of the Kodak company, and the lavish mansion houses one of the best photography exhibits in the state.

Continue west to Buffalo with its Frank Lloyd Wright homes, Albright-Knox Art Gallery and proximity to Niagara Falls – time your visit to see the falls in the late afternoon light, from the Canadian side. Allow ample time to cross the border, even though it's only a short drive. Southwest New York is notable for the Chautauqua Institution, on the shore of Chautauqua Lake: It's an American classic, having served as a center for education and the arts since 1874.

From there you can enter northern Pennsylvania and the Allegheny National Forest.

However, to return to New York City, take Route 17 east to Salamanca, just north of New York's Allegany State Park, and onto Route 417. This is one of the state's most scenic roads, passing through Corning, home of the Corning Glass Center.

Continuing east, Ithaca, Cooperstown and the western Catskills are on the return route to New York City.

New Jersey In New Jersey, seven spare days provide enough time to visit the gambling tables of Atlantic City and, assuming you haven't lost all your money, a restful day or two in the charming town of Cape May, which is at the state's southern tip. From there you can walk along New Jersey's whitest (and cleanest) beach or track migratory birds at Cape May Point State Park.

Pennsylvania In Pennsylvania, after visiting Pennsylvania Dutch Country head west to Gettysburg and spend a full day wandering around the historic town and touring the Civil War sights of Gettysburg National Military Park.

Pittsburgh is a few hours' drive west from Philadelphia, and it requires a couple of days to take in the views from Mt Washington, tour the Andy Warhol Museum and visit the Carnegie complex in Oakland. The Laurel Highlands are southeast of the city, and the main attractions there are whitewater rafting, canoeing and hiking. Rafting is at its best in spring when the rivers are at their highest and whitest. Allow at least a couple of days. Frank Lloyd Wright's Fallingwater and Kentuck Knob are also here.

Another four or five days allows you to devote time to outdoor recreational pursuits in the huge Allegheny National Forest, in northern Pennsylvania, before heading east along scenic Route 6 to the Pocono Mountains, also rife with natural beauty and a wide range of outdoor activities. This trip is particularly worthwhile in autumn when the forest foliage changes color. From northern Pennsylvania you can head north to see the attractions of western New York, and from the Poconos it's only a few hours drive to New York City.

PLANNING
When to Go

The region has many events and festivals throughout the year, and it may be worth planning your itinerary around some of them. See the Public Holidays & Special Events section later in this chapter and the Special Events sections in the regional chapters.

The least hospitable months are November to February, when it's cold and rainy and daylight hours are short. For skiers, however, that's when many of the best snowfalls occur, and in the cities many cultural institutions, such as symphony orchestras, operas and theaters, are the most active.

In the Adirondacks, 'mud season' arrives after the first thaw of spring. And, anywhere from late May to early July, the 'fifth season' arrives with its prominent, hungry guest, the black fly. It bites.

Summers can get really hot, and warm air from the Gulf of Mexico can make the humidity stifling. 'Tourist season' is Memorial Day (last Monday in May) to Labor Day (first Monday in September). From mid-July through August summer resorts are busy, accommodations fully booked and restaurants crowded. But in numerous communities along the Jersey Shore, summer is the only time to visit: Many accommodations, amusements and restaurants that can't survive on local trade shut down by mid-September.

Mid-September through October is also busy, when people come to see the magnificent fall colors of the forests. Visitors often combine this with some early Christmas shopping in New York City's department stores or the factory outlets of New Jersey and Pennsylvania.

Perhaps the best time to travel is late spring (late April to May) before schools close and families hit the road, and early fall (early September) after the summer rush and before the fall-foliage tourists arrive. Especially during the week at these times, accommodations are more readily available and there's less traffic. The weather is generally mild and pleasant, though storms sometimes occur, particularly along the coast.

What Kind of Trip

This largely depends on your interests and the amount of time and money at your disposal. The longer you stay, the more likely you'll step outside the often-superficial world of the tourist, and the lower your relative daily expenses will be. If you're visiting from abroad and able to work or study here, make the most of the opportunity.

Try to allow enough time to do a walk or two through the countryside, and spend a couple of days somewhere off the beaten track. New York City and Philadelphia are great cities, but they can be expensive and are only part of what there is to experience.

Outside major cities there's often limited public transportation, so you may want to consider renting or buying a car. Alternatively, you can visit most attractions by guided tour from the metropolitan centers. That way, you get an overview of the region and an idea of where you might want to return to spend more time.

Traveling alone is fine, provided you follow the normal precautions, and it is a great way to meet new people. Hostels and campgrounds are good places to meet fellow travelers, and B&Bs are a good way to meet locals who may offer insights unavailable at the nearby tourist office.

Maps

The maps in this book provide a useful first reference, and excellent maps are available throughout the USA.

Street & Highway Maps Lonely Planet publishes a useful laminated foldout map of New York City with bus and subway information. City and town maps are available, free or low cost, from local tourist offices and chambers of commerce. These vary from useless to very detailed. Free, detailed state maps are distributed by state governments. Before you leave, you can order maps from the state tourism boards (see the Tourist Offices section that follows) or pick them up at highway tourist offices (known as welcome centers or thruway centers). See the Local Tourist Offices section.

The American Automobile Association (AAA) issues comprehensive, dependable highway maps, free to members or for a few dollars to nonmembers. These range from national, regional and state maps to detailed maps of cities, counties and even relatively small towns.

Publishers providing a similar range of maps are Hagstrom, Rand McNally and Gousha Travel Publications; these can be bought at bookstores, convenience stores, gas stations, etc.

Topographical Maps The US Geological Survey (USGS) topographical maps cover the USA at a scale of 1:24,000. They're superb close-up maps for hiking, backpacking or intensive exploration by car. Information on ordering maps is available from the USGS National Center (☎ 703-648-4000, 888-275-8747), Map & Book Sales, 12201 Sunrise Valley Drive, Reston, VA 20192. You can also order maps from its website (www.usgs.gov). Camping stores, National Park Service (NPS) visitor centers and US Forest Service (USFS) ranger stations sell USGS maps of their immediate area.

The NPS provides maps of parks, National Recreation Areas (NRAs), national reserves and national trails. USFS ranger stations sell maps of national forest areas for a few dollars.

Jimapco (☎ 518-899-5091), 2095 Route 9, Round Lake, NY, 12151, publishes the best commercial topographic maps for all hiking regions in New York state. It maintains a website (www.jimapco.com).

Atlases If you plan to do a lot of traveling – especially hiking or biking – in a particular state, you might want to purchase a state atlas.

The DeLorme Mapping Company (☎ 207-865-4171), PO Box 298, Yarmouth, ME 04096, publishes large-format atlases and gazetteers of all New York, New Jersey and Pennsylvania. They contain detailed topographic and highway maps at a scale of 1:150,000, as well as helpful listings of campgrounds, historic sites, parks, natural features

and even scenic drives. The atlases cost $17 each, and DeLorme maintains a website (www.delorme.com).

ADC The Map People (☎ 703-750-0510, 800-232-6277), 6440 General Green Way, Alexandria, VA 22312, sells state and city atlases for Pennsylvania; the website is www.adcmap.com.

What to Bring

It's better to start light and pick up items along the way as you need them.

A travel pack – a combination of backpack and shoulder bag – is a good item for carrying gear. A travel pack's straps can be tucked inside the pack when not needed, making it easy to handle in airports and on crowded public transportation. It also looks reasonably smart and can be made reasonably theft-proof with the addition of a small combination lock, or even just a safety pin, that holds the zip tags together.

The clothing that you pack will depend on the season. Bring a raincoat or an umbrella any time of year, and some warm clothes even in summer if you intend to visit areas of higher elevation. Insulation works on the principle of trapped air, so several layers of thin clothing are warmer than a single thick one (and are easier to dry). Dress is usually casual.

A packing list might include a warm sweater; solid, comfortable, waterproof shoes; shower shoes for shared bathrooms; waterproof jacket; combination padlock; neck pouch or money belt; small daypack; wide-brimmed hat; gloves; water bottle; and toiletry bag.

A sleeping bag is useful in hostels and when visiting friends; get one that can also be used as a quilt. A sleeping sheet with a pillow cover is necessary if you're staying in hostels, though you can buy or rent one at the hostel.

Other possible items include a compass (for orientation on walks), alarm clock or watch with an alarm function, adapter plug for electrical appliances and a shortwave radio with the capability to tune-in to the region's hundreds of radio stations.

TOURIST OFFICES
Local Tourist Offices

Each state is divided into tourism regions, each with its own tourist bureau to provide information on the local area. The bureaus' addresses are given in the state's vacation guide, available from the state tourist office (see below). Each state also maintains a series of tourist offices (called 'welcome centers' in New Jersey and Pennsylvania and 'thruway centers' in New York) strategically positioned on the turnpikes and interstate highways.

In many towns free visitor information is given by the chamber of commerce (sometimes called Convention and Visitors' Bureau or CVB). These are membership organizations for local businesses (hotels, restaurants, etc). Although they often provide maps and other useful information, they usually don't tell you about nonmember establishments which are often the smallest and cheapest, and they may be unaware of public transportation options.

In this book, addresses and phone numbers for tourist offices and chambers of commerce are given in the Information section under individual town headings.

State Tourist Offices

State tourist offices will send you excellent detailed road maps and colorful vacation guides listing each state's main attractions, plus listings for accommodations and other useful information.

The state authorities are as follows:

New York State Division of Tourism
(☎ 800-225-5697)
PO Box 2603, Albany, NY 12220-0603
The website is iloveny.state.ny.us.

New Jersey Commerce & Economic Growth Commission
(☎ 609-777-0885, 800-847-4865)
PO Box 820, Trenton, NJ 08625
The website is www.visitnj.org.

Pennsylvania Center for Travel, Tourism & Film Staff
(☎ 717-787-5453, 800-847-4872)
453 Forum Building, Harrisburg, PA 17120
The website is www.state.pa.us/visit.

Tourist Offices Abroad

US embassies and consulates abroad may have some tourist information (see the Embassies & Consulates section later in this chapter).

Some US cities, states and regions have tourism offices in the UK that can only be contacted by phone. A list of phone numbers is available from the US embassies or consulates. There's no number for New York state or Pennsylvania, but there are telephone numbers for the Port Authority of New York & New Jersey (☎ 020-7659-0320) and New Jersey state (☎ 0125-272-7325).

VISAS & DOCUMENTS

To make replacing lost or stolen documents easier, photocopy important travel documents and keep copies in a separate, safe place from the documents themselves.

Passports & Visas

To enter the USA, Canadians must have proof of Canadian citizenship, such as a citizenship card with photo ID or a passport. Visitors from other countries must have a valid passport, and most visitors also require a US visa. Check out the US State Department's website for visa information (travel.state.gov/visa_services.html).

However, there's a reciprocal visa-waiver program that allows citizens of certain countries to enter the USA without a US visa for stays of 90 days or less. The countries include: Andorra, Argentina, Australia, Austria, Belgium, Brunei, Denmark, Finland, France, Germany, Iceland, Ireland, Italy, Japan, Liechtenstein, Luxembourg, Monaco, the Netherlands, New Zealand, Norway, San Marino, Slovenia, Spain, Sweden, Switzerland and the UK. Under this program you must have a roundtrip ticket that's nonrefundable in the USA, and you're not allowed to extend your stay beyond 90 days.

Other travelers need to obtain a visa from a US embassy or consulate. In most countries the process can be done by mail.

Your passport should be valid for at least six months longer than your intended stay in the USA, and you'll need to submit a recent photo (37mm x 37mm) with the application. Documents of financial stability and/or guarantees from a US resident are sometimes required, particularly for those from developing countries.

Visa applicants may be required to 'demonstrate binding obligations' that will ensure their return home. Because of the requirement, those planning to travel through other countries before arriving in the USA are generally better off applying for their US visa while they are still in their home country rather than when on the road.

The most commonly issued visa is a Non-Immigrant Visitors Visa (B1 for business purposes, B2 for tourism or visiting friends and relatives). A visitor's visa is good for one or five years with multiple entries, and it specifically prohibits the visitor from taking paid employment in the USA. If you're coming to the USA to work or study, you'll probably need a different type of visa, and the company or institution to which you're going should make the arrangements. Allow six months (in advance of your trip) for processing the application. (See also the Work section later in this chapter.)

Visa Extensions If you want to stay in the USA past the date stamped on your passport, contact the local office of the Immigration & Naturalization Service (INS; ☎ 800-375-5283, or look in the local telephone directory's white pages under 'US Government – Immigration & Naturalization Service') *before* your visa expires (see the stamped date on your visa). If you remain more than a few days past the expiration date, the INS may assume you want to work illegally. At an interview with the INS, you'll need to explain why you didn't leave by the expiration date, and you'll have to convince officials that you're not looking for work and that you have enough money to support yourself until you do leave. It's a good idea to bring a US citizen with you to vouch for your character, and to bring some

HIV/AIDS & Entering the USA

Anyone entering the USA who isn't a US citizen is subject to the authority of the Immigration & Naturalization Service (INS). The INS can prevent someone from entering or staying in the USA by excluding or deporting them. This is especially relevant to travelers with HIV (human immunodeficiency virus) or AIDS (acquired immune deficiency syndrome). Though being HIV-positive isn't a ground for deportation, it is a 'ground for exclusion,' meaning that the INS can invoke this rule and refuse to admit an HIV-positive visitor to the country.

Although INS officers don't test people for HIV or AIDS at the point of entry into the USA, they may try to exclude anyone who answers 'yes' to the following question on the non-immigrant visa application form: 'Have you ever been afflicted with a communicable disease of public health significance?' An INS officer may also stop someone who seems sick, is carrying AIDS/HIV medicine or appears to be from a 'high-risk group' (ie, gay), though sexual orientation itself isn't a legal ground for exclusion. Visitors may be deported if the INS later discovers that they are HIV-positive but didn't declare it. Being HIV-positive isn't a 'ground for deportation,' but failing to provide correct information on the visa application is.

If you can prove to consular officials that you're the spouse, parent or child of a US citizen or legal permanent resident (green-card holder), you are exempt from the exclusionary law, even if you're HIV-positive or have AIDS.

Immigrants and visitors who may face exclusion should discuss their rights and options with a trained immigration advocate within the USA before applying for a visa. For legal immigration information and referrals to immigration advocates, contact the National Immigration Project of the National Lawyers Guild (☎ 617-227-9727), 14 Beacon St, suite 506, MA 02108, or the Immigrant HIV Assistance Project, Bar Association of San Francisco (☎ 415-782-8995), 465 California St, suite 1100, San Francisco, CA 94104.

proof that you have enough currency to support yourself.

Short-Term Departures & Re-Entry It's easy to make trips across the border to Canada, but upon return to the USA, non-Americans may be subject to full immigration examination. Always take your passport when crossing the border. If your immigration card has plenty of time left on it, you'll probably be able to re-enter with the same one, but if it has nearly expired, you'll have to apply for a new one, and border control may want to see your onward air ticket, sufficient funds, etc.

Citizens of most western countries don't need a visa for Canada, so it's no problem to cross to the Canadian side of Niagara Falls or to Quebec. All foreign travelers entering the USA by bus from Canada may be closely scrutinized – a roundtrip ticket that takes you back to Canada will make the INS less suspicious.

Travel Insurance

A travel insurance policy to cover theft, loss and medical problems is a good idea. This should cover you not only for medical expenses and luggage theft or loss, but also for cancellations or delays in your travel arrangements, and everyone should be covered for the worst possible case, such as an accident requiring hospital treatment and a flight home. Coverage depends on your insurance and type of ticket, so ask both your insurer and ticket-issuing agency to explain the finer points.

Many travel agencies sell medical and emergency repatriation policies but these can be relatively expensive for what you get. It's advisable to discuss travel insurance with your health care provider or regular insurance agent for comparison of coverage and costs. Make sure you have a separate record of all your ticket details or, better still, a photocopy of the ticket. Also, make a copy of your travel insurance policy in case you lose the original.

Purchase travel insurance as early as possible. If you buy it the week before you fly,

you may find, for example, that you're not covered for delays to your flight caused by strikes or industrial action. Insurance may seem expensive, but it's nowhere near the cost of a medical emergency in the USA.

The following companies offer various sorts of travel and health insurance:

Access America, Inc
  (☎ 212-490-5345, 800-284-8300)
  600 Third Ave, New York, NY 10116
  The website is www.accessamerica.com.

Tripguard Plus
  (☎ 800-423-3632, fax 818-892-6576)
  16933 Parthenia St, North Hills, CA 91343
  The website is www.tripguard.com.

In the UK contact:

Europ Assistance
  (☎ 020-8680-1234)
  252 High St, Croydon, Surrey CR0 1NF
  The website is www.europassistance.com.

Driver's License & International Driving Permits

Most foreign visitors can legally drive in the USA for up to a year with their home driver's license. An International Driving Permit (IDP) is a useful adjunct and may have more credibility with US traffic police, especially if your home license has no photo or is in a foreign language. Your home automobile association can issue an IDP, valid for one year, for a small fee. You must carry your home license together with the IDP.

Automobile Association Card

If you plan on doing a lot of driving in the USA, it might be beneficial to join your national automobile association. Members of the American Automobile Association (AAA) or an affiliated automobile club may be entitled to lodging, car rental and sightseeing admission discounts. More importantly, membership gives you access to AAA road service in an emergency. See the Car & Motorcycle section in the Getting Around chapter for additional information on AAA.

Hostel Card

Most hostels in the USA are members of Hostelling International-American Youth

Hostel (HI-AYH). For more information see the Hostels section under Accommodations later in this chapter.

Student & Youth Cards

If you're a student, bring your school or college identification or get the International Student Identity Card (ISIC) so that you can take advantage of student discounts. The GO 25 card, issued to those ages 12 to 25 can help you get a reduced rate on airfares, car rental and other travel expenses. Both the ISIC and GO 25 card are issued at many budget travel agencies, colleges and universities.

Seniors' Cards

For information on senior discounts, see the Senior Travelers section later in this chapter.

EMBASSIES & CONSULATES
US Embassies & Consulates Abroad

US diplomatic offices abroad include:

Australia
Embassy: (☎ 02-6214-5600, www.usis-australia .gov/embassy.html) 21 Moonah Place, Yaralumla, ACT 2600
Consulate: (☎ 02-9373-9200, www.usconsydney .org) Level 59 MLC Center, 19-29 Martin Place, Sydney, NSW 2000
Consulate: (☎ 03-9526-5900, www.usis-australia .gov/melbourne) Level 6, 553 St Kilda Rd (PO Box 6722), Melbourne, VIC 3004
Consulate: (☎ 08-9231-9400, www.usis-australia .gov/perth) St George's Court, 13th floor, 16 St George's Terrace, Perth, WA 6000

Austria
Embassy: (☎ 1-31339-0, www.usembassy-vienna.at) Boltzmanngasse 16, A-1090, Vienna

Canada
Embassy: (☎ 613-238-4470, 800-283-4356, www.usembassycanada.gov) 100 Wellington St, Ottawa, ON K1P 5T1
Consulate: (☎ 902-429-2485) 2000 Barrington St, Cogswell Tower, suite 910, Halifax, NS B3J 3K1
Consulate: (☎ 514-398-9695) 1155 rue Saint-Alexandre, Montreal, Quebec H2Z 1Z2
Consulate: (☎ 416-595-1700) 360 University Ave, Toronto, ON M5G 1S4
There are also consulates in Calgary, Quebec City and Vancouver.

Denmark
Embassy: (☎ 35-55-32-44, wwwusembassy.dk) Dag Hammarskjölds Allé 24, 2100 Copenhagen

Finland
Embassy: (☎ 9-171-931, www.usembassy.fi) Itäinen Puistotie 14, 00140 Helsinki

France
Embassy: (☎ 01 43 12 22 22, www.amb-usa.fr) 2 rue Saint-Florentin, 75382 Paris Cedex 08

Germany
Embassy: (☎ 228-339-1, www.usembassy.de) Deichmanns Aue 29, 53170 Bonn
Embassy: (☎ 030-932-0233) Clayallee 170, 14195 Berlin
There are also consulates in Dusseldorf, Frankfurt, Hamburg, Leipzig and Munich.

Greece
Embassy: (☎ 10721-2951, www.usisathens.gr) 91 Vasilissis Sophias Blvd, 10160 Athens
There is a consulate-general in Thessaloniki.

Ireland
Embassy: (☎ 01-688-7122, www.indigo.ie/usembassy-usis) 42 Elgin Rd, Ballsbridge, Dublin 4

Israel
Embassy: (☎ 3-519-7575, www.usis-israel.org.il) 71 Hayarkon St, Tel Aviv
There is a consulate in Jerusalem.

Italy
Embassy: (☎ 6-46-741, www.usis.it) Via Vittorio Veneto 119/A, 00187 Rome

Japan
Embassy: (☎ 3-224-5000) 1-10-5 Akasaka Chome, Minato-ku, Tokyo

Mexico
Embassy: (☎ 5-209-9100, www.usembassy.org .mx) Paseo de la Reforma 305, Colonia Cuauhtémoc, 06500 México, DF
There are consulates in Ciudad Juárez, Guadalajara, Hermosillo, Matamoros, Mérida, Monterrey, Nuevo Laredo and Tijuana.

Netherlands
Embassy: (☎ 70-310-9209, www.usemb.nl) Lange Voorhout 102, 2514 EJ The Hague
Consulate: (☎ 20-575-5309) Museumplein 19, 1071 DJ Amsterdam

New Zealand
Embassy: (☎ 9-3003-2724) General Bldg, 29 Shortland St, Auckland

Spain
Embassy: (☎ 1-906-421431 from Spain only, fee payable; US passport holders can call ☎ 91587-2251) Calle Serrano 75, 28006 Madrid

Sweden
Embassy: (☎ 08-783-53-00, fax 660-58-79) Strandvägen 101, S-115 89 Stockholm
Switzerland
Embassy: (☎ 31-157-1-54, 357-72-34, fax 357-73-98) Jubiläumsstrasse 95, 3005 Bern

UK
Embassy: (☎ 020-7499-9000, www.usembassy.org.uk) 24 Grosvenor Square, London W1A 1AE

Consulate: (☎ 0131-556-8315, fax 557-6023) 3 Regent Terrace, Edinburgh EH7 5BW
Consulate: (☎ 028-90328-239, fax 90248-482) Queen's House, 14 Queen St, Belfast BT1 6EQ

Embassies & Consulates in the USA

Embassies are in Washington, DC. The presence of the United Nations in New York City means that nearly every country in the world maintains diplomatic offices in Manhattan. Some also have diplomatic representation in Philadelphia. To obtain the telephone number of an embassy or consulate not listed below call directory assistance for the city in which you hope to find a consulate (Washington ☎ 202-555-1212, New York City ☎ 212-555-1212, Philadelphia 215-555-1212). For information you can also check the yellow pages telephone directory under the listing for 'Consulates.'

Australia
Embassy: (☎ 202-797-3000, fax 797-3168, www.austemb.org) 1601 Massachusetts Ave NW, Washington, DC 20036
Consulate: (☎ 212-245-4000) International Bldg, 636 Fifth Ave, New York, NY 10011

Canada
Embassy: (☎ 202-682-1740, www.cdnemb-washdc.org) 501 Pennsylvania Ave NW, Washington, DC 20001
Consulate: (☎ 212-596-1700) 1251 Ave of the Americas (Sixth Ave), 16th Floor, New York, NY 10020-1175
Consulate: (☎ 412-392-2308), 1 Gateway Center, 9th Floor, Pittsburgh, PA 15222

France
Embassy: (☎ 202-944-6200) 4101 Reservoir Rd NW, Washington, DC 20007-2171
Consulate: (☎ 212-606-3699) 934 Fifth Ave, New York, NY 10021
Consulate: (☎ 215-851-1474) 1 Liberty Place, Philadelphia, PA 19103-2793

Germany
Embassy: (☎ 202-298-4000, fax 298-4249, www.germany-info.org) 4645 Reservoir Rd NW, Washington, DC 20007-1998
Consulate: (☎ 212-308-8700) 460 Park Ave, New York, NY 10022

Ireland
Embassy:
(☎ 202-462-3939, www.irelandemb.org) 2234 Massachusetts Ave NW, Washington, DC 20008
Consulate: (☎ 212-319-2555) 515 Madison Ave, New York, NY 10022

Israel
Embassy: (☎ 202-364-5500, fax 364-5423, www.israelemb.org) 3514 International Drive NW, Washington, DC 20008
Consulate: (☎ 215-546-5556) 230 S 15th St, 8th Floor, Philadelphia, PA 19102

Italy
Embassy: (☎ 202-328-5500, fax 462-3605, www.italyemb.nw.dc.us/italy) 1601 Fuller St NW, Washington, DC 20009
Consulate: (☎ 212-737-9100) 690 Park Ave, New York, NY 10021
Consulate: (☎ 215-592-7329) Public Ledger Building, 6th and Chestnut Sts, suite 1026, Philadelphia, PA 19106

Japan
Embassy: (☎ 202-238-6700, fax 238-2187, www.embjapan.org) 2520 Massachusetts Ave NW, Washington, DC 20008
Consulate: (☎ 215-553-2170) Mellon Bank Center, 1735 Market St, Room 731, Philadelphia, PA 19101

Mexico
Embassy: (☎ 202-728-1600, www.embassyofmexico.org) 1911 Pennsylvania Ave NW, Washington, DC 20006

Netherlands
Embassy: (☎ 202-244-5300, fax 362-3430, www.netherlands-embassy.org) 4200 Linnean Ave NW, Washington, DC 20008
Consulate: (☎ 212-246-1429) 1 Rockefeller Center, New York, NY 10020
Consulate: (☎ 215-520-9591) 45 Brennan Drive, PO Box 8047, Bryn Mawr, PA 19101-8047

New Zealand
Embassy: (☎ 202-328-4800, fax 667-5227, www.emb.com/nzemb) 37 Observatory Circle NW, Washington, DC 20008
Consulate: (☎ 212-832-4038) 80 Third Ave, Suite 1904, New York, NY 10017

UK
Embassy: (☎ 202-588-6500, fax 588-7850, britain-info.org) 3100 Massachusetts Ave NW,

Washington, DC 20008
New York British Information Services:
(☎ 212-745-0444, 752-5747) 845 Third Ave,
New York, NY 10017

Your Own Embassy

As a foreign visitor, it's important to realize what the embassy of the country of which you're a citizen can and can't do.

Generally speaking, it won't help much in an emergency situation if the trouble you're in is your own fault. Remember that while here, you're bound by US state and federal laws. Your embassy won't be sympathetic if you're jailed for committing a crime locally, even if such an action is legal in your own country.

In genuine emergencies you might get some assistance, but only if other channels are exhausted. If your tickets, money and documents are stolen, your embassy might help get you a new passport, but it won't give you a free ticket home or a loan for onward travel – you're expected to have insurance. Your embassy will help someone in your home country get in touch with you.

Embassies no longer operate mail holding services for travelers.

If you're going to be spending any length of time in a remote area it's a good idea to register with your embassy.

CUSTOMS

US customs allows each person over the age of 21 to bring 1 liter of liquor and 200 cigarettes duty free into the USA. US citizens are allowed to import, duty-free, $400 worth of gifts from abroad, and non-US citizens are allowed to bring in $100 worth. If you're carrying more than $10,000 in US and foreign cash, traveler's checks, money orders and the like, you need to declare the excess amount. There is no legal restriction on the amount that may be imported, but undeclared sums may be subject to confiscation.

MONEY
Currency

The US dollar is divided into 100 cents (¢). Coins come in denominations of 1¢ (penny), 5¢ (nickel), 10¢ (dime), 25¢ (quarter), 50¢ (half dollar – rare) and $1 (the silver dollar and the gold coin). Notes ('bills') come in denominations of $1, $2 (rare), $5, $10, $20, $50 and $100.

Exchange Rates

At press time, exchange rates were as follows:

country	unit		US dollars
Australia	A$1	=	$0.63
Canada	C$1	=	$0.69
Euro	€1	=	$0.99
France	FF1	=	$0.15
Germany	DM1	=	$0.50
Hong Kong	HK$1	=	$0.10
Japan	¥100	=	$0.91
New Zealand	NZ$1	=	$0.50
United Kingdom	UK£1	=	$1.61

Exhanging Money

Banks in cities exchange cash or traveler's checks in major foreign currencies, though banks in outlying areas don't do so very often, and it may take them some time. Nearly all banks buy and sell Canadian currency. If you're changing US to Canadian dollars, you're more likely to get a better rate at a Canadian bank. Almost any business on either side of the US–Canadian border will honor a fair exchange rate, so you should be aware of what it is. Some businesses near the border accept Canadian dollars 'at par,' meaning they'll accept Canadian dollars as though they were US dollars, in effect giving you a substantial discount on your purchase.

Thomas Cook and American Express offices and exchange counters at airports also exchange foreign currencies, though you'll probably get a better rate at a bank. Thomas Cook and American Express usually don't charge a fee for changing their traveler's checks into cash. In the main cities avoid cash-exchange kiosks, which charge a hefty currency-exchange fee.

Cash & Traveler's Checks Though carrying cash is more risky, it's still a good idea to travel with some for the convenience. It's useful to help pay all those tips and some smaller, more remote places may not accept credit cards or traveler's checks. Traveler's checks offer greater protection from theft or loss and in many places can be used as cash. American Express and Thomas Cook are widely accepted and have efficient replacement policies. Keep a record of the check numbers and the checks you have used and keep the record separate from the checks themselves. The numbers are necessary to obtain a refund of lost checks.

It's best to bring traveler's checks in US dollars, which can be used at most restaurants, hotels, gas stations and big stores as if they were cash. Get them in $50 and $100 denominations. Traveler's checks in a foreign currency can only be changed at a bank or at one of the few exchange counters. This can be inconvenient and might require an exchange fee, and you may not get a good exchange rate. If you're reluctant to buy US dollar traveler's checks up front because you think your currency might appreciate against the dollar, it would be better to rely on credit cards and ATMs.

ATMs Automatic teller machines (ATMs) are open 24 hours a day at most banks, as well as at shopping centers, airports, train stations, grocery stores, busy streets and casinos. You can withdraw cash from an ATM using your credit card (Visa, Master Card, etc); this will usually incur a fee. Alternatively, most ATMs are linked with one or more of the main ATM networks (Plus, Cirrus, Exchange, Accel), and you can use them to withdraw funds from an overseas bank account if you have a card affiliated with the appropriate network. The exchange rate on ATM transactions is usually as good as you'll get.

Check with your bank or credit card company for exact information about using its cards at ATMs in the USA. If you'll be relying on ATMs, bring more than one credit card and keep them separate. Don't forget your security code or PIN (personal identification number), but don't write it on the card. Contact your bank immediately if you lose your ATM card.

In Pennsylvania ATMs are known as money access centers (MACs).

Credit & Debit Cards Major credit cards are accepted by car rental agencies and most hotels, restaurants, gas stations, shops and larger grocery stores. Many recreational and tourist activities can also be paid for by credit card. The most commonly accepted cards are Visa, MasterCard (EuroCard, Access) and American Express. However, Discover and Diners Club are also accepted by a fair number of businesses.

You'll find it hard to perform certain transactions without one. Ticket buying services, for instance, won't reserve tickets over the phone unless you offer a credit card number, and it's difficult to rent a car without a credit card (you may have to put down a cash deposit of several hundred dollars). Even if you prefer traveler's checks and ATMs, it's a good idea to have a Visa or MasterCard for emergencies.

Places accepting Visa and MasterCard are also likely to accept debit cards. A debit card deducts payment directly from the user's savings account and users are charged a small fee for the transaction. Check with your bank to confirm that your debit card is accepted in the USA.

Carry copies of your credit card numbers separately from the cards. If you lose your credit cards or they are stolen, contact the company immediately. The following are toll-free numbers for the main credit cards:

American Express	☎ 800-528-4800
Diners Club	☎ 800-234-6377
Discover	☎ 800-347-2683
MasterCard	☎ 800-826-2181
Visa	☎ 800-336-8472

International Transfers You can instruct your bank back home to send you a draft. Specify the city, bank and branch to which you want your money directed, or ask your home bank to tell you where a suitable one is, and make sure you get the details right. The procedure is easier if you've authorized someone back home to access your account.

Money sent by telegraphic transfer should reach you within a week; by mail, allow at least two weeks. When it arrives it will most likely be converted into local currency – you can take it as it is or buy traveler's checks.

You can also transfer money through American Express, Thomas Cook or Western Union, though the latter has fewer international offices. These transfer services are expensive.

Security

Usually, there's nothing to worry about, but if you're being cautious, don't carry more cash than you need for the day. Carry your money in an inside pocket, money belt or your socks, rather than in a handbag or in an outside pocket. It's a good idea to divide your money and credit cards and stash them in several places. Most hotels and hostels provide safekeeping, so you can leave your money and other valuables with them. A safety pin or key ring to hold the zipper tags of a daypack together can help deter theft.

Costs

You can travel reasonably cheaply in this region if you know how. What you spend depends upon several factors, when and where you travel, how you travel and your age. When calculating costs remember to factor in taxes and tipping.

Seasonal Costs The busiest travel seasons are July and August (high summer or in-season), and late September through mid-October (fall foliage season, also considered in-season). Prices for hotels, transportation and attractions are generally highest at these times.

City vs Country Generally speaking, accommodations in cities are more expensive during the week, less expensive on Friday, Saturday and sometimes Sunday nights. In small towns, resorts and the countryside, inns and motels are cheaper during the week, more expensive on weekends. Thus, you should plan to visit cities on weekends,

and venture out into the country during the week, if possible.

Sightseeing & Attractions Admission prices to museums and other attractions run from free to $15. Children are usually charged half to three-quarters of the adult price, and seniors and students often get discounts of 10% or more. Some public museums have a free period, free day or cheaper entry once a week or month. Unless otherwise stated, prices in this book are for adults/children.

Accommodations Camping is the cheapest option if you're on a limited budget and mainly interested in non-urban adventure. You can camp for free in many places and cook for yourself in these campgrounds. Some full-service campgrounds charge up to $30 a night for a site with recreational vehicle (RV) hookups, but most of them are less expensive.

Hostels exist, but they're relatively few, sometimes inconveniently located and usually charge around $13 per person (except in New York City where the cost is almost double). The cheapest motels, usually in commercial strips outside town, start around $45/55 for a single/double. You can find satisfactory mid-range accommodations for $70 to $90 a double in most places, and some towns have luxury hotels with rooms from $100 to infinity. There are also world-class resorts where you can pay more than $230 a day. B&Bs start at about $60 for a single, but most are in the $75 to $150 range.

In hotels, beware of grossly inflated charges for some services, especially telephone and laundry. Ask about these before you incur any extra expenses. Many hotels have pay phones (cheaper than calling from your room), and cheap coin-operated laundries outside the hotel are an alternative to expensive hotel laundry charges.

Food & Drink Food is reasonably priced. If you buy food at markets you can get by quite cheaply; in small corner stores food items tend to be 20¢ to 30¢ more expensive. Even the smallest town has a fast-food restaurant where you can get a large hamburger, soft drink and french fries for about $4 or $5. Good restaurant meals can be found for $10 or less. Many towns have all-you-can-eat restaurants where you can fill up for $6 to $12. You can eat well any night in any town for less than $25 per person. Interestingly, dining in a restaurant outside major cities where the choices are limited can be more expensive.

Soft drinks are cheap and a cup of brewed coffee costs around $1. A six-pack (of 12oz bottles) of domestic beer costs $6 to $8 in a supermarket or liquor store, but a bottle of the same beer ranges from $2 to $5 in a bar or restaurant.

Transportation Intercity transportation is inexpensive considering the distances involved. Buses are normally the cheapest way to get around, especially with bargain-priced special deals. Standard train fares are usually more expensive than buses, but advance purchase fares, rail passes and other deals might make it less expensive. Fares on buses and trains are cheaper Monday to Thursday. The cost of flying varies greatly, but cheap tickets are sometimes available and air passes can be a good value.

In some areas a car is the only way of getting around. Car rental is available in most towns, and weekly rates can be about $120 a week for the smallest (sub-compact) cars, but more often rentals begin around $150 for a week. In New York City, car rental can be very expensive, starting at $60 a day for a compact car and rising sharply. Liability and collision insurance can add $16 or more a day. Gasoline (petrol) is cheap, ranging from about $1.15 to $1.75 for a US gallon, depending on the location and grade of fuel.

Special Deals At some tourism information centers there are racks of brochures for hotels, motels, inns, restaurants, tours and attractions. Some of these offer discounts to travelers who present handbills or coupons given out at information centers. For some lodgings you must call and make a reservation from the information center to obtain the discount. Also, contact the state tourism office for publicity materials, which will be mailed to you and may contain discount coupons for attractions, car rentals, lodging and meals.

If you're a member of an auto club affiliated with the American Automobile Association (see the Car & Motorcycle section in the Getting Around chapter for details), many roadside motels and some inns and hotels may offer you rate discounts of 10% to 15%. Car rental agencies sometimes offer discounts in tandem with national motel chains. Most hotels and motels allow one or two children to share their parents' room at no extra charge.

Sunday newspapers typically have discount coupons that can be used at some supermarkets and department stores. Supermarkets also run specials on tickets for local attractions, especially 'family' attractions, such as amusement parks or professional sporting events (usually baseball). If there's downhill skiing nearby, discount lift tickets are often available at supermarkets as well.

Bulk warehouse stores and New York City discounters sell everything you could want at a discount. These are good places for items like batteries and film.

Tipping

Tipping is expected in restaurants and better hotels, as well as by taxi drivers, hairdressers and baggage carriers. Americans tend to be liberal tippers. (Not giving the appropriate tip may even earn you scorn from the untipped or under-tipped service provider.)

If you sit down in a restaurant, bar or lounge, be prepared to tip 10% for mundane service, 15% for good service or up to 20% for exceptional service. If you leave less than 10%, it will be interpreted as foreign ignorance or a purposeful insult (which may be what you intend). Tip in cash on the table, or add it to your credit card slip in the appropriate space.

At take-out food counters, there may be a jar or other container labeled 'tips' into which you may throw a few coins if you like. Never tip in fast-food restaurants.

Taxi drivers expect 12% to 18% of the fare, and hairdressers get 15% if their service is satisfactory. Baggage carriers (skycaps in airports, bellboys in hotels) receive 75¢ to $1 per piece. Most hotels and inns allow you to carry your bags and find your room by yourself if you prefer, instead of having to tip the staff-person accompanying you. In budget hotels tips aren't expected.

Taxes

There's no national sales tax in the USA. Some states levy sales taxes, and states, cities and towns may levy taxes on hotel rooms and restaurant meals. Room and meal taxes aren't included in prices quoted even though (or because) they may substantially increase your final bill. Be sure to ask about taxes when you ask for hotel room rates. Unless otherwise stated, the prices given in this book don't reflect the addition of taxes.

Taxes on transport services (bus, rail and air tickets, gasoline, taxi rides) are usually included in the prices quoted. For details on tax rates see the Taxes section in the Facts about chapter for each state.

POST & COMMUNICATIONS

The US Postal Service (USPS) is reliable and inexpensive, though Americans often complain about it. For 24-hour postal information call ☎ 800-275-8777 or check www.usps.gov. Private shippers such as United Parcel Service (UPS; ☎ 800-742-5877) and Federal Express (FedEx; ☎ 800-463-3339) ship much of the nation's parcels and important time-sensitive documents to both domestic and foreign destinations.

Postal Rates

Rates for 1st-class mail within the USA are 33¢ for letters up to 1oz, 22¢ for each additional ounce and 20¢ for postcards. The cost for parcels airmailed anywhere within the USA is $3.20 for 2lbs or less, increasing by $1 per pound up to $6 for 5lbs. For heavier items, rates differ according to the distance mailed. Books, periodicals and computer disks can be sent by a cheaper 4th-class rate.

International airmail rates (except Canada and Mexico) are 60¢ for a half-ounce letter and 40¢ for each additional half an ounce. International postcard rates are 50¢. Letters to Canada are 46¢ for a half-ounce letter and 72¢ for a letter weighing up to 2oz. Postcards are 40¢. Letters to Mexico are 40¢ for a half-ounce letter and 46¢ for a 1oz letter. Postcards to Mexico are 35¢. Aerograms are 50¢.

Sending Mail

If you have the correct postage, you can drop your mail into any blue mailbox. To buy stamps, weigh your mail or send a package 16oz or heavier, go to a post office. There are branch post offices and post office centers in some shopping centers and drugstores. For the address of the nearest office, call ☎ 800-275-8777 or the main post office listed under 'Postal Service' in the 'US Government' section in the local white pages telephone directory.

Usually, post offices are open 8 am to 5 pm weekdays and 8 am to 3 pm on Saturday. Major cities such as New York and Philadelphia have extremely convenient 24-hour service in their main branch.

Receiving Mail

Poste restante is called 'general delivery' in the USA. If you're sending (or expecting) mail to be held at the post office in a city or town, it should be addressed:

Your name
c/o General Delivery (*Optional:* Station Name)
Town, State, ZIP Code
USA

Mail is usually held for 10 days before it's returned to the sender: You might request your correspondents to write 'hold for arrival' on their letters.

In large cities, it's a good idea to add the optional station (branch) name if you know it. If you don't, add the ZIP code or station name, your mail will be held at the main station (central post office). It may not be the most convenient, but it'll have the longest hours of operation.

When you pick up mail, bring some photo identification. Your passport is best.

Alternatively, you may be able to have mail sent to the local representative of American Express or Thomas Cook, which often provide mail service for their clients.

Telephone

Telephone service is usually good, convenient and not particularly expensive, but the plethora of phone companies, policies and rates is very confusing, even for Americans.

Telephone Numbers If you're calling from abroad, the international country code for the USA is '1.'

Phone numbers within the USA consist of a three-digit area code followed by a seven-digit local number. If you're calling locally, just dial the seven-digit number. If you're calling a town in another area code, dial ☎ 1 + the three digit area code + the seven-digit number.

For local directory assistance, dial ☎ 411. For directory assistance outside your area code, dial ☎ 1 + the three digit area code of the place you want to call + 555-1212. If you don't know the area code, dial ☎ 0 (zero) for operator assistance (it's free).

Due to the increasing demand for phone numbers (for faxes, cellular phones, etc), some metropolitan areas are being divided into multiple area codes. New codes are being added or changed in patches all over the country.

The 800, 877 and 888 area codes designate toll-free numbers within the USA and sometimes from Canada. Some toll-free numbers may be limited to calls from within a given region. For toll-free directory assistance call ☎ 800-555-1212.

Some area codes, including 550, 554, 900, 920, 940, 976 and others beginning with 5 and 9 designate information services for which you may pay a premium rate.

To make an international call direct, dial ☎ 011 + country code + area code + the phone number.

Call Charges Local calls cost 25¢ to 35¢ for three minutes or more, depending on the town from which you are calling.

Because of the complex rate structure and multitude of phone companies, regional calls (anywhere from 2 miles to 200 miles) are often the most expensive domestic calls, costing from 60¢ to $1 and up per three-minute call. Long-distance domestic calls can cost as little as 9¢ per minute if dialed from a home phone, but 25¢ to 75¢ per minute from a public coin telephone. Telephone company credit card calls may cost several dollars for the first minute, but only 25¢ to 35¢ for subsequent minutes.

Foreign calls and rates vary by the country called, telephone used (public or private), company providing the long-distance service, the time of day and the day of the week.

For rate information call the operator (☎ 0). Don't ask the operator to put your call through, however, because operator-assisted calls are much more expensive than direct-dial calls. Generally, nights (11 pm to 8 am), all day Saturday and 8 am to 5 pm Sunday are the cheapest times to call (60% discount). Evenings (5 to 11 pm Sunday to Friday) are mid-priced (35% discount). Day calls (8 am to 5 pm weekdays) are full-price calls within the USA.

Paying for Calls Most public telephones accept only coins (5¢, 10¢, 25¢), but some accept credit cards. For local and short calls within the USA, using coins is easy enough. However, there are more convenient ways than feeding a stack of quarters into the phone.

Some telephones in airports and large hotels allow payment by credit card. There may be a slot to slide your card into, or you may have to punch in your credit card number. An alternative is phone debit cards that allow purchasers to pay in advance. However, these can be confusing, cumbersome and are often expensive.

Buy a telephone debit card from a convenience store, phone company office, post office or tourist office. Cards are usually sold in denominations of $5, $10, $20, $40 or $50, and offer calls in the USA for anywhere from 20¢ to 60¢ per minute; 70¢ to $1.80 per minute to Canada and the UK; $1 to $2.40 per minute to Europe; or $2 or $3 per minute to Asian and Pacific countries.

Unfortunately, it's usually impossible to tell how much a call may cost when buying a card. To learn per-minute call costs, you must call a customer service number (on the card) and ask. When dialing, follow the calling instructions on the card, which usually require that you punch in 35 or so digits altogether. As you talk, your time on the line is deducted from your account.

Lonely Planet's eKno Communication Card is aimed specifically at travelers and offers cheap international calls, a range of messaging services and free email. For local calls, you're usually better off with a local card. You can join online at the websitse www.ekno.lonelyplanet.com, or by phone from the continental USA by dialing ☎ 800-707-0031. Once you've joined the service, to use eKno from the continental USA dial ☎ 800-706-1333.

Phone cards often have no magnetic stripe or microchip: instead they have an account number. So when you use your card in public places, be careful – you're vulnerable to thieves who'll watch you punch in the account number. They memorize numbers and use them to make costly international calls. New York airports and especially the Port Authority are notorious for this scam. Shield the telephone with your body when punching in the number.

In addition, when you buy a phone debit card, the account number should be covered (by scratch-off paint or paper wrapper) in order to keep it secret. If it's exposed to view when you buy the card, you must assume that it has already been used and that it is worthless.

Fax & Telegram
Fax machines are easy to find in the USA at shipping companies like Mail Boxes Etc, hotel business-service centers and photocopy services, but be prepared to pay high prices (over $1 a page). Telegrams can be sent from Western Union offices. For additional information call ☎ 800-325-6000.

Email & Internet Access
Most public libraries have a computer with Internet access that allows you to surf the Web or send the occasional email message. Other options are an Internet cafe (for worldwide lists of cybercafes, browse www.traveltales.com or www.netcafeguide .com); a copy center (such as Kinko's, which charges about $10 an hour); or a hotel that caters to business travelers. Some hostels also offer Internet access to their guests. The cheapest way to have email access while traveling is to get a free web-based email account with Lonely Planet's eKno Communication Card (see Paying for Calls, earlier) or from Hotmail (www.hotmail.com), Yahoo (www.yahoo.com) or Netscape (www.netscape .com) that you can access from any online computer with a browser.

INTERNET RESOURCES
The World Wide Web is a rich resource for travelers. You can research your trip, hunt down bargain airfares, book hotels, check on weather conditions or chat with locals and other travelers about the best places to visit (or avoid!).

There's no better place to start your Web explorations than the Lonely Planet website (www.lonelyplanet.com). Here you'll find summaries on traveling to most places on earth, postcards from other travelers and the Thorn Tree bulletin board, where you can ask questions before you go or dispense advice when you get back. You can also find travel news and updates to many of our most popular guidebooks, and the subWWWay section links you to the most useful travel resources elsewhere on the web.

State governments and tourist offices have websites, usually with hyperlinks to more specific and detailed information on destinations, accommodations, attractions, etc. Each state also has hundreds of sites and homepages, run by local chambers of commerce, small businesses and resorts. website addresses are given throughout this book for many of these state and city information services and other helpful organizations and businesses.

Always check the date of the last site update. Despite the seeming immediacy of the Internet, the information on it may be out of date.

BOOKS

Many books are published in different editions by different publishers in different countries. A book might be a hardcover rarity in one country but readily available in paperback in another. To find out about the availability of the recommendations below, check your library, local bookstore or the online bookstore www.amazon.com or the websites of Borders (www.borders.com), Barnes & Noble (www.bn.com) or your local bookstore.

Lonely Planet

Lonely Planet's *New York City*, *New England*, *Virginia & the Capital Region* and *Hiking in the USA* are good supplementary guides for travelers exploring the northeast, and *Canada* is useful for those continuing their journey north. If you're traveling extensively in the USA you may want to consider Lonely Planet's *USA* guide.

Guidebooks

Most guidebooks focus on New York City or New York state, but there are also guides to other parts of the region as well. For recommendations of books covering outdoor pursuits see the Outdoor Activities chapter in this book.

The classic US travel series is the *WPA Guides to America*, published in the 1930s as part of the New Deal Federal Writers Project to employ writers. The guides to New York and to New Jersey were published in 1939. They're so wonderful that they stand on their own today as good reading.

The Mid-Atlantic States, part of the Smithsonian Guides to Historic America series, is a glossy, beautifully photographed account of historically important places and buildings in all three states.

Organized into tours, *National Parks of the Mid-Atlantic* is a guide to NPS sites in the region (plus Maryland, Virginia and West Virginia). *State Parks of the Northeast*,

by Vici Dehaan, is a guide to camping, sightseeing and outdoor activities in state parks in eleven states including New York, New Jersey and Pennsylvania.

New York For those interested in New York City's architecture, the American Institute of Architects' recently updated *Guide to New York City* (2000), edited by Norval White, is the classic text on the subject.

Ethnic New York (1995), by Mark Leeds, is a good neighborhood-by-neighborhood guide. *Wonderful Weekends* (1999), by Marilyn Wood, has information on trips within a 200-mile radius of New York City; it's a good trip planner, but has little on public transportation.

The *Traveler's Guide to the Hudson River Valley* (1999), by Tim Mulligan & Stan Skardinski, is a thorough guide to attractions and amenities from Saratoga Springs to New York City.

New Jersey Rutgers University Press has republished a series of guides by Henry Charleton Beck (1902-65), originally written in the 1930s and '40s. The guides include *Forgotten Towns of Southern New Jersey* as well as *Tales and Towns of Northern New Jersey*.

Guide to the Jersey Shore (1998), by Robert Santelli, describes the attractions, history and activities found there. *New Jersey Day Trips* (1998), by Barbara Hudgins, lists attractions within the state as well as New York, Pennsylvania and Delaware.

Pennsylvania *Fun with the Family* (1998), by Emily & Faith Paulsen, steers parents to attractions that'll keep children amused when exploring Pennsylvania. *Philadelphia Magazine* publishes an annual guide to the best the city has to offer, called *Best of Philly*. *City Smart Guidebook: Pittsburgh* (1999), by Doina Locke who lives in the city, gives a rundown of Pittsburgh attractions, lodging and restaurants.

Travel

Some past literary luminaries from across the Atlantic left written records of their travels through this region. In the 19th century, Charles Dickens wrote *American Notes* (1842); William Russell, a journalist with the London *Times* described his odyssey in *My Diary North and South* (1850); Robert Louis Stevenson recounted his journey from New York City to Pittsburgh in *Across the Plains* (1984); and Oscar Wilde gave his *Impressions of America* in 1883. Early in the 20th century, GK Chesterton described his visit in *What I saw in America* (1923).

The poet Walt Whitman wrote of his travel experiences in *Specimen Days* (1882). Beat author Jack Kerouac wrote about his peregrinations across the country in *On The Road* (1957) and of his life in New York City in *Lonesome Traveler* (1960). John Steinbeck, in his last full-length book, *Travels with Charley* (1962), described his three-month journey in a truck from New York to the West Coast with his wife's pet poodle. More recently Bill Bryson wrote humorously of his travels across 38 states in search of the perfect American small town in *The Lost Continent* (1989) and about his hike along the Appalachian Trail in *A Walk in the Woods* (1998). Sean Condon's pilgrimage from New York to San Francisco is humorously chronicled in *Drive Thru America* (1998), published by Lonely Planet.

History

Patriots (1989), by AJ Langguth, is a narrative history of the personalities, battles and treacheries of the American Revolution. Shelby Foote's three-volume *The Civil War: A Narrative* (1986) is considered one of the most authoritative on its subject.

New York *The Epic of New York City* (1966), by Edward Robb Ellis, is a massive (600 pages), sweeping, personality-based history of the city from the days when Native Americans were the region's only residents to the mid-1960s.

Christopher Morley's New York City (1988) contains accounts of his travels in and around the city in the 1930s and '40s. *The Lost World of the Fair* (1939), by David Gelernter, is an engaging, well-written popular history of the 1939 World's Fair that captures the post-Depression, prewar prominence of New York. *Here is New York* (1949) is a classic, novella-sized essay on New York by the elegant *New Yorker* writer EB White. His observations on the city remain insightful – even today.

Manhattan 45 (1987), by Jan Morris, is a quick look at New York City at its postwar heights, before the country fell in love with suburban living and city centers began a two-generation decline. *New York Days, New York Nights* (1985), by Stephen Brook, is a humorous account of aspects of life in the city.

New York Days (1993), by Willie Morris, tells how, as a young man, he moved from the South to New York City in search of his literary fortune, and how he found it when he became editor of *Harper's Magazine* in its heyday. It's wonderfully descriptive of the 1960s literary era and new journalism, as well as the backstabbing in the profession.

The Power Broker (1974), by Robert Caro, is an authoritative account of the life and times of town planner and public official Robert Moses (1888-1981), who largely created modern New York City, with all its flaws and glories. *New York When I Was Young* (1995), by Mary Cantwell, is a sharply written memoir of life and love in the city during the 1960s by a prominent *New York Times* editorial writer.

The massive *Gotham: A History of New York City to 1898* (1998), by Edwin G Burrows & Mike Wallace, is the result of over two decades of research by its authors. It chronicles the city from the early days of the Lenape Indians to the era when it became regarded as 'Capital of the World.'

Among the many excellent histories of New York's cultural and political development, check *The Common Landscape of America (1580-1845)* by John Stilgoe.

Writing New York (1998), edited by Phillip Lopate, is the single best overview on New York City's role in literature.

The following two small book presses in New York's Catskills region publish works on the history, natural history and folklore of New York: Purple Mountain Press

(☎ 914-254-4062, purple@catskill.net), PO Box E3, Fleischmanns, NY 12430-0378; its website is www.catskill.net/purple; and Black Dome Press (☎ 518-734-6357, black-domep@aol.com), RR 1, Box 422, Hensonville, NY 12439; it maintains a website at www.mhonline.net/~black.

New Jersey *This is New Jersey* (1994), by John Cunningham, is a brief, straightforward history of the state. *New Jersey: A History* (1984), by Thomas Fleming, examines the divisions that have characterized the state's history since the 17th century.

The Powerticians (1980), by Thomas FX Smith, a former mayor of Jersey City, is an entertaining, popular history of the Democratic Party's 'machine politics' that dominated the state's northern cities.

Patrimony: A True Story (1996), by novelist Philip Roth, deals with the life and death of the author's father and contains a good series of cameo images on growing up in Depression-era Newark. *Growing Up* (1984), by Russell Baker, also deals with living in the state (and other locales) during the Depression and is one of the best childhood memoirs ever written.

Pennsylvania For colonial Pennsylvania, check out *William Penn's Holy Experiment: The Founding of Pennsylvania, 1681-1701* (1978), by Edwin Bronner, or JE Illick's *Colonial Pennsylvania* (1976). For the history of Pennsylvania during less-booming times, read *People, Property and Politics: Pennsylvania During the Great Depression* (1981), by Thomas Coode & Benjamin Bauman. *Philadelphia – A 300 Year History* (1982) is a series of essays on the city's history from 1681 to 1982 edited by Russell E Weigley.

Originally published in 1862, *Incidents in the Life of a Slave Girl* (1987), by Harriet Jacobs, tells her real-life story as she moved from Philadelphia to New York and New England.

There are numerous books on the Battle of Gettysburg. Some of the best are Bruce Catton's *Gettysburg: The Final Fury* (1974); Edward Stackpole's *They Met at Gettysburg*

(1995); and George Rippey Stewart's *Pickett's Charge* (1991).

Information on Pennsylvania's immigrants is found in John E Bodnar's *The Ethnic Experience in Pennsylvania* (1973).

For biographical information about Andrew Carnegie see James Howard Bridge's *The Inside Story of the Carnegie Steel Company* (1992), a republished 1903 attack on Andrew Carnegie, or Harold C Livesay's *Andrew Carnegie and the Rise of Big Business* (1975). The rise of Andrew Carnegie and the steel industry wasn't without incident – most notably the strike at Homestead in Pittsburgh in 1892. There are several books on the subject. *Homestead: The Glory & Tragedy of an American Steel Town* (1993), by William Serrin, and *The Battle for Homestead, 1880-1892, Politics, Culture, & Steel* (1992), by Paul Krause, are good histories. *The River Ran Red: Homestead 1892* (1992), edited by David Demarest and Fannia Weingartner, is a collection of excerpts from newspapers of the time. For a contemporary view see Arthur G Burgoyne's *The Homestead Strike of 1892* (1979).

A detailed retelling of the Johnstown flood in southwest Pennsylvania, the worst in US history, can be found in David McCullough's *The Johnstown Flood* (1968). *Christopher Morley's Philadelphia* (1993), like his New York title, details his Philadelphia travels in the 1930s and '40s.

Route 40, once called the National Rd, was the main route west until the 1850s, and its interesting story is told in *The National Road: Main Street of America* (1975) by Norris Schneider.

General

The Encyclopedia of New York City (1995), edited by Kenneth T Jackson, is a mammoth record of the city. *New York Cookbook* (1992), by Molly O'Neil, is the ultimate New York nosh (The author – the food columnist for the *New York Times* – spent years asking New Yorkers, both famous and obscure, for their favorite recipes.)

The *Pennsylvania Almanac* (1997), by Jere Martin, is replete with facts and figures about the state. *Pittsburgh – An American City* (1991), with photos by Walt Urbina and text by Sally Webb, is a good paperback photographic record of Pittsburgh.

A wide selection of books on the Amish and Mennonites is available in the Pennsylvania Dutch region. Many are published by Good Books in Intercourse, PA. Several paperbacks that will answer most of your questions are *The Puzzles of Amish Life*, by Donald B Kraybill; *The 20 Most Asked Questions about the Amish and Mennonites*, by Merle Good & Phyllis Pellman Good; and Merle Good's *Who Are the Amish?*, which has lots of photographs.

For a more in-depth study, try Stephen M Nolt's *A History of the Amish – from the Reformation to Today*. Daniel & Kathryn Mc-Cauley's *Decorative Arts of the Amish of Lancaster County* is aimed specifically at crafts. *Amish Society*, by John Hostatler, examines Amish culture, explains their religious beliefs and ceremonies, their community and family life, and the tension and interaction with outsiders. *The Amish and the State*, edited by Donald B Kraybill, looks at conflicts between people practicing their traditional beliefs and the demands of the modern state.

The Riddle of Amish Culture, by Donald B Kraybill, and *The Amish Struggle with Modernity*, edited by Kraybill and Marc A Olshan, explore how these people survive and thrive in the modern world while living outside it. *Old Order Amish – Their Enduring Way of Life* is a photographic account of Amish life. *An Introduction to Mennonite History*, by Cornelius J Dyck, is a history of the Mennonites from the 16th century to the present day.

NEWSPAPERS & MAGAZINES

The USA supports a wide spectrum of newspapers and magazines, many of which are based in this region. New York City is the main magazine- and book-publishing center in the country and is a major proving ground for journalists and editors. It's the headquarters for such publishing giants as Condé Nast, Hachette Filippacci, Hearst, K-III, Time & Life and Time Warner. The city's

multibillion dollar industry produces more magazines per month than any other city in the nation.

Published in New York City, two well-respected, influential newspapers are the *Wall Street Journal* and the *New York Times*; the latter is also published in several regional editions. The populist tabloid *USA Today* has lots of color and sports coverage (it's the country's highest circulating newspaper though it's not published in the city). The loud, Rupert Murdoch-owned tabloid the *New York Post* is *the* oldest newspaper in the US.

The *New Jersey Gazette* is the state's oldest newspaper, but the most influential is the *Newark Star Ledger*.

Important daily newspapers in Pennsylvania are the well-regarded *Philadelphia Inquirer*, plus the *Philadelphia Daily News*, the *Pittsburgh Press* and the *Pittsburgh Post-Gazette*.

Many smaller cities and large towns have their own newspapers (including ethnic ones), published daily or weekly.

Many nationally distributed magazines are published in New York City, including *Vanity Fair, Cosmopolitan, Esquire, GQ* and *Vogue*. These contain a significant amount of New York-centric information and often describe the latest trends in chic clothing, food, music and design as they emerge in the city. To people living even as close as Pittsburgh, these developments often appear decidedly foreign.

As a major financial center, New York City also publishes the most prominent magazines relating to business and industry. If you're looking for employment, the end pages in these publications provide a glimpse of what's on offer. For the buzz on Wall St, pick up *Forbes, Money, Crain's New York Business* or *Fortune*. *Publishers Weekly* gives you the lowdown on book publishing in the city. *Advertising Age* is Madison Ave's tell-all for the advertising industry, and *Magazine Age* does the same for magazine publishing. *Women's Wear Daily* and *W* are New York City fashion-industry musts.

Distributed nationally, *New York* and the *New Yorker* magazines publish information on city happenings. See also Newspapers &

Magazines in the Information section of the New York City chapter.

Philadelphia Magazine is an influential monthly magazine and the *Farm Journal*, a Philadelphia publication, is one of the nation's leading farm magazines.

RADIO & TV

Radio first appeared in the US when its inventor, Guglielmo Marconi, broadcast a commentary from New York Harbor on the America's Cup yachting race in 1899. Then, in the early 20th century, two major advances occurred at New York's Columbia University. In 1913, Edwin H Armstrong, a student there, invented the speaker – up till that time transmissions could only be heard through earphones. Over the next two decades Armstrong successfully developed frequency modulation (FM), although it didn't become widely available until much later. Amplitude modulation (AM) was the most common form of transmission until the 1960s and 1970s.

In the meantime, KDKA, the first permanent commercial broadcasting radio station in the world, opened in Pittsburgh in 1920. Soon after, companies such as the Radio Corporation of America (RCA) set up radio stations in the region. Several networks were founded in New York City, which remains the location of their headquarters today. The National Broadcasting Company (NBC) and the Columbia Broadcasting System (CBS) were formed in the 1920s, and the American Broadcasting Company (ABC) was formed in the 1940s.

The influence of radio at this time was graphically displayed in 1938 when Orson Welles broadcast a play about a Martian invasion of New Jersey. It was misinterpreted as a report on a real event and threw people into a panic.

From the 1960s onward the number of radio stations proliferated, and today most communities have their own local radio station. You can choose from literally hundreds of them. In and near major cities, there is a wide variety of music and entertainment, especially in New York City. The listening market there is so large, a radio station can maximize its profits by 'narrowcasting' – specializing in a particular type of music (rock, country, etc) or news or talk radio.

There are numerous talk radio stations, especially on the AM dial, and they are very popular. One manifestation of talk radio is 'shock' radio, typified by New York's Howard Stern, who is heard nationally over hundreds of radio stations. National Public Radio (NPR) features a more level-headed approach to discussion, music and news. NPR's *Morning Edition* and its afternoon *All Things Considered* are the most worthwhile programs on the radio.

New York City pioneered a number of innovations in TV, including the first mobile unit and the broadcasting of the first sporting event. WNBC-TV, which began operating in New York City in 1941, was the country's first commercial TV station. After WWII the popularity of TV mushroomed and network companies such as ABC, CBS and NBC started broadcasting regularly.

Until the 1950s, New York City dominated much of national TV programming, most of which was broadcast live. But during that decade Hollywood movie studios began filming TV series and the production of most programs shifted to the West Coast, though news programming has remained in New York. Nevertheless, since that period, some of the most successful programs in American TV have been produced in the city. See also TV under the Arts section of the Facts about the Region chapter.

New York wasn't the only city in the region where important changes occurred. In Pittsburgh, the TV station WQED pioneered community-sponsored educational TV when it began broadcasting in 1954.

The main US TV networks have affiliated stations throughout the country. In addition to ABC, CBS and NBC in New York City, there is also FOX and the Public Broadcasting Service (PBS). New York City is also an important center for network news and Cable News Network (CNN), a cable channel providing continuous news coverage. Cinemax, the Movie Channel and

Viacom are three important cable-TV companies based in New York City.

PHOTOGRAPHY & VIDEO
Film & Equipment
All major brands of film are available at reasonable prices. Every town of any size has at least one photo shop that stocks a variety of fresh film, cameras and accessories. Slide film is not as easily available, and black and white film is rarely sold outside major cities.

In most towns and tourist centers, some shops can develop your color print film in one hour (that can end up being two or so), or at least the same day, for an extra charge. Processing a roll of 100 ASA 35mm color print film with 24-exposures will typically cost about $7 for regular service.

Film can be damaged by excessive heat, so don't leave your camera and film in the car on a hot summer day or place your camera on the dashboard while you're driving.

It's worth carrying a spare battery for your camera to avoid disappointment when your camera dies in the middle of nowhere. If you're buying a new camera for your trip, do so several weeks before leaving and practice using it.

Technical Tips
When the sun is high, photographs tend to emphasize shadows and wash out highlights. It's best to take photos during early morning and late afternoon hours, when the light is softer. This is especially true of landscape photography. Protect camera lenses with a haze or ultraviolet (UV) filter. At high altitudes, the UV filter may not adequately prevent washed-out photos; a polarizing filter can correct this problem and dramatically emphasize cloud formations.

Video Systems
Overseas visitors should remember that the USA uses the National Television System Committee (NTSC) color TV and video standard. It isn't compatible with Phase Alternative Line (PAL) and Système Electronique Couleur avec Mémoire (SECAM) standards used in Africa, Europe, Asia and Australia unless converted.

Restrictions
There are few restrictions on photography, except within art galleries, museums and at musical and artistic performances.

Photographing People
You can't generalize about how people will react to being photographed, but politeness and chatting beforehand will make things easier for you. The Amish, in particular, don't like having photographs taken of them. Also, many foreign-born street-stall owners and residents in ethnic neighborhoods are reluctant to be photographed by strangers. Sometimes it's due to cultural reasons, but often it's because they're in the US illegally.

In cities, street performers enjoy being photographed provided you give them some money (it's their livelihood). Don't take photographs of any person acting crazily or suspiciously on the street.

Airport Security
Air passengers must pass their luggage through X-ray machines, which are said to pose no danger to most films. To bypass the X-ray scanner, unpack your film from the boxes and plastic film cans and have all film canisters readily visible in a plastic bag. You really only need to do this for very high-speed film (1600 ASA and higher).

TIME
Excluding Hawaii and Alaska, the USA has four time zones. New York, New Jersey and Pennsylvania are on US Eastern Time – five hours behind GMT/UTC, two hours ahead of US Mountain Time and three hours ahead of US Pacific Time. When it's noon in New York City, it's 5 pm in London and 9 am in San Francisco. Most of the US observes daylight-saving time: clocks go forward one hour from the first Sunday in April to the last Saturday in October, when the clocks are turned back one hour. It's easy to remember by the popular phrase 'spring ahead, fall back.'

In the US, dates are usually given with the month first, then the day, then the year.

ELECTRICITY

Electric current is 110 to 120 volts, 60-cycle. Appliances built to take 220- to 240-volt, 50-cycle current (as in Europe and Asia) will need a converter (transformer) and a US-style plug adapter with two flat pins, or three (two flat, one round) pins. Plugs with three pins don't fit into a two-hole socket, but adapters are easy to buy.

WEIGHTS & MEASURES

The USA uses a modified version of the British Imperial measuring system.

Distances are in feet (ft), yards (yd) and miles. Three feet equal one yard, which is 0.914 meters; 1760 yards (or 5280 feet) equal one mile. Near the Canadian border you may see some distances marked in kilometers (km) as well as miles.

Dry weights are measured in ounces (oz), pounds (lbs; 16oz equal 1lb) and tons (2000lbs equal 1 ton).

Liquids are measured by the fluid ounce – the cup (8oz), the pint (16oz), the quart (32oz, 2 pints) and the gallon (1 gallon equals 4 quarts). Note that the US pint equals 16 fluid oz, not 20 as in the Imperial system. The US gallon, at 64oz, is 20% less than the Imperial gallon (it takes 1.2 US gallons to make an Imperial gallon). Gasoline is measured in US gallons.

Although the metric system has made some inroads (for example, wine bottles tend to be 70 centiliters or 750 milliliters), most Americans continue to resist its imposition. There's a conversion chart on the inside back cover of the book.

LAUNDRY

Self-service, coin-operated laundry facilities are in most towns of any size, in hostels, in better campgrounds and some hotels. Washing a load costs about $1.50, and it is another $1.50 for 30 minutes in the dryer. Coin-operated vending machines sell single-wash-size packages of detergent, but it's usually cheaper to pick up a small box at the supermarket. Some Laundromats have attendants who wash, dry and fold your clothes for an additional charge. To find a laundry, look under 'Laundries' or 'Laundries – Self-Service' in the yellow pages of the telephone directory. Dry cleaners are also listed under 'Laundries' or 'Cleaners.'

RECYCLING

It's illegal to litter highways, streets, sidewalks or other public spaces. Fines can be stiff, though enforcement is usually lax. Litter clean-up costs governments millions of dollars annually.

Virtually all commercial beverage containers sold in the USA are recyclable. Many highway rest stops and other public facilities (such as airports and bus and train stations) have trash and recycling bins side by side; the recycling bins are usually labeled 'cans and bottles.' In places where many newspapers may be discarded, such as airports and train stations, there are newspaper recycling bins.

Although recycling is great, an even better option is reducing your use of these products. Many gas stations and convenience stores sell large, inexpensive, insulated plastic cups with lids, which are reusable and ideal for hot and cold drinks. In addition, you can usually save a few cents by using your own cup when you buy drinks.

When you're hiking and camping in the wilderness, take out everything you bring in – including *any* garbage you create.

TOILETS

Americans have different names for public toilet facilities. The most common names are 'rest room' and 'bathroom.' Other names include 'ladies'/men's room,' 'comfort station,' 'facility' and 'sanitary facility.'

You'll find relatively clean public toilets in airports, bars, large stores, museums, state parks, restaurants, hotels and tourist offices. Ones in bus, train and highway gas stations and rest stops may or may not be clean, but most are still usable. Most facilities turn away nonpatrons from bathrooms, but it's possible to walk into many hotel lobbies, or into a crowded bar or restaurant if you're discreet and reasonably well dressed. Not all gas stations have toilets; among those that do, the quality varies considerably. Public toilets in city parks and other public places have mostly closed due to criminal and sexual misuse.

On a long drive in New York's Adirondacks, when each curve of the road promises hope for a rest stop, or at least a turnout with a shade tree, remember Stewart's Convenience Stores. Its toilets are free and clean.

HEALTH

Generally speaking, the USA is a healthy place to visit. There are no prevalent diseases, and the country is well served by hospitals and clinics. However, due to the high cost of health care, international visitors should consider taking out comprehensive travel insurance.

Hospitals, medical centers, walk-in clinics and referral services are found easily. Ask the staff of your hotel to recommend a local doctor or clinic. In an emergency, call ☎ 911 for an ambulance to take you to the nearest hospital emergency room (ER), but note that both the ambulance and the ER will be incredibly expensive. Many city hospitals have 'urgent care clinics,' which are designed to deal with less-than-catastrophic injuries.

For comprehensive health information and advice for travelers, browse the US Centers for Disease Control & Prevention's website (www.cdc.gov/travel). Lonely Planet's website has lots of good travel health advice (www.lonelyplanet.com/health), and many other travel health sites are listed. There's also dir.yahoo.com/Health/Travel.

Predeparture Preparations

Make sure you're healthy before traveling. If you're embarking on a long trip, make sure your teeth are in good condition. If you wear glasses, take a spare pair and your prescription. You can get new spectacles made up quickly and competently for around $100. If you require a particular medication, take an adequate supply and bring the prescription with you. Pharmaceuticals are expensive in the USA.

Medical Kit Check List

Following is a list of items you should consider including in your medical kit – consult your pharmacist for brands available in your country.

❏ **Aspirin or paracetamol (acetaminophen in the USA)** – for pain or fever

❏ **Antihistamine** – for allergies, eg, hay fever; to ease the itch from insect bites or stings; and to prevent motion sickness

❏ **Cold and flu tablets, throat lozenges and nasal decongestant**

❏ **Multivitamins** – consider bringing some for long trips, when dietary vitamin intake may be inadequate

❏ **Antibiotics** – consider including these if you're traveling well off the beaten track; see your doctor, as they must be prescribed, and carry the prescription with you

❏ **Kaolin preparation (such as Pepto-Bismol or Lomotil)** –blocks diarrhea

❏ **Prochlorperazine or metaclopramide** – for nausea and vomiting

❏ **Rehydration mixture** – to prevent dehydration, which may occur, for example, during bouts of diarrhea; particularly important when traveling with children

❏ **Insect repellent, sunscreen, lip balm and eye drops**

❏ **Calamine lotion, sting relief spray or aloe vera** – to ease irritation from sunburn and insect bites or stings

❏ **Antifungal cream or powder** – for fungal skin infections and thrush

❏ **Antiseptic (such as Betadine)** – for cuts and grazes

❏ **Bandages, Band-Aids (plasters) and other wound dressings**

❏ **Water purification tablets or iodine**

❏ **Scissors, tweezers and a thermometer** – note that mercury thermometers are prohibited by airlines

Generally, no immunizations are required for entry, though cholera and yellow fever vaccinations may be necessary for those coming from infected areas.

Health Insurance Travel health insurance is essential – some hospitals refuse care without evidence that the patient is covered. If you have a choice between lower or higher medical expenses options, take the higher one for visiting the USA.

Some policies specifically exclude 'dangerous activities' such as scuba diving, motorcycling and even hiking. If these activities are on your agenda avoid this sort of policy.

You may prefer a policy that pays doctors or hospitals directly, rather than requiring you to pay first and file a claim with the insurance company later. If you have to file a claim later, keep all documentation. Some policies ask you to call collect ('reverse charge') to a center in your home country for an immediate assessment of your problem.

Check whether the policy covers ambulance fees or an emergency flight home. If you have to stretch out, you'll need two seats and somebody has to pay for them!

See also Travel Insurance under Visas & Documents, earlier in the chapter.

Food & Drink

Stomach upsets are the most common health problems for travelers, but these will be minor in the US, where places serving food and drink have high standards of cleanliness. Tap water is usually okay to drink, though it may smell or taste of chlorine. It may also contain some bacteria to which your gut may not be accustomed, at least for the first few days. Bottled drinking water is widely available.

Travelers on a tight budget may resort to a junk-food diet that's not well balanced. Fast food is low in dietary fiber, so try to get some fresh fruit and vegetables every day. Overcooked food can lose much of its nutritional value, so eat eggs, tofu, beans, lentils and nuts (or meat) for protein and plenty of grains and bread.

In hot weather make sure you drink enough – don't rely on feeling thirsty to indicate when you should drink. Excessive sweating may lead to loss of salt and therefore muscle cramping. Adding salt to food will help.

Climatic & Geographical Ailments
Sunburn You can get sunburned quickly, even through clouds, especially if you're on water, snow or ice. Use a sunscreen with a high protection factor, wear a hat and cover up with a long-sleeved shirt and trousers. Calamine or aloe vera lotion provide some relief for mild sunburn.

Heat Exhaustion Dehydration or salt deficiency can cause heat exhaustion, which is characterized by fatigue, lethargy, headaches, giddiness and muscle cramps. Always carry – and use – a water bottle on long trips.

Heat Stroke Long, continuous periods of exposure to high temperatures can leave you vulnerable to this serious, sometimes fatal, condition. It occurs when the body's heat-regulating mechanism breaks down and the body temperature rises to dangerous levels. Avoid excessive alcohol intake or strenuous activity.

Symptoms include feeling unwell, lack of perspiration and a high body temperature of 102° to 105°F (39° to 41°C). Hospitalization is essential for extreme cases, but meanwhile get out of the sun, remove clothing, cover with a wet sheet or towel and fan continuously to bring down body temperature.

Fungal Infections Fungal infections such as athlete's foot, jock itch or ringworm occur more often in hot weather. To prevent these, wear loose, comfortable clothes, wash frequently and dry carefully. If you get an infection, wash the infected area daily with a disinfectant or medicated soap and water, and rinse and dry well. Apply an antifungal cream or powder and try to expose the infected area to air or sunlight as much as possible to promote healing.

Hypothermia Skiers and winter hikers will find that temperatures in the mountains can drop quickly to below freezing, or a sudden soaking and high winds can lower your body temperature rapidly. Travel with a partner whenever possible, or, if you're alone, be sure someone knows your route and when you expect to return.

Seek shelter when bad weather is unavoidable. Woolen clothing and synthetics that retain warmth even when wet are superior to cotton clothing. Carry a good quality sleeping bag and high-energy, easily digestible snacks such as chocolate or dried fruit.

Get hypothermia victims out of bad weather as quicly as possible and make sure they're in dry, warm clothing. Give hot liquids (not alcohol) and high-calorie, easily digestible food. In advanced stages, place victims in warm sleeping bags and get in with them. Don't rub victims – place them near a fire or, if possible, in a warm (not hot) bath.

Motion Sickness Eating lightly before and during a trip reduces the chances of motion sickness. If you're prone to motion sickness, try to sit near the wing on an aircraft or near the center of a bus. Fresh air usually helps. Commercial antimotion sickness preparations, which can cause drowsiness, have to be taken before you start your trip. If you wait until you feel sick, it's too late. Ginger, a natural preventative, is available in capsule form.

Jet Lag Jet lag occurs because many of the body's functions (such as temperature, pulse rate and emptying of the bladder and bowels) are regulated by internal 24-hour cycles called circadian rhythms. When we travel long distances rapidly, our bodies take time to adjust to the 'new time' of our destination, and we may experience fatigue, disorientation, insomnia, anxiety, impaired concentration and loss of appetite. These effects are usually gone within three days of arrival, but there are ways of minimizing the impact of jet lag:

- Rest for a couple of days prior to departure; try to avoid late nights and last-minute dashes for traveler's checks, passport, etc.
- Select flight schedules that minimize sleep deprivation; arriving late in the day means you can sleep soon after you arrive. For long flights, try to organize a stopover.
- Avoid excessive eating and alcohol during the flight. Instead, drink plenty of noncarbonated, nonalcoholic drinks such as fruit juice or water.
- Make yourself comfortable by wearing loose-fitting clothes and perhaps bringing an eye mask and ear plugs to help you sleep.

Sexually Transmitted Diseases

Sexual contact with an infected sexual partner spreads sexually transmitted diseases (STDs). Although abstinence is the only 100% preventative, practicing safe sex and using latex condoms can reduce the chance of infection by diseases such as gonorrhea and syphilis (the most common STDs) and HIV/AIDS.

Gonorrhea and syphilis can be cured but can be debilitating if left untreated. Herpes can be treated but not cured. If you suspect that you've caught an STD, have an examination and explore your options.

The Human Immunodeficiency Virus (HIV) may develop into Acquired Immune Deficiency Syndrome (AIDS). Exposure to blood, blood products or bodily fluids may place you in danger of contracting HIV/AIDS. In addition to unprotected sex, infection can come from sharing contaminated needles, including needles re-used for acupuncture, tattooing or body piercing (a clean-looking needle or tool, or a healthy-looking person, may be carrying HIV). HIV/AIDS can also be spread through infected blood transfusions, though the blood supply in the USA is screened and presumably safe. Symptoms may appear only months after infection, so it is impossible to detect a person's HIV status without a blood test.

A good resource for help and information is the US Centers for Disease Control HIV/AIDS hotline (CDC; ☎ 800-342-2437, 800-344-7432 in Spanish). The CDC also has a website (www.cdc.gov). See the 'HIV/AIDS

& Entering the USA' boxed text, earlier in this chapter.

Insect-Borne Diseases

Ticks are parasitic arachnids that may be present in brush, forest and grasslands, where hikers often get them on their legs or in their boots. An adult tick sucks blood from the host by burying its head into the host's skin, but ticks are often found unattached and can simply be brushed off. To remove an attached tick, use a pair of tweezers, grab it by the head and pull it straight out – don't twist it. (If no tweezers are available, use your fingers, but protect them from contamination with a piece of tissue paper.) Don't touch the tick with hot object such as a match or a cigarette – this can cause it to regurgitate noxious gut substances or saliva into a wound. And don't rub oil, alcohol or petroleum jelly on it. If you become sick in the next couple of weeks, consult a doctor.

Bedbugs live in various places, but particularly in dirty mattresses and bedding. Spots of blood on bedclothes or on the wall around the bed suggest the presence of bedbugs, and it's wise to find another hotel. Bedbugs leave itchy bites in neat rows. Calamine lotion may help.

Lice cause itching and extreme discomfort. They make themselves at home in your hair (head lice), your clothing (body lice) or in your pubic hair (crabs). You can catch lice through direct contact with infected people or by sharing combs, clothing and the like. Powder or shampoo treatment kills the lice; wash infected clothing in hot water. See Insects, later in this chapter.

WOMEN TRAVELERS

Women often face different situations from men when traveling and, especially if they're traveling alone, should maintain a little extra awareness of their surroundings. People in the region are generally friendly and happy to help travelers, but consider the following suggestions, which might help reduce or eliminate your chances of encountering problems. The best approach is to trust your instincts.

Precautions

In general, exercise more vigilance in large cities than in rural areas. Try to avoid the 'bad' or unsafe neighborhoods or districts; if you go into or through these areas, it's best to go in a private vehicle (car or taxi). It's more dangerous at night, but in the worst areas crime can occur even in the daytime. If you're unsure which areas are considered unsafe, ask at your hotel or telephone the tourist office for advice. Tourist maps can sometimes be deceiving, compressing non-touristed areas and making distances seem shorter than they really are.

New York City is a reasonably safe city for women travelers; lesbian visitors will also feel safe and generally welcome. Given the low crime figures of the past few years, the subway needn't be shunned by solo female travelers, though it's wise to ride in the conductor's car (in the middle of the train). If someone stares or acts in an annoying manner, simply move to another part of the car. Women are far more likely to encounter obnoxious behavior on the street, being greeted with whistles and muttered 'compliments.' Any engagement amounts to encouragement – so simply walk on.

Even in rural areas, women may still be harassed by men unaccustomed to seeing women traveling solo. Try to avoid hiking or camping alone, especially in unfamiliar places. The 'buddy system' may not only help protect you from other humans, but may also help if you're injured or become ill.

The best way to deal with the threat of rape is to avoid putting yourself in vulnerable situations; using common sense will help avoid most problems. For example, you're more vulnerable if you've been drinking or using drugs than if you're sober; you're more vulnerable alone than with company; and you're more vulnerable in a high-crime urban neighborhood.

Some men may interpret a woman drinking alone in a bar as an invitation for male company, whether it's intended that way or not. If you don't want the company, most men respect a firm but polite 'no thank you.' If you're the object of catcalls, don't engage the caller.

Hitchhiking isn't advisable; but if you decide to hitch, do so with a companion. If you're driving alone, don't pick up hitchhikers. If you get stuck on a road and need help, have a pre-made sign to signal for help. At night avoid getting out of your car to flag down help; turn on your hazard lights and wait for the police to arrive. Be extra careful at night on public transit, and remember to check the times of the last bus or train before you go out at night.

To deal with potential dangers, many women protect themselves with a whistle, mace (a chemical spray), cayenne pepper spray or some self-defense training. If you decide to purchase a spray, contact a police station to find out about regulations and training classes. Note that laws regarding sprays vary from state to state, though mace and other sprays are legal in New York. However, because of its combustible nature, it's a federal felony to carry a spray can on an airplane.

If, despite your precautions, you are assaulted, call the police (☎ 911). In some rural areas where 911 is not active, just dial ☎ 0 (zero) for the operator. Many cities have rape-crisis centers to aid rape victims. For the telephone number of the nearest center, call directory information (☎ 411 or 1 + area code + 555-1212).

Organizations & Resources

The headquarters for the National Organization for Women (NOW; ☎ 202-331-0066, now@now.org), 1000 16th St NW, suite 700, Washington, DC 20036, is a good resource for information and can refer you to state and local chapters. NOW's website is www.now.org. Planned Parenthood (☎ 212-541-7800, communications@ppfa.org), 810 Seventh Ave, New York, NY 10019, can refer you to clinics throughout the country and offers advice on health concerns and issues. Its website is www.plannedparenthood.org. Check the yellow pages under 'Social & Human Services,' 'Clinics' and 'Health Services' for local resources.

Maiden Voyages is a print and online magazine for women travelers. Its website, www.maiden-voyages.com, has a comprehensive database of travel services owned, run by and/or geared toward women. Also visit www.journeywoman.com, another good website for women travelers.

GAY & LESBIAN TRAVELERS

New York City has one of the largest gay populations in the country, and Philadelphia's gay population is also sizeable. In the cities it's easier for gay men and women to live their lives with a certain amount of openness, but gay travelers should be careful in rural areas. However, upstate New Yorkers seem to be a fairly accepting, if not approving, group. Like their nearby New England neighbors, they may be skeptical of noticeably different lifestyles, but are not overtly critical.

Organizations & Resources

Several national organizations can provide you with information. They include the national AIDS/HIV hotline (☎ 800-342-2437), the National Gay/Lesbian Task Force (☎ 202-332-6483) in Washington, DC, and the Lambda Legal Defense Fund (☎ 212-995-8585) in New York City and Los Angeles (☎ 213-937-2727).

Women's Rights Sights

Those interested in the history of the women's movement may enjoy a visit to Seneca Falls, NY, where Elizabeth Cady Stanton met with a group of friends in 1848 and drafted a declaration calling for the right to vote and proclaiming that 'all men and women are created equal.' Here you'll find the Women's Rights National Historical Park and the National Women's Hall of Fame commemorating the achievements of American women. You can also visit Cady Stanton's house.

In Rochester, NY, you can visit the home of Susan B Anthony (see the Finger Lakes Region chapter for details). She was the first American woman to vote, though this was illegal in 1872, and Anthony was arrested.

Most cities have a gay paper or alternative paper that lists what's happening or at least provides phone numbers of local organizations. Another good resource is the *Gay Yellow Pages* (☎ 212-674-0120), PO Box 533, Village Station, NY 10014-0533, which has a national edition as well as regional editions and a website (gayyellowpages.com). A useful website is www.gay.com with information on travel to gay friendly cities, accommodations and entertainment.

Some good national guidebooks are *The Women's Traveller*, providing listings for lesbians; *Damron's Address Book*, for men; and *Damron Accommodations*, with gay-owned/gay-friendly hotel, B&B and guesthouse listings nationwide. All three books are published by the Damron Company (☎ 415-255-0404, 800-462-6654), PO Box 422458, San Francisco, CA 94142-2458. The company's website is www.damron.com. Ferrari's *Places for Women* and *Places for Men* are also useful, as are guides to specific cities. For example, check out *Betty & Pansy's Severe Queer Reviews* to various cities, available in some bookstores; it's also available online at www.gaymart.com.

DISABLED TRAVELERS

The USA is a world leader in providing facilities for the disabled. The Americans with Disabilities Act (ADA) is a federal law that requires public buildings (including hotels, restaurants, theaters and museums) and public transit to be wheelchair accessible. Telephone companies are required to provide relay operators for the hearing impaired and many banks provide ATM instructions in Braille. You'll find audible crossing signals, and at busier roadway intersections there are curbs with wheelchair ramps.

Larger private and chain hotels have suites for disabled guests. Major car-rental agencies offer hand-controlled models at no extra charge. Major airlines, intercity buses and Amtrak trains allow guide dogs to accompany passengers and frequently sell two-for-one packages when seriously disabled passengers require attendants. Airlines also provide assistance for connecting, boarding and disembarking the flight – mention that you will need assistance when making your reservation. (Note: airlines must accept wheelchairs as checked baggage and have an onboard chair available, though some advance notice may be required on smaller aircraft.) The more populous the area, the greater the likelihood of facilities for the disabled. Wherever you're headed, it is always a wise idea to call ahead to arrange your accommodations and transportation.

For New York residents with permanent disabilities, the Access Pass provides free admission to New York parks and recreation areas. To obtain an application for a pass, call ☎ 518-474-0456, or write to Access Pass, State Parks, Albany, NY 12238.

Organizations & Resources

The following organizations and tour providers specialize in the needs of disabled travelers:

Access-Able Travel Source (☎ 303-232-2979, fax 239-8486, www.access-able.com) PO Box 1796, Wheat Ridge, CO 80034

Mobility International USA (MIUSA) (☎ 541-343-1284, fax 541-343-6812, info@miusa.org, www.miusa.org) PO Box 10767, Eugene, OR 97440. It advises disabled travelers on mobility issues and runs educational exchange programs.

Moss Rehabilitation Hospital's Travel Information Service (☎ 215-456-9600, 456-9602) 1200 W Tabor Rd, Philadelphia, PA 19141-3099

Society for the Advancement of Travel for the Handicapped (SATH) (☎ 212-447-7284, fax 725-9253, sathtravel@aolcom) 347 Fifth Ave, suite 610, New York, NY 10016. It publishes *Open World* magazine.

Travelin' Talk (☎ 615-552-06670, fax 552-1182, trvlntlk@aol.com) PO Box 3534, Clarksville, TN 37047

Twin Peaks Press (☎ 360-694-2462, 800-637-2256) PO Box 129, Vancouver, WA 98666. It publishes several handbooks for disabled travelers.

SENIOR TRAVELERS

Though the age when the benefits begin varies, travelers from 50 years and up can receive cut rates and benefits unknown to their younger fellows. Be sure to inquire about such rates at hotels, museums and restaurants.

The National Park Service issues Golden Age Passports to people 62 or older (see the boxed text 'Golden Passports,' below). New York state residents 62 or older score free access to state parks, state historic sites and arboretums.

In the Adirondacks, the Sagamore Institute operates a fine Elderhostel (see Organizations, below) program for seniors. The program encourages continuing education for retired people in unusual settings, stressing cultural and natural history. One popular program is the Grandparents' & Grandchildren's Summer Camp, a one week 'intergenerational' gathering. Reservations a year in advance are recommended. For information, contact Sagamore Great Camp (☎ 315-354-5311, Sagamore@Telenet.net), PO Box 146, Raquette Lake, NY 13436, or visit its website (www.sagamore.org). See also Sagamore Great Camp under the Lake George section in the Adirondack Region chapter.

Organizations & Resources

National advocacy groups that can help in planning your travels include the following:

American Association of Retired Persons (☎ 800-227-7737, www.aarp.org) 601 E St NW, Washington, DC 20049. The AARP is an advocacy group for Americans 50-plus and is a good resource for travel bargains. Annual membership for US/non-US residents costs $8/10.

Elderhostel (☎ 617-426-8056, 877-426-8056, www.elderhostel.org) 75 Federal St, Boston, MA 02110-1941. Elderhostel is a nonprofit organization offering seniors the opportunity to attend academic college courses throughout the USA and Canada. Programs last one to three weeks, include meals and accommodations and are open to people 55-plus and their companions.

Grand Circle Travel (☎ 800-248-3737, www.gct.com) 347 Congress St, Boston, MA 02210. This organization offers escorted tours and travel information in a variety of formats and distributes a free useful booklet, *Going Abroad: 101 Tips for Mature Travelers*.

TRAVEL WITH CHILDREN

Many establishments and services offer discounted fees and fares for children. Age limits for discounts vary. Hotels and motels may count anyone under 18 as a child, though B&Bs rarely offer discounts and may not welcome children at all. At museums, a child may be considered as someone aged three to nine, or five to 12. If it's not posted, you'll have to ask.

Some restaurants offer a limited selection of inexpensive child-friendly foods; ask for the children's menu. Airlines sometimes discount international fares for children's tickets, but these are often more expensive than the cheapest APEX adult tickets. Many buses and tours have discounted children's prices (often 50%). Car rental companies provide infant seats for their cars on request.

Various children's activities are mentioned in this book. For general information on traveling with kids, read Lonely Planet's *Travel with Children* by Maureen Wheeler.

DANGERS & ANNOYANCES
Crime

The USA has a widespread reputation as a dangerous, violent place because of the availability of firearms. This is true to some extent, but the image is propagated and exaggerated by the media. New York City's

---

> ## Golden Passports
>
> The **Golden Age Passport** allows permanent US residents 62 years and older lifetime entry to sites in the NPS system and other federally operated facilities, with 50% discounts on camping and other fees. It costs $10 and you must apply in person. The **Golden Access Passport** offers the same to US residents who are medically blind or permanently disabled. You can apply for these at any NPS or USFS office or site.
>
> A **Golden Eagle Passport** costs $50 annually and offers one-year entry into national parks to the holder and accompanying guests. You can get this at any NPS or USFS site or by sending a check or money order to: Golden Eagle Passport, NPS, 1100 Ohio Drive SW, Room 138, Washington, DC 20242.

crime rates have fallen dramatically since the 1970s (and continue to decline), and Philadelphia is ranked first by the Federal Bureau of Investigation (FBI) as the safest of the nation's 12 largest metropolitan areas. Nevertheless, all cities suffer to some degree from the crimes of pickpockets, muggers (robbers), carjackers and rapists.

As in other cities throughout the world, the majority of crimes take place in the poorest neighborhoods among the local residents. The signs of a bad or dangerous neighborhood are obvious, and pretty much the same as in any other country. Observe the following standard common-sense urban safety rules and you should have no trouble.

- Avoid unnecessary displays of money or jewelry. Carry valuables in a money belt or pouch underneath your clothing for maximum safety from pickpockets (split up your money and credit cards to avoid losing everything). This is usually only necessary in crowded areas such as airports, subways, city buses, markets or concerts, but it doesn't hurt to do it all the time.
- Lock valuables in your suitcase in your hotel room or put them in the hotel safe when you're not there.
- Don't leave anything visible in your car when you park it in a city, particularly at night. Always lock your car when you leave it. While driving, if your car is bumped from behind, don't stop – keep going to a well-lit area, service station or even a police station.
- Avoid walking or driving through poorer neighborhoods, especially at night. Don't walk in parks at night. Avoid walking along any empty street at night. Aim to use ATMs in well-trafficked areas. Well-lit streets busy with walkers are usually all right.

Street People & Begging

Street people and panhandlers may approach visitors in the larger cities and towns – nearly all are harmless. It's an individual judgment call as to whether you believe their stories and offer them money or anything else, though it's immensely preferable to give to a recognized charity. If a stranger approaches you and doesn't ask for the time or directions and doesn't get to the point immediately, they will ask for money – it's a hard and fast rule. If it is a

scam, they've probably had a lot of practice and will sound very convincing.

If you do give, don't wave a full wallet around – carry some change in a separate pocket. See also Dangers & Annoyances in the New York City chapter.

Guns & Hunting

Unregistered guns are banned in New York City and New Jersey, but not in Pennsylvania.

Residents of rural areas often carry guns, mainly to use on animals. Avoid forests – or indeed anywhere where game and hunters roam – during the fall hunting season, especially at dawn and dusk, when game is most active. 'No Hunting' signs are widely ignored and are not a guarantee of safety.

Wildlife

If you're camping in the woods, beware of animals, mostly bears, looking for an easy snack. Keep your food in nylon bags; a sleeping-bag sack is good. Tie the sack to a rope and sling it high over a branch away from your tent and away from the trunk of the tree, as some bears can climb. Don't leave food scraps around the site and never keep food in the tent. Don't try to get close-up photographs of bears and never come between a bear and its cubs. If you see a bear, try to get upwind so it can smell you and you won't startle it. When hiking in bear country, making a noise, talking loudly or singing as you go warns the animals of your presence.

Drivers should watch for animals on highways. Hitting a deer at 55 mph will total your car, kill the animal and may kill you and/or other people.

Insects

In some rural areas you will be plagued by mosquitoes and black flies, and if you're camping or hiking an insect repellent is a necessity. Lemon or orange peel rubbed on your skin helps if you have no repellent. As a rule, darker clothes are said to attract biting insects more than lighter ones. Try to minimize the amount of skin exposed by wearing a long-sleeved shirt, long pants and a close-fitting cap or hat.

Insects are at their worst deep in woods. In clearings, along shorelines or anywhere there's a breeze you'll be safer. Mosquitoes come out around sunset; building a fire, if it's allowed, will help keep them away.

EMERGENCY

Dial ☎ 911 if you need emergency assistance of any kind. This is free from any phone. A few rural phones might not have this service, in which case dial ☎ 0 (zero) for the operator, who'll connect you to the necessary local emergency service.

Travelers Aid Society (☎ 202-546-1127, fax 202-546-9112), 1612 K St NW, suite 506, Washington, DC, is an organization of volunteers who do their best to help travelers solve their problems. It has a website (www.travelersaid.org) and offices at JFK airport (☎ 718-656-4870), Newark airport (☎ 973-623-5052), in Philadelphia (☎ 215-523-7580) and in Pittsburgh (☎ 412-281-5466). Offices are listed in the local yellow pages phone book, or you can call directory assistance at ☎ 411 and ask for the Travelers Aid Society.

LEGAL MATTERS

If you're stopped by the police for any reason, bear in mind that there's no system of paying on-the-spot fines. For traffic offenses, the police officer will explain your options to you. Attempting to pay the fine to the officer is frowned upon at best and may lead to a charge of bribery to compound your troubles. Should the officer decide that you should pay up front, he or she can take you directly to the magistrate instead of allowing you the usual 30-day period to pay.

If you're arrested for more serious offenses, you're allowed to remain silent, entitled to have an attorney present during interrogation and are presumed innocent until proven guilty. There's no legal reason to speak to a police officer if you don't wish to. Any arrested person is legally allowed (and given) the right to make one phone call. If you don't have a lawyer or family member to help you, call your embassy or consulate. The police will give you the number on request.

Drinking & Driving

The minimum age for drinking alcohol is 21. You'll need a government-issued photo ID (such as a passport or US driver's license) to prove your age. Stiff fines, jail time and other penalties may be incurred if you're caught driving under the influence (DUI) of alcohol or providing alcohol to minors. The blood alcohol limit is 0.08%. During festive holidays and special events, road blocks with breathalyzer tests are sometimes set up to deter drunk drivers. Refusing a breathalyzer, urine or blood test is treated as if you'd taken the test and failed.

BUSINESS HOURS

Generally, public and private office hours are 8 or 9 am to 5 or 5:30 pm weekdays. Customary banking hours are 9 am to 3 pm weekdays, but many banks have extended customer service hours until 5 pm (or even 8 or 9 pm on Thursday) and on Saturday 9 am to 2 pm or later. In most areas, post offices are open 8 am to 4 or 5:30 pm weekdays, and some are open 8 am to 1 or 3 pm on Saturday.

In large cities, a few supermarkets, convenience stores, restaurants and the main post office are open 24 hours a day. Some stores are open until 9 pm, especially those in shopping malls, and many stores are open shorter hours on Sunday (typically from noon to 5 pm).

Service stations on major highways are open 24 hours a day, and city service stations are open 6 or 7 am to 8 or 9 pm. In small towns and villages, hours may be only 7 or 8 am to 7 or 8 pm.

Most museums open at 9 or 10 am and close at 5 pm, Tuesday to Sunday. Check entries in this book or call to be sure. Some smaller museums and exhibitions are seasonal and only open in the warmer months.

Many attractions close on Thanksgiving Day (the fourth Thursday in November), Christmas Day and New Year's Day.

PUBLIC HOLIDAYS & SPECIAL EVENTS

On national public holidays banks, schools and government offices (including post offices) are closed, and transportation, museums and other services are on a Sunday schedule. Many stores, however, maintain regular business hours. Holidays falling on weekends are usually observed the following Monday. Public holidays are denoted by an asterisk (*) in the month-by-month listing below.

Some national holidays are less official: these include Halloween and Mother's Day. In some cities with strong ethnic cultures, traditional holidays of other countries are also celebrated with fanfare, such as St Patrick's Day in New York City. Some of these are local public holidays and therefore local banks, schools and government buildings close.

As well as national holidays, residents celebrate hundreds of regional special events, from highbrow arts festivals to down-home country fairs. Such events are covered in the regional chapters.

January

New Year's Day* is January 1.

Mummers Parade is on January 1 (Philadelphia).

Martin Luther King Jr Day* is the third Monday of the month; it celebrates the civil rights leader's birthday (January 15, 1929).

Chinese New Year begins at the end of January or beginning of February and lasts two weeks; the first day is celebrated with parades, firecrackers, fireworks and food.

February

Presidents' Day* is the third Monday of the month; it celebrates the birthdays of Abraham Lincoln (February 12, 1809) and George Washington (February 22, 1732).

Black History Month is observed nationally for the entire month; it recognizes the history and the achievements of African Americans.

March

St Patrick's Day is March 17; it honors the patron saint of Ireland; many wear something green, stores sell green bread, bars serve green beer and towns and cities put on parades with participation by marching bands and community groups. The region's premier parade is held in New York City.

Easter* is the first Sunday after a full moon in March or April; celebrates the resurrection of Christ; travel during this weekend is usually expensive and crowded. Incidentally, Good Friday (the Friday before Easter) isn't a public holiday.

April

Passover is in March or April (depending on the Jewish calendar); Jewish families gather for a symbolic seder dinner to remember God's deliverance of the ancient Hebrews from bondage in Egypt.

May

Cinco de Mayo is May 5; it is the day the Mexicans wiped out the French army in 1862. Americans now celebrate with festivals, Mexican food and margaritas.

Mother's Day is the second Sunday of the month.

Memorial Day* is the last Monday in the month; it honors the war dead (and is also the unofficial first day of the summer tourist season); there's a parade in Atlantic City, NJ.

June

Father's Day is the third Sunday of the month.

July

Independence Day* is July 4; more commonly called fourth of July, this day celebrates the adoption of the Declaration of Independence in 1776; notable fireworks demonstrations are held at New York Harbor, in the New Jersey shore towns and in Philadelphia.

September

Labor Day* is the first Monday of the month; it honors working people (and is the unofficial end of the summer tourist season).

October

Columbus Day* is the second Monday of the month; commemorates the landing of Christopher Columbus in the Bahamas on October 12, 1492; though it's a federal holiday, many Native Americans don't consider this day a cause for celebration.

Halloween is October 31; kids and adults dress in costumes; in safer neighborhoods children go 'trick-or-treating' for candy.

November

Day of the Dead is November 2; observed in areas with Mexican communities; it's a day for families to honor dead relatives.

Veterans' Day* is November 11; it honors the nation's war veterans.

Thanksgiving* is the fourth Thursday of the month; it's a day of giving thanks and is traditionally celebrated with a turkey dinner; there are parades in New York City and Philadelphia.

December

Christmas* is December 25; Christmas Eve (Dec 24) is as much of an event as the day itself, with church services, caroling in the streets and last-minute shopping.

Kwanzaa is December 26 to 31; it is an African American celebration of cultural heritage.

New Year's Eve is December 31 and is celebrated with dressing up and drinking champagne.

WORK

Seasonal work is possible, in summer at resorts, camps and on the Jersey Shore, and in the winter at the ski areas. For information contact local chambers of commerce. It's also possible to find year-round work in city bars, restaurants, fast-food outlets and local newspapers. If you're coming from abroad and want to work in the USA, you need to apply for a work visa from the US embassy in your home country before you leave. The type of visa varies depending on how long you're staying and the kind of work you plan to do. Generally, you'll need either a J-1 visa, which you can obtain by joining a visitor-exchange program, or an H-2B visa, which you receive when being sponsored by a US employer. The former is issued mostly to students for work in summer camps or as au pairs.

The latter can be difficult to procure unless you can show that you already have a job offer from an employer who considers your qualifications unique and not readily available in the USA. There are, of course, many foreigners working illegally in the country. Controversial laws prescribe punishments for employers giving jobs to 'aliens' (foreigners who don't have the proper visas). INS officers can be persistent and insistent as they enforce the laws.

Voluntary work is available with environmental organizations such as Earthwatch; see Ecology & Environment in the Facts about the Region chapter.

ACCOMMODATIONS

The region offers a comfortable array of accommodations. In the countryside, these range from simple campsites to lavish country inns. In cities, both mid-range and top-end hotels are usually plentiful, but truly inexpensive accommodations are rare. The most comfortable accommodations for the lowest price are usually found in that great American invention, the roadside motel. These are plentiful around highway exits on the outskirts of cities.

To keep the cost of accommodations down, visit cities on weekends (when hotels offer lower rates Friday to Sunday) and the countryside during the week (when country and resort lodgings reduce rates Monday to Thursday). There's also a vast difference between high- and low-season rates. Prices in this book are generally the high-season prices and are only a guideline. Discounts are available at some motels and hotels for senior citizens, members of AAA and those with coupons (see also the Cost section, earlier in this chapter). Most hotels and motels have smoking and nonsmoking rooms.

Reservations

Many cheaper places may not accept reservations, but you can phone ahead to see what's available – even if they don't take reservations, they'll often hold a room for an hour or two. With the exception of busy holiday times and local events, it's possible to just pull into a motel or hotel in New Jersey (even Atlantic City) and Pennsylvania without a reservation. You simply can't do that in New York City, where it's always a good idea to book ahead.

Chain motels and hotels take reservations days or months in advance. Normally, you have to give a credit-card number to hold the room. If you don't show and don't call to cancel, you'll be charged the first night's rental. Cancellation policies vary – some let you cancel at no charge 24 hours or 72 hours in advance; others are less forgiving. Find out about cancellation policies when you book. Also, let the establishment know if you plan to arrive late, because many will rent your room if you haven't arrived or called by 6 pm. Chains often have a toll-free number, but their central reservation system might not be aware of local availability and special discounts (see the Motel & Hotel section, below).

Some places, especially B&Bs and some cabins, won't accept credit cards and want a check as deposit before they reserve a room.

Camping

Visitors with their own transportation and a tent can camp on many public lands or use one of the hundreds of public and private campgrounds.

Public Campgrounds These are on public lands, such as national and state forests, National Park Service (NPS) areas, state parks and US Army Corps of Engineers' land.

Free dispersed camping (meaning you can camp almost anywhere) is permitted in many public backcountry areas. Sometimes you can camp right from your car along a dirt road, and sometimes you can backpack in with your gear. Information on where camping is permitted and detailed maps are available from many local ranger stations (addresses and telephone numbers are given in the text) and may be posted along the road. Sometimes a (free) camping permit is required.

Camping in an undeveloped area, whether from your car or backpacking, entails basic responsibility. See the Outdoor Activities chapter for more on wilderness camping.

Basic campgrounds usually have toilets, fire pits (or charcoal grills), picnic tables and drinking water (it's always a good idea to have a few gallons of water with you anyway). These sites are often available on a first-come, first-served basis, fill up on Friday nights and usually cost about $7 to $12 a night. More-developed camping areas may have showers or recreational vehicle (RV) hookups and accept or require reservations. Sites in these campgrounds usually cost several dollars more.

A site normally accommodates up to six people (or two vehicles). Public campgrounds often have seven- or 14-night limits.

Private Campgrounds These are usually more expensive and less spacious, with sites closer together and less shade, but with lots more entertainment facilities. Most of the sites are for RVs and have water and electric hookups and perhaps sewage hookups. A small grassy area without hookups is usually set aside for tent campers, who are distinctly in the minority and pay the lowest rate.

Sometimes hot showers are free, sometimes not. Private campgrounds usually have small shops and snack bars for essentials. Recreation facilities are usually elaborate, with playgrounds, swimming, game rooms and even miniature golf. Some private campgrounds open late May to early September, some from mid-April through November; a few are open all year.

Woodall's North American Campground Directory is a huge tome listing campgrounds throughout the USA and Canada. It has a website at www.woodalls.com. Kampgrounds of America (KOA; ☎ 406-248-7444), PO Box 30558, Billings, MT 59114-0558, a national network of private campgrounds, publishes a free annual directory of its sites and has a website at www.koa.com.

Hostels

The hostelling network is less widespread in America than in Australia, Canada or Europe. New York City has a reasonable selection, but even some prime travel destinations such as Gettysburg, don't have a hostel. The Internet guide to hostelling (www.hostels.com) lists hostels worldwide.

HI-AYH US citizens/residents can join Hostelling International-American Youth Hostels (HI-AYH; ☎ 202-783-6161, fax 783-6171, hiayhserv@hiayh.org) PO Box 37613, Washington, DC 20013, by calling and requesting a membership form or by downloading a form from their website (www.hiayh.org) and mailing or faxing it. Membership can also be purchased at regional council offices and at many (but not all) youth hostels. Non-US residents should buy a HI-AYH membership in their home countries. If not, you can still stay in US hostels by buying 'Welcome Stamps' for each night you stay in a hostel. Six stamps on your stamp card qualifies you for a valid one-year HI-AYH membership throughout the world. The HI-AYH card may be used to get discounts at some local merchants and services, including some intercity bus companies.

Strictly, you must have a sheet sleeping bag, but many hostels accept a regular sleeping bag if they're convinced it doesn't harbor bugs. Dorms are segregated by sex. Some hostels have a curfew (around 10 pm). Most prohibit alcohol and some require you to do a small housekeeping chore. Most also have kitchen and laundry facilities, information and advertising boards, TV room and lounge area.

Reservations are accepted and advisable during the high season (there may be a limit of a three night stay then). You can call HI-AYH's head office (see above) to make reservations for any HI-AYH hostel, or use their toll-free, code-based reservation service at ☎ 800-909-4776. You need the access code for the hostels to use the code-based service (available from any HI-AYH office or their handbook), but not all hostels participate in the service. For additional information write or call HI-AYH at its head office or one of the following regional offices:

Delaware Valley Council
 (☎ 215-925-6004, fax 925-4874, hitravelphl@
 compuserve.org, www.hi-dvc.org) 624 S 3rd St,
 Philadelphia, PA 19147

Hudson Mohawk Council
 (☎ 518-472-1914, fax 472-1544) PO Box 7066,
 Albany, NY 12206

New York City Hostel
 (☎ 212-932-2300, www.HInewyork.org) 891
 Amsterdam Ave, New York, NY 10025-4403

Niagara Frontier Council
 (☎ 716-852-5222, fax 852-1642, af060@freenet
 .buffalo.net) 667 Main St, Buffalo, NY 14203

Pittsburgh Council
 (☎ 412-431-4910, fax 431-2625, ayh@trfn.clpgh
 .org, www.trfn.clpgh.org/orgs/ayh) 830 East Warrington Ave, Pittsburgh, PA 15210

Syracuse Council
 (☎ 315-472-5788, wfrancis@mailbox.syr.edu) 535
 Oak St, Syracuse, NY 13203-1609

Independent Hostels There's a small number of independent ('backpacker') hostels, mostly in New York City. Rates are similar to HI-AYH, but they don't have curfews or housekeeping chores. Standards are variable. Dorms are often mixed, male and female (coed), and some have a few private single/double rooms, although bathroom facilities are usually shared. Kitchen, laundry, notice board and TV facilities are also available.

University Accommodations

Some universities and colleges offer student accommodations to visitors during vacations, usually June to mid-August. Most rooms are comfortable, functional single/ double rooms with shared bathroom. Prices start at $15 per person. For general information contact the Council on International Educational Exchange (CIEE; ☎ 212-661-1414), 205 E 42nd St, New York, NY 10017, or visit its website (www.ciee.org).

Guesthouses

Accommodations at a guesthouse may be simply a spare room in someone's home, but can more commonly be in commercial lodging houses and are normally found in places with a large tourist trade, such as Gettysburg. Rooms range in size and have varying amenities; some include private bathrooms. Prices start at about $35 per person.

B&Bs

North American B&Bs aren't the casual, inexpensive accommodations found in Britain or Ireland. Usually family run, cheaper establishments may have clean, but plain, rooms with a shared bathroom. Pricier places offer private bathrooms and feature fireplaces, balconies and private gardens. Others may be in historical buildings, quaint country houses or luxurious urban homes. Most include a substantial breakfast in the price, but sometimes it's self-serve continental. The best are distinguished by a friendly, personal attention to detail by the owners/hosts who can provide you with local information, contacts and other amenities.

Most B&Bs fall in the $60 to $120 price range, but some go way over this – especially in New York City and at peak times in popular resorts. Many require reservations and don't take walk-in customers. In fact, in larger urban centers, for security reasons there may be no external indication that a place is a B&B. Many B&Bs don't accept children or smokers, and pets are usually unwelcome; some prohibit alcohol or may have a curfew.

Motels & Hotels

Motel and hotel prices vary tremendously. A hotel charging $50 for a double in the high season may drop to $35 in the low season and may raise its rates to $75 for a special event when the town is overflowing. Hotels may charge single and double rates during the week, but a flat, cheaper room rate on the weekends. At times, rates may depend on the size of the bed and/or the view from the room rather than the number of occupants. This guidebook gives rates for one or two people but, unless otherwise stated, the rates don't include taxes. Extra people are charged $5 to $15 per person.

Children are often allowed to stay free with their parents, but rules vary. Some hotels allow children under 18 to stay free, others allow children under 12. Others may charge a few dollars extra per child, especially if the child uses an extra bed. Ask when you book.

Advertised prices are called 'rack rates' but can be negotiable. If you ask about any 'specials,' you can often save money. Booking through a travel agent can be cheaper, and seniors, students, AAA members and business travelers may get a discount or 'corporate' rate. Many tourist publications, brochures and flyers have discount coupons for hotels and motels, but such discounts are usually only valid for off-peak times (see also Costs, earlier in this chapter).

Budget Motels with $35 rooms are found in small towns along major highways and along motel strips on the outskirts of larger towns – often at the intersection of highways. Popular destinations won't have rock-

bottom budget motels therefore, what may be a budget motel in one town may be mid-range in another.

Budget motels are very standardized. Rooms are usually small, and beds may be soft or saggy, but the sheets should be clean. A minimal level of cleanliness is maintained, but expect scuffed walls, atrocious decor, old furniture, dim lighting and the smell of stale tobacco. Even these places, however, normally have a private shower, toilet and TV. Most have air-con and heat. Even the cheapest motels may advertise 'efficiencies,' which cost a few dollars more but give you the chance to cook a meal. Efficiencies vary from those with a two-ring burner to those with a spiffy little mini-kitchen, and they may or may not have utensils.

Downtown hotels tend to be either very expensive or very seedy, with little in between. Cheap, old hotels often double as transient rooming houses and tend to cluster near train and bus stations. Though not usually dangerous, they're often in undesirable parts of town. The cheapest hotels have shared bathroom and toilet and no parking lot.

Chain Motels & Hotels Motel and hotel chains offer a standardized level of quality and style, though with variations in facilities and prices depending on location. Members of frequent guest programs may get discounts and priority reservations.

Motel chain room prices start in the $30s in smaller towns, in the $40s in larger or more popular places. Beds are reliably firm, decor fairly attractive, a 24-hour desk is often available, and little extras such as free coffee, cable TV, or a bathtub with your shower may be offered. Some may have swimming pools. Chains in this range are Super 8 Motel, Days Inn or Econo Lodge.

Chains with rooms in the $50 to $85 range (depending on location) have noticeably nicer rooms; on-site or adjacent cafe, restaurant or bar; and perhaps an indoor swimming pool, spa or exercise room. Best Western offers good rooms in this price range. Often they're the best available in a given town. Less widespread but also good are the Red Roof Inn and Comfort Inn.

Chains with widespread representation in the area include the following:

Best Western	☎ 800-528-1234
Comfort Inn	☎ 800-228-5150
Days Inn	☎ 800-329-7466
Econo Lodge	☎ 800-424-4777
Red Roof Inn	☎ 800-843-7663
Super 8 Motel	☎ 800-800-8000
Travelodge	☎ 800-578-7878

At the top end, hotel chains have in-house restaurants, bars, swimming pools, fitness centers, room service and 24-hour reservation numbers. Prices usually range from $90 to $150, but are much more in big cities such as New York and Philadelphia. Such chains include the following:

Hilton	☎ 800-445-8667
Hyatt	☎ 800-233-1234
Marriott	☎ 800-228-9290
Radisson	☎ 800-333-3333
Ramada	☎ 800-228-2828
Sheraton	☎ 800-325-3535
Westin	☎ 800-228-3000

Nonchain Hotels There are nonchain establishments that charge prices similar to those charged by the chain motels and hotels. A few of them are funky, historical hotels, full of early-20th-century furniture. In New York City and Philadelphia there are many boutique hotels, some on the pricier side, some on the lower end. Those that represent a good value are listed in the text. They are less common outside major cities.

Lodges & Resorts

Lodges are found throughout the Poconos, Adirondacks and the Catskills. They're often rustic looking, but usually quite comfortable inside. They often have restaurants and excellent services, but they're not cheap, with most rooms going for around $100 for a double during the high season. Many lodges are fully booked months in advance.

Luxury resorts have so much to do that they're often destinations in themselves. Some are devoted to skiing, and others

include recreational activities such as golf, tennis, horseback riding and swimming. Accommodations range from motel rooms to condominiums ('condos'). Skiing resorts may charge $230 or so for a condo in mid-season, then drop prices to less than half that in the snowless summer.

FOOD

The long Atlantic coastline and the many lakes and fertile valleys with their orchards and farms provide a variety of high-quality, locally caught and grown food. Clams and oysters are found on the coast, and fresh fruits and vegetables are available from the market gardens of New Jersey. The Pennsylvania Dutch Country is known for its meat and dairy products.

The different immigrant groups that make up the USA's cultural mosaic contribute enormously to the diversity of ethnic cuisine. Chinese restaurants have been around a long time, but Japanese, Indian, Thai, Vietnamese and other Asian alternatives are also available. Italian food is common, and French and other European cuisine are found in some areas. Mexican-style restaurants are also fairly common.

New York City and Philadelphia offer the widest variety of restaurants, including some of the best in the country.

Fast Food

Almost every settlement big enough to support a restaurant has at least one of the many fast-food franchises (their neon-lit logos are visible from many blocks away). They're usually on or near the main drag downtown, close to major tourist attractions or along the highway commercial strips on the edges of towns. Because these eateries are so abundant and conspicuous, they're rarely mentioned specifically in the text.

Vegetarian

If you're a vegetarian or just want to avoid red meat, you won't have much trouble finding alternatives – most restaurants are service oriented and try to give customers what they want. You'll find vegetarian restaurants in the larger cities, especially

New York and Philadelphia, and most regular restaurants, including some chains, offer nonmeat choices. Elsewhere, salads are a standard offering and often big enough to be a complete meal. At roadside diners, you might be eating a lot of eggs or grilled-cheese sandwiches. Restaurants serving ethnic cuisine – Chinese, Mexican, Middle

Local Grub

Many of the region's local dishes derive from those brought in or created by immigrants. New York City is the pizza capital of the world, but initially the dish was a staple of some of Italy's poorer people. The average pizza slice is doughy and covered with sweet tomato sauce and gooey cheese. The city's Jewish community first introduced the immensely popular bagel to the nation. The best are water bagels, made of sweet dough and boiled before baking so that their crusty shells hide a springy center. Most New Yorkers have their bagels for breakfast, often with sweet butter or cream cheese.

The humble, ubiquitous hot dog was originally produced in Coney Island, and pastrami sandwiches are a quintessential New York item. Manhattan clam chowder is a local dish made with clams, carrots, celery, green pepper and tomatoes.

Buffalo, NY, is the home of buffalo wings – spicy chicken wings. These are covered in a spicy red chili sauce and served with creamy blue cheese dressing and celery. Another Buffalo specialty is beef on weck – sliced roast beef on *kummelweck*, a hard, salty bread roll.

New York cheesecake is served plain or with a pineapple or strawberry topping. The best way to combat a sweltering New York City summer day is to try an Italian ice, a rich, creamy treat, halfway between an ice cream and a granita. At some of the better places the Italian ices come with chunks of real fruit. Another icy sweet is custard, a super rich ice cream that originated in the beach resort of Coney Island.

Submarine sandwiches (sliced meats, cheeses and condiments on a large bread roll) are known as heroes in New York City and grinders in New Jersey. Philadelphia produces its own submarine sandwich called a hoagie, which is made with ham, provolone and salami and adorned with onions, lettuce, mayonnaise, pickle, tomato and olive oil – not a good choice if you're on a diet.

In the Southern Tier of the Finger Lakes region the local specialty is the spiedie sandwich that consists of marinated pork, chicken or lamb, grilled and served on a large roll.

Although imitated throughout the country, the best cheese steak – a long sandwich roll filled with slices of steak and covered in cheese and onion – is found in Philadelphia (popularly know as a Philly cheese steak). Philadelphia is sometimes jokingly called the Big Scrapple, because of another local dish called scrapple. It's made of cornmeal and ground meat fried together. You'll also find water ice, a mixture of crushed ice and fruit pulp (a variation on New York City's Italian ice).

Pennsylvania is famous for its pretzels, the best of which are reputedly made by the Amish of the Pennsylvania Dutch Country. In addition, the region is noted for its baked fruit and pies (such as shoo-fly pie, a tart filled with molasses and brown sugar), as well as cooked meats, especially Lebanon bologna.

Eastern, Indian, etc – usually have a vegetarian selection. Health-food stores and delis are found in cities and some small towns.

Markets & Roadside Stalls

Many towns have farmers' markets two to three days a week where you can purchase fresh produce and cooked goods at reasonable prices. In the region's many rural areas, farmers' stalls sit beside highways and secondary roads, offering the crops of the season. Pumpkin, corn and fruit are items that are worth keeping an eye out for.

The ubiquitous supermarkets, often open 24 hours, have about the lowest food prices and a wide variety of fresh and prepared foods. These are good places to stock up on supplies for camping trips or a stay in a summer resort, because outlying or local grocery stores may inflate prices.

Mealtimes

Breakfast is typically served between 6 and 11 am, and it's an affordable way to fill up, provided you can stomach large quantities of greasy food. A breakfast of pancakes, eggs and sausage or a hearty omelet costs around $5 and usually includes home fries (sliced potatoes fried with spices) or hash browns (shredded potatoes, often mixed with onions and fried), toast and coffee. Some places serve breakfasts all day.

Lunch, usually between 11 am and 2 pm, is often the best-value meal. Prices may be 30% to 50% less than the dinner menu, though the food and portions are identical. Fixed-price specials are common.

Dinners, served between about 5 and 10 pm, are more expensive. In larger towns some restaurants offer 'early-bird' specials that feature a complete meal for around $5 or $6. Spending a few dollars on a drink during 'happy hour' (usually before 7 pm) will often get you free appetizers. Some of the better restaurants require reservations.

DRINKS
Nonalcoholic Drinks

Most restaurants provide customers with free ice water – tap water is safe to drink, though it can smell of chlorine. The usual soft drinks are available, although you may be asked if you drink Coke instead of Pepsi and vice-versa. Lemonade is a mixture of lemon, sugar and ice water. If you want the clear, carbonated variety, ask for a Sprite or 7-Up. Less familiar to foreign visitors are Dr Pepper, a kind of sarsaparilla, and Mountain Dew, a yellow liquid that is high in sugar and caffeine.

Many restaurants serve milk, including low-fat varieties. You can often get freshly squeezed orange juice at better restaurants, but packaged juices are common.

Coffee is served more frequently than tea, usually with a choice of regular or decaf (decaffeinated), with milk or cream, or without (black). In many cities and towns there's a wide, sometimes bewildering, choice of coffee drinks: from a single espresso to a decaf latte grande or a mocha made with soy milk.

Tea is usually a cup of hot water with a tea bag next to it – milk isn't normally added but a slice of lemon often is. Iced tea, with lemon and sugar, is available in cans as a soft drink. Better restaurants and cafes serve herbal teas.

Alcoholic Drinks

Persons 21 and over are allowed to consume alcohol. To enter a bar, order alcohol at a restaurant or buy alcohol, carry a driver's license or passport as proof of your age.

Big-name brands of domestic beers are available everywhere alcohol is sold, though many people find that these beers lack flavor. To order beer, specify the type you want: if you just ask for a beer, you'll get a rapid-fire list to choose from.

A growing number of microbreweries (or brewpubs) offer beers brewed on the premises. Their brews echo British or German brewing styles. These breweries include the Pennsylvania Brewing Company in Pittsburgh, Park Slope Brewing Company in New York City and the Chapter House Brewpub in Ithaca. The beers are naturally brewed and sometimes cask conditioned. The beers are also available in bottles or on tap. Supermarkets and liquor stores stock a huge array of imported beers, which are more expensive but may be more to your taste.

California wines compete well with their European and Australian counterparts, but you'll also find good local wines from the vineyards of the Finger Lakes, Lake Erie, Hudson Valley and eastern Long Island regions of New York and the Lake Erie region of Pennsylvania.

Bars have a big range of 'hard liquor,' invariably served with lots of ice (on the rocks) unless you ask for it 'straight up.' Whiskey is called bourbon if it's from Kentucky (ie, Jim Beam), or whiskey if it's not (ie, Jack Daniels). If you want Scotch whiskey, ask for Scotch.

There are thousands of cocktail recipes. Some well-known ones first appeared in New York, the most famous of which is probably the Bloody Mary, a mixture of vodka and spicy tomato juice. New Jersey bars tend to feature highly calorific (and sometimes highly alcoholic) specialty drinks such as Long Island Iced Tea, a potent, dark-rum drink made without tea (despite the name, you don't really see it on Long Island), and Sea Breeze, a cranberry and vodka drink.

Alcohol is sold in liquor stores in New Jersey and Pennsylvania, but is available in food stores in New York. New York laws prohibit the sale of package beer, wine and liquor on Sunday.

ENTERTAINMENT

The main centers for opera, theater, classical music and ballet are mentioned in the Arts section of the Facts about the Region chapter. In addition, many smaller towns have their own local amateur performance-art companies and venues. Generally, the quality and variety increases with the size and affluence of the city. Often, there's at least one free weekly newspaper listing the entertainment options in town, and local newspapers often have a section with entertainment listings.

Cinemas

Despite video and cable TV, most small towns still have a movie theater. The main venues are multiscreen complexes, typically in suburban shopping malls. Admission is about $7 to $9, often with discounts on Monday or Tuesday, or for matinees the first show of the day, and seniors are frequently entitled to a discount at all performances. Larger cities have art house cinemas showing foreign, alternative and underground films.

Bars & Nightclubs

For young adults, the mainstay of American nightlife is bars, which range from sleazy booze joints to slick cocktail lounges. The distinction between bars and nightclubs can be blurred. In general, a bar serves alcohol and may offer live music on occasion, and a nightclub is a more formal venue that depends on live entertainment, but also serves alcohol. In bigger cities this blurring extends to restaurants, because most pubs and clubs offer food and some are worth going to just to eat. On the other hand, some restaurants provide regular entertainment in order to attract customers.

In cities, bars and nightclubs present a variety of performances, ranging from rock, jazz, blues, folk, alternative and country music to lounge singers and comedians. Some bars (known as sports bars) also have big-screen TVs that show major sporting events. In rural areas the regular attraction is a local dance band, playing a variety of styles, but usually country-music based. In small towns, a bar might be the best place to have a beer, shoot some pool and meet the locals.

New York City has the biggest bar and club scene of course, but Philadelphia's is also extensive, and Hoboken has a reputation as a popular weekend party town.

Cafes

In the cities and college towns there are many coffeehouses serving Italian-style coffee as well as varieties of brewed coffee blends from South America and Asia. Some double as bars and/or have live music one or more nights a week and offer book or poetry readings. Cafes are also found in larger bookstores.

SPECTATOR SPORTS

Baseball, football and basketball are the cornerstones of spectator sports in the USA. In the fall, regardless of the temperature or class of play, an American football game is an exhilarating experience. The same is true of baseball in the spring, summer and fall. Minor-league and college team games are sometimes significantly less expensive, yet more fun than those of professional teams.

The major football teams in this region are the New York Jets and New York Giants, although they actually play at the Meadowlands Sports Complex in East Rutherford, NJ, 5 miles west of New York City. The other main team in New York is the Buffalo Bills, with wildly loyal fans who brave sub-zero temperatures to watch their team play in upstate New York. In Pennsylvania the teams are the Philadelphia Eagles and Pittsburgh Steelers. The football season is from August through December, and the Super Bowl is played on the third Sunday in January.

In basketball the region's major clubs are the New York Knickerbockers (Knicks), New Jersey Nets and Philadelphia 76ers (Sixers), and the season is from October through July.

Two of the most famous baseball clubs in the US are the New York Yankees, the most successful team in baseball history, who play at Yankee Stadium in the Bronx, and the New York Mets, who play at Shea Stadium in Queens. In Pennsylvania the major teams are the Philadelphia Phillies and Pittsburgh Pirates. The season is from April through October, when the World Series is played. Minor league teams in the region include the Buffalo Bisons (NY), Hudson Valley Renegades (NY), Oneonta Yankees (NY), Rochester Red Wings (NY), Syracuse Chiefs (NY), Utica Blue Sox (NY), New Jersey Cardinals (NJ), Princeton Reds (NJ), Trenton Thunder (NJ), Erie Seawolves (PA), Harrisburg Senators (PA), and Reading Phillies (PA).

Ice hockey is also popular, and teams compete in the National Hockey League (NHL) for the Stanley Cup, which is awarded to the champions. The main clubs are the New York Rangers, New York Islanders, Buffalo Sabers, New Jersey Devils, Philadelphia Flyers and Pittsburgh Penguins. The NHL season is from October through April.

Though popular with school aged children, soccer hasn't enjoyed much success as a spectator sport. The tide may be turning, however, due to the 1999 victory of the US team in the Women's World Cup. Even President Bill Clinton turned out to watch them win the final match. The Major League Soccer (MLS) competition began in 1996 with teams playing from April to October. This region is represented by the New York–New Jersey Metrostars.

In New York City, Madison Square Garden is a world-famous sports venue. Flushing Meadows, in Queens, NY, is the site

Ticket Scalpers & Brokers

You'll find 'ticket scalpers' hovering about at major events – theaters, concerts, sporting venues, etc. Scalping (selling already purchased tickets at inflated prices) is legal in New Jersey, but banned everywhere else. Where it is banned, transactions occur illegally, but the perpetrators are rarely busted.

Nevertheless, the buyer should be very cautious: the bigger the event, the bigger the chance that the scalper is selling counterfeit tickets well above the ticket's face value. If you use a scalper, it's best to engage them only during regular season events and offer money close to game time when prices can drop drastically.

Alternatively, you can contact a ticket broker, a licensed ticket retailer and a more secure bet (or, if you're desperate, a concierge in the major metropolitan hotels). Newspapers' sports pages are a good place to find brokers for major sporting events. In New York, they often take out small ads in the *New York Post* or *Daily News*. No matter how big the sporting event, show or concert, good seats are usually available up to starting time, though you will, of course, pay more.

for pro-tennis' US Open tournament, which is held in September.

Thoroughbred horseracing is popular, and national events are held in summer at the Belmont Race Track on Long Island, NY, and at the Saratoga Race Course, Saratoga Springs, NY, also home of the National Museum of Racing. Horseracing is also popular at well-kept Monmouth Park near the Jersey Shore.

SHOPPING

The sheer variety and quantity of consumer goods in the USA is staggering, and prices of many goods are lower than in other western countries. At the center of this consumerism sits New York City, the nation's shopping capital. Here, and in other big cities with their shopping malls, department stores, galleries, antique stores and markets, you'll be able to buy just about anything you could want or need.

New York City is the best place for cutting edge and traditional fashion. Stores on Madison Ave have the best international designs, and there are signature shops from 30th St northwards. Both Saks Fifth Ave and Bloomingdale's have designer areas, and though Macy's sells designer clothes too, it's more downmarket. Hip and chic clothes and antique clothes are found in Greenwich Village, East Village and SoHo – in the summer check out the street fairs there, where clothing basics go for around $10 to $20. Century 21, a large store near the World Trade Center, has great discounts on designer clothes. And don't forget to visit the Fashion District (Seventh Ave and Broadway between 34th and 42nd Sts) for sample sales – designer clothing discounted directly from the manufacturer's offices. Sample sales are often advertised by flyers handed out in the street or in building lobbies.

New York City is also the best place to shop for professional-level photographic equipment; you can get good deals, but be sure to patronize a reputable dealer. See Cameras under Shopping in the New York City chapter.

A wide variety of ethnic food items, which are largely unavailable elsewhere in the country, can also be readily found in New York City. For more information on shopping in NYC, check out the Shopping section in the New York City chapter.

New Jersey has numerous craft fairs, and many people head there to buy clothes because there's no state tax on clothing. Secaucus Outlet Center in Hackensack, a short ride from New York City, is noted for its discount factory outlets.

Philadelphia has centers for antiques, jewelry and commercial arts and crafts. In Pennsylvania Dutch Country you can buy hex signs (painted geometric designs, usually on the side of barns and originally used to ward off witches) and crafts made by the Amish, notably quilts, wooden furniture and faceless dolls. Pennsylvania also has no tax on clothing, and there are numerous discount factory outlets, particularly in Reading. Civil War memorabilia is available in Gettysburg, PA, and Hershey, PA, is the place to fill up on chocolate.

Outdoor Activities

Although this region is heavily urbanized, the pursuit of outdoor activities opens up some of its most beautiful and fascinating corners away from cities. Many activities are within the reach of the tightest budget, and a walk or cycle in the countryside will almost certainly be a highlight of your vacation. The region's mountains are popular destinations for rock climbing, mountain biking and hiking, while its lakes and rivers draw white-water rafters and canoeists. Wildlife enthusiasts can chose from dense woodlands, glacial lakes or coastal wetlands. For those who have the money, activities like skiing, golf or fishing are available as part of holiday packages that include bed, board and transportation.

New York's natural treasures include the 6-million acre Adirondack Park, which is wild and remote mountain country; and the long, narrow lakes, waterfalls and gorges of the Finger Lakes region. New Jersey's physical variety can be found in the forests of the Pine Barrens, the most unpopulated part of the state; Great Swamp National Wildlife Refuge in the north; and the Gateway National Recreation Area (NRA), which straddles the coast between New York and New Jersey. Pennsylvania has the white-water Youghiogheny River in the Laurel Highlands, dense forests in the Allegheny National Forest and popular summer resorts in the Poconos.

A variety of government and independent organizations provide information on all types of outdoor activities. For contact information of national and state government agencies see the Parks & Forests section in the Facts about the Region chapter. Private clubs and associations can also give visitors invaluable information. Many have national or international affiliations, so check before leaving home. The state and county tourist offices put out information covering many activities, and these can be a starting point for further research. For information about New York, New Jersey and Pennsylvania's public lands, see the State Parks & Forests section of each state's Facts about chapter. An Outdoor Activities section in the Long Island, Catskills Region, Adirondack Region and Northern New Jersey chapters gives more information about popular natural destinations. The Jersey Shore, Southern New Jersey and Northern Pennsylvania chapters give information about popular outdoor activities available in those areas.

New York and New Jersey Coastal Adventures, by Betsy Frawley Haggerty, has information on activities along the shore, including sailing and whale watching. Pennsylvania – a Guide to Backcountry Travel & Adventure, by Diana Rupp, gives an excellent overview of activities in the state. New Jersey Outdoors is a periodical produced by New Jersey's Department of Environmental Protection. Other resource guides are mentioned under the specific activities, later in this chapter.

Recreational programs for handicapped people are offered by Disabled Sports USA (☎ 301-217-0960/0963), 451 Hungerford Drive, Suite 100, Rockville, MD 20850, which also maintains a website (www.nas .com/~dsusa). New York's Department of Environmental Conservation distributes the publication Opening the Outdoors to People with Disabilities.

HIKING & BACKPACKING

On foot and on the trail is one of the best ways to appreciate the mountains, public forests, wildlife sanctuaries, wilderness areas and river and coastal areas of New York, New Jersey and Pennsylvania. Every weekend thousands of people take to the parks and countryside. Perhaps because the region is so crowded, a high premium is placed on open space and the chance to find fresh air.

A vast network of trails traverses the region's most stunning scenery and wilderness. The 2158-mile **Appalachian Trail** – which passes through 14 states, from Maine to Georgia, following mountain ridges ranging in height from about 500 feet to 1200 feet – enters New York State from Connecticut in the rural area north of Pawling and heads southwest through the small farm communities of the Hudson Valley, rocky cliffs of the Hudson Highlands and weather-beaten Ramapo Mountains. From there it passes through the Pocono Mountains and Delaware Water Gap NRA into central Pennsylvania then Maryland.

The 4200-mile **North Country National Scenic Trail** – 1500 miles have been completed – is planned to run from Lake Champlain in New York to Lake Sakakawea in North Dakota, and will link the Appalachian Trail with the West Coast's Lewis & Clark and Pacific Crest trails. The trail runs through the Adirondack Mountains and connects with the 552-mile **Finger Lakes Trail**, which runs east-west from the Catskill Mountains, through the state's southern tier into the Allegheny Mountains and the wooded Allegany State Park. This park spills over into Pennsylvania and becomes the Allegheny National Forest, which offers over 80 miles of hiking trails.

Many abandoned railroad lines that belonged both to railroad and mining companies are being converted to trails for public recreational use. There are now over 700 trails nationwide and close to 150 in New York, New Jersey and Pennsylvania. The same process is occurring along 338 miles of the Erie Canal, which is being converted into a trail that will ultimately link the Hudson and Niagara Rivers.

Information

Hikers seeking true wilderness should contact the organizations in the boxed text 'Useful Outdoor Organizations' in the Facts about the Region chapter. For travelers with little hiking experience there are many short, well-marked, well-maintained trails, which often have restroom facilities at either end and interpretive displays along the way. These trails give access to natural features and are usually marked on maps as nature trails or self-guided interpretive trails.

The following private clubs can provide hiking information:

Adirondack Mountain Club
(☎ 518-668-4447, 800-395-8080, www.adk.org) RR 3, Box 3055, Lake George, NY 12845; maintains trails and leads excursions and workshops in New York's Adirondack and Catskill Parks.

Appalachian Mountain Club
(☎ 212-986-1430, www.outdoors.org) Manhattan Resource Center, 5 Tudor City Place, New York, NY 10017; America's oldest conservation and recreation organization, sponsors a wide variety of outdoor activities.

Appalachian Trail Conference
(☎ 304-535-6331, www.nps.gov/aptr) PO Box 807, Harper's Ferry, WV 25425-0807; maintains portions of the trail and provides hiker information.

Delaware Valley Orienteering Association
(☎ 610-792-0502, www.dvoa.us.orienteering.org) 14 Lake Drive, Spring City, PA 19475; holds orienteering (map and compass navigation) events across the region.

Finger Lakes Trail Conference
(☎ 716-288-7191) 202 Colebourne Rd, Rochester, NY 14609-6733; maintains trails in New York's Finger Lakes region.

Keystone Trails Association
(www.pennaweb.com/kta) PO Box 251, Cogan Station, PA 17728; organizes hikes in Pennsylvania and monitors forest-related legislation.

New York-New Jersey Trail Conference
(☎ 212-685-9699, www.nynjtc.org) 232 Madison Ave, New York, NY 10016; maintains over 1300 miles of trails in southeastern New York and northern New Jersey; sells maps.

New York State Canal System
(☎ 518-471-5011, www.canals.state.ny.us) PO Box 189, Albany, NY 12201; working on the conversion of the Erie Canal towpath into hiking trails.

North Country Trail Association
(☎ 616-454-5506, NCTAssoc@AOL.com, www.northcountrytrail.org) 49 Monroe Center, NW suite 200B, Grand Rapids, MI 49503; maintains North Country National Scenic Trail.

Rails-to-Trails Conservancy
(☎ 202-797-5400, www.railtrails.org) 1400 16th St NW, suite 300, Washington, DC 20036; a private nonprofit organization that manages public trails created from former rail lines.

Western Pennsylvania Conservancy
(☎ 412-288-2777) 209 4th Ave, Pittsburgh, PA 15222; preserves natural lands in western Pennsylvania for public use.

Other organizations and outfitters can be great sources of information as well as providers of equipment, hiking partners and organized walks. The Sierra Club (☎ 415-977-5500), 85 2nd St, 2nd floor 2F, San Francisco, CA 94105, publishes guides, is involved in conservation projects and maintains a website at www.sierraclub.org. The club also has local chapters in the region:

New York
(☎ 518-426-9144) Atlantic Chapter, 353 Hamilton St, Albany, NY 12210

New Jersey
(☎ 609-924-3141) New Jersey Chapter, 57 Mountain Ave, Princeton, NJ 08540

Pennsylvania
(☎ 717-232-0101) Pennsylvania Chapter, 600 N 2nd St, PO Box 663, Harrisburg, PA 17108

REI (☎ 800-426-4840, www.rei-outlet.com) has outfitting stores in most major cities in the region, as does Eastern Mountain Sports (www.easternmountainsports.com).

HI-AYH hostels are often in areas where hiking and other activities are available. You can request a membership form or make reservations by contacting the head office (☎ 202-783-6161, fax 783-6171, hiayhserv@ hiayh.org), PO Box 37613, Washington, DC 20013, or by downloading a form from its website (www.hiayh.org). For additional information see Hostels under Accommodations in the Facts for the Visitor chapter, earlier in this book.

What to Bring The following equipment list is only a general guide for serious backcountry hiking of at least several days duration. Know yourself and what special things you may need on the trail, and consider the area and seasonal climatic conditions you'll be traveling in. This list is inadequate for snow country or backpacking in winter.

- Boots – light to medium boots for day hikes, sturdy ones for extended trips with a heavy pack; most importantly, they should be well broken in and have a good heel.
- Alternative footwear – flip-flops/mucklucks/ sandals/running shoes for wearing around camp (optional) and canvas sneakers for crossing streams.
- Socks – heavy polypropylene or wool stays warm even if wet; frequent changes during the day reduce the chance of blisters, but that is usually impractical.
- Colors – subdued tones are recommended, though if you're hiking during hunting season, blaze orange is a necessity.
- Shorts, light shirt – for everyday wear; heavy cotton takes a long time to dry and is cold when it is wet.
- Long-sleeve shirt – light cotton, wool or polypropylene; button-down front makes layering easy and can be left open when the weather is hot, and the long sleeves protects your arms from the sun.
- Long pants – heavy denim jeans take forever to dry; sturdy cotton or canvas pants are good for trekking through brush, and cotton or nylon sweats are comfortable to wear around camp; long underwear with shorts over them is a good combination – warm but not cumbersome – for trail hiking where there isn't much brush.
- Wool/polypropylene/polar fleece sweater – essential in cold weather.
- Rainwear – light, breathable and waterproof is the ideal combination.
- Hat – wool or polypropylene is best for cold weather, a cotton hat with a brim is good for sun protection; about 80% of body heat escapes through the top of the head – keep your head (and neck) warm to reduce the chances of hypothermia.
- Bandana/handkerchief – as well as its normal use, it's good for carrying a picnic lunch or as a flag (especially a red one).
- Small towel – one that's indestructible and will dry quickly.
- First-aid kit – should include self-adhesive bandages, disinfectant, antibiotic salve or cream, gauze, tape, small scissors and tweezers.
- Knife, fork, spoon and mug – a double-layer plastic mug with a lid is best; a mug acts as an eating and drinking receptacle, mixing bowl and washbasin; the handle protects you from getting burned; bring an extra cup if you like to have a drink with your meal.
- Pots and pans – aluminum cooking sets are best, but any sturdy one-quart pot is sufficient; a pot scrubber is helpful, especially using cold water and no soap.
- Stove – one using butane or propane gas, should be lightweight and easy to operate; test the stove before you head out.
- Water purifier – optional; water can be purified by boiling for at least 10 minutes.

- Matches/lighter – waterproof matches and several lighters are useful.
- Candle/lantern – candles are easy to operate, but hazardous in a tent; test the lantern before you hit the trail.
- Flashlight – one per person; make sure to have fresh batteries and extra bulbs.
- Sleeping bag – goose-down bags are warm and light, but useless when wet; outdoors stores rent synthetic bags.
- Sleeping pad – optional; use a sweater or sleeping bag sack stuffed with clothes as a pillow.
- Tent – should be waterproof or have waterproof cover; know how to put it up before you start out; remember your packs will be sharing the tent with you.
- Camera/binoculars – store film in waterproof film canisters (sealable plastic bags work well).
- Compass and maps – each person should have their own.
- Eyeglasses – contact-lens wearers should bring a back-up set.
- Sundries – toilet paper, small sealable plastic bags, insect repellent, sunscreen, lip balm, unscented moisturizing cream, moleskin for foot blisters, dental floss, sunglasses.
- Food – keeping your energy up while hiking is important, but so is keeping your pack light. Some staple foods are oatmeal, bread (the denser the better), rice or pasta, instant soup or ramen noodles, dehydrated meat (jerky), dried fruit, energy bars, chocolate, trail mix (raisins and peanuts mixed with various other goodies), peanut butter and honey or jam and also beverages such as coffee, tea and hot chocolate.

What is Wilderness?

The 1964 Wilderness Act, the first major act of Congress to set aside large roadless areas as federally administered wilderness, defined wilderness as:

… an area where the Earth and its community of life are untrammeled by man, where man himself is a visitor who does not remain… . It is a region which contains no permanent human inhabitants, no possibility for motorized travel, and is spacious enough so that a traveler crossing it by foot or horse must have the experience of sleeping out of doors.

Books Countryman Press (☎ 802-457-4826, 800-245-1451), PO Box 748, Woodstock, VT 05091-0175, publishes a series of backcountry hiking books on New York, New Jersey and Pennsylvania; each contains 50 walks. These titles are available in bookstores or directly from the publisher; its website is www.countrymanpress.com.

The Rails-to-Trails Conservancy publishes a series of directories of multiuse paths created from abandoned railroads. These include *40 Great Rail-Trails in New York & New England*, *40 Great Rail-Trails in the Mid-Atlantic* and *Pennsylvania's Rail Trails*, which has 79 trails covering over 700 miles.

Hikes in the Mid-Atlantic States, by Don Hopey and Glenn Scherer, details 32 hikes in the Appalachians. A book dealing with walks at high altitudes in the region is *High Ground: Peak Hikes of the Mid-Atlantic States* by Bill Rozday.

In Pennsylvania the Keystone Trails Association publishes *Pennsylvania Hiking Trails* and *Appalachian Trailguide Pennsylvania*, which are updated regularly. *Hiking Pennsylvania*, by Rhonda & George Ostertag, lists 75 walks, day hikes and overnight trips.

Maps A good map is essential. National Park Service (NPS) and US Forest Service (USFS) ranger stations usually stock topographical maps costing about $3 to $6. State park and forest bureaus also provide maps. Alternatively, try the local stationery or hardware store. Longer hikes require two types of maps: US Geological Survey (USGS) Quadrangles and USFS maps. Excellent topographic maps of New York State are available from Jimapco. For a price list and map index of USGS maps or to order Jimapco maps, see Topographic Maps in the Maps section of the Facts for the Visitor chapter.

Safety

The main things to reckon with are the changeable weather and your own frame of mind. Weather conditions and terrain vary significantly from one region, or even from one track or trail, to another. Seasonal changes can significantly alter any track or

Local musicians get it on in Intercourse, PA.

TOM SMALLMAN

Are you ready to rock? Lake Chatauqua, NY

MICHAEL CLARK

A couple of swingers in Cape May, NJ

PHILIP GAME

ANGUS OBORN

Pedalling preppies, Princeton, NJ

TOM SMALLMAN

Vista from Grandview Ave, Pittsburgh, PA

BRIGITTE BARTA

The Wall that Went for a Walk at the Storm King Art Center in NY's Hudson Valley

trail. These differences influence the way you should dress and the equipment you should carry, and may warrant a decision not to undertake a walk or hike at a given time. Carry a rain jacket and light pair of long underwear at all times, even on shorter hikes. Backpackers should have a pack-liner (heavy-duty garbage bags work well), a full set of rainwear and food that doesn't need cooking. A positive attitude is helpful in any situation.

Obtain reliable information about physical and environmental conditions along the route you intend to take (eg, from park authorities or a reputable local guiding operation). Before you set out ask about environmental considerations that can affect your trip and how local, experienced hikers deal with these considerations. Regardless of location, there may be special requirements for walking in that area.

If possible never hike alone, but if you travel solo let someone know where you're going and how long you plan to be gone. Use sign-in boards at trailheads or ranger stations. Travelers seeking hiking companions can inquire or post notices at ranger stations, outdoors stores, campgrounds and hostels.

Forging rivers and streams is another potentially dangerous, but often necessary, part of hiking. On maintained trails bridges are usually available for crossing bodies of water, but not in wilderness areas where bridges are taboo.

If you have to cross a river in a wilderness area, on reaching it unclip all your pack straps – your pack is expendable, you are not. Avoid crossing barefoot – river cobblestones suck body heat out of your feet, numbing them and making it impossible to navigate. Bring a pair of lightweight canvas sneakers to avoid sloshing around in wet boots for the rest of your hike. Although cold water makes you want to cross as quickly as possible, don't rush; take small steps, watch where you put your feet and keep your balance. Using a staff for balance is helpful, but don't rely on it to support all your weight. Don't enter water higher than mid-thigh; any higher and your body gives the current a large mass to work against.

If you get wet, wring out your clothes immediately, wipe off as much excess water from your body and hair as you can and put on some dry clothes. Synthetic fabrics and wool retain heat when they get wet, cotton doesn't.

People with little hiking or backpacking experience shouldn't attempt to do too much too soon. Know your limitations, know the route you're going to take and pace yourself accordingly. Remember, it's OK to turn back or not go as far as you originally intended. Plan your water supply and be careful with fires. Be very careful when walking during the hunting season (Thanksgiving to mid-December).

Contact with poisonous snakes is rare, but you should always check where you tread or place your hands.

Laws & Regulations

Most NPS areas, such as the Delaware Water Gap NRA, require overnight hikers to carry backcountry permits, available from visitors' centers or ranger stations. These must be obtained 24 hours in advance and require you to follow a specific itinerary. Most wilderness areas don't require permits for hiking and backpacking.

State game lands don't allow fires, and in other areas during periods of fire hazard (usually summer and early fall) there are constraints on building open fires.

Don't assume that animals in huts are nonindigenous vermin and attempt to exterminate them. In wild places, they are likely to be protected native animals.

Discourage the presence of wildlife by not leaving food scraps behind you. Place gear out of reach and tie packs to rafters or trees. Do not feed wildlife, as this can lead to animals becoming dependent on handouts, to unbalanced populations and to other problems.

Responsible Hiking

The popularity of hiking places great pressure on the natural environment. Backcountry areas, especially, are composed of fragile environments that can't support a flood of human activity. A code of ethics has evolved to deal with the growing numbers of people in the wilderness. Most conservation organizations and hikers' manuals have their own backcountry codes, which outline the same important principles: minimizing impact, leaving no trace and taking nothing but photographs and memories. Above all, even if it means walking through mud or crossing a patch of snow, stay on the main trail.

Please, consider the following tips when hiking and backpacking, and help preserve the ecology and beauty of New York, New Jersey and Pennsylvania.

Garbage Carry out all your garbage. Don't overlook those easily forgotten items such as silver paper, orange peel, cigarette butts and plastic wrappers. Empty packaging weighs little anyway and should be stored in a dedicated garbage bag. Make an effort to carry out garbage left by others.

Never bury your garbage: digging disturbs soil and ground cover and encourages erosion. Buried garbage will more than likely be dug up by animals, who may be injured or poisoned by it. It may also take years to decompose, especially at high altitudes.

Minimize the waste you'll have to carry out by taking minimal packaging and no more food than you will need. If you can't buy in bulk, unpack small-portion packages and combine their contents in one container before your trip. Take reusable containers or stuff sacks.

Don't rely on bought water in plastic bottles, because disposal of them creates a major environmental problem; use iodine drops or purification tablets instead.

Sanitary napkins, tampons and condoms should also be carried out despite any inconvenience. They burn and decompose poorly.

Human Waste Disposal Contamination of water sources by human feces can lead to the transmission of hepatitis, typhoid and intestinal parasites such as Giardia, amoebas and roundworms. It can cause severe health risks not only to members of your party, but also to local residents and wildlife.

Where there is a toilet, please use it. Where there is none, bury your waste. Dig a small hole 6 inches deep and at least 320 feet from any watercourse. Consider carrying a lightweight trowel for this purpose. Cover the waste with soil and a rock. Use toilet paper sparingly and bury it with the waste. In snow, dig down to the soil; otherwise, your waste will be exposed when the snow melts.

If the area is inhabited, ask locals if they have any concerns about your chosen toilet site.

Washing Don't use detergents or toothpaste in or near watercourses, even if they are biodegradable.

For personal washing, use biodegradable soap and a water container (or even a lightweight, portable basin) at least 160 feet away from the watercourse. Disperse the waste water widely to allow the soil to filter it fully before it finally makes it back to the watercourse.

Wash cooking utensils at least 160 feet from watercourses, and use a scourer, sand or snow instead of detergent.

Erosion Hillsides and mountain slopes, especially at high altitudes, are prone to erosion. It is important to stick to existing tracks and avoid shortcuts that bypass a switchback. If you create a new trail straight down a slope, it will turn into a watercourse with the next heavy rainfall and eventually cause soil loss and deep scarring.

If a well-used track passes through a mud patch, walk through the mud: walking

around the edge will increase the size of the patch.

Avoid removing plant life that keeps topsoils in place.

Fires & Low-Impact Cooking You should not depend upon open fires for cooking. The cutting of wood for fires in popular trekking areas can cause rapid deforestation. It's best to cook on a lightweight kerosene, alcohol or Shellite (white gas) stove and avoid those powered by disposable butane gas canisters.

Fires may be acceptable below the tree line in areas that get very few visitors. If you light a fire, use an existing fireplace rather than creating a new one. Don't surround fires with rocks, as this creates a visual scar. Use only dead, fallen wood. Remember the adage 'the bigger the fool, the bigger the fire.' Use minimal wood, just what you need for cooking. In huts, leave wood for the next person.

Ensure that you fully extinguish a fire after use. Spread the embers and douse them with water. An extinguished fire is only truly safe to leave when you can comfortably place your hand in it.

BICYCLING & MOUNTAIN BIKING

The many smaller highways (not interstates) crisscrossing the region offer cyclists access to an assortment of topographies from the steep river valleys and mountain ranges of the Adirondacks to the gently undulating farmland of Pennsylvania Dutch Country. In addition, there are several thousands of miles of trails, either multi-use or bicycle only, in NPS sites, Allegheny National Forest, various state parks, forests and game lands and areas operated by the Rails-to-Trails Conservancy.

Information

You can either bring your bike with you, or there are many places where you can rent one from about $5/15/50 per hour/day/week. Spare parts are widely available and repair shops are numerous, but it's still important to be able to do basic mechanical work yourself.

Members of the national organization the League of American Bicyclists (☎ 202-822-1333), 1612 K St NW, suite 401, Washington, DC 20006-2082, may transport their bikes for free on selected airlines. Members also receive a list of hospitality homes in each state that offer simple accommodations to touring cyclists. Visit the league's website (www.bikeleague.org) for information about becoming a member.

The Adventure Cycling Association (☎ 406-721-1776), PO Box 8308P, Missoula, MT 59807, a nationwide bicyclists' club, encourages cycle travel, publishes maps, helps develop bike trails and maintains a website at www.adv-cycling.org.

For information about cycling in Pennsylvania contact the Bicycling Federation of Pennsylvania (☎ 717-975-0888), PO Box 11625, Harrisburg, PA 17018-1625, or visit its website at trfn.clpgh.org/wpw/paorg.html. The Bicycle Touring Club of North Jersey (☎ 973-284-0404, www.Btcnj.org), PO Box 839, Mahwah, NJ 07430-0839, is one of the best resources for tours of the state and the northeast. The North Jersey Mountain Bike Club (☎ 201-225-1525), 223 Taylor Rd, Paramus, NJ 07652, specializes in more strenuous rides in the region. It also maintains a website at www.dwmorrison.com/njmbc.htm.

Transportation Alternatives (☎ 212-629-8080, www.transalt.org), 115 West 30th St, 12th Floor, New York, NY 10001, promotes cycling and offers weekend trips in and around New York City. The Five Borough Bicycling Club (☎ 212-932-2300), based at New York International Hostel, 891 Amsterdam Ave, New York, NY, also offers day and weekend trips.

A number of other operators organize cycling vacations; state tourist offices can supply you with a list of reputable operators. HI-AYH and the Adventure Cycling Association are two national organizations that also offer cycling holidays.

What to Bring For any long-distance cycling, your bike should be in good condition; make sure the brakes work properly. For night cycling it should be fitted with amber side reflectors, a rear reflector and a headlight visible from 500 feet. Other things to bring include a helmet, water bottles, panniers, tools, spare parts and maps. (See also What to Bring under Hiking & Backpacking earlier in this chapter.)

Books The *Cyclist Yellow Pages* is an international directory of bicycling resources published by the Adventure Cycling Association. The League of American Bicyclists publishes an annual *Almanac*, listing contacts in each state along with information about bicycle routes and special events; it also publishes the *Tour Finder*, which gives details of touring events in the US and abroad.

Globe Pequot Press publishes a series on short bicycling trips. *Short Bike Rides in New Jersey* (1998) by Robert Santelli, has descriptions of 30 bike tours of the state. Similar is *Short Bike Rides in and around New York City* (1999), by Phil & Wendy Harrington, *Short Bike Rides in and around Philadelphia* (1997), by Ann Lembo, and *Short Bike Rides in Eastern Pennsylvania* (1998), by William Simpson.

Countryman Press publishes books on cycling in the region, and the Rails-to-Trails Conservancy publishes directories of multiuse paths created from abandoned railroads (see Books under Hiking & Backpacking earlier).

Maps The Adventure Cycling Association publishes trail maps with information on topography, nature, history, lodging, food and bicycle stores. DeLorme's topographic *Atlas & Gazeteer* for each state is a good tool for planning trail rides. A map of the 35-mile Mohawk-Hudson Trail is available from the Schenectady City Department of Planning, Schaffer Heights, 107 Nott Terrace, suite 303, Schenectady, NY 12308. (See also Maps under Hiking & Backpacking earlier and in the Facts for the Visitor chapter.)

Maps are also available from the following:

New York State Department of Transportation
(☎ 888-245-3697, punch.dot.state.ny.us) State Campus, Building 4, Room 105, Albany, NY 12232-0415

New Jersey Transportation Department
(☎ 609-530-2000, 800-537-7397, www.state.nj.us) 1035 Parkway Ave, CN 600, Trenton, NJ 08625

Pennsylvania Department of Transportation, Pedestrian & Bicycle Coordinator
(☎ 717-787-6746, www.dot.state.pa.us) Forum Place, 555 Walnut St, Harrisburg, PA 17101-1900

Transporting Your Bike Bicycles can be transported by air. You *can* disassemble them and put them in a bike bag or box, but it's easier simply to wheel your bike to the check-in desk, where it should be treated as a piece of baggage, although airlines often charge an additional fee. You may have to remove the pedals and front wheel so that the bike takes up less space in the aircraft's hold.

Check any regulations or restrictions on the transportation of bicycles with the airline well in advance, preferably before you pay for your ticket. While some airlines welcome bicycles, others consider them a nuisance and try to discourage them.

You can also take bicycles on Greyhound buses and Amtrak trains, but again, check with them in advance. For full protection, bicycles must be boxed.

Bikes are usually allowed on metropolitan public transportation, but are sometimes subject to Byzantine restrictions that may be known only to the transit police who are empowered to write you a ticket. Call the local transit authority to determine whether you must avoid trains at rush hour or obtain a special pass.

Safety

On the road, bicyclists are generally treated courteously by motorists. You may, though, encounter the occasional careless one who passes too closely or too fast (or both). Helmets should be worn to reduce the risk of head injury. Always keep at least one hand on the handlebars. Stay close to the edge of roads and don't wear anything, such as headphones, which can reduce your ability to hear. Always lock your bicycle securely and be cautious about leaving bags on the bike, particularly in larger towns or more touristed locations.

Carry at least two full bottles of water and refill them at every opportunity.

Laws & Regulations

Bikes are restricted from entering wilderness areas and some designated trails but may otherwise ride in NPS sites, state parks, national and state forests and Bureau of Land Management (BLM) single-track trails. Trail etiquette requires that cyclists yield to other users, such as walkers or horses. Passing is typically done on the left and it is a courtesy to politely inform others as you pass (cyclists commonly say 'on your left' or 'passing' as they move around slower traffic). You need a permit to camp overnight along forest trails, but no camping is allowed on state game lands.

Bikes aren't allowed on interstate highways. In cities, obey traffic lights and signs and other road rules; yield to pedestrians; in downtown areas don't ride on the sidewalk unless there's a sign saying otherwise and don't ride two abreast unless in a cycle lane or path.

Trails

In Manhattan Central Park isn't a bad place for a ride on the weekend – otherwise leave the city-street cycling to the insane bike messengers. Near Saratoga the spectacular 35-mile Mohawk-Hudson Bike-Hike Trail, on former railroads and canal towpaths, is at the confluence of the Mohawk and Hudson Rivers. For information contact the Schenectady City Department of Planning (see Maps earlier). Other popular cycling areas are the Old Erie Canal State Park and stretches of the 454-mile Seaway Trail, the nation's longest scenic byway, which runs parallel to the St Lawrence River, Lake Ontario, the Niagara River and Lake Erie.

For the placid biker the best area to bicycle in New Jersey is the flat terrain around Cape May; you can pick up local maps and information from Shield's Bike Rentals (☎ 609-884-1818), 11 Gurney St, in the town of Cape May. The back roads of northern New Jersey provide challenges for the more experienced rider. The Bicycle Touring Club of North Jersey and the North Jersey Mountain Bike Club (see Information earlier in this section) can advise you on these.

In Philadelphia the 25-mile Fairmount Park Bikeway heads northwest from the Philadelphia Museum of Art along the Schuylkill River and Wissahickon Creek. Contact the Fairmount Park Commission (☎ 215-685-0111), Memorial Hall, Philadelphia, PA 19131, or visit its website at www.phila.gov/departments/fairpark. The southern section of this trail joins the 21½-mile Schuylkill River Rail-Trail that connects historic sections of Philadelphia with Valley Forge National Historic Park. For information, contact the park (☎ 610-783-1077, www.nps.gov/vafo) PO Box 953, Valley Forge, PA 19482-0953.

Pennsylvania's state parks have some great trails. Moraine State Park, in western Pennsylvania north of Pittsburgh, has a 7-mile track beside Lake Arthur. Southeast of Pittsburgh in Ohiopyle State Park, there is a 25-mile trail beside the Youghiogheny River. In Presque Isle State Park on the shores of Lake Erie, a gentle 5.8-mile trail affords great views of Presque Isle Bay and the lake.

In the Pocono Mountains a 25-mile mountain-bike trail along a former railroad track through Lehigh Gorge State Park connects Jim Thorpe and White Haven. The rugged 15-mile Switch Back Gravity Railroad Trail runs across the valley from Mauch Chunk Ridge to Pisgah Mountain via Jim Thorpe. For more details write to Switch Back Gravity Railroad Foundation (☎ 570-325-8255), PO Box 73, Jim Thorpe, PA 18229-0073, or consult their website at www.switchbackgravityrr.org.

DOWNHILL SKIING

The Adirondacks, Catskills and Poconos provide the region's best skiing. There are dozens of resorts offering great opportunities for skiing as well as other snow-related sports. Facilities range from day-only ski areas to resorts that are self-contained mini-cities and offer gentle slopes for the learner and challenging verticals for more accomplished skiers.

Information

The skiing season lasts from about mid-December to early April, though it's sometimes possible to ski as early as November and as late as May. State tourist offices have information on resorts, and travel agents can arrange full-package tours that include transport and accommodations. Many resorts are close to towns so it's quite feasible to travel on your own to the slopes for the day and return to town at night. If you have travel insurance make sure that it covers you for winter sports.

Ski areas are often well equipped with accommodations, eateries, shops, entertainment venues, child-care facilities (both on and off the mountain) and transport. In fact, it's possible to stay a week at some of the bigger places without leaving the slopes. Ski areas have at least one comfortable base lodge with a rental office, ski shop and lockers. There are also cafeterias and lounges or bars where visitors can relax in warmth. You don't have to buy a lift ticket or pay to enjoy the base lodge.

Major ski areas sell lift tickets for $25 to $50 a day. Three-day or week-long lift passes are often more economical, especially if they don't need to be used on consecutive days.

Equipment rentals are available at or near even the smallest ski areas, though renting equipment in a nearby town can be cheaper if you can transport it to the slopes.

For information on skiing nationally contact the US Recreational Ski Association (☎ 209-539-6332), PO Box 397, Springfield, CA 93265. Updated regularly, *Skiing America*, by Charles Leocha, Hilary Nangle and Diane Scholfield, has facts and figures about all the US's big ski resorts. *Ski* and *Skiing* are year-round magazines. *Snow Country* magazine ranks ski resorts in the US using criteria that include terrain, ski school, nightlife, lodging and dining.

Ski Schools & Resorts

Visitors planning on taking lessons should rent equipment on the mountain since the price of a lesson, around $30 for a half a day, usually includes equipment rentals, with no discount for having your own gear. Children's ski schools are popular places to stash the kids for a day, offering lessons, day-care facilities and lunch for around $40 per child.

New York has numerous downhill ski resorts. The Adirondacks have many prime winter destinations including Whiteface Mountain near Lake Placid, which has hosted Winter Olympic alpine competitions. In the Catskills fairly close to New York City, Belleayre Mountain, Hunter Mountain and Ski Windham are the best known.

Within a few hours' drive of New York City, northern New Jersey has Mountain Creek (formerly Vernon Mountain Creek), the state's ski capital. Both offer good slopes for skiing and snowboarding and are rarely crowded.

Pennsylvania has more than 30 downhill ski areas, many of them in the northeast in the Pocono Mountains. These ski areas include Camelback, Shawnee Mountain, Big Boulder and Jack Frost Mountain. Further west, along Route 6 near Coudersport, is the ski resort Denton Hill. In southwestern Pennsylvania, two popular ski areas are Seven Springs Mountain Resort and Hidden Valley in Laurel Highlands, southeast of Pittsburgh. Blue Knob Ski Resort, 20 miles east of Johnstown, is quite popular with skiers and snowmobilers.

Snowboarding

Boards are allowed at most ski areas and many have half-pipes, snowboard lessons and rental equipment. Snowboarders stand sideways, strapped to a board 4 or 5 feet long, to cruise down mountains. The motion is comparable to surfing or skateboarding, rather than skiing.

CROSS-COUNTRY SKIING

Cross-country skiing (also called ski touring or Nordic skiing) allows you to experience quiet, natural beauty at close quarters and escape the crowds and relatively expensive lift tickets at ski resorts. The sport appeals to beginners in particular, because they can be on their way with only a few lessons.

Public lands operated by NPS, USFS and the US Army Corps of Engineers, in addition to state parks and forests, Rails-to-Trails

Conservancy and private lands support hundreds of cross-country trails; some trails are operated under special-use permits by private industries. New York's Finger Lakes region provides some of the best views; trails near Ithaca, Buttermilk Falls State Park, Keuka Lake State Park and Finger Lakes National Forest are popular. Among the best places is Robert Moses State Park in the Thousand Islands region. In the Hudson Valley, good spots are Bear Mountain, Mills-Norrie and James Baird State Park, while in the Capital District & Mohawk Valley you'll find decent trails in Saratoga National Historic Park and Chenango Valley State Park.

The main spots for cross-country skiing in New Jersey are the parks and forests in the north of the state including High Point State Park.

Prime areas in Pennsylvania are Allegheny National Forest in the northwest and the parks and forests of the Laurel Highlands in the southwest. State parks in the Poconos have a variety of good trails as do the state forests around Williamsport.

Many ski resorts also provide groomed ski trails, but most cross-country skiers prefer to avoid the downhill crowds by visiting dedicated cross-country areas and back-country trails.

Equipment rentals are available at outfitters like REI, Eastern Mountain Sports and other places near the trails. The Cross-Country Ski Areas Association (☎ 603-239-4341), 259 Bolton Rd, Winchester, NH 03470, has information on guided tours and publishes *The Best of Cross-Country Skiing*, a guide to the sport in North America. Its website is at www.xcski.org. Most cross-country trail distances are given in kilometers (to convert trail distances into miles, see the conversion chart on the inside back cover of this book).

ROCK CLIMBING & MOUNTAINEERING

The premier rock-climbing destination is the Shawangunk Mountains of the Catskills region – especially popular are spots in the Minnewaska State Park, near the village of New Paltz, and the Mohonk Preserve. In the Adirondacks, Lake George and Lake Placid have many worthwhile climbing areas.

In Pennsylvania some popular rock-climbing spots are Wissahickon Creek in Fairmount Park in northwest Philadelphia,

Delaware Water Gap NRA, McConnell's Mill State Park north of Pittsburgh (in southwestern Pennsylvania) and Lehigh Gorge State Park in the Poconos (in northern Pennsylvania).

The Access Fund (☎ 303-545-6772), 2475 Broadway, Boulder, CO 80304, is a nonprofit organization working to keep climbing areas open to the public by purchasing or negotiating access to key sites. Action alerts on legislation affecting climbing are posted on its website (www.outdoorlink .com/accessfund).

Safety

Rock climbing and mountaineering are demanding activities requiring top physical condition. They also require an understanding of the composition of rock types, their hazards and other hazards of the high country and familiarity with equipment including ropes, chocks, bolts, carabiners and harnesses.

Rock climbers and mountaineers categorize routes on a scale of one to five. Class I is hiking, while Class II involves climbing on unstable materials like talus and may require use of the hands for keeping balance, especially with a heavy pack. Class III places the climber in dangerous situations involving exposed terrain, with the likely consequences of a fall being a broken limb. Class IV involves steep rock, smaller holds and great exposure, with obligatory use of ropes and knowledge of knots and techniques like belaying and rappelling; the consequences of falling are death rather than injury. Class V divides into a dozen or more subcategories based on degree of difficulty and requires advanced techniques, including proficiency with rope.

Climbing is potentially hazardous, though serious accidents are more spectacular than frequent. Nevertheless, climbers should be aware of hazards, which can contribute to falls and very serious injury or death. Weather is an important factor, as rain makes rock slippery and lightning can strike an exposed climber; hypothermia is an additional concern. In dry weather, lack of water can lead to dehydration.

Minimum Impact

Many climbers follow guidelines similar to those established for hikers to preserve the resource on which their sport relies. These include concentrating impact in high-use areas by using established roads, trails and routes for access; dispersing use in pristine areas and avoiding the creation of new trails; refraining from creating or enhancing handholds; and eschewing the placement of bolts wherever possible. Climbers should also take special caution to respect archaeological and cultural resources, such as rock art, and refrain from climbing in such areas.

Instruction

Travelers wishing to acquire climbing skills can do so at several schools and guide services, including:

Adirondack Mountain Club
(☎ 518-668-4447, 800-395-8080) RR3, Box 3055, Lake George, NY 12845

Alpine Adventures
(☎ 518-576-9881) PO Box 179, Route 73, Keene, NY 12942

Ascents of Adventure
(☎ 518-475-7519) 147 Cherry Ave, Delmar, NY 12054-2522

Mountain Skills Climbing School
(☎ 914-687-9643) 595 Peak Rd, New Paltz, NY 12484

WHITE-WATER RAFTING & TUBING

The rivers of the region offer a number of opportunities for this most exhilarating of sports. The Delaware River, which connects all three states, is a popular Wild & Scenic River – particularly scenic stretches pass through the Catskill towns of Narrowsburg and Barryville. The Genesee River in Letchworth State Park, in the Finger Lakes region, runs for 17 miles beneath a 600-foot gorge. Other New York options include the Hudson River, where early spring rapids provide some of the most challenging opportunities; Esopus Creek, which is a center for tubing, near Phoenicia in the Catskills; and Lake Placid in the Adirondacks.

In Pennsylvania's Laurel Highlands the Youghiogheny River has beginner to expert rapids. In the Poconos, white-water trips on the Lehigh River are best March through June and from mid-September through mid-December. Pine Creek, which flows through the north central mountains, has 20 miles of rapids.

White-water trips take place in either large rafts seating a dozen or more people, or smaller rafts seating half a dozen; the latter are more interesting and exciting because the ride over the rapids can be rougher and because everyone participates in rowing. Some trips may only be suitable for experienced rafters, while some may have restrictions regarding age and/or weight.

Tubing is popular on smaller streams and rivers, but is often available only when spring runoff has quieted and the current isn't as rough. Often, you rent a 'tube' – or the innertube of a tire – which may or may not be fitted with handles or seats. Then, much like white-water rafting, tubers (people, not the root vegetables) are 'put in' at the head of a river and they float downstream.

Outfitters provide white-water experiences ranging from short, inexpensive morning or afternoon trips to overnight stays and three or four-day expeditions. Outfitters on NPS, USFS, US Army Corps of Engineers (see the boxed text 'Useful Outdoor Organizations' in the Facts about the Region chapter), state park or state forest lands operate with permits from the appropriate agency. Individuals and groups with their own or rented equipment sometimes also need a permit.

For information on white-water rafting and tubing contact the American White-Water Affiliation (☎ 301-589-9453), 1430 Fenwick Lane, Silver Spring, MD 20910. The organization works to conserve and restore the nation's white-water resources and promote white-water activity. Visit its website (www.awa.org) for more information.

Safety

While white-water trips aren't without danger and it's not unusual for participants

Wild & Scenic Rivers

Congressional legislation establishes certain criteria for the preservation of rivers with outstanding natural qualities; these are called Wild & Scenic Rivers. Wild rivers are, simply speaking, free-flowing and remote, while scenic rivers enjoy relatively natural surroundings and are free of impoundments, but have better access by road. Recreational rivers are more developed and usually have roads close by.

to fall out of the raft in rough water, serious injuries are rare and the huge majority of trips are without incident. Outfitters give orientation and safety lectures before heading off; trips have at least one river guide experienced in white-water rafting and trained in safety procedures and lifesaving techniques. You don't have to be able to swim to participate, but you must wear a US Coast Guard-approved life jacket and should be in reasonably good physical condition. Keep your feet and arms inside the raft.

CANOEING & KAYAKING

Canoeing and kayaking offer travelers the chance to see things – river gorges, lake edges, remote sections of wilderness and local wildlife – they might otherwise miss doing other watersports. Many rafting rivers are just as good for canoeing or kayaking, and for those who prefer still water there are numerous lakes. Sea kayaking is also common along the coast and bays. St Regis Canoe Area, a network of 58 lakes and ponds connected primarily by the Raquette, St Regis and Saranac Rivers in New York's Adirondacks Forest Preserve, is the best-known area in the state, and, best of all, is off-limits to power boats. The Adirondack Canoe Route follows a series of lakes, ponds, rivers and portages from Old Forge to Tupper and the Saranac Lakes. Also in the Adirondacks, the Ausable River carves its way through the sandstone cliffs that rise several hundred feet. Other areas that attract canoeing enthusiasts are Chautauqua Lake in western New York, the North/South Lake Area in the Catskills and the Hudson River in the Hudson Valley.

In New Jersey canoeing/kayaking is a great way to explore Pinelands National Preserve, the Pine Barrens and the wetlands and rivers of southern New Jersey.

The 500 miles of the Susquehanna River and its tributaries begins at Otsego Lake in New York and flows south through central Pennsylvania into Chesapeake Bay in Maryland. The river is particularly beautiful in north-central Pennsylvania just north of Harrisburg. The Allegheny River (which heads north into New York) and its many branches offer opportunities to explore Allegheny National Forest. There's also canoe-

ing on Lake Erie around Presque Isle State Park in northern Pennsylvania, the many lakes of the Poconos and the Schuylkill River in Philadelphia.

If you don't have your own equipment it can often be rented from rafting outfitters or other small operations, which may double as campgrounds or summer resorts on the shore of a calm body of water. Wear woolen or polypropylene clothing or a wet suit; take spare paddles, a first-aid kit, a whistle and rescue line. State park-controlled waters usually require a permit to launch a boat.

Maps and guides are available and you should study these to plan your route before setting off. As well as from the American White-Water Affiliation (see Canoeing & Kayaking) you can get useful information

River Difficulty Rankings

River trips are classified on a scale of I to VI according to difficulty. On any river, classifications can vary during the year, depending on the water level. Higher water levels, usually associated with spring runoff, can make a river trip either easier or more difficult by covering up hazards or increasing the velocity of the river. Lower water levels can expose hazards like rocks and whirlpools, making the river more exciting. Some rivers depend on water releases from upstream dams.

Class I (easy) – Ranges from flatwater to occasional series of mild rapids.

Class II (medium) – Frequent stretches of rapids with waves up to 3 feet high and easy chutes, ledges and falls. The best route is easy to identify and the entire river can be run in open canoes.

Class III (difficult) – Features numerous rapids with high, irregular waves and difficult chutes and falls that often require scouting; for experienced paddlers who either use kayaks and rafts or have a spray cover for their canoe.

Class IV (very difficult) – Long stretches of irregular waves, powerful back eddies and even constricted canyons. Scouting is mandatory and rescues can be difficult in many places. Suitable in rafts or whitewater kayaks, and paddlers are equipped with helmets.

Class V (extremely difficult) – Continuous violent rapids, powerful rollers and high unavoidable waves and haystacks; these rivers are only for white-water kayaks and paddlers who are proficient in the Eskimo roll.

Class VI (highest level of difficulty) – Rarely run except by highly experienced kayakers under ideal conditions.

from the American Canoe Association
(☎ 703-451-0141) 7432 Albany Station Blvd,
Suite B-232, Springfield, VA 22150, or visit
its website at www.aca-paddler.org.

The US Army Corps of Engineers, responsible for administering various lakes
and rivers, produces brochures and navigational and nautical charts. Nautical charts
can also be obtained from the National
Ocean Service (☎ 301-713-3074, www.nos
.noaa.gov), 1305 East West Highway, Silver
Spring, MD 20910.

Safety

Paddlers should be able to swim, and occupants should wear a US Coast Guard-
approved life jacket. As in hiking try not to
canoe/kayak alone and let someone know
where you're heading and for how long.
Keep a reasonable distance between your
and other canoes.

If you fall into the water stay upstream of
the craft to avoid being hit by it. Lie on your
back with your feet facing downstream and
up where you can see them. Hold on to your
paddle, as this helps make you more visible.
Relax and breathe when you aren't going
through waves. Turn over and swim when
the water becomes calmer and don't try to
stand in moving water in case your foot gets
caught in a rock.

FISHING

The Atlantic coastline, the hundreds of lakes
and ponds and the thousands of miles of
rivers and streams make this a prime fishing
region. Freshwater fish include varieties of
trout, salmon, bass and pike, as well as
muskellunge (muskie), sauger, shad and
walleyed pike; in the Atlantic you'll find
bluefish, flounder, giant tuna and even shark.

The streams of the Catskill Mountains are
said to have some of the country's best trout
fishing, and the lakes of the Adirondacks, including the 469 sq miles of Lake Champlain,
are home to bass, pike and salmon. Some of
the best bass and muskellunge fishing is reputedly found along the St Lawrence River
in the northwest of New York. Lake Chautauqua in the far southwest corner of the
state is noted for its giant muskellunge.

Stream and ice-fishing is popular in Allegany State Park. Anglers are drawn to the
Thousand Islands region, for muskie, northern pike and largemouth bass.

Bluefish, salmon, sturgeon and striped
bass are common in the Atlantic waters
around New Jersey's Belmar, Cape May,
Island Beach, Long Beach and Point Pleasant. The Delaware Water Gap NRA supports bass and pickerel in its lakes, and trout,
bass and walleye in the Delaware River.

Yellow Breeches is a trout stream in
Pennsylvania that attracts anglers from interstate and abroad. Lake Erie, once too polluted, is now visited by spawning salmon.
The lakes and rivers of Allegheny National
Forest have some of the best fishing in the
country's northeast.

Anglers are required to have the appropriate state license and to abide by whatever
seasonal or territorial regulations are in
place. The same stream may have several
sections with quite different restrictions on
types of hooks, bait, seasons and what size
and type of fish can be kept. It can be complicated so ask for current regulations at bait
or sporting-goods stores or fish and wildlife
offices or some state campgrounds where
you can also buy a license.

Fishing licenses are issued to resident and
out-of-state anglers (the latter are more expensive) and can be bought for a year or
shorter intervals. There are numerous types
of licenses (New Jersey has no fewer than 22
freshwater licenses) and generally speaking,
you'll pay about $20/35 for a day/seasonal
out-of-state license, with discounts for students and seniors. A license for fishing in the
Delaware River is valid from any of the
three states. In New Jersey, recreational
fishers using ocean charter boats don't need
a license, but there are 'bag limits' on the
amount of fish you can catch, depending on
the type of fish being pursued. Up-to-date
information on licenses, regulations, charter
boats and publications is available from:

New York
(☎ 518-457-3521) Department of Environmental
Conservation, Licensing Sales, 50 Wolf Rd,
Room 111, Albany, NY 12233-4790

New Jersey
(☎ 609-292-2965) Fish, Game & Wildlife Commission, CN-400, Trenton, NJ 08625-0400

Pennsylvania
(☎ 717-657-4518) Fish & Boat Commission, PO Box 67000, Harrisburg, PA 17106

OTHER WATERSPORTS

The coastal waters and numerous lakes are havens for sailing, scuba diving, swimming and windsurfing. Popular sites for watersports are the Finger Lakes region south of Rochester and Syracuse; Oneida Lake northeast of Syracuse; the lakes of the Adirondacks, especially Lake George; the Atlantic waters around Long Beach, Island Beach, Point Pleasant and Cape May in New Jersey; and Lake Arthur in Moraine State Park north of Pittsburgh.

Rentals and training can be found in many centers. The American Sailing Association (☎ 310-822-7171, www.asa.com), 13922 Marquesas Way, Marina del Rey, CA 90292, promotes safe recreational sailing and is a good place to start your research. The New York City Community Sailing Association (☎ 212-222-1405), 545 West 111th St, New York, NY 10025, provides instructional and recreational sailing more cheaply than commercial companies.

The Aqua Lung School of New York (☎ 212-0582-2800), 1089 Second Ave, New York, NY 10021, offers pool-based, scuba diving orientation courses. Also check out New Jersey Scuba Diving (www.njscuba.com), 1050 Highway 35, suite 225, Shrewsbury, NJ 07702.

The US Windsurfing Association (☎ 541-386-8708), PO Box 978, Hood River, OR 97031, has a list of affiliated clubs in the region and maintains a website at www.uswindsurfing.gorge.net.

WILDLIFE & BIRD-WATCHING

Despite the heavy urbanization of the region, the sanctuaries, preserves, wildlife management areas and vast number of state and federal public lands make bird and wildlife watching a rewarding pastime. Many species are protected by law. The Gateway NRA, which includes the marshes and

estuary between New Jersey and New York, provides habitat for various wildlife species.

The headlands and capes of New York and New Jersey also offer glimpses of sea turtles, dolphins and migrating gray whales. Favorite watching spots include Montauk on Long Island in New York, and Wildwood and Cape May in New Jersey. You can also take boats out from Atlantic City. And in the Finger Lakes region of New York, the Beaver Lake Nature Center is a resting stop for Canada geese.

In Pennsylvania some of the best spots for bird-watching are Hawk Mountain Sanctuary north of Reading, Presque Isle State Park on Lake Erie and Moraine State Park north of Pittsburgh. In the northwest, Pymatuning Wildlife Management Area houses some nesting bald eagles. Allegheny National Forest is full of wildlife, including black bears; nearby is a herd of wild wapiti (elk). Erie National Wildlife Refuge has around 40 species of mammals and is a stopover for migratory birds. River otters can be seen in the Poconos.

See the Flora & Fauna section in the Facts about the Region chapter for common and endangered species in each state.

The various relevant federal and state bodies (see the boxed text 'Useful Outdoor Organizations,' in the Facts about the Region chapter) can provide information about wildlife watching. The National Audubon Society has regional offices as well as local clubs and nature centers that often sponsor educational programs, hikes and trips to bird-watching areas. The society is interested in ecology, conservation and wildlife, and publishes the magazine *Audubon*. Contact the society's head office (☎ 212-979-3000), 700 Broadway, New York, NY 10003, or visit its website (www.audubon.com). The National Wildlife Federation (☎ 202-797-6800) 1400 16th St NW, Washington, DC 20036-2266, publishes the magazine *National Wildlife*. Visit its website at www.nwf.com.

HORSEBACK RIDING

Hundreds of miles of trails traverse the region on public lands. In addition, there are scores of horseback riding ranches, stables, associations and clubs offering services from guided trips of a few hours to multi-day treks along mountain or forest trails.

In New York City, Claremont Riding Academy (☎ 212-724-5100), 175 W 89th St, NY 10024, is the nation's oldest continuously operated stable. It arranges indoor lessons and rides in Central Park, as well as riding lessons and events in northern New Jersey. In upstate New York popular bridle trails are found in the Catskill and Adirondack mountains, Connetquot State Park Preserve, Allegany State Park, Rockefeller State Park Preserve and Highland Forest Park.

In New Jersey, popular areas are the Pine Barrens, Liberty State Park, High Point State Park, Washington Crossing State Park and Island Beach State Park.

In Pennsylvania the 140-mile Horse-Shoe Trail leads from Valley Forge National Historic Park to join the Appalachian trail northeast of Harrisburg. There are many more trails in Pennsylvania's state parks and forests.

For information about riding facilities or lessons, contact local tourist offices or see Planning under Hiking & Backpacking earlier in this chapter for addresses to contact for maps and details.

HANG GLIDING & PARAGLIDING

Hang gliding and paragliding are great ways to experience the thrills of flight. Some favorite spots are Ellenville in the Catskills and the Delaware Water Gap NRA. A number of schools cater to both novices and experienced fliers. The US Hang Gliding Association (☎ 719-632-8300), PO Box 1330, Colorado Springs, CO 80901-1330, produces a directory of instructors and clubs nationwide. You can also or visit its website at www.ushga.org.

CAVING

Experienced spelunkers can explore caves in several areas, and some caves are open to the casual visitor for guided interpretive tours. In New York, a popular caving spot is Secret Caverns near Binghamton. Laurel Caverns in the Laurel Highlands is Pennsylvania's largest cave.

Because of the delicate and tightly circumscribed subterranean environments, cavers must make special efforts to respect the ecosystem: leave no trace of human presence, avoid contact with sensitive formations and refrain from disturbing bats and other animals. Cavers should also travel in groups, with a minimum of three persons. Hazards associated with caving include poisonous gases and dangerous spores.

For general information, enthusiasts can get in touch with the National Speleological Society (☎ 256-852-1300, www.caves.org), 2813 Cave Ave, Huntsville, AL 35810-4413. A guide to Pennsylvania's caves is available from the Pennsylvania Caves Association (☎ 814-643-1558, www.cavern.com), RR1, Box 280, Huntingdon, PA 16652. *Going Underground* (1994), by Sharon Hernes Silverman, is a guide to caves in New York and Pennsylvania, as well as Maryland, Virginia and West Virginia.

GOLF

There are hundreds of public and private golf courses, often in beautiful settings, which range from the modest to the deluxe and expensive. State tourist boards produce lists of many of them and have information on packaged golfing vacations that include food and accommodations.

It's advisable to book in advance, especially for public courses in the suburbs, which tend to be crowded on weekends and holidays. Most private clubs give members priority in booking tee-off times; it's usually easier to book a tee-off time on a public course, but on weekends, public holidays and days when the weather is good, it's often busy on all courses. You should also check whether there's a dress code and whether the course has golf clubs for rent if you don't have your own.

Getting There & Away

New York, New Jersey and Pennsylvania sit at the crossroads between the northeastern states of New England and the rest of the continental USA. New York City is one of the country's major entry and exit points for international traffic.

Whether you're coming from a domestic location or from abroad, obviously, the easiest, quickest way to travel is by airplane. Within the USA you can also travel by bus, train or car, but that eats into your vacation time! This chapter focuses on getting to the main transportation hubs in the region from the major US ports of entry and other parts of the world.

Whichever way you're traveling, make sure you take out travel insurance (see Visas & Documents in the Facts for the Visitor chapter).

AIR
Airports & Airlines
Most air travelers to the region arrive at John F Kennedy, LaGuardia or Newark airports (the latter is the hub for Continental Airlines). For more information on these airports and the airlines that service them, see Getting There & Away under New York City. In Pennsylvania the major airports are Philadelphia and Pittsburgh (the home of US Airways). See the Getting There & Away sections under those cities for more information.

Smoking is prohibited on all domestic flights within the USA and on many international flights. Many airports in the USA also restrict smoking (some have special smoking rooms).

Buying Tickets
Numerous airlines fly to the region, and a wide variety of fares are available. It pays to do some research first. Start by perusing travel sections of magazines such as *Time Out* and *TNT* in the UK, or the Saturday editions of newspapers such as the *New York Times*, *Los Angeles Times* in the US, or *Sydney Morning Herald* and *The Age* in

> ## Warning
>
> The information in this chapter is particularly vulnerable to change: Prices for international travel are volatile, routes are introduced and/or canceled, schedules change, special deals come and go, and rules and visa requirements are amended. Airlines and governments seem to take a perverse pleasure in making price structures and regulations as complicated as possible. The travel industry is highly competitive and there are many hidden costs and benefits.
>
> Get opinions, quotes and advice from as many airlines and travel agents as possible and make sure you understand how a fare (and any ticket you may buy) works before you part with your hard-earned money. The details given in this chapter should be regarded as pointers and are not a substitute for your own careful, up-to-date research.

Australia. Ads in these publications offer cheap fares, but don't be surprised if they're unavailable or sold out when you contact the agents: they're usually low-season fares on obscure airlines with conditions attached.

Start shopping for a ticket early – some of the cheapest tickets must be purchased months in advance and some popular flights sell out early. Talk to recent travelers, contact a few travel agents and watch newspapers and magazines for special offers.

Also, check out online reservation services. To get an idea of fares visit some of the following websites:

www.onetravel.com
www.atevo.com
www.bestfares.com
www.cheapfares.com
www.previewtravel.com
www.priceline.com
www.travelocity.com

Airlines can supply information on routes and timetables, but unless there's a price war, they won't offer the cheapest tickets. However, airlines often have competitive low-season, student and senior citizens' fares. Find out the fare, route, duration of the journey and any restrictions on the ticket. Fare levels change constantly and some fares that include accommodations may be as cheap as roundtrip fares.

The high season is from mid-June to mid-September. At holiday times it can be difficult, if not impossible, to get the flights you want unless you plan – and purchase your ticket – well in advance. Holiday times include Christmas, New Year's, Easter, Memorial Day, Labor Day and *especially* Thanksgiving. During these times, planes fill up early and discounts are virtually impossible to find. Outside these times, the best rates for travel are found November through March.

Cheap tickets are available in two distinct categories: official and unofficial. Official tickets have a variety of names, including 'APEX,' 'excursion,' 'promotional' or 'advance-purchase' fares. Unofficial tickets are simply discounted tickets that airlines release through selected travel agents (not through airline offices). The cheapest ones are often nonrefundable and require an extra fee for changing your flight. Many insurance policies cover this loss if you have to change your flight for emergency reasons. Roundtrip (return) tickets are often much cheaper than two one-way fares.

Use the fares quoted in this book as a guide only. They're approximate and based on rates advertised by travel agencies and airlines at press time. Quoted fares aren't necessarily a recommendation for the carrier.

In some places, especially the UK, the cheapest flights are advertised by obscure bucket shops. Many are honest and solvent, but some will take your money and disappear. If you feel suspicious, don't give them all the money at once – leave a deposit of 20% or so and pay the balance on receiving the ticket. If they insist on cash in advance, go elsewhere. Once you have the ticket, phone the airline to confirm that you are booked on the flight.

You may decide to pay more than the rock-bottom to opt for the safety of a better-known travel agent. Established firms such as Council Travel (www.counciltravel.com) or STA Travel (www.statravel.com), which have offices internationally, or Travel CUTS (www.travelcuts.com) in Canada, offer competitive prices to most destinations.

Once you have your ticket, make a copy of it, and keep the copy separate from the original ticket. This will help you get a replacement if your ticket is lost or stolen. Remember to buy travel insurance as early as possible.

Special Fares for Foreign Visitors Most domestic carriers offer special fares to visitors who are non-US citizens. Typically, you must purchase a booklet of coupons in conjunction with a flight into the USA from a foreign country other than Canada or Mexico. Each coupon in the booklet entitles you to a single flight segment on the issuing airline. However, you may have to use all the coupons within a limited period of time, and there may be other restrictions, such as a limit of two transcontinental flights (ie, flights all the way across the USA).

Continental Airlines' Visit USA pass costs $489 for three coupons (minimum purchase), $959 for 10 coupons (maximum purchase) in high summer. Changes of itinerary incur a $50 penalty. Northwest Airlines has a similar program. On American Airlines, you must reserve your flights one day in advance.

Delta has two different programs. Visit USA grants discounts on fully planned itineraries; Discover America allows purchase of coupons good for standby travel anywhere in the continental USA. Four coupons cost $549, 10 coupons $959 (maximum purchase). Children's fares cost about $40 less.

When flying standby, call the airline one or two days before the flight and make a standby reservation. This way you get priority over all the others who just appear and hope to get on the flight the same day.

Round-the-World Tickets Round-the-World (RTW) tickets are popular and are often real bargains. They can work out to be no more expensive – or even less expensive – than an ordinary roundtrip ticket to the USA, so you get the extra stops for nothing. They're of most value for trips that combine the USA with Europe, Asia and Australia or New Zealand. RTW itineraries that include stops in South America or Africa can be substantially more expensive.

Official RTW tickets are usually put together by a combination of two or three airlines and permit you to fly a specified number of stops on their routes as long as you do not backtrack. You must usually book the first sector in advance, and cancellation penalties apply. The tickets are valid for a fixed period, usually one year. An alternative type of RTW ticket is one put together by a travel agent using a combination of discounted tickets.

Most airlines restrict the number of sectors that can be flown within the USA and Canada to three or four, and some airlines don't allow travel on a few heavily trafficked routes (such as Honolulu to Tokyo). In most cases a 14-day advance purchase is required. After the ticket is purchased, travel dates can be changed without penalty, and tickets can be rewritten to add or delete stops for $50 each.

From Australia, an RTW ticket that uses United, Lufthansa and Thai, with several stops in the USA, costs about A$2500. A cheap deal with Qantas and Air France flies to Los Angeles, has an open-jaw segment (enabling you to fly into one city and leave from another city) across the USA, then includes flights from New York to Europe, Asia and back to Australia for A$1880. There are many other possibilities with Qantas and various partner airlines, ranging from A$1500 to A$3200.

From New Zealand, a RTW ticket via North America, Europe and Asia with Air New Zealand and other airlines costs NZ$2300 and up.

Getting 'Bumped'

Airlines routinely overbook flights, knowing that there are usually 'no-shows' (people with reservations who don't take the flight).

When no-shows leave empty seats, the seats become available to standby passengers. When there are few no-shows and there are more people than seats, the airline must 'bump' excess passengers onto later flights.

If it appears that passengers will be bumped, the gate agent first asks for volunteers. Those willing are booked on the next available flight to their destination and are also offered an incentive, which can be a voucher good for a roundtrip flight on the airline, or at least a discount on a flight, at a later date. In extreme circumstances or when faced with a hard bargainer, the airlines may even offer cash, or both cash and a flight pass.

If your schedule is flexible (the next available flight may not be until the next day), getting bumped can be a bonanza. When you check in at the gate, ask if the plane is oversold and if there may be a call for volunteers. If so, leave your name so you'll get first choice. When it comes time to collect your incentive, keep in mind that you don't have to accept the airline's first offer. You can haggle for a better reward.

However, you should be aware that under this same system, being just a little late for boarding could get you bumped with none of the benefits.

Baggage & Other Restrictions

On most domestic and international flights you may check in two bags, or three if you don't have carry-on luggage. There could be a charge if you bring more or if the size of the bags exceeds the airline's limits. It's best to check with the individual airline if you're worried about this. On some international flights the luggage allowance is based on weight, not numbers; again, check with the airline.

If your luggage is delayed upon arrival (which is rare), some airlines give a cash advance to purchase necessities. If sporting equipment is misplaced, the airline may pay for rentals. Should the luggage be lost, it's important to submit a claim. The airline doesn't have to pay the full amount of the claim, but can estimate the value of your lost items. It may take them anywhere from six

Air Travel Glossary

Cancellation Penalties If you have to cancel or change a discounted ticket, there are often heavy penalties involved; insurance can sometimes be taken out against these penalties. Some airlines impose penalties on regular tickets as well, particularly against 'no-show' passengers.

Courier Fares Businesses often need to send urgent documents or freight securely and quickly. Courier companies hire people to accompany the package through customs and, in return, offer a discount ticket which is sometimes a phenomenal bargain. However, you may have to surrender all your baggage allowance and take only carry-on luggage.

Full Fares Airlines traditionally offer 1st class (coded F), business class (coded J) and economy class (coded Y) tickets. These days there are so many promotional and discounted fares available that few passengers pay full economy fare.

Lost Tickets If you lose your airline ticket an airline will usually treat it like a travellers cheque and, after inquiries, issue you with another one. Legally, however, an airline is entitled to treat it like cash and if you lose it then it's gone forever. Take good care of your tickets.

Onward Tickets An entry requirement for many countries is that you have a ticket out of the country. If you're unsure of your next move, the easiest solution is to buy the cheapest onward ticket to a neighbouring country or a ticket from a reliable airline which can later be refunded if you do not use it.

Open-Jaw Tickets These are return tickets where you fly out to one place but return from another. If available, this can save you backtracking to your arrival point.

Overbooking Since every flight has some passengers who fail to show up, airlines often book more passengers than they have seats. Usually excess passengers make up for the no-shows, but occasionally somebody gets 'bumped' onto the next available flight. Guess who it is most likely to be? The passengers who check in late.

Promotional Fares These are officially discounted fares, available from travel agencies or direct from the airline.

Reconfirmation If you don't reconfirm your flight at least 72 hours prior to departure, the airline may delete your name from the passenger list. Ring to find out if your airline requires reconfirmation.

Restrictions Discounted tickets often have various restrictions on them – such as needing to be paid for in advance and incurring a penalty to be altered. Others are restrictions on the minimum and maximum period you must be away.

Round-the-World Tickets RTW tickets give you a limited period (usually a year) in which to circumnavigate the globe. You can go anywhere the carrying airlines go, as long as you don't backtrack. The number of stopovers or total number of separate flights is decided before you set off and they usually cost a bit more than a basic return flight.

Transferred Tickets Airline tickets cannot be transferred from one person to another. Travelers sometimes try to sell the return half of their ticket, but officials can ask you to prove that you are the person named on the ticket. On an international flight tickets are compared with passports.

Travel Periods Ticket prices vary with the time of year. There is a low (off-peak) season and a high (peak) season, and often a low-shoulder season and a high-shoulder season as well. Usually the fare depends on your outward flight – if you depart in the high season and return in the low season, you pay the high-season fare.

weeks to three months to process the claim and pay you.

Your ticket folder usually gives details of items that are illegal to take on a plane, either checked in with your baggage or as hand luggage. These may include weapons, aerosols, tear gas, pepper spray, camp stove fuel canisters, full oxygen tanks and fire-crackers. You may carry matches and lighters on your person, but don't put them in checked baggage.

Travelers with Special Needs

If you have a special need – a broken leg, dietary restrictions, dependence on a wheel-chair, responsibility for a baby, fear of flying – airports and airlines can be surprisingly helpful, but you should let them know as soon as possible so that they can make arrangements accordingly. Remind them when you reconfirm your booking (at least 72 hours before departure) and again when you check in at the airport. It may also be worth phoning several airlines before you make your booking to find out how they handle your particular needs.

Most international airports provide escorts from the check-in desk to the air-plane if needed, and there should be ramps, accessible toilets and reachable phones. Air-craft toilets, on the other hand, are likely to present a problem; travelers should discuss this with the airline at an early stage and, if necessary, with their doctor.

Guide dogs for the blind often have to travel in a specially pressurized baggage compartment with other animals, away from their owner, though smaller guide dogs may be admitted to the cabin. Guide dogs are not subject to quarantine as long as they have proof of being vaccinated against rabies.

Deaf travelers can ask for airport and in-flight announcements to be written down for them.

Children

Children younger than two travel for 10% of the standard fare (or free, on some airlines), as long as they don't occupy a seat, but they usually don't get a baggage allowance. 'Skycots' may be provided by the airline if requested in advance; these hold a child weighing up to about 22lb. Children between the ages of two and 12 can sometimes occupy a seat for half to two-thirds of the full fare, and they do get a baggage allowance. Strollers usually must be checked at the aircraft door; they're returned to you at the door after the aircraft lands.

Within the USA

Domestic airfares vary tremendously depending on the season you travel, the day of the week you fly, the length of your stay, how far in advance you pay and the flexibility of the ticket (in allowing for flight changes and refunds). There's also much competition and at any given time any one of the airlines could have the cheapest fare.

See the Getting There & Away sections in the New York City, Philadelphia and Pittsburgh chapters for information on domestic airlines that service the region. The following list contains some sample discount roundtrip fares from various US cities to New York City:

from	discount roundtrip fare
Atlanta, GA	$138
Boston, MA	$179
Chicago, IL	$182
Dallas-Fort Worth, TX	$241
Denver, CO	$265
Indianapolis, IN	$194
Los Angeles, CA	$288
Miami, FL	$227
Minneapolis-St Paul, MN	$199
Phoenix, AZ	$314
San Francisco, CA	$215
Seattle-Tacoma, WA	$390
Washington, DC	$169

The *Boston Globe*, *New York Times*, *Los Angeles Times*, *Chicago Tribune*, *San Francisco Examiner* and other major newspapers have weekly travel sections with many advertisements for discounted airfares. Council Travel (☎ 800-226-8624) and STA Travel (☎ 800-777-0112) have offices in major cities nationwide and may offer good fares. The website for Council Travel is www.counciltravel.com and for STA Travel is www.statravel.com.

The magazine *Travel Unlimited*, PO Box 1058, Allston, MA 02134, publishes details on the cheapest air fares and courier possibilities.

Canada

Major Canadian newspapers such as the *Globe & Mail* and *Vancouver Sun* carry travel agencies' advertisements. The magazine *Great Expeditions*, PO Box 8000-411, Abbotsford BC V2S 6H1, is also useful. Travel CUTS (www.travelcuts.com), the Canadian Federation of Students travel agency, offers low fares and has offices in major cities.

Most of the airline connections between Canada and the region are through New York City. Roundtrip fares from Toronto with US Airways and Delta Air Lines start from around C$520. Fares from Montreal start around C$555.

The UK & Ireland

Check the ads in magazines such as *Time Out* and *City Limits*, plus the Sunday papers and *Exchange & Mart*. Also check the free magazines widely available in London – start by looking outside the train and tube stations. Also the Globetrotters Club (www.globetrotters.co.uk), BCM Roving, London WC1N 3XX, publishes the *Globe* newsletter that covers obscure destinations and can help you find traveling companions.

Most British travel agents are registered with the Association of British Travel Agents (ABTA; www.abta.com). If you've paid for your flight at an ABTA-registered agent who then goes out of business, ABTA will guarantee a refund or an alternative.

London is arguably the world's headquarters for the no-frills discount travel agencies called bucket shops. These are well advertised and invariably have fares below the airlines' published standard rates. Two reliable agents for cheap tickets in the UK are

---

International Visitors

Arriving in the USA Even if you're continuing immediately to another city, the first airport that you land at is where you must carry out immigration and customs formalities. If your luggage is checked from, say, London to Buffalo, you'll still have to take it through customs if you first land in New York City.

Passengers aboard the airplane are given standard immigration and customs forms to fill out. After the plane lands, you first go through the immigration procedure. There are two lines: one for US citizens and residents, the other for nonresidents. After immigration you collect your baggage then pass through customs. If you have nothing to declare, you'll probably clear customs quickly and without a luggage search, but don't count on it. (See also Customs in the Facts for the Visitor chapter.)

If your flight is continuing to another city or you have a connecting flight, it's your responsibility to get your bags to the right place. Normally, there are airline counters or an airline official outside the customs area to help you.

Leaving the USA You should check in for international flights at least two hours early. During check-in procedures, you'll be asked questions about whether you packed your own bags, whether anyone else has had access to them since you packed them and whether you've received any parcels to carry. These questions are for security purposes.

Airport Taxes There's a $6 airport departure tax on all passengers bound for a foreign destination, plus a $6.50 North American Free Trade Agreement (NAFTA) tax on passengers entering the USA from a foreign country. There may also be smaller airport usage and security fees depending upon which airport you fly to or from. Airport departure taxes are normally included in the cost of tickets purchased in the USA. If you purchased your ticket outside the USA, you may have to pay the tax when you check in for your departing flight.

Trailfinders (☎ 020-7937-5400), 194 Kensington High St, London W8 7RG, and STA Travel (☎ 020-7937-9971), 86 Old Brompton Rd, London SW7 3LQ. Trailfinders also has offices in Manchester, Glasgow and Dublin.

Virgin Atlantic is an airline with consistently low fares. Its standard high-season roundtrip fare from London to New York City is $676; its 21-day advance-purchase fare allowing a one-month maximum stay costs $432. Aer Lingus has direct flights from Shannon and Dublin to New York City, but because competition on flights from London is fiercer, it's generally cheaper to fly to London first.

Continental Europe

There are many nonstop flights to New York. Amsterdam is one of the best places to purchase cheap airfares. The official student agency, NBBS Reizen (☎ 020 624 0989), Rokin 38, is good, but may not have the lowest prices, so check some of the discount travel agencies along Rokin. In Paris, Council Travel (☎ 1 44 41 89 89) is at 16 rue des Vaugirard. In Germany, Council Travel has an office (☎ 211 36 30 30) at Graf Adolf Strasse 64, 40212 Dusseldorf and in Munich (☎ 089 39 50 22) at Adalbert Strasse 32, 80799 Munich.

The newsletter *Farang*, La Rue 8 à 4261 Braives, Belgium, deals with exotic destinations, as does the magazine *Aventure du Bout du Monde*, 116 rue de Javel, 75015 Paris, France.

On Virgin Atlantic, flights from Paris to New York are usually cheaper than alternatives. A standard roundtrip weekday high-season fare costs FF8190, but cheaper advance-purchase fares start from around FF4000.

Australia & New Zealand

In Australia and New Zealand, STA Travel (www.statravel.com.au, www.statravel.co.nz) and Flight Centre (www.flightcentre.com) are the main discount travel agencies. They usually have rates to the USA that are within a few dollars of each other. It's also worth checking the online agency www.travel.com.au. Qantas flies to Los Angeles from Sydney, Melbourne (via Sydney or Auckland) and Cairns, with onward connections to Pittsburgh, Philadelphia and New York City on US Airways. United Airlines flies to San Francisco and Los Angeles from Sydney with onward flights to the same East Coast cities.

The cheapest tickets have a 21-day advance-purchase requirement, a minimum stay of seven days and a maximum stay of 60 days.

Qantas flies from Melbourne or Sydney to New York for A$2808 in the high season. Flying with Air New Zealand is slightly cheaper, and both Qantas and Air New Zealand offer tickets with longer stays or stopovers, but you pay more. Roundtrip flights from Auckland to Los Angeles on Qantas cost NZ$1999 in the low season.

Asia

Bangkok is the discount-plane-ticket capital of the region, but its bucket shops can be unreliable. Hong Kong, Kuala Lumpur and Singapore are also competitive. STA Travel has branches in Hong Kong, Tokyo, Singapore, Bangkok and Kuala Lumpur. These cities all have good connections to the US West Coast, many of which go via Honolulu, HI. A standard roundtrip high-season fare from Hong Kong to New York costs around US$1200.

Central & South America

Most flights from Central and South America go via Miami, Dallas/Fort Worth or Los Angeles and some fly direct to New York City. American, Continental, Delta, Northwest and United all have routes connecting Mexico and Central and South America to the US. Aeroméxico, Mexicana and the airlines of Central America (Aeroquetzal, Aeronica, Aviateca, COPA, LACSA and TACA) have flights to either Miami or New York City.

LAND

Although major rail lines and interstate highways connect New York, New Jersey and Pennsylvania with the rest of the US, public transportation to remote areas is limited.

Bus

Big, comfortable, air-conditioned buses connect most cities and some towns in the USA. However, as the private auto is king, and air service is faster in this large country, bus service is limited. Bus lines don't serve places off the main routes, so you won't find buses to most NPS areas, for example, or important tourist towns such as Gettysburg. Fares are relatively high and discount airfares can undercut buses on some long-distance routes. On the other hand, long-distance bus trips are often available at bargain prices by purchasing or reserving tickets at least three days in advance. See also Buses in the Getting Around chapter.

Greyhound connects most major Canadian centers with the main continental US cities, but often with a bus transfer at the border or the nearest town to it. Greyhound does, however, run directly from Toronto (via Niagara Falls and Buffalo) and Montreal to New York City.

New York City is the region's major hub for buses. The Port Authority Bus Terminal (☎ 212-564-8484, www.panynj.gov/tbt/pabframe.HTM), Eighth Ave and W 42nd St in Manhattan, is the city's main bus terminal.

Greyhound (☎ 800-231-2222) operates cross-country buses from Los Angeles, San Francisco and Seattle on the West Coast and from southern cities such as Atlanta and Miami to Philadelphia and New York City. Its website is www.greyhound.com. Bonanza Bus Lines (☎ 800-556-3815) operates routes between New York City and various destinations in New England. Its website is www.bonanzabus.com. Peter Pan Bus Lines (☎ 800-343-9999) and Capitol Trailways (☎ 800-444-2877) are two other major interstate bus lines serving the region. Their websites are www.peterpan-bus.com and www.capitoltrailways.com, respectively.

See also Green Tortoise under Organized Tours, below.

The one-way/roundtrip fare from New York City to Washington, DC, is only $39/74, which definitely beats air and train prices; the trip should take about 4½ hours, though this depends on the volume of traffic. From Miami the fare is $117/162 (seven hours); from Toronto $75/125 (three hours); and San Francisco to Philadelphia is $159/308 (27½ hours).

Bus Passes Passes can be economical if you're doing a lot of traveling, but the relatively high prices may impel you to travel more than you would normally, simply to get your money's worth. The passes are for unlimited travel on consecutive days, not for a number of days spread over a longer period. Greyhound's passes are also valid on regional bus lines that are affiliated with Greyhound.

Greyhound's **Ameripass** can be purchased in the USA and costs $169 for seven days of unlimited travel year-round; $249 for 15 days; and $349 for 30 days. Children younger than 11 travel for half price. You can get on and off at any Greyhound stop or terminal, and the Ameripass is sold at every Greyhound terminal.

Greyhound's **International Ameripass** is available only to foreign tourists and foreign students and lecturers (with their families) staying less than a year. A seven-day pass with unlimited travel costs $149; a 15-day pass costs $229; and a 30-day pass costs $319.

The International Ameripass is usually purchased abroad at a travel agency. The only place you can buy it in the USA is through the Greyhound International Office (☎ 212-971-0492, 800-246-8572) in New York City. Purchases can be made over the phone from anywhere in the US, but you'll need to give your passport number, your country and date of entry. This information will be written on your International Ameripass when you receive it.

Train

Amtrak operates most of the passenger rail services (☎ 800-872-7245), and this region, part of the northeast rail system, features some of the most heavily traveled routes. Long-distance travelers, from the west and southwest, must make connections in Chicago. Amtrak maintains a website (www.amtrak.com).

By the time you read this, Amtrak's new high-speed Acela 'tilt' trains (www.acela.com)

should be fully operating. The trains run on electric lines at up to 150mph between Boston, New York City and Washington, DC, cutting travel time from New York City to Boston to less than three hours; to Washington to about 2½ hours. It's cheaper and more comfortable than a plane, and about as fast from city center to city center. The New York City-Boston fare is around $135 one way for premium service.

In summer, extra trains run to/from popular tourist destinations, but throughout the year most services remain constant. See also Getting There & Away in the New York City chapter for information on the Metro North Rail Road.

The *Metroliner* is a daily, fast-shuttle service between New York City and Washington, DC, via Newark, Trenton, Philadelphia, Wilmington and Baltimore. Seats must be reserved. The *Northeast Direct* also connects the two cities (and Boston), but only some of its services need to be reserved.

The *Twilight Shoreliner* is a daily overnight service between Boston and Newport News, VA, via New York City and Washington, DC. These cities are connected with Niagara Falls and Toronto on the *Empire Service* (via Philadelphia, Trenton and Newark) and with Montreal on the *Adirondack* (from New York City via Saratoga Springs). The *Vermonter* also connects Washington, DC, and Montreal, running via Connecticut and Vermont, stopping daily at Philadelphia, Newark and New York City.

Finally, the *Ethan Allan Express* runs daily between Rutland, VT, and Washington, DC, via Albany, New York City and Philadelphia. Reservations are required for travel north of Albany.

From Washington, DC, you can connect with trains south to Miami and New Orleans.

In some areas, Amtrak operates a coordinated train/bus connecting service known as Amtrak Thruway. You must have an onward ticket before you can board the bus.

Tickets & Fares Fares are complex but rail travel is generally cheaper midweek and if you buy special fares in advance. A reservation can be held under your surname only.

You can buy tickets by credit card over the phone, from a travel agent or at some (but not all) Amtrak stations. Tickets may be purchased aboard the train without penalty if the station isn't open 30 minutes prior to boarding; otherwise, there's a $7 surcharge. There are discounts of 15% for seniors 62 and over, students and disabled persons; 50% for children two to 15; and 25% for military personnel. Roundtrip fares are the best bargain, but even some of these may be as expensive as airfares.

Some examples of unreserved, midweek, roundtrip fares from New York City are: Boston $54 (four hours), Chicago $151 (20 hours), Miami $162 (22½ hours) and Washington $116 (nine hours).

Note that most small train stations don't sell tickets; you have to book them with Amtrak over the phone or online. Some small stations have no porters or other facilities, and trains may stop there only if you've purchased a ticket in advance.

Train Passes The USA Rail Pass is available from travel agents outside North America, but foreign passport holders can purchase them from Amtrak once inside the USA. The pass offers unlimited coach-class travel within a specific region for either 15 or 30 days, with the price depending on the region and whether it's the high/low season (high season is June to Labor Day in early September). The Northeast pass costs $195/175 for 15 days, $230/215 for 30 days. The national pass costs $425/285 for 15 days, $535/375 for 30 days.

Amtrak's North America Rail Pass, operated in conjunction with Canada's VIA Rail, offers unlimited travel on US and Canadian railways for 30 consecutive days for $645/450 in the high/low season. The high season is July and August and the pass can be purchased by anyone. But the Northeast North America Rail Pass, like the USA Rail Pass, is available only to foreign visitors. It's valid for 15 days and costs $400/300.

Car & Motorcycle

For information on buying or renting a car, or using a drive-away (driving a car for someone else), see the Getting Around chapter, later in this book.

If you plan on driving from outside the region, I-95 is the major north-south route along the East Coast and stretches from the Canadian (Maine-New Brunswick) border to Miami, FL. I-95 becomes a toll road between New York City and the Delaware Memorial Bridge (this portion is the NJ Turnpike); it's well traveled by trucks and badly pockmarked. The other main north-south route, I-81, runs from the New York-Ontario border through Pennsylvania to Maryland, Virginia and Tennessee. I-79 also heads north-south, off I-90 near Erie, PA, to West Virginia. I-87 leads north from New York City to the Quebec border.

I-90 extends east-west from Boston, MA, across New York state along the southern shore of Lake Erie, through Pennsylvania to Ohio and on to Seattle, WA, on the Pacific Northwest coast. I-80 runs from New York City through northern New Jersey and central Pennsylvania to San Francisco on the West Coast. Finally, I-70/76 stretches from Philadelphia through southern Pennsylvania to Ohio and meets I-15 in Utah.

If you're coming from Canada, automobile drivers and motorcyclists need the vehicle's registration papers and liability insurance. (See also Driver's License & International Driving Permit under Visas & Documents in the Facts for the Visitor chapter.) I-95 connects with the Trans-Canada Hwy at the Maine-New Brunswick border; at the New York-Quebec border I-87 meets Hwy 15, which leads north to Montreal. Near Kingston, Ontario, at the New York state border northeast of Lake Ontario, I-81 meets Hwy 401; southeast of Lake Ontario, I-90/I-190 connect with the Canadian highway system at Niagara Falls.

SEA

Cunard's *Queen Elizabeth II* makes transatlantic voyages from Southampton, UK, to New York City, but the cruise itself is really the vacation. Seabourn Cruise Line (☎ 800-929-9595), 55 Francisco St, San Francisco, CA 94133, offers cruises from Montreal to New York City via Boston. The standard

reference for passenger ships is the *PAG Cruise & Ferry Guide*, published by Reed Travel Group (☎ 0158-260-0111), Church St, Dunstable, Bedfordshire, LU5 4HB, UK.

Some ocean-going freight lines also allow passengers on board. The *ABC Passenger Shipping Guide* is a good source of information. Also, contact the Cruise & Freighter Travel Association (☎ 800-872-8584), PO Box 580218-D1, Flushing, NY 11358.

A ferry service connects this region with Canada. On the St Lawrence River, Wolfe Island Ferries (☎ 315-783-0638) runs between Cape Vincent, NY, and Wolfe Island, Ontario, from early May to late October.

A number of ferries cross Lake Champlain between Vermont and New York state: from Grand Isle to Plattsburgh, Burlington to Port Kent, Charlotte to Essex and Shoreham (Larabees Point) to Ticonderoga. See Getting There & Around in the Adirondack Region chapter for more information.

There is a year-round ferry service across Delaware Bay connecting Cape May in New Jersey with Lewes, DE. See Cape May in the Southern New Jersey chapter for additional information.

ORGANIZED TOURS

For those with limited time, organized tours can be an efficient and relatively inexpensive way to go. Tours of the USA are so numerous that it's impossible to attempt a comprehensive listing. See your travel agent and check the small ads in newspaper travel pages.

A number of companies offer standard guided tours of the region, usually by bus, and include accommodations. Any travel agent can tell you about these and arrange air, train or bus tickets to get you to the beginning of the tour.

Green Tortoise (☎ 415-956-7500, 800-867-8647), 494 Broadway, San Francisco, CA 94133, offers alternative bus transportation to New York from the West Coast with stops at places such as hot springs and national parks. Meals are cooperatively cooked, and you sleep on bunks on the bus or camp. This isn't luxury travel, but it's more relaxing than Greyhound and a lot more fun. Fares are $349 to $399, plus a food fund of $111 to $121 per person. The company has a website (www.greentortoise.com).

Trek America (☎ 973-983-1144, 800-221-0596), PO Box 189, Rockaway, NJ 07866, offers roundtrip camping tours of the different areas of the country. In Britain contact the company (☎ 01295-256777, fax 01295-257399) at 4 Waterperry Court, Middleton Rd, Banbury, Oxon, OX16 8QG. These tours last from one to nine weeks and are designed for small, international groups (13 people maximum) ages 18 to 38. Tour prices vary with the season, and are highest from July to September. Sample prices, including food and occasional hotel nights, are about $770 for a 14-day tour to $3200 for a nine-week tour of the entire country. Some side trips and cultural events are included in the price, and participants help with cooking and camp chores. It also has 'Footloose' camping and walking trips for older travelers. Its nine-day Appalachian Trail Walk costs $579/669 in the low/high season. The company has a website (www.trekamerica.com).

Contiki (www.contiki.com) is similar and caters to 18 to 35 year olds. Its seven-day tour of the eastern states costs $715. Globus & Cosmos (www.globusandcosmos.com) is more suited to older travelers. Its nine-day tour of the northeast starts at $1559.

AmeriCan Adventures (☎ 800-864-0335), 6762A Centinela Ave, Culver City, CA 90230, offers a 19-day tour of the East Coast that costs about $899. The company's website is www.americanadventures.com. For worldwide sales, contact its UK headquarters (☎ 1-892-511894), 45 High St, Tunbridge Wells, Kent TN1 1XL.

Peter Pan Bus Lines (☎ 800-343-9999) is one of the largest organized bus-tour operators in the northeast. It offers day-trip and overnight packages from Boston and Washington, DC. The company's website is www.peterpan-bus.com.

Getting Around

Airfares aren't cheap, but for those with a little extra money and not much time, the occasional flight may be useful. Land travel is generally less expensive and, of course, more interesting than flying. Buses provide the most extensive public transportation and are generally cheaper than the more limited train service, though train travel can be quicker.

Public transportation doesn't reach many of the interesting, more isolated places, so having your own transportation can be a major advantage. It's worth considering car rental for at least a part of your trip. You can use public transportation to towns and cities, then rent a car locally to get to places not served by public transportation. This option is usually more expensive than just renting a car and driving yourself everywhere, but it can cut down on long-distance driving.

AIR

The region is served by most domestic airlines (see the Getting There & Away chapter). Regular fares are expensive, but you can save money if you book in advance. Fares also drop considerably if you avoid peak times and fly early in the morning or late at night, or on specific flights. Ask about special fares when making reservations.

If you're arriving from abroad or another major US airport, it's usually much cheaper to buy a through ticket to small airports as part of your fare rather than buying them separately.

Another alternative is an air pass, available from the major airlines flying between the USA and Europe, Asia and Australia. (See Special Fares for Foreign Visitors in the Getting There & Away chapter.)

Domestic Airports

For information on airlines and JFK, La Guardia and Newark airports, see the Getting There & Away chapter. Buffalo-Niagara international airport (☎ 716-630-6000) is busy serving upstate New York. Other New York

state airports include Syracuse's Hancock International Airport (☎ 315-454-4330), Adirondack Airport (☎ 518-891-4600) and Albany County Airport (☎ 518-869-9611).

In addition to the Newark airport, other New Jersey airports are Atlantic City International (☎ 609-645-7895), Princeton (☎ 609-921-3100) and Teterboro (☎ 201-288-1775), one of the nation's leading hubs for private aircraft.

For Philadelphia and Pittsburgh airports, see the Getting There & Away sections for those cities. Other Pennsylvania airports serve Johnstown/Cambria County (☎ 814-536-0002), Harrisburg (☎ 717-948-3905), Lancaster (☎ 717-569-1221) and Reading (☎ 610-372-4666).

Domestic Airlines

The following airlines serve the region (all phone numbers are toll-free and may be dialed only from North America):

Air Tran www.airtran.com	☎ 800-825-8538
America West www.americawest.com	☎ 800-235-9292
American Airlines www.aa.com	☎ 800-433-7300
Continental Airlines www.continental.com	☎ 800-525-0280
Delta Air Lines www.delta-air.com	☎ 800-221-1212
Midwest Express www.midwestexpress.com	☎ 800-452-2022
Northwest www.nwa.com	☎ 800-225-2525
Shuttle America www.shuttleamerica.com	☎ 888-999-3273
Spirit Airlines www.spiritair.com	☎ 800-772-7117
Trans World Airlines www.twa.com	☎ 800-221-2000
United Airlines www.ual.com	☎ 800-241-6522
US Airways www.usairways.com	☎ 800-428-4322

BUS

Buses go to more places than airplanes or trains, but the routes still leave a lot out, bypassing some prime destinations. Towns that aren't on major routes are generally served by local carriers. Greyhound and other bus lines often share the same terminal.

Buses normally provide the cheapest form of public transportation, and fares are even cheaper if you travel Monday to Thursday; Friday to Sunday, any fare goes up several dollars. For specific fares, check the information given under specific towns and cities.

Carriers

Greyhound (☎ 800-231-2222) is the main long-distance carrier for the region; its website is at www.greyhound.com. It has the most extensive routes, and it usually has its own terminal, though they are sometimes in undesirable parts of town. However, the buses are reasonably comfortable, and they usually run on time. The company has a good safety record.

Greyhound connects large towns one or two times a day along major highways, stopping at smaller towns on the way. In many small towns, Greyhound doesn't maintain terminals but merely stops at a given location, such as a service station, grocery store or fast-food restaurant (which may be the only choice for a meal – bring your own food if burgers and fries are unappealing). At these 'terminals,' passengers may be able to buy a ticket, but usually you pay the driver (with exact change) upon boarding. Note that all buses are nonsmoking.

Greyhound works in conjunction with Bonanza Bus Lines (☎ 800-556-3815), which has a website at www.bonanzabus.com, and Peter Pan Bus Lines (☎ 800-343-9999), which has a website at www.peterpanbus.com. Bonanza connects New York City with upstate New York and New England. Peter Pan operates between Washington, DC, and Boston via Philadelphia and New York City, and it also runs to Atlantic City, New Jersey.

Other bus lines operate in the region. Capitol Trailways (☎ 800-333-8444) runs between Washington, DC, and Baltimore, Maryland; it has many stops in central and eastern Pennsylvania, as well as in New York state, at New York City, Syracuse, Binghamton and Buffalo. The company's website is at www.capitoltrailways.com.

Martz Trailways connects Philadelphia and other towns in eastern Pennsylvania with New York City and several towns in New Jersey, including Atlantic City. For information on Pennsylvania, call ☎ 800-432-8069, and for New York and New Jersey, call ☎ 800-233-8604. The company's website is at www.martztrailways.com.

Adirondack Trailways (☎ 518-436-9651, 800-225-6815) runs to many major towns in New York state. Fullington Trailways (☎ 800-942-8287) runs between Buffalo in New York and Pittsburgh and Harrisburg in Pennsylvania. Also, Susquehanna Trailways (☎ 800-692-6314) runs west from New York City and Philadelphia to Williamsport, Pennsylvania; the company's website is at www.susquehannabus.com.

New Jersey Transit (NJ Transit; ☎ 973-762-5100, 800-772-2222 in New Jersey) has a regular bus service from Atlantic City along the coast, extending north to New York City and south to Cape May; its website is www.njtransit.state.nj.us. Regional lines such as Shortline (☎ 201-529-3666), Academy (☎ 201-420-7000) and Community Coach (☎ 800-522-4515) run many buses between New York City's Port Authority Bus terminal and cities in the northern New Jersey suburbs.

Buying Tickets

Tickets can be bought over the phone with a credit card. The tickets can be mailed to you if you bought them at least 10 days in advance, or they can be picked up at the terminal (make sure to bring proper identification). Greyhound terminals also accept American Express, traveler's checks, post-office money orders and cash. Reservations are made with ticket purchases only. Fares can vary tremendously; it's best to call Greyhound for current details.

Sometimes you can get discounted tickets if you buy them seven or 21 days in advance.

Greyhound occasionally introduces a mileage-based discount-fare program that can be a bargain, especially for long distances, but it's a good idea to check the regular fare anyway. As with regular fares, these promotional fares are subject to change.

TRAIN
Amtrak
Amtrak (☎ 800-872-7245) connects the major cities in the region with stops at smaller towns along the routes. For information on fares, train passes and services beyond New York, New Jersey and Pennsylvania, see the Getting There & Away chapter. You can find Amtrak's website at www.amtrak.com.

The main Amtrak routes radiate from New York City: north to the New York cities of Albany, Schenectady and Rouses Point (near the Quebec border) and to Montreal, Quebec; northwest to the New York cities of Utica, Syracuse, Buffalo and Niagara Falls; and southwest to the New Jersey cities of Newark, Princeton and Trenton and to the Pennsylvania cities of Philadelphia, Harrisburg and Pittsburgh. From Philadelphia, there's a connecting bus service north to the Pennsylvania cities of Bethlehem and Allentown.

Other Services
In addition to its bus services, NJ Transit (☎ 973-762-5100, 800-772-2222 in New Jersey) has a number of rail lines; its website is at www.njtransit.state.nj.us. The Northeast Corridor Line connects New York City's Penn Station with New Jersey's western towns (including Newark, Hoboken, New Brunswick, Princeton, Trenton); there are also direct links to the Jersey Shore. The Atlantic City Line runs directly between Atlantic City and Philadelphia; it also connects with Port Authority Transit Corporation (PATCO) at Lindenwold in New Jersey. PATCO's New Jersey phone number is ☎ 856-772-6900, and its Philadelphia number is ☎ 215-922-4600; you can find its website at www.drpa.org/patco.

The Long Island Rail Road (LIRR; ☎ 516-822-5477, 718-217-5477) joins New York City with Long Island. Metro-North Railroad (☎ 212-532-4900) serves New York City's northern suburbs (Westchester) and Connecticut. You can find more information about these two and other New York City transportation services at www.mta.nyc.ny.us. Port Authority Trans-Hudson (PATH; ☎ 800-234-7284) connects the city to New Jersey's northern cities (including Newark, Hoboken and Jersey City).

Philadelphia's Southeastern Pennsylvania Transportation Authority (SEPTA; ☎ 215-580-7800) covers its suburbs extensively and connects with New Jersey at West Trenton, Trenton and Newark; you can find its website at www.septa.org. The SEPTA network links with PATCO in central Philadelphia. From there, PATCO runs east as far as Lindenwold in New Jersey, where it connects with NJ Transit.

For specifics on services and fares, check the Getting There & Away sections under the location you're interested in. Also see the Local Transport section, later in this chapter.

In some areas, privately owned tourist trains offer scenic day trips through the countryside or other attractions. Some of the trains travel on narrow-gauge railroads built by former mining companies; these are usually steam powered.

CAR & MOTORCYCLE
Driving or motorcycling are undoubtedly convenient ways of getting around the countryside, seeing small towns and visiting out-of-the-way places. With your own mode of transportation, you have independence and flexibility. Driving can work out reasonably cheaply if two or more people share the cost. With a car, it's feasible to carry camping and cooking gear, so that some of its cost can be offset by savings in accommodations and food.

On the debit side, the independence you enjoy using your own vehicle tends to isolate you from the local people. The larger cities, with their one-way traffic systems and complex network of highways into, through and around town, can be confusing and wearing on the nerves. Finding a convenient

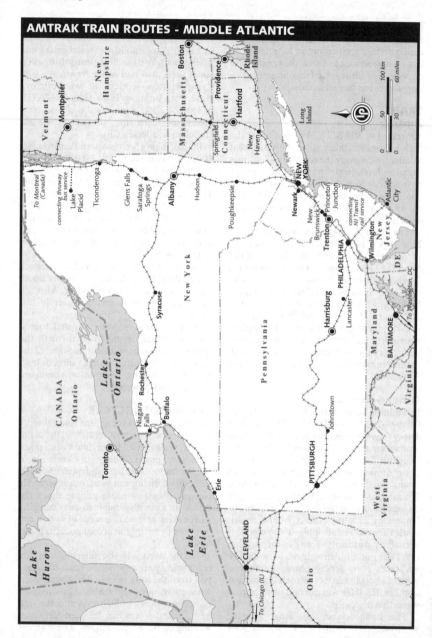

AMTRAK TRAIN ROUTES - MIDDLE ATLANTIC

Distance Chart (in miles)

	Albany, NY	Alexandria Bay, NY	Atlantic City, NJ	Buffalo, NY	Cape May, NJ	Erie, PA	Gettysburg, PA	Harrisburg, PA	Lake Placid, NY	Lancaster, PA	New York, NY	Philadelphia, PA	Pittsburgh, PA	Rochester, NY	Scranton, PA	Syracuse, NY
Alexandria Bay, NY	245															
Atlantic City, NJ	285	530														
Buffalo, NY	284	247	461													
Cape May, NJ	319	564	49	495												
Erie, PA	387	356	473	103	508											
Gettysburg, PA	341	404	189	380	222	300										
Harrisburg, PA	312	357	164	319	180	317	39									
Lake Placid, NY	156	146	428	345	463	448	500	456								
Lancaster, PA	342	394	134	379	147	351	58	36	492							
New York, NY	150	395	144	394	179	428	223	170	292	179						
Philadelphia, PA	248	347	56	405	86	413	125	103	382	69	96					
Pittsburgh, PA	490	472	351	224	386	128	193	211	569	234	376	308				
Rochester, NY	231	194	407	70	442	180	266	289	301	338	342	294				
Scranton, PA	191	235	182	273	217	295	168	125	332	125	121	123	297	217		
Syracuse, NY	141	105	312	143	347	250	298	254	200	290	246	255	367	87	142	
Trenton, NJ	217	377	90	371	125	432	156	121	360	91	59	33	333	353	135	277

place to park in unfamiliar city centers can be difficult and expensive.

Many US cities and towns owe their sprawl to the popularity of the automobile. Satellite communities – with their shopping malls, fast-food restaurants and motels – exist along highways and at the intersections of important routes. The attractions you've come to see may be downtown, but the only affordable accommodations may well be a number of miles away in one of these commercial strips, and the only means of access will be a car or motorcycle. Pittsburgh is a good example of this.

For young travelers (under 25 and especially under 21), car travel is scarcely an option. Car rentals are expensive or unavailable, and if you buy a car, insurance can be prohibitive.

If you're not a resident of the US, you may want to consider getting an International Driving Permit to supplement your normal driver's license (see the Visas & Documents section in the Facts for the Visitor chapter).

Road Rules

You must be at least 16 years of age to drive; in New York City, you *must* be at least 18 years of age, regardless of whether you are licensed to drive in other states. Speed limits are 65mph on interstate highways and freeways unless otherwise posted (but you're likely to find traffic moving at around 70mph); some interstate highways have limits of 55mph. On undivided highways, speed limits vary from 30 to 50mph. In cities and towns, they're usually 25 to 35mph, lower near schools and medical facilities.

Wearing a seat belt is compulsory, and children under four must use approved safety seats. No child should sit in the front-passenger seat of a car equipped with a front-passenger seat air bag. Air bags, which inflate at 200mph, are designed to protect a full-size, full-weight adult and can seriously injure or kill a small or light person.

Motorcyclists and their passengers must wear helmets. Also see Drinking & Driving under Legal Matters in the Facts for the Visitor chapter.

Road Safety

To minimize the chance of theft, always lock your car and don't leave valuables (or anything) in view inside a parked car. Tuck items under a seat or, better still, put them in the trunk. If the car has trunk entry through the back seat or if you can pop open the trunk using a device (a lever or button) in the car, consider taking the items with you. Don't leave valuables in a car overnight.

In more isolated areas, wild animals may be seen foraging along the highways. Many, such as raccoons, are small, but a collision with a large animal such as a deer can wreck a car. It may also severely injure or kill the occupants, as well as the animal. Pay attention to the roadside, especially at night.

Road conditions are particularly difficult in winter. In an emergency, dial ☎ 911. Tire chains are useful and sometimes required on snowy or icy roads. (Note that rental companies specifically prohibit the use of chains on their vehicles.) Other cold-weather precautions include keeping a warm blanket, jumper cables, a jack, a windshield ice-scraper, a spade or snow shovel, flares and an extra pair of gloves and boots in the trunk.

Rental

To rent a car, you must have a valid driver's license (your out-of-state or home license will do) and present a major credit card or else a large cash deposit. You normally need to be at least 25 years of age, but some companies rent to drivers aged 21 to 24 for an additional daily fee.

The major rental agencies are as follows:

Alamo	☎ 800-327-9633
Avis	☎ 800-831-2847
Budget	☎ 800-527-0700
Dollar	☎ 800-800-4000
Enterprise	☎ 800-325-8007
Hertz	☎ 800-654-3131
National	☎ 800-227-7368
Thrifty	☎ 800-367-2277

Rent-a-Wreck (☎ 800-535-1391) offers older vehicles at lower prices. Smaller local companies sometimes offer better prices than the major companies; consult the yellow pages under 'Automobiles.'

Rental prices vary greatly in relation to region, season, day of the week and the type or size of the car. Some rental agencies have bargain rates for weekend or weeklong rentals, especially outside peak season or in conjunction with airline tickets. If you're arranging a rental before you get to the USA, check the options with your travel agent. If you get a fly-drive package, local taxes may be an extra charge when you collect the car. The cheapest car is usually a 'subcompact' or 'compact,' which generally cost about $50 per day.

It's also possible to rent an RV (recreational vehicle; also known as a motor home), which is basically a vanlike vehicle that usually has beds, a stove or microwave oven, a toilet and a shower. They can range in size from a camper slightly bigger than a pickup truck to a 30-foot behemoth.

The benefits of renting an RV are that it can be fun to do it with friends or family, and you can conceivably save money on accommodations and food, especially if you're in a large group. Many campgrounds throughout the US have special sites designated for RVs, with electrical, water and sewage hookups. The downside is that RVs can be very expensive to rent, especially when you consider the hefty amount of gas they require (and don't forget the cost of the campsites). They are cumbersome, difficult to drive and even more difficult to park. If you're planning on spending much time in cities, parking and driving an RV will probably turn out to be more trouble than it's worth. If you are thinking about renting an RV, be sure to consider the total cost, and if you or no one in your group has ever driven a very large vehicle, you might want to reconsider your choice.

One of the more common RV rental companies is Cruise America (☎ 800-327-7799); its website is www.cruiseamerica.com. The pricing scheme is very complicated and depends on the size of the vehicle and where, when and how long you'd like to rent. A standard RV that sleeps up to five people could be $380 to $670 for three nights with a mileage allowance of 500 miles, whereas a large RV that sleeps up to seven people could be $460 to $830 for the same rental period and mileage allowance. Check with the rental company for details and special deals.

You're normally expected to return any rental, car or otherwise, to where you picked it up; you can arrange to drop the vehicle off elsewhere, but you'll have to pay a surcharge to do so.

In addition, there are several types of insurance to consider. Liability insurance, which covers damage you may cause to another vehicle, is required by law but isn't always included in rental contracts because many Americans are covered for rental cars under their regular car liability insurance policy. You do need liability coverage, but don't pay extra if the coverage already included with the rental is sufficient. Liability insurance is also called 'third-party coverage.'

A Collision Damage Waiver (CDW), also called a Loss Damage Waiver (LDW), is usually optional; you don't need to buy this waiver to rent, but it does cover the full value of the vehicle in case of an accident, except when the accident is caused by acts of nature or fire. For a mid-sized car, the cost for this extra coverage is around $15 per day. Agencies also add a daily fee for each additional driver.

Some credit cards cover your CDW if you rent for 15 days or less and charge the full cost of rental to your card. If you opt to do that, you'll need to sign the waiver, declining the coverage. If you already have collision insurance on your personal policy, the credit card covers the large deductible. To find out extents and details, contact your credit card company.

Purchase

If you're spending three or more months in the USA, you may want to consider buying a car, which may work out to be cheaper than renting one. However, buying one can be complicated and requires plenty of research.

First, contact AAA (☎ 800-477-1222) for some general information (you need to be a member for this service). Then contact the Department of Motor Vehicles (DMV) to find out about registration fees and insurance, which can be confusing and expensive.

Cars bought at a dealer cost more, but may come with warranties and/or financing options. Dealers are often concentrated in certain areas so you can see lots of vehicles in a short time and compare prices. Buying from an individual is usually cheaper; look in the newspaper classified ads or in special publications for used vehicles. Check the *Kelley Blue Book* (available at public libraries or online at www.kbb.com) for the average value of the model and year of vehicle you're considering. Have it checked out by a mechanic or diagnostic service before you buy. Some AAA offices have diagnostic centers where they do this on the spot for local members and those of foreign affiliates.

If you buy from a dealer, the dealer should submit to the DMV the required forms for the car's registration and transfer. If you buy from an individual, you (the buyer) must register the vehicle with the DMV within 10 days of purchase. To register the vehicle, you'll need the bill of sale, the title to the car (the 'pink slip') and proof of insurance or other financial responsibility.

Insurance Every owner or driver of a motor vehicle must 'maintain financial responsibility' to protect the health and property of others in the event of an accident. The easiest way to do this is to have Auto Liability Insurance. For rental cars, the company will arrange insurance if you're not already covered – it can cost almost as much as the rental.

If you buy a car, you must take out liability insurance, and this can be difficult if you don't have a local license. A car dealer or AAA may be able to suggest an insurer. Even with a local license, insurance can be expensive and difficult to obtain if you don't have evidence of a good driving record. Bring copies of your home auto-insurance policies if they can help establish that you are a good risk. Drivers under 25 will have big problems getting insurance. Rates are generally lower if you register the car at an

Accidents Do Happen

It's helpful to know the following appropriate protocol when involved in a 'fender-bender:'

- Remain at the scene of the accident until you have given information to the police or exchanged it with the other driver(s) involved, especially if there has been substantial damage or personal injury. It may be necessary to move your car off the road for safety's sake, but leaving the scene of an accident is illegal.

- Call the police (and an ambulance, if needed) immediately, and give the operator as much specific information as possible (your location, injuries etc). The emergency phone number is ☎ 911.

- Get the name, address, driver's license number, license plate number and insurance information of the other driver(s). Be prepared to provide the same information, including any documentation you have, such as your passport, International Driving Permit and insurance documents.

- Tell your story to the police carefully. Refrain from answering any questions until you feel comfortable doing so (with a lawyer present, if need be). That's your right under the law. The only insurance information needed is the name of your insurance carrier and your policy number.

- If you've hit a large animal, such as a deer or moose, and it's badly injured, call the police to report it immediately. If your car is damaged in any way, report it to your insurance company or rental agency.

- If a police officer suspects that you're under the influence of alcohol, he or she may request that you submit to a breath-analysis test. If you don't, you may have your driving privileges suspended until a verdict is delivered in your court case. If you're driving a rental car, call the rental company promptly.

---

address in the suburbs or in a rural area rather than in a city center, and avoid registering it in New Jersey, which has a notorious car-theft problem.

American Automobile Association

AAA ('Triple A'; ☎ 800-222-4357) is an umbrella organization uniting a variety of local and regional auto clubs that use the AAA name. Members belonging to one club may also use the facilities of any other AAA club in the USA. AAA has offices in all major cities and many resort towns; the offices provide useful information, free maps, routine road services, such as tire repair and towing (free within a limited radius), and diagnostic tests.

AAA members often receive discounts on attraction admission fees and on lodging. The annual membership fee depends upon the particular club you join but ranges from about $35 to $63. Members of its foreign affiliates are entitled to reciprocal services in the USA. The organization's website is at www.aaa.com.

Drive-Away Cars

This is a cheap way to get around if you like long-distance driving and meet eligibility requirements. A drive-away is a car belonging to an owner who can't drive it to a specific destination but is willing to allow someone else to drive it for them. For example, if someone moves from Boston to Pittsburgh, they may elect to fly and leave the car with a drive-away agency. The agency will find a driver and take care of all the necessary insurance and permits. If you happen to want to drive from Boston to Pittsburgh, are over 21 and have a valid driver's license and a clean driving record, you can apply to drive the car. Normally, you have to pay a small refundable deposit. You pay for the gas (though sometimes a gas allowance is given).

You must deliver the car to its destination at a specified time; the time allotted for a trip

Fruit and friends, Hudson Valley, NY

Casual Friday in Woodstock, NY

A meal that will stick to your ribs, Ticonderoga, NY

Visit an old-fashioned diner for a slice of Americana, Hudson, NY

View from Route 28, near Cooperstown, NY

Antique stores on Main Street in Catskill, NY

usually works out at about six hours of driving per day. You're also allowed a fixed number of miles, based on the shortest route.

Drive-away companies often advertise in the classified sections of newspapers under 'Travel.' They're also listed in the yellow pages of the telephone directory under 'Automobile Transporters & Drive-Away Companies.' You need to be flexible about dates and destinations when you call. If you're going to a popular area, you may be able to leave within two days or less, or you may have to wait over a week before a car becomes available. The most readily available routes are coast to coast, though intermediate trips are certainly possible.

HITCHHIKING

Travelers who hitch should understand that they're taking a serious risk. It's potentially dangerous and definitely not recommended. Most Americans don't do it and drivers are reluctant to pick up hitchhikers anyway. This may be less so in rural parts, but traffic can be sparse, and you might get stranded.

If you do hitch, be extremely careful when accepting a lift. If in doubt, don't. Ask the driver where they're going rather than telling them where you want to go. Hitching in pairs may be a fraction safer, and you should let someone else know where you're planning to go.

Hitching on freeways is prohibited – there's usually a sign at the on-ramp stating 'no pedestrians beyond this point,' and anyone caught hitching past there can be arrested. Police routinely check hitchhikers' identification, and you may be asked to show some money to prove you aren't destitute.

Even hitching to and from a hiking trailhead should be avoided – try to arrange something at a ranger station or with other hikers. If you're broke, there are alternatives to hitching – look for rideshares at hostels or ask at campgrounds.

WALKING

Because of the great distances, few people use their feet as a primary means of transportation. However, it's possible to traverse the region along sections of long-distance trails, such as the North Country National Scenic Trail and the Appalachian Trail, and to cover other interesting areas on foot. For more information, see Hiking & Backpacking in the Outdoor Activities chapter.

BOAT

You can rent boats to travel New York State's 524-mile canal system, which is made up of four waterways: the Erie, Cayuga-Seneca, Oswego and Champlain Canals. These link with lakes and rivers across the state and connect the Hudson River with the Great Lakes and the waterways of the northeast. The Champlain Canal heads north from Albany to Lake Champlain and west along the Erie Canal to Buffalo and the Great Lakes. The Erie Canal meets the Oswego Canal at Three Rivers, west of Syracuse. For more information, contact the New York State Canal System (☎ 800-422-6254), PO Box 189, Albany, NY 12201-0189; alternatively, you can visit the website at www.canals.state.ny.us.

From New Jersey, ferries connect Hoboken with Manhattan and Camden with Philadelphia.

LOCAL TRANSPORT

Comprehensive local bus networks exist in big cities and most larger towns, though some popular destinations, such as Gettysburg in Pennsylvania, have no public transportation. Other towns have bus systems with limited hours and routes, which make them unreliable as a primary means of local transportation.

New York City (which has an extensive subway and bus system, plus the Metro North Railroad and the Long Island Rail Road) and Philadelphia (which has SEPTA; see Train, earlier), have extensive urban and suburban transportation systems. Also, the PATCO subway line runs across central Philadelphia on route to New Jersey.

Most towns of any size have a taxi service. Taxis can be expensive but aren't so outrageous if shared with two or three people. You can hail them on the street when their center roof-light is lit. Check the yellow pages under 'Taxi' for phone numbers and services. Drivers almost always expect a tip of about 12% to 18% of the fare.

New York City is serviced by the Staten Island Ferry, but most ways of getting around a town by boat or ferry are as part of a guided tour.

ORGANIZED TOURS

City tours by bus or 'trolley' (actually a bus disguised as a light-rail trolley) are popular in the major cities, tourist towns and resort areas. Most are useful for getting a look at the major sights, but don't expect too much from the commentary. There are some adventurous exceptions such as Just Ducky Tours in Pittsburgh, where an amphibious vehicle cruises the city streets, then glides into the river for a nautical cruise.

Regional tours are the way to go if your time is limited. You can book these through a travel agent, tourist office, sometimes through your hotel or directly through the tour companies themselves. Some of the larger bus companies, such as Gray Line or Peter Pan Bus Lines, offer trips of varying lengths, some of which include accommodations. Amtrak provides a similar service. Tours to see the fall foliage are very popular and are often fully booked early on.

Many small companies offer a variety of activity-based trips – you can hike, camp, bike, canoe or raft rivers, or bird-watch. Many of these companies are listed under their specific locations.

See also Organized Tours in the Getting There & Away chapter.

New York

Facts about New York

New York State is a world apart from its better known cousin, New York City. One of the original thirteen English colonies, upstate New York still retains some of the character associated with New England – its people are self-reliant, often stoic and proud of their close knit communities and relationship to the land.

Once a traveler manages to move beyond the gravitational pull of New York City, the state opens up in ways unimaginable from midtown Manhattan. An ongoing debate, of course, is what constitutes 'upstate' New York. Folks in the Adirondack's North Country refer casually to 'down-staters' as occupants of a different reality. On the other hand, it's not unusual to hear New York City dwellers discuss a trip 'upstate,' only to find out they went to Poughkeepsie, where commuter trains carry people in and out of the Big Apple every day of the week. A resident of Westchester County had the best definition of upstate: 'Any place north of where you are.' Indeed, the land and its recent history continually alter as you travel away from New York City's throbbing hub.

New York's early European history – much of it revealed through encounters with the indigenous Native Americans – begins in the lower Hudson River Valley, along the banks of the river that Henry Hudson hoped was the long sought Northwest Passage to the Pacific and the storied lands beyond. He could hardly be blamed for his error in navigation; the Hudson estuary is one of the largest on the continent, with the salty waters of the Atlantic extending more than 50 miles upriver.

Navigation by water, in fact, shaped the state's evolution. The Hudson River, the Mohawk River, the canal system that connected Albany and Buffalo, Lake Ontario and Lake Erie, as well as the extensive network of rivers and ponds that cover much of the Adirondacks, were all vital to the state's economic and social development. The state's four coastlines – Lake Erie, Ontario, the Atlantic and St Lawrence Seaway – all contributed to a 19th-century economic boom that saw New York ranked first in wealth and population well into the 20th century. From Buffalo to New York City, a series of industrial and manufacturing centers developed along the most navigable waterways.

In addition, the vast system of lakes, streams and falls confer impressive and fascinating physical beauty, from the roar of Niagara Falls in the northwest corner to the slender beauty of Taughannock Falls in the Finger Lakes region. Many of New York's waterways have also been fertile ground for the cultural, intellectual and artistic character of New York. Aside from the sparkle and international flavor of New York City, the upstate region has its own unique offerings. These include the gorges of Ithaca and the Ivy League ambience of Cornell University, and the charm of Saratoga Springs – where the New York City Ballet and the Philadelphia Philharmonic Orchestra make their summer home, and strolling musicians entertain the winners and losers at the Saratoga racetrack.

Summer in the Adirondacks might put you in the middle of a storytelling festival, with musicians providing sweet accompaniment and local cooks providing sustenance. And for a bit of elegant nostalgia, New York

State Trivia

State motto: Excelsior (Ever Upward)
State nickname: Empire State
State flower: rose
State bird: bluebird
State tree: sugar maple
State song: I Love New York
State fish: native brook trout
State fruit: apple
State muffin: apple muffin

is home of the National Baseball Hall of Fame in Cooperstown, positioned appropriately on Main St.

To the west, the 11 elegantly shaped Finger Lakes are home to a well-established wine region. Several of these are popular summer destinations for swimming, boating and fishing. The largest of the Finger Lakes are Cayuga, Seneca, Keuka, Canandaigua, Owasco and Skaneateles. In the southwest corner of the state, on the shore of Chautauqua Lake, the Chautauqua Institution hosts a series of lectures and arts performances, continuing a 19th-century tradition of enlightenment and entertainment in which enterprising speakers and performers crisscrossed the country as part of the Chautauqua Circuit, now an indelible part of American, and New York, history.

But clearly, the state and, indeed, the entire Middle Atlantic region is dominated by New York City, which will serve as the departure and entry point for most travelers who will use this book. In a sense, Henry Hudson was but the first of many millions to build a future on the small island of Manhattan and its surrounding area. The city's reputation as an intellectual, economic and creative capital and place of opportunity for newcomers seems destined to continue to draw settlers and travelers alike in perpetuity.

INFORMATION

See the Facts for the Visitor chapter for listings of New York state tourist offices. For a free copy of the *I Love New York* travel guide, call Empire State Development (☎ 800-225-5697), which administers New York's tourism office.

The Empire State Development office divides New York state into 11 tourist regions; the regions often subdivide themselves into sub-regions by county or geographical features such as islands (Long Island) or mountains (Adirondacks). See the regional chapter information headings and destination headings for chambers of commerce or convention and visitor bureaus.

Rural New York is well known for a variety of quality farms and orchards, road-side markets and stands and 'pick-your-own' farms. The New York State Department of Agriculture and Markets, 1 Winners Circle, Albany, NY 12235, issues a fruit and vegetable harvest calendar called the *New York State Guide to Farm Fresh Food*, which is available by region. The information on farm stands, and information about travel, attractions and events throughout the state, is also accessible through the state's travel website (www.iloveny.state.ny.us).

HISTORY
Original Peoples

New York's history begins with the influence that various Native American tribes held over the would-be colonial empires of France, Holland and England. A Native American confederacy known as the Five Nations and consisting of the Mohawk, Oneida, Onondaga, Cayuga and Seneca peoples controlled most of present-day New York, from the Hudson River in the east to the Genessee River west of the Finger Lakes. This powerful tribal alliance was also known as the Iroquois Confederacy or Iroquois League and was joined in 1722 by the Tuscaroras to form the Six Nations.

The less powerful Algonquians occupied the lower Hudson River area and parts of the seacoast. The power of the Iroquois peoples, their knowledge of the land and their propensity to trade with their early European counterparts put them in a unique position to leverage power among the quarreling European factions.

European Arrival

Giovanni da Verrazano, representing France, was the first European to sail into New York's waters. Exploration and trade were sporadic until 1609, when Samuel de Champlain of France, fresh from founding the colony of Quebec and naming a lake for himself, unwisely decided to fight the Iroquois, allying himself with the weaker Algonquians. The British were the eventual winners, managing to convince the Iroquois that protection and prosperity would result from an alliance with England. Of course, the Iroquois were the eventual losers.

NEW YORK

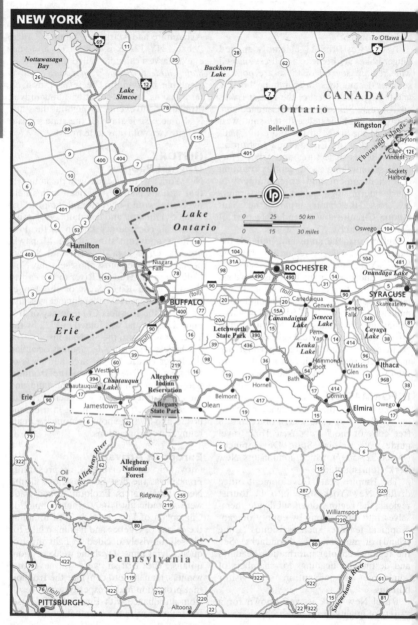

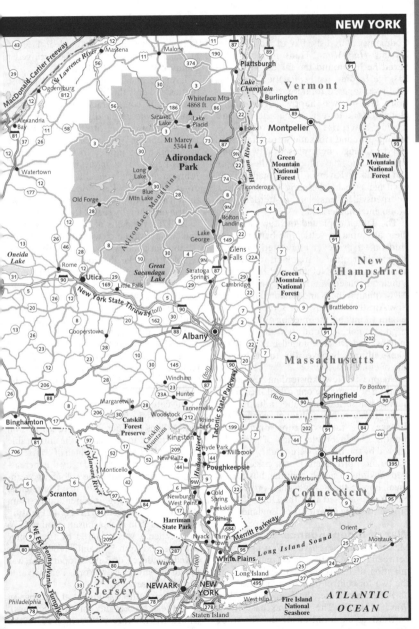

That same year (1609) Henry Hudson, in the employ of the Dutch East India Company, entered the bay of New York in his ship *Half Moon*. Hudson initially believed he had found the fabled Northwest Passage leading to the Pacific. When the tidal river tapered to more modest proportions, Hudson was happy to report that Holland stood to reap the benefits of a vast trading enterprise with the Iroquois. A trading post and stockade were established at Fort Orange, near present-day Albany, and the strategic confluence of the Hudson and Mohawk Rivers. (Today, many of the town names echo the early Dutch settlers: Voorheesville, Rensselaer, Rotterdam, Half Moon and Guilderland.)

The Dutch exploited the fur trade, but their attempts to settle the banks of the Hudson River never amounted to much, despite their offer of free land to 'all good inhabitants of the Netherlands.' In 1626, the Dutch purchased Manhattan from the local Algonquian Indians and renamed the island New Amsterdam. However, settlers were reluctant to inhabit the interior of the region in great numbers. Conflicts with the 'River Indians' and Dutch colonial interests elsewhere ultimately gave way to an English takeover in 1664.

No one in New Amsterdam seemed to mind terribly, and no one asked the Algonquians, whose numbers and influence had been greatly reduced through conflict and disease. The takeover took only a few months. The favorable terms of surrender offered by the British were readily accepted by the most prominent Dutch citizens, who were anxious to simply continue business as usual, now in the newly named province of New York – named after the Duke of York, brother of King Charles II of England.

War of Independence

Meanwhile, the Seven Years War in Europe between France and England (really the culmination of 150 years of struggle between the two for control of North America) had its American phase: the French & Indian War (1754–63). The war was basically a battle over exploitation of the fur trade

between the French and English. The British were losing to the French until Sir William Johnson won an important battle in 1755–56 at Lake George, for which he received a bonus of £5000 from Parliament.

Even so, the British continued to lose battles, and only the Mohawk group (part of the Iroquois confederacy) did not question their loyalty to England; this was apparently due to Johnson's efforts. In 1758, British Prime Minister William Pitt provided more men and more money to the effort, and things began to favor the British. In 1761, Johnson convinced (possibly bribed) several other tribes to switch sides, and that was that: The Iroquois finally sided with the British and thereby sealed the outcome.

By 1765, residents of Britain's new colonial empire were increasingly unhappy with the mother country's stern ways. Britain attempted to make the colonies pay for the war by means of the Stamp Act, a revenue tax passed by the British Parliament requiring that all legal documents and newspapers carry stamps indicating that a tax had been paid. Some people never learn. In 1766, American protesters organized the Stamp Act Congress, the first intercolonial congress, to peacefully petition the British monarch to repeal the act. The request was wisely granted that same year, but the damage was done.

Boycotts of British goods increased and riots occurred, often at the instigation of the radical Sons of Liberty. In 1773, the Boston Tea Party led to passage of the Intolerable Acts Law by Parliament, which of course led to numerous intolerable acts by the increasingly militant patriots. The colonial governments began to fail, and the first Continental Congress operating independently from Britain was convened in 1774. Fighting began in 1775 in Massachusetts, and in 1776 independence was declared by the former colonies, and from 1776 until 1780, the War of Independence, or Revolutionary War, was fought mostly in New York, Pennsylvania and New Jersey.

The key battle was fought at Saratoga in 1777 (near present-day Saratoga Springs), where British forces surrendered to the

American patriots on October 7. The American victory at Saratoga convinced France to enter the war on the side of the revolutionaries. The following year, New York ratified the Articles of Confederation. In 1783, the British finally evacuated New York City.

The Revolutionary War was also the final blow to the influence of the Iroquois Confederacy, which had consistently sided with the British. In 1778, fighting bands of British Loyalists and their Iroquois allies carried out a massacre at the Scotch-Irish community of Cherry Valley, just east of Otsego Lake in the Mohawk Valley. The following year, a punitive expedition under the command of Generals John Sullivan and James Clinton marched through the Mohawk Valley, destroying the Iroquois villages and in the process, the Iroquois Confederacy as well. The road was literally about to be paved for European settlement.

Early Independence & War of 1812

Many influential New Yorkers were reluctant to approve a federal constitution after the colonies won independence from Britain. Supporters of a national government, known as Federalists, were led by John Jay, James Madison and Alexander Hamilton (Hamilton's eloquent essays were instrumental in convincing delegates to ratify the Constitution in July of 1788). George Washington was inaugurated as the first US president in April 1789 in New York City.

Conflicts between France and Britain damaged US trade interests. During the Napoleonic Wars (1799–1815) the US was officially neutral, but France needed US supplies in order to maintain its ascendancy in Europe. Britain, as part of its economic blockade of Napoleonic Europe, began stopping and searching US ships. Ultimately, the USA declared war on Britain and attempted to invade Canada. Despite important victories on Lake Erie and in New York state, the Americans were stalled near Detroit by Oneida Indians (the British had formed alliances with them and with other Native Americans, as they all opposed US

expansion). The British navy blockaded US ports, and in 1814 captured Washington and burned the Capitol and the White House.

The Treaty of Ghent (1814) ended the war without a clear winner, though Native Americans lost any hope of an independent Indian nation. The war did result in a rise of nationalism and confidence in the USA, and soon the entire state of New York experienced a massive economic boom. Because of its strong transportation links, available labor and capital, New York quickly became the nation's center for trade, finance and manufacturing. The population soared, and factories and foundries sprang up across the state.

But the most dramatic economic development of the era was the completion in 1825 of the Erie Canal, an artificial waterway that connected Buffalo and Albany and, more significantly, the Hudson River to Lake Erie and the ports of the western Great Lakes. Its impact on the country was monumental. It was not only an engineering marvel, but an economic one as well, which greatly accelerated the development of the country's expanding Northwest (now Midwest). However, with the expansion of the country's rail system later in the 19th century, the influence of the Erie Canal began to diminish.

The regions surrounding the canal were recently granted $160 million for renovation and revival for recreation, primarily boating.

Civil War

The debate over the nature of the new American government did not end with the celebration at Washington's 1789 inauguration. Longstanding social and economic differences between the North and the South led to inevitable economic conflicts that eventually escalated to military opposition. Both sides generally agreed that blacks were not the equal of whites. Thus, the impetus of war wasn't really a civil rights issue, but an issue of whether slave labor would be introduced in the territories and provide a cheap alternative to products produced by whites in the new factories of the northern states. The territorial explosion of the early 19th century was the main reason slavery became an important issue in the 1850s. When Abraham Lincoln was elected president in 1860, South Carolina became the first of 11 southern states to secede from the Union.

The Civil War ended in 1865, partly due to the superior industrial resources of the North (New York in particular). Over 500,000 troops from New York fought for the preservation of the Union. Of these, nearly 60,000 died on the battlefield – ironically, about the same number of Americans who died a hundred years later in Vietnam. A controversy over the practice of drafting the poor (in this case, mostly poor Irish) to serve in the army, while the rich were able to buy their way out for $300, resulted in one of the country's most deadly riots ever, the Draft Riots of 1863 in New York City.

21st Century

Today, though much of New York's stormy past has dimmed, the state remains a vital region, full of contrasts. The prosperity that arose along the Erie Canal and made it a corridor of commerce eroded in this century, and the region became better known as 'the rust belt.' Today, many of the former industrial cities are working to revitalize themselves as cultural and economic centers.

The pristine beauty of the state's mountains and lakes is also being recaptured as civic groups from the Alleghenies to the Adirondacks work to maintain the land's splendid natural features.

Taxes

New York state imposes a sales tax of 7% on goods, most services and prepared foods.

New York City imposes an additional 1.25% tax, bringing the total surcharge to 8.25%. Several categories of so-called luxury items – including dry cleaning and rental cars – carry an additional city surcharge of 5%, so you wind up seeing 13.25% added to those bills.

Hotel rooms in New York City are subject to 13.25% tax plus a flat $2 per night occupancy tax. Believe it or not, that reflects a reduction in the previous hotel tax.

GEOGRAPHY

New York's total land area comprises 47,939 sq miles, and its total inland water area is 1637 sq miles. The addition of New York's share of Lakes Erie and Ontario adds another 3140 sq miles to the total.

The most striking feature of New York's waterways is their variety: the Atlantic seacoast, two of the Great Lakes (Erie and Ontario), the Finger Lakes of central New York, Lake George, Lake Champlain and thousands of smaller lakes and ponds across the state, the St Lawrence Seaway and its 'Thousand Islands' and an engineered canal system that connected many of the natural waterways and sustained much of New York's westward expansion.

The most striking topographical feature of the state is the Adirondack mountain range in the northeast. Though not particularly high in elevation, the Adirondacks are striking for their range, beauty and age. The ancient range was once covered by a continental glacier, resulting in a gently worn landscape of low relief highlighted by a number of dramatic peaks, known collectively as the High Peaks. The highest of the High Peaks is Mt Marcy (5344 feet), and the rest range from 4000 to 5000 feet. Much of the Adirondack range is covered by forests, and most areas are protected from extensive development.

As the continental glacier receded roughly 10,000 years ago, it left its dramatic legacy across the region. Valleys were carved and broadened, hills were rounded and gorges and waterfalls were created. Glaciers sculpted the Finger Lakes.

Just south of the Adirondacks, the Appalachian Plateau stretches between the Allegheny Mountains and the Catskills. This plateau extends to the shores of Lake Erie and Lake Ontario, where it forms a fertile plain that has been the basis of extensive agriculture.

The drainage of New York makes its way in several directions. Most of the Adirondack waterways drain into the St Lawrence system. Parts of the Catskills drain into the Delaware River and into Delaware Bay. The source of the Hudson River is Lake Tear of the Clouds in the Adirondacks, the highest lake in the state. From there, the Hudson ranges over 306 miles until it reaches New York Bay.

CLIMATE

Like much of the northern US, New York state has a climate of extremes – hot and muggy in the summer, cold and wet in the winter. The Atlantic Ocean and the Great Lakes moderate the temperatures somewhat, but in the high Adirondacks severe winter storms and sub-zero temperatures are not unusual.

The phenomenon known as 'lake-effect snow' is famous from Syracuse to Buffalo, both for its quantity and its wet quality. Storms gain strength as they blow from the northwest to the southeast over the Great Lakes and tend to dump all the accumulated precipitation on the eastern shores.

Average mean temperatures in the state range from 21°F in January, 50°F in April, 70°F in July and 49°F in October. See also the Climate Chart in the Facts about the Region chapter.

ECOLOGY & ENVIRONMENT

Much of upstate New York's outdoor sparkle – from the high peaks of the Adirondacks to the shimmering Finger Lakes – dims a bit when the impact of a modern industrial society is taken into full account. The good news is that several organizations are working to check this impact, including efforts to bring environmentalists and commercial enterprises closer together; land use, wildlife preservation and agricultural practices are now topics for debate and compromise.

Acid rain is a continuing problem in the industrial northeastern US and the Great Lakes region, as well as much of New York state. Airborne pollutants from as far away as Chicago, Detroit and Cleveland join the airstream, finding their way eventually to waterways. Most of the alpine areas in the Adirondacks are affected not only by acid rain, but by human activity as well. There are vigorous efforts to arrest erosion and to educate hikers and others who enjoy the land.

Newcomers to acid-rain impact need to know a deceptive fact: The acid affects all life forms, from plankton to minnows to dazzling brook trout – so much so that a small lake may look 'clearer' than ever. But clear does not mean clean, despite what the advertisers tell us; a little murky algae on the edges is what we want. (Algae is a living organism quite vulnerable to acid pollutants.) Many of the mountain lakes, in addition to the larger Finger Lakes, have increased acid levels, though acid rain isn't the only villain. In Lake Ontario, a combination of pollutants have led to contaminated fisheries; although locals continue to fish, ongoing studies suggest that nearly half of all the fish in the lake are unsafe to consume on a regular basis.

There are positive signs that environmental efforts are working. In the Adirondacks, moose are returning in greater numbers, mostly from Canada. The same is true for many birds of prey, including the bald eagle, peregrine falcon and osprey.

The ongoing efforts to preserve many of the wilderness areas of the Adirondacks and elsewhere call to mind the definition of wilderness as stated in the national Wilderness Act (1964):

A wilderness is hereby recognized as an area where the Earth and its community of life are untrammeled by man, where man himself is a visitor who does not remain.

State Parks & Forests

Among New York state's extensive system of public lands, the **Adirondack Forest Preserve** (established in 1885) is pristine wilderness, protected by the 'Forever Wild' clause in the state's constitution (see the boxed text 'Forever Wild'), and roughly 40% of the much larger Adirondack Park, a mixture of public and private lands. The region is a year-round center not only for wilderness exploring, but also for hiking, canoeing, rock climbing and skiing. Lake Placid is in the heart of the High Peaks region.

Just northwest of the Adirondacks, in the Thousand Islands region, **Wellesley Island State Park** is a wildlife sanctuary, popular camping area and home to an excellent nature center.

Closer to New York City, **Bear Mountain State Park** and **Harriman State Park** are popular hiking and mountain-biking destinations. Also close to New York City is the **Rockefeller State Park Preserve**, about three miles north of Tarrytown, a peaceful and secluded wooded area, great for walking and bird-watching.

Further north, but less than two hours by car from New York City, one of Washington Irving's favorite haunts, the **Catskill Forest Preserve**, is home to Kaaterskill Falls and the art- and music-lovers' town of Woodstock. **Minnewaska State Park** is nearby, near

the town of New Paltz, and is a popular hiking and rock-climbing area.

Further west, in the Finger Lakes region, **Taughannock Falls State Park** is home to the highest waterfall in the state. **Letchworth State Park**, south of Rochester, is referred to as the 'Grand Canyon of the East' – rather unfair, because it is a stunning site on its own merits – and takes in the 600-foot-deep Genesee River Gorge. Continuing west, **Niagara Reservation State Park** is home to Niagara Falls, the largest (not the highest) waterfall of all.

A free *Guide to New York State Operated Parks, Historic Sites and Their Programs* identifies hikes and other cultural and

Forever Wild

A too common story by now, of course, is the impact that rapid industrialization has on the land, water and natural resources of any region on earth. In the late 1800s, when commerce and industry were in full swing in New York and much of America, the land was suffering. Destructive logging practices and the pollution of lakes and rivers by careless manufacturing interests were taking their toll on New York's abundant wildlife.

In the 1890s, the citizens of New York acted to make the Adirondacks and the Catskills part of a publicly owned forest preserve. The spirit of this effort is found in the 'Forever Wild' clause of the New York state constitution. It proclaims: 'The land of the state, now owned or hereafter acquired, constituting the Forest Preserve as now fixed by law, shall be forever kept as wild forest lands. They shall not be leased, sold or exchanged, or be taken by any corporation, public or private, nor shall the timber thereon be sold, removed or destroyed.'

Briefly, more than half of New York state is covered in forests, with over 150 varieties of trees, including several types of pine, spruce, mountain ash, maple and oak. The alpine areas of the Adirondacks remain the most vulnerable to airborne pollutants and damage from hikers and others who visit the area. The boots rattlesnake root and the alpine birch are two suffering species in particular that are drawing attention.

Much of the forest habitat of New York has improved quite a bit over the years, due primarily to the great efforts of volunteers and nature lovers of all kinds who treat the land with the respect it requires. The habitat is so improved, in fact, that the beaver, once trapped to near-extinction, is now returning in numbers great enough to allow it to be hunted. The same is true for wild turkeys and even Canada geese, whose steadily increasing population is unpopular with farmers who blame them for increasing crop damage.

According to the New York State Department of Environmental Conservation (DEC), other waterfowl, such as the mallard, are dwindling in number due to general environmental factors. As more has been learned about the effects of acid rain, fish restocking efforts have grown. Pike, bass, perch and minnows are among the species being restocked in great number. To help restore the plankton to the ponds and lakes of the Adirondacks, the DEC is liming these bodies of water. Plankton accumulates near the surface, and its absence in an otherwise clear pond is not a good sign; the sighting of a mallard on the pond is a much better sign.

outdoor activities. Request it by writing to this simple address: State Parks, Albany, NY 12238. The website for the state park system is www.nysparks.state.ny.us.

GOVERNMENT & POLITICS

Just as it has long been prominent in the arts, culture and business, New York state has always played an outsized role in national politics. Six New Yorkers have been elected president, including two of the country's most important chief executives, Theodore Roosevelt and his cousin Franklin D Roosevelt. Although population shifts in the '70s led to the loss of several seats in the US House of Representatives, today the state has an impressive 33 electoral votes, with its congressional delegation of two senators and 31 representatives, the second largest voting block in the country behind California (though Texas is poised to displace New York as the second largest US state following the 2000 census).

New York is politically split between a heavily Democratic New York City and Republican-leaning voters in the rest of the state, and candidates of both parties can do well here in both national and local elections. In 1998, voters elected Democrat Charles Schumer to the US Senate to join Democrat Daniel Patrick Moynihan. The fussy, professorial Moynihan, a four-term liberal Democrat, isn't running for re-election. In a political first, a first lady, Hillary Clinton, is running for his seat (opposing New York City Mayor Rudolph Giuliani). The results of this race are not yet known as this book goes to press, but the state's swing voters will no doubt cast the winning votes.

New York's governor serves a four-year term, as do the people elected to the three other state-wide offices: lieutenant governor, attorney general and comptroller (chief budget director). There is also a popularly elected legislature. In the state's 62 counties, local issues are decided by a board of supervisors or 'county executive.' The exception to this rule are the five counties – or boroughs – of New York City that are each headed by powerless borough presidents.

For rural politicians who had long complained about being overshadowed by the interests of 'down-state' – a barely polite euphemism for New York City – Governor Pataki's election heralded a new political climate. Pataki came to office promising to slash taxes and social services. Despite the rhetoric, he has moved more to the center, frequently working with rival Democrats on key issues. In the spring of 2000, the more centrist Pataki took a controversial stand in favor of new gun control measures – in stark contrast to the hot feelings of ultra-conservative Republicans, including Mayor Giuliani. The two often clash in public on key issues.

Nevertheless, the political tensions between upstate and down-state have renewed the notion, first floated in the '30s, that New York City break away from upstate and declare itself the 51st state. That will never happen, if only because office-holders on both sides of the divide would then find themselves left with a greatly diminished political landscape.

ECONOMY

New York is still a national leader in agriculture, commerce and manufacturing. The state's production of printed reading materials, precision electronics and heavy machinery contributes $80 billion to the economy and employs more than a million people.

There are more than 35,000 farms in the state producing dairy products, apples and a variety of root vegetables. Many of these small farms have been able to supply the demand for organically grown farm products. The Finger Lakes region and northeastern Long Island are known for wine grape production and their vineyards are tourist attractions.

Surprisingly, slightly more than half of New York's landmass is woodland, and forestry contributes $4 billion to the economy annually through the harvesting of timber for furniture and paper. The state is also the country's leading producer of magazines and books, as well the most important market for literature (the majority of quality hardcover books sold in the US are bought in the metropolitan area). Mining of minerals such as salt, sand and gravel add to the economic picture.

While New York City remains the nexus of world finance, computer technology has made 'Wall Street' more of an email address than a physical location. Companies are increasingly moving their support operations out of expensive, crowded Manhattan to the suburbs and beyond. That has prompted the state to offer large tax incentives – some would even say bribes – for corporations to remain.

One consistently bright spot is tourism, which has been a vitally important part of the local economy since the introduction of the 'I Love New York' ad campaign in the mid-1970s. Visitors now spend more than $32 billion each year, and the travel industry already employs some 725,000 people.

POPULATION & PEOPLE

With 18 million residents, New York is the third most populous state in the nation, behind California and booming Texas. Seventy percent of that total are white; 15% are African American and 11% are Hispanic. Asians make up 4% of the state's population.

Approximately half of all state residents live in the New York City area, and 28% of the city's residents are foreign-born, buttressing its reputation as the nation's 'melting pot,' though that term seems somewhat quaint and misapplied in this era of enduring ethnic division.

Still, New York City is an example of racial diversity. The city is home to the largest Chinese population in the US, along with the country's largest bloc of Asian Indians. On Labor Day, hundreds of thousands of Caribbean-born immigrants attend the West Indian festival. New York City claims to have the largest Jewish population outside of Israel; more native Greeks than anywhere outside Athens; more native Russians than anywhere outside Moscow; and perhaps more native Irish than anywhere outside Ireland and Britain. Given both differences in culture and undocumented immigration, these claims are difficult to prove

using statistics, but a walk through several of the city's neighborhoods leaves the impression that these assertions are probably not far off the mark.

African Americans

There are 1.8 million African Americans living in New York City today. That figure rises to 3 million blacks – more than any other state – when one includes the large number of recent immigrants from Haiti and other Caribbean islands.

African slaves first arrived in New York in 1644, when it was still the Dutch colony of New Netherland. A few were able to obtain freedom. By the time the colonies went to war with Britain, the African population numbered about two thousand, and slaves fought on both sides of the conflict in the hope of winning greater freedom. (After the war, New York state freed those who fought in the local armed forces.) New York City and other towns around the state became station stops on the Underground Railroad. By the early 19th century, the abolitionist movement had been established in New York City, along with *Freedom's Journal*, the nation's first black newspaper. But voting rights were not bestowed on black males until well after the Civil War, when the Fifteenth Amendment was enacted in 1870. At the same time, blacks found themselves losing economic ground to growing numbers of immigrants from Ireland and Eastern Europe.

By the early 20th century, migrating African Americans from the South triggered the development of Harlem in northern Manhattan, helping to create a well-defined community with churches, black-owned businesses and nightclubs that welcomed whites from other neighborhoods. For the first time, a number of West Indian blacks became a significant part of the area's population. But the 'Harlem Renaissance' of the '20s ended abruptly with the Depression.

After WWII, it became clear that blacks were again economically behind more entrenched second- and third-generation white ethnic groups. Not to mention that American white society was still barring them from schools and businesses. Yet city officials did little to address the situation until riots broke out in Harlem in 1964. By the 1970s, what was left of the black middle class had abandoned Harlem, following the path paved by whites to the suburbs.

Latin Americans

Hispanics make up 11% of the state's 18 million residents, about 2.1 million people.

About half of New York City's 1.8 million Latin American residents are of Puerto Rican descent and began migrating from the island in significant numbers during the Depression. Throughout the '60s, political activism by 'Nuyoricans' (noor-EE-cans) led to increasing recognition of their contribution to city life, as well as the establishment of several important cultural institutions, including the Museo del Barrio near East Harlem, also known as Spanish Harlem.

Over the past 20 years there has been an influx of Latinos from many other countries. Immigrants from Ecuador and Colombia have created new communities in Queens, and the Washington Heights section of Manhattan, even further north of Harlem, is home to many former citizens of the Dominican Republic and El Salvador. In fact, Washington Heights has seen the greatest influx of immigrants in the entire city.

Jewish Americans

The first Jews, a group of 24 refugees fleeing persecution in Brazil, came to New York in 1654, when it was still a Dutch colony. They have been an important part of the city's population and politics ever since. Until the early 20th century, most of the Jewish population lived in Manhattan's Lower East Side, and the neighborhood still retains its traditional character, even though most New Yorkers of Jewish background live elsewhere. In Brooklyn, the neighborhoods of Crown Heights and Williamsburg are still home to large numbers of Orthodox Jews, and an influx of immigrants from the former Soviet Union during the '80s added to their numbers.

Today, the Jewish population comprises 15% of New York City's total population.

They are the city's second-largest ethnic voting bloc (African Americans are first). In some neighborhoods, most prominently the Crown Heights section of Brooklyn, there have been violent and long-standing tensions between the neighborhood's African American community and the growing community of Orthodox Jews, many of whom have emigrated from the former Soviet Union.

RELIGION

Roman Catholics make up the largest single religious group in New York state, at 44% of the population, followed by Protestants at 10%, Jews at 7%, Baptists at 6%, Moslems at 2%, and a mixture of other Christian religions make up 10%.

Religious groups and fringe sects have found a home in Sullivan County, nestled among the Catskill Mountains, on the sites of several abandoned Jewish summer camps and resort hotels. The region is now home to Korean fundamentalist Christians, Zen Buddhists, Branch Davidians (followers of the late Texas cult leader David Koresh) and at least one ashram.

In New York City alone, often derided by outsiders as some sort of modern-day Sodom, there are over 6000 places of worship, including everything from Buddhist temples to kingdom halls used by Jehovah's Witnesses. Muslims have been part of the city's religious landscape since the late '50s and now number more than 500,000. Most adherents follow the Sunni Islam tradition. In 1991, a huge new mosque, the Islamic Cultural Center, opened at 96th St and Third Ave. It is a monument to the city's fastest growing religion.

LANGUAGE

New York is such a varied and large place that it is ludicrous to identify state-wide language patterns. In general, people who live in rural areas and fisherman on the eastern end of Long Island tend to speak in a clear but more deliberate manner. Terms of language tend to change as you move about the state – in New York City, if you want a soft drink, you ask for a 'soda.'

You will immediately recognize the elongated vowels of New York City dwellers; the reality sounds like a much milder version of the 'Noo Yawk Tawk' popularized in films and TV. 'Corner' is often pronounced 'CAWnah' as in 'I'll meet ya on the CAWnah.' Similarly, 'God' tends to come out 'Gawd' as in 'Oh, my Gawd!' Or that popular expression 'Forget about it' or, actually, more like 'FAWget about it' said in a particular tone of voice and inflection that indicates beyond all possible doubt that there is no way something is ever going to happen or that something is just not worth considering.

Older residents often have a strange cadence in their voices, pronouncing 'Broadway' and 'receipt' with a heavy emphasis on the *first* syllable. The New York accent grows stronger in the outer boroughs, provided the person you're speaking to wasn't born in another country! Its melting-pot history is partly the reason the city has such an interesting dialect – who knows whether Italian, Yiddish, Russian, French, Irish or whatever has had the most influence?

The city's huge Hispanic population has led to the emergence of Spanish as a semi-official second language. But so far, a Spanish-English hybrid has not developed for popular use, though everyone knows that a *bodega* is Spanish for a street corner convenience store.

Many phrases that have roots in working-class bars and delis are now an indelible part of the sound of the city. People working the counter at downtown delis say 'You GOT it!' to mean 'It's coming up' or 'I'm getting it for you right away' – after you order a sandwich, for instance. People working in delis also like to ask the unusual question, 'Is anyone next?' meaning 'Can I help the next person?' or 'Who's next?' Deli-speak also includes frequent use of the word 'boss,' as in, 'What can I get you, boss?' or 'Do you want lettuce on that, boss?'

City dwellers use the expression 'bridge and tunnel' as an adjective to describe those from greater New York who come to Manhattan (via bridge and tunnel) but are provincial and garishly unsophisticated. For example, 'The bridge and tunnel crowd flock to my neighborhood on the weekend,' or 'a bridge and tunnel hairstyle (also known as 'big hair'). New Jersey residents are the lucky recipients of most of these jokes. If asked where you live and your answer is 'New Jersey,' the next question might be, 'Which exit?'

There are New Yorkisms translated from the Dutch. Buildings, for example, have stoops (from the Dutch for steps) where people used to hang out in the summertime. Grammar gets a makeover at times. Many native New Yorkers actually say, 'I'm working here for 5 years.'

It's easier to identify common phrases used, or at least recognized, by most New Yorkers, though even this is tricky because rap music is changing English in profound, but as yet uncharted, ways. The meaning of phrases changes from neighborhood to neighborhood. Asking for a 'regular' coffee in Midtown means you'll get it with milk and a bit of sugar. The same request at a coffee shop near Wall St will result in the server immediately throwing three heaping spoonfuls of the sweet stuff in the cup, because that's the way the hyper stock brokers and lawyers like it served.

New York City

The dawn of the millennium is something of a golden age for New York City. Business is booming, crime rates are very low and hotels are enjoying historically high occupancy rates (at equally high prices). Sure, there's a growing blandness – even a 'Disneyfication' – of some formerly hard areas such as Times Square, but you have to take some bad with the good.

Other, more modest, municipalities can claim to be centers of manufacturing, or even the biggest city in their nation. However, only New York City reserves for itself the title of 'The Capital of the World,' and it has the arrogance to hang banners saying so along its avenues.

That boast has some validity: Long after it ceased to be the geographic and political center of its nation, New York has continued to dominate the popular imagination. It has gained, then lost, primacy in many different important endeavors, including politics, agriculture, manufacturing and shipping, as well as film and TV production. Thus, New Yorkers are conditioned by history to expect that their city will soon find a new activity to exploit, and they remain ever-confident that no rival city will ever equal theirs as a center for cultural and intellectual pursuits.

Numbers tell much of the story: With 7 million residents, New York City has more than twice as many people as Los Angeles (the second largest US city). All of these people are packed into 309 sq miles of space. New York's intensity comes from this density.

Not that New Yorkers much notice it. Every day they blithely stroll past – or live in – buildings that would dominate the skylines of almost any other major city. Yet this immensity of scale – and the crowding of so many colors and cultures within its borders – is what stuns people from more homogeneous locales. Many of the 30 million people who visit annually are conditioned by Hollywood (and lazy journalists) to assume that New York is a mayhem-ridden nightmare, so

Highlights

- A spectacular skyline – the one you've seen in all those movies
- The astounding array of cultures on the city's streets
- World-class museums, spectacular theatrical events and concerts of every kind
- More than 18,000 restaurants – a food-lover's paradise, offering every cuisine, often at bargain prices
- Shopping, shopping and more shopping

they often arrive gripped by a caution that borders on paranoia.

Yes, some of the clichés are true: a New Yorker talks faster – and closer to your face – than just about anyone else. The European *pension* tradition never took hold, making it difficult, and at some times of the year nearly impossible, to find low cost accommodations. To survive in this crowded atmosphere, people close in on themselves. One could argue that the city's reputation for rudeness – such as its citizens' habit of never standing to the right and walking to the left on escalators or thoughtlessly burying their faces in books – is simply the survival instinct carried to the *nth* degree. But contrary to New York's tough image, locals are regularly gracious and helpful to tourists. Sometimes, they even excuse themselves if they bump into you, and they love to give directions, if only because visitor queries cater to their self-perceived expertise on the city.

Thanks to community policing, along with a general decline in crime nationwide, New York City is the safest big city in the country. It is not even in the top 10 of the major US cities for violent crimes. The bottom line is that you should exercise sensible caution when visiting – just as you would in any city.

New York is an exhausting holiday destination. This megacity demands that you assault it with a game plan. Define your sightseeing priorities and get to them ahead of everyone else. Along the way, serendipitous occurrences will unfold, if only because some of the city's best entertainment can be found for free on the streets.

HISTORY

The area now known as New York City was occupied by Native Americans for more than 11,000 years before Giovanni da Verrazano, a Florentine hired by the French to explore the American northeastern coast, arrived in 1524. After his brief visit, no serious attempt was made to document the area or its people until 1609 when English explorer Henry Hudson, on a mission to find the Northwest Passage, anchored *Halve Maen* (Half Moon) in the harbor for 10 days before continuing up the river. 'It is as beautiful a land as one can hope to tread upon,' reported Hudson.

The local Munsee tribe had several names for the region, including *Manahatouh* (Place of Gathering Bow Wood), *Manahactanienk* (Place of General Inebriation) and *Menatay* (the Island). The name of Manhattan can be traced to any one of these words.

Colonial Era

By 1625 the first Dutch settlers were dispatched to establish a trading post they eventually called New Amsterdam, the seat of a much larger colony called New Netherland. Historians generally agree that the story behind the purchase of the island from local tribes for goods worth 60 guilders ($24), although myth-like, may actually be true (though a more accurate exchange rate for the goods would be about $600 – still a bargain).

In 1647 a new governor named Peter Stuyvesant arrived to impose order on what the Dutch government considered an unruly colony. His ban on alcohol and curtailment of religious freedoms caused unrest among the settlers, and few regretted the bloodless takeover of New Amsterdam by the English in 1664.

Renamed New York in honor of King Charles II's brother the Duke of York, the port town retained much of its Dutch character well into the mid-18th century. By that time, opposition to the excesses of British colonial rule had developed and was given voice by John Peter Zenger's influential newspaper the *Weekly Journal.* Though many influential New Yorkers resisted a war for independence, New York's Commons – where the city hall stands today – was the center of many anti-British protests. King George III's troops controlled New York for most of the Revolutionary War and took their time going home, finally withdrawing in 1783, a full two years after the fighting ended.

Boom Years

By the time George Washington was sworn in as president of the new republic (on the balcony of Federal Hall on Wall St) in 1789, New York was a bustling seaport of 33,000 people. The new congress abandoned the city after establishing the District of Columbia the following year. The move was probably driven by a dislike of the city by the founding fathers – Thomas Jefferson later said that he regarded New York to be a 'cloacina (sewer) of all the depravities of human nature.'

New York boomed in the early 19th century, and by 1830 its population approached a quarter million, though it had no police force to speak of until the Civil War period. The Croton Aqueduct, completed in 1842 (at a then phenomenal cost of $12 million), brought 72 million gallons of fresh water to the city each day; this not only improved public health conditions but finally allowed residents the opportunity to bathe regularly.

New York has always had wide gaps between the rich and the poor and tensions between different racial groups. In the summer of 1863, poor Irish immigrants launched the 'draft riots,' in large part because of a provision that allowed wealthy men to pay $300 in order to avoid being conscripted to fight in the Civil War. Within days the rioters turned their anger on black citizens, who they considered the reason for the war and their main competition for work. More than 11 men were lynched in the streets and a black orphans' home was burned to the ground.

The years following the Union victory in the Civil War were a gilded age for both private and public figures. William Magear Tweed, notorious boss of the city's Tammany Hall Democratic organization, used public works projects to steal millions of dollars from the public treasury before being toppled from power. Meanwhile, robber barons, such as railroad speculator Jay Gould, were able to amass tax-free fortunes that approached $100 million.

Growing Pains

New York City's population more than doubled from 515,500 in 1850 to 1,164,600 in 1880. This was largely due to a huge influx of poor immigrants from Ireland and Central Europe, all seeking the storied 'streets of gold.' But for those with little money, there was merely a life of manual labor and isolation at the end of the journey. Inevitably, a tenement culture developed: The poorest New Yorkers invariably worked in dangerous factories and lived in squalid apartment blocks. The work of crusading journalist Jacob Riis, who chronicled how this 'other half' lived through his writings and pictorials, shocked the city's middle class and led to the establishment of an independent health board as well as a series of workplace

reforms. At the same time, millionaires such as Andrew Carnegie, John D Rockefeller and John Jacob Astor began pouring money into public works, leading to the creation of institutions such as the New York Public Library in 1895.

The burgeoning of New York's population beyond the city's official borders led to the consolidation movement, as the city and its neighboring districts struggled to accomodate the growing numbers. Residents of the independent districts of Queens, Staten Island, the Bronx and financially strapped Brooklyn voted to become 'boroughs' of New York City in 1898.

This new metropolis absorbed a second huge wave of European immigrants, and its population exploded once again, from more than 3 million in 1900 to 7 million in 1930. During this period, horse-drawn trolleys were abandoned as a major network of underground subways and elevated trains ('els') made the city's outer reaches easily accessible.

During the Depression, crusading mayor Fiorello La Guardia fought municipal corruption and expanded the social service network. Meanwhile, civic planner Robert Moses used his politically appointed position

---

The Big Apple Gets its Name

It has long been thought that New York City was dubbed 'The Big Apple' by jazz musicians who regarded a gig in Harlem as a sure sign that they had made it to the top. But Barry Popik, an amateur historian, did extensive research into the phrase and came up with a surprising answer. He discovered that the term first appeared in the 1920s when it was used by a writer named John FitzGerald who covered the horse races for the *Morning Telegraph*. Apparently, stable hands in a New Orleans racetrack called a trip to a New York racecourse 'the Big Apple' – or greatest reward – for any talented thoroughbred. The slang passed into popular usage long after the newspaper – and FitzGerald – disappeared.

as a parks commissioner to wield power without the obligation of answering to voters. He used that influence to remake the city's landscape through public works projects and highways that glorified the car culture and disdained public transportation. Unfortunately, Moses had the power of a modern-day Baron Haussmann but none of the master's aesthetic sense; his projects (which included the Triborough Bridge, Lincoln Center and several highways and projects on the Lower East Side) often destroyed entire neighborhoods and routed huge numbers of residents.

Tailspin & Renewal

Although New York emerged from WWII proud and ready for business, the middle class began abandoning the city for its suburbs. Television production, manufacturing jobs and even the fabled Brooklyn Dodgers baseball team moved to California, along with the Dodgers' cross-town rivals the New York Giants.

By the 1970s the unreliable, graffiti-ridden subway system became an internationally recognized symbol of New York's psychic and economic tailspin. Only a massive federal loan program saved the city from bankruptcy. The city's prominence as a world financial center also provided a lifeline – and set the stage for the booming '80s.

During the anything-goes Reagan years, the city regained much of its swagger as billions of dollars were made on Wall St. The era was presided over by Ed Koch, the colorful and opinionated three-term mayor, who seemed to embody the New Yorker's ability to charm and irritate at the same time. But in 1989, Koch was defeated in a Democratic primary election by David Dinkins, who went on to became the city's first African American mayor. Dinkins, consistently criticized for merely presiding over a city government in need of reform, was narrowly defeated for a second term by moderate Republican Rudolph Giuliani.

A City Emergent

The Giuliani era, helped by the nationwide economic boom, has fashioned New York into the city of today's popular imagination. The current mayor, now in his second (and legally mandated) final term, conveys all the charm of a high school detention officer, and he is more respected than liked. Crime has been effectively tamed, the subway is efficient and cheap, and New York is statistically the safest big city in the US. The '90s stock market boom fuelled building and spending. The city may even get around to making a huge investment in infrastructure and build a much-needed new subway line under Second Ave. But the city is by no means in a state of nirvana: the gap between rich and poor has widened, and housing is phenomenally expensive, which probably hampers the inflow of new residents.

Still, with great bargains, great food and world class cultural attractions, this is a very good time to visit New York City.

ORIENTATION

New York City consists of five 'boroughs' – entities that came together in 1898 to form 'Greater New York City.' A series of islands make up the city's 309-sq-mile land mass. Manhattan and Staten Island stand alone; Queens and Brooklyn comprise the western end of Long Island. Only the Bronx is connected to the US mainland.

The water gap between Brooklyn and Staten Island – the narrows through which the first Europeans entered the area – serves as the entrance to New York Harbor, which is also accessible to ships from the north via Long Island Sound. Manhattan itself is bordered by two bodies of water: on the west it is bordered by the Hudson River and on the east it is bordered by the East River, both technically estuaries subject to tidal fluctuations.

Served by three major airports, two train terminals and a massive bus depot, New York City is the most important transportation hub in the northeast. I-95, which runs from Maine to Florida, cuts through the city as the Cross Bronx Expressway. Via I-95, Boston is 194 miles to the north, Philadelphia is 104 miles to the south and Washington, DC, is 235 miles south.

Manhattan

Most of Manhattan is easy to navigate, thanks to a street plan for the area north of Houston St that was imposed by a city planning commission in 1811. It created the current grid system of 14 named or numbered avenues running the north-south length of the island, crossed by east-west numbered streets. (If you intend to do a lot of walking, be aware that along the avenues, 20 blocks equal approximately 1 mile.)

Because the grid system was established long before the advent of the automobile, modern Manhattan suffers from tremendous traffic congestion, giving rise to the term 'gridlock.' The street plan had at least one other unintended consequence: the narrow streets precluded the creation of grand avenues in the European tradition and discouraged the creation of buildings set back on large tracts of property. There was nowhere to go but up, and by the late 19th century, Manhattan had a cluster of 'skyscrapers,' as prominent multistory office buildings were called.

Above Washington Square, Fifth Ave serves as the dividing line between the 'East Side' and the 'West Side.' Cross-street numbers begin there and grow higher toward each river, generally (but not exclusively) in 100-digit increments per block. Therefore, the Hard Rock Cafe, at 221 W 57th St, is slightly less than three blocks west of Fifth Ave.

Most New Yorkers give out addresses in shorthand by listing the cross street first and the avenue second, eg, 'we're at 33rd and Third.' If you are given an address on an avenue – such as '1271 Sixth Ave' – be sure to ask for the nearest cross street to save time.

In the oldest part of New York City, from 14th St to the southern tip of Manhattan, travel becomes a bit trickier. Streets that perhaps began as cow paths or merchants' byways snake along in a haphazard manner, which is why it is possible today to stand at the corner of W 4th St and W 10th St in Greenwich Village.

Broadway, the only avenue to cut diagonally across the island, was originally a woodland path used by Native Americans; it runs, in some form, from the tip of the island all the way to the state capital of Albany, 150 miles away. Today, Wall St stands at the place where, in 1653, the Dutch residents of New Amsterdam constructed a wooden barrier at the town's northern border to ward off attacks from hostile natives.

Neighborhoods There's no method to the names that New Yorkers have given their neighborhoods. They can be purely geographical (the Lower East Side), ethnically descriptive (Chinatown) or just plain scary (Hell's Kitchen). Tribeca is the name given to the 'Triangle Below Canal St' that passed into popular use. A similar thing happened with SoHo, the area south of Houston St (unrelated to London's Soho, which is named after a fox hunting call.)

Some neighborhoods have long outgrown their designations. Few residents of Chelsea know their area was named after an 18th-century farm owned by a British army officer. Turtle Bay, a fashionable enclave surrounding the United Nations on the East Side of Manhattan, is named after a riverside cove that was drained in 1868.

The Upper East Side and Upper West Side include the areas above 59th St on either side of Central Park. Midtown generally refers to the largely commercial district from 59th St south to 34th St, an area that includes Rockefeller Center, Times Square, the Broadway theater district, major hotels, Grand Central Terminal and the Port Authority Bus Terminal.

Significant neighborhoods in the outer boroughs include Brooklyn Heights, Park Slope, Williamsburg and Brighton Beach in Brooklyn; Arthur Ave, Riverdale and City Island in the Bronx; and Astoria, Jackson Heights, Forest Hills and Flushing Meadows in Queens.

Maps

Lonely Planet publishes a pocket sized laminated map of New York City available at all bookstores. Decent downtown Manhattan maps are also given away free in the lobby of any decent hotel. If you want to explore the city at large, buy a five-borough street atlas.

Geographia and Hagstrom both publish paperback-sized editions that cost under $12.

Most subway stations in Manhattan have a Passenger Information Center (next to the token booth) with a wonderfully detailed map of the surrounding neighborhood and all points of interests clearly marked. Taking a look at it before heading to the train platform may save you from getting lost.

You can purchase maps at the Hagstrom Map & Travel Center (☎ 212-398-1222), 57 W 43rd St, and the Rand McNally Travel Store (☎ 212-758-7488), 150 E 52nd St, which ships globes and atlases worldwide. Both stores sell colorful wall maps of Manhattan made by the Identity Map Company for $30. Though not practical for walking around the city, these wonderfully detailed maps make a great souvenir of your trip.

INFORMATION
Tourist Offices

The NYC & Company – the Convention & Visitors' Bureau (☎ 800-692-8474, 212-397-8222 outside the US) has a sleek new Information Center at 810 Seventh Avenue at 53rd St. It's open weekdays 8:30 am to 6 pm and on weekends 9 am to 5 pm. The 24-hour line offers information on special events and reservations. The center has hundreds of brochures available for cultural events, and it maintains a website (www.nycvisit.com). To speak directly with a multilingual counselor, call ☎ 212-484-1222.

The Big Apple Greeters Program (☎ 212-669-2896, fax 212-669-4900) with the help of 500 volunteers welcomes visitors to the city by offering free tours of lesser-known neighborhoods. Some greeters are multilingual and specialize in helping the disabled. Reservations must be made in advance, and these tours have been praised by visitors. The website (www.bigapplegreeter.org) has links in French, German and Spanish.

The New York State Travel Information Center (☎ 800-225-5697), 810 Seventh Ave at 53rd St, issues books for other areas upstate.

Money

Given the prevalence of automated teller machines (ATMs) in New York City, you can draw cash directly from a home bank account, provided it is linked with the Cirrus or Plus networks. ATM fees for foreign banks are usually about $3 to $5; foreign-currency exchange commissions range from $5 to $7. Most New York banks are linked by the NYCE (New York Cash Exchange) system, and you can use local bank cards interchangeably at ATMs.

Chase Manhattan Bank's branch at the corner of Liberty and William Sts downtown offers a commission-free foreign-currency exchange service weekdays 8 am to 3 pm. A Midtown branch directly across the street from the Empire State Building at 34th St and Fifth Ave also offers foreign exchange during the same hours.

The main American Express travel office (☎ 212-421-8240), 374 Park Ave, has a reliable foreign exchange service, but there are long lines during the afternoons. It's open weekdays 9 am to 5 pm.

Thomas Cook Foreign Exchange has eight locations in the city. The Times Square office (☎ 212-265-6049), 1590 Broadway at 48th St, is open Monday to Saturday 9 am to 6 pm and Sunday 9 am to 5 pm. American Express has an office in Bloomingdale's (☎ 212-705-3171), 59th St and Lexington Ave, as well as offices at 374 Park Ave (☎ 212-421-8240), 65 Broadway (☎ 212-493-6500) and 150 E 42nd St (☎ 212-687-3700).

Chequepoint (☎ 212-750-2400), 22 Central Park South, offers less-favorable rates; it has several locations.

Banks are normally open weekdays, usually 9 am to 3 pm. The Chase Manhattan branch at the corner of Mott and Canal Sts in Chinatown is open daily. Several other banks along Canal St also have weekend hours.

Post

Poste restante mail is accepted at the main post office provided it is marked 'General Delivery.' This method is not recommended or reliable, especially in the era of email and wire money transfers. The main post office (☎ 212-967-8585), 421 Eighth Ave, New York, NY 10001, is at the corner of W 33rd St and is open 24 hours a day. The Rockefeller Center post office, in the basement of

610 Fifth Ave, NY, NY 10022, is open weekdays 9:30 am to 5:30 pm.

The Franklin D Roosevelt Station (☎ 212-330-5549), 909 Third Ave, NY, NY 10022, at 55th St, is open for most postal business weekdays 9 am to 8 pm.

The following American Express offices offer a mail drop for cardholders: 420 Lexington Ave, NY, NY 10170, at 42nd St; 374 Park Ave, NY, NY 10022, at 53rd St; and 822 Lexington Ave, NY, NY 10021, at 63rd St.

Telephone & Fax

There are thousands of pay telephones on the streets, but those maintained by Bell Atlantic, the local utility company, are much more reliable than the others. However, a dwindling number take coins, and those that do are often vandalized. It's best to buy a pre-paid Bell Atlantic phone card from a drug store or other small shop.

Be particularly careful about dialing long distance with a credit card on an unaffiliated phone; you may end up with a whopping bill from an unscrupulous long distance firm. It's much better to use the access lines of major carriers such as AT&T (☎ 800-321-0288) or MCI (☎ 800-888-8000). Lonely Planet's eKno Communication Card is aimed specifically at travelers and provides cheap international calls, a range of messaging services and free email. You can join online at www.ekno.lonelyplanet.com, or by phone from the continental USA by dialing ☎ 800-707-0031. Once you've joined, to use eKno from the continental USA dial ☎ 800-706-1333.

Directories are no longer provided at outdoor phone booths, so if you're unsure of a number, dial ☎ 411 for telephone number information. It's a free call.

Kinko's (☎ 212-308-2679), 16 E 52nd St, offers 24-hour fax service as well as computer and photocopying services. There are approximately 20 other locations in Manhattan. Check the yellow pages in the phone book under 'Copying' for the nearest Kinko's location or equivalent service.

Email & Internet Access

The New York Public Library's main branch, (☎ 212-930-0800) on Fifth Ave at 42nd St, offers free half-hour Internet access, though there may be a wait in the late afternoon.

There are several cyber cafes in the city where you can surf the Internet for an hourly fee that ranges from $8 to $12. The Internet Café (☎ 212-614-0747), 82 E 3rd St, is open daily 11 am to 2 am. Also try Cyberfeld's (☎ 212-647-8830), 20 E 13th St off Fifth Ave, which also has computer rentals, and Cyber Café (☎ 212-334-5140), 273 Lafayette St.

Internet Resources

The following websites are particularly useful for finding out information about the city:

NYC & Company – the Convention & Visitors' Bureau
www.nycvisit.com
(general information and a rush hotel reservation line)

New York Today
www.nytoday.com
(the city site from the *New York Times*, offering entertainment listings and an archive of reviews)

The *New York Times*
www.nytimes.com
(the 'newspaper of record's' home site, with a complete version of the daily paper and additional cyber content)

Chowhound
www.chowhound.com
(web restaurant reviewer Jim Leff's eclectic *vox populi* site offering feedback for eateries at all income levels; worth bookmarking if you live in New York)

Discount Hotels
www.new-york-city-hotels.com
(discount and last-minute room bookings and direct links to the hotels)

City Search
newyork.citysearch.com
(a comprehensive roundup of city happenings)

NYC Subways
www.nycsubway.org
(unofficial site detailing the transit system, from practical information to historical trivia)

Scenetrack
www.scenetrack.com
(a club and bar listing with up-to-the-minute information on New York's nightlife)

The Mark of the Outsider

For years, the prefix '212' marked all New Yorkers' telephone lines. The code was chosen back in the days of rotary phones because it was the fastest combination to dial, perfectly in keeping with New York's fast lifestyle. (The same reasoning gave Los Angeles the '213' area code.)

In the 1980s, the surge in telephone use in Manhattan led to the introduction of the '718' area code that eventually was assigned for the four outer boroughs. But in the late '90s the use of cells phones and faxes finally exhausted the 9.2 million phone numbers that could be assigned under these codes. At first '917' was assigned to new business numbers and cell phones. But now the unthinkable has happened: New residences in Manhattan are being given phone numbers with a '646' area code. At the moment, few numbers have this area code, but 646 is already dismissed as the sign of the new arrival, something totally uncool and to be avoided.

Perhaps Wall St traders will find a way of creating a secondary market for numbers in the desirable '212' zone. Until then, newcomers must grin and bear it.

Travel Agencies

Council Travel offers bookings at three sites: (☎ 212-254-2525), 148 W 4th St; (☎ 212-666-4177), 895 Amsterdam Ave; and (☎ 212-661-1450), 205 E 42nd St. STA Travel (☎ 212-627-3111) is at 10 Downing St on Sixth Ave. American Express (☎ 212-421-8240), 374 Park Ave, offers package deals. AAA (☎ 212-757-2000), the 'auto club,' has an office at 1881 Broadway, where you can obtain an International Driver's License, good throughout the US.

Bucket Shops Consolidators, or 'bucket shops,' are travel agencies that sell last-minute flights on scheduled carriers. There are plenty of consolidators on the World Wide Web, so check your local server for deals. In New York City, consolidators are in Midtown office buildings and advertise weekly in the *Village Voice* and the Sunday *New York Times*. Try to deal with a travel agency that accepts credit cards – it's a sign of reliability.

You should also check with several places in order to get the best price, because some agencies have deals only with specific airlines. TFI Tours (☎ 212-736-1140), 34 W 32nd St, accepts credit cards. Airforce Travel (☎ 212-219-8478) and Air-Tech (☎ 212-219-7000) are phone-based travel services.

Now Voyager (☎ 212-431-1616) books courier flights and sells last-minute domestic specials. It's best to call its busy office after business hours (after 7 pm) to hear a voice menu of locations and conditions.

Bookstores

General New York City has several Barnes & Noble superstores, including the following locations: Union Square (☎ 212-253-0810); Astor Place (☎ 212-420-1322); (☎ 212-727-1227) 675 Sixth Ave at 22nd St; and (☎ 212-362-8835) 2289 Broadway at 82nd St. The stores are open daily 9 am to 10 pm.

Borders Books (☎ 212-839-8049) has three locations: 461 Park Ave (☎ 212-980-6785); 550 Second Ave (☎ 212-685-3938); and 5 World Trade Center (☎ 212-839-8049), at the corner of Church and Vesey Sts.

The Gotham Book Mart (☎ 212-719-4448), 41 W 47th St, is one of the city's premier stand-alone shops; its trademark shingle declares that 'wise men fish here.' Coliseum Books (☎ 212-757-8381), 1771 Broadway, has a huge selection of paperback fiction and out-of-print titles. Shakespeare and Co is a general interest shop with three locations: downtown (☎ 212-529-1330) at 716 Broadway; in the financial district (☎ 212-742-7025) at 1 Whitehall St; and on the Upper East Side (☎ 212-570-0201) at 939 Lexington Ave.

Three Lives (☎ 212-741-2069), a Greenwich Village institution at 154 W 10th St, stocks a good number of biographies. Books and Co (☎ 212-737-1450), 939 Madison Ave, is a distinguished store that attracts major authors for readings – their photos line the walls. It's open 10 am to 7 pm Monday to Saturday and 12 pm to 6 pm Sunday.

St Marks Book Shop (☎ 212-260-7853), 31 Third Ave, specializes in political literature, poetry and academic journals.

The handsome Rizzoli store sells art books and general interest titles at two locations: (☎ 212-759-2424) 31 W 57th St, and (☎ 212-674-1616) 454 West Broadway, in SoHo.

Travel Books Travel titles and maps can be found at the Traveller's Bookstore (☎ 212-664-0995) in the Time Warner building, 22 E 52nd St in Manhattan. The Complete Traveller (☎ 212-685-9007), 199 Madison Ave (at the corner of 35th St), also offers an interesting selection of first editions and old Baedecker guides.

Used Books Strand Bookstore (☎ 212-473-1452), 828 Broadway, a true and well-loved New York institution, boasts of having 8 miles of used books and review copies. The Argosy (☎ 212-753-4455), 116 E 59th St, features books from estate sales and rare prints (it's closed Sunday). The dusty and colorful Chelsea Books & Records (☎ 212-465-4340) is at 111 W 17th St.

A&S Magazines (☎ 212-947-6313), 308 W 40th St, sells secondhand books and old magazines.

Libraries

The main branch of the New York Public Library (☎ 212-930-0800), on Fifth Ave at 42nd St, is a significant architectural attraction and worth visiting, if only to see the famous 3rd-floor reading room. The library also offers free Internet access, though there tends to be a wait for terminals, and the connection to the Internet tends to be slow. Those looking for periodicals and book information will find fewer crowds at the Midtown Manhattan annex (☎ 212-340-0830), directly across Fifth Ave, or at the Jefferson Market branch (☎ 212-243-4334), 425 Avenue of the Americas at 10th St.

The yellow pages lists all city library branches (closed Sunday).

Newspapers & Magazines

Even in the age of the Internet, New York is bursting with periodicals, both homegrown and foreign. It's hard to determine a single best source for entertainment listings – it's best to buy two or three upon arrival for a fuller picture of what's happening in the city.

The *New York Times* is the nation's premier newspaper, with more foreign bureaus and reporters than any other publication in the world. Its Friday Weekend Section is an invaluable guide to cultural events. Reading the *Wall Street Journal* is a must for financial workers. The *Village Voice* (distributed free in Manhattan each Wednesday), is well known for its nightlife listings for the mainstream clubs and music venues. It's also the best-known source for fee-free rental apartments and roommate situations. *New York* magazine does the same thing for its restaurant-obsessed readers. The *New York Observer*, a weekly newspaper for people obsessed with the local media and politics, strives for quirkier listings of literary readings and parties.

Time Out New York, published Wednesday, has the same format as its London cousin and has the most comprehensive listings of any publication. *Where New York* is the best free monthly guide to mainstream city events. Available at most hotels, it's more useful than *The New York Quick Guide*, a monthly guide, or *City Guide*, published weekly.

Radio

There are more than 100 radio stations in the city. On FM, classical music lovers turn to WNYC (93.9) and WQXR (96.3), which also include reviews and news reports. WBGO (88.3) carries National Public Radio in the morning and commercial-free jazz the rest of the day. WNEW (102.7), one of the nation's pioneering rock stations, abandoned the format in 1999 in favor of male-oriented (ie, silly and smutty) talk slots. The best rock mixture is on WHTZ (100.3). WBLS (107.5) is a premier spot for mainstream and light-soul music, and WQHT (97.1) is known as 'Hot 97' for its hip-hop and rap programming. Those seeking the widest musical variety should listen to WKCR (89.9) and WFMU (90.1), fringe stations with eclectic programming.

AM frequencies typically carry talk and news stations. WCBS (880) and WINS (1010) have news and weather updates, and WNYC-AM (820) broadcasts National Public Radio programs.

Other AM stations include WABC (770) is a conservative pundit/radio-shrink outlet. WOR (710), one of the nation's oldest stations, has a calmer talk shows, and WFAN (660) is a 24-hour sports station. WQEW (1560) broadcasts big band music and crooner standards. Spanish speakers listen to WKDM (1380) and WADO (1280). WWRL (1660) is a talk radio station aimed at the city's black community, with an emphasis on immigrant issues.

TV

The flagship stations of all four major US networks – NBC, CBS, ABC and FOX – are in New York City and carry national prime-time fare.

Cable networks include CNN, MTV and HBO. Channels dedicated to sports, culture, history and old movies are available. News broadcasts from Britain, Ireland, France, Mexico, Greece, Korea, Japan and Germany also appear on different Manhattan cable channels between 7 and 11 pm. Cable also carries dozens of local amateur programs on the 'public access' channels. The most famous shows are essentially soft-core porn, carrying strip shows and ads for escort services. Because they are covered by the First Amendment, they are not pay-per-view shows, and most hotels carry this regardless of whether their clientele want it or not.

Universities

New York City is home to many world class private universities and fine public colleges, including Columbia, New York and Fordham Universities. There are also New School for Social Research (which has extensive evening adult classes), Cooper Union and various colleges of the City University of New York (CUNY). These urban educational centers are not physically sepa-

rated from the city – in fact NYU's campus and dorm facilities are distributed throughout Greenwich Village. Columbia's main campus is on Broadway on Manhattan's Upper West Side. The City College campus of CUNY at St Nicholas Terrace is significant for its neo-Gothic design and worth a visit (subway: 137th St-City College).

Cultural Centers

New York City's major cultural centers include the following:

Alliance Française
    (Map 7; ☎ 212-355-6100) 22 E 60th St
Asia Society
    (Map 7; ☎ 212-288-6400) 502 Park Ave
Czech Center
    (Map 7; ☎ 212-288-0830) 1109 Madison Ave
Goethe Institute
    (Map 7; ☎ 212-439-8700) 1014 Fifth Ave
Hispanic Society of America
    (☎ 212-926-2234) 613 Broadway and 155th St
Italian Cultural Institute
    (Map 7; ☎ 212-879-4242) 686 Park Ave
Japan House
    (Map 5; ☎ 212-832-1155) 333 E 47th St
Spanish Institute
    (Map 7; ☎ 212-628-0420) 684 Park Ave
Swiss Institute
    (Map 4; ☎ 212-925-2035) 495 Broadway, 3rd floor

Laundry

Many New Yorkers live in apartments without laundry rooms, so neighborhoods have an abundance of laundries. Suds Cafe and Laundromat (☎ 212-741-2366), 141 W 10th St, has a reputation as a social scene. It is open daily 7 am to 10 pm.

Washing machines generally cost $2 for a 25-minute cycle. Dryers cost $2 for 30 minutes. Many facilities offer pick-up laundry services at the rate of about $2 per pound of clothing.

Toilets

New York City doesn't have a lot of public toilets, and you should head to department stores such as Macy's, Saks Fifth Avenue and Bloomingdale's or use a hotel lobby. If you're discreet and well dressed, it's also possible to walk into a crowded bar or restaurant to use the bathroom. At the moment, there are a few modern outdoor public toilets, the best-known is behind City Hall near the entrance to the Brooklyn Bridge; it costs 25¢.

Left Luggage
There are no public facilities for left luggage at train stations or the airports. All hotels will keep an eye on bags for guests, but do remember to take all items of value out beforehand, because hotels will never assume responsibility for lost items.

Medical Services
All hospital emergency rooms are obligated to accept sick visitors without regard to an ability to pay. However, showing up without insurance or money will virtually guarantee a long wait unless you are in extremis. The New York University Medical Center (☎ 212-263-5550), 462 First Ave at 33rd St, is easily reached by taxi. You can also go to the nearest hospital; check the yellow pages for the phone number of the emergency room near you.

New York is practically busting with 24-hour pharmacies, which is really the term for a convenience store with a drugs counter. The main chains are Duane Reade and Rite Aid. The Duane Reade locations that have pharmacy facilities include the Midtown store (☎ 212-541-9708) on the corner of W 57th St and Broadway, as well as a store in Greenwich Village (☎ 212-674-5357) at Sixth Ave and Waverly Place (near the W 8th St subway entrance).

For birth control and advice, Planned Parenthood has several facilities, including clinics at 26 Bleecker St (☎ 212-965-7000) and 44 Court St (☎ 212-965-7111), and it has its offices at 810 Seventh Ave, 12th floor (☎ 212-541-7800). For appointments at any New York City Planned Parenthood call ☎ 800-230-7526.

Emergency
For police, fire and ambulance calls, dial ☎ 911 – it's a free call from any phone. The police department can be reached for non-

emergencies at ☎ 212-374-5000 weekdays from 7:30 am to 6 pm (this line will also direct you to the nearest station).

Useful Organizations
The following is a list of some organizations that can help travelers in trouble:

AIDS Hotline	☎ 212-447-8200
Alcoholics Anonymous	☎ 212-647-1680
Crime Victims Services	☎ 212-577-7777
Dept of Consumer Affairs	☎ 212-487-4444
Gay & Lesbian Nat'l Hotline	☎ 212-989-0999
Legal Aid Society	☎ 212-577-3300
Public Transport to Airports	☎ 212-247-7433

Dangers & Annoyances
Panhandlers camp out at subway stops and, most threateningly, at ATMs. It's impossible to differentiate between those truly in need and someone on the hustle, and many tourists assuage their guilt by giving money. But New Yorkers know that money handed out to beggars will probably go to support a drug or alcohol habit.

Requests for money come in dozens of forms, including appeals for a dubious support group ('I'm a member of the United Homeless Organization'), unsubtle appeals to tourist fear ('I don't want to hurt or rob anybody'), to the shoulder-shrugging appeal for help ('I just got locked out of my car and need money for a cab'). When approached by anyone with a sad story, remember that the person is asking a tourist for help because the police and most locals are wise to scams.

If you wish to donate to a legitimate organization that helps people in need, contact Citymeals-on-Wheels (☎ 212-687-1234), which reaches out to feed hundreds of hungry people each day.

Hustlers often set up three-card-monte games – 'players' try to pick the red card out of three shuffled on the top of a cardboard box. This variation on the shell game is widely known to be a no-win scam. Yet, enough tourists play along (or get their wallets lifted while watching) to make it a common sight on downtown streets during the weekends. Readers have written us with tales of friends who have been taken in by this, and as long as there's a gullible player willing to shell out money, this scam will continue.

The bottom line is never, under any circumstances, give money to a stranger.

Manhattan

For most visitors, Manhattan (population 1,487,500) *is* New York City. Even the residents of the outer boroughs refer to it as 'the city,' a tacit acknowledgment of the island's primacy. But it's important to remember that the Bronx, Brooklyn, Queens and Staten Island each have their own attractions. Only visitors who include at least one excursion out of Manhattan are truly taking advantage of what the entire city has to offer.

The following sections divide Manhattan into neighborhoods, organized from the island's southern tip to the north. Remember, the most popular sites attract large crowds year-round.

A Note on Prices

As any department store owner or Hollywood agent knows, if you have a hot commodity, you can always increase the price the public must pay for it. New York City, with its 30 million annual visitors, is certainly a hot property. That's why prices in this book will be subject to greater change than usual. It is now the habit of museums and tourist attractions to raise prices in $5 increments rather than by just a dollar or two. Please factor a few unpleasant price surprises in your budget, especially if you want to see a Broadway musical, where top prices are already in the $75-per-seat range.

The upside is that you can eat very cheaply in New York, and the dollar is a bargain against many foreign currencies, so shopping still offers real opportunities for savings.

LOWER MANHATTAN (MAP 3)
Statue of Liberty

The most enduring symbol of New York City – and indeed, the New World in general – can trace its origins to a Parisian dinner party in 1865. There, a group of intellectuals opposed to the government of Napoleon III gathered in the house of political activist Edouard René Lefebvre de Laboulaye to discuss ways to promote French Republicanism. The notion of building a monument honoring the American conception of political freedom intrigued sculptor Frédéric-Auguste Bartholdi, a fellow dinner guest, and he dedicated most of the next 20 years to turning the dream into a reality.

Laboulaye and Bartholdi decided that the structure should end up in the US. Bartholdi traveled to New York in 1871 to choose a site for the work (modeled on the Colossus of Rhodes). Soon afterward, the pair held a lottery to raise $250,000 to cover the cost of construction of the statue, which, incidentally, included a metal skeleton by railway engineer Alexandre Gustave Eiffel, who later became world-famous for his eponymous Parisian tower. Meanwhile, in the US, a campaign by the New York *World* newspaper beat the drum for the project. In 1883, poet Emma Lazarus published a work called *The New Colossus* in support of a fund for a pedestal for the statue. Her words have long since been associated with the monument:

Give me your tired, your poor
Your huddled masses yearning to breathe free
The wretched refuse of your teeming shore
Send these, the homeless, tempest-tost to me
I lift my lamp beside the golden door!

Ironically, these famous words were added to the base only in 1901, 17 years after the poet's death.

On October 28, 1886, the 151-foot *Liberty Enlightening the World* was finally unveiled in New York Harbor before President Grover Cleveland and a harbor full of tooting ships.

By the 1980s a restoration of the statue was in order, and more than $100 million was spent to shore up Liberty for its centennial. Substantial work was required to restore the rotting copper skin, and a new gold-plated torch, the third in the statue's history, was installed. The older stained-glass torch is now on display just inside the entrance to the staircase, near a fine museum that describes the statue's history and its restoration.

Getting There & Away The trips to the Statue of Liberty and Ellis Island (☎ 212-363-3200) are pleasant 15-minute ferry rides, and each site attracts well over 2 million visitors a year. Millions more take the boat ride just for the spectacular view of Manhattan but pass on taking the 354 steps to the statue's crown, the equivalent of climbing a 22-story building. (No one is allowed onto the statue's torch balcony.)

Circle Line, which runs the boat service, strongly advises that visitors show up at noon if they intend on climbing to the statues' crown. A trip taking in both the Statue of Liberty and Ellis Island is an all-day affair. In the summer you may wait up to an hour to embark on an 800-person ferry, only to be confronted with a three-hour trek to the crown, followed by a bottleneck getting off both islands. Ferries run every day except Christmas.

Though there is no charge to get off at Liberty Island, the ferries from Manhattan (☎ 212-269-5755) cost $7 for adults, $3 for children and $6 for seniors. They leave every 30 minutes from Battery Park from 9 am to 5 pm, with boats leaving as early as 8 am during the summer. The ticket office for the Statue of Liberty/Ellis Island boats is in **Castle Clinton**, the fort built in 1811 to defend Manhattan from the British. Originally located 300 yards offshore before landfill engulfed it, Castle Clinton was converted to a theater in 1823, and it also served as an immigration station and aquarium. Today, the castle is literally just a shell of its former self – there's no roof on the building anymore (subway: South Ferry; Bowling Green).

Ferries (☎ 201-435-0499) also leave from Liberty State Park on the New Jersey side of

the harbor for the same price and on the same schedule.

If the crowds are too much, why not try the nearby Staten Island ferry, which doesn't take you to the statue itself, but it does provides a great view of the statue and downtown Manhattan, and, best of all, it's free! (See the Staten Island section, later in this chapter, for details.)

Ellis Island

Ferries to the Statue of Liberty make a second stop at Ellis Island, New York's main immigration station from 1892 to 1954. More than 15 million people passed through here before the island was abandoned.

A $160 million restoration project turned the impressive redbrick building into an **Immigration Museum** covering the history of the island. The exhibitions begin at the Baggage Room and continue on the second floor where medical inspections took place and foreign currency was exchanged.

At all points, the exhibits emphasize that, contrary to popular myth, most of the ship-borne immigrants were processed within eight hours, and conditions were generally clean and safe. The 338-foot long Registry Room includes a beautiful vaulted-tile ceiling made by immigrants from Spain. But walking though the registry today – described as 'light and airy' in museum literature – surely can't compare to days when the same room housed a queue of 5000 confused and tired people waiting to be interviewed by overworked immigration officers and inspected by doctors.

There is a 50-minute audio tour of the facility available for a small charge of $6. Much more moving are the recorded memories of real Ellis Island immigrants that were taped in the 1980s and are available through phone banks in each display area. Visitors can also take in *Ellis Island Stories*, a 30-minute play about the experience of arriving at Ellis Island. Admission to the play is $3 for adults and $2.50 for seniors and children older than 14. (You can purchase the tickets there.) The show (☎ 212-883-1986, ext 742) plays five times daily on the half-hour from 10:30 am to 3:30 pm.

There is a 30-minute film on the immigrant experience that is also worth checking out. Also interesting is the exhibition describing the influx of immigrants who arrived just before WWI and changed the ethnic population of the US.

Barely visible up the slip from the boat docks are the rotting remains of *Ellis Island*, a passenger ferry that sank in 1968 after years of neglect.

Getting There & Away The Circle Line ferries are $7/6/3 for adults/seniors/children. See Getting There & Away under the Statue of Liberty section, above, for additional details.

Lower Manhattan's Architectural Landmarks

Students of architecture will no doubt be drawn to New York City's far-flung landmarks: the brownstones of Brooklyn Heights, the marvelous medieval quiet of the Cloisters, or the sleek modernism of Ludwig Mies van der Rohe's Seagram Building (built in 1958) in Midtown. But if you want a short but comprehensive tour of the city's man-made landscape, it's best to spend a day downtown near Wall St. Though famous as the world's financial capital, this area of urban canyons is an unrivaled museum of architecture. Along the cramped and circuitous side streets and the grand avenue of Broadway you will find Federal homes, Greek Revival temples, Gothic churches, Renaissance palazzos and one of the finest collections of early-20th-century skyscrapers.

Although no Dutch buildings survive from the early 17th century, the paths and lanes mapped out by the engineer Cryn Fredericksz in 1625 have restrained and influenced every architect who ventured to build here. Likewise, little lasts from the more than 100 years of British rule. Indeed, seven years of British military occupation during the Revolutionary War and major fires in 1776 and 1778 ruthlessly altered the face of the city. By the end of the war, a quarter of the settled area – more than 1000 shops and homes – lay in burnt decay. According to the diarist William Duer, 'The skeletons of the remaining walls cast their grim shadows upon the pavement, imparting an unearthly aspect to the street.'

Thankfully, during one of the blazes citizens climbed to the roof of **St Paul's Chapel**, on Broadway between Vesey and Fulton Sts, and extinguished the flames that threatened the schist-and-brownstone church. Designed in 1764 by Thomas McBean, the chapel is now the last remaining colonial building in the area and one of the greatest Georgian structures ever built in the country. It was here, within the airy interior of fluted Corinthian columns and Waterford chandeliers, that President George Washington attended services when New York served as the nation's capital. His personal pew is still on display. (See Fraunces Tavern in the Lower Manhattan section for more on existing traces of colonial architecture.)

On State St (between Pearl and Whitehall Sts), at the southern tip of the island, stands the **Shrine to St Elizabeth Ann Seton**, the first American Catholic saint. This delicate Georgian home, set in redbrick, dates from 1793 and is the lone survivor of a series of graceful row houses that once hugged the shoreline (due to landfill, it's now set well back from the river). Today, the shrine occupies the eastern portion of 7 State St. A Federal-style west wing was added in 1806, reputedly by John McComb, the first major New York-born architect. This section of the structure is enlivened with a curved porch and a double colonnade of attenuated Doric and Ionic columns that were supposedly made from recycled ship masts.

In Battery Park, just to the west, looms the shell of **Castle Clinton**. Built in 1811 and indisputably designed by McComb, the imposing fortress, with its 8-foot-thick walls and rusticated gate, once brimmed with 28 guns set in the embrasures. Back then, the fort stood on an island that was hundreds of feet from the shore; landfill has since joined it with Manhattan. Its guns were never fired in anger, and in the 1820s the government decommissioned the fort and turned it into Castle Garden,

Museum of Jewish Heritage

The new facility (☎ 212-945-0039), 18 First Place in the Battery Park City business complex in the shadow of the World Trade Center, gives prominence to all aspects of Jewish New York, from immigration to assimilation. Recent exhibitions include a holographic history of the museum's establishment and a display of Jewish-owned art that was stolen by the Nazis and eventually returned to the surviving family members. Audio tours of the museum are available for $5.

It's open Sunday to Wednesday and on Friday from 9 am to 5 pm; Thursday 9 am to 8 pm (closed Saturday). Admission is $7 for

Lower Manhattan's Architectural Landmarks

a concert hall-cum-resort that is said to have hosted up to 6000 people beneath a domed roof. Castle Clinton has had a colorful history: In 1855 the government turned it into a processing center for immigrants, and in 1896 the renowned architecture firm of McKim, Mead & White converted the building into an aquarium (a purpose it served until 1941). Today, it is the site of the ticket office for the Statue of Liberty ferry.

As Americans sought a way to define their new nation, they looked to the ancient democracy of Greece and the republic of Rome for examples to emulate. Classical architecture, it was felt, gave expression to the aspirations of the young republic. The finest surviving example in Lower Manhattan is **Federal Hall**. Standing on Wall and Nassau Sts on the site of the old British City Hall where Washington took his oath of office, the 1842 design, with its hefty Doric porticoes, two-story rotunda, circular colonnade and paneled dome, is truly a temple to purity.

By the mid-19th century, everything new, from courthouses and banks to privies, was designed to look like Greek temples, and people quickly tired of the austerity of the ancients. When British-born Richard Upjohn built **Trinity Church** on Broadway and Wall St in 1846, the brownstone church, with its buttresses, finials and octagonal spire, was the tallest and most richly decorated building in the city. Its appearance proved a revelation to a citizenry craving more transcendental and less rationalist forms. Upjohn's church helped launch the picturesque neo-Gothic movement in America.

By the early 1900s, as New York remained the center of US commercial trade, the federal government decided it needed a new **Customs House** to collect its revenues. Located on Bowling Green near the foot of Broadway, the Customs House (now the home of the National Museum of the American Indian) was completed in 1907. Cass Gilbert's vast seven-story limestone building melds art and architecture in a tribute to the grandeur of trade. Walls, doors, ceilings and floors are festooned with marine ornamentation, shells, sails, sea creatures and other sea imagery. Dormers are the prows of galleons, and the glorious elliptical rotunda is a 135-foot-long room encircled by Reginald Marsh's murals (added in 1937) portraying everything from the great explorers of America to Greta Garbo at an impromptu dockside press conference. It is simply one of the most sumptuous beaux arts buildings ever built.

The Customs House inspired a rash of new buildings near Bowling Green, most of them monuments to particular companies, and these skyscrapers started to dwarf neighboring landmarks. The 41-story **Equitable Building**, on Broadway between Pine and Cedar Sts, is a rather undistinguished, but nevertheless influential, example of the form. When it opened just before WWI, its sheer, unapologetic bulk changed the shape of Manhattan – and world architecture – forever. At 1.2 million sq feet, it was the largest office building on the planet. Its size created such an uproar that four years after its opening, New York enacted the nation's first zoning laws requiring building setbacks, thus stimulating countless architects to reinterpret the nature of the skyscraper. Their dizzyingly tall towers have sprung up all over Manhattan – and have subsequently filled other cities throughout the world.

adults and $5 for students and seniors (subway: Rector St).

New York Stock Exchange

Though 'Wall Street' is the widely recognized symbol of American capitalism, the New York Stock Exchange (NYSE; ☎ 212-656-5167), 8 Broad St, the world's best-known stock exchange, is actually around the corner. It has a portentous facade reminiscent of a Roman temple.

A visitor's gallery overlooks the frenetic trading floor and the 'Big Board' that lists share activity. The gallery also includes an exhibit describing the exchange's history. Free tickets to view the NYSE are distributed at a booth at 20 Broad St, weekdays from 9:15 am to 4 pm. The tickets, which allow entrance to the visitors' center in 45-minute increments throughout the day, are usually snapped up by noon, so head to the office early (subway: Cortland St).

Trinity Church

This former Anglican parish (☎ 212-602-0872), at the corner of Broadway and Wall St, was founded by King William III in 1697 and once had several constituent chapels, including the still-existent St Paul's Chapel at the corner of Fulton St and Broadway. Trinity's huge land holdings in Lower Manhattan made it the city's wealthiest and most influential church during the 18th century.

The current Trinity Church, built in 1846 by English architect Richard Upjohn, is the third structure to sit on this site. Before the advent of skyscrapers, its 280-foot bell tower made it the tallest building in New York City. A pamphlet describing the history of the parish is available for a small donation.

The long, dark interior of the church includes a beautiful stained glass window over the altar. Trinity, like other Anglican churches in America, became part of the Episcopal faith following US independence.

The church is open to visitors Monday through Friday 9 am to 4 pm, Saturday 10 am to 3:45 pm, and Sunday 1 to 3:45 pm, excluding lunchtime services (subway: Rector St or Wall St).

Federal Hall

Marked by a huge statue of George Washington, Federal Hall (☎ 212-767-0637), 26 Wall St, is on the site where the first US Congress convened and where Washington later took the oath of office as the first president of the United States. These events took place in the former city hall built by the British (replaced by the Greek Revival structure in 1842) that also served as the US Customs House.

Today, there is a small museum dedicated to post-colonial New York. It's open 9 am to 5 pm weekdays. Free guided tours of the building leave every hour on the half hour from 12:30 to 3:30 pm (subway: Rector St or Wall St).

Federal Reserve Bank

The only reason to visit the Federal Reserve Bank (☎ 212-720-6130), 31 Liberty St, is to see the high-security vault that is 80 feet below ground and contains more than 10,000 tons of gold reserves. You will only see a small part of the fortune, but the tour and the exhibit of coins and counterfeit currency are informative. The bank prefers that you call ahead for a tour reservation, but it's likely you can get on a tour by just showing up at the bank (subway: Cortland St).

National Museum of the American Indian

This museum (☎ 212-668-6624), an affiliate of the Smithsonian Institution, abandoned its uptown spot at 155th St in 1994 and moved to the former US Customs House on Bowling Green. The Beaux Arts monument to commerce was built to collect federal duties imposed on foreign goods in the days before income tax; it is a grand but somewhat incongruous space for the US's leading museum on Native American art, established by oil heir George Gustav Heye in 1916. The facility's information center is found in the former collection office, with computer banks next to old wrought-iron teller booths.

continued on page 180

Metropolitan Transportation Authority

MTA New York City Subway

June 2000
© 2000 Metropolitan Transportation Authority
Design: Michael Hertz Associates, New York City
Map is subject to change
Used with permission

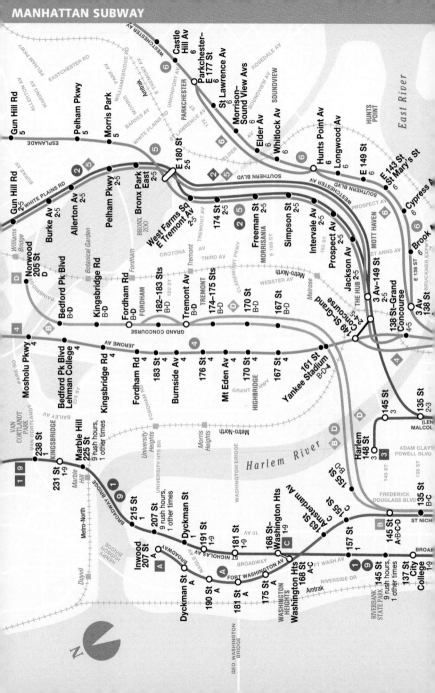

BROOKLYN

STATEN ISLAND

Atlantic Ocean

Jamaica Bay

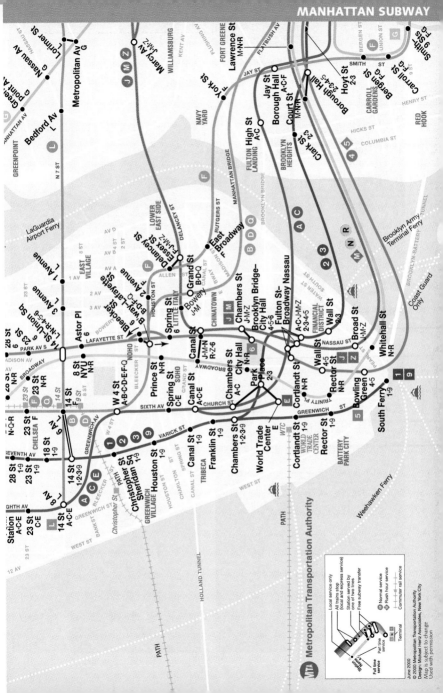

MANHATTAN SUBWAY

Times Square never naps.

Chrysler Building and beyond

'Give me your tired, your poor...'

ROBERT REID

Durians for sale in New York's Chinatown

VERONICA GARBUTT

Harlem tour guide welcomes visitors.

LIZ BARRY

Young Hasidic boy

Wonder Wheel, Coney Island

American Museum of Natural History

Hanging out in Central Park

New York City Map Section

ANGUS OBORN

MAP 1 FIVE BOROUGHS

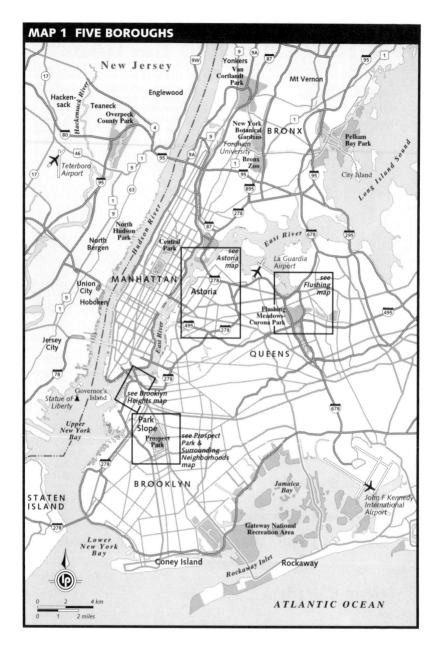

Prometheus watches over the plaza at Rockefeller Center.

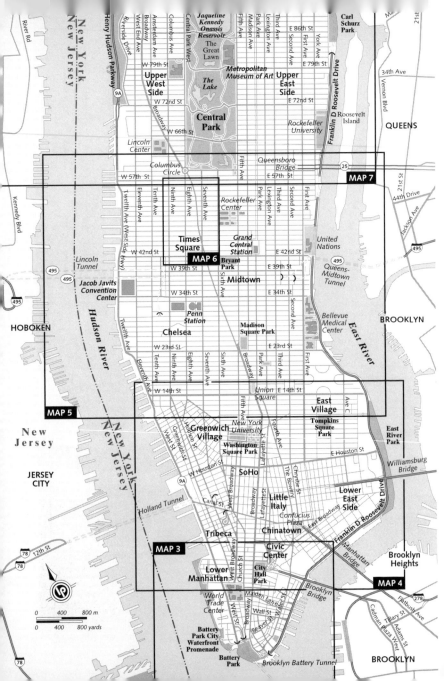

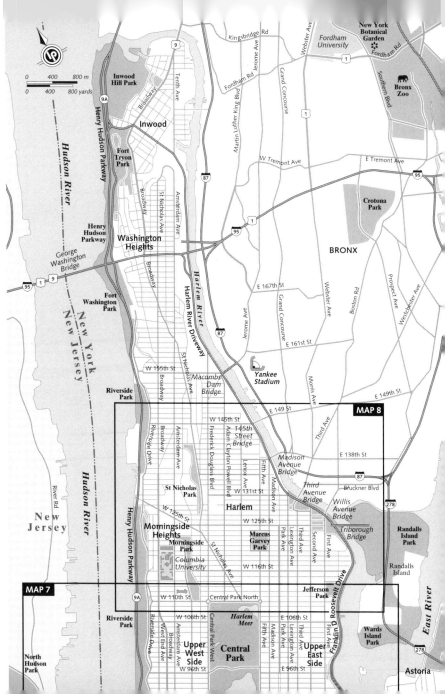

MAP 3 LOWER MANHATTAN

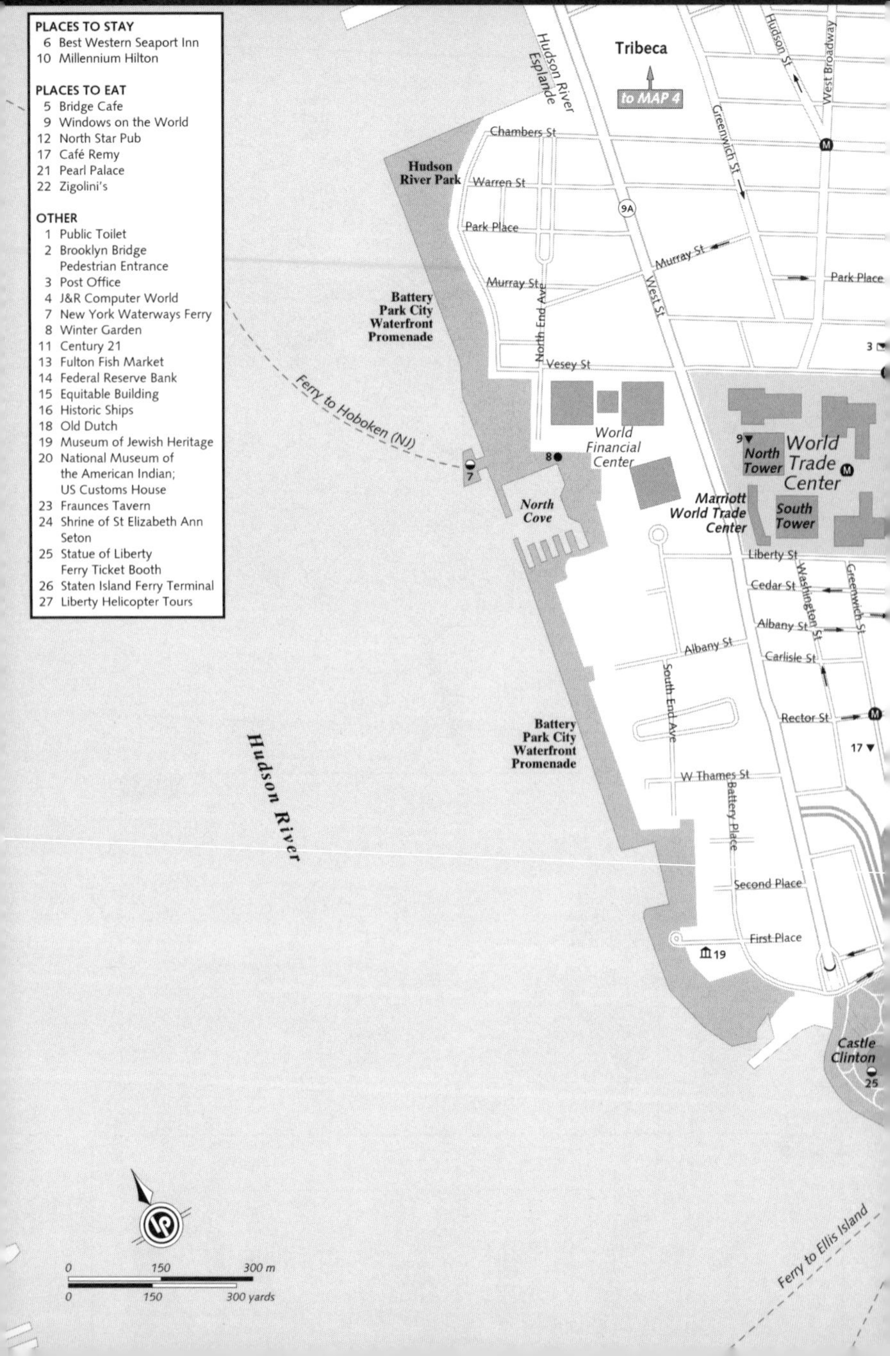

PLACES TO STAY
6 Best Western Seaport Inn
10 Millennium Hilton

PLACES TO EAT
5 Bridge Cafe
9 Windows on the World
12 North Star Pub
17 Café Remy
21 Pearl Palace
22 Zigolini's

OTHER
1 Public Toilet
2 Brooklyn Bridge
    Pedestrian Entrance
3 Post Office
4 J&R Computer World
7 New York Waterways Ferry
8 Winter Garden
11 Century 21
13 Fulton Fish Market
14 Federal Reserve Bank
15 Equitable Building
16 Historic Ships
18 Old Dutch
19 Museum of Jewish Heritage
20 National Museum of
    the American Indian;
    US Customs House
23 Fraunces Tavern
24 Shrine of St Elizabeth Ann
    Seton
25 Statue of Liberty
    Ferry Ticket Booth
26 Staten Island Ferry Terminal
27 Liberty Helicopter Tours

Tribeca

to MAP 4

Hudson River Esplanade

Hudson St

West Broadway

Chambers St

Hudson River Park

Warren St

Greenwich St

Park Place

9A

Murray St

Park Place

Battery Park City Waterfront Promenade

Murray St

West St

North End Ave

Vesey St

3

World Financial Center

8

North Tower

9

World Trade Center

North Cove

7

Marriott World Trade Center

South Tower

Liberty St

Cedar St

Washington St

Greenwich St

Albany St

Carlisle St

South End Ave

Albany St

Rector St

17

Hudson River

Battery Park City Waterfront Promenade

W Thames St

Battery Place

Second Place

First Place

19

Castle Clinton

25

Ferry to Hoboken (NJ)

Ferry to Ellis Island

0   150   300 m
0   150   300 yards

Thomas St

Thomas Paine Park

Duane St

African Burial Ground

Foley Square

Pearl St

Park Row

Oliver St

Monroe St

Catherine St

Cherry St

Market St

to MAP 4

meade St

Sun Building

Civic Center

Surrogate's Court

St James Place

Madison St

Water St

Lower East Side

Chambers St

Municipal Building

Warren St

Tweed Courthouse

City Hall

Municipal Building

Ave of the Finest

Robert F Wagner Place

1

2

Franklin D Roosevelt Drive

NYC Info Booth

NYC Info Booth

Murray St

Frankfort St

Pearl St

Brooklyn Bridge

City Hall Park

Spruce St

Woolworth Building

Barclay St

Beekman St

Dover St

Park Row

4

Nassau St

Ann St

William St

Gold St

5

6

Peck Slip

Jersey St

St Paul's Chapel

Fulton St

William St

Cliff St

Ped Mall

Pearl St

Water St

Front St

South St

13

Lower Manhattan

11

Cortlandt St

Maiden Lane

John St

Platt St

Water St

Pearl St

Ped Mall

Fulton St

12

Schermerhorn Row

14

Liberty St

Burling Slip

South Street Seaport

Pier 17

Thames St

Cedar St

15

Pine St

Fletcher St

Maiden Lane

16

Pier 16

Trinity Church

Morgan Guaranty Building

Nassau St

Federal Hall

Wall St

Maiden Lane

Front St

Bank of New York

New York Stock Exchange

Wall St

South St

East River

Exchange Place

Broadway

New St

Pearl St

Gouverneur Lane

Morris St

Standard Oil Building

William St

Stone St

Old Slip St

Franklin D Roosevelt Drive

Bowling Green

Beaver St

Broad St

18

Coenties Slip

Vietnam Veterans Plaza

20

Whitehall St

Stone St

Bridge St

23

Water St

State St

Pearl St

21 22

Battery Park

24

Peter Minuit Plaza

27

26

Ferry to Statue of Liberty

Brooklyn Battery Tunnel

Ferry to Staten Island

to MAP 5

East River

Franklin D Roosevelt Drive

E 14th St
E 13th St
E 12th St
E 11th St
E 10th St
E 9th St
St Marks Place
E 7th St
E 6th St
E 5th St
E 4th St
E 3rd St
E 2nd St
E 1st St

Third Ave
Second Ave
First Ave
Ave A
Ave B
Ave C
Ave D

East Village

Tompkins Square Park

Alphabet City

East River Park

105
108 ● 110 ▼ ● 111
▼109
▼113   E 9th St   ▼114
■ 116
▼ 117   118
▼125
128 ▼
129
131 ● ● 132
133 ●
▼ 134

106 ▼
107 ▼

119 ●
122 ▼   ▼ 123

■ 120

The Bowery

Second Ave

First Ave

E Houston St

Houston St
The Bowery
Mott St
Elizabeth St
Prince St
Spring St
▼ 313
▼ 314
Kenmare St

Sara D Roosevelt Parkway

Chrystie St

304 305
▼303   ▼▼ Ludlow St
306 ▼ ▼ 307
309 ●
310 ▼
315 ▼ 316
Delancey St
319

308 ▼

Stanton St

311 ●

Eldridge St
Forsyth St
Allen St
Orchard St
Essex St
Norfolk St
Suffolk St
Clinton St
Attorney St
Ridge St
Pitt St
Columbia St

Rivington St

317 ●

Williamsburg Bridge

Lower East Side

318 ■

Broome St

320   ▼ 321
▼ 322
Grand St

Little Italy

323 ▼
Hester St

324 ■

Grand St

325 ●
Hester St

East Broadway

Henry St
Madison St
Montgomery St
Gouverneur St
Water St

Jackson St
Cherry St

Canal St

326 328
▼▼327   ▼ 329
Bayard St
332 ▼
333 ▼ 337
335 ▼ 336 ▼

Chinatown

330

Confucius Plaza

Columbus Park
334
Moss St
Chatham Square
Worth St
339 ●

331

Division St
Rutgers St
Jefferson St
Clinton St
Cherry St
South St

East Broadway
Henry St
Madison St
Market St
Pike St
Catherine St
Cherry St
Water St
South St

▼ 338

Oliver St
James St

Pell St
Doyers St
Mott St

East Broadway

Pearl St
Park Row
St James Place

East River

Frankfort St
Gold St
Pearl St

Brooklyn Bridge

Manhattan Bridge

Franklin D Roosevelt Drive

Brooklyn Heights

John St
Water St
Gold St
Bridge St

to MAP 3

Greenwich Village

PLACES TO STAY
7 Incentra Village
12 Larchmont Hotel
13 Riverview Hotel
26 Washington Square Hotel

PLACES TO EAT
2 Jon Vie
4 Florent
5 El Faro
9 Benny's Burritos
10 'Original' Ray's Pizza
11 Bar Six
17 Sammy's Noodles
18 French Roast
27 Gourmet Garage
36 Cones
38 Bleecker Street Pastry
42 Café Reggio
44 Grange Hall
45 Trattoria Spaghetto
46 Minetta Tavern
50 Marinella
51 Le Figaro
52 Cafe Lure
53 Rocco
54 Tomoe Sushi

BARS/CLUBS
6 Hudson Bar & Books
8 Corner Bistro
14 Village Vanguard
21 Small's
23 55 Bar
28 Washington Square Church
30 Bottom Line

31 Sweet Basil
32 Blue Note
35 Chumley's
43 Bar d'O
48 Back Fence

OTHER
1 Gay & Lesbian Community Service Center
3 Strand Bookstore
15 Patchin Place
16 Jefferson Market Library
19 Second Cemetary of Spanish & Portugese Synagogue
20 Andrew Lockwood House
22 Stonewall Place
24 Northern Dispensary
25 Shoe Stores
29 Arch in Washington Square Park
33 Judson Memorial Church
34 Tower Records
37 Route 66 Records
39 Triton
40 Electric Lady Studios; Kettle of Fish
41 Café Wha?
47 Café Borgia
49 Urban Outfitters
55 Angelika Film Center

East Village

PLACES TO STAY
116 St Mark's Hotel
120 East Village B&B

PLACES TO EAT
106 DeRobertis

107 Lanza's
109 Sharaku
110 Second Ave Deli
113 Hasaki
114 Veselka
122 Roetelle AG
123 Benny's Burritos
130 Time Cafe
131 Astor Restaurant & Lounge
134 Lucky Cheng's

BARS/CLUBS
104 Webster Hall
117 McSorley's
118 Tribe
125 Scratcher
128 KGB
129 Swift Bar
132 CBGB

OTHER
101 Footlight Records
102 Post Office
103 Grace Church
105 St Marks in-the-Bowery
108 Renwick Triangle
111 10th St Baths
112 Astor Place
115 Cooper Union
119 Resurrection Vintage
121 Colonnade Row
124 Joseph Papp Public Theater
126 Other Records
127 Old Merchant's House Museum
130 Fez
133 Anthology Film Archives

TONY WHEELER

Manhattan cabs

DOWNTOWN MANHATTAN

SoHo • Tribeca

PLACES TO STAY
227 Soho Grand Hotel

PLACES TO EAT
203 Souen Restaurant
204 Helianthus Vegetarian
 Restaurant
213 Fanelli Cafe
224 Lupe's East LA Kitchen
226 Gourmet Garage
228 Lucky Strike
231 Riverrun
232 Nobu
233 Bubby's
234 Walker's
235 Chanterelle
237 Odeon

BARS/CLUBS
201 SOB's
215 Ear Inn
216 Don Hill's
225 Cafe Noir
229 Bubble Lounge

OTHER
202 Film Forum
205 Rizzoli Bookstore
206 Post Office; Edward Thorpe
 Gallery
207 African Museum

208 New Museum of
 Contemporary Art
209 Guggenheim/SoHo
210 Leo Castelli Gallery
211 Howard Greenberg Gallery
212 Haas Mural
214 Singer Building
217 Fire Museum
218 Enchanted Forest
219 St Nicholas Hotel
220 Balthazar
221 Canal Jeans
222 Swiss Institute
223 Haughwout Building
230 Post Office
236 Harrison Street Houses

Little Italy • Chinatown • Lower East Side

PLACES TO STAY
315 Off SoHo Suites
318 Pioneer Hotel
324 World Hotel

PLACES TO EAT & DRINK
303 Yonah Schimmel Bakery
304 Bereket
305 Katz's Deli
307 Mercury Lounge
308 Far Side
312 Spring Street Natural
313 Lombardi's Pizza
314 Vincent's

321 Cafe Roma
322 Benito I Restaurant
323 Puglia
326 New Pasteur
327 Thailand Restaurant
329 House of Vegetarian
332 Peking Duck House
333 Hay Wun Loy
334 Vegetarian Paradise
336 Hong Ying Rice Shop
338 Nice Restaurant

OTHER
301 Puck Building
302 Old St Patrick's
306 Luna Lounge
309 Surf Reality
310 147 Ludlow Street
311 Schapiro's Wines
316 First Roumanian-American
 Congregation
317 Streit's Matzoh Co
319 Lower East Side Tenement
 Museum
320 Old Police Headquarters
325 Essex Pickles
328 Chinatown History Museum
330 Eastern States Buddhist Temple
331 Eldridge St Synagogue
335 Church of the Transfiguration
337 Post Office
339 First Shearith Cemetery

Ice-skating at Wollman Rink in Central Park

ANGUS OBORN

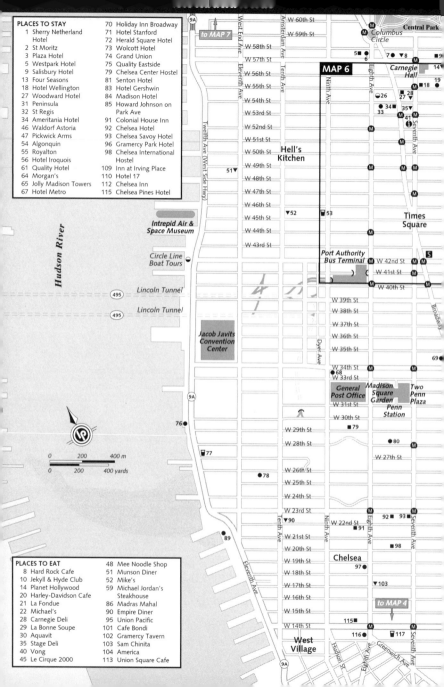

PLACES TO STAY

1 Sherry Netherland Hotel
2 St Moritz
3 Plaza Hotel
5 Westpark Hotel
9 Salisbury Hotel
13 Four Seasons
18 Hotel Wellington
27 Woodward Hotel
31 Peninsula
32 St Regis
34 Ameritania Hotel
46 Waldorf Astoria
47 Pickwick Arms
54 Algonquin
55 Royalton
56 Hotel Iroquois
61 Quality Hotel
64 Morgan's
65 Jolly Madison Towers
67 Hotel Metro
70 Holiday Inn Broadway
71 Hotel Stanford
72 Herald Square Hotel
73 Wolcott Hotel
74 Grand Union
75 Quality Eastside
79 Chelsea Center Hostel
81 Senton Hotel
83 Hotel Gershwin
84 Madison Hotel
85 Howard Johnson on Park Ave
91 Colonial House Inn
92 Chelsea Hotel
93 Chelsea Savoy Hotel
96 Gramercy Park Hotel
98 Chelsea International Hostel
109 Inn at Irving Place
110 Hotel 17
112 Chelsea Inn
115 Chelsea Pines Hotel

PLACES TO EAT

8 Hard Rock Cafe
10 Jekyll & Hyde Club
14 Planet Hollywood
20 Harley-Davidson Cafe
21 La Fondue
22 Michael's
28 Carnegie Deli
29 La Bonne Soupe
30 Aquavit
35 Stage Deli
40 Vong
45 Le Cirque 2000
48 Mee Noodle Shop
51 Munson Diner
52 Mike's
59 Michael Jordan's Steakhouse
86 Madras Mahal
90 Empire Diner
95 Union Pacific
101 Cafe Bondi
102 Gramercy Tavern
103 Sam Chinita
104 America
113 Union Square Cafe

MAP 6

to MAP 7

to MAP 4

Central Park
Columbus Circle
Carnegie Hall
Hell's Kitchen
Times Square
Port Authority Bus Terminal
Intrepid Air & Space Museum
Circle Line Boat Tours
Hudson River
Lincoln Tunnel
Lincoln Tunnel
Jacob Javits Convention Center
General Post Office
Madison Square Garden
Two Penn Plaza
Penn Station
Chelsea
West Village

Central Park W
West End Ave
Amsterdam Ave
Eleventh Ave
Tenth Ave
Ninth Ave
Eighth Ave
Seventh Ave
Broadway
Twelfth Ave (West Side Hwy)
Dyer Ave
Hudson St
Greenwich Ave

W 60th St
W 59th St
W 58th St
W 57th St
W 56th St
W 55th St
W 54th St
W 53rd St
W 52nd St
W 51st St
W 50th St
W 49th St
W 48th St
W 47th St
W 46th St
W 45th St
W 44th St
W 43rd St
W 42nd St
W 41st St
W 40th St
W 39th St
W 38th St
W 37th St
W 36th St
W 35th St
W 34th St
W 33rd St
W 31st St
W 30th St
W 29th St
W 28th St
W 27th St
W 26th St
W 25th St
W 24th St
W 23rd St
W 22nd St
W 21st St
W 20th St
W 19th St
W 18th St
W 17th St
W 16th St
W 15th St
W 14th St

495
9A

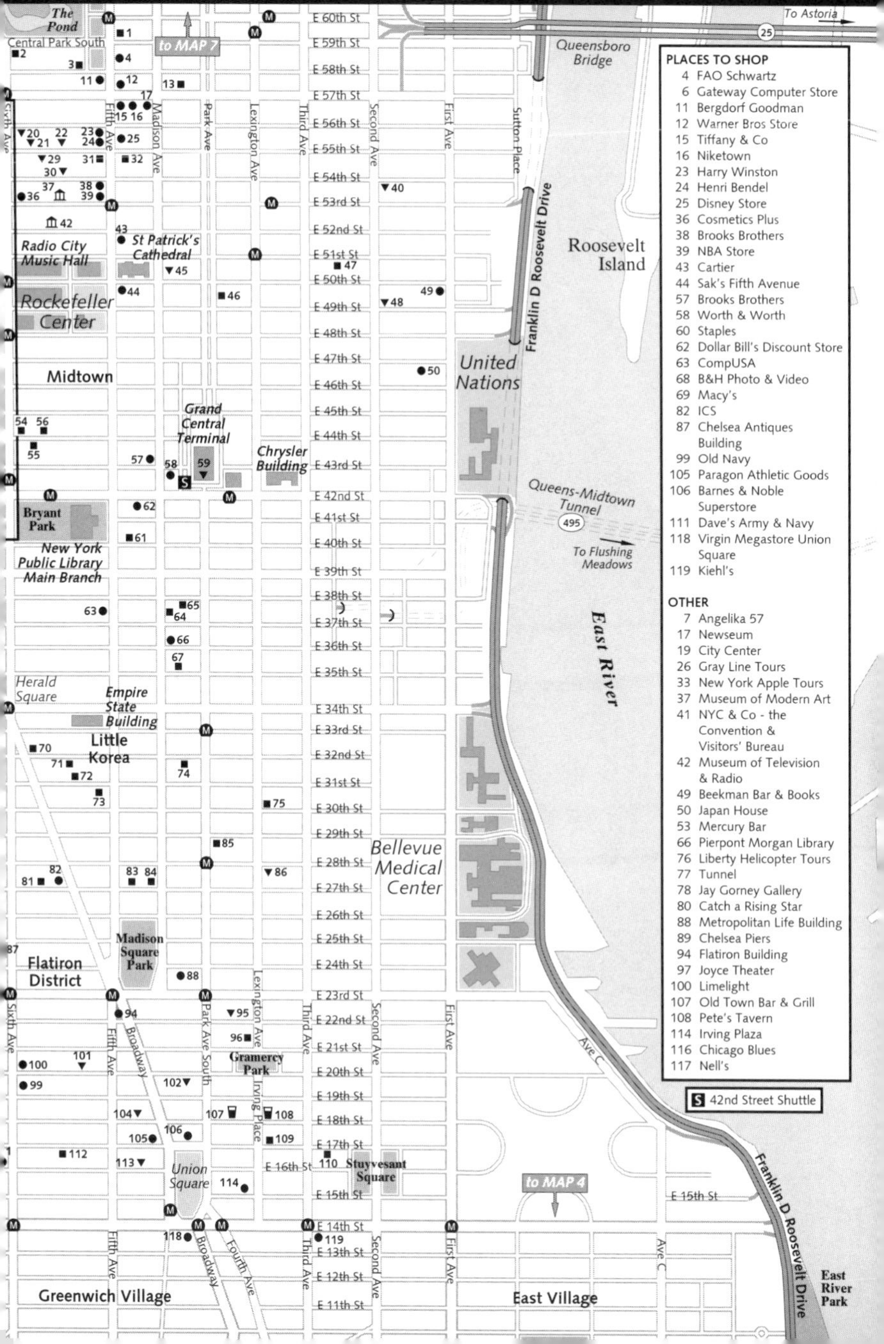

The Pond
Central Park South
to MAP 7

E 60th St
E 59th St
E 58th St
E 57th St
E 56th St
E 55th St
E 54th St
E 53rd St
E 52nd St
E 51st St
E 50th St
E 49th St
E 48th St
E 47th St
E 46th St
E 45th St
E 44th St
E 43rd St
E 42nd St
E 41st St
E 40th St
E 39th St
E 38th St
E 37th St
E 36th St
E 35th St
E 34th St
E 33rd St
E 32nd St
E 31st St
E 30th St
E 29th St
E 28th St
E 27th St
E 26th St
E 25th St
E 24th St
E 23rd St
E 22nd St
E 21st St
E 20th St
E 19th St
E 18th St
E 17th St
E 16th St
E 15th St
E 14th St
E 13th St
E 12th St
E 11th St

Queensboro Bridge
To Astoria
Roosevelt Island
United Nations
Queens-Midtown Tunnel
To Flushing Meadows
East River
Sutton Place
Franklin D Roosevelt Drive
East River Park

Radio City Music Hall
Rockefeller Center
Midtown
St Patrick's Cathedral
Grand Central Terminal
Chrysler Building
Bryant Park
New York Public Library Main Branch
Herald Square
Empire State Building
Little Korea
Madison Square Park
Flatiron District
Gramercy Park
Union Square
Stuyvesant Square
Bellevue Medical Center
Greenwich Village
East Village

Central Park South
Park Avenue
Lexington Ave
Third Ave
Second Ave
First Ave
Ave C
Madison Ave
Fifth Ave
Sixth Ave
Broadway
Park Ave South
Irving Place
Fourth Ave

to MAP 4

PLACES TO SHOP
- 4 FAO Schwartz
- 6 Gateway Computer Store
- 11 Bergdorf Goodman
- 12 Warner Bros Store
- 15 Tiffany & Co
- 16 Niketown
- 23 Harry Winston
- 24 Henri Bendel
- 25 Disney Store
- 36 Cosmetics Plus
- 38 Brooks Brothers
- 39 NBA Store
- 43 Cartier
- 44 Sak's Fifth Avenue
- 57 Brooks Brothers
- 58 Worth & Worth
- 60 Staples
- 62 Dollar Bill's Discount Store
- 63 CompUSA
- 68 B&H Photo & Video
- 69 Macy's
- 82 ICS
- 87 Chelsea Antiques Building
- 99 Old Navy
- 105 Paragon Athletic Goods
- 106 Barnes & Noble Superstore
- 111 Dave's Army & Navy
- 118 Virgin Megastore Union Square
- 119 Kiehl's

OTHER
- 7 Angelika 57
- 17 Newseum
- 19 City Center
- 26 Gray Line Tours
- 33 New York Apple Tours
- 37 Museum of Modern Art
- 41 NYC & Co - the Convention & Visitors' Bureau
- 42 Museum of Television & Radio
- 49 Beekman Bar & Books
- 50 Japan House
- 53 Mercury Bar
- 66 Pierpont Morgan Library
- 76 Liberty Helicopter Tours
- 77 Tunnel
- 78 Jay Gorney Gallery
- 80 Catch a Rising Star
- 88 Metropolitan Life Building
- 89 Chelsea Piers
- 94 Flatiron Building
- 97 Joyce Theater
- 100 Limelight
- 107 Old Town Bar & Grill
- 108 Pete's Tavern
- 114 Irving Plaza
- 116 Chicago Blues
- 117 Nell's

S 42nd Street Shuttle

The bright lights of Times Square

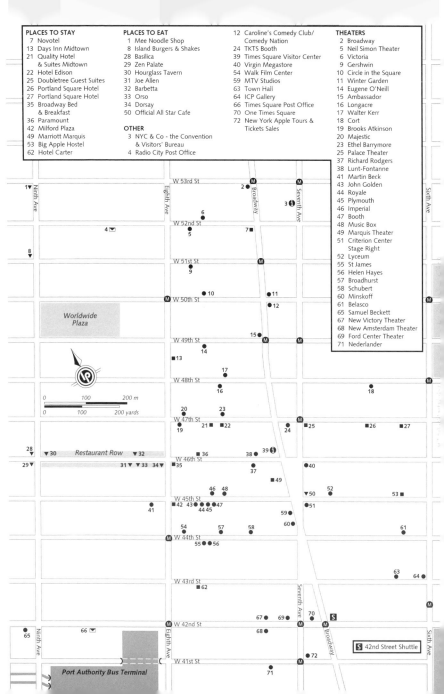

PLACES TO STAY
7 Novotel
13 Days Inn Midtown
21 Quality Hotel
& Suites Midtown
22 Hotel Edison
25 Doubletree Guest Suites
26 Portland Square Hotel
27 Portland Square Hotel
35 Broadway Bed
& Breakfast
36 Paramount
42 Milford Plaza
49 Marriott Marquis
53 Big Apple Hostel
62 Hotel Carter

PLACES TO EAT
1 Mee Noodle Shop
8 Island Burgers & Shakes
28 Basilica
29 Zen Palate
30 Hourglass Tavern
31 Joe Allen
32 Barbetta
33 Orso
34 Dorsay
50 Official All Star Cafe

OTHER
3 NYC & Co - the Convention
& Visitors' Bureau
4 Radio City Post Office

12 Caroline's Comedy Club/
Comedy Nation
24 TKTS Booth
39 Times Square Visitor Center
40 Virgin Megastore
54 Walk Film Center
59 MTV Studios
63 Town Hall
64 ICP Gallery
66 Times Square Post Office
70 One Times Square
72 New York Apple Tours &
Tickets Sales

THEATERS
2 Broadway
5 Neil Simon Theater
6 Victoria
9 Gershwin
10 Circle in the Square
11 Winter Garden
14 Eugene O'Neill
15 Ambassador
16 Longacre
17 Walter Kerr
18 Cort
19 Brooks Atkinson
20 Majestic
23 Ethel Barrymore
25 Palace Theater
37 Richard Rodgers
38 Lunt-Fontanne
41 Martin Beck
43 John Golden
44 Royale
45 Plymouth
46 Imperial
47 Booth
48 Music Box
49 Marquis Theater
51 Criterion Center
Stage Right
52 Lyceum
55 St James
56 Helen Hayes
57 Broadhurst
58 Schubert
60 Minskoff
61 Belasco
65 Samuel Beckett
67 New Victory Theater
68 New Amsterdam Theater
69 Ford Center Theater
71 Nederlander

MAP 7 UPPER WEST SIDE, UPPER EAST SIDE & CENTRAL PARK

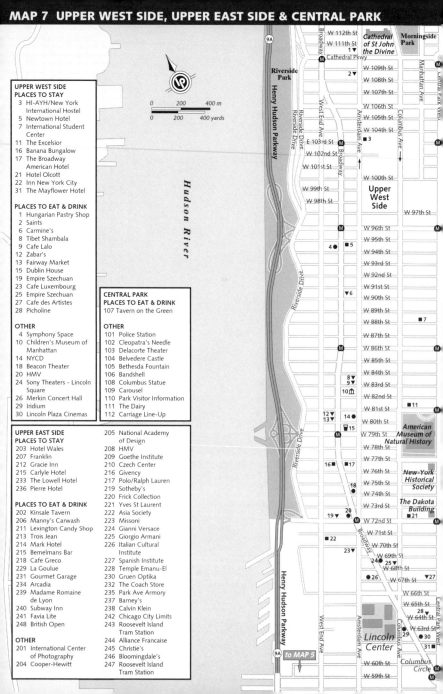

UPPER WEST SIDE
PLACES TO STAY
3 HI-AYH/New York International Hostel
5 Newtown Hotel
7 International Student Center
11 The Excelsior
16 Banana Bungalow
17 The Broadway American Hotel
21 Hotel Olcott
22 Inn New York City
31 The Mayflower Hotel

PLACES TO EAT & DRINK
1 Hungarian Pastry Shop
2 Saints
6 Carmine's
8 Tibet Shambala
9 Cafe Lalo
12 Zabar's
13 Fairway Market
15 Dublin House
19 Empire Szechuan
23 Cafe Luxembourg
25 Empire Szechuan
27 Cafe des Artistes
28 Picholine

OTHER
4 Symphony Space
10 Children's Museum of Manhattan
14 NYCD
18 Beacon Theater
20 HMV
24 Sony Theaters - Lincoln Square
26 Merkin Concert Hall
29 Iridium
30 Lincoln Plaza Cinemas

CENTRAL PARK
PLACES TO EAT & DRINK
107 Tavern on the Green

OTHER
101 Police Station
102 Cleopatra's Needle
103 Delacorte Theater
104 Belvedere Castle
105 Bethesda Fountain
106 Bandshell
108 Columbus Statue
109 Carousel
110 Park Visitor Information
111 The Dairy
112 Carriage Line-Up

UPPER EAST SIDE
PLACES TO STAY
203 Hotel Wales
207 Franklin
212 Gracie Inn
215 Carlyle Hotel
233 The Lowell Hotel
236 Pierre Hotel

PLACES TO EAT & DRINK
202 Kinsale Tavern
206 Manny's Carwash
211 Lexington Candy Shop
213 Trois Jean
214 Mark Hotel
215 Bemelmans Bar
218 Cafe Greco
229 La Goulue
231 Gourmet Garage
234 Arcadia
239 Madame Romaine de Lyon
240 Subway Inn
241 Favia Lite
248 British Open

OTHER
201 International Center of Photography
204 Cooper-Hewitt
205 National Academy of Design
208 HMV
209 Goethe Institute
210 Czech Center
216 Givency
217 Polo/Ralph Lauren
219 Sotheby's
220 Frick Collection
221 Yves St Laurent
222 Asia Society
223 Missoni
224 Gianni Versace
225 Giorgio Armani
226 Italian Cultural Institute
227 Spanish Institute
228 Temple Emanu-El
230 Gruen Optika
232 The Coach Store
235 Park Ave Armory
237 Barney's
238 Calvin Klein
242 Chicago City Limits
243 Roosevelt Island Tram Station
244 Alliance Francaise
245 Christie's
246 Bloomingdale's
247 Roosevelt Island Tram Station

0 200 400 m
0 200 400 yards

Cathedral of St John the Divine
Morningside Park
Riverside Park
Henry Hudson Parkway
Riverside Drive
West End Ave
Amsterdam Ave
Broadway
Columbus Ave
Central Park West
Manhattan Ave

W 112th St
W 111th St
Cathedral Pkwy
W 109th St
W 108th St
W 107th St
W 106th St
W 105th St
E 103rd St
W 104th St
W 102nd St
W 101st St
W 100th St
W 99th St
W 98th St
W 97th St
W 96th St
W 95th St
W 94th St
W 93rd St
W 92nd St
W 91st St
W 90th St
W 89th St
W 88th St
W 87th St
W 86th St
W 85th St
W 84th St
W 83rd St
W 82nd St
W 81st St
W 80th St
W 79th St
W 78th St
W 77th St
W 76th St
W 75th St
W 74th St
W 73rd St
W 72nd St
W 71st St
W 70th St
W 69th St
W 68th St
W 67th St
W 66th St
W 65th St
W 64th St
W 63rd St
W 60th St
W 59th St

Hudson River
Upper West Side
American Museum of Natural History
New-York Historical Society
The Dakota Building
Lincoln Center
Columbus Circle

9A
to MAP 5

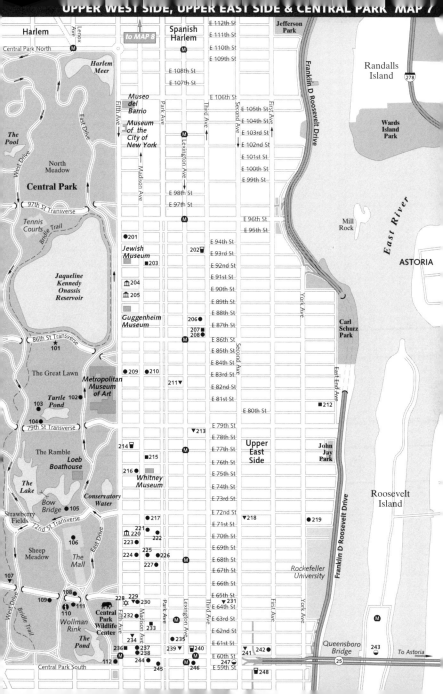

Harlem

Central Park North Ⓜ

Spanish Harlem

Ⓜ

E 112th St
E 111th St
E 110th St
E 109th St

Jefferson Park

Randalls Island
278

Harlem Meer

E 108th St
E 107th St

Lenox Ave

Fifth Ave

Park Ave

Third Ave

Museo del Barrio

E 106th St

Second Ave

First Ave

E 105th St
E 104th St
E 103rd St
E 102nd St
E 101st St
E 100th St
E 99th St

Wards Island Park

Museum of the City of New York

Ⓜ

The Pool

North Meadow

Central Park

Madison Ave

Lexington Ave

E 98th St
E 97th St

Franklin D Roosevelt Drive

East River

Mill Rock

Ⓜ

97th St Transverse

E 96th St
E 95th St

Tennis Courts

Bridle Trail

●201

E 94th St
E 93rd St
E 92nd St
E 91st St
E 90th St
E 89th St
E 88th St

202▜

ASTORIA

Jewish Museum

■203

Jaqueline Kennedy Onassis Reservoir

🏛204
🏛205

York Ave

Carl Schurz Park

Guggenheim Museum

206●
207■
208●

E 87th St
E 86th St
E 85th St
E 84th St
E 83rd St
E 82nd St
E 81st St

Ⓜ

86th St Transverse

101

Second Ave

●209 ●210

211▼

The Great Lawn

Metropolitan Museum of Art

East End Ave

■212

Turtle Pond 102●
103●

E 80th St
E 79th St
E 78th St

104●

79th St Transverse

▼213

The Ramble

Loeb Boathouse

214▜

Ⓜ

E 77th St
E 76th St

Upper East Side

John Jay Park

■215

216●

Whitney Museum

E 75th St
E 74th St
E 73rd St

The Lake

Bow Bridge ●105

Conservatory Water

Roosevelt Island

Strawberry Fields

72nd St Transverse

●217

E 72nd St

▼218

●219

Sheep Meadow

106●

221■
220🏛
223●

222●

225●
224● 226●

227●

E 71st St
E 70th St
E 69th St
E 68th St
E 67th St
E 66th St

Ⓜ

Rockefeller University

Franklin D Roosevelt Drive

107▼

The Mall

East Drive

109●

108●
111●
110

228● 229
▼●230

232■

233●

234●

237■
236■■238

239▼ 240▜

E 65th St
▼231
E 64th St
E 63rd St
E 62nd St
E 61st St
E 60th St
247▜

Central Park Wildlife Center

Ⓜ

First Ave

York Ave

●219

Ⓜ

Queensboro Bridge

243●

To Astoria

Wollman Rink

The Pond

112●

244●

235●

245

246●
Ⓜ

E 59th St

241▼ 242●

Central Park South

248▜

25

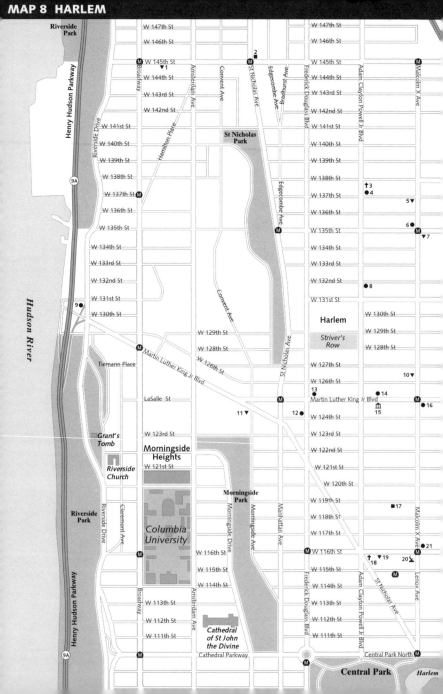

MAP 8 HARLEM

Riverside Park

Henry Hudson Parkway

9A

Hudson River

Riverside Park

Henry Hudson Parkway

9A

Broadway

Riverside Drive

Amsterdam Ave

Hamilton Place

Convent Ave

St Nicholas Ave

Edgecombe Ave

St Nicholas Park

Edgecombe Ave

Convent Ave

St Nicholas Ave

Frederick Douglass Blvd

Adam Clayton Powell Jr Blvd

Malcolm X Ave

W 147th St
W 146th St
W 145th St ▼1
W 144th St
W 143rd St
W 142nd St
W 141st St
W 140th St
W 139th St
W 138th St
W 137th St
W 136th St
W 135th St
W 134th St
W 133rd St
W 132nd St
W 131st St
W 130th St
W 129th St
W 128th St
W 126th St
W 123rd St

W 147th St
W 146th St
W 145th St
W 144th St
W 143rd St
W 142nd St
W 141st St
W 140th St
W 139th St
W 138th St
W 137th St
W 136th St
W 135th St
W 134th St
W 133rd St
W 132nd St
W 131st St
W 130th St

2 ■

†3
●4
5 ▼
6 ●
▼7
●8

Harlem

Striver's Row

W 129th St
W 128th St
W 127th St
W 126th St

10 ▼

13
●

14
●

Martin Luther King Jr Blvd

15

16
●

11 ▼

12 ●

W 124th St
W 123rd St
W 122nd St
W 121st St
W 120th St
W 119th St
W 118th St
W 117th St
W 116th St
W 115th St
W 114th St
W 113th St
W 112th St
W 111th St

Tiemann Place

Martin Luther King Jr Blvd

LaSalle St

Grant's Tomb

Riverside Church

Morningside Heights

W 123rd St
W 121st St

Riverside Drive

Claremont Ave

Columbia University

Broadway

Amsterdam Ave

Morningside Drive

Morningside Ave

Manhattan Ave

Morningside Park

9 ●

17 ■

■17

●21

18 †

▼19

20

Frederick Douglass Blvd

Adam Clayton Powell Jr Blvd

St Nicholas Ave

Malcolm X Ave

Lenox Ave

Cathedral of St John the Divine

Cathedral Parkway

Central Park North

Central Park

Harlem

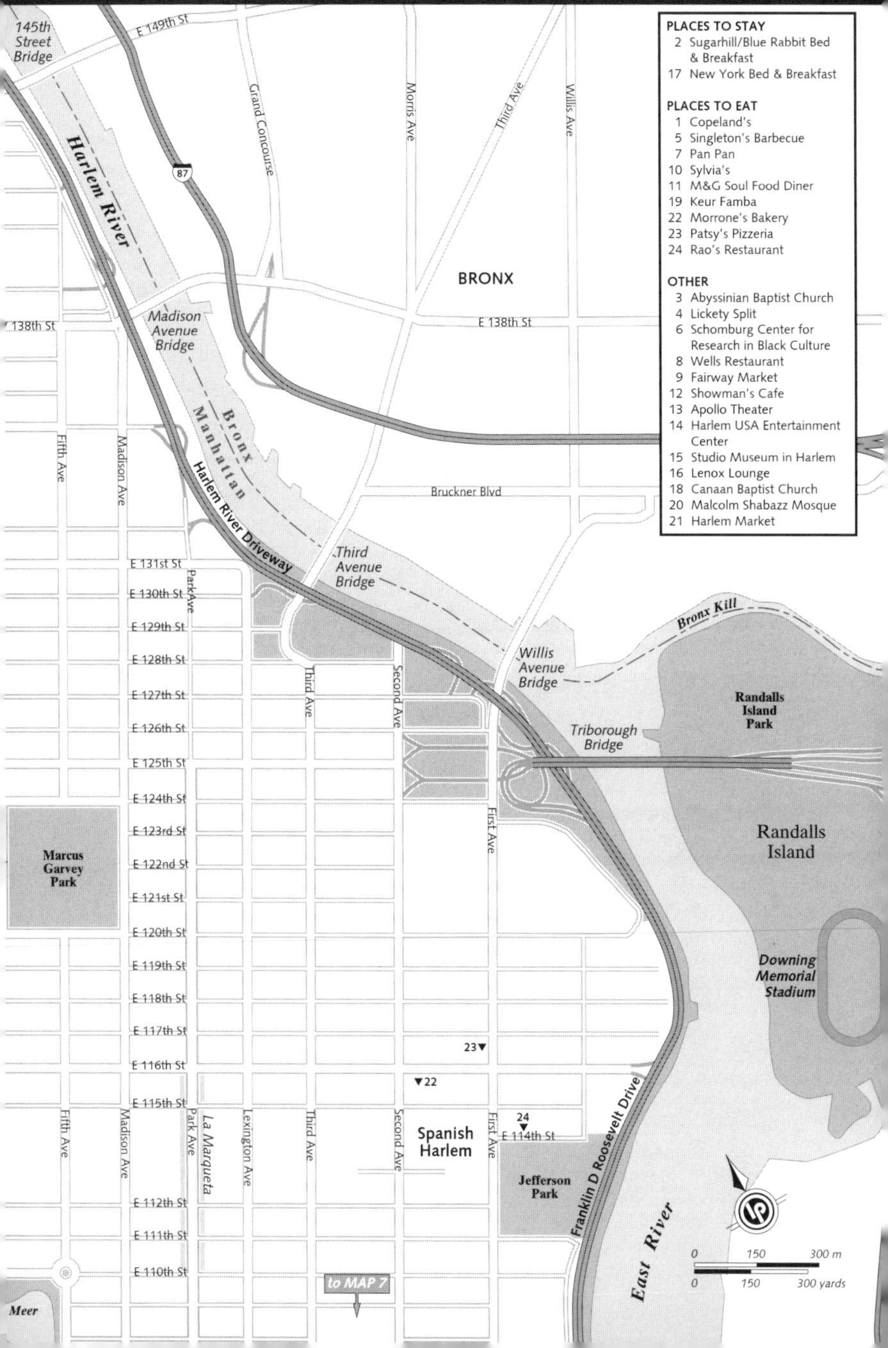

PLACES TO STAY
2 Sugarhill/Blue Rabbit Bed & Breakfast
17 New York Bed & Breakfast

PLACES TO EAT
1 Copeland's
5 Singleton's Barbecue
7 Pan Pan
10 Sylvia's
11 M&G Soul Food Diner
19 Keur Famba
22 Morrone's Bakery
23 Patsy's Pizzeria
24 Rao's Restaurant

OTHER
3 Abyssinian Baptist Church
4 Lickety Split
6 Schomburg Center for Research in Black Culture
8 Wells Restaurant
9 Fairway Market
12 Showman's Cafe
13 Apollo Theater
14 Harlem USA Entertainment Center
15 Studio Museum in Harlem
16 Lenox Lounge
18 Canaan Baptist Church
20 Malcolm Shabazz Mosque
21 Harlem Market

145th Street Bridge
E 149th St
E 145th St
Grand Concourse
Morris Ave
Third Ave
Willis Ave
Harlem River
87
BRONX
E 138th St
Madison Avenue Bridge
138th St
Bronx Manhattan
Harlem River Driveway
Bruckner Blvd
Bronx Kill
Fifth Ave
Madison Ave
Park Ave
Third Avenue Bridge
Third Ave
Second Ave
Willis Avenue Bridge
Triborough Bridge
Randalls Island Park
E 131st St
E 130th St
E 129th St
E 128th St
E 127th St
E 126th St
E 125th St
E 124th St
E 123rd St
E 122nd St
E 121st St
E 120th St
E 119th St
E 118th St
E 117th St
E 116th St
E 115th St
First Ave
Randalls Island
Downing Memorial Stadium
Marcus Garvey Park
Fifth Ave
Madison Ave
Park Ave
La Marqueta
Lexington Ave
Third Ave
Second Ave
Spanish Harlem
First Ave
23▼
▼22
24
E 114th St
Jefferson Park
Franklin D Roosevelt Drive
E 112th St
E 111th St
E 110th St
Meer
East River

to MAP 7

0   150   300 m
0   150   300 yards

continued from page 160

The galleries are on the 2nd floor, beyond a vast rotunda featuring statues of famous navigators and murals celebrating shipping history. This museum does little to explain the history of Native Americans, but instead concentrates its collection on Native American identity as reflected in its million-item collection of crafts and everyday objects. Computer touch-screens offer views on Native American life and beliefs, and working artists are often available to explain their techniques. A gift shop offers Native American jewelry for sale.

This facility will no doubt be overshadowed somewhat by a museum being constructed in Washington, DC. But for New York visitors, it's worth a look. It's open daily 10 am to 5 pm, with free admission (subway: Bowling Green).

South Street Seaport

This 11-block enclave of shops and historic sights (☎ 212-732-7678) is visited each year by over 12 million people, and combines the best and worst in historic preservation. **Pier 17**, beyond the elevated FDR Drive, is a waterfront development project that's home to a number of shops and overpriced restaurants. But the area also contains a number of genuinely significant buildings from the 18th and 19th centuries. These buildings once surrounded this old East River ferry port, but the port fell into disuse when the Brooklyn Bridge was built and deep-water piers were established on the Hudson River.

Schermerhorn Row is a block of old warehouses bordered by Fulton, Front and South Sts. It contains novelty shops, seafood restaurants and a pub. The **Fulton Market Building**, built across the street in 1983 to reflect the redbrick style of its older neighbors, is nothing more than a glorified fast-food hall and shopping arcade.

The **South Street Seaport Museum** (☎ 212-748-8600) runs several interesting sights in the area, including three galleries, an antique printing shop, a children's center, a maritime crafts center and historic ships.

These are all open daily 10 am to 5 pm, and admission to the collection of buildings costs $6 for adults, $5 for seniors, $4 for students and $3 for children. Permanent exhibitions offer a glimpse of the seaport's history and a survey of the world's great ocean liners (subway: Fulton St).

Harbor Tours Just south of Pier 17 stands a group of tall-masted sailing vessels, including the *Peking*, the *Wavertree*, the *Pioneer* and the lightship *Ambrose*. All can be inspected with the price of admission to the museum. A booth on Pier 16 also sells tickets for the Seaport Liberty Cruise Line's (☎ 212-630-8888) hour-long riverboat excursion that highlights Manhattan's maritime history. Tours run at least three times each day from April to the end of November and cost between $12 and $25. Pioneer Sail (☎ 212-748-8590) offers sailing trips on the East River and sunset tours.

New York Waterways (☎ 800-533-3779) has 45-minute river cruises on the river that depart from Pier 17 (prices range from $25 to $45, depending on the trip). It also offers direct service by water taxi to New York Yankee and New York Mets baseball games during the summer. (See Lower Manhattan map for location.)

Fulton Fish Market Pier 17 is also the site of the Fulton Fish Market (☎ 212-669-9416), where most of the city's restaurants get their fresh seafood. The market is a perfect example of how this area maintains its old character while still catering to tourists. The facility has long been thought to be controlled by an organized crime family, and a federal and city government crackdown on corruption led to months of labor unrest and a suspicious 1995 fire that destroyed a part of the market.

Nevertheless, visitors can see the nightly workings of the market from midnight to 8 am, and guided tours (☎ 212-664-9416) are available from April to October.

City Hall

City Hall (☎ 212-788-6865), along Park Row near the entrance to the Brooklyn Bridge, has been home to New York's government since 1812. In an example of the half-baked civic planning that has often plagued big New York projects, officials neglected to finish the building's northern side in marble, betting that the city would not expand uptown! The mistake was finally rectified in 1954, completing a structure that architecture critic Ada Louise Huxtable has called a 'symbol of taste, excellence and quality not always matched by the policies inside.' On either side of the building stands 'The Key to City Hall,' an interactive video center with information on local landmarks and visitor services.

Walk to the 2nd floor to the spot at the top of the stairs where, in 1865, Abraham Lincoln's coffin was placed on its way from Washington, DC, to Springfield, IL, so that New Yorkers could pay their respects to the defender of the Union. The Governor's Room, a reception area used by the mayor for important guests, contains 12 portraits by John Trumbull of the founding fathers, several examples of Federal furniture, including George Washington's writing table, and the remnants of a flag flown at his 1789 presidential inaugural ceremony. Peeking into the City Council chambers may reveal the lawmakers deliberating the renaming of a city street in someone's honor, an activity which accounts for about 40% of all the bills passed by the 51 member body.

The steps of City Hall's are a popular site for demonstrations and press conferences by politicians, including the mayor. Don't be discouraged by the less than welcoming security presence – the building is open to the public weekdays 10 am to 4 pm (subway: City Hall).

Brooklyn Bridge

This was the first steel suspension bridge ever built; the 1596-foot span between its two support towers was the world's longest when it opened in 1883. It is regarded by many to be the most beautiful bridge in the world and is a magnificent example of fine urban design.

Plans for a suspension bridge spanning the East River were drawn up by the Prussian-born engineer John Roebling. Unfortunately, he was knocked off a pier by a ferry in Fulton's Landing in June 1869 and died of tetanus poisoning before construction of the bridge began. His son Washington Roebling supervised construction of the bridge, which took 14 years to build and was plagued by budget overruns and the deaths of 20 workers. The younger Roebling was stricken by the bends while helping to excavate the riverbed for the bridge's western tower and supervised the project largely from his bed. There was one final tragedy to come in June of 1883, when the bridge opened to pedestrian traffic: Someone in the crowd shouted, perhaps as a joke, that the bridge was collapsing into the river, setting off a mad rush in which 12 people were trampled to death.

There's no fear of collapse today. The bridge enters its second century following an extensive renovation in the early 1980s. The pedestrian walkway that begins just east of City Hall affords a wonderful view of Lower Manhattan, and you can stop at observation points under both stone support towers and view brass panorama histories of the waterfront at various points in New York's past. Once you reach the Brooklyn side (about a 20-minute walk) you can bear left to walk down to Cadman Plaza West to a park that will bring you to Middagh St, which runs east to west in the heart of Brooklyn Heights. Bearing right brings you to Brooklyn's downtown area, which includes the ornate Borough Hall and the Fulton St pedestrian mall (subway: Fulton St). See the Brooklyn Heights map and the Brooklyn section of this chapter for more coverage.

Fraunces Tavern Museum & Restaurant

Fraunces Tavern (☎ 212-425-1778), 54 Pearl St, is on a block of historic structures that, along with nearby Stone St and the South Street Seaport, are the final examples of colonial-era New York that remain largely intact – the buildings here can be traced to the early 18th century.

Here stood the Queen's Head Tavern, owned by Samuel Fraunces, who changed the name to Fraunces Tavern after the American victory in the War for Independence. It

Museum Bargains

First time visitors especially are advised to buy the CityPass. This card is good for nine days and costs $32 ($24 for children 13 to 18 and $21.75 for seniors). With it, you will receive admission to the American Museum of Natural History, the World Trade Center observation deck, the observatory of the Empire State Building, the galleries of the Solomon R Guggenheim Museum, the Intrepid Sea, Air & Space Museum and the Museum of Modern Art. (These sites are all described in detail in this chapter.) You can save up to $32 by using the pass, which can be purchased at any of the museums mentioned above or at the Information Center at 810 Seventh Ave, between 52nd and 53rd Sts.

was in the 2nd-floor dining room on December 4, 1783, that George Washington bade farewell to the officers of the Continental Army after the British relinquished control of New York City. In the 19th century, the tavern closed and the building fell into disuse. It was also damaged during several massive fires that swept through old downtown areas and destroyed most colonial buildings and nearly all structures built by the Dutch. In 1904, the building was bought by the Sons of the Revolution historical society and returned to an approximation of its colonial-era look – an act believed to be the first major attempt at historic preservation in the US.

The museum is open weekdays 10 am to 4:45 pm and Saturday noon to 4 pm. Admission is $2.50/1 for adults/children.

Just across the street from the tavern are the excavated remains of the Old Dutch **Stadt Huys**, which served as New Amsterdam's administrative center, courthouse and jail from 1641 until the peaceful British takeover in 1664. This building, destroyed in 1699, was originally on the city's waterfront until landfill added a few more blocks to southern Manhattan (subway: Whitehall St).

World Trade Center

The massive twin towers of the World Trade Center (WTC; ☎ 212-323-2340) rise 1350 feet above the square at the corner of Church and Vesey Sts. The towers are part of a complex that houses more than 350 different businesses employing 50,000 people. Built at a cost of $700 million from 1966-73, the sleek WTC has never stirred people's hearts in the same manner as the Empire State Building. But the project did change the city in a profound way: the 1 million cubic yards of rock and dirt unearthed for its foundation became the landfill on which the 24-acre Battery Park City development was constructed.

The WTC's twin towers attract daredevils: George Willig, who used mountain climbing equipment to scale the side of one building, and circus performer Philippe Petit, who used a crossbow to run a tightrope across both buildings and – without authorities stopping him – put on a show a quarter-mile above the ground. The observation deck also attracted two parachutists who got away with jumping off the building and landing in Battery Park.

The WTC's array of federal and state government offices made it a tempting target for the terrorists who set off a truck bomb in the underground parking garage on February 26, 1993, killing six people. A discreet memorial to those who perished in the blast is on the WTC plaza.

The ticket booth for the WTC observation decks is open daily 9:30 am to 11:30 pm June to September and 9:30 am to 9:30 pm the remainder of the year. Admission is $13 for adults, $6.50 for children younger than 12 and $9.50 for seniors. One way around the charge is to be well dressed and visit the Greatest Bar on Earth (☎ 212-524-7011), at Windows on the World on the 107th floor of One World Trade Center. It offers a great view for the price of a drink. (Although the Empire State Building offers similar views, cheaper admission prices and a Midtown location, it is a more popular choice, and, as a result, it has longer lines.)

The **Commodities Exchange Center** (☎ 212-938-2025) is within the complex on the 9th floor of 4 World Trade Center, but no longer offers views of its trading floor. The shopping plaza located on the subway level underneath the buildings was the first indoor mall to open in New York City (subway: Cortland St).

World Financial Center This complex, at West and Vesey Sts, just behind the WTC, stands on the landfill created by the excavation of the WTC's foundation. This group of four office towers surrounds the **Winter Garden**, a glass atrium and ostentatious centerpiece that is the site of free concerts during the summer and exclusive black-tie events year-round. During good weather it's pleasant to visit the Winter Garden or walk, run or bike down the mile-long esplanade that runs from the Battery Park City apartments to the north, past the World Financial Center, to the tip of Manhattan. When it's rainy you can pass an hour in the shopping area and art gallery next to the Winter Garden. The Liberty St Gallery, 225 Liberty Place, has a number of worthwhile exhibitions and there's a museum-quality autograph store in the enclosed shopping plaza.

TRIBECA (MAP 4)
This neighborhood of old warehouses, loft apartments and funky restaurants derives its name from its geographical location: the 'TRIangle BElow CAnal' St, an area roughly bordered by Broadway to the east and Chambers St to the south. Though not as touristed or architecturally significant as SoHo, its northern neighbor, Tribeca is the place for a fair number of 'scene' restaurants and bars, along with actor Robert De Niro's Tribeca Films production company.

Most of the warehouses retain long truck-loading platforms covered by metal awnings and make great apartment spaces. As such, the neighborhood is not yet overrun with the boutiques and chain stores that have driven some art galleries and plenty of well-heeled residents out of SoHo. Tribeca is now well known as the neighborhood where the late John F Kennedy Jr resided. In the winter it's not unusual to spot a movie star

such as Harvey Keitel or Robert De Niro hanging out at a local restaurant.

The eight townhouses on the block of Harrison St immediately west of Greenwich St were all built between 1804 and 1828 and constitute the largest collection of Federal architecture left in the city. But they were not always neighbors: Six of them once stood two blocks away on a stretch of Washington St that no longer exists. In the early 1970s, that area was the site of Washington Market, a wholesale center that was the fruit and vegetable equivalent of the Fulton Fish Market. A new home had to be found for the row houses when the market was relocated uptown to allow the development of the waterfront, including Manhattan Community College and the unattractive concrete apartment complex that now looms over the townhouses. Only the buildings at 31 and 33 Harrison St remain where they were originally constructed.

The Franklin St subway station is in the heart of Tribeca, or you can get to the neighborhood's northern border by taking the A, C or E train to Canal St and walking south on West Broadway.

New York City Fire Museum
The museum (☎ 212-691-1303), 278 Spring St, occupies a grand old firehouse that dates back to 1904. There's a well-maintained collection of gleaming gold horse-drawn fire fighting carriages as well as modern-day fire engines. The development of the New York City fire fighting system, which began with the 'bucket brigades,' is also explained. All the colorful equipment and the museum's particularly friendly staff make this a great place to bring children, even though they are not allowed to hop on any of the engines.

The museum is open 10 am to 4 pm Tuesday to Saturday; suggested admission is $4 for adults and $1 for children (subway: Spring St).

CHINATOWN & LITTLE ITALY (MAP 4)
Chinatown and Little Italy are renowned as ethnic enclaves just north of the Civic

Center and the financial district; Chinatown largely sprawls south of Canal St, and Little Italy is a narrow sliver extending north of the same thoroughfare.

There are about 130,000 Chinese-speakers in Chinatown. This community, with its own rhythms and traditions, is catered to in different ways: Some banks along Canal St keep Sunday hours, and no fewer than six Chinese newspapers are available on newsstands. Since the mid-1990s, Chinatown has also been home to a growing community of Vietnamese immigrants who have set up their own shops and incredibly cheap restaurants here.

In contrast, Little Italy is confined largely to Mulberry St north of Canal St. This was once a very strong Italian neighborhood (film director Martin Scorsese grew up on Elizabeth St), and although many of the apartment buildings in this 10-block radius are still owned by Italian Americans, there was an exodus from Little Italy in the mid-20th century to the Cobble Hill section of Brooklyn and to the city's suburbs.

For that reason, there are few cultural sites, and most people come to Little Italy specifically to eat, even though there are dozens of good restaurants elsewhere that serve Italian cuisine at all price levels.

Off Mulberry St, on Elizabeth and Lafayette Sts, Little Italy begins to take on a more cosmopolitan character, as the overflow of SoHo-style shops, cafes and restaurants make their way into the area. This is now known as 'NoHo.'

Walking Tour

For a tour of Chinatown, start on Canal St (subway: Canal St). West of Lafayette St, Canal St maintains a decidedly seedy character, with hardware and electrical supply stores co-existing with street vendors selling phony designer clothing and bootleg videos of films still playing in theaters. If you buy anything off a street-seller, make sure it's something you can wear or check out on the spot – a hat, a book or a leather jacket.

The Chinese shopping district begins east of Baxter St, with several stands selling fresh fish and exotic produce, including guavas

and durians, the infamously smelly fruit banned from the subways of Singapore.

Crossing Mott St (east of Lafayette St) brings you to most of the district's restaurants. The **Eastern States Buddhist Temple** (☎ 212-966-4753), in a storefront at 64B Mott St, is a busy shrine with dozens of golden and porcelain Buddhas on display. You can buy a fortune for a donation and watch the devout make their offerings.

The **Church of the Transfiguration**, at 29 Mott St, began as an Episcopal church in 1801 and was purchased by the Roman Catholic Church 50 years later to meet the needs of what was then an Irish and Italian neighborhood. In the 1890s the ascendant and spiteful Irish church leaders forced Italian patrons to worship in the basement. The church got its first Chinese pastor in the 1970s and today holds services in Chinese.

Turning left on Pell St, an old road named for a butcher who plied his trade here in the colonial period, brings you to Doyers St. Chinatown began in this small enclave in the 1870s when Chinese railway workers, fed up with racial discrimination in the American West, moved to New York City in large numbers. During Chinese New Year celebrations in late January and early February, papier-mâché dragons snake their way around this corner to the sounds of firecrackers shooing away evil spirits.

Exiting Doyers St brings you toward two examples of the neighborhood's previous ethnic history. **Chatham Square** is where public auctions took place to sell the goods of Irish debtors in the early 19th century. Walking 150 yards south on St James Place brings you to **First Shearith Israel Graveyard**. This cemetery, which dates back to the 1680s, served early Portuguese and Spanish immigrants and is the oldest Jewish cemetery in the US.

Turning around and heading north brings you up to the Bowery and to the grand but pollution-marred entrance to the Manhattan Bridge. Heading four blocks west of Mulberry St on Canal St brings you to **Cortlandt Alley**, a perfectly preserved four-block enclave of gloomy old factories and warehouses that is often featured in movies – it's worth a quick exploration.

Museum of Chinese in the Americas

The nonprofit Museum of Chinese in the Americas (☎ 212-619-4785), 70 Mulberry St, is on the 2nd floor of a former public school building. The museum sponsors walking tours and crafts workshops (paper lantern-making and other creative endeavors). Recent exhibits include 80 works (made while in captivity) by the survivors of the *Golden Venture*, a ship full of illegal immigrants from China that ran aground near New York Harbor in 1993. Thirty-three of the Chinese who crossed over on the ship were detained by the US immigration service for more than three years.

The museum is open noon to 5 pm Tuesday to Sunday. Admission is $3/1 for adults/children; it is free for children younger than 12 (subway: Canal St).

Little Italy Sights

The **Old Police Headquarters** at 240 Centre St is an example of how public officials in New York often approved the construction of European-style monuments without providing proper setback space or park land to allow passersby to fully appreciate the buildings' grandeur. This building overwhelms its neighbors, just as it did upon its completion in 1909. It was converted into apartment units in 1988.

The **Old St Patrick's Cathedral** (☎ 212-226-8075), 263 Mulberry St, appears bland and unimpressive due to a fire that destroyed much of its exterior. But the structure served as the city's first Roman Catholic Cathedral from 1809-78, until its more famous successor was built uptown on Fifth Ave. The old cathedral and its damaged Georgian interior can be viewed only during weekend services, Saturday at 5 pm and Sunday at 9:30 am and 12:30 pm. In 1999, the cathedral was the site of the memorial mass for John F Kennedy Jr, who lived nearby.

As you continue up Mulberry to Houston St, you will reach the back of the stunning redbrick **Puck Building**, the home of the turn-of-the-century American humor magazine. The building, with its two gold-leaf statues of the portly Puck, is a popular spot for wedding receptions and film shoots; it is not open to the public.

The subway station at Grand St makes a good starting point for touring Little Italy.

LOWER EAST SIDE (MAP 4)

The Lower East Side is probably one of the most desirable entry-level neighborhoods in the city. More than a dozen no-name bars and late-night lounges have opened in the four-block area on and around Ludlow St, which runs south from Houston St. On Saturday night, the streets are packed with grunge rockers, dance-club addicts and underage drinkers.

Architecturally, this storied old-tenement area still retains its hardscrabble character, with block after block of crumbling buildings. You can still see why early-20th-century residents – about half a million Jews from Eastern Europe who worked in factories in the area – lamented that 'the sun was embarrassed to shine' on their benighted neighborhood.

But like Little Italy, the Lower East Side has lost most of its traditional ethnic flavor. There is a small Jewish community left here, served by several traditional businesses. The people living behind the crumbling doorways of the contemporary Lower East Side are more likely to be young people living in their first city apartment or long-term residents holding onto rent-controlled apartments. Also, a growing Latino community has spilled across the Lower East Side's northern border, and the Chinese have been moving into the area south of Delancey St.

The subway station at Second Ave (reached via the F train) makes a good starting point for touring the Lower East Side.

Orchard St

The 'Orchard St Bargain District' is the market area above Delancey St defined by Orchard, Ludlow and Essex Sts (it runs east to west). This is where Eastern European merchants set up pushcarts to sell their wares when this was still a largely Jewish neighborhood. A free tour of the district leaves each Sunday at 11 am from Katz's Deli, which is on the corner of Ludlow and Houston Sts.

Today, the 300-odd shops in this modern-day bazaar sell sporting goods, leather belts, hats and a wide array of off-brand 'designer fashions.' Although the businesses are not exclusively owned by Orthodox Jews, they still close early on Friday afternoon and remain shuttered Saturday in observance of the Sabbath. There's an unspoken rule that shop owners should offer their first customer of the day a discount – usually 10% – for good luck, so it helps to arrive at 10 am if you're serious about buying something. Offering to pay in cash may also attract a discount.

There's not much for sale in the Lower East Side that you couldn't pick up elsewhere in the city, with the exception of **kosher food products**. You can buy kosher wine at Schapiro's Wines (☎ 212-674-4404), 126 Rivington St. This winery offers a tour of its facilities each Sunday (call ahead for information). You can pick up unleavened bread at Streit's Matzoh Company, 150 Rivington St; potato knishes at Yonah Shimmel Bakery, 137 E Houston St, and sweet and sour pickles directly out of the wooden barrels at Essex Pickles, on Essex St.

Lower East Side Tenement Museum

The neighborhood's heartbreaking heritage is preserved at this museum. The gallery (☎ 212-431-0233), 90 Orchard St, is open 11 am to 5 pm Tuesday through Sunday. It includes a video presentation on the difficult life endured by the people who once lived in the surrounding area – often in buildings that did not even have running water or electricity.

Across the street, the museum has recreated a turn-of-the-20th-century tenement owned by Lucas Glockner, a German-born tailor. This building, in which an estimated 10,000 people lived over a 72-year period, is accessible only by guided tour. The tours leave Tuesday through Friday at 1, 2 and 3 pm and every half-hour on the weekend

from 11 am to 4:45 pm. On weekends from April through December there is an interactive display and walking tour of the neighborhood; tours leave at 1 pm and 2:30 pm (reservations are recommended).

Tickets to the museum, including the tenement tour, are $8/6 for adults/seniors and children. A combination ticket for a walking tour and admission to the museum is $14 for adults and $10 for seniors and children.

Synagogues

Nearby, the tenement museum, near the corner of Rivington and Orchard Sts, is the **First Roumanian-American Congregation** (☎ 212-673-2835), 89 Rivington St, one of the few remaining Orthodox synagogues in the Lower East Side (400 once thrived in the neighborhood in the early 20th century). The building, somewhat restored to past glory, features a wonderfully ornate wooden sanctuary that can hold 1800 of the faithful, but membership has dwindled.

The landmark **Eldridge St Synagogue** (☎ 212-219-0888), 12 Eldridge St, east of the Bowery between Canal and Division Sts, is another struggling place of worship in an area that is now completely part of Chinatown. The Moorish-style synagogue faces one of the oldest surviving blocks of tenements in New York City (subway: Grand St).

SOHO (MAP 4)

This neighborhood is not named after its London counterpart but is a geographic conceit for the rectangular area 'SOuth of HOuston St' that extends as far down as Canal St. No one really knows for sure why Houston St is pronounced HOW-ston, though it is assumed that a man named William Houstoun who lived in the area pronounced his surname in that manner. (Somewhere along the line the second 'u' in the spelling of the street was dropped.)

SoHo is a paradigm of inadvertent modern urban renewal. The district is filled with block after block of cast-iron industrial buildings that date to the period just after the Civil War, when the area was the city's leading commercial district. These multi-story buildings housed linen, ribbon and clothing factories, and there were often showcase galleries on the street level. But the area fell into disfavor as retail businesses relocated uptown and manufacturing concerns moved out of the city. By the 1950s the huge lofts and cheap rents attracted artists and other members of the avant-garde. Their political lobbying not only saved the neighborhood from destruction but assured that a 26-block area was declared a legally protected historic district in 1973. Today, SoHo is the city's leading area for art galleries, clothing stores and boutiques.

It's preferable to visit SoHo on a weekday morning, when the neighborhood is populated largely by the people who work in the galleries and assorted offices. True to the downtown clichés, these office workers are dressed invariably in sleek black outfits and wear some of the most adventurous eyewear you'll see in the city. On Saturday and Sunday, West Broadway (a separate street from Broadway) becomes a sea of suede, and it, and nearby Prince St, are packed with tourists and street artists selling homemade jewelry and paintings in defiance of the laws requiring a city license to sell such wares. A few vendors have been arrested for this, and a democracy wall covered with handbills protesting the police crackdown is on Prince St near the corner of Mercer St (subway: Spring St, Houston St or Lafayette St).

Walking Tour

Begin your exploration of SoHo by taking the subway to the Broadway-Lafayette St station and walking south down Broadway.

On the very first block you will encounter three fine art museums described in detail further on: the African Museum, the New Museum of Contemporary Art and the Guggenheim SoHo. Just past Prince St, on the right side of Broadway, is the **Singer Building**, 561-563 Broadway, a very attractive iron-and-brick structure that was the main warehouse for the famous sewing machine company. At 521-523 Broadway, above the fabric store and gourmet food shop, you can see what's left of the marble-faced **St Nicholas Hotel**, the 1000-room

The Gallery Scene

New York's art galleries used to be clustered in SoHo and on the Upper East Side on Madison Ave above 59th St. But as the downtown neighborhood became popular with tourists, the gallery owners began looking for new neighborhoods.

Art dealer Mary Boone, who launched the careers of Julian Schnabel, David Salle and Jean-Michel Basquiat, has moved her gallery from SoHo to 745 Fifth Ave (☎ 212-752-2929). Paula Cooper followed the trend outwards by going to Chelsea (☎ 212-255-1105), 524 W 21st St, as did Jay Gorney (☎ 212-966-8545), 526 W 26th St.

However, some of SoHo's other stalwarts still have a presence in SoHo, starting with the gallery of the late-art titan Leo Castelli (☎ 212-431-5160), 420 W Broadway. Castelli, who died in 1999, represented many contemporary greats at this location and at his other gallery at 59 E 79th St (☎ 212-249-4470). Ileana Sonnabend (☎ 212-966-6160) is at the same address on the 3rd floor.

There are also a number of influential galleries on Wooster St, which parallels West Broadway immediately to the east, including the Howard Greenberg Gallery (☎ 212-334-0010), 120 Wooster St, which specializes in photography, and Edward Thorpe (☎ 212-431-6880), 103 Prince St.

Information on current displays is available in the free monthly *NY/SOHO* map that is available in downtown galleries, or scan the 'Goings on about Town' section in the *New Yorker* or the entertainment section of the Sunday *New York Times*. The best Internet resource for information on galleries is www.artseensoho.com.

luxury hotel that was *the* place to stay when it opened in 1854. The hotel, which closed in 1880, was the headquarters of Abraham Lincoln's War Department during the Civil War years.

As you walk through SoHo, stop to look up at the buildings you're passing – many still have elaborate, decorated flourishes that have been obscured or destroyed on the street level. A perfect example is the **Haughwout Building** that houses the Staples office supply store at 488 Broadway. This was once the headquarters of the EV Haughwout Crockery Company. Built in 1857, it was the first building to use the exotic steam 'elevator' developed by Elisha Otis.

One block further south, at Grand St, you will encounter a parking lot that is the site of an unremarkable antique market on Sunday. Turning right and walking west four blocks will bring you to West Broadway; near this corner you will find a half dozen late-night restaurants and bars that are worth checking out for a drink.

On the southeast corner of the intersection of Prince and Greene Sts, you will see a local landmark: Artist Richard Haas' now fading mural of the front of an apartment building is painted on the bare brick wall of 112 Prince St.

Museum for African Art

This facility (☎ 212-966-1313), 593 Broadway, is the city's only space dedicated solely to the works of African artists, and there's a heavy concentration on tribal crafts, musical instruments and works depicting spirituality. The interior of the museum was designed by Maya Lin, the young architect who first gained fame for her stunning Vietnam Memorial in Washington, DC. It's open 10:30 am to 5:30 pm Tuesday to Friday and noon to 6 pm weekends; admission is $5 for adults and $2.50 for students.

New Museum of Contemporary Art

This museum (☎ 212-219-1222), 583 Broadway, is at the vanguard of the contemporary SoHo scene and exhibits art works that are less than 10 years old. Therefore, you may see the works of artists that you aren't familiar with. The museum is open Sunday and Wednesday noon to 6 pm and Thursday to Saturday noon to 8 pm. Admission is $6 for adults, $3 for artists, students and seniors and free for those younger than 18.

Guggenheim Museum SoHo

The Solomon R Guggenheim Museum's downtown branch (☎ 212-423-3500), 575 Broadway, was part of the extensive renovation and expansion that tripled the museum's showcase space. The SoHo branch also lent legitimacy to the neighborhood's claim of being the center of the US arts scene. In addition to featuring works by living artists in mid-career, the museum's two floors sometime offer works from the uptown Guggenheim's permanent collection. A recent exhibition featured Andy Warhol's *Last Supper* – a series of works inspired by the Da Vinci masterpiece; it was Warhol's last work before his death in 1987.

The Guggenheim SoHo is open 11 am to 6 pm Thursday to Monday and is closed Tuesday and Wednesday. Admission is free (subway: Spring St).

GREENWICH VILLAGE (MAP 4)

This storied neighborhood is one of the city's most popular, and it was once a symbol for all things outlandish and bohemian. Today, it's more associated with clubs, restaurants and exclusive, expensive brownstone apartments.

Generally defined by a northern border on 14th St and a southern demarcation on Houston St, Greenwich Village runs from Lafayette St all the way west to the Hudson River. The area just south of Washington Square Park (including Bleecker St running west all the way to Seventh Ave) is a lively and somewhat overcrowded collection of cafes, shops and restaurants. Beyond Seventh Ave is the West Village, a pleasant neighborhood of winding streets and townhouses (subway: W 4th St or Christopher St).

History

Greenwich Village began as a trading port for the Native Americans who liked the easy access to the shores of what is now Hoboken, NJ, just across the Hudson River. Dutch settlers established a number of tobacco plantations, and the peaceful wooded area was named Greenwich Village by their English successors. As the city began to develop a large servant class, Greenwich Village became New York's most prominent black neighborhood; just before the 1920s, many of those residents moved to Harlem in search of better housing.

Its reputation as a creative enclave can be traced back to at least the early 20th century when artists and writers moved in, and by the '40s the neighborhood was known as a gathering place for gays. The center of 'the Village' is dominated by New York University, which owns most of the property around Washington Square Park, and the brownstone buildings abandoned by blacks all those years ago are now some of the most fashionable and valuable properties in the city.

Walking Tour

The best place to start is the arch at **Washington Square Park**. Head south on Thompson St past a series of chess shops where Village denizens meet to play the game at the cost of $2 an hour. At the intersection of Thompson and Bleecker Sts (Bleecker being the main east-west thoroughfare in Greenwich Village), look up at the southwest corner and you will see the old sign for the legendary jazz club **Village Gate**, which has since relocated to Midtown.

Turn right on Bleecker St and head east for two blocks, which will bring you to two old coffeehouses associated with New York's '50s beatnik culture: **Le Figaro**, which still has a worthwhile weekend jazz brunch, and **Cafe Borgia**. You're better off taking a quick look around Bleecker St and then taking a right onto MacDougal St. There, you'll find a great cup of cappuccino at **Caffe Reggio**, 119 MacDougal St, which still retains some Old World character thanks to its dark walls and massive trademark espresso machine.

Double back a half block to **Minetta Tavern**, at the corner of MacDougal and Minetta Lane, an old Village hangout with a decent restaurant. It's a great place to stop for a beer and to admire the old photos of the '50s-era celebrities that used to hang out there. On the opposite corner is **Cafe Wha?**,

a legendary old club where Jimi Hendrix once played. Head west down Minetta Lane, making a left onto Minetta St, which will bring you past a block of 18th-century slums that have been preserved and improved into desirable row houses. The old Minetta Brook still runs under some of the houses.

Crossing Sixth Ave and walking west on Bleecker St brings you past a three block stretch of record stores, leather shops, restaurants and shops that sell delicious Italian pastry. Turn right on Seventh Ave, noting the famous jazz club **Sweet Basil** on the left, and head north three blocks to Grove St, where a right turn will lead to **Stonewall Place**, site of the historic 1969 gay rebellion.

Heading east (right) on Waverly Place brings you to the oddly shaped **Northern Dispensary** at 165 Waverly Place. It was built in 1831 to combat a cholera epidemic that was then sweeping through the neighborhood. New York's oldest public health facility until 1989, it's now awaiting renewal. The triangular Dispensary building creates one of the strangest spots in New York City: the corner of Waverly Place and Waverly Place!

Back on Sixth Ave you will want to turn left and examine the redbrick **Jefferson Market Courthouse**, now a public library, and the **Jefferson Market Gardens**, which are open to the public. Just behind the courthouse building, on W 10th St, is **Patchin Place**, an enclosed block of flats that was home to both journalist John Reed and poet e.e. cummings.

Double-back to Sixth Ave and head two blocks to W 11th St and then head east. On the right you'll find the tiny **Second Cemetery of the Spanish and Portuguese Synagogue** that was used from 1805–29. Continue along W 11th St and you'll pass a series of traditional row houses, including builder **Andrew Lockwood's House** at No 60. It was built in 1842 on a lot that was originally part of the larger Wouter Van Twiller Farm. Turn right when you reach Fifth Ave and you'll be heading directly back toward the arch in Washington Square Park.

Washington Square Park

Washington Square Park, like many public spaces in the city, began as a 'potter's field' – a burial ground for the penniless. Its status as a cemetery protected it from development. It was also the site of public executions, including the hanging of several petty criminals to honor a visit to New York by the French statesman Marquis de Lafayette in 1824. The magnificent old tree near the northwestern corner of the park has a plaque stating it was the 'Hangman's Elm,' though no one is quite sure if it was actually used for executions.

Pay particular attention to the **Stanford White Arch**, originally designed in wood to celebrate the centennial of George Washington's inauguration in 1889. The arch proved so popular that it was replaced in stone six years later and adorned with statues of the general in war and in peace (the latter work is by A Stirling Calder, the father of artist Alexander Calder).

In 1916, artist Marcel Duchamp climbed to the top of the arch by its internal stairway with a few friends and declared the park the 'Free and Independent Republic of Washington Square.' Today, the anarchy takes place on the ground level, as comedians and buskers use the park's permanently dry fountain as a performance space. The site was once used as the terminus and turnaround for the Fifth Ave buses that ran under the arch.

The **Judson Memorial Church** graces the park's south border. This yellow-brick Baptist church honors Adoniram Judson, an American missionary who served in Burma in the early 19th century. Designed by Stanford White, this national historic site features stained-glass windows by muralist John La Farge, who was born near the park, and marble frontage designed by Augustus Saint-Gaudens.

One block east of the park, at 245 Greene St, is the building where the Triangle Shirtwaist Fire took place on March 25, 1911. (A plaque declares it the 'site' of the fire, but it is the actual building.) This sweatshop had locked its doors to prevent the young seamstresses who toiled there from taking unau-thorized breaks. The inferno killed 146 young women, many of whom jumped to their deaths from the upper floors because the fire department's ladders did not extend to the top floors of the 10 story building. Every year, the New York Fire Department holds a solemn ceremony to commemorate the city's most deadly factory fire.

The row of townhouses at Washington Square North, the street that comprises the north border of the park, was the inspiration for *Washington Square*, Henry James' novel of late-19th-century social mores, though James did not live here as is popularly assumed. A hundred yards up Fifth Ave, to the right, is the **Washington Square Mews**, a quiet, cobblestone street of stables that now houses New York University offices.

Greenwich Village's Rock Landmarks

In addition to checking out Cafe Wha? on the corner of MacDougal St and Minetta Lane, rock and roll fans will want to take note of 161 W 4th St, where Bob Dylan once lived and was inspired to write 'Positively 4th St.' He often performed (and reputedly smoked his first joint) at Gerdes Folk City, which originally stood at 11 W 4th St. Folk City moved to 130 W 3rd St in 1969 and closed in 1986. The site is now occupied by a bar called Kettle of Fish, but the old, half-lit Folk City neon sign remains above the building. Jimi Hendrix lived and recorded at the **Electric Lady Studios** at Sixth Ave at 55 W 8th St. The brown brick building is now a shoe store.

EAST VILLAGE (MAP 4)

Attitudes are a bit different on the eastern edge of Greenwich Village. The 'East Village' is generally defined by 14th St to the north and E Houston St to the south, and from Lafayette St east to the East River. Historically, this neighborhood doesn't have much in common with Greenwich Village.

The area was once a series of rich and large farm estates that were overtaken by urban development in the late 19th century as New York became more industrial and moved northward from Lower Manhattan.

By the early 20th century, this region was considered the northern section of the Lower East Side, a poorer cousin to Greenwich Village. But it certainly came into its own during the 1990s. The East Village has been gentrified, and even so-called **Alphabet City**, an area marked by Aves A, B, C and D has seen tenements turned into pricey housing.

The Ukrainian and Polish communities settled here more than 100 years ago, and they are still very much in evidence today. Senior citizens from these groups hang out in **Tompkins Square Park** alongside punks, junkies, anarchists, and dog-walking yuppies.

In the East Village, E 8th St is called **St Mark's Place**, and it's a nexus for the artistic fringe. This stretch of street east of Astor Place contains a community center and stalls selling books, illegal concert tapes, and T-shirts. On St Mark's Place, east of Second Ave, there are many lively late-night cafes and bars.

The best way to explore the East Village is by simply walking up or down First Ave between E 14th and Houston Sts. On this 15-minute walk you will see the neighborhood in lively transition. The short buildings that line both sides of the avenue house a succession of laundries, bars, coffee shops, Eastern European meat stores, pharmacies and restaurants offering a virtual world tour of cuisines – there are places serving Italian, Polish, Indian, Lebanese, Japanese and Thai fare. The same array of gastronomic choices can be found along Second Ave, though the bars and cafes are a bit more upscale.

Boutiques selling all-natural products, antiques, furniture and both new and used clothing are springing up all over the East Village, but a good number of them are clustered on E 9th St just east of Second Ave. There are also a number of herbal medicine stores nearby.

The subway stations at Astor Place and Second Ave are good starting points for exploring this neighborhood.

Astor Place

This square is named after the Astor family, who, in the city's early years, built a fortune on beaver fur trading and lived at 429-434 Lafayette St on **Colonnade Row**, just south of Astor Place. Four of the original nine marble-faced Greek Revival residences still exist, but they are entombed beneath a layer of black soot. Across the street, in the public library built by John Jacob Astor, stands the **Joseph Papp Public Theater**. This building was built in 1848 for the then-phenomenal sum of $500,000. The theater is now one of the city's most important cultural centers and home to the New York Shakespeare Festival.

Astor Place itself is dominated by the large brownstone **Cooper Union**, the public college founded by glue millionaire Peter Cooper in 1859. Just after its completion, Abraham Lincoln condemned slavery in his 'Right Makes Might' speech that he delivered in the Union's Great Hall. The fringed lectern he used still exists, but the auditorium is only open to the public for special events.

Walking two blocks north and turning west on W 10th St to Broadway brings you to **Grace Church**, an Episcopal church designed by James Renwick. This Gothic Revival building is made of marble quarried by prisoners at Sing Sing, the state penitentiary in the upstate town of Ossining. At night, its floodlit white marble makes for a strangely elegant sight in this neighborhood of dance clubs, record stores and pizza parlors. The same architect is thought to have designed **Renwick Triangle**, a movie-set-perfect group of brownstone Italianate houses one block to the east at 112-128 E 10th St.

Another significant church is **St Mark's-in-the-Bowery** at Second Ave and E 10th St, also an Episcopal place of worship. It stands on the site of the farm, or *bouwerie*, owned by Dutch Governor Peter Stuyvesant, whose crypt is under the church grounds. The church, damaged by fire in 1978, has been restored with abstract stained-glass windows. It's open 10 am to 6 pm weekdays.

Old Merchant's House

Not much remains of the neighborhood that existed here before the tenement boom, but this museum (☎ 212-777-1089), 29 E 4th St, in the 1831 house of drug importer Seabury Tredwell is a remarkably well-preserved example of how the business class lived. Occupied by Tredwell's youngest daughter Gertrude until her death in 1933, its original furnishings were still intact when it began life as a museum three years later.

The Old Merchant's House is open 1 to 4 pm Sunday to Thursday. Admission is $3 for adults and $2 for seniors and students.

10th St Baths

The waning of Eastern European traditions on the Lower East Side led to the closure of many old bath houses in Manhattan, and the AIDS crisis prevented their continuation as gay gathering places. But these historic old steam baths (☎ 212-674-9250), 268 E 10th St, still remain. Here you can get a Russian-style oak-leaf massage followed by a plunge in an ice-cold bath, provided your heart can stand the strain. There's also a small cafe on the premises.

The 10th St Baths are open daily 9 am to 10 pm. Both sexes are admitted on Monday, Tuesday, Friday and Saturday. Thursday and Sunday are for men only, and women have exclusive entry on Wednesday. General admission is $20, with massage rates starting at around $45.

CHELSEA (MAP 5)

Chelsea has overtaken Greenwich Village as the city's most prominent gay neighborhood. Roughly bordered by 14th St to the south, 23rd St to the north, the Hudson River to the west and Broadway to the east, this neighborhood was the dry goods and retail area for the gilded age, and many of the emporia built to attract well-heeled shoppers are now office buildings. Closer to the Hudson River on Eighth and Ninth Aves, Chelsea is dominated by housing projects and warehouses.

The prime sight on noisy 23rd St is the **Chelsea Hotel** (for details, see Chelsea & Gramercy Park in the Places to Stay section, later in this chapter) the redbrick residential hotel with ornate iron balconies that is dominated at street level by no fewer than seven

plaques declaring it a literary landmark. Even before Sid Vicious murdered his girlfriend there, the hotel was notorious for being a literary hangout for the likes of Mark Twain, Thomas Wolfe, Dylan Thomas and Arthur Miller. One famous anecdote about the Chelsea has Jack Kerouac typing *On the Road* on a single roll of teletype paper during one marathon session at the Chelsea.

The subway station at 23rd St is a good starting point for those wishing to explore this neighborhood.

Union Square

Union Square is one of the city's most active nighttime neighborhoods, bursting with bars, microbreweries and restaurants (see Places to Eat and Bars, later in this chapter). This square, on the convergence of 14th St and Broadway, was one of New York City's first uptown business districts, and throughout the mid-19th century it was the site of many workers' rallies and political protests, thus its name. By the 1960s, this was something of a depressed part of town and a hangout for junkies. But the '90s heralded a big revival, with the Greenmarket farmers' market on Wednesday, Friday and Saturday throughout the year (subway: Union Square).

Flatiron District

This neighborhood, part of Chelsea, but somewhat distinct in character, is named after the **Flatiron Building** at the intersection of Broadway, Fifth Ave and 23rd St. Built in 1902, the Flatiron Building was featured in a famous and haunting 1905 color-tinted photograph by Edward Steichen. The building dominated this plaza when the neighborhood was home to the city's prime retail and entertainment establishments. Until 1909 the Flatiron was also renowned as the world's tallest building, but it was overtaken by the nearby **Metropolitan Life Tower** at 24th St and Madison Ave, which has an impressive clock tower and golden top. For a 10-block radius the Flatiron District, loaded with loft buildings and boutiques, does a good imitation of SoHo, but without the European pretensions and crowds. **Madison**

Square Park, just across from the Flatiron Building, defined the northern reaches of Manhattan until the city's population exploded after the Civil War.

The subway station at 23rd St (reached via the N and R lines) is a good starting point for exploring this neighborhood.

GRAMERCY PARK (MAP 5)

Gramercy Park is one of New York's loveliest spaces, the kind of garden area commonly found dotted throughout Paris and other European cities. Unfortunately, when the neighborhood was designed on the site of a marsh in 1830, admission to the park was restricted to residents. The tradition still holds, and mere mortals must peer through iron gates at the foliage.

Two other exclusive institutions here are worth noting for their architecture. The **National Arts Club** (☎ 212-475-3424), 15 Gramercy Park South, was designed by Calvert Vaux, one of the men behind the creation of Central Park. It holds exhibitions that are sometimes open to the public. The club has a beautiful vaulted stained-glass ceiling above its wooden bar.

The **Players Club**, 16 Gramercy Park, is an actors' hangout that was created in 1888 by Shakespearean actor Edwin Booth (brother of Abraham Lincoln's assassin John Wilkes Booth) and designed by Stanford White. Its warm wooden interiors, high ceilings and sumptuous leather seating are the epitome of a late-19th-century mansion and give a glimpse of how the rich once lived (subway: Union Square).

TIMES SQUARE (MAPS 5, 6)

Once again, Times Square is the 'Crossroads of the World.' Before television Times Square was the nation's largest space for glittery advertising directed at a mass audience. Once called Long Acre Square, it was renamed after the famous newspaper that is still located there – the *New York Times*. Dubbed the 'Great White Way' after its bright lights, the area fell into a well-known decline in the 1960s, as once-proud first-run movie palaces turned into 'triple X' porn theaters.

Over the years, the city reversed Times Square's fortunes by offering big tax breaks to businesses as an incentive to relocate there. Today, the square draws 27 million annual visitors, who spend something over $12 billion in Midtown.

TV networks such as MTV and ABC have opened studios there, and theme palaces such as the Virgin Megastore and the Official All Star Café are also smack in the middle of the square. The combination of color, zipping message boards and (at last count) six massive color TV screens makes for quite a sight. Several media companies – among them Reuters, the US magazine group Condé Nast and German publisher Bertelsmann, – have built headquarters in and around Times Square recently, and the storied *New York Times* is also moving to a new skyscraper there.

Up to a million people gather here every **New Year's Eve** to see a brightly lit ball descend from the roof of One Times Square

Getting on TV

It's not hard to wave to the folks back home via television, because New York is a popular backdrop for network morning shows broadcast daily 7 am to 9 am. The NBC *Today* show started it all with a windowed studio in Rockefeller Center. Fans (many with elaborate signs) show up at Rockefeller Plaza every morning hoping that Katie, Matt, Al and Anne, the show's chummy hosts, will turn their attention to them. This format proved so successful that ABC unveiled a studio for *Good Morning America* that overlooks Times Square. CBS's *The Early Show* is at ground level in the General Motors Building on Fifth Ave across from the Plaza Hotel. Tickets are not necessary – fans just show up.

It's not just the morning shows that call New York City home. MTV's US network overlooks Times Square, and *Late Night with David Letterman* is famous for outside events and man-in-the-street gags from the Ed Sullivan Theater at Broadway and 53rd St.

at midnight. Although this event garners international coverage, it lasts just 90 seconds.

The Times Square Visitor Center (☎ 212-768-1560), 1560 Broadway between 46th and 47th Sts, sits right in the middle of the famous crossroads of Broadway and Eighth Ave. More than 1 million visitors use the center's ATMs, video guides to the city and computer terminals that provide free access to the Internet. The center also offers free walking tours of the neighborhood several times a week. It's open daily 8 am to 8 pm.

E Walk Film Center

This massive 13-screen cinema complex (☎ 212-505-6397), on 42nd St between Broadway and Eighth Aves, was opened by the Loews Theater group in what was once the nation's cinema showplace. The block became the quintessential porn district in the '70s, and this facility celebrates its restoration to cleaner entertainment.

MIDTOWN (MAP 5)

You'll wind up spending a great deal of time in New York's teeming Midtown area, because it's the place where many of the city's most popular attractions are located. Very few people live in the center of Manhattan, and most apartment houses are found east of Third Ave and west of Eighth Ave. Midtown isn't the most dangerous part of town, but as in any similar district in cities around the world, you should be particularly savvy as you move about, because you'll meet up with some of the city's most aggressive panhandlers.

Herald Square

This crowded convergence of Broadway and Sixth Ave at 34th St is the location of **Macy's** department store, which for years has inaccurately claimed to be the world's largest department store (a title that probably belongs to massive GUM in Moscow). The busy square doesn't offer much in the way of cultural landmarks. There are two indoor malls on Sixth Ave south of Macy's that offer a boring array of shops and an HMV record store across the street.

Far more interesting is **Little Korea**, the small enclave of Korean-owned shops on 31st to 36th Sts between Broadway and Fifth Ave. Over the past few years this little neighborhood (particularly 32nd St) has seen an explosion of restaurants that serve Korean fare.

The **Garment District**, where most of New York's fashion firms have their design offices, stands to the west of Herald Square on Seventh Ave from 34th St to Times Square. During workdays the side streets are packed with delivery trucks picking up racks of clothing. Broadway between 23rd St and Herald Square is called the **Accessories District** because of the many ribbon and button shops located there to serve the fashion industry. There are a number of stores on 36th and 37th Sts immediately west of Seventh Ave that sell so-called designer clothing at wholesale prices.

Empire State Building

New York's original skyline symbol (☎ 212-736-3100), at the corner of W 34th St and Fifth Ave. is a limestone classic built in just 410 days during the depths of the Depression at a cost of $41 million. Located on the site of the original Waldorf-Astoria Hotel, the 102-story, 1454-foot Empire State Building opened in 1931 and was immediately the most exclusive business address in the city. The famous antenna was originally intended to be a mooring mast for zeppelins, but the Hindenburg disaster put a stop to that plan. One airship accidentally met up with the building: a B25 crashed into the 79th floor on a foggy day in July 1945 and killed 14 people.

Since 1976, the building's top 30 floors have been floodlit in seasonal and holiday colors (eg, green for St Patrick's Day in March, red and green for Christmas, pink for Gay Pride weekend in June). This tradition has been copied by many other skyscrapers, lending elegance to the night sky.

Looking down on the city from the building's 102nd floor means standing in line for an elevator on the concourse level and sometimes being confronted with another line at the top. Getting there very early or very late helps you avoid this. Don't bother with the other exhibits on the concourse – they thrive purely on their proximity to the ticket office.

The Empire State Building's observatories on the 86th and 102nd floors are open 9:30 am to midnight daily, with the last tickets sold at 11:25 pm. Admission is $7 for adults and $4 for seniors and children younger than 12. The Empire State Building is part of the CityPass scheme – see the 'Museum Bargains' boxed text, earlier in this chapter, for more information (subway: 33th St or 34th St).

Pierpont Morgan Library

The Pierpont Morgan Library (☎ 212-685-0008), 29 E 36th St, off Madison Ave, is part of the 45-room mansion owned by steel magnate JP Morgan. This formerly private collection features cold temperatures (the better for the Morgan's manuscripts, tapestries and books), a study filled with Italian Renaissance art works, a marble rotunda and the three-tiered East Room main library. Morgan spared little expense in his pursuit of ancient works of knowledge or art: There are no fewer than three Gutenberg Bibles in residence here.

The Morgan Library has long had a stuffy reputation, but its curator has livened things up with a year-round program of lectures and concerts in the Garden Court. This lovely glass-enclosed space also contains a cafe and bookstore. The Morgan is open 10:30 am to 5 pm Tuesday to Friday, 10:30 am to 8 pm Saturday and noon to 5 pm Sunday. Admission is $7/5 for adults/children (subway: 33rd St).

Grand Central Terminal

This is one of New York's grandest public spaces. The station is well worth visiting because of its huge Romanesque south facade (marred a bit by an ugly car ramp), as well as the huge main concourse and its vaulted celestial ceiling depicting the constellations of the zodiac. The famous ceiling was recently restored, as were the lower levels of the terminal, including the **Oyster Bar**, a famous seafood restaurant that's quite noisy thanks to its vaulted tile ceiling. A nice

bar – on a balcony on the western side – overlooks the concourse and its central clock and passenger information center. On the other side, a new staircase was built to mirror its partner and provide new observation space.

When the New York Central Rail Road built this terminal in 1913, the 'cut and cover' installation of tracks for its new electric trains created the unusually wide expanse of Park Ave. Grand Central is no longer a romantic place to begin a cross-country journey – today it serves as a terminus for the Metro North commuter trains to the northern suburbs and Connecticut. It is also home to a large community of street people who live in the track areas under Park Ave.

The Municipal Art Society conducts free walking tours through Grand Central every Wednesday at 12:30 pm. During the hour-long tour, you will cross a glass catwalk high above the concourse and learn that the ceiling constellation was mistakenly laid out in a 'god's eye view,' with the stars displayed from above rather than below. The tours meet at the visitor information booth in the middle of the terminal.

Chrysler Building

Just across from Grand Central Terminal, at Lexington Ave and 42nd St, is the 1048-foot Chrysler Building, an art deco masterpiece designed by William Van Allen in 1930. It briefly reigned as the tallest structure in the world until it was superseded by the Empire State Building. The Chrysler Building, a celebration of the car culture, features gargoyles that resemble hood ornaments (barely visible from the ground) and a 200-foot steel spire that was constructed as one piece and placed at the top of the building as a distinctive crowning touch. At the top is the Cloud Club, a businessmen's club that closed years ago, and a private apartment built for Walter Chrysler, head of the company.

There have long been plans to convert part of the building into a hotel, but at the moment it doesn't offer much in the way of interest for visitors – there's no restaurant or observation deck. Until one is established, the Chrysler will be known primarily as the landmark most often mistaken by tourists for the Empire State Building.

United Nations

The United Nations (UN; ☎ 212-963-7713), with its visitors' entrance at First Ave and 46th St, is technically considered international territory. It overlooks the East River. Tours of the facility show you its **General Assembly**, where the annual autumn convocation of member nations takes place, the **Security Council** chamber, where crisis hearings are held year-round and the **Economic & Social Council** chamber. A park south of the complex includes Henry Moore's *Reclining Figure* and several other sculptures with a peace theme.

The UN was created in 1945 by an international conference that convened in San Francisco, CA. The organization subsequently met for two years in Flushing Meadows Park in Queens, NY, before the Rockefeller family donated $8.5 million for the purchase of the land where it sits today. The complex, appropriately enough, was designed by a large international committee of architects.

For years there have been complaints in the US about the UN's spendthrift ways, but they are not much in evidence at the head-quarters. The buildings have a dated, late-1950s feel to them, with a lot of Norwegian wood, and the carpeting is woefully worn.

It's open 9:15 am to 4:45 pm daily, March to December and maintains the same hours Monday to Friday in January and February. English-language tours of the complex leave every 45 minutes and are available on a limited basis in several other languages. Admission is $7.50 for adults, $4.50 for students, and it is $3.50 for seniors. Children aged five to 17 are $3.50, and children younger than five are not admitted. Reservations are not required, but the lines grow long later in the day (subway: Grand Central/42nd St).

New York Public Library

The main branch of the New York Public Library (☎ 212-930-0800), at 42nd St and Fifth Ave, recently celebrated its centennial. The library contains a massive 3rd-floor reading room, large enough for 500 people, that still has its original lamps, more than 11 million books in its permanent collection and display galleries of precious manuscripts by just about every author of note in the English language. The library's famous stone lions are adorned by Christmas wreaths each holiday season.

ANGUS OBORN

Lion statue guards the New York Public Library.

It's open from 11 am to 6 pm Tuesday and Wednesday, from 10 am to 6 pm Monday and Thursday to Saturday.

Located just behind the library, **Bryant Park** (☎ 212-883-2476) was once overrun by drug-dealers, but it has been impressively restored and is a pleasant place to sit if you can claim one of the park's marble benches or folding chairs. It's a popular midday sun-bathing site, and a free outdoor movie festival is held there on Monday night during the warm summer months (subway: Grand Central/42nd St).

Rockefeller Center

Rockefeller Center is one of America's most attractive and architecturally coherent projects. It consists of 19 buildings situated on more than 22 acres. Construction started in 1931 at the height of the Depression. The complex took nine years and 70,000 construction workers to build, and they were watched by 'sidewalk supervisors' – the many passers-by who peered through holes cut into the fence around the site.

The completion of the center was tainted by a controversy over artwork. A mural painted by Mexican artist Diego Rivera for the lobby of the 70-story RCA (now GE) Building was rejected by the Rockefeller family because it featured the face of Lenin. The fresco was covered during the opening ceremony and was later destroyed. Its replacement (not painted by Rivera) features the more acceptable figure of Abraham Lincoln.

In 1989, controlling interest in Rockefeller Center was sold to a Japanese consortium, triggering lamentations in the press about the selling of American icons to foreigners, as if the buildings were in danger of being relocated to Tokyo. (The Japanese holding company actually went broke when real estate values plummeted.)

But the center's money travails have not resulted in a lack of exterior maintenance. Take special note of the tile work above the Sixth Ave entrance to the GE building, the three flood-lit cameos along the side of Radio City Music Hall, and the back-lit gilt and stained-glass entrance to the East River

Savings Bank building at 41 Rockefeller Plaza – immediately to the north of the skating rink/outdoor-garden cafe in the heart of the complex (subway: 47-50 Sts/ Rockefeller Ctr).

Christmas Tree Lighting In the 1930s, construction workers building the center set up a small Christmas tree on the site during the holidays. They inadvertently started a tradition that continues to this day. Every year during the Christmas season a huge pine tree is set up overlooking the Rockefeller Center skating rink. The annual lighting of the Rockefeller Center Christmas tree, the Tuesday after Thanksgiving, attracts thousands of visitors to the area and semi-officially kicks off the city's holiday season.

Radio City Music Hall The interior of this 6000-seat art deco movie palace (☎ 212-247-4777) is a protected landmark. It reopened after extensive renovation to restore the velvet seats and furnishings to the exact state they were in when the building opened in 1932. (Even the smoking rooms and toilets are elegant at the 'Showplace of the Nation.') Today it's used for live performances, and concerts and the occasional movie premiere. Tickets to the annual Christmas pageant featuring the hokey (but enjoyable) dancers, the Rockettes, now run up to $70. But you can see the interior by taking a tour that leaves every half hour Monday to Saturday 10 am to 5 pm and Sunday 11 am to 5 pm. Admission is $15 for adults and $9 for children.

TONY WHEELER

The Rockefeller Legacy

Perhaps no family has had a larger influence on 20th-century American history than the Rockefellers, who have left their stamp on business, domestic politics and international relations. Their works and deeds have had a particular impact upon New York, New Jersey and Pennsylvania.

It all started when the wily Ohio-born patriarch John D Rockefeller (1839–1937) bought into an oil refinery in 1859 with three partners, including his brother William (1841–1922). In the years following the end of the Civil War, John successfully built an empire of oil refineries in the Midwest, while William, a genius with money, organized the finances in New York (which included shady stock dealing). By the 1880s, their Standard Oil Company had a hammer-lock on crude oil processing and sales in the US. (See the Oil City & Around section in the Northern Pennsylvania chapter.)

However, John D's ruthless behavior attracted the attention of state and federal officials who normally gave the corporate chieftain free rein on business matters. By the time the Standard Oil Company was broken into 34 different companies by the US Supreme Court in 1911, John D Rockefeller had amassed a fortune worth more than $1 billion. (Standard Oil's constituent parts are now huge businesses in their own right and include Exxon, Mobil, Texaco, Amoco, British Petroleum, Shell, Chevron and Atlantic Richfield.) Rockefeller spent the rest of his days looking after the various charitable and educational institutions he founded, including the University of Chicago and Rockefeller University, a medical research facility based in New York City.

John D Rockefeller Jr (1874–1960) took over control of the family's fortune after his father retired, and he also left his mark on society, particularly on New York City. At the height of the Depression, the younger Rockefeller proposed the building of a new Metropolitan Opera House on property occupied by hundreds of small brownstone apartment blocks. When that plan fell through, Rockefeller proceeded with a massive project that became known as the Rockefeller Center, the limestone office and shop complex that changed the face of central Manhattan. He also built Riverside Church in upper Manhattan and donated valuable land on the East Side for the headquarters of the United Nations.

John D Jr's six children all played prominent roles in public life. Among them were John D III (1906–1978), one of the founders of New York City's Lincoln Center; Winthrop (1912–1973), who was Arkansas' Republican governor from 1967 to 1970; and David (born 1925), the chairman of Chase Manhattan Bank and a recognized leader of the American business establishment.

But perhaps the most famous scion was Nelson Rockefeller (1908–1979). He served Presidents Roosevelt, Truman and Eisenhower in a variety of positions and helped establish the current site of the Museum of Modern Art in New York City. He was also elected governor of New York state for four terms and built the massive Empire State Plaza complex (see the Albany section in the Capital District & Mohawk Valley chapter). Rockefeller was a socially liberal Republican who was so self-conscious of his wealth that he used the phrase 'thanks a thousand' to express gratitude. A leading contender for the Republican presidential nomination in the 1960, 1964 and 1968 elections, Nelson was appointed by President Gerald Ford to serve as vice president following Richard Nixon's resignation in 1974. Even today, the left-wing GOP is known derisively as 'Rockefeller Republicans.'

Today, the Rockefeller billions are spread among dozens of cousins, and the family name is not as prominent in the public eye. But John D IV, the great-grandson of the patriarch, continued the tradition of public service by moving to West Virginia to work with the poor in Appalachia. Known as 'Jay' Rockefeller, he served as Democratic governor of that state and is now a US senator, and he is considered one of the most articulate liberal voices in the country.

The $2.5 billion New York-based Rockefeller Foundation, created by John D Sr in 1913, continues to award more than $100 million in grants every year to promote world-wide policy reforms in education, health and the environment.

NBC Studios The NBC TV network has its headquarters in the 70-story GE building that looms over Rockefeller Center, and the *Today* show broadcasts from there daily 7 to 9 am. Tours of the NBC studios (☎ 212-664-4000) leave from the lobby of the GE Building Monday to Saturday 9:30 am to 4:30 pm. Admission is $10, and children younger than six are not permitted. Tours leave four times an hour and reservations are not taken in advance.

St Patrick's Cathedral

St Patrick's Cathedral (☎ 212-753-2261), on Fifth Ave at 50th St, just across from Rockefeller Center, is the main place of worship for the 2.2 million Roman Catholics in the New York diocese. (The diocese of Brooklyn, a separate district, serves 1.7 million more Catholics.)

The cathedral, built at a cost of nearly $2 million during the Civil War, originally didn't include the two front spires (added in 1888). The well-lit St Patrick's isn't as gloomy as its Old World counterparts, and the new TV monitors in restricted view seats are testimony to the church's determination to have its place in the modern world.

Passing by the eight small shrines along the right side of the cathedral brings you past the main altar to the quiet **Lady Chapel**, dedicated to the Virgin Mary. From here you can see the handsome stained-glass **Rose Window** above the 7000 pipe church organ. A basement crypt behind the altar contains the coffins of every New York cardinal. The crypt is visible from the altar but closed to the public.

Unfortunately St Patrick's is not a place for restful contemplation during the day because of the constant buzz from visitors. It's also a regular site for protests by gays who feel excluded by the church hierarchy. Protests frequently occur here in March due to the exclusion of Irish gays from the St Patrick's Day Parade since 1993 (an event not sponsored by the Catholic Church per se, but identified with Catholic traditionalists).

It's open 6 am to 9 pm daily. Masses are held frequently on the weekend, and the res-ident cardinal presides over the service at 10:15 am Sunday (subway: 47-50th Sts/Rockefeller Ctr).

Fifth Ave

Immortalized in both film and popular song, Fifth Ave's reputation as a high-class area dates back to the early part of the 20th century. It's uptown portion was known as Millionaire's Row due to the series of mansions that extended all the way up to 130th St. The avenue's southern end at Washington Square Park in Greenwich Village are home to a number of high-rise apartment buildings that date back to the '30s, giving way to retail clothing stores and carpet wholesalers in the Flatiron District from 14th to 42nd Sts.

In Midtown, the street is the site of offices, high-end shops and hotels, including the garish **Plaza Hotel** at Grand Army Plaza overlooking the corner of Central Park and Fifth Ave. The huge institution really doesn't have much of a grand lobby, but it is worth a walk through just to say you've been there. The fountain in front of the hotel features a statue of the Roman goddess Diana. It faces the southeastern entrance to **Central Park** and is a good spot for a rest and a bit of lunch – provided you're not downwind from the horse-drawn carriages that line 59th St during the summer months.

Most of the heirs of the millionaires that built mansions on Fifth Ave above 59th St either sold them for demolition or converted them to the cultural institutions that make up **Museum Mile** (see the Upper East Side section, later in this chapter). The **Villard Houses**, actually on Madison Ave behind St Patrick's Cathedral, are surviving examples of these grand homes. The six townhouses were built by financier Henry Villard in 1881; they eventually became the property of the Catholic Church and later were sold to become part of the 1000-room Mayfair hotel and the chic and famous restaurant Le Cirque 2000.

Most of Manhattan's exclusive boutiques are uptown on Madison Ave (see Shopping, later in this chapter), but Liz Claiborne, Henri Bendel and Tiffany & Co are all still on Fifth Ave above 50th St. On 57th St nearby, you can shop at Burberry's, Hermès and Charivari, among several other designer boutiques.

Newseum New York

This museum (☎ 212-317-7596), 580 Madison Ave between 56th and 57th Sts, is dedicated to journalism. Established by the Gannett newspaper-publishing group, it features exhibitions of photojournalism and various publications. It's also the site of debates on current affairs. The museum is open Monday through Saturday from 10 am to 5:30 pm, and admission is free.

Museum of Modern Art

The Museum of Modern Art (☎ 212-708-9480), 11 W 53rd St, known as MoMA, is in the midst of an extensive renovation that will more than double its current exhibition space by 2005.

Among the first-rate sculptures and paintings are a number of works by Picasso, Van Gogh's *Starry Night* and Matisse's *Dance 1*. A quiet gallery is dedicated solely to Monet's paneled *Water Lilies*, and the Abby Aldrich Rockefeller Sculpture Garden is the setting for a summer series of concerts during July and August.

At least once a year, MoMA puts on an important exhibit of one major artist's work – recent retrospectives focused on the abstractionist Piet Mondrian, Picasso's portraiture and American painter Jasper Johns.

The museum places a special emphasis on photography and film, two areas of visual expression that get short shrift at the larger Metropolitan Museum of Art. There are daily film screenings in MoMA's two basement theaters, and an Academy Award given to the museum's film department in 1978 is on permanent display along with an impressive collection of film posters.

If you're pressed for time or simply undecided on where to go, it's a good idea to rent the audio tour of the museum – it is delivered via a cell phone that you can program to get more information about specific works of interest.

The museum is one of the few major cultural institutions in New York City that is open Monday (closed on Wednesday). Hours 11 am to 5:45 pm Saturday to Tuesday and 10:30 am to 8:15 pm Thursday and Friday. Admission is $10 for adults, $6.50 for seniors and students; children younger than 16 are free. The museum offers free admission on Friday after 5:30 pm. MoMA is part of the CityPass scheme; see the 'Museum Bargains' boxed text, earlier, for more information (subway: E, F trains to Fifth Ave/53 St; B, D to Seventh Ave).

Museum of Television & Radio

This couch potato's paradise (☎ 212-621-6800), 25 W 52nd St, contains a collection of more than 50,000 American TV and radio programs – available with the click of a mouse from the museum's computer catalog. It's a great place to head when it's raining or when you're simply fed up with walking. Nearly everybody checks out their favorite childhood TV programs on the museum's 90 consoles, but the radio-listening room is an unexpected pleasure.

It's open noon to 6 pm Tuesday to Sunday and to 8 pm on Thursday. Admission is $6 for adults, $4 for students and seniors, $3 for children younger than 12 (subway: 47-50th Sts/Rockefeller Ctr).

Intrepid Sea, Air & Space Museum

The Intrepid Sea, Air & Space Museum (☎ 212-245-2533), located on the waterfront at W 46th St, is on an aircraft carrier that served in WWII and in Vietnam. The carrier's flight deck has many fighter planes, and the pier area contains the Growler, a guided-missile submarine, an Apollo space capsule and Vietnam-era tanks, along with the 900-foot destroyer *Edson*. The Intrepid is the nexus for the **Fleet Week** celebrations each summer, when thousands of the world's sailors descend upon Manhattan for their own version of *On the Town*.

The museum is open daily 10 am to 5 pm June to August and Wednesday to Sunday 10 am to 5 pm the rest of the year. Refreshingly, it hasn't raised its prices in recent years.

Admission is $10 for adults, $7.50 for seniors, veterans, students and persons 12 to 17, and $5 for children aged six to 11 years old. The museum is part of the CityPass scheme – see the 'Museum Bargains' boxed text, earlier, for more information.

CENTRAL PARK (MAP 7)

This 843-acre rectangular park in the middle of Manhattan was designed to be an oasis from the urban bustle, but on weekends it's packed with joggers, in-line skaters, musicians and tourists. Its quieter areas are found above 72nd St, where the crowds thin out and the landscaping becomes more apparent to the visitor. The park is currently in the midst of a restoration program that has led to the re-seeding of many open spaces.

A good stroll through the park begins on the west side at the Columbus Circle entrance, through the **Merchants' Gate** and up to **Sheep Meadow**, a wide expanse of green for sunbathers and Frisbee players. Turning right, a pathway (called a transverse) runs along the south side of the meadow to the Carousel, and then the Dairy building, where the park's visitors' center is not far from the Wollman ice-skating rink.

Just north of the Dairy, past the statue of Christopher Columbus, is **The Mall**, enclosed on both sides by a group of 150 American elms. These trees, which have not suffered from the Dutch elm disease that destroyed most of the country's elms, are believed to be the largest surviving stand in the country. At the end of The Mall is **Bethesda Fountain**, a '60s hippie hangout that has been restored. Continue on the path to the right to Bow Bridge. You can cross the

bridge to **The Ramble**, a lush wooden expanse that is still a gay pickup area and is also a meeting place for dog owners of all sexual persuasions.

The Ramble gives way to Belvedere Castle and the **Delacorte Theater**, where the public theater holds free Shakespeare productions each summer. (You line up for tickets at about 5:30 pm each performance day.) Immediately beyond is **The Great Lawn**, where the occasional free concert is held, along with annual open-air performances of the New York Philharmonic and Metropolitan Opera in June and July. (The Lincoln Center information line at ☎ 212-875-5400 lists dates for these events.) The Great Lawn is undergoing a much needed re-seeding, temporarily moving the concerts to **North Meadow** above 97th St.

At the W 72nd St park entrance is **Strawberry Fields**, the 3-acre landscape dedicated to the memory of John Lennon; it contains plants from more than 100 nations. This spot was frequently visited by the former Beatles member, who lived in the massive Dakota apartment building across the street. He was shot to death in front of the building on December 8, 1980.

Park Activities

There are many activities in the park, and more information on what's happening is available at the visitors' center in the **Dairy** (☎ 212-794-6564) in the middle of the park along the 65th St pathway. It's open Tuesday to Sunday from 11 am to 4 pm and has park maps and lists of activities.

The Central Park roadway that loops around the park for 6 miles is closed to

Canines meet and greet at The Ramble in Central Park.

traffic in the evenings and on weekends, and is a popular track for runners, in-line skaters and bikers. (The wicked S-shaped curve near E 106th St and the Lasker Pool should be avoided by beginner rollerbladers.)

A soft, 1.6-mile cinder path encircles the **Jacqueline Kennedy Onassis Reservoir,** named in 1994 in her honor because she regularly used the track. The New York Road Runners Club (☎ 212-860-4455) sponsors regular runs through the park and operates an information booth near the reservoir entrance at E 90th St.

The **Central Park Wildlife Center** (☎ 212-861-6030) is a small zoo built in the 1930s. It has been renovated for the comfort of the animals housed there. Zoo residents include a lazy polar bear and several seals, whose frequent feedings delight the children who visit. The zoo is open April to October Monday to Friday from 10 am to 5 pm and Saturday and Sunday from 10:30 am to 5:30 pm. In the winter the zoo is open daily 10 am to 4:30 pm. Admission is $3.50 for adults, $1.25 for seniors, 50¢ for children aged three to 12 (and free for toddlers).

Carriage Rides
Without a doubt, the most touristy thing to do in the park is to rent a horse-drawn carriage for a spin along the carriage paths. It's expensive and a bit smelly in the summer months. Carriages line up along 59th St (Central Park South) and cost $40 for a half hour and $10 for every 15 minutes thereafter; see Map 7. Drivers expect a tip on top of that charge.

UPPER EAST SIDE (MAP 7)
The Upper East Side is home to New York's greatest concentration of cultural centers, as Fifth Ave above 57th St is called **Museum Mile.** The neighborhood is filled with many of the city's most exclusive hotels and residential blocks. From 57th to 86th Sts, the streets between Fifth Ave and Third Ave have some stunning townhouses and brownstones, and walking through this area at nightfall affords a voyeuristic opportunity to peer into the interiors and see the grand libraries and living rooms in these homes.

The East Side is served by just three subway lines running up and down Lexington Ave, and the stations listed for sites in this section are served by the 6 local train and the 4 and 5 express trains.

Frick Collection
The Frick Collection (☎ 212-288-0700), 1 E 70th St (just off Fifth Ave), is in a mansion built in 1914 by businessman Henry Clay Frick, one of the many such residences that made up Millionaire's row. Most of these mansions proved too expensive for succeeding generations and were eventually destroyed, but the wiley and very wealthy Frick, a Pittsburgh steel magnate, established a trust to open his private collection as a museum. (Frick's home in Pittsburgh is also a museum; see the Southwest Pennsylvania chapter.)

It's a shame that the 2nd floor of the residence is not available for viewing, though the 12 rooms on the ground floor are grand enough. The Frick's Oval Room is graced by Jean-Antoine Houdon's stunning figure *Diana the Huntress* and you'll find works by Titian, Vermeer, Bellini, Gilbert Stuart, Sir Joshua Reynolds, Thomas Gainsborough and John Constable. It's worth picking up the guide to the galleries ($1) to fully appreciate the significance of the works on display.

It's open Tuesday to Saturday from 10 am to 6 pm and Sunday from 1 to 6 pm. Admission is $7 for adults and $5 for students and seniors. Children younger than 10 are not permitted (subway: 68th St/Hunter College).

Temple Emanu-El
Five blocks south of the Frick, at E 65th St and Fifth Ave, stands Temple Emanu-El (☎ 212-744-1400), the world's largest Reformed Jewish synagogue, which is significant for its Byzantine and Near-Eastern architecture. It's open to the general public daily from 10 am to 5 pm (it closes at 4 pm on Friday for services).

Whitney Museum of American Art
This museum (☎ 212-570-3600/3676), 945 Madison Ave at 75th St, was established to

house cutting-edge American art, but in recent years it seems to have lost its way somewhat and become overshadowed by The Museum of Modern Art downtown, and even the Brooklyn Museum. The Whitney is housed in an ugly yet functional structure by Marcel Breuer that virtually defines the institution's mission to provoke.

Gertrude Vanderbilt Whitney established its collection in the 1930s; she hosted a salon of prominent artists, including Edward Hopper, in Greenwich Village. Recent major exhibits included a retrospective of Dadist art and a survey of 20th-century American art trends.

The Whitney is open Wednesday 11 am to 6 pm; Thursday 1 to 8 pm; and Friday and Sunday 11 am to 6 pm. Admission is $12.50 for adults, $10.50 for seniors and students and free for children under 12. Admission is free on the first Thursday of the month from 6 to 8 pm (subway: 77th St).

The Whitney has smaller exhibits at its branch in the Philip Morris Building, 120 Park Ave, across the street from Grand Central Terminal. Hours are Monday to Wednesday, Friday to Sunday 11 am to 6 pm and Thursday 11 am to 7:30 pm; admission is free (subway: 77th St).

Metropolitan Museum of Art

With more than 5 million visitors each year, the Metropolitan Museum of Art (☎ 212-879-5500), at Fifth Ave and 82nd St, is New York's most popular single-site tourist attraction. Like the city of its location, it is powerful, popular and sometimes arrogant in its approach. The Met is virtually a self-contained cultural city-state with 2 million individual objects in its collection and a budget of over $120 million. The museum has restored the galleries housing its amazing collection of Greek antiquities, and in 1999 it received a $300 million donation of works by modern masters, including Picasso and Matisse.

Once inside the **Great Hall**, pick up a floor plan and head to the ticket booths, where you will find a list of exhibits closed for the day along with a line-up of special museum talks. The Met presents more than 30 special

exhibitions and installations each year, and clearly marked floor plans show you how to get to them. To the right of the hall, there is an information desk that offers guidance in several languages (these change depending on the volunteers) and audio tours of the special exhibits ($7 to $10).

It's best to target exactly what you want to see and head there first, before culture and crowd fatigue set in (usually after two hours). Then, put the floor plan away and let yourself get lost as you make your way through the galleries. It's a virtual certainty that you will stumble across something interesting along the way. The Met offers free guided walking tours of museum highlights and specific galleries. Check the calendar, which is given away free at the Great Hall information desk for the specific schedule. Met crowds are impossible on rainy Sunday afternoons in the summer, though during horrible winter weather, you might find the 17-acre museum nearly deserted in the evening.

It is open 9:30 am to 5:30 pm Tuesday to Thursday and Sunday; 9:30 am to 9 pm Friday and Saturday. Suggested admission is $10 for adults, $5 for seniors and students, and free for children younger than 12 and accompanied by an adult. (You may pay as little as a penny to get in.) Admission to The Cloisters (see the Washington Heights section) is included with admission to the Met. Visit the museum's website at www.metmuseum.org (subway: 6 train to 77th St).

Walking Tour – Permanent Galleries If you do not want to see anything in particular, begin by making a loop of the 1st floor. Entering the **Egyptian Art** section in the north wing, you will pass the tomb of Pernebi (circa 2415 BC), several mummies and incredibly well-preserved wall paintings before seeing the **Temple of Dendur**. The temple, threatened with submersion during the building of the Aswan dam, found a home in New York under this glass enclosure. If you look closely at its walls, you can see the graffiti left by European visitors to the site in the 1820s. (The accompanying history makes plain that the temple was a gift to the US in exchange for building a permanent space for it.) This room, with a wall of windows overlooking Central Park, is popular for museum fundraisers and corporate Christmas events.

Exiting the gallery through the door behind the temple brings a culture shock, as you see the Met's collection of **baseball cards**, including the rarest and most expensive card in existence: a 1909 Honus Wagner worth some $200,000. Continuing on to the left brings you to the **American Wing**, which displays furniture and architecture and has a quiet, enclosed garden space that serves as a respite from Met hordes. Along the garden walls are several stained glass works by Louis Comfort Tiffany, as well as an entire two-story facade of the Branch Bank of the US, preserved when the downtown building was destroyed in the early 20th century.

You then pass through the dark **Medieval Art** galleries, where at Christmas, the museum displays its famous crèche. Turning right, you reach a pyramid-like addition that houses the **Robert Lehman Collection** of **impressionist and modern art**, including several works by Pierre August Renoir (including *Young Girl Bathing*), Georges Seurat and Pierre Bonnard. An unexpected bonus in this gallery is the rear terra-cotta facade of the original 1880 Met building, now completely encased by later additions and standing mutely on view as its own piece of architectural art.

Heading back toward Fifth Ave brings you through the Rockefeller collection **Arts of Africa, Oceania and the Americas**. At the museum cafe, turn left and wander through the **Greek and Roman Art** section before winding up back at the south side of the Great Hall.

On the 2nd floor, you will see the Met's famous collection **European Paintings**, located in some of the museum's oldest galleries, with colonnaded entryways. Here you will see works by every artist of note, including self-portraits by Rembrandt and Van Gogh, *Portrait of Juan de Parej* by Velazquez, and a suite of rooms dedicated to impressionist and post-impressionist art. The new collection of modern masters is housed

on this level, as well as the photographs recently purchased by the Met.

Solomon R Guggenheim Museum

The Solomon R Guggenheim Museum (☎ 212-423-3500), 1071 Fifth Ave, is the distinctive spiral art space designed by Frank Lloyd Wright to hold one of the 20th century's greatest private bequests. A 1993 renovation added a 10-story building behind Wright's structure, and many complained it made the museum resemble a commode, but it did add space for the 5000 work Guggenheim collection, including the major donation in 1976 of impressionist and modern works by Justin Thannhauser.

The museum is open Sunday to Wednesday from 9 am to 6 pm and Friday and Saturday from 9 am to 8 pm. Admission is $12/7 for adults/children, and children under 12 are admitted for free. A pay-as-you-wish policy is in effect Friday 6 to 8 pm. This museum is part of the CityPass scheme; see the 'Museum Bargains' boxed text, earlier, for more information (subway: 4, 5, 6 trains to 86th St).

National Academy of Design

The National Academy of Design (☎ 212-369-4880), 1083 Fifth Ave, was founded by painter-inventor Samuel Morse and has a permanent collection of paintings and sculptures. The academy's works have been housed since 1940 in a big mansion designed by Ogden Codman, who also designed the Breakers mansion in Newport, RI. The academy's house is notable for its marble foyer and spiral staircase.

The academy is open Tuesday to Sunday from 11:30 am to 5:30 pm, with late hours Friday until 8 pm. Admission for adults/students is $8/5; for seniors and children under 16 it's free. The museum is free for all from Friday 5 pm to 8 pm.

Cooper-Hewitt National Museum of Design

The Cooper-Hewitt National Museum of Design (☎ 212-860-6868), 2 E 91st St, stands in the 64-room mansion that billionaire

Andrew Carnegie built in 1901 in a spot then far away from the downtown bustle. Within 20 years, the country surroundings that Carnegie sought disappeared as other wealthy men followed his lead and built palaces around his.

The museum, a branch of the Smithsonian Institution, is a must for anyone interested in architecture, engineering, jewelry or textiles. For example, it has held exhibits on topics such as modern design in advertising campaigns and household-item design. If you only have a passing interest in any of this, the place is still worth a visit for its garden.

It's open Tuesday 10 am to 9 pm, Wednesday to Saturday 10 am to 5 pm and Sunday noon to 5 pm. Admission is $8 for adults, $5 for seniors and students, and free for children. There is no admission 5 to 9 pm on Tuesday (subway: trains 4, 5, 6 to 86th St).

Jewish Museum
The Jewish Museum (☎ 212-423-3200), 1109 Fifth Ave, is really an art facility, examining 4000 years of Jewish ceremony and culture. The building, a 1908 banker's mansion, has more than 30,000 items of Judaica, and it underwent a substantial expansion in 2000.

It's open Sunday to Thursday 11 am to 5:45 pm and Tuesday 11 am to 8 pm. Admission is $8 for adults, $5.50 for students and seniors, and free for children under 12; admission is free Tuesday 5 to 8 pm (subway: trains 4, 5, 6 to 86th St).

International Center of Photography
The International Center of Photography (ICP; ☎ 212-860-1777), 1130 Fifth Ave, is the city's most important showplace for exhibitions on the careers of major figures in photography such as fashion photographer and filmmaker William Klein and French photojournalist Henri Cartier-Bresson.

It's open Wednesday to Sunday 11 am to 6 pm and Tuesday 11 am to 8 pm. Admission is $6 for adults, $4 for seniors and students and $1 for children under 12. Friday 5 pm to 8 pm is pay-as-you-wish day (subway: 96th St-Lexington).

There is also an ICP Gallery in Midtown (☎ 212-768-4682), 1133 Sixth Ave, that has the same opening hours and admission prices (subway: 42nd St-Seventh Ave).

Museum of the City of New York
The Museum of the City of New York (☎ 212-534-1672), at Fifth Ave and 103rd St, doesn't seem to have a coherent plan to its displays, and it somewhat duplicates the function of the older New-York Historical Society across town (see Upper West Side section, later in this chapter). Consequently, both institutions attract fewer visitors than their world-class neighbors and have suffered financially.

Nevertheless, this museum expanded its facility and offers a lot of Internet-based historical resources. The museum itself has a notable 2nd-floor gallery that displays entire rooms from demolished homes of New York grandees, an excellent collection of antique doll houses, teddy bears and toys, along with and an exhibition dedicated to Broadway musicals.

It's open Wednesday to Saturday 10 am to 5 pm and Sunday 1 to 5 pm. Admission is $5/4 adults/children, or $10 for an entire family (subway: 103rd St-Lexington Ave).

Roosevelt Island
New York's most planned neighborhood is on a tiny island that's no wider than a football field and sits in the East River between Manhattan and Queens. Once known as Blackwell's Island after the farming family that lived there, the island was purchased by the city in 1828 and became the location of several public hospitals and an insane asylum. In the 1970s the state of New York built apartments for 10,000 on the island. The planned area along the cobblestone roadway resembles an Olympic Village, or, as some less kindly put it, a college dorm complex.

Most visitors take the three-minute aerial tramway over, admire the stunning view of the East Side of Manhattan framed by the 59th St Bridge and head straight back. But it's worth spending an hour or so on the island during good weather, if only to enjoy the quiet and the flat roadway and paths that circle it, making it a perfect spot for both running and picnicking. Roosevelt Island Tours (☎ 212-223-0157) offers group excursions of the island and its six landmarks for $10 per person. (For more information, such as where to meet for the tours, call ahead.)

The Roosevelt Island tramway station (☎ 212-832-4543) is at 59th St and Second Ave. Trips leave every 15 minutes on the quarter hour from 6 am to 2:30 am daily ($1.50). Roosevelt Island has its own subway station that's accessible from Manhattan via the Q train during the day and the B train on nights and weekends. Just make sure the train you get on lists '21st St-Queensbridge' as its final destination (subway: 63rd St-Lexington).

UPPER WEST SIDE (MAP 7)

The Upper West Side begins as Broadway emerges from Midtown at Columbus Circle. A number of middle to top-end hotels are along Central Park South, and many celebrities live in the massive apartment buildings that line Central Park West all the way up to 96th St.

Lincoln Center

Lincoln Center (☎ 212-875-5400), at Columbus Ave and Broadway, is a complex of seven large performance spaces built in the 1960s, replacing a group of tenements that were the real-life inspiration for the musical *West Side Story*. There's a clean, if architecturally uninspired look to Lincoln Center during the day, but at night the chandeliered interiors look simply beautiful from across Columbus Ave. For more information on the performance companies, see the Entertainment section or call the center's events line at ☎ 212-546-2656.

If you are at all interested in high culture, Lincoln Center is a must-see, because it contains the **Metropolitan Opera House**, adorned by two colorful lobby tapestries by Marc Chagall; the **New York State Theater**, home of the New York City Ballet; and the New York City Opera, the low-cost, more daring alternative to the Met. The New York Philharmonic holds its season in **Avery Fisher Hall**.

The Lincoln Center Theater group calls the 1000-seat **Vivian Beaumont Theater** home. The lower levels of the building also contain the smaller and more intimate, **Mitzi Newhouse Theater**. To the right of the theaters stands the **New York Public Library for the Performing Arts**, containing the city's largest collection of recorded sound, video and books on film and theater.

The Juilliard School of Music, attached to the complex by a walkway over W 65th St, contains **Alice Tully Hall**, home to the Chamber Music Society of Lincoln Center and the **Walter Reade Theater**, the city's most comfortable film revival space and the major screening site for the New York Film Festival that is held every September.

Tours of the complex begin at the concourse level each day and explore at least three of the theaters, though just which ones you see depends on production schedules. It's a good idea to call ahead to make a reservation (☎ 212-875-5350). Tours costs $9.50 for adults, $8 for students and seniors, $4.75 for children aged six to 17 (subway: 66th St).

New-York Historical Society

As the antiquated, hyphenated name implies, the New-York Historical Society (☎ 212-873-2400), 2 W 77th St, is the city's oldest museum. It was founded in 1804 to preserve artifacts of history and culture. It was also New York's only public art museum until the founding of the Metropolitan Museum of Art in the late 19th century, and in this capacity, it obtained John James Audubon's original watercolors for his *Birds of America* survey (they are on display in a 2nd-floor gallery).

The museum is somewhat overshadowed by its neighbor, the American Museum of Natural History, and it has suffered severe financial problems in recent years. But it is well worth a visit, because viewing its quirky permanent collection is a bit like traipsing through New York City's attic.

It's open Wednesday to Sunday noon to 5 pm. Admission is free, but donations are very welcome (subway: 81st St).

American Museum of Natural History

The American Museum of Natural History (☎ 212-769-5100), with its entrance at Central Park West and 79th St, was founded in 1869, and today it has over 30 million artifacts in its collection. It is no doubt most famous for its three large dinosaur halls which present the latest knowledge on how these behemoths behaved and theories on why they disappeared. Knowledgeable guides roam the dinosaur halls ready to answer questions, and there are 'please touch' displays that allow you to handle, among other items, the skullcap of a pachycephulasaurus, a plant-eating dinosaur that roamed the earth 65 million years ago.

In February 2000, the giant new **Rose Center for Earth and Space** opened after an extensive renovation that includes a new Hyden Planetarium, a place popular with school groups.

The museum is open daily, except on Thanksgiving and Christmas. Hours are 10 am to 5:45 pm Sunday to Thursday and 10 am to 8:45 pm Friday and Saturday. Admission is $9.50 for adults, $6 for children and $7.50 for seniors and students. It is part of the CityPass scheme; see the 'Museum Bargains' boxed text, earlier, for more information (subway: 81st St).

Children's Museum of Manhattan

The Children's Museum of Manhattan (☎ 212-721-1223), 212 W 83rd St, features discovery centers for toddlers and a postmodern Media Center for children under 16. There, technologically savvy kids can work in a TV studio. The museum also runs crafts workshops on weekends. The museum is open 10 am to 5 pm Wednesday and Sunday. Admission is $5 for adults, $2.50 for seniors and free for children under two (subway: 86th St).

Columbia University

Columbia University (☎ 212-854-1754) and the affiliated Barnard College are on upper Broadway at W 116th St, in a spot once far removed from the downtown bustle. Today, the city has definitely enveloped and moved beyond Columbia's gated campus. But the school's main courtyard, with its statue *Alma Mater* perched on the steps of the Low Library, is still a quiet place to enjoy the sun and read a book. Hamilton Hall, in the southeast corner of the main square, was the famous site of a student takeover in 1968, and since then, it's periodically a place for protests as well as pretty wild student parties. As you would expect, the surrounding neighborhood is filled with inexpensive restaurants, good bookstores and cafes (subway: 116th St-Columbia).

Cathedral of St John the Divine

The Cathedral of St John the Divine (☎ 212-316-7540) dominates Amsterdam Ave at W 111th St, just behind the Columbia University campus. It is the largest place of worship in the US, a massive and dark 601-foot-long Episcopal cathedral that, upon completion, will be the third largest church in the world (after St Peter's Basilica in Rome and the newly built Our Lady at Yamoussoukro in the Ivory Coast).

But it's unlikely that St John, which had its cornerstone laid in 1892, will be finished in your lifetime. Work has yet to begin on the stone tower on the left side of the west front or the crossing tower above the pulpit. In 1978, the Episcopal Diocese of New York began training local young people in stone cutting. Other features that are shown on the church's cutaway floor plan near the front entrance, such as a Greek amphitheater, are merely wistful visions of the distant future.

Still, the cathedral is a flourishing place of worship and community activity, the site of holiday concerts, lectures and memorial services for famous New Yorkers. There's even a Poet's Corner just to the left of the front entrance – though, unlike Westminster Abbey, no one is actually buried there. You should also check out the altar designed and built by the late artist Keith Haring.

The cathedral is open 7 am to 5 pm Monday to Saturday and 7 am to 8 pm on Sunday. There is also a 9:30 am mass in Spanish (subway: Cathedral Parkway or 116th St-Columbia).

General US Grant National Memorial

Popularly known as Grant's Tomb (☎ 212-666-1640), this landmark monument at Riverside Drive and W 122nd St is where Civil War hero and President Ulysses S Grant and his wife Julia are buried. Completed in 1897 – 12 years after Grant's death – the granite structure cost $600,000 and is the largest mausoleum in the country. The building was a graffiti-marred mess for years until the general's relatives threatened to move his body somewhere else and shamed the National Park Service into cleaning it.

It's open Wednesday to Sunday 9 am to 4:30 pm. Admission is free (subway: 116th St-Columbia).

Riverside Church

Riverside Church (☎ 212-222-5900), 490 Riverside Drive at 122nd St, is a gothic marvel overlooking the Hudson River; it was built by the Rockefeller family in 1930. The observation deck, 355 feet above the ground, is open to the public during good weather ($2), and its 74 carillon bells, the largest grouping in the world, are rung every Sunday at noon and 3 pm.

It's open daily from 9 am to 4 pm, with interdenominational services on Sunday at 10:45 am (subway: 116th St-Columbia).

HARLEM (MAP 8)

New York's best-known African American neighborhood is going through a real transition. Tourist dollars are flowing in thanks to the many Japanese and European travelers who are eager to learn about Harlem's significant history. But the many bus tours give off an unseemly vibe – much like an urban safari undertaken by people too fearful to move about on foot.

The city has aggressively promoted Harlem to developers, and the plan seems to be working. The new Harlem USA entertainment and retail complex (☎ 212-316-2500), 300 West 125th St, near the Apollo Theater, opened in 2000. It has a dance club, 12-screen cinema, a rooftop-skating rink and a Disney store.

The best time to visit Harlem is on a Sunday morning when people head to services at the dozens of small churches in the neighborhood. Wednesday is also good, because you can end the day at the Apollo Theater and watch its famous amateur night.

As you explore Harlem, you should note that the major avenues have been renamed in honor of prominent African Americans, but many locals still call the streets by their original names, making getting around a little confusing. From west to east: Eighth Ave/Central Park West is Frederick Douglass Blvd; Seventh Ave is Adam Clayton Powell Jr Blvd, named for the controversial preacher who served in Congress during the 1960s; Lenox Ave has been renamed for the Muslim activist Malcolm X; and 125th St is also known as Martin Luther King Jr Blvd.

First time visitors will probably be surprised to discover that Harlem is but one express stop away from the Columbus Circle-59th St station downtown. The trip on the A and D trains takes just five minutes, and the station is only one block from the Apollo Theater and two blocks from Lenox Ave, where there are many soul food restaurants. The 2 and 3 trains from the West Side stop on Lenox Ave at 116th St (site of the Harlem open-air market) and at Lenox and 125th St.

Apollo Theater

The Apollo Theater (☎ 212-749-5838), on W 125th St just east of Douglas Blvd, has been Harlem's leading space for political rallies and concerts since 1914. Virtually every major black artist of note in the 1930s and '40s performed there, including Duke Ellington and Charlie Parker. After a brief desultory spell as a movie theater and several years of darkness, the Apollo was bought in 1983 and revived as a live venue. It still holds its famous weekly amateur night – 'where stars are born and legends are made' – on Wednesday at 7:30 pm. Watching the crowd call for the 'executioner' to yank hapless performers from the stage is often the most entertaining part of amateur night.

On other nights the Apollo hosts performances by established artists such as

NEW YORK

Check out amateur night at the Apollo.

KIM GRANT

the crafts and culture of African Americans for nearly 30 years, and it provides working spaces to promising young artists. Its photography collection includes works by James VanDerZee, the master photographer who chronicled the Harlem Renaissance of the 1920s and '30s.

It's open Wednesday to Friday from 10 am to 5 pm and Saturday and Sunday from 1 to 5 pm. Admission is $5 for adults, $3 for seniors and students and $1 for children under 12.

Schomburg Center for Research in Black Culture

The nation's largest collection of documents, rare books and photographs recording black history is at the Schomburg Center for Research in Black Culture (☎ 212-491-2200), 515 Lenox Ave. Arthur Schomburg, born in Puerto Rico to a white father and black mother, started gathering works on black history during the early 20th century while becoming active in the movements for civil rights and Puerto Rican independence.

His collection was purchased by the Carnegie Foundation and eventually expanded and stored in this branch of the New York Public Library. The Schomburg Center has a theater where lectures and concerts are regularly held.

It's open Monday to Wednesday noon to 8 pm and Friday and Saturday 10 am to 6 pm. The center's gallery spaces are also open Sunday 1 to 5 pm. Admission is free.

Gospel Services

Some of the churches in Harlem have cut deals with bus operators, and their services are packed with visitors who attempt to take pictures during the services or even leave early. It's much better to go on your own to a place that welcomes visitors but not tour groups.

The **Abyssinian Baptist Church** (☎ 212-862-7474), 132 W 138th St, was a downtown institution started by an Ethiopian businessman. It moved north to Harlem in 1923, mirroring the migration of the city's black population. Its charismatic pastor Calvin O Butts is an important community activist

Whitney Houston and comedian Chris Rock, to name a few.

Striver's Row

While you're in Harlem, check out Striver's Row, also known as the St Nicholas Historic District, just east of St Nicholas Park. These row houses and apartments, many designed by Stanford White's firm in the 1890s, were much prized (check out the alleyway signs advising visitors to 'walk their horses'). When whites moved out of the neighborhood, the buildings were occupied by Harlem's black elite, thus giving the area its colloquial name. Striver's Row is one of the most visited blocks in Harlem – so try to be a bit discreet, because the locals (modern-day Harlem elites) are a little sick of all the tourists. Streetside plaques explain more of the area's history.

Studio Museum in Harlem

The Studio Museum in Harlem (☎ 212-864-4500), 144 W 125th St, has given exposure to

whose support is sought by politicians of all parties. The church has a superb choir and holds services every Sunday at 9 and 11 am and 3 pm.

The **Canaan Baptist Church** (☎ 212-866-0301), 132 W 116th St, may be Harlem's friendliest church. It's considerate to show up a bit early and introduce yourself to the parishioners before the Sunday 10:45 am service (10 am during the summer) and to refrain from taking pictures during the service.

Harlem Market

Vendors at the semi-enclosed Harlem Market, at W 116th St and Lenox Ave, do a brisk business selling tribal masks, oils, traditional clothing and assorted African bric-a-brac. Most of the people at the market used to sell their wares from tables set up along 125th St, but were moved to the open-air site, amid great controversy, in 1995 after retailers complained about their presence. You can also find cheap clothing, leather goods, music cassettes and bootleg videos of films still in first-run theaters. The market is operated by the **Malcolm Shabazz Mosque**, the former pulpit of Muslim orator Malcolm X, which stands across the street.

The market is open daily from about 10 am to 5 pm.

Spanish Harlem

Spanish Harlem is the name given to the area from Fifth Ave above 96th St east to the river. Formerly an Italian neighborhood, it now contains one of the biggest Latino communities in the city. There, on Park Ave above 110th St, you will find **La Marqueta**, a colorful, ad-hoc collection of produce stalls that is a signature attraction in 'El Barrio.'

El Museo del Barrio (☎ 212-831-7272), 1230 Fifth Ave, in an unprepossessing office block, began in 1969 as a celebration of Puerto Rican art and culture and has since expanded its brief holdings to include the folk art of Latin America and Spain. Its galleries now feature pre-Columbian artifacts and a collection of more than 300 *santos*, hand-carved wooden saints in the Spanish Catholic tradition. Temporary exhibits

feature the work of local artists who live in Spanish Harlem.

El Museo del Barrio is the best starting point for any exploration of Spanish Harlem. It's open Wednesday to Sunday 11 am to 5 pm, with extended summer hours on Thursday to 7 pm. Admission is $4 for adults, $2 for seniors and students, and children under 12 get in free.

Every January 5, the museum holds a **Three Kings Parade** in which hundreds of schoolchildren, along with camels, donkeys and sheep, make their way up Fifth Ave to 116th St, the heart of the neighborhood (subway: 103rd St-Lexington).

Organized Tours

Harlem Spirituals (☎ 212-757-0425) offers several black heritage excursions that cost $15 to $75. It maintains a website at www.harlemspirituals.com. Harlem, Your Way! (☎ 212-690-1687, 800-382-9363) has tours from $25 to $55. Its website is www.harlemyourway.com. Walking tours ($12 to $15) are also sponsored by the Municipal Art Society (☎ 212-935-3960) and Urban Explorations (☎ 718-721-5254). The Municipal Art Society's Harlem tours are more informative and are cheaper.

WASHINGTON HEIGHTS

Near the northern tip of Manhattan, Washington Heights is named after President George Washington, who set up a Continental Army fort there during the War for Independence. An isolated rural spot until the late 19th century, Washington Heights is today an unremarkable neighborhood of large apartment buildings. In the 1990s, the neighborhood saw the arrival of thousands of new immigrants from the Dominican Republic. The area around the Cloisters, which includes **Fort Tryon Park**, is quite beautiful in warm weather.

Free shuttle buses run between the area's museums from 11 am to 5 pm. (Call one of the following places to find out the schedule.)

Audubon Terrace

Audubon Terrace, at Broadway and 155th St, is the former home of naturalist John

James Audubon and the site of three little known, free museums.

The **American Numismatic Society** (☎ 212-234-3130) has a large permanent collection of coins, medals and paper money. It is open Tuesday to Saturday 9 am to 4:30 pm and Sunday 1 to 4 pm. Admission is free.

The **Hispanic Society of America** (☎ 212-690-0743) has furniture and artifacts of Spanish and Portuguese culture, including significant artworks by El Greco. Few people make the journey up here – guards often outnumber visitors, and they'll have to come upstairs to turn on the lights so you can see the paintings. There are also some nice statues in the courtyard. It's open Tuesday to Saturday 10 am to 4:30 pm and Sunday 1 to 4 pm; admission is free.

The **American Academy & Institute of Arts & Letters** (☎ 212-368-5900) opens its bronze doors to the public several times a year for temporary exhibitions related to literature; call ahead for the schedule. Admission to exhibitions is free (subway: 155th St-St Nicholas Ave).

Morris-Jumel Mansion

Built in 1765, the columned Morris-Jumel Mansion (☎ 212-923-8008), 65 Jumel Terrace at 160th St east of St Nicholas Ave, served as George Washington's Continental Army headquarters. After the war it returned to its former function as the summer residence of a wealthy local family. The mansion's interior is a designated landmark (a rarity for an interior) and contains many of the original furnishings, including a bed on the 2nd floor that reputedly belonged to Napoleon. The ghost of Eliza Jumel, the woman who lived here until her death in 1865, is said to still move about the place.

It's open Wednesday to Sunday 10 am to 4 pm; admission is $3 for adults, $2 for seniors and students and free for children under 10 (subway: 163rd St-Amsterdam Ave).

The Cloisters

Built in the 1930s, the Cloisters (☎ 212-923-3700), in Fort Tryon Park, is partially constructed of fragments of old French and Spanish monasteries. It houses the Metropolitan Museum of Art's collection of medieval frescos, tapestries (including the famous Unicorn tapestries) and paintings. In summer, the best time to visit, concerts and are held on the grounds, and more than 250 varieties of medieval flowers and herbs grow in the courtyard garden. The museum and the surrounding gardens in Fort Tryon Park are very popular with European visitors, so get here early during the warm months.

It's open Tuesday to Sunday 9:30 am to 4:45 pm. Admission is $10/3.50 for adults/children, and free for those under 12 (subway: 190th St).

Dyckman House Museum

The Dyckman House (☎ 212-304-9422), 4881 Broadway, was built in 1783 on the site of a 28-acre 17th-century farm and is the only remaining Dutch farmhouse to survive in Manhattan. Excavations of the property have turned up valuable clues about colonial life.

It's open Tuesday to Sunday 11 am to 4 pm, and admission is free, although donations are welcome (and needed for funding).

To get to the Dyckman House, take the subway to the 207th St station and walk one block south – many people mistakenly get off one stop too soon at Dyckman St.

The Bronx

The Bronx – a geographic area that has a curious article before its name, like The Hague – is named after the Bronck family, Dutch farmers who owned a huge tract of property in the area. They, in turn, gave their name to Bronck's River, which led to the derivation used today.

The Bronx was a metaphor for urban decay and the birthplace of America's rap music industry. But even the southwestern part of the borough – the area unofficially referred to as the South Bronx – doesn't quite live up to its reputation, thanks to a 10-year, multibillion dollar program to build low income housing.

The borough, once a forest-like respite from the rest of the city, but now home to 1.2 million people, is a study in contrasts. The

Morrisania section of the lower Bronx is still riddled with abandoned buildings, while Fieldston, in the northern reaches of the borough, is a privately owned community of Tudor homes occupied by some of the city's richest residents. The Bronx also boasts the quiet and isolated fishing community of City Island as well as the 2764-acre Pelham Bay Park, the city's largest.

The Bronx Tourism Council (☎ 718-590-3518) offers a visitors' guide to the borough and keeps track of community events. The Bronx County Historical Society (☎ 718-881-8900) sponsors weekend walking tours of various sites. Call ahead for details.

Yankee Stadium

The legendary ballpark at 161st St and River Ave (☎ 718-293-6000) is called 'the most famous stadium since the Roman Coliseum.' Throughout the summer it hosts 81 home games for the New York Yankees (see the 'Team of the Century' boxed text). Gates open 90 minutes before game time, and fans can visit the left field **Memorial Park** where plaques are dedicated to such baseball greats as Babe Ruth, Lou Gehrig, Mickey Mantle and Joe DiMaggio. Several bustling memorabilia shops and restaurants stand across from the stadium. **Stan's Sports Bar** gets particularly raucous when the Yankees play the arch-rival Boston Red Sox. Tickets cost between $12.50 and $30, with distant bleacher seats priced at $5 (to be avoided on hot days, because there is no shade).

Yankee Stadium is 15 minutes from downtown via the 4 and D trains (subway: Yankee Stadium).

New York Botanical Garden

The 250-acre New York Botanical Garden (☎ 718-817-8700) features several beautiful

---

Team of the Century

Major sports leagues are often dominated by a single franchise, and no team has loomed larger in American baseball history than the New York Yankees. The 'Bronx Bombers' are arguably the most famous sports team in the world, and millions recognize their team symbol, an interlocking 'NY' on a navy blue hat. Yankees caps can be found on top of heads in cities as diverse as London, Beijing, Sydney and Cairo.

Even their ballpark is famous: Yankee Stadium has been the site of numerous heavyweight title fights, a famous National Football league championship match, and it was the site of masses celebrated by two Popes (Pope Paul VI and John Paul II).

The turning point for the Yankees came in 1920 when they picked up a pitcher named George Herman 'Babe' Ruth from the Boston Red Sox. Ruth's spectacular home run hitting drew huge crowds, and he helped the Yankees win their first American League pennant in 1921 and their first World Series in 1923. Yankee Stadium was built in 1923 and renovated in 1976. It is still referred to as the 'House that Ruth Built,' because it was partly designed to suit his hitting style and was made large enough to fit the many fans who came just to see him.

In 1927 Babe Ruth hit 60 homers, which remained a record for a single season until 1961. His career total of 714 home runs (659 for the Yankees) wasn't surpassed until Hank Aaron beat it in 1974.

From the 1920s through the 1960s, the Yankees had a talent for seamlessly handing the club from one major star to another. These men – Lou Gherig, Joe DiMaggio and Mickey Mantle – became popular cultural icons, even to people who didn't follow baseball. Although the Yankees hit a fallow period in the '80s, they came roaring back at the end of the century, capturing three World Series victories between 1996–1999 and setting several records in the process. In 1999, the Yankees handily won their 25th World Series title, marking them as the most successful baseball club of all time.

The world-famous NY Botanical Garden

gardens and the restored Victorian **Enid A Haupt Conservatory**, a grand iron and glass edifice.

There's also an outdoor **Rose Garden**, next to the conservatory, and a **Rock Garden** with a multitiered waterfall. It's open Tuesday to Sunday 10 am to 6 pm, with the same hours on national holidays that fall on Monday. Admission is $7 for adults and $2 for children.

You can reach the garden by taking the D train to Bedford Park Blvd and walking east down the hill for seven blocks to the gate. Metro North trains (☎ 212-532-4900) leave hourly from Grand Central Terminal to the Botanical Garden stop; it costs $4 each way and is faster – and closer to the garden – than the subway.

Bronx Zoo

The Bronx Zoo (☎ 718-367-1010), also known by its more politically correct title Bronx Wildlife Conservation Society, attracts more than 2 million visitors annually to its 265-acre site. Nearly 5000 animals are on exhibit, all in naturalistic settings. It's best to visit the zoo in warm weather, because many of the outdoor rides are closed during the winter months and the animals retreat into sheltered areas.

The usual array of lions, tigers and bears can be viewed from the Bengali Express Monorail (tickets: $2), which is open May to October and offers a 25-minute narrated journey through the Wild Asia areas. The Jungle World indoor exhibit, which is open year-round, is a 37,000-sq-foot re-creation of the Asian tropics with a hundred different species of animals and tropical plants. You'll either be delighted or terrified by the World of Darkness, where bats hover nearly unseen (but not unsmelled).

The zoo is open daily 10 am to 5 pm weekdays and to 5:30 pm on weekends; but it closes at 4:30 pm November through March. Admission costs $9 for adults, $5 for seniors and children aged two to 12. Admission is less November through March and free on Wednesday and Saturday from 10 am to noon.

Liberty Lines Express (☎ 718-652-8400) runs buses to the Bronx Zoo. The buses pick up passengers along Madison Ave (at 26th, 47th, 54th, 63rd, 69th and 84th Sts) for $5. You can also reach the zoo via the subway (2 or 5 trains) or with a car by taking the Bronx River Parkway. Parking at the zoo costs $6 (subway: Pelham Pkwy).

Arthur Ave

Just south of Fordham University is the Belmont section of the Bronx, the most authentic Italian neighborhood in the city. This is a neighborhood for pure gastronomic exploration (see the Places to Eat section, later in this chapter), and a place to soak up true Italian American culture.

Belmont is the perfect place to head on a Saturday (some shops are closed Sunday) to stock up on Italian provisions, including live chickens at the Arthur Ave Poultry Market, 2356 Arthur Ave, and Teitel Brothers Wholesalers (☎ 718-733-9400), on the corner of 186th St and Arthur Ave. The **Arthur Ave Retail Market** contains indoor food stalls, including Mike & Sons, a cheese shop with heartbreakingly good aged parmesan and prosciutto. The Cosenza fresh fish store, 2354 Arthur Ave, sells clams on the half shell to pedestrians from a small table on the street, and clerks at the Calabria Pork Store (☎ 718-367-5145), 2338 Arthur Ave, offer free samples of hot and sweet homemade sausages that age on racks that are suspended from the ceiling.

The **Belmont Italian American Playhouse** (☎ 718-364-4700), 2384 Arthur Ave, is the neighborhood's most lively performance spot. It's the site of a season of new theatrical works that run from April to December, and it's a place where local authors and musicians perform year-round.

You can reach Arthur Ave by taking the Metro North trains from Grand Central to Fordham Rd or the 4 train to the stop of the same name and walking east 11 blocks, then turning right at Arthur Ave and continuing south for three blocks.

City Island

Surely the oddest and most unexpected neighborhood in the Bronx is City Island, a 1½-mile-long fishing community 15 miles from Midtown Manhattan. City Island has numerous boat slips, is home to three yacht clubs, and it's the place to go if you're interested in diving, sailing or fishing in Long Island Sound. Perhaps the strangest thing about this self-contained little spot cut off from the rest of the Bronx by Pelham Bay Park is that there's hardly a trace of the New York accent found in conversation between the locals – in fact their inflections and accents betray a New England influence.

All of its shops and 20-odd seafood restaurants are along City Island Ave, which runs the length of the island. The short side streets are filled with attractive clapboard houses that overlook the surrounding water, and the main marinas are found on the western side.

You can reach City Island by taking the 6 subway train to its terminus at Pelham Bay Park and getting on the Bx29 bus that runs directly to City Island Ave, or by taking an express bus from Madison Ave in Midtown directly to City Island ($6 one-way).

Brooklyn

This is the only 'outer borough' that rivals Manhattan in the popular imagination. For years a sign on the eastern side of the Brooklyn Bridge welcomed visitors to the 'fourth-largest city in the America.' The sign has been replaced by one with a less separatist sentiment, but Brooklyn's pride – and right to claim big-city status – still remains (it is home to 2.3 million people). The borough even makes the claim that 'one out of every seven famous people' in America was born in Brooklyn!

Brooklyn, officially called Kings County, derives its name from *breucklen*, the Dutch word for marshland. For most of its 350-year history Brooklyn was a collection of farming villages, and its citizens joined greater New York City with great reluctance. Even after the 1898 consolidation the borough remained independent in spirit: Citizens enjoyed Prospect Park, Brooklyn's own version of Central Park, followed the fortunes of the Brooklyn Dodgers baseball team and sun worshipped at the ritzy resort hotels on Coney Island. But much of Brooklyn's separate city pretensions were destroyed in the late 1950s, when the Dodgers moved to the West Coast and many of the borough's residents began moving to the suburbs.

Today Brooklyn's inner neighborhoods are home to newer immigrants from the Caribbean, Eastern Europe and the former Soviet Union. The old carriage houses and brownstones in neighborhoods along the eastern part of the borough have been snapped up by professionals looking for a nice space within commuting distance of Manhattan.

INFORMATION

The Brooklyn Tourism Project (☎ 718-855-7882) issues a free calendar of events called *Meet Me in Brooklyn*. It's updated every three months and is available at all Brooklyn cultural institutions. *Brooklyn Bridge*, a monthly magazine on sale in shops and newsstands throughout the borough, has a more extensive list of happenings. There are also a number of free neighborhood newspapers that list events.

BROOKLYN HEIGHTS

This neighborhood of brownstones and mansions near the mouth of the East River

BROOKLYN HEIGHTS

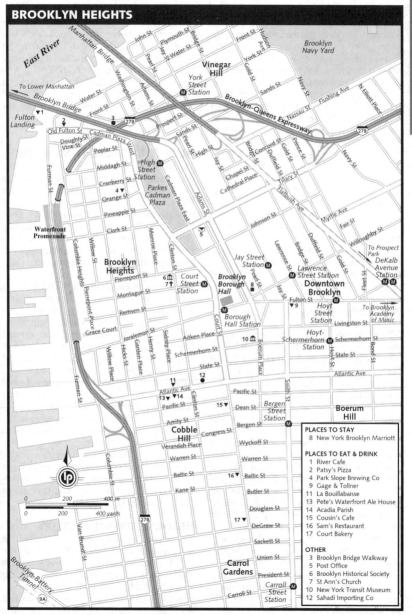

PLACES TO STAY
8 New York Brooklyn Marriott

PLACES TO EAT & DRINK
1 River Cafe
2 Patsy's Pizza
4 Park Slope Brewing Co
9 Gage & Tollner
11 La Bouillabaisse
13 Pete's Waterfront Ale House
14 Acadia Parish
15 Cousin's Cafe
16 Sam's Restaurant
17 Court Bakery

OTHER
3 Brooklyn Bridge Walkway
5 Post Office
6 Brooklyn Historical Society
7 St Ann's Church
10 New York Transit Museum
12 Sahadi Importing Co

developed as a ferry departure point for Lower Manhattan in the early 19th century. Walking along its promenade, you get a stunning view of Manhattan's skyscrapers (framed at the bottom by the far less impressive buildings and warehouses that sit along the waterfront).

You can begin a tour of 'The Heights' at the 1848 beaux arts **Brooklyn Borough Hall** (☎ 718-875-4047), 209 Joralemon St. If you are particularly energetic, you can get to Borough Hall from downtown Manhattan via a 20-minute walk across the Brooklyn Bridge, then bear right on the bridge's pedestrian walkway and it will bring you south along Adams St to the building. Borough Hall is open weekdays during business hours; a free tour of the facility is given every Tuesday at 1 pm (subway: Jay St-Borough Hall).

From behind Borough Hall, continue down Montague St, the main avenue for cafes and bars. One block north runs the parallel Pierrepont St (pronounced 'PIER-pont'), site of the Brooklyn Historical Society (see immediately following this section).

Montague St ends at Pierrepont Place and the waterfront promenade, and here you can turn right and continue north on Columbia Heights to **Fulton Landing**, the old ferry dock at the base of the Brooklyn Bridge. This was the main departure point for Manhattan-bound ferries before the bridge was completed in 1883. Now classical music concerts are held on a barge here, and it's a perfect place to watch the sun set beyond Manhattan.

Heading back up the hill along Old Fulton St (which becomes Camden St), turn right and go up Henry St. At Middagh St, turn right again and check out the old wood-frame houses before returning to **Atlantic Ave**, the busy thoroughfare featuring several Middle Eastern spice shops and an array of restaurants. Sahadi Importing Co (☎ 718-624-4550), 187-189 Atlantic Ave, sells its dried fruits and nuts all over the country, and it's worth stopping in to pick up some snacks or simply to enjoy the exotic smells and atmosphere.

BROOKLYN HISTORICAL SOCIETY

This research library (☎ 718-624-0890, 718-254-9830 for walking tours), 128 Pierrepont St, also has a museum dedicated to borough history. The museum is housed in a fine terra-cotta auditorium that's a national landmark. Its digitized collection of 31,000 photographs and prints is available for browsing in the 2nd-floor library. Hours are noon to 5 pm Tuesday to Saturday.

NEW YORK TRANSIT MUSEUM

The transit museum (☎ 718-243-8601) is in a decommissioned subway station from the 1930s. Located at the corner of Boerum Place and Schermerhorn St, a block north of Atlantic Ave, it has a distinctly low-tech look. Virtually unchanged since its opening in 1976, the museum does not have a video presentation, let alone any computer-driven exhibits, and it's in bad need of an update.

What it does have is an impressive collection of subway cars from the transit system's first hundred years; most have their original ads still intact. Keep an eye out for the silver car used in the 1995 film *Money Train*, along with the model R-1, the vintage that inspired Duke Ellington's *Take the A Train*. You will also see the 1947 R-11 model that featured 'germicidal' lighting designed to sterilize tunnel air. The cars were discontinued amid fears that the lights would also sterilize subway conductors and trainmen.

The transit museum also runs tours of the system in antique subway cars several times a year; call for a schedule.

It's open Tuesday, Thursday and Friday 10 am to 4 pm, Wednesday 10 am to 6 pm and Saturday and Sunday noon to 5 pm. Admission is $3/1.50 for adults/children (subway: Jay St-Borough Hall).

HIDDEN SUBWAY HISTORY

The ornate City Hall subway station, built in 1904, was the crown jewel of the first subway line. The station went out of active service in 1945 and was replaced by the adjacent Brooklyn Bridge-City Hall station, now servicing the 4, 5 and 6 Lexington Ave lines. But it's possible to catch a glimpse of the older station even today, because it's used as a turnaround for the local 6 line that terminates at the Brooklyn Bridge-City Hall station.

Get on (or stay on) the last car of a 6 train on the downtown platform. (That way, the conductor who occupies the middle car won't see you and reveal that the train has reached the end of the line.) Within a few minutes the train will begin its turnaround – press your face to the windows on the right-hand side of the car. You'll get a ghostly glimpse of the old City Hall station's terracotta walls and cathedral-like roof structure.

BROOKLYN ACADEMY OF MUSIC

The Brooklyn Academy of Music (BAM; ☎ 718-636-4100), 30 Lafayette Ave, the oldest concert center in the US, consists of the **Majestic Theater** and the **Brooklyn Opera House**. BAM hosts visiting opera companies from around the world and is home to the Mark Morris dance troupe.

You can take public transportation to BAM or call to reserve a spot on the bus that leaves from the corner of 51st St and Lexington Ave in Manhattan an hour before the performance; it costs $10 roundtrip (subway: Atlantic Ave).

PROSPECT PARK

Created in 1866, the 526-acre park is considered the greatest achievement of Frederick Law Olmsted and Calvert Vaux, the same landscaping duo that designed Central Park. Though less crowded than its more famous Manhattan sister, Prospect Park offers many of the same activities along its broad meadows, including **ice-skating** at the Kate Wollman Rink (☎ 718-287-6431), which is open daily October to early March. Admission costs $2.50/1 for adults/children, with skate rental for $3.50. There is also the **Lefferts Homestead Children's Museum** (☎ 718-965-6505), open only on weekends, and a small **zoo** (☎ 718-399-7339), open 10 am to 4 pm; admission costs $2.50/50¢ for adults/children. Information on other activities, including park walks, carousel rides and art exhibitions, is available at the boathouse

(subway: Prospect Park) or by calling ☎ 718-965-8999.

Grand Army Plaza stands at the northwest entrance to the park, marked by an 80-foot **Soldiers' and Sailors' Monument** constructed in 1898 to commemorate the Union Army's triumph during the Civil War. In the summer, you can visit a gallery in the arch that's dedicated to local artists. You can also visit the observation deck that's just below the four horse bronze chariot ($2). New York City's only structure honoring President John F Kennedy is in a small park with a fountain, just north of the Grand Army arch. The immense art deco **Brooklyn Public Library** faces the arch on its south side.

On weekends year-round, a free hourly trolley service makes a loop from Prospect Park to points of interest around the museum, including the park zoo, ice rink, botanical garden, and library. Ask at the museum information desk what time it passes by the entrance (subway: Grand Army Plaza or Prospect Park).

PARK SLOPE

This rectangular-shaped residential neighborhood is immediately west of Prospect Park, and most of its shops and restaurants are along the 18 blocks of Seventh Ave flanked by two subway stations. Novelist Paul Auster and essayist Ian Frazier live here, and there's a literary atmosphere to the area, with four book shops within easy walking distance. Booklink (☎ 718-965-9122), 320 Seventh Ave, features the work of local writers. Park Slope is a pleasant place to have a meal or just linger over coffee. Ozzie's (☎ 718-398-6695), 57 Seventh Ave, is a coffee-shop-cum-literary hangout patronized by local celebrities, and there are several more cafes along the street (subway: D, Q trains to Seventh Ave; F train to Seventh Ave-Park Slope).

EASTERN PARKWAY

Named after the six-lane boulevard that runs along the north end of Prospect Park, this area was once one of the most exclusive neighborhoods in Brooklyn. The area cuts through Prospect Heights and Crown

NEW YORK

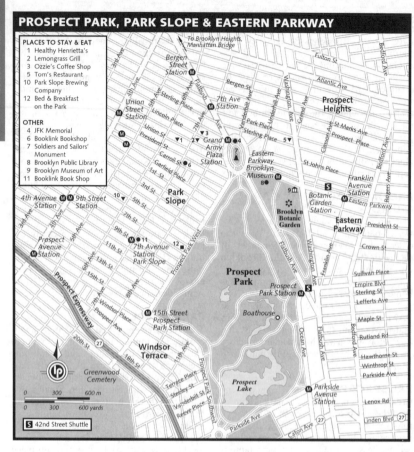

PROSPECT PARK, PARK SLOPE & EASTERN PARKWAY

PLACES TO STAY & EAT
1 Healthy Henrietta's
2 Lemongrass Grill
3 Ozzie's Coffee Shop
5 Tom's Restaurant
10 Park Slope Brewing
    Company
12 Bed & Breakfast
    on the Park

OTHER
4 JFK Memorial
6 Booklink Bookshop
7 Soldiers and Sailors'
    Monument
8 Brooklyn Public Library
9 Brooklyn Museum of Art
11 Booklink Book Shop

Heights, home to the Lubavitch sect of Orthodox Jews and a large Caribbean community. There have been major tensions
between the two groups in recent years, but
it is quite safe to explore shops and restaurants along Washington Ave, which runs in
front of the Brooklyn Museum of Art.

Brooklyn Museum of Art

Were it located anywhere else, the Brooklyn
Museum of Art (☎ 718-638-5000), 200
Eastern Pkwy, would be considered a
premier arts institution. Even though it is
shadowed by the Met, this museum is very

much worth a visit. It's never really
crowded, even on Sunday, and you can take
up an entire day exploring its collection and
seeing the nearby botanical gardens and
Brooklyn Children's Museum (see those
sections, later in this section).

The museum received a lot of publicity in
1999 when it sponsored the Sensation exhibition of young British artists. One the featured artist, Chris Ofili, uses elephant dung
for his paintings. Ofili's portrait of the Virgin
Mary was attacked by Mayor Giuliani,
giving the exhibition (and the mayor) a lot
of press coverage.

The permanent galleries are dedicated to African, Islamic and Asian art. Particularly good are the modern 3rd-floor galleries containing colorful Egyptian cartonnages (mummy casings) and funerary figurines. The 4th floor, which overlooks a tiled court crowned by a skylight, has period rooms, including a reconstruction of the Jan Schenck House, a 17th-century Dutch settlement in Brooklyn. The 5th floor has colonial portraiture, including a famous Gilbert Stuart painting of George Washington in which the general looks particularly uncomfortable wearing his false teeth and a collection of 58 Auguste Rodin sculptures.

The Brooklyn Museum of Art is open Wednesday to Friday 10 am to 5 pm, Saturday 11 am to 9 pm and Sunday 11 am to 6 pm. Admission is free, except for admission charges for the special exhibitions (subway: Eastern Pkwy-Brooklyn Museum).

Brooklyn Botanic Garden

The 52-acre botanic garden (☎ 718-623-7200), 1000 Washington Ave, has more than 12,000 different plants in its 15 gardens. There's a fanciful Celebrity Path with slate steps honoring famous Brooklynites and a Fragrance Garden that makes for a wonderful walk. Unfortunately, someone recently made off with several of the Steinhardt Conservatory's bonsai trees, a few of which were 250 years old or more.

The botanic garden is open Tuesday to Friday 8 am to 6 pm and Saturday and Sunday 8 am to 4:30 pm from April to September. Winter hours are Tuesday to Sunday 10 am to 4:30 pm. Admission for adults and seniors/children is $5/2 (subway: Eastern Pkwy-Brooklyn Museum).

Brooklyn Children's Museum

The Brooklyn Children's Museum (☎ 718-735-4400), 145 Brook Ave at St Mark's Ave, is the world's first museum designed expressly for children. This small facility is full of hands-on exhibits and play programs, but it is not worth a separate trip given that a bigger facility is located in Manhattan. It is worth checking out, though, if you are taking in the Brooklyn Art Museum with kids in tow. Its website is www.bchildmus.org.

CONEY ISLAND

Now somewhat desolate and unattractive, Coney Island was once a bustling showplace where sweating city dwellers came to enjoy the fun house, minor games of chance and bumper car rides in the Dreamland amusement park before WWI. Coney Island is very dead after Labor Day, when the storied **Cyclone** roller coaster closes for the season. But it's still worth the 60-minute trip from Manhattan, especially because it's also the site of the New York Aquarium (see below) and just a quarter-mile boardwalk stroll from Brighton Beach, the nation's largest grouping of Russian immigrants.

As you emerge from the colorfully decrepit subway station, you'll see a 24-hour coffee shop right in the middle of the station. Hard-bitten patrons sit at a countertop hunched over their meals and dozens of menu items are advertised on the bright yellow walls of the shop. Meanwhile, your nose is assaulted by the smell of sausages, hot dogs, home fries and other greasy delights. Then pass through the doors to Surf Ave, where Russian residents pick up odd tools and electronic equipment at **flea market** stalls along the street.

Not far from here is the **Coney Island Sideshow** (☎ 718-372-5159), 1208 Surf Ave, a small museum and freak show where you can see snake charmers, tattooed ladies and sword swallowers for a small admission charge.

Nathan's, the city's prototypical fast-food stand, has been open at the same Surf Ave site for more than 75 years and still sells its famous hot dogs ($2.50) from 8 am to 4 am daily.

Along the Boardwalk you will see two relics of Coney Island's past glory: the bright red parachute jump, moved here from the 1939 World's Fair in Queens, and the ivy covered **Thunderbolt** roller coaster that operated from 1925 to 1983. It's older than the more famous Cyclone in the Astroland Amusement Park just up the boardwalk (subway: Coney Island).

NEW YORK

JENNIFER STEFFEY

Working off the hot dogs at Nathan's

New York Aquarium

The New York Aquarium (☎ 718-265-3400), along the Coney Island Boardwalk is now called the Aquarium for Wildlife Conservation. Its manageable scale makes it a wonderful place for young children. There's a touch pool where kids can handle starfish and other small forms of sea life, and there is a small amphitheater with Sea World-style dolphin shows several times daily. Most children love observing whales and seals from the outside railing that overlooks the tanks or from the observation windows that afford views of the animals in their underwater habitats. You can spend the better part of a day at the aquarium viewing its 10,000 specimens of sea life.

It's open every day in summer, and in the winter it is open on weekends from 10 am to 6 pm. Admission to the aquarium is $8.75 for adults and $4.50 for seniors and children (subway: W 8th St-NY Aquarium).

BRIGHTON BEACH

There's more than a little bit of Russia to be found in Brighton Beach, just a five-minute walk north via the Boardwalk. Russian shops, bakeries and restaurants line Brighton Beach Ave, which runs parallel to the Boardwalk and is just one block from the beach.

Brighton Beach has been identified as the main money laundering spot in the US for the Russian mafia. But there's no reason to worry about crime on the street – just about the only criminal behavior you'll observe are the *babushkas* selling illegal prescriptive medicine Moscow-style on the street corner. This community is so close-knit that a non-Russian speaker will stick out like a sore thumb. But the restaurants and shops are tolerant and friendly to outsiders, a category that includes Brooklynites from any other neighborhood (subway: Brighton Beach).

WILLIAMSBURG

This neighborhood, just over the namesake Williamsburg Bridge, is home to a large Orthodox Jewish community – a living embodiment of what Manhattan's Lower East Side once was in the early 20th century. But the windswept northern area of Williamsburg, is much different and varied in character. The north has long been home to a large population of Central European immigrants, mostly from Poland. In recent years, this aging community has been augmented by many aspiring artists and writers who are taking advantage of the cheap rents and large loft spaces. The two distinct communities coexist quite peacefully. On sunny Sunday afternoons, you can see Polish senior citizens hanging out on just about every other doorstep, exchanging greetings in their native language after church services, while paint-splattered younger folks gather in the local bars for brunch, beer and cigarettes.

Though the local press has noted Williamsburg's growing popularity with the cutting edge art crowd, there has yet to be an invasion of art galleries or Manhattan-level rents. A college campus atmosphere prevails along Bedford St, where locals looking for apartment shares post signs on mini 'democracy walls,' and musicians advertise for band mates.

Though Williamsburg doesn't have much to offer culturally as yet, it's only a five-minute subway trip from Manhattan's Union Square and worth seeing in good weather – you can grab a good meal here and admire the sunset view of Manhattan from Kent Ave along the waterfront (subway: L to Bedford Ave).

Brooklyn Brewery

Since 1988, the Brooklyn Brewery has made its award-winning Brooklyn Lager under contract at breweries outside the borough. But the beer 'came home' to Brooklyn in 1996 with the opening of a microbrewery in Williamsburg (☎ 718-486-7422), 79 N 11th St. Housed in a series of buildings that once made up the Hecla Ironworks factory (the firm that made the structural supports for the Waldorf-Astoria Hotel), the brewery has become a Williamsburg institution.

There is a non-smoking tasting room with a display of historical beer bottles and monthly specials. There is often entertainment at night and a happy hour every Friday between 6 pm and 9 pm. On Saturday, there are free tours from noon to 4 pm that include a free tasting. During the summer, call in advance to find out if the tours are booked.

Queens

Manhattan has the fame. Brooklyn has the pride. The Bronx has the attitude. Staten Island, the temperament of the put upon. Where does that leave Queens, a borough of boring, low slung row houses and a transitional zone between Manhattan urban and Long Island suburban? Only as the most ethnically diverse spot in the Untied States. The area's cheap rents and proximity to the airports has long made Queens attractive to the newest New Yorkers.

With a landmass of 282 sq miles, Queens is the largest borough in New York City. A strange phenomenon has happened over the years – most of the newer immigrant groups have augmented, rather than replaced, those already in Queens. More than 100 minority groups now live in this borough, speaking over 120 different languages or dialects – and its population is over 2 million.

The Queens Council on the Arts has a 24-hour hotline (☎ 718-291-2787) on community cultural events; in keeping with the multicultural demographics of the borough, it provides information in English, Spanish, Korean and Chinese.

ASTORIA

This residential neighborhood is home to the largest Greek community in the US; it also has a smattering of Eastern European immigrants. Astoria was a mid-19th century ferry depot named after millionaire fur merchant John Jacob Astor. It soon developed into a neighborhood of factories, including

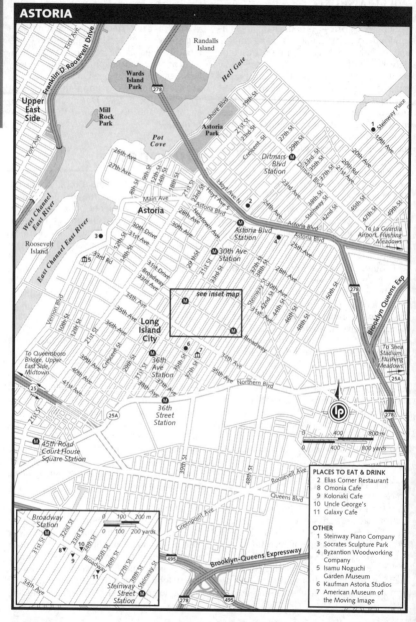

ASTORIA

Randalls
Island

Wards
Island
Park

Hell Gate

Upper
East
Side

Mill
Rock
Park

Pot
Cove

Astoria
Park

Ditmars
Blvd
Station

Main Ave

Astoria

Roosevelt
Island

West Channel East River

East Channel East River

Astoria Blvd
Station

Astoria Blvd

To La Guardia
Airport, Flushing
Meadows

30th Ave
Station

see inset map

Long
Island
City

To Queensboro
Bridge, Upper
East Side,
Midtown

36th Ave
Station

Northern Blvd

To Shea
Stadium,
Flushing
Meadows

36th
Street
Station

45th Road
Court House
Square Station

Roosevelt Ave

Queens Blvd

Broadway
Station

Greenpoint Ave

Brooklyn-Queens Expressway

Steinway
Street
Station

PLACES TO EAT & DRINK
2 Elias Corner Restaurant
8 Omonia Cafe
9 Kolonaki Cafe
10 Uncle George's
11 Galaxy Cafe

OTHER
1 Steinway Piano Company
3 Socrates Sculpture Park
4 Byzantion Woodworking
   Company
5 Isamu Noguchi
   Garden Museum
6 Kaufman Astoria Studios
7 American Museum of
   the Moving Image

the Steinway Piano Company, which still operates there. The German and Italian craftsmen who lived in Astoria were replaced by Greek immigrants in the years following WWII.

Today, Astoria is proudly a working-class neighborhood of brick and concrete apartment blocks and two story wooden homes (subway: N train to Broadway; R train to Steinway St).

American Museum of the Moving Image

The American Museum of the Moving Image (☎ 718-784-0077), at 35th Ave and 36th St, stands in the middle of the Kaufman Astoria Studio complex. This 75-year-old film production center has been the shooting site of everything from the Marx Brothers' *Coconuts* to *Glengarry Glen Ross* and TV's *Cosby Show*.

Unfortunately, the studios are not open to public tours, but this museum makes a good effort at showing the mastery behind filmmaking, with galleries showing the makeup

and costumes from films such as *The Exorcist* and movie sets from the 1987 *Glass Menagerie*, directed by Paul Newman. Film and TV serials are played in a small theater built by conceptual artist Red Grooms, inspired by the 1930s Egyptian-theme movie palaces.

The museum also holds interesting film retrospectives year-round, with several movies screened daily. If you decide to make the short 15-minute subway ride out to Queens, go when there's an interesting film on offer, and end your day with a Greek meal on Broadway.

It's open Tuesday to Friday noon to 5 pm and Saturday and Sunday noon to 6 pm. Admission is $8.50/5.50 for adults/seniors, and $4.50 for children and students (subway: Steinway St).

Isamu Noguchi Garden Museum

Tucked away among the East River warehouses in Long Island City, the cinder-block Isamu Noguchi Garden Museum (☎ 718-721-1932), 32-37 Vernon Blvd, stands on the site of a studio designed by the Japanese-American sculptor who died in 1988, three years after the museum opened. The 12 galleries and garden contain more than 300 examples of his work.

It's open April to November only on Wednesday, Saturday and Sunday 11 am to 6 pm, and a tour of all the galleries takes place at 2 pm. Admission is $4/2 for adults/children.

Just two blocks north, where Broadway meets Vernon Blvd, is the **Socrates Sculpture Park** (☎ 718-545-5707), a free, year-round, open-air public space with changing works by local artists on a former illegal waste dump overlooking the East River. The displayed works, including the five wind chimes along the shoreline, have a stark industrial look to them that's in keeping with its location right next to a steel company. It's open 10 am to dusk; admission is free (subway: N to Broadway).

FLUSHING & AROUND

It's hard to imagine that the bustling neighborhood of Flushing – right in the middle of

---

Artisans at Work

You can view two very different examples of skilled craftsmanship in Astoria. The **Byzantion Woodworking Company** (☎ 718-932-2960), 37-20 Astoria Blvd, doesn't offer tours, but you can drop by Monday to Saturday to see artisans at work carving elaborate Greek Orthodox religious items for clients from around the US and Canada.

The **Steinway Piano Company** (☎ 718-721-2600, ext 164), at 19th Ave and 38th St, has been making world-class pianos in Queens for more than 100 years. Steinway is the leading concert piano; in Manhattan, there's a showroom near Carnegie Hall just across from Planet Hollywood. The factory in Astoria offers free 90-minute tours of its facility every Thursday. It's vital to call ahead to reserve a place, because the tours are often booked by school groups months in advance (subway: Ditmars Blvd).

NEW YORK

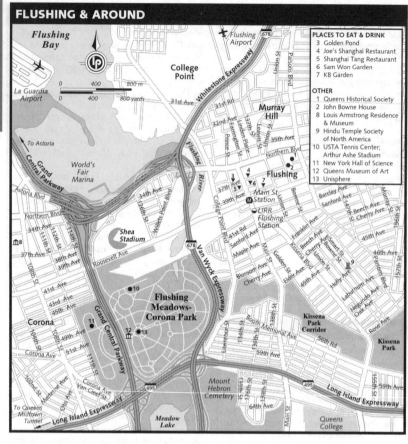

FLUSHING & AROUND

Flushing Bay

Flushing Airport

678

College Point

La Guardia Airport

To Astoria

Grand Central Parkway

Astoria Blvd

Northern Blvd

34th Ave

37th Ave

Corona

Corona Ave

To Queens Midtown Tunnel

Long Island Expressway

World's Fair Marina

Shea Stadium

Roosevelt Ave

678

Van Wyck Expressway

Flushing Meadows-Corona Park

Grand Central Parkway

495

Meadow Lake

Whitestone Expressway

31st Ave
31st Rd

32nd Ave

35th Ave

Murray Hill

Northern Blvd

Flushing River

College Point Blvd

Main St Station

LIRR Flushing Station

Flushing

Barclay Ave
Sanford Ave

Beech Ave
Cherry Ave

45th Ave

46th Ave

Kissena Park Corridor

Kissena Park

Mount Hebron Cemetery

495 Long Island Expressway

59th Ave

Queens College

PLACES TO EAT & DRINK
3 Golden Pond
4 Joe's Shanghai Restaurant
5 Shanghai Tang Restaurant
6 Sam Won Garden
7 KB Garden

OTHER
1 Queens Historical Society
2 John Bowne House
8 Louis Armstrong Residence & Museum
9 Hindu Temple Society of North America
10 USTA Tennis Center; Arthur Ashe Stadium
11 New York Hall of Science
12 Queens Museum of Art
13 Unisphere

Queens – was once the secluded forest that the mid-17th-century Quakers used as a secret meeting place to circumvent Dutch Governor Peter Stuyvesant's religious intolerance. The country village was also the site of the first commercial nursery in the US, visited by George Washington soon after his inauguration as president.

Flushing eventually became an urban eyesore, the site of a huge commercial ash heap (mentioned in F Scott Fitzgerald's *The Great Gatsby*) and a series of junkyards often noted by travelers to Long Island. The area was reclaimed as parkland for the 1939 World's Fair, and it saw a huge influx of Korean and Chinese immigrants in the 1980s.

Packed as it is with discount shops, 24-hour coffee shops and municipal offices, Flushing is anything but architecturally charming. But at some spots, with the prevalent signage in Korean, you could possibly believe you're in a residential neighborhood in Seoul. Although some of the older residents resent the incursion of new Asian immigrants, so far Flushing has not suffered from any outward tensions between the various communities.

Flushing's center is at the corner of Roosevelt Ave, which runs east-west, and Main St, which runs north-south – right at the subway exit (subway: Main St-Flushing).

Nearby neighborhoods include Woodsie, Jackson Heights and Corona. This area, with its cheap rents and direct subway connection to Midtown Manhattan, has long been a bastion of first generation immigrants. Recent arrivals from Ireland, Uruguay, Panama, Korea, China and many other countries often head straight to Queens and stay with friends or family before they get on their feet.

These neighborhoods don't have tourist attractions yet, but they are full of cheap, tasty ethnic restaurants. In recognition of this fact, the US government has identified the No 7 train that cuts through the heart of Queens as a National Historic Trail. The Queens Council on the Arts (☎ 718-647-3377), 1 Forest Park, Woodhaven, NY 11421-1166, offers information on what has been dubbed the 'International Express.' Call or send $1 to the organization for more information.

Architecturally, most of these neighborhoods are uniformly bland, a landscape of brick buildings punctuated by wooden, single-family houses. What changes from one stop to another is the ethnic character found around the subway station. (Check out restaurants in this area in the Places to Eat section.)

After leaving Manhattan on the No 7 train (catch it at Grand Central Station or Times Square), you can reach the different neighborhoods by disembarking at subway stations along the line and exploring the blocks nearby. You won't get lost if you keep to Roosevelt Ave, which runs directly under the elevated train tracks for the final third of the line, as a reference point. The journey from Manhattan to the very end of the line at Main St-Flushing takes about 35 minutes.

Flushing Walking Tour

The historical society has maps of the 'Freedom Mile,' listing 19 places of religious significance. The tour is a bit of a cheat, because some of the sites are really the locations of important places that no longer exist. But you can still see the 1661 **John Bowne House**, which stands today at 37-01 Bowne St, near the Kingsland Homestead. Quakers met in the house, which is the oldest residence in Queens, and brochures published in English, Korean, Spanish and Chinese, available for a small donation.

You can obtain maps and brochures (in English, Korean, Spanish and Chinese) for a small donation from the Queens Historical Society (☎ 718-939-0647), 143-35 37th St, housed in the Kingsland Homestead, a wooden 1765 estate house, just beyond Margaret Carmen Green. You can get there by traveling two blocks east on Roosevelt Ave, turning left, and walking two more blocks north.

A 10-minute walk south on Bowne St will bring you to what must be Flushing's most exotic sight: the **Hindu Temple Society of North America** (☎ 718-460-8484), 45-57 Bowne St. The temple, complete with carved elephant-headed gods, was designed and built in India and reconstructed here in 1977. Taking your shoes off and entering the 2nd floor of the temple, you can observe devotees offering coconut milk to the deity Maha Vallabha Ganapati. There are daily services at the temple, which is open 8 am to 9 pm, and at the side of the building a cafe serves yogurt drinks and light fare.

In late August the temple holds a festival to the god Ganesh that lasts nearly two weeks and includes visiting performers from India and a parade through Flushing.

Leaving the temple, you should turn right on Holly Ave, then right again on Kissena Blvd, which will eventually bring you back to Main St.

Louis Armstrong Home & Archives

Corona, once an Italian neighborhood, was also a place where well known black jazz musicians bought comfortable houses in the 1920s and '30s. Louis Armstrong lived at 34-56 107th St (☎ 718-997-3670) from 1929 until his death in 1971; it's open 10 am to 5 pm weekdays. Queens College will be opening his former home as a museum in the near future, so it's best to call ahead for details.

NEW YORK

Flushing Meadows-Corona Park & Shea Stadium

Flushing Meadows Park is the site of **Shea Stadium**, the ballpark of the New York Mets (see Spectator Sports). It is also the location of the **National Tennis Center**, home of the US Open and its **Arthur Ashe Stadium**. The spectacular 1939 and 1964 World's Fairs were also held here.

The center of the park is dominated by the distinctive, 380-ton **Unisphere** globe, built for the 1964 fair by US Steel. A few of the old buildings constructed for the fair are still in use, though Philip Johnson's New York State Pavilion is a mess – rusty, overgrown with weeds and closed to the public (subway: Willets Point-Shea Stadium).

New York Hall of Science

This former World's Fair pavilion (☎ 718-699-0005), which resembles a Stalin-era concrete block, houses a children's museum dedicated to technology. It stands next to an outdoor park with a few early space-age rockets.

It's open Wednesday and Friday to Sunday 10 am to 5 pm, Thursday 2 pm to 5 pm. Admission for adults/children is $7.50/5; free on Wednesday (subway: Willets Point-Shea Stadium).

Queens Museum of Art

The former New York City building for the 1939 World's Fair has been completely renovated as a museum (☎ 718-592-9700) and contains displays dedicated to both fairs held in the park. The building was also the site of the first sessions of the UN before the body moved into its permanent quarters on Manhattan's East Side (a gallery explains the history of those early peacemaking meetings).

The major attraction of the museum is the **Panorama of New York City**. This 9335-sq-foot model of the metropolis debuted at the '64 fair and was a big hit with visitors who marveled at its details reproduced at a scale of 1200:1. In 1994 the panorama was cut up into 273 four-by-10-foot sections and updated to include all of the significant new additions to the local skyline. Today, it's a stunning sight with more than 835,000 tiny buildings. A glass-bottomed observation deck encircles the panorama, and every 15 minutes there's a mock sunset, prompting thousands of tiny lights to flicker on across the diorama.

The Queens museum is open Wednesday to Friday 10 am to 5 pm and weekends noon to 5 pm; admission is $4 for adults and $2 for seniors and students (subway: Willets Point-Shea Stadium).

Staten Island

Residents of the 'forgotten borough' of Staten Island have long entertained thoughts of secession from greater New York City. Its tiny population of 378,900 is primarily white, middle class and politically Republican, and historically, its had little clout in predominately Democratic New York City. Most politicians have made little secret of their disdain for this suburban tract of land close to the New Jersey shoreline. What's worse, the borough is home to the city's largest garbage dump – a fact snickered about in Manhattan and deeply resented on Staten Island. (The dump is scheduled to be closed permanently by 2001.) The borough's image is not helped by the gray, dirty and unimpressive waterfront near the ferry terminal.

Staten Island grew when railway magnate Cornelius Vanderbilt established a ferry service between it and the port of New York in the early years of the 19th century. The island retained its character for verdant farmlands and large estates for the rich, and there was little development there until the 1960s when the construction of the Verrazano Narrows Bridge finally forged a land link with the rest of New York City. Even still, most New Yorkers know the borough as the place to turn around after a pleasantly breezy ferry ride when the weather turns hellish in the summer, or simply as the starting point of the New York City Marathon. Of course, there's more to Staten Island than that, and it's worth a day trip.

The Staten Island Chamber of Commerce (☎ 718-727-1900) provides information on cultural events and attractions weekdays 9 am to 5 pm. The daily *Staten Island Advance* covers local news and events.

Eighteen bus routes converge on the St George Ferry Terminal in Staten Island; from there you can pick up buses to all the major sites. The buses leave within minutes of the ferry's arrival; the fare is $1.50.

STATEN ISLAND FERRY

The ferry (☎ 718-814-2628) is one of New York's best bargains, taking 70,000 passengers each day on the free 20-minute, 6-mile journey from Lower Manhattan to Staten Island. The return trip to Manhattan used to be 50¢, but because Staten Island is a Republican-supporting district, Mayor Rudolph Giuliani abolished the fee. It operates on the half hour, 24 hours a day, and only the most brutal weather will keep the ferries in their slips. (Ferries that carry cars operate from early morning until 9:30 pm and charge $4 per vehicle.)

This is the low-cost, hassle-free alternative to the crowded boat trips to the Statue of Liberty and Ellis Island. You'll pass within a half mile of both on the way out to Staten Island, and the views of Manhattan and Brooklyn Heights are breathtaking. It's best to pack a lunch or snack before heading out to the ferry, because the food on the boat itself is dreadful, and the South Ferry terminal, an outdated facility slated for replacement within a few years, doesn't have a decent restaurant (subway: South Ferry).

Now, *that's* a Kodak moment.

SNUG HARBOR CULTURAL CENTER

The Snug Harbor Cultural Center (☎ 718-448-2500), 1000 Richmond Terrace, is on the site of a retirement complex for sailors that was built between 1831 and 1917. The five buildings just inside the north gate are some of the finest small-scale Greek Revival structures left in the US. Two of the buildings on the site, the Great Hall and the Veterans Memorial Chapel, have impressive interiors.

In 1976 the city took control of the rundown 83-acre site that overlooks the oil tankers and container ships docking in New Jersey and restored it as a complex for the borough's cultural institutions. You can easily spend a day exploring the **Botanical Garden** (☎ 718-273-8200), the **Staten Island Children's Museum** (☎ 718-273-2060), which charges $4 for general admission and the **Newhouse Center for Contemporary Art** (no phone). All three are open Wednesday to Sunday from noon to 5 pm. A free tour of the 28 landmark buildings on the site leaves from the visitors' center on weekends at 2 pm.

You can get to the Snug Harbor Cultural Center by taking the S40 bus from the ferry terminal 2 miles west.

JACQUES MARCHAIS CENTER OF TIBETAN ART

Home to the largest collection of Tibetan art outside China, the Jacques Marchais Center (☎ 718-987-3478), 338 Lighthouse Ave, was built by art dealer Edna Koblentz, who collected the works under an alias that did not betray her gender. It opened to the public in 1947, a year before her death, and includes a number of golden sculptures and religious objects made of human bone. Just about the only authentic thing missing from the home, built in the style of a Tibetan temple, is the smell of yak butter. The museum holds its annual weekend-long Tibetan cultural festival in the early part of October in the outdoor garden amongst the stone Buddhas.

The Marchais Center is open Wednesday to Sunday 1 to 5 pm, with concerts and demonstrations Sunday at 2 pm. Admission for adults/children and seniors is $7/$4.

To get to the Marchais Center by public transportation, take the S74 bus from the ferry terminal (it travels along Richmond Rd and is about a 25-minute ride) and ask the driver to let you off at Lighthouse Ave. The museum is at the top of a hill.

There's a bonus in store for those who make the trek out to the museum – just across Lighthouse Ave from the museum, you can get a glimpse of the **Wright Residence**, the only private home designed by **Frank Lloyd Wright** ever built in New York City. It's the low-slung, cliff-side residence at 48 Manor Court, constructed in 1959 for a private couple.

HISTORIC RICHMOND TOWN

The village of Richmond (☎ 718-351-1611) was once the county seat of Staten Island, and 11 original buildings still stand in what is now a borough preservation project, including the 300-year-old-redwood **Voorlezer's House**, believed to be the oldest surviving school building in the country. In the 1960s, 11 other historic structures from around the island were moved here in an ambitious attempt to protect local history.

Historic Richmond Town is best seen in warm weather to enjoy the surrounding landscape along Richmond Creek. During the summer, volunteers dressed in period garb roam around the grounds ready to explain the ways of 17th-century rural colonial life.

You can begin an exploration of the 100-acre site at the village courthouse that serves as a visitors' center. Every hour, there's a guided tour of the 15 buildings open to the public. There's also a historical museum in the former county clerk's office.

Historic Richmond Town is open during the summer months Wednesday to Friday 11 am to 5 pm and weekends 1 to 5 pm. From September to June it's open Wednesday to Sunday 1 to 5 pm. Admission is $4/2.50 for adults/children and free for children five and younger free. You can reach the center by taking the S74 bus from the ferry to Richmond Ave and St Patrick's Place, a journey of about 35 minutes.

GREENBELT NATURE WALKS

The 2500-acre Greenbelt environmental preserve (☎ 718-667-2165) in the middle of Staten Island encompasses several parks with five different ecosystems, including swamp areas and freshwater wetlands. It's one of New York City's unexplored nature treasures, offering some spectacular walks not far from the bustle of downtown Manhattan. Casual walkers and aggressive hikers are served by its 28 miles of trails. Bird-watchers should also head to the Greenbelt to track its 60 different species of birds.

The **High Rock Park** section of the Greenbelt offers six trails through hardwood forest as well as three gardens. You can get there by taking the S74 bus from the ferry to Rockland Ave, walking up Rockland and then bearing right at Nevada Ave to the park entrance.

The **William T Davis Wildlife Refuge** once housed the wells that gave Staten Islanders their drinking water; today, it is a sanctuary for migrating birds and the site of the Greenbelt Native Plant Center. You can reach the refuge walking trails by taking the S62 or S92 buses from the ferry along Victory Blvd to Travis Ave.

ACTIVITIES

The **Chelsea Piers Complex** (☎ 212-336-6000) on the Hudson River and 23rd St offers a range of activities. This huge complex has a four-level driving range overlooking the river and an indoor ice-skating rink. A huge sports and fitness center there offers a running track, swimming pool, workout center, even sand volleyball and rock-climbing. A day pass costs $26. The complex is open weekdays 6 am to 11 pm, Saturday 7 am to 8 pm and Sunday 8 am to 8 pm (subway: 23rd St).

Gyms all over the city offer day rates for about $15. Many advertise in the *Village Voice*. One well-located, no-frills gym to keep in mind is the Prescriptive Fitness Gym (☎ 212-307-7760) at 250 W 54th St. It offers $15 daily rates for its well-maintained machines, and there's no 'scene' at the club (subway: 50th St-Eighth Ave).

Running

The New York Road Runner's Club (NYRRC; ☎ 212-860-4455), 9 E 89th St, organizes weekend runs all over the city as well as the annual October New York Marathon. Information and assistance for runners can be found at the NYRRC booth at the Engineer's Gate entrance to Central Park at E 90th St.

There are three good spots for solo runs in Manhattan: Central Park's 6-mile roadway loops around the park and is closed to cars each weekday from 10 am to 3 pm and all weekend. If you don't want to jockey for space with rollerbladers and bikers, try the Jacqueline Kennedy Onassis Reservoir (subway: 86th St on either side of the park), which is encircled by a soft 1.6-mile path.

West St has a runner's pathway along the Hudson River from 23rd St all the way down to Battery Park City, which passes a very pleasant stretch of public park and offers great views of the Jersey shoreline and the Statue of Liberty. The Upper East Side boasts a path that runs along FDR Drive and the East River from 63rd St to about 115th St. If you're alone, it's not advisable to run further north than 105th St, because the path isn't well lit beyond that point.

Bicycling

If you hit the city's pockmarked streets, use a trail bike with wide wheels. Also, wear a helmet and be alert so you don't get 'doored' by a passenger exiting a taxi. Transportation Alternatives (☎ 212-475-4600), 92 St Marks Place, is a bike advocacy group that sponsors free or low-cost weekend trips to the outskirts of the city – its newsletter is available at major bike shops.

Many places rent bicycles for the day, including Metro Bicycle. It has seven stores, with one at 6th St and Broadway (☎ 212-663-7531). Other stores include Sixth Ave Bicycles (☎ 212-255-5100), 545 Sixth Ave, and Frank's Bike Shop (☎ 212-533-6332), 533 Grand St, an out-of-the-way shop in the Lower East Side that attracts many customers thanks to its helpful staff and very low prices (subway: Grand St).

ORGANIZED TOURS
Bus Tours

Gray Line (☎ 212-397-2620) offers more than 29 different tours of the city from its main bus terminal at Eighth Ave and 54th St, including a hop-on, hop-off loop of Manhattan. The cheapest tours begin at $15/7.50 for adults/children and go as high as $50/37.50. There is a downside to these tours: you may get a non-native guide who knows far less about the city than some of the passengers. (See Chelsea & Midtown Manhattan map for location.)

New York Apple Tours (Map 5; ☎ 800-876-9868), 53rd St and Broadway next to the Ameritana Hotel, offers tours on rumbling old London double-decker buses that sometimes break down in mid-tour. Buses leave on a loop of Manhattan from the Plaza Hotel and W 50th St and Eighth Ave; it costs $25/16 for adults/children for two days of unlimited use of the buses. (See Chelsea & Midtown Manhattan map for location.)

Walking Tours

There are many companies and organizations that conduct urban treks, and their phone lines offer detailed information on the latest schedules. Big Onion Walking Tours (☎ 212-439-1090), established by two Columbia University history doctoral candidates, operates year-round. It specializes in ethnic New York and runs an annual Christmas Day tour of the Jewish Lower East Side. Its walks cost $10 for adults, $7 for students and seniors. Adventures on a Shoestring (☎ 212-265-2663) charges $5 for tours of historic houses and other places of interest.

New York City Food Tours (☎ 732-636-4650) arranges $20 'walking and tasting tours' of SoHo and Village food shops; samples of the fare are included in the price.

Citywalks (☎ 212-989-2456) has two-hour tours of specific neighborhoods from March to November at a cost of $12 per person. The Municipal Art Society (☎ 212-439-1043) is famous for its free tours of Grand Central Terminal each Wednesday at 12:30 pm; other regularly scheduled tours cost $10 a person.

Boat Tours

More than 1 million people a year take the three-hour, 35-mile Circle Line cruise around Manhattan (☎ 212-563-3200) that leaves from Pier 83 at 42nd St on the Hudson River, from March to December. This is *the* tour to take, provided the weather is good and you can enjoy the waterside breezes on an outside deck. The quality of the narration depends on the enthusiasm of the guide; be sure to sit well away from the narrator to avoid the inevitable 'Where are you from?' banter. Tickets for adults/children/seniors cost $18/9/16.

Circle Line also runs a 2½-hour Tuesday night Jazz Cruise from Pier 83 and a Thursday night Country Music Cruise during the summer; call for reservations.

World Yacht (☎ 212-563-3347) has well-regarded culinary cruises around Manhattan year-round that leave from Pier 81 at W 41st St. Reservations and proper dress are required, and tickets start at $30 for a two-hour lunch to $75 for a three-hour dinner.

Helicopter Tours

Liberty Helicopter Tours (☎ 212-967-4550) has bird's-eye views of the city that depart from two locations: Midtown at W 30th St and Twelfth Ave, and Pier Six on the East River near Whitehall St. Tickets costs $49 to $150, depending on the duration of the tour. Gray Line also offers tours of Manhattan that depart on the half hour from the heliport (☎ 212-397-2600) at E 34th St and First Ave. Island Helicopter Sightseeing (☎ 212-683-4575) has departures from the same site from 9 am to 9 pm daily.

SPECIAL EVENTS

Hardly a week goes by without a special event taking place in New York. In fact, there are some 50 officially recognized parades each year honoring certain causes or ethnic groups, along with several hundred street fairs. Most of New York's street fairs offer a rather unremarkable selection of fast food, houseplants, athletic socks and cheap belts. You're bound to come across one as you stroll through town during the summer months.

The best source for information on upcoming festivals and cultural happenings are some of the Internet sites listed in the Internet Resources section under the Information heading, earlier in this chapter.

Fifth Ave shuts down several times a year for the elaborate major parades, including the granddaddy of all ethnic celebrations, the St Patrick's Day Parade on March 17th. All of the following events are generally celebrated in Manhattan unless otherwise specified:

January

First Night – December 31 – January 1

Chinese New Year – late January or early February

February

Black History Month

March

St Patrick's Day Parade – March 17

April

Antiques Show

French Film Festival

May

Naval Ships Fleet Week

Ninth Ave International Food Fair

East Village Carnival

June

New York City Jazz Festival

Comedy Festival

Buskers Festival

Puerto Rican Day Parade

NY Shakespeare Festival – June to September

Gay Pride Day

Celebrate Brooklyn, Brooklyn

July

Independence Day Fireworks – July 4

Lincoln Center Festival – July to August, every other year, with festivals scheduled for 2000, 2002 and 2004

Mostly Mozart

Central Park Summerstage – July to August

August

Harlem Week

September

New York is Book Country

New York Film Festival

Caribbean Day Parade, Brooklyn

US Open Tennis Tournament, Flushing Meadows, Queens

Queens Fall Festival, September to November, Queens

October

Halloween Parade

Greenwich Village Jazz Festival

New York Marathon

November

International Poster Fair

Thanksgiving Day Parade

December

Rockefeller Center Christmas Tree Lighting

Singing Christmas Tree Celebration, South Street Seaport

PLACES TO STAY

Although New York City has more than 70,000 hotel rooms, it can barely keep up with its continued and growing popularity as a tourist destination. With visitor numbers running at 30 million a year, many hotels have a 70% occupancy rate or more year round.

Indeed, the average cost of a room is a whopping $245 a day, compared to the US average of $80 a night. If you come from a part of the world where a decent, clean room runs about $50, you're in for a shock, because the New York City equivalent will certainly be a flophouse.

The bottom line is that a decent hotel room will run $150 or more a night. If you want to find a good, cheap place to stay in New York City, the best thing is to find a friend who lives there. Failing that, you must plan this part of your trip very carefully. Keep in mind that two phone calls made before your arrival could turn out to be the smartest money spent on the vacation – one to make a reservation as far in advance as possible, the other confirming the booking just before you arrive. If you do come to New York on-the-fly and with a limited budget, you might want to front load your costs by taking a first night in a hotel. The next day, after a shower and a good night's sleep, go in person to a select few cheaper choices; be sure to go well before noon if you expect to find a room.

The hotels listed here are arranged by neighborhood, with the less expensive places generally listed first.

Hotel Discounts

The city realizes that tourists have problems booking cheaper hotels and has set up a discount line (☎ 800-692-8474, fax 212-245-5943) that offers rooms at 100 hotels for $125 a night.

Consolidators are copying the patterns of the airline travel industry by serving as last-minute clearinghouses for unsold rooms. Quickbook (☎ 800-789-9887) discounts moderate Midtown hotels; the office is open 9 am to 5 pm. You can ask them about room availability in many of the hotels listed below.

The Hotel Reservations Network (☎ 800-964-6835) books rooms in 20 US cities, and their service includes nearly 100 Manhattan hotels that cost as little as $70 a night. As with airline consolidators, you must pay in advance, though the room can be canceled on 24 hours' notice. (Do ask questions about

---

Booking In

Remember to confirm your reservation with a phone call before you arrive, and beware of lower cost hotels that ask you to pay with a credit card for your full stay in advance. That's usually a sign of a hotel with a lot of early customer check-outs, and the payment policy could be a ploy to keep you there. Insist on paying only for the first night, so you have the option of finding other accommodations should you find yourself unsatisfied with your room.

Please remember that rates quoted do not include the city's taxes, which are 13.25% plus $2 per night room charge.

where the room is in the hotel – last minute booking can be the rooms that no one else wants.)

Accommodations Express (☎ 800-444-7666) offers smaller discounts – around 15%, but it deals with a larger number of rooms in every price category; it's open from 7 am to 11 pm.

Hostels

HI-AYH/New York International Hostel (Map 7; ☎ 212-932-2300, fax 212-932-2574, 891 Amsterdam Ave), is the HI-AYH facility in the city, and it books its 480 beds quickly during the summer season. As it is open for check-in 24 hours a day, it is a good place to head if you land in town at an odd time of the day. A bed costs $26 for members, with a small $3 surcharge for nonmembers (subway: 103rd St).

There are a few alternatives to the HI-AYH facility further uptown: the *International Student Center* (Map 7; ☎ 212-787-7706, 38 W 88th St) welcomes non-US residents under age 30 for $12 a night (subway: W 86th St). The *Big Apple Hostel* (Map 6; ☎ 212-302-2603, fax 212-302-2605, 119 W 45th St) is a spare facility just off Times Square that's open all day and has a laundry; beds cost $30 (subway: Times Square). *Banana Bungalow* (Map 7; ☎ 212-769-2441, 250 W 77th St), in an old hotel on the Upper West Side, sleeps six in a room and has a poor reputation on cleanliness and policing of the rooms.

Harlem offers the *New York Bed & Breakfast* (Map 8; ☎ 212-666-0559, 134 W 119th St). Its five rooms cost $20 per person and share a bath. There have been some disturbing reports of overbooking and lack of cleanliness at this location. Stick with the reliable *Sugar Hill International House* (Map 8; ☎ 212-926-7030, fax 212-283-0108, 722 St Nicholas Ave) and *Blue Rabbit* (Map 8; ☎ 212-491-3892, 730 St Nicholas Ave), sister hostels with 30 beds in each facility. Dorm beds are $20 and private rooms that sleep two are $25 per person per night. Reader feedback on Blue Rabbit and Sugar Hill is generally very favorable (subway: B, C trains to W 145th St).

The *Chelsea International Hostel* (Map 5; ☎ 212-647-0010, 251 W 20th St) has a party atmosphere with a limited number of private rooms at $40. A few blocks up and to the west is the quieter *Chelsea Center Hostel* (Map 5; ☎ 212-643-0214, fax 212-473-3945, 313 W 29th St); its 22 beds are $27 each.

Despite its name, the *Larchmont Hotel* (Map 4; ☎ 212-989-9333, fax 212-989-9496, 27 W 11th St) is more of an inn with shared baths. Located on a great block just off Fifth Ave, the hotel's 52 rooms have sinks (baths and kitchens in the hallways) and cost about $80-$120.

B&Bs

The city does not have a single clearinghouse for B&B reservations, and so several rival companies vie for the business, many offering spots in 'outlaw' B&Bs not registered with the city or any organization. Rooms tend to be the same price as at the cheapest hotels, about $75 to $120 a night, with two night minimum stays in the summer. To avoid disappointments and misunderstandings, reservation services should be prepared to describe the level of contact you will have with a host and also give a detailed description of the neighborhood and its nearest attractions. Most services offer reduced rates for monthly room rentals.

The *Broadway Bed & Breakfast* (Map 6; ☎ 212-997-9200, 264 W46th St), near Times Square, is a very popular choice that edges into the hotel category with accommodation and rates that are $100 to $190, with breakfast included.

At Home New York (☎ 800-692-4262) is a service connecting visitors to 300-odd private properties, with a range of $50 to $120 per night hosted single rooms (minimum stay two nights).

Urban Ventures (☎ 212-594-5650) has 600 rooms in its registry; the cost is $75 to $125 for double occupancy. *New York Bed & Breakfast* (☎ 800-900-8134) has singles/doubles starting at $60/90, with a good selection of rooms in Greenwich Village. *Manhattan Bed and Breakfast* (☎ 212-879-4229) is a newer, smaller service with 250 rooms with private baths that range from $70 to $110 a night.

The Fund for the Borough of Brooklyn has information on Brooklyn B&Bs and mails out a list of locations; call ☎ 718-855-7882. Brooklyn's premier B&B is the romantic *Bed & Breakfast on the Park* (☎ *718-499-8961, fax 718-499-1385, 113 Prospect Park West*), between 6th and 7th Sts, in a beautiful brownstone in Park Slope. (See Prospect Park map for location.) Rates range from $125 to $225.

On City Island in the Bronx, there's *Le Refuge Inn* (☎ *718-885-2478, fax 718-885-1519, 620 City Island Ave*), a B&B run by transplanted French chef Pierre Saint-Denis. It's open year-round and has eight rooms (four with shared bath) at rates of $96 and upward.

Long Stay Apartments

In addition to the B&B services, there's *Manhattan East Side Suites Hotels* (☎ *800-637-8483*), a group of ten East Side locations offering kitchen-equipped suites from $170 weekdays and $150 on weekends. *City Lights Bed and Breakfast* (☎ *212-737-7049*) offers private apartments in uptown locations up to $245 a night.

Hotels

Lower Manhattan (Map 3) Most of the available hotels below Houston St cater to a business clientele, thus most of them offer very good deals on weekends. The downside is that the neighborhood is quite dead once the office workers go home. Best Western's *Seaport Inn* (☎ *212-766-6600, 800-468-3569, fax 212-766-6615, 33 Peck Slip*) sits in the shadow of the Brooklyn Bridge at the South Street Seaport. Rates for singles are $150.

The business-oriented *Millennium Hilton* (☎ *212-693-2001, 800-445-8667, 55 Church St*) rises above the street like a black plinth, but it's still dwarfed by the World Trade Center across the street. It's good for free-spending travelers who want great views but care little about nightlife; weekday prices start at $400 for a single. On weekends, however, the rates drop to $250 and include buffet breakfast (subway: Cortlandt St).

Chinatown & Lower East Side (Map 4) If you're on a strict budget and have ever stayed in a Chinese-run hotel in Southeast Asia, you might try the *World Hotel* (☎ *212-226-5522, fax 212-219-9498, 101 Bowery*). This transient place is relatively clean, with 130 tiny rooms running $50/60 with shared bath. There are several other closet-like 'hotels' near here – they are flophouses to be avoided.

If you can ignore the garish interior design, the *Off SoHo Suites* (☎ *800-633-7646, 11 Rivington St*), two blocks south of E Houston St, has efficiencies starting at $129, though you may have to share a kitchen with another room. A party of four can book adjoining rooms in suites with aircon, voicemail and a good-sized kitchen and bathroom, for $199. The *Pioneer Hotel* (☎ *212-226-1482, 800-737-0702, fax 212-226-3525, 341 Broome St*) is a nice find on the outskirts of Chinatown with tidy doubles for about $175, slightly more in summer (subway: Grand St).

SoHo (Map 4) Zoning laws kept hotels out of this neighborhood for years, until a savvy real estate magnate built the *SoHo Grand* (☎ *212-965-3000, 800-965-3244, fax 212-965-3244, 310 West Broadway*) just outside the restricted zone; it's a well-located spot near Canal St. The exterior of this 367-room facility looks like a college dorm. Inside you'll find Eurotrash central: a cast-iron staircase, a staff dressed in black and models lounging on overstuffed couches along the 2nd-floor bar area. Singles cost $250 to $300, and doubles start at $250.

The *Cosmopolitan Hotel* (☎ *212-566-1900, fax 212-566-6909, 888-895-9400, 85 W Broadway*), near Chambers St, is also taking advantage of the boom in SoHo tourism. This 103-room hotel, above the Chambers St stop on the subway, is cheap for the location – doubles are $109 to $140.

Greenwich Village & East Village (Map 4) *St Mark's Hotel* (☎ *212-674-2192, 2 St Marks Place*) has a great location in the East Village, but the block is noisy and you won't want to inquire about the activities of your neighbors; rates begin at $90. **Incentra Village** (☎ 212-206-0007, fax 212-604-0625, 32 Eighth Ave) is a charming 12-room inn that's gay and lesbian friendly and booked

Gay & Lesbian Accommodations

Several hotels cater exclusively to gays and lesbians, but laws designed to protect the gay community from discrimination also prevent them from specifically excluding straight people. Gay-friendly hotels are mainly found in SoHo and Greenwich Village.

It's necessary to make reservations at least a month in advance for all of these popular spots. The *Washington Square Hotel* (see Greenwich Village listings), the *Grand Union* (Map 5; ☎ 212-683-5890, 34 E 32nd St) and the *Gramercy Park Hotel* (see Chelsea & Gramercy Park listings) offer comfortable accommodations starting at $130 a night.

Incentra Village (see Greenwich Village listings) is a charming 12-room inn that's booked solid every weekend. *Chelsea Pines Inn* (Map 5; ☎ 212-929-1023, 317 W 14th St) and *The Colonial House Inn* (Map 5; ☎ 212-633-1612, 318 W 22nd St) have rooms for around $150 a night. *East Village B&B* (Map 4; ☎ 212-260-1865, 252 E 7th St) caters to lesbians. The famous *Chelsea Hotel* (see Chelsea, & Gramercy Park listings) is a pricier option in New York City's most popular gay neighborhood.

Assistance can be obtained through the Gay & Lesbian Community Center (Map 4; ☎ 212-620-7310), which is temporarily located at 1 Little W 12th St; its website is www.gaycenter.org. (The center will move back to its headquarters at 208 W13th St following a renovation.) *Our World* is a Florida-based bimonthly magazine on gay and lesbian travel destinations. (You can subscribe by calling ☎ 904-441-5367.) The *Out & About Newsletter* (☎ 800-929-2268) also provides information about gay-friendly hotels, restaurants, clubs, gyms and shops in New York City; its informative website is www.outandabout.com.

solid every weekend. This well-maintained, quiet place has a lovely parlor; rates are $100 for smaller rooms and $170 for suites.

The best feature of the **Riverview Hotel** (☎ 212-929-0060, 113 Jane St) is its location in the West Village overlooking the Hudson River just west of some of the neighborhood's most beautiful blocks. The hotel's 220 rooms are very sparse and cheap. This transient hotel has a $5 key fee refunded upon checkout (subway: 14th St-Eighth Ave).

With 160 rooms, **Washington Square Hotel** (☎ 212-777-9515, 800-979-8373, 103 Waverly Place) has earned a good reputation for its location and price, but its popularity makes last-minute booking difficult. This used to be a mid-range choice, but rates have zoomed in recent years: singles/ doubles cost $150/200 (subway: W 4th St).

Chelsea & Gramercy Park (Map 5) The **Senton Hotel** (☎ 212-684-5800, 39-41 W 27th St) has attracted patronage because of its central location, but readers' overwhelming complaints about its staff and the condition of the rooms mean we cannot recommend it, even at just $50 a night.

The **Hotel Gershwin** (☎ 212-545-8000, 3 E 27th St) is more a hostel than a hotel, and has aura of a performance space. Just four blocks north of the Flatiron Building, this increasingly popular spot features a funky lobby that's a shrine to Andy Warhol. Dorm beds are $35 per person; private rooms start at $95. In many ways, it's more bohemian in character than the far more famous (and pricey) Chelsea Hotel. The Gershwin's reputation and popularity make reservations a must, and it's becoming a popular hangout for young travelers who are staying in hostels and hotels elsewhere in the city.

Just a few steps away from the Gershwin is the gamier but cheap **Madison Hotel** (☎ 212-532-7373, 800-962-3476, fax 212-686-0092, 21 E 27th St) – an alternative only for those without reservations or looking to get a booking into the Gershwin the next day when a room frees up. Very spare rooms with private bath are provided for $60/80. (Do not accept their demand of paying for your entire stay in advance.)

Hotel 17 (☎ 212-475-2845, 225 E 17th St) is a popular Gramercy Park choice with rates starting at $100 a night for rooms with shared baths, $110 with private baths. This hotel is getting a reputation for overbooking and has triggered off a lot of negative feedback from readers. *Gramercy Park Hotel* (☎ 212-475-4320, 800-221-4083), at the corner of E 21st St and Lexington Ave, overlooks Gramercy Park and has a dark bar off the lobby that's worth checking out. Singles start at $165 a night.

The *Chelsea Hotel* (☎ 212-243-3700, fax 212-675-5531, 222 W 23rd St) was once a low-cost hangout and is now cashing in on its fame as a literary landmark. The rooms are uneven in quality and the front desk clerk will snicker if you ask for Sid Vicious' room (since remodeled and renumbered). There are some shared bath for $99 a night, but they're nearly always booked. Rooms with private baths have climbed in price in recent years and now start at $135.

The *Chelsea Inn* (☎ 212-645-8989, 46 W 17th St) is a set of joined townhouses that offer private or shared bath. It's clean and popular. Rates start at $100, and private suites top off at $160.

Just near the Chelsea Hotel is the lower-priced *Chelsea Savoy Hotel* (☎ 212-929-9353, fax 212-741-6309, 204 W 23rd St). Singles/doubles cost $115 to $180 per night.

The *Inn at Irving Place* (☎ 212-533-4600, 56 Irving Place), at E 17th St, is a charming and more expensive 12-room townhouse with a reputation for romance. Rates begin at $250.

Midtown (Map 5) There are several inexpensive places near Herald Square. The non-chain choices are generally okay, and if you're paying under $85 a night, it certainly won't be for luxury accommodations.

The no-frills *Herald Square Hotel* (☎ 212-279-4017, 800-727-1888, 19 W 31st St) has rates of $50 for a small room with a shared bath, $55 for private bath. Double rooms begin at $75. *Hotel Stanford* (☎ 212-563-1500, 800-365-1114, fax 212-643-0157, 43 W 32nd St) is a good choice right in the middle of Little Korea near Herald Square.

Rooms run $110/$160 for a single/double with continental breakfast, and there's a 24-hour restaurant on the premises. A sign indicating just how much this neighborhood has improved is the *Holiday Inn Broadway* (☎ 212-736-3800, 800-465-4329, fax 212-631-0449, 39 W 32nd St), at the corner of Broadway and 32nd St. This was once a notoriously filthy welfare hotel, and now it offers decent, clean, yet uninspiring rooms. Room rates begin at $100.

The *Wolcott Hotel* (☎ 212-268-2900, 4 W 31st St) is a 280-room beaux art hotel designed by John Duncan, the architect of Grant's Tomb. Rates start at $100. The furnishings are a bit frayed at the 400-room *Pickwick Arms Hotel* (☎ 212-355-0300, 800-742-5945, Fax 212-755-5029, 250 E 51st St), but the place is popular with European budget travelers. Rates start at $100.

The area around Park Ave south of Grand Central Terminal is an unremarkable but busy stretch between Midtown and the Flatiron District that has a number of reasonably priced hotels. *Howard Johnson on Park Ave* (☎ 212-532-4860, 800-446-4656, fax 212-545-9727, 429 Park Ave S) is a comfortable place with rooms starting at $119.

Just around the corner from the main branch of the New York Public Library is the *Quality Hotel* (☎ 212-447-1500, 3 E 40th St), a 186-room business hotel that reduces its $180 weekday rates on weekends, when occupancy drops. *Hotel Metro* (☎ 212-947-2500, 800-356-3870, fax 212-279-1310, 45 E 35th St), off Madison Ave, combines 1930s art deco with the comfort of a gentlemen's club. It has an attractive lounge and library area. Upstairs, you'll find rather plain rooms, but the price ($145 to $195) and location (near the Morgan Library and the Empire State Building) make this 160-room hotel a worthy choice.

The *Hotel Iroquois* (☎ 212-840-3080, 800-332-7200, fax 212-398-1754, 49 W 44th St) is a poorer version of the more famous Algonquin and charges $200 and up depending on the season. *The Jolly Madison Towers* (☎ 212-685-3700, 800-225-4340, fax 212-447-0747, 22 E 38th St), just off Madison Ave, is very popular with Latin American tourists who hang out in its wonderfully tacky Whaler Bar. Rates start at $220. The *Ameritania Hotel* (☎ 212-247-5000, 800-664-6835, fax 212-207-4800, 1701 Broadway), next door to the Ed Sullivan Theater (where the *Late Show with David Letterman* is taped), is popular with bus tours. It's decorated like a futuristic disco, and the desk clerks usually knock off 10% from the room rates, which start at $245/265 for singles/doubles, if they are told you heard about the hotel in a guidebook.

The following mid-range hotels are near or on Central Park South:

The *Woodward Hotel* (☎ 212-247-2000, 800-336-4110, fax 212-581-2248, 210 W 55th St), a quiet and efficient Best Western property, is near Carnegie Hall and has singles/doubles from $159/179; there's access to a good local gym. The *Hotel Wellington* (☎ 212-247-3900 871 Seventh Ave), and 55th St, is a block south of Carnegie Hall and has 700 unremarkable rooms at $155. The *Salisbury Hotel* (☎ 212-246-1300, 123 W 57th St) is virtually across the street from icons of both high- and low-culture: Carnegie Hall and Planet Hollywood.

Just south of Columbus Circle is the *Westpark Hotel* (☎ 212-246-6440, 800-248-6440, fax 212-246-3131, 308 W 58th St). It's tough booking a room there in the summer because of its word-of-mouth popularity with European travelers. Suites are available for as low as $180. Like all the hotels on Central Park South, the *St Mortiz* (☎ 212-755-5800, 50 Central Park South) has a great location, but has lost quite a bit of its good reputation these past few years.

Most of the expensive Midtown hotels have rates starting at $200 that fluctuate greatly according to seasonal demand, ie, they often go up, but don't go far down from that mark. Publishing executives still love to lunch at the *Royalton* (☎ 212-869-4400, 800-635-9013, Fax 212-869-8965, 44 W 44th St), keeping the hotel's restaurant an A-list must, but the hotel itself is easier to book. Rooms are $315 and up for doubles. Across the street, the *Algonquin* (☎ 212-840-6800, 800-555-8000, fax 212-944-1419 59 W 44th St), still attracts people thanks to its reputation as the site of the 1930s' Algonquin Round Table of writers, but some of the $305-plus rooms are small and a bit cramped.

Morgan's (☎ 212-686-0300, 800-334-3408, fax 212-779-8352, 237 Madison Ave) is a sleek hotel with no sign indicating a name or purpose to the building, and it's consistently popular with the European *glitterati*. Rates are $280 and up for singles and $320 to $365 for doubles, with suites beginning at $350.

The legendary *Waldorf-Astoria* (☎ 212-355-3000, 800-925-3673, fax 212-872-4859, 301 Park Ave) is the place where members of the British Royal Family turn up for fundraising dinners; singles/doubles start at $275/300, though weekend specials bring the price down to about $200. The lobby is quietly elegant but, surprisingly, not as grand as you would expect; the restaurants and bars within are suitably expensive, and the smoky Bull & Bear pub at the back is a prime pickup spot for middle-aged executives looking for a bit of company for the evening.

The *Peninsula* (☎ 212-247-2200, 700 Fifth Ave), at 55th St, once known as the Gotham Hotel, is one of the oldest surviving grand hotels in Midtown, dating back to 1904. It's totally renovated and has a spa and athletic club that sprawl over three floors. Rates are $340 and up for doubles only.

Across the street the *St Regis* (☎ 212-753-4500, 800-759-7550), at Fifth Ave and 55th St, is well-known for its huge electronic taxi call sign, first-class service and King Cole bar, which features a mural by Maxfield Parrish. (This mural was moved here from the old Knickerbocker Hotel in Times Square.) Its large, comfortable rooms start at $545.

The *Plaza Hotel* (☎ 212-759-3000, 800-527-4727, fax 212-546-5324, 768 Fifth Ave) is famous for its Oak Room and the many celebrities who have stayed there (the Beatles, Cary Grant, Grace Kelly). Rates are $350 and up. The equally elegant *Sherry Netherland Hotel* (☎ 212-355-2800, 800-247-4377, 781 Fifth Ave) is just a block north on Fifth Ave. Rates at the elegant limestone IM Pei–designed *Four Seasons* (☎ 800-332-

3442, 57 E 57th St) begin at $585 for rooms, $1200 for suites.

Times Square (Map 6) The *Broadway Bed and Breakfast (☎ 212-997-9200, 800-826-6300, fax 212-768-2807, 264 W 46th St)*, just across the street from Restaurant Row, is a former run-down Times Square area hotel that has been turned into a reasonably priced and well-located small inn with 42 neat rooms. If you need a Midtown space on short notice, try the *Hotel Carter (☎ 212-944-6000, fax 212-398-8541, 250 W 43rd St)*, a huge old hotel that has steadfastly lagged behind the rest of the neighborhood in gentrification. Rates run as low as $100 a night.

The *Milford Plaza (☎ 212-869-3600, 800-272-6232, fax 944-8357, 270 W 45th St)* is a Ramada-owned, 1300-room, standard hotel that is a favorite for out of town bus tours and airline crews. Rooms are $129 and up, and it offers special three-day weekend deals. *Days Inn Midtown (☎ 800-572-6232, 790 Eighth Ave)*, off 48th St, and *Quality Hotel and Suites Midtown (☎ 212-768-3700, 157 W 47th St)* are bland chain hotels with rates from $120.

The renovated and clean *Portland Square Hotel (☎ 212-382-0600, 800-388-8988, fax 212-382-0684, 132 W 47th St)* is just steps away from the middle of Times Square and has shared rooms; private rooms start at $99. *Hotel Edison (☎ 212-840-5000, 800-637-7070, fax 212-596-6850, 228 W 47th St)* was once a high-class spot for Broadway stars, but it caters to tourists now, though its colorful coffee shop is still a hangout for theater people. Rates begin at $130.

Top-end hotels around Times Square charge $200 or more a night, but they don't really offer much distinction; they are charging for their location. All are rather loudly lit, and the lobbies are set back from the street to discourage outsiders. They include the *Marriott Marquis (☎ 212-398-1900, 1535 Broadway)*; the *Novotel (☎ 212-315-0100, 226 W 52nd St)*; and the *Doubletree Guest Suites (☎ 212-719-1600)* at 47th St and Seventh Ave. For more character, try the *Paramount (☎ 212-764-5500, 800-225-7474, fax 212-764-4892, 235 W 46th St)*. This was a

hip place in the early '90s, but it's no longer difficult to get into the Whiskey Bar on the street level. Singles start at $200.

Upper East Side (Map 7) The *Quality Eastside (☎ 800-567-7720, 161 Lexington Ave)*, at E 30th St, starts at $120 a night. The 12-room *Gracie Inn (☎ 212-628-1700, 800-404-2252, fax 212-319-4230, 502 E 81st St)* is an undiscovered country-style inn near the East River with singles/doubles starting at $175. You get a good breakfast with the room. The *Franklin (☎ 212-369-1000, 164 E 87th St)* is a standard hotel with 53 rooms running from $125.

Some of New York's most elegant and expensive hotels are on the Upper East Side. For around $300 or more a night, you can enjoy the quiet elegance of the *Pierre Hotel (☎ 212-838-8000, 800-332-3442, fax 212-758-1615, 2 E 61st St)*, at Fifth Ave. Steps away from Madison Ave is the intimate and quiet 61 room *The Lowell Hotel (☎ 212-838-1400, 800-221-4444, fax 212-319-4230, 28 E 63rd St)* is the of-the-moment place to stay for celebrities such as Brad Pitt. Rates start at $350 a night.

A slightly cheaper East Side alternative is the *Hotel Wales (☎ 212-876-6000, 877-847-4444, fax 212-894-5220, 1295 Madison Ave)*, at 92nd St, a century-old hotel restored to its former glory. Its 100 rooms start at $249 a night and include a continental breakfast.

Upper West Side (Map 7) There's a good selection of mid-range hotels here with rooms from $90 to $200 a night. *The Broadway American Hotel (☎ 212-362-1100, 2178 Broadway)* attracts visitors with its $60 rooms with shared baths. The *Hotel Olcott (☎ 212-877-4200, 27 W 72nd St)* is an old residence hotel well known as a bargain spot on the Upper West Side. The hotel is just steps away from the Dakota apartment building and the 72nd St entrance to Central Park, and you'll have to book early to get singles that start at $90.

The Mayflower Hotel (☎ 212-265-0060, 15 Central Park West), at W 61st St, though a bit stodgy, has more than 500 rooms and often offers special deals for three-day weekends.

The 96-room **Newtown Hotel** (☎ 212-678-6500, 2528 Broadway) is a smaller-sized alternative to the big West Side hotels. Room rates start with a single room at $99 and a double room at a reasonable $105 (higher in summer).

The Excelsior (☎ 212-362-9200, 800-368-4575, fax 212-721-2994, 45 W 81st St) is an old, 169-room hotel that overlooks the Museum of Natural History. Rates run from $159 for a single, and two-room suites begin at $199. The **Inn New York City** (☎ 212-580-1900, fax 212-580-4437, 266 W71st St) is an elaborate and well-regarded town house with four beautifully appointed suites. Luxury, however, comes at a price – daily rates start at $415 (with a free night on every weekly stay).

Brooklyn It's a real indication of the hotel boom that Brooklyn has gotten its first new full-service hotel in more than 50 years. The **New York Brooklyn Marriott** (☎ 718-246-700, 800-436-3759, fax 718-246-0563, 333 Adams St), between Tillary and Willoughby Sts, is an impressive 376-room facility with a restaurant and health club. The hotel, which occupies the lower floors of an office building, is easily accessible by subway and is actually closer to JFK airport than the Midtown hotels. With rooms averaging $145 to $310 a night, it's well worth trying to get a discount room here. The Brooklyn Heights location guarantees that you're as close to Midtown via the subway as you would be from the Upper East or West Sides of Manhattan.

PLACES TO EAT

New York is a food-lover's paradise, and in many ways a bargain. You can find any kind of cuisine, and if you decided to eat in a different restaurant every night in New York City, 46 years would pass before you ran out of options. Only Paris offers a greater selection of elegant culinary experiences; but at the opposite end, absolutely no other city can beat New York's selection of reasonably priced restaurants.

Don't be shy about asking about cost – most waiters, whatever the price level of a restaurant, neglect to tell you the cost of off-menu 'specials' or recommended wines. And if you're looking for a night of drinking, do it at a bar, not a restaurant, because proprietors gouge on alcohol prices, especially for specialty drinks such as margaritas.

The single best source for restaurants is the Zagat Survey, available at bookstores all over the city. Restaurant reviews also appear weekly in Time Out and New York magazine, and in the Friday section of the New York Times.

As for grocery stores, New York City's food stores are uniformly small and over priced, but you can cobble together a decent and healthful lunch from one of the fruit stands set up on major avenues all over the city. There are numerous stands on the Upper West Side along Broadway, where you can stock up on provisions for a picnic or quick snack. (Remember that grapes and the like should be washed because they've been exposed to pollution all day.)

Lower Manhattan (Map 3)

Café Remy (☎ 212-267-4646, 104 Greenwich St) has an array of good Latin dishes. **Pearl Palace** (☎ 212-482-0771, 60 Pearl St) is a no-frills Indian restaurant open 24 hours a day, everyday. It fuels workers from nearby Wall St firms. Weekdays from 11 am to 2:30 pm, they offer a bargain all-you-can-eat buffet lunch ($7) that includes a salad bar. **Zigolini's** (☎ 212-425-7171, 66 Pearl St) specializes in focaccia sandwiches, all for less than $8. (Some of the specials are creatively named after the customers who suggested them.)

There are dozens of places to eat in South Street Seaport, few of them better than an average McDonald's. The **North Star Pub** (☎ 212-509-6757, 93 South St) is a passable imitation of a British pub, with traditional fare such as bangers and mash. It's packed with office workers on weekdays.

Slightly more expensive, but worth the detour, is the **Bridge Café** (☎ 212-227-3344, 279 Water St), which is underneath the Brooklyn Bridge. Certified as the oldest pub in the city, the restaurant offers an extensive wine list and main dishes in the $15 range.

Windows on the World (☎ 212-524-7011), on the 107th floor of 1 World Trade Center, has a good menu and, of course, spectacular views all day – with prices to match.

Chinatown (Map 4)

In general, Chinatown is a bargain. Most starters run about $5, and the most expensive main course will set you back no more than $10. Finding the right place is the only task; everyone in New York has a favorite restaurant in Chinatown. Former mayor Ed Koch is a proud patron of *Peking Duck House* (☎ 212-227-1810, 22 Mott St), although this restaurant may have seen better days (stick with the standard fare if you visit). *Vegetarian Paradise* (☎ 212-406-6988, 33 Mott St) is a good and very cheap option for the meat-wary.

Hay Wun Loy (☎ 212-285-8686, 28-30 Pell St) specializes in fresh fish right out of the tank and dim sum. *Hong Ying Rice Shop* (☎ 212-349-6126, 11 Mott St) is a prototypical basement-level Chinatown eatery, serving dishes such as shrimp with black bean sauce for $8.95. Vegans should check out the *House of Vegetarian* (☎ 212-226-6572, 68 Mott St). The barbecue 'pork' and 'duck' dishes for $7 to $12 taste so much like the real thing, you'll wonder if the entire menu is a put on.

Just a bit further afield, on East Broadway running directly east from Chatham Square to the Manhattan Bridge, there are a number of restaurants and food stands that cater to locals. Visitors tend to flock to Mott St. You'll find moderately priced Hong Kong–style food at the *Nice Restaurant* (☎ 212-406-9779, 35 East Broadway). Its 2nd-floor banquet room is a popular spot for wedding receptions.

In recent years a number of Vietnamese restaurants have found a home in Chinatown. *Nha Trang* (☎ 212-233-5948, 87 Baxter St) is often packed at lunch with jurors and lawyers from the nearby city courthouses; they eat at crowded tables with other strangers. A filling meal can be had for less than $10 if you stick with dishes such as the $3.50 barbecued beef on rice vermicelli and the $2.75 shrimp spring rolls.

ROBERET REID

If you're Daffy or Donald, don't go.

The super-rich but delicious Vietnamese-style coffee with condensed milk is available for $1.50. A virtually identical menu is available next door at *New Pasteur* (☎ 212-608-3656, 85 Baxter St).

The *Thailand Restaurant* (☎ 212-349-3132, 106 Bayard St) serves up the most authentic Thai dishes outside of Bangkok. Particularly good is the $7.95 spicy vegetarian soup for two – it's the closest thing to a cure for the common cold.

Little Italy (Map 4)

A good rule of thumb while looking for a restaurant in Little Italy is to avoid any place where the manager hangs out in the street trying to drum up business. During summer months, the two blocks of Mulberry St north of Canal St are closed to traffic to allow the small restaurants more space for outdoor seating. Most of the places with al fresco dining offer main dishes for $15 or less, and if you stick with pasta, you can't go too wrong. Please note, however, that Little Italy restaurants are notorious for adding a 25% service charge onto the bills of people they suspect of being tourists (while providing service that does little to justify that percentage tip).

Benito 1 (☎ 212-226-9171, 174 Mulberry St) is one of the better-known choices here. By far the best spot to sit down for a while is *Cafe Roma* (☎ 212-226-8413, 385 Broome St), where you can have cannoli and espresso in a quiet setting after a Chinatown or SoHo meal.

Pizza War

An odd little pizza war has been waged in New York among several unrelated pizzerias named Ray's. Legend has it that one of the Ray's was 'the best pizza joint in the city' – the only problem is, no one can decide which one it is!

While all claim to be the 'original Ray's,' that distinction is generally thought to belong to the one at Sixth Ave and 11th St (Map 4). Oddly enough, no one quite seems sure what it was about this Ray's that prompted the good word of mouth. One decent Ray's claimant is in Little Italy near the Puck Building on Prince St, but you're better off passing it by and patronizing the truly legendary **Lombardi's** (☎ 212-941-7994, 32 Spring St), indisputably the oldest pizza restaurant in New York. Established in 1905, this brick-oven pizzeria serves only pizza pies and huge calzones, delicious half-moon dough shells stuffed with ricotta cheese and herbs. The fresh-mushroom pie is made with three different types of mushrooms.

Many of the storied old eateries in this neighborhood, such as **Puglia** (☎ 212-226-8912, 189 Hester St), with its raucous singing and huge crowds, and **Vincent's** (☎ 212-226-8133, 199 Mott St), are directed at tourists.

Tribeca (Map 4)

In recent years Tribeca has overtaken SoHo as the trendiest dining spot in the city, but there is still a healthy selection of moderately priced restaurants.

Odeon (☎ 212-233-0507, 145 West Broadway) is an amazing phenomenon: a once trendy 1980s restaurant that has not only survived, but thrived in the 1990s. It serves bistro fare such as lamb sandwiches and steak frites for less than $20; it is open until 2 am every day.

Riverrun (☎ 212-966-3894, 176 Franklin St) has seriously declined as a restaurant, but it's still a great neighborhood bar – the juke box is the cheapest in the city at 10¢ per

play. (subway: Franklin St). **Walker's** (☎ 212-941-0142, 16 N Moore St) is a dark watering hole with three dining rooms and a very reasonable Sunday brunch. It serves straightforward fare – sliced turkey sandwiches and hamburgers for $6.95. Jazz combos play Sunday nights, and there's no cover charge.

Bubby's (☎ 212-219-0666, 120 Hudson St) is always packed on weekends for their breakfast. Reservations are required weeks in advance at **Chanterelle** (☎ 212-966-6960, 2 Harrison St), which offers a fixed-price dinner menu for around $80 per person. Its changing menu often features a heavenly seafood sausage, and the combined experience of service and cuisine in the sparse dining room is world class. The highly overrated **Nobu** (☎ 212-219-0500, 105 Hudson St) is next door.

SoHo (Map 4)

For gourmet groceries, try **Gourmet Garage** (☎ 212-941-5850, 453 Broome St).

Lupe's East LA Kitchen (☎ 212-966-1326, 110 Sixth Ave) is a reasonably priced Mexican restaurant that is popular among locals for lunch. It offers good burritos and enchiladas in the $7 to $8 range.

SoHo offers three notable vegetarian restaurants. **Souen** (☎ 212-807-7421, 219 Sixth Ave) has a wide selection of macrobiotic items, as well as less stringent vegetarian dishes. **Helianthus Vegetarian** (☎ 212-598-0287, 48 MacDougal St) features Chinese and Japanese food and offers a lunch deal that includes a dumpling and rice with dishes such as lemon mock chicken and sautéed udon (Japanese noodles) for around $5.50. **Spring Street Natural** (☎ 212-966-0290, 62 Spring St) is a louder and busier restaurant with a large menu that, in addition to vegetarian selections, includes healthy fish and organic chicken dishes for $15 or less.

Lucky Strike (☎ 212-941-0479, 59 Grand St) features French bistro fare, and the menu, painted on mirrors above the table, has remained unchanged for several years. It gets very crowded late on Friday and Saturday when a DJ plays the front room. **Fanelli's Cafe** (☎ 212-226-9412, 94 Prince St) is one of the grittier places in the neighborhood. It's a dark, smoky bar with a pressed-tin ceiling and burgers for a reasonable $10.

The exclusive **Balthazar** (☎ 212-965-1785, 80 Spring St) is a celebrity studded, mock-Parisian bistro that's famous for not picking up its main phone and having an exclusive reservation line for friends only. Nobodies such as us can try to get in during the day.

Greenwich Village (Map 4)

There's a branch of **Gourmet Garage** (☎ 212-941-1664, 117 Seventh Ave) that has a good selection of fruit, breads and cheeses.

There are dozens of cafes in Greenwich Village, and one of the best is **Bleecker Street Pastry** (☎ 212-242-4959, 245 Bleecker St), where you can linger over a cappuccino and sweet Italian croissant for $4 among locals reading their morning papers.

Jon Vie (☎ 212-242-4440, 492 Sixth Ave) is a traditional French bakery where you can get a caloric pastry and a coffee for $1.95 before 11 am. **French Roast** (☎ 212-533-2233, 78 W 11th St) is a 24-hour cafe serving sandwiches and desserts at reasonable prices. It's a good place to peruse the New York newspapers.

Benny's (☎ 212-727-0584, 113 Greenwich St), in the West Village, has super-filling burritos and enchiladas for $8 or less and there are plenty of options for vegetarians. But watch out for the lethal margaritas.

Cones (☎ 212-414-1795, 272 Bleecker St) is run by self-proclaimed 'ice cream artisans.' Their Italian-style ice creams and sorbets are a great respite from the summer heat and costs $2 for a double scoop.

Passers-by can watch homemade noodles being prepared at **Sammy's Noodles** (☎ 212-924-6688, 453-461 Sixth Ave), which sprawls over several storefronts. Lunch specials start at $4.50 and none of the noodle dishes are more expensive than $6.95.

Despite its trendiness, **Bar Six** (☎ 212-645-2439, 502 Sixth Ave) is a reasonable place to stop for lunch. Grilled chicken or rockfish sandwiches cost just $7 and include soup or salad.

Grange Hall (☎ 212-924-5246, 50 Commerce St), just off Barrow St a block from Sixth Ave, is a renovated neighborhood tavern once called the Blue Mill. It still has a beautiful wooden bar, and it serves organic foods. It's very popular and the wait can be as long as an hour without a reservation, but the prices are reasonable – the $7.95 smoked trout salad appetizer is a meal in itself. **Caffe Lure** (☎ 212-473-2642, 169 Sullivan St) is a cramped and popular French bistro with a wood-burning oven. It's popular with celebrities, especially models such as Naomi Campbell and film heartthrob Leonardo DiCaprio. Yet, amazingly enough, they let mere mortals in, too (no reservations).

El Faro (☎ 212-929-8210, 823 Greenwich St) is a classic old Spanish restaurant that's quiet during the week, and impossibly crowded on Friday and Saturday nights. The decor hasn't changed in 20 years, nor have the waiters. Main dishes such as the spicy shrimp diablo may seem pricey at $16, but they're enough to feed two people.

In the heart of the meat-packing district, off Washington St, sits **Florent** (☎ 212-989-5799, 69 Gansevoort St), a 24-hour French-run bistro offering hanger steak, hamburgers and breakfast selections. On the weekend closest to July 14th, the restaurant takes over Gansevoort St for an open-air Bastille Day celebration.

There are many mid-range Italian restaurants in Greenwich Village. Among the best is **Trattoria Spaghetto** (☎ 212-255-6752, 232 Bleecker St), at the corner of Carmine St, a converted old coffee shop with traditional red-checked vinyl tablecloths. Almost all the pasta dishes cost $10.

Slightly more expensive, and certainly more colorful, is **Rocco** (☎ 212-677-0590, 181 Thompson St), just north of Houston, where the friendly and attentive staff will be happy to provide your favorite dish, even if it's not on the menu. This gathering place for local Village eccentrics has been around for 60 years.

Marinella (☎ 212-807-7472, 49 Carmine St) not only has a multipaged menu, but displays extensive daily specials on a blackboard that is wheeled from table to table. The chicken, fish and veal main dishes cost about $14.

East Village (Map 4)

Astor Restaurant & Lounge (☎ 212-253-8644, 316 Bowery) is a sleek new place with a great open-air dining area just across from the legendary CBGB club. It's a perfect place to meet for a long night out in the Village.

Benny's Burritos (☎ 212-254-2054, 93 Ave A), decorated in 1960s kitsch (lava lamps, pink walls and Formica tables), is a local pioneer in low-fat Cal-Mex food. The super-filling burritos and enchiladas are $8 or less and include plenty of options for vegetarians. But watch out for the lethal margaritas.

Bereket (☎ 212-475-7700, 187 E Houston St), on the corner of Orchard, is a 24-hour kebab eatery with a good selection of vegetarian dishes. It's a favorite with hungover and drunk clubbers (subway: Second Ave).

South and to the east of the Union Square subway station are many delis and diners that will provide you with a filling meal at low prices. Some that stand out are: *Veselka* (☎ 212-228-9682, 144 Second Ave), a Polish diner with a strong local following. It's decorated with murals by local artists, has great soups and grill chefs who treat making pancakes as a performance art. The *Second Ave Deli* (☎ 212-677-0606, 156

Little Tokyo

In recent years, E 9th St has become something of a Little Tokyo with excellent sushi restaurants lining the street. *Hasaki* (☎ 212-472-3327, 210 E 9th St) has the best reputation. Try there first, but if you find you have a long wait ahead of you, then go next door to *Sharaku* (☎ 212-598-0403, 14 Stuyvesant St), where there are plenty of tables and a large menu featuring many Japanese specialties in addition to sushi.

In the center of the Village, the best choice by far is *Tomoe Sushi* (☎ 212-777-9346, 172 Thompson St), a wildly popular place that always seems to have a line. Its sushi is reputed to be the best in the city, and a meal costs between $15 to $25.

Second Ave) is a quintessential deli offering great fare (the matzo ball soup comes with sprigs of fresh dill).

Time Cafe (☎ 212-533-7000, 380 Lafayette St) is a pleasant surprise: a trendy nightspot, popular with models, that actually serves very good organic food, although the service can sometimes be inattentive. There's a good selection of pizzas at $10 to $12 and other main dishes top out at about $18. *Roettelle AG* (☎ 212-674-4140, 126 E 7th St) is a Swiss restaurant incongruously located on a block in the East Village that retains much of its Polish character.

With its pressed-tin ceilings and faded paintings, *Lanza's* (☎ 212-674-7014, 168 First Ave) is a throwback to an earlier time in the East Village. Its five-course Italian dinner (for just $11.95) includes a selection of delicious desserts. If you're not hungry but want a strong espresso and an Italian pastry, try the nearby *DeRobertis* (☎ 212-674-7137, 176 First Ave), a *pasticceria* (bakery) which has been in business since 1904.

Lucky Cheng's (☎ 212-473-0516, 24 First Ave) is a Thai restaurant that features drag queen 'waitresses,' so it has been overrun by curious out-of-towners. Note that reservations often are not respected – you can encounter an hour-long wait. Entrees start at $12, but prices average $35 per person.

Chelsea (Map 5)

It could be argued that Chelsea has the best and most varied dining experiences in the city. But for some of its more popular (and expensive) restaurants, you'll need to make weekend reservations weeks in advance.

One of New York's oddest hybrid cuisines, serving the best of the Cuban-Chinese food in Chelsea, is *Sam Chinita* (☎ 212-741-0240), on Eighth Ave and 17th St, with its diner atmosphere and items such as plantains and *ropa vieja*, shredded beef in a spicy sauce. Most dishes are $7 or less. This cheap and filling fare was developed by Chinese immigrants who once lived in Cuba and moved to the US following the revolution in the late 1950s.

The *Empire Diner* (☎ 212-243-2736, 210 Tenth Ave) is one of the most prominent

Theme Restaurants

Once dubbed the 'restaurant trend of the '90s,' it appears that the theme restaurant has had its day. Even in an era when the tourist trade is booming in New York, many of these tourist traps have had severe drops in business. Places such as Television City and the Fashion Café have closed, and the company controlling Planet Hollywood has gone bust. Only the original theme restaurant, the Hard Rock Café, seems to be fully holding its own. Expect to be steered, if not pressured, into buying merchandise – these places see a profit margin of 15% on the food, but realize a 50% gain on the T-shirts.

Hard Rock Cafe (☎ 212-459-9320, 221 W 57th St) is the granddaddy of all theme restaurants. Started in London, it has been in New York since 1983 and offers glimpses of rock memorabilia of dubious provenance. Just how many times did Elvis really strum that guitar, anyway? It's open Sunday to Thursday 11:30 am to midnight and Friday and Saturday 11 am to 2 am. (See Chelsea & Midtown Manhattan map for location.)

Harley-Davidson Cafe (☎ 212-245-6000, 1370 Sixth Ave) is a shrine to the Wisconsin-based motorcycle company and features gas tanks signed by celebrities and pictures of anyone who owned, rode on or even stood near a Harley-Davidson. It's so commercial the menu's available for sale ($10), and drinks are a whopping $8 to $10. Open 11 am to 2 am daily. (See Chelsea & Midtown Manhattan map for location.)

The *Jekyll & Hyde Club* (☎ 212-541-9505, 1409 Sixth Ave) is refreshingly free of celebrity connections. It features a trick elevator, waiters dressed as vampires and a flashy show where Frankenstein comes to life. Complain about the long wait to get in, and your waiter will point to a skull and say, 'That guy was dying to get in.' If that's your idea of a funny line, this place is for you. It's open Monday, Tuesday and Thursday 11:30 am to 2 am; Wednesday and Sunday 11 am to 2 am; and Friday and Saturday 11 am to 3 am. (See Chelsea & Midtown Manhattan map for location.)

Official All Star Cafe (☎ 212-840-8326, 1540 Broadway), at 45th St, is an enormous restaurant-cum-sports stadium in Times Square with sports memorabilia such as Andre Agassi's ponytail, a backboard smashed by Shaquille O'Neal and Monica Seles' tennis racquets. It's open daily 11 am to 2 am. (See Times Square map for location.)

Planet Hollywood (☎ 212-333-7827, 140 W 57th St) is the flagship of a theme empire that has fallen on hard times. The restaurant displays film artifacts and costumes in a noisy, flashing-light atmosphere that resembles a futuristic disco. Reservations aren't taken, and you stand in line outside for about 45 minutes just to get to another line inside. There are enough movie items visible through the window and on display in the gift shop next door to get your fill of the experience without actually eating in the restaurant. It's open 11 am to 1 am every day. (See Chelsea & Midtown Manhattan map for location.)

all-night hangouts in the neighborhood. The *America* (☎ 212-505-2110, 9 E 18th St), with its multipage menu, is a huge, noisy restaurant that is worth checking out because of its elevated bar in the back that is covered by a skylight. Nearby is *Cafe Bondi* (☎ 212-691-8136, 7 W 20th St), which is an isolated restaurant with a garden in the back of the building; it specializes in Sicilian cooking.

Union Square (Map 5)

There are several sublime places near Union Square, including the famous *Union Square Cafe* (☎ 212-243-4020, 21 E 16th St), and the *Gramercy Tavern* (☎ 212-477-0077, 42 E 20th St). These sister restaurants are renowned for providing five-star dining at three-star prices; as a consequence, it's necessary to make reservations several weeks beforehand to eat on a weekend. Gramercy

Tavern serves a $60 fixed-price menu every night.

The extraordinary **Union Pacific** (☎ 212-995-8500, 111 E 22nd St) is a newly opened venue that's designed like an old-style railway station. The food, though expensive, is the last word in fresh American cuisine, with an emphasis on seafood dishes.

Midtown (Map 5)

Madras Mahal (☎ 212-684-2788, 104 Lexington Ave) is but one of 10 Indian restaurants between 27th and 29th Sts, but this vegetarian restaurant is the only one in the city that conforms to kosher rules of preparation. There's a lunch buffet available for a reasonable $6.95.

La Fondue (☎ 212-581-0820, 43 W 55th St) offers very reasonable lunches in a narrow dining space off Sixth Ave. Fondue for one costs $7.95, and daily lunch specials ($8.95) include a main course, salad and a glass of wine. Across the street, the slightly more expensive **La Bonne Soupe** (☎ 212-586-7650, 48 W 55th St) has similar lunch specials with a French flavor.

There are more than two dozen delis, pubs and moderately priced restaurants on 55th and 56th Sts between Sixth and Fifth Aves that serve Midtown office workers. It's also worth checking out the **JP French Bakery** (☎ 212-765-7575, 54 W 55th St), which offers coffee, Gallic pastries and sandwiches on fresh baguettes for $6 or less.

Mike's (☎ 246-4115, 650 Tenth Ave) is a Cajun-influenced bistro with cheap food and ever-changing decorative themes that have turned the place into a pinball machine/Christmas shrine to Madonna (the singer, not the Virgin).

Michael Jordan's Steakhouse (☎ 212-655-2300, 23 Vanderbilt Ave) is smack in the middle of Grand Central Station, on a balcony overlooking the concourse. Despite its celebrity owner (usually a sign of poor food), this place is getting raves for its steak and lobster, though you pay for the setting and the name – about $50 per person.

One of the most authentic restaurants in the city must be the **Munson Diner** (☎ 212-246-0964, 600 W 49th St), at Eleventh Ave,

where cab drivers hang out before and after their shifts. (The burgers are greasy, and the waitress will call you 'Hon.')

Le Quercy (☎ 212-265-8141, 52 W 55th St) is an unpretentious, but authentic French bistro where you can get a good glass of steely Vouvray or Sancerre.

There are plenty of restaurants that rely on expense account executives in Midtown, but few have the quality to match their prices. One that certainly does is **Aquavit** (☎ 212-307-7311, 13 W 54th St). The main dining room is in a stunning six-story glass-enclosed atrium complete with a silent waterfall. The $60 fixed-price menu may seem steep, but it's worth every penny considering that the main dishes, such as venison with berry sauce, are sublime.

Vong (☎ 212-486-9592, 200 E 54th St) offers pricey Asian fare to office workers in an elegant setting. It's best to go there for the lunch specials, all of which cost around $20.

Times Square (Maps 5, 6)

Two popular delis are the **Carnegie Deli** (☎ 212-757-2245, 854 Seventh Ave), at W 54th St, and **Stage Deli** (☎ 212-245-7850, 834 Seventh Ave), at W 53rd St. The Carnegie is a tourist trap that nonetheless offers huge sandwiches for about $12. The Stage is a similar venue.

The side streets off Times Square are filled with hamburger joints and a variety of mid-range ethnic restaurants of varying quality. You'll do okay if you stick to unambitious food choices or patronize the following selections. A typical one is **Basilica** (☎ 212-489-0051, 676 Ninth Ave), between 46th and 47th Sts. Homemade pasta main dishes cost about $10, and meat dishes cost $10 to $12.

Mee Noodle Shop (☎ 212-765-2929, 795 Ninth Ave) is part of the city's best chain of cheap Chinese restaurants, serving a hearty bowl of broth, noodles and meat for just $5. Mee serves the same menu at two other locations: 922 Second Ave at 49th St, and 219 First Ave at 13th St. **Island Burgers and Shakes** (☎ 212-307-7934, 766 Ninth Ave), which specializes in churascos, a juicy breast of chicken sandwich that comes in

Restaurant Row

Restaurant Row is officially the block of W 46th St between Eighth and Ninth Aves, but locals use the name to refer to almost all the restaurants west of Times Square.

Some mediocre places – usually those serving glorified pub grub – survive thanks to their proximity to the theater district, but there are a few gems here too. *Joe Allen* (☎ *212-581-6464, 326 W 46th St)* serves salads, sandwiches and soup in a brick-walled room lined with the posters of famous Broadway flops. It's impossible to get into the place before the theater without a reservation, but it clears out completely for walk-ins by the 8 pm curtain time. *Orso* (☎ *212-489-7212, 322 W 46th St)*, also run by Joe Allen, serves more expensive Tuscan-style food for about $17 to $20 per main dish. It's popular with theater people and has a daily late-night seating at 10:30 pm for those coming out of performances. *Barbetta* (☎ *212-246-9171, 321 W 46th St)* is in an old townhouse that may have once been a brothel. You can get a $30 price-fixed meal in its quiet garden.

Closer to Eighth Ave is *Dorsay* (☎ *212-586-5900, 320 W 46th St)*, a sleek art deco lounge with a nice restaurant. *Hourglass Tavern* (☎ *212-265-2060, 373 W 46th St)* is a tiny place with reasonably priced stews and fish dishes; it figures in the John Grisham novel *The Firm*. Just around the corner is *Zen Palate* (☎ *212-582-1669, 663 Ninth Ave)*, which serves an exclusively vegetarian menu.

more than 50 different varieties for less than $8.

An expensive option off Sixth Ave near the Museum of Modern Art is *Michael's* (☎ *212-767-0555, 24 W 55th St)*, which is popular with the media crowd for its California cuisine.

Upper East Side (Map 7)

If you'd like to buy some groceries on the East Side, try the *Vinegar Factory* (☎ *212-987-0885, 431 E 91st St)* for a good range of gourmet food choices. There's also a branch of *Gourmet Garage* (☎ *212-535-5880, 301 E 64th St)*, just east of Second Ave; it has a good selection of fruit, bread and cheese.

Favia Lite (☎ *212-223-9115, 1140 Second Ave)* is a healthy Italian restaurant near the 59th St Bridge that serves surprisingly tasty pasta main dishes, listing calories and fat

content for every menu item. The large grilled-chicken pizza costs $15; skimmed milk or soy mozzarella is available at no extra charge.

The *Lexington Candy Shop* (☎ *212-288-0057, 1226 Lexington Ave)*, at 83rd St, is a picture-perfect lunch spot (complete with an old-fashioned soda fountain) that serves some of the most reasonable fare in one of the city's most expensive neighborhoods.

There are dozens of moderately priced restaurants on Second and Third Aves between 60th and 86th Sts that offer lunch specials for less than $10. *Cafe Greco* (☎ *212-737-4300, 1390 Second Ave)*, between 71st and 72nd Sts, is a typical example of the norm, serving continental dishes and a good brunch on the weekend.

Many small, wood-paneled restaurants with a French flavor line Madison Ave (north of 60th St) and several nearby side streets. Two fine places to find a bit of Paris (including slightly pricey main dishes ranging from $18 to $30 and a well-dressed clientele) are *La Goulue* (☎ *212-988-8169, 746 Madison Ave)*, near 64th St, and *Madame Romaine de Lyon* (☎ *212-759-5200, 132 E 61St)*, off Park Ave. It's possible to have a moderately priced and pleasant meal at either by sticking to the appetizer side of the menu or having lighter fare such as omelettes.

Arcadia (☎ *212-223-2900, 21 E 62nd St)* is one of best dining experiences in the city – well worth every penny you spend (which can top $80 per person). The food has a French American taste to it; you can't go wrong with anything on the menu, and the service is attentive, but not intrusive. It's an intimate space, adorned by a mural of the four seasons by Paul Davis, and it can be a little crowded if you're seated in the middle; when making reservations, ask for a side banquet.

Upper West Side (Map 7)

If you'd like to buy some groceries, *Zabar's* (☎ *212-787-2000)*, Broadway at W 80th St, is the city's most popular food emporium, with very good prices on items such as smoked salmon. A few blocks south, *Fairway Market* (☎ *212-595-1888, 2127 Broadway)*, at W 74th St, has the lowest prices on cheese and prepared salads. Fairway has a massive Harlem outlet at 125th St, just under the Henry Hudson Parkway.

The Upper West Side has dozens of cheap Chinese restaurants, pubs and coffee shops. The most reliable Chinese selection is *Empire Szechuan* with seven city locations, including *251 W 72nd St* (☎ *212-496-8460)* and *193 Columbus Ave* (☎ *212-496-8778)*, above 68th St. These bustling places serve generally healthy fare and offer lunch specials for around $7.

Tibet Shambala (☎ *212-721-1270, 488 Amsterdam Ave)* has a menu split evenly between meat and vegetarian dishes ($8.95).

Cafe Lalo (☎ *212-496-6031, 201 W 83rd St)* has a 14-page menu of expensive pastries, but you can spend an entire rainy afternoon here reading the dozens of newspapers and magazines on offer.

This neighborhood's moderate restaurants tend to have mediocre food and inattentive service. If you're in that price range head a little further south on Ninth Ave to 40th St and pick a place with an interesting window-displayed menu. But if you're looking to splurge, try either of the neighborhood's well-known and expensive restaurants. *Cafe Luxembourg* (☎ *212-873-7411, 200 W 70th St)* is impossible to get into without a reservation before performances at Lincoln Center. *Carmine's* (☎ *212-362-2200, 2450 Broadway)*, at 90th St, is a zoo-like Italian restaurant popular with big crowds, because the community-style pasta dishes are huge.

The romantic *Cafe des Artistes* (☎ *212-877-3500, 1 W 67th St)* has seen countless marriage proposals over the years, and it's a favorite of President Bill Clinton. The restaurant features a famous mural of naked nymphs prancing through Central Park – it almost obscures the generally high-quality main dishes ($20 range). Men must wear jackets after 6 pm.

Picholine (☎ *212-724-8585, 35 W 64th St)* offers Mediterranean-flavored cuisine and is one of the few restaurants in the city to maintain an after-dinner cheese course, with cheeses kept in a purpose-built cellar on the premises. Dinner for two, with wine, will hover around the $100 mark, and you will discover it's worth it.

Tavern on the Green (☎ *212-873-3200)*, at W 67th St and Central Park West, is the most profitable restaurant in the US, pulling in an astounding $35 million annually from visitors who want to admire its floodlit topiary statues in the back garden. Yes, it's a tourist trap.

The landmark *Hungarian Pastry Shop* (☎ *212-866-4230, 1030 Amsterdam Ave)* is a famous Columbia University hangout.

Harlem (Map 8)

Harlem is justifiably famous for its soul food, but there's also a growing West African influence in the neighborhood. Vegetarians or those seeking low-fat choices will have a hard time. All the following restaurants are within walking distance of the 125th St subway stations. Most places serve big portions at incredibly cheap prices.

By far the most famous restaurant in Harlem is *Sylvia's* (☎ 212-996-0660, 328 Lenox Ave), which has a gospel brunch on Sunday afternoon (reservations required; cost is about $25 per person). *Copeland's* (☎ 212-234-2357, 549 W 145th St), just off Broadway, is famous for its $12.95 nighttime buffet (open until midnight daily); eating à la carte (main courses run as high as $17) means a higher tab.

You can get the real deal at much better value at *Singleton's Barbecue* (☎ 212-694-9442, 525 Lenox Ave), where the $6 lunch specials offer pigs feet, 'smother' chicken livers, other delicacies and a choice of two vegetables.

Keur Famba (☎ 212-864-6161, 120-126 W 116th St), off Lenox Ave, is considered the best French African restaurant in the neighborhood thanks to its spicy fish stews that start at $7. *Pan Pan* (☎ 212-926-4900, 500 Lenox Ave) offers spicy Jamaican meat patties for $1.25 and coffee-and-roll breakfasts for $1.

The *M&G Soul Food Diner* (☎ 212-864-7326, 383 W 125th St) is just a short stroll from the Apollo Theater and one of the cheapest options in a low-cost neighborhood Try the delicious fried chicken. It's about $8 per person for a huge amount of food.

Several landmark remnants of Italian East Harlem remain in business: *Rao's Restaurant* (pronounced 'RAY-o's') (☎ 212-722-6709, 455 E 114th St), a tiny 12-table restaurant open weekdays; and *Patsy's Pizzeria* (☎ 212-534-9783, 2287 First Ave). Check out *Morrone's Bakery* (☎ 212-722-2972, 324 E 116th St) for great peasant bread.

The Bronx

The Bronx's most famous culinary neighborhood is in Belmont. Some of the restaurants in this eight-block neighborhood have been in business since WWI, including *Mario's* (☎ 718-584-1188, 2342 Arthur Ave)

and *Ann & Tony's* (☎ 718-933-1469, 2407 Arthur Ave), a family-style Neapolitan restaurant with pasta specials for $12 or less. There are often lines outside of the more famous *Dominick's* (☎ 718-733-2807, 2335 Arthur Ave), a cash-only place where the crusty waiters serve large portions of food at long tables; meals cost around $12 a dish. (There are no menu prices – the waiters present you with a final figure at the end of the meal. It usually winds up at about $15 per person, depending on your wine consumption.)

In City Island, locals hang out at *Rhodes Restaurant* (☎ 718-885-1538, 288 City Island Ave), which is open every day until 2 am and serves standard pub specials and burgers for under $10.

Brooklyn

Brooklyn Heights This neighborhood has two excellent bring-your-own-bottle restaurants: *Acadia Parish* (☎ 718-624-5154, 148 Atlantic Ave), near Clinton St, serves filling Cajun fare. Nearby is *La Bouillabaisse* (☎ 718-522-8275, 145 Atlantic Ave), where the signature dish and other French fare often attract lines out the door. At about $15 an entrée, it's expensive for this neighborhood, but cheap on the Manhattan scale.

For those who don't want to bother with shopping around for something to drink with a meal, there's an outpost of the *Park Slope Brewing Co* (☎ 718-522-4801, 62 Henry St) that serves a dozen local microbrews and sandwiches for $7 or less. You can enjoy a cheap pint during happy hour (4 to 7 pm) at *Pete's Waterfront Ale House* (☎ 718-522-3794, 136 Atlantic Ave), which proclaims itself the 'home of warm beer, lousy food and an ugly owner.'

There's also *Cousin's Café* (☎ 718-596-3514, 160 Court St), a bar serving sandwiches for lunch, and it features jazz combos on weekend nights. You can also get a good value meal at the no-frills *Sam's Restaurant* (☎ 718-596-3458, 238 Court St). It has a '40s-style atmosphere, including the menu recommendation 'if your wife can't cook, don't divorce her – eat at Sam's.' The *Court Bakery* (☎ 718-875-4820, 298 Court St) is famous for filling pastries, including the cream-filled lobster tail.

There are two storied places near each other in the Heights, close to the Brooklyn Academy of Music. *Junior's* (☎ 718-852-5257), at the corner of Flatbush and DeKalb Aves, is the place to get New York's best cheesecake. *Gage & Tollner* (☎ 718-875-5181, 372 Fulton St) is one of New York's oldest restaurants (established 1879). It's the place to go for a romantic, gaslight atmosphere and solid fare.

At Fulton Landing stands the famous *River Cafe* (☎ 718-522-5200, 1 Water St), a romantic restaurant with delicately prepared American cuisine and a $65 price-fixed dinner menu – you'll need to make reservations early for a window seat. Just as good, but much cheaper, is *Patsy's Pizza* (☎ 718-858-4300, 19 Old Fulton St), a wonderfully friendly family place that's great for children.

Park Slope Vegetarians are served by *Healthy Henrietta's* (☎ 718-622-2924, 787 Union St), with specialties such as scrambled tofu and vegetable burritos for less than $8. The *Lemongrass Grill* (☎ 718-399-7100, 61A Seventh Ave) has spicy and generous Thai dishes, including a wide selection of meatless choices, for $12 or less. The original *Park Slope Brewing Co* (☎ 718-788-1756, 356 Sixth Ave), at 5th St, serves hearty pub grub and local brews.

Eastern Parkway The streets near the Brooklyn Museum of Art have a number of West Indian restaurants, including the *Wizard* (☎ 718-399-9141, 806 Washington Ave), which serves pumpkin soup and $3 West Indian meat patties. *Tom's Restaurant* (☎ 718-636-9738, 782 Washington Ave) is a legendary, 70-year-old place that is a must for its egg cream sodas and its filling and hearty breakfasts.

Coney Island Two blocks away from the boardwalk is *Totonno's* (☎ 718-372-8606, 1524 Neptune Ave), one of the city's best and oldest brick-oven pizza restaurants. Totonno's is open only Thursday to Sunday

from noon to whenever he runs out of fresh mozzarella cheese. *Gargiulos* (☎ 718-266-4891, 2911 W 15th St) is a noisy family-style place once famous for its huge Styrofoam Octopus, reputedly stolen from the aquarium. The octopus is gone, but you can get filling Southern Italian dishes for about $15 a person.

Brighton Beach Some of Brighton Beach's restaurants cater to regional sectors of the Soviet émigré population, such as *Cafe Pearl* (☎ 718-891-4544, 303 Brighton Beach Ave), which serves Georgian specialties for about $12, or the *Winter Garden* (☎ 718-934-6666), on the Boardwalk, which attracts Muscovites. The bakeries on Brighton Beach Ave sell fantastic Russian dark-sourdough bread for $1.50 a loaf. You can enjoy a sticky, sweet cherry drink while watching videos of Russian variety programs at *Caffe Cappuccino* (☎ 718-646-6207, 290 Brighton Beach Ave).

At night, two raucous nightclub-restaurants offer set menus and elaborate floor shows. The *National* (☎ 718-646-1225, 273 Brighton Beach Ave) charges $55 per person on Friday, Saturday and Sunday nights for its completely over-the-top variety show and dinner, well-oiled by carafes of vodka. *Primorski* (☎ 718-891-3111, 282 Brighton Beach Ave) has a cheaper set menu ($20 during the week and $25 on the weekend), but if you lose track of your vodka consumption, the bill is sure to be much larger.

Williamsburg This neighborhood is home to the most famous steak house in the city: *Peter Luger's* (☎ 718-387-7400, 178 Broadway), an old warehouse of a restaurant that has a reputation for serving New York's best beef. This out-of-the-way place takes cash only, and dinner can cost up to $60 per person with wine (subway: Marcy Ave).

In northern Williamsburg you can visit *Plan-eat Thailand* (☎ 718-599-5758, 184 Bedford Ave) and enjoy Southeast Asian dishes for $8 to $10 while listening to live jazz and checking out work by local artists (subway: Bedford Ave).

At **Oznot's Dish** (☎ 718-599-6596, 79 Berry St), the Mediterranean-style menu offers dishes for less than $10. **Teddy's** (☎ 718-384-9787, 96 Berry St) is a great old bar with all the old reliables – primarily burgers and strong beer. **Bean** (☎ 718-387-8222, 167 Bedford Ave) is a bustling and inexpensive vegetarian restaurant.

Queens

Astoria You can have an inexpensive dinner at the 24-hour **Uncle George's** (☎ 718-626-0593, 33-19 Broadway), which serves daily specials of barbecued pork and potatoes for $8 and red snapper for $12. The taste of the restaurant's *tzatziki*, the delicious Greek dip made of yogurt, garlic and cucumber, will last in your mouth for hours. Just across the street is the smoky and sleek patisserie **Omonia Cafe** (☎ 718-274-6650, 32-20 Broadway), where it's possible to linger over an espresso, close your eyes and hear nothing but Greek spoken all around you as you eat.

A similar experience can be found at the **Galaxy Cafe** (☎ 718-545-3951, 34-02 Broadway) and **Kolonaki Cafe** (☎ 718-932-8222, 33-02 Broadway), which is named after Kolonaki Square in Athens, the meeting place for Greece's idle rich.

The more expensive and out-of-the-way **Elias Corner** (☎ 718-932-1510, 24-02 31st St) is worth a trip to the Astoria Blvd subway stop. It's famous in the Greek community for its floppingly-fresh grilled fish and bracing *retsina*, a potent Greek wine (cash only).

Jackson Heights This is the neighborhood to find the legendary **Jackson Diner** (☎ 718-672-1232, 37-03 74th St), which many consider the city's best southern Indian restaurant. This dingy converted coffee shop is famous for its *masala dosa* appetizer, a massive crepe with potato, onion and peas, and the *seekh kabob*, a long sausage made of tender lamb.

Around the corner from the Jackson Diner is **La Porteña** (☎ 718-458-8111, 74-25 37th Ave), which serves Buenos Aires–style barbecue. Meals come to the table with *chimichurri*, a garlic-laden oil and vinegar sauce.

There's also a large population of Colombians that frequent such restaurant-nightclubs as **Chibcha** (☎ 718-429-9033, 79-05 Roosevelt Ave), which has salsa and jazz shows on Friday and Saturday nights beginning at 11 pm. **Taco Mexico** (☎ 718-899-5800, 88-12 Roosevelt Ave) is a fast-food restaurant that has homemade salsa and tortilla chips. **Inti Raymi** (☎ 718-424-1938, 86-14 37th Ave) serves Peruvian specialties such as grilled cow's heart (open only Thursday to Sunday).

Corona Several Latino subcultures exist side by side at the dividing line between Jackson Heights and Corona. The **Broadway Sandwich Shop** (☎ 718-898-4088, 96-01 Roosevelt Ave) serves garlicky toasted Cuban pork sandwiches for less than $5 and steaming hot cups of strong *cafe con leche*. One block away is **Quisqueya Restaurant** (☎ 718-478-0704, 97-03 Roosevelt Ave), which offers sweet-plantain plates and Dominican specialties such as young goat stew for $8.

Tomas Gonzalez offers a taste of Mexico at **La Espiga** (☎ 718-779-7898, 42-13 102nd St), which is a combination bakery, taco bar and grocery store. People line up for the fresh tortillas (two pounds for $1) that are made several times a day. The shop also sells Mexican embroidery and foodstuffs for home cooking.

The Lemon Ice King of Corona (☎ 718-699-5133, 52-02 108th St) is open year-round until 6 pm in winter, 10 pm in summer, and serves homemade ices. The signature ice has chunks of lemon and is the perfect refresher for a summer day. The Lemon Ice King is about a mile from the subway. Walk south on 104th St to Corona Ave, turn left and walk two blocks to 52nd Ave; or take the Q23 bus to Forest Hills and get off on 108th St and 52nd Ave on the opposite corner from the shop.

Flushing It's hard to offer a comprehensive list of the best of Flushing's many restaurants, but **Joe's Shanghai** (☎ 718-539-3838,

136-21 37th Ave) is known throughout the city for its noodle dishes and steaming bowls of handmade dumplings. The sleekest place in Flushing is the inexpensive *Shanghai Tang* (☎ 718-661-0900, 135-20 40th Rd), between Roosevelt and 41st Aves. The staff enthusiastically guides newcomers thorough the Shanghai-style menu choices.

Fish is the specialty at *Golden Pond* (☎ 718-886-1628, 37-17A Prince St), west of the Flushing-Main St subway station. Try a Sunday afternoon dim sum feast at *KB Garden* (☎ 718-961-9088, 136-28 39th Ave). Most of the dim sum choices are $4, leaving nary a dent in your wallet.

Sam Won Garden (☎ 718-321-0101, 136-17 38th Ave) is open 24 hours and offers a menu of sushi and Korean barbecue.

Staten Island

It's bleak and unattractive near the ferry terminal. The *Sidestreet Saloon* (☎ 718-448-6868, 11 Schuyler St), just a few minutes walk from the ferry, is a popular lunch spot for workers from the borough courthouse across the street. The *Cargo Cafe* (☎ 718-876-0539), Slossen Terrace and Bay St, three blocks east of the ferry terminal, has inexpensive lunch specials.

La Caleta (☎ 718-447-0397, 75 Bay St) has Spanish seafood specials and chicken dishes for $8 or less. Nearby, the *Clipper* (☎ 718-273-5100, 38 Bay St) is a diner with most dishes less than $10. It is open 6 am to midnight daily and until 3 am Friday and Saturday. *Gilly's Luncheonette* (☎ 718-448-0579, 9 Hyatt St), immediately behind Staten Island Borough Hall, is a classic working-class breakfast and lunch spot. *RH Tug's* (☎ 718-447-6369, 1115 Richmond Terrace) is a nice spot for waterfront al fresco lunching; it's just a few minutes walk west from the Snug Harbor Cultural Center.

ENTERTAINMENT

No single source could possibly list everything that happens in the city, but *Time Out* is the single best guide to nightlife. High-culture events get big play in the Sunday and Friday *New York Times* and the *New*

Yorker; dance clubs and smaller music venues take out numerous ads in the *Village Voice*. The free papers such as *Metro* and *New York Press* all roundup cultural events. NYC On Stage (☎ 212-768-1818) is a 24-hour information line listing music and dance events.

Tickets

The Broadway Line (☎ 212-302-4111) provides descriptions of plays and musicals both on and off the Great White Way; you can use it to obtain information on ticket prices and make credit card purchases.

Discount Tickets The TKTS booth in the middle of Times Square (☎ 212-768-1818) sells same-day tickets to Broadway and Off-Broadway musicals and dramas. Tickets sell at either half price or 75% off regular box office rates, plus a $2.50 service charge per ticket. The booth's marquee lists available shows; ticket availability depends on the popularity of the show – check out the Friday *New York Times* and *Time Out* for ticket availability.

On Wednesday and Saturday, matinee tickets go on sale at 10 am, and on Sunday the windows open at noon for afternoon performances. Evening tickets go on sale every day at 3 pm, and a line begins to form up to an hour before the booth opens. Note that TKTS accepts cash or traveler's checks only. Touts offering last-minute discounts to off-Broadway events also canvass the TKTS line with flyers.

The nearby Times Square Visitor Center (☎ 212-869-5453), 1560 Broadway between 46th and 47th, also sells discounted tickets and vouchers to certain shows.

Tickets by Phone Telecharge (☎ 212-239-6200) is the main contact for Broadway and off-Broadway ticket sales by telephone. Ticketmaster (☎ 212-307-7171 for concerts, 307-4100 for the performing arts) has a lock on sales for most major concerts and sporting events. Beware: Ticketmaster adds 'handling,' 'venue' and 'postage' fees to orders, which can add a whopping $20 to the cost of a top-price ticket.

Broadway & Other Theater

Although Times Square is ostensibly the center of New York's legitimate theater (the 'theater district'), the productions around Times Square have been dominated by musicals produced by Andrew Lloyd Webber *(Cats, Phantom of the Opera)*, and film spin-offs from Disney *(The Lion King, Beauty and the Beast)*. Some of that began to change in the late 1990s, with serious plays arriving from Britain and Ireland, some to great acclaim *(The Weir, The Blue Room* and *Closer)*. Some new musicals saw success, too – among them *Titanic* and revivals such as *Chicago* and *Fosse*.

All of this has added up to a great era of success for Broadway. More than 11 million people buy tickets to shows each year, and the average age of patrons has finally begun to drop after years of worries about the graying of the audience. Now there's even a shortage of theaters to meet the demand. In fact, the high cost of putting a serious play (ie, nonmusical) on Broadway forced even Broadway giant Neil Simon – who has a theater named after him on 52nd St – to debut his **London Suite** in Union Square.

In general, 'Broadway' productions are those showing in the large theaters around Times Square. (For theater locations, see the Times Square map.) 'Off Broadway' usually refers to dramas that are performed in smaller (200 seats or fewer) spaces elsewhere in town. A big business in itself, it now boasts an annual attendance of 4 million people a year. Prominent spots for off-Broadway performances include the following: **PS 122** (☎ *212-477-5288, 150 First Ave*) (subway: Union Square); **Circle in the Square Theater** (☎ *212-307-2705, 1633 Broadway)*, at 50th St (subway: Rockefeller Center); **Samuel Beckett Theater** (☎ *212-594-2826, 410 W 42nd St)*, near Ninth Ave (subway: Times Square); **Performing Garage** (☎ *212-966-3651, 33 Wooster St)* (subway: Spring St).

'Off-off-Broadway' events are readings, experimental performances and improvisations held in spaces for less than 100. The *Village Voice, New York* magazine and *Time*

Out are the best resources for finding out about fringe shows.

Cinemas

New York offers the cineast plenty of choices, and you can still duck into a movie house on a rainy or hot afternoon. New Yorkers take film very seriously, so going to the cinema can be a trying experience in the evening and on weekends. Though prices are now $9.50, and it's just a matter of time (or the next popular big-budget film) before the city breaks the $10 per ticket mark.

Most first-run films sell out a half-hour early on Friday and Saturday nights. You're likely to have to stand in one line to buy a ticket and another to get into the theater. What's worse, movie chains publish semi-fictitious start times in order to leave about 20 minutes to sell you popcorn and soda. You can at least avoid one queue by calling ☎ 212-777-3456 and prepaying for the movie of your choice ($1 service charge per ticket); you pick up your ticket by swiping a credit card through a machine upon arrival.

Independent films and career retrospectives are held at the three screen *Film Forum* (☎ *212-727-8110, 209 W Houston St)* (subway: Houston St), and Lincoln Center's *Walter Reade Theater* (☎ *212-875-5600)*, which has wide, screening-room-quality seats (subway: 66th St). At *Anthology Film Archives* (☎ *212-505-5181, 32 Second Ave)*, you can see fringe and low-budget European works (subway: Second Ave).

The 12 screen *Sony Theaters – Lincoln Square*, Broadway and 68th St (Map 7), includes a 3D IMAX theater and first-run features. Sony (☎ *212-336-5000)* and Cineplex Odeon (☎ *212-505-2463)* have multiplexes throughout Manhattan.

The following specialize in foreign and low-budget independent films: the *Angelika Film Center* (☎ *212-995-2000)*, at Mercer and Houston Sts (subway: Broadway-Lafayette St); *Angelika 57* (☎ *212-586-1900)*, at 57th and Broadway (subway: N, R trains to 57th St); and the *Lincoln Plaza Cinemas (Map 7; ☎ 212-757-2280)*, at Broadway and 63rd St (subway: 66th St-Lincoln Center).

Bryant Park (☎ 212-883-2476), at 42nd St and Sixth Ave, right behind the New York Public Library, is the site of open-air film screenings on Monday evenings throughout the summer. The park's information booth provides a schedule.

Classical Music & Opera

Manhattan The **New York Philharmonic** has been getting rave reviews under the direction of German-born conductor Kurt Masur, though its audience at *Avery Fisher Hall* (☎ 212-721-6500), in Lincoln Center, still resists deviations from the standard repertoire. Tickets range from $15 to $70. It also performs 'rush hour' concerts (lasting just 90 minutes) during the season (subway: 66th St-Lincoln Center).

The **American Symphony Orchestra**, the **Chamber Music Society of Lincoln Center** and the **Little Orchestra Society** also hold their seasons at *Alice Tully Hall* (☎ 212-721-6500) in Lincoln Center (subway: 66th St-Lincoln Center).

The *Metropolitan Opera* (☎ 212-362-6000), holds its season from September to April in its namesake Lincoln Center theater. It's nearly impossible to get into the first few performances of operas that feature such big stars as Jessye Norman and Placido Domingo, but once the B-team moves in, tickets become available. Tickets for center orchestra seats start at $125, but you can get in the upper balcony for $16. Standing room is also available on a limited basis (subway: 66th St-Lincoln Center).

The *Merkin Concert Hall (Map 7;* ☎ 212-362-8719, 129 W 67th St) is a more intimate venue for classical music (subway: 66th St-Lincoln Center), as well as *Symphony Space (Map 7;* ☎ 212-864-5400, 2536 Broadway), at 95th St (subway: 1, 2, 3, 9 trains to 96th St), and *Town Hall (Map 6;* ☎ 212-840-2824, 123 W 43rd St), in Times Square, which is also the site for lectures and readings (subway: Times Square).

Visiting philharmonics and the **New York Pops** orchestra perform at storied *Carnegie Hall (Map 6;* ☎ 212-247-7800), at 57th St and Seventh Ave (subway: N, R trains to 57th St). A schedule of monthly events is available in the lobby next to the box office, and you can usually get tickets for as low as $12 for nonsubscription events.

The more daring and lower-cost **New York City Opera** (☎ 212-870-5630) takes the stage at the Philip Johnson-designed *New York State Theater*, in Lincoln Center (see Map 7), for a split season that runs for a few weeks in early autumn and picks up again in the late spring (subway: 66th St-Lincoln Center). For other events at the theater, call ☎ 212-870-5570.

Brooklyn The prime outer-borough spot for entertainment is the *Brooklyn Academy of Music* (☎ 718-636-4100, 30 Lafayette Ave). It consists of the **Majestic Theater** and the **Brooklyn Opera House**, and it hosts concerts, operas and plays all year (subway: Atlantic Ave).

Other Brooklyn venues include *St Ann's Church* (☎ 718-858-2424), Montague and Clinton Sts in Brooklyn Heights, with a year-round calendar of concerts; tickets run about $25. *Bargemusic* (☎ 718-624-4061), at Fulton Landing, is the name for the chamber music program held under the Brooklyn Bridge during the summer. Concerts and performances by small dance companies are held at the *Brooklyn Center for the Performing Arts* (☎ 718-951-4500), at the Brooklyn College at Campus Rd and Hillel Place (subway: Flatbush Ave-Brooklyn College).

Dance & Ballet

New York is home to more than half a dozen world-famous dance companies. The *New York City Ballet* (☎ 212-721-6500), established by Lincoln Kirstein and George Balanchine in 1948, performs at the **New York State Theater** in Lincoln Center during the winter. During the spring, the **American Ballet Theater** (☎ 212-477-3030) takes over at the *Metropolitan Opera House* in Lincoln Center for a summer season (subway: 66th St-Lincoln Center).

City Center (Map 5; ☎ 212-581-1212, 131 W 55th St), between Sixth and Seventh Aves, is home to the **Alvin Ailey American Dance**

Theater every December and hosts engagements by foreign companies.

The most offbeat dance venue is the *Joyce Theater (Map 5; ☎ 212-242-0800, 175 Eighth Ave)* at 19th St. The Merce Cunningham and Pilabolus dance companies make annual appearances here (subway: A, C, E trains to 14th St).

Popular Music

When major singers and 'super groups' that regularly fill arenas play a smaller venue in New York, their record company usually buys up all the tickets and hands them out as freebies, so don't feel disappointed if you miss your favorite performer's surprise club appearance. It's easier to get tickets to see lesser lights.

Madison Square Garden (Map 5; ☎ 212-456-6000) is a venue for major concerts (subway: 34th St). *Radio City Music Hall (Map 5; ☎ 212-247-4777)* also hosts big events (subway: Rockefeller Center), and the *Beacon Theater (Map 7; ☎ 212-496-7070, 2124 Broadway)* does too (subway: 72nd St).

The Concert Hotline (☎ 212-249-8870) tells you who's playing in the music clubs.

Jazz The basement-level *Village Vanguard (Map 4; ☎ 212-255-4037, 178 Seventh Ave)* may be the world's most famous jazz club; it has hosted literally every major star of the past 50 years. The cover charge runs $15 to $20 with a two-drink minimum (subway: Christopher St).

There is a well-known Sunday jazz brunch at *Sweet Basil (Map 4; ☎ 212-242-1785, 88 Seventh Ave South)*, but the music's better than the food (subway: Christopher St). The club also hosts week-long visits by jazz stars such as McCoy Tyner. *Smalls (Map 4; ☎ 212-929-756, 183 W 10th St)* is a unique place (without a liquor license) that hosts an incredible $10, 10-hour jazz marathon every night from 10 pm to 8 am that attracts top talent coming off gigs in mainstream joints (subway: Christopher St).

By far the most expensive club is the *Blue Note (Map 4; ☎ 212-475-8592, 131 W 3rd St)*, featuring big stars playing short sets, with music charges up to $60 for the most storied

names in jazz (subway: W 4th St). You can hear fringe jazz and folk at the *Knitting Factory (☎ 212-219-3055, 74 Leonard St)* in Tribeca.

The popular **Mingus Big Band** plays every Thursday at *Fez (Map 4; ☎ 212-533-2680, 380 Lafayette St)*, which hosts experimental music the rest of the week (subway: Bleecker St). *Iridium (Map 7; ☎ 212-219-3055, 48 W 63rd St)* breaks new jazz acts (subway: W 66th St-Lincoln Center).

Harlem's Cotton Club era is long gone, but there are still several places to hear jazz, both modern and traditional. Because of declining patronage, most have performances only on weekend nights; call ahead to check times and possible cover charges. The old *Lenox Lounge (Map 8; ☎ 212-722-9566)*, Lenox Ave and 125th St, is worth visiting anytime for its remarkable art deco interior. *Showman's Cafe (Map 8; ☎ 212-864-8941, 2321 Frederick Douglass Blvd)* features jazz combos and R&B vocalists. The same mix of styles, along with a late-night menu, can be found at *Wells Restaurant (Map 8; ☎ 212-234-0700, 2247 Powell Blvd)*. *Lickety Split (Map 8; ☎ 212-283-9093, 2361 Powell Blvd)* specializes in Caribbean bands (subway: A train to 125th St).

Rock Well-known, intimate concert spaces include the *Bottom Line (Map 4; ☎ 212-228-6300, 15 W 4th St)* in the Village (subway: W 4th St). The prototypical punk club *CBGB (Map 4; ☎ 212-982-4052, 315 Bowery)* is still going strong after 25-plus years (subway: Bleeker St). At the small *Mercury Lounge (Map 4; ☎ 212-260-4700, 217 E Houston St)*, big names turn up (subway: Second Ave) and *Irving Plaza (Map 5; ☎ 212-777-6800, 17 Irving Place)*, too (subway: Union Square). *Webster Hall (Map 4; ☎ 212-353-1600, 125 E 11th St)* has five levels and holds exclusive dance parties and last-minute surprise events with big stars (subway: Union Square).

Blues, Folk & World Music The *55 Bar (Map 4; ☎ 212-929-9883, 55 Christopher St)* is an authentic, smoky joint that never charges a cover (subway: Christopher St). Visiting blues masters play at *Chicago Blues*

(Map 5; ☎ 212-924-9755, 73 Eighth Ave), between 13th and 14th Sts (subway: A, C, E trains to 14th St) and at *Manny's Car Wash (Map 7; ☎ 212-369-2583, 1558 Third Ave)*, uptown (subway: 86th St).

International artists are brought to New York by the World Music Institute for concerts at the *Washington Square Church (☎ 212-545-7536, 135 W 4th St)* and other venues throughout the city.

College radio favorites play at *Far Side (Map 4; ☎ 212-673-9143, 269 E Houston St)* on the Lower East Side (subway: Second Ave). The *Back Fence (☎ 212-475-9221, 155 Bleecker St)*, which never charges a cover, is the best folk venue among many in the center of Greenwich Village.

SOB's (Map 4; ☎ 212-243-4940, 204 Varick St) specializes in Afro-Cuban sounds (subway: Houston St). Uptown, the place to go is the *Latin Quarter (☎ 212-864-7600)*, at Broadway and 95th St.

Bars

New York's bars can stay open until 4 am, and on weekends, most of them do. A proper listing of New York City's best bars is worth an entire separate book – here's a highly selective list of bars that are open until 2 am most nights.

Lower Manhattan (Map 3) *The Greatest Bar on Earth (☎ 212-524-7011)*, at Windows on the World on the 107th floor of One World Trade Center, has an unparalleled view.

SoHo & Tribeca (Map 4) *The Ear Inn (☎ 212-226-9060, 326 Spring St)* is in the old James Brown House (not the Godfather of Soul). This old place near the Hudson River attracts sanitation workers and office dwellers with its great shepherd's pie and inexpensive lunch choices (subway: Spring St). *Cafe Noir (32 Grand St)* is a good place to munch on North African appetizers while watching the passing SoHo parade from the open-air bar railing (subway: Grand St).

Union Square (Map 5) *Pete's Tavern (☎ 212-473-7676, 124 E 18th St)* is a place patronized by short-story writer O Henry, who is said to have written his Christmas story *The Gift of the Magi* in a front booth. You can get a decent burger and beer here or find the same fare by walking a block away to the equally popular *Old Town Bar and Grill (☎ 212-529-6732, 45 E 18th St)*, a wood-paneled 1892 pub with grumpy barmen but decent food in its booths and upstairs dining area (subway: Union Square).

Greenwich Village & East Village (Map 4) *Chumley's (86 Barrow St)* is a hard-to-find, storied speakeasy serving decent pub grub (cash only). It was among the first places in the city to serve American microbrews exclusively (subway: Christopher St). *The Corner Bistro (331 W 4th St)* is a famous West Village bar where you can eat charred hamburgers and other pub fare until 2 am (subway: Christopher St).

In the East Village *The Scratcher (209 E Fifth St)* is a true Dublin-style pub, a quiet place to read the newspaper during the day over coffee, but crowded and raucous at night (subway: Astor Place). *Swift (34 E 4th St)*, just off the Bowery, is another wildly popular Irish bar with live bands and probably the best pint of Guinness in New York City. *KGB (85 E 4th St)* is a bar that also serves as a site for literary meetings. *McSorley's Old Ale House (5 E 7th St)* is the well-known setting for Joseph Mitchell's *New Yorker* short stories. A cramped and stodgy old bar, it refused to admit women until the 1970s; today, it often has a long line of tourists waiting to get in.

Times Square (Maps 5, 6) *Mercury Bar (☎ 212-262-7755, 659 Ninth Ave)*, between 45th and 46th Sts, is a sleek new bar-restaurant in this up-and-coming West Side neighborhood near Port Authority. It's packed on Thursday and Friday nights, and there's a decent menu, too.

Upper East Side (Map 7) *Kinsale Tavern (☎ 212-348-4370, 1672 Third Ave)* is a gathering place with more than 20 beers on tap; it attracts European rugby and soccer fanatics with live, early-morning satellite broad casts of European matches during the winter months (subway: 96th St). In a city packed with Irish pubs, *The British Open* (☎ 212-355-8467, *320 E 59th St*), in the shadow of the Queensboro Bridge, draws fans of golf and the British Royal Family (subway: 59th St-Lexington Ave). *The Subway Inn* (☎ 212 223-8929, *143 E 60th St*), just above the 59th St-Lexington Ave subway station, is an old bar that looks like it hasn't changed in 40 years, right down to the barmen's white shirts and thin black ties.

Upper West Side (Map 7) *Dublin House* (☎ 212-874-9528, *225 W 79th St*) shouldn't be remarkable, but it is, thanks to the odd combination of old men and Columbia University undergrads who patronize the place (subway: 79th St). Columbia's grad students tend to hang out at the *Night Cafe* (☎ 212-864-8889, *938 Amsterdam Ave*) at 106th St.

Lounges
As the economy boomed in New York City in the late 1990s, some of the newly wealthy found that a mere bar just wouldn't do for high-end nightlife. That desire for some sort of ill-defined 'class' led to a big growth in lounges, catering to both gay and mixed crowds. Moreover, some once-stuffy classic cocktail lounges got a new lease on life, particularly in hotels and on the East Side. Lounges tend to be defined by their clientele – those downtown offering cigars and bourbon attract office workers; uptown, it's mainly old money; SoHo attracts the arts crowd; Chelsea lounges are mostly gay.

Tribeca & Greenwich Village (Map 4) The *Café Remy* (☎ 212-267-4646, *104 Greenwich St*) has a great lounge area and a wild dance floor with salsa and other Latin music nightly. *The Bubble Lounge* (☎ 212-431-3433, *228 West Broadway*) is the place to drop $2000 on a bottle of champagne. It's patronized by the well-heeled Wall Street crowd.

Hudson Bar & Books (*636 Hudson St*) is a narrow, faux library that has free jazz on weekend evenings. This place has an uptown cousin: *Beekman Bar and Books* (*889 First Ave*), near the UN, which has an elaborate cigar-smoking room. *Bar d' O* (*29 Bedford St*) is a sleek lounge with drag acts several nights a week. It attracts a chic mixed crowd of gays and straights (subway: W 4th St).

East Village (Map 4) *Tribe* (☎ 212-979-8965, *132 First Ave*), at St Marks Place, tells you everything you need to know about the East Village today. This was the location of the storied old St Marks Bar & Grill. Now it has a DJ, dance floor lighting and pricey pints. *147 Ludlow St*, at that address, is a place so cool it doesn't have a name. A DJ plays from 7:30 pm to 4 am nightly (subway: Delancey St). There are many bars in the Ludlow street area.

Midtown (Map 5) At the Rainbow Room's *Promenade Lounge* (☎ 212-632-5000, *30 Rockefeller Plaza*), on the 65th floor of the GE Building, you must wear a jacket. However, for about the same cost as visiting the top of the Empire State Building, you get a stunning view that includes that very landmark and a drink to go along with it (subway: Rockefeller Center).

Upper West Side & Upper East Side (Map 7) *Saints* (☎ 212-222-2431, *992 Amsterdam Ave*), between 109 and 110 Sts, is a quiet gay bar that welcomes a mixed crowd. *Bemelmans Bar* (☎ 212-744-1600, *35 E 76th St*) is an elegant space in the Carlyle Hotel where you'll feel uncomfortable without a jacket – there's a cover charge (usually $25) for evening performances (subway: 77th St). The lounge at *The Mark Hotel* (☎ 212-744-4300, 800-843-627522, fax 212-744-2749, *E 77th St*) is a quiet space that epitomizes Upper East Side elegance.

Clubs
If a club is around long enough to be listed here, it's by definition no longer hot. The monthly magazine *Paper* is the best source for clubs. You should also keep an eye out for club and band flyers on walls and billboards while walking through the East Village – it's often the only current way to find out about some clubs that for legal

Crash of a Club King

These are tough times for New York City's dance clubs. Now that the cops have cracked down on the street drug trade, the city government has set the law authorities loose on the clubs. Unfortunately for the club owners and those who love partying all night, there seems to have been something to Mayor Rudolph Giuliani's claims that the facilities are nothing more than all-night drug supermarkets. Things weren't helped by press revelations about the city's 'club kids,' an odd mixture of the idle rich, drug addicts and hangers-on who live for the nightlife.

No one has suffered more from the crackdown than Peter Gatien, the self-proclaimed 'Club King' and owner of Limelight and the Tunnel. A Canadian entrepreneur, with an eye patch that lends him an air of malevolent mystery, Gatien has long been a target of the crackdowns. Things went bad when a club kid named Angel Melendez disappeared following a dispute over drug debts. (His mutilated body was later found floating in the river.) A Limelight party planner named Michael Alig was convicted of the murder and turned on Gatien in exchange for a lesser sentence. Gatien survived the accusation of drug dealing, but he served a 90-day sentence for not paying $1.4 million in taxes.

Both the Limelight and Tunnel reopened but were again shuttered when a teenager died after a taking both ecstasy and Special K. (At the trial, the judge uttered the immortal line: 'You mean Special K is not a cereal?') Several club employees have also been arrested on suspicion of drug dealing.

Today, the Tunnel and Limelight open only when lawyers can hold off the latest legal attack. But denizens of all clubs ought to be forewarned that the cops are keeping a close eye on who sells what to whom.

Most of the clubs listed here are downtown, below 14th St, and they attract a mixed gay and straight crowd. It generally costs about $25 to $35 to get into the clubs from Thursday to Saturday. Don't even think about going to any of these places before 11 pm, even on a weeknight; things don't truly pick up until 1 am or later. Some of the phone numbers listed here are pretty much useless, because the clubs don't generally answer the phone. Also, note that some clubs have had real legal difficulties stemming from drug investigations (see the 'Crash of a Club King' boxed text).

Rockstar (☎ 212-714-7153) is a monthly party held in a different secret location, usually a West Side loft. Call the number, and the operators will ask you a series of questions about your music tastes. If they think you're cool enough for inclusion, you'll be told where to show up.

Tribeca, Chelsea & Greenwhich Village (Maps 4, 5) ***Tunnel*** (☎ 212-695-7292, 220 Twelfth Ave), at 27th St, is a massive three-floor club (subway: 23rd St-Eighth Ave). ***Limelight*** (☎ 212-807-7850, 660 Sixth Ave), like other Limelights around the world (London, Montreal), is in a disused church (subway: 23rd St). It has been opened and closed frequently, because the city has been trying to effectively shut down the club culture after a series of drug incidents. ***Don Hill's*** (☎ 212-334-1390, 511 Greenwich St), at Spring St, is a favorites with transvestites (subway: Spring St).

Union Square (Map 5) ***Nell's*** (☎ 212-675-1567, 246 W 14th St) was once a European velvet lounge, but now it brings in a rougher hip-hop crowd (subway: 14th St-Eighth Ave). ***Webster Hall*** (☎ 212-353-1600, 125 E 11th St) is a huge, five-level club (subway: Union Square).

Comedy Clubs

Those looking for more cutting edge comedy should head to the Lower East Side and try the nightly shows at ***Surf Reality*** (Map 4; ☎ 212-673-4182, 172 Allen St), between Stanton and Rivington Sts, and the

reasons do not have phones or advertise. You can also check out the latest club information on the Internet at Scenetrack (www.scenetrack.com).

Luna Lounge (*Map 4;* ☎ *212-260-2323, 171 Ludlow St*), where edgier comedians, such as Marc Marron and Janeane Garafalo, try out their stuff, sometimes for free (subway: Second Ave).

If you're looking for mainstream material, stick with the top-level comedians. The lounges offer pub fare and beer during the shows. Try *Caroline's Comedy Club/ Comedy Nation* (*Map 6;* ☎ *212-757-4100, 1626 Broadway*), in Times Square, or *Chicago City Limits* (*Map 7,* ☎ *212-888-5233, 1105 First Ave*). *Catch a Rising Star* (*Map 5;* ☎ *212-244-3005, 253 W 28th St*) is the legendary launching ground for many comedy stars of the '70s, but it's not at its original location.

SPECTATOR SPORTS
New York's baseball teams have had good years lately, and tickets can be hard to obtain for certain games. However, the Yankees and the Mets play a combined 162 home games during the summer months, so if you're in town for more than a few days, it should be easy to walk up to the stadium and buy day tickets ($5 to $32.50).

The National League New York Mets (☎ 718-507-8499) play in windswept old *Shea Stadium* in Flushing Meadows, Queens; it's a 40-minute journey from Midtown (subway: Willets Point-Shea Stadium). The American League New York Yankees (☎ 718-293-6000) play at their legendary namesake stadium in the South Bronx, just 15 minutes from Midtown (subway: 161st St-Yankee Stadium).

Most games begin at 7:30 pm and the two crosstown rivals play a limited number of regular season inter-league games. See the Uptown Manhattan map for the location of Yankee Stadium. (For more on the stadiums and their surrounding neighborhoods, see the Queens and Bronx sections, earlier in this chapter.)

Although New York is a baseball town, its high profile basketball and hockey teams play in the famous 19,000-seat *Madison Square Garden* arena. The NBA New York Knicks (☎ 212-465-6741) and the NHL New York Rangers (☎ 212-465-6741) sell a huge

number of season tickets, and so generally, visitors must book seats through Ticketmaster (☎ 212-262-3424) or Madison Square Garden's box office (☎ 212-456-6741), or deal with the many scalpers who hover around the area on game nights (subway: 34th St).

Scalpers try to get a premium price for seats that already cost up to $200 for big games. When dealing with scalpers, the best strategy is to wait until after the 7:30 pm game time, when prices drop – or merely head to a nearby bar. All the Knicks and Rangers games are on cable television.

SHOPPING
What to Buy
Antiques Top-level auctions are held at Christie's (Map 7; ☎ 212-546-1000), 502 Park Ave, which has sold items from John F Kennedy's estate, Marilyn Monroe's dresses and Frank Sinatra's personal items. Sotheby's (Map 7; ☎ 212-606-7000), 1334 York Ave, specializes in paintings and fine furniture.

Friday's edition of the *New York Times* contains announcements of exhibitions of sale items, and there are frequent antique shows at the Park Ave Armory at 61st St (Map 7).

There are antique furniture stores on 59th St between Third and Second Aves. More stores are on Broadway, just below Union Square, and along E 12th St.

Vendors selling lighting, rare books, prints and other items of interest can be found at the Metropolitan Art Auction (☎ 212-463-0200), 110 W 19th St, and the Chelsea Antiques Building (Map 5; ☎ 212-929-0909), 110 W 25th St.

Cameras New York's camera prices are hard to beat, but some of the camera stores in Midtown have reputations for bait-and-switch tactics, so if you go in to buy a Canon lens and the salesman begins offering a cheaper, no-name alternative that's supposedly 'better,' beware. And because the sector is dominated by shops owned and operated by Orthodox Jews, they usually close early Friday and all day Saturday in observation of the Sabbath, early Friday and all day Saturday and they are shuttered during all major Jewish holidays.

You should know what kind of camera you want, because most of the places offer cheap prices, but not patient service.

B&H Photo-Video (Map 5; ☎ 800-606-6969, 212-444-6615), 420 Ninth Ave between 33rd and 34th Sts, is New York's most popular camera store, but it suffers from zoo-like crowding and a pay-first, pick-up-second bureaucracy. It's open Monday and Tuesday 9 am to 6 pm, Wednesday and Thursday 9 am to 7:15 pm, Friday from 9 am to 1 pm and Sunday 10 am to 5 pm. It does a brisk business with international clients, and it even accepts personal checks (drawn on US banks) of up to $15,000.

Toys It may not be the only toy store in the city, but you wouldn't know it from the weekend crowds at FAO Schwarz (Map 5; ☎ 212-644-9400), 767 Fifth Ave. There's usually a 25-minute wait to get in during the holiday season. The Barbie salon at the back of the store (entrance on Madison Ave) is wildly popular. The store is open Monday to Saturday from 10 am to 6 pm (Thursday to 8 pm) and Sunday from 11 am to 6 pm.

The Enchanted Forest (Map 4; ☎ 212-925-6677), 85 Mercer St, is a smaller and delightful store catering to kids in SoHo. It specializes in teddy bears and hand puppets from ($25 and under or less). It's a perfect place to avoid 'brand name' toys and commercial tie-ins.

Computers Gateway Computers, the mail order firm, has opened a New York retail outlet at 4 Columbus Circle (☎ 212-246-5575). If you're staying at an address in New York, you can have a computer delivered and realize great savings over European prices. J&R Computer World (Map 3; ☎ 212-238-9100), 15 Park Row, has a good reputation for selection and price, but the level of service depends on the salesperson you encounter. Try to avoid shopping there on busy weekends (subway: City Hall). ICS (Map 5; ☎ 212-924-5579), 1123 Broadway, has some

of the best deals on Apple products and laptops. It's open weekdays 9 am to 6 pm and Saturday noon to 4 pm.

CompUSA (Map 5; ☎ 212-764-6224), 420 Fifth Ave, has a good range of printers and aisles of computer software. The Staples (Map 5; ☎ 212-944-6744), 1075 Sixth Ave, is one of several branches selling computer peripherals, fax machines, printers and office supplies at decent prices.

Cosmetics Perfumes and colognes can be had at a great discount from many stores. But the Cosmetics Plus chain seems to have the most reliable supply of the popular scents. Its main store is at Sixth Ave and 53rd St (☎ 212-247-0444).

The popular French chain Sephora has Manhattan stores in the following locations: Rockefeller Center at 636 5th Ave, suite 300; SoHo at 555 Broadway; Times Square at 1500 Broadway; and the World Trade Center at 204 World Trade Center Mall, Concourse Level.

Shoes & Handbags Low-cost knockoffs of Coach bags and leather backpacks are available in numerous stores along Broadway just above Houston St, on Bleecker St and on W 4th St immediately off Sixth Ave. More than a dozen stores selling Doc Martens, hiking boots and other sturdy walkers can be found on W 8th St between Fifth and Sixth Aves – check ads in the *Village Voice* for specials.

Higher-priced shoe stores can be found in SoHo among the clothing boutiques. See also Where to Shop, below.

Jewelry High-end jewelry shoppers should visit Cartier, Harry Winston and Tiffany and Co, all on Fifth Ave between 52nd and 57th Sts. If you're looking for diamonds and pearls at lower prices, you should visit the Diamond District on W 47th St off Fifth Ave (closed weekends). The vendors here are very skilled in looking pained while offering you the best deal possible – while still making a healthy profit. There's also a stretch of diamond shops on Canal St just north of Chinatown.

Vintage & Cheap Clothing Dozens of shops sell off-brand clothing at wholesale prices in the Garment District, mainly on W 37th St between Eighth and Ninth Aves. Resurrection Vintage Clothing has two sites: 123 E Seventh St off Avenue A (☎ 212-228-0063), off Avenue A, and 217 Mott St (Map 4; ☎ 212-625-1374). Both outlets have summer-long sales.

For jeans, many people head to Canal Jeans (Map 4; ☎ 212-226-1130), 504 Broadway, and the nearby Urban Outfitters (Map 4; ☎ 212-475-0009), 628 Broadway. But these stores now sell an array of accessories and are no longer the cheapest places in town. For true bargains on casual wear, go to Old Navy (several locations, including Sixth Ave and 20th St; Map 5), and Dave's Army and Navy (Map 5; ☎ 212-989-6444, 800-543-8558) at its new location at 581 Sixth Ave (between 16th and 17th Sts). Dave's does an extremely brisk business selling jeans and construction boots to tourists, and as it closes its doors at 6 pm on Saturday, there's usually a long line of airplane-bound foreign visitors stocking up on $35 pairs of Levi's.

Music & Videos Tower Records (Map 4; ☎ 212-505-1500), with its main branch at 692 Broadway, has the best selection of music, but you pay generally higher prices (about $15) there than at HMV, which has a downtown store in Herald Square and uptown branches on Lexington Ave and E 86th St and Broadway at 72 St (Map 7).

Both chains are being given a run for their money by the massive Virgin Megastore (Map 6; ☎ 212-921-1020), at 45th and Broadway in Times Square, with a new location on the south side of Union Square.

J&R Music World (Map 3; ☎ 212-238-9100), 15 Park Row, just across from City Hall, is the best mainstream store and has a very large selection of jazz and hip-hop (subway: City Hall).

Shops specializing in CDs for less than $10, along with bootlegs and imported music, are found on Bleecker St in the West Village. Triton, 247 Bleecker, and Route 66 Records, across the street at 258 Bleecker, are among the best in the city. NYCD (Map 7; ☎ 212-724-4466), 426 Amsterdam Ave, runs a permanent special where if you buy four CDs, you get the fifth one free. Other Music (☎ 212-477-8150), 15 E 4th St, brazenly opened right across the street from a Tower Records outlet, and thrives thanks to its selection of offbeat CDs.

Traditionalists should head to Carmine St in Greenwich Village, where stores still sell old LPs. Footlight Records, 113 E 12th St, has a magnificent collection of out-of-print albums and foreign-movie soundtracks.

Sporting Goods Paragon Athletic Goods (☎ 212-255-8036), 867 Broadway, not only has the best selection of sports merchandise, but it regularly beats prices found at chain stores such as Sports Authority. Particularly notable for its end-of-season sales on tennis racquets and running shoes, Paragon also has the best selection of in-line skates in the city and helpful staff (subway: Union Square).

Foot Locker, a nationwide chain, sells athletic shoes at many Manhattan locations.

Where to Shop
If you can't get it in New York, it's not available. But it helps to know the places where you can get the best or the cheapest.

A Day Trip for Bargains

Woodbury Common Premium Outlets (☎ 914-928-4000) in Central Valley, NY, is one of area's largest discount shopping centers, with 120 different stores. You can find cut-price offerings from Betsey Johnson, Next, Esprit, French Connection and many others. The facility, some 90 minutes away from New York City, attracts many bargain hunters and offers a bus service during the week. Shortline buses run from Port Authority (☎ 800-631-8405) and a roundtrip ticket costs $31.95 and includes a book of coupons to use in the outlet. To reach Woodbury Common by car, take the New York State Thruway to exit 16 (Harriman) and follow the signs.

Century 21 Century 21 (Map 3; ☎ 212-227-9092), 25 Church St, is a legend among savvy New York shoppers. Located across from the World Trade Center, this store has big bargains on designer clothing, perfume, sportswear and kitchen products. It's one of the few discount places in New York City where the selection of men's wear is as extensive as the women's department. You never know exactly what's on offer, but you will be guaranteed to find marked down Armani shirts and Donna Karan dresses on the racks.

Shopping at the store, – which doesn't advertise and opens early for the Wall St crowd, is also a ritual for people serving their two weeks of jury duty at the nearby courthouses.

It's open Monday to Wednesday 7:45 am to 7 pm;, Thursday 7:45 am to 8:30 pm, Friday 7:45 am to 8 pm, Saturday 10 am to 7 pm and Sunday 11 am to 6 pm (subway: Cortlandt St).

Dollar Bill's Discount Store This store (Map 5; ☎ 212-867-0212), 32 E 42nd St, just near Grand Central Station, is a smaller version of the Century 21 concept: designer closeouts at knockdown prices. It's open weekdays 8 am to 7 pm, Saturday 10 am to 6 pm and Sunday noon to 5 pm (subway: 42nd St-Grand Central).

Bloomingdale's 'Bloomie's' (Map 7; ☎ 212-705-2000), at 59th St and Lexington Ave, may think of itself as a New York version of Harrods, but this incredibly cramped, crowded and badly designed department store matches it in attitude and almost nothing else. It does not duplicate the famous London emporium's architectural splendor, magnificent food hall or grand selection of merchandise.

Still, it's worth visiting if there's a good advertised clothing sale and to see the designer shops. It's also entertaining – in a weird way – to walk through the bizarre first-floor perfume section, where dozens of clerks try to spray you with the latest scent while repeating the sales pitch in an automaton-like fashion.

Bloomingdale's is open weekdays 10 am to 8:30 pm, Saturday 10 am to 7 pm, and Sunday 11 am to 7 pm.

Kiehl's This quirky downtown pharmacy (Map 5; ☎ 212-475-3400), 109 Third Ave between 13th and 14th Sts, has a patient staff that has been selling organic skin-care products since 1851. This precursor to the Body Shop has a very loyal clientele, and celebrities are sometimes spotted in the place buying products and admiring the late owner's eccentric collection of antique Harley-Davidson motorcycles.

Macy's Most New Yorkers have an affectionate regard for Macy's (Map 5; % 212-695-4400), at 34th St and Seventh Ave, one of the city's last surviving general interest retailers, in large part because of its sponsorship of a fireworks festival on the 4th Fourth of July and the annual Thanksgiving Day Parade. Though Macy's has experienced financial problems in recent years, the store's stock hasn't diminished and it continues to hold its famous Wednesday 'One Day Sales.'

Fifth & Madison Aves The funkiest boutiques may be in SoHo, but more formal shopping can be found on Fifth and Madison Aves above 42nd St. Madison Ave is as close as New York comes to a *Place Vendome* Parisian experience, as designers try to outdo each other in their showplace stores. There are fewer crowds on Sunday, but you won't be able to drop in on any of the avenue's 1st-rate art galleries, which are closed that day.

Walking north on Madison Ave from 42nd St, you will see the following shops:

Brooks Brothers
  (☎ 212-682-8800) 346 Madison Ave
  This is a legendary store selling conservative clothing and formal wear for men; includes a smaller department for women. (Another store is at 666 Fifth Ave, at 51st St.)

Worth & Worth
  (☎ 212-867-6058) 331 Madison Ave
  This is the place for men's hats, custom-made umbrellas and scarves.

Barney's
(☎ 212-826-8900) 660 Madison Ave
This is the flagship of the hip and haughty clothing chain store that's famous for treating potential customers as too fat, too poor, and, in the men's department, too straight.

Calvin Klein
(☎ 212-292-9000) 654 Madison Ave
The media savvy designer opened this flagship store in early 1995.

The Coach Store
(☎ 212-319-1772) 710 Madison Ave
This is the place for expensive leather bags, wallets and belts that never go on sale.

Gruen Optika
(☎ 212-988-5832) 740 Madison Ave
This is the best store in the city for one-of-a-kind eyewear.

Giorgio Armani
(☎ 212-988-9191) 815 Madison Ave
Not to be outdone by anyone, Armani opened his own massive store at 65th St and Madison.

Gianni Versace
(☎ 212-744-5572) 816 Madison Ave
The late, over-the-top Italian stylist opened his own shop just before his death.

Missoni
(☎ 212-517-9339) 836 Madison Ave
The popular Italian designer's expensive knitwear is sold here.

Yves St Laurent
(☎ 212-472-5299) 855 Madison Ave
Selections from the legendary master of French couture are sold here.

Givenchy
(☎ 212-772-1040) 954 Madison Ave
This is the place for traditional French suits and accessories.

Polo/Ralph Lauren
(☎ 212-606-2100) Madison Ave and 72nd St
An old mansion makes an appropriate setting for Lauren's clothing aimed at aristocratic wannabes.

Here are a few Fifth Ave stores worth noting:

Warner Bros Studio Store
(☎ 212-754-0300) E 57th St and Fifth Ave
This is one of the most profitable retail outlets in New York City.

Disney Store
(☎ 212-702-0702) 711 Fifth Ave
This store is for fans of Mickey Mouse and friends.

Saks
(☎ 212-753-4000) Fifth Ave at 50th St

NBA Store
(☎ 212-515-6221) 645 Fifth Ave
The National Basketball Association is cashing in on the game's worldwide popularity.

Brooks Bros
(☎ 212-682-8800) 666 Fifth Ave
Just a few doors away from the NBA store, this is the outlet for the traditional men's store.

Among the other stores in the immediate area:

Niketown
(☎ 212-891-6453) 6 E 57th St

Henri Bendel
(☎ 212-247-1100) 712 Fifth Ave at 55th St

Tiffany & Co
(☎ 212-755-8000) 727 Fifth Ave at 57th St

Bergdorf Goodman
(☎ 212-753-7300) 754 Fifth Ave at 57th St

GETTING THERE & AWAY
Air
New York is served by three major airports. John F Kennedy (JFK), 15 miles from Midtown Manhattan in southeastern Brooklyn, is where most international flights land. La Guardia airport in northern Queens is 8 miles away and services mostly domestic flights, including the air shuttles to Boston and Washington, DC. Newark International Airport is in New Jersey, 10 miles directly to the west. It's the hub for Continental Airlines and is also used by international and domestic flights of all major carriers.

For more about getting to/from the airports, see the Getting Around section.

The following international airlines have offices downtown or at the airports:

Aer Lingus
(☎ 212-557-1110) 509 Madison Ave

Aeromexico
(☎ 212-754-2140) 37 W 57th St

Air Canada
(☎ 800-776-3000) 15 W 50th St

Air France
(☎ 800-321-4538) 120 W 56th St

American Airlines
(☎ 800-433-7300) 18 W 49th St

British Airways
(☎ 800-247-9297) 530 Fifth Ave

Continental Airlines
(☎ 212-319-9494) 100 E 42nd St

Delta Airlines
(☎ 212-239-0700) 100 E 42nd St

Finnair
(☎ 212-499-9000) 228 E 45th St

Japan Air Lines
(☎ 800-525-3663) JFK Airport

Korean Air
(☎ 800-438-5000) 609 Fifth Ave

Olympic
(☎ 800-838-3825) 647 Fifth Ave

Philippine Airlines
(☎ 800-435-9725) JFK Airport

Qantas
(☎ 800-227-4500) 712 Fifth Ave

Singapore Airlines
(☎ 212-644-8801) 55 E 59th St

Swissair
(☎ 800-842-2201) 608 Fifth Ave

Tower Air
(☎ 718-553-8500) JFK Airport

TWA
(☎ 800-893-5436) 1 E 59th St

United Airlines
(☎ 800-241-6522) 100 E 42nd St

US Airways
(☎ 800-428-4322) 101 Park Ave

Virgin Atlantic
(☎ 212-242-1330) 125 Park Ave

JFK This airport, in Brooklyn some 15 miles from Midtown, serves 35 million passengers a year. It's sprawling and unpopular, and the airport's international arrivals terminal rivals London's Heathrow for crowding and chronic underinvestment.

The terminals are linked by the JFK Expressway and a free shuttle bus. American Airlines, British Airways, Delta and TWA have their own terminals; most other airlines use the crowded international arrivals building.

The airport information line (☎ 718-244-4444) will tell you if the airport is closed in bad weather. The airlines themselves, however, are usually reluctant to give honest information about flight delays over the phone.

Until the airport undergoes a much-needed renovation, set to be completed in 2005, it's a place best used only for transit. JFK's Duty Free shops, such as those in most US cities, are useless – you can get alcohol, electronics and clothes cheaper in town, so don't expect to embark on a last minute purchasing spree for anything other than cartons of cigarettes.

La Guardia If you're arriving or departing in the middle of the day, La Guardia (☎ 718-533-3400) is a more convenient choice than JFK. US Airways and Delta Shuttle each have dedicated terminals; all other airlines use the central terminal building in front of the parking garage. (La Guardia does not serve wide-body jets, so cross-country or transatlantic flights don't land there. The airport largely serves Northeastern and Canadian destinations.)

Newark Newark is the best choice at the moment for foreign visitors, thanks to a new, well-organized international terminal. The best feature: a large immigration hall that speeds up passport checks. Moreover, flights to/from Newark International Airport (☎ 201-961-6000) are usually a bit cheaper because of the erroneous perception that the airport is less accessible than JFK. Most arrivals do have to endure a bus journey into Manhattan – but JFK arrivals are subject to similar delays from Brooklyn. The airport's four terminals will soon be linked by a monorail system that connects it to the NJ Transit train system, offering a traffic-free trip to the airport from Manhattan.

Bus

All suburban and long-haul buses leave and depart from the Port Authority Bus Terminal (☎ 212-564-8484), at 41st St and Eighth Ave. Greyhound (☎ 212-971-6300, 800-231-2222) links New York with major cities across the country. Peter Pan Trailways (☎ 800-343-9999) run buses to the nearest major cities, including a daily express to Boston for $24.95/47.95 one-way/roundtrip.

Short Line (☎ 212-736-4700) has numerous departures to towns in northern New

Jersey and upstate New York. New Jersey Transit buses (☎ 201-762-5100) serve the entire state, with direct service to Atlantic City for $15 one way. Port Authority has been modernized and is much improved in recent years. Though it's not as rough as its reputation, you can still be hassled by beggars asking for handouts or offering to carry your bags for tips (subway: 42nd St-Port Authority).

Short-haul buses also leave for New Jersey from the terminal (☎ 212-568-5323) near the George Washington Bridge (subway: 175th St).

Train
Pennsylvania Station (Penn Station), at 33rd St between Seventh and Eighth Aves, is the departure point for all Amtrak trains (☎ 212-582-6875, 800-872-7245), including the *Metroliner* service to Princeton, NJ, and Washington, DC. (Note: the *Metroliner* is a slightly faster and more expensive train than the *Northeast Direct* service to the same points). The Long Island Rail Road (LIRR; ☎ 718-217-5477) serves several hundred thousand commuters each day from a newly renovated platform area to points in Brooklyn, Queens and the suburbs of Long Island, including the resort areas. New Jersey Transit (NJ Transit; ☎ 973-762-5100) also operates trains from Penn Station to the suburbs and the Jersey Shore.

Only one company still departs from Grand Central Terminal, at Park Ave and 42nd St: Metro North Rail Road (☎ 212-532-4900 in NYC; 800-638-7646 outside NYC), which serves the northern suburbs and neighboring Connecticut.

GETTING AROUND
It's hard to exaggerate the problem of gridlock in Manhattan's streets. The entire center of the island's grid system is packed with cars during the day, and major avenues, primarily Lexington and Broadway, get tied up by double-parked trucks making deliveries to stores. The subway is the fastest way to get between uptown and downtown points, and contrary to popular belief, taking it is

statistically safer than walking the streets in broad daylight.

Like most New Yorkers, you should use the city buses exclusively to get to points along the same avenue, when it's easy to calculate the amount of travel time by looking at the traffic.

The best overall plan is to use the subway all day until about 9 pm, then use taxis at night. It's very important to note that taxis are obligated to take you anywhere you want to go within the five boroughs, as well as to the airport in Newark (though you must pay tolls each way). During rush hours, taxi drivers often brazenly refuse fares from airport-bound customers (particularly during bad weather) because they can pick up easier fares in town. *Do not* ask permission to get into the cab if you're going to the airports, and *do not* negotiate a higher price above the metered fare. If the cabbie refuses your business, threaten to report his/her license number to the Taxi & Limousine Commission. Even if this is an empty threat, the cab driver will take it seriously enough to relent.

Under no circumstances should you take an unlicensed taxi – these are, by-and-large, rip-off merchants who target tourists, usually at the airport, and there is little cost savings to justify the risk.

To/From the Airports
Gray Line (☎ 800-451-0455) runs minivans to many prominent hotels in Manhattan from JFK, La Guardia and Newark airports. The fare runs between $13 to $16 depending on the airport; a return fare is just a dollar or two more.

When departing for the airports in the middle of the day, allow at least one hour's travel time. The Port Authority of New York and New Jersey's Air Ride line (☎ 800-247-7433) offers comprehensive information on ground transportation to and from all three airports.

No matter what airport you fly into, there are several advantages to ordering car service by phone for an airport journey. The cars are newer and larger than yellow cabs and you do not have to tip the driver. You can also order a pickup a day in advance and pay by credit card. If you ask for a 'price check' while ordering the taxi, the dispatcher can tell you the exact cost of the journey, which should run between $35 to $50, depending on your departure point and the airport destination.

JFK Gray Line (☎ 800-451-0455) runs minivans to many hotels in Manhattan from JFK. The fare is $14 into the city and $19 back, or you can purchase a roundtrip ticket for $28. For more information, the company's website is www.graylineny.com.

Carey Transportation buses (☎ 718-632-0500) runs to/from JFK at least every 30 minutes from 5 am to 1 am daily. Buses leave from 125 Park Ave, just a block south of Grand Central Terminal, and from the Port Authority Airport Bus Center near the 42nd St and Eighth Ave entrance, from 7:15 am to 11:15 pm each day. One-way fare to JFK is $13, with half-price tickets available for students. The journey takes at least one hour.

You can also take the subway to the Howard Beach-JFK station on the A line, which takes at least an hour, and then switch to a free yellow and blue bus at the long-term parking lot to the terminals, which takes another 15 minutes. (You have to haul your luggage up and over several flights of stairs at the Howard Beach terminal.)

Taxi fare from JFK is a flat rate of $32 to any location in Manhattan. (You must pay for tolls, bringing it to $35.50 without tip.)

The long-term parking lot at JFK costs $6 a day; short-term parking (closer to the terminals) costs $4 for four hours.

La Guardia Gray Line (☎ 800-451-0455) runs minivans to many hotels in Manhattan from La Guardia. The fare is $13 into the city and $16 back, or you can purchase a roundtrip ticket for $26. The company's website is www.graylineny.com.

Carey Transportation (☎ 718-632-0500) buses leave from Port Authority Airport Bus Center from 7:15 am to 12:45 am daily and from 125 Park Ave (near Grand Central Terminal) from 5 am to 1 am daily. Buses depart at least every 30 minutes and cost $10 one

way; the trip to the airport takes 45 minutes to an hour.

The Delta Water Shuttle (☎ 800-221-1212) leaves frequently for La Guardia with two pickups: Pier 11 at South and Wall Sts and at E 34th St on the East River. The fare is $20 one way, $30 roundtrip.

La Guardia is also accessible via public transportation by taking the subway to the Roosevelt Ave-Jackson Heights and 74th St-Broadway stops in Queens (two linked stations served by five lines). You then take the Q33 bus to the La Guardia main terminals or the Q47 bus to Delta Shuttle's Marine Air Terminal. Because this journey takes well over an hour and costs two tokens ($3), it is recommended only for those who absolutely can't afford the additional $7 for the direct Carey bus. In Upper Manhattan, pick up the M60 bus at one of the signed stops along 125th; it goes directly to La Guardia for the cost of a subway token, Metrocard or $1.50 in change.

Taxis to La Guardia from Midtown cost about $45.

Newark Gray Line (☎ 800-451-0455) runs minivans to many hotels in Manhattan from Newark. The fare is $14 into the city and $19 back, or you can purchase a roundtrip ticket for $28 For more information, the company's website is www.graylineny.com.

Olympia Trails (☎ 212-964-6233) travels to Newark from a stop near Grand Central Terminal (Park Ave and 41st St) from 5 am to 11 pm daily. Another bus departs to Newark from Lower Manhattan at One World Trade Center on West St from 6 am to 8 pm weekdays and 7 am to 8 pm weekends. Both buses cost $10.

NJ Transit (☎ 973-762-5100) runs bus No 300 from Port Authority Airport Bus Center to the airport 24 hours a day; cost is $7 one way and $12 roundtrip.

A taxi to Newark will cost about $55.

Subway

The 656-mile New York City subway system is used by 4 million people every day. Quite a few tourists shun the subway because of its reputation, but you'd be foolish to pass up the opportunity to get around town quickly, and only for $1.50 per trip.

Indeed, the subway is the fastest and most reliable way to travel, especially for trips totaling more than 20 blocks in north-south directions during the day. Taking a bus or a taxi guarantees that you'll hit traffic choke points at places such as Times Square and wind up arriving at your destination only after a long and frustrating ride.

Most major Manhattan attractions (especially those on the West Side and downtown) are easily accessible by several subway lines. Madison Square Garden, for example, is within walking distance (four blocks) of three subway stations on 34th St (serving 12 different lines). Throughout this chapter, the subway station, when listed for a site, is selected for being the closest to the destination.

As for safety, standing in the middle of the platform will bring you to the conductor's car. The conductor – who rides in the middle car of all trains – can direct you through the system (when he/she is not closing the doors of the train).

There are free copies of the subway map, available at any subway station booth.

SUBWAY
SARDINES
Packed in Stagnant Air

The Cheapest Way to Travel

Currently there are two ways to get on the subway: by individual tokens, which are sold at staffed booths for $1.50 each, or by Metrocard. The plastic Metrocard keeps track of your credits and is swiped at turnstiles. (You can buy one at token booths, off automated machines in the stations or at convenience stores.) The card also offers free transfers to city buses within 20 minutes of leaving a subway station. If you purchase one Metrocard for $15, you can get 11 trip credits (ie, one free trip).

But the best deal is the weekly Metrocard that costs $17. It offers unlimited travel on subways and buses for seven days. One and 30-day cards are also available. It appears likely that the transit authority will eventually phase out token sales.

For subway information call ☎ 718-330-1234 or 330-4847 for non-English speakers.

PATH

New Jersey PATH trains (☎ 800-234-7284) are part of a separate subway system that runs along Sixth Ave, with stops at 34th, 23rd, 14th, 9th and Christopher Sts to Hoboken, Jersey City and Newark. A second line runs from northern New Jersey to the World Trade Center. These reliable trains run every 15 minutes and the fare is $1 (machines take dollar bills).

Bus

City buses operate 24 hours a day, generally along avenues in a south or north direction, and cross-town along the major thoroughfares (including 34th, 42nd and 57th Sts). Buses that begin and end in a certain borough are prefixed accordingly: ie, M5 for Manhattan, B39 for Brooklyn, Q32 for Queens, Bx29 for the Bronx. For bus information, call ☎ 718-927-7499.

Bus maps for each borough are available at subway and train stations, and each well-marked bus stop has 'Guide-a-Ride' maps showing the stops for each bus and nearby landmarks. Remember that some 'Limited Stop' buses along major routes pull over only every 10 blocks or so at major cross streets. 'Express' buses are generally for outer borough commuters and cost about $5 and should not be used for short trips.

As a safety precaution, you can request to be let off at any location along a bus route from 10 pm to 5 am – even if it is not a designated bus stop.

Taxi

Taxi drivers may be the butt of jokes, but most cabs are clean and, compared to most international destinations, pretty cheap.

Taxis cost $2 for the initial charge, with 30¢ for every additional quarter mile and 20¢ a minute while stuck in traffic. There's an additional 50¢ surcharge for rides after 8 pm. Tampered meters turn over every 20 seconds or so while the cab is stopped in traffic or at a light, and if you notice it happening, don't hesitate to ask if it is 'running too fast.' If the driver apologizes a bit too energetically, you've probably busted him and can negotiate a lower fare than the meter. Tips are expected to run 10% to 15%, with a minimum of 50¢. If you feel ripped off, ask for a receipt and note the driver's license number. The city's Taxi & Limousine Commission (☎ 212-302-8294) is particularly aggressive.

For hauls that will last 50 blocks or more, it's a good idea to instruct the driver to take a road well away from Midtown traffic. Suggest the West Side Highway or Eleventh Ave if you hail a taxi west of Broadway; on the East Side, the best choice may be Second Ave (heading downtown) or First Ave (uptown), because you can hit a string of green lights in either direction.

There is a flat rate to Manhattan *from* JFK airport of $32, plus $3.50 tolls. Please be aware that this flat rate does *not* apply to trips to the airport – you will pay for time spent in traffic.

Car & Motorcycle

It's a nightmare to have a car in New York, unless you're rich. Parking garages in Midtown usually charge at least $30 for a day's parking. Cheaper lots can be found in Manhattan along West St in Chelsea, but even those $10 to $15 daily deals aren't a bargain after the 18.25% parking tax is added. Using a hotel lot is no bargain – Midtown hotels can charge $40 a day, even for their guests.

Car rental rates start at $60 a day for a compact, and zoom higher. (You usually get 100 miles free a day and pay 15¢ for every mile over the limit.)

Car rental companies regularly gouge New Yorkers, and unless you have a special deal offering a cheap car rental (booked *before* your arrival in conjunction with an air ticket), expect to pay $80 or more a day, with rates of about $300 per weekend.

Long Island

Long Island (population 2.6 million in Nassau and Suffolk Counties) is a study in social contrasts. This is the largest island (120 miles from end to end) in the US and begins with Brooklyn (Kings County) and Queens (Queens County) on the western shore. The island then gives way to the suburban housing and strip malls in neighboring Nassau County. The terrain becomes flatter and less crowded in rural Suffolk County, which comprises the eastern end of the island. Suffolk County itself contains two peninsulas – commonly called the North and South Forks – divided by Peconic Bay.

The island was first a series of whaling and fishing ports, as well as the exclusive outpost for the ultra-rich, who built estates along the secluded coves on the north shore. In the years following WWII, Nassau County became increasingly more populated as thousands of middle-class families moved to the suburbs. One prime location was Levittown, built in 1947 in the center of Nassau County. It features thousands of low-cost homes in huge tracts near major highways and railway lines leading into Manhattan. Named after the Levit & Sons company that developed it, the town attracted 55,000 residents and became the model for hundreds of similar and boring suburban communities across the US.

In Suffolk County, things were reversed: the rich settled on the south shore while the north side of the island became home to working class, salaried workers and owners of small farms. Today, the South Fork is dominated by several villages (Hampton Bays, Southampton, Bridgehampton, East Hampton and Amagansett) known collectively as the Hamptons. It's the place where actors, writers and entertainment executives gather to schmooze away the summer season on private estates and in expensive restaurants.

For most visitors, a trip to Long Island means a trip to the beach, whether the

Highlights

- Frolicking on the beach at Fire Island, New York's prime gay resort, or the more family-dominated beaches of Robert Moses State Park

- East Hampton, a trendy yet elegant refuge for vacationing celebrities

- The quiet charms of Shelter Island and the Mashomack Nature Preserve

- Sampling white wine in the North Fork vineyards

- Numerous science museums and children-oriented centers offering lots of educational activities for the inquisitive visitor

destination is crowded Jones Beach, quiet Shelter Island or the more showy enclaves of the Hamptons. All of these beaches are within easy reach of New York City via public transportation, which is the best option for summer weekends, when traffic jams are particularly hellish. But if you're interested in exploring Long Island's historic mansions or sampling wine in the vineyards of the North Fork, it's best to have a car.

INFORMATION
Tourist Offices

The Long Island Convention and Visitors Bureau (☎ 516-951-3440) publishes a free travel guide. You can obtain maps, restaurant listings and lodging guides from the local chamber of commerce by calling:

Southampton	☎ 516-283-0402
Shelter Island	☎ 516-749-0399
Parks Information	☎ 516-669-1000
East Hampton	☎ 631-324-0362
Montauk	☎ 631-668-2428
Greenport-Southold	☎ 631-477-1383

OUTDOOR ACTIVITIES

It's possible to bike along Route 25 on the North Fork, and along the Hamptons' side roads, especially along the 7-mile Route 114 (the Sag Harbor Turnpike) from East Hampton to Sag Harbor. The Long Island Greenbelt follows the Connetquot and Nissequoque Rivers for 34 miles from Long Island Sound to Sunken Meadow State Park, passing through wetlands and forest.

There are excellent opportunities for guided walks in the Sunken Forest, located in the middle of the Fire Island National

LONG ISLAND

Seashore (☎ 516-597-6183). You can also enjoy strolls in the Mashomack Nature Preserve on Shelter Island. Off-season, it's possible to embark on long, uninterrupted walks along the shoreline from East Hampton to Montauk.

Surfers frequently head to the Georgica Jetties, Montauk and Shinnecock Inlet. Directions and information on weather conditions can be obtained in season by calling ☎ 516-283-7873.

Two-hour kayak explorations of Peconic Bay are offered by Shelter Island Kayak Tours (☎ 516-749-1990) for $50 a person.

GETTING AROUND

The Long Island Expressway (I-495, known as the L–I–E) cuts through the center of the island, and turns into Route 25 and a series of crowded smaller roads. The older Route 25 (also known as the Jericho Turnpike) runs roughly parallel to I-495, then continues to the end of the North Fork at Orient Point. Route 27 (also known as the Sunrise Highway) runs along the bottom of Long Island from the Brooklyn border and eventually becomes the Montauk Highway, and ends up at the end of the South Fork at Montauk Point. A trip to the end of Long

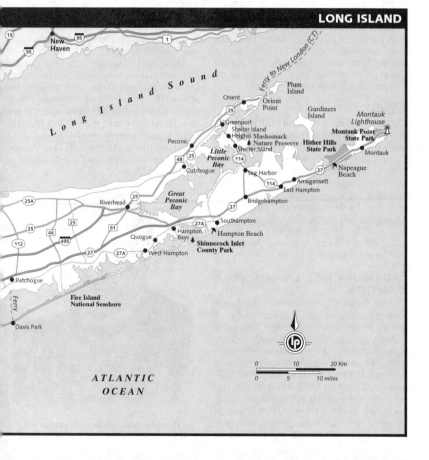

LONG ISLAND

Island takes at least three hours, but on weekends, traffic jams can turn it into a six hour ordeal.

Bus

The Hampton Jitney (☎ 800-936-0440, 516-283-4600) leaves several times daily for Long Island's South Fork from three locations on the East Side of Manhattan, including 41st St between Lexington and Third Aves. Sunrise Coach Lines (☎ 800-527-7709) departs for the North Fork from its stop at 44th St and Third Ave. The fare is $22 one-way and $40 roundtrip. Drivers usually know ways of circumventing summer weekend traffic, making these buses a good alternative to driving a car.

A number of private bus companies serve many destinations within Long Island; for information on bus transportation in Nassau County, call ☎ 516-766-6722, for Suffolk County call ☎ 516-360-5700.

Train

The Long Island Rail Road (LIRR; ☎ 516-822-5477, 718-217-5477) carries 275,000 passengers daily to 134 stations throughout Long Island from New York City's Penn Station. Trips to the furthest points on the railroad – Greenport in the North Fork and Montauk in the South Fork – cost about $20 each way. In the summer the LIRR offers roundtrip deals to the south shore beaches, but be aware that the lines at the station ticket office are very long on Friday night and Saturday morning.

SAGAMORE HILL & VANDERBILT MANSION

Driving through the toney, secluded waterside spot of Oyster Bay brings reminders of robber barons and the Jazz Age. This quiet village – just one hour away from New York City – is a refuge for the rich and the location of **Sagamore Hill**, the 23-room mansion built in 1885 by Theodore Roosevelt. Sagamore Hill (☎ 516-922-4447) eventually served as the summer White House during his tenure in office from 1901-09. It was in this dark Victorian mansion that Roosevelt brokered an end to the Russo-Japanese War, an effort for which he won the Nobel Peace prize.

Roosevelt was in many ways the first president of the modern era – he used a telephone (which is still on view in his study) to remain in contact with Washington. Though Roosevelt was also the first chief executive to concern himself with conservation, animal rights activists will no doubt turn pale at the many mounted heads, antlers and leopard skins on display, along with the inkwell made from a rhinoceros foot.

Roosevelt died at Sagamore Hill in 1919 and is buried in a cemetery a mile away. A redbrick Georgian house on the grounds displays his gold Nobel medal. The home was later occupied by Theodore Roosevelt Jr, and is now a museum charting the 26th president's political career.

Sagamore Hill is open daily from April to October and Wednesday to Sunday during the winter from 9 am to 5 pm. Tours of the Roosevelt home leave on the hour; admission is $2, seniors and children under 17 are free. To get there, take the 41N exit from the Long Island Expressway (I-495) and travel on Route 106; turn right on E Main St, and follow the road signs on Cove Neck Rd to Sagamore Hill.

Theodore Roosevelt used Sagamore Hill as the summer White House from 1901-09.

The **Vanderbilt Mansion & Planetarium** (☎ 516-854-5555) is in Centerport (look for the sign for Route 25A east, which will bring you to the mansion). Also known as Eagle's Nest, this was the estate of Willie Vanderbilt, one of the last major heirs to the Staten Island family railroad fortune. Willie spent most of his life – and money – collecting sea creatures and curiosities from the South Pacific and Egypt, many items of his collection are on display. A planetarium (☎ 516-854-5533) was added to the grounds in 1971, featuring a 60-foot 'Sky Theater' and telescope. The mansion is now owned by Nassau County, which holds community events on the 43-acre site. It's open Tuesday to Sunday from 10 am to 4 pm. Admission to the mansion is $5/3, with a $1 charge for children; a planetarium laser show costs $7.50.

JONES BEACH STATE PARK

Jones Beach (☎ 631-785-1600) is the most crowded public beach in the area. Though it's always mobbed, the sand at Jones Beach is clean and it's an enjoyable respite from the city heat. The LIRR offers $15 roundtrip fares from Penn Station in the city to the Freeport station on Long Island; the trip takes under 40 minutes and includes a shuttle bus to Jones Beach.

ROBERT MOSES STATE PARK & FIRE ISLAND

This park, at the westernmost end of the Fire Island National Seashore (☎ 631-289-4810), is the only spot on Fire Island accessible by car. The park is similar in scale (and popularity) to neighboring Jones Beach.

The rest of Fire Island is a summer-only cluster of villages accessible only by ferry from three points on mainland Long Island. Though the tourist board tries to play down the fact, Fire Island is probably the country's leading gay resort area. The scene tends to be a bit wild, and straights may not feel entirely comfortable.

Places to Stay

There are not many places to stay, and you really wouldn't want to stay on the mainland and travel in and out.

Camping spots include **Heckscher Park** (☎ 631-581-4433) in East Islip, and **Watch Hill** on Fire Island as part of the national Seashore.

The hotels and lots of other places in eastern Long Island and the beaches have the affectation of no street numbers. The Ocean Beach zip (11770) will ensure delivery of mail (during the summer months). **Houser's Hotel** (☎ 631-583-7799), on Bay Walk in Ocean Beach, has 12 rooms with rates from $135 to $200 a night. **Ocean Beach Hotel** (☎ 631-583-9292) is a 21-unit facility, and is open from May to September; it charges up to $225 per room.

Getting There & Away

By car you can get there by taking exit 53 of the Long Island Expressway and traveling south across the Robert Moses Causeway.

The three ferry terminals are all close to the Bay Shore, Sayville and Patchogue (pronounced 'Patch-oog') LIRR stations. The ferry season runs from early May to November; trips take about 20 minutes and cost an average of $12/6 adults/children roundtrip, with discounted seasonal passes available. Most ferries depart in order to link directly with a train to/from New York.

Fire Island Ferries
(☎ 631-665-3600) runs from Bay Shore to Saltaire, Fair Harbor and Ocean Beach

Sayville Ferry Service
(☎ 631-589-8980) runs from Sayville to Cherry Grove and the Pines

Davis Park Ferry Company
(☎ 631-475-1665) travels from Patchogue to Davis Park and Watch Hill

THE HAMPTONS

Prominent artists, musicians and writers have long been attracted to the beautiful beaches and rustic Cape Cod-style homes in the Hamptons, but the easy-money of the '80s brought an influx of showier summertime visitors who made their fortunes in the fashion industry and on Wall St. In recent years, the Hamptons have become truly 'hot' as West Coast entertainment moguls purchased large homes here, following in the footsteps of Steven Spielberg. Year-round residents seem annoyed and amused by the show in equal measures. If you're celebrity obsessed, you're better off heading to the Hamptons instead of standing in line at Planet Hollywood in New York City.

Many of the attractions, restaurants and hotels in the Hamptons close the last week in October and remain shut until late April. About two weeks after Labor Day B&B prices drop and traffic jams along the Montauk Highway disappear.

Southampton

Southampton village doesn't have half the flash of its neighbors to the east, but it's a pleasant place to spend an afternoon in search of history and art. You can get maps and brochures about the town at the chamber of commerce office at 76 Main St. Maps and books are available at the well-stocked Bookhampton shop (☎ 631-283-0270), at 93 Main St.

Just a few steps away from the tourist office is **Halsey Homestead**, a saltbox house built in 1648, just eight years after the first European settlers arrived in the area. It's open to the public from June to September, Tuesday to Saturday from 11 am to 4:30 pm and Sunday from 2 to 4:30 pm.

The **Parrish Art Museum** (☎ 631-283-2111), 25 Jobs Lane, is just a short walk away from Main St. It has been open to the public since 1898, and its gallery features the work of major artists like the late Roy Lichtenstein, who had a house nearby. The museum is open Wednesday to Saturday from 11 am to 5 pm and Sunday from 1 to 5 pm. In the winter the museum is closed on Tuesday and Wednesday. Suggested admission is $3.

The Duck Walk winery (☎ 631-726-7555) in Southampton can be visited for tastings.

Sag Harbor

On Peconic Bay Sag Harbor, 7 miles north from Bridgehampton on Route 27, is an old whaling town that's far less beach-oriented than the other Hampton towns. The **Whaling Museum** (☎ 631-725-0770) is just west of the shops on its Main St, and it celebrates this history. The museum is open May to October, Monday to Saturday from 10 am to 5 pm and Sunday from 1 to 5 pm; admission is $3/1.

East Hampton & Amagansett

The heart of trendy Long Island is East Hampton, where you can shop at the Coach leather store, catch readings and art exhibitions at the **Guild Hall** (☎ 631-324-0806) and indulge in elegant dining. Maps and books are available at the well-stocked Bookhampton (☎ 631-324-4939), 20 Main St.

Driving or biking down Main Beach along Ocean Ave will afford glimpses of the larger saltbox estates with water views. You can see some other grand (private) houses by turning right at **Lilly Pond Lane** and peeking through the breaks in the high shrubbery.

Amagansett is basically an extension of East Hampton distinguished by the huge flagpole in the center of the Montauk Highway.

Montauk

Montauk is a long, flat 13-mile drive away from Amagansett along Route 27. If you're a biker looking for a challenge, peel off to the right and take the **Old Montauk Highway**, an undulating road overlooking the ocean that passes by several resorts.

Montauk itself is more honky-tonk than the rest of the Hamptons, and has more reasonable restaurants and a rougher bar scene. From the LIRR train terminus it's a 10-minute walk to the center of town.

Montauk Downs State Park (☎ 631-668-3781) has a fine public golf course that charges $25 per person for a round; there are long waits for tee times in the summer.

If you drive out to **Montauk Point State Park** stop at the scenic overlook. But avoid the parking lot at the very end; it charges for a view that's not really worth the money. You will have to park if you intend to visit the unimpressive **Montauk Lighthouse Museum**, which is an additional fee of $2.

Places to Stay

There's camping at *Hither Hills State Park* (☎ 631-668-2461), southwest of Montauk.

There's virtually no price difference between places calling themselves B&Bs and smaller inns – most have rates well over $150 a night in high season. In Sag Harbor, the *American Hotel* (☎ 631-725-3535, Main St) has only eight rooms starting at $200 a night. The ground-floor restaurant and bar is a hangout for weekending media types.

In East Hampton, the renovated *Mill House Inn* (☎ 631-324-9766, 33 N Main St) is run by Dan and Katherine Hartnett and has eight rooms starting at $100 a night off season and $200 in summer. East Hampton's *Sea Breeze Inn* (☎ 631-267-3692, 30 Atlantic Ave) is just a block away from the LIRR station, and its 12 rooms are all clean (some rooms have shared bath). Rates are $60 to $140, with weekly discounts available.

The motels in more isolated Montauk run a bit cheaper during the summer – about $125 a night – but many are booked solid on a monthly basis by groups of students employed at the resorts and restaurants. You can get a list by calling the Montauk tourist office at ☎ 516-668-2428.

The top choices are *Montauk Yacht Club Resort,* (☎ 888-692-8668, 32 Star Island Rd), with suites in summer running up to $400. *Gurney's Inn* (☎ 631-668-3203, 290 Old Montauk Hwy) is a 175-room facility with a spa; rates are from $300.

Places to Eat & Drink

It's easier to find reasonably priced places to eat than reasonably priced lodging, though that is not saying much in the Hamptons.

There are relatively inexpensive seafood stands on Route 27 near Napeague Beach (between Amagansett and Montauk) that serve fish sandwiches, fresh steamers and fried clams for $10 and under during the summer. The most popular are *Lobster Roll* (☎ 631-267-3740), with its distinctive 'Lunch' sign, and *Clam Bar*, which also does a brisk business selling T-shirts to its BMW- and Mercedes-driving clientele. *Cyril's*, a restaurant started by an ex-Marine with a handlebar mustache, serves excellent sesame shrimp.

In Montauk *Shagwong Restaurant* (☎ 631-668-3050), on Main St, serves good tavern-style meals year-round.

The *Laundry* (☎ 631-324-3199, 31 Race Lane), one block from the East Hampton train station, was among the first celebrity-spotting restaurants to open in the Hamptons. There's less attitude here than in other places, and the food – generally fresh-fish main dishes in the $20 to $25 range – is actually quite good. *Maidstone Arms* (☎ 631-324-5006, 207 Main St) is the most elegant and expensive restaurant in town.

Stephen Talkhouse (☎ 631-267-3117, 161 Main St) is a 25-year-old concert venue (Billy Joel and James Taylor have appeared here) that has an active bar scene on non-performance nights. *Rowdy House* (☎ 631-324-8555, 10 Main St), in East Hampton, is a microbrewery that gets very crowded during the summer months.

SHELTER ISLAND

Nearly a third of quiet Shelter Island's land mass is dedicated to the **Mashomack Nature Preserve**, and there's an attractive town center in Shelter Island Heights, a cluster of Victorian buildings on the north side of the island. It's a perfect place to explore nature and a true respite from the crowds in the Hamptons.

Just beyond the Shelter Island Heights Bridge is Piccozzi's Bike Shop (☎ 631-749-0045), on Bridge St. Bikes can be rented for $18 a day, and are sturdy enough for a strenuous trek across Shelter Island, or take the ferry to Greenport to explore the North Fork and Orient Point. Call ahead in the summer to reserve bikes.

Places to Stay & Eat

For such a small place, Shelter Island is well served by B&Bs, including *Azalea House* (☎ 631-749-4252, 1 Thomas Ave), which has five rooms with rates from $50 to $125. *Shelter Island B&B* (☎ 631-749-0842, 7 St Mary's Rd) has four rooms for $60 on weekends.

You can get very good off-season rates at the *Ram's Head Inn* (☎ 631-749-0811), on Ram Island Drive, a large, columned place overlooking the water. It charges $70 for a room with a private bath in midweek (off peak); during the summer rates jump to $200 or more a room.

The dining choices on Shelter Island are very seasonal. **Dory** (☎ 631-749-8871), near the Shelter Island Heights Bridge, is a smoky bar that serves simple fare on a waterfront patio. **Shelter Island Pizza** (☎ 631-749-0400), on Route 114, is just about the only place open every day year round.

Getting There & Away

The North Ferry Company (☎ 631-749-0139) runs boats from the North Fork terminal (near the LIRR station in Greenport) to Shelter Island every 15 minutes from 6 am to 11:45 pm; a car and driver are charged $6.50, additional passengers $1. The trip takes seven minutes.

South Ferry Inc (☎ 631-749-1200) leaves from a dock 3 miles from Sag Harbor. To get to the dock go north on Route 114 and follow the signs. Ferries leave from 6 am to 1:45 am; a car and driver are charged $7, additional passengers $1.

NORTH FORK

Rural and picturesque, the North Fork is dotted with vineyards, sleepy villages and white sand beaches. Greenport is the main town in the North Fork, where you can catch a ferry to/from nearby Shelter Island. It used to be packed with farmers and workers from the Grumman company, but economic change forced a downturn in the '80s; Greenport is now shaking off some of that slump.

Greenport is still far more working class than the Hamptons, but real estate in the area is being snapped up by weekending city dwellers, changing the character of the town.

The staple of Route 25

Efforts to revitalize the slumping farming and manufacturing economy in the North Fork led to the establishment of several local vineyards during the 1980s. Now, Greenport is the perfect base from which to begin an exploration of the area's wineries.

Long Island Wineries

Today there are 14 full-scale wineries and 50 vineyards totaling 1400 acres of land on eastern Long Island. Most of the major wineries are in the North Fork on Route 25. Just look for the distinctive green 'wine trail' road signs that crop up past Riverhead; nine of the vineyards are clustered within 2 miles of the town of Cutchogue (pronounced 'kutch-oog').

Long Island seems to have perfected the art of making white wine, but its reds lag behind because the soil and climate aren't conducive to those heartier grapes. Judge for yourself by visiting a few – the wine makers are more than happy to pour out a few free glasses of their product.

You can get more information on touring the wine trail by contacting the Long Island Wine Council (☎ 631-369-5887), PO Box 74, Peconic, NY 11958. A *Winery Guide* can be obtained by calling ☎ 800-441-4601.

The following wineries offer tastings, usually 11 am to 5 pm during the summer months:

Bedell Cellars (☎ 631-734-7537)
Duck Walk (☎ 631-726-7555) near Southampton
Hargrave (☎ 631-734-5158)
Lenz (☎ 631-734-6010)
Osprey's Dominion (☎ 631-765-6188)
Palmer (☎ 631-722-9463)
Paumanok (☎ 631-722-8800)
Peconic Bay Vineyards (☎ 631-734-7361)
Pelligrini (☎ 631-734-4111)
Pindar Vineyards (☎ 631-734-6200) near Peconic

Pindar Vineyards is the largest facility and offers tours of its 250 acres of vines. It also hosts evening wine festivals several times a year.

Orient Point

The far tip of the North Fork is where the ferry departs for the casinos in New London, CT. Three miles from the docks is the tiny hamlet of **Orient**. There's not much of a business district in this tiny 17th-century hamlet, just an old wooden post office and a general store, but Orient is a well-preserved collection of white clapboard houses and former inns. To get to Orient follow the signs for the 'Orient Business District' at the Civil War monument on the side of Route 25.

Further out of town, you can bike past the Oyster Ponds just east of Main St and also check out the beach at Orient Beach State Park, which offers some great bird-watching opportunities.

Places to Stay & Eat

The best place to stay in Greenport is **White Lions Inn** (*☎ 631-477-8819, 433 Main St*). This large old home, adorned by two huge stone lions, has five rooms (two with shared bath), and is a four-block walk from the Shelter Island ferry dock and LIRR train station. Rates are $70 to $110, with free parking.

Seafood Barge (*☎ 631-765-3010*), on Route 25, 3 miles from Greenport, is one of the best places in the area to taste the sweet Peconic Bay scallops, a local specialty that was devastated by brown tide in 1994. The restaurant, which overlooks the Port of Egypt Marina, charges $18 for dinner main dishes, and offers a selection of lunch specials for $8.95.

In Greenport restaurants are clustered around the marina. **Claudio's** (*☎ 631-477-0715*), on the ferry dock, is a landmark with a noisy bar; the food is considered to be expensive by locals. A better option is **Aldo's** (*☎ 631-477-1699, 103-105 Front St*), which is also pricey but serves sublime food, and is known for its desserts, which are made in the small bakery next to the restaurant. Reservations are essential.

Getting There & Away

The Cross Sound Ferry Company (*☎ 631-323-2525; 860-443-5281*) takes passengers and cars from Orient Point, at the tip of the North Fork, to New London, CT, several times a day; reservations are recommended and can be held with a credit card. Cars cost $32, including driver; passengers cost an extra $9 one-way. The company also offers a pedestrian only hydrofoil shuttle from the terminal to the Foxwoods Casino and Resort in Connecticut for $14 one-way, $22 same day return.

See Getting There & Away in the Shelter Island section for information about ferry service from Shelter Island to North Fork.

Hudson Valley

NEW YORK

Highlights

- Legend of Sleepy Hollow author Washington Irving's Sunnyside cottage, south of Tarrytown
- Val-Kill, Eleanor Roosevelt's humble home near Hyde Park
- Olana, the ornate mansion of Hudson River school artist Frederick Church, with views to match the owner's famous landscape paintings
- The wetland ecology center and arboretum at Institute of Ecosystem Studies, Millbrook
- The Storm King Art Center, an outstanding contemporary-sculpture park between Newburgh and West Point, with works by Calder, Moore and other modern masters
- Pick-your-own apple orchards and berry farms in the Mid-Hudson Valley
- Panoramic views and architectural gems at the US Military Academy at West Point

From a riverbank along the Hudson, it's easy to imagine a New York of another era – when New York City itself was (by today's measure) a relatively small port, and the skyline was dotted with tall buildings, some even reaching four or five stories. In fact, history is a major attraction here. Stone fences and Victorian cottages, along with opulent and extravagant mansions, seem commonplace.

Today New Yorkers who live in the upstate region closest to the Big Apple still boast of their active but bucolic environment. Small towns dot the river, river traffic is abundant, and dairy farms, roadside produce stands and dirt roads adorn the landscape. This is the same landscape, by the way, captured in the luminous paintings by the famous artists of the Hudson River school (whose work is on view in galleries from New York City to Albany).

'Pick-your-own' fruit and vegetable farms, horseback-riding stables, hiking and biking trails compliment the valley's historic landmarks, which range from Washington Irving's 19th-century Sleepy Hollow haunts near Tarrytown to President Franklin D Roosevelt and Eleanor Roosevelt's home in Hyde Park.

The Hudson Valley generally refers to the area south of Albany that follows the Hudson River and lies between the Catskill Mountains to the west and the Taconic highlands and the Connecticut state border to the east. The river itself begins in the Adirondacks at Lake Tear-of-the-Cloud, atop Mt Marcy. It flows south (over 300 miles) to New York Bay, where it forms an estuary so large that Dutch navigator Henry Hudson mistook the river for the object of his 17th-century search – the Northwest Passage across the continent to the Far East. The spot where the river begins and the inlet ends changes with the tides, making the Hudson more like a fjord than a river. The Hudson Valley is often divided into the lower, mid- and upper sections of the valley; the bridges that cross the river help define each area to some degree.

Just over New York's eastern border are Connecticut's Litchfield Hills, and further north are Massachusetts' Berkshire Hills. These are very popular tourist destinations, especially in the summer, when outdoor activities and festivals abound. The area is dotted with inns and B&Bs, and all of it is detailed in Lonely Planet's *New England* guidebook. However, most of the same variety of attractions and scenery are found in New York in the mid- and upper Hudson Valley – with fewer tourists to compete for space.

HISTORY

In 1609, Henry Hudson, contracted by the Dutch East India Company, sailed up a river known to the Native Americans of the upper Hudson as Muhheakunnuk ('Great Waters in Motion') in search of a northern passage to the Pacific. Hudson's ship, *Half Moon*, got as far as present-day Albany. (Two years later, in the Canadian bay that bears his name, he was set adrift with eight others by his own crew and never seen again.)

The Native Americans that Hudson and subsequent Europeans encountered were Algonquian (Mohican) and the more powerful Iroquois, who controlled much of the fur trade from which the Dutch, English and French all sought to profit. The Iroquois, or Six Nations, Confederacy remained intact until the American Revolution.

During the Revolutionary War, General George Washington made his headquarters at Newburgh on the west bank of the river. In 1802, the US Military Academy – better known as West Point for its position on the river – was established a few miles below Newburgh. The strategic value of the river soon turned commercial, and it contributed to the prosperous early days of the nation. When the Erie Canal was completed in 1825 between Albany and Buffalo, the state of New York essentially became the port for the farms and factories of the nation's Midwest.

When Washington Irving moved to Sunnyside, just south of Tarrytown, it was to combine the watery solitude of this Sleepy Hollow by the river with proximity to the bustling metropolis of New York City. Many

residents of the valley today try to achieve the same balance. Many also have suffered some of the same disappointments: 10 years after building Sunnyside on a serene hillside, the railroad came up the river and could not be stopped, even by America's most famous author. Irving cursed the coal-burning steam engine as it passed his home, shaking the ground. He made a compromise of sorts by finally using the train to venture into New York City.

INFORMATION

Dutchess County Tourism (☎ 845-463-4000, 800-445-3131), 3 Neptune Rd, Poughkeepsie, has information on Dutchess County, Poughkeepsie and most of the Hudson Valley (see Information in the Poughkeepsie section, later in this chapter).

Hudson Valley Tourism (☎ 800-232-4782) has its own free guide with information on regional special events. Alternatively you can call for a free visitors' guide to Orange County (☎ 800-762-8687), which includes West Point and the Storm King Art Center; Rockland County (☎ 800-295-5723), which includes Harriman and Bear Mountain State Parks; Westchester County (☎ 800-833-9282), which includes Tarrytown and Peekskill.

There's a state information center at Harriman (☎ 845-938-2638); take exit 16 off I-87 (the New York State Thruway).

Post offices, hospitals and banks or ATMs are easily found and widely available throughout the region, especially in the larger towns such as Newburgh, Millbrook, Tarrytown and Poughkeepsie. Banks and post offices are obvious, as they are usually on the main street; hospitals are seldom on the main street, but nearby.

GETTING THERE & AROUND

If you fly or take the train into this region, be prepared to arrange for automobile transportation to get around, especially in the smaller towns.

Air

The main airports in the region are La Guardia in New York City and Albany International Airport to the north (see the

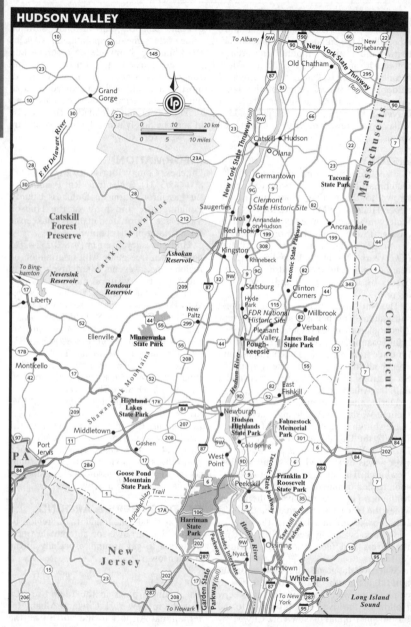

HUDSON VALLEY

Capital District & Mohawk Valley chapter). Several carriers serve Newburgh's Stewart International Airport, including United Express, American, Delta, Midway and US Airways.

Bus

Short Line Bus Co (☎ 800-631-8405) offers the best service to West Point and the surrounding area. Short Line buses stop in front of Thayer Gate. Buses to New York City (2 hours) cost $11/21. Buses to Albany (2.5 hours) cost $13/24.

Short Line also serves nearby Bear Mountain. The bus stops at the Bear Mt Inn; the fare to New York City is $10/20.

Short Line service between Newburgh and New York City costs $14/26. The bus stop is at the junction of Route 17K and I-87.

Train

Amtrak's (☎ 800-872-7245) Adirondack line runs the length of the river and connects several of the communities along the eastern shore, from Penn Station in New York City north to Croton-on-Hudson, Poughkeepsie, Rhinecliff, Hudson and beyond to Albany and towns in the Adirondacks.

Metro-North (☎ 212-532-4900, 800-638-7646) runs frequent commuter trains (its Hudson Line) from Grand Central Station in New York City. The trains stop at Tarrytown, Ossining, Peekskill and Poughkeepsie terminals. One-way fares are $7.50 to $9.50.

Car & Motorcycle

To get around, a car is essential, especially to see the countryside and small towns.

Route 9, the principle scenic north-south road in the Hudson Valley, hugs the east side of the river for the most part; when it strays, Route 9D near Cold Spring and Route 9G near Rhinebeck continue the scenic riverside drive. On the west side of the river is Route 9W.

The area further east of the river is paralleled by the Taconic State Parkway, which connects the towns of Old Chatham, southeast of Albany, and East Fishkill, southeast of Poughkeepsie in Dutchess County. The Saw Mill River Parkway diagonally traverses the lower eastern valley from southwest to northeast. There it turns into I-684, which runs into I-84 as well as Route 22, an eastern north-south valley route straddling the state borders of Connecticut, Massachusetts and Vermont.

The lower Hudson Valley further west of the river is traversed by east-west I-287, which runs into north-south I-87 (the New York State Thruway – often called the 'Northway'). I-87 continues north into the Catskills region. Also on the river's west side is the Palisades Interstate Parkway, which begins at Ft Lee, NJ, and runs north through Harriman State Park and ends at Route 9W in Bear Mountain State Park.

East-west routes include Routes 17 and 6 in the lower Hudson Valley; I-84 in the mid-Hudson; and Routes 44, 199 and 308 in the upper Hudson Valley.

Car Rental There are rental companies in towns such as Poughkeepsie, but the best rates are from the larger towns with airports, in this case Albany – but not Newburgh, which is very expensive.

Bicycle

The country roads east of the Hudson River are perfect for biking. There are several well-traveled bike trails in the region and two in particular near Millbrook. A 39-mile tour connects the villages of Millbrook, Verbank, Pleasant Valley and Clinton Corners. A shorter 27-mile trip takes in Clinton Corners, Pleasant Valley and Schultzville.

For further information, consult *Mountain Biking Destinations in the NY Metropolitan Area*, by Joel Sendek, or *25 Bicycle Tours in the Hudson Valley*, by Peter Kick.

Lower Hudson Valley

Heading north from New York City, the lower Hudson Valley stretches north and west from the Tappan Zee Bridge, connecting Nyack and Tarrytown to Cold Spring

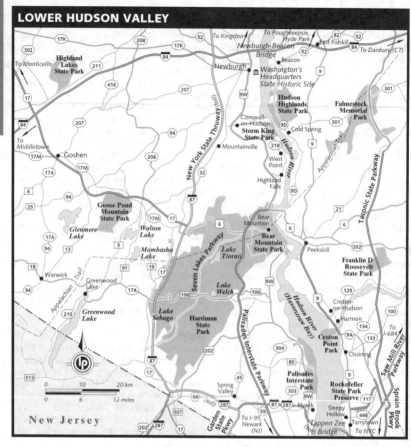

LOWER HUDSON VALLEY

just below the Newburgh-Beacon Bridge. It also takes in West Point, Newburgh and Goshen.

NYACK

Nyack sits on the west bank across the river from Tarrytown (see this section later in the chapter) and the Tappan Zee Bridge. A ferry once connected both towns. Nyack has always been a sort of commuter village for New York City. But, it's still a pleasant place to walk, with lots of antiques, several good eateries, shops and bookstores within a few blocks of the Main and Broadway intersec-

tion. Five times a year, the intersection is closed off to host street fairs.

From New York City, take I-87 north to I-287 and go west over the Tappan Zee Bridge. Nyack is at the junction of I-287 and Route 9W.

Information

The Nyack Chamber of Commerce (☎ 845-353-2221), 92 Main St, near the corner of Cedar St, is in the Rockland County Building and has walking-tour maps of Nyack.

Bookstores include the Pickwick Bookshop (☎ 845-358-9126), 8 S Broadway, which is a browser's delight. There is a rumpled air to the place and a sprawling corner for children's books. You can easily lose track of time here, as the owner himself does. Official hours are daily from 10 am to 6 pm, but the store is often open later.

A tidy shop opposite Pickwick's, Ben Franklin Bookshop (☎ 845-358-0440), 17 N Broadway, is another great place to browse. There is a good selection of local history and literature, but the specialty is rare mystery and science fiction. It is open daily from 11 am to 5:30 pm, Saturday and Sunday from 11 am to 6:30 pm.

Places to Stay

Best Western Nyack (☎ *845-358-8100, 26 Route 59*) is just off the I-87/I-287 New York State Thruway at (northbound) exit 11. From town, it's at the top of Main St and walking distance to the main drag. Room rates are $89 to $95.

Super 8 Motel (☎ *845-353-3880, 47 Main St*), next to McDonald's, is a bit cheaper, charging $75 to $85 for a room.

Places to Eat

Runcible Spoon Bakery Café (☎ *845-358-9398, 37-9 N Broadway*), at High St, is a very inviting place, roomy and comfortable. Open-faced sandwiches called 'scans' are a big summer item and go for $3 to $5. In the fall and winter, homemade soups make a steamy appearance. It is open Monday to Friday from 7 am to 7 pm and until 5 pm on Sunday.

Next to Ben Franklin Bookshop, *Vintage Deli* (☎ *845-353-0609*) is a low-priced diner serving authentic Cuban-American dishes, such as chicken, rice and beans, pork stews and the like. It is open daily for breakfast, lunch and dinner.

Encore (☎ *845-358-2900, 3 Broadway*), near the corner of Main St, is an attractive and casual French-style bistro, which is open daily for dinner. Entrees cost $11 to $16, and the restaurant is closed on Tuesday.

HARRIMAN & BEAR MOUNTAIN STATE PARKS

Just outside of New York City, Harriman State Park and the adjacent Bear Mountain State Park have several well-maintained hiking trails. The Appalachian Trail (see the Outdoor Activities chapter) passes through both parks on its way from New Jersey to Connecticut. Admission to the parks is free, but parking is not; parking is $5 at Harriman's beaches, $3 at other lots, and it's $4 at Bear Mountain.

Harriman State Park is large (72 sq miles) and a good place for a swim; it has three lakes with sandy beaches. Hiking and swimming are the most popular activities in Harriman. For free trail maps, visit the Harriman Park Visitor Center (☎ 845-786-5003), which is open daily from mid-April to mid-October from 8 am to 6 pm, and to 5 pm during the winter.

The three lakes in Harriman are used for both boating and swimming. The good news for swimmers is that no gas motors are permitted; still, lots of rowboats plus a few electric motorboats are available for rent.

Near the eastern edge of the park (exit 14 off the Palisade Parkway, near Willow Grove), **Lake Welch** has the only campground in either Harriman or Bear Mountain. Parking is included if you camp, but day-use parking is $5. **Lake Tiorati** (☎ 845-351-2568) is just below the Appalachian Trail and is another good spot for hiking, swimming, boating, picnicking and, in the winter, ice-skating. At **Lake Sebago** (☎ 845-351-2583), there are a good swimming beach, hiking trails and rowboats for rent, but only for those staying in the state cabins. Boats rent for $3 per hour.

Bear Mountain State Park (☎ 845-786-2701) borders the western bank of the Hudson River. It was once the designated spot for Sing Sing Prison, until President Teddy Roosevelt intervened in 1910. The view from Bear Mountain's peak (1305 feet) takes in the Manhattan skyline on a clear day, as well as the river and surrounding mountain greenery. Hiking, spring wildflower viewing, fall foliage viewing, pool swimming and fishing are the popular activities; in the winter, cross-country skiing, sledding and ice-skating take over. Bear Mountain is open all year, from 8 am until sunset.

The **Trailside Museum & Zoo** (☎ 845-786-2701) is across the road from the Bear Mountain Inn (see Places to Stay) and has several exhibits on the geological and natural history of the area. The zoo is a refuge of sorts for rescued and wayward animals of the region. Both the museum and zoo are open daily from 9 am to 4:30 pm, and admission is free.

Places to Stay

At Harriman, tent camping is at Lake Welch, and cabins are at Lake Sebago. Lake Welch's *Beaver Pond Campground* (☎ 845-947-2792) is open from mid-April to mid-October. Basic campsites are $13, and for $16, you get a 14-sq-foot wooden platform with tent stakes. For reservations, call the New York State Camp (☎ 800-456-2267).

Lake Sebago Cabins (☎ 845-351-2360) are a great deal for families or groups of four to six. There are 38 rough cabins here, each with four cots (you can add two more for a fee). You must bring your own bedding and towels. The cabins are open from mid-April to mid-October, and the rates are $50 a night (two-night minimum) or $200 for a week.

Bear Mountain does not have campgrounds but does offer *Bear Mountain Inn* (☎ 845-786-2731). This mountain stone and timber inn has been around since the 1920s, and the giant stone fireplaces in the lobby area are worth a visit, even if you stay elsewhere. There are 15 rooms in the main building and four lodges down the road. Rooms (with one or two beds) cost $89 per night. The restaurant is open for lunch and dinner daily from 11:30 am to 9 pm.

Getting There & Away

Bear Mountain and Harriman State Parks are adjacent to one another. They lie between I-87 to the west and the Palisades Interstate Parkway to the east. I-287 runs to the south of the park system, and Route 6 marks the northern boundary. To reach Bear Mountain from the south, take Route 9W to the Bear Mountain exit. You can also take the Palisades Parkway north to exit 19 and follow signs to Bear Mountain State Park.

To reach Harriman State Park, take exit 16 from the Palisades Parkway and follow signs to Harriman State Park.

GOSHEN

Goshen, about 17 miles west of Harriman State Park on Route 17, is among the more appealing towns of the lower Hudson region. The old Federal and Victorian structures are well maintained, and the town is perfect for walking. Except for the modern and rather grotesque county building (an example of early 'industrial park' style), Goshen's colonial roots are intact. The gem of the bunch, **Goshen Court House** (☎ 845-294-6644), 101 Main St, has been in continuous use as a court of law since 1841; it's open to the public weekdays from 9 am to 4 pm.

Walking-tour maps are available from the Goshen Chamber of Commerce (☎ 845-294-7741), 44 Park Place, and the kiosk in the town square.

The **Goshen Historic Track** (☎ 845-294-5357), 44 Park Place, dates from 1854 and features trotter horse racing from the Independence Day (July 4) to Labor Day (first Monday in September). There is no betting, and the $2 admission is all you'll lose here. Opening day (July 4) also features a big fair with bed-races and a few jokes if it rains. The nearby **Trotting Horse Museum and Hall of Fame of the Trotter** (☎ 845-294-6330), 240 Main St, is open daily.

Places to Stay

Dobbs Stagecoach Inn (☎ 845-294-5526, 268 Main St) is comfortable, full of English antiques and in the center of town (three short blocks from the free public tennis courts). The four rooms cost $95 to $150 per night. Children are welcome, if you can maintain that they are at least 12 years old.

WEST POINT

Dedicated to duty, honor and country, the castle-like turrets of the US Military Academy at West Point jut out of the landscape in irregular and imposing tiers, as if carved from the rocky shore. Before an academy was established here, West Point was a key fortification during the Revolutionary War. Sometime between 1778 and 1780, a massive wrought-iron chain (with a log-boom to protect it) was stretched across the river to Constitution Island to prevent British ships from attempting to control river navigation. In 1802, the military academy, the oldest of its kind in the nation, was founded. Notable graduates include famous military heroes, astronauts and presidents.

Though the cadets – men and women – still live a strict military life, it's possible to visit and tour the sprawling complex at your own pace. You might even imagine the plight of a young Edgar Allen Poe, a cadet in 1830, who was dismissed for insubordination after only eight months of less than military endeavor.

The campus is impressive. Miles of pathways crisscross a grand preserve of redbrick and gray-stone Gothic- and Federal-style campus buildings, churches and temples, stadiums, a boat landing and panoramic views of the Hudson River. If at first you didn't realize that this was a military establishment, the landscaping might offer a clue; anything hinting at disorder has been neatly trimmed. Just walking around can make you yearn for a needless haircut.

The main routes into the area are the Palisades Parkway and Route 9W. Signs for West Point are hard to miss. From Harriman State Park, take Palisades Parkway to the junction with Route 9W, and then continue north for about 7 miles to West Point.

Information
West Point Visitors' Center (☎ 845-938-2638) is actually in Highland Falls, about 100 yards south of the military academy's Thayer Gate. It's open daily from 9 am to 4:45 pm and can provide maps and tour information. West Point Museum is open from 10:30 am to 4:15 pm. The village of Highland Falls and the nearby town of Fort Montgomery are unique to the Hudson Valley; the atmosphere around West Point reflects the rather prim (shined shoes), blue-collar aesthetic of a professional military operation, with just a touch of New England.

Places to Stay & Eat
The five-story *Hotel Thayer* (☎ 845-446-4731), on Route 218, will satisfy any cravings for military ambience. Once operated by the US Military Academy, the hotel sits on a beautiful perch overlooking the Hudson River and history past. Weekday/weekend rates are $150 to $180. A good and cheaper alternative is the 50-room *Best Western Palisades Motel* (☎ 845-446-9400, 17 Main St), which charges $75/85 for most rooms.

In addition to the fancier restaurant at the Hotel Thayer, try *Park Restaurant* (☎ 845-446-8709, 451 Main St); it is open daily (except Monday) from 8:30 am to 11 pm. Next door is *Shades Restaurant* (☎ 845-446-2626, 457 Main St), which is open daily for lunch and dinner, and has an Italian-American menu.

Shopping
The Toy Soldier Gallery (☎ 845-446-6731, 800-777-9904), 501 Main St, Highland Falls, is a fascinating store to browse through and certainly helps put the entire area in perspective. A brightly colored assortment of mostly metal toy soldiers includes ancient Romans, modern Zulus and uniformed warriors from just about any war you can name – from the Civil War to several 20th-century varieties. The toys are not cheap – an individual piece costs $5 to $20, and sets start at about $100. It is open Tuesday through Saturday from 10 am to 4:30 pm.

STORM KING ART CENTER
This art center (☎ 845-534-3115) is a beautiful outdoor walk-through sculpture park featuring some of the finest modern and contemporary sculpture in North America, including works by modern masters Calder, Moore and Noguchi. The setting matches the artwork, angle for angle. There is also a fine indoor museum with a gift and bookshop. Several picnic areas are available, but the nicest is near Parking Lot B. On weekends only, there is an open-air cafe that sells sandwiches and soft drinks.

Walking tours depart the gift shop daily at 2 pm, and take 50 minutes. On Saturday, a shuttle bus tour is also available. Tours are included with the admission price.

Storm King is open from April to mid-November daily from 11 am to 5 pm. Admission is $7/5/3 for adults/seniors/students and children, and free for children under five years of age.

Storm King is in Mountainville (not Storm King State Park), about 9 miles southwest of Cornwall-on-Hudson and 4 miles from West Point. From I-84, I-87 or Route 9W, exit to Route 32, where blue-and-white signs will point you to Storm King Art Center on Old Pleasant Hill Rd.

NEWBURGH

Once upon a time, Newburgh was an important whaling village, as were its neighbors Poughkeepsie and Hudson. The small industrial city is mostly remembered today as General George Washington's headquarters during the Revolutionary War.

Newburgh could serve as a textbook of American architecture from the Revolutionary War period to the present. Unfortunately, one chapter of the book would include the demise of such historical towns. The oldest of the town's remaining commercial and residential buildings are in disrepair, and the best views are looking east across the river. Nevertheless, there is distinct historic sense to Newburgh, and nearby Downing Park is a good spot for a picnic by the pond.

Washington's Headquarters State Historic Site

Washington's headquarters (☎ 845-562-1195), 84 Liberty St, is the home of a small museum and **Hasbrouck House**, where Washington stayed from 1782–83; he was there until the end of the war. The site features several galleries, period furniture and a 50-foot map that wraps around an entire room. Plan to spend about an hour here.

Both the museum and house are open from mid-April to late October Wednesday through Saturday from 10 am to 5 pm and Sunday 1 to 5 pm. The site maintains weekday winter hours for families or small groups, but you must call ahead. Admission is $3 for adults; $2 for seniors; $1 for children.

Places to Eat

26 Front Street (☎ 845-569-8035, at – yes – 26 Front St) is a handsomely converted warehouse on the waterfront with a wonderful river-and-valley view from the deck, where you can eat and dance in the evening until the wee hours. There's even a small dock, in case you'd prefer to arrive by boat. The restaurant is open at 11:30 am for lunch, and dinner is served from 5 to 9 pm. After that, they stay open for dancing until 4 am. On weekends only, there is a $5 cover charge.

Getting There & Away

Stewart International Airport (☎ 845-564-7200), 2 miles west of Newburgh on Route 17K, is served by several carriers including Delta (☎ 800-221-2121), United (☎ 800-241-65220), American (☎ 800-433-7300) and US Airways (☎ 800-428-4322). US Airways has the most flights from this airport. The fare from Newburgh to Rochester is $272; Newburgh to Buffalo is $389; Newburgh to Boston is $328; and Newburgh to Philadelphia is $308.

By car, Newburgh is north of West Point via Route 9W.

Driving Tip: River Views

If you're driving north from Newburgh, Route 9W (between the Newburgh-Beacon Bridge and the Mid-Hudson Bridge at Poughkeepsie) is not as scenic as you might expect. The infrequent river view is hardly worth the string of strip malls, light industry and local traffic you will encounter. Either jump onto the Northway (I-87), or cross the river and proceed north on Routes 9D and 9 to the Poughkeepsie area.

Across the river, views are more spectacular, but Washington's Headquarters is only 12 miles north of popular West Point. It's common to visit West Point, drive north to Newburgh, see George and Martha's place, then cross the river at the Newburgh-Beacon Bridge to the other side.

NEW YORK

TARRYTOWN, SLEEPY HOLLOW & AROUND

Washington Irving once stated that Tarrytown got its name from the Dutch farm wives who complained that their husbands tarried a bit too long at the village tavern after selling their farm produce at the nearby markets. The more likely, but less appealing, linguistic explanation finds it a variation of the Dutch 'tarwe,' meaning wheat.

Peaceful, picturesque Tarrytown is the first of the historic Hudson River towns on the east bank of the river and makes a good base for visiting the many historic homes of the lower valley, all of which are within a few miles of each other. A town landmark is the **Music Hall Theater** near the corner of Broadway and Main St, a classic old brick edifice with a bright marquee listing current theater and music events. **Marymount College** (☎ 914-332-8209), 100 Marymount Ave, was started in 1907 and is one of more than 80 remaining women's colleges in the US.

In December 1996, the village of North Tarrytown decided that it might do better to attract tourists if it changed its name to Sleepy Hollow – and so it did. Look out for old maps that might bear the old North Tarrytown name.

The Sleepy Hollow/Tarrytown Chamber of Commerce (☎ 914-631-1705), 54 Main St, Sleepy Hollow, is open Monday to Friday, 11 am to 4 pm; you can also visit their website at www.sleepyhollowchamber.com.

Historic Homes & Churches

Historic Hudson Valley (☎ 914-631-8200, 800-448-4007) is a nonprofit organization that maintains five of the most historic sites in the Lower Hudson Valley: Sunnyside, Philipsburg Manor, Kykuit, Van Cortlandt Manor and the Union Church of Pocantico Hills. All of these sites are open daily (except Tuesday). The organization maintains a website (www.hudsonvalley.org).

The sites below are listed from south to north.

Sunnyside This cottage (☎ 914-591-8763), which Washington Irving described as being

'made up of gable ends and full of angles and corners as an old cocked hat,' is 3 miles south of Tarrytown, just off Route 9 on W Sunnyside Lane. Even today, it's easy to imagine Irving staring into the deep forests and ravines and envisioning the Headless Horseman of Sleepy Hollow chasing poor Ichabod Crane.

As the costumed tour guide will surely tell you, Irving's old Dutch cottage was 'cute, cozy, quiet and charming.' It's easy to see the age of Romanticism at work on the grounds, just as it worked on Irving's imagination. Like all romantics, he found a divine spirit in

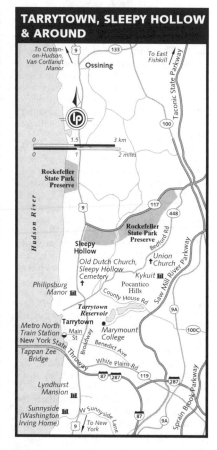

Sleepy Hollow's Headless Horseman

nature. The formal English hedges are gone, replaced by a carefully designed 'natural' look. The climbing wisteria that Irving planted over a century ago still clings to the house. The house tour reveals how people of leisure spent time at home, took advantage of the daylight hours and often gathered round the piano in the evening.

To see Irving's home, you must take the one-hour tour that begins in the gift shop near the parking lot. Tours leave every half-hour, beginning at 10:30 am; the last tour begins at 4 pm in the summer and 3 pm in the fall and spring (the combination of earlier sunsets and small windows make it too dark to see late in the day). Sunnyside operates daily (except Tuesday) from March through December from 10 am to 5 pm; and admission costs $8/7/4 for adults/seniors/children.

Lyndhurst This historic home (☎ 914-631-4481), 635 S Broadway (Route 9), is a classic 19th-century Gothic Revival mansion designed by the leading architect of the genre, Alexander Jackson Davis, in the 1830s. The home, which overlooks the Hudson, was built for the mayor of New York City, William Paulding. The landscaping is as spectacular as the building, particularly the rose garden. A small map identifying most of the flora is available for free at the entrance gate when you drive in.

Lyndhurst is open daily (except Monday), from April 15 through October from 10 am to 5 pm and Saturday and Sunday from 10 am to 5 pm the rest of the year. Tours are conducted throughout the day. Admission is $9/8/3 for adults/seniors/children (ages 12 to 17), free for children six and under.

Philipsburg Manor Two miles north of Tarrytown on N Broadway (Route 9), this manor (☎ 914-631-3992), also called the Philipsburg Restoration, dates from 1865 and is one of the most accessible of the lower valley mansions. Like many wealthy Europeans, the Dutchman Frederick Philipse was awarded a large tract of land here, on which he built a family home, a water-powered gristmill and a Dutch church. Visitors will see farm workers in period dress performing the chores of the day, from tending the vegetable garden to milking the cow.

There is a museum shop and a good lunch counter cafe. Philipsburg is also the starting point for tours to Kykuit (see that section, later in this chapter). The manor is open weekdays (except Tuesday) from 11 am to 5 pm, Saturday from 10 am to 5 pm and Sunday 2 to 5 pm. Admission costs $8/7/4 for adults/seniors/children (ages six to 17), and it's free for children 5 and under.

Old Dutch Church & Sleepy Hollow Cemetery Across the road from Philipsburg Manor, this 1865 church (☎ 914-631-0081) was part of the original manor.

Adjacent to the church is the Sleepy Hollow Cemetery, formerly the Tarrytown Cemetery until Washington Irving petitioned to rename it to 'keep that beautiful and umbrageous neighborhood sacred from the anti-poetical and all-leveling axe' and 'to secure the patronage of all desirous of sleeping quietly in their graves.'

In fact, Washington Irving is buried here in a section called Beekman Mound; other section names include Poet's Mound and Sunnyside. The whole place has a sort of mysterious air about it. It's hilly, and the roads are narrow and curvy – it's easy to get lost for a moment.

Kykuit Home to several generations of Rockefellers, Kykuit (☎ 914-631-9491) only recently opened to public tours. The house is essentially a fine art gallery with a kitchen, furniture and staff. Fine porcelain and famous paintings – including several by modern masters – adorn the interior. Outside, the exquisite garden overlooking the Hudson River ('Kykuit' is the Dutch word for 'lookout') is home to modern sculptures by Henry Moore, Alexander Calder, Jacques Lipchitz, Alberto Giacometti, Pablo Picasso and others. And despite its expensive patina, it must be said of Kykuit that it avoids the ostentatiousness of many Hudson Valley mansions.

Reservations are essential to visit Kykuit; chances are slim that you will join a tour if you simply show up in a hopeful mood (though the steamy month of August is probably your best bet for a last-minute visit). If you do decide to trust your luck, go in the morning, get on the day's wait list, and wait around on the deck in back, or stroll across the bridge to the mill to get away from the mob scene in the gift shop.

All tours leave by shuttle bus from nearby Philipsburg Manor. The basic tour is $20 per person; seniors and students are $19, but there are no discounts for children, a policy no doubt meant to blunt the natural attraction between small children and porcelain. The tour lasts about two hours and includes the house, galleries and garden. The hectic scene at the shuttle bus area improves dramatically once you reach Kykuit. It is open April 24 to November 7 (call for hours).

There is a good cafe inside the gift shop area, which is open daily from 9:30 am to 8 pm; you can eat on a covered deck, or take away a picnic lunch for $6.

Union Church at Pocantico Hills This old stone church (☎ 914-631-2069), on River Rd in Pocantico, must be seen from the inside out. It's home to several stained-glass windows by Henri Matisse and Marc Chagall; the modern art treasures were commissioned by the Rockefeller family and were completed between 1954 and 1965.

Most of Chagall's nine windows are dedicated to Old Testament prophets. Matisse's beautiful rose window was his last completed work of art.

The church is open to visitors April through December Monday through Thursday 11 to 5pm, Friday from 11 am to 4 pm, Saturday from 10 to 2pm and Sunday from 2 to 5 pm; it is closed on Tuesday. To reach the church, go north from Tarrytown about 2 miles, and turn right (east) just before Philipsburg Manor onto Route 448. The church is about 3 miles away on your right.

Van Cortlandt Manor This manor (☎ 914-271-8981, 914-631-8200 for reservations), on S Riverside Ave in Croton-on-Hudson, was built in 1748 by one of the most influential Dutch families of the day. The home and 200 year old gardens overlook both the Hudson and the Croton rivers. The furnishings are a major attraction; perhaps three quarters of the family's original possessions are on display, from Queen Anne and Chippendale furniture to the colonial kitchen – complete with pots and pans, jugs, mixing bowls and graters. There's not a microwave in sight.

American Manors

The aristocratic land system that arrived with the Europeans certainly exacted its price from the general population, who had to make do with humble farmhouses and old stone churches. Nevertheless, the monuments of wealth and power are scattered up and down the Hudson River. They often lie deep within a manicured park, where even the gardeners seem to carry the authority of the past.

A word on the word 'manor': in the 17th and 18th centuries, it carried a specific legal meaning similar to its medieval European use, complete with hereditary rights granted by royal charter. With few exceptions, most of these New World mansions are Gothic in mood and proportion – good settings for a scary fireside story.

There is even a milk room with a stone floor for cold storage.

For a telling sign of the politics of the day, notice the gun-slits built into the sides of several outer walls, a reminder of the failure to live peacefully with the native inhabitants of the area.

The manor is open daily (except Tuesday) from April through December from 10 am to 5 pm. Admission is $8/7/4 for adults/seniors/children (ages six to 17); or $4 for a grounds pass with no tour. The first tour begins at 10:30 am and the last tour of the manor begins at 4 pm.

Rockefeller State Park Preserve

Three miles north of Sleepy Hollow (formerly North Tarrytown) is the entrance to Rockefeller Preserve (☎ 914-631-1470), a peaceful and beautiful getaway from the hustle and bustle that historic touring can stir up. The preserve is a rolling, woodsy expanse of solitude and old fields and pastures marked by low stone walls. A free-walking tour map is available at the small administrative building, and a large notice board tells some of the area's history, from the earliest Munsee-speaking Indian people, to the developers of the New Netherlands to the Rockefeller benefactors.

A short trail from the entrance will put you on the edge of the small Swan Lake. The preserve is free, but it costs $5 to park in the adjacent lot. It is open from 8 am to sunset. The area is closed in the winter, usually from December to mid-April.

The preserve's entrance is just off Route 117, 1 mile east of Route 9, about a mile north of Philipsburg Manor.

River Cruises

New York Waterway (☎ 800-533-3779) offers several tour packages to historic sites in the area as well as a transportation service between Tarrytown and New York City (see Getting There & Away, below). Most cruise boats depart Pier 78 in Manhattan, and one boat departs the Tarrytown docks at the end of W Main St.

The **Sleepy Hollow Cruise** departs Pier 78 and visits both Washington Irving's Sunny-side home and Philipsburg Manor. The $35 price (half for children ages three to 12) includes boat and ground transportation and admission prices. There is a good lunch counter in the gift shop area at Philipsburg Manor.

The **Kykuit Cruise** departs Pier 78 and only visits Kykuit. The price (all transportation and admission) is $60 for everyone from adults to infants; small children are really discouraged, in fact, from visiting Kykuit – something about noise and vast wealth being incompatible.

New York Waterways also offers a two-hour **North Hudson Cruise** that departs Tarrytown and takes in the Peekskill mountains to the north. The river cruise runs daily (except Tuesday) from May to November and departs at 1:15 pm. The cost is $10 for adults; half price for children.

Places to Stay

Courtyard by Marriott (☎ 914-631-1122, 475 White Plains Blvd/Hwy 119), south of town, has rooms and several larger suites for $119 to $159. Rooms at the nearby *Hampton Inn* (☎ 914-592-5680, 200 Tarrytown Rd), in Elmsford, cost $120.

Tarrytown Hilton Inn (☎ 914-631-5700, 455 S Broadway/Hwy 9) is one of the more attractive Hiltons to be found and seems to have acknowledged its historic locale, even the bar has a homey-antique touch. Rooms are pricier here and cost $115 to $175; large suites cost $200 to $400.

Places to Eat

One of best diners in the valley is *Bella's Restaurant & Donut Shop* (☎ 914-332-0444, 5 S Broadway), near the corner of Main St. The donuts will tempt those who swore off donuts years ago. They are fresh, homemade and they go early. Bella's also serves goulash, pot roast, hearty soups and sandwiches. Prices are reasonable. It is open Monday to Saturday from 5 am to 9 pm, Sunday from 7 am to 3 pm.

For good homemade Greek food, try *Lefteri's Gyro Restaurant* (☎ 914-524-9687, 1 N Main St), near the corner of Broadway. This small, family-run business serves big pita sandwiches (chicken, beef or veggie), homemade Greek pastries, and the 'small' Greek salad is a meal in itself. Most lunch items are under $6, and dinners are only slightly more. This restaurant is open daily from 11 am to 10 pm.

Main Street Café (☎ *914-332-9834, 24 Main St*) is a moderately upscale American bistro with interesting sandwiches (portabello mushrooms or London broil, for example) and half orders of seafood pasta, all costing about $7. Broiled salmon and fresh-pasta dinners cost around $13. In the summer, there are outside tables on the Main St sidewalk. It is open Tuesday to Saturday for lunch from noon to 3 pm, for dinner from 5 to 10 pm, and Sunday from noon to 9 pm.

Entertainment
If you start feeling depressed from visiting too many mansions, you can return to 'architectural Earth' with a quick visit to the *Tarrytown Music Hall* (☎ *914-631-3390, 13 Main St*). The theater is an 1885 Queen Anne–style building and listed in the National Register of Historic Places. It is now a performing arts center with frequent jazz, classical and folk concerts, as well as dance, opera, musicals, dramas and children's theater.

Getting There & Away
Tarrytown is just off the Tappan Zee Bridge at the junction of Route 9 and I-87. If you're coming across the bridge from the west (Nyack), take the first exit (exit 9) after the tollbooth and go to Route 9, which is the main north-south road in the area.

To reach Tarytown from Manhattan (about 30 miles), take the West Side Hwy north, which first turns into the Henry Hudson Parkway and then into the Saw Mill River Parkway. Follow the Saw Mill River Parkway to I-287 and go west on it. I-287 merges with I-87, and Tarrytown is at exit 9.

Metro-North (☎ 212-532-4900, 800-638-7646), the Hudson Valley commuter train, also offers train and shuttle-bus packages to several historic sites in the area. The Tarry-

town station is just south of the New York Waterways dock at the end of W Main St.

However, there's a more interesting way to arrive if you don't have, or want to be, carless. New York Waterway (☎ 800-533-3779) operates one-way and roundtrip boat transportation from Pier 78 in Manhattan daily (except Tuesday) during the summer and on weekends only in May and October, weather permitting. Boats leave Manhattan at 10:30 am and Tarrytown at 4:30 pm; the trip takes about 90 minutes. Fares are $15.00/$25.00 for adults; $8.00 for children (ages three to 12).

OSSINING
This is a handsome riverside village between Tarrytown and Peekskill on Route 9. The **Ossining Historical Museum** (☎ 914-941-0001), 196 Croton Ave, houses Indian artifacts, antique dolls and items from nearby Sing Sing Prison. The museum is open Monday, Wednesday and Sunday from 1 to 4 pm and daily by appointment. Sing Sing fans can see more prison items at the nearby **Ossining Urban Cultural Park** (☎ 914-941-3189), 95 Broadway, including an old electric chair and life-size replicas of prison cells. The center is open Tuesday to Saturday from 9 am to 7 pm.

The Metro-North train station in Tarrytown is on Green St between Main and White Sts (most people enter from Main St).

PEEKSKILL
Peekskill doesn't have the spiffy antique look of other riverside towns, but it does have an active arts scene, reasonable accommodations and eateries and a few very interesting shops.

One of the most interesting stores for used books in the Hudson Valley is the Bruised Apple (☎ 914-734-7000), 923 Central Ave, featuring floor-to-high-ceiling stacks of used, rare and out-of-print books. There are good sections on local history, travel and exploration and art. This bookstore is open Tuesday, Wednesday and Thursday from 10 am to 6 pm, Friday and Saturday from 10 am to 8 pm and Sunday from noon to 6 pm.

Paramount Center for the Arts (☎ 914-739-2333), 1008 Brown St, shows excellent international and independent films, which generally change every two days. The theater is also the setting for occasional concerts and plays.

The Metro-North station is on Hudson Ave at Railroad Ave, on the riverfront. It's about a half mile to the downtown area. To reach Croton-on-Hudson to the south, follow Route 9A south for about 10 miles. To reach Cold Spring to the north, follow Route 9D north for about 15 miles.

Places to Stay & Eat
Peekskill Inn (☎ *914-739-1500, 634 Main St*), near the junction of Routes 9 and 6, is a large (over 50 rooms) motel-inn with a view of the river and charges $80 to $93 for rooms.

Susan's (☎ *914-737-6624, 12 N Division St*) serves good American bistro-style food for lunch and dinner. Prices are $5 to $10 for lunch and $10 to $16 for dinner. Susan's is open daily from noon to 2:30 for lunch and 5:30 to 9 pm for dinner, and to 10 pm on weekends; it is closed on Sunday and Monday.

COLD SPRING
Cold Spring, on Route 9D, is still a good place to find a meal, and its peaceful Main St is filled with old inns and several antique shops (including the honestly named Possibly Antique). A walking tour sponsored by the Putnam County Historical Society (☎ 914-265-4010) begins at 72 Main St. The tour is offered on Sunday at 2 pm from mid-May to mid-November. Call for additional information, or inquire at any of the antique shops on Main St.

Places to Stay & Eat
There are several very nice, if pricey, B&Bs here, including *Pig Hill B&B* (☎ *914-265-9247, 73 Main St*), a pink-brick Victorian in the middle of the village. Summer rates vary for rooms with private bath and fireplace ($150/125 on weekends/weekdays), to rooms with a shared bath ($130/100). Non-summer rates drop by about 20% and start at $80.

Lincoln's Appetite

When President Abraham Lincoln visited Cold Spring during the Civil War to inspect cannons made in the village, their inventor proudly demonstrated the cannons' power by firing a round at the facing cliffs across the river. According to the WPA *Guide to New York* (1940), Lincoln was unimpressed, remarking: 'I'm confident you can hit that mountain over there, so suppose we get something to eat. I'm hungry.'

The restaurant *The Depot* (☎ *914-265-5000, 1 Depot Rd*) is right by the Amtrak tracks, as you'll definitely discover at some point during your stop here (it's a converted train lounge). In the summer, several umbrella-shaded outdoor tables vibrate slightly as the train goes by. Inside, a lovely horseshoe bar also affords a quick glimpse of the passing trains. Food options range from fish and chicken to burgers and pasta; dishes cost $6 to $18.

Henry's-on-the-Hudson (☎ *914-265-3000, 184 Main St*) is a small bistro-style restaurant with sandwiches, burgers, fish & chips, ribs, chops and the like. Lunches cost $6 to $10, dinners $10 to $20. They are open Sunday to Thursday from noon to 10 pm, Friday and Saturday until midnight.

Mid-Hudson Valley

The mid-Hudson Valley extends from the Newburgh-Beacon Bridge (and I-84) north to the area east of the Kingston-Rhinecliff Bridge. It includes Rhinebeck, Red Hook, Poughkeepsie, and Hyde Park.

POUGHKEEPSIE
Poughkeepsie ('pooh-KIP-see,' population 28,000), the largest town on the east bank of the Hudson, has suffered the same urban fate as many towns in New York; as industry moved out, decay moved in. But like many of those same communities, there is an

active effort to revitalize the town (the old historic districts are usually the first to feel the paint brush).

Information

One of the organizations most responsible for efforts to improve conditions in the valley is headquartered here. Scenic Hudson, Inc (☎ 845-473-4440), 9 Vassar St in the old downtown section, is a nonprofit group that has done much to slow the thoughtless development of the open rural spaces that for so long characterized the entire valley.

The Poughkeepsie Area Chamber of Commerce (☎ 845-454-1700), 1 Civic Center Plaza, is open all year Monday through Friday from 8:30 am to 4 pm. The Dutchess County Tourism Office (☎ 845-463-4000, 800-445-3131), 3 Neptune Rd, is open all year Monday to Friday from 9 am to 5 pm. The office also maintains a website at www .dutchesstourism.com.

The Poughkeepsie train station is at the bottom of Main St, next to the river, in the downtown area called the Riverfront District. It's less than a mile from the Bardavon Opera House.

Vassar College

This well-respected liberal arts school (☎ 845-437-7000), 124 College Ave at the corner of Raymond Ave, was established as a private women's college in 1861 and remained so until 1969 (when it went co-ed). Tours of the 125-acre campus are conducted daily during the summer months.

Vassar is home to a fine and recently refurbished art gallery, the **Francis Lehman Loeb Art Center** (☎ 845-437-5632, 437-5237), which contains several paintings from the Hudson River school (see the boxed text 'Hudson River School of Landscape Painters,' later in this chapter). It's open daily (except Monday) from 10 am to 5 pm and 1 to 5 pm on Sunday, and admission is free.

Samuel FB Morse Historic Site (Locust Grove)

This privately-owned 1830 mansion (☎ 845-454-4500), 370 South Rd (Route 9), about 2 miles south of the Mid-Hudson Bridge, is the former home of telegraph inventor and artist Samuel FB Morse. The house, built in the Tuscan Villa style popular in the mid-19th century, has its picture windows designed to showcase the 150-acre manicured grounds whose carriage roads wind through locust, hemlock and larch trees and gardens galore. It's also home to a beautiful wildlife and bird sanctuary with easy hiking trails and a visitors' center, a gallery and a museum shop on the grounds. In addition to the ornate mansion furnishings, some of Morse's old telegraph equipment and paintings are displayed. Check out the mirror in the butler's pantry and kitchen that is carefully positioned for the staff to follow progress at the dining table without disturbing the family or guests.

Although Morse is remembered as one of the great inventors, his passion was painting. He seems to have invented things in order to support his painting. For an eight-year period, he was in and out of court over patent rights, but he continued painting the entire time.

The home is open daily May through November from 10 am to 4 pm, but the gardens and trails stay open from 8 am to dusk. The home is also open in December, March and April by appointment. Admission for the one-hour home tour is $5/4/2 for adults/seniors/children (ages six to 18) and free for children under six. There is no charge to view the grounds.

Places to Stay

There are a number of motel chains along Route 9 just south of the Mid-Hudson Bridge, including *Sheraton Civic Center* (☎ 845-485-5300, 40 Civic Center Plaza), at Washington St, which charges $129 for rooms; *Best Western Inn & Conference Center* (☎ 845-462-4600, 800-528-1234, 679 South Rd), which charges $69 to $130; and *The Courtyard by Marriot-Poughkeepsie* (☎ 845-485-6336, 800-321-2211, 408 South Rd), which has a breakfast-only cafe, indoor pool and charges about $130. Rates at *Holiday Inn Express* (☎ 845-473-1151, 341 South Rd) are $109 to $149. On Route 55 the

100-room *Travelodge of Poughkeepsie* (☎ 845-454-3080, 313 Manchester Road) offers single/double budget rooms for $73/83 during the peak months of May to October, and $63/68 during the rest of the year.

Fancier accommodations can be had just south of town at *Inn at the Falls* (☎ 845-462-5770, 50 Red Oaks Mill Rd), overlooking the Wappinger Creek falls. The rooms ($150 to $185) are lavish and done in several extremely different styles, from quilted Victorian to black-tile modern; see your room before deciding.

Places to Eat

There are several decent eateries, bakeries and pubs across from Vassar's campus on Raymond Ave, including *Juliet's Café & Billiards* (☎ 845-452-2234, 60 Raymond Ave), which serves brick-oven pizza, subs and sandwiches from 11 am until after midnight. Across the street is *Julie's Restaurant* (☎ 845-452-6078, 49 Raymond Ave), a popular Vassar eatery. The reliable *Palace Diner* (☎ 845-473-1576, 194 Washington St), downtown, is open 24 hours daily.

Entertainment

Bardavon Opera House (☎ 845-473-2072, 35 Market St) is one of the premier theaters in the Hudson Valley and the oldest operating theater in New York. Performances at the restored 1869 venue include touring dance and opera companies, symphony and chamber music, a young people's theater series and silent films with live Wurlitzer organ accompaniment.

HYDE PARK

Hyde Park, a few miles north of Poughkeepsie on Route 9, is forever associated with the Roosevelts and their homes; other than the main tourist sights described here, there's not much else for tourists.

Franklin D Roosevelt Home National Historic Site

This historic site (☎ 845-229-8114, 800-967-2283 for reservations) is at 519 Albany Post Rd (Route 9) and includes FDR's home, gravesite and rose garden. Tours are available by reservation only. It is open daily from 9 am to 5 pm, and is closed from January to mid-March.

Museum of the Franklin D Roosevelt Library

This library (☎ 845-229-8114, 800-967-2283 for reservations), 511 Albany Post Rd, is the nation's first Presidential Library and the only one that was ever put to use by a sitting president.

Roosevelt came from a prominent and wealthy Hudson Valley family, but the former governor of New York made his mark with his promise of a New Deal to help bring the country out of the tailspin of the 1930s Great Depression. Several exhibits at the museum highlight these relief programs, along with exhibits about Pearl Harbor and America's entry into WWII.

The museum features old photos, FDR's voice on tape (from the fireside chats and several speeches), a special wing in memory of Eleanor Roosevelt and FDR's famous 1936 Ford Phaeton car – equipped with special hand controls so he could drive despite the restricted mobility caused by his bought with polio. Roosevelt's White House Desk is also here, supposedly just as he left it on his last day at work in 1945, less than a year after he was elected to a record fourth term as president.

The museum is open daily April to October from 9 am to 6 pm and November to March from 9 am to 5 pm. Admission is $10 for adults and free for children under 17.

Eleanor Roosevelt National Historic Site

Better known as **Val-Kill**, Dutch for 'Valley Stream,' (☎ 845-229-9115, 800-967-2283 for reservations), this site is 2 miles east of Hyde Park. Eleanor herself used to make the drive frequently, but townspeople apparently pulled over to the curb quickly when she came by – not so much out of their respect and admiration for the popular First Lady, but rather due to their knowledge of her erratic driving habits.

Eleanor Roosevelt used Val-Kill as a retreat from the main house at Hyde Park,

Eleanor Roosevelt

in part to pursue her own interests and maintain her own identity. The cottage, as she called it, was her own place – not FDR's and not his mother's. After the president's death, Eleanor made this her permanent home. The grounds are dotted with sugar maple and pine trees, and a road leads to the cottage from the entrance off Route 9G.

The first impression of the cottage is how unpretentious it is. Unlike many of the famous residences up and down the Hudson, Val-Kill was not meant to impress anyone; comfort was a priority, and you see it immediately in the comfortable and non-matching furniture, the everyday chinaware and the plain restaurant water glasses. This was the dinnerware she used to entertain statesmen, kings and queens and the local students she invited for dinner.

Eleanor was involved in human rights before the term was coined, and she helped establish the International Declaration of Human Rights, earning her the designation 'first lady of the world.' Instead of great works of art, the wood-paneled walls of the cottage are crammed with family photos.

Val-Kill is open daily from May through October and weekends only in April, November and December. Admission is $5.

Vanderbilt Mansion National Historic Site

This mansion (☎ 845-229-9115, 800-967-2283) is about 2 miles north of Hyde Park on Route 9. It's another valley spectacle of wealth and lavish architecture in the beaux arts style – an eclectic mix of classical Greek, Roman and Baroque lines. Country palaces like the Vanderbilt Mansion are all the more amazing when you realize they were essentially weekend or seasonal getaways – even though they resemble old banks, post offices or libraries. The mansion is open daily 9 am to 5pm. Admission is $8 for adults, and children younger than 17 are admitted for free.

Mills Mansion & State Park

About 5 miles north of Hyde Park on Albany Post Rd (Route 9) in Staatsburg, Mills Mansion (☎ 845-889-8851) is an updated Greek Revival-style building with requisite white columns in front. It was built in 1832 and remodeled in 1896. This is no ordinary addition – it's ostentatious in the extreme. There are guided house tours every half-hour (otherwise, you'd get lost amid the 65 rooms). The palatial grounds at Mills Mansion are open all year. The mansion is open from April to early September Wednesday through Saturday from 10 am to 5 pm and Sunday from noon to 5 pm; and again from mid-September to the end of October Wednesday to Sunday from noon to 5 pm. Admission is $3/2/1 for adults/seniors/children (ages five to 12).

About 2 miles from the entrance to Mills Mansion, the Mills-Norrie State Park (☎ 845-889-4646), on Old Post Rd, is 1000 acres and has camping, a marina, a boat launch, bicycle paths, sledding, cross-country skiing, nature trails and museum. It's open dawn to dusk. Camping costs $13 per night, cabins $234 per week. At the park, **Norrie Point Environmental Site** (☎ 845-889-4830) has an aquarium that replicates conditions of the Hudson River, a museum of New York State wildlife and nature trails.

Places to Eat

The *Culinary Institute of America* (☎ 845-471-6608) must bear the nickname of CIA, but this is the best student cooking you'll find, and the institute has a solid reputation in the region. Reservations are recommended for the four restaurants on the campus – the Italian *Caterina de Medici* and French *Escoffier*, as well as the *American Bounty* and *St Andrew's Café*, which is the least formal (and least expensive) of the bunch and where you have the best chance of getting a good meal without a reservation. Lunch is served from 11:30 am to 1 pm sharp, and dinner is served from 6:30 to 8:30 pm sharp. Escoffier and American Bounty are open Tuesday through Saturday, Caterina and St. Andrew's Café are open Monday through Friday. The newest addition to CIA's spread is the informal *Apple Pie Bakery and Café*, a student-staffed eatery open Monday to Friday from 8 am to 8 pm. It maintains a website (www.ciachef.edu).

The menu at the busy art-deco *Eveready Diner* (☎ 845-229-8100), on Route 9 between Poughkeepsie and Hyde Park, has a bit of everything at reasonable prices. Nearby is the *Hyde Park Brewing Company* (☎ 845-229-8277), with a selection of microbeers and pub fare.

RHINEBECK

Rhinebeck is one of the prettier villages along the Hudson and was once a well-known stagecoach stop. It's probably the only town in the valley to sport both a New Age bookstore and a cigar shop on the same street. The town also boasts the famous Beekman Arms, America's oldest continuously operating inn. Rates have changed over the years, and a sign in the lobby recalls another era:

Lodging 3 pence
With breakfast, 4 pence
Only 5 lodgers to a bed
No boots can be worn in bed.

The **Old Rhinebeck Aerodrome** (☎ 845-758-8610), on Stone Church Rd, between Rhinebeck and Red Hook, is a combination museum and air-show with vintage planes from WW1; you can even take a ride in an open cockpit plane for $30, but you have to provide your own scarf. It is open daily mid-May through October from 10 am to 5 pm. Weekend airshows at 2:30 pm from mid-June through mid-October. Admission is $10 for adults and $5 for children (ages six to 10). Weekday (non-airshow) admission is $5 for adults and $3 for children.

Places to Stay & Eat

Beekman Arms (☎ 845-876-7077, 6387 Mill St), Route 9 at the intersection of Route 308 in the middle of town, got its start in 1766 and has been expanded with succeeding generations. Rates are $85 to $110 for a room in the main building. The two adjacent suites go for $135 a night, but expect to pay about $10 more during the fall foliage season, from the end of September until the end of October (or until all the leaves drop). From May through October, there is generally a two-night minimum stay.

The restaurant adjacent to the lobby is a very good and rather expensive dining spot. Its specialty is cedar plank salmon with garlic mashed potatoes. Entrees begin at $20. The atmosphere is friendly, dimly lit and woodsy.

The *Cripple Creek Restaurant* (☎ 845-876-4355, 22 Garden St) offers American regional cuisine, a long bar with an international flavor, classical music and art work (check out the Chagall on the wall). It is open daily (except Tuesday) for lunch and dinner, with main dishes costing $15 to $20.

Calico Restaurant & Patisserie (☎ 845-876-2749, 9 Mill St/Route 9) has the best pastries in a town that likes pastries. It is open Wednesday through Sunday for breakfast, lunch and dinner. *Blondie's Café* (☎ 845-876-7271, 34 East Market St) is a popular breakfast and lunch spot.

NORTH OF RHINEBECK

Red Hook is a small community hidden among the winding roads and greens, about 5 miles north of Rhinebeck via Route 9. It offers a few B&Bs and several restaurants. Another interesting village is Annandale-on-Hudson, which is just west of Red Hook on Route 9G. This town is home to Bard College and the impressive Montgomery Place mansion.

Bard College

Located on Route 9G near Montgomery Place is Bard College's 600-acre campus. It was founded in 1860 as a school for men, though today it is coed and best known for its devotion to the creative arts. The Avery Center for the Arts and the Edith C Blum Art Institute both feature exhibits that change throughout the year.

On campus, visitors can see contemporary arts at the Center for Curatorial Studies Museum, musical performances, film festivals and various special events, such as the acclaimed Bard Musical Festival (☎ 845-758-7410) in mid-August.

Montgomery Place

In Annandale-on-Hudson, you'll find this 1805 neo-classical riverside villa (☎ 845-758-5461), which is impressive, but the grounds are among the prettiest of any of the great estates. Among the 434 acres are gardens, a waterfall, walking trails, and views of the Catskill Mountains and the Hudson River. It is open from April to October Wednesday to Monday 10 am to 5 pm; weekends in November from 10 am to 4:30 pm; and the first two weekends in December from noon to 5 pm. Admission is $6/5/3 for adults/seniors/children (ages six to 17); $3 for a grounds pass. Montgomery Place is north of Rhinebeck, just west of Route 9G on River Rd, before the entrance to Bard College.

Clermont State Historic Site

Between Annandale-on-Hudson and Germantown off Route 9G, this site (☎ 518-537-4240) is the early-18th-century home of the Robert Livingston family; part of the attraction here is the history of the home and its occupants. The original manor was burned to the ground by the British during the Revolutionary War, but rebuilt soon after. Born in Scotland, the Livingstons made a fortune in the new nation, and a great grandson, Robert R Livingston, was a delegate to the Continental Congress that produced the Declaration of Independence. He also negotiated the Louisiana Purchase of 1803 from Napoleon for Thomas Jefferson. In Paris he also met and became partners with Robert Fulton, who was busy working on a contraption called a steamboat. In 1807, the first steamboat, *North River*, made its appearance on the Hudson River. Later, it was called *Clermont*.

The house is Georgian in style, and original furnishings are on view. The grounds, which extend down to the river, offer a fine view of the Catskill Mountains across the river. The grounds are open daily all year from 8:30 am to sunset. The mansion and visitors' center are open from mid-April through October, Wednesday to Sunday from 10 am to 5 pm. Admission is free.

Places to Stay & Eat

In Red Hook, *Grand Duchess B&B* (☎ 845-758-5818) is a quiet and elegant spot with rooms from $85 to $125. Nearby, *Santa Fe Restaurant* (☎ 845-757-4100, 52 Broadway), west of Red Hook in the one-block village of Tivoli, is a good Cal-Mex place (and a genuine cut above the spaghetti-sauce diners with Mexican names that abound on the East Coast). Sante Fe is open for dinner nightly (except Monday), and most of the regional items cost $6 to $12.

Across the street in Tivoli, check out *Café Pongo* (☎ 845-757-4403, 69 Broadway), an excellent dinner spot and late-night Bard hangout, with homemade pastas and bakery goods. Dinner items range from pasta and seared greens ($10) to lamb stew ($13). It is open for dinner from 5:30 to 10 pm and is closed Monday. A $10 brunch is served on Saturday and Sunday, and it goes from 9 am to 3 pm.

MILLBROOK & AROUND

Millbrook lies east of the Hudson in the Taconic Region, midway between the river and the Connecticut border on Route 44. The area has long been an upscale alternative to the Hamptons in Long Island, and there's a privileged, old-money feel about the area. A maze of backroad retreats, riding trails and genteel country homes seem to appear and disappear among the winding country roads. Nearby Route 22, which runs north-south near the Connecticut and Massachusetts borders, is also one of the state's most bucolic corridors, dotted with farms and pastures, antique stores and blue-plate family diners.

Millbrook itself is as pretty a little town as you'll find, complete with a village green, shiny fire station and spiffy Main St diner. This is a town with a center, and it's an easy place to linger. The area counts among its more famous visitors one Timothy Leary, who spent some of his early LSD-experimenting days around Millbrook at the nearby Hitchcock estate. Some of the townsfolk were scandalized, but it's hard to tell these days if they're bragging or if they're complaining.

Innisfree Garden

This garden (☎ 845-677-8000), on Tyrell Rd, is one of the most beautiful in the valley – and there are many. When the great Irish poet William Butler Yeats wrote 'The Lake Isle of Innisfree,' he described a spot in the imagination that is always alive. The 200-acre garden here was designed by Walter Beck, who designed a series of cup gardens, with terraces, streams and stones arranged in meticulous fashion, all of which comes to a delicate rest on the edge of Tyrell Lake – all reminiscent of Yeats' 1893 poem, part of which reads:

And I shall have some peace there,
for peace comes dropping slow,
Dropping from the veils of the morning
to where the cricket sings…

Innisfree is open from May through October, Wednesday to Friday from 10 am to 4 pm, and Saturday and Sunday from 11 am to 5 pm. Admission is $2 and $3 on weekends. To find Innisfree from Millbrook, head west on Route 44 at the traffic light, and turn left on Tyrell Rd and follow the signs.

Institute of Ecosystem Studies

This center for the study of ecology is between the Taconic State Parkway and the town of Millbrook, just off Route 44A where a sign will point the way. The institute is a combination arboretum, gardening-education and wetland-ecology center. In addition to being a lovely spot to walk through, you can sign up for courses that last from one day or weekend to a week or six weeks. Courses include Natural Science Illustrating and Drawing in the Greenhouse. There are also canoe excursion trips to study wetland ecology, as well as other trips; these cost $30 to $50 for half and full-day trips.

The arboretum is open October to April Monday to Saturday from 9 am to 4 pm and Sunday from 1 to 4 pm; May to September, the hours extend to 6 pm. The greenhouse closes at 3:30 pm all year. Call for more information (☎ 845-677-5359), or write for a brochure: Institute of Ecosystem Studies, Box R, Millbrook, NY 12545.

James Baird State Park

This park (☎ 845-452-1489), 122 Freedom Rd, off the Taconic State Parkway in Pleasant Valley, is about a 10-minute drive southwest from the Millbrook area, and it's a great day-use park (no camping). It's popular for short hiking, picnicking and biking in the summertime; a nature center is open Friday, Saturday and Sunday during July and August. From mid-June through October there is a popular farmers' market and concert series on Sunday from 1 to 5 pm. Winter activities include cross-country skiing (over the golf course) and getting warm by the fireplace at *Restaurant in the Park* (☎ 845-473-0744), which is open weekends from 9 am to 6 pm. Park admission is free.

Places to Stay

Cottonwood Motel (☎ 845-677-3283), on Route 44 just outside town, is a sparkling white motel, set back from the road a comfortable distance; room rates are $105 to $145.

Mill at Bloomvale Falls B&B (☎ 845-266-4234) is 3 miles west of Millbrook at the junction of Routes 82 and 13. Look for a small wood sign announcing the Mill, which is an 18th-century stone cider mill that used the adjacent falls for power. At night, the only sound you hear is the rushing water; sleep comes quickly here. You can also borrow the house canoe to explore the stream. There are four rooms sharing two baths. Prices (including a fine breakfast, with apple muffins) are $85 to $115. The Mill is open from the end of May through November, and there is a two night minimum on weekends.

Cat in Your Lap B&B (☎ *845-677-3051*) is the cutesy name for another fine B&B right in the village of Millbrook. It's an old Victorian with five rooms divided between the main house and the barn. Prices are similar to the Mill.

Places to Eat

For basic diner fare, try the handsome *Millbrook Diner* (☎ *845-677-5319*) near the village green, an occasional backdrop for TV commercials. The diner's old wooden figurehead is a local landmark. The tables inside are adorned with jukebox units, and the food – especially breakfast – is just right. It is open daily from 6 am to 9 pm.

For pricier and fancier fare, try *Allyn's Restaurant & Café* (☎ *845-677-5888*), on Route 44 about 4 miles east of Millbrook. Dinner main dishes range from $15 to $22, and international is the theme. Allyn's is open Monday, Wednesday and Thursday from 11:30 am to 9:30 pm, Friday and Saturday from 11:30 am to 10:30 pm, and Sunday brunch is served from 11:30 am to 3 pm.

MID-VALLEY FARMS

The Hudson Valley has long been a rich agricultural area. Small farms are abundant, and gardening is a common activity. There are hundreds of local farms, produce stands and 'pick-your-own' farms in the region, though the number of family-run farms is dwindling. Mid- to late summer is the best time to visit, of course, but check on the harvest schedule; depending on the weather, rain and so forth, harvest times vary. Most farms are open daily during the summer.

Greig Farm

This farm (☎ 845-758-1234) occupies the whole of Pitcher Lane in Red Hook, between Routes 9 and 9G. It's a one-stop produce market with a bakery and education center. The pick-your-own system works like this: They give you a container (tray or basket), you pick what you want from the seasonal fruits and vegetables, then you weigh your pickings at the register and

pay wholesale prices. There is also a cut-your-own flower garden, as well as a picnic area and a weekend snack bar.

Popular produce pickings in the mid- to late summer include asparagus, peas, strawberries, blueberries, blackberries, raspberries and a dozen varieties of apples (Empire, Jonathan, Rome, etc) and pumpkins – especially popular in the fall before Halloween.

There are also farm education programs, which are very popular locally; the summer sessions for children fill up by spring, and they don't advertise. If you're visiting the area for several days, you may want to ask about the children's summer day-camp programs. A three-day session for preschool children costs $75 per child; children in grades 1 to 3 can do an additional five-day program for $150; and children in grades 3 to 6 can do five longer days for $210. Greig Farm is open daily April through December from 9 am to 5 pm, though summer hours usually extend to 6 or 7 pm.

Ronnybrook Farm Dairy

This farm (☎ 518-398-6455) is in Ancramdale near the junction of Routes 82 and 199. Ronnybrook's milk, sold in glass bottles, can be found in local stores here, not far from the Massachusetts and Connecticut borders. There are no tours as such, but a telephone call will usually produce an invitation to see a working dairy farm, especially if children are involved.

Keepsake Farms

This is a very good produce market and pick-your-own farm (☎ 845-897-2266), on

Hudson River School of Landscape Painters

The Hudson River school is the name given to the group of landscape painters who made the rural Hudson Valley and the wilderness of the Catskill Mountains across the river an important subject of American art. The expansion and prosperity that came in the first decades of the 19th century – especially after the completion of the Erie Canal in 1825 – gave the country a strong national consciousness, and along with it, the freedom to begin exploring distinctly American (that is, non-European) themes. The new artists shunned popular historical themes along with formal portraiture in favor of scenes from everyday life – romanticized to be sure, but with a detailed realism that was new to the American art scene around New York. Like Washington Irving, author of *The Legend of Sleepy Hollow*, the romantic impulse was at work.

Thomas Doughty was the self-taught founder of the school, but its leading spirit was Thomas Cole, whose detailed landscapes included such canvases as 'Catskill Mountain House' and 'Sunday Morning on the Hudson.' Cole was followed by Asher Durand, John Kensett and Frederick Church (who turned his home at Olana into a 'real' landscape painting). Both Cole and Church injected allegorical elements into their work, but most members of the school worked using a purely representational style, one which some critics found to be uninspired and tedious. By the end of the century, some members of the school seemed to agree, having dispersed to even more spectacular scenery in the American West; Albert Bierstadt, for example, chose the Rocky Mountains as his new inspiration. The school did succeed in elevating the status of landscape painting in the US and in immortalizing the mountain slopes, valleys, streams and falls of the Catskill and Adirondack mountains. Even John James Audubon's famous *Birds of America* bears the influence of the school's detailed recording of nature.

Today, a bright day in the Hudson Valley is sure to bring out a few painters to sit by a quiet riverbank or budding hillside with brush in hand and eye on the same landscapes that inspired their famous predecessors.

E Hook Cross Rd, just south of I-84 and a mile west of the Taconic Parkway (the nearest town is Fishkill). Apples, pumpkin, berries and more are available, but if you are after a certain fruit or vegetable, call ahead to be sure it's harvest time. It is open all year, daily from 9 am to 6 pm; until 5 pm in the winter.

Upper Hudson Valley

The upper Hudson Valley extends roughly from the area east of the Kingston-Rhinecliff Bridge north to the area between Hudson and New Lebanon. This chapter covers only a portion of the upper Hudson Valley. Communities along the west bank of the Hudson, including the town of Kingston, will be found in the Catskills Region chapter.

OLANA

Olana (☎ 518-828-0135) was the home of landscape painter Frederic Edwin Church (1826–1900). Church set out to create a three-dimensional landscape painting using the grounds around his home as a canvas. Church originally planned to build a French chateau on the land he bought in the mid-19th century. But after a two year trip to the Middle East, he changed his plans and commissioned Calvert Vaux to design a villa with influences of Moorish architecture; the Persianesque project was finished in the late 1870s.

Although some of the views are now spoiled by industrial eyesores along the Hudson's west bank, the house and grounds are still breathtaking and the view from the 'front porch' on a summer afternoon resembles some of the large canvases of the Hudson River school of landscape painters.

Olana is open only for guided tours that begin on the hour Wednesday to Sunday from around 10 am to 5 pm (hours vary depending on the season). Call ahead for reservations; tickets ($3/2 for adults/seniors) sell out quickly.

Olana is about 5 miles south of Hudson, across the Hudson River from the town of Catskill. Take the New York State Thruway (I-87) to exit 21, cross the Rip Van Winkle Bridge to Route 9G south. The entrance to Olana is on Route 9G, 1 mile south of the bridge. Look for the sign on the left and go up the hill.

HUDSON

Hudson is a beautiful old town given over to antique shops – the light industry of the Hudson Valley. Hudson is another former whaling village, and the architecture is worth a trip through town. Warren St in particular is part of the classic-Americana downtown of small family-owned businesses selling everything from charming junk to the family jewels. Hudson's other claim to fame is its (former) red-light district, said to be the first in the country.

There's a AAA travel services office (☎ 518-828-4537), 179 Healy Blvd; it is open from 9 am to 5 pm Monday through Friday with later hours (to 7 pm) on Thursday.

American Museum of Firefighting (☎ 845-828-7695), 125 Harry Howard St, is a one-of-a-kind exhibit, with an antique fire apparatus dating from 1731, paintings, old photos and the works. The museum is open daily from 9 am to 4:30 pm, and admission is free.

SHAKER MUSEUM & LIBRARY

About 20 miles from the town of Hudson via Route 66, Old Chatham is home of the Shaker Museum & Library (☎ 518-794-9100), Shaker Museum Rd. Its location, however, must be put in context: It's even closer to the border of Massachusetts, home of the Pilgrims and several early religious movements.

The Shakers were an early experimental communal group, one of many to follow the trail of New England religious migration. The original group, known as the United Society of Believers in Christ's Second Appearing, came from England with Mother Ann Lee in 1774. In 1792, the first Shaker community was established in nearby New Lebanon (NY), near the Massachusetts state line.

The Shakers got their nickname from their love of music and dance, all in the name of religious ritual and harvest celebration. The moniker took hold as word spread of their excited religious services in which members often shook with emotion when seized with the Holy Spirit. The Shakers also had the unique ability to simultaneously entertain the notions of communal living and celibacy.

Even though their numbers have dwindled over the years, their legacy is preserved in the fascinating museum in Old Chatham. It's open daily from May through October, except Tuesday and Wednesday from 10 am to 5 pm. Admission is $8/7/3 for adults/seniors/children (ages eight to 17). The family rate is $14, in the communal tradition.

Catskills Region

Highlights

- Browsing through art galleries on Woodstock's village green
- Taking in the view of the Hudson Valley from Overlook Mountain
- Skiing, hiking and rock climbing in the Shawangunk Mountains near New Paltz
- Spending a mellow afternoon in Bethel, site of the 1969 Woodstock Festival
- Strolling through Kingston's historic Stockade District, a 17th-century Dutch neighborhood

The Catskills, named after the mountain range, refers to an entire region of small towns, farms, resorts, streams and hiking trails north and west of the Hudson Valley. Despite this large territory, even the far reaches of the Catskills are still within a day's drive from New York City; the heart of the area is about 2½ hours north of Manhattan.

Two large rivers border the Catskills, with the Hudson River on the eastern edge and the Delaware River on the southwest border with Pennsylvania. The region's name, bestowed by Dutch immigrants, comes from the Dutch *Katsbergs*, meaning mountain cats, and *kill*, meaning stream. But don't expect to find any mountain cats today.

The Catskill Mountains, which are part of the Appalachian Range, are older than the Adirondacks and more worn, with few peaks over 3000 feet. The tallest are in the north, where excellent downhill and cross-country skiing opportunities attract visitors from throughout the northeastern states. Both the Catskill Mountains and the older Shawangunk Mountains to the southeast are havens for hikers, and numerous trails criss-cross the area.

The Catskills region includes the 1094-sq-mile Catskill Park, 40% of which is publicly owned and protected. Like the Adirondack Forest Preserve, the Catskill Forest Preserve was established in the late 19th century, when the governor of New York signed a law that required these lands 'be forever kept as wild forest lands.' During the same period, developers built deluxe hotels in the southern Catskill Mountains, transforming the area into a popular destination for affluent city dwellers wanting to escape to the wilderness. Most of the hotels have since disappeared, but the site of the most famous one to have burned down – Catskill Mountain House – still attracts hikers.

The southern Catskill foothills (which are actually outside the boundaries of the park) are still home to the remaining 'Borscht Belt' resorts. In their heyday in the 1950s and '60s, these huge resorts were packed with New York's Jewish families drawn here by the tightly scheduled activities, sports, food and 'name' entertainment offered nearly around the clock. Wilderness this was not.

The Catskill Park provides the region with its essential identity. Most towns in the preserved area retain the qualities of small villages, laid out along a single main street. The towns covered in this section form a loop of sorts, beginning at Woodstock, then proceeding west on Route 28 from I-87

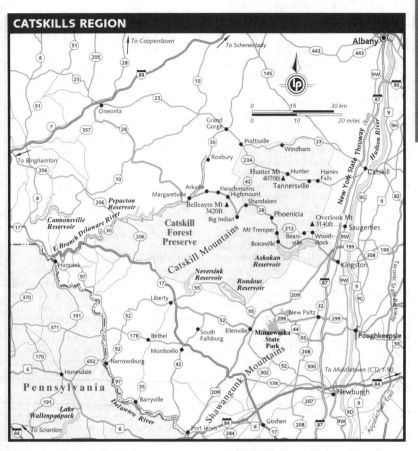

CATSKILLS REGION

through Boiceville, Mt Tremper, Phoenicia, Shandaken, Big Indian, Highmount, Fleischmanns and Arkville. From Arkville, Route 30 travels west to Margaretville and north to Roxbury. At Route 23A, you head east to Hunter, Windham, Tannersville and Haines Falls, completing the loop in the town of Catskill. Restaurants and lodgings are scattered throughout the area.

The west bank of the Hudson River includes the towns of Catskill, Saugerties and Kingston, all along Route 9W; and the village of New Paltz, in the foothills of the Shawangunk Mountains near the junction of I-87 and Route 299. Each lies outside the Catskill Forest Preserve.

The area between the Pennsylvania border and the preserve contains the famous Catskill resorts; the Borscht Belt is concentrated among the towns of Liberty, Monticello and Ellenville. Along the Delaware River at the Pennsylvania border, Narrowsburg and Barryville are popular spots for white-water rafting and hiking.

INFORMATION

The Ulster County Information Office (☎ 800-342-5826) offers information on

Kingston, Woodstock, Saugerties, Boiceville, Mt Tremper, Phoenicia, Shandaken and Big Indian.

The Greene County Promotion & Tourism Department (☎ 800-355-2287) covers Hunter, Windham, Tannersville, Haines Falls and Catskill.

The Delaware County Tourism Board (☎ 800-642-4443) handles Fleischmanns, Arkville, Margaretville and Roxbury.

The Sullivan County Info Center (☎ 800-882-2287) has information on the large resorts in the southern Catskill foothills.

The New York State Dept of Environmental Conservation (DEC; ☎ 518-357-2234), 1150 N Westcott Rd, Schenectady, NY 12306, is an excellent source of information about the region's ecology.

For entertainment information, pick up one of the weekly papers: the *Catskill Mountain News*, the *Woodstock Times* and the *Mountain Eagle*.

An excellent book on the Catskills region is *Route 28: A Mile-by-Mile Guide to New York's Adventure Route* by Rob Scharpf (Big Pencil Publishing; Melbourne, Florida). For a complete and personal account of Woodstock history, read *Woodstock Gatherings: Apple Bites & Ashes* by Jean Lasher Gaede.

OUTDOOR ACTIVITIES

Most of the towns mentioned here are detailed later in this chapter.

Hiking

There is excellent hiking throughout the Catskills. Two of the most popular areas are outside Haines Falls. High Land Flings (☎ 800-453-6665) leads guided hiking trips and offers walking tours of several towns.

Good maps are available from:

New York/New Jersey Trail Conference (☎ 212-685-9699) 232 Madison Ave, suite 802, New York, NY 10116

US Geological Survey (USGS) Map Distribution Branch Box 25286, Denver, CO 80225

Timely Discount Topos (☎ 800-821-7609)

Catskill Center for Conservation & Development (☎ 845-586-2611, 586-3044) Arkville, NY 12406

Jimapco (☎ 518-899-5091) PO Box 1137, Clifton Park, NY 12065

Delorme Mapping (☎ 800-335-6763) 276 US Route 1, Freeport, ME 04032

The Catskill Center for Conservation & Development is devoted to protecting and preserving the Catskill environment and is an excellent source of information. The center's Erph House in Arkville (see the Route 28 to Margaretville section, later in this chapter) hosts cultural events and sells copies of the Catskill history book, *Kaaterskill: From the Catskill Mountain House to the Hudson River School*, published in 1993 by Black Dome Press Corp (☎ 518-734-6357), RR1, Box 422, Hensonville, NY 12439.

Backcountry Publications (☎ 802-457-1049), PO Box 175, Woodstock, VT 05901, also publishes detailed guides.

Downhill Skiing

The northern Catskills offer some of the best downhill skiing in the state. Lift ticket prices vary according to the day of the week (children seven to 12 get discount tickets). The resorts below are among the best known:

Belleayre Mountain (☎ 845-254-5600) Highmount, NY; just off Route 28, 37 miles west of I-87 exit 19. Belleayre offers a casual, rustic state park atmosphere. The ski area has a vertical drop of 1340 feet; lift fees are $25 to $33.

Hunter Mountain (☎ 518-263-4223) Hunter, NY; on Route 23A, 20 miles west of I-87 exit 20. It has great ski runs and caters to the party crowd. The vertical drop is 1600 feet; lift fees are $22 to $45.

Ski Windham (☎ 518-734-4300) on Route 23, 25 miles west of I-87 exit 21. Ski Windham is a popular family and singles destination. It has a vertical drop of 1600 feet; lift fees are $34 to $43.

Cross-Country Skiing

The gentle and worn terrain of the Catskills is ideal for cross-country skiing and snowshoeing, another popular winter activity.

Belleayre Mountain (☎ 845-254-5600) Highmount, NY; off Route 28, 37 miles west of I-87 exit 19; 4 miles of trails; free

Villagio Resort (☎ 518-589-5000) Haines Falls, NY; 12 miles west of I-87 exit 21 on Route 23A; 8½ miles of trails; free

GETTING THERE & AWAY
Air
Stewart International Airport, to the south in Newburgh, is 20 miles from New Paltz and is the nearest airport to the region. Slightly further and to the north is Albany International Airport (60 miles from New Paltz).

Bus
Adirondack Trailways (☎ 800-225-6815) offers daily service to many Catskill area towns, including Kingston, Saugerties, Catskill, Hunter and Woodstock, as well as to Boston, New York City and Albany. The Ulster County Rural Transportation (UCRT; ☎ 845-340-3333) offers local bus transportation to Kingston, New Paltz, Woodstock, Ellenville and Saugarties.

Train
Amtrak (☎ 800-872-7245) runs north and south along the east bank of the Hudson River. Two stations are near the Catskills: Rhinecliff, across the river from Kingston, and Hudson, opposite the town of Catskill. One-way/roundtrip fares to Kingston are $24/36 from New York and $48/91 from Montreal. Both locations offer bus service around the region via Adirondack Trailways.

Car & Motorcycle
Part of the Catskills' charm is the clustering of small villages and towns, most of which are easily accessible by car or motorcycle.

Eastern Catskills

From south to north, the towns of New Paltz, Kingston and Catskill can easily be reached by car or motorcycle from I-87 (New York State Thruway).

NEW PALTZ
New Paltz (population 11,000), 9 miles west of the banks of the Hudson River, is a recreation center and home to a branch of the State University of New York (SUNY-New Paltz). From I-87 exit 18, head west on Route 299.

The New Paltz Chamber of Commerce (☎ 845-255-0243), at 259 Main St, is open 10 am to 4:30 pm weekdays.

Founded by French Huguenot religious refugees in 1677, New Paltz still shows off its original stone architecture on **Huguenot St**. The difference between Huguenot St and Main St is easy to spot; about 300 years of architecture separate the elegant old stone facades on Huguenot St from the typical roadside shops and franchises along Main St (Route 299).

To get the flavor of the original village, visit the Huguenot Street Visitors' Center (☎ 845-255-1889, 255-1660), 6 Broadhead Ave, which conducts tours of six preserved stone structures from June until October 31. Tours take place 9:30 am to 4 pm Tuesday through Sunday. Guides lead a rather thorough two-hour tour twice daily for $7/3.50 adults/children; a one-hour tour costs half that much.

About 4 miles outside New Paltz, the **Mohonk Mountain House** (☎ 845-255-1000), 1000 Mountain Rest Rd, reminds some of California's lavish Hearst Castle. Even if you don't choose to stay at this expensive resort, the National Historic Landmark is worth visiting. The resort grounds are popular with day hikers in the summer and snowshoers in the winter. Day passes cost $9/7 for adults/children. From Route 299/Main St in New Paltz turn right immediately after crossing the bridge over the Wallkill River and follow the 'Mohonk' signs.

New Paltz is also a center for outdoor recreation, including rock climbing at nearby Minnewaska State Park and the Mohonk Preserve. **Minnewaska State Park** (☎ 845-255-0752) is open year-round, and offers cross-country skiing (groomed trails), snowshoeing, biking (40 miles of trails), hiking, picnicking and swimming in the summer. It's very popular for rock climbing as well as bouldering (climbing without ropes). There is no camping and no snowmobiling. Entrance fees are $5 per car in the summer, and $6 per person ($4 for children under 12) in the winter. Take Route 299 west to Route 44/55, go west for 4 miles to the marked entrance.

Mohonk Preserve (☎ 845-255-0243) is a full-time conservation, education, research and recreation center situated on 6400 acres of woods. There is no camping allowed, but there is picnicking, great rock climbing, hiking, biking and cross-country skiing (on ungroomed trails). A visitors' center has interactive weather exhibits for children.

The preserve is open year-round and entrance costs $5/7 for day/weekends and holiday use. Take Route 299 west and go right (west) on Routes 44/55, to the entrance, which is a half mile on the right.

By rail or bus, Amtrak and MetroNorth trains arrive and depart from Poughkeepsie, while Adirondack Trailways coaches serve New Paltz directly (Albany to New Paltz, $12/23).

Places to Stay & Eat

Several chains are just east of town, including Super 8 and Econo Lodge. *Days Inn* (☎ *845-883-7373, 601 Main St*) is typical of the bunch, with most single/double rooms in the $60 to $90 range.

If you're looking for something more upscale, try the *Mohonk Mountain House* (☎ *845-255-1000, 1000 Mountain Rest Rd*). Room rates begin at $300. Hotel guests can sign up for a variety of events, ranging from music workshops to weekend language classes.

Foley's Square Public House (☎ *845-255-9718, 107 Main St*) is a convivial spot for subs, burgers, tap beer, and TV sports.

KINGSTON

Like most Hudson River communities on the eastern edge of the Catskills, Kingston (population 23,000) is built on a fairly steep slope that ends at the waterfront, where a ubiquitous maritime theme dominates what used to be an early Dutch trading post. It was the state capital for a brief period in 1777, when New York's provincial congress was driven from New York City by the British. A gateway to the Catskills, the region's largest town is laid out along pleasant narrow streets with old stone homes.

The best source of information, including free walking tour brochures, is the Kingston Urban Cultural Park Visitors' Center, which maintains two locations: downtown, in the Rondout Historic District (☎ 845-331-7517, 800-331-1518) at 20 Broadway; and in the Stockade District (☎ 845-331-9506) at 308 Clinton Ave. Both are open weekdays 9 am to 5 pm year-round, and weekends 11 am to 5 pm May through October.

Adirondack Trailways stops at Dietz Stadium Diner (☎ 845-331-0744), 400 Washington Ave. For those coming by car, Kingston is at exit 19 on I-87, about 90 miles north of New York City. Plan on a two-hour drive from Manhattan.

Things to See & Do

At the southeastern end of town, you'll find the interesting **Rondout Historic District**. Once a bustling 19th-century terminal port of the Delaware and Hudson Canal, the Rondout today is a revived neighborhood and shopping area, boasting restaurants and exhibits.

Within the historic district, **Trolley Museum of New York** (☎ 845-331-3399), 98 E Strand St, offers rides on old trolleys ($3/2 for adults/children). And across the street at 1 Rondout Landing, the **Hudson River Maritime Center** (☎ 845-338-0071) celebrates the history of life on the river. The center is open every day (except Tuesday) from 11 am to 5 pm early May through October. Admission is $2/1 for adults/children. River excursions on the Hudson operate daily from Rondout Landing during the summer. To get to the Rondout, take Route 587 from I-87 to Route 28 (Broadway), which runs through the heart of the district.

Another historic Kingston neighborhood is the 17th-century district called the **Stockade**, a fortification built by Peter Stuyvesant. An early senate house, the **Senate House State Historic Site** (☎ 845-338-2786), 296 Fair St, is here, along with **Beavier House** and other historic homes. Senate House is open April 15 to October 31, Wednesday through Saturday from 10 am to 5 pm and Sunday 1 to 5 pm. The Senate House tour costs $3/2/1 for adults/seniors/children (ages five to 12).

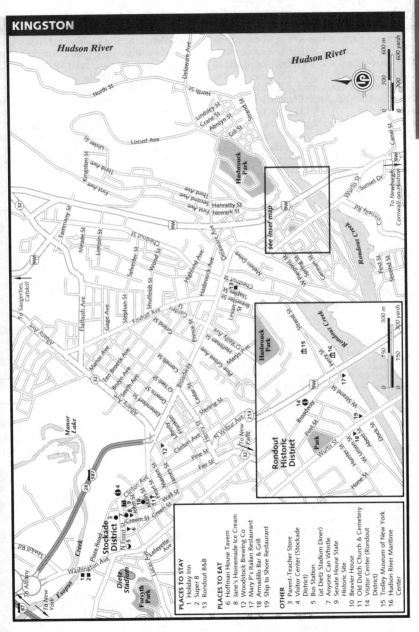

KINGSTON

Hudson River

Hudson River

see inset map

Rondout Historic District

Stockade District

PLACES TO STAY
1   Holiday Inn
2   Super 8
13 Rondout B&B

PLACES TO EAT
6   Hoffman House Tavern
8   Jane's Homemade Ice Cream
8   Woodstock Brewing Co
12 Mary P's Italian Restaurant
17 Armadillo Bar & Grill
19 Ship to Shore Restaurant

OTHER
3   Parent-Teacher Store
4   Visitor Center (Stockade District)
5   Bus Station (at Dietz Stadium Diner)
7   Anyone Can Whistle
9   Senate House State Historic Site
10 Beaver House
11 Old Dutch Church & Cemetery
14 Visitor Center (Rondout District)
15 Trolley Museum of New York
16 Hudson River Maritime Center

In addition, a guided walking tour is offered the first Saturday of the month, May through October. The cost is $3 for adults and $1 for children under 16. You can also do a self-guided tour for free; information is available from either location of the Kingston Urban Cultural Park Visitors' Center. The **Old Dutch Church & Cemetery** (☎ 845-338-6759), on Main St, is free and open Monday to Friday from 9 am to 4 pm. To find the Stockade, take Washington Ave from the traffic circle after exiting I-87 (exit 19), drive south a few blocks, and then make a left on Main St.

Places to Stay & Eat

The **Holiday Inn** (☎ 845-338-0400, 503 Washington Ave), just off I-87 at exit 19, boasts a large indoor atrium with a whirlpool. Single/double rooms are $109/139 from late May to mid-October; rates are about 15% less during the winter. A **Super 8** (☎ 845-338-3078, 800-800-8000, 487 Washington Ave) motel is next to the Holiday Inn, with rooms in the $65 to $85 range.

Rondout B&B (☎ 845-331-8144, 88 W Chester St) is a classy Federal-style home with broad porches, two private rooms ($100 per night) and two rooms with shared bath ($85).

Kingston offers a number of restaurant choices. In the Stockade, try a scoop of **Jane's Homemade Ice Cream** (☎ 845-338-8315, 305 Wall St). A short walk away, the **Hoffman House Tavern** (☎ 845-338-2626, 94 N Front St) is housed in a sturdy 1711 stone building, now an official historic landmark. It has a full bar and serves good pub food.

In the Rondout, the **Armadillo Bar & Grill** (☎ 845-339-1550, 97 Abeel St) serves a good New York version of Tex-Mex food. It's open Tuesday through Sunday from 11:30 am to 11 pm.

Across the street, **Ship to Shore Restaurant** (☎ 845-334-8887, 15 W Strand St), is a popular local eatery with fishnet decor. The basic food is good, with burgers for $3 to $6, seafood salad for $4 and great fish-and-chips for $4. It's open daily from 11 am to 10 pm.

Mary P's Italian Restaurant (☎ 845-338-0116, 1 Broadway), also in the Rondout,

serves northern Italian fare. Weather permitting, sit on the garden deck overlooking a small inlet of the Hudson River. Pasta, veal and seafood dishes are priced around $16, with daily lunch items around $10. It's open daily from 11 am to 10 pm.

The **Woodstock Brewing Co** (☎ 845-331-2810, 20 James St) is not in Woodstock, but in Kingston, in an 1830 brick structure. The brewery conducts free tours that include samples of freshly made beer. A restaurant is planned to open by summer (food would be pub fare, sandwiches, salads, etc).

Shopping

Kingston touts its history, but its shops are up-to-date. One of the most modern-minded is the Parent-Teacher Store (☎ 845-339-1442), 63 N Front St, which sells books, games and kits for children curious about science, music, art and history. It's open Monday to Thursday from 10 am to 6 pm, Friday from 10 am to 7 pm, Saturday from 10 am to 5 pm and Sunday from noon to 4 pm.

Outback Antiques (☎ 845-331-4481), 72 Hurley Ave, resembles a musty old barn on the outside but is really a charming vintage clothing store inside, complete with lace pillows. You may have to ring the doorbell to rouse the owners even during regular hours. The shop's open 10 am to 5 pm daily except Tuesday.

Anyone Can Whistle (☎ 845-331-7728), 323 Wall St in the heart of the Stockade, is a fascinating try-anything-you-want music and musical arts store. It's open daily from 10 am to 6 pm.

CATSKILL

About 15 miles north of Kingston on I-87, you'll reach the town of Catskill (population 4700), where the Hudson-River-school painter Thomas Cole lived during the 19th century, when the town and surrounding area were more scenic.

Today, most of Catskill's attractions appeal to children. You'll come upon them, one after the other, west of town on Route 32. A Wild West re-creation, **Carson City & Indian Village** (☎ 518-678-5518, 800-622-

2489) features gun shows, country music shows, Native American exhibits and train and stagecoach holdups. Admission is $11/7 for adults/children.

Clyde Peeling's Reptileland (☎ 518-678-3557), Route 32, is the home of pythons, crocodiles and cobras – in other words, it's not for the thin-skinned. It's open Memorial Day to Labor Day, from 10 am to 6 pm, and then on weekends until Columbus Day. Admission is $6.50/4.25 for adults/children.

Catskill Game Farm (☎ 518-678-9595), 2 miles south of Clyde Peeling's Reptileland on Route 32, has more of a zoological bent than its carnival-like neighbor. It started in the 1930s as a conservation project to protect rare and endangered animals from around the world, both tame and wild. Today, the family-operated complex tends to approximately 2000 animals and runs a successful nursery that breeds wild horses from Mongolia. It is open daily 10 am to 6 pm from the end of May (Memorial Day) to the beginning of September (Labor Day), and on weekends 10 am to 6 pm for all of May and September and the first two weeks of October. It is closed the rest of the year. Daily animal shows are part of the schedule. Admission is $13.95/9.95 for adults/children ages four to 11. The farm's several amusement rides cost 90¢ each.

Northern Catskills

Although much of the central and southern Catskills serve as the nearest weekend getaway from New York City, the northern 'Cats' feels more remote and bucolic. It serves as a watershed, recreation area, and ecological and scenic reserve. Much of the land here (Greene county and the northernmost parts of Sullivan and Ulster counties) is part of the Catskill Forest Preserve, protected in the famous 1894 'forever wild' clause of the New York State Constitution. Tannersville, Haines Falls and North-South Lake are popular destinations here. The area is known for being rugged, with waterfalls, cliffs, fire towers, old farmsteads, bears, rattlesnakes and rare plant species.

WOODSTOCK

Ten miles northwest of the Catskills' largest town of Kingston, Woodstock (population 6200) is best known for the 1960s event that actually didn't happen here. The Woodstock music festival really took place more than 40 miles southwest near the town of Bethel, where a simple roadside plaque marks the spot.

Woodstock today is not so simple. This attractive village is a charming cross between quaint and hip. You will still see a few tie-dyed locals who look like they're in a 1960s time warp, and a handful of shops and businesses retain the names of that magical era: Sunflower, Hibiscus, Pegasus, Once Possessed, Pondicherry and Not Fade Away (from the Buddy Holly song recorded in 1958).

But Woodstock's reputation as a legitimate arts colony goes back to the early 1900s, and it's fast returning to its New England small-town roots. Most of today's residents appear to be artists, musicians or well-heeled folks from downstate who own summer homes here. Chain stores are virtually nonexistent, and many quality one-of-a-kind shops line both sides of Tinker St and Mill Hill Rd. With art galleries, fashionable clothing stores, theatrical and musical productions – not to mention a good selection of places to stay and eat – Woodstock should be at the top of your list of towns to visit in the region.

Seeing Woodstock means strolling about town, enjoying the friendly feel of the place, browsing through the galleries and crystal shops. It also means people-watching. The small village green at the center of town offers the perfect vantage point. If you happen to be in town on Christmas Eve, you'll be one of the first to know how Santa Claus arrives on the village green. This is the best-kept secret around, and it's never dull; Santa's been known to travel by camel and hang-glider – on separate occasions, of course.

Information

The active Woodstock Chamber of Commerce (☎ 845-679-6234) has an enthusiastic

NEW YORK

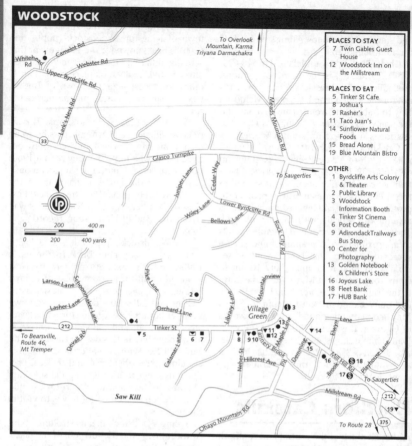

WOODSTOCK

To Overlook
Mountain, Karma
Triyana Darmachakra

PLACES TO STAY
7   Twin Gables Guest
    House
12 Woodstock Inn on
    the Millstream

PLACES TO EAT
5   Tinker St Cafe
8   Joshua's
9   Rasher's
11 Taco Juan's
14 Sunflower Natural
    Foods
15 Bread Alone
19 Blue Mountain Bistro

OTHER
1   Byrdcliffe Arts Colony
    & Theater
2   Public Library
3   Woodstock
    Information Booth
4   Tinker St Cinema
6   Post Office
9   AdirondackTrailways
    Bus Stop
10 Center for
    Photography
13 Golden Notebook
    & Children's Store
16 Joyous Lake
18 Fleet Bank
17 HUB Bank

voice-mail system that will record your requests for information. The chamber maintains a website at www.woodstock-online.com. For more information, you can also stop at Woodstock's two staffed information booths: on Rock City Rd, just north of the village green, and at the junction of Tinker St and Mill Hill Rd on Route 212.

The HUB Bank (formerly First Union Bank), Route 212 (Mill Hill Rd), and Fleet Bank, Bradley Meadows, both have ATMs.

The post office is on Tinker St.

The Golden Notebook (☎ 845-679-8000, www.goldennotebook.com), on Tinker St, is

an excellent small bookstore with helpful staff who are knowledgeable about local attractions. It's open weekdays from 10:30 am to 7 pm, Saturday from 10:30 am to 9 pm and Sunday from 10:30 am to 6 pm. Next door is a children's store, which is an extension of the bookshop.

The public library (with an excellent reference section on art and local history) is at 5 Library Lane. The library is closed Sunday and Monday and is open Tuesday through Saturday 10 am to 5 pm.

Woodstock has its own radio station, WDST (100.1 FM), which plays everything from classical to folk to rock and roll and is known locally as Radio Woodstock. The *Woodstock Times* is a weekly newspaper (which is published on Thursday) with regional news and comprehensive local events information.

Things to See & Do

Within town, the attractions include the **Center for Photography**, (☎ 845-679-9957), 59 Tinker St, which offers contemporary and historical exhibits, lectures and photography workshops year-round. This attractive and serious gallery is open noon to 5 pm Wednesday through Sunday; it's closed in January and February. Admission is free.

The little **Tinker St Cinema** (☎ 845-679-6608) has a loyal following, and for good reason. It features the best in recent and classic international and independent film, with an occasional nod to a good commercial film.

North of town, you'll find the **Byrdcliffe Arts Colony & Theater** (☎ 845-679-2079), a 1500-acre complex founded in 1902 by American artists Bolton Brown and Hervey White with the substantial financial backing of Englishman Ralph Radcliffe Whitehead. For generations before the 1969 Woodstock Festival, artists and concertgoers traveled to Byrdcliffe to share their common vision of peace and justice. Their hopeful message

The Woodstock Festivals

About half a million people descended on Max Yasgur's farm in Bethel, New York (40 miles southeast of the town of Woodstock), from August 15 to 17, 1969, for a music festival billed as 'Three Days of Peace & Music.' The lineup of musicians for the Woodstock Festival – Joan Baez; Joe Cocker & the Grease Band; Country Joe & the Fish; Crosby, Stills & Nash; Arlo Guthrie; Richie Havens; Jimi Hendrix; Santana; John Sebastian; Sha-Na-Na; Sly & the Family Stone; Ten Years After; and The Who – has never been matched.

Festival promoters sold tickets for a remarkable $7 for one day and $18 for three days. The entire event cost only $3 million to stage; unfortunately, less than one quarter of the half-million concertgoers paid for admission, and the festival had trouble paying its bills.

Despite numerous setbacks ranging from broken toilets to a serious mud problem after a day of rain (earning the festival its 'Hog Farm' nickname), there were no riots and no violence. It was the most successful hippie gathering in the world. The most violent scene probably occurred when activist Abbie Hoffman ran on stage to make a speech, only to be greeted by The Who's Pete Townshend, who promptly bashed him over the head with his electric guitar. Lucky he didn't run into Jimi Hendrix, who often set his guitar on fire.

If anyone needed to be reminded that the 1990s were not the 1960s, the 1994 Woodstock II Festival did the job. Promoted as a 'commemoration concert' on an 840-acre dairy farm in the nearby town of Saugerties (where the 1969 festival planners had originally hoped to hold their concert), Woodstock II promised 'two more days of Peace and Music.' And it delivered: performers included Aerosmith; Crosby, Stills & Nash; Cypress Hill; Peter Gabriel; Red Hot Chili Peppers; and Spin Doctors. The concert was broadcast on pay-per-view cable, and tickets were $135. The 1994 concert cost $30 million and is still waiting to turn a profit with CD sales. Hundreds of shuttle buses brought folks to the field from parking lots throughout the Hudson Valley, but only 250,000 tickets were sold. Meanwhile, the original 'Woodstock Generation' was at home, waiting for the video.

In 1999, another Woodstock concert happened even farther away in Rome, between Utica and Syracuse. For nostalgia buffs, it was definitely the 'late Roman stage' of Woodstock. The overhyped event took place on a plot of land with ties to the military, which displeased anyone hoping for a speedy return to the past. The concert ended badly, with fights and a bonfire.

was set to music by songwriters and performers, including Pete Seeger; Peter, Paul & Mary; and Louisiana bluesman Leadbelly.

Today, the colony still hosts artist residencies, craft demonstrations, exhibitions and performances at the Byrdcliffe Theater. Performances are announced in the *New York Times* and the local *Woodstock Times*. To get there, take Rock City Rd north from the village green to the Glasco Turnpike, head west to Upper Byrdcliffe Rd, then turn right and head north to the colony.

While you're north of town, you can hike to the top of **Overlook Mountain** for views of the surrounding countryside and the Hudson River. To get to the trail from the village green, drive up Rock City Rd (it turns into Meads Mountain Rd) for 2 miles and park across from the Tibetan monastery Karma Triyana Dharmachakra. Hike up the path from the parking lot 2.4 miles to the top and see what the monks see.

Karma Triyana Dharmachakra, a popular Buddhist center (☎ 845-679-5906), 352 Meads Mountain Rd, regularly offers teachings that range from the introductory to the advanced. Meditation instruction is available by appointment free of charge. Meditation retreats and lectures are also offered year-round.

For more spiritual edification, visit the **Zen Mountain Monastery**, (☎ 845-688-2228), a 200-acre sanctuary on S Plank Rd. Guests and staff maintain the grounds, eat together and meditate. The discipline is fairly rigorous, but it is well worth the investment in time and effort. Retreats of various lengths are offered and can be as short as a weekend. To reach the sanctuary, take Route 212 north from Route 28 to the first four-way intersection and then go left on S Plank Rd and look for the monastery a block up on your right. Or take Route 212 west toward Phoenicia, which is about 10 miles west of Woodstock. Before Route 28 (1/4 mile), turn right at S Plank Rd (by LaDuchess Anne Restaurant) and go 1/8 mile, over the bridge to the monastery on the right.

The landscape sculpture **Opus 40** (☎ 845-246-3400) features 6½ acres of amazing man-made pathways, pools, steps and an obelisk. Creator Harvey Fite, who meticulously carved and set the bluestone from an abandoned quarry, named it Opus 40 because he expected it to take 40 years to finish. That should have been a tip-off; Fite worked on the quarry his entire life. The **Quarryman's Museum** displays many of Fite's tools. It's open 10 am to 4 pm weekdays and noon to 5 pm Sunday, May through October. Admission is $5. Take Route 212 east from Woodstock to County Rd 32 east and look for the signs.

The **Overlook Observatory** (☎ 845-246-4294), on W Saugerties Rd between Saugerties and Woodstock, is the home and workshop of astronomer and writer Bob Berman, who conducts free guided tours of the night sky for small groups by appointment. Individuals can sometimes join a group, but it is essential to call ahead. To get to the observatory from the village green, take Rock City Rd north to Glasco Turnpike. From the turnpike turn onto W Saugerties Rd, go about 5 miles until you see the sign on the left for Bob Berman's house/observatory.

Places to Stay

For campers, the *Saugerties-Woodstock KOA* (☎ 845-246-4089) offers 100 sites at about $20 each. It's open from April to November. From I-87 exit 20, follow Route 212 west for 2¼ miles to the campground.

The *Rip Van Winkle Campground* (☎ 845-246-8334) has 90 sites ($18) and is open from early May to early October. Take Route 212 west 2 miles from I-87 exit 20 and then go half a mile north on County Rd 32 to Blue Mountain Rd.

If you'd rather sleep in a bed, *Twin Gables Guest House* (☎ 845-679-9479, 73 Tinker St) is a good bet at a fair price. The house is right in the middle of town, and the nine nicely furnished rooms are roomy. Singles/doubles with shared bath are $48/60. A double with private bath is $82.

The *Woodstock Inn on the Millstream* (☎ 845-679-8211, 38 Tannery Brook Rd), a block behind Tinker St, is an attractive and quiet motel with weekday/weekend rooms for $69/110, which includes a continental breakfast.

Places to Eat

Tinker St, Woodstock's main street, has an abundance of good restaurants, cafes and bakeries. These include the following, from west to east.

Joshua's (☎ 845-679-5533, 51 Tinker St) serves Middle Eastern and Israeli dishes, as well as bacon and cheese baguette sandwiches (hey, it's Woodstock). The hummus, babaganoush and tabouli are good, along with potato latkes, several pasta dishes and a mixed meat grill of lamb, chicken, shrimp, beef and vegetable; generous portions of food cost $12 to $16.

Rasher's (☎ 845-679-5449, 13 Tinker St), is a favorite for breakfast and lunch, with excellent soups, sandwiches, veggie chili, omelets and bargain lunch specials. It's open weekdays from 8 am to 4 pm and weekends from 8 am to 9 pm.

On the same side of the street, *Taco Juan's* (☎ 845-679-9673, 31 Tinker St) has good knishes, enchiladas and burritos for under $5 and an arty 'psyche-deli' menu on the wall.

If you bear right onto Mill Hill Rd as Tinker St ends, you'll find even more choices. Try *Sunflower Natural Foods* (☎ 845-679-5361), in the small Bradley Meadows Shopping Center on Mill Hill Rd, for a decent selection of health food items, fresh juices and produce. It's open Monday through Saturday from 9 am to 9 pm, Sunday from 10 am to 7 pm.

Bread Alone (☎ 845-679-2108, 22 Mill Hill Rd) is a landmark for bread lovers. Since most folks cannot live by bread alone, though, the shop also offers fine pastries, morning burritos and eggs (in the $2 to $4 range), and several gourmet deli items. Bread Alone is open weekdays from 7:30 am to 5 pm and weekends from 7:30 am to 7 pm.

There are also several excellent restaurants just a short drive from the village of Woodstock. Two miles west of the village green on Route 212 is the small town of Bearsville, where you'll find the *Bear Cafe* (☎ 845-679-5555), serving American and French bistro fare in a rather serene brookside setting. The food is excellent, on the pricey side ($20 for an entree) but popular with local and New York City celebrities.

The adjacent *Little Bear* (☎ 845-679-8899), which shares the forest setting with the Bear Cafe, has a well-deserved reputation for serving the best Chinese food north of New York City at mid-range prices. The menu offers a few Thai dishes, too.

Also a bit out of town, the *Blue Mountain Bistro* (☎ 845-679-8519), at the junction of Routes 212 and 375, is a popular upscale cafe with Mediterranean cuisine, serving lunch and dinner Tuesday through Sunday. It's about a mile east of town at the Woodstock Golf Club.

The *New World Home Cooking Co* (☎ 845-246-0900), on Route 212 halfway between Woodstock and Saurgerties, is a hip country gourmet eatery specializing in a Caribbean-Thai-down-home mix; Jamaican jerk chicken is a local favorite, along with *ropa vieja* (Cuban pot roast). Big servings in deep-dish plates are the order of the day. This spot is open for lunch Monday to Friday from noon to 3 pm and for dinner daily from 4 to 11 pm. On weekends, it's best to call ahead for reservations.

Entertainment

Gone is the Tinker Street Cafe, where Bob Dylan often played during the early 1960s, but Woodstock continues to be home to a thriving arts and music scene.

Woodstock and its environs support a concentration of performing arts programs and concert series, including the *Bearsville Theater* (☎ 845-679-2100), which puts on plays, concerts and stand-up comedy acts. The theater is on Route 212 in Bearsville, next to the restaurants Little Bear and The Bear.

During the summer, the *Byrdcliffe Arts Colony & Theater* (see Things to See & Do, above) holds craft demonstrations, art exhibits and theatrical performances.

Maverick Concerts (☎ 845-679-7558), Maverick Rd off Route 375, is the oldest chamber music series in the US, dating from 1916. Sunday concerts with top performers take place at 3 pm from mid-June to early September. Concerts are listed in the Sunday *New York Times* during the summer; people often drive up from the city for this.

Local clubs include *Joyous Lake* (☎ 845-679-1234, 42 Mill Hill Rd), a popular restaurant and nightclub with dancing. It's open nightly.

Getting There & Around

Adirondack Trailways (☎ 845-679-2115, 800-225-6815) stops at Houst & Sons hardware store (☎ 845-679-2115), 4 Mill Hill Rd.

Motorists can reach Woodstock from I-87. Take exit 19 to Route 28 west, then Route 375 north, or take exit 20 to Route 32 west to Route 212 to town. If you're coming from Mt Tremper in the west, follow Route 212 east past Bearsville to town.

For bicycle rentals, try Overlook Mountain Bikes (☎ 845-679-2122), 93 Tinker St.

ROUTE 28 TO MARGARETVILLE

The route from Woodstock to Margaretville begins on Route 375 south (at the junction with Route 212 in Woodstock), which dead-ends at the Ashokan Reservoir and the junction with Route 28. Turn right, and you're on your way. As you travel west on Route 28, you will pass several small towns all close together – something to consider if you're planning lodging or dining in the area.

About 15 miles of the road follows the northern edge of the Ashokan Reservoir, which supplies New York City with drinking water. Route 28A loops around the more

This is a good region for fishing.

deserted southern side of the reservoir. West of **Boiceville** (notable for its bakery, see below), Route 28 meets Route 212. **Mt Tremper** is less than a mile north on Route 212 and offers skiing, fishing, camping and hunting.

Places to Stay & Eat

The *Kenneth L Wilson Public Campground* (☎ 845-679-7020) is on County Rd 40 in the state park of the same name, about 4 miles east of Mt Tremper. County Rd 40 crosses Route 28 a little over a mile west of Boiceville in the town of Beresford. The campground is open from mid-May to late October. Sites cost $12.

La Duchesse Anne (☎ 845-688-5260, 4 Miller Rd), in Mt Tremper, is one of several good French restaurants in the Catskills, set in an old house in a wooded setting. You can eat dinner here for $15 to $20. Basic rooms with shared bath are available for $40 to $60; with private bath, $90.

When you get to tiny Boiceville, pull off at *Bread Alone* (☎ 845-657-3328), on the north side of Route 28. This bakery, which has another branch in Woodstock, prepares the best baked goods anywhere in the Catskills.

Catskill Rose (☎ 845-688-7100), next door to La Duchesse Anne on Route 212, is one of the better-known restaurants in the area and a favorite among locals. The kitchen features a good selection of both vegetarian and meat dishes; the smoked duck receives rave reviews. Most dinners range from $12 to $18.

Phoenicia

On Route 28 west of Mt Tremper, Phoenicia is the center of tubing in the Catskills. Visitors can tube on the Esopus Creek, which runs along Route 28. The more exciting tubing starts 5 miles northwest of town, where water is released from the Schoharie Reservoir, and ends 5 miles downstream at the bridge in Phoenicia. The floating trip takes about two hours. There is also an easier course that runs southeast from Phoenicia and takes about 1¾ hours. Tubes can come with seats and handles, and outfitters rent paddles and life jackets. The outfitters will drive you to the put-in site.

FS Tube & Raft Rental (☎ 845-688-7633), at 4 Church St behind the Phoenicia Inn, rents tubes with/without seats for $13; this includes transportation to the site.

The Town Tinker Tube Rental (☎ 845-688-5553), on Bridge St half a block south of Main St, rents tubes with/without seats for $15/16, including transportation and life jackets. You can also rent wet suits and helmets.

For more information, contact the American White Water Affiliation (☎ 845-586-3050) in Margaretville. It is a national organization dedicated to promoting whitewater rafting.

The Adirondack Trailways bus stops in front of Morne Imports (☎ 845-688-7738), 52 Main St.

Places to Stay & Eat The *Hide-A-Way Campsite* (☎ 845-688-5109) is open from mid-April to mid-October. From Route 28, take the Phoenicia/Woodland Valley detour. When you come to the railroad tracks, make a right onto High St (which is also Woodland Valley Rd here), and follow it for about 3½ miles to the campground. Rates are $15 to $20 per site, per night.

Sleepy Hollow Campsite (☎ 845-688-5471) is on Route 28 about a mile east of the Phoenicia Hotel. The camping options also include the *Woodland Valley Campground* (☎ 845-688-7647, 1319 Woodland Valley Rd), 6 miles southwest of Phoenicia, and *Uncle Pete's Campsite* (☎ 845-688-5000) in the hamlet of Phoenicia.

The *Phoenicia Hotel* (☎ 845-688-7500), Main St, is the place to stay in town. The large and popular bar downstairs and the patio area are great for hanging out. The 24 rooms (three with shared baths) are all air-conditioned with TV. The weekday/weekend rates are $45/60; weekly rates are available. If you're hungry for a bite to eat, *Sweet Sue's* (☎ 845-688-7852), Main St, is as famous throughout the Catskills for its pancakes as Folkert's is for its fly-fishing equipment. Sue's creates more pancake combinations ($5) than you could possibly dream up on a snowy week in the Catskills. French toast, burgers and standard lunch fare are also available.

Shandaken

The town (pronounced 'shan-DAY-ken') is at the heart of an area (also called Shandaken) that runs along Route 28 and includes the towns of Phoenicia, Mt Tremper and Big Indian. Also known as the French Catskills, this region offers fine dining at several French restaurants and inns – welcome refreshment after a day spent enjoying the area's excellent hiking and outdoor opportunities.

Popular hiking trails include Woodland Valley Denning Trail, Wittenberg Slide Trail, Phoenicia Trail to Mt Phoenicia, and Overlook Mountain area.

Shandaken's most famous inn, *Auberge Des 4 Saisons* (☎ 845-688-2223), provides what is perhaps the best dining experience in the northern Catskills. Located in a secluded setting on Route 42 about half a mile off Route 28, the restaurant features delicious appetizers, including smoked salmon, paté and goat cheese on French beans for $6 to $7. The entrees (about $15 to $20) are equally good; standouts include poached salmon with mustard sauce on spinach, mussels with thyme, roasted duck in three-peppercorn sauce and rabbit with flageolets. The restaurant also offers a good selection of wines. Rooms are available for $135 to $195 per person, including meals.

The nearby inn *Val D'Isere* (☎ 845-254-4646) is decorated in an eclectic mix of modern and traditional – shag carpets and old oak furniture. Rooms are $65. The restaurant is unpretentious, and the menu includes frogs' legs ($14), lamb ($13) and duck ($13).

Highmount

Just before you enter Fleischmanns on Route 28, you'll pass through the village of Highmount. This small town attracts skiers who come to try out the slopes and trails of the Belleayre Mountain ski area. For more information, see the Outdoor Activities section at the beginning of this chapter.

On a hill overlooking the main road (you'll have to look up to see it) is the *Gateway Lodge* (☎ 845-254-4084). It's a warmly furnished house with a wood-burning fireplace and a piano. The nine rooms (four with private baths, five with shared baths) are tastefully furnished. Rates range from $65 to $75.

Fleischmanns

Fleischmanns is on Route 28, not long before the junction with Route 30. The town was originally known as Griffin Corners but was renamed in 1913 to honor Charles Fleischmann, a Hungarian immigrant who developed a bit of land here in the 1880s and assembled a band to greet family members as they arrived at the old train station. The Fleischmann family later gave a park to the town. But Fleischmanns' most famous resident was baseball great Honus Wagner, who played ball here before going on to become one of the all-time great shortstops with the Pittsburgh Pirates.

Today, the little town is home to **Purple Mountain Press**, on Main St, an excellent press that specializes in regional history and folklore.

Roberts' Auction (☎ 845-254-4490), also on Main St, auctions everything from nuts and bolts to antiques every Saturday night at 7 pm. You can find items here for as little as a dollar. Come early because seats fill up fast.

Adirondack Trailways stops at Petry's Store (☎ 845-254-4010) on Main St.

Places to Stay & Eat On Main St, *River Run* (☎ 845-254-4884) is an unusual inn, in that host Larry Miller welcomes pets. The large, restored house has an inviting front porch complete with Adirondack chairs. The four rooms on the 2nd floor come with private baths, while three rooms on the top floor share a bath. Rates range from $65 to $105. The best deal here is the 'retro wing,' a space with a private bath, twin beds, shared kitchen and television for a very reasonable $65. River Run also has a two-bedroom apartment with a private entrance, kitchen and barbecue for $105.

La Cabana (☎ 845-254-4966) is a Mexican restaurant with several unusual menu items, like *pollo en Pipian* (chicken in chile-and-pumpkin-seed sauce), *huachinango a la Veracruzana* (red snapper with tomato, onion and pepper sauce) or pork loin in wine.

Arkville

Arkville is home to the **Catskill Center for Conservation & Development** (☎ 845-586-2611). Located on Route 28 in the Erph House, a white house perched on a hill, this organization can provide information on hiking and environmental preservation in the Catskills. (See Hiking at the beginning of the chapter.)

In warm weather, the **Delaware & Ulster Rail Ride** (☎ 845-586-3877, 800-225-4132) offers a one-hour roundtrip train ride ($10/5 for adults/children).

The Adirondack Trailways bus stops at the Delaware & Ulster Rail Ride, which is on Route 28.

MARGARETVILLE

Margaretville, at the junction of Routes 28 and 30, is the major commercial town in the northern Catskills area and is a good place to stop for supplies. The former theater on Main St is now the **Margaretville Antique Center** (☎ 845-586-2424).

The Adirondack Trailways bus stops at the Inn Between Rest Stop (☎ 845-586-4265).

Places to Stay & Eat

The *Margaretville Mountain Inn* (☎ 845-586-3933) is an 1886 slate-roofed home on top of the mountain overlooking the town. The 2nd-floor rooms have the best views and are more expensive than the 1st-floor rooms. Rates range from $65 to $125, including a full breakfast. After entering Margaretville from Route 28, make a left at the first light and then make the first right onto Walnut St. Drive up the hill for 1½ miles to the inn.

Merritt's Motel (☎ 845-586-4464), on Route 28, has singles/doubles for $35/45. It's across the road from the East Branch of the

John Burroughs Memorial

Roxbury, a small town along Route 30 about 12 miles north of Margaretville, is the site of Boyhood Rock, a huge glacial boulder marking the John Burroughs Memorial. A plain bronze plaque, dedicated to the prolific naturalist writer, portrays Burroughs looking over the land he loved and bears an inscription from his poem 'Waiting': 'I stand amid the eternal ways.' To find the modest memorial, go north from Roxbury to Hardscrabble Rd, then west for about a mile to Burroughs Memorial Rd, then 1½ miles to the memorial itself.

Delaware River, about a half mile east of Margaretville.

Buswell's Bakery & Restaurant (☎ 845-586-3009), on Granary Lane, serves great pies, muffins and other baked goods daily from 8 am to 8 pm. Breakfast and lunch selections include pancakes, omelets and sandwiches. Dinner service begins at 2 pm – hot turkey, roast beef and Reubens are some of the house specials. To reach the restaurant, make the first left onto Granary Lane after you cross the green bridge into town from Route 28 west.

HUNTER

Hunter Mountain is by far the most popular ski resort in New York. The town of Hunter itself (population 500), perched in the northern reaches of Hunter Forest Park, has little to recommend it, but the skiing and summer festivals – and the accompanying party atmosphere – make it an interesting place to stay. What little there is of Hunter is strung out along Route 23A.

To get there, follow Route 30 north to Route 23 at Grand Gorge, turn right (south) and drive about 6 miles to Prattsville, where Route 23 branches off to Route 23A, which will bring you to Hunter.

Adirondack Trailways stops at Peter's Hunter Auto Repair (☎ 518-263-4713) on Main St.

Hunter Mountain Ski Area

Hunter Mountain (☎ 518-263-4223) ski resort probably makes more snow than any other mountain in the US. The resort's 24-hour snowmaking capacity is almost as impressive as the skiing. Hunter has it all: 15 lifts, a network of 50 trails and restaurants featuring everything from sushi to burgers. During the summer, Hunter operates one chairlift that affords great views of the Catskills' slopes and valleys. An interesting book, *The Sleeping Giant* by Paul E Pepe, traces the development of the mountain into a commercial sports area.

Hunter Mountain also sponsors a series of **summer festivals** (☎ 518-263-3800) from July to early September every year, the biggest of which is the German Alps Festival in late August.

Places to Stay & Eat

Devil's Tombstone Campground (☎ 845-688-7160) is on Route 214, 4 miles south of Hunter. The cost is $9 per night for a very basic site with toilets but no showers. The campground is open from mid-May to early September.

The ***Forester Motor Lodge*** (☎ 518-263-4555), on Route 23A, has a good view of the mountain. Large but basic rooms cost $65/$150 on weekdays/weekends during summer; winter rates are $65/85.

The best place to stay in town is ***Scribner Hollow*** (☎ 518-263-4211, *Route 23A*), which offers magnificent views of the mountain. Each room is individually decorated in styles ranging from 17th-century Spanish adobe to 21st-century futuristic; all of the rooms have cathedral ceilings, some have fireplaces and many have bedroom lofts. 'Future World' features a fireplace and a tiered bathtub with a waterfall; the 'Hunting Lodge' includes log-cabin walls and a bear carpet. Ask to see a few so you can pick one you like. Below the hotel is a grotto with an indoor heated pool, small waterfall and faux-stone columns. Most basic single or double rooms cost $160 to $225. More elaborate rooms, suites and townhouses range from $225 to $450. Rates include breakfast and dinner, and all rates are cheaper in spring and summer.

Scribner Hollow's restaurant, which is called *The Prospect* (☎ 518-263-4211), overlooks Hunter Mountain. It features good American and Italian dishes (including roasted herbed chicken, duck á l'orange and veal, all served with salad, potato and vegetable) in the $15 to $20 range.

Hunter Mountain Bagels (☎ 518-263-5022), on Route 23A, sells bagels and sandwiches. It's a sit-down deli and a very good unofficial information center for the Hunter area; it provides helpful maps and friendly advice.

Entertainment
Hunter is a town for partying. Check out *Hunter Village Inn* (☎ 518-263-4788) on Main St, which features music and happy hours, as well as *Tequila's* (☎ 518-263-4863) and *Pete's Place* (☎ 518-589-5021). The bar in Scribner Hollow is a bit mellower than the rest.

WINDHAM
Ten miles up Route 296 from Hunter, you'll come to the more family-oriented ski resort town of Windham (population 1700).

The resort **Ski Windham** (☎ 518-734-4300, 800-729-4766) has a helpful staff and facilities that are open year-round. In the winter, the resort operates a system of 33 trails and five lifts. Lift fees range from $35 to $43. In the summer, these same trails are used by mountain bikers. The resort is also the site of craft fairs and antique shows. From I-87 get off at exit 21 (for the town of Catskill) and take Hwy 23 west for 25 miles to Windham.

The Adirondack Trailways bus stops at the Four Star Food Center (☎ 518-734-4600), which is on Main St.

Places to Stay & Eat
The *White Birches Campground* (☎ 518-734-3266) has 130 sites ($20) open from mid-May to mid-October. Follow Route 23 one-tenth of a mile west of the junction with Route 296, then go north on Old Rd to Nauvoo Rd and follow the signs.

The *Hamilton Motel* (☎ 518-734-3190) on Route 23 has doubles for $65/75 on weekdays/weekends.

The *Kopper Kettle Motel* (☎ 518-734-3575), at the intersection of Routes 23 and 296 (across the bridge), rents singles and doubles for $50 to $70, slightly less during the summer.

The *Brooklyn Bridge Restaurant* (☎ 518-734-5219), on Route 23 off Route 296, offers good burgers, and steak, chicken or pork chop dinners for $10 to $12. *Tequila's Restaurant* (☎ 518-263-4863), in the middle of town, serves good Tex-Mex and Cajun dishes for lunch and dinner.

TANNERSVILLE
East of Hunter on Route 23A, Tannersville is named for the leather tanning industry that once thrived here. Before the introduction of chemical substitutes, hemlock bark was required in the tanning process. The Catskills, whose hillsides were once covered with hemlocks, provided a convenient source of the raw material. However, the mountains were quickly stripped of hemlock in the early days of the industry, and now Tannersville and the surrounding areas are home instead to several exclusive residential developments. For visitors, the town offers a few good restaurants and bars for after-ski entertainment.

If you're up for a pleasant hike along a stream punctuated by small waterfalls, visit **Platte Clove**, a nature reserve run by the Catskill Center for Conservation & Development (☎ 845-586-2611). The reserve gets few visitors, making it an ideal stop for those wanting a bit of solitude. Take County Rd 16 south from Route 23A near Tannersville (turn at Pete's Place) for about 5 miles. About a mile after you pass Hutterian Brothers on your left, you'll see a tiny sign for Platte Clove.

Adirondack Trailways stops at Warms Restaurant (☎ 518-589-9871) on Main St.

Places to Stay & Eat
The *Sun View Motel* (☎ 518-589-5217) on Route 23A, has rooms for $78 during the week and $95 on weekends.

The **Eggery Inn** (☎ 518-589-5363), in a large house, features great views, a big dining room and a woodstove. To reach the inn, turn south on County Rd 16 at the Tannersville traffic light and follow the road for 1½ miles to the inn. Rooms cost $75 to $85 on weekdays, $95 to $125 on weekends.

As the name suggests, the **Last Chance Antiques & Cheez Cafe** (☎ 518-589-6424) on Main St specializes in cheese dishes, including fondue, nachos and chili with cheese. Most lunch selections are under $6; it is also open for dinner. The restaurant also sells the antiques and collectibles that cover every inch of its wall space.

Maggie's Krooked Cafe (☎ 518-589-6101), on Main St, has a funky atmosphere, small tables and good food. The breakfasts are great, including a local favorite, the 'SOB Omelet' ('south of the border'), made with grilled veggies and salsa. The cafe is open for breakfast and lunch.

KAATERSKILL FALLS HIKES

The 260-foot falls are the highest in New York and actually make two plunges on Spruce Creek. The Laurel House Hotel, which used to stand at the headwaters of the falls, dammed the creek and released the water over the falls periodically for groups of people who paid 25¢ to watch. The falls inspired generations of painters, including Thomas Cole – one of the Hudson River school painters – who immortalized the falls in his work *View of Kaaterskill Falls*.

To get to the base of the falls, drive 1 mile east of Haines Falls on Route 23; as the highway begins to dip, you'll see a small parking area on the right. Park here, cross the highway and walk east along the north shoulder for a quarter mile to the trailhead. The rocky and slightly steep trail travels a half mile from the highway to the falls. Since this is a popular hike, you should arrive early on weekends.

To get to the top of the falls from Route 23A, look for a sign in Haines Falls indicating the turnoff for North/South Lake. The trailhead is off Laurel House Rd on the way into North/South Lake.

NORTH/SOUTH LAKE AREA

This is probably the most popular outdoor destination in the Catskills. A trail from the North/South Lake area leads up to the site of the Catskill Mountain House. To get there from Haines Falls, take the marked turnoff for North/South Lake and follow the signs.

The **North/South Lake Campground** (☎ 518-589-5058), 3 miles northeast of Route 23A, is a large area with showers, canoe and boat rentals, play areas and trailheads. It has over 200 sites ($16) and is open from early May to early November. It's open early May through late October for $16 per night; reservations are essential in summer and also in the fall when the leaves are ablaze with color.

The Late, Great Catskill Hotels

The area around Haines Falls was home to three of the biggest 19th-century Catskill hotels, the most famous of which was the Catskill Mountain House. Built in the mid-19th century, this resort was the first of its kind: a deluxe hotel built in a remote wilderness on a cliff, with breathtaking views of North and South Lakes and the Hudson Valley.

Part of the resort's attraction was its inaccessibility. After a long and difficult journey to the hotel by stage coach, guests were rewarded with spectacular scenery and elegant accommodations. However, the introduction of the automobile allowed vacationers to travel even greater distances from the cities in search of even more magnificent surroundings. By the 1920s, the Catskill Mountain House showed signs of disrepair, and in 1943 it closed permanently. In 1963, the state bought the abandoned hotel and burned it.

Two other deluxe hotels in the area, the 800-room Kaaterskill Hotel and the Laurel House, built at the top of Kaaterskill Falls, met with similar fates. The former burned accidentally in a fire in 1924; the abandoned remains of the latter were burned by the state of New York in 1966.

Southern & Western Catskills

In the southern foothills of the Catskill Mountains, the famous **Catskill resorts** are clustered around Monticello and Liberty along Route 17 and near Minnewaska State Park and Ellenville on Route 209, north of Route 17.

These resorts evolved from the boarding houses that sprang up here in the late 19th and early 20th centuries, when Jewish immigrants sought an escape from the poverty and crowded conditions of New York City. The area became known as the 'Borscht Belt,' and the small boarding houses grew into enormous (although not especially graceful) resorts, offering guests every imaginable kind of activity, from swimming in Olympic-size pools to skiing to golfing. As the resorts grew, so did the program of activities, which catered to whole families, from children and teenagers to parents and grandparents. Two major ingredients of the Borscht Belt experience were the food (and lots of it) and the comedians. Woody Allen captures some of this scene in his movies *Annie Hall* and *Broadway Danny Rose*. The 1990 hit film *Dirty Dancing* takes place at one of these resorts during the Borscht Belt's final glory days.

With the advent of jet travel, the resorts went into decline, and many closed as guests chose to travel to Florida, the Caribbean and Europe instead. More recently, Atlantic City has been drawing away a lot of their business. The surviving resorts have redefined themselves with big-name entertainment (from singers and bands like Tom Jones, Neil Sedaka and Frankie Valli & the Four Seasons to such comedians as Jackie Mason, George Carlin and Brett Butler), special-interest promotions (singles, golfers, tennis players, families celebrating Mother's and Father's Day) and conference facilities. Gurumaya and her Siddhi Yoga organization have even bought up a former Borscht Belt hotel in South Fallsburg. The ones that remain, such as the huge *Grossingers* in Liberty, prove the Darwinian maxim of survival of the fittest.

The other survivors include *Kutsher's* (☎ 800-431-1273) in Monticello, *Raleigh* (☎ 800-446-4003) in South Fallsburg and *Villa Roma* (☎ 800-533-6767) in Callicoon.

ALONG THE DELAWARE RIVER

The Delaware River, dividing New York and Pennsylvania, offers some of the best recreation in the region. For more information on the area, see also the Delaware Water Gap sections in the Northern Pennsylvania and Northern New Jersey chapters.

The town of **Narrowsburg** on Route 97 sits at a once-strategic bend in the Delaware River. Its 18th-century stockade history is on display at the **Fort Delaware Museum of Colonial History** (☎ 845-252-6660), open daily during July and August, and weekends in June, from 10 am to 4:30 pm. Admission is $4/2.25 for adults/children.

Narrowsburg is also one of several points along the river that offers opportunities for **rafting** and **canoeing**. Lander's Delaware River Trips (☎ 800-252-3925) runs raft and canoe trips daily from April to mid-October. Reservations are suggested. Trips range from three to six hours, cover 5 to 10 miles of river (depending on river and weather conditions) and cost $28/14 for adults/children.

Another summer river destination is **Barryville**, at the junction of Routes 97 and 55, along an especially beautiful part of the Delaware River. Wild & Scenic River Tours (☎ 800-836-0366) offers rafting, canoeing and tubing trips daily from May to October (or whenever it gets too cold to coax people onto the water). Trips can last two to six hours and cost $26 per person on weekdays, $28 on weekends, including shuttle transportation. **Tubing** is a bargain at $12 per person. Children ages 12 and under get a discount, according to the 'Pay What They Weigh' plan: 10¢ a pound when accompanied by two adults per raft.

Capital District & Mohawk Valley

Much of New York's history unfolds near the confluence of the Hudson and Mohawk Rivers, only a few miles from the state's modern capital at Albany. Points of interest in the region include Saratoga Springs, the summer home of the US's oldest thoroughbred racetrack; Cooperstown, pristine home to the National Baseball Hall of Fame; and Binghamton, a sleepy college town on the Susquehanna River near the Pennsylvania border.

I-90, the primary east-west highway in the state, follows the Mohawk Valley from Oneida Lake – between Syracuse and Rome – and links the towns of Cazenovia, Utica, Herkimer, Canajoharie, Amsterdam and Rotterdam to Albany. From Albany, I-90 dips south to join I-87 (for 8 miles), then crosses the Hudson River and continues to the southeast into Massachusetts. I-88 is the other major east-west highway in the region, connecting Binghamton to Albany, 140 miles to the northeast.

I-87, also known as the Northway, runs from north-south and connects Albany to Saratoga Springs, Glens Falls, Lake George and the Adirondacks. The other principle north-south route in the region is Route 28, which links Oneonta (at the junction of I-88) to Cooperstown and the Adirondacks.

ALBANY

Located on the west bank of the Hudson River, Albany (population 100,000) is the state capital of New York. It is a city that has managed to retain, and retrieve, the historic charm of an old and vibrant northeastern city. Ornate state buildings and brownstone houses grace the downtown and the tree-lined streets of the neighborhoods. The marble and glass buildings of the enormous Empire State Plaza dominate downtown and stand in sharp contrast to the otherwise historic surroundings.

Albany's character is largely defined by its role as the seat of the nation's second largest state government. Although it con-

Highlights

- Albany's Empire State Plaza – impressive architecture, museums and performing arts events

- Saratoga Springs, home to active mineral springs, the nation's oldest thoroughbred racetrack and Caffé Lena, America's oldest continuously operating coffeehouse

- National Baseball Hall of Fame, Fenimore Art Museum and the Farmers' Museum in quaint Cooperstown

tinues to be a manufacturing center, it is the city's service economy that allowed Albany to escape the economic devastation that accompanied the decline of basic manufacturing in other northeastern cities. In fact, the city enjoys a relatively healthy economy that supports excellent restaurants, revitalized neighborhoods, architectural gems and an array of amenities that make Albany worth a visit.

History

The Albany plateau was once the heart of the Five Indian Nations, which included the

CAPITAL DISTRICT & MOHAWK VALLEY

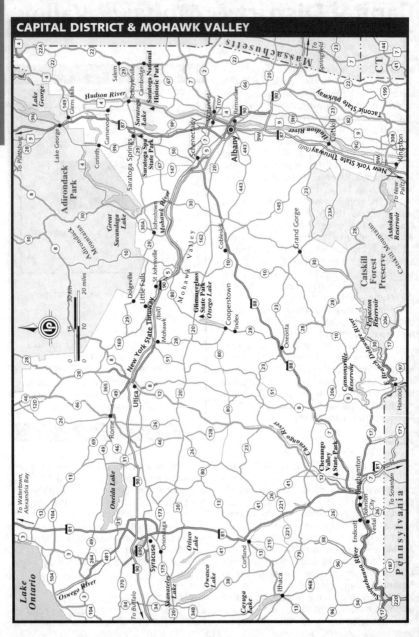

Iroquois and Mohawk tribes. The plateau runs for 18 miles northwest to the Mohawk Valley.

The first Europeans to arrive in the area in the 1500s were French trappers. In 1609, Henry Hudson sailed the *Half Moon* up the river that bears his name, opening the area to Dutch fur traders, who built a fort and developed a trading center. The first permanent settlement was established by a handful of Walloon families, French Protestants who fled the Spanish Netherlands looking for religious freedom and converts. They called their settlement Fort Orange.

The town that grew up around the fort was known as Beverwyck (Beaver Town) and was controlled jointly – and with considerable contention – by the Dutch West India Company and a powerful diamond merchant, Kiliaen Van Rensselaer. In 1652, Peter Stuyvesant, who was – at that time – a director for the Dutch West India Company, declared Beverwyck an independent town.

Twelve years later, Stuyvesant was forced to surrender the town and fort to the English, who once again renamed it, this time in honor of the Duke of York and Albany. Albany was officially granted a charter in 1686. The Dutch were allowed to keep their own language, religions and customs, all of which are still in evidence in Albany today.

Throughout the 17th and 18th centuries Albany remained an important link in the fur trade, and its strategic location made it a logical meeting place for representatives from the various colonies. The British tried to capture it during the Revolutionary War, but they failed. It became the state capital in 1797.

With the opening of the Erie Canal between Buffalo and Albany in 1825, the city grew dramatically. Albany built a 4000-foot pier to service canal boats to transport people, wheat, salt, glass and other items. The railroad reached town in 1851, and the city soon became an important transportation crossroads and manufacturing center.

The city's strategic location and its diverse economic base have helped it – in more recent times – to maintain a vibrant economy and to launch a preservation and renewal movement for much of the city.

Orientation

Albany is completely surrounded by interstate highways. The New York State Thruway (I-90) enters from the east and circles the city westward. I-87 comes in from the south, and I-787 completes the circle to the east.

The 98-acre Nelson A Rockefeller Empire State Plaza sits at the center of the city. (For more on Rockefeller, see 'The Rockefeller Legacy' boxed text in the New York City chapter.) Its white, gleaming marble buildings and sculpture gardens are bounded by Madison Ave to the west and State St to the east. Another major street, Washington Ave, runs northwest and soon forks into Western and Central Aves. State St divides many street addresses into north and south. Within walking distance of downtown are several historic residential neighborhoods and the 84-acre Washington Park.

Albany is an easy town to get around, by foot or by car. There's even free parking downtown.

Information

The Albany Heritage Area Visitor Center (☎ 518-434-0405), 25 Quackenbush Square at the northeast corner of Broadway and Clinton Aves, has the usual vast assortment of brochures, including a self-guided walking tour of the historic downtown area. It is open daily Monday through Friday from 9 am to 4 pm and Saturday and Sunday from 10 am to 4 pm. You can visit its website at www.albany.org.

Trolley tours run periodically in the summer on Friday afternoons and Saturday mornings. Tours are 1½ hours and cost $10/8.50/5 for adults/seniors/children.

The Albany County Convention & Visitor Bureau (☎ 518-434-1217, 800-258-3582) is in the same building as the visitors' center and is open Monday through Friday from 9 am to 5 pm. The main post office (☎ 518-462-1359) is at 45 Hudson St, at the corner of Pearl St. There are other post

NEW YORK

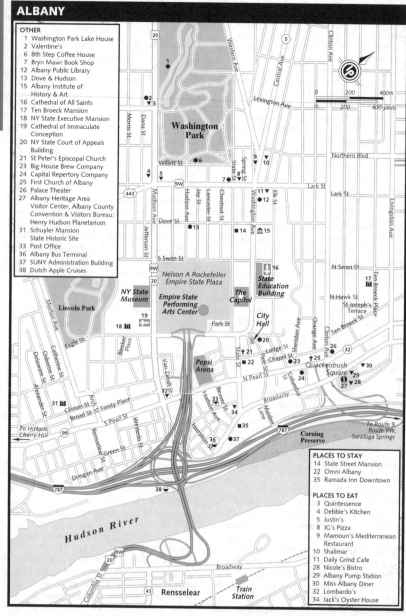

ALBANY

OTHER
1 Washington Park Lake House
2 Valentine's
6 8th Step Coffee House
7 Bryn Mawr Book Shop
12 Albany Public Library
13 Dove & Hudson
15 Albany Institute of History & Art
16 Cathedral of All Saints
17 Ten Broeck Mansion
18 NY State Executive Mansion
19 Cathedral of Immaculate Conception
20 NY State Court of Appeals Building
21 St Peter's Episcopal Church
23 Big House Brew Company
24 Capital Repertory Company
25 First Church of Albany
26 Palace Theater
27 Albany Heritage Area Visitor Center, Albany County Convention & Visitors Bureau; Henry Hudson Planetarium
31 Schuyler Mansion State Historic Site
33 Post Office
36 Albany Bus Terminal
37 SUNY Administration Building
38 Dutch Apple Cruises

PLACES TO STAY
14 State Street Mansion
22 Omni Albany
35 Ramada Inn Downtown

PLACES TO EAT
3 Quintessence
4 Debbie's Kitchen
5 Justin's
8 JG's Pizza
9 Mamoun's Mediterranean Restaurant
10 Shalimar
11 Daily Grind Cafe
28 Nicole's Bistro
29 Albany Pump Station
30 Miss Albany Diner
32 Lombardo's
34 Jack's Oyster House

offices in Empire Plaza on the concourse level and in the capitol.

There are two good stores for used books in town: Dove & Hudson (☎ 518-432-4518), 296 Hudson at the corner of Dove, and the Bryn Mawr Book Shop (☎ 518-465-8126), 115 Lark St. Both stores are open Tuesday through Saturday. The Albany Public Library (☎ 518-427-4300) is on Washington Ave between Dove and Lark Sts.

The *Times Union* is the daily newspaper, and *Metroland* is the giveaway alternative news weekly.

Henry Hudson Planetarium

Attached to the visitors' center is the child-friendly Henry Hudson Planetarium, which offers a 45-minute tour of the solar system every Saturday at either 11:30 am or 12:30 pm. Admission is $4.50 for adults and $3 for students, seniors and children.

Empire State Plaza

Elevated slightly above the surrounding streets and buildings, the Empire State Plaza is 98 acres of brilliant white marble-and-glass buildings and sculpture gardens, which afford great views of the surrounding city and country. The plaza houses legislative offices, courtrooms, various state agencies, a collection of modern art and a performing arts center (referred to by locals as 'the Egg' because of its curvy modern silhouette). Empire Plaza is bounded by Madison Ave and State St on the north and south and Eagle and Swan Sts on the east and west. On weekends, when the plaza isn't crowded, people come here to roller-skate and play roller-hockey on the hundreds of feet of marble tiles.

For a quick orientation to the city and surrounding region, check out the view from the **observation deck** on the 42nd floor of the Corning Tower Building (☎ 518-474-2418). It is open daily (except Christmas, New Year's Day and Thanksgiving) from 9:30 am to 3:30 pm.

A collection of modern art is on display along the concourse below the plaza and in the buildings surrounding the plaza. Guided tours of the artwork are available daily upon request. Call ☎ 518-473-7521 for additional information.

New York State Museum

This museum (☎ 518-474-5877) is in the Cultural Education Center at the south end of Empire Plaza, but the entrance is at street level on Madison Ave. The museum might be better described as an experience, with installations built to scale, sound effects and interactive exhibits that highlight the political, cultural and natural history of New York City and state. The museum is free (but a $2 donation is suggested) and open daily from 10 am to 5 pm.

Albany Institute of History & Art

Located a block east of the plaza at 125 Washington Ave is the Albany Institute of History & Art (☎ 518-463-4478), which was founded in 1791. Browsing the institute's collection of period furnishings, silver and pewter, decorative arts and fine arts from the Hudson Valley is an excellent way to gain knowledge and insight into the history and culture of the region.

The Hudson River school of landscape painters is represented here with works by Thomas Cole, Asher Durand, James and William Hart and Jasper Cropsey. Artwork and exhibits are well displayed and thoughtfully annotated, making this museum a pleasure to visit – allow plenty of time. It is open Wednesday to Sunday from noon to 5 pm. General admission is $3/2 for adults/seniors and students, free for children under 12; Wednesday is free to all.

Note: The museum is closed for renovations until May 2001. Many of the Hudson landscape paintings are touring other museums in the state.

New York State Capitol

The capitol (☎ 518-474-2418) is next to the plaza between State St and Washington Ave. Built between 1867 and 1899, it is a fascinating mixture of Italian and French Renaissance and Romanesque architecture, a combination that makes it fun to explore the building. Inside, beyond the pink granite facade, is the Million Dollar Staircase, a series of intersecting stairs and landings. Alongside one of the staircases, there are 300 carved portraits of famous New Yorkers and friends of the sculptor. On the senate staircase, carvings depict the evolutionary chain, with simpler organisms at the bottom and more complex ones at top. (Not surprisingly – given the era in which the building was constructed – neither men nor apes are represented in the carvings.) The capitol is free to visit and is open daily. One hour tours are offered daily at 10 am, noon and 2 and 3 pm.

Facing the capitol, across Washington Ave, is the **State Education Building**, which has 90-foot columns – the tallest in the world according to the *Guinness Book of World Records*.

New York State Court of Appeals

This gold-domed building (☎ 518-455-7711) is at the intersection of Washington Ave and Eagle St. The white marble and masonry structure, built in 1842, is an interesting example of Greek Revival architecture. At the center of the massive structure is a large rotunda that is decorated with Greek columns. Guided tours are available, but you should call ahead.

Historic Houses & Buildings

Albany has a number of interesting churches within walking distance of the plaza. They're more impressive inside than you might imagine if you were to only view them from the outside. The 1852 **Cathedral of the Immaculate Conception** (☎ 418-463-4447), at the corner of Eagle St and Madison Ave, and the 1884 **Cathedral of All Saints** (☎ 418-465-1342), 62 Swan St, are both Gothic Revival structures containing stone carvings, stained glass and displays of religious and historic decorative art. Both are open daily.

First Church of Albany (☎ 518-463-4449), 110 N Pearl St at Clinton Square, has a pulpit that was constructed in 1656 and is said to be the oldest in America. The floor of **St Peter's Episcopal Church,** (☎ 518-434-3502), at State and Lodge Sts, is intricately laid with mosaics. Built in 1859, the church is

an excellent example of the Gothic architecture made popular in America by the English architect Richard Upjohn, who also designed Trinity Church in New York City. Organ recitals are offered here Friday at 12:30 pm. Admission is free.

The **Schuyler Mansion** (☎ 518-434-0834), 32 Catherine St, was the home of Philip Schuyler ('SKY-ler'), a Revolutionary War general and senator. During the war, he commanded forces for the northern frontier from his home. As a result, the mansion was visited by many prominent political and military figures of the day, including George Washington and Benjamin Franklin. It was here that his daughter Betsy married Alexander Hamilton. British General John Burgoyne was held captive in the mansion after defeat by American forces at the Battle of Saratoga in 1777.

The state of New York bought the house in 1912 and carefully restored it. It contains excellent examples of colonial furnishings. It is open mid-April through October from Wednesday to Saturday from 10 am to 5 pm and Sunday from 1 to 5 pm. Admission costs $3/1 for adults/children.

Built in 1787, **Historic Cherry Hill** (☎ 518-434-4791), S Pearl St between First and McCarty Aves, was the home of the powerful Dutch diamond merchant Philip Van Rensselaer and was once the center of a 900-acre farm. You can tour the grounds and the home, which contains an excellent collection of decorative arts, including silver, china and glassware, as well as colonial furnishings and paintings. It is open Tuesday through Saturday from 10 am to 3 pm and Sunday from 1 to 3 pm, with guided tours on the hour. Admission is $3.50/2/1 for adults/students/children (ages six to 17).

Although the home is only a mile from downtown, the neighborhood is not considered safe to walk through; you should consider taking a cab.

Eight blocks from Empire Plaza is **Ten Broeck Mansion** (☎ 518-436-9826) on Ten Broeck Place. The house was built in 1798 by Revolutionary War general Abraham Ten Broeck and currently houses the Albany County Historical Society. Tours of the house are given April through December from Wednesday to Sunday from 1 to 4 pm. The house features period rooms furnished in precise detail, as well as changing displays on old Albany. Admission is $3/1 for adults/ children under 12.

New York State Executive Mansion (☎ 518-474-2418), 138 Eagle St, was the governor's home and is conveniently adjacent to Empire Plaza on the west. This enormous redbrick Victorian was built in 1856 and altered many times, first by private owners and then by successive political administrations. It's open to the public on Thursday by appointment.

While you are in the area, stroll down **Bleeker Place**, which runs perpendicular to the entrance to the Executive Mansion. The street is lined with rows of wooden colonial houses built in the 1850s.

The two-winged neo-Gothic monster that now houses the **SUNY Administration Building** was once the office of the Delaware & Hudson Railroad. On top of its central tower is a weathervane in the shape of Henry Hudson's ship *Half Moon*. The 6-by-9-foot weathervane is the largest working one in the country and weighs a ton – 'and yet it spins,' as Galileo once said. The administration building is on Broadway St near the river.

Lark St

Downtown, Lark St between Madison and Washington Aves is an interesting street of counter-culture establishments, restaurants and even an upscale tattoo parlor, all of which helped it earn the saintly nickname of 'Greenwich Village North.'

Cruises

Dutch Apple Cruises (☎ 518-463-0220), 139 Broadway at the snow dock, conducts two-hour narrated cruises along the Hudson River from April through October. Lunch and dinner cruises are available and ticket prices start at $9.

Special Events

As the name suggests, the Annual Tulip Festival in early May is a three-day celebration of the city's Dutch heritage. It is held in Washington Park and includes food vendors, crafts and the crowning of a Tulip Queen.

The Altamont Fair in mid-August is a week long country fair at the nearby Altamont Fairgrounds (☎ 518-861-6671).

Places to Stay

Budget & Mid-Range There are a number of independently owned motels along Central Ave within the first 3 miles northwest of the intersection with I-87 (exit 2). The rooms are very basic and generally clean, but a spot check of the bathrooms is advisable. Most rooms range from $25 to $35 a night.

Of these, a favorite is *Jack's Motel & Chinese Restaurant* (☎ 518-456-5522, 1881 Central Ave). Check in at the restaurant; the desk closes at 11 pm. Another motel in the same category is *Skylane Motel* (☎ 518-456-1330, 1927 Central Ave). *Northway Inn* (☎ 518-869-0277, 1517 Central Ave) offers well-kept, clean rooms and free continental breakfast. Some rooms have refrigerators, and there is a nice outdoor pool and bar. Rooms range from $50/69 for singles/ doubles.

On Western Ave, 3 miles from downtown, is *Capital Lodge* (☎ 518-489-4423, 1230 Western Ave). Small, typical motel rooms are $40 to $50. *Western Motel* (☎ 518-456-7241, 2019 Western Ave), north of Washington Park and the downtown area, offers basic rooms with cable TV and showers. Rates are $30.

Close to the downtown area, *Pine Haven B&B* (☎ 518-482-1574, 531 Western Ave) has rooms that are furnished with antique dressers, iron bedframes, featherbeds and other Victorian amenities. Rates for singles/ doubles without bath are $50/65, with private bath $65/80. These rates include a continental breakfast that is served in a dining room that features a fireplace that is lit on cold mornings.

Also downtown, just east of Empire Plaza, is *State Street Mansion* (☎ 518-462-6780, 281 State St). This renovated guesthouse was formerly a seminary. Rooms have private or shared baths and rates typically start at $50.

Top End Across from the state university, **Ramada Inn Downtown** (☎ 518-434-4111, 300 Broadway) has an indoor pool, exercise room and saunas, and they provide cof-feemakers and TVs in every room. It's almost as comfortable as the pricier Omni – and with rates of $69 to $89, including full breakfast in their restaurant – it's more reasonable. **Omni Albany** (☎ 518-462-6611), at the corner of State and Lodge Sts, is in the heart of downtown Albany, and offers a large indoor pool, two restaurants and bar with nightly entertainment. Rates are $120 to $150.

Closer to the airport, you'll find **The Desmond** (☎ 518-869-8100, 660 Albany-Shaker Rd), at exit 4 off I-87, an elegant colonial-style hotel with lavishly decorated rooms. This hotel includes an indoor pool, exercise room and two restaurants – one casual, the other formal. Rates range from $90 to $160.

Century House Hotel & Restaurant (☎ 518-785-0931, 987 New Loudon Rd), in Latham, is just 10 minutes from Albany on Route 9. This is a charming hotel in an old Dutch farmhouse that dates back to 1810 and has tastefully decorated rooms and ex-quisite grounds (and nature trail), as well as a complimentary breakfast and newspaper each morning. There's a full-service restaurant and pub, tennis courts and a pool. Rates are $95 to $105.

Places to Eat

Budget Several eateries are on Madison Ave (Route 20), a pleasant part of town that is frequented by students from the College of St Rose and SUNY-Albany.

Shalimar (☎ 518-434-0890, 31 Central Ave) serves inexpensive Pakistani-Indian food in modest surroundings. Vegetable curries and several meat dishes with rice cost $5. **Mamoun's Mediterranean Restaurant** (☎ 518-434-3901, 206 Washington Ave), near the corner of Lark St, serves tasty and authentic Middle Eastern food daily from 11:30 am to 10 pm.

Miss Albany Diner (☎ 518-465-9148, 893 Broadway) was designed as an old railroad car and is best known for breakfast. Try the

Irish Toast, which is thick French toast bread with pecan cream cheese filling, topped with an Irish whiskey butterscotch sauce ($6). The MAD Eggs concoction is also a favorite at $4.50. It is open for breakfast and lunch weekdays from 7 am to 2 pm and weekends from 9 am to 2 pm.

Along Lark St between Madison and Washington Aves, you can choose from several inexpensive eateries, including **Debbie's Kitchen** (☎ 518-463-3829, 456 Madison Ave), a popular take-out (or sit-in) spot with excellent sandwiches ($4.50), deli salads and desserts. **JG's Pizza** (☎ 518-465-1922, 195 Lark Street), one of the best pizze-rias in town, serves whole pies or just slices. Try the hot meatball sub for $4. It is open daily, except Sunday. **Daily Grind Cafe** (☎ 518-427-0464, 204 Lark St) serves decent cappuccino, homemade muffins, croissants and sandwiches. Try the $6 Belgian waffle and refillable coffee special. It is open daily from 7 am to 10 pm and Sunday from 8 am to 8 pm.

Mother Earth's Cafe (☎ 518-434-0944, 217 Western Ave) offers great vegetarian and international dishes in a pleasant setting. Choose from Mexican, Indian, Middle Eastern and Caribbean entrees. Live music is featured every night of the week, and no menu item is more than $7. It is open daily 11 am to 11 pm.

Mid-Range & Top End Several miles west of downtown, **Grandma's Country Restaurant** (☎ 518-459-4585, 1273 Central Ave) serves American food with freshly prepared side dishes. Entrees include liver and onions, pot roast and chicken. The food is good, plentiful and reasonable ($9 to $14). Be sure to leave room for great pies that are baked on the premises; big slices cost $2.75 to $3.25.

Quintessence (☎ 518-434-8186, 11 New Scotland Ave) is a trendy stainless-steel diner with a tuxedoed host and a bar where one might expect a counter. The restaurant features international theme menus; selections include burgers and teriyaki chicken and beef for around $6. There's dancing Wednesday through Saturday, and there is a band on Sunday. Usually, reservations are needed for dinner.

Lombardo's (☎ 518-462-9180, 119 Madison Ave), near S Pearl St, is a neighborhood family Italian eatery; unfortunately for Lombardo's, the atmosphere of the neighborhood has enjoyed better days. The front room has a high, decorative tin ceiling with a long bar and wooden booths. Lombardo's serves traditional pastas with tomato sauce ($10) and special pastas such as linguine with butter shrimp, fish and white beans ($14). There are also good fish, veal and chicken dishes. It is open Monday to Saturday from 4 to 11 pm.

Justin's (☎ 518-436-7008, 301 Lark St) has an upscale, creative menu and jazz brunches, and it is very popular with the college crowd. You have a choice of two menus: the reasonably priced cafe menu that features grilled andouille sausage ($6.50) and beans and rice ($4); or the more upscale menu that includes basil pepper salmon ($18), Thai coconut shrimp ($15) and jerk chicken ($12), to name a few dishes.

For a taste of typical Albany, try *Jack's Oyster House* (☎ 518-465-8854, 42 State St). The restaurant's namesake, Jack Rosenstein, opened his first oyster house in 1913 and the present one in 1937. The food is as good as the atmosphere, especially if you like clams and oysters, which are served on the half shell ($5 to $6) or in stews ($6.50). Jack's also serves other seafood dishes, most in the $12 to $14 range. Pulitzer Prize winner William Kennedy, author of *Iron Weed*, immortalized Jack's in a 1985 *Esquire* article called 'Jack and the Oyster.'

Nicole's Bistro (☎ 518-465-1111), at the corner of Clinton and Broadway, is Albany's oldest Dutch landmark, dating back to the 1600s. Located in historic Quackenbush Square, this very popular French bistro specializes in steak au poivre, homemade pastas and rack of lamb. Dine in the outdoor garden for lunch or dinner. Entrees average $18 (some half portions are available), and a special three-course meal is offered each night of the week for $25. It is open for lunch and dinner Monday to Saturday from 11:30 am to 10pm and is closed Sunday.

Albany Pump Station (☎ 518-447-9000, 19 Quakenbush Square) is an old warehouse converted into a hip, upscale brewpub and restaurant. The menu of American fare includes everything from sandwiches and burgers to filet mignon, grilled chicken and ribs. Entrees range from $6 to $18. It is open daily for lunch and dinner from 11:30 am to 11 pm; the bar stays open later, usually until the crowd clears.

Entertainment

The *8th Step Coffee House* (☎ 518-434-1703, 14 Willett St), holds poetry readings, features local folk and acoustic performers, and it has a weekly mike night.

For late night jazz, check out *Justin's* (☎ 518-436-7008, 301 Lark St). Weekend sets start at about 10:30 pm, with a $3 cover and $7.50 food or drink minimum.

Big House Brewing Company (☎ 518-445-2739, 90 N Pearl St) is a renovated warehouse turned into a lively three-story brewpub with several bars, a restaurant, pool, darts and weekend deejay. Dancing takes place on the third floor most nights of the week. It is open until 2 am during the week, 3 am on weekends. *Valentine's* (☎ 518 432-6572, 17 New Scotland Ave), at Dana St, has great drink specials and is a haven for local bands with big followings. It has two floors, with bars on each, and at least two bands play most nights of the week. It is open until 2 am during the week, 3 am weekends.

Theater and classical music events are held at *Empire State Performing Arts Center* (☎ 518-473-1845), which features two theaters. *Palace Theatre* (☎ 518-465-4663, 19 Clinton Ave) is the home of the Albany Symphony Orchestra, Berkshire Ballet and Theatreworks USA and a venue for visiting acts. *Capital Repertory Company* (☎ 518-462-4531, 462-7469, 111 N Pearl St) does a six-play season through the year, featuring mostly contemporary American playwrights.

Washington Park Lake House (☎ 518-434-4524), on Washington Ave, puts on a play every night of the week for six weeks beginning in early July. There is free seating on the lawn or reserved seating for $6. In the summer, paddleboat rentals are available, or you can just enjoy a walk in the park and feed the ducks. ***Corning Preserve***, downtown between the river and I-787, is a large park that hosts the 'Alive at Five' free-concert series every Thursday night in the summer. The area also has paved running and bike trails and fishing.

Getting There & Away
Air Albany International Airport (☎ 518-869-9611) is served by American, Continental, Delta, Mohawk, Northwest, United and US Airways. Roundtrip fares are about $469 to Chicago and $341 to Washington, DC.

Bus Adirondack Trailways, Bonanza and Greyhound stop at the Albany Bus Terminal (☎ 518-427-7060), 34 Hamilton St at the corner of Broadway. Adirondack Trailways (☎ 518-436-9651, 800-858-8555) has service to/from New York City, Long Island, the Catskills, the Adirondacks and points west. Bonanza Bus Lines (☎ 800-556-3815) runs from Albany to Connecticut and Massachusetts. Greyhound (☎ 518-434-8095, 800-231-2222) runs regular buses to Atlantic City, Buffalo, New York City and Montreal. One-way/roundtrip fares are typically $19/34 to New York City, $29/58 to Buffalo and $49/98 to Montreal.

The Capital District Transportation Authority (CDTA; ☎ 518-482-8822) runs buses to/from Schenectady, Troy and Saratoga Springs. It costs 75¢ plus zone charges of 20¢ or 30¢.

Train The Amtrak station (☎ 518-462-5763, 800-872-7245) is across the Hudson River in Rensselaer, about 5 minutes by car from downtown Albany. Amtrak has daily service along the Hudson River Valley.

Car & Motorcycle Albany is accessible via I-90 from western New York or Massachusetts and I-87 from southern or northern New York.

Getting Around
CDTA buses No 1 and 31 run to/from the airport and various stops in downtown. It costs 75¢ plus zone charges of 20¢ or 30¢. Taxis cost about $15 for the same route.

Albany's airport is in the town of Colonie on Albany-Shaker Rd and is about 10 miles from downtown; the drive takes about 15 minutes.

SARATOGA SPRINGS
Famous for its mineral springs and thoroughbred horseracing, Saratoga Springs (population 25,000) is a gracious town with Victorian architecture, manicured gardens, luxurious spas, classic pavilions, modern museums and a renowned program of concerts and dance performances.

Here, you can 'take the cure,' as visitors have been doing for more than a century, which is to say that – even on a modest budget – you can pamper yourself with mineral baths, unwind in beautiful surroundings and check out the restorative powers of the spring water. In August, however, the atmosphere is far from relaxing, as the town is packed with boisterous-race fans who travel long distances to enjoy some of the world's best thoroughbred horseracing. Just 35 miles north of Albany, Saratoga Springs is easily accessible and worth exploring.

History
Before the arrival of Europeans, the springs at Saratoga attracted wild animals, making this area a favorite hunting spot of the Mohawk Indians, who called it *Saraghoha*, meaning 'Fast Water Place.' Legend has it that Europeans were first introduced to the curative powers of the springs in 1771, when Mohawks brought Sir William Johnson, superintendent of Indian Affairs for the British, here to recover from a variety of war-related ailments. Johnson was a trapper and, as the story goes, he developed a close relationship with several of the tribes of the Five Nations.

The commercial development of the springs began only two decades later. Gideon Putnam arrived in the area in 1789 and bought the land around what later became known as Congress Spring (now in Congress Park). In 1802, he built the first hotel here.

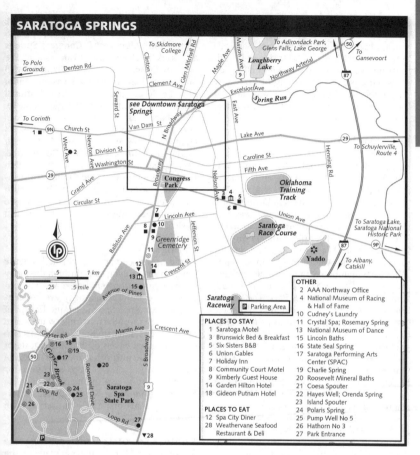

SARATOGA SPRINGS

To Skidmore College
To Polo Grounds
Denton Rd
To Corinth
Clement Ave
see Downtown Saratoga Springs
Van Dam St
Church St
Division St
Washington St
Grand Ave
Circular St
Ballston Ave
Lincoln Ave
Greenridge Cemetery
Jefferson St
Crescent St
Avenue of Pines
Geyser Rd
Marrin Ave
Crescent Ave
Roosevelt Drive
Loop Rd
Saratoga Spa State Park
Loop Rd
Maple Ave
Marion Ave
Clinton St
Glen Mitchell Rd
Loughberry Lake
Northway Arterial
To Adirondack Park, Glens Falls, Lake George
To Gansevoort
Excelsior Ave
Spring Run
East Ave
Lake Ave
Caroline St
Fifth Ave
Henning Rd
To Schuylerville, Route 4
Oklahoma Training Track
Union Ave
Saratoga Race Course
To Saratoga Lake, Saratoga National Historic Park
Yaddo
To Albany, Catskill
Congress Park
Saratoga Raceway
Parking Area

PLACES TO STAY
1 Saratoga Motel
3 Brunswick Bed & Breakfast
5 Six Sisters B&B
6 Union Gables
7 Holiday Inn
8 Community Court Motel
9 Kimberly Guest House
14 Garden Hilton Hotel
18 Gideon Putnam Hotel

PLACES TO EAT
12 Spa City Diner
28 Weathervane Seafood Restaurant & Deli

OTHER
2 AAA Northway Office
4 National Museum of Racing & Hall of Fame
10 Cudney's Laundry
11 Crystal Spa; Rosemary Spring
13 National Museum of Dance
15 Lincoln Baths
16 State Seal Spring
17 Saratoga Performing Arts Center (SPAC)
19 Charlie Spring
20 Roosevelt Mineral Baths
21 Coesa Spouter
22 Hayes Well; Orenda Spring
23 Island Spouter
24 Polaris Spring
25 Pump Well No 5
26 Hathorn No 3
27 Park Entrance

Other commercial developments followed quickly. The first horse races began in 1847.

During the Civil War, John Morrissey, a champion bare-knuckle heavyweight boxer and US congressman, took over one racetrack and built another, along with a casino (still standing in Congress Park). Saratoga had arrived. The resorts were visited by President Ulysses S Grant, Cornelius Vanderbilt and Jay Gould, as well as the likes of Diamond Jim Brady and Boss Tweed. An early guidebook described visitors as a mixture of 'gentlemen of the turf, connoisseurs of the odd trick, and the amateurs of poker.'

Shortly after the turn of the century, New York state began buying the springs and the land surrounding them in order to begin a program of conservation and preservation. Construction began on a complex of buildings, pools and bathhouses designed to rival those found in European health spas. The facilities opened to the public in 1935, and the area officially became a state park in 1962. The result is the 2000-acre Spa State Park, which contains beautifully landscaped grounds, spas, outdoor pools and pavilions.

The grounds of the state park also house the Saratoga Performing Arts Center.

Orientation

From I-87, exit 13N (Route 9) goes right into town, where it becomes Broadway. Saratoga Spa State Park is on the west side of Broadway before you hit the town center. The racecourse is a few blocks east of Broadway off Union Ave. You can easily walk around the town, although you may want to drive through the state park.

Information

Saratoga Springs has several visitor and tourist information spots. The most visible is the Urban Heritage Area and Visitors Center (☎ 518-587-3241) across from Congress Park at 297 Broadway in Drink Hall, a 1916 beaux arts trolley station that was converted to a public springwater drinking building in 1941. It's open Monday through Saturday from 9 am to 4 pm and Sunday during July and August from 9 am to 4 pm. They also maintain a summertime information booth (☎ 518-584-4471) at the Broadway entrance to Congress Park. The helpful Saratoga County Chamber of Commerce (☎ 518-584-3255), 28 Clinton St, is open from 9 am to 5 pm Monday to Friday. Its website is www.saratoga.org.

The post office is on Broadway at the corner of Church St.

The public library (complete with cafe) is across from Congress Park on Henry St; there is also an entrance on Putnam.

Lyrical Ballad Bookstore (☎ 518-584-8779), 7 and 9 Phila St, is an inviting old bookshop. It is open daily from 10 am to 6 pm and Sunday from 11 am to 5 pm.

The AAA Northway office (☎ 518-587-8449), 26 West Ave, has maps and travel services. It is open Monday, Wednesday and Friday from 9 am to 5 pm and to 6pm on Tuesday and Thursday.

Cudney's Laundry (☎ 518-584-8460) is at 126 S Broadway, just south of Lincoln Ave. S&S Friendly Laundry is at 57 Church St, two blocks off Broadway.

Walking Tour

This walking tour takes you to the major natural and man-made sights in Saratoga Springs; descriptions of these sights occur later in this section. Begin at **Congress Park** on Broadway. Walk east through the park to sample the **Columbian & Congress Springs** and look at the **casino**. Come out at the back of the park and cross Circular St to proceed up Union Ave. Walk east on Union past the decent old houses to the **National Museum of Racing and the Race Course**. Walk back west on Union to Nelson Ave, and go north to Lake Ave, then west to High Rock Ave. Walk north on High Rock to the **High Rock Cone** and **Governor & Peerless Springs**. Continue north on High Rock Ave to the **Old Red Spring** at the intersection with Excelsior Ave. Walk south on Excelsior Ave until it becomes Maple Ave, and then cut one block west to return to Broadway.

Springs

There are public springs throughout the town – a spring even runs through the lobby of the information building – and in Congress Park, but the majority are concentrated in Saratoga Spa State Park. Except in the coldest weather, spring waters are pumped constantly, spilling from spigots into concrete catch basins or drains. The taste of each and the purported medicinal effects vary greatly. Carry a cup with you for tasting. There is also the helpful guide *The Springs of Saratoga*, which provides information the history and location of each spring.

Saratoga Spa State Park If you have time for only one stop in the park, go to the Geyser area parking lot on Loop Rd from where you can walk to several springs. At the north end of the parking lot is the **State Seal Spring**, which pumps non-mineral well water.

Across Loop Rd and about 50 feet southeast of the parking lot are the unmarked **Polaris Spring** and **Pump Well No 5**. These are also piped, but they bubble up very close to the ground, so you may have to clear away questionable-looking vegetation to taste the water.

Across Loop Rd to the northwest of the parking lot is Geyser Brook. Running along the edge of the stream, you'll find **Hayes Well**, which is immediately across Loop Rd and is marked by a square cobblestone block about 4 feet high and capped with a stone. A spring pours out of one side of the block, and on the other side there is a 1-inch pipe from which you can inhale carbon dioxide – for that 'special' feeling. However, do not inhale deeply or your nasal passages will be burned.

Walk north a few feet and you'll find **Island Spouter**, a geyser next to the brook that spouts a continuous stream of water 10 to 20 feet into the air above a large mound of calcified minerals. If you walk north on the asphalt path above the west side of Geyser Brook, you will come to **Orenda Spring**. Its highly mineralized water contains so much radium that a sign has been posted that warns drinkers not to overindulge. If you walk along the dirt trail below the asphalt path on the west side of the creek, you come to a mound of minerals created by

the build up from the Orenda runoff as it heads into the brook.

Elsewhere in the park, **Coesa Spouter** is visible from the northwest corner of the Coesa parking area. It spouts 10 feet up from a pipe in the middle of a small creek, and its water is said to be valuable in curing digestive ailments. **Hathorn No 3**, at the intersection of Route 50 and the park's east-west road, is purported to be a laxative. Another freshwater spring is at the north end of the park, south of Geyser Rd and next to the old bottling plant. **Charlie Spring** flows out of a wall near Saratoga Performing Arts Center.

In addition to the spring waters, the park features a full range of resort-like amenities, including two swimming pools: the Olympic-sized Peerless Pool and the Victoria Pool. If you don't want to swim, check out Victoria's gracious surroundings and arched pavilions. You can spend an entire afternoon relaxing here for $6 ($3 for children ages five to 11).

DOWNTOWN SARATOGA SPRINGS

PLACES TO STAY
4 Willow Walk
21 Adelphi Hotel

PLACES TO EAT
5 Olde Bryan Inn
9 Compton's
11 Esperanto
12 Sperry's
14 Uncommon Grounds Coffee & Tea
15 Scallions
18 Four Seasons Natural Food Café
19 Hattie's

OTHER
1 Old Red Spring
2 High Rock Cone; Peerless & Governor Springs
3 Peerless & Victoria Pools
6 S & S Friendly Laundry
7 Saratoga County Chamber of Commerce
8 Post Office
9 One Caroline Street
13 Parting Glass Pub
16 Public Library
17 Lyrical Ballad Bookstore
20 Caffe Lena
22 Urban Heritage Area & Visitors' Center
23 Congress Spring
24 Casino
25 Columbian Spring
26 Regent St Antique Center

The park also has walking trails, a golf course, tennis courts and picnic areas. It is open daily 8 am to dusk. Admission is $4 per car and free if you walk or bicycle in.

Congress Park The small, formally landscaped Congress Park is directly across from the visitors' center, just off Broadway. The park was developed in 1823 and houses Morrissey's restored 1870 Victorian casino, which is now a museum and art gallery. Around the casino there are Italian sculpture gardens and three springs, including **Congress Spring**, which is inside a Greek Revival-style pavilion. The spring was 'improved' by Gideon Putnam in the late 1700s and its water bottled and sold in the 1820s. **Columbian Spring**, a freshwater spring, also runs through the park.

You can drive into the park from Broadway and park on the road just past the entrance gate.

High Rock Park High Rock Park is a narrow park two blocks east of Broadway. The park itself isn't particularly attractive and is bordered by a few modern townhouses. However, the park's springs are of historical interest. It was here, according to legend, that in 1767 the Mohawk Indians introduced Sir William Johnson to the restorative powers of the highly mineralized water. In doing so, the area was opened to commercial development.

Around 1800, Alexander Bryan built a public house of logs on the ridge above the springs and filled a water trough 'similar to those in use for feeding swine' for the use of his customers. By the 1830s, Bryan had built a stone house, which is now a restaurant called Olde Bryan Inn (see Places to Eat, later in this section).

High Rock Cone is a cone formed by the mineral deposits of the spring water pumped through it. The cone sits inside a semicircular cement and cobblestone grotto that has a pavilion roof. The water bubbles out very slowly from the top of the cone. **Governor Spring**, about 50 feet to the south of the cone, was drilled in 1908 and is named for former New York Governor Charles Evans

Hughes, who signed a bill protecting the springs. The spring has a strong mineral taste. Behind it is the very mild tasting **Peerless Spring**, and its water is actually pumped from across High Rock Ave.

Other Springs in Town The **Old Red Spring** is at the northern end of High Rock Ave near the intersection with Excelsior Ave, a few blocks from High Rock Park. In 1784, a bathhouse was built here. The spring, which has a high iron content, was called the 'beauty water spring' because it was said to be good for the complexion and as a cure for eye problems.

Outside the downtown area, **Rosemary Spring** is behind the Crystal Spa and in front of the Grand Union Motel at 120 S Broadway; although it looks as if it is on private-motel property, it is open to the public.

Mineral Baths

The **Roosevelt Baths** (☎ 518-584-2011) are inside Saratoga Spa State Park. Although the baths are closed for renovation (as of this writing), the stately Georgian-style building is worth a look when you visit the park. For an old-fashioned mineral bath, people still go to the nearby Lincoln Baths.

The **Lincoln Baths** (☎ 518-583-2880), on S Broadway between the park entrance and the National Museum of Dance, are operating year round until the renovation at Roosevelt Baths is completed. The Lincoln Baths started in 1911 in a remodeled gas company building and moved to its present home in 1935. In the Georgian building, there are men's and women's sections with semiprivate soaking rooms. Each has a deep tub and a massage table. The customary treatment here is to sit in the bubbly water (which contains 16 minerals) for 20 minutes, and then relax on a table for another 20 minutes. Moving around in the tub increases the amount of carbonation, just like shaking a bottle of soda. Weekday/weekend rates are $23/26 for massage only, $35/40 for bath and massage and $13/15 for bath only.

Crystal Spa (☎ 518-584-2556), 120 S Broadway, is the only private-bath facility in town. It pumps water from the publicly accessible Rosemary Spring, located behind the building. The facilities and treatments here are more luxurious than those in the public baths in the park. The 15 soaking rooms have tile floors. A mineral bath, sauna treatment and 30-minute massage costs $47. Other services include body wraps and seaweed treatments. The spa is closed on Wednesday and Thursday except during the summer.

Saratoga Race Course

From late July to August, the town is transformed as fans flock to the Saratoga Race Course (☎ 518-584-6200), the oldest active thoroughbred racetrack in the US. Hotel prices soar, the streets are jammed with fancy cars, and the nights are long, as gamblers celebrate or commiserate over their wins and losses. You don't have to be a high-stakes gambler to enjoy the racetrack. General admission is only $2 ($5 for clubhouse admission), and the minimum bet is $1. On the way in, pick up a copy of the *Post Parade*, which lists each horse's record by race and describes how to place bets.

Once inside, you can walk right up to the fence and stand a few feet from the horses as they charge past. You can also stand near the winner's circle and watch the congratulations bestowed on jockey, owner and horse. Even if you lose all your money, you can still cheer the horses, take in the crowds and enjoy the great musical entertainment. Jazz and folk groups change on a daily basis, and the house Dixieland band guarantees that there is never a lull in the fast-paced, spirited atmosphere.

The track is closed on Tuesday, steeplechase is on Wednesday and Thursday; post time is generally at 1 pm. Parking near the track runs in the neighborhood of $3 to $5. There is free admission from 7 am to 9:30 am. This is the time to come and watch the horses' morning workouts and get a free tour of the stables. Many people bring their own breakfast and coffee, or splurge at the trackside cafe for a $12 breakfast buffet.

There are plenty of outdoor-food concessions at the track where you can buy typically overpriced food. Picnic tables are available in the grassy areas near the Victorian clubhouse, or you can sit under the grandstand and watch the races on television while you eat. As an alternative, you can eat at one of the several $15-minimum clubhouse dining rooms, but only if you are properly attired – 'collared shirts for men, no shorts or abbreviated wear.'

National Museum of Racing & Hall of Fame

This state-of-the-art museum (☎ 518-584-0400), on Union Ave across from the track, contains exhibits on the history of horseracing in England and America and on jockeys, thoroughbreds and breeding. In addition to paintings, sculptures and memorabilia, the museum has interactive exhibits built to scale and a multimedia center where you can watch a famous race of your choice in one of the video booths that line the walls. It is open Monday to Saturday from 10 am to 4:30 pm and Sunday from noon to 4:30 pm, and during the racing season, it is open from 9 am to 5 pm. Admission is $5 for adults, $3 for children and seniors and free for children under 5. Admission is free on Sunday, except during July and August.

National Museum of Dance

This dance museum (☎ 518-584-2225) is on S Broadway next to the Lincoln Baths in the former Washington Baths building. This is the country's only museum dedicated to preserving the history and art of American dance; the building has a hall of fame and changing exhibits. A must for dance fans, it's open year round Tuesday through Sunday from 10 am to 5 pm. Admission price is $3.50/2.50/1 for adults/students/children under 12.

Yaddo

Yaddo (☎ 518-584-0746), on Union Ave east of the racecourse, is a private estate that has served as a retreat for writers, poets, artists and composers since the 1920s. The massive cut-stone mansion and lush grounds were built and developed by industrialist Spencer Trask and his wife. After their four children were killed in a smallpox epidemic, the

Trasks converted the estate into a working community where they hoped artists might 'find the Sacred Fire and light their torches at its flames.' The mansion is still an artists' retreat and is, therefore, off limits to the public. However, the beautifully landscaped gardens – including a mysterious wooded area and formal rose garden – are open to visitors during the day.

Special Events
The Saratoga Polo Association (☎ 518-584-8108) hosts polo events from mid-June to mid-August at Bostwick Field at the Saratoga Equine Sports Center or at Whitney Field 2 miles from town. To reach Whitney Field, go north on Broadway, left on Church St for a half mile to Seward, right on Seward for 1 mile to the railroad overpass, and then turn right and look for the field on your left. Adult/senior admission to events is $5/3.

Places to Stay
Every August hotel prices double or even triple as the town fills up for the six-week thoroughbred racing season. You need to make reservations a year in advance to be sure of getting a room during this time. Rooms can also be scarce, and prices accordingly high, in May during commencement ceremonies at Skidmore College. Any other time of year – with the exception of the mid-winter – is a good time to visit Saratoga.

Budget The nearest campground to Saratoga is *Cold Brook Campsites* (☎ 518-584-8038), about 10 miles north in Gansevoort. Open May to early October, the campground has 272 sites, laundry facilities and hot showers. There's a $20 daily fee. Take I-87 to exit 16 and go north 1 mile on Gurn Springs Rd, or follow Route 50 north out of town.

Further north in Corinth is *Rustic Barn Campsites* (☎ 518-654-6588). It is open May through September and has 55 sites, hot showers and laundry facilities for $15 to $17 a day. Take Route 9N north from Corinth for 12 miles.

Mid-Range The cheapest places to stay are the independently owned motels outside of town, between I-87 exits 12 and 13N, and along Route 9 north of town. Slightly more expensive places are between exit 13N and town.

Kimberly Guest House (☎ 518-584-9006, 184 S Broadway), at Lincoln Ave just outside of downtown, rents eight rooms with kitchens and televisions. Some rooms share baths. During the winter, rates are $35. As the summer approaches and the temperature rises, so do the rates. In July, they're $55; by August, $99. *Saratoga Motel* (☎ 518-584-0920, 440 Church St), 2 miles west of town, charges $55 for a single and $85 to $95 for a double during racing season, making it one of the best deals in town during peak season.

The renovated *Holiday Inn* (☎ 518-584-4550), Broadway at Circular St, is near the south end of Congress Park. Rooms are spacious and rates vary from $52 to $75. During the racing season, expect to pay around $190 a night.

Brunswick Bed & Breakfast (☎ 518-584-6751, 143 Union Ave) is a rooming house that is transformed during racing season into a makeshift B&B. Weekly rates for rooms with shared/private bath are $65/80. In July and August, daily rates are almost as high as weekly rates are during the rest of the year. Rooms rates are about $80/95.

Top End *Willow Walk* (☎ 518-584-4549, 120 High Rock Ave), across from the High Rock Park springs, is one of the newest B&Bs in Saratoga. There are four rooms with private baths and a living room with a wood-burning fireplace. Two of the bedrooms have twin beds, and two rooms have queens. Off-season rates are $60 to $80; summer rates $85 to $95; and racing season $135 to $145.

Union Gables (☎ 518-584-1558, 800-398-1158, 55 Union Ave), just before the racecourse, is one of the loveliest B&Bs in town. The restored turn-of-the-century Victorian has 10 spacious, individually decorated rooms with private baths and refrigerators. Rates from November to April are $80; $90 from September to October and May to July; and $200 in August.

If you have transportation and like personal attention, try *Saratoga B&B* (☎ 518-584-0920, 434 Church St). There are actually two houses here, each with four rooms. One house was built in 1850 and has been lovingly restored. Each room is a suite with gas fireplace, television and phone. In the other house, the spacious rooms are decorated with period furnishings and handmade quilts. All rooms have private baths, and two rooms have fireplaces. Rates, which include full breakfast, run $65 to $135 and $95 to $195 during racing season. From downtown, go west on Church St for 2 miles; Saratoga B&B is on the left.

Six Sisters B&B (☎ 518-583-1173, 149 Union Ave) has four rooms, several with porches. All rooms have refrigerators and air-conditioning. Rates include a full breakfast. From November to March, rooms cost $60 to $89; April to October, $85 to $105; and in August, they go up from there.

Its location in the middle of Saratoga Spa State Park makes *Gideon Putnam Hotel* (☎ 518-584-3000, 800-732-1560) the most famous hotel in town. Owned by the state of New York, the Georgian colonial hotel was renovated in keeping with the vintage elegance of Saratoga. Guests approach the hotel – as one might expect – up a grand driveway. The lobby is expansive, with marble floors, potted palms and period furnishings. Rooms are extremely comfortable, and the hotel has several restaurants and bars and easy access to all the recreational activities in the park. The hotel is in a beautiful setting right off the Avenue of Pines. From May 1 to October 31, rates are $94 to $147; in August, $236 to $433.

Adelphi Hotel (☎ 518-587-4688, 365 Broadway) is old Saratoga personified – including its seasonal schedule (it's only open May to October). The Adelphi was built in 1877 and is elegantly Victorian throughout. Rates vary from $100 to $150 during the off season, but rise to $200 to $300 during May graduation at nearby Skidmore College and the August racing season.

Places to Eat
Budget The town diner is *Compton's* (☎ 518-584-9632, 457 Broadway), between Caroline St and Lake Ave. It's open Monday to Friday from 4 am to 2:45 pm and weekends from 3 am to 2:45 pm. Just a bit south of downtown is *Spa City Diner* (☎ 518-584-9833, 133 S Broadway), which has been around since 1948 and is open 24 hours daily.

Weathervane Seafood Restaurant (☎ 518-584-8157), on S Broadway a mile south of Congress Park, serves fresh and moderately priced seafood. It is open daily for lunch and dinner.

Uncommon Grounds Coffee & Tea (☎ 518-581-0646, 402 Broadway) is a convivial morning or late-night spot for good coffee, pastries, fresh bagels, soups and sandwiches. It is open daily from 7 am to 11 pm, and midnight on Friday and Saturday. Around the corner is *Esperanto* (☎ 518-587-4236, 6 1/2 Caroline St), a tasty budget eatery with an international flavor.

Mid-Range A wide variety of food is offered at *Scallions* (☎ 518-584-0192, 404 Broadway), which serves very good sandwiches with fresh turkey breast, salmon and hummus ($6.50). There are also several chicken dishes with sun-dried tomatoes, artichoke hearts, curry and other stuff for $11.

Hattie's (☎ 518-584-4790, 45 Phila St) has been serving Southern cooking since 1938. The restaurant is a Saratoga landmark and a very good eatery. Southern fried chicken costs $11, ribs $13 and pork chops $12. *Four Seasons Natural Foods & Café* (☎ 518-584-4670, 33 Phila St), a short block east of Broadway, serves excellent buffet-style vegetarian fare, with homemade soups, deserts and cornbread. The cafe is open daily from 11 am to 8 pm.

Olde Bryan Inn (☎ 518-587-2990, 123 Maple Ave), behind the Sheraton, is a popular place because of its 'rustic' look – stone walls, exposed beams and fireplaces. The look would seem fake if it weren't in fact a 19th-century building. There are more tables than the space warrants, but the atmosphere is pleasant and no one minds.

Grilled sandwiches and hot and cold salads cost around $7. Chicken, meat and fish entrees range from $12 to $17.

Sperry's (☎ 518-584-9618, 30½ Caroline St) has excellent fish and meat dishes for $15 to $20 and a fine wine list. The food and service are quite good and the atmosphere is very casual.

Entertainment

As if there weren't already enough to draw visitors to town, the *Saratoga Performing Arts Center (SPAC; ☎ 518-587-3330)* offers world-class entertainment. Located in Saratoga Spa State Park, SPAC is the summer home for both the New York City Ballet and the Philadelphia Orchestra. In addition, the outdoor amphitheater draws big-name entertainment, ranging from Tony Bennett to Twyla Tharp's Dance Company. Tickets cost $15 to $35, and you can often get lawn seats for $12.50 to $15.

Caffe Lena (☎ 518-583-0022, 47 Phila St) is the 'oldest continuously operating coffeehouse in America.' Now run as a nonprofit, the cafe is a wonderful throwback to the 1960s folk scene, and it is an authentic Saratoga original. It still books top acoustic musicians and is a venue for young performers. The cafe is open Thursday through Sunday.

One Caroline Street (☎ 518-587-2026, 1 Caroline St) is a fine jazz and blues bistro with live jazz four nights a week. One Caroline also serves excellent food including a Sunday brunch. *Parting Glass Pub (☎ 518-583-1916, 40-42 Lake Ave)* is a block east of Broadway near the fire department, and in addition to the extensive beer selection, the big attraction is the traditional Irish music. The club draws top performers from Ireland and the US.

Shopping

The Regent St Antique Center (☎ 518-584-0107), 153 Regent St, a block east of Congress Park, houses 30 antique dealers in one building. This is a great place to hunt for regionally produced stoneware and crockery as well as silver, glassware, paintings and books. It is open daily from 10 am to 5 pm

year-round. Many other interesting antique shops, clothing stores as well as music shops can be found off of Broadway on Phila and Caroline Sts.

Getting There & Away

Both Greyhound and Adirondack Trailways stop at the Spa City Diner (☎ 518-584-0911), 153 S Broadway. CDTA buses go to Albany, Schenectady and Troy. From Saratoga Springs to New York City, the four-hour trip typically costs $32/60; to Albany, the 35-minute trip costs $6/11.

The Amtrak station (☎ 518-587-8354), West Ave at Station Lane, is a couple of miles outside of town. Saratoga Springs is on the Montreal to New York City line, with one train going north and one south daily. Fares from New York's Penn Station to Saratoga Springs are $34/68 one-way/roundtrip, except Friday and Sunday, when it jumps to $56/112.

Saratoga is off I-87 at exit 13N. The exit leads you along Route 9 past Saratoga Spa State Park and onto Broadway. Enterprise Rent-A-Car (☎ 518-587-0687), 180 S Broadway near the Hilton Inn, is a national car-rental agency.

Getting Around

The CDTA Saratoga Springs bus No 98 makes a big loop through town Monday to Saturday. It costs 75¢.

During August racing season, Upstate Transit (☎ 518-584-5252) runs a shuttle bus to/from the track and Broadway (downtown) for $1.

Saratoga Horse Carriage Co (☎ 518-695-3359) runs carriage rides to/from the Gideon Putnam Hotel and points in Saratoga Spa State Park for $20.

AROUND SARATOGA SPRINGS
Saratoga National Historic Park

In October 1777, British forces were defeated at the Battle of Saratoga, a major turning point in the campaigns of the Revolutionary War. The battle is commemorated at various sites within the 2800-acre Saratoga National Historic Park (☎ 518-664-9821), PO Box 648, Route 32, Stillwater, NY

The Battle of Saratoga

For many Europeans, the American victory over British General Burgoyne's army at Saratoga was proof that Americans could fight successfully against the British. The battle is often characterized as a turning point in the war because the American victory led to France's entry into the war on behalf of the US.

Burgoyne believed that the key to defeating the colonies was to control the Hudson River. He left St Johns (now St Jean) in Canada in mid-June 1777 with a 9000-man army of British, German, Canadian and Iroquois troops. Burgoyne's strategy involved acting in concert with other British forces, specifically Colonel St Leger's troops marching from Lake Ontario in the east and General Howe's coming from New York City to the south. However,
in early August, Colonel St Leger's forces, fearing attack by a larger American force led by Benedict Arnold, retreated back to Canada after penetrating 50 miles east. Meanwhile, General Howe had moved his army against Philadelphia, not leaving enough troops in New York City to aid Burgoyne in the north.

In spite of setbacks, Burgoyne pushed on through Saratoga (now Schuylerville) and was engaged by American troops in the town of Stillwater. The American troops were now commanded by General Horatio Gates, who was aided by Polish engineer Thaddeus Kosciuszko. In two battles on September 19 and October 7, Burgoyne's forces suffered heavy casualties and retreated to Saratoga. An American force of 20,000 men surrounded them there, and on October 17, Burgoyne surrendered.

MICHAEL CLARK

12170, 14 miles east of Saratoga Springs via Route 29. At the visitors' center you can pick up a guide to key battle sites along a 9-mile driving tour. The route is open from early May to late November. There is a $4 vehicle fee; bicycles are also permitted on the route for $2. Or, you can hike the trails for $2. The park is open year round and is a popular spot for cross-country skiing.

Seven miles north of the visitors' center – and still within the park boundaries – is **Schuylerville**, formerly the town of Saratoga. Located on Route 4 at the southern end of the town is the **Philip Schuyler House** (☎ 518-695-3664). Schuyler was a Revolutionary War general who commanded the northern frontier from his home in Albany. Schuylerville was the site of his summer house, which was burned by British General Burgoyne's retreating forces. The present house was rebuilt in 30 days on the same

site. The house, which has been carefully restored with period furnishings, is open Memorial Day through Labor Day Wednesday through Sunday from 9 am to 5 pm. From the day after Labor Day until the end of September, the house is open Saturday and Sunday from 9 am to 5 pm. Guided tours are available.

Also in Schuylerville is **Saratoga Monument**, a 155-foot obelisk commemorating this decisive battle. Dedicated in 1912, the monument sits upon a 300-foot hill that affords spectacular views of the surrounding countryside. The monument is currently closed for renovations.

COOPERSTOWN

With a population of only 2300, Cooperstown must be the most popular small-town destination in the state. It is a mix of kitsch and culture with shops dominated by tacky souvenirs such as baseball cards and T-shirts, as well as good bookstores, opera and theater. The draw for most visitors is an equally disparate but interesting mix of museums – the Fenimore Art Museum, Farmers' Museum and National Baseball Hall of Fame and Museum.

Don't let the commercialism associated with baseball deter you from stopping here. The town has a great deal to recommend it, including the museums, its location on the forested banks of Otsego Lake, its attractive 19th-century architecture and excellent accommodations and restaurants.

Cooperstown was founded in 1786 by William Cooper, a wealthy land agent and the father of novelist James Fenimore Cooper, author of *The Last of the Mohicans*, The Leatherstocking series, *The Pathfinder* and *The Deerslayer*. Cooper spent much of his childhood here as did Stephen Clark, a descendent of Edward Clark who made his money in Singer sewing machines. Stephen Clark was the fortune behind the creation of the three museums that have turned Cooperstown into a popular tourist spot.

An earlier local resident, General Abner Doubleday, was falsely credited with in-

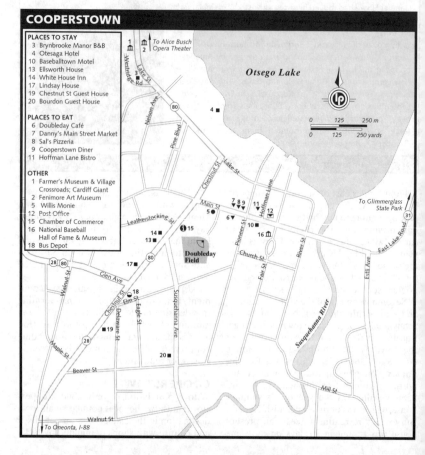

COOPERSTOWN

PLACES TO STAY
3 Brynbrooke Manor B&B
4 Otesaga Hotel
10 Baseballtown Motel
13 Ellsworth House
14 White House Inn
17 Lindsay House
19 Chestnut St Guest House
20 Bourdon Guest House

PLACES TO EAT
6 Doubleday Café
7 Danny's Main Street Market
8 Sal's Pizzeria
9 Cooperstown Diner
11 Hoffman Lane Bistro

OTHER
1 Farmer's Museum & Village
  Crossroads; Cardiff Giant
2 Fenimore Art Museum
5 Willis Monie
12 Post Office
15 Chamber of Commerce
16 National Baseball
  Hall of Fame & Museum
18 Bus Depot

venting the game of baseball in 1839. Despite the historical inaccuracy, Cooperstown has been the home to the National Baseball Hall of Fame and Museum since its opening in 1939. This is the most popular sports museum in the US, attracting more than 400,000 devoted visitors annually. In late July or early August, the town is even more crowded than usual as baseball fans make a pilgrimage here for the annual inductions into the Hall of Fame and the Hall of Fame Game.

Information

The Cooperstown Chamber of Commerce (☎ 607-547-9983) is in the Higgins Cottage at 31 Chestnut St on the way into town. The office has information on the town and limited details on accommodations. It is open daily from 9 am to 7 pm from late May to early September; during the rest of year, it is open daily from 9 am to 5 pm. Its website is www.cooperstownchamber.org.

The post office is on Main St opposite the National Baseball Hall of Fame. Willis Monie (☎ 607-547-8363, 800-322-2995), 139 Main St, is an excellent bookstore that sells used books.

National Baseball Hall of Fame & Museum

The Hall of Fame (☎ 607-547-7200), 25 Main St, is baseball's national shrine and houses all the important baseball artifacts, such as famous players' bats, gloves and uniforms and balls hit by Babe Ruth, Willie Mays and Reggie Jackson, just to name a few. Plaques honoring the players – and a handful of managers, umpires and others – who have been voted into the hall are on display. In addition to the thousands of artifacts, the museum has its own movie theater and offers exhibits on every imaginable aspect of baseball. There are many superb interactive statistical exhibits and, for the more serious fans, a library.

From May to September, the museum is open daily from 9 am to 9 pm. From October to April, the doors close at 5 pm. Admission is $9.50/4 for adults/children (ages seven to 12), free for children six and under.

If you intend to visit Cooperstown's other museums (the Fenimore Art Museum and Farmers' Museum) in addition to this museum, you can buy a combination ticket and save 20% to 25% off the price of a single ticket. A combination ticket for two of the museums is $15/6.50 for adults/children (ages seven to 12); for three of the museums, $22/9.50.

Farmers' Museum & Village Crossroads

The Farmers' Museum (☎ 607-547-1450) and adjacent Village Crossroads are holdings of the New York State Historical Association. The museum is comprised of a dozen 19th-century buildings built in the region and moved to Cooperstown on land donated by the Clark estate. The village's buildings – which include a working blacksmith shop, general store, printing office, barn and more – have been very realistically assembled to capture the atmosphere of rural life and to exhibit rural trades and skills. Demonstrations range from farming practices to baking bread to printing.

The nearby **Cardiff Giant** is a 2990-pound carving that, in the 19th century, was passed off as the petrified skeletal remains of a giant dug up in nearby Cardiff. In fact, cigar maker George Hull had the giant sculpted out of gypsum. Even after the hoax was discovered, people continued to line up – as they do today – to see the 'petrified giant.'

From June 1 through Labor Day, the museum is open daily from 10 am to 5 pm; and from April to May and October to November, it is open daily from 10 am to 4 pm. Admission is $9 for adults, $4 for children (ages seven to 12), and free for children six and under.

Fenimore Art Museum

Across from the Farmers' Museum is the stone Fenimore Art Museum (☎ 607-547-1420), formerly Fenimore House, which was the home of Edward Clark, of Singer sewing-machine fame and the town benefactor. Heirs to his estate converted an Iroquois bark house into a museum, which now displays quite an outstanding collection of

The Origin of Baseball

Although Cooperstown is popularly considered the birthplace of baseball, it almost certainly was not. In 1907, baseball's owners, attempting to establish the American origins of baseball, set up the Mills commission to investigate the issue. The commission took their task seriously and came up with a story establishing baseball as a truly 'American' game, complete with a deceased military hero as its inventor. The inconvenient fact that baseball developed almost directly from the British game of 'rounders' was ignored.

The commission announced that baseball was invented in Cooperstown in 1839 by Abner Doubleday (who, at that time, was not in his hometown of Cooperstown but was instead studying at West Point). Doubleday, who died in 1893, was unavailable to comment.

Doubleday or not, the commission's findings were not completely unfounded. Baseball was being played in the 1840s in the urban areas of the northeast, with many organized baseball clubs. In 1876 the National League was formed, giving birth to truly professional ball in the sense that players were now openly paid for their services.

Baseball gained in popularity, and in 1902 the American League was formed, challenging the monopoly of the old National League. The first World Series was played a couple of years later, and modern baseball was in full swing.

Although there were a handful of black players in the National League during the late 1800s, professional baseball was strictly segregated and remained so until after WWII. The major leagues (and their minor league 'farm teams') were reserved for whites only. Black players were relegated to the Negro Leagues, playing under harsh conditions and for little money. In 1947, Jackie Robinson signed with the Brooklyn Dodgers and became the first black player in modern baseball. He was quickly followed by other young players from the Negro League, and baseball became integrated. However, many of the finest players of that era never had the chance to test their skills against 'all comers.'

Baseball has long been a game of tradition, with statistics and records playing an important part in helping to build its popularity and its place in American mythology. The more recent developments of TV marketing, free agency, player strikes, lockouts, escalating salaries and astronomical profits have often frustrated the game's broad appeal with spectators, but it is still the irrevocable symbol of the National Pastime.

For an extensive overview of the sport, look for Ken Burns' *Baseball*, a PBS documentary series available on videotape.

folk art, Native American artifacts and masks, contemporary photography and paintings from the Hudson River school of landscape painters. Included here are Thomas Cole's *Last of the Mohicans* and Gilbert Stuart's *Joseph Brandt*.

The museum also houses memorabilia of the author James Fenimore Cooper. Ironically, Cooper's work is far more popular in other countries than it is in the US, where it came under sharp attack as early as the late 19th century. American writers and poets of that time – most notably Mark Twain and Walt Whitman – were breaking with the British literary traditions and developing a truly authentic American voice in their writing. Cooper's romanticized characters, his unrealistic and contrived dialogue and the conservative views he expressed in his essays were harshly criticized, especially by the sharp-witted Twain.

More recently, however, Cooper's work gained some favor when his *Last of the Mohicans* was made into a popular movie. Whatever your views of the writer and his work, it's fascinating to view the country's history – as is done at the Fenimore Art Museum – through the lives of one of its literary figures. The museum is open July 15 to Labor Day daily from 9 am to 5 pm. After Labor Day until October 31 and the week after Christmas, it is open daily from 10 am to 4 pm. From December 1 to 24, the museum is open Friday through Sunday. The price of admission is $9.

Otsego Lake

According to local lore, Judge William Cooper founded the village of Cooperstown in 1786 because of the pristine lakeside setting. He also purchased a colonial land grant and sold plots of land adjacent to the lake. His son, author James Fennimore Cooper, called the lake Glimmerglass in his novel *The Deerslayer,* describing it as 'a broad sheet of water, so placid and limpid that it resembled a bed of pure mountain atmosphere compressed into a setting of hills and woods.' There are three parks for swimming and fishing, two small public boat launches, along with two golf courses, though most of the shoreline is protected from development.

Places to Stay

Budget The nearest campground is ***Cooperstown Beaver Valley Campground*** (☎ 800-726-7314, Route 28 Box 704), about 4 miles south of Cooperstown near the town of Index. The campground has 100 sites and complete facilities, including laundry, hot showers and boat rentals. Sites are $21 and they offer a free shuttle bus to town on weekends in July and August.

There's also ***Cooperstown Famous Family Tent & Trailer Campground*** (☎ 607-293-7766), 4 miles south of Cooperstown. From Route 28, take County Rd 11 west for 4 miles. Sites with laundry facilities and hot showers cost $18.

On the northeast side of Otsego Lake, ***Glimmerglass State Park*** (☎ 607-547-8662, RR 2 Box 580) offers campsites with hot showers and laundry facilities for $10.

Mid-Range *Bourdon Guest House* (☎ 607-547-9387, 60 Susquehanna Ave) has the best bargain in town. There is a single, small, clean, dormered room on the second floor of this old Cooperstown home, with two beds, a television and fridge. The bathroom is in the room, but the shower is a short walk down some stairs and through the house. The single/double occupancy rate is $30/35 in the summer and $25/30 in the winter.

Ellsworth House (☎ 607-547-8367, 52 Chestnut St) is a three-room B&B. Single/double rates, with breakfast, are $30/55. ***Lindsay House*** (☎ 607-547-5618, 56 Chestnut St) has three small studios with private entrances for $45 to $55.

Chestnut St Guest House (☎ 607-547-5624, 79 Chestnut St) has two rooms. One is decorated with baseball memorabilia and has a shared bath for $65, including continental breakfast. The other is a one-bedroom suite with a kitchen and sleeping porch for $90. You cook for yourself if you rent the suite. The hosts are friendly and knowledgeable about the area.

The downtown ***Baseballtown Motel*** (☎ 607-547-2161, 61-63 Main St) has unremarkable but large rooms with TVs for $45 to $59 for singles and $48 to $98 for doubles.

Lake & Pines Motel (☎ 607-547-2790, 800-615-5253, 7102 Hwy 80), a few miles north of Cooperstown on Otsego Lake, offers nice rooms and cottages to rent daily or weekly. Amenities include both an indoor and outdoor pool, whirlpool, sauna, rowboats and paddle boats. A good time to visit is during the off season when rooms are $50/60 for a single/double and range up to $125 on summer weekends.

Major League Motor Inn (☎ 607-547-2266), on Route 28 about 3 miles north of Cooperstown, is a good value, with family rates at $80 in the summer season and $55 in the off-season.

Top End The B&B, ***White House Inn*** (☎ 607-547-5054, fax 607-547-1100, 46 Chestnut St), is a circa 1835 classic Greek Revival home that has gardens and a pool. For two people, room rates are $85 in the low season and $125 in the high season; both rates include complete breakfast. Rooms have private baths, phones and TVs.

Brynbrooke Manor B&B (☎ 607-547-2893, 6 Westridge Rd), near Lake and Nelson

Sts, is a lovely renovated Victorian mansion set back on a quiet lane, with four large rooms, all with private bath. Rooms cost about $100, and rates include full breakfast. Call ahead for reservations.

Located right on Otsego Lake, *Otesaga Hotel* (☎ 607-547-9931, 800-678-8946, 60 Lake St) is a beautiful Georgian resort with manicured lawns, a golf course, tennis courts, fishing, pool and boat rental. Built in 1909, this stately landmark is well worth visiting for a drink or a meal, even if you don't choose to stay here. A trolley runs from the hotel to downtown. It is open from late April to late October only, room rates include breakfast and dinner. Most room rates range from $230 to $320, with a few suites priced at $400 to $500.

Places to Eat

Cooperstown Diner (☎ 607-547-9201, 136½ Main St) and, a few doors down, *Sal's Pizzeria* (☎ 607-547-5721, 110 Main St) generally serve inexpensive 'family style' basics.

Danny's Main Street Market (☎ 607-547-4053, 92 Main St) is a very good deli, with sandwiches made to order, fresh coffee and pastries. *Doubleday Café* (☎ 607-547-5468, 93 Main St) is a good choice for reliable family dining. It is open year-round for breakfast, lunch and dinner. Lunch costs $3 to $7 and dinner $4 to $7.

Dining at *Otesaga Hotel* (☎ 607-547-9931, 60 Lake St) is a lovely experience and a good value considering the elegant surroundings. They have a $12.50 lunch buffet and a set dinner for $27 (including tax and gratuities) and a Sunday brunch for $15 (served from 11 am to 2 pm). Jackets are required for men in the evening.

Hoffman Lane Bistro (☎ 607-547-7055, 2 Hoffman Lane) has lunch and dinner menus with seasonal specials. Lunch entrees cost $6 to $7 and dinner entrees range from $11 to $18. It is open 11:30 am to 3 pm and 5 pm to 9 pm daily, except Sunday.

Fly Creek Cider Mill & Orchard (☎ 607-547-9692), on Route 28 about 3 miles northwest of town, is a water-powered cider press that uses original equipment to make great tasting cider.

Entertainment

In addition to supporting three excellent museums, this tiny town is home to the Glimmerglass Opera, which stages performances at *Alice Busch Opera Theater* (☎ 607-547-2255; box office at 18 Chestnut St), about 8 miles north of Cooperstown on Route 80, opposite the lake. The theater is partially open to the outdoors in the summer. The season is July and August.

A trio performs nightly, except Sunday, throughout the season in the lounge at *Otesaga Hotel* (see Places to Stay, earlier in this chapter).

Getting There & Away

Pine Hills Trailways and Adirondack Trailways (☎ 800-858-8555 for both bus lines) stop in front of the Chestnut St Deli (☎ 607-547-5829), 75 Chestnut St. Pine Hills goes to New York City's Port Authority bus terminal via Woodstock in the Catskills. The one-way/roundtrip fare from Cooperstown to Albany is $18/34.

By car from I-88, take exit 16 and then Route 28 north for 18 miles to town. From I-90, take exit 30 to Route 28 south for 28 miles to town.

Getting Around

A trolley runs throughout town on weekends daily from June 27 through Labor Day. From Memorial Day weekend to June 27 and after Labor Day through Columbus Day, the trolley runs on weekends only. Service is from 8:30 am to 9 pm and costs $2 for the entire day.

In the summer Cooperstown is packed and parking is scarce. The town makes a tidy sum dispensing parking tickets to the unwary. You can park all day for free at Doubleday Field, but the lot is usually full by 8:30 am.

AROUND COOPERSTOWN

Soccer fans love the **National Soccer Hall of Fame** (☎ 607-432-3351), at Brown St in Oneonta, 22 miles from Cooperstown. Both the men's and women's games are highlighted with lots of interactive stuff for children. It is open Thursday to Monday from

10 am to 5 pm and closed Tuesday and Wednesday. Admission is $7.50/4.50 for adults/children.

To get there take from Cooperstown, take Route 28 south to I-88, exit 13. Adirondack Trailways (☎ 800-858-8555) and Vermont Transit (☎ 800-451-3292) operate buses between Cooperstown and Oneonta. The cost for the 30-minute trip is $4/8.

BINGHAMTON & AROUND

When the Chenango Canal was completed in 1837, Binghamton (population 53,000) became a busy link connecting the nearby Pennsylvania coal fields to the Erie Canal and ports beyond. SUNY-Binghamton (formerly Harper College) adds about 12,000 students to the area and provides an active theater and arts scene. The area is also known for several gold-domed Russian Orthodox and Ukrainian Catholic churches.

The Broome County Chamber of Commerce (☎ 607-772-8860, 800-836-6740), 49 Court St, has walking- and driving-tour maps of Binghamton and nearby Endicott and Johnson City – collectively known as the Triple Cities.

Cyber Cafe (☎ 607-723-2456), 176 Main St, offers Internet access.

Discovery Center of the Southern Tier

This is a great children's museum (☎ 607-773-8661), 60 Morgan Rd, with several hands-on exhibits, including a flight simulator. It is open daily during July and August, and Tuesday through Sunday during the rest of the year.

Ross Park Zoo

Established in 1875, this zoo (☎ 607-724-5454), at Park Ave and Morgan Rd, is the fifth oldest in the country. Today, it features picnic facilities, a gift shop and over 200 animals, including birds, reptiles and mammals from around the world. It is open 10 am to 5 pm daily (closed December to February). Admission is $4 adults, $2.75 children and seniors, children two and under free.

Within the park, **Carousel Museum** (☎ 607-724-5461), 60 Morgan Rd, is home to a beautifully restored merry-go-round. There are five others in and around the town – all wood carved and all working – but this is a good place to start. The carousels operate from the end of May until early September, weather permitting, and are free.

Roberson Museum & Science Center

This museum (☎ 607-772-0660), 30 Front St, features displays of regional history and folk art, and has a child-friendly science exhibit and planetarium. The museum is open daily, and admission is $4 for adults and $3 for children (ages five to 17). The planetarium is an additional $1.

Kopernik Space Education Center

The center (☎ 607-748-3685) is at Underwood Rd off Route 26, Vestal Center, Vestal. This is the largest public observatory in New York state and offers hands-on exhibits, lectures and observation sessions. It is open year round on Friday evenings starting at 8 pm, weather and clouds permitting.

Finch Hollow Nature Center

The nature center (☎ 607-729-4231), 1394 Oakdale Rd, Johnson City, offers fishing, hiking, guided nature walks, cross-country skiing, snowshoeing, exhibits and a pond. Trails are open daily during daylight hours. Free tours are given Monday to Friday by appointment. To reach Finch Hollow from Binghamton, take I-86 (formerly Route 17) west about 7 miles to the Johnson City exit and Oakdale Rd.

Making tracks at Finch Hollow

Parks

There are several county parks in the area and **Otsiningo County Park** is one of the closest; it is right in Binghamton on Bevier and Front Sts. The park (☎ 607-778-8826) has a playground and bike and walking trails and is ideal for rollerblading and picnicking.

Chenango Valley State Park (☎ 607-648-5251), a 20-minute drive northeast of town via I-88, is a popular recreation spot for swimming, biking, hiking and cross-country skiing.

Special Events

Dating from 1986, the Binghamton Summer Music Festival (☎ 607-777-4777) runs from mid-July to August and draws some of the best jazz, pop, classical and dance groups in the country. Shows are at the Anderson Center for the Arts (see Entertainment, later in this section), or at parks throughout the area.

Places to Stay

Clean, basic rooms ranging from $45 to $75 can be found at *Super 8 Motel* (☎ 607-775-3443), at Upper Court St and Route 11. *Parkway Motel* (☎ 607-785-3311, 900 Vestal Parkway E), in Vestal, is open all year, with clean rooms and the basic necessities, plus a heated outdoor pool. Rates are $30 to $50. From Binghamton, take Route 434 about 5 miles to Vestal.

Best Western Binghamton Regency Hotel (☎ 607-722-7575, 225 Water St) is the newest big hotel in Binghamton and doubles as a conference center. It is downtown, has a pool and charges reasonable rates ($70 to $80).

The Grand Royale (☎ 607-722-0000, 80 State St) is Binghamton's only upscale hotel and is conveniently located in the downtown business district. The rooms are large and come complete with coffeemaker and refrigerator. Rates are $95 to $125 and include complimentary breakfast.

Places to Eat

Born in Binghamton, 'spiedies' are the sandwiches of choice here, but they never quite gained national notoriety. If you haven't heard of a spiedie, it is made of pork, chicken or lamb in a special marinade, grilled and served on a hoagie roll. You'll find many places – including *Lupo's Char-Pit* (☎ 607-723-6106, 6 West State St) and *Spiedie & Rib Pit* (☎ 607-724-7085, 49 Court St) – that make the sandwich, usually for around $5.

The reliable *Spot Diner Restaurant* (☎ 607-723-8149, 1062 Front St) is a Binghamton institution and tour-bus stop. It is open for breakfast, lunch and dinner 24 hours daily and has good service and food.

A popular student hangout, restaurant and late-night coffeehouse is *Lost Dog Cafe* (☎ 607-771-6063, 222 Water St), which is open Sunday through Thursday from 11 am to 11 pm and until midnight on Friday and Saturday. The Lost Dog features a good Sunday brunch that's a bargain ($6 for Texas-style eggs). Other menu items include Greek chicken, pita pizzas, big salads and Italian sodas.

The historic *Ritz Restaurant* (☎ 607-773-8876, 27 Chenango St) dates back to the 1920s, and was renovated in 1999. The menu is largely Greek, but it also includes everything from gyros to pasta and prime rib. Reasonably priced entrees cost $7 to $12 for items such as stuffed lobster and a glass of wine. It is open from 7 am to 10 pm weekdays and 24 hours on weekends.

Whole in the Wall (☎ 607-772-5138, 43 South Washington St) offers all natural foods prepared from scratch with Middle Eastern and Mexican influences. Try the stir-fry vegetable dishes or anything made with their original pesto sauce. Lunch and dinners range from $5 for a sandwich to $17 for the seafood platter. It is open Tuesday to Saturday from 11:30 am to 9 pm.

Cyber Cafe (☎ 607-723-2456, 176 Main St) is a trendy coffeehouse featuring online computers, plus a good selection of pastries, danishes and a variety of coffee blends. There is live entertainment most evenings. It is open 11am to midnight and until 1 am on weekends (closed Monday).

Mekong Vietnamese Restaurant (☎ 607-770-9628, 29 Willow St), in Johnson City, serves authentic Vietnamese fare in large, inexpensive portions. Try the coffeehouse afterwards where there are homemade pastries for dessert. Entrees range from $6 to $12. It is open for lunch and dinner Tuesday to Saturday from 11 am to 10 pm and Sunday from 5 to 10 pm.

Entertainment

Forum & Playwright Theater (☎ 607-778-2480, 236 Washington St) features a free *Twilight Zone* exhibit about writer Rod Sterling, who grew up in Binghamton.

Located on the Binghamton University campus, *Anderson Center for the Arts* (☎ 607-777-2787) features both indoor and outdoor shows. It draws many major performers and attractions. There's an art gallery with free tours and experimental theater programs. For tour information, call ☎ 607-777-6802.

For more than 20 years, *Cider Mill Playhouse* (☎ 607-748-7363, 2 S Nanticoke Ave), a former apple warehouse in Endicott, has served as a professional theater presenting plays and musicals, ranging from Shakespeare to Neil Simon. There are roughly nine different performances each season, from September to June, Thursday through Sunday. Tickets cost around $22. Endicott is 10 miles west of Binghamton via I-86.

Getting There & Away

The bus station in Binghamton is located in the downtown area at 81 Chenango St. Adirondack Trailways (☎ 800-858-8555) has service to Binghamton from New York City ($31/58, 3½ hours), Albany ($23/45, three hours) and Syracuse ($11/19, 1½ hours). Other bus companies include Short Line Bus Co (☎ 800-631-8405), with service to New York City, and Vermont Transit (☎ 800-451-3292), with service to Albany.

There is no direct bus service between Binghamton and Cooperstown.

Binghamton is reached most easily by car. To reach the town, take I-86 from New York City, I-88 from the Albany area or I-81 from Syracuse. Car rentals are available in Syracuse and Albany, as well as the Amtrak station in Albany.

Adirondack Region

- Canoeing and cross-country skiing in the St Regis Wilderness Canoe Area

- Lake Placid, site of the 1932 and 1980 winter Olympics, and home to year-round hiking, skiing, cycling and fishing

- The No Octane Boat Regatta, a summer-time gathering of human- and wind-powered watercraft on Blue Mountain Lake in mid-June

- Six Nations Indian Museum, near Saranac Lake, representing the lasting culture of the Iroquois Confederation

The beautiful Adirondack region covers most of the northern triangle of New York State. When people refer to the 'Adirondacks,' they are speaking not only of the mountains, but also of the park and the region, all of which are inextricably woven together.

The Adirondack Park, established in 1892, is six million acres of private and public land covering 20% of the entire state. Inside the park are roads, villages and ski resorts – including Lake Placid, site of the 1932 and 1980 Winter Olympics – as well as

mountain trails, jewel-like lakes and rivers. The Adirondack Forest Preserve is the 40% of the Adirondack Park that is owned by the state and protected from development by the designation 'forever wild' in the state Constitution. This is one of the least densely populated regions in the country. A five hour drive from New York City, the region offers visitors spectacular scenery and sublime solitude.

Within the park, which is the largest outside Alaska, are 46 mountains over 4000 feet high, including New York's tallest, Mt Marcy (5344 feet); 2800 lakes and ponds, 6000 miles of rivers, and many thousands more of streams. The Hudson River begins on Mt Marcy at Lake Tear-of-the-Clouds. There are only about 1300 miles of roadway in the park, but there are also over 2000 miles of hiking trails attracting both casual and avid hikers. When the park was first established, a blue line was used on an official map to designate the borders. Residents who live within the park's boundaries speak with understandable pride of living within the 'Blue Line.'

The Adirondack region described here extends beyond the Blue Line and includes the area north and east of the park boundary. Occasionally, people will include Saratoga Springs (near the state capital of Albany) in the region, though most residents of that town would wonder why. I-87 runs the length of the Adirondacks from the Lake George area north to Plattsburgh and the Canadian border 20 miles beyond. Together, Lake George and Lake Champlain form a contiguous border that separates the Adirondack region from neighboring Vermont to the east; several ferries connect the lakes' shores.

There are relatively few roads within the Adirondacks. In addition to I-87, the main north-south road is Route 30, which begins at the Canadian border in Quebec and connects the villages of Malone, Saranac Lake, Tupper Lake and Blue Mountain Lake. The term 'North Country' is a bit elusive (like 'upstate'), but tends to refer to the Blue Mountain Lake area northward; as with the Blue Line designation, North Country residents are proud of the term, even if it does mean that they shovel more snow and ice during the long winters. (How long? In Lake Placid, July is the only 'killing-frost-free' month.)

Route 73, which goes through narrow Keene Valley between the Northway (I-87) and Lake Placid, is a short and dazzling drive, curving past rocky ledges and ponds surrounded by stands of white birch. Route 22 is a particularly scenic route that skirts the west edge of Lake Champlain and connects the historic towns of Ticonderoga, Crown Point and Essex. Lake Placid of Winter Olympics fame is a year-round recreation center, close to the rugged High Peaks region. Route 3 connects Plattsburgh and the Tupper Lake area, and continues westward to Lake Ontario. Route 28 is a mostly east-west route that runs through Blue Mountain Lake and connects Old Forge in the southwestern portion of the park to Lake George in the southeast.

There are three primary drainages for the Adirondacks: the St Lawrence River, the Hudson River and Lake Champlain.

HISTORY

The Adirondack Mountains are not, as is popularly believed, part of the Appalachian chain. They're actually an outcropping of the Canadian Shield, a much older rock formation that lies mostly underneath Canada, but which surfaces in New York State as the Thousand Islands and the Adirondacks. The eastern Adirondacks, south of Lake Placid, are the most mountainous and the most spectacularly scenic. Looking at a map of the entire region, you'll note that many of the lakes and streams run in a northeast to southwest direction. This is because they were carved out by glaciers moving in that direction about 10,000 years ago. In the southwestern section of the park, many of the lakes are interconnected, providing over 100 miles of excellent canoeing.

The Adirondack region includes ecosystems that range from alpine to wetlands. Forest cover includes white pine, red spruce, maple, beech, birch and other species. Park fauna includes white-tailed deer, black bear, raccoons and, in a few places, moose. You can easily spot hawks and, of course, waterfowl. Fishing for trout, salmon, pike and other species is still considered excellent, despite the acid rain that has harmed these populations. Swarms of insects – in particular, the infamous black flies – can be a nuisance, especially during June and July, so bring plenty of bug repellent, or 'bug dope,' as the locals say.

The origin of the name 'Adirondack' is unclear. A widely believed explanation is that the name is an Iroquois word – *ha-de-ron-de* or *rat-eh-ron-tak* – meaning 'bark eaters,' a term which the Iroquois used pejoratively to describe the poor hunting skills of the Algonquians. A Williams College professor and surveyor, Ebenezer Emmons, mistook the word for a Huron term meaning 'they of the Rock Clan,' and thus christened the mountains while on an expedition, believing that he was commemorating the Native Americans of the region. Native Americans did, in fact, use the Adirondacks to hunt, fish and gather forest products, but moved south during the winter to escape the rugged terrain and harsh, sometimes violent, weather.

Early Europeans and Americans settled in the Adirondacks; many were especially interested in exploiting the area for its natural resources, specifically beaver for fur and pine trees for ship masts. During the 1800s, the forests were logged mercilessly. White pine was cleared for building, hemlock bark for leather tanning and spruce for making paper. The Adirondacks were denuded of much of their original timber by the early 1900s, but have since managed to recover. Today, logging – now referred to as 'managed forestation' – is once again a big business in the region and the source of an ongoing debate.

In the 19th century, during the period of the heaviest logging, the Adirondacks were also being exploited as a tourist destination

French & Indian War

The French & Indian War, which lasted from 1754 to 1763, is known in Europe as the Seven Years' War. In the early 1750s, fur traders and land speculators in the American colonies began to express interest in lands claimed by France east of the Appalachian Mountains. The French had built a line of forts from Lake Erie to western Pennsylvania from which they controlled their territory. In 1754, the British colonial government sent young George Washington and 150 troops to dislodge the French. Washington failed, as did a force of 1500 men under British General Braddock (see the boxed text 'The Battle of Fort Necessity' in the Southwestern Pennsylvania chapter).

The British and American troops fared poorly against the French and their Indian allies until 1757, when William Pitt became prime minister of England. Pitt borrowed heavily to pay for a vast infusion of troops and ships that helped change the course of the war. In 1759, the Anglo-American forces captured Fort Niagara on eastern Lake Erie, Fort Crown Point on southern Lake Champlain and Quebec. When British and American troops captured Montreal in July 1760, French resistance in the New World collapsed. In 1763 the Peace of Paris agreement gave Britain all of North America east of the Mississippi, as well as Florida and Canada.

for those seeking to escape to the wilderness. In the decades after the Civil War, entrepreneurs opened large hotels throughout the Adirondacks. At the same time, conservationists urged that the land be saved to protect the watershed. The region's remoteness and beauty attracted millionaires – among them, the Rockefellers, Morgans and Vanderbilts – who built luxurious estates running into the tens of thousands of acres. These vast complexes, arrogantly referred to by their owners as 'camps,' popularized the notion of the region as a playground for the rich.

The battle between developers and conservationists continues to this day. For many residents, development means sorely-needed jobs. For environmentalists and part-time residents fleeing New York City, development continues to threaten the pristine wilderness. The Adirondack Park Agency (APA) regulates land use, both public and private, within the park. It's hard to find a landowner who doesn't dislike the APA because of its restrictions or a conservationist who doesn't wish the agency would do more to preserve the region.

INFORMATION
Tourist Offices

There are two Visitors' Interpretive Centers that feature indoor and outdoor exhibits about the park. One is in Paul Smiths (☎ 518-327-3000) on Route 30, a mile north of Paul Smith's College. The other is the Newcomb Center (☎ 518-582-2000), 14 miles east of the town of Long Lake on Route 28. Both are open daily all year, except Christmas and Thanksgiving, from 9 am to 5 pm (until 7 pm from May 1 to October 1). The centers also sponsor various educational programs and lectures.

There are also local and regional tourist offices in just about every major town.

Local papers can also provide important tourist information. The *Adirondack Journal* and *Chronicle* are free weeklies available in the Adirondack region. They contain news, community information and ads. The *Adirondack Daily Enterprise* is the only daily published in the park. The paper is published in Saranac Lake and available in most towns.

Adirondack Mountain Club

Those who are interested in seriously exploring the park should contact the Adirondack Mountain Club (ADK). The club, which has been around since 1922, promotes conservation, hiking, canoeing and other outdoor activities in the Adirondacks. It also offers educational programs, guided hikes, senior getaways, nature courses (on birds, mushrooms and plants), photography, rock climbing, fly-tying, kayaking and more. ADK

ADIRONDACK REGION

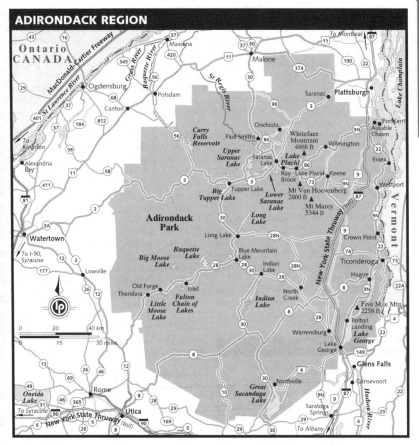

headquarters (☎ 518-668-4447, 800-395-8080), RR3, Box 3055, Lake George, NY 12845, is on Route 9 south of exit 21 off of I-87 at the street address 814 Goggins Rd. There is also an Adirondak Loj & ADK High Peaks Information Center (☎ 518-523-3441, www.adk.org), Box 867, Lake Placid, NY 12946, in the northern Adirondacks.

ADK members will receive a 10% discount on everything sponsored by the organization, including accommodations, and the *Adirondack* magazine every other month. Adult/senior/student membership costs $35/25/20.

OUTDOOR ACTIVITIES
Hiking

Whether you're interested in an easy day-hike or a far more adventurous wilderness backpacking experience, the Adirondacks offer the best hiking trails in New York, and some of the best in the entire New York, New Jersey, Pennsylvania region. The New York State Department of Environmental Conservation (DEC) maintains the Adirondack trails with assistance from conservation groups. It's easy to find the trail heads, which are marked by brown wooden signs with yellow lettering. You can set up camp anywhere on state land as long as it isn't above 4000 feet, within 150 feet of water or within 100 feet of a trail. Much of the Adirondacks is privately owned and only a few owners allow public access, so be sure to look for 'No Trespassing' signs.

Hiking Guidebooks There are several excellent books on the Adirondack trail networks. Lonely Planet's *Hiking in the USA* covers a three-day loop in the High Peaks region, a day hike to Mt Marcy and a brief description of the Northville-Lake Placid Trail. The Adirondack Mountain Club ADK (see Tourist Offices, earlier in this chapter) publishes *Adirondack* magazine six times a year. *Discover the Adirondacks* is a fine series by Backcountry Publications (☎ 802-457-1049), PO Box 175, Woodstock, VT 05901. *Longstreet Highroad Guide to the New York Adirondacks*, by Phil Brown, is an excellent all-around guide to enjoying the natural history of the region.

The ADK also publishes guides that break up the region into seven parts. Each book includes a large, removable topo-graphical map. The club also publishes guides on rock and ice climbing, natural history, literature about the Adirondacks and a good field guide.

The Discover series includes 11 books – one for each of the 11 different parts of the region – that describe hiking, snowshoeing and cross-country skiing trails and include topographical maps.

Maps The *Adirondack North Country Regional Map* shows all state-owned land as of 1986. It's available free or for $1.25 by mail from the Adirondack North Country Association (☎ 518-891-6200), 183 Broadway, Saranac Lake, NY 12983.

The US Geological Survey (USGS) Map Distribution Branch, Box 25286, Denver, CO 80225, publishes maps on different parts of the region. You'd need to buy quite a few to cover the entire park. USGS maps are also available from outdoor stores in New York City and the Adirondacks or from Timely Discount Topos (☎ 800-821-7609).

Jimapco maps (☎ 518-899-5091), Box 1137, Clifton Park, NY 12065, is a good source of Adirondack hiking and boating maps. The ADK also publishes maps that can be purchased separately from their guides.

Downhill Skiing

The weather, elevation and comfortable facilities combine to make much of the Adirondack Park prime ski country. Lake Placid was chosen twice to host the Winter Olympics and another bid is likely. Meanwhile, there's great skiing across the park, though the Lake Placid-Whiteface Mountain area is the most famous.

Big Tupper Lake (☎ 518-359-7902) 3 miles south of Tupper Lake on Route 30; vertical drop of 1150 feet; lift fees $18 to $20

Gore Mountain North Creek (☎ 518-251-2411) Off Routes 8 and 28, 16 miles north of Warrensburg; 2100 feet; $24 to $33

Whiteface Mountain Wilmington (☎ 518-523-1655) Route 86, 10 miles east of Lake Placid; 3200 feet; $28 to $34

Willard Mountain Greenwich (☎ 518-692-7337) Route 40, 16 miles southeast of Saratoga Springs on Route 29; 500 feet; $16 to $20

Warning to Hikers

Be careful hiking in the Adirondacks. Although the mountains are deceptively gentle in appearance, the terrain is, in fact, difficult. Add to this the sheer size of the wilderness, and the result is the nearly annual tragedy, often involving an experienced, lone hiker who wanders from the established trails. In the summer of 1990, 38 year old David Boomhower got lost while on a solo 10-day hike along the popular 130-mile Northville-Lake Placid Trail. He left on June 5 and died in early August after trying to survive on insects, snails and plants. One of the final entries in his journal, found after his death, reads 'Just what happened? I didn't bring enough food, ran out, and also encountered a string of bad weather. Took (unreadable) trail…Somehow got lost off that…I'm surprised they haven't found me… .'

Cross-Country Skiing

Cross-country skiing is for experts and beginners alike. Ask at the following ski centers about trail difficulty and weather conditions as novice Nordic skiers can roam far from any community before realizing their predicament. This is not the lift-and-lodge experience. Most cross-country trail distances are given in kilometers (to convert trail distances into miles, see the conversion chart on the inside back cover of this book).

Adirondack Park Visitors Interpretive Center (☎ 518-327-3000) Paul Smiths, Route 30, 1 mile north of the junction of Routes 192 and 30; 17 kilometers of trails; free

Adirondak Loj (☎ 518-523-3441) off Route 73, 8 miles southeast of Lake Placid; 20 kilometers; $6

Ausable Chasm Cross Country Ski Center (☎ 518-834-9990) Ausable Chasm; about 12 miles from Plattsburgh at exit 34 off I-87 on Route 373; 12 kilometers; $4

Bark Eater Keene (☎ 518-576-2221) 17 miles north of exit 30 off I-87, half mile off Route 73 on Alstead Hill Rd; 20 kilometers; $5 to $8

Cascade Ski Touring Center (☎ 518-523-9605) 5 miles south of Lake Placid on Route 73; 20 kilometers; $5 to $6

Cold River Ranch (☎ 518-359-7559) Tupper Lake, 13 miles west of Saranac Lake on Route 3; 10 kilometers; free

Gore Mountain (☎ 518-251-2411, 800-342-1234) North Creek, 16 miles north of Warrensburg on Route 28; 11 kilometers; $2 to $4

Mt Van Hoevenberg (☎ 518-523-2811, 800-462-6236) 7 miles south of Lake Placid off Route 73; 50 kilometers; $4 to $8

Whiteface Inn Nordic Ski Center (☎ 518-523-2551) 1½ miles west of Lake Placid's Main St off Route 86; 30 kilometers; $6 to $10

Canoeing

To a canoeist, the Adirondacks are heaven on water. The terrain is hilly, but the base is often gentle and level, and ideal for canoeing. Adirondack Park offers some of the best canoeing in the northeast. Canoe trips can vary from a dilettante afternoon to several days of canoeing, camping and portaging – or carrying – your canoe and supplies. A wealth of information providers, outfitters and guides can help. The state's Department of Environmental Control (DEC; ☎ 914-255-5453, 518-897-1309), in Albany, distributes a short pamphlet, *Adirondack Canoe Routes*, describing many popular canoe routes. Obtaining a detailed map, such as those from the USGS, not to mention advice from local canoeists, is also advisable when planning a trip.

Prices You can bring your own equipment, rent the equipment you need or sign on for a complete guided tour, including meals and shuttle service. Prices, of course, vary accordingly. Basically, there are four ways to go:

• Bring your own equipment, maps, food, experience and knowledge of the terrain. Instruction and paddling programs are available for adults and children.

• Rent the necessary equipment from a good canoe outfitter who will also help you plan a comfortable itinerary (canoes rent for $25 to $50 a day, depending on weight).

• Rent a complete (or partial) outfitting kit, including canoe, car racks, portage and camping/cooking gear, food, shuttle transportation and itinerary; prices range from $40 to $80 per person, per day; a four-day family camp and canoe package for two adults and two children costs about $500.

• Sign up for a guided trip that includes all of the above plus your own expert. Prices range from $80 to $100 per person for a one day excursion to about $200 a day for small groups on trips of more than a day.

GETTING THERE & AROUND
Air

US Airways (☎ 518-891-2290, 800-428-4322) has regular service into Adirondack Airport in Saranac Lake, 10 miles west of Lake Placid. Roundtrip from Albany to Saranac Lake is about $300; service is daily except Saturday. Flights from Saranac Lake to New York City are routed through Albany and cost $270. US Airways also serves Plattsburgh and Syracuse airports, mostly from their Pittsburgh, PA, hub.

Bus

The main bus company in the region is Adirondack Trailways (☎ 800-858-8555).

Destinations within the Adirondacks include Plattsburgh, Glens Falls, Keene Valley, Lake George, Lake Placid, Saratoga Springs, Saranac Lake, Schroon Lake, Ticonderoga and Tupper Lake. Buses also serve New York City, Montreal and Albany. The summer (from June to October) schedule is fairly extensive, but winter is more limited. Sample fares are included in coverage of Adirondack destinations later in this chapter.

Greyhound (☎ 800-231-2222) has a few routes within the region, and both bus companies offer information about the other's schedules.

The company Lake Placid Sightseeing (☎ 518-523-4431) runs a shuttle (called Champ) between Lake Placid and Saranac Lake. The same company also has a bus (Champ Express) that meets arriving train passengers in Westport.

Train

Amtrak's Adirondack line (New York to Montreal) stops at Westport (☎ 518-962-8730, 800-872-7245), 37 miles east of Lake Placid on Route 22. The one-way/roundtrip fare from Albany is $24/48, New York City $48/96 and Montreal $17/34 (service is once a day, either direction). The journey is quite scenic; the train goes along the Hudson River on and off until Albany, and then through quite a bit of forests.

The train also stops in Plattsburgh to the north, and in Saratoga Springs to the south (see Getting There & Away in the Saratoga Springs section of the Capital District & Mohawk Valley chapter). The fare for Plattsburgh to Westport is $11/22.

During the summer, the pink-and-white Champ Express shuttle meets arriving trains at the small Westport station and will take passengers to Lake Placid (see the Getting There & Away section for Lake Placid for more information).

Car & Motorcycle

I-87 runs north-south from New York City through the eastern portion of the Adirondacks and into Canada. Almost every road through the Adirondack Park could be called a scenic route and most are only two lanes wide. Route 30 is an especially beautiful road that runs for 160 miles from the Great Sacandaga Lake in the south to Malone outside the northern boundary of the park. Routes 28 and 3 both enter from the west and intersect with Route 30 near the middle of the park. The village of Blue Mountain Lake and the Adirondack Museum are at the intersection of Routes 30 and 28. Routes 73 and 86, in the northeastern part of the park near Lake Placid and the Saranac Lakes, are also lovely byways.

Ferry

Lake Champlain Ferries (☎ 802-864-9804) runs three routes across Lake Champlain between Vermont and the low plain of the eastern Adirondacks. The northernmost ferry crosses between Grand Isle, VT, and Plattsburgh, NY. The 12-minute trip is done all year from 5 am to 1 am. The one-way/roundtrip car and driver fare is $7/12.75; additional adult passengers, $2.25/3.75; children (ages six to 12), 50¢/$1. From Plattsburgh you can take Route 3 south through the northern Adirondacks to Saranac Lake, a distance of about 50 miles.

Another ferry travels between Burlington, VT, and Port Kent, NY. The one-hour crossing is daily from mid-May to mid-October from 7:30 am to 7:30 pm. One-way/roundtrip car and driver fare is $13/23; additional adult passengers, $3.25/5.75; children (ages six to 12), $1.25/2.25. Port Kent is 40 miles from Lake Placid. From Port Kent (which is inside the Blue Line of the park) take Route 373 west to Route 9N west and then Route 86 west into Lake Placid.

A third ferry connects Charlotte, VT, and Essex, NY (see the Essex section, later in this chapter, for more information).

The Fort Ti Ferry runs to and from Shoreham (Larabees Point), VT, and Ticonderoga, NY (see the Ticonderoga section, later in this chapter, for more information).

LAKE GEORGE

Lake George, at the southeastern entrance to the park, is the largest lake completely

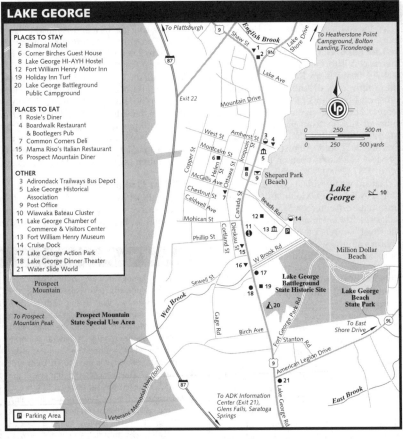

LAKE GEORGE

PLACES TO STAY
2   Balmoral Motel
6   Corner Birches Guest House
8   Lake George HI-AYH Hostel
12 Fort William Henry Motor Inn
19 Holiday Inn Turf
20 Lake George Battleground
    Public Campground

PLACES TO EAT
1   Rosie's Diner
4   Boardwalk Restaurant
    & Bootlegers Pub
7   Common Corners Deli
15 Mama Riso's Italian Restaurant
16 Prospect Mountain Diner

OTHER
3   Adirondack Trailways Bus Depot
5   Lake George Historical
    Association
9   Post Office
10 Wiawaka Bateau Cluster
11 Lake George Chamber of
    Commerce & Visitors Center
13 Fort William Henry Museum
14 Cruise Dock
17 Lake George Action Park
18 Lake George Dinner Theater
21 Water Slide World

within the park boundaries. The 32-mile-long lake – dotted with 365 islands – is often described as the 'Queen of America's Lakes,' in part for its deep-blue, crystal-clear water and wild shorelines. Called Lac du Saint Sacrement by Jesuit missionary Isaac Jacques when he was led here by Native American guides in 1646, the lake was of strategic importance during the French & Indian War. In 1755, British General William Johnson renamed the lake after King George. More recently, during the mid-20th century, the lake became the haunt of city-weary artists, among them the artist Georgia

O'Keeffe and her husband, photographer Alfred Steiglitz, who managed to capture with his camera their quotidian existence along the lake's forested shores.

At the southern end of the lake is Lake George Village (population 900), a town crammed with motels and tacky souvenir shops, all of which stand in marked contrast to the otherwise scenic surroundings. Don't let Lake George Village discourage you from visiting the lake. As tourist towns go, it isn't that bad and, as a major tourist destination, it offers a variety of inexpensive places to stay.

Orientation & Information

From I-87 (the Northway), exit 21 lets you off at the south end of town on Route 9, and exit 22 puts you at the north end.

The Lake George Chamber of Commerce & Visitors Center (☎ 518-668-5755, 800-705-0059) is on Route 9/Canada St at the south end of the village (opposite Prospect Mountain), on the east side of the street. They are open daily during the summer season from 9 am to 5 pm, and Monday to Friday the rest of the year. During July and August another office (☎ 518-668-2846) is open on Route 9N right off of I-87, exit 22. You can also visit their website at www.visitlakegeorge.com.

The Adirondack Mountain Club (ADK) Information Center (☎ 518-668-4447, www.adk.org), 814 Goggins Rd, south of town, is the best source of information on the region's natural wonders – including hiking, canoeing, camping and skiing. This well-informed center is dedicated to the responsible use of the forest and waterways. It's a good source of trail guidebooks, maps and more.

The post office (☎ 518-668-3386) is on Canada St a block north of Beach Rd, right at the center of town.

Parking is something neither the Native Americans nor the English of the 18th century had to deal with. Now they do, along with everyone else who comes to Lake George Village. A good place to park is the big lot across the street from the steamboat landing. It's metered parking, but – good news – you can feed the meter for 10 hours at a time, for 50¢ an hour. Bad news: The meters operate 24 hours daily, seven days a week. There is another lot nearby with an attendant where the standard charge is $5 a day (you get $2 back if you ride the steamboat).

Fort William Henry Museum

This fort (☎ 518-668-5471) is a re-creation of the 'site of the *Last of the Mohicans*' as the banners and plaques tirelessly note. The fort was built in 1755 by the order of British General William Johnson. A victorious French and Indian force burned it to the ground in 1757. It was rebuilt by Americans

seeking tourist dollars in 1953. Inside are reconstructed barracks and other rooms and artifacts. During July and August, a 'living history' program includes cannon firing and musket ball making. The fort is at the center of town off Route 9/Canada St as part of the Fort William Henry Motor Inn complex. You can also get to it by staircase from the southern shore of the lake, above the stores. It is open daily during July and August from 9 am to 10 pm; in May and June and from Labor Day to Columbus Day from 10 am to 5 pm. Admission costs $8; for adults over 60 and children (ages three to 11) it is $6.

Million Dollar Beach

This small, sandy beach (☎ 518-668-3352) in Lake George Beach State Park is a short walk south of Fort William Henry along the

---

Last of the Mohicans

Much of James Fenimore Cooper's book *Last of the Mohicans* takes place during the French & Indian War in the 18th century. During August of 1757, forces under French General Montcalm attacked the British Fort William Henry. Inside, General George Munro eventually surrendered and was given safe passage with his men to Fort Edward. However, Native Americans fighting with the French attacked the surrendered British and killed many of them. Their reasons for doing so and what actually transpired are quite a bit different from the popular image of bloodthirsty savages massacring unarmed Anglos. Ian Steele's *Betrayals: Fort William Henry and the 'Massacre'* gives a more balanced portrayal of events.

In any case, in his book James Fenimore Cooper told the story of Uncas and Chingachgook and Anglo guide Natty Bumppo, or 'Hawkeye,' who safely hid the daughters of Colonel Munro in a cave. This cave is under the Route 9 bridge over the Hudson River between Glens Falls and South Glens Falls. The circular staircase that once lead into the cave is now closed to the public.

shore of the lake. The beach was originally developed (and so named) for the wealthy clientele of the bygone era of big resorts along the lake. There are picnic facilities here, a bathhouse and on-duty lifeguards daily from 9 am to 6 pm from mid-June to Labor Day. Admission costs $1 for those over six years old; parking is $3.

You can find other nice (and free) places to swim by heading further north around the lake.

Prospect Mountain
You can drive up the Veterans Memorial Hwy to the top of Prospect Mountain (2021 feet) for dramatic views of the lake and surrounding mountain ranges, including Vermont's Green Mountains and New Hampshire's White Mountains. The entrance to this two lane toll road is on Route 9 south of Lake George Battleground State Historic Site. From here, it's a 5-mile drive to a crest, where you can take a free, open-air trolley pulled by a jeep to the summit (it takes three minutes) or you can hike for even more spectacular views. There are picnic sites at the summit. It is open daily from 9 am to 5 pm from Memorial Day to the end of October; the toll is $5 per vehicle.

Lake George Shipwrecks
History buffs, boating enthusiasts and divers will enjoy viewing the remains of seven boats used on the lake during the French & Indian and Revolutionary Wars in the 18th century. These boats were typical of the flat-bottomed transport vessels called *bateaux* by English as well as French speakers. Bateaux, which were about 30 feet long, were poled or oared across the lake in order to transport troops and supplies. In the summer of 1758, after the British failed to take Fort Ticonderoga (Fort Carillon) from the French, British and American forces sunk over 200 boats to store them for retrieval after the winter. The troops returned in the spring of 1759 to retrieve the bateaux, but they missed many, including those on display.

The best-known group is referred to as the Wiawaka Bateau Cluster, which is on the state register of historic places. What's left of the seven boats is submerged in 25 to 40 feet of water about 150 feet northeast of the Camp Wiawaka boat house on the eastern side of Lake George off of Route 9L (East Shore Drive) near Lake George Village. Visitors are allowed to dive to the lake bottom for a *look* at the boats' remains, but not to touch them.

Scuba diving here is rather popular, but the old diving paradox remains: the colder the water the clearer the view. Lake George is 200 feet deep in parts, and old war-wrecks are the viewing prize.

For more information, contact the Lake George Historical Association (☎ 518-668-4644); Bateaux Below (☎ 518-587-7638), PO Box 2134, Wilton, NY 12866; or the DEC, Region 5 (☎ 518-891-1370), Route 86, Box 296, Ray Brook, NY 12977.

For organized cruises of the lake, see Lake George Cruises, below.

Lake George Cruises
A cruise, even one as short as an hour, is a good way to enjoy the lake and take in the scenery along its shores. Several tour boats (☎ 518-668-4644) leave from Beach Road on the southern shore of the lake opposite Fort William Henry. From late June to Labor Day, one hour sightseeing cruises leave daily about every hour, and from May 1 to the end of June and from Labor Day to October 31, four times daily. Basic sightseeing cruises cost $7; $6.50 for seniors and $3.50 for children (three to 11). There are also less-frequent 2½-hour cruises.

From late June to Labor Day, dinner cruises leave daily at 6:30 pm. From May 1 to late June and Labor Day to October 31, they leave on Saturday at 6:30 pm. There is also a 10 pm entertainment cruise. The dinner cruise costs $27/17 for adults/children. The entertainment cruise is $7.75/5.

The Lake George Steamboat Co (☎ 518-668-5777, 800-553-2628) offers cruises on their paddleboat *Minne-ha-ha*, and on the *Mohican* and dinner cruises on the *Lac de Saint Sacrement*. You can get on or off at Baldwin Landing in Ticonderoga on the north end of the lake if you just want to go one way. The 4½ hour cruise leaves from late June to Labor Day, daily at 9 pm. The roundtrip fare is $14.50/7.25. The one-way fare is $10.50/5.25.

From mid-May to Columbus Day in early October, lunch cruises leave daily at 11:30 am for $24.50/12.25. From late June to Labor Day, a dinner cruise leaves at 6:30 pm; tickets cost $34.40/17.25. From July 3 to the end of August, moonlight cruises leave at 10 pm for $12.50/6.25.

Other Things to Do

The **Lake George Historical Association Museum** (☎ 518-668-5044), at the corner of Canada and Amherst Sts in the old courthouse building, has a well displayed collection of memorabilia ranging from ice harvesting and logging equipment to quilts and medieval-looking doctors' tools for treating the tuberculosis patients who once frequented the Adirondacks to 'take the cure.' A doctor's bag on display still smells of old medicines from the early 20th century. The museum is open year-round from 10 am to 4 pm Monday to Friday, and also on weekends from 1 to 5 pm from July through September.

The **Lake George Dinner Theatre** (☎ 518-668-5781) is located in the Holiday Inn Turf on Canada Street, opposite the Tiki Lounge. This is an equity theatre that does one play each summer, usually a Broadway or off-Broadway musical or comedy. Performances run from mid-June to mid-October, nightly except Sunday, and there are lunch shows on Wednesday and Saturday. Rates range from about $32 to $42 per adult.

For serious amusement-park-type fun, you can head for **Lake George Action Park** (☎ 518-668-5459), at West Brook Rd on Route 9, an 1890s theme park with rides and shows; and **Water Slide World** (☎ 518-668-4407), just south of town on Route 9, which features a wave pool, 13 water slides and hot tubs. Both are open from mid-June through Labor Day.

Before heading back to the wilderness, you can make one more stop along Route 9 and take in the attractions at New York's largest amusement park, **Great Escape Fun Park** (☎ 518-798-1084, 792-3500), with raft rides, roller coasters and live shows – and a nice Adirondack backdrop. It is open Memorial Day to Labor Day daily from 9:30 am to 6 pm, later on weekends. Expect big crowds in the summer. Admission costs $22 for adults, $18 for children (ages three to 11), and free for children two and under.

Special Events

The Lake George Opera Festival (late July to mid-August; ☎ 518-793-3858) is a professional opera company that stages performances at the Little Theatre in Saratoga State Park. Tickets range from $10 to $60.

The Lake George Jazz Festival draws national jazz artists on the second weekend in September in Shepard Park. There are various other special events in the park throughout the summer, including Family Week in mid-August. Call the Lake George Arts Project (☎ 518-668-2616) for schedule details.

Places to Stay

The largest and one of the most impressive of the Adirondack resorts, the Sagamore, is 10 miles north of Lake George Village (see Bolton Landing in the Around Lake George section, later in this chapter).

Camping The State of New York maintains *campgrounds* on 92 of the islands in Lake George. For information and reservations in any New York state park, call the camping reservation system (☎ 800-456-2267). In addition, *Lake George Islands Public Campgrounds* (☎ 518-668-5441) are on three islands, each accessible by boat from nearby shore points. All the island campsites are open from mid-May to mid-September. Canoeing parties sometimes get a tow at the marina to one of the islands, and then paddle around from there.

Long Island (☎ 518-656-9426) is on the southern end of the lake, and has 90 sites at $11 per site. You can get there by boat from Lake George Village, on the eastern side of the lake from Cleverdale, Kattskill Bay and Pilot Knob or from the western side from Diamond Point or Bolton Landing.

Glen Island (☎ 518-644-9696) is in the narrows of Lake George (not to be confused with Narrow Island) and is accessible from Bolton Landing. It has 213 sites at $13 each. Glen Island also has a camp store. To get to Bolton Landing, drive north from Lake George Village on Route 9N for about 10 miles.

Narrow Island (☎ 518-499-1288) is in the Mother Bunch of Islands in the northern half of the lake. It has 96 sites for $13 each. You can get there from Silver Bay on the west side of the lake or Hulett's Landing on the east.

There are a fair number of busy campgrounds around Lake George Village. *Lake George Battleground Public Campground* (☎ 518-668-3348) is at the south end of town on Route 9. It has 50 sites in a shady pine grove with showers and bathrooms. Rates are $10 to $16. It's a good place to shower at the day-use rates ($3 per car or $1 for walkins), and it is open from mid-May to mid-October.

Adirondack Camping Village (☎ 518-668-5226), on Route 9, is on a shaded hill and has 150 sites and full amenities, including hot showers, camp store, recreation room and laundry. Sites cost $18 to $22. Go north on Route 9 for three-quarters of a mile from I-87 exit 22. It is open mid-May to mid-September.

Hearthstone Point Campground (☎ 518-668-5193), on Route 9N, has 250 tent and trailer sites near the lakeshore at $11 per site for up to six people (a bargain by camping standards). It is open from mid-May to mid-September. Take Route 9N, 2 miles north of Lake George Village.

Guesthouses *Corner Birches Guest House* (☎ 518-668-2837, 86 Montcalm St)*, at Helen St, offers four small, but comfortable and clean rooms that share one bathroom and a living room with TV. Year-round rates, including a breakfast of coffee, juice and toast, are $35 to $45.

Motels & Efficiencies Route 9/Canada St is lined with motels from one end of town to the other. Rates are highest from late June through Labor Day weekend. *Balmoral Motel* (☎ 518-668-2673, 444 Canada St) is at the north end of town in the middle of the Route 9/9N fork. There are 25 nicely furnished rooms; the management is friendly and the swimming pool – with an island in the middle – is the largest in town. Off-season rates are typically $30 to $54; in season, $55 to $90.

Fort William Henry Motor Inn (☎ 518-668-3081, 800-234-0267, 48 Canada St) is at the center of town in the Fort William Henry complex. There are wonderful views of the lake from the property, but not – unfortunately – from all of the rooms. Rooms here are not much better than those in other motels in town, but it has some resort-like features, including terraces, indoor pool and miniature golf courses. There are several types of rooms, with rates for each; standard off-season rates are $65 to $90, in season $150 to $180.

The 100-room *Holiday Inn Turf* (☎ 518-668-5781) is opposite the lake; rates vary according to the view and start at $80 (off season) and $180 to $210 (in season). There are heated indoor and outdoor pools, a restaurant and a playground for children.

Places to Eat

The food in Lake George Village doesn't begin to compare with the scenery, but there are some fair choices. The village is walkable, and most places do not have street numbers.

The *Prospect Mountain Diner* (☎ 518-668-9721) is at the south end of the village on the west side of Canada St, near the visitors' center. This traditional chrome and vinyl diner offers typical diner fare, pancakes, steak & eggs, chicken parmesan and great pie ($2 a slice).

Rosie's Diner (☎ 518-668-2499) is at the north end of the village by the fork in the road for Routes 9 and 9N (Lake Shore Drive). Rosie's is open daily from 7 am to 10 pm, and is very popular with local residents. It's also one of the last places where the ice cream list is happily limited to the basic three ice cream groups: chocolate, vanilla and strawberry.

The Meeting Place Restaurant (☎ 518-792-9565), on Route 9, is just in front of the Days Inn next to the sprawling outlet mall. This is a cut above coffee-shop food, and the restaurant serves breakfast, lunch and dinner daily from 7 am. Breakfast specials start at $3 and dinner entrees at $9 to $15; the bargain, however, is brick oven pizza for $4.

There are several Italian restaurants along the Route 9 strip. *Mama Riso's Italian Restaurant* (☎ 518-668-2550) is at the south end of town. The food is good, as the menu will remind you. Most dishes range from $12 to $15. It is open daily for dinner from 4 pm.

Boardwalk Restaurant & Bootleggers Pub (☎ 518-668-5324), on Lower Amherst St, overlooks the lake. Specialties include ribs, and there is a Sunday champagne brunch. It is open daily with live music in the summer.

Common Corners Deli (☎ 518-745-1171, 16 McGillis St), at the corner of Ottawa, is a popular local eatery, with excellent soups, sandwiches, salads and homemade baked goods. It is open all year for breakfast and lunch.

Shopping

Nearby, and somehow surviving the outlet mall phenomenon, is the unique Doll Shop (☎ 518-792-0393) on Route 9 just east of the mall's fringe. The shop's sloping front lawn is remarkable for the array of large doll figures that adorn the green in the spring and summer. Inside, the shop is small, cramped and charming and the owner (Peggy) can tell you about every item on display, including figurines and paper dolls. The shop is open all year, daily except Monday, from 10 am to 5 pm, but you may have to ring the doorbell to get in.

The 'Million $ Half Mile' (☎ 518-793-2161) is a factory outlet strip at I-87 exit 20. There are actually four malls here, with 50 stores and counting, open every day to cater to various forms of shopping fever.

Getting There & Away

Adirondack Trailways (☎ 800-858-8555) stops at the corner of Canada and Amherst Sts, in front of Wagar's Soda Fountain and across the street from a gas station. Tickets must be purchased by paying the driver with the exact fare amount. There are three buses that go north and three that go south daily during the summer. One-way/roundtrip tickets to Plattsburgh are $33/64, Albany $10/20, New York City $40/77 and Montreal $34/64. The 30-minute trip to Glen Falls and Bolton Landing costs $2 one way.

See the Route 9N: Lake George to Ticonderoga section, later in this chapter, for driving directions to other towns along Lake George.

AROUND LAKE GEORGE
Glens Falls

The village of Glens Falls houses the **Hyde Collection** (☎ 518-792-1761), 161 Warren St, a remarkable collection of art amassed with a thoughtful and expert eye by Charlotte Pryun Hyde, heiress to a local paper fortune. The collection is on display in her rambling Florentine Renaissance mansion. Here you can view works from European and American artists spanning five centuries, from Rembrandt and Reubens to Matisse and Eakins. Also on display from the permanent collection are tapestries, sculpture and period furnishings. A new educational wing serves as a space for temporary exhibits and lectures. From January to April, the museum is open Tuesday through Sunday, 10 am to 5 pm. During the rest of the year, it is open Wednesday through Sunday, noon to 5 pm. Admission is free. From Lake George take Route 9 to Glens Falls and go east on Warren St.

Lox of Bagels & Moor (☎ 518-793-8681, 89 Main St), just east of I-87 at exit 18, is a good spot for fresh bagels and lox and other yummy deli specialties. It is open daily from 7 am to 4 pm.

Bolton Landing

This tiny village, 10 miles from Lake George Village, is on the western shore of Lake George and is home to the impressive Sagamore Resort. **Marcella Sembrich Memorial Studio** (☎ 518-644-9839), home of the 20th-century opera singer, is also here. The studio contains mementos of the singer's career during the early part of the century. It's open to visitors from mid-June to mid-September. As you drive up Route 9N just before entering Bolton, you'll pass the iron gate of Sembrich's house on the east side of the road.

Places to Stay *Hilltop Cottage B&B* (☎ *518-644-2492, 6883 Lakeshore Drive)* is on Route 9N opposite Carey's Lakeside Motel, about half a mile south of the first of two traffic lights in town; be warned, you won't see any building numbers. This B&B is the former caretaker's cottage for the Sembrich estate across the street. Anita and Charlie Richards rent out three rooms in the comfortable and well-maintained home and adjacent cabin. Rooms with shared bath are $50, one with a private bath is $65. The single cabin, which has a television, fridge and microwave, is $75.

The *Sagamore Resort* (☎ *518-644-9400, 800-358-3585, 110 Sagamore Rd)* is on a private island, accessible by a bridge, east of town. The main building, with its dramatic approach up a sweeping driveway, is stunning. The white structure with green shutters was built as an inn in the 1920s, and has suffered two major fires during its history. It was completely renovated in 1985.

Everything about this resort speaks of luxury and opulence: the restaurants, indoor pool, tennis courts, ornate furnishings, professional service and breathtaking views of Lake George. The Sagamore's reputation as the most lavish resort in the Adirondacks is well-deserved. Not surprisingly, the price tag for such an experience is high. From July through August, there is a three-night minimum stay. Prices begin at $190 for a room without a view and rise to $390 for a suite overlooking the lake. The resort is open all year; room rates drop dramatically from early November until late December, and can be had for $90 to $100 a night.

Places to Eat The odds of getting a decent meal are better in Bolton Landing than the sprawling village scene down the road at Lake George.

Bolton Diner (☎ *518-644-3522)*, a blue-and-yellow diner at the center of town, is on the site formerly occupied by the Bill Gates Diner, which was taken apart and reassembled in the Adirondack Museum (see the Blue Mountain Lake section, later in this chapter). It serves comforting diner food, and the prices are reasonable; a breakfast special with three eggs, pancakes, meat, toast, homefries and coffee costs $6. The diner is open daily in the summer for breakfast, lunch and dinner; in the winter, for breakfast and lunch only.

Algonquin Restaurant (☎ *518-644-9442)*, on Lake Shore Drive, is a local eatery, popular with boaters who pull into the nearby docks for lunch or dinner. Good sandwiches and soups (black bean soup is a specialty) for lunch cost $5 to $8, bistro fare for dinner costs $10 to $15. It is open from May to mid-October.

Pumpernickel's (☎ *518-644-2106)*, on Lake Shore Drive, is adjacent to the Bolton Pines Motel, about 8 miles north of Lake George Village. The menu tries to be international, with a pronounced German flavor. Entrees range from $12 to $20, and include a salad bar. It is open daily May to early October for dinner from 5 to 9 pm.

There are five restaurants at the Sagamore Resort – six if you count the converted steamship/dinner cruise. *Mr Brown's Pub* has good bar food, including sandwiches, burgers and salads that cost $7 to $10, and is open from 11 am to midnight. *Sagamore Dining Room* serves breakfast from 7 to 11 am, and offers standard dinners of steak, seafood and pasta in the $15 to $25 range, from 5:30 to 9:30 pm. The changing menu at *Trillium* is far more adventurous. Selections might include peppered mahi mahi, seared breast of duckling or a seafood ragout. Entrees start at $20, and formal attire is expected. A Sunday brunch (requiring reservations) happens from 10 am to 1 pm and costs $26 for adults, $13 for children six to 12 years old and $4 for children one to five.

Getting There & Away Adirondack Trailways (☎ 800-858-8555) stops at Neuffer's

Citgo gas station (☎ 518-644-2561) at the southern end of town. There's one bus that travels north and one that travels south daily during the summer. One-way/roundtrip fares from Bolton Landing to Glens Falls are $3/6, Lake George $4/7, Albany $13/22, New York City $40/77, Montreal $34/65 and Boston $53/106. There is no service to Westport.

ROUTE 9N: LAKE GEORGE TO TICONDEROGA

The 39 mile drive (via Route 9N) along the western shore of Lake George from Lake George Village north is a pleasant one. There's a spectacular view of the lake at a scenic overlook after you drive over Five Mile Mountain (2258 feet).

After passing Bolton Landing, you will drive through the small towns of **Silver Bay** and **Hague**. *Indian Kettles* restaurant (☎ *518-543-6576*) in Hague has a good view of the lake. The 'kettles' in the name refers to the depressions in the large rock surfaces of the surrounding mountains. The depressions were formed when smaller rocks tumbled about in a single spot, eventually eroding the surface to create a hole. You can eat lunch at the restaurant for under $10 and enjoy the view.

TICONDEROGA

On the northern tip of Lake George is Ticonderoga. Visitors – particularly history buffs – stop here to visit Fort Ticonderoga. Other than the fort, there's little to recommend the town. Ferries to Larrabee's Point, VT, offer an additional possible excursion (see the Lonely Planet guide, *New England*).

Some visitors might connect the name Ticonderoga to a long-familiar brand of yellow No 2 pencils, and – in fact – from the mid- to late-18th century, the town was an important graphite mining center.

Route 9N intersects Montcalm St at a traffic circle around the Liberty Monument, a depiction of early multiculturalism showing a Native American, Green Mountaineer (a member of Ethan Allen's Vermont rebels), French soldier and Royal Scottish Highlander. You can follow the signs from here through town to get to Fort Ticonderoga.

Fort Ticonderoga

The fort (☎ 518-585-2821) is a mile northeast of town on Route 74. Originally named Fort Carillon, it was built by the French in 1755 to control the southern reaches of their conquests in America and was strategically located at the southern end of Lake Champlain and the northern end of Lake George. (Its name is a variation on *Cheonderoga*, a Native American term meaning 'Between Two Waters.') So critical was its location that the fort was attacked a record six times and nicknamed 'Key to the Continent.' In 1758, a French force of only 3500 – under the command of the Marquis de Montcalm – defended the fort against 15,000 British and American colonial troops. However, the following summer, British forces under General Jeffrey Amherst captured and renamed the fort.

Sixteen years later, in 1775, Ethan Allen and his Green Mountain Boys captured the fort for the Americans in a surprise attack. Two years after that, General John Burgoyne captured the fort for the British, who abandoned the fortifications and burned the buildings. This historic fort would have been commemorated today with little more than an historical marker if it had not been for the family of William Ferris Pell, who bought the grounds in 1820 and began a complete restoration. Today, it is one the country's few major historical sites that is privately owned.

Inside the reconstructed buildings are collections of weapons, tools, uniforms and documents from the colonial and revolutionary periods. While the fort is open, there are weekly events, including fife and drum concerts, historical drills and craft demonstrations.

It is open from early May to mid-October daily from 9 am to 5 pm, until 6 pm during July and August. Admission is $8 for adults, $6 for children seven to 12 and free for children under seven. MV *Carillon* (☎ 802-897-5331) conducts short history cruises on the lake near the fort. Narrated tours leave the fort four times a day, weather permitting, on a replica of a 1920s cruise boat. Tickets are $7.50/4.50 for adults/children.

As a side trip on a clear day, you might drive up to **Mt Defiance** (☎ 518-585-2821). It was at the summit that British General John Burgoyne mounted cannons and forced the American forces at Fort Ticonderoga to surrender in 1777. There are fine views from here of Lake Champlain, the valleys and the Green Mountains. It is open daily mid-May to mid-October from 9 am to 5 pm. Admission is free.

Places to Stay

Most visitors to Fort Ticonderoga do not opt to stay over in the town. There is a campground outside town and a few motels on the main road, Montcalm St.

Brookwood Park Campsites *(☎ 518-585-7113)*, on Route 9N, situated in a shaded campground in the countryside, has 65 sites, laundry facilities and a small store. The sites are $15 each; open from early May to mid-October. The campground is south of Ticonderoga on Route 9N, 5 miles south of the intersection of Route 74.

Super 8 Motel *(☎ 518-585-2617)*, on Route 9N at Route 74, is open all year and has rooms for $45 to $65. ***Stone House Motor Lodge*** *(☎ 518-585-7394, 429 Montcalm St)* has about 20 rooms in two buildings, one a motel and the other a converted restaurant, now referred to as a 'lodge.' Rooms in the lodge are slightly nicer. Rooms rates are $40 to $70. It is closed in winter. ***Circle Court Motel*** *(☎ 518-585-7660, 440 Montcalm St)* is on the small traffic circle (with the arresting Liberty Monument sculpture in the middle), and open all year. Rates for singles/doubles are about $50 to $60; slightly lower rates are available in the winter.

Places to Eat

Your best bet, if you're staying over, is to check the menus in the lobby at either of the two motels near the traffic circle. There are fancier dinner spots in the area, but a very decent eatery is ***Hot Biscuit Diner*** *(☎ 518-585-3483, 428 Montcalm St)*, two doors down from the Circle Court Motel.

Getting There & Away

Adirondack Trailways (☎ 800-858-8555) stops at Hank's General Store (☎ 518-585-6680), 112 Champlain Ave. There is one bus north, and one south daily during the summer. One-way/roundtrip fares from Ticonderoga to Plattsburgh are $26/50, Lake Placid $21/40, Albany $18/33, New York City $46/87 and Montreal $59/119. There is no bus service to the nearby towns of Essex, Blue Mountain Lake, Long Lake and Old Forge.

The Fort Ti Ferry (☎ 802-897-7999) runs to and from Shoreham (Larabees Point), VT, and Ticonderoga, NY, from early May to late October. This is a cable ferry (nonmotorized). A tug boat pushes and pulls the ferry back and forth along the cable guides. The ferry can handle up to 15 cars and the crossing takes six minutes. In May, June, September and October it runs from 8 am to 6 pm; in July and August it runs from 7 am to 8 pm. The one-way/roundtrip fares are $6/10 for a car and up to four passengers, $2 for bikes and 50¢ for pedestrians (the same as it was 150 years ago). The Fort Ti ferry is the oldest business in Vermont (in continuous operation since 1799), and was originally a military crossing in use during the French & Indian War.

Today, on the Fort Ti side, some people are content to spend part of a summer afternoon by the small sandy parking lot just watching the ferry and its small assortment of people come and go. There is even a converted trailer-snack shop under a shady group of trees for refreshments while you wait.

ESSEX

The village of Essex is between Ticonderoga and Plattsburgh along the very scenic Route 22, which follows along the western shore of Lake Champlain and is certainly one of the prettiest drives in all of upstate New York; even the occasional satellite dish blends easily with the gentle terrain here.

The little hamlet of Essex is picturesque, starting with the mural on the fire station; this old firehouse dates from the early 1800s, and is one of several 'village architecture' highlights.

Essex Inn (☎ 518-963-8821), on Main St, is an historic site, dating from about 1810; it's open all year. There are five rooms with private bath, two with shared bath. Prices are from $85 to $115. The small restaurant here serves good homemade soups and pizza. Fancier entrees are $9 to $18.

Several good restaurants can be found here, including *Old Dock House* (☎ 518-963-4232), on the small marina, just down the alleyway between the firehouse and the ice cream shop. It is open daily from mid-May to mid-October from 11:30 am to 10 pm, and features fresh fish, pasta and grilled meats.

The Ice Cream Shop (☎ 518-963-7951), on Main St, is open from 11 am to 9 pm daily, late May to mid-September.

Getting There & Away

Lake Champlain Ferries (☎ 802-864-9804) connects Charlotte, VT, and Essex, NY. The 20-minute crossing is done daily, year-round from 6:30 am to 7 pm and in the summer until 9:30 pm. In the summer there are over 20 crossings throughout the day; but fewer crossings are made in the winter, spring and fall. The one-way/roundtrip car and driver fare is $7/12.75; additional adult passengers, $2.25/3.75; children (ages six to 12), 50¢/$1.

All schedules are subject to change due to ice and weather conditions. Essex is on Route 22, which runs along the western shore of Lake Champlain south to Ticonderoga, a distance of about 40 miles. You can also head south for 12 miles to Route 9N, which runs west into Route 73 and then to Lake Placid.

BLUE MOUNTAIN LAKE & AROUND

Blue Mountain Lake is a tiny village of 200 people in the geographic center of the Adirondacks. Despite its size, the town houses several important cultural attractions, including the Adirondack Museum and Adirondack Lake Center for the Arts. In addition, the town serves as a gateway to the Fulton Chain of Lakes in the southwestern Adirondacks (see Fulton Chain of Lakes in the Old Forge section later in this chapter) and to a network of excellent hiking trails, including the trail up Blue Mountain. Blue Mountain Lake can only be reached by car.

Information

The Indian Lake Chamber of Commerce (☎ 518-648-5112) has a small office about 11 miles east on Route 28. The post office at Blue Mountain Lake is in the middle of the village; it is open Monday to Friday from 8 am to 4:30 pm but is closed for lunch.

The closest laundry facilities are in Long Lake (see that section later in this chapter).

Adirondack Museum

One of the finest regional museums in the US, the Adirondack Museum (☎ 518-352-7311), on Route 30 just north of the intersection with Route 28, is housed in a complex of 22 buildings overlooking Blue Mountain Lake. Each building focuses on different aspects of Adirondack life. You can wander through indoor and outdoor exhibits of rustic Adirondack furniture displayed in a restored Victorian cottage, a typical 19th-century luxury resort hotel room, a hermits' camp, or the reassembled Bill Gates Diner (a former private railroad car – doubtfully related to the Microsoft billionaire), originally located in Bolton Landing. In addition, there are exhibits depicting the history and lore of the logging and mining industries of the region. Boating enthusiasts in particular will want to explore the popular exhibit on boat building, which includes fine examples of watercraft, ranging from dugout and birch-bark canoes to speedboats.

The museum is open from Memorial Day weekend to mid-October, daily from 9:30 am to 5:30 pm. Allow at least three hours. Admission for adults/seniors/children (ages seven to 16) is $10/9/6.

Blue Mountain

You can get a spectacular 360° view from the summit of this mountain (elevation 3759 feet, nearly 2000 feet above Blue Mountain Lake). The hike to the top takes about two hours (about 2 miles) each way, and gets steep at the top. The trail head is 1.6 miles

The Fifth Season: Blackflies, Head Nets & Bug Dope

Summer in the Adirondacks is a favorite time of year for bugs as well as humans. During the month of June, give or take a week, blackflies can change your life.

Blackflies are tiny, the size of a poppy seed, and they swarm. They definitely discourage summer recreation for the unprepared hiker, canoeist or swimmer. They can be fierce, and the only remedy is preparation – either chemical or fashion. Head nets are considered a must by local outfitters, especially if you want to do anything but dive into your tent cursing the day you expressed interest in the wilderness.

You can buy bug suits, hooded bug sweatshirts, or simple head nets in almost any sporting goods or general store in the Adirondacks.

An alternative is chemical lotions and sprays. Some contain DEET, which many people consider too strong for prolonged application. Candles with citronella also help at campsites.

With any of the chemical applications, take extreme care with children, who should not be allowed to apply such lotions or sprays; many can cause adverse reactions if swallowed or smeared in the eye.

north from the junction of Routes 28 and 30 and about an eighth of a mile past the Adirondack Museum. The road crests at the top of the hill, and there is a parking lot on the right. Bring water. For more information contact New York Department of Conservation (☎ 518-863-4545), 701 S Main St, Northville, NY 12134, or Blue Mt Outfitters (☎ 518-352-7306), 144 Main St, Blue Mountain Lake, NY 12812.

Sagamore Great Camp

This wilderness retreat was one of many 'great camps' built between the end of the Civil War and the beginning of WWI, when the rich and stylish built expensive and exclusive getaways. Sagamore, which was built in 1897, is typical in its architectural layout: there are servant and worker complexes and guest complexes. The buildings designed for the workers are in the board and batten style. Comfortable enough, but no match for the guest quarters, which defined the rustic wood and stone style of architecture still popular throughout the region. The interior of the buildings is covered in bark sheathing and log railings.

The camp is now a National Historic Site that provided the model for subsequent National Park Service sites. The camp offers residential programs ranging from mountain music to camps for grandparents and their grandchildren. Also, visitors can go on two-hour guided tours of the 27 rustic buildings on the grounds. For residential program information, call ☎ 315-354-5311, or visit its website at www.sagamore.org. Tours ($9/3 for adults/children) take place daily at 10 am and 1:30 pm, July 4 to Labor Day, and weekends through Columbus Day.

From Blue Mountain Lake, take Route 28 west 12 miles to Raquette Lake, and take Sagamore Rd 4 miles south to the camp.

Organized Tours & Outfitters

At nearby Raquette Lake, Bird's Boat Livery (☎ 315-354-4441), on Route 28, takes on paying passengers ($10 each) for the daily and scenic Mail Boat ride. It takes about two hours to drop off everyone's mail and enjoy the lake.

Blue Mt Outfitters (☎ 518-352-7306), 144 Main St, is just north of the junction of Routes 28 and 30, and functions as a complete outfitters, general store and information clearing house for the area. Ernie and Kim LaPrairie know the area well. They rent equipment and provide guided canoe and kayak trips and canoe instruction. Camping and canoe trips are individually planned. Rates average $75 a day per person including food. Family rates are slightly cheaper.

Special Events

The No Octane Boat Regatta (☎ 518-352-7311) is a gathering of human and wind-powered watercraft on Blue Mountain Lake in mid- to late June. There are races, canoe jousting, a clam bake and parade. Call the Development Office (☎ 518-352-7311) for exact dates.

Places to Stay

For more places to stay in the area, see the Old Forge section, later in this chapter.

Potter's Wilderness Resort & Restaurant (☎ 518-352-7331, 888-352-7331), at the junction of Routes 28 and 30 on the lake, has motel units and lakeside cottages for two to eight people, one of which has recently been winterized and is available all year. The resort charges $80 to $90 for a room. Seasonal weekly cottage prices range from $750 to $1250; off-season rates are $90/$550 per night/week.

LaPrairie's Lakeside Cottages (☎ 518-352-7675) is an extension of Blue Mt Outfitters, about a quarter mile north of the junction of Routes 28 and 30. There is a private sandy beach that is good for swimming in the summertime. Cottage room rates are in the $50 to $60 range. Like several motels in the area, LaPrairie's is a 'full housekeeping' cottage, meaning a full kitchen or kitchenette.

Hemlock Hall B&B (☎ 518-352-7706, winter ☎ 518-359-9065) is a large lodge with eight rooms in the main building, 10 cabins and four motel units in a shaded pine forest overlooking the lake. The main lodge has an enormous stone fireplace and an inviting porch. Hemlock Hall has its own beach and canoes. All room rates are double occupancy with breakfast and dinner, and you eat family-style at tables with other guests. Rooms cost $80 to $110. Most of the cottages are on the hill right above the lake. These rent for $100 to $125 a night. It's open mid-May to mid-October. To get there take Route 30 north from the intersection with Route 28; after a quarter mile you should see the sign for the lodge and Maple Lodge Rd. If you get to the Adirondack Museum, you've gone too far.

Places to Eat

There is a scarcity of restaurants and cafes in Blue Mountain Lake. For alternatives, go west to Old Forge, east to Indian Lake, or north to Long Lake for more options.

Potter's Restaurant (☎ 518-352-7331), at the junction of Routes 28 and 30, serves American food in a dining room full of artifacts from the Adirondacks. They are open during the summer daily except Tuesday from 7 am to 8:30 pm; they close from mid-September to mid-May. The *cafe* at the Adirondack Museum (☎ 518-352-7311) is a good spot for lunch.

For a good breakfast or lunch ($3 to $5 plates), try *Burkes Diner*, on Route 28 about 4 miles west of the Route 30 junction, on the south side of the road across from the Mobil gas station. (Look for a faded sign, 'Good Food Here.') If you get to Raquette Lake, you missed it.

The dining room at *Hemlock Hall* (☎ 518-352-7706, winter ☎ 518-359-9065) is open to the public for breakfast and dinner, but you must call ahead for reservations.

Shopping

Blue Mt Designs (☎ 518-352-7361), 200 yards north of the junction of Routes 28 and 30, offers a good selection of quality local crafts, painting, pottery, weavings, jewelry, and Adirondack furniture (including the region's famous Adirondack chairs). It is open May through October from 10 am to 5 pm or by appointment.

Entertainment

Adirondack Lakes Center for the Arts (☎ 518-352-7715, PO Box 205, Blue Mountain Lake, NY 12812) is a visual and performing arts center near the junction of Routes 28 and 30. Evening performances include folk music, classical music and storytelling. During the day, the center runs a series of workshops – for children and adults – that include canoe construction, wildlife photography and basket making. Email the center at alca@telnet.net for schedules. There is a gallery and gift shop. The center is open all year, Monday through Friday, from 9 am to 4 pm; during the summer season (late May to early September), they are also open weekends from 10 am to 4 pm. Admission to the gallery is free.

LONG LAKE

Eleven miles north of Blue Mountain Lake on Route 30 sits the small town of Long Lake. The Long Lakes Park & Recreation Department (☎ 518-624-3077) in the town office building has information on nearby trails and waterways. Laundry facilities are available at Long Lake Laundromat, next to Rockwell's Garage on Route 30.

If you drive through, stop at *Adirondack Hotel* (☎ 518-624-4700), by the small bridge north of the center of town. Look for the boulder out front with 'Adirondack Hotel' painted on it. There has been a hotel on this site since the 1800s, although most of the original one burned down in 1900. Its current owners keep it open all year. The hotel has white halls with pine floors and basic, clean rooms. Rooms with shared/private bath are $35/45 to $50/60 for double occupancy. Rooms without bathrooms have sinks. There are two restaurants in the hotel, one serving sandwiches and burgers in the $5 to $7 range, and a slightly fancier and more expensive dining room.

The *Long Lake Diner* (☎ 518-624-3941), just off Route 30 (by Hoss' Corner), is open daily from 6 am to 8:30 pm all year. It's got good diner food, fresh salads, turkey and gravy and homemade soups.

OLD FORGE

Old Forge (and the neighboring village Thendara) sits in the southwest corner of the Adirondacks, at the western edge of Fourth Lake in the Fulton Chain of Lakes. The area is the snowmobiling capital of the region during the winter, and the summer attracts canoe and hiking buffs. Contact the Old Forge Tourist Information Center (☎ 315-369-6983), PO Box 68, Old Forge, NY 13420 (across the road from McDonald's), for seasonal events information; the center is open daily from 8 am to 5 pm and Sunday from 9 am to 5 pm. Most motels, B&Bs and restaurants in the area are also good sources of information on recreation spots, hiking trails and canoe trips through the Fulton Chain of Lakes.

Most shops and businesses are along Route 28 (Main St), including the post office, coin laundry and two banks with ATMs. Buses do not service Old Forge.

Adirondack Scenic Railroad

This scenic railroad (☎ 315-369-6920) is a project of the Adirondacks Railway Preservation Society in nearby Thendara (just west of Old Forge) and operates vintage open-window coaches through some very pretty country between the old Thendara and Minnehaha stations, complete with fake, weekly train robberies. The twice-daily trips take about an hour, run from early May to late November, and cost $7 for adults, $4.75 for children (ages three to 12).

Fulton Chain of Lakes

Made up of eight lakes – from the pond at Inlet to Fourth Lake – this cluster of lakes covers over 2000 acres and stretches for about 20 miles from Old Forge to Raquette Lake. Carved out over 10,000 years ago by massive glaciers, the Fulton lakes were once the way into the interior of the Adirondacks. Native Americans used these lakes, which run southwest to northeast, to crisscross the region, carrying their canoes from lake to lake.

In the early 1800's, the railroad opened the region to development as a resort area, and the early trappers and hunters of the region often became the guides of rich sportsmen from the industrial capitals of the East Coast. Today, the area draws all sorts of watersports enthusiasts. Old Forge to Third Lake is popular with boaters. Canoeists are often advised to begin elsewhere to avoid the heavy motorized traffic.

The Adirondack Canoe Route, a 90-mile scenic journey through the Fulton lakes, begins at Old Forge to the Raquette River and all the way up to the Saranac Lakes. The route goes through a number of northern lake towns including Tupper Lake, Saranac Lake and Paul Smiths. Some portage is required.

The Wilderness Letter

In 1960 naturalist author Wallace Stegner wrote 'The Wilderness Letter,' which urged federal protection of America's wild spaces and was later used to introduce a bill that would establish national legislation protecting wilderness areas. Here is an excerpt:

> Something will have gone out of us as a people if we ever let the remaining wilderness be destroyed; if we permit the last virgin forests to be turned into comic books and plastic cigarette cases; if we drive the few remaining members of the wild species into zoos or to extinction; if we pollute the last clean air and dirty the last clean streams and push our paved roads through the last of the silence, so that never again will Americans be free in their own country from the noise, the exhausts, the stinks of human and automotive waste.

For a more leisurely day trip, you can canoe down the North Branch of the Moose River, beginning at the North Street Bridge near Old Forge. The trip, which takes about four hours, is easy and scenic as the river twists its way along the gently curved banks of hardwood forests and grassy wetlands. Take along a picnic to enjoy on one of the many small, sandy beaches. There is one portage of about 300 yards along the route. For an even easier canoeing trip, you might try Nick's Lake, 2 miles from Old Forge.

Third Lake to Seventh Lake, and Seventh Lake to Raquette Lake, are popular with canoeists. Most portages are under a mile.

If you arrive in the area without a boat, you can rent one at the marinas on most lakes, or try Tickner's Adirondack Canoe Outfitters (☎ 315-369-6286), 1 Riverside Drive, Old Forge, or Adirondack Canoes and Kayaks (☎ 518-359-2174), 96 Old Piercefield Rd and Route 3, Tupper Lake.

For information about routes, contact the New York State DEC (☎ 518-897-1200)

office in Ray Brook, or the local tourist office in Old Forge (☎ 315-369-6983).

Special Events

The Adirondack Canoe Classic (☎ 518-369-6983, 347-1992) is a 90-mile race (and party) from Old Forge to Saranac Lake. It takes place in early September, on the weekend following the Labor Day holiday.

Places to Stay

There is no shortage of basic motels along Route 28 between the towns of Blue Mountain Lake and Old Forge. Restaurants aren't as common.

Camping Between Old Forge and Blue Mountain Lake there are several good campsites, including **Limekiln Lake Campground** (☎ 315-357-4401), about 3 miles southeast of the town Inlet and Route 28. This is a big public campground, with room for RVs. It's open from May to November, weather permitting. Rates are $11 per site, and boat rentals are available.

A more interesting campsite is available for boaters only. **Alger Island Campground** (☎ 315-369-3224) is about 8 miles east of Old Forge near the foot of Fourth Lake, open from late May until early September. Minimal facilities include toilets but no showers. There are 15 lean-tos and two tent sites, in addition to a picnic area and hiking trail that circles the 40-acre island. Rates are $12 per site.

Eighth Lake Campground (☎ 315-354-4120) is midway between Inlet and Raquette Lake on Route 28. There are 125 tent and trailer sites, a beach and picnic area, showers and toilets. Rates are $12 per site. It is open mid-April to mid-November.

Year-round camping is available at **Old Forge KOA** (☎ 315-369-6011), off Route 28 about a half mile north of Old Forge. This site has the usual array of KOA commercial facilities, including several cabins, laundry, grocery store and playground. Rates are $20 for campsites, $35 for cabins for two.

B&Bs & Inns The **Cinnamon Bear B&B** (☎ 315-357-6013), on Route 28, is a charming bargain in the village of Inlet; just look for the circular sign. This refurbished old farmhouse has four upstairs rooms, larger than most B&Bs, with two semi-private shared baths between the rooms. The year-round rates are $65 for two adults; add a few dollars more for children to cover their breakfast.

Moose River House B&B (☎ 315-369-3104, 12 Birch St) is in the village of Thendara. There are four rooms here, two with private bath. Year-round rates are $65 and $85 a night.

Van Auken's Inne & Restaurant (☎ 315-369-3033), at Forge St in Old Forge, is across the street from the Adirondack Scenic Railroad in a beautiful old white Victorian building with a long front porch. It has 12 rooms, all with private bath, TV and telephone, ranging from $65 to $85 for singles or doubles. You can also have lunch or drinks in the evening on the front porch. The restaurant offers grilled dinner entrees like pork tenderloin, duck and fresh fish for $12 to $20. Van Auken's restaurant is open daily in the summer season from 11:30 am to 9 pm, and until 10 pm on weekends. The rest of year they are usually closed on Sunday.

In Eagle Bay you'll find *Big Moose Inn* (☎ 315-357-2042, 1510 Big Moose Rd). This B&B has 16 rooms, 12 with private baths. Double occupancy rates are $88 to $160.

Places to Eat

Seventh Lake House Restaurant (☎ 315-357-6028, 479 Route 28), above the village of Inlet, at the west edge of Seventh Lake (part of the Fulton Chain), is one of the best dinner spots west of Blue Mountain Lake. The fare is contemporary American, but the owners call it 'civilized dining in the wilderness.' Entrees range from $10 to $20. It is open for dinner daily from June through September from 5 to 9 pm; weekends only during the rest of year.

Across the street from the post office is *Farm Restaurant* (☎ 315-369-6199, Route 28) in Thendera, a small village 2 miles west of Old Forge. This place has character written all over it, from the food to the antiques to Frank, the owner. The Farm is open daily for breakfast and lunch only from 7 am to 2 pm.

LAKE PLACID

Lake Placid Village (population 2800) is actually situated on Mirror Lake. Lake Placid – the lake, not the town – is nearby. The town Lake Placid was the site of the 1932 and 1980 winter Olympics. Only two other towns – Innsbruck, Austria and St Moritz, Switzerland – have hosted two Winter Games.

This resort town isn't as swank as many other major winter sports destinations, but it has a great deal to offer in summer as well as winter. Sports enthusiasts come in the winter to ski the High Peaks (of which there are 46, some measuring over 4000 feet) or for ice skating and other winter sports (see the Outdoor Activities section earlier in this chapter). In the summer, the region offers excellent cycling, mountain biking, hiking, golf and boating. You can also see Olympic athletes training in the various facilities.

Lake Placid became an Olympic center because Dr Melvil Dewey, of Dewey Decimal System fame, opened the Lake Placid Club as a resort here in 1895. The club began winter sports in 1904.

Orientation & Information

Lake Placid is in the middle of the High Peaks region on Routes 73 and 86. It's accessible from the north and south on Route 30, from the west on Route 3 and from the east via I-87 on Route 73.

The Lake Placid Visitors Bureau (☎ 518-523-2445, 800-447-5224), 216 Main St, is in the large brownstone building connected to the new Olympic Center building at the south end of town. It's open Monday to Saturday from 9 am to 5 pm, and Sunday from Christmas to mid-March from 9 am to 5 pm. You can pick up the helpful booklet that lists all the places to stay in Lake Placid and surrounding towns or check out its website at www.lakeplacid.com.

The post office is in the fork between Main St and Parkside Drive downtown (☎ 518-523-3071). The local biweekly newspaper is the *Lake Placid News*.

NEW YORK

LAKE PLACID

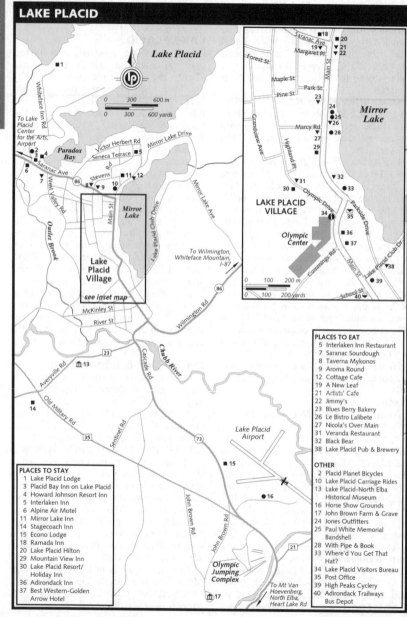

PLACES TO EAT
5 Interlaken Inn Restaurant
7 Saranac Sourdough
8 Taverna Mykonos
9 Aroma Round
12 Cottage Cafe
19 A New Leaf
21 Artists' Cafe
22 Jimmy's
23 Blues Berry Bakery
26 Le Bistro Lalibete
27 Nicola's Over Main
31 Veranda Restaurant
32 Black Bear
38 Lake Placid Pub & Brewery

OTHER
2 Placid Planet Bicycles
10 Lake Placid Carriage Rides
13 Lake Placid-North Elba
   Historical Museum
16 Horse Show Grounds
17 John Brown Farm & Grave
24 Jones Outfitters
25 Paul White Memorial
   Bandshell
28 With Pipe & Book
33 Where'd You Get That
   Hat?
34 Lake Placid Visitors Bureau
35 Post Office
39 High Peaks Cyclery
40 Adirondack Trailways
   Bus Depot

PLACES TO STAY
1 Lake Placid Lodge
3 Placid Bay Inn on Lake Placid
4 Howard Johnson Resort Inn
5 Interlaken Inn
6 Alpine Air Motel
11 Mirror Lake Inn
14 Stagecoach Inn
15 Econo Lodge
18 Ramada Inn
20 Lake Placid Hilton
29 Mountain View Inn
30 Lake Placid Resort/
   Holiday Inn
36 Adirondack Inn
37 Best Western-Golden
   Arrow Hotel

Olympic Center & Sites

The Olympic Center (☎ 518-523-1655, 800-462-6236), the large white building next to the visitors bureau on Main St, was used for the 1980 Olympics and houses four ice skating rinks. It was on the adjacent speed-skating oval that speed skater Eric Heiden made history by winning five individual gold medals. You can watch athletes training here for free or take in an ice show or hockey game. Bring a jacket or sweater; even in the summer the ice is cold.

You can visit the following Olympic sites separately or all together on the all-inclusive **Olympic Site Tour Package**, which costs $16 for adults, free for children (ages six and under), and is available from mid-June to mid-October.

Olympic Jumping Complex (☎ 518-523-1655, 523-2202), located southeast of town on Route 73, is the training facility for the US Olympic ski jump teams. Thanks to artificial surfaces, ski jumpers train here all year. When there is no snow, ski jumping takes place on a porcelain in-run and plastic-covered landing hill. You can take a chair lift followed by an elevator ride to the top of the 26-story viewing room. During the peak seasons, mid-December to mid-March, and again from mid-May to mid-October, the jumping complex is open daily from 9 am to 4 pm, and the cost is $8/5 for adults/children and seniors; free for children under six. During the off-season (mid-March to mid-May and mid-October to mid-December), it is closed Monday and Tuesday, and the cost is $5/3.

Admission also includes **Kodak Sports Park** and the freestyle ski jump training center. Skiers jump, then flip and turn, into a 17-foot-deep (750,000 gallon) pool of water. It's right next to the jumping complex.

Olympic Sports Complex at Mt Van Hoevenberg (☎ 518-523-4436) is the site of bobsled, luge and cross-country skiing events. Tours of both the bobsled and luge areas are also available. It is open from mid-December to mid-March, and from mid-May to mid-October, Wednesday through Sunday from 9 am from to 4 pm, and Monday from 12:30 to 4 pm. It is closed Tuesday during these periods. The complex is closed entirely from mid-March to mid-May and mid-October to mid-December. Admission for adults/seniors and children (ages five to 12) is $4/3. Mt Van Hoevenberg is 4 miles east of the jumping complex on Route 73.

Winter and summer bobsled rides are available to the public. During the winter (mid-December to mid-March), bobsled rides on the half-mile 1980 Olympic track reach speeds of over 50 mph (as compared to speeds of over 80 mph during professional competitions on a newer track); the cost is $30 per person, and rides are available Wednesday to Sunday from 10 am to 3 pm. During the summer (mid-June to mid-October) 'wheeled' bobsleds run on a concrete track, reaching speeds over 45 mph; the cost is $25 per person. All bobsled rides are piloted by professional drivers and brakemen. Good luck anyway.

Whiteface Mountain, in nearby Wilmington, also hosted several Olympic events in 1980 (see Whiteface Mountain in the Wilmington section, later in this chapter).

John Brown Farm & Grave

The famous American abolitionist who was hanged for leading the raid on the US Arsenal at Harpers Ferry, WV, is buried outside Lake Placid in North Elba. The historic site (☎ 518-523-3900) includes Brown's farm and his gravestone, as well as those of two of his sons and nine other men killed in Harpers Ferry.

Brown was born in Connecticut in 1800 and lived in Ohio for a number of years; he moved to North Elba in 1849 to participate in a radical social experiment led by Gerrit Smith. The plan was to give land to any free black man who wished to farm it. Brown moved to North Elba to teach farming practices. It was here that he and his followers organized the raid, hoping to use the captured arms to launch a general rebellion. On October 16, 1859, Brown and a group of followers attacked the federal arsenal. They were captured on October 18, and hanged on December 2.

There is a self-guided tour of the farm building, the 244-acre farm and the graves.

The house is open from late May to late October, Wednesday through Saturday from 10 am to 5 pm. You can walk around the grounds and look at the graves any time of year. Take Route 86 from town to Route 73 south. Drive 1.7 miles to the fork with a sign noting the 'John Brown Historic Site.' Drive half a mile down this road (John Brown Rd) to the farm.

ADK Adirondak Loj

At the base of many of the region's tallest mountains, the Adirondak Loj ('lahj') is a large house situated on Heart Lake and surrounded by 20 kilometers of cross-country and snowshoe trails that connect to hundreds of miles of state trails. Inside, there is a common room with rocking chairs in front of a large fireplace, over which is hung a moose head; there's also a good library of books and magazines on the Adirondacks. The year-round loj has bunks and private rooms for guests, both ADK members and nonmembers alike. There are also two cabins, 14 lean-tos and 46 campsites (see the Places to Stay section for details).

Take Route 73 south of Lake Placid for about 2 miles to Adirondak Loj Rd (also known as Heart Lake Rd). Drive on Adirondak Loj Rd for 5 miles and you're at the combination campground and lodge (the Adirondak Loj) and ADK High Peaks Information Center (☎ 518-523-3441), PO Box 867, Lake Placid, NY 12946. Here, you have immediate access to the lake and numerous trails. The center has an information number (☎ 518-523-3518) for daily weather and trail conditions in the North Country.

Hiking

With hundreds of lakes, rivers, ridges and mountains, there seems to be no end to the walking and hiking possibilities. Contact the Adirondak Loj's ADK High Peaks Information Center (☎ 518-523-3441) on Heart Lake for hiking maps and advice on the best seasonal hiking and nature trails. (See also Hiking in the Outdoor Activities section, near the beginning of this chapter, for helpful hiking resources.)

One of the best short hiking options in the area is a 2.3 mile loop to Mt Jo, named in 1877 after Josephine Schofield, who was engaged to Henry Van Hoevenberg. She died before they were to be married. The trail to the summit rises dramatically over Heart Lake. Take the short steep trail up the mountain and the long gentler trail down, or the long trail both ways with small children. Red pine, silver birch, and maple adorn the way, and both routes take roughly the same time. From the boulder ledge at the summit, you can see Indian Pass and half a dozen of the High Peaks, including Mts Marcy and Algonquin (5114 feet).

One of the best known trails is **Phelps Trail**, which covers 9.5 miles from Keene Valley to the summit of Mt Marcy, the highest of the 46 High Peaks. Another well-known trail is the 130-mile-long **Northville-Lake Placid Trail**, which starts near Great Sacandaga Lake in the southern Adirondacks and winds through high meadows and dense pine forests. The trail that follows **Ausable River** in the Adirondacks passes through some superb scenery of pine and birch forests, rivers and rock outcrops.

Other hikes of moderate difficulty in the Lake Placid area include **Avalanche Lake** (10 miles roundtrip) and **Rocky Falls** (4.5 miles roundtrip).

Debates are endless about which peak affords the best view. Among the perennial favorites are Mts Haystack, Algonquin, Marcy, Nippletop and Santanoni.

Bicycling

The Lake Placid area is great bicycling country. Country-road and off-road trails are abundant, and road shoulders tend to be wide enough for cars to safely pass. Any of the several bike shops in town can provide you with maps and rentals. A half day of cycling, for example, could take you around the River Rd loop, a trip of about 12 miles.

Bike rental rates are competitive and usually start at $7/15/20 for an hour/half day/full day. Each shop also rents helmets, car racks and children's safety equipment. Placid Planet Bicycles (☎ 518-523-4128), 200 Saranac Ave at the corner of Whiteface Inn Rd, does sales, repairs and rentals, and they'll help you with maps and suggestions for either off-road or country-road cycling.

High Peaks Cyclery (☎ 518-523-3764), 331 Main St, rents bikes, in-line skates, rock climbing equipment and camping supplies (but not sleeping bags).

In the summer, the cross-country ski trails at Mt Van Hoevenberg are open to mountain bikers, both experienced and novice. Trail fees are $5 and bikes and helmets are available to rent at the High Peaks Mountain Biking Center (☎ 518-523-3764), 331 Main St, which is open daily.

Other Things to See & Do
The **Lake Placid-North Elba Historical Museum** (☎ 518-523-1608), on Averyville Rd two blocks from Route 73, is housed in a former railroad station. The station's waiting room now displays old farm implements, furnishings and photographs of the region, as well as memorabilia from the Olympics. It is open from June to September, Tuesday through Sunday, noon to 4 pm. To get there, take Route 73 south to Averyville Rd, go right to the museum. It's free.

There is also a **nature trail** with interpretive signs identifying various plants and trees along Lake Placid. The trail starts behind the Howard Johnson's Restaurant off Route 86. Pick up a trail guide from the Lake Placid Visitors Center (☎ 518-523-2445) in the Olympic Center on Main St.

Outfitters
Jones Outfitters (☎ 518-523-3468), 37 Main St, rents canoes, paddleboats and kayaks. They also teach fly fishing and lead fishing and boating trips all year. In addition to the lake, which is just out the front door, they also go to the good fishing rivers, such as Ausable, Chubb, Saranac and Bog. Half and full day trips range from about $100 to $150. Overnight canoe trips, complete with guide, equipment and food, are also available. It is open daily.

You'll understand how serious these folks are about fish with a quick glance at the chalk board outside the shop. In the summer, it lists the names of hatch flies that

the fish are biting; poetic entries include Yellow Sallys, Red Quills, Olive Caddis and Stonefly Nymphs.

Middle Earth Expeditions (☎ 518-523-9572), on Route 73, is a year-round outfitter specializing in wilderness canoe and fishing trips and whitewater rafting in the spring, summer and fall; call for directions from Lake Placid.

Organized Tours
The Adirondack Flying Service (☎ 518-523-2473) offers 20-minute flights year round at $23 per person. Sail-plane rides are $45 for 20 minutes and $55 for 30 minutes.

Lake Placid Carriage Rides (☎ 518-523-2483), 1 Main St, takes folks on carriage rides around Mirror Lake from mid-June to Labor Day.

Special Events
Sporting events, particularly ice skating, hockey and skiing, take place all winter long in Lake Placid. The events and schedules change every year; the Olympic Regional Development Authority (☎ 518-523-1655, 800-462-6236) can provide a schedule and answer questions. In June, the Lake Placid Horse Show is a main event.

Places to Stay
A note on seasons and prices: Lake Placid is a premier resort area, and the press of the Olympic stamp is everywhere. There are bargains to be had, but prices are the highest in the Adirondacks. The high season is generally the summer months from mid-June to early September, followed by the winter ski season from about a week before Christmas until March 15; weekends can be higher year-round. Rates are lower, often considerably so, after mid-October and mid-March – unless a 'special event' is scheduled. It's often worth asking about possible discounts during off-season.

Wilmington, 12 miles east of Lake Placid, offers additional (and sometimes cheaper) accommodations, as does Saranac Lake.

Budget The shared rooms at *ADK Adirondak Loj* have wooden bunks, thick and firm mattresses and, if you're lucky enough to get a bunk facing the lake, great views. Private rooms have double beds. This is your best choice in the bottom-end accommodations bracket – if not in any bracket – and it's open to members and nonmembers.

All room rates include breakfast; if you want dinner, arrange it in advance; it's $12.50 more. The food is good and served family-style at long tables. The menu is creative and different each night, but usually includes soup, salad, fish or chicken, pasta or rice and dessert. A favorite detail of the Loj: there are 46 beds to match the 46 high peaks of the Adirondacks. Weekday/weekend rates for bunk rooms are $25/32 for the 18 bunk room or $32/41 for the six bunk room. Private rooms cost $42/52 and cabins cost $75/95 or $12/16 per person with a minimum of 10 people required. Lean-tos are $12/16 in winter/summer for two people and $2.50 for each additional person. Campsites are $8/13 in winter/summer and $1.50 for each additional person. Breakfast is $5 for those in cabins, lean-tos and campsites. Trail lunches can be ordered in advance for $4.50.

About 3½ miles by foot from the Adirondak Loj is the *John Brooks Loj (JBL)*. It has bunk rooms for $34 in the family bunkroom and $28 in the co-ed bunkroom. Breakfast is included and dinner is $12.50. JBL lean-tos are $13 for the first two and $2.50 for each extra person; breakfast/dinner is $5.50/12.50.

ADK also maintains two backcountry cabins, *Grace Camp*, which sleeps six, and *Camp Peggy O'Brien*, which sleeps 12. These camps are a 3¼ mile walk from the town of Keene Valley on Route 73, about 15 miles southeast of Lake Placid. They're open all year and have bunks, tables, firewood, cooking stoves (you bring the fuel) and cooking equipment. There are also lean-tos around Camps Grace and O'Brien. Rates for Grace Camp are $80; for O'Brien, $125.

ADK members get a 10% discount on everything. See the Adirondack Mountain Club section at the beginning of this chapter for contact information, or visit their web site at www.adk.org.

Whispering Pines Campground (☎ 518-523-9322), on Route 73, has 80 sites ranging from $7.50 to $17.50 for two. You can choose between sites in the open or ones in the shade. It is open from May 1 to the end of October. To get there by car take Route 73 for 6 miles south of Lake Placid from the junction with Route 86.

Most of the cheaper motels extend along Saranac Ave on the way into town from Route 86 to the west. Rooms facing the road can be noisy because of all the traffic, so get a back room if you need quiet. *Alpine Air Motel* (☎ 518-523-9261, 99 Saranac Ave) has rooms in several motel buildings spread out along the roadside property. There's a large pool in the middle of the complex, and the atmosphere is convivial. Single/double rates range from $45 to $85 depending on season and demand. Alpine Air also rents suites at $99/150.

The well-managed *Econo Lodge* (☎ 518-523-2817), Route 73, is on Cascade Rd about a mile south of the Olympic Center in town. In-season room rates for singles/doubles range from $60/95, off-season rates from $45/85 a night.

Mid-Range The *Stagecoach Inn* (☎ 518-523-9474, 370 Old Military Rd) just south of town, is the oldest hotel in Lake Placid. Originally a stagecoach stop, it was converted into a hotel in 1833, and later into a B&B. There's a big front porch, fireplaces and antique furniture, all in a beautiful country setting. A room with private bath and fireplace is $80 to $95; other private rooms cost $70 to $85; and shared bath $60 to $70. A full breakfast is included. You reach the inn by traveling south from town on Route 73; make a right at the sign for the John Brown Historic Site, then another immediate right onto Old Military Rd (Essex County Route 35). Go 1.3 miles and the inn is on your left.

Placid Bay Inn on Lake Placid (☎ 518-523-2001, 70 Saranac Ave), on Route 86 as you enter Lake Placid from the west, is open all year. The sky-blue building with carved birds on the facade makes it hard to miss. The decor here is a bit severe: shag carpeting, bright gold velour bed covers and low ceilings. But the rooms are neat and good sized, and there is a pool. Seasonal rates vary from $45 to $85 for a double.

The *Mountain View Inn (☎ 518-523-2439, 800-499-2668, 140 Main St)* is on a hill across from the Best Western. Standard rooms, with psychedelic orange doors, have views of nothing in back or across Main St to the lake in front. Rates are $58 to $95; they're cheapest from November to mid-December and from April through July.

Adirondack Inn (☎ 518-523-2424, 800-556-2424, 217 Main St) is across the street from the Olympic Center, in the middle of town. The place is modern, clean and the rooms are large and each one has a small fridge. The inn has an indoor and outdoor pool, in addition to the small sandy beach facing Mirror Lake. Rooms range from $69 to $144, depending on the season.

Best Western-Golden Arrow Hotel (☎ 518-523-3353, 150 Main St) is right on the lake and has a beach, heated pool, saunas, Jacuzzi and racquetball court. Rooms are furnished in upmarket motel style. Single or double rates range from $70 to $170, depending on the view.

Ramada Inn (☎ 518-523-2587, 8-12 Saranac Ave) offers a greenhouse lounge with a lake view. Rates from mid-June to late October range from $79 to $125. The rest of the year, room rates are $59 to $109. *Howard Johnson Resort Inn (☎ 518-523-9555, 90 Saranac Ave)* offers a lovely view of the lake and mountains. The hotel charges $75 to $120 for a room.

Top End *Interlaken Inn (☎ 518-523-3180, 800-428-4369, 15 Interlaken Ave)* is just north of Mirror Lake, and it's the closest thing to a Victorian country inn that you'll find in the area. There are only 11 rooms, all with private bath, and rates range from $150 to $210 for two persons, and include a full-course dinner. On Tuesday and Wednesday, when the restaurant is closed, room rates drop by $30 per person.

Mirror Lake Inn (☎ 518-523-2544, 5 Mirror Lake Drive) is just north of Swiss Rd. This is an Adirondack classic, and one of the most elegant retreats in upstate New York. It offers afternoon tea, a restaurant,

private beach, canoeing, tennis, spa, lakeside dining and the list goes on. Prices range from a modest off-season $105 to the in-season high of $355.

Lake Placid Lodge (☎ 518-523-2700), on Whiteface Inn Rd, is rustic, remote and expensive. The lodge overlooks the west end of Lake Placid and offers everything from stone fireplaces and sunset cruises to swimming and snowshoeing. Rates range from $300 for rooms without fireplace to suites for $700.

Lake Placid Hilton (☎ 518-523-4411, 800-755-5598, 1 Mirror Lake Drive), near the junction of Main St and Saranac Ave, is really a complex of several buildings. The best rooms – all of which have a view of Mirror Lake or the mountains – are in the tallest of these buildings, located on the hill at the corner of Main St and Saranac Ave. The hotel complex offers a vast number of amenities, including indoor and outdoor pools, a restaurant, lounge and game room. Rooms are big, nicely furnished and each has a balcony.

Room rates range from $120 to $190 in the summer high season, and from $90 to $140 in the off-season. Rates vary according to whether you have a view of Mirror Lake. Ask for information about ski packages that include lift tickets to Whiteface Mountain and about late January and spring specials.

Lake Placid Resort/Holiday Inn (☎ 518-523-2556, 1 Olympic Drive) has many rooms with fireplaces and balconies looking out over Mirror Lake and the mountains. Also available are two chalets with fireplaces accommodating up to four people. Rates range from $70 to $330 for rooms and $125 to $325 for chalets.

Places to Eat
Budget & Mid-Range *The Cottage Cafe (☎ 518-523-9845, 5 Mirror Lake Rd)* is a very popular local spot for lunch and dinner. The menu includes hot sandwiches, chicken burritos and feta salad, all under $8. Best value on the lake. It is open from 11:30 am to 1 am.

For good deli sandwiches, try *Saranac Sourdough (☎ 518-523-4897, 89 Saranac*

Ave), across the street from Howard Johnson's. This is a good place to put together a picnic basket. It is open daily from 8 am to 8 pm during July and August, and until 5 pm the rest of the year.

There are several places serving good American fare on Main St along Mirror Lake, including the ***Black Bear*** *(☎ 518-523-9886, 157 Main St)*, with a nicely varied menu that includes fish sandwiches and Reubens (about $5) and ribs, scampi and pasta ($10 to $14). It also serves great pie. The tables at the rear of the restaurant look out over the lake. The restaurant is open from 6:30 to 10 pm weekdays, and around the clock on Friday and Saturday.

The ***Artist's Cafe*** *(☎ 518-523-9493, 1 Main St)*, on the corner of Saranac Ave, is a cozy place down a long staircase. Tables in the back of the dining area look directly over Mirror Lake. You can get a sandwich, omelet or burger here for $6 to $7. Dinner selections include scampi and New York strip steaks, ranging from $7 to $19, and they also have an artsy kids' menu.

Nicola's Over Main *(☎ 518-523-4430, 90 Main St)* is a big and busy restaurant with an open kitchen and a long bar, serving good steaks, lobster, pasta, brick-oven pizza, big Greek salads and appetizers. It is open daily from 5 to 11 pm. ***Aroma Round*** *(☎ 518-523-3818, 18 Saranac Ave)* is a nice spot to begin the day or hang out in. It has a fireplace, books, puzzles to play and a good coffee bar. It is open daily for breakfast and lunch and evenings for desert and coffee.

Taverna Mykonos *(☎ 518-523-1164, 38 Saranac Ave)* is a pleasant and small Greek eatery with good soups and salads, moussaka, pilaf and kebobs. It is open daily for lunch and dinner in the summer, and daily for dinner and weekend lunches the rest of the year.

Lake Placid Pub and Brewery *(☎ 518-523-3813)* features English-style microbrews. The pub menu ranges from nachos to steak sandwiches and a veggie stir-fry. Try the Ubu Ale, a local favorite. It is open from 11:30 am to 2 am.

A New Leaf *(☎ 518-523-1847, 8 Main St)*, at the bottom of Hilton Plaza, is a good combination bookstore/gift shop, and they serve decent coffee and muffins. It is open daily from 6:30 am to 7 pm. ***Blues Berry Bakery*** *(☎ 518-523-4539, 26 Main St)* has a fine mix of breads and sweets. It is open Sunday through Thursday from 8 am to 6 pm, Friday and Saturday from 8 am to 8 pm.

Top End The restaurant at ***Interlaken Inn*** *(☎ 518-523-3180, 15 Interlaken Ave)* serves a five-course, fixed-price meal for $25, Thursday through Monday with seating between 6 and 8 pm. There is also a full a la carte menu. The food here is excellent and entrees change daily. The inn is in an old Victorian house with appropriately dark walls and furnishings and has accommodations (see Places to Stay, above). Expect to spend a minimum of $20 per person for a la carte dinner. Reservations are advised.

Le Bistro Lalibete *(☎ 518-523-3680, 51 Main St)* is a fine French restaurant. Specialties include escargot, duck and salmon. It is open daily in the summer from 5 to 10 pm. The rest of the year, it closes on Monday and Tuesday. ***Veranda Restaurant*** *(☎ 523-3339, 1 Olympic Drive)* is a very good French eatery opposite the Holiday Inn. It is open daily for dinner. Two can eat for about $50, including a bottle of wine.

Entertainment

The ***Lake Placid Center for the Arts*** *(☎ 518-523-2512)*, on Saranac Ave, is a year-round, multi-purpose center that presents professional theatrical, music and dance performances, shows films and conducts workshops.

The Lake Placid Sinfonetta *(☎ 518-523-2051)* is a summer orchestra of 19 professional musicians. They present a six-week season of concerts in July and August at a variety of locations, including Sunday night performances at the Lake Placid Center for the Arts. Free outdoor 'cushion concerts,' which some boaters attend by floating over to listen, are performed Wednesday nights at ***Paul White Memorial Bandshell*** downtown along Mirror Lake.

Shopping

With Pipe & Book *(☎ 518-523-9096)*, 91 Main St, sells fine pipes and natural blended tobaccos. They also have a great selection of new, rare and used books, as well as scenic prints and good hiking and driving maps of the Adirondack region. This is a great browsing store, with more rooms upstairs and downstairs. The shop is open daily from 9:30 am to 6 pm, and Sunday from 10 am to 4 pm.

Where'd You Get That Hat? (☎ 518-523-3101), 155 Main St, has a vast assortment of headgear from near and far.

Getting There & Away

Air Adirondack Airport in Saranac Lake is the closest commercial airport; it is 16 miles west of Lake Placid. (See the Getting There & Around section at the beginning of this chapter for fares and contact information.) US Airways Express has regular 19-seater service. Taxis meet arriving flights, and the fare to Lake Placid is about $15. Rental cars are also available from the Hertz office in Lake Placid (☎ 518-891-9044, 800-654-3131). There is also a private airport in Lake Placid.

Bus Adirondack Trailways (☎ 800-858-8555) stops at 324 Main St, home of Lake Placid Video. There's one bus in and out each way daily. A one-way/roundtrip ticket from Lake Placid to Saratoga Springs costs $18/34, from Lake Placid to Montreal costs $54/108.

Champ (☎ 518-523-4431) runs a daily shuttle between Lake Placid Hilton and Saranac Lake's Hotel Saranac during the day. Check with either hotel for the daily schedule, which varies according to events in town. Fares are around $3.

Train Amtrak stops at Westport (☎ 518-962-8730, 800-872-7245), 37 miles east of Lake Placid on Route 22. (See the Getting There & Around section, earlier in this chapter, for fare information.)

The same company that operates Champ also runs a shuttle between Westport train station and Lake Placid on Friday, Saturday and Sunday. The fare is an additional $15 each way, and according to Amtrak, must be purchased when purchasing your Amtrak train ticket. The connection is guaranteed; the bus will wait for a late train.

If arriving at the train station at other times you should call ahead to Rick's Taxi (☎ 518-523-4741). Taxi fare for two people from the train station to Lake Placid costs about $40.

Car & Motorcycle From New York City, take the Palisades Parkway to I-87 north to exit 24 (Albany). Continue on I-87 to Route 9N (exit 30). Follow Route 9N north to Route 73, then 30 miles west to Lake Placid. From Montreal, Take Autoroute 15 south to the Champlain crossing, where it connects with I-87 south. Take exit 34 west to Route 9N and east to Route 86.

WILMINGTON

About 12 miles east of Lake Placid is the small village of Wilmington (population 1000), home to Whiteface Mountain. This is a good place to stop over if you plan to ski or hike on the mountain, or if you want to visit Lake Placid but not pay the higher prices to stay there.

Whiteface Mountain

Whiteface Mountain (4868 feet) is a popular ski destination for its 65 miles of trail and the greatest vertical drop (1200 feet) in the eastern part of the US. (See the Outdoor Activities section, earlier in this chapter, for resort contact information.)

In the summer and fall, you can drive the Whiteface Mountain Memorial Highway up Whiteface Mountain, the only Adirondack High Peak accessible by car. To get there, drive 17 miles north on Route 86 to Wilmington and then take Route 431 for roughly 8 miles up the 4900-foot mountain. On clear days, you can view the surrounding peaks and mountain ranges as far off as Montreal and Vermont. The highway is open from late May to mid-October 9 am to 4 pm. The toll is $8 for each car and driver and an additional $4 for each passenger (with a $25 maximum).

You can also take a **chair lift** up another 3600 feet to the Whiteface Mountain summit. The entrance is on Route 86 before you get to Wilmington; it's open from mid-June to mid-October, 9 am to 4 pm and costs $7/5 for adults/children and seniors.

Other Things to See & Do

Geology buffs will be particularly interested in a hike in **High Falls Gorge** (☎ 518-946-2278), 4½ miles southwest of Wilmington on Route 86. The marked interpretive trail, which is privately owned and operated, is a deep ravine cut by ice, wind and the Ausable River at the base of Whiteface Mountain. Markers along the trail describe the geology, flora and fauna of the surrounding mountain area. Along the trail, you can enjoy waterfalls and the only remaining stand of virgin forest in the Adirondacks, the rest of the forest having been devastated by massive logging operations at the turn of the century. The trail is open from Memorial Day to mid-October, daily from 8:30 am to 4:30 pm. Admission for adults is $4.95; seniors over 62, $3.95; children ages 12 to 17, $3 and ages four to 11, $1.50.

The North Pole theme park, **Santa's Workshop** (☎ 518-946-2211), is on Route 431, just 1½ miles west of Wilmington and 12 miles east of Lake Placid. Children can meet Santa Claus and his helpers, pet live reindeer and go on amusement park rides. This is billed as the oldest theme park in the US. It's open June 10 through October 14, Monday through Sunday, from 9:30 am to 4:30 pm in July and August and reduced hours during other times. In July and August, admission for adults is $11.95 and children ages three to 17, $7.95 and under three, free. Rates are slightly cheaper at other times of the year.

Places to Stay & Eat

Wilmington Notch Campground (☎ 518-946-7172) is a simple public camp between Lake Placid and Wilmington on Route 86. There are 54 tent and RV sites, with water and toilets. Sites are $9 a day. It is open from mid-April to mid-October. The *Lake Placid-Whiteface KOA* (☎ 518-946-2171), on Fox Farm Rd, is an enormous private campground open all year. There are 200 sites, a pool, laundry facilities, canoes, minia-

ture golf, tennis and more. Sites range from $20 to $30, depending on season. From Route 86, take a right on Fox Farm Rd and you'll come to the campground in less than half a mile.

Wilkommen Hof (☎ 518-946-7669, 800-541-9119) is on Route 86, south of the four-way stop in town. This B&B is a converted farmhouse with a German theme. It has a comfortable common area with fireplace and television, a sauna and hot tub. There are nine rooms. During the winter the weekday/weekend rate for rooms with private bath is $70/80; during summer it's $60/70. For the rooms with shared bath the rates are from $50 to $63.50. Rates include a full breakfast. In the winter the Yosts family serves a German dinner for $15. In the summer you can swim in the Ausable River, located directly across the road.

Getting There & Away

From Lake Placid, Wilmington can only reached by car via Route 86, or by taxi ($12 one way).

AUSABLE CHASM

Traveling east on Route 86/9N for 35 miles from Lake Placid, you'll come to the town of Ausable Chasm near I-87. The chasm (☎ 518-834-7454, 800-537-1211) is a gorge formed 5 million years ago as the Ausable River carved through layers of sandstone, leaving cliffs, waterfalls and rapids. Today visitors walk through the chasm on a series of walkways, bridges and stone steps (which can be slippery). The walk is three-quarters of a mile, followed by a 10-minute boat ride through the grand flume. From late May to late October, the chasm is open daily from 9:30 am to 5 pm. Admission for the walk and boat ride is $12.95/10.95/7.95 for adults/seniors/children.

SARANAC LAKE

Situated in the middle of a chain of lakes, including the Upper, Middle and Lower Saranac, the village of Saranac Lake (population 5400) is 10 miles northwest of Lake Placid on Routes 86 and 3. The town was settled early in the 19th century and became

lation 5400) is 10 miles northwest of Lake Placid on Routes 86 and 3. The town was settled early in the 19th century and became a major tuberculosis treatment center later in the century. With the alarming resurgence of the disease in the US, it's of value to note that as late as 1930, tuberculosis – or consumption, as it was more commonly referred to then – killed more Americans than heart disease.

The first sanitarium for the treatment of tuberculosis was established here in 1884 by Dr Edward Livingston Trudeau, a young New York physician who was diagnosed with tuberculosis at the beginning of his career. Instead of heading to the tuberculosis sanatoria of Europe, he decided to return to a place he had once visited for pleasure, the Adirondacks. After a great deal of hardship, he opened the Adirondack Cottage Sanitarium, just northeast of the remote village of Saranac Lake (in the 1880s the village was a 32-mile stagecoach ride from the nearest railroad station).

The sanitarium was on the wooded slopes of Mt Pisgah, with views of the Saranac River and Whiteface Mountain. By 1890, 25 patients had traveled here to take the cure,

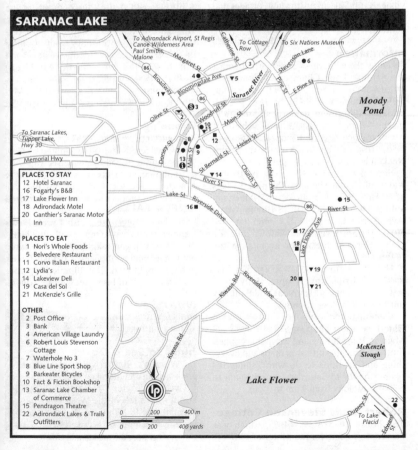

SARANAC LAKE

PLACES TO STAY
12 Hotel Saranac
16 Fogarty's B&B
17 Lake Flower Inn
18 Adirondack Motel
20 Ganthier's Saranac Motor Inn

PLACES TO EAT
1 Nori's Whole Foods
5 Belvedere Restaurant
11 Corvo Italian Restaurant
12 Lydia's
14 Lakeview Deli
19 Casa del Sol
21 McKenzie's Grille

OTHER
2 Post Office
3 Bank
4 American Village Laundry
6 Robert Louis Stevenson Cottage
7 Waterhole No 3
8 Blue Line Sport Shop
9 Barkeater Bicycles
10 Fact & Fiction Bookshop
13 Saranac Lake Chamber of Commerce
15 Pendragon Theatre
22 Adirondack Lakes & Trails Outfitters

and by 1898 that number had quadrupled. Health-seekers were drawn here in the hopes that the same climate and landscape that invigorated pleasure seekers would prove as virtuous for them. Today, Trudeau's original sanitarium, known as Little Red, survives on the grounds of the Trudeau Institute, which is on Algonquin Ave near Lower Saranac Lake.

The area around Saranac Lake continues to offer visitors – in a far more accessible manner – the pleasures of the wilderness: small lakes and ponds, ancient forests and wetlands. You can also wander along the village's winding streets to view cottages and treatment centers dating from the late 19th century.

Information

To enjoy the wilderness experience, contact the Saranac Lake Chamber of Commerce (☎ 518-891-1990, 800-347-1992), in the municipal building at 30 Main St. They publish booklets describing wilderness areas and places to stay, and maintain a website at www.saranaclake.com. It's open Monday to Friday from 8:30 am to 5:30 pm, and summer weekends from 10 am to 3 pm.

Several banks and ATMs are on Broadway, Church and Main Sts. The post office is at 60 Broadway. For laundry, try American Village (☎ 518-891-2150), 28 Bloomingdale Ave. Adirondack Medical Center (☎ 518-891-4141), northwest of downtown on Lake Colby Drive, is the major hospital in the region.

Fact & Fiction Bookshop (☎ 518-891-8067), 17 Broadway, is open daily from 9:30 am to 6 pm, and Thursday and Saturday until 8 pm. It's closed Sunday.

General outdoor supplies can be found at Blue Line Sport Shop (☎ 518-891-4680), 82 Main St. It has hiking and camping supplies, footwear and bugsuits, area maps and everything and anything to do with fishing. It's open Monday to Saturday from 8:30 am to 5:30 pm, Sunday from 9 am to 3 pm.

Robert Louis Stevenson Cottage

The house (☎ 518-891-1462), which was Stevenson's home for the winter of 1887–88, contains the largest collection of Stevenson memorabilia in the US, including old photos, clothing, ice skates and a lock the author's hair. Stevenson wrote the essays 'The Master of Ballantrae,' 'The Wrong Box' and 'A Christmas Sermon' here. It is open from July 1 to September 15, Tuesday to Sunday from 9:30 am to noon and from 1 to 4:30 pm. Admission for adults is $5, for children under 12, free. Take Main St north to Bloomingdale Ave, turn south on Pine St to Stevenson Lane.

Cottage Row

A little-known area on the outskirts of the town should be of interest to history buffs. There are a number of historic 'cure cottages' dating from the days when Saranac Lake was a mecca for people (Stevenson and baseball great Christie Mathison) seeking a cure for tuberculosis. The best restored houses are on Park Ave and Old Military Rd, from Catherine St up to Grove St.

Canoeing

Around Upper Saranac Lake, the St Regis Canoe Wilderness Area (designated by New York State) is prized by canoeists. This area is composed of 58 lakes and ponds where you can canoe for weeks, or put in for a leisurely afternoon. There are no motorized boats, cars or roads in the area.

In the St Regis area, Fish Creek Ponds Loop is a good trip to make with small children. This trip can take from one to three days, and begins and ends at Fish Creek public campground. The 10-mile loop connects the ponds of Fish Creek, Little Square,

MICHAEL CLARK

Far from the maddening crowd

Floodwood, Rollins, Whey and Copperas. There are only three portages, each less than a quarter mile.

Another modest 10-mile trip through the area is between Saranac Inn and Paul Smith's College. Also known as the Seven Carries route, the trip begins with a 1½ mile portage to Little Green Pond, and crosses the ponds of Little Clear, St Regis, Green, Little Long, Bear and Bog, and the lakes of Upper St Regis and Spitfire. The average portage here is no more than a quarter mile.

Other popular trips include the St Regis area to Tupper Lake, a trip of three to four days.

Outfitters There are many outdoor outfitters in the area that can help you organize a canoe trip (see Canoeing in the Outdoor Activities section, earlier in this chapter, for additional tips). Adirondack Lakes & Trails Outfitters (☎ 518-891-7450, 800-491-0414), 168 Lake Flower Ave (Route 86), on the south end of town across from Pizza Hut, has a retail store and gives guided tours and has equipment rentals for canoeing, kayaking, skiing, hiking and camping. It is open daily in summer and in winter peak seasons.

Mac's Canoe Livery (☎ 518-891-1176) is one of the best sources in the area for canoes in the summer (and cross-country skiing and snowshoeing in winter). Mac's concentrates on the adjacent St Regis area and is about a mile west of Lake Clear on Route 30, near the New York State Fish Hatchery. Canoe rentals range from $25 to $40 a day.

Also in Lake Clear, you can rent canoes and arrange for a guide or car shuttles from outfitters such as McDonnell's Adirondack Challenges (☎ 518-891-1176), on Route 30, and St Regis Canoe Outfitters (☎ 518-891-1838), on Floodwater Rd. The same services are available in Lake Tupper from Raquette River Outfitters (☎ 518-359-3228), 131 Moody Rd.

Horseback Riding

The Cold River Ranch (☎ 518-359-7559), midway between Saranac Lake and Tupper Lake on Route 3, is open all year and offers

The Wilderness Cure

In 1882, one in every seven human deaths was from tuberculosis (TB). The disease was thought to be hereditary until the 1882 discovery of the bacillus. Quickly, a public health question arose: how could this highly communicable disease be confined to the already infected patients? The doctors presented TB patients with the following simple choices:

- pay $25 a week to stay at one of Saranac Lake's modest 'cure cottages'
- go to a crowded hospital
- go to a sanitarium where they don't want you to die on the premises: Hence the inevitable advice, 'seek a warmer climate,' ie, go home to die

In 1939, a doctor told his patients: 'We never use the word 'cured.' When you leave here you are not even arrested (as in, the disease is under control). You are called 'quiescent' if we discharge you...If you continue to be all right for a couple of years you are arrested, but you are cured of TB only when you die of some other disease.'

Reminiscences of patient Eva Milbover in 1896 give a glimpse of life in the cottages: 'I obeyed regulations – up in the morning, to the main building to breakfast, back to Nathan Cottage, undressed and back to bed...Then up and dressed for the midday meal in the main building, back to the cottage, undressed, to bed; up and dressed for dinner in the main building, a short social hour, back to bed in the cottage – while I did that, others were doing all sorts of hanky-panky.'

one-day trail rides through a wilderness area to Raquette Falls, which is also reachable by canoe or hiking. They also do two-to-four day wilderness pack trips. Emerald Springs Ranch (☎ 518-891-3727), Route 186 in Saranac Lake, offers trail rides. Rates begin at about $25 an hour, and both stables offer lessons for beginners and children.

Bicycling

Barkeater Bicycles (☎ 518-891-5207, 800-254-5207), 49 Main St, sells, rents and repairs bikes, and is a good source of information about local bike trails. Free bike trail maps, from beginning to expert, are available by the front door. Bikes rent for $15 a day to about $75 for a full week. Barkeater is open for business Monday through Saturday from 10 am to 5 pm.

Special Events

The Adirondack Guideboat Show in July displays classic Adirondack boats. The Can-Am Rugby Tournament in August has over 100 Canadian and American teams playing in the largest North American tournament.

Places to Stay

Budget There are camping facilities in the Saranac Lakes area to accommodate large boaters, small canoeing parties and wilderness hikers. There are around 20 primitive *campsites*, which are free, maintained by the state around Upper Saranac Lake. Contact the state DEC (☎ 518-897-1200) on Route 86 in nearby Ray Brook about availability.

Saranac Lakes Islands Campground (☎ 518-891-4590, 800-456-2267) is a collection of 87 state-maintained campsites in and around Lower and Middle Saranac Lakes. Sites are considered primitive, but have tables, pit fireplaces and toilets. Small power boats are permitted on Lower Saranac Lake, so canoeists and hikers tend to prefer Middle Saranac Lake. It's also where you'll find a fine little sandy beach reachable by an easy half-mile trail. To get there, head west on Route 3 from the village of Saranac Lake at the junction of Route 86. Go 8½ miles, and look for a small parking lot and trail on the right (north).

Adirondack Motel (☎ 518-891-2116, 23 Lake Flower Ave/Route 86) is a clean and quiet spot on the lake with a dozen rooms, some with kitchenettes. Rates in the late fall and spring are $40 to $60 for doubles and efficiencies; in the summer and peak winter season, $60 to $85.

Ganthier's Saranac Motor Inn (☎ 518-891-1950, 143 Lake Flower Ave/Route 86) is a good budget choice, with singles and doubles for $55 to $85 . Two family rooms with kitchenettes are $105. *Lake Flower Inn* (☎ 518-891-2310, 15 Lake Flower Ave) is cozy and clean, and most of the 14 rooms face the lake. Rooms rates are $45 to $85, depending on the season.

B&Bs *Sunday Pond B&B* (☎ 518-891-1531), on Route 30 in the village of Saranac Inn, is a 10- to 15-minute drive from Saranac Lake and just opposite the St Regis Wilderness Canoe Area (which has excellent cross-country ski trails). Visitors can go mountain biking, fishing, canoeing and hiking from here. (They'll make you a trail lunch.) Sunday Pond is clean and rustic and decorated with old quilts, antiques and two screened-in porches. There are five rooms, one with private bath. Dinner is available with 24-hour notice. It's open all year and rates are $59 to $64 double, plus $15 per extra person. To get there from Saranac Lake take Route 86 to Route 186 for 7 miles to Route 30.

Fogarty's B&B (☎ 518-891-3755, 800-525-3755, 37 Riverside Drive) has five rooms, all with shared bath, and some with a view of Flower Lake. The single/double rate is a reasonable $55/65, $5 extra for children. The helpful owners will bring your luggage up the 73 steps from the street. The payoff is the view. They'll also set you up with a canoe to explore nearby lakes and ponds at a cost of about $20.

Top End The *Hotel Saranac* (☎ 518-891-2200, 800-937-0211, 101 Main St) is a large red-brick Italianate hotel run by hospitality management students of Paul Smith's College. When the hotel was built in 1927 it was noticed for its big city non-woodsy look. The hotel is spotless and the service good, if somewhat anxious. There are 92 modestly furnished and comfortable rooms. The ones on higher floors have good lake views. Rates are reasonable and range from $59/69 in the off-season (mid-October to mid-June) to $89/99 during the summer high season. B&B and modified American plans are also available.

are two large living rooms, each with fireplace. Rooms range from $85 to $110; children are not allowed.

Places to Eat

Budget & Mid-Range *Lakeview Deli* (☎ 518-891-2101, 102 River St) serves excellent sandwiches made to order, along with its own fresh breads and soups and a few other deli items. Most items are under $5. There are a few tables, but most people order to go. It is open Monday to Friday from 7 am to 8 pm, and weekends from 9 am to 6 pm.

Nori's Whole Foods (☎ 518-891-6079, 70 Broadway) is a good, friendly, neighborhood health-food store for self-catering. They also sell some prepared items and fresh soups that you can eat at the one table up front. Nori's is open Monday to Friday from 9 am to 7 pm and Saturday from 10 am to 5 pm all year.

Belvedere Restaurant (☎ 518-891-9873, 57 Bloomingdale/Route 3) is a very good Italian family diner. Prices are reasonable and the food and service are good. It is open for dinner from 5 to 8:30 pm. It is closed on Monday. *Corvo Italian Restaurant* (☎ 518-891-0510, 94 Main St), across from the Hotel Saranac, is clean and attractive. Lunches are a bargain, with pasta dishes and sandwiches under $5, dinners from $10 to $15. It's open daily from 11 am to 10 pm and on Sunday from 2 to 9 pm.

Casa del Sol (☎ 518-891-0977, 154 Lake Flower Ave), on Route 86 just outside town as you arrive from Lake Placid, is the best Mexican food for many miles around. All the selections – burritos, tostadas, flautas, chimichangas – are good, and ingredients fresh. Portions are large and prices hover around $5 to $7. But forego the salsa, which is really a bland tomato topping.

Nearby, *McKenzie's Grille* (☎ 518-891-9920, 148 Lake Flower Ave) serves family-style fare, including pasta, barbecue, fresh fish and salads. McKenzie's is open daily from 7 am to 10 pm.

Top End Inside the Hotel Saranac is *Lydia's* (☎ 518-891-2200, 101 Main St), a restaurant run by chefs and hospitality folk from Paul Smith's College. Lydia's has a Sunday buffet brunch with waffles, omelets, eggs, meat, salad and desserts for $10. Children under 12 eat for $5. Lydia's also serves American lunches, such as Reubens, tuna melts and other sandwiches, for about $5 to $7. Dinners can include grilled lamb, Thai-style duck and Adirondack trout from $11 to $14. The food is good, as is the service. The students also make the house wine during summer stints in the south of France.

Just a 20-minute drive out of town, *Wawbeek's Restaurant* (☎ 359-2656, 553 Panther Mountain Rd), 1 mile north of Route 3 near Upper Saranac Lake is a fancy lodge and restaurant in the great camp tradition. It is open daily.

Entertainment

Waterhole No 3 (☎ 518-891 -9502, 43 Main St) is upstairs and across the street from the town hall. The Waterhole features good local music from rock to folk. Admission ranges from $3 to $10.

Pendragon Theatre (☎ 518-891-1854, 148 River St) is a year-round professional theatre and arts center for the Adirondack region. Ticket prices for adults/students are $15/13, and a family rate for one or two parents and children under 17 is $6 per person.

Getting There & Away

US Airways serves Adirondack Airport, which is 5 miles from Saranac Lake. (See the Getting There & Around section at the beginning of this chapter for fares and contact information.) Taxis meet arriving flights, and the fare into Saranac Lake is approximately $10.

Adirondack Trailways (☎ 800-858-8555) stops at Hotel Saranac (☎ 518-891-3300), 101 Main St. Champ (☎ 518-523-4431) public transportation runs a daily shuttle between Saranac Lake's Hotel Saranac and Lake Placid Hilton. Fares are around $3. Check with either hotel for the daily schedule, which varies according to special events occurring in town.

Poetry of the Woods

The pastoral poetry of many famous American poets, including Walt Whitman and Henry Wadsworth Longfellow, was inspired by the rugged and wild country of the northeast. It often evokes the mystery Americans found in the thick woods and Native American ways; below is a portion of *The Adirondacks*, a poem written in 1858 by Ralph Waldo Emerson (1803–82).

…we swept with oars the Saranac,
With Skies of benediction, to Round Lake,
Where all the sacred mountains drew around us,
Tahawus, Seaward, MacIntyre, Baldhead,
And other Titans without muse or name.
Please with these grand companions, we glide on…
Through gold-moth-haunted beds of pickerel-flower,
Through scented banks of lilies white and gold,
Where the deer feeds at night, the teal by day…
The wood was sovran with centennial trees –
Oak, cedar, maple, poplar, beech and fir,
Linden and spruce. In strict society
Three conifers, white, pitch and Norway pine.
Five-leaved, three-leaved, and two-leaved, grew thereby…
'Welcome!' the wood gods murmured through the leaves –
'Welcome, though late, unknowing, yet known to me'…

Enjoy the scenery from an Adirondack chair.

AROUND SARANAC LAKE
Six Nations Indian Museum

The museum (☎ 518-891-2299), 14 miles north of Saranac Lake and a mile from Onchiota on County Rd 30, helps to preserve the culture of the Iroquois Confederation, originally comprised of the Mohawk, Seneca, Onondaga, Oneida and Cayuga tribes, and later, the Tuscaroras. On display in the museum are artifacts, historic documents and models of typical Iroquois villages, as well as contemporary Iroquois crafts. The museum stands as a reminder to visitors that the Native American culture and history long predates their contact with Europeans.

This small, excellent museum has been carefully managed by four generations of the Fadden family; John Fadden will most likely greet you and if you show the least bit of curiosity, he is happy to discuss the museum's extensive collection. There are four rooms, all in a row in longhouse style, and each one is rich with artifacts, clothing, artwork and historic scenes, quotations and photos. One display includes this excerpt from the 1940 speech by Chief Joseph Hill (Big White Owl) to the First Inter-American Congress, which was held at Patxcuaro, Michoacan, Mexico:

When we are unable to relate the heroic deeds of our great nobles, chieftain sages, prophets and warriors; when the Indian mother cannot lull her children affectionately in her arms and against her breast, then the white man shall have definitely strangled us and we will no longer be deserving of the designation 'American Indian.'

The Six Nations Museum is open July to Labor Day, daily except Monday, from 10 am to 6 pm, and by appointment in May, June, September and October. Admission for adults/children is $2/1. The family used to allow dogs inside, until one went after a pelt on the wall.

Thousand Islands & St Lawrence Seaway

The lower part of the St Lawrence River, at the outflow of Lake Ontario, is dotted with 1864 small islands known as the Thousand Islands. Some of these islands are so small that they appear only as specks on a map. Appearances, in this case, are not deceiving: most of the islands are home to a few solitary trees, a jumble of rocks, or a single – albeit magnificent – vacation house. A few islands are large enough to support small towns, summer camps, state parks and dense growths of pines, birches and oaks. All of the islands are surrounded by the St Lawrence's deep blue waters.

There are competing legends as to how the region came to be known as the Thousand Islands. An Iroquois legend has it that the Great Spirit, or Master of Life, created a bountiful and beautiful land for the Indian nations that had agreed not to fight each other. When the nations broke their promise, the Great Spirit sent messengers to retrieve the paradise in a huge blanket. As the land was being lifted into the sky, it fell out of the blanket and broke into thousands of pieces, creating the Thousand Islands. Modern geologic legend suggests that the islands are part of a granite mass that was crushed, twisted and pushed above the surface over time.

The islands straddle both sides of the US-Canadian border. The greatest concentration of islands is at the source of the St Lawrence river, near Lake Ontario and between the New York towns of Alexandria Bay and Clayton.

Camping at one of the region's many scenic island state parks draws US and Canadian visitors alike. Some of the best camping is on the Canadian side of the river in St Lawrence Islands National Park. The waterfront towns offer visitors a few interesting sights and activities. But the big draw here, especially in Clayton, is fishing for muskie, northern pike and largemouth bass. The Thousand Islands International Bridge,

Highlights

- Watching ships passing through the Eisenhower Lock at Massena, on the St Lawrence Seaway

- Outdoor activities, such as canoeing and bird-watching, in Wellesley Island State Park

- Camping in Canada's St Lawrence Islands National Park

- Boldt Castle, a Rhineland-inspired castle built on a heart-shaped island across from Alexandria Bay

- Tibbets Point Lighthouse in Cape Vincent

- Summer produce stands along the roadside from Clayton to Sackets Harbor

the gateway to Canada, crosses near Alexandria Bay, where the wealthy once built huge estates on privately owned islands.

Running through the center of the river is the St Lawrence Seaway, a major transit line for huge oil, grain and ore transports traveling from the Atlantic through the Great Lakes. Residents and visitors alike enjoy watching the ships as they pass by at night, their lights twinkling in the darkness.

To truly enjoy the islands and the sense of escape they afford, you need to travel the St Lawrence by boat. You can rent a houseboat, take auto ferries between the islands or take one of the boat tours that leave frequently from Alexandria Bay. You can also drive, bike and camp along the river's shore.

HISTORY

Little permanent settlement of the area by Native Americans predated white exploration. The region was under the influence of the Iroquois Confederacy. The Oneida Nation claimed lands in Jefferson County, and the Mohawk still maintain a reservation in St Lawrence County. The French first explored the region, with Father Simon Lamoine making a trip up the river to Lake Ontario in 1654. Control of the region remained with the French until 1758, when an English force swept down the upper St Lawrence.

INFORMATION

The 1000 Islands International Council, in Alexandria Bay, provides tourist informa-

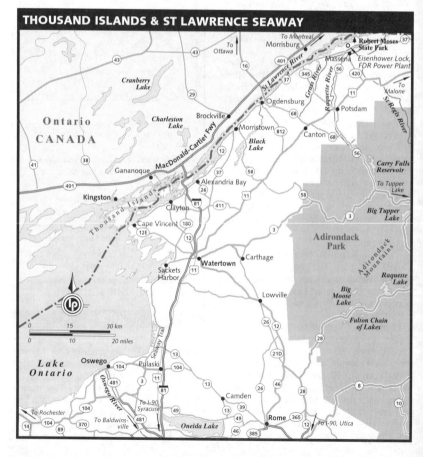

THOUSAND ISLANDS & ST LAWRENCE SEAWAY

tion for both sides of the St Lawrence River (see Alexandria Bay for contact information). For regional information on fishing license fees, contact the regional office of the New York State Department of Environmental Conservation (☎ 315-785-2262), 317 Washington St, Watertown, NY 13601. In Canada, contact the Ministry of Natural Resources (☎ 613-258-8204), PO Bag 2002, Kemptville, Ontario K0G 1S0. Local chambers of commerce can also provide information (see Information under each town later in this chapter).

If planning a trip to Canada from the Thousand Islands region, see the Lonely Planet guide *Canada*. For information on Canadian and US currency, see Money, in the Facts for the Visitor chapter. For information on getting into Canada, see the boxed text 'Crossing International Borders,' in the Western New York chapter.

GETTING THERE & AROUND
Air
The region has limited commercial-airline service. US Airways (☎ 800-428-4322) has daily routes from its hub in Pittsburgh, PA, and Watertown, NY. United, American and Delta serve Syracuse, which is 45 miles south of Watertown via I-81.

Bus
Both Greyhound (☎ 800-231-2222) and Adirondack Trailways (☎ 800-858-8555) serve parts of the Thousand Islands region; call their offices for schedules and bus-depot locations. The one-way/roundtrip fare to travel from Watertown to Syracuse is $10/16, from Massena to Plattsburgh is $16/30 and from Watertown to Massena is $21/$42. During the summer, Thousand Islands Bus Line (☎ 315-788-8146) runs from Watertown to several Thousand Islands towns, including Alexandria Bay and Clayton.

Train
Syracuse, 45 miles south of Watertown, has the nearest Amtrak terminal to the region. VIA rail in Canada makes a stop at nearby Cornwall (a Canadian city across from Massena) and continues to Montreal.

Car & Motorcycle
A car is almost essential to explore much of the Thousand Islands region. I-81 is the main north-south road in the region and connects Syracuse to Watertown and the St Lawrence Seaway at the international border with Canada and the US via the Thousand Islands International Bridge. From I-81, the primary road heading northeast is Route 12/37, which connects Alexandria Bay, Ogdensburg and Massena. Route 11 is another southwest-northeast road connecting Watertown to Malone in the northern Adirondacks.

From New York City, take I-80 west to 380 north to I-81 north; or take I-87 north to I-90 west to I-81 north. From Philadelphia, take I-476 north to I-81 north. From Boston, take I-90 west to I-81.

Boat
The only auto ferry across the St Lawrence River leaves from Cape Vincent, NY, at the source of the river, and goes to Wolfe Island, where another ferry travels to the Canadian mainland.

Thousand Islands

ALEXANDRIA BAY & AROUND
At the turn of the century, Alexandria Bay (population 1200) was a bustling resort town boasting several large hotels. Today these grand hotels are gone, but many of the estates – built during the same time on privately owned islands – remain. The largest of these estates is George Boldt's castle on Heart Island, located outside of town.

Alex Bay or just the Bay, as locals call it, is still pleasant enough, with tree-lined streets, old buildings and a welcome arch on Church St. Even the commercial strip of James St – lined with tour-boat companies, small galleries, sandwich shops and tacky souvenir shops – is only four blocks long and relatively low-key.

Alex Bay does get crowded with tourists from mid-June to August. But its location – near the Thousand Islands International

Bridge, 4 miles north of I-81 on the St Lawrence River – makes it a good base from which to explore the region. If you have a limited amount of time, you can take a boat tour from here to explore the nearby islands.

If time is not a factor, rent a boat and meander the waterways. For more information on boat and houseboat rentals, contact Remar Shipyard (☎ 315-686-4170), 510 Theresa Street, Clayton, NY. Smaller boat rentals are available at a number of marinas; the 1000 Islands International Council (see Information, later, for contact information) publishes a complete directory.

Information

The Alexandria Bay Chamber of Commerce (☎ 315-482-9531, 800-541-2110), on Market St off James St, is open from mid-May to early October daily from 9 am to 5 pm and during the rest of the year on weekdays from 9 am to 5 pm. The 1000 Islands International Council (☎ 315-482-2520, 800-847-5263), PO Box 400, Collins Landing (under the Thousand Islands Bridge), Alexandria Bay, NY 13067, promotes tourism along the St Lawrence River in both New York and Ontario. The visitors' center is open daily April through October (on Wednesday

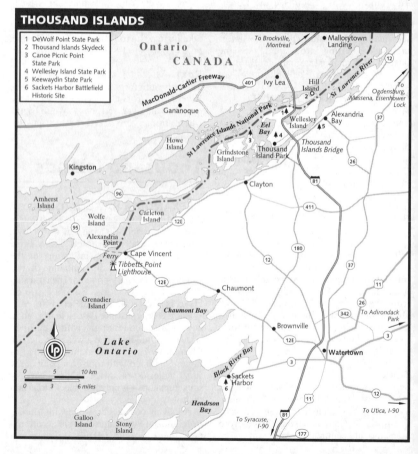

THOUSAND ISLANDS

1 DeWolf Point State Park
2 Thousand Islands Skydeck
3 Canoe Picnic Point State Park
4 Wellesley Island State Park
5 Keewaydin State Park
6 Sackets Harbor Battlefield Historic Site

only during the rest of the year) from 8 am to 5 pm and is a source of information on fishing, camping and attractions for the entire region.

Across the river, another very helpful source is the 1000 Islands-Gananoque Chamber of Commerce (☎ 800-561-1595), at 2 King St, Gananoque, Ontario.

The post office is on Bethune St. The local weekly newspaper is the *Thousand Islands Sun*. There is a 24-hour laundry at the intersection of Route 12 and Church St.

Boldt Castle

This 120-room, Rhineland-inspired stone castle (☎ 315-482-2501), on Heart Island, across from Alex Bay, is billed as the site of the 'saddest true love story ever told.' The story begins in 1900, when George Boldt, who had worked his way up from the kitchen to ownership of New York City's Waldorf-Astoria Hotel, decided to have a castle built for his wife, Louise. He bought Heart Island and had it reshaped into a heart. In 1904, as the castle was nearing completion, and with $2.5 million invested, Louise died. Boldt stopped all work on the estate, and the building and grounds were left to decay until 1977, when the Thousand Islands Bridge Authority took over the castle and began the slow process of renovation.

The castle, with its numerous towers, is quite dramatic from the outside. However, during its long period of abandonment, much of the interior was stripped of its marble and exotic wood detailing, leaving only bare walls. A recent renovation has managed to preserve much of the original feel to the place. The castle and its grounds – including a five-story playhouse and a boathouse – make an interesting visit. From late May to mid-October, it's open daily from 10 am to 6 pm. Admission for adults/ children (ages six to 12) costs $3.75/2. Uncle Sam Boat Tours has a ferry that is the only way to get to the island; see Organized Tours, later in this chapter.

Wellesley Island

Wellesley Island is home to the town of **Thousand Island Park**. The town was origi-

nally a Methodist camp meeting ground. Today it's home to summer residents, who carefully maintain elaborate 19th-century Victorian homes. Visitors enjoy driving through the town and admiring the architecture. Residents, however, seem to find the experience less than enjoyable.

North of Thousand Island Park, **Wellesley Island State Park** spreads over 2600 acres and has hiking trails, a beach, a campground, miniature and nine-hole golf courses and a marina. The land used to be a working farm run by Edison Bradley, who also owned Old Grand Dad distillery. On the southeast end of the park is **Minna Anthony Common Nature Center** (☎ 315-482-2479), which includes a museum and wildlife sanctuary and encompasses a 600-acre peninsula. There are fascinating collections of (live) fish, amphibians and an 'observation hive' of busy honeybees. The nature center is open Monday to Saturday from 8 am to 8 pm and Sunday from 8 am to 5 pm. (See Places to Stay, later in this section, for information about the campground.)

One of the best activities offered by the center is the Ecology Canoe Paddle, a daily ride in a 36-foot canoe along river shorelines with a guide who is knowledgeable about the natural history of the St Lawrence River. The trip lasts about two hours, and the cost is $2 for adults and $1 for children (ages 13 and under).

Bird-watchers will be kept busy looking for loons, geese, eagles, robins and bluejays, among others. Canoe rentals are available in nearby Alex Bay from Aqua Marina (☎ 315-482-4678), on Route 12, and from O'Brien's (☎ 315-482-9548), at 51 Walton St.

Wellesley Island can be reached from both the US and Canadian mainlands. To get to there, take I-81 to the Thousand Islands Bridge (a $2 toll going northbound, free southbound). For Thousand Island Park, take exit 51 (the first exit after the bridge) and follow the signs to Thousand Island Park Resort Community.

Attractions in Canada

Thousand Islands Skydeck, a 395-foot observation tower (☎ 613-659-2335) is on Hill

Island, Canada, which is reached via the Thousand Islands Bridge. It offers excellent views of the islands and the river. It is open June 1 to Labor Day daily from 8:30 am to 9 pm, May from 8:30 am to dusk and after Labor Day to October 31 from 9 am to 6 pm. Admission for adults/children (ages six to 12) is C$7/C$4.

For travel information, stop at Hill Island Information Center (☎ 613-382-3250), or at Kingston Visitor Center (☎ 613-548-4415), 209 Ontario St, Kingston, Ontario, about a mile from the Thousand Islands Bridge on the Canadian mainland. It's open daily from 8:30 am to 6 pm in-season, and Monday to

Friday from 10 am to 3 pm otherwise. US citizens may be asked to show valid ID at the border; international visitors need a passport.

Organized Tours

Uncle Sam Boat Tours (☎ 315-482-2611, 800-253-9229), 2 James St, cruises the island region on triple-deck paddle wheelers. They offer a variety of tours and cruises from Alex Bay to Clayton. From May through October, daily tours depart regularly. Two-hour tours cost $13/6.50 (children 4 to 12); the Heart Island-Boldt Castle ferry trip is $6/4 for adults/children.

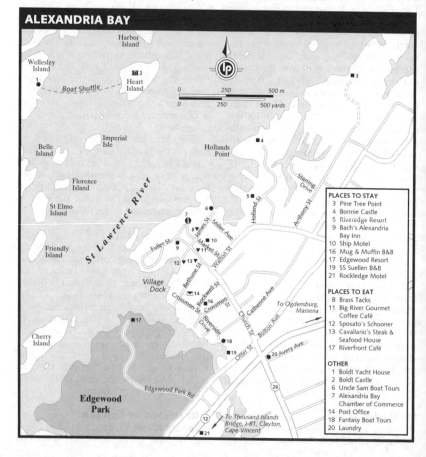

ALEXANDRIA BAY

Harbor Island

Wellesley Island

Boat Shuttle

Heart Island

🏛 2

■ 3

0   250   500 m
0   250   500 yards

Belle Island

Imperial Isle

Hollands Point

■ 4

Florence Island

St Elmo Island

St Lawrence River

Sterling Drive

Holland St

Anthony St

5 ■

Friendly Island

7
❶
James St   Miller Ave
9
■ 10
▼ 11
6 ●

Market St

Walton St

12 ▼ 13 ▼

Bethune St

Village Dock

■ 14
Rockwell St

Crossmon St   Crossmon St

Riverside Drive

Catherine Ave

Church Ave

Bolton Ave

To Ogdensburg, Massena

■ 17

Cherry Island

■ 18
■ 19
20 ● Avery Ave

Otter St

Edgewood Park

Edgewood Park Rd

26

12
To Thousand Islands Bridge, I-81, Clayton, Cape Vincent

■ 21

PLACES TO STAY
3 Pine Tree Point
4 Bonnie Castle
5 Riveredge Resort
9 Bach's Alexandria Bay Inn
10 Ship Motel
16 Mug & Muffin B&B
17 Edgewood Resort
19 SS Suellen B&B
21 Rockledge Motel

PLACES TO EAT
8 Brass Tacks
11 Big River Gourmet Coffee Café
12 Sposato's Schooner
13 Cavallario's Steak & Seafood House
17 Riverfront Café

OTHER
1 Boldt Yacht House
2 Boldt Castle
6 Uncle Sam Boat Tours
7 Alexandria Bay Chamber of Commerce
14 Post Office
18 Fantasy Boat Tours
20 Laundry

Fantasy Boat Tours (☎ 315-482-6415), 24 Otter St, Alexandria Bay, NY 13607, takes small groups on tours to the less-visited islands. The emphasis here is on exploring the history of the region in a 30-foot antique boat named *Joshua*. Two- and three-hour cruises range from $20 to $30. This is a rather more relaxed trip than Uncle Sam's.

For those who wish to view the islands from the air rather than by water, 1000 Island Helicopter Tours (☎ 315-639-4950, 782-6642), Route 12, will take you up in a chopper on weekends in May and October and daily from mid-June to mid-September. It's closed Wednesday.

Places to Stay

There are plenty of inexpensive motels, resorts and a few B&Bs in Alex Bay. Other options are the excellent campgrounds on some of the nearby islands.

Camping US and Canadian state parks on the various islands of the St Lawrence River make scenic campgrounds. For general information about camping in the Thousand Islands area, call ☎ 315-482-2593 (for US parks) and ☎ 613-923-5261 (for Canadian parks).

The US The largest US campground in the area is at *Wellesley Island State Park* (☎ 315-482-2722), on I-81. The park has 430 sites (including 10 cabins) and hot showers. The campground extends from the St Lawrence River to Eel Bay. Fees are collected from April 24 to October 12 and are $13 per campsite for up to six people. Follow the signs after crossing the Thousand Islands Bridge onto Wellesley Island. The campground is 2 miles west of exit 51 on I-81. *DeWolf Point State Park* (☎ 315-482-2012) is on Wellesley Island, 4 miles north of the Thousand Islands bridge. There are 13 sites for $13 each. It is open from mid-May to Labor Day.

Other campsites include *Canoe Picnic Point State Park* (☎ 315-654-2522), 3½ miles southwest of Wellesley Island and accessible by boat only. The 30 sites are open from May 16 to September 14 and cost $10. *Keewaydin State Park* (☎ 315-482-3331), on Route 12, is

half a mile west of Alex Bay and is one of the prettiest parks in the region, with several old gazebos. There are 41 sites at $13 each, and they are available from late May to early September.

Canada If you'd like to camp in Canada, *St Lawrence Islands National Park* (☎ 613-923-5261, Box 468, RR 3, Mallorytown Landing, Ontario K0E 1R0, Canada) is a collection of about 20 islands and has 21 sites – 15 of which are open for camping and the rest of which are for day use. The islands extend for some 45 miles from Brockville, in the east, to Kingston, in the west. All of the sites are easily accessible by boat from either side of the river, but only one is accessible by car. They all have outhouses, and almost all have water pumps and shelter, usually cabins with camp stoves. The Canadian government even provides firewood.

The one car-accessible site is at Mallorytown Landing, at the park headquarters. This site has flush toilets, running water and a boat launch for getting to Grenadier Island. It is 15 miles north of the Thousand Islands Bridge, on the Canadian mainland. Take Canada Route 401 north and look carefully for the sign for Mallorytown Landing, which is easy to miss. You'll see a parking area and boat launch on your right along the river. The park's headquarters is hidden behind the greenery on the side of the road opposite the parking area.

As for the other island camping sites along the St Lawrence River, you'll find *Stovin*, off the coast of the Canadian city of Brockville; *East*, *West*, *North* and *Centre Grenadier* and *Adelaide*, on or near Grenadier Island; *Georgina*, between Hill Island and the Canadian mainland near the town of Ivy Lea; *Mulcaster*, between Wellesley Island and Canada; *Camelot*, *Endymion* and *Gordon*, between Grindstone Island, offshore from Clayton, NY, and the Canadian city of Gananoque; *Thwartway*, *Mermaid*, *Aubrey*, *Beaurivage* and *McDonald*, between Gananoque and Grindstone Island; and *Milton* and *Cedar*, off the shore of the Canadian town of Kingston.

There is no reservation system for the St Lawrence Islands National Park campsites.

On summer weekends, many sites fill up by Friday, so you may want to think about arriving on Thursday night. All payments are done on a self-registration system. You calculate camping and mooring fees and put them in an envelope and deposit it in a slot at the site.

Camping fees are C$10 at Mallorytown and C$7 at Grenadier Island, because they both have running water and flush toilets. Camping on the other islands is C$6. Day mooring fees are C$3 to C$9; overnight fees are C$6 to C$18, depending on the size of your boat. A seasonal mooring pass is C$17 per meter. Firewood is included in overnight camping fees or is otherwise C$3. Parking at Mallorytown Landing costs C$3 per day; launch and leave also costs C$3. Fees are in effect and firewood is provided from late May to Canadian Thanksgiving, but the campgrounds are open year-round. There is a ferry from Mallorytown Landing to Grenadier Island (see Getting Around, later in this chapter).

Motels The *Rockledge Motel* (☎ 315-482-2191, 45302 Clayton Rd/Route 12) is a good, friendly budget spot with clean rooms at an off-season low of $35 and reaching a summer peak of $75. The *Ship Motel* (☎ 315-482-4503, 12 Market St) is similar but a bit more expensive because of the downtown location. Both motels are open May to October.

B&Bs *Mug & Muffin B&B* (☎ 315-482-2188, 18 Crossmon St) is a clean and renovated Cape Cod home with three rooms (one with private bath) ranging from $50 to $75. It is open from May to mid-October.

SS Suellen B&B (☎ 315-482-2137, 26 Otter St) is a renovated and compact suburban-style house. Accommodations include three bedrooms with private baths, a heated pool and dock access. July and August rates, including continental breakfast, are $75/$85 on weekdays/weekends. Subtract about $20 from those rates during off-season (from October to May).

Inns & Resorts The *Hart House* (☎ 315-482-5683), on Wellesley Island, is an elegant

B&B with seven rooms, each with a comfortable canopy bed.

Bach's Alexandria Bay Inn (☎ 315-482-9697, 2 Church St) is just off the downtown area, across from the St Lawrence River. This is a lovely Italianate Victorian (painted pale lavender with purple trim). There are several handsomely furnished rooms with private bath. The year-round rates range from $70 to $130, depending on the number of guests and the day of the week.

Edgewood Resort (☎ 315-482-9922, 888-334-3966), on Edgewood Park Rd, is just west of downtown on the river. The grounds are beautifully landscaped. A wonderful old hotel stands unused in the middle of the grounds, and the resorts' 160 rooms are in motel buildings. The decor here is contemporary, if unexceptional. There is a restaurant and bar, an outdoor pool, a beach and a dock. Rates are $29 to $99 for rooms away from the river and $49 to $159 on the river. The highest rates apply from late June to early September.

Of the four major resorts in or around town, the nicest is *Riveredge* (☎ 315-482-9917, 800-365-6987, 17 Holland St), which was rebuilt in the late 1980s after a devastating fire. The 129 rooms all have views of the river. Rooms have been named to describe particular views, including 'castle-view,' 'bayview,' and 'channel view.' Of these, the channel-view rooms open up to the most spectacular scenery. Rooms have private balconies, are furnished with armoires and double beds and are decorated with paintings by local artists. There are two restaurants, indoor and outdoor pools, an exercise room and a boat dock. In-season (July through August) rates range from $125 to $200 on weekdays and $175 to $250 on weekends. Off-season rates drop to $95 to $165 weekdays and $130 to $220 weekends. Rates vary according to views.

Pine Tree Point (☎ 315-482-9911, 70 Anthony St) offers a variety of accommodations ranging from cabins to suites, all set on tree-covered grounds. There are 95 guest rooms, a restaurant, a pool and a picnic area. The rate schedule is relatively complicated.

Waterfront rates range from $105 to $170; off-water rooms range from $55 to $115.

Bonnie Castle (☎ 315-482-4511, 800-955-4511), on Holland St, is the most expansive of the motel-like resorts and is one of the most popular locally. Rooms come with wet bars, tiled bathrooms and free cable TV. Resort amenities abound, including tennis courts, indoor and outdoor pools and a restaurant. The landscaped grounds are spread out over several acres, with parking lots in between. In-season rates range from $85 to $150.

Places to Eat

Many visitors to Alex Bay dine in the restaurants in the Riveredge or Edgewood resorts. There are several informal dining spots in the downtown area and a string of fast-food joints.

Brass Tacks (☎ 315-482-9805, 24 James St) is a tavern that serves salads, burgers and sandwiches ranging from $3 to $5. It also offers a few Mexican dishes, such as deep-fried jalapenos for $5 and fajitas for $8. ***Sposato's Schooner*** (☎ 315-482-3000, 59 James St) is a popular pub and eatery.

Worth trying is ***Big River Gourmet Coffee Café*** (☎ 315-482-5046, 19 Church St). The Edgewood resort's ***Riverfront Café*** (☎ 315-482-9922) has good food and a great view of the river.

If you are looking to spend a bit more money, check out ***Cavallario's Steak & Seafood House*** (☎ 315-482-9867), which is on Church St half a block south of James St. The facade here has been made to look like a castle, and the interior is decorated in a red-velvet 'knight' motif, including armor and weapons. The pricey dinner selections are standard medieval fare – steak and seafood in the $16 to $22 range. It is open for dinner 4 to 10 pm.

Getting There & Away

From the south, take I-81 to just before its northern terminus at the Thousand Islands Bridge and exit at Route 12. Alex Bay is 4 miles to the east. From the northeast, take Route 37 along the St Lawrence Seaway to Alex Bay.

CLAYTON

Just 11 miles southwest of Alex Bay, on the St Lawrence River, is the quieter town of Clayton. This town of 2100 people was once a shipbuilding and lumbering port. Today, the town mostly provides services for summer island residents and fishermen. The small downtown area is appealing, but the big draw is fishing, and the town is home to the Muskie Hall of Fame, which contains fishing paraphernalia and a replica of the world-record muskellunge that weighed 69lb, 15oz.

The chamber of commerce (☎ 315-686-3771, 800-252-9806) can give you lists of licensed fishing guides.

Antique Boat Museum

This museum (☎ 315-686-4104), 750 Mary St, houses 150 freshwater boats, ranging from Native American dugout and birch-bark canoes to examples of the St Lawrence Skiff to the thickly varnished Kris-Kraft pleasure boats that once belonged to the region's millionaire summer residents. It is open from mid-May to mid-October daily from 9 am to 4 pm. Admission for adults is $6; for children, (ages five to 17) $2.

Places to Stay & Eat

Try ***Bertrands Motel*** (☎ 315-686-3641, 229 James St), a two-story motel in the middle of town with basic rooms for $60 in-season and $50 or less off-season. Across the street is the ***Koffee Kove*** (☎ 315-686-2472), a sandwich-shop/diner where you can get a sandwich for under $4.

A bit fancier is the ***Thousand Island Inn*** (☎ 315-686-3030, 335 Riverside Dr), an old brick hotel with large rooms in the $60 to $80 range. The hotel's restaurant is open daily for breakfast, lunch and dinner. The inn operates seasonally only, from May through September. This inn lays claim to being the restaurant where the Thousand Island dressing originated. But as might be expected, there are different versions of where the dressing originated. Another version claims that the dressing was developed by a chef employed by George Boldt, of Boldt Castle fame.

The Clipper Inn (☎ 315-686-3842), on Route 12, is one of the finest dining spots in the Thousand Islands region. It's certainly worth the drive from Alex Bay. Daily specials generally feature fresh seafood, prime rib and pasta, all in the $14 to $18 range. It is open from April through December from 4 to 10 pm.

CAPE VINCENT

Cape Vincent, or simply 'the Cape,' is a lovely village (population 700) on the cape where the St Lawrence River meets Lake Ontario. The town was named for Vincent LeRay de Chaumount, who came here seeking asylum for the failing Napoleonic government. Napoleon's brother and sister lived here briefly before returning to France. The village celebrates its French heritage at the Annual French Festival.

Although its location at the convergence of Lake Ontario and the St Lawrence provides for a wide variety of fishing, the town is particularly famous for black-bass fishing. Cape Vincent is on Hwy 12E, 28 miles southwest of Alex Bay. Cape Vincent Chamber of Commerce (☎ 315-654-2481), 175 James St, near the ferry dock, can give information about fishing licenses and guides.

There aren't many attractions in Cape Vincent; the town's main street, Broadway, is lined with towering trees and big old houses, and there is a very nice playground at the end of James St. The Breakwater Gallery, next to the Village Dock, displays works by local artists.

Tibbetts Point Lighthouse (☎ 315-654-2700) marks the entrance to the St Lawrence River from Lake Ontario. The present 69-foot, white, conical, stucco tower was constructed in 1854. It is still an active light maintained by the Coast Guard. Tibbets Point is open from May to October from 10 am to 4 pm, and also from 6 to 8 pm for the often dazzling sunset.

The only auto ferry across the river leaves from Cape Vincent; you can travel by ferry from here to Wolfe Island's Point Alexandria and then take another ferry to the historic city of Kingston, Ontario.

Places to Stay

The HI-AYH *Tibbetts Point Lighthouse Hostel* (☎ 315-654-3450) is one of the most picturesquely located hostels in the country. It's on the grounds of a lakeside lighthouse that was built in 1854. It's located 3 miles west of the town, and the dorm rooms are in two white houses that used to be the lighthouse keepers' quarters. It's friendly and quiet. The hostel is open from mid-May to late October, following the Wolfe Island ferry schedule that runs from town. Beds in dorm rooms for members/nonmembers are $10/$13. Check-in is from 5 to 9:30 pm, with a 10 pm curfew. The hostel is closed from 9:30 am to 5 pm.

To get there, take Route 12E west from Clayton into Cape Vincent. Where 12E turns south in the middle of town, keep going west on Broadway, which becomes Lighthouse Rd and leads you to the lighthouse/hostel.

The *Buccaneer Motel* (☎ 315-654-2975, 230 N Point St), on the river, has 10 rooms that extend along a single corridor in a motel building a few steps from the water. There are four more rooms (with a shared bath) in the main house. The main floor of the house has large floor-to-ceiling windows. Motel rooms are $60 to $80; the rooms in the main house go for $120 and include a big breakfast.

Places to Eat

As in Alex Bay, there are several taverns and cafes that serve burgers, salads and sandwiches. *Anchor Inn* (☎ 315-654-3566, 790 E Broadway) and *Aubrey's Inn* (☎ 315-654-3754, 126 St James St) are good diners serving breakfast, lunch and dinner. You could also try *Captain Jack's* (☎ 315-654-3333, 361 Club St), near the ferry.

Roxie Hotel (☎ 315-654-2456, 111 E Broadway) is open year-round from 7 am to 10 pm and has a good Friday-night fish fry. *The Cape Restaurant* (☎ 315-654-4900, 592 E Broadway) is considered by locals to be the best eatery in the cape area.

Getting There & Away

Wolfe Island Ferries (☎ 315-783-0638) make 11 trips daily each way between Cape

Vincent and Wolfe Island, Canada, from early May to late October (weather permitting) daily from 8 am to 7 pm. The 10-minute crossing between Cape Vincent and Wolfe Island costs $6 per car and driver and $1 per passenger. The ferry continues from Wolfe Island to Kingston, Canada, takes another 35 minutes and is free. The schedule may change slightly each year. The ferry dock in Cape Vincent is at the north terminus of James St.

You can then drive 7 miles across Wolfe Island and take another ferry (☎ 613-544-2231) to Kingston, Canada. The crossing here takes 25 minutes and runs year-round. Currently, the ferry is free, but it may cost C$3 to C$4 in the future. The ferry makes about 15 trips each way daily in summer, fewer in winter.

SACKETS HARBOR

On the shores of Lake Ontario, Sackets Harbor is a picturesque village with a strong sense of history. A key naval battle was won by the Americans here at the expense of the British during the War of 1812. After the war, the harbor's strategic importance made it a major shipping point. That lasted until the 1850s, when the railroad arrived. Today much of the town depends on seasonal tourism. Guides working out of nearby Lake Ontario ports feature trophy fishing for salmon and lake trout. An annual Octoberfest celebrates the town's history during the second week of October.

Information

The Sackets Harbor Chamber of Commerce (☎ 315-646-1700) and the Sackets Harbor Visitors Center (☎ 315-646-2321) share the same location on Broad St overlooking the harbor. The chamber of commerce can provide information on fishing guides and licenses. Both operate daily in the summer – this far north, summer is only from July to Labor Day – from 10 am to 4 pm. During the month of June and from Labor Day until mid-October, the tourist information center is open from Wednesday through Saturday 10 am to 4 pm.

Sackets Harbor Battlefield Historic Site

Two battles were fought at this former naval base (which was maintained until the 1870s in case of a military attack by Canada) during the War of 1812. The site (☎ 315-646-3634), 505 W Washington St, has a small house-museum tour through the commandant's 1850s four-story residence, as well as a hands-on exhibit of the naval battles, so children can pretend to shoot at the British boats. The tours operate daily from 10 am to 4:30 pm. The cost is $3 for adults, $2 for seniors and $1 for children (ages five to 12).

The **Madison Barracks** (☎ 315-646-3374) is both historical and contemporary – that is, it's a residential community with about 200 year-round residents who make their homes in the renovated Army barracks. The small visitors' center at 85 Worth Rd is open daily from June through September from 8 am to 8 pm during the week, 10 am to 5 pm on Saturday and 11 am to 4 pm on Sunday. They have free walking-tour maps of the area.

Places to Stay & Eat

Cheaper accommodations are available in nearby Watertown, 8 miles west. But in town, *Ontario Place* (☎ 315-646-8000, 103 General Smith Drive) is a classy old waterfront hotel with very nice rooms in the $60 to $75 range.

The Barracks Inn Restaurant (☎ 315-646-2376) is part of the old Madison Barracks. The feeling is historic here – the barracks date from the War of 1812 – but the food is fresh. Seafood and steak entrees with an Italian flavor dominate. There is also a nice outside dining area overlooking the lake and harbor. Dinners cost $14 to $18, and lunches cost $6 to $12. As with many establishments in the area, the restaurant is only open from June until Labor Day weekend. It is open daily for lunch and dinner from 11 am to 10 pm.

Tin Pan Galley (☎ 315-646-3812, 110 Main St) is a great spot for breakfast, lunch and dinner and is less formal and expensive than its upstairs partner, *One Ten Main Street*, owned by the same folks. *Sackets Harbor Brewing Company* (☎ 315-646-2739,

212 W Main St) is open Tuesday through Sunday from 4:30 pm to around midnight.

St Lawrence Seaway

In 1959, the St Lawrence Seaway opened – the long-sought joint effort of the Canadian and US governments to create a deepwater channel between the Atlantic Ocean and the Great Lakes. The Canadians actually led the effort, and the US joined in when it became apparent that the canal might be built without its involvement – or benefit.

Now operated jointly by both countries, the seaway is a system of 15 locks that allows large cargo vessels to travel 2350 miles (8.5 sailing days) from the Atlantic Ocean to Duluth, Minnesota, on Lake Superior. Along the way, the water level rises 602 feet. The channel is extremely narrow in some places, notably off Alexandria Bay, where a disastrous 1976 oil spill wreaked havoc on the ecosystem. The area has never fully recovered. Of the 15 locks, two belong to the US, including the Dwight D Eisenhower Lock near Massena, NY. From here, you can watch ships passing through the lock and learn how the system works.

SEAWAY TRAIL

The New York State Seaway Trail is a 450-mile driving and bicycling route on a series of highways following the seaway through New York (and northern Pennsylvania) along the St Lawrence River, Lake Ontario and Lake Erie. The well-marked trail includes Routes 104, 3, 12E, 12 and 37 (from Oswego to Massena) and provides an interesting alternative to superhighways. Green and white 'Seaway Trail' signs help guide you along the historic and scenic route, which leisurely makes its way through small towns and villages. There are also 42 brown and white interpretive signs along the trail, marking events that took place here during the War of 1812.

MASSENA

Before the engineering marvel of the St Lawrence Seaway and Eisenhower Lock, Massena was a small industrial town dominated by an aluminum plant. In 1900, Henry Warren led an ambitious canal-digging enterprise between the Grass River and the St Lawrence River. The water in the new canal dropped 45 feet in about 3 miles, creating a power source that spurred the town's growth.

Dwight D Eisenhower Lock

To see a 700-foot oceangoing ship (or 'laker') passing through the narrow canal at Massena is stunning. The best place to see it happen is at the **Eisenhower Lock Visitor Center** (☎ 315-769-2049), just off Route 37 (follow the signs). There are two viewing decks, one above the other, and the cost is 25¢ per person. The center is open daily during the summer from 8 am to 9 pm, but you can see the ships easily from the adjacent parking lot anytime.

To make sure you get to see a ship passing through, call Seaway Eisenhower (☎ 315-769-2422) to hear a 24-hour recorded message giving the estimated arrival times (and ship names) of both ocean-bound and lake-bound ships.

St Lawrence-Franklin D Roosevelt Power Project

The Power Project Visitors Center (☎ 315-764-0226) is hard to miss. It sits atop the 3200-foot dam that spans the St Lawrence River between the US and Canada (look for the different colors of brick used by each country's builders). The power project is part of the same scheme that delivered the Eisenhower Lock and Robert Moses State Park in the mid-1950s.

There are several highlights here. The 5th-floor glass-enclosed observation deck offers a four-way view of the entire region, including the seaway's shipping channel. There are also several energy-related exhibits, including several of the hands-on variety. On the 3rd floor, you can stand in front of a large picture window to view the control room and power plant. There are also two large murals by American painter Thomas Hart Benton depicting 17th-century French explorer Jacques Cartier's early voyages and meetings with members of the Mohawk tribes.

Admission and parking are free, and the visitors' center is open late May to early September daily from 9:30 am to 6 pm, September to mid-October until 4:30 pm and the rest of the year weekdays from 9 am to 4:30 pm.

Robert Moses State Park

Robert Moses State Park (☎ 315-769-8663) is one of the prettiest parks in the northeast, situated on both the mainland and Barnhart Island. The park is spacious and serene. White-tailed deer, beaver, shy (they say) bobcat and coyote live here, along with several songbirds, waterfowl and birds of prey. The park (and beach) is open year round, and the entrance fee is $5 per car. There is a visitors' center and a nature interpretive center with wildlife, natural history and environmental displays, as well as a campground (see Places to Stay, later in this section). Robert Moses State Park is one of several 'carry in – carry out' parks in New York. Trash barrels have been removed from day-use areas, with faith in the visitors to hang on to their own garbage. The park is reached via a tunnel that passes under the Eisenhower Lock.

Places to Stay

Robert Moses State Park (☎ 315-769-8663) is open for camping from mid-May to mid-October. Campsites are $13 per day. There are also about a dozen cabins available by the week only for $265 (reservations are required for the cabins).

Robert Moses State Park is home to many birds.

Super 8 Motel (☎ 315-764-1065), at Route 37 and Grove St, is about three blocks from downtown Massena. The motel is decent enough, and rates are relatively low: $42 to $52. ***EconoLodge Motor Inn*** (☎ 315-764-0264, Route 37W) is about 2½ miles west of the downtown area. This is a relatively upscale EconoLodge and is not part of a motel strip. Room rates range from $60 to $85 year-round. There is also a good German restaurant on the premises.

Places to Eat

For good northern Italian food, try ***Viola's Restaurant*** (☎ 315-764-0329, 209 Center St). The ***Village Inn*** (☎ 315-769-6910), on Maple St, is a good family-style eatery in town. ***Loran Restaurant*** (☎ 315-358-4535), on Route 37 at the Ananwate Marina on the St Lawrence Seaway, has fine food and lovely views of the seaway.

Baurenstraube Restaurant (☎ 315-764-0246), in the EconoLodge on Route 37W (see Places to Stay, earlier), is one of the nicest motel eateries you'll find, and specializes in German fare. The Friday and Saturday all-you-can-eat dinner buffet for $10 is the best deal around. It is open daily for breakfast from 6 am to 10 am and for dinner from 5 pm to 10 pm, and Sunday from 6 am to 3 pm.

Getting There & Away

Adirondack Trailways (☎ 800-858-8555) serves Massena from Plattsburgh. The fare is $16/30. Massena to Lake George is $30/57. The trip takes about four hours. Greyhound (☎ 800-231-2222) operates bus service between Massena and Syracuse via Canton and Watertown. The cost for the four-hour trip is $37/75.

Massena is on Route 37, and most people reach the town by car via I-81 and Route 12 from the west, via I-87 and Route 374 from Plattsburgh and via Routes 20 and 401 from Montreal.

OGDENSBURG

Following the banks of the St Lawrence, Ogdensburg is roughly midway between Alexandria Bay and Massena. The town traces its settlement back to 1748, when the French established Fort La Presentation. The town is named after Colonel Samuel Ogden, who acquired the land in 1796 under the provisions of Jay's Treaty.

There is a regional AAA office (☎ 315-393-4280, 800-244-4280 toll-free in the region) in Ogdensburg, at Route 37 and Park St. It's open weekdays 8:30 am to 5 pm.

Frederic Remington Museum

The Remington Museum (☎ 315-393-2425), 303 Washington St, is in the artist's boyhood hometown. The museum houses the largest collection of Remington's bronze sculptures, oil paintings and pen-and-ink sketches, as well as many of the artist's personal effects. Born in 1861, Remington is best known as a chronicler of the American Western experi-ence. He left Yale at 19 and moved to the West, where he spent five years capturing what he saw (frontiersmen and cowboys riding on horseback, soldiers fighting and Native Americans hunting) in photographs, illustrations for newspapers and sketches that would later serve as the basis for his work in bronze and on canvas.

Remington died in 1909 at his home in Connecticut. After his death, his widow returned to Ogdensburg and rented a home, which opened as a museum shortly after her death in 1923. Admission to the museum is $3 for adults and $2 for seniors and youth. From May 1 to October 31, it is open 10 am to 5 pm Monday to Saturday and 1 to 5 pm Sunday; from the beginning of November to April 30, it's open 10 am to 5 pm Tuesday to Saturday.

Finger Lakes Region

The Finger Lakes region derives its name from the 11 long, slender, finger-like bodies of water running north to south in the western part of the state. Named for several of the tribes of the Six Nations of the Iroquois Confederacy, the largest lakes are the Cayuga, Seneca and Keuka at 39, 35 and 19 miles long, respectively. These are also among the deepest glacial lakes on the continent, with Seneca Lake being the deepest at 650 feet.

The region's spectacular natural sites include the many gorges and waterfalls in Watkins Glen State Park and in the state parks around Ithaca. Taughannock Falls, at 215 feet, is the highest waterfall around, even higher than its better known counterpart in Niagara. All of this water creates a multitude of boating, fishing and swimming opportunities. Cycling, hiking and cross-country skiing round out the area's recreational offerings.

The Finger Lakes region is often divided into the Northern Tier – including the towns of Canandaigua, Geneva and Seneca Falls – and the Southern Tier – including Ithaca, Corning and Watkins Glen. Stretching north and south between the tiers are the lakes and 'wine trails' that lead to dozens of wineries on the hills above the lakes (see the boxed text 'Wine Trails').

This broad area contains both charming small towns such as Ithaca, the home of Cornell University, and Seneca Falls, the birthplace of America's women's rights movement, and the larger cities of Rochester, home to a lively arts and photography scene, and Syracuse, a former industrial center on the Erie Canal.

But much of the region remains pastoral, with a rolling countryside dotted by numerous wineries, often in restored farm buildings. The area's glacier-carved geography has created a surprisingly productive wine region. The lakes themselves produce microclimates that protect the vines by preventing extreme temperatures, while sloping hills

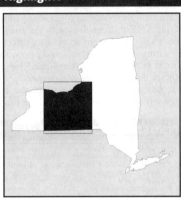

Highlights

- Winery hopping on the shores of Seneca, Keuka and Cayuga Lakes
- Charming, lush Ithaca, home to Cornell University
- Excellent state parks and camping, including Letchworth State Park and Watkins Glen State Park
- Taughannock Falls, the highest waterfall in the US
- Rochester's excellent Strong Museum, and Eastman House Museum of Photography

and glacial soils provide the high-drainage terrain ideal for grape growing.

As a result, New York is now the second-largest wine-producing state in the US, after California, with annual sales of over $300 million. More than half of the state's wineries are concentrated in the Finger Lakes, and half of those have only opened in the past 20 years. The long-held opinion that New York wines were too 'grapey' is changing as premium vineyards appear and occasionally win awards once conceded to California wines.

HISTORY

Before it was settled by Europeans, the Finger Lakes region was home to much of the Iroquois Confederacy, a political union of the Cayuga, Mohawk, Onondaga, Oneida, Seneca and later Tuscarora Indian nations. During the Revolutionary War, many of the Iroquois allied themselves with the British. Though not the first group in history to pick the wrong side, the Iroquois paid a far worse price than the average lottery loser. Beset by military defeats, disease and continuing encroachment by European settlers, the Iroquois communities around the Finger Lakes were devastated for good in 1779, when General George Washington sent a heavily armed expedition to punish the Indians for their isolated and brutal attack on a Scotch and Irish community near Otsego Lake. Entire communities were wiped out, and much of the land was deeded to Revolutionary War veterans as payment for service.

With the completion of the Erie Canal in 1825, the economy of the region changed dramatically. From Albany to Buffalo, towns and cities prospered along with the canal's economic promise (see the Erie Canal Museum in the Syracuse section). Today,

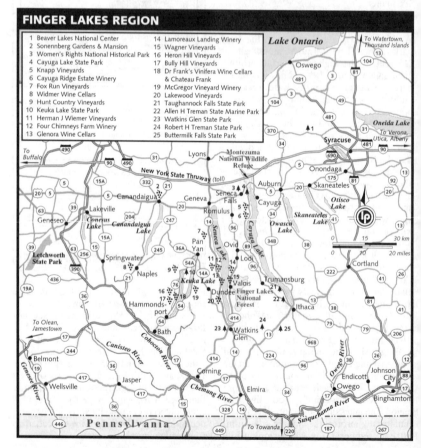

FINGER LAKES REGION

1 Beaver Lakes National Center
2 Sonennberg Gardens & Mansion
3 Women's Rights National Historical Park
4 Cayuga Lake State Park
5 Knapp Vineyards
6 Cayuga Ridge Estate Winery
7 Fox Run Vineyards
8 Widmer Wine Cellars
9 Hunt Country Vineyards
10 Keuka Lake State Park
11 Herman J Wiemer Vineyards
12 Four Chimneys Farm Winery
13 Glenora Wine Cellars
14 Lamoreaux Landing Winery
15 Wagner Vineyards
16 Heron Hill Vineyards
17 Bully Hill Vineyards
18 Dr Frank's Vinifera Wine Cellars
   & Chateau Frank
19 McGregor Vineyard Winery
20 Lakewood Vineyards
21 Taughannock Falls State Park
22 Allen H Treman State Marine Park
23 Watkins Glen State Park
24 Robert H Treman State Park
25 Buttermilk Falls State Park

parts of the canal attract recreational boaters and history buffs, who can visit several old cobblestone buildings. The roads south of the old canal now weave through family farms, orchards and vineyards scattered among the low hills and along valleys of the Finger Lakes.

At about the same time that the canal was being built, another local enterprise enjoyed more modest beginnings. During the 1820s, a Hammondsport minister started making sacramental wine in the Finger Lakes. Apparently, this was a sacrament with broad appeal; in 1860, Hammondsport businessmen opened the first commercial winery – the Pleasant Valley Wine Company – near the shores of Keuka Lake. A few years later the company hired French Champagne makers. A Boston taster gushed that the Pleasant Valley's bubbly was 'the great Champagne of the Western World,' and the owners adopted the name Great Western for the company. Great Western is now part of Taylor Vineyards, the largest producer in the state and second-largest in the US.

But the biggest revolution in New York winemaking came when the Ukrainian immigrant Dr Konstantin Frank discovered that European vinifera grapes – far superior to New York labrusca (not lambrusca) varieties, which make good grape juice but bad wine – could be grown in New York. (See the boxed text 'Konstantin Frank,' later in this chapter.) Today's vineyards tend to favor vinifera and hybrid varieties, though many wineries still make grape juice and other sparkling fruit juices, along with the sparkling wine that US producers call 'champagne,' even though European purists know that only wine produced in the Champagne region of France counts as the true stuff.

For more about the history of the Finger Lakes region, pick up a copy of *Country Towns of New York* (Country Roads Press).

GETTING THERE & AROUND

For motorists, the area is easily accessible by car. The trip from Ithaca to New York City is a 5½-hour drive; from Ithaca to Philadelphia is a 6½-hour drive.

In the Northern Tier, Route 20 runs east to west and skirts the northern fringe of most of the lakes. I-90 (the New York State Thruway) links Rochester and Syracuse. On the region's southern edge, Route 17 connects the towns of Bath, Corning, Elmira and Oswego. In the west, I-390 drops south from Rochester, and in the east I-81 links Syracuse with Cortland. The primary north-south routes within the region are Routes 21, 14 and 89, which parallel the western shores of Canandaigua, Seneca and Cayuga Lakes.

Public transportation outside Rochester, Syracuse and Ithaca is limited. You must have a car to explore many of the lakeside communities.

If traveling to this region by air or train, see Getting There & Away in the Syracuse and Rochester sections.

Southern Tier

The towns of the Southern Tier – including Ithaca, Corning and Watkins Glen – derive their appeal from their proximity to the lakes, their village greens and their rural pace. Route 17 runs through many of them, linking Bath, Corning, Elmira and Oswego. Route 13 connects Ithaca with these southernmost towns.

ITHACA

Like its ancient Greek namesake, Ithaca recalls a somewhat bygone time. This handsome college town of 30,000 people is dominated by distinguished Cornell University, which overlooks it, and Cayuga Lake. Cornell is an integral part of Ithaca; the hilltop Ivy League campus is adjacent to the downtown area, flanked by Cascadilla Gorge to the south and Fall Creek Gorge to the north, both of which wind their way to Cayuga Lake. The local population nearly doubles when combined with Cornell's student body of 18,000 and the 6000 students at nearby Ithaca College, a music conservatory and fine arts school.

Though small, Ithaca is culturally rich, the quintessential college town; bookstores and

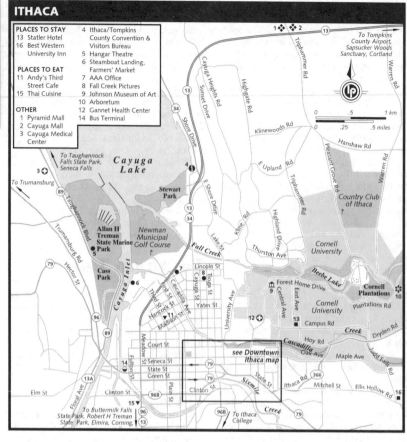

ITHACA

PLACES TO STAY	4	Ithaca/Tompkins
13	Statler Hotel	County Convention &
16	Best Western	Visitors Bureau
	University Inn	5 Hangar Theatre
		6 Steamboat Landing,
PLACES TO EAT		Farmers' Market
11	Andy's Third	7 AAA Office
	Street Cafe	8 Fall Creek Pictures
15	Thai Cuisine	9 Johnson Museum of Art
		10 Arboretum
OTHER		12 Gannet Health Center
1	Pyramid Mall	14 Bus Terminal
2	Cayuga Mall	
3	Cayuga Medical	
	Center	

eateries abound, and foot traffic fills the small streets and arcades. Ithaca's idea of a shopping mall, for example, is the DeWitt Mall – a converted turn-of-the-century schoolhouse without a single national franchise. Not that Ithaca lacks modern conveniences: the roads are paved, the traffic lights work and dogs must be on leashes.

Ithaca sparkles like few other upstate New York communities its size; it's a recreational hub and gateway to the Finger Lakes region. Residential and business districts share the space with creeks, waterfalls and gorges and several town and lakeside parks,

museums and theaters. On fall afternoons, you may see university rowing shells sliding through the calm water at the south end of Cayuga Lake. Ithaca Falls, Buttermilk Falls and Taughannock Falls are close by.

Ithaca marks the beginning of the Cayuga Lake Wine Trail (see the boxed text 'Wine Trails'). The surrounding countryside also produces fruits and vegetables, all available at the town's farmers' market.

Information

Tourist Offices The Ithaca/Tompkins County Convention & Visitors Bureau

(☎ 607-272-1313, 800-284-8422, fax 272-7617, www.visitithaca.com), 904 E Shore Drive off Route 13, is open Monday through Friday from 9 am to 5 pm; in summer and fall (from mid-May until November), it's also open on weekends from 10 am to 5 pm.

The AAA office (☎ 607-273-6727), 303 W Lincoln St, has maps (free for members) and offers auto club and travel services.

Post & Communications The downtown post office (☎ 607-272-5455) is at the corner of Buffalo and Tioga Sts.

For Internet access, try Oak-Internet Cafe & Books (☎ 607-273-1140), 107½ Dryden Road. Or try the Tompkins County Public Library (☎ 607-272-4557), 312 North Cayuga St, which offers free Internet access.

Bookstores Two of the best bookstores in town are The Bookery I and The Bookery II (☎ 607-273-5055), in the DeWitt Mall, 215 N Cayuga St. Bookery I is the more esoteric of the two; used, rare and out-of-print books are its specialty. It's open Monday to Saturday from 10 am to 6 pm. Bookery II offers a rambling collection of contemporary prose, poetry, travel and children's books. It's open Monday to Saturday from 9:30 am to 9:30 pm, Sunday from 11 am to 6 pm.

Borealis Bookstore (☎ 607-272-7752), 111 N Aurora St, specializes in literature, mystery, philosophy and New Age titles. It's open Monday to Saturday from 10 am to 6 pm, Sunday from noon to 6 pm.

For a large selection of discounted and remaindered books, try the Corner Bookstore (☎ 607-273-6001), 115 S Cayuga St, inside a 160-year-old building complete with tin ceiling. It's open Monday to Saturday from 9:30 am to 9 pm, Sunday from noon to 5 pm. Logos Bookstore (☎ 607-273-6360), 115 the Commons, has a good cross section of new and used books.

Library The Tompkins County public library (☎ 607-272-4555), 312 N Cayuga St at Court St, is open Monday to Thursday from 10 am to 9 pm and Friday and Saturday from 10 am to 5 pm.

Media The *Cornell Daily Sun* is an independent, reliable, student-run morning newspaper featuring international as well as campus news. The *Ithaca Journal* is the

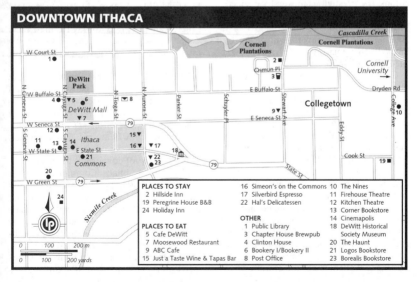

DOWNTOWN ITHACA

PLACES TO STAY		16 Simeon's on the Commons	10 The Nines
2 Hillside Inn		17 Silverbird Espresso	11 Firehouse Theatre
19 Peregrine House B&B		22 Hal's Delicatessen	12 Kitchen Theatre
24 Holiday Inn			13 Corner Bookstore
		OTHER	14 Cinemapolis
PLACES TO EAT		1 Public Library	18 DeWitt Historical
5 Cafe DeWitt		3 Chapter House Brewpub	Society Museum
7 Moosewood Restaurant		4 Clinton House	20 The Haunt
9 ABC Cafe		6 Bookery I/Bookery II	21 Logos Bookstore
15 Just a Taste Wine & Tapas Bar		8 Post Office	23 Borealis Bookstore

regular town paper, published daily except Sunday. The *Ithaca Times* is a free weekly arts and entertainment guide.

WICB, at 91.7 FM, is Ithaca's college radio station and carries NPR. For news and weather, try WHCU 870 AM.

Laundry The Cayuga Mall Laundromat & Cleaners (☎ 607-257-4922), in the Cayuga Mall (on the north side of Ithaca near the intersection of Route 13 and Triphammer Rd), offers self-service and drop-off service. It's open daily from 7 am to 11 pm.

Medical Services Cayuga Medical Center at Ithaca (formerly Tompkins Community Hospital; ☎ 607-274-4011), 101 Dates Drive, is near Cayuga Lake in the northwest corner of town. Cornell University's Gannett Health Center (☎ 607-255-5155) is on the campus' Central Ave.

Cornell University

Founded in 1865, Cornell (☎ 607-254-4636) boasts several notable departments, from the Colleges of Agriculture, Architecture, and Human Ecology to the Schools of Hotel Administration and Industrial & Labor Relations. The prestigious university even contains its own particle accelerator, located beneath the school's football field – a juxtaposition that some regard with irony. Call the **Wilson Synchrotron Lab** (☎ 607-255-3480) for tour information.

Cornell is a lovely and inviting campus. The mixture of old and new architecture, shaded arcadian walkways and the panoramic view of Cayuga Lake make it a common destination for tourists. For one of the best views of the lake and beyond, go to the fifth floor of the **Johnson Museum of Art** (☎ 607-255-6464), University at Central Aves, which houses a major Asian collection, as well as pre-Columbian, American and European exhibits. This striking modern structure, designed by acclaimed architect IM Pei, is known on campus as 'the sewing-machine building.' See for yourself. The museum is open Tuesday through Sunday 10 am to 5 pm. Admission is free. Metered parking is available near the entrance.

Cornell's classic Ivy League landscaping includes the **Cornell University Plantations** (☎ 607-255-3020), on Plantations Rd near the eastern end of campus. This is not merely a large greenhouse in a far campus corner, but an elaborate and diverse complex with an arboretum, a botanical garden that houses an array of poisonous plants and the ever-popular 'weed garden.' The plantations contains miles of nature trails, including paths through Cascadilla and Fall Creek Gorges. The complex is open daily from sunrise to sunset, and admission is free. A gift and book shop near the entrance is open weekdays from 9 am to 4 pm year-round, and daily during most of the spring and summer.

Things to See & Do

The **Sapsucker Woods Sanctuary** (☎ 607-254-2473), 159 Sapsucker Woods Rd, might turn you into a bird-watcher. The Cornell Lab of Ornithology operates an observatory overlooking a bird-feeding garden and a 10-acre pond full of waterfowl and other wildlife. You can also stalk birds on the 4 miles of trails, which are open year round from dawn to dusk. A visitors' center (featuring the bird art of Louis Agassiz Fuertes) is open Monday through Thursday 8 am to 5 pm, Friday 8 am to 4 pm, Saturday 10 am to 4 pm. To get to the sanctuary, head north of town on Route 13 and turn right at Sapsucker Woods Rd.

The **DeWitt Historical Society Museum** (☎ 607-273-8284), 401 East State St, has a fine collection of historical photos. Permanent and revolving exhibits examine local folk art and immigration. It's open Tuesday through Saturday 11 am to 5 pm. Admission is free.

In the heart of downtown, the pedestrian mall known as **Ithaca Commons** occupies two blocks of State St between Cayuga and Aurora Sts. The Commons is attractive and people-friendly, in keeping with Ithaca's genteel charm, and is home to several restaurants, galleries, crafts shops and clothing stores. During summer, Ithaca Commons hosts a free Thursday-evening music series (see Entertainment, below). Parking is available on adjacent streets, and it's an easy stroll to nearby Cascadilla Creek.

The city's parks include **Stewart Park** (☎ 607-272-1718), just off Route 13 on Meadow St, adjacent to the visitors' bureau. This large park at the southern edge of Cayuga Lake has picnic tables, lighted tennis courts, a real carousel and plenty of room to play. It's open daily until 10 pm. **DeWitt Park** (☎ 607-272-1718), 116 N Cayuga St, just north of the Commons near the corner of Buffalo and Cayuga Sts, is one of two locations for Ithaca's popular farmers' market (see Shopping, later in this chapter).

Hiking

Two miles south of Ithaca on Route 13, **Buttermilk Falls State Park** (☎ 607-273-5761) features five hilly woodland and deep gorge trails; adjacent to the park is the Larch Meadows Trail, a 1-mile wetlands trail.

Taughannock Falls State Park (☎ 607-387-6739), 8 miles north of town on Route 89, contains two major trails, one following the streambed to the falls, the other following the ridge and crossing over the falls. The 215-foot-high Taughannock Falls drops down a steep gorge. You can see it from the two lookout points on the trails.

Robert H Treman State Park (☎ 607-273-3440), on Route 13 south of the city, features a 3-mile winding gorge trail that passes 12 cascades, including Devil's Kitchen and Lucifer Falls. This trail is part of the Finger Lakes Trail (☎ 716-288-7161), which connects the Appalachian Trail with Canada's Bruce Trail. The entire 776-mile footpath, bordered by waterfalls, glens and glacial lakes, is off-limits to motor vehicles.

Circle Greenway (☎ 607-274-6570) refers to a 10-mile walking circuit that links a series of half-hour to three-hour walks in and around Ithaca, including Fall Creek, the Waterfront, the Commons and Six Mile Creek Gorge, a mostly level walk that winds through a wildflower preserve. A map is available from either city hall, at the corner of Green and Cayuga Sts, or from the convention & visitors bureau (see Information, earlier in this chapter).

For information about accommodations at these parks, see Places to Stay, below.

Cayuga Lake Cruises

Several luxury and charter boat companies offer Cayuga Lake day trips, along with dinner and moonlight cruises, generally from May through October. The MV *Manhattan* (☎ 607-273-8043), 704 Buffalo St, offers a nightly dinner cruise for about $30. *Loon-A-Sea* (☎ 607-387-5474) runs fishing excursions for small groups. To simply enjoy the beauty of the lake, try Alcyone Charters (☎ 607-272-7963), which offers a four-hour (half-day) tour aboard a 35-foot sloop for $30.

Places to Stay

Camping For information and reservations in any New York state park, call ☎ 800-456-2267. Three nearby state parks provide excellent camping, and sites cost $13.

Buttermilk Falls State Park (☎ 607-273-5761), 2 miles south of town on Route 13, has 60 campsites and seven cabins. It's open from mid-May to mid-October.

Robert H Treman State Park (☎ 607-273-3440), 5 miles south of Ithaca on Route 13, features over 70 campsites and 14 cabins. It's open from mid-May through November.

Taughannock Falls State Park (☎ 607-387-6739), 8 miles north of town on Route 89, is one of the state's most popular parks. The grounds include 76 campsites, 16 cabins, boat facilities, a small swimming beach and picnic areas with fire pits. You can also fish here. Camping is available from late March to mid-October.

You'll find two private campgrounds nearby, but don't expect to get away from it all at either one: *Willowood Resort, Campground & Cabins* (☎ 607-272-6087, 28 Rockwell Rd), a half mile north of Robert H Treman State Park off Route 327, and *Spruce Row Camp & RV Resort* (☎ 607-387-9225, 2271 Kraft Rd) is off Route 89.

Motels The 41-room *Hillside Inn* (☎ 607-272-1000, 518 Stewart Ave) is adjacent to the Cornell University campus. Clean and basic rooms cost $55 to $75, with continental breakfast included.

Wine Trails

Most vineyards and wineries dotting the Finger Lakes region remain open year-round, and many offer a chance to enjoy splendid lake views, as well as an opportunity to taste the latest vintages. To visit the wineries, follow the 'wine trails' – usually lakeside roads with wineries left and right. Most trails have signs directing drivers to specific wineries; some signs simply picture a bunch of grapes to indicate a nearby vineyard.

But before you embark on the grand tour, a word of advice: The road signs may be missing, and getting lost can become an adventure in itself. When in doubt, ask about distances and landmarks. The New York Wine & Grape Foundation (☎ 315-536-7442), 350 Elm St, Penn Yan, NY 14527, can provide information about all the Finger Lakes wineries and brochures for various wine trails.

On the west side of Keuka Lake, take Route 54A north between Hammondsport and Branchport and then Route 54 to Penn Yan at the top of Keuka Lake.

On the west side of Seneca Lake, take Route 14 north from Watkins Glen to Geneva. On the east side of Seneca Lake, follow Route 414 north to Route 96A. On the west side of Cayuga Lake, take Route 89 north from Ithaca.

Wineries near Canandaigua Lake

At the westernmost edge of New York's wine country, the **Widmer Wine Cellars** (☎ 716-374-6311), 1 Lake Niagara Lane in Naples, makes Manischewitz Wines and offers free 45-minute tours of the winery daily. It's open 10 am to 4:30 pm during the summer and fall, 1 to 4 pm in winter.

Wineries near Keuka Lake

Several of the area's oldest wineries are along the western side of Keuka Lake. **Bully Hill Vineyards** (☎ 607-868-3610), on Route 76 off Route 54A in Hammondsport, used to be the original Taylor wine company, founded by Walter S Taylor. But Walter isn't allowed to tell you this – a 1977 lawsuit by Coca-Cola, which bought the newer and larger Taylor Wine Company in nearby Pleasant Valley, prevents him from using his name or the paintings of any ancestors on his wine labels. So he's responded by putting paintings of his goat on many labels and proclaiming: 'They have my name and heritage, but they didn't get my goat.' Bully Hill offers free 45-minute tours in the summer. It's open daily year-round. Its restaurant is open for lunch from mid-May to mid-November.

Between Hammondsport and the Route 54 junction, **Dr Frank's Vinifera Wine Cellars & Chateau Frank** (☎ 607-868-4884), 9749 Middle Rd (Route 76), is the home of the vinifera revolution in Finger Lakes winemaking. Run by Dr Konstantin Frank's son and grandchildren, the winery is known for its Johannesburg Riesling, Pinot Noir and champagne. It's open daily.

The small, family-owned **Heron Hill Vineyards** (☎ 607-868-4241), on Middle Rd (Route 76) 3 miles north of Hammondsport, specializes in vintage varietals and specialty wines, including late-harvest wine. It's open daily from May through November.

On the east side of Keuka Lake, **McGregor Vineyard Winery** (☎ 607-292-3999), 5503 Dutch St on Route 54 between Hammondsport and Penn Yan, offers a clear view of Bluff Point. It's open year-round.

On the northwestern side of Keuka Lake, **Hunt Country Vineyards** (☎ 315-595-2812), 4021 Italy Hill Rd, is well-known for its whites. Its Classic White is a very drinkable bargain, and its superb icewine is said to resemble the best European dessert wines.

Wineries near Seneca Lake

The largest number of quality wineries in the Finger Lakes are on the western and eastern shores of Seneca Lake. **Four Chimneys Farm Winery** (☎ 607-243-7502), on Hall Rd in Himrod, is a small but important organic winery; lately, organically produced wines are catching the attention of larger winemakers interested in sustaining their vineyards. Four Chimneys offers tastings daily from May through November.

Herman J Wiemer Vineyards (☎ 607-243-7971), Route 14 in Dundee, is known for its excellent Riesling wines, produced by a winemaking family from Germany. It's open daily from April through November and weekdays from December to April.

Glenora Wine Cellars (☎ 607-243-5511), 5435 Route 14 in Dundee, is the largest producer of vinifera wines in the eastern US; its output includes excellent sparkling wines and Rieslings. Glenora enjoys a commanding view of Seneca Lake. It's open year-round.

Lakewood Vineyards (☎ 607-535-9252), 4024 Route 14, north of Watkins Glen, offers a good view of the lake and surrounding countryside, as well as an icewine made from frozen grapes and a fruity mead. It's open daily from May through December, on Friday and weekends from January to April.   **Wagner Vineyards** (☎ 607-582-6450), 9322 Route 414 in Lodi, lies on the eastern shore of Seneca Lake. The premises contain the Ginny Lee Cafe. The vineyard is open daily year-round.

The relatively new **Lamoreaux Landing Winery** (☎ 607-582-6061), County Rd 137 in Valois on the southeast shore of Seneca Lake, already has a reputation as a premium producer. Both its vinifera wines and its lake view are splendid. It's open daily year-round.

Wineries near Cayuga Lake

You'll find several vineyards and wineries on the western shore of Cayuga Lake between Seneca Falls and Ithaca. **Knapp Vineyards & Restaurant** (☎ 607-869-9271), 2770 County Rd 128 in Romulus, produces some of the best white wines in the region. It's open daily from April to December, weekdays from January to March. Its restaurant is open from April until mid-December.

Cayuga Ridge Estate Winery (☎ 607-869-5158), 6800 Route 89 in Ovid, gives hands-on seminars in grape growing and winemaking, in addition to the usual tastings. It's open daily from mid-May to December.

Special Events along the Wine Trail

Glenora Wine Cellars (☎ 607-243-5511), on Route 14 in Dundee on the western shores of Seneca Lake, hosts two summer jazz performances, on the third Sunday in July and again in August. Across the lake to the east, the Hector Jazz Festival goes into full Dixieland mode the last weekend of August, in the town of Hector, near Finger Lakes National Forest.

Some of the other regularly scheduled events include the Seneca Lake Wineries Frühling Wein Fest (Spring Wine Festival) in early April, the Cayuga Wine Trail Fresh Herb & New Wine Festival in early May, the Keuka Lake Winery Route Picnic & Summer Wine Festival in June, the Keuka Lake Winery Route Harvest Festival in late September and the Grape Festival in Naples in late September.

For information on any of these, contact the NY Wine & Grape Foundation (☎ 315-536-7442), which distributes a *Wine Country Calendar* that lists the events planned at each winery during the year, as well as promotional events throughout the summer.

Grayhaven Motel (☎ 607-272-6434, *657 Elmira Rd*) is on Route 13, 3 miles south of town. Rates for the clean and roomy accommodations run from $60 to $90 during the summer peak season and on special-event weekends; rooms go for $40 to $50 from December to April.

Best Western University Inn (☎ 607-272-6100, *1020 Ellis Hollow Rd*) is at the corner of Ellis Hollow and Pine Tree Rds, within walking distance of Cornell. Single or double rooms range from $65 to $101; they're slightly cheaper from December to March. Amenities at this attractive motel include continental breakfast, a swimming pool and room refrigerators.

Holiday Inn (☎ 607-272-1000, *222 S Cayuga St*), just off the Commons, features the usual full-service chain hotel amenities. Rates range from $89 to $149, with higher prices on special-event weekends.

The 150-room *Statler Hotel* (☎ 607-257-2500, 800-541-2501), on Campus Rd, is Cornell University's hotel management training school, and it matches the campus in quality, not to mention price. Amenities include three restaurants, big banquet rooms, a 93-seat amphitheater and rooms with VCRs and computer modem hookups, as well as free transportation from the airport. Rooms range from $139 for a single to $179 for a double with a west view of Ithaca and Cayuga Lake.

B&Bs There are quite a few B&Bs around Ithaca; the visitors' bureau will be able to help you find one.

The well-managed *Peregrine House B&B* (☎ 607-272-0919, *140 College Ave*) is an 1870s Victorian near the Cornell campus. All eight rooms have private baths and telephones, and children are welcome. Rooms range from $60 to $100.

The Archway Bed & Breakfast (☎ 607-387-6175, 800-387-6175, *7020 Searsburg Rd*), on the west side of Cayuga Lake in Trumansburg, 10 miles north of Ithaca via Route 96, is an 1861 Greek Revival home with a hammock on the porch overlooking the garden. This historic home is adjacent to the Trumansburg Golf Course and wel-

comes children. Rooms range from $60 to $85.

Hanshaw House Inn (☎ 607-257-1437, 800-257-1437, *15 Sapsucker Woods Rd*) is a few miles out of town in northeast Ithaca, just off Route 13. This remodeled 1830s farmhouse, complete with antique furnishings and private baths, contains four rooms, priced from $65 to $120. Its proximity to Cornell's Sapsucker Woods Sanctuary is a peaceful plus.

La Tourelle Country Inn (☎ 607-273-2734, 800-765-1492, *1150 Danby Rd*), 2 miles south of town on Route 96B, is very comfortable, unpretentious, inviting and convenient. The inn sits on a hill with great views of Cayuga Lake, and walking trails are nearby. The facilities include a year-round tennis court known as the 'bubble.' Rates range from $80 for a basic room during the week to $135 for a weekend stay in the biggest room.

The Rose Inn (☎ 607-533-7905, *813 Auburn Rd*), about 10 miles north of Ithaca via Route 34, is an elegant 15-room 1850s Italianate mansion. The inn has candlelight dining and marble fireplaces. Room prices range from $120 for a midweek off-season (December to April) double to $325 for an in-season weekend suite.

Places to Eat

Ithaca might have the best variety of restaurants in all of upstate New York, and you can even get a late dinner on a weeknight. Many area restaurants use fresh and seasonal ingredients to prepare international, gourmet and vegetarian fare fit for every budget. The Ithaca farmers' market is a great place to look for lunch items. See Shopping, later in this chapter, for more information.

For great omelettes, open-faced sandwiches and meatball dinners, try *Andy's Third Street Cafe* (☎ 607-277-0007, *425 Third St*), which is open daily for breakfast, lunch and dinner.

The *ABC Cafe* (☎ 607-277-4770, *308 Stewart Ave*) is a popular vegetarian restaurant in the Collegetown neighborhood, featuring fresh pastries, daily international specials for the hip at heart and live weekend music. ABC is open Tuesday to Sunday from 11 am until about midnight.

The New York-style deli **Hal's Delicatessen** (☎ 607-273-7765, 115 S Aurora St) offers big sandwiches at reasonable prices. It's open daily from 6:30 am to 8 pm.

Silverbird Espresso (☎ 607-277-3805, 302 E State St), at the corner of State and Aurora Sts, is a cozy cafe with good pastries. It's open daily 8 am to 10 pm.

Around the corner you'll find **Simeon's on the Commons** (☎ 607-272-2212, 224 W State St), which features excellent sandwiches and soups ($5 to $8), an elegant long bar in a Victorian setting and a good people-watching view of the Commons. It's open daily from 11 am to 11 pm.

Just a Taste Wine & Tapas Bar (☎ 607-277-9463, 116 N Aurora St), near the Commons, serves an assortment of tasty Spanish tapas along with a good selection of wines; meals range from $5 to $15.

The **Cafe DeWitt** (☎ 607-273-3473, 215 N Cayuga St), at the corner of Buffalo and Cayuga Sts, is one of several eateries in the DeWitt Mall. The cafe spreads across the old schoolhouse walkway, adjacent to the eclectic shops. Always busy, it's open for breakfast and lunch (8:30 am to 2:30 pm) Monday through Saturday; from October through May, the cafe serves Sunday brunch (11 am to 2 pm). The prices here range from $5 to $10.

Also in the DeWitt Mall, you'll find the **Moosewood Restaurant** (☎ 607-273-9610, 215 N Cayuga St). The source of the popular Moosewood cookbooks, this restaurant rightly takes some credit for elevating vegetarian cooking to a loftier plane. Despite its vegetarian roots, Moosewood offers a fresh fish dish Thursday through Sunday. Several spicier ethnic dishes are available on Sunday only. Dinners range from $10 to $15. Be forewarned: There is usually a line to get in, made less tiresome by reading the flyers on the long bulletin board by the inside entrance. Moosewood is open Monday through Saturday for lunch (11 am to 2 pm) and daily for dinner (5:30 to 8:30 pm). In summer, the hours are slightly longer, and you can dine outside.

On Route 13 in south Ithaca, **Thai Cuisine** (☎ 607-273-2031, 501 S Meadow St) serves authentic, if upscale, Thai dishes, with an additional vegetarian menu. Entrees range from $10 to $18. Thai Cuisine is open daily except Tuesday from 5 to 9:30 pm; it's also open for lunch (11 am to 2 pm) on Saturday and Sunday. Reservations are recommended on the weekend.

Main Moon Chinese Buffet (☎ 607-277-3399, 401 Elmira Rd) is about 2 miles south of town on Route 13. For travelers on a budget, it's a reliable spot to fill up on decent Chinese food.

Set in a 150-year-old restored country farmhouse, **John Thomas Steakhouse** (☎ 607-273-3464, 1152 Danby Rd), adjacent to La Tourelle Country Inn on Route 96B south of town, features dry-aged beef, as well as lamb, seafood and chicken entrees, priced from $18 to $30 – expensive, but a bargain when matched with comparable restaurants down-state. This is one of Ithaca's best dining spots, with everything prepared fresh on the premises. Dinner is served from 5:30 to 10:30 pm.

Entertainment

Ithaca supports a thriving theater and performing arts scene. Call the Ticket Center at Clinton House (☎ 607-273-4497, 800-284-8422, 116 N Cayuga St), for more information about most Ithaca theater and performing arts activities.

Theater The **Hangar Theatre** (☎ 607-273-8588), on Route 89, runs a popular summer theater series that includes the Kiddstuff summer children's theater. Look for the bright red building in Cass Park, just off Route 89 west of the inlet to Cayuga Lake. Two other highly regarded theater groups are the **Kitchen Theatre Company (KTC)** (☎ 607-272-0403, 116 S Cayuga St) and the **Firehouse Theatre** (☎ 607-277-7529, 136 W State St).

Cinema The **Cinemapolis** (☎ 607-277-6115, 171 E State St), in the Commons, contains two small theaters that generally feature foreign and independent films. **Fall Creek**

Pictures (☎ 607-272-1256, *1201 N Tioga St*), at Lincoln St, shows specialty and Hollywood films after they complete their big cineplex runs. *Hoyt's Theater* (☎ 607-257-2700), at the Pyramid Mall on the north end of town, shows first-run commercial releases on seven screens. The *Cornell Cinema* (☎ 607-255-3522, *104 Willard Straight Hall*), on Cornell's campus, presents a different double feature every night, often showcasing independent and foreign films.

Brewpubs The *Chapter House Brewpub* (☎ 607-277-9782, *400 Stewart Ave*), at Osmun Place, is a popular and lively town brewpub (with a good jukebox). It's open from 4 pm to midnight.

Music During summer, head to *Ithaca Commons* (☎ 607-277-8679) for free outdoor concerts at 7 pm on Thursday evenings; the music ranges from classical to rockabilly. The Taughannock Falls Concert Series (☎ 607-387-6739) takes place every Saturday evening at Taughannock Falls State Park, weather permitting.

The Nines (☎ 607-272-1888, *311 College Ave*), in the Collegetown area, is a popular rock, reggae and blues club featuring the best local and touring bands. *The Haunt* (☎ 607-275-3447, *114 W Green St*), near the Commons and Holiday Inn, is similar. The cover charge is usually around $5 for either club.

Shopping

Ithaca Farmers' Market The Ithaca farmers' market (☎ 607-273-7109, during market hours) is a wonderful outdoor market where you can pick up organic produce and dairy products. It's a great place to sample summer berries, autumn apples, Finger Lakes wines, bread and cookies just out of the oven, as well as hot meals that range from Mexican to macrobiotic dishes.

The market doubles as a local arts-and-crafts showcase featuring painters, quilters, jewelers and musicians. Everything sold here has been made within a 30-mile radius of town. Most weekends feature free performances by everyone from bluegrass musicians to belly dancers, from ping-pong players to turkey callers.

A 'moveable feast,' the market takes place at two locations, each with its own schedule.

The Steamboat Landing site (with a covered pavilion), at the Cayuga Inlet near Route 13 and Third St, operates on Saturday from 9 am to 2 pm, April through December; and on Sunday from 10 am to 2 pm, May through December.

DeWitt Park, the other location, handles the midweek demand. It's open on Tuesday from 9 am to 2 pm, mid-May until the end of October.

Farms & Food Ithaca and much of the surrounding countryside contain a wealth of quality farms and orchards, roadside stands and 'pick-your-own' farms; several offer tours. The fruit and vegetable harvest calendar, *New York State Guide to Farm Fresh Food (Central Region)*, is available from the New York State Department of Agriculture and Markets, 1 Winners Circle, Albany, NY 12235.

Just north of Ithaca is **Ludgate Farms** (☎ 607-257-1765), 1552 Hanshaw Rd, about 1 mile east of Route 13. Fresh fruits and vegetables, cider, honey and chestnuts fill the shelves, but the Hollywood Restaurant Pasta Sauce wins the name-of-the-week prize. It's open daily from 9 am to 9 pm year-round.

CRS Growers (☎ 607-257-2195), 2622 Triphammer Rd, 1½ miles north of Route

Why bears and horses never meet

13, enjoys a view of Cayuga Lake. It's open from May through October.

Grisamore Farms (☎ 607-497-1347), on Goose St near the junction of Routes 34 and 90 in Locke, is about 20 miles northeast of Ithaca. It's popular in the summer months for 'u-pick' berries and apples, and in the winter for maple syrup and Christmas trees.

Getting There & Away

Tompkins County Airport (☎ 607-257-0456) is 5 miles northeast of Ithaca via Route 13. Served by Continental Airlines and US Airways, this modest airport offers daily service to Newark, New York City, White Plains, Syracuse, Pittsburgh, Philadelphia and Boston. To travel from the Tompkins County Airport to town by taxi, contact Ithaca Dispatch (☎ 607-277-2227) or Cayuga Taxi (☎ 607-277-8294). The fare from downtown Ithaca to the airport is about $8.

To travel from Ithaca to Hancock International Airport in Syracuse, contact Ithaca Airline Limousine Shuttle Service (☎ 607-273-3030) or Cayuga Taxi (☎ 607-277-8294). The fare is $85.

The bus terminal (☎ 607-277-8800), 710 W State St at Fulton St, serves as a depot for Adirondack Trailways (☎ 800-858-8555), Greyhound (☎ 800-231-2222) and Hudson Transit (☎ 607-734-8007). A one-way trip from Ithaca to New York City takes about five hours ($35/69 for one-way/roundtrip). Ithaca to Syracuse takes about 1½ hours ($10/19). From Ithaca to Philadelphia, via Scranton, PA, takes 9 hours, with layovers ($60/119).

The nearest Amtrak train terminal (☎ 800-872-7245) is 60 miles north in Syracuse. (Service between Syracuse and Ithaca is provided by Greyhound.)

Those traveling by car will find Ithaca at the crossroads of Routes 13 and 96, about 50 miles northwest of Binghamton and 55 miles southeast of Syracuse. If you're coming from the southeast (ie, New York City), take I-88 west to Route 17; at exit 64, head north on Route 96 to 96B and follow that into Ithaca. From I-81 to the east, take exit 11 or exit 12 to Route 13 west. From the west, take Route 224 east to Route 13 north, which brings you to the south of town. From Watkins Glen, take Route 414 north to Route 79 east, which takes you right into Ithaca.

Getting Around

Ithaca Transit, T-CAT and Cornell University (CU) Transit (☎ 607-277-7433) all offer regular town bus service, with rides costing 30¢ to 60¢. Transfers are available between Ithaca Transit and all T-CAT routes.

Taxi service is available 24 hours a day from Cayuga Taxi (☎ 607-277-8294).

Ithaca and the surrounding countryside make for great mountain and road biking. Cayuga Mountain Bike Shop (☎ 607-277-6821), 138 W State St, rents bikes and offers route advice. It's open daily and has evening hours.

TRUMANSBURG

Trumansburg is a small town about 15 miles north of Ithaca on Route 96 on the west side of Cayuga Lake.

In the winter the Podunk Ski Touring Center and Ski Shop (☎ 607-387-6716), 6383 Podunk Rd, has many cross-country trails. Reasonably priced rentals, including trail fees, are $11 for the day or $18 for the weekend. The center also gives lessons for $6 per hour per person for a group of four or $18 for an individual. And guests can use the sauna and then roll in the snow.

To reach the ski center from Ithaca, take Route 96 north past Jacksonville and then make a left on Cold Springs Rd and a left on Podunk Rd. From the north, take Route 96 south to Trumansburg, follow South St to the end and turn left on Podunk Rd. The center is about a quarter mile up the road. Look for the sign.

If you're hungry for a bite to eat, you have only a few choices in this one-street town. Try the ***Rongovian Embassy to the USA*** (☎ *607-387-3334, 1 W Main St*), a restaurant with an insane wall map, a bar (with 200 beers) and pizza for $10. The menu also features unusual items like sautéed catfish. Children under 12 eat free on Thursday nights; timing is everything.

Three doors down is ***Ron Don's*** (☎ *607-387-5622, 19 W Main St*), serving breakfast and burgers from 5 am to midnight. You have to look hard to find anything for more than $4 on the menu. *Falls Restaurant & Tavern* (☎ 607-387-9761, 214 E Main St) is a popular local spot with good pub food.

A little further afield, you'll find *Taughannock Farms Inn* (☎ 607-387-7711, 2030 Gorge Rd), a Victorian estate 8 miles north of Ithaca on Route 89, directly across from Taughannock Falls State Park. The Inn, which overlooks Cayuga Lake, offers American cuisine and fine wines from the Finger Lakes region. It's open for breakfast and dinner from April through December, but only on weekends after mid-October.

If you are traveling by public transportation, T-CAT (☎ 607-274-5370) bus No 41 serves the route from Ithaca to Trumansburg. The trip takes about half an hour and costs 60¢.

WATKINS GLEN

The modest town of Watkins Glen is on the southern tip of Seneca Lake. Although once well-known for its salt wells, today Watkins Glen is famous for an unlikely duo of attractions: an international auto-racing track and a spectacular natural gorge with waterfalls. Both attract tourists to the area, but the town itself offers little to see. Route 14 becomes Franklin St as it travels through the commercial center of town. Route 414 from Corning runs into Franklin St at 15th St.

Information

The Schuyler County Chamber of Commerce (☎ 607-535-4300, 800-607-4552), 1000 N Franklin St, keeps the following hours: Monday to Wednesday from 9 am to 5 pm, Thursday and Friday from 9 am to 8 pm, Saturday from 10 am to 5 pm and Sunday from 1 to 4 pm during the summer months of May through October; winter hours are Monday through Friday from 9 am to 5 pm.

An information booth at Watkins Glen State Park is open daily 10 am to 6 pm from late May to mid-October. During the rest of

the year, it's open daily from 9 am to 5 pm. There's no phone at the park.

Things to See & Do

Watkins Glen International (☎ 607-535-2481) is a well-known car-racing track that is 3 miles outside town. Cars used to race on a 6.6-mile course through town streets, but saner minds built a 2.3 mile course in its present location in 1956. Since then, the track has gone through some ups and downs, but today it hosts major NASCAR and Grand Prix races, including the Winston Cup Race in August.

The season runs from June to October, and most tickets cost $10 to $50 depending on the race and how close you want to be to cars trying to break the sound barrier. You can also bring your RV and park next to the track during some races for $35 to $110. To reach the track, take Route 414 north through town to County Rd 16 and then follow the signs 3 miles to the track.

Watkins Glen State Park (☎ 607-535-4511) operated as a private tourist attraction until the state bought it in 1906. The park has 19 waterfalls, grottos and lots of summer tourists, who walk along a dazzling self-guided 1½-mile gorge trail with 832 stone steps. The entrance to the park is on Franklin St between 10th and 11th Sts. You can camp here, too (See Places to Stay, later in this section). The park stays open from May until the first snow, which is usually some time in October or November.

Captain Bill's Seneca Lake Cruises (☎ 607-535-4541/4680), at the foot of Franklin St, takes people by the boatload onto the lake. A one hour, 10-mile roundtrip tour costs $7.50/3.50 for adults/children ages two to 12. More expensive brunch, lunch and dinner cruises are also offered. Cruises start on the hour from 10 am to 8 pm daily from mid-May to mid-October.

Places to Stay

On big race weekends during the summer, the town is booked and prices jump up; if you're not planning on a race weekend visit, you'll have more choices.

Camping The campground at *Watkins Glen State Park* (☎ 607-535-4511) has 300 sites that cost $13 to $17, depending on electric hookups. It's open from mid-May until the park closes at the first snowfall, usually by late October. The sites are near the park entrance, at Franklin St between 10th and 11th Sts.

Watkins Glen KOA (☎ 607-535-7404), on Route 414, features more than 100 sites on 90 acres. The rates are $22 for a tent site, $25 for a site with electric hookup, $29 for a site with electricity and water. A one-room cabin is $40, a two-room cabin $50. The amenities include laundry facilities, pool, rental boats and a camp store. The KOA is open from late April to late October. To reach it, take Route 414 about 4½ miles south of the junction with Route 14.

Finger Lakes National Forest (☎ 607-546-4470), 8 miles north of Watkins Glen via Route 414, between Cayuga and Seneca Lakes, is the smallest national forest in the country (and the only one in New York state). The 16,000-acre site has more than 20 miles of hiking trails, fishing ponds and a basic campground (Blueberry Patch Camp) that costs $5 per night; it's open year round. A visitors' center with maps and wildlife information is open weekdays 8 am to 4:30 pm. (From May to early September it's also open Saturday noon to 4 pm.)

Motels & B&Bs The *Seneca Lodge* (☎ 607-535-2014) is in Watkins Glen State Park, nestled in a pine forest. You can choose between small, inexpensive duplex-style cabins and basic motel rooms with two beds, a table and a TV. The dining room resembles a giant log cabin. Single/double cabins are $60/90; motel rooms are $58; two/three bedroom A-frame rentals are $88/98. The lodge is open from late April through November.

In town, *Queen Catherine Motel* (☎ 607-535-2441, 436 S Franklin St) contains 15 rooms in a holiday-green building with red trim. The rooms have TVs, shag carpeting and no phones. Summer rates are $55/65; winter prices come down to around $50.

Clarke House B&B (☎ 607-535-7965, 102 Durand Place), at Franklin St, features four rooms sharing two bathrooms in a Tudor home. Rates are $75 to $85, including a full breakfast in the dining room.

Seneca Lake Watch B&B (☎ 607-535-4490) rents private rooms for $85 to $105 in summer peak season, $65 to $85 off-season.

The 18-room *Idlwilde Inn* (☎ 607-535-3081, 1 Lakeview Ave) is a distinctive pink-roof Victorian with a wraparound porch overlooking Seneca Lake. All rooms have private bath, and a full breakfast is included. Prices range from $85 off-season to $225 from May to mid-October, the peak season. The inn doesn't allow children under 12.

Places to Eat

You'll find several delis and fast-food outlets along Franklin St. The *Wildflower Cafe* (☎ 607-535-9797, 301 N Franklin St) features light American cuisine, often with fresh local ingredients. It's open daily for lunch and dinner. The Chinese *House of Hong* (☎ 607-535-7024), 4th St at Franklin St, serves lunch specials ($4.50 and up).

Professors' Place (☎ 607-535-8000, 2 N Franklin St) is one of the more unique eateries in Watkins Glen, serving very good pasta, seafood and veggie dishes. It also includes a small wine-tasting room and bookstore. Summer weekends often feature a touch of live folk music and tasty mead beer from the bar. It's closed from December to April.

If you want to splurge on a fancy meal, try *Seasons Restaurant* (☎ 607-535-4619, 1008 N Franklin St), in the Watkins Hotel. Continental main courses average about $20 during dinner, served from 5 to 9 pm nightly. A Sunday brunch, from 11 am to 2 pm, is a bargain at $15 per person.

Jerlando's Italian Restaurant (☎ 607-535-4254, 400 N Franklin St) serves very good Sicilian dishes at reasonable prices ($6 to $11). A pizzeria on the premises is open daily.

The *Franklin Street Grill* (☎ 607-535-2007, 413 N Franklin St) is an upscale grill with a good atmosphere and live piano jazz on Friday and Saturday evenings. It's open daily for lunch and dinner.

CORNING

This town owes its name to Erastus Corning of Albany, who bought land here to build a railroad for the transportation of Pennsylvanian anthracite to the nearby Chemung Canal. The town is better known as the home of the Corning Glass Works, a company that moved here from Brooklyn after the Civil War. Corning is still the largest employer in the town and surrounding area.

After the Chemung River flooded downtown Corning in 1972, the Market St area was carefully restored to resemble its 19th-century origins. The downtown cobblestone and brick arcade sets the tone for this old company town, and the official street name – Historic Market St – sums up the scene.

Most tourists just stop for the day. For tourist information, visit the Greater Corning Chamber of Commerce (☎ 607-936-4686), 42 E Market St. It's open from 9 am to 5 pm weekdays.

Things to See & Do

The **Corning Glass Center** (☎ 607-974-8271), on Cedar St about a quarter mile west of Route 17, has become a major tourist attraction, with a series of exhibits that relates the fascinating history of glass. The first is the Corning Museum of Glass, which houses glass objects from 1400 BC to the present. The collection contains 26,000 items, including a Baccarat table and the largest piece of glass in the world – a 20-ton yellow honeycomb monstrosity cast for the telescope at the Mt Palomar Observatory.

The center's ever-popular Hall of Science & Industry features working glass welders and plenty of hands-on exhibits to explain such technology as fiber optics and binary coding. In the Steuben Glass Factory, an actual working factory, you can observe a small team of glass blowers transforming molten glass to finished object – one of the few places in the age of automation where art glass is still handcrafted. Steuben crystal is often used for gifts of state. The center is open daily from 9 am to 5 pm. Admission is $10/9/5 for adults/seniors/children ages six to 17. A family pass is $30.

The **Rockwell Museum** (☎ 607-937-5386), 111 Cedar St at Route 17 (in the Historic Market St area), primarily contains American Western art, early examples of Steuben glass and antique toys. The displays by Frederic Remington, Charles M Russell and 1830s landscapes by the 'explorer artists' are especially noteworthy. It's open Monday to Saturday from 9 am to 5 pm and Sunday from noon to 5 pm. Admission is $5/2.50 for adults/children, or $12.50 for families.

The **Mark Twain Study & Exhibit** (☎ 607-735-1941), at Elmira College (1 Park Place, Elmira), is dedicated to the legacy of Samuel Clemens, whose better-known pen name, Mark Twain, is synonymous with the very best American storytelling. Twain was a humorist, newspaperman, lecturer and the author of *The Adventures of Tom Sawyer* among other titles. Famous for reporting the world as he found it, he once wrote: 'Tell the truth – that way you don't have to remember anything.'

In 1952, a gallery of photos, along with Twain's original study, was moved to the current location from nearby Quarry Farm, where Twain spent 20 summers with his wife Livy (Olivia Langdon), a graduate of Elmira College. The study contains his 1880s Remington Rand typewriter; Twain claimed to be the first author in the world to submit typewritten manuscripts to a publisher.

The exhibit is open Monday through Saturday 9 am to 5 pm and Sunday noon to 5 pm, from mid-June to early September, or by appointment at other times. Admission is free. Elmira College lies between Corning and Ithaca, just off Route 17 exit 56.

Places to Stay & Eat

You'll find a few inexpensive motels in and around town. *Lando's Hotel* (☎ 607-936-3612), at the corner of William and Bridge Sts, offers clean and basic singles/doubles for $35/45. The 20-room *Gate House Motel* (☎ 607-936-4131, 145 E Corning Rd charges $38/52. As in Watkins Glen, prices go up during racing weekends.

Rosewood Inn B&B (☎ 607-962-3253, 134 E First St) is an elegant restored Victorian home with seven rooms, each with private bath. Peak-season rates (June to October) range from $85 to $155, including a full breakfast.

The plush **Radisson Hotel Corning** (☎ 607-962-5000, 125 Denison Parkway East) is centrally located, close to Historic Market St. Its 177 spacious rooms range from $80 to $150.

Most of Corning's eateries are in the downtown historic area, a block west of Route 17. **Medleys** (☎ 607-936-1685, 61 E Market St) is a bakery and restaurant serving good sandwiches, vegetarian chili and pasta salads, accompanied by occasional live music. It's open from 10 am to 5 pm (later on weekends). A Sunday brunch is only $6.

Pelham's Upstate Tuna Co (☎ 607-936-8862, 73 E Market St) lets customers cook for themselves. You buy your favorite chicken teriyaki or fish kabobs for about $10 and start cooking on a grill with your fellow diners. The restaurant is open for dinner from 5 to 10 pm nightly; the bar, which features dozens of imported and domestic beers, stays open until 1 am.

If you're just passing through and want a good, quick, cheap meal, try **Wegman's Market Cafe** (☎ 607-937-8346, 1 Bridge St). Wegman's is an upscale supermarket, and its deli and cafes have a reputation for fresh food, ranging from Caesar salads to sushi to subs. It's open daily around-the-clock.

Getting There & Away

About 20 miles southwest of Watkins Glen, Corning is at the intersection of Route 414 and Route 17, a short hop west of the intersection of Routes 17 and 15. It's served by Capitol Trailways (☎ 800-444-2877) and Chenango Valley Transit (☎ 800-647-6471). The fare from Corning to Rochester is $19/34 one-way/roundtrip; to Syracuse, $18/33; to Ithaca, $11/20.

HAMMONDSPORT

At the southern tip of Keuka Lake, Hammondsport lies on Route 54A, just off Route 54. From here, you can explore the nearby wineries, such as Dr Frank's Vinifera Wine Cellars (the best) and Bully Hill Vineyards

Konstantin Frank

New York is famous for its native labrusca grapes – Delaware, Concord, Catawba and Niagara – which make great jam but mediocre wine. For years, New York winemakers used labrusca grapes because they believed that European vinifera grapes could not survive in the state. Enter Dr Konstantin Frank, born of German parents in the Ukraine in 1899. Frank held a doctorate in plant sciences and had been director of a large state-owned vineyard in the Ukraine. In 1953, he came to the US speaking many languages – though not English – and went to Geneva, near Seneca Lake, to ask for work at the New York State Experimental Station. He was allowed to hoe blueberries and work as a janitor.

A few years later Charles Fournier, who was working at the Urbana Wine Co (which later became Gold Seal), hired Frank. Fournier and Frank experimented with grafting native American rootstock to European vinifera buds to prove the latter could grow in New York. Frank's successful experiments led to the growth of the state's huge wine industry. He later opened his own winery – Dr Frank's Vinifera Wine Cellars – although it wasn't until his son Willy Frank took over in the 1980s that the business expanded beyond experimentation to the production of fine wines.

(the most interesting). For more information on the wineries, see the boxed text 'Wine Trails.'

The town of Hammondsport itself has a pleasant village square. For tourist information, contact the Hammondsport Chamber of Commerce (☎ 607-569-2989), PO Box 539, Hammondsport, NY, 14840; during the summer, it's open Monday and Wednesday from 1 to 5 pm; Tuesday, Thursday and Friday from 9 am to 5 pm; and weekends from 10 am to 4 pm. You can also visit the helpful information booth at the northwest corner of Liberty and Main Sts.

The post office is on Sheather St on the square. You'll find a self-service laundry one block south of the square on Sheather St.

Things to See & Do

The **Wine Museum of Greyton H Taylor** (☎ 607-868-4814), on the grounds of the Bully Hill Vineyards, sits in one of the original Taylor Winery buildings. It features old wine-making equipment and artwork by Walter S Taylor, the owner and founder of Bully Hill. Admission is $1. To reach the winery, head 1½ miles north of town on Route 76, off Route 54A.

The **Glenn H Curtis Museum** (☎ 607-569-2160), a half mile south of town on Route 54, displays airplanes, motorcycles and engines. From May to October, it's open Monday to Saturday from 9 am to 5 pm, Sunday from 11 am to 5 pm; from November to April, it's open Monday to Saturday from 10 am to 4 pm, Sunday from noon to 5 pm. Admission is $5/3.50/2.50 for adults/seniors/children.

While you're in town, you can take a **Keuka Lake cruise**. The *Keuka Maid* (☎ 607-569-2628/3631) sails from Hammondsport between May and October. Fares range from $10 to $20, depending on whether you opt for a lunch or dinner cruise, or just a cruise.

Places to Stay & Eat

There are some cheap chain motels around the Route 17 exit at Bath, 8 miles south of Hammondsport. The *Budget Inn* (☎ 607-776-7536, 330 W Morris St) is a bit battered but functional enough at $26/33 in winter and $33/44 in summer. You get coffee and a Danish in the morning. The more expensive but definitely superior *Days Inn* (☎ 607-776-7644) is next door, with rooms from $60 to $90 a night.

Another Tyme (☎ 607-569-2747, 7 Church St) features three immaculate rooms named after important people and times in the owner's life – the Douglas Room for her deceased husband, Mimi's Room for her mother-in-law and the Kamakwie Room for her stint in the Peace Corps in Africa. It's a couple of blocks from the town square. Rates are around $50 and include breakfast.

Half a block north of the square and half a block from the lake, *JS Hubbs B&B* (☎ 607-569-2440, 17 Sheather St) is in a big green house built in 1840. It has four large rooms all with private bath, though some of the toilets are a little cramped. The B&B includes two very large common rooms with a TV and piano, a small greenhouse and a parking area. Rooms are $79 to $99, including a full breakfast.

Park Inn (☎ 607-569-9387, 37 Sheather St) is opposite the village green, next to the Crooked Lake Ice Cream shop. The inn charges $50 to $80 for its five rooms, which are all on the 2nd floor, above a small tavern/restaurant that serves lunch and dinner.

If you're hungry for a bite, try *Crooked Lake Ice Cream Co* (☎ 607-569-2751, 35 Sheather St), which serves breakfast, lunch and great ice cream in an old-fashioned setting on the town square. *Village Tavern* (☎ 607-569-2528, 30 Mechanic St), also on the square, features a good tavern atmosphere and tavern fare. Lunch and dinner entrees cost $6 to $11.

Northern Tier

An indelible part of this area's history begins with the construction of the legendary Erie Canal. When it first opened in 1825, it was the engineering marvel of its day. A great wave of westward migration followed, along with the construction of several lateral canals. Route 20, which connects many of the towns at the northern ends of the lakes, is a direct descendent of the canal's development, and it's also considered among the loveliest drives in New York state. (Incidentally, Route 20 and I-90 form the northern borders of the Finger Lakes region.)

Towns with the most notable historical architecture in this region, particularly Greek Revival mansions, tend to be in the Northern Tier, a more citified and urban environment than the southern half of the region. The Northern Tier encompasses the industrial centers of Syracuse and Rochester, in addition to smaller towns such as Canandaigua, Geneva and Seneca Falls.

PENN YAN

Ideally situated for winery visiting, Penn Yan lies on Route 54 at the northern tip of Keuka Lake, between the Northern and Southern Tiers. The town's name is an amalgamation of 'Pennsylvania' and 'Yankee' because most of the early settlers came from Pennsylvania and New England. Today it's the world's largest producer of buckwheat and home of the Buckwheat Harvest Festival (☎ 315-536-7434), held the fourth weekend in September, when the National Buckwheat Institute serves buckwheat ice cream, buckwheat pizza, buckwheat shortcake and other buckwheat delights. The festivities also include amusement games, arts and crafts and a parade.

The town's limited attractions include the **Windmill Farmers' Market**, (☎ 315-536-3032), on Route 54, 6 miles south of the Elm St intersection downtown. Mennonites (see Pennsylvania Dutch Country chapter), who still use horse and buggy to travel, come from the surrounding area to sell good produce, jams, molasses and baked goods at this indoor-outdoor farmers' market. From May to December, it's open every Saturday (plus Memorial Day, the 4th of July and Labor Day) from 8 am to 4:30 pm.

If you're looking for some local history books, Eileen O'Reilly's Belknap Hill Books (☎ 315-536-1186), 106 Main St, is one of the better used bookstores in the region.

Places to Stay & Eat

Keuka Lake State Park (☎ 315-536-3666), 3370 Pepper, Bluff Point, includes 150 campsites on 620 acres, and it has a good view of the lake. Campsites are $13, and the campground is open May to mid-October. In the winter, there are hiking and cross-country skiing opportunities. In the summer a gravel-covered beach is open for swimming and there are a few boat launches. The park is reached via Hwy 54A.

Towne Motel (☎ 315-536-4474, 206 Elm St) is a low-end motel in town. It's worn but not dirty or unpleasant. Rooms come with phones and air-con. Singles/doubles are $37/47.

Colonial Motel (☎ 315-536-3056, 800-724-3008, 175 W Lake Rd) has unremarkable rooms, but it's nicer than the Towne Motel and is across from the lake. Take 14A south to W Lake Drive, then go 1.4 miles to get there. The rooms are $75, or $85 with kitchenette.

Fox Inn (☎ 315-536-3101, 158 Main St) contains four rooms with private baths, a two-bedroom suite, and, best of all, the ghosts of two former inhabitants, according to the 19th-century diary of a Penn Yan dentist. You can't miss its yellow facade and two-story white columns. There's a huge garden out back. Single/double rooms are $80/90 and a large suite is $150. Rates include a full breakfast.

The local dining choices include *Lloyd's Ltd* (☎ 315-536-9029, 3 Main St), which sells pub food like hamburgers, onion rings ($3), sandwiches ($4) and pizza ($5 to $16). It also has a vast selection of imported bottled beer.

CANANDAIGUA

Canandaigua sits on the northern tip of Canandaigua Lake, at the intersection of Routes 5 and 20. The name Canandaigua comes from the Seneca '*Kanandarque*,' which means 'Chosen Spot,' and the site was the main village in the Seneca nation. In the 19th century, this was where Susan B Anthony was tried for voting, found guilty and fined $100. She refused to pay and the authorities didn't have the nerve to imprison her. When the Susan B Anthony dollar coin was issued in the 1980s, the Canandaigua National Bank paid her fine with 100 of the new coins. (Despite her legacy, though, this dollar coin has never caught on with the American public.)

The late Victorian-looking town, oddly enough, gets more interesting the farther north you go from the lake. You'll find particularly nice houses along Main St and on the side streets around the Sonnenberg Mansion, which is a handsome country estate and Canandaigua's principal tourist attraction.

A 50-acre estate, **Sonnenberg Gardens & Mansion** (☎ 716-394-4922), 151 Charlotte St, includes nine formal gardens, an arboretum and an 1887 stone mansion with a tasting room for the Canandaigua Wine Co. The grounds are regarded as some of the finest Victorian gardens in the US. The site is open daily from 9:30 am to 5:30 pm, mid-May to mid-October. Admission is $7/5/4 for adults/seniors/children ages six to 16.

While you're in town, you can also visit the **Granger Homestead & Carriage Museum** (☎ 716-394-1472), 295 N Main St, a magnificent 1816 Federal-style house with a collection of carriages. It's open Tuesday to Saturday from 10 am to 5 pm and Sunday from 1 pm to 5 pm, May to October.

For more tourist information, contact the chamber of commerce (☎ 716-394-4400), 113 S Main St, which is in an A-frame building on the south side of Route 20 east of town.

Places to Stay & Eat

The Route 20 commercial strip east of town has a string of cheap and uninteresting motels. Try the **Budget Lodge** (☎ 716-394-2800), which has doubles with one/two beds for $49/69.

For good pizza, wings, subs and pasta, try **Pudgie's Pizza & Barbecue Shack** (☎ 716-394-6720, 520 N Main St), open daily from 11 am to 10 pm. You'll find the usual complement on Routes 5 and 20 as they pass by town.

GENEVA

Geneva lies at the intersection of Routes 20 and 14 at the northern tip of Seneca Lake. It's the home of Hobart & William Smith College, which sits on a low bluff overlooking the lake. It is a convenient place to stay if you're passing through the area, but the town offers little to see. However, if you're looking for some entertainment, two downtown movie theaters (one on Exchange St, one on Seneca St) show decent films.

For tourist information, contact the Geneva Area Chamber of Commerce (☎ 315-789-1776), 1 Lakeside Drive. It's open weekdays from 9 am to 5 pm.

Places to Stay & Eat

Cheerful Valley Campground (☎ 315-781-1222), on Route 14, has 160 sites ($18) near the river. Services include a coin laundry and pool. The campground is 7 miles north of town on Route 14. It's less than 1 mile north of I-90 exit 42.

If Geneva is known for anything, it's the **Belhurst Castle** (☎ 315-781-0201), on Route 14 south of town. Belhurst is a large, red 1889 Medina stone castle on the lake. It was originally built for Carrie Harron Collins, a descendent of Henry Clay. The 13 rooms come complete with polished woodwork, stone and plaster walls, solid oak doors and gas fireplaces. Guests get a continental breakfast in the winter but nothing extra during summer. Room rates are $85 to $240 in the off-season, $125 to $315 during peak times. The restaurant on the main floor serves lunch-time sandwiches and pasta from $5 to $7 and fish for about $10. Dinners are lavish, like the lakeside surroundings, and prices range from $15 to $25.

The *farmers' market* (666 S Exchange St), at the Geneva Recreation Complex, offers a good selection of local produce and baked goods. It's open Thursday from 7:30 to 11:30 am, late June to mid-October.

SENECA FALLS

Seneca Falls is on Route 20, 3 miles west of Cayuga Lake. In 1915, the 43-foot high falls, along with 60 homes and 116 businesses and factories, were flooded to make way for the state's Barge Canal – a spur of the Erie Canal. For area information, stop by the Heritage Area Visitors Center (☎ 315-568-2703), 115 Fall St. The center, adjacent to the canal, features exhibits on the fight for women's suffrage.

Things to See & Do

The **Women's Rights National Historical Park** is actually a federal complex composed of a visitors' center (☎ 315-568-2991), 136 Fall St; what's left of the Wesleyan Chapel, site of the 1848 Women's Rights Convention; the M'Clintock House in nearby Waterloo; and the Elizabeth Cady Stanton

House in Seneca Falls. The Stanton House, 32 Washington St, has been restored in the spirit of historical accuracy. The original wallpaper has been copied and replaced, and the few pieces of original furniture that could be located, including her writing desk and piano, have been placed in the house. Missing is a wing of the house that once held the kitchen.

The historical park is open daily from 9 am to 5 pm. In the summer the Suffrage Press Print Shop is also open. Admission to the visitors' center is $2, which includes a short lecture about the history of the suffrage movement. For $3, you can also take a 30-minute ranger-led tour of the Stanton House.

The **National Women's Hall of Fame** (☎ 315-568-8060), 76 Fall St, is a small private museum with large wall plaques describing the achievements of an expanding number of women in the arts, athletics and humanitarian fields – everyone from Elizabeth Bailey and 'Mother' Seton to Jane Adams, Marian Anderson, Sojourner Truth and Emily Dickinson. It's a good place to come if you like a quiet, reflective museum experience. The museum is open daily from 9:30 am to 5 pm, May to October. From November to April, it's open Wednesday to Saturday from 10 am to 4 pm, Sunday noon to 4 pm. Admission is $3/1 for adults/students, or $7 per family.

The **Montezuma National Wildlife Refuge** (☎ 315-568-5987), about 5 miles east of Seneca Falls, sits at the north end of Cayuga Lake. Once part of a broad marsh system that's largely been drained, the refuge is still a major stopover point for waterfowl on their way south from Canada. Because it's in the middle of a busy flyway, it sees a lot of avian traffic. From the middle of September until the ponds freeze, Canada geese and ducks stop by, many of them arriving in November. From mid-August to mid-October (with a mid-September peak), shorebirds like herons, egrets and sandpipers come through. From late February to April, Canada and snow geese and some ducks come back. Mid-May is peak warbler season.

The refuge is on Routes 5 and 20. To get there from Route 89, turn east onto Routes 5 and 20. From I-90, take exit 41 to Route 414 south to Route 318 east to Routes 5 and 20 east. For more information, visit the website www.fws.gov/r5mnwr.

Places to Stay & Eat

Cayuga Lake State Park (☎ 315-568-5163), on Route 89, contains almost 300 sites ($15 to $17). It's open from May to November. To get there, take Lake Rd east from town for 3 miles, then go 4 miles south on Route 89.

Holiday Inn of Waterloo/Seneca Falls (☎ 315-539-5011, 2468 Route 414), in Waterloo, features a heated outdoor pool, restaurant and lounge. Single/double rooms cost $99/129 in the peak summer season, $69/89 the rest of the year. About 5 miles west of Seneca Falls, the hotel is one block north of Route 20.

Downtown Deli (☎ 315-568-9943, 53 Fall St) offers a long menu of big sandwiches and subs for around $4. Standard deli-diner

---

> ### Elizabeth Cady Stanton
>
> Seneca Falls would be an unexciting town to visit except that it's the birthplace of the organized women's movement in the USA, thanks to Elizabeth Cady Stanton, who moved to Seneca Falls from Boston in 1847. While her husband Henry was away, Cady Stanton managed her family and home. On July 9, 1848, when gathered with a group of friends, she expressed discontent about the confinement of women to 'the women's sphere.' A couple of days later, the group met at Mary Ann M'Clintock's home and drafted a *Declaration of Sentiments* modeled on the *Declaration of Independence*. The declaration called for the right to vote and said that 'all men and women are created equal.' On July 19 and 20, 1848, more than 300 women and men gathered at the Wesleyan Chapel on Fall St for the first Women's Rights Convention, where 68 women and 32 men signed the declaration.
>
>

items include hot pastrami, chili, pizza and (on the children's menu) macaroni and cheese.

SKANEATELES

Picturesque, small and quiet, Skaneateles ('skinny-atlas'), on Route 20, sits at the top of one of the prettiest, deepest and smallest of the Finger Lakes. There's not much to do here, which makes it attractive to a lot of people. A mail-boat cruise (☎ 315-685-8500) makes the delivery rounds beginning at 10 am on summer weekdays. The three-hour cruise, with running commentary, costs $21 per person.

The town has a number of good eateries, inns and motels, most in the small and walkable downtown area. Two in particular represent the range of peculiar possibilities here. **Sherwood Inn** (☎ 315-685-3405, 26 W Genesee St) is a classic New York colonial inn that dates back to 1807, when it was a stagecoach stop. Each of the 20 rooms is a bit different, though all feature antique furnishings and private baths. Prices range from $90 to $160. It's open year-round, and children are welcome.

At the other end of the Skaneateles spectrum, **Doug's Fish Fry** (☎ 315-685-3288, 8 Jordan St) is good, greasy, loud and cheap ($4 for a big fish sandwich and fries). The fish is trucked in from Boston daily, and the menu includes seafood gumbo, steamed clams, baked beans and fries. Doug's is open daily from 11 am to 10 pm.

SYRACUSE

Syracuse (population 152,000), laid out around the southern end of Onondaga Lake, stands in sharp contrast to the more pastoral portions of the Finger Lakes region. The salt industry that prospered here in the 19th century made Syracuse a working-class town at heart. With the completion of the Erie Canal in 1825, the city's image as an industrial center took hold.

Syracuse is enlivened by the presence of Syracuse University's large student body, but commerce and industry still dominate the city's image. Railroads and highways crisscross each other. The downtown skyline is really more of a 'brickline,' with striking examples of Victorian Gothic, art deco and limestone Romanesque. There's no mistaking Syracuse for suburbia.

History

The Onondaga Indians chose Syracuse as the site of the capital of the Iroquois Confederacy in 1570. French Jesuits came into the region in the mid-1600s and established a mission called Fort Sainte Marie de Gannentaha in 1656, which they abandoned two years later after repeated conflicts with the Onondaga.

Indian guides showed French Father Simon LeMoyne a local spring that they believed was occupied by an unfriendly spirit. LeMoyne saw the spirit of an untapped resource after tasting the briny water. Commercial salt production began in the last decade of the 18th century, when newcomers settled around Onondaga Lake. In 1797, the state administered (and taxed) the salt fields and leased them out to producers who made salt by boiling or evaporation. Today, you can visit the Salt Museum, which describes the process as it took place in 'Salt City.'

Syracuse was chosen as a name for the city in 1805, when the city's first postmaster noted that the Greek city of the same name in Sicily had been founded around salt springs. In the mid-19th century, spurred by the success of the Erie Canal, Syracuse became a manufacturing and transportation center. In the 1960s and '70s, however, it suffered the same fate as many of its rust belt neighbors; employers and workers discovered the suburbs and the downtown decayed. Today, the Armory Square neighborhood, a collection of trendy shops and cafes, represents the downtown's revival. A symbol of Syracuse's transformation, a pre-Civil War National Guard Armory now houses the Rubenstein Museum of Science and Technology, home of the Bristol Imax Omnitheater.

Orientation & Information

Salina ('sa-**lie**-na') St divides the east side of the city from the west, and Erie Blvd splits the city's northern and southern halves. I-81

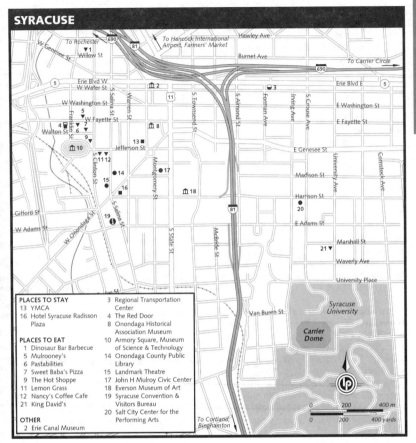

SYRACUSE

PLACES TO STAY
13 YMCA
16 Hotel Syracuse Radisson Plaza

PLACES TO EAT
1 Dinosaur Bar Barbecue
5 Mulrooney's
6 Pastabilities
7 Sweet Baba's Pizza
9 The Hot Shoppe
11 Lemon Grass
12 Nancy's Coffee Cafe
21 King David's

OTHER
2 Erie Canal Museum
3 Regional Transportation Center
4 The Red Door
8 Onondaga Historical Association Museum
10 Armory Square, Museum of Science & Technology
14 Onondaga County Public Library
15 Landmark Theatre
17 John H Mulroy Civic Center
18 Everson Museum of Art
19 Syracuse Convention & Visitors Bureau
20 Salt City Center for the Performing Arts

and I-690 pass right through town, to the dismay of many.

The Syracuse Convention & Visitors Bureau (☎ 315-470-1910, 800-234-4797), 572 S Salina St, provides walking tour maps of downtown. Its website is at www.syracusecvb .org and it is open weekdays 8:30 am to 5 pm. There's also a Tourist Information Center at Carousel Center, a big shopping mall off I-81 north at the Hiawatha exit. The Erie Canal Museum (☎ 315-471-0593), 318 Erie Blvd E, also houses a visitors' center.

In addition to numerous banks and ATMs in the downtown area, the major malls (Carousel Center, Shoppingtown) also have some ATMs.

The main post office (☎ 315-452-3401) is at 5640 E Taft Rd.

For travel agency services, members of AAA can go to the main area office (☎ 315-451-2000, 800-222-4357), 7485 Henry Clay Blvd in Liverpool, just northwest of Syracuse on Route 370. The office is open Monday to Friday from 9 am to 5:30 pm (later on Thursday) and from 9 am to 3 pm on Saturday.

Onondaga County's public library (☎ 315-435-1900) is at 441 S Salina St.

The *Post-Standard* and the *Herald-Journal* are the local daily newspapers; the Sunday paper is called the *Herald American*. For arts and entertainment information, consult the *Syracuse New Times* and *The Guide*. The *Pink Paper* is a free bimonthly newsletter with articles and information of interest to the gay and lesbian community.

Things to See & Do

Erie Canal Museum The museum (☎ 315-471-0593), 318 Erie Blvd E at Montgomery St, is housed in the 1850 Weighlock Building. Boats were once towed along the canal (now Erie Blvd) into the building; locks at the front and rear were closed and the water drained out. Each boat then lay on a huge wooden cradle and scale, which weighed it and determined the tax. The museum features a restored 65-foot canal boat that you can board and explore and a 12-minute video on the canal's history. It's open daily from 10 am to 5 pm, and admission is free.

Onondaga Historical Association Museum This excellent small museum (☎ 315-428-1864), 321 Montgomery St, is a short walk from the Erie Canal Museum, and history buffs should make time for both. Nineteenth-century fashion, old photos, Iroquois culture and antique typewriters are among the featured displays. The museum is open Tuesday through Friday from noon to 4 pm, Saturday from 11 am to 4 pm. Admission is free.

Everson Museum of Art Syracuse's art museum (☎ 315-474-6064), 401 Harrison St, includes a fine collection of ceramics and American art. Noted modern architect IM Pei designed the striking and austere 1968 building. It's open Tuesday through Friday and Sunday from noon to 5 pm, Saturday from 10 am to 5 pm.

Sainte Marie among the Iroquois This living history museum (☎ 315-453-6767), in Onondaga Lake Park on the northeastern side of Onondaga Lake, recreates the 'fateful meeting' of the Iroquois Nation and the French in the 17th century. The living-history exhibit features costumed interpreters who portray Jesuit missionaries, blacksmiths, cooks and other workers of the time; visitors can talk to any of them in French or English about their work – from converting the local Indians to Christianity to hammering horseshoes. It's popular with children, if a bit bizarre.

The Sainte Marie complex is open Wednesday to Thursday from 10 am to 5 pm, Sunday from 12:30 to 5 pm. To get there, take I-81 north to exit 24 (Onondaga Lake Pkwy/Route 370 West). Go about 1½ miles to the entrance on the right. Admission is $3.50/1.50 for adults/children ages five to 14.

Salt Museum Opposite Sainte Marie, the Salt Museum (☎ 315-453-6715) is built on the site of a former salt works in Onondaga Lake Park. The small wooden building displays the salt-making process, in which brine was pumped into masses of boiling kettles or evaporation pans through wooden pipes, which wouldn't rust. The museum is open daily from 10 am to 5 pm, May to mid-October. Admission is 50¢.

Milton J Rubenstein Museum of Science & Technology (MOST) Housed in the old armory at the corner of Franklin and W Jefferson Sts, this museum (☎ 315-425-9068) has several exhibits designed for children, including the Silverman Planetarium, which features daily star shows. The MOST's newest edition is the Bristol Omnitheater, New York state's only IMAX Dome Theater. The museum is open Sunday to Thursday from 11 am to 5 pm, Friday and Saturday from 9:30 am to 5 pm. Admission is $4.75/3.75 for adults/seniors and children. The IMAX films and planetarium shows cost extra.

Special Events

The New York State Fair (☎ 315-487-7711), with lots of food and music (and salt), takes place at the Empire Expo Center in Syracuse, just west of I-690, for 12 days, including the Labor Day weekend in September.

Places to Stay

The HI-AYH *Downing International Hostel* (☎ *315-472-5788, 535 Oak St*) is a mile northeast of downtown in a residential neighborhood. It's a big house with 31 beds in several male and female dorm rooms, a couple of private rooms, a large basement kitchen and a small library. There's a 9 am to 5 pm lockout and an 11 pm curfew. The cost is $15 ($12 for members). Sleeping bags are not permitted, but bedding is only $1 per stay.

Also for budget travelers, the downtown *YMCA* (☎ *315-474-6851, 340 Montgomery St*) costs $30 a night or $86 a week for a room with a shared bath; it's fairly clean, if a bit run-down. Long-term residents often fill the place, so it may be hard to get a room.

There are a few moderately priced motels at Carrier Circle. (To reach the area, take I-690 east about 2½ miles to Thompson Rd north.) The *John Milton Inn* (☎ *315-463-8555*), on Carrier Circle, has about 50 standard rooms for $35 to $60. The nearby *Red Roof Inn* (☎ *315-437-3309, 800-843-7663*) charges $35 to $55 for its rooms. There are similarly priced places along Thompson Rd.

The *Wyndham Syracuse* (☎ *315-432-0200, 800-782-9847*) is the luxury hotel at Carrier Circle. It has a heated indoor-outdoor pool, sauna, whirlpool, tanning salon and more. Weekday single/double rooms are $129/139; weekend rates are slightly lower.

Downtown, the *Hotel Syracuse Radisson Plaza* (☎ *315-422-5121, 800-333-3333, 500 S Warren St*) was recently remodeled and expanded. Built in the 1920s, the hotel is registered with Historic Hotels of America. Room rates start at $109.

On a quiet residential street, the *Bed & Breakfast Wellington* (☎ *315-474-3641, 800-724-5006, 707 Danforth St*) is housed in a 1914 Tudor home designed by Ward Wellington Ward. The sturdy wood-and-stucco house contains a fireplace and four porches, as well as a fridge stocked with sodas and juices. Each of the four rooms has a private bath. Room prices range from $55 to $95, including a full breakfast.

Places to Eat

Without question, Syracuse's most unique eatery is the funky *Dinosaur Bar Barbecue* (☎ *315-476-4937, 246 W Willow St*), at Franklin St. This blues bar and restaurant attracts an unlikely mix of bikers, tattooed waitresses, students, business professionals and anyone else who likes to eat ribs while gazing at the walls crowded with old signs, car parts and bumper stickers ('No Feeding the Cooks'). Most dishes are under $8, including racks of ribs (pork or beef), chili, red beans and sausage, chicken sandwiches and homemade desserts. At night, the Dinosaur draws crowds with live blues and recorded music.

The Armory Square area is a trendy restaurant row that includes several cafes and restaurants within a few blocks of each other. *Pastabilities* (☎ *315-474-1153, 311 S Franklin St*) makes a wide variety of its own pastas in unusual flavors, such as paprika lasagna. The dining area is a crisply designed narrow room lined with booths and a bar; music in a garden courtyard adds to the summertime atmosphere. Lunch and dinner are served Monday through Saturday.

Mulrooney's (☎ *315-479-6163, 239 W Fayette St*) is a sports bar with pub food that's served weekdays from 11:30 am to 3 pm. Come hungry – the servings are plentiful. Prices range from $1.50 (appetizers) to $8.75 (full lunch). The pub is open from 11:30 am to 2 am weekdays and from 3 pm to 2 am on Saturday.

For good coffee, espresso drinks, homemade gourmet desserts and a good view of the people coming and going around Armory Square, try *Nancy's Coffee Cafe* (☎ *315-476-6550, 290 W Jefferson St*). Nancy's is open Monday through Thursday from 10 am to 9 pm, Friday and Saturday from 10 am to midnight.

For excellent (and expensive) Thai cuisine, try *Lemon Grass* (☎ *315-475-1111, 238 W Jefferson St*), near the Armory. It's open for lunch and dinner Monday through Saturday and for dinner only on Sunday.

Sweet Baba's Pizza (☎ *315-472-2227, 218 Walton St*) offers excellent wood-fired pizza, with toppings ranging from the traditional to smoked salmon with brie, for $5 to $8, in addition to a good in-house dessert menu. Sweet Baba's opening hours are Monday through Thursday from 11 am to 10 pm, Friday and Saturday from 11 am to midnight, Sunday from 3 to 9 pm.

If you like it hot, check out **The Hot Shoppe** (☎ 315-424-1010, 142 Walton St), a Cajun-Caribbean-Southwestern deli with spicy concoctions from around the world. It's open daily from 8 am to 6 pm, Friday and Saturday from 8 am to 9 pm.

The Syracuse University campus area, particularly Marshall St, has dozens of mostly fast-food outlets. One of the more interesting eateries here is **King David's** (☎ 315-471-5000, 129 Marshall St), which serves good Middle Eastern dishes, including steak shawarma, stuffed cabbage, grape leaves and baba ghanoush.

You'll also find dozens of restaurants, many of them chains, along Erie Blvd E. For the freshest food, head to the regional farmers' market (see Shopping, below).

Entertainment

The Syracuse Symphony (☎ 315-424-8200) and the Syracuse Opera (☎ 315-475-5915) perform at the **John H Mulroy Civic Center** (☎ 315-435-3155, 411 Montgomery St).

The **Landmark Theatre** (☎ 315-475-7979, 362 S Salina St) is a flourishing 1928 architectural leftover from Hollywood's make-believe tropical-vaudeville movie-palace days. The Landmark showcases everything from touring stage shows to rock-and-roll concerts.

Like the Landmark Theater, the **Salt City Center for the Performing Arts** (☎ 315-474-1122, 601 S Crouse Ave) presents musicals, dramas and comedies year-round. **Syracuse Stage** (☎ 315-424-8210, 820 E Genessee St), the area's only professional theater, presents seven main-stage productions each year. The **Famous Artists Series Ltd** (☎ 315-424-8210) makes its home at the Onondaga Country Library (☎ 315-435-1900), adjacent to Hotel Syracuse Radisson Plaza. It brings nationally touring Broadway shows to town (most performances take place at the various performing centers around town).

The Red Door (☎ 315-472-2665, 314 S Franklin St) is a live music and dance club inside a warehouse across from the Pastabilities restaurant in Armory Square. The music, which plays Thursday to Sunday from 9 pm to 2 am, ranges from blues to hardcore metal and acid jazz. During the summer a courtyard barbecue pit adds to the festive atmosphere.

For live music, try **Dinosaur Bar Barbecue** (see Places to Eat), a Syracuse landmark that features live blues and all-around honky-tonk surroundings.

Shopping

The hungry and the curious alike should stop in at the Central New York Regional Farmers' Market (☎ 315-422-8647). Originally a WPA project, the market dates from 1938. It's still one of the largest and oldest regional markets in the country, with more than 300 stalls selling agricultural products from the US and abroad. You can buy baked goods, jams, cheeses, a huge selection of New York state apples, all types of produce and more. The May-to-October period is the busiest. The market is open from 7 am to 2 pm on Saturday year-round; from May to October, it's also open from 11 am to 7 pm on Thursday. To get there, take I-81 to exit 23 (Hiawatha Blvd) and exit at the market.

Getting There & Away

Hancock International Airport (☎ 315-454-4330; ground transportation ☎ 455-6351) offers daily service by a number of airlines, including American, Continental, Delta, Mohawk, Northwest, TW Express, United and US Airways. Regular fares from Philadelphia and Chicago are about $400 roundtrip, but weekend specials can range from $99 (Philadelphia) to $168 (Chicago). The airport is north of the city; take I-81 and exit at 27.

A new Regional Transportation Center (☎ 315-478-1936) houses both the bus and train station. It's served by Greyhound/Trailways (☎ 800-231-2222) and Amtrak (☎ 800-872-7245). Located on the north side of town, near the farmers' market, the center is only a five-minute drive from downtown.

You'll find a visitors' information center located there.

Those traveling by car will have no trouble reaching Syracuse. Two major highways cross it: I-81 and I-90 (the NY State Thruway).

Getting Around

The Centro bus system (☎ 315-442-3400) runs all over the city, with central stopping points at the downtown four-corners intersection of Fayette and Salina Sts, as well as at the Regional Transportation Center (see above).

If you need a taxi anywhere in the Syracuse area, call Dependable Taxi (☎ 315-475-0030). It costs about $14 to get from the airport to downtown.

AROUND SYRACUSE

Syracuse and New York state maintain several exhibits, parks and centers dedicated to the Erie Canal. Many of these offer recreational possibilities. Twelve miles west of Syracuse, the **Erie Canal Parkway** (☎ 315-689-3278), in Jordon, is a 7-mile stretch of land and towpath along the original canal route. Three miles east of the parkway, the 300-acre **Camillus Erie Canal Park** (☎ 315-672-5110) includes another 7 miles of navigable canal. In the summer, the park hosts a boat-building display. From Syracuse, take I-690 west to Route 695 toward Auburn/Camillus and exit at Camillus. Follow the signs to the park (5250 DeVoe Rd).

East of Syracuse, **Old Erie Canal State Park** (☎ 315-687-7821) encompasses 36 miles of enlarged canal stretching from the DeWitt Canal Center (☎ 315-471-0593), 10 miles east of Syracuse, to the Erie Canal Village (☎ 315-337-3999), 30 miles east of Syracuse in Rome. This outdoor living-history museum, situated on an original portion of the canal, is open from May to September. In between, you'll find **Chittenango Landing Canal Boat Museum** (☎ 315-687-3801), about 12 miles east of Syracuse, on the site of a dry dock where canal boat construction and repair took place. The museum (and interpretive center) is open weekends from 1 pm to 4 pm, April to June;

daily from 10 am to 4 pm, July to September; and the first Saturday of the month from 1 to 4 pm, October to March. From Syracuse, take I-690 east to Route 290 east and exit at Fayetteville onto Genessee St. Follow signs to the boat museum.

Other area attractions include the **Turning Stone Casino** (☎ 315-361-7711), which is 35 miles east of Syracuse in Verona. The first legalized gambling casino in the state is owned and operated by the Oneida Indian Nation. To get there, take I-90 (the NY State Thruway) to exit 33 and follow the bright signs to the nearby casino.

Canal Cruises

Mid-Lakes Navigation Co (☎ 315-685-8500, 800-545-4318) offers a variety of Erie Canal cruises from mid-April to early November, depending on the infamous weather (which includes much precipitation). The shortest excursions are the lunch tours ($19) and champagne dinner cruises ($35); a Sunday brunch cruise costs $30. A better value might be the four-hour cruise for $29 ($20 for children), with a buffet lunch that includes salads and sandwiches.

For the more adventurous, two and three-day overnight cruises are available. These range from about $250 to $375 per person, including all meals and transportation to and from area hotels. Two-day cruises, in particular, sell out early; reservations are necessary during the busy summer season.

Cruises depart from Dutchman's Landing, about 7 miles northwest of Syracuse via Route 370. From Syracuse, take I-81 to I-90 west to exit 38 (Route 57). Turn left to reach Route 370, then right at River Rd and right at Hillsdale Rd.

Beaver Lake Nature Center

For those who enjoy outdoor activities, the Beaver Lake Nature Center (☎ 315-638-2519), 8477 E Mud Lake Rd, Baldwinsville, is northwest of Syracuse (between Plainville and Baldwinsville) via Route 370. It is especially child-friendly place. The relatively small county preserve (600 acres) is a resting stop for Canada geese and parents and children fascinated by the outdoors. Naturalists lead trail tours and conduct workshops in canoe making and maple sugaring. Many of the activities here are free. Organized day camps for children are offered throughout the summer, and the cost ranges from $50 for a half-day camp to $95 for a full day. Admission is $1 per car.

ROCHESTER

Rochester (population 230,000) spreads across and around the Genesee River in western New York, a few miles south of Lake Ontario. The city has a small, modern (but somewhat deserted at night) downtown encircled by an expressway and a number of neighborhoods with old homes and mansions from its industrial glory days. Rochester is home to Eastman Kodak, Bausch & Lomb and the Eastman School of Music. Xerox's manufacturing presence adds to the city's high-tech image. But the town also contains several fine museums, including George Eastman House and International Museum of Photography and Film.

History

The Seneca Indians called the Genesee River *Casconchiagon* (River of Many Falls).

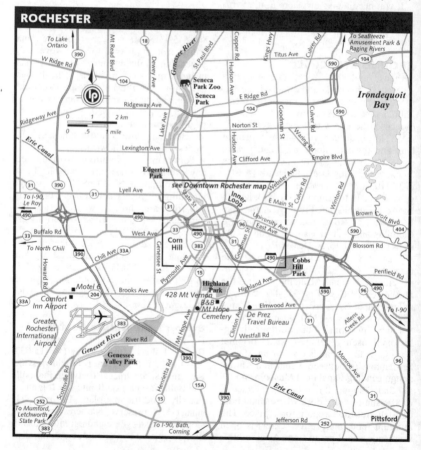

ROCHESTER

The power of the river and its 96-foot downtown waterfall fueled Rochester's early industries. But the city grew slowly from 1789, when the first European settlers arrived, until the 1824 arrival of the Erie Canal, which passed through what is now Broad St. The canal turned Rochester into a booming mill town. So many flour mills sprang up along the Genesee River in the early 19th century that the town was called 'Flour City.' By mid-century, the nickname evolved to 'Flower City,' as nurseries and horticulture supplanted flour mills as the major Rochester industry. The city's impressive garden and park system dates to these early efforts.

During its 19th-century glory days, Rochester attracted several important cultural figures. The abolitionist Frederick Douglass published his *North Star* newspaper here beginning in 1847, and Susan B Anthony was arrested for voting here in 1872.

Today, the city happily bills itself as the 'world's image center,' with some justification. In 1853, John Bausch and Henry Lomb opened a small optical shop that grew to global dimensions. In the 1880s, a curious bank clerk named George Eastman experimented with photographic techniques in his mother's kitchen; the Eastman Kodak Company followed. Even the Xerox Corporation got its start in Rochester, as the Haloid Company in 1906.

The prosperity of Kodak and others benefited Rochester throughout most of the latter 19th and 20th centuries. Beginning in the 1960s, however, Rochester experienced the hard economic times of many industrial cities, earning its place along the rust belt. During the late '90s, the economy rebounded, and the city has a lively feel to it.

Orientation & Information

The central downtown area of Rochester is encircled by the 'Inner Loop,' part of I-490. The Genesee River runs north-south through the western portion of downtown. The High Falls are two blocks north of the Inner Loop. Park Ave, a popular restaurant

and shopping district, is just east of downtown. East Ave is Rochester's 'museum and mansion row.'

The Greater Rochester Visitors' Association (☎ 716-546-3070, 800-677-7282), 45 East Ave, maintains a 24-hour events line (☎ 716-546-6810) and has a website at www.visitrochester.com. The office is open weekdays from 8:30 am to 5:30 pm (until 6 pm from mid-May to mid-October), Saturday 9 am to 5 pm, Sunday 10 am to 3 pm.

You'll find a number of banks and ATMs throughout downtown. Wegmans, a supermarket chain with stores all over the place, has a 24-hour ATM service.

The main post office (☎ 716-272-5952) is at 1335 Jefferson Rd; the downtown post office is located in the Midtown Plaza, off Clinton Ave.

For travel services (including maps), AAA members can contact the local office (☎ 716-461-4660), 777 Clinton Ave S. DePrez Travel Bureau (☎ 716-442-8900), 145 Rue deVille, is a full-service travel agency.

World Wide News (☎ 716-546-7140), 100 St Paul St, features a large selection of domestic and foreign newspapers. Brownbag Bookshop (☎ 716-271-3494), 678 Monroe Ave, and Gutenberg Books (☎ 716-442-4620), 675 Monroe Ave, sells used books and are worth a visit. Barnes & Noble (☎ 716-586-6020), 3349 Monroe Ave, is at the corner of Clover Ave, southeast of the downtown loop.

Rochester's main public library is the Rundell Library (☎ 716-428-7300), 115 South Avenue, a block south of the Hyatt and Sheraton hotels. It's open daily.

The daily newspaper is the *Democrat & Chronicle*. Pick up the *Freetime* for comprehensive entertainment listings.

The Center at High Falls

The center (☎ 716-325-2030), 60 Brown's Race St, sits on the site of a 19th-century industrial water diversion, or 'race,' from the Genesee River. Interactive 3-D exhibits trace Rochester's development from its founding in the early 1800s. A computer-graphic video telegraphs thousands of years of geology and natural history into a

NEW YORK

DOWNTOWN ROCHESTER

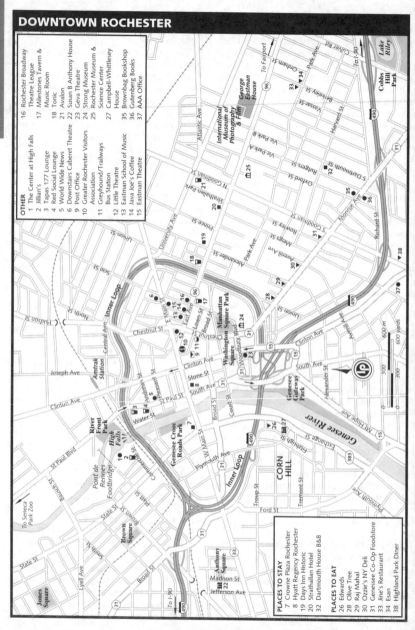

OTHER
1 The Center at High Falls
2 Jillian's
3 Tapas 177 Lounge
4 Red Social Lounge
5 World Wide News
6 Downstairs Cabaret Theatre
10 Greater Rochester Visitors Association
11 Greyhound/Trailways Bus Station
12 Little Theatre
13 Eastman School of Music
14 Java Joe's Coffee
15 Eastman Theatre
16 Rochester Broadway Theatre League
17 Milestones Tavern & Music Room
18 Tonic
21 Avalon
22 Susan B Anthony House
23 Geva Theatre
24 Strong Museum
25 Rochester Museum & Science Center
27 Campbell-Whittlesey House
35 Brownbag Bookshop
36 Gutenberg Books
37 AAA Office

PLACES TO STAY
7 Crowne Plaza Rochester
8 Hyatt Regency Rochester
19 Days Inn Historic
20 Strathallan Hotel
32 Dartmouth House B&B

PLACES TO EAT
26 Edwards
28 Olive Tree
29 Raj Mahal
30 Ozzie's NY Deli
31 Genessee Co-Op Foodstore
33 Jine's Restaurant
34 Esan
38 Highland Park Diner

minute's imaginary taxi ride through Rochester's past. Most of the exhibits are especially suitable for children.

The center overlooks the 96-foot High Falls, which Sam Patch and his reluctant pet bear jumped over in 1829 (the bear made it, Patch didn't). Patch gained attention earlier that year with two successful jumps into the gorge at the foot of Niagara Falls.

The Pont de Rennes, a pedestrian bridge next to the center, spans the Genesee River opposite the falls. During the summer, the center puts on a laser and light display that dazzles the chasm walls and cascading water. This free event, held on Thursday, Friday and Saturday, can be enjoyed from May until early September.

George Eastman House & International Museum of Photography & Film

The house that Kodak built, 900 East Ave, is a 1905 Colonial-Revival mansion. Daily docent tours begin at 10:30 am and 2 pm (only 2 pm on Sundays), but you can easily explore the exhibits on your own with a self-guided map.

The museum (☎ 716-271-3361), connected to the house by a long corridor filled with photos and history, boasts the world's largest collection of historic films, photographs, cameras and books about photography and film. There are rotating exhibits of original photographs and equipment – such as the one revealing a cross section of a four-snapshot automatic portrait booth.

Serious students of photography can also make an appointment to view some of 400,000 photographs dating from 1839 to the present (via videodisk or actual images), the motion-picture collection of 23,000 films and 5 million publicity stills and posters, the 15,000 cameras and pieces of equipment in the 'technology vault' and the 43,000 titles in the Menschel Library. Visitors can also step outside to take in the restored gardens on this 12-acre estate.

Eastman House is open Tuesday through Saturday from 10 am to 5 pm, Thursday

George Eastman

George Eastman was born in 1854 in Waterville, NY, and his family moved to Rochester in 1860. Eastman's version of an American success story began when he dropped out of school at 14 to take a $3-a-week messenger job to help support his family. In 1874, he began working as a bank clerk for $15 a week. Three years later, Eastman bought a cumbersome camera and, being a curious fellow, began to investigate ways to simplify the development process. In 1880, he invented and patented a dry-plate coating machine. A year later, with the financial support of Henry Strong, Eastman opened a factory to make dry plates.

In 1884, Eastman Dry Plate and Film Co patented a rollable film alternative to glass negatives. Four years later, the first Kodak (Eastman made up the name) cameras were sold for $125. They came with 100 exposures and had to be sent back to the company to be developed. The relatively high price of the camera didn't deter people who were fascinated with the new technology. Within 10 years, Eastman was a millionaire, and soon after that, a multimillionaire. During his lifetime, he gave over $100 million to charities. George Eastman died in 1932.

from 10 am to 8 pm, Sunday from 1 to 5 pm. Admission is $6.50/5/2.50 for adults/seniors and students/children ages five to 12.

Strong Museum

The Strong Museum (☎ 716-263-2700), which is at 1 Manhattan Square at the corner of Monroe Ave and Woodbury Blvd, is both a hands-on history center for children and the home of an enormous collection of middle-class Americana. A working 1918 carousel and an operating 1950s diner at the museum's glass atrium entrance set the tone for a whimsical and interactive learning environment made up of Sesame Street characters, whaling ships, cooking shows and time labs.

NEW YORK

MICHAEL CLARK

Wheee! Carousel at the Strong Museum

The museum also features several excellent exhibitions on popular culture. For example, past exhibits included the history of Jell-O and an exhibit on American sign language. The collection of Americana and folk art – toys, dolls and doll houses and household furnishings – was accumulated by Margaret Woodbury Strong. Strong's father made his money in the buggy-whip business and then smartly invested very early in George Eastman's new photography industry. Margaret Strong used her own wealth to acquire about 300,000 objects (27,000 dolls alone), many of which are displayed on a rotating basis in row after row of glass cases.

Although it's not officially described as a children's museum, the Strong is very popular with kids, probably because it offers a great deal for them to do – including trying on clothes from other eras. But it does manage to bridge the generation gap with such ongoing exhibits as 'When Barbie Dated GI Joe – Toying with the Cold War.' Plastic godzillas, trigger-happy cowboys,

dainty dolls and tiny cooking sets from the 1950s and '60s speak to period stereotypes of boys and girls.

The museum is open Monday through Thursday from 10 am to 5 pm, Friday from 10 am to 8 pm, Saturday from 10 am to 5 pm, Sunday from noon to 5 pm. Admission is $6/5/4 for adults/seniors and students/children ages three to 17.

Other Things to See & Do

The **Rochester Museum & Science Center** (☎ 716-271-4320), 657 East Ave, contains a first-rate exhibit about the interaction between Seneca Indians and colonial Europeans. 'At the Western Door' documents the devastation and transformation of Native American culture. This excellent regional museum also includes an extensive collection of art from the Seneca Iroquois Arts Project, as well as permanent geology and natural science exhibits. The center is open Monday through Saturday from 9 am to 5 pm, Sunday and holidays (except Christmas) from noon to 5 pm. Admission is $6/5/3 for adults/seniors/students.

Mt Hope Cemetery, at the corner of Mt Hope and Elmwood Aves south of downtown, features a rolling expanse of 196 acres that attracts walkers, cyclists or sun lovers. Dating from 1838, the chapel, crematorium and other buildings represent neo-Gothic, Moorish Revival and Italianate styles. Mt Hope is the final resting place of Frederick Douglass, Susan B Anthony, Buffalo Bill's children and George Washington's drummer boy, among other luminaries. The Friends of Mt Hope Cemetery (☎ 716-461-3494) provide free one- to two-hour tours of the grounds and buildings on Sunday at 2 and 3 pm. You can also get a pocket guide to the grave sites from the Greater Rochester Visitors Association (☎ 716-546-3070).

The **Susan B Anthony House** (☎ 716-235-6124), 17 Madison St, was the famous feminist's home from 1866 to 1906. She helped write the *History of Woman Suffrage* in her attic, and she was arrested here in 1872 after she tried to vote. The historic home is open Wednesday to Sunday from 11 am to 4 pm.

Jell-O

Jell-O, the trademark for a gelatin desert and metaphor for the weak of knee, was invented in 1897 in the town of LeRoy, southwest of Rochester, by Paul B Wait, a carpenter. Orator Woodward bought the rights for Jell-O for $450 in 1899, and in 1925 the Woodward family sold them for $60 million.

The Jell-O Gallery at the LeRoy House Historic Museum (☎ 716-768-7433), 23 E Main St in LeRoy, tells the story of this original bit of Americana. It's open Sunday through Friday from 10 am to 4 pm. Admission to the gallery is $3; the historical museum is free. LeRoy is about a 30-minute drive southwest of Rochester (about 3 miles south of exit 47 off I-90).

Admission is $6/4.50/3/2 for adults/seniors/students/children.

The Corn Hill neighborhood was once known as the 'ruffled shirt district,' after the 19th-century residents who built many of Rochester's largest homes near the Genesee River. One of the most notable of these structures is **Campbell-Whittlesey House**, which was built in 1835 (☎ 716-546-7029), 123 S Fitzhugh St. It's open Friday, Saturday and Sunday from noon to 4 pm. Admission is $3/1 for adults/children.

Seneca Park Zoo (☎ 716-342-2744), 2222 St Paul Blvd, is open daily from 10 am to 4 pm, with extended hours from mid-May to mid-October. Admission is $4/3/2 for adults/seniors/children ages three to 15.

Cruises

Two companies run cruises along the Genesee River into Lake Ontario during warmer months. For more information, contact The Spirit of Rochester (☎ 716-865-4930) or Riverview Cruise Lines (☎ 716-865-4930), 18 Petten St Extension, one block south of the intersection of Lake Ave and Stutson St.

The Colonial Belle (☎ 716-223-9470), 400 Pocket Landing in Fairport, southeast of

Rochester, offers Erie Canal sightseeing cruises from mid-May to mid-October for $12 to $15. The company's lunch and dinner cruises cost $19 to $35.

Special Events

In mid-May, the 10-day Lilac Festival celebrates 22 acres of lilacs and other spring flowers throughout the 155-acre Highland Park. Events include a parade, an arts and crafts fair and daily entertainment. Call ☎ 716-256-4960 for more information.

The Corn Hill Arts Festival, held the first weekend after July 4, features arts and crafts, music and entertainment in the historic Corn Hill neighborhood.

Places to Stay

Decent, and usually cheaper, motels are outside town near the highways. Near the airport, take I-390 to exit 18 west (Brooks Ave/Airport exit). Go one block to Buell Rd and turn right. Several discount motel chains line the first block of Buell, including **Motel 6** (☎ 716-436-2170, 155 Buell Rd), with rooms for $40/50. The nearby **Comfort Inn Airport** (☎ 716-436-4400, 395 Buell Rd) charges $50 to $65, with slightly cheaper rates from November to May.

The in-town motels and hotels include the **Days Inn Historic** (☎ 716-325-5010, 384 East Ave), which rents rooms for $60/75, including a continental breakfast. It's within walking distance of several restaurants, museums and galleries.

Nearby, the 150-room **Strathallan Hotel** (☎ 716-461-5010, 800-678-7284, 550 East Ave) is set among several mansions and boasts of service to match the neighborhood. All rooms have balconies and fridges, and most have small kitchenettes. Rates range from $110 to $165, including a full breakfast buffet.

The downtown **Crowne Plaza Rochester** (☎ 716-546-3450, 70 State St) overlooks the Genesee River and contains an outdoor pool and a fitness center. Rooms range from $100 to $140.

But the best large hotel in town is the **Hyatt Regency Rochester** (☎ 716-546-1234, 125 E Main St), connected to the convention center by an enclosed skyway. Amenities include excellent service, a pool, health club and the Palladio restaurant. Weekday rooms range from $130 to $195; weekends are a better value, ranging from $80 to $110.

Rochester also contains several B&Bs. **Dartmouth House B&B** (☎ 716-271-7872, 215 Dartmouth St) is an ideally located spot between Monroe and East Aves, within walking distance of several restaurants and museums. The 1905 English Tudor home has four rooms, two with shared bath and two with private bath, with rates ranging from $60 to $110, including a generous candlelit breakfast.

428 Mt Vernon B&B (☎ 716-271-0792, 428 Mt Vernon) is a roomy and well-appointed Victorian on 2 wooded acres at the edge of Highland Park. The seven rooms, all with private bath and in-room phone, range from $95 to $115, including a full breakfast.

Places to Eat

You'll find several good, inexpensive eateries along Monroe Ave, a popular restaurant-row destination southeast of the Inner Loop between Union and Alexander Sts. Monroe Ave is a popular street to stroll, with its variety of restaurants, herb shops and used clothing and antique stores. To prepare your own food, stop in at the **Genesee Co-Op Foodstore** (☎ 716-244-3900, 713 Monroe Ave), which sells an assortment of natural foods.

Raj Mahal (☎ 716-546-2315, 324 Monroe Ave), at the corner of Alexander St, prepares excellent and mostly North Indian food (tandoori, etc) and several vegetarian dishes, most from $10 to $15. It's open daily for lunch and dinner.

Ozzie's NY Deli & Bar (☎ 716-244-7077, 470 Monroe Ave) is a deli serving over-stuffed sandwiches with famous Hollywood names. The food is good, so if you don't mind ordering a 'Pita Sellers' instead of saying 'turkey and Swiss on a pita,' eat here. All basic sandwiches cost $5 or $6.

Olive Tree (☎ 716-454-3510, 165 Monroe Ave) is a fancier Greek spot housed in a re-stored 1864 brick storefront with a summer garden. The menu features nouvelle Greek cuisine, including the ever-popular retsina wine. The Olive Tree is open for lunch on weekdays and for dinner Monday through Saturday from 5 to 9 pm.

On nearby Clinton Ave, **Highland Park Diner** (☎ 716-461-5040, 960 S Clinton Ave) is a restored 'Orleans' style diner whose nostalgic motto is 'real food at real prices.' It's open daily.

Less than a mile from Monroe Ave is Park Ave, a rather recent addition to the restaurant scene in Rochester. Several interesting eateries and shops near the corner of Park Ave and Berkeley St are worth a look, including **Esan** (☎ 716-271-2030, 696 Park Ave), a very good Thai café with moderate prices. It's open Tuesday to Sunday from 11 am to 10 pm.

Jine's Restaurant (☎ 716-461-1280, 658 Park Ave), in the heart of Park Ave's lively restaurant scene, offers an eclectic menu, though Greek is the specialty. Prices range from $3 for a sandwich to $13 for a dinner entrée, with the great breakfasts falling in between. It's open Monday to Saturday from 7 am to 10 pm, Sunday from 7 am to 8 pm.

At the top end of the spectrum, the Society of Rochester Landmark Restaurants is a group of seven more expensive area restaurants, all in restored historic buildings. Of these, **Edwards** (☎ 716-423-0140, 13 S Fitzhugh St), in the 1873 Academy Building, is among the most popular. The decor is a mix of mirrors and marble, but the food is creative, with meat and seafood entrees ranging from $12 to $20.

Richardson's Canal House (☎ 716-248-5000, 1474 Marsh Rd) has a fixed-price dinner for $38. The menu changes seasonally. Richardson's is near the Victor Rd exit of I-490.

Entertainment

Theater The Geva Theatre (☎ 716-232-4382, 75 Woodbury Blvd), at the corner of Clinton Ave S, is Rochester's premiere professional theater. The performance season runs from September through June. Other live theater productions include the **Downstairs Cabaret Theatre** (☎ 716-325-4370,

20 Windsor St), and the *Rochester Broadway Theatre League (☎ 716-325-7760, 100 East Ave)*. In the East End theater district, Java Joe's Coffee, 16 Gibb St, makes a good late-night stop after a show.

Cinema The *Little Theatre (☎ 716-232-4699, 240 East Ave)* shows revivals and new independent movies on five screens in a classic art deco building in the East End district. The *Curtiss & Dryden Theatres (☎ 716-271-4090, 900 East Ave)*, at the George Eastman House, show classic films that cost $5 for adults and $4 for children.

Music Between Main and Scio Sts, *The Eastman School of Music (☎ 716-274-1100, 26 Gibbs St)* has regularly scheduled jazz and classical concerts by students and visitors.

The *Eastman Theatre (☎ 716-222-5000)*, at the school, hosts performances by the Rochester Philharmonic Orchestra.

Clubs Rochester's downtown club scene is spread among three areas, starting with the hip East End district around the Eastman Theatre and Eastman School of Music. *Tonic (☎ 716-325-7720, 336 East Ave)* is a club and restaurant that overlooks East Ave from a loft-like upper floor. *Milestones Tavern & Music Room (☎ 716-325-6490, 170 East Ave)* offers nightly live music, usually with local bands, plus moderately priced food. *Avalon (☎ 716-473-7250, 274 N Goodman St)*, near the Memorial Art Gallery, features a DJ dance mix and a huge dance floor.

In the city's St Paul Quarter, check out *Tapas 177 Lounge (☎ 716-262-2090, 177 St Paul St)*, where you can enjoy late-night tapas and flamenco guitar. *Red Social Lounge (☎ 716-234-0888, 171 St Paul St)* attracts dancers.

In the High Falls district, you can get a bit of everything at *The Center at High Falls (☎ 716-423-0000, 60 Browns Race)*, including three nightclubs with jazz and dance music, plus a sports bar. Around the corner is *Jillian's (☎ 716-454-6530, 61 Commercial St)*, an unlikely combination of restaurant, bowling alley, billiard room and dance spot.

Getting There & Away

The Greater Rochester International Airport (☎ 716-464-6000) is on Brooks Ave, at I-390 exit 18. Most major carriers serve Rochester, including American, Delta, United, Continental, Northwest and US Airways. The typical roundtrip fare from Chicago is around $240; from New York City, $200; from Philadelphia, $280.

The bus terminal (☎ 800-295-5555) is at 187 Midtown Plaza (on the corner of Broad and Chestnut Sts). Trailways buses go to Buffalo, Syracuse, Niagara Falls and points further east like Albany and New York City. Greyhound also offers similar routes. Daily service from Rochester to Buffalo is $14/26 one-way/roundtrip; to Syracuse, $16/30; to New York City, $52/99.

The Amtrak train station (☎ 716-454-2894, 800-872-7245) is at 320 Central Ave. Trains run east through Syracuse to New York City, west to Buffalo and other points. Fares from Rochester to Buffalo are $16/38 one-way/roundtrip; to New York City, $89/178. Excursion discounts are often available, so be sure to inquire.

If you're coming by car, Rochester is about 10 miles north of I-90 via I-390 (Genesee Expressway) or I-490, which circles the center of town.

Getting Around

Regional Transit Service (RTS; ☎ 716-288-1700) buses will take you anywhere you want to go in town. The fare is $1.25.

The Skyway system is an enclosed network of walkways connecting downtown buildings. The Skyway begins at Main St near the Genesee River, runs three blocks east to Elm St and then three blocks south to a parking garage on Woodbury Blvd.

AROUND ROCHESTER

Charlotte-Genesee Lighthouse (☎ 716-621-6179) is 8 miles north of Rochester at 70 Lighthouse St, off Latta Rd east of Lake Ave. The lighthouse stands at the mouth of the Genesee River and once welcomed ships traveling Lake Ontario. It's no longer a working lighthouse, but visitors do have access to the tower. It's open weekends from mid-May to mid-October from 1 to 5 pm. Admission is free.

Seabreeze Amusement Park & Raging Rivers Water Park (☎ 716-323-1900), in Irondequoit on Lake Ontario, combines old-fashioned attractions (a classic wooden roller coaster and carousel) with a modern water park. The complex is open from mid-June to Labor Day. Admission is $15/11 for adults/children. Take I-490 east through Rochester to Route 590 north to the lake. You'll drive about 10 miles total.

Twenty minutes west of Rochester is the **Victorian Doll Museum and Chili Doll Hospital** (☎ 716-247-0130), 4332 Buffalo Rd in North Chili ('chai-lai'). It's open Tuesday to Saturday from 10 am to 4:30 pm and Sunday in December only from 1 to 4:30 pm; it's closed in January. Admission is $2/1 for adults/children ages three to 12.

Genesee Country Village & Museum (☎ 716-538-6822), 1410 Flint Hill Rd in Mumford, 20 miles west of Rochester, is a living-history collection of 57 buildings representing most of the 19th century. The staff dresses in period costumes, and the museum houses a large collection of sporting and wildlife art. On the grounds are a 4½-mile hiking trail system and a nature center. The village is open mid-May to mid-October. Admission is $11/9.50/6.50 for adults/seniors/children ages four to 16.

A 15-minute drive south of Rochester via Route 31 (Monroe Ave), the town of **Pittsford** is a good place to spend part of the day walking or biking along the Erie Canal or even taking a cruise aboard one of the canal boats. The *Sam Patch* (☎ 716-262-5661) stops at Pittsford on summer weekends.

The original barge canals of New York weren't built with bike paths in mind, but it's hard to find a better place to take a leisurely ride. Towpath Bikes (☎ 716-381-2808), at 7 Schoen Place, gets its name from the days when mules were used to tow the barges along the canal. Bikes (helmets included) rent for $7 to $10 an hour, or $15 to $20 for three hours – ample time to check out the canal. Have lunch at *Aladdin's Natural Eatery* (☎ 716-264-9000, 8 Schoen Place), which overlooks the canal and serves good sandwiches and salads for $5 to $7.

Letchworth State Park (☎ 716-493-3600), a one-hour drive southwest of Rochester, is often called the Grand Canyon of the East – an unfair comparison given its spectacular and unique views. In addition to the vistas, the park also features cabins, trails through dense forests, waterfalls, canoeing and white-water rafting opportunities and hikes along the Genesee River gorge. The William Pryor Letchworth Museum inside the park showcases Native American artifacts and presents a pictorial history of the park. To get there from Rochester, take I-390 south to exit 7 at Mt Morris and follow Route 408. For more information, visit the park's website at www.nysparks.com.

Western New York

Western New York boasts the state's most famous tourist destination after New York City – Niagara Falls.

The Seneca were the first people to populate the area around the falls, and among the Iroquois, they were known as 'the keepers of the western door.' When the Erie Canal was completed in 1825, another path to the western frontier was opened. The canal was the engineering marvel of its day (completed without the benefit of a professional engineer) and the primary trade route from New York City to Buffalo, now the second largest city in the state. Most of the 10 million annual visitors to Niagara Falls bypass Buffalo, which may be a good reason in itself to visit this vital city. Buffalo is home to the acclaimed Albright-Knox Art Gallery and magnificent architecture ranging from 19th-century mansions to homes designed by Frank Lloyd Wright.

South of Buffalo, Chautauqua Institution (on Chautauqua Lake) hosts a well-known summer retreat, which includes lectures and courses on music, dance, theater and art. The courses attract about 180,000 visitors to this tranquil lake community. A few miles east of Chautauqua along scenic Route 17/I-86 lies the 65,000 acre Allegany State Park, with over 80 miles of hiking trails, stream fishing and year-round camping.

GETTING THERE & AWAY
Air
The major airport in the region is Buffalo Niagara International Airport (see Getting There & Away in the Buffalo section, later in this chapter). The Greater Rochester International Airport (see the Rochester section of the Finger Lakes chapter) is also nearby.

Bus
The Niagara Frontier Transportation Authority runs buses to and from Buffalo, Buffalo airport and Niagara Falls. The area is also served by New York Trailways and Greyhound.

Highlights

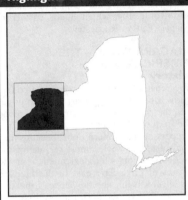

- Niagara Falls, including roaring Horseshoe and misty Bridal Veil Falls, and the panoramic view from the Canadian side

- Buffalo's bustling theater district and numerous Frank Lloyd Wright–designed homes as well as other architectural treasures

- Chautauqua Institution's quiet charm, famous porches and summer educational series

- Year-round outdoor activities – such as camping, hiking, and ice-fishing – at Allegany State Park

Train
Several Amtrak trains make daily runs between Buffalo and Rochester to the east; Buffalo and Niagara Falls and Toronto, Canada, to the north; and between Buffalo and Erie, PA, to the southwest.

Car & Motorcycle
I-90 stretches from New York's southwest corner to Buffalo, then runs east toward Rochester. The other major east-west road is

Route 17/I-86 near the Pennsylvania border; Route 417, which branches off Route 17/I-86 just east of Allegany State Park, is certainly one of the prettiest drives in all New York. Other east-west roads are Route 20, which heads east from Buffalo to the Finger Lakes; and Route 104, which heads east from Niagara Falls to Rochester.

NIAGARA FALLS – THE AMERICAN SIDE
History

The Seneca, largest of the confederated Iroquois tribes, were the first people to populate the area around Niagara Falls. Among the Iroquois, the Seneca were known as 'the keepers of the western door' because they controlled the westernmost regions of the Iroquois nation, which extended from the shores of Lake Erie east to the Hudson Valley. It was through the Seneca tribal territories that Iroquois warriors and hunters passed to attack and later exploit the western and southern nations. In 1678 Seneca guides led Father Louis Hennepin, a French priest serving under explorer Robert LaSalle, to the falls. Hennepin was, perhaps, the first to call attention to the cataracts as a natural wonder. In his account of his travels, which were widely read in Europe, he made reference to the falls, observing that 'the universe does not afford its parallel.'

For early Europeans, control of the portage around the falls was vital since they were the only break in the St Lawrence River to the Great Lakes waterway. The French were the first to build a fort in 1687 at the nexus of the Niagara River and Lake Ontario. In 1726, they built Fort Niagara north of the present-day falls. Throughout the French & Indian War of the 18th century, the French and British fought for control of the portage and the surrounding region. Finally, in 1759, the British took Fort Niagara and held it until 1796.

During this period, farming settlements sprang up on both sides of the Niagara River, only to be burned and looted during the War of 1812. After the war the region rebounded, particularly after the arrival of the Erie Canal in 1825. In 1855 the Roe-

bling family (who later designed the Brooklyn Bridge in New York City) and backers built the Roebling Suspension Bridge across the Niagara Gorge. The two level bridge supported trains below and carriages above.

In the mid-19th century, the area around the falls became increasingly commercialized. Private owners went so far as to block off views of the falls with fences and then charged frustrated visitors to view the magnificent cataracts through small holes in the fences. Angered by such blatant exploitation of a natural resource, the Free Niagara Movement arose in 1869. Led by men such as Frederick Law Olmsted, the group launched a well-organized campaign to force the state government to buy back land around the falls and create a public park. Finally, in 1885 the NY State Legislature created the Niagara Reservation parks system to preserve the area around the falls. Olmsted designed the gorge-front Prospect Park, which is the oldest state park in the US. It is still considered a well-designed park, although the modern additions of a visitors center building and the large metal Observation Tower might not meet with Olmsted's approval if he were to come back for a look.

The world's first commercial hydroelectric alternating-current-generating facility opened at the falls in 1895, proving that electricity could be reasonably and cheaply produced and sent miles away for use. Today, the Niagara Power Project in nearby Lewiston produces about 17% of New York's electricity.

The sheer power and beauty of the falls – a spectacular 40 million gallons of water per minute hurtling downward and extending outward into a cloud of mist – have made them a popular destination for honeymooners, daredevils and other seekers of romance. As early as 1803, Napoleon's nephew Jerome Bonaparte is said to have made a visit here with his bride. And the challenge of surviving a trip over the falls has attracted a number of curious and daring individuals. Even for the less adventurous, simply viewing and experiencing the

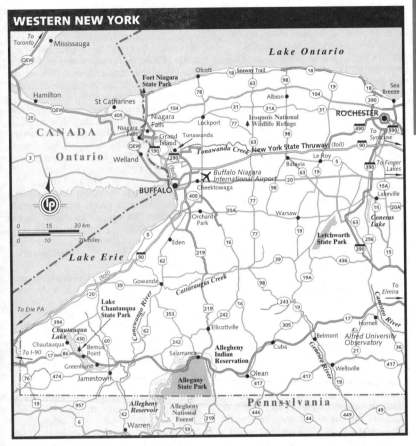

WESTERN NEW YORK

falls up close can be an exciting and memorable experience.

Orientation

There are actually two towns of Niagara Falls: Niagara Falls, NY, and Niagara Falls, Ontario (Canada), situated across from one another on the opposite banks of the Niagara River. The town of Niagara Falls, NY (population 62,000), is fairly easy to navigate. Its downtown is laid out on a grid pattern with numbered streets running north to south and named ones running east to west, with the exception of a few streets

that run diagonally. Prospect Park extends along the Niagara River, creating a vast green strip. Niagara St runs east-west to the Rainbow Bridge gateway to Canada. Most of the major attractions are south of Niagara St, along the river.

See the Niagara Falls – the Canadian Side section, later in this chapter, for coverage across the river.

Information

Throughout the town, you'll come along privately-owned information centers that offer accommodations and tour packages.

Services vary in quality, but the staff can be helpful in answering questions and providing more general assistance.

The best source of information is the Niagara Falls Official Information Center (☎ 716-284-2000), next to the large convention center, adjacent to the bus terminal at 4th and Niagara Sts. During the summer months (mid-May to mid-September), it's open daily from 8:30 am to 7:30 pm; during the rest of year, daily from 9 am to 5 pm.

Another official visitors' center is operated by the state of New York, the Orin Lehman Visitor Center (☎ 716-278-1796), in Prospect Park adjacent to the falls. It is open daily during the summer from 8 am to 10 pm and in the winter from 9 am to 6 pm.

The post office (☎ 716-285-7561) is at 615 Main St. The library (☎ 716-286-4881) is at 1425 Main St. The *Niagara Gazette* is the local daily paper. There are several banks in the downtown vicinity around 4th and Main Sts. You can park for free in the lot of the Rainbow Mall right downtown and walk to everything you'll need to see.

The Falls

Writing about the falls, the French missionary, Father Hennepin, observed that 'the waters which fall from this horrible precipice do foam and boil after the most hideous manner imaginable.' In a more irreverent vein, Oscar Wilde remarked that he would have been more impressed if the falls had flowed upward. It's unlikely the two gentlemen had much in common.

When describing the falls, it is important to note that there are actually two cataracts, or high waterfalls. The Canadian, or **Horseshoe Falls**, are the larger and more impressive. They are 2500 feet across and plunge 170 feet down. The smaller **American Falls** are 1100 feet across and fall 180 feet. Sometimes referred to as a separate cataract, **Bridal Veil Falls** actually forms the western portion of the American Falls. The parkland called Goat Island sits in the middle of the Niagara River. The middle of the river makes up part of the international border between Canada and the US, the longest unprotected border in the world.

Originally about 200,000 cubic feet per second (or 5.5 billion gallons per hour) of water flowed over the falls, but today between a half and three-quarters of the water is diverted to run power turbines in the US and Canada. About 10% of the water flows over the American Falls and 90% over the Canadian Horseshoe.

The falls were formed about 12,000 years ago as glaciers melted, releasing water from the Great Lakes along what became the Niagara River. The 37-mile-long Niagara River connects Lake Erie and Lake Ontario. As it flows through the city of Niagara Falls, the river is actually flowing northward. The water cut through rock over time creating a waterfall. When they were formed, the falls were 7 miles downstream from their present location. The edge of the falls continues to erode upstream at the rate of about one inch every year. Note the piles of boulders at the base of the falls.

In 1969 the American Falls were actually shut off for a period of time. A dam was built across the river and the flow diverted to the Horseshoe Falls because the Army Corps of Engineers wanted to study how to prevent further erosion. Gleeful tourists walked along the dry river bed, and among the things found were 12 buckets of coins and two bodies.

The falls are illuminated at night throughout the year on a changing monthly schedule, but roughly according to the sunset times. The Festival of Lights refers to the lighting of all the trees in the parks adjacent to the falls, and runs from late November to the first week in January.

Viewing the Falls

'Both sides' is the answer to the most often asked question 'which is the best side for viewing?' For the best panoramic view, cross over to the Canadian side. Views from the American side are considered less satisfactory because you're generally standing too close for comfort, or at an angle that makes viewing difficult. One exception is the view from Prospect Observation Tower, which was erected to improve the view from the American side, thus revealing an insecurity

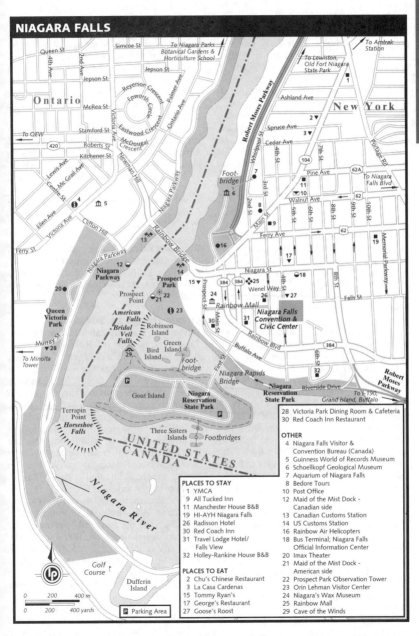

NIAGARA FALLS

Queen St
Simcoe St
To Niagara Parks
Botanical Gardens &
Horticulture School
To Amtrak
Station

To Lewiston,
Old Fort Niagara
State Park

Jepson St
Jepson St
Ashland Ave

Reyerson Crescent

Ontario

McRea St
Epworth Circle
Spruce Ave
New York

Stamford St
Victoria Ave
Eastwood Crescent
Cedar Ave

To QEW
420
Roberts St
McDougal
Crescent
104
4th St
7th St
Portage Rd

Kitchener St
Newman Hill
62A
To Niagara
Falls Blvd

Lewis Ave
Centre McGrail Ave
Niagara Parkway
Foot-
bridge
7
Pine Ave
62

Ellen Ave
Victoria Ave
4
5
6
11
10
Walnut Ave

To QEW
Clifton Hill
8
2nd St
Main St
6th St
8th St
9th St
10th St

Ferry St
13
9
Ferry Ave
62

16
17
19

Niagara Parkway
Niagara St
Memorial Parkway

12
14
Niagara
Parkway
15
384
384
25
18
4th St

20
Prospect
Park
24
Wenel Way
26
27
Falls St

Prospect
Point
22
21
23
Rainbow Mall
30
31
Niagara Falls
Convention &
Civic Center
8th St

Queen
Victoria
Park
American
Falls
Bridal
Veil
Falls
Robinson
Island
Rainbow Blvd
384

Murray St
28
29
Bird
Island
Green
Island
Buffalo Ave
32

To Minolta
Tower
Foot-
bridge
Niagara Rapids
Bridge
Niagara
Reservation
State Park
Riverside Drive
Robert
Moses
Parkway

Terrapin
Point
Horseshoe
Falls
Goat Island
Niagara
Reservation
State Park
To I-190,
Grand Island, Buffalo

Three Sisters
Islands
Footbridges

UNITED STATES
CANADA

Niagara River

Golf
Course

Dufferin
Island

0   200   400 m
0   200   400 yards

P Parking Area

PLACES TO STAY
1 YMCA
9 All Tucked Inn
11 Manchester House B&B
19 HI-AYH Niagara Falls
26 Radisson Hotel
30 Red Coach Inn
31 Travel Lodge Hotel/
Falls View
32 Holley-Rankine House B&B

PLACES TO EAT
2 Chu's Chinese Restaurant
3 La Casa Cardenas
15 Tommy Ryan's
17 George's Restaurant
27 Goose's Roost

28 Victoria Park Dining Room & Cafeteria
30 Red Coach Inn Restaurant

OTHER
4 Niagara Falls Visitor &
Convention Bureau (Canada)
5 Guinness World of Records Museum
6 Schoellkopf Geological Museum
7 Aquarium of Niagara Falls
8 Bedore Tours
10 Post Office
12 Maid of the Mist Dock -
Canadian side
13 Canadian Customs Station
14 US Customs Station
16 Rainbow Air Helicopters
18 Bus Terminal; Niagara Falls
Official Information Center
20 Imax Theater
21 Maid of the Mist Dock -
American side
22 Prospect Park Observation Tower
23 Orin Lehman Visitor Center
24 Niagara's Wax Museum
25 Rainbow Mall
29 Cave of the Winds

deeper than the river gorge itself. On the other hand, the American side allows you (you have no choice) to feel the immense power of the falls. You can easily walk or drive across Rainbow Bridge to Canada. (If you drive, prepare to pay about C$8 to park; see Entering Canada, later in this chapter.)

If you plan to visit a number of attractions in Niagara Falls, consider buying a Master Pass, which covers entry to the Cave of the Winds, *Maid of the Mist*, Prospect Park Observation Tower, Viewmobile Tour, Aquarium, Prospect Park Visitors Center film and Schoellkopf Geological Museum. It costs $21 ($16 for children ages six to 12) and is available at the centers, Viewmobile stops and other sights.

Goat Island Goat Island is a half-mile-long island connected to the US mainland by free pedestrian and car bridges. From the island you can walk to **Three Sisters Islands**, a series of rapids approaching Horseshoe Falls. You can also walk down to **Terrapin Point**, the closest viewing point to Horseshoe Falls. From this spit of land you can imagine 17-year-old Deanne Woodward being rescued from shooting over the brink after her boat capsized (see the boxed text, 'Niagara Falls Daredevils').

To experience the falls up close, take an elevator down from Goat Island to the **Cave of the Winds** (☎ 716-278-1730), where you'll walk along wooden walkways within 25 feet of the cataracts. You'll be provided with a yellow rain coat to protect you from the heavy mist. Admission is $6/5 for adults/children. It is open Memorial Day to Labor Day daily from 10 am to 7 pm; from Labor Day until early October it's open from 10 am to 6 pm.

There is free parking at the eastern end of Goat Island close to Three Sisters Islands, or a $5 parking lot near Terrapin Point on the western side of the island.

Prospect Park Observation Tower As if craning its neck to get a better view, the green metal platform of the Prospect Park Observation Tower stands out as a reminder of the inferior views of the falls afforded vis-

itors from the American side. The platform does provide excellent views of both the river canyon and falls and is well worth the modest 50¢ admission. You can take an elevator to the base of the falls or up to the top of the observation tower. You can also walk out on the observation deck at town level. The *Maid of the Mist* also leaves from here at the river level.

At the base of the falls, visitors can climb up a rickety cement and stone staircase and along a path that takes them reasonably close to the north side of the American Falls, at least close enough to get wet from the mist and spray. The view from the top is also spectacular; it is open daily mid-May to mid-September from 8 am to 11 pm, otherwise from 8:30 am to 4:30 pm.

Rainbow Bridge Travelers can drive across this bridge for $2.50 (roundtrip) or walk across for 25¢ (each way). You'll get a magnificent view of the falls from the Canadian side.

Other Things to See

Schoellkopf Geological Museum (☎ 716-278-1780), in Niagara Reservation State Park, overlooks the Niagara Gorge and houses exhibits and nature trails explaining the geology of the region. A 15-minute three-screen slide show sketches the geology of the gorge. You can take a free guided tour along the rim or descend to the base of the falls. Walks vary in length and difficulty, but all are designed to be both informative and fun. It is open daily from late May to early September and Monday to Wednesday during winter. Admission costs $1 (free to children under six).

The Aquarium of Niagara Falls (☎ 716-285-3575), 701 Whirlpool St, is open daily from 9 am to 5 pm and until 7 pm during the summer. Admission is $6.50/4.50 for adults/children (ages six to 12). A footbridge connects the aquarium and the geological museum. A free shuttle operates every 10 minutes between the Observation Tower and the aquarium and museum.

The Niagara Power Authority (☎ 716-285-3211) is at 5777 Lewiston Rd in the attractive village of Lewiston, NY, north of the falls. The power project is one of the largest in the world. You'll find a visitors' center and a good view of the Niagara Gorge. The power complex is open daily in July and August from 9 am to 5 pm, and 10 am to 5 pm the rest of the year. Admission is free.

Niagara's Wax Museum of History (☎ 716-285-1271), 303 Prospect St opposite Prospect Park, has several authentic historical exhibits. The museum is open daily during the summer from 10 am to 10 pm; winter hours are from 11 am to 5 pm. The admission cost is $5/3 for adults/children (ages 6-12).

Maid of the Mist Tours

Since 1846, Niagara Falls' biggest tourist attraction has been a boat ride on the *Maid of the Mist* (☎ 716-284-8897, Canada ☎ 905-358-5781), which leaves from the base of the Prospect Park Observation Tower. If you only have time for one attraction, this should be it. You'll be supplied with a raincoat before heading for the base of the American Falls and Horseshoe Falls, where you can best experience the power and the fury of the water hurtling over the cliffs above. Even with a raincoat, expect to get wet. The trip lasts half an hour and costs $8.50/4.80 for adults/children. In season, from mid-May to October 24, boats leave every 15 minutes from 10 am until early evening.

Maid of the Mist also leaves from the dock at Clifton Hill St and River Rd in Canada.

Organized Tours

Although you can view the falls by walking or by a combination of driving and walking, many visitors prefer to take in the sights on a narrated bus tour. Typically, organized tours include stops on both sides of the border. On the US side, the major sights generally include a boat ride on the *Maid of the Mist* and visits to the Prospect Park Observation Tower and Goat Island. On the Canadian side, you will visit the tunnels behind the falls, the Minolta Observation Tower and also take a ride on *Maid of the Mist*. Check to see what the current tour

stops are and compare the package rate with the costs for admission to the individual sights (don't forget about the Master Pass, which is detailed in the Viewing the Falls section) and the time you'd need to get there on your own.

Bedore Tours (☎ 716-285-7550, 800-538-8433) offers tours with stops at the major attractions on the Canadian and/or US sides of the falls for $35 to $40. Bilingual tours are also offered.

For informal and very inexpensive sightseeing, hop on The Viewmobile (☎ 716-278-1730), an open trolley operated by the NY State Park office. The tour goes around Goat Island and over to Prospect Park in a loop, stopping at five various sights. Riders can get on and off at any stop and pick up the next one. The cost is $4.50/3.50 for adults/children (ages six to 12).

Niagara River Guide Service (☎ 716-297-9424) operates all-day fishing trips out of Lewiston, which is about 3 miles north of Niagara Falls. The cost is $360 for up to three people. Depending on the season, they fish for salmon, walleye, muskie and bass.

You can arrange to fly over the falls by contacting Rainbow Air Helicopters (☎ 716-284-2800), 454 Main St, near the Howard Johnson and Bedore Tours. The cost is $45 per person for a 10-minute flight.

Places to Stay

Budget There are several campsites on Grand Island, 5 to 7 miles south of Niagara Falls. *Niagara Falls KOA Campground* (☎ 716-773-7583, 2570 Grand Island Blvd) is on Grand Island next to Fantasy Island amusement park; take exit N-19 from I-190 on Grand Island. The campground has a pool, laundry facilities, camp store, miniature golf and more. It is open from April to mid-November; sites are $18 to $25. Nearby, *Cinderella Campsite* (☎ 716-773-4095) offers sites for $18 year-round.

Niagara Falls Campground (☎ 716-731-3434, 800-525-8505, 2405 Niagara Falls Blvd/Route 62), is about 7 miles east of Niagara Falls. Sites cost $16 to $21.

The HI-AYH *Niagara Falls* (☎ 716-282-3700, 1101 Ferry Ave) has dormitory rooms

Niagara Falls Daredevils

Since early in the 19th century, stuntsters have been attracted to the falls, challenging the raging waters on tightropes and in barrels, kayaks and rubber inner tubes. Some not-so-daring visitors have even gone over the falls unintentionally. In recent years, police have been fining daredevils for attempting to perform a stunt without a license.

In 1829, Sam Patch leaped twice from a platform about 100 feet above the gorge at the foot of the falls.

The first recorded woman plunger was Anna Edson Taylor, a Michigan teacher who, at 63, decided the way to fame was to go over the falls in a barrel. On October 24, 1901, friends strapped her into an oak barrel, towed it out in the stream and cast it loose. Taylor and her barrel went over. Less than 20 minutes later, the barrel was pulled to shore and Taylor told a reporter, 'I would sooner walk up to the mouth of a canon knowing it was going to blow me to pieces.' Although Taylor got the fame she had sought, she ended up in court – not to

Anna takes the plunge.

pay a fine, but to sue her manager for the return of her famous barrel. It seems her manager dumped Taylor for a younger and prettier woman who then posed in Taylor's place for photographs. Taylor got her barrel back, but ended up broke, selling postcards of herself on the streets of Niagara Falls.

The next person to challenge the falls was Englishman Bobby Leach, who went over in a steel barrel on July 25, 1911. He was so battered and bruised that he needed six months in the hospital to recuperate. Fifteen years later, while on a lecture tour in New Zealand, Leach slipped and fell on an orange peel, broke his leg and died from ensuing complications. Another Brit, Charles Stephens, tried the falls in an oak barrel on July 11, 1920. Unfortunately, when his barrel hit the water, Stephens was catapulted out its bottom. Only his arm was recovered.

Jean Lussier of Quebec designed an innovative vehicle with a steel frame and 32 inner tubes and went over the top on July 4, 1928. He emerged an hour later in perfect health. For years afterwards Lussier sold small pieces of his inner tubes for 50¢ apiece. In 1961, Nathan T Boya duplicated Lussier's rubber ball and also made the drop successfully.

George Stathakis, a Buffalo chef, built a 2000-pound, wood-and-steel contraption and made the plunge on July 4, 1930. He lived through the drop but suffocated when his vehicle was trapped behind the falls for 22 hours.

with four, six or eight bunks to a room (a total of 46 beds). There is a large living room, and the hostel has laundry and kitchen facilities. A Tops food store is just three blocks away. During the summer, guests receive discount coupons for the *Maid of the Mist* boat tours and other attractions. You can also rent a bike for $10 a day. There's a 9:30 am to 4 pm lockout and an 11:30 pm curfew. The cost is $14 for

members, $17 for nonmembers. If you're staying at the hostel, bring a sleeping bag or rent one for $1.50. The hostel is closed from December 16 to January 30.

YMCA (☎ 716-285-8491), Portage Rd and Main St, has rooms for men only. The rooms, which are minimally furnished with a single bed, a florescent light and small desk, rent by the day/week for $25/95. Both men and women can rent floor space for $15 in an ex-

Niagara Falls Daredevils

Red Hill, Jr, built a shoddy craft christened 'The Thing' out of 13 inner tubes, fish net and canvas straps and launched it and himself into the rapids on August 5, 1951. The Thing began to fall apart even before it reached the brink. What was left of it floated to the surface soon after it hit the bottom. Hill's body was fished out the next day.

Only one person is recorded to have gone over the falls unintentionally – and lived. On July 9, 1960, Jim Honeycutt took 17-year-old Deanne Woodward and her seven-year-old brother Roger out for a boat ride on the upper Niagara River above the falls. To give the children a thrill, Honeycutt maneuvered the boat close to the falls, but when he turned it around, the engine failed. The boat wallowed and then flipped, hurtling all three into the waters rushing towards the edge of the falls. Deanne was pulled out at Terrapin Point on Goat Island very close to the brink. Honeycutt and Roger Woodward went over. Amazingly, Roger survived and was picked up by the *Maid of the Mist* tour boat, but Honeycutt died.

Canadian Karl Soucek made the plunge in a red barrel on July 3, 1984, and emerged with bruises, a hurt arm and a chipped tooth. Less than a year later, Soucek dropped 180 feet from the top of the Houston Astrodome in a specially designed barrel heading for a 10-foot-deep pool of water. The barrel hit the edge of the tank and Soucek died of his injuries.

Steve Trotter survived the falls in a homemade rubber barrel on August 19, 1985, and did it again in 1995. David Munday is another person to have gone over twice and survived, in 1985 and 1993. Peter DeBernardi and Jeffrey Petkovich, from Niagara Falls and Ottawa, respectively, went over head to head in the same barrel on September 27, 1989. Both lived.

The most daring – and, perhaps, the stupidest (though the competition is stiff) – attempt of all was that of Tennessee's Jessie W Sharp, who shot the falls in a 12½-foot polyethylene kayak on June 5, 1990. Sharp had planned to ride the rapids beyond the falls to Lewiston, NY, where he had made dinner reservations. He skipped wearing a helmet so his face would be recognizable on film. It was, but his body was never found.

Tightrope walkers have also challenged the falls. The most famous, Jean François Gravelet – known as 'Blondin' – walked across many times beginning in the summer of 1859. Each time, Blondin would vary his routine, so as to continue to attract attention. On some attempts, he might somersault on the rope, ride a bicycle, push a wheelbarrow, cook an omelet or pull up a bottle of champagne from the *Maid of the Mist* to refresh himself. He even once carried his trusting manager across on his back.

In case you have daredevil ideas of your own, the current maximum fine for performing a stunt without a license (and they don't grant licenses anyway) is $10,000. This fine is payable if you live to tell about it.

---

ercise room covered with mats. You share a clean bathroom and have free use of the gym. If you stay in the mat room during the summer, you have to get up early because the room is in use for activities beginning at about 7 am and continuing until 7 pm. There are lockers for personal belongings, and you can come and go throughout the day, unlike the hostel, which has a lockout. There is a $10 key deposit charge.

Mid-Range Route 62 (Niagara Falls Blvd), as it nears Niagara Falls, is over-loaded with inexpensive motels. Off-season rates are typically $25 to $40 and in-season (during the summer) rates are $40 to $60. The **Red Carpet Inn** (☎ 716-283-2010, 6625 Niagara Falls Blvd) has off-season single/double/triple rates of $39/49/59; in-season rates range from $59 to $149 a night for a double room.

All Tucked Inn (☎ 716-282-0919, 574 3rd St) has 10 clean rooms with basic furnishings. Two rooms have private baths and the others have sinks and share three clean bathrooms. There are no phones or televisions, and there is generally a 1 am curfew. From May 16 to September 14 the rates are $40 to $65, and off-season $35 to $55.

Manchester House B&B (☎ 716-285-5717, 800-489-3009, 653 Main St) is a private home built in 1903. There are four rooms that share two baths. This is a pleasant place, and the owners know the area well. You can also take advantage of the sitting room with its gas fireplace, television and music. From Memorial Day to Labor Day rates are $65 to $90, a bit cheaper in the winter.

The old Niagara Hotel, built in 1924, is now the *Travel Lodge Hotel/Falls View* (☎ 716-285-9321, 201 Rainbow Blvd). The 193 redecorated guest rooms can't restore the hotel to its former charm, but it's still a decent value. The grand lobby is a dim reminder of better days. There is a cocktail lounge and restaurant. Prices vary according to weekday/weekend and views of the falls (best from the 6th floor and up). From November to March rates are $39 to $99 and during summer, $79 to $199.

Top End The *Holley-Rankine House B&B* (☎ 716-285-4790, 800-845-6649, 525 Riverside Drive) is a large Gothic stone house across from the Niagara River. The long, comfortable living room with fireplace looks out over the river. There's also a nice stone terrace. The B&B has five rooms ranging from $65 for the 'maid's quarters' to $120 with private bath and a view. A full breakfast is included.

Near the bridge to Goat Island, the *Red Coach Inn* (☎ 716-282-1459, 2 Buffalo Ave) offers one- and two-bedroom suites furnished with European antique reproductions. The inn is above the Red Coach restaurant in a 1920s Tudor-style building. The suites at the front of the inn have views of the street and river; rooms in the back of the building have a view of the parking lot. From November 1 to April 30 rates are $75 for a room and $95/150 for one/two bedroom

suites. From May 1 to October 31, rates increase by $20 to $30.

The *Radisson Hotel* (☎ 716-285-3361, fax 285-3900), on 3rd St near the Rainbow Mall, has over 400 rooms in a brown, brick building adjacent to the convention center. It's the newest and nicest of the full-service hotels. From mid-May to mid-September rates are $80 to $110; other times of the year, $120 to $175.

Places to Eat

Food isn't the main attraction in Niagara Falls. Choices are few, and tend to be spread out.

George's Restaurant (☎ 716-284-5766, 420 Niagara St) is a simple neighborhood restaurant with $4 breakfast specials, sandwiches for under $5 and dinners with selections such as meatloaf with mashed potatoes for $5.50. You can't miss George's: it's the color of a bright pumpkin.

La Casa Cardenas (☎ 716-282-0231, 921 Main St) is a Mexican restaurant in a red house with green trim and turrets near the armory. The food here is unexceptional, but it provides a respite from diner food. Fajitas and a slew of chicken dishes are $9; burritos, enchiladas and taco plates are $4 to $6.

Chu's Chinese Restaurant (☎ 716-285-7278, 1019 Main St) is quite good and serves both Szechwan and Mandarin dishes. It is open daily from 11 am to 11 pm.

And *Tommy Ryan's* (☎ 716-282-5025, 1 Prospect Point) is a '50s-style diner with very decent food. It is open from 11 am to 10 pm daily.

Goose's Roost (☎ 716-282-6255, 343 4th St) is next to the Convention Center. The food is quite good, somewhat on the Italian side; most dinners are under $10. It is open daily from 7 am to 11 pm.

The restaurant at *Red Coach Inn* (☎ 716-282-1459, 2 Buffalo Ave) is more expensive. The dining room is decorated with faux wood beams and chandeliers, and diners are seated in comfortable captain's chairs at oak tables. Lunch selections include sandwiches, fish & chips and salads for $6 to $9. Dinners feature London broil, pork chops, veal and fresh fish for $15 to $20.

Getting There & Away

Air Buffalo's airport, which is 30 miles away, is the nearest. To reach the airport from Niagara Falls, go to the bus stop in front of the Niagara Falls Official Information Center at 4th and Niagara Sts, and get the No 40 bus to downtown Buffalo (ask for a transfer). From Buffalo, take the No 24 bus to the airport. The entire trip takes nearly two hours, and the cost is $2.

Alternately, the ITA Buffalo Airport Shuttle (☎ 800-551-9369) runs three times a day between Niagara Falls and the Buffalo airport for $18/31 one-way/roundtrip. ITA runs an extended schedule during the summer. A taxi between the airport and Niagara Falls is about $45 one-way. Be sure to fix the price first because these cabs are not metered.

Bus The Niagara Frontier Transportation Authority (NFTA; ☎ 716-285-7211, 285-9319) runs bus No 40 between Niagara Falls and Buffalo every day all day long. Express bus No 60 runs between Niagara Falls and Buffalo five times a day from Monday to Friday. Two express buses leave Niagara Falls for Buffalo before 7 am and three buses leave Buffalo for Niagara Falls roughly between 4:30 and 5 pm. The fare for both buses is $1.90. The bus terminal is next to the visitors' center at 4th and Niagara Sts.

For buses further afield you should consider taking either Greyhound or Trailways from Buffalo.

Train Amtrak (☎ 716-285-4224) stops at Lockport Rd and 27th St, one block east of Hyde Park Blvd. There is daily service to Buffalo (one-way/roundtrip for $6/12) and to Toronto ($17/32).

Car & Motorcycle You can get to Niagara Falls by I-190 from the south, a toll road from Buffalo, or by Route 62, a commercial strip that extends all the way from Buffalo to the falls. From Canada, the QEW (Route 420) highway leads to the Rainbow Bridge, which dumps cars right downtown next to the American Falls.

Getting Around

NFTA (see Getting There & Away) runs buses through the town. The base fare is $1.20, add another 20¢ for each extra zone crossed or for a transfer. Route maps are available at the bus terminal and the information center at 4th and Niagara Sts.

The tourist information center distributes a *Bicycle Route Guide* of the Buffalo-Niagara Falls area. You can rent bikes at the HI-AYH Niagara Falls hostel (see Places to Stay earlier in this section) or try the yellow pages in the phone book for a rental place near your accommodations.

FORT NIAGARA STATE PARK

This state park is about 15 miles north of the town of Niagara Falls, and contains Old Fort Niagara (☎ 716-745-7611). The fort was built by the French in 1726, but was captured by the British during the French & Indian War in 1759. The US took over in 1796 after the British retreated across the river to Fort George in Canada. The fully restored fort is open year-round and also contains a historic museum, which is called Old Fort Niagara. Admission to the museum is $6.75/4.50 for adults/children (ages six to 12). Park entrance costs $5 per car from May to November and is free the rest of the year. In July and August the opening hours are daily from 9 am to 7 pm; the rest of the year, opening hours are 9 am to 5 pm.

To reach the park from downtown Niagara Falls, travel north on Robert Moses Parkway for 12 miles and take the Fort Niagara State Park exit.

NIAGARA FALLS – THE CANADIAN SIDE

It's not surprising that two cities in two countries share one name to describe their proximity to the falls. Both towns are essentially dedicated to serving the needs of the millions of annual visitors. Queen Victoria Park affords the best view of the falls from either side of the river, and it's a short drive, or short walk, across the bridge. In fact, weather permitting, pedestrians often arrive sooner than drivers due to the long line of cars at the international border.

In addition to the views (including nightly illumination of the falls) other notable attractions include Lundy's Lane Historical Museum and the Niagara Falls Museum.

For information on getting to the falls, see Getting There & Away in the Niagara Falls – The American Side section, above.

History

Following the established presence of the Seneca who originally settled the area, many British settlers took up residence around the falls – especially those who had opposed the American Revolution and were obliged to move on. The War of 1812 between the US and Britain didn't improve matters, and in July 1814, one of the bloodiest battles of the war was fought along the Niagara River at Lundy's Lane. In the early part of the 19th century, in fact, the battlefields were a major tourist attraction.

Information

The Niagara Parks Commission (☎ 905-356-2241) maintains over 3000 acres of parkland from Lake Erie to Lake Ontario (including the Niagara Glen Nature Preserve), and operates a helpful tourist center near Horseshoe Falls. The center is open daily from 9 am to 6 pm and until 10 pm during the summer. The parks commission also maintains a website at www.niagaraparks.com.

The Niagara Falls Visitor & Convention Bureau (☎ 905-356-6061, 800-563-2557), 5433 Victoria Ave, has restaurant and lodging information, and suggestions for enjoying the falls and other parts of the region. Ontario Travel & Tourist Information (☎ 905-358-3221), 5355 Stanley Ave, also provides travel advice.

Entering Canada Despite its casual appearance and heavy tourist traffic, the US-Canadian border is a proper international boundary, and the normal rules apply.

Most Americans and Canadians will encounter little trouble as they cross from one side to the other. Nevertheless, you should have proof of citizenship with you. A driver's license is not always enough; passports, birth certificates, voter registration cards and green cards may be requested by border guards. Citizens of other countries, of course, should possess proper documents, visas, etc. If you're renting a car in the US and considering crossing the border, ask the rental agency if you'll need any additional documents.

Just because you are going over the bridge to get a better view, or a better photo, doesn't mean you won't be stopped, questioned or even searched – either upon entering Canada or upon reentering the US.

From the US side of Rainbow Bridge, it's a quick walk into Canada; the toll is light: 25¢ per person (each way). If you take a car over, you may pay up to C$8 to park at Queen Victoria Park. Walkers can enjoy the advantage of riding on the **People Mover**, an open-air tram that makes frequent trips from the falls to Queenston Park. You can get on and off at any stop, and resume your ride 15 to 20 minutes later when the tram comes around again. The fare is a bargain ($4.50/2.25 for adults/children).

As for currency, prices in Canada are routinely given in Canadian dollars, but most businesses accept US currency. Exchange rates vary widely, however, and banks – believe it or not – give the best rates. Credit-card exchange rates are also fair. See Money in the Facts for the Visitor chapter for more information.

Queen Victoria Park

While the US side can boast of offering the most thrilling proximity to the falls, the Canadians can rightly claim the best panorama. The long perspective across the river is magnificent and perhaps easier to take in, like a long leisurely breath – as opposed to the powerful gasp of the roaring water at the US vantage point.

In addition to the various tours (such as *Maid of the Mist*, among others), the Victoria Park Dining Room & Cafeteria (☎ 905-356-2217) affords a great view of the falls, and the cafeteria food is very good and reasonably priced.

Other Things to See

The Canadian government has developed the **Niagara Parkway**, a beautiful scenic drive along the Niagara River north to Lake Ontario, and it is a worthwhile drive. If you are driving a rental car from the US to Canada, mention this to the rental company, which may provide you with additional documents for the car.

Close to the river, the town of Niagara Falls is lined with fast food spots and hotels; traffic signals and neon lights are a sharp contrast to the falls. Nevertheless, the town can be inviting and the people helpful.

Lundy's Lane Historical Museum (☎ 905-358-5082), 5810 Ferry St, takes its name from one of the bloodier battles of the War of 1812; the 1814 battle is remembered here, along with military exhibits and Seneca artifacts. The museum is open daily May through November from 9 am to 4 pm, and Monday through Friday from noon to 4 pm the rest of the year.

The **Imax Theater** (☎ 905-374-4629), 6170 Buchanan Ave, is home to the spectacular giant screen (six stories tall), which – among other things – dramatizes (and occasionally eulogizes) the daredevils, tightrope walkers and others of questionable decision-making powers who have pitted their wits and bodies against the power and splendor of the falls. (For more information, see the boxed text, 'Niagara Falls Daredevils' earlier in this chapter.) Imax is open daily 11 am to 6 pm, but does open earlier and close later in the summer months. Admission is $8 for adults, $7 for seniors and children (ages 12 to 18) and $6 for children (five to 11).

Niagara Parks Botanical Gardens & Horticulture School (☎ 905-356-8554) is 5 miles north of the town of Niagara Falls on the Niagara Parkway (which is also called River Rd), and operated by the Niagara Parks Commission year-round from dawn to dusk. Admission is free.

Guinness World of Records Museum (☎ 905-356-2299), 4943 Clifton Hill, is like walking through the book; you can stand face to face with the tallest, fastest and most ridiculous. It is open year-round daily from 9 am to midnight during the summer; other months have slightly shorter hours. Admission is $7/6/4 for adults/seniors and students/children (ages six to 12).

Summertime Friday evenings feature the **fireworks display**, and the **Winter Festival of Lights** takes place every winter from late November until the first week of January.

BUFFALO

New York State's second largest city, Buffalo (population 328,000), is not a major tourist destination, but it is a city of uncommon historical interest and magnificent architecture. This famous port city is on Lake Erie in the far northwestern corner of the state, 20 miles from Niagara Falls and a few minutes from Canada by the Peace Bridge.

It is Buffalo's proximity to Canada that is partly responsible for the recent boom to the city's economy. With the passage of the North American Free Trade Agreement (NAFTA), tariffs between the US and Canada are being phased out, and Buffalo is once again becoming a major trading center. In addition, the city continues to be a manufacturing center, producing glass, rubber, auto parts, machinery and medical instruments. The economic boom is helping to fund a major renovation of the city's downtown and neighborhoods.

Historic buildings – from early skyscrapers to 19th-century residences – are perhaps Buffalo's greatest treasure. Only Chicago boasts a larger collection of buildings by American's foremost architects, Frank Lloyd Wright, Louis Sullivan and Henry Hobson Richardson. (Coincidentally perhaps, Buffalo is closer to Chicago than to New York City.) In addition, Buffalo's park system – the first of its kind in the US – was designed by the renowned landscape architect Frederick Law Olmsted.

Buffalo is an interesting town to explore, and its moderately priced accommodations and the accessibility of Niagara Falls make it a good stopover in western New York. Of course, if you're stopping over in the winter, be prepared for not only the snow, but the inevitable conversation it generates – especially how much heavier it is over in Syracuse.

History

The town of Buffalo was originally a French settlement, established in 1758. In 1800, the

Holland Land Co purchased the land and made plans for a town to be called New Amsterdam. The settlers, however, demanded that the town be called Buffalo.

The derivation of the name is unclear. The most romantic explanation is that the name is a mispronunciation of the French *beau fleuve*, meaning 'beautiful stream,' a reference to the Niagara River. Other theories are that the name is a British mistranslation of the Indian word for beaver or that there was a Seneca Indian named Buffalo who once lived here. A more serious suggestion traces the name to the buffaloes that roamed the region before being exterminated, and which were – around the time of the early settlement – attracted to a salt lick along a creek.

It was the completion of the Erie Canal in 1825 that spurred Buffalo's growth. The city became the center of the shipping trade between the Great Lakes region and the eastern US. The arrival of the railroads – some 10 years later – was a further boost to the city's economy. Beginning in the 1970s, Buffalo's manufacturing base began to decline, but NAFTA promises to help Buffalo regain its former status as a major trading center.

Buffalo is home to the largest university in the state, the State University of New York at Buffalo (SUNY-Buffalo), as well as 17 other educational institutions. The town boasts several important former residents, including two US presidents, Millard Fillmore and Grover Cleveland. Also, Samuel Clemens (Mark Twain) resided briefly in Buffalo, editing the *Buffalo Morning Express*. It was also here that Theodore Roosevelt was sworn in as US president after the assassination of President William McKinley at the city's Pan-American Exposition in 1901.

Orientation

Buffalo's major streets radiate outward from its downtown business district. Because Lake Erie forms the city's western and southern borders, most of the city's major streets begin in the downtown area and run to the north and the east. Niagara Square serves as a point of orientation in the downtown. The visitors bureau and city hall are nearby.

From Niagara Square in the downtown area, Niagara St branches out to the northwest and Delaware Ave to the north. Main St is three blocks east of Delaware Ave and runs north to south. Main St is closed to traffic downtown from the Buffalo & Erie County Naval & Military Park (Naval Park) to near Goodell St. A Metro rail public transportation line runs up the center of Main St and this car-free pedestrian area is designated 'Buffalo Place.'

North of downtown is the historic district of Allentown. Good walking tour maps are available from the visitors' bureau. Just north of Allentown is the Elmwood strip, a trendy and lively area of shops, eateries and bookstores.

Buffalo is a city where it helps to have a car to see things; the most interesting sights are far apart.

Information

The Greater Buffalo Convention & Visitors Bureau (☎ 716-852-2356, 800-283-3256, 617 Main St) houses a visitors' center in the Market Arcade. The center provides a wide selection of travel brochures and maps. It's open Monday to Friday from 9 am to 5 pm, and weekends from May to October. You can also get more information from its website at www.buffalocvb.org.

The post office is at 701 Washington St; another branch is near Niagara Square. The Buffalo and Erie County Public Library (☎ 716-858-8900) is on Lafayette Square. There are at least half a dozen banks on Main St, downtown. The local newspaper is the *Buffalo News*; *Art Voice* is the giveaway arts paper in town.

For laundry, try Kenmore Cleaners & Coin-Op (☎ 716-875-8270), 3197 Delaware Ave. Buffalo General Hospital (☎ 716-859-5600) is at 100 High St near the corner of Goodrich and Ellicott Sts.

Albright-Knox Art Gallery

Housed in a wonderful Greek Revival building adjacent to the location of the 1901

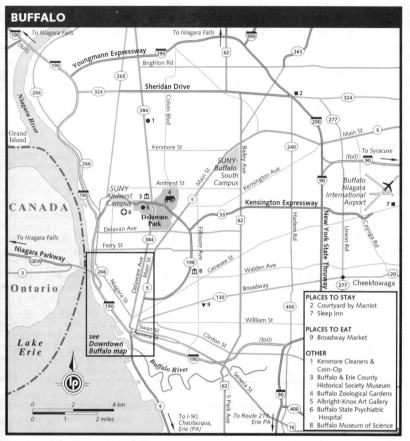

BUFFALO

Map labels:
- To Niagara Falls
- To Niagara Falls
- Youngmann Expressway
- Brighton Rd
- Sheridan Drive
- Colvin Blvd
- Grand Island
- Kenmore St
- SUNY Amherst Campus
- Amherst St
- Delaware Park
- CANADA
- To Niagara Falls
- Niagara Parkway
- Delavan Ave
- Ferry St
- Ontario
- Lake Erie
- see Downtown Buffalo map
- Swan St
- Seneca St
- Buffalo River
- SUNY-Buffalo South Campus
- Bailey Ave
- Kensington Ave
- Kensington Expressway
- Main St
- Fillmore Ave
- Genesee St
- Walden Ave
- Broadway
- William St
- Clinton St
- Harlem Rd
- New York State Thruway
- Union Rd
- Cayuga Rd
- Buffalo Niagara International Airport
- Cheektowaga
- To I-90, Chautauqua, Erie (PA)
- To Route 219, Erie PA
- To Syracuse
- Main St

PLACES TO STAY
2 Courtyard by Marriot
7 Sleep Inn

PLACES TO EAT
9 Broadway Market

OTHER
1 Kenmore Cleaners & Coin-Op
3 Buffalo & Erie County Historical Society Museum
4 Buffalo Zoological Gardens
5 Albright-Knox Art Gallery
6 Buffalo State Psychiatric Hospital
8 Buffalo Museum of Science

0   2   4 km
0   1   2 miles

Pan-American Exposition in Delaware Park, the Allbright-Knox Art Gallery (☎ 716-882-8700), 1285 Elmwood Ave, is best known for its collection of 20th-century art including works from all the major currents, from abstract expressionism to pop art. The collection also contains paintings and sculpture from other historic periods. The gallery is open Tuesday to Saturday from 11 am to 5 pm, Sunday from noon to 5 pm. Admission is $4/3 for adults/seniors and children, free on Saturday from 11 am to 1 pm. Metered parking is available.

Buffalo & Erie County Naval & Military Park

Naval Park (☎ 716-847-1773, fax 716-847-6405), 1 Naval Park Cove on Lake Erie at Main St, displays scale models of ships, airplanes and armored vehicles, as well as some of the real things. The destroyer USS *The Sullivans*, named after five brothers who went down with their ship near Guadalcanal during WW2, is here, as are the guided missile cruiser USS *Little Rock* and the submarine USS *Croaker*. Everything is docked on a small inlet off of Lake Erie just south of I-190, where you'll also find a small museum.

It is open daily April 1 to October 31 from 10 am to 5 pm; in November, weekends only. Admission for adults/children (ages six to 16) is $6/3.50.

City Hall Observation Tower

Visitors are welcome to take an elevator to the 25th floor of the very large city hall building at 65 Niagara Square and then walk three flights to the observation tower (☎ 716-851-5891). It's free and open from 9 am to 4 pm.

QRS Music Rolls

The largest and oldest player-piano roll maker in the country is QRS (☎ 716-885-4600, 800-247-6557), 1026 Niagara St. The factory is in the historic 1885 Buffalo Electric Railway Co generating station building. In the 1920s, when player pianos were far more popular than they are today, QRS made 10 million rolls a year. Today they make between 200,000 and 300,000 rolls annually. Guests are welcome to tour the small factory and watch the production process. Tours are limited to 15 people, and take place Monday to Friday at 10 am and 2 pm; admission costs $2.

On the premises is a one-of-a-kind 1912 Melville-Clark marking piano, a piano used as a recording device. A musician would play a tune on the piano, causing the music to be marked on the roll. The American Society of Mechanical Engineering designated the machine a national historical mechanical engineering landmark.

One-song piano rolls are on sale for $10.25 to $15.75. QRS also sells player pianos, which are priced at about $6500 new, but better deals for used pianos in need of refinishing are available by consulting western New York classified ads.

Architectural Sights

You can explore Buffalo's architectural treasures in greater depth if you take advantage of one of the excellent self-guided or guided architectural tours (see Organized Tours, later in this chapter) sponsored by the Theodore Roosevelt Inaugural National Historic Site. If you are already versed in American architecture and would prefer going at it alone, you might pick up a copy of Reyner Banham's book *Buffalo Architecture: A Guide*, which is available in many local bookstores.

The largest concentration of **Frank Lloyd Wright homes** is north of the downtown area near **Delaware Park**, which was designed by landscape architect Frederick Law Olmsted. Most of these residences are privately owned except Darwin Martin House, 125 Jewett Pkwy at the corner of Summit, which is owned by SUNY-Buffalo (☎ 716-831-3485). Others include the William Heath House, 76 Soldiers Place at the corner of Bird Ave; George Barton House, 118 Summit, which is definitely worth a look; Gardiner's Cottage, 285 Woodward Ave; and Walter Davidson House, 57 Tillinghast Place. The homes can be distinguished from others in the neighborhood by their sleek and strong horizontal lines.

Frank Lloyd Wright's mentor, architect Louis Sullivan, and his partner Dankmar Adler, designed the **Prudential Building** on Church St. Sullivan is generally regarded as the father of the skyscraper. One of the finest examples of early skyscraper design is Sullivan's **Guaranty Building**, at 28 Church St near Pearl St. Built in 1895, the building was beautifully restored in 1983. Tours are available.

There are a number of other interesting buildings downtown, such as the art deco **city hall** on Niagara Square, the **old post office** on Ellicott and Swan Sts, and the former **Buffalo Savings Bank** building at Main and Huron Sts. Henry Hobson Richardson designed nine of the buildings at the **Buffalo State Psychiatric Hospital**, 400 Forest Ave. These red sandstone buildings are excellent examples of the Romanesque Revival that Richardson championed in the latter half of the 19th century. The **McKinley Monument**, designed by Carrère and Hastings and sculpted by A Philmister Proctor, is in the middle of Niagara Square.

The beautiful residential neighborhood of Allentown is just south of the intersection of Delaware and North Sts. The streets of this National Historic District are lined

Cave of the Winds, Niagara Falls, NY

Cascadilla Creek, Ithaca, NY

Mashomack Nature Preserve, Shelter Island, NY

Bottled mineral water - a tonic for what ails you (Saratoga Springs, NY)

Olana, built by Frederic Erwin Church to resemble his famous Hudson Valley landscape paintings

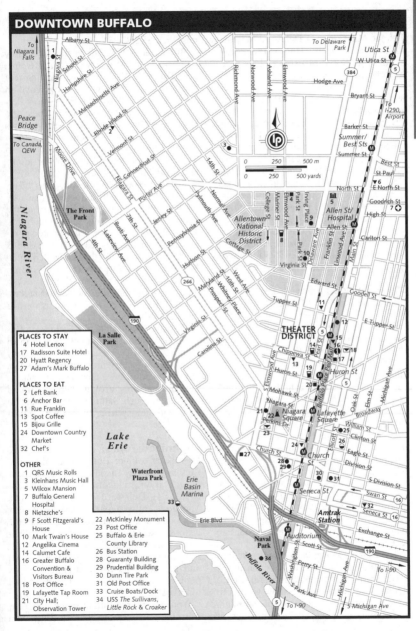

DOWNTOWN BUFFALO

PLACES TO STAY
4 Hotel Lenox
17 Radisson Suite Hotel
20 Hyatt Regency
27 Adam's Mark Buffalo

PLACES TO EAT
2 Left Bank
6 Anchor Bar
11 Rue Franklin
13 Spot Coffee
15 Bijou Grille
24 Downtown Country Market
32 Chef's

OTHER
1 QRS Music Rolls
3 Kleinhans Music Hall
5 Wilcox Mansion
7 Buffalo General Hospital
8 Nietzsche's
9 F Scott Fitzgerald's House
10 Mark Twain's House
12 Angelika Cinema
14 Calumet Cafe
16 Greater Buffalo Convention & Visitors Bureau
18 Post Office
19 Lafayette Tap Room
21 City Hall; Observation Tower
22 McKinley Monument
23 Post Office
25 Buffalo & Erie County Library
26 Bus Station
28 Guaranty Building
29 Prudential Building
30 Dunn Tire Park
31 Old Post Office
33 Cruise Boats/Dock
34 USS The Sullivans, Little Rock & Croaker

with restored 19th-century homes, galleries and restaurants. Walk by the 1869 **Dorsheimer Mansion**, 434 Delaware St, which was designed by Henry Hobson Richardson, and the 1899 **Butler Mansion**, 672 Delaware St, designed by Stanford White.

The Finnish architects Eliel and Eero Saarinen designed the modernist **Kleinhans Music Hall** (☎ 716-883-3560) on Symphony Circle. The building is famous for its modern curving lines and acoustical excellence.

F Scott Fitzgerald's childhood home is 29 Irving Place. **Mark Twain** lived at 472 Delaware Ave while working for the *Buffalo Morning Express*. The one historic home open it visitors is the **Wilcox Mansion** (☎ 716-884-0095), 641 Delaware Ave. Now it is a national historic site and museum, but was the site of Teddy Roosevelt's inauguration following President William McKinley's assassination. Admission is $6/3 for adults/seniors; free for children ages three to 14.

Other Things to See & Do

The **Buffalo Zoological Gardens** (☎ 716-837-3900), 300 Parkside Ave, is in Delaware Park and was part of Frederick Law Olmsted's original design for the park in 1875, making it the third oldest zoo in the country. The 23-acre site is home to a white tiger, rare Indian rhinoceros and, of course, bison. There is also a Lowland gorilla exhibit, a children's zoo and exhibits in the World of Wildlife Building. The zoo is open May through September Monday to Friday from 10 am to 5 pm and weekends 10 am to 5:30 pm, and October through April daily from 10 am to 4 pm. Admission costs $6/3 for adults/children (ages three to 14).

The **Olmstead Winter Carnival** (☎ 716-856-3150) takes place in February. Shakespeare in Delaware Park (☎ 716-876-7430) has free, fully staged Shakespeare performances Tuesday through Sunday from late June to August.

The **Buffalo Museum of Science** (☎ 716-896-5200), 1020 Humboldt Pkwy, outside of the downtown area, contains natural science exhibits and activities that allow visitors to investigate the natural world of dinosaurs and insects or unravel the principles of action and reaction. It is open Tuesday through Sunday from 10 am to 5 pm. Admission is $5.25/3.25.

Buffalo & Erie County Historical Society (☎ 716-873-9644), 25 Nottingham Court, near Delaware Park, is in the building that once served as the New York State Pavilion at the 1901 Pan-American Exposition. Permanent and changing exhibits trace the history of Buffalo and explore the city's diverse cultures and traditions. It's open Tuesday through Saturday from 10 am to 5 pm; admission costs $3.50/2/1.50 for adults/seniors/children (ages seven to 15).

Pedaling History Bicycle Museum (☎ 716-662-3853), 3943 N Buffalo Rd, in nearby Orchard Park, is the only museum in the country devoted exclusively to bicycles. There are 300 bikes and other related paraphernalia on display, as well as exhibits tracing the history of bicycling. It's open Monday through Saturday 11 am to 5 pm; on Sunday it opens at 1:30 pm. The cost of admission is $4.50/4/2.50 for adults/seniors/children (ages seven to 15); admission for families of six is $12.50.

Original American Kazoo Factory (☎ 716-992-3960) is about 30 minutes south of town in Eden, at 8703 S Main St. It's the only metal kazoo factory in the world. This is a one-of-a-kind place, a combination factory, museum and gift shop. It is open year-round Monday through Saturday from 10 am to 5 pm and Sunday from 12 to 5 pm. Admission is free.

Organized Tours

A walking tour of Buffalo's architectural sites is offered by Theodore Roosevelt Inaugural National Historic Site (☎ 716-884-0095), 641 Delaware Ave in the Wilcox Mansion. Tours depart from the Wilcox Mansion and go through downtown and the historic residential neighborhood of Allentown. There are one-hour, self-guided cassette tours (which are offered year-round) and guided tours for a minimum of six people (available April to October). All tours cost $5.

You can also see Buffalo and its environs from Lake Erie or the Niagara River on a cruise boat. The *Miss Buffalo* and *Niagara Clipper* (☎ 716-856-6696, 800-244-8684) depart from Buffalo dock and North Tonawanda dock, respectively. *Miss Buffalo* runs narrated sightseeing tours through the canal, taking in the sights around Lake Erie; *Niagara Clipper* sails on the upper Niagara River and around Grand Island. From May to September cruises depart throughout the afternoon and evening. A two-hour tour costs $9/6.50 for adults/children (ages five to 12); music, lunch, dinner and murder mystery cruises cost $23 to $39. Visit the company's website at www.missbuffalo.com for information and directions.

If you're without a car, you might want to consider a tour package that includes both Buffalo and Niagara Falls. Gray Line Buffalo (☎ 716-625-1603, 800-695-1603) gives tours of Buffalo and Niagara Falls on both sides of the border from May through October. The tour lasts for three and a half hours and goes quickly around Buffalo and then to Niagara Falls. Tickets cost $58/28 adults/children (ages five to 11). Gray Line Buffalo is located at 3466 Niagara Falls Blvd in North Tonawanda, 6 miles north of downtown Buffalo.

Places to Stay
Near the airport, there are several places to stay, including *Sleep Inn* (☎ 716-626-4000, 100 Holtz Rd). Rates are $50 to $125.

Hotel Lenox (☎ 716-884-1700, 800-825-3669, 140 North St) is an old classic in the city's historic Allentown district. The good-sized rooms are furnished with mismatched, but sturdy furniture. There is a student rate of $49 for up to four people in a room. Otherwise singles/doubles are $59/69; fancier suites go for $80/90 with kitchenette. *Courtyard by Marriott* (☎ 716-874-8000, 4100 Sheridan Drive) is a few minutes from downtown off I-290. Accommodations include indoor pool, whirlpool and exercise room. Room rates are $98 to $144.

Hyatt Regency (☎ 716-856-1234, 2 Fountain Plaza) is truly a luxurious place. It's in the theater district on the Buffalo Place pedestrian mall along Main St. The brick and stone building was originally an office tower that was converted into a hotel in 1984. Even if you don't stay here, it's a fun place to explore. The lobby is a plant-filled atrium. There are three restaurants, a bar, indoor pool and sun garden. Rooms are equally luxurious and rates start at $89 to $149 and up.

The largest hotel in western New York, *Adam's Mark Buffalo* (☎ 716-845-5100, 120 Church St), at the corner of Lower Terrace, is a luxurious complex overlooking Lake Erie and the entire downtown. Year-round rates are $99 to $170; ask about discounts and weekend specials.

Also downtown is the *Radisson Suites Hotel* (☎ 716-854-5500, 601 Main St), adjacent to the historic Market Arcade annex. Weekend rate specials are as low as $89 and standard suites cost $99 to $159.

Places to Eat
In culinary terms, Buffalo is best known for its Buffalo-style chicken wings and beef on weck. Buffalo wings are covered in a spicy red chili sauce (unlike the honey-mustard sauce of lesser-known Rochester wings) and are served with creamy blue cheese dressing and celery sticks. Beef on weck is sliced roast beef on *kummelweck*, a hard roll impregnated with salt and sometimes caraway seeds. Both items are featured on menus throughout the city.

Budget & Mid-Range The *Anchor Bar* (☎ 716-886-8920, 1047 Main St), at E North St, claims to have invented Buffalo chicken wings. Located in a marginal neighborhood, the bar still packs in the crowds on the weekends. (Oscillating video cameras scan the parking lot and nervous bar patrons watch their cars on indoor video screens.) Inside the red-brick building is a tin-ceilinged bar backed with a hundred baseball caps and other memorabilia. You can also dine in one of the two modern – but less imaginative – dining rooms. Wings come in single and double orders ($5/7). For lunch, the restaurant serves – in addition to Buffalo chicken wings – sandwiches and Italian specialties, including pizza, spaghetti and meatballs and vegetarian lasagna, all ranging from $4 to $6. Dinners include homemade ravioli, chicken and fish selections, barbecued ribs and – of course – Buffalo chicken wings. Dinner can cost up to $16.

On Thursday from June to September you can stop by *Downtown Country Market* (☎ 716-856-3150, *Main St*) between 8 am and 2:30 pm to pick up fresh produce and baked goods. The market is on Main St between Court and Church Sts.

Broadway Market (☎ 716-893-0705, *999 Broadway*), at Fillmore St, is in the heart of the city's Polish neighborhood, outside of downtown. In this indoor market, over 40 small concessions serve an array of ethnic specialties. It is open Monday to Friday from 8 am to 5 pm, and Saturday 7 am to 5 pm.

Bijou Grille (☎ 716-847-1512, *643 Main St*), across from Theater Place, is a good and informal eatery with excellent desserts and a longbar, and there's outdoor dining in the summertime.

Chef's (☎ 716-856-9170, *291 Seneca St*), at Chicago St, is an Italian restaurant a few blocks east of Main St in an industrial neighborhood. This is another Buffalo institution. The main building is an unpretentious three-story brownstone connected to two one-story additions. The decor is simple and the food is good. Dishes (most with tomato sauce) are offered in small and large portions and cost $5 to $10. Typical dishes are spaghetti with meatballs or sausages, or ravioli stuffed with meatballs, mushrooms or sausages. It is open Monday through Saturday from 11:45 am to 9 pm.

For good coffee or chai and dessert, check out *Spot Coffee* (☎ 716-854-7768), which is at Delaware Ave and Chippewa St. Pastries are baked from scratch on-site. It is open 24 hours daily.

Top End If you want to splurge and enjoy excellent French cuisine, try *Rue Franklin* (☎ 716-852-4416, *341 Franklin St*), a bit north of downtown. Appetizers such as rabbit galantine or fois gras terrine cost around $7; entrees include trout with leeks, veal provençal and lamb shanks, and prices range from $16 to $21. It is open Tuesday through Saturday for dinner only from 5:30 to 10 pm.

On the west side is *Left Bank* (☎ 716-882-3509, *511 Rhode Island St*), which usually serves garlicky Italian food in a pub-like atmosphere, despite the Sunday brunch with a string quartet.

Entertainment

Buffalo has a thriving entertainment scene, and visitors can find worthwhile offerings every night.

Theater Buffalo's theater district extends primarily along Main St between Tupper and Chippewa Sts. Several theaters are to the west, on Franklin St and Delaware Ave. You can make reservations from most hotels and motels, as well as through Ticketmaster (☎ 716-852-2000).

Alleyway Theatre (☎ 716-852-2600, *1 Curtain Up Alley*) is a small, intimate theater company that showcases new plays. *Buffalo Ensemble Theatre* (☎ 716-855-2225, *220 Delaware Ave*) is a small professional theater. Its repertory includes both new and classic works. *Paul Robeson Theater* (☎ 716-884-2013, *350 Masten Ave*) is in the African American Cultural Center, between Utica and Ferry Sts, east of the downtown area.

The Theater of Youth at the newly renovated *Allendale Theatre* (☎ 716-884-4400, *203 Allen St*), in historic Allentown, has staged plays for children and young adults for 20 years. Performances are held year-round, Friday at 10 am and 7 pm, and weekends at 2 pm. The summer hours vary. Admission is $10.

Ujima Theater Co, in the *Theater Loft* (☎ 716-883-0380, *545 Elmwood Ave*) is a professional company dedicated to performing works by African-American and other playwrights.

Irish Classical Theatre (☎ 716-853-4282, *625 Main St*) is a new, state-of-the-art center that mounts productions by renowned Irish and international playwrights.

Other theaters include the *Katharine Cornell Theatre* (☎ 716-645-2038) at the Ellicott Complex of SUNY-Buffalo on the Amherst Campus. *Studio Arena Theatre* (☎ 716-856-5650, *710 Main St*) performs modern and contemporary works. *Pfeifer Theatre* (☎ 716-847-6761, 681 Main St) is a small, intimate house in the heart of the theater district.

Classical Music The Buffalo Philharmonic Orchestra (☎ 716-885-5000) performs at the Saarinen-designed *Kleinhans Music Hall* (☎ 716-883-3560, Symphony Circle). Kleinhans is one of five acoustically perfect concert halls in the country.

Lancaster Opera House (☎ 716-683-1776, 21 Central Ave) is a restored 350-seat, early 20th-century theater that hosts plays, musicals and concerts.

Clubs *Calumet Cafe* (☎ 716-855-2220, 54 W Chippewa St), in the theater district, features top jazz performers in a classic bistro atmosphere. It also serves dinner on Thursday, Friday and Saturday night. This club is closed for renovations until 2001.

Nietzsche's (☎ 716-886-8539, 248 Allen St) showcases popular rock and blues bands and has a good little dance floor. There are free open-mike nights (usually Monday), and cover charges of about $5, depending on the act.

Lafayette Tap Room (☎ 716-885-8800, 320 Pearl St) is a good jazz and blues club and restaurant near the Chippewa Strip, which features an assortment of clubs and restaurants.

Thursday at the Square, Main at Court Sts in Lafayette Square, offers outdoor concerts free to the public from late May through August. Headliners range from local favorite The Flutie Brothers Band (with footballer Doug on drums) to the Marshall Tucker Band and Spyro Gyra. Events typically run from 5 to 8:30 pm.

Spectator Sports

Buffalo is a sports town. Get tickets either from Ticketmaster (☎ 716-852-5000) or from the stadiums.

The Buffalo Bills football team (☎ 716-649-0015) plays at Ralph Wilson Stadium in Orchard Park from September to December, barring yet another trip to the Superbowl. This team is well known for playing

great games until the national championship comes along.

Marine Midland Arena (☎ 716-885-4100), 1 Seymour H Knox Plaza, hosts National Hockey League's Buffalo Sabres (October to April), the Buffalo Bandits lacrosse team (January to March), Buffalo Blizzard soccer team (November to March) and Buffalo Destroyers arena football team (April to July).

The Buffalo Bisons minor league baseball team (☎ 716-852-4700) plays its games at downtown Dunn Tire Park, Washington and Seneca Sts, throughout the spring and summer.

Several buses depart from the bus station (Metro Transportation Center), at the corner of Ellicott and Eagle Sts, for Ralph Wilson Stadium. To Dunn Tire Park and to Marine Midland Arena, you can take the Metro rail.

Getting There & Away

Air Buffalo Niagara International Airport (formerly named Greater Buffalo International Airport; ☎ 716-630-6000), at Genesee St, in Cheektowaga, is served by American, Continental, Delta, Northwest, Shuttle America, United, US Airways as well as Vanguard Airlines.

Some average roundtrip fares are from Buffalo to Philadelphia, $228; to New York City (JFK), $238; and to Chicago, $204. Vanguard has fares to Chicago for as low as $49 one-way.

Bus The Metro Transportation Center, 181 Ellicott St at the corner of Eagle St, is served by New York Trailways (☎ 716-855-7531, 800-295-5555), Greyhound (☎ 800-231-2222) and NFTA.

NFTA (☎ 716-285-7211, 285-9319) operates bus No 40 between Niagara Falls and Buffalo every day. Express bus No 60 runs between Niagara Falls and Buffalo five times a day from Monday to Friday. Two express buses leave Niagara Falls for Buffalo before 7 am and three buses leave Buffalo for Niagara Falls roughly between 4:30 and 5 pm. The fare for both buses is a reasonable $1.90.

Train Amtrak stops in Buffalo at the downtown Buffalo Exchange Station (☎ 716-683-8440), Exchange and Oak Sts, and at the Depew Station (☎ 716-856-2075), 55 Dick Rd in nearby Cheektowaga, near the airport (about 16 miles from downtown).

A cab from Depew Station to downtown Buffalo is about $20 (see the Getting Around section, below).

Car & Motorcycle Buffalo is reached by I-90 from the east and south and by I-190 from Niagara Falls to the north. The QEW in Canada to the west leads to the Peace Bridge over the Niagara River and into Buffalo at Niagara St.

Several major car rental companies are at the airport, including Hertz, Alamo, National, Budget, Dollar Rent a Car, Thrifty and Avis.

Getting Around
To/From the Airport Bus No 24 runs from the airport to the Metro Transportation Center.

The ITA Buffalo Airport Shuttle (☎ 716-633-8318, 800-551-9369) runs between Buffalo airport, major hotels and the bus terminal for $11/18 one-way/roundtrip. Buses leave the airport every hour on the hour. A taxi is about $25.

Bus & Light Rail The Metro bus and rail system (☎ 716-855-7211) have the same fare structure. The basic fare is $1.25 in exact change and an additional 25¢ for each zone crossed beyond the basic zone. On the bus, you pay when boarding, but on the rail line you buy a ticket from a self-serve machine *before* boarding. If you're caught by roving inspectors without a ticket on the rail line, you get fined $20. The rail is free to/from the six southernmost above-ground stops on the line, from the theater district to the last stop south on Main St, almost at Lake Erie. North of the theater district stop, continuing to the SUNY-Buffalo campus, the train goes underground and riders start paying. Buffalo's buses run from about 5 am to midnight; light rail runs from 6:30 am to 11:30 pm.

Taxi Taxi companies include:

Airport Taxi Service/ITA Shuttle (☎ 716-633-8318, 800-551-9369)

City Service Taxi (☎ 716-852-4000, 800-439-7006)

Liberty Cab (☎ 716-877-7111, 800-455-8294)

CHAUTAUQUA
The township of Chautauqua (pronounced 'sha-TAW-kwah') is 65 miles southwest of Buffalo on Chautauqua Lake (named by the Seneca tribe and meaning 'bag tied in the middle,' referring to the shape of the lake) in western New York's bucolic wine and farm country. While 400 to 1100 people live here year-round, the majority of activity takes place during the nine-week summer tourist season.

Chautauqua includes several villages, the lake and Chautauqua Institution, which hosts lectures, concerts, workshops, dance and theater for approximately 180,000 visitors each summer. Comprising 215 acres inside its gates, the institution has been designated a National Historic District because of its small winding streets and beautifully maintained Victorian buildings and gardens, as well as the tranquil atmosphere, which is a throwback to a bygone era. Between attending lectures, taking music classes or swimming, visitors loll about on front porches and garden benches or stroll the locust-tree-covered grounds. Cars are banned (except for loading and emergencies), and given its 'Sunday School' roots, alcohol is permitted but it is not sold, and no drinking is allowed in public. Life here is as unstructured as you wish to make it. The psychologist William James, brother to Henry James, referred to Chautauqua – in a less than complimentary tone – as a 'middle-class paradise, without a sin, without a victim, without a blot, without a tear.'

The institution does appeal to a broad audience through its diverse course offerings, ranging from writing to puppetry, from personal interaction and adjustment to archery. Lectures and entertainment are also designed to attract people of different ages and backgrounds.

You can visit the town in one day, but most visitors arrange for longer stays of a weekend, a week or longer. In fact, many visitors return year after year for generations, bringing with them children and grandchildren. To receive information about the upcoming summer session, a schedule of entertainment and the various packages offered by the institution, write or call them at the Chautauqua Institution (☎ 716-357-6200, 800-836-2737), PO Box 28, 1 Ames Ave, Chautauqua, NY 14722.

History
Chautauqua's austere beginnings and cobblestone walkways can be traced to the Chautauqua movement of adult education, which offered cultural, religious and recreational activities. Chautauqua was founded in 1874 by Lewis Miller, an Ohio inventor and manufacturer, and John Heyl Vincent, a Pennsylvania Methodist minister, as a vacation school for Sunday-school teachers. The institution quickly became a place for the public discussion of a wide range of contemporary issues, including religion, women's rights and new inventions (like electricity).

Traveling tent 'chautauquas,' not actually connected to the institution, toured the country in the early 20th century presenting lectures, concerts and sermons. William Jennings Bryan appeared on the chautauqua circuit many times to give his *Cross of Gold* speech. The Chautauqua Institution grew and eventually adopted its present mission: to encourage and present discussions of religious, social and political issues in a community environment.

Orientation
The village is between Route 394 and Chautauqua Lake. There are five gates to the Chautauqua Institution, but visitors must enter through the main gate. At the center of the community is Bestor Plaza. Around the plaza are the Colonnade (a building housing the institution's offices), the post office, library and a few restaurants. Brick Walk extends along the north side of the plaza. One block east of Bestor Plaza is the amphitheater. Going around the lake, little

Jamestown (population 34,000) seems to be an urban center compared to most of the lakeside hamlets, such as picturesque Bemus Point, a recreation and boating hub.

Information
The institution's business offices (☎ 716-357-6200, 800-836-2787) are in the Colonnade building. There is an information desk in the Colonnade lobby (☎ 716-357-6257) and at the main gate (☎ 716-357-6263).

Be sure to contact or stop at the Chautauqua Country Visitors' Bureau (☎ 716-357-4569, 800-242-4569), PO Box 1441, Route 394, Chautauqua, NY 14722, located in the Welcome Center, Chautauqua Institution Main Gate.

The post office (☎ 716-357-3275) on Bestor Plaza is open in-season from 9 am to 5 pm weekdays and 9 am to noon on Saturday, with reduced hours in the off-season. Throughout the summer, the *Chautauquan Daily* newspaper is published out of the post office building. The institution bookstore is downstairs from the post office.

The Smith Memorial Library (☎ 716-357-6296) on the plaza is open year-round. Summer hours are Monday to Saturday from 9 am to 5 pm, Sunday 2 to 4 pm. There are exhibits on Chautauqua's past in the library and Chautauqua historian Alfreda L Irwin had her offices there. Her book *Three Taps of the Gavel: Pledge to the Future, the Chautauqua Story* is the institution's definitive history.

The use of cars on the grounds is restricted. Parking lots near the entrance gates charge $4 a day and long-term parking ($111 per season) is available at the main gate parking office (☎ 716-357-6225).

Narrated bus tours of the institution (☎ 716-357-6263) typically cost $3/1 for adults/children.

Activities & Entertainment
Everyone over 13 who enters the institution, including residents, must buy a gate ticket at the main gate. The ticket entitles its bearer to attend every event with the exception of operas, plays and special study courses. These require an additional ticket or fee.

Tickets are free on Sunday, in keeping with Chautauqua's Christian roots. Otherwise, prices for adults/children (ages 13 to 17) are as follows during their season from mid-June through August:

a day (7 am to 8 pm)	$11
noon to 8 pm	$6
an evening (4 pm to midnight; includes concert)	$22 to $29
a day and evening	$33
a weekend	$47
one week	$190
two weeks	$260/67
three weeks	$390/75
four weeks	$515/85
five weeks	$640/92
six weeks	$760/101
nine weeks (full season)	$760/125

Large events in the amphitheater have festival seating, and popular performances and lectures fill up quickly. The amphitheater is a 5000 seat, roofed outdoor structure that houses an enormous massey pipe organ.

Lectures The lecture series at Chautauqua enjoys national renown. President Franklin D Roosevelt gave his *I Hate War* speech at the Chautauqua Amphitheater in 1936. Nine other US presidents, from Ulysses S Grant to Bill Clinton, have lectured here, as have Leo Tolstoy and William Jennings Bryan. Today, every weekday morning during the nine-week season a different lecture is given in the amphitheater. Lectures are organized around broad seasonal or weekly themes, such as racism and ethnicity, emerging democracies, science and technology and ethics and public life. The lectures are followed by question-and-answer sessions. In addition, the Chautauqua Literary & Scientific Circle invites authors to speak on their work, as does the School of Art.

Chautauqua Literary & Scientific Circle Founded in 1878, making it the oldest book club in America, the Circle is a four-year home-study program. In its early years, the circle served as correspondence courses

do today. In particular, they reached out to men and women from small rural towns who had little access to formal advanced study. The circle also played an important role in the creation of adult education programs in the US. Today, each graduating class comes to the **Hall of Philosophy**, an open-air plaza, for a graduation ceremony. On the floor of the hall are tile plaques representing many Circle classes of the past.

Music The Chautauqua Symphony Orchestra is comprised of American and international musicians and is conducted by Uriel Siegel, as well as guest conductors. The institution also presents a nine-concert chamber music series, guest recitals and student recitals.

Larger concerts and performances take place in the amphitheater. Past performers include Glenn Miller, Peter, Paul & Mary, 10,000 Maniacs (originally from the local Jamestown area), the Beach Boys, Bill Cosby and Natalie Cole.

The Chautauqua Opera stages four operas each season. Tickets are $16 to $39 or all four for $60 to $140.

Dance Jean-Pierre Bonnedoux, a former dancer with the New York City Ballet and the Paris Opera, is the artistic director of the Chautauqua Dance Company. Each season they put on performances of modern dance and ballet.

Theater The Chautauqua Conservatory Theater Company presents four plays each season in Normal Hall. Tickets are available at the Opera/Theater Ticket Office (☎ 716-357-6250) at the Main Gate and cost $10 to $16.

Religion There are morning Christian services most days of the week. On Sunday, sermons are given by visiting theologians. Throughout the season, lectures and discussions on religion and spirituality are far more ecumenical. Past speakers have included Norman Vincent Peale, Jesse Jackson, Elie Wiesel and Mrs Coretta Scott King.

Summer Schools The institution houses four schools of fine and performing arts for art, dance, music and drama. Auditions are required and competition is rigorous. There are also over 200 **Special Studies** courses (☎ 716-357-6234/6255) that do not require participants to audition. These one-week courses include studies in literature, languages, art, dance and music. They cost $40 to over $100, depending on materials fees.

Parents who bring their children to Chautauqua can enroll them in a variety of programs geared to children of different ages and interests. There is day care, children's school, boys' and girls' clubs and youth activities. Contact the Chautauqua Institution business office (☎ 716-357-6200) for current listings.

Recreation On Chautauqua Lake fishing is probably the most popular summertime activity, along with water-skiing and boating. Fish that abound in Chautauqua Lake include muskellunge, walleye, northern pike, crappie, carp, perch, sunfish, bass and trout.

The sports club (☎ 716-357-6281) on the lake rents sailboats and canoes, and there is also dock space for those who bring their own boats (☎ 716-357-6288). The club also fields a number of softball, volleyball and basketball teams in the Chautauqua leagues.

There are several fishing supply and boat rental shops all around the lake, including Redwood Ranch Bait & Tackle (☎ 716-386-4275), South Harold Ave, in Bemus Point; Hogan's Hut General Store (☎ 716-789-3831), Route 394, in Stow; and Chautauqua Marina (☎ 716-753-3913), Route 394, in Mayville.

The Chautauqua Yacht Club (☎ 716-357-4001) has weekly races during the summer and teaches sailing through the Special Studies program (☎ 716-357-6255).

There are four public swimming beaches (☎ 716-357-6255/6309) on the lake within the grounds of the institution and eight tennis courts near the main gate.

Bike Rent (☎ 716-357-9032) does just that on Massey Ave Monday to Saturday from 9 am to 6 pm and Sunday from 11 am to 6 pm.

Palestine Park

The park, which is reflective of the institution's religious beginnings, is a to-scale replica of the Holy Land complete with the Sea of Galilee, Dead Sea and other topographical features. The park is near Miller Bell Tower on Lake Street, the road that runs along the lake.

Places to Stay

The Chautauqua CVB Accommodations Referral Service (☎ 716-357-6373, 800-242-4569) can assist you in finding housing for your stay at the institution. Or, you can drop by the information office in the Colonnade and pick up a copy of the *Accommodations Directory* that is updated before each season. The best budget options are generally rooms in houses or guest houses. At the upper end are the hotels and condos, some of which offer vacation packages ranging from one weekend to one week. The packages include accommodations, a gate ticket and tickets for selected events. These cost $125 to $600 depending on length of time and kind of accommodations.

Budget *Grace Cottage* (☎ *716-357-2802, off-season 815-235-7267, 10 Ames Ave*) rents rooms by the day for $15 to $30 and by the week for $104 to 400. Guests may use the kitchen.

Rates at *27 Scott* (☎ *716-357-3011, off-season 716-484-1438*) are $28 to $40 a day. Rooms at *9 Whitfield* (☎ *716-357-3925, off-season ☎ 309-828-6874*) have lake views and rates are $22 to $45 a day and $88 to $190 a week.

If you're a student planning to stay the entire season, check out *CLSC-Alumni Hall* (☎ *716-357-3105, off-season 716-357-4839*), at Cookman and Wyeth Sts. Rooms here are only $55 to $175 a week.

Mid-Range *Gleason* (☎ *716-357-2595, 12 N Lake Drive*) is a large lakefront house with a porch. Daily rates are $45 to $65 and weekly rates are $225 to $375. *Rose Cottage* (☎ *716-357-5375, 2 Roberts*) is an 1877 cottage just one house from the amphitheater in the middle of town. Daily rates are $32 to $36.

Lakeside Cottages (☎ 716-386-2535, 50 Lakeside Drive) has 20 cottages, one row of white, one row of green. The rooms are clean and attractive and are available by the day or week. Daily rates range are $80 to $100 (for two to four people). Weekly rates are $450 to $500. There is also a B&B with single/double rooms for $40/50. It is open April through October, sometimes longer for the B&B.

Sheldon Hall B&B (☎ 716-664-4691), on Main St in the hamlet of Greenhurst, 5 miles west of Route 17/I-86 at the Jamestown exit, is a restored turn-of-the-century summer home once favored by boat captains who dropped in from Lake Erie. Sheldon Hall has a 50-foot boathouse and an upstairs ballroom. There are 10 guest rooms, most with private bath; all include a full breakfast. Prices range from $60 to $100 a night. It is open summers only from Memorial Day to Labor Day.

Top End The *Athenaeum Hotel* (pronounced 'a-thu-NEE-um') (☎ 716-357-4444, 800-821-1881) is, for many, a hotel that helps define the Chautauqua experience. The large white-and-green Victorian building overlooks the lake. Originally built in 1881, the hotel was renovated in 1983. The rooms all have high ceilings and are comfortably furnished in Victorian period reproductions. Room rates include three meals a day (at dinner the hotel suggests that 'ladies are to be dressed in their loveliest and gentlemen, neckties and jackets, please'). The hotel charges $120 to $158 for single rooms and $180 to $282 for doubles. The more expensive rooms have lake views. The hotel offers discounts for longer stays.

Places to Eat
During the summer session, you can pick up fresh produce and baked goods at the farmers' market Monday through Saturday from 7 to 11 am. The market is at the main gate building.

Sadie J's (☎ 716-357-5245), at Pratt and Ramble Sts next to the Colonnade, is open year-round. You can buy reasonably priced soup and deli sandwiches here. *The Refectory* restaurant next to the post office allows customers to cook food on a hot rock at the table. You can eat here for $10 to $15. You can also sit out front and eat ice cream.

Athenaeum Hotel (see the Places to Stay section, above) serves a fixed-price breakfast/lunch/dinner for $13/16/30, and is rather formal. The tradition is to get two desserts with every meal. The all-you-can-eat daily brunch is an especially good deal.

Getting There & Around
The Chautauqua Institution is in the middle of the town of Chautauqua about 65 miles south of Buffalo. Take I-90 to the Westfield exit and then Route 394 to the entrance. From the south it's 16 miles north of Jamestown on Route 394. Niagara Scenic (☎ 800-695-0086) runs buses between the two towns,

There is a free shuttle bus and tram service running around the grounds from 8:20 am to 8:20 pm, as well as after amphitheater and Norton Hall events.

AROUND CHAUTAUQUA
Bemus Point
About 5 miles east of Chautauqua Institution is the summer resort of Bemus Point, with restaurants and lodgings, shops and galleries, fishing facilities, a golf course and jet-ski and parasailing rentals.

Hotel Lenhart (☎ 716-386-2715, 20 Lakeside Drive), is a must-stay, with a late-night bar and a long porch of brightly painted rocking chairs. Tradition is the theme at the Lenhart, and any summer evening will see the porch gradually fill up with patrons, diners, drinkers and storytellers. It's a local institution and an eavesdropper's dream. The same families return summer after summer (usually taking the same room). A waitress was once overheard responding tongue-in-cheek to a customer who inquired about the possibility of adding yogurt to the very traditional menu, 'THAT would be wrong.'

Dinner at *Hare & Hound Inn and Restaurant* is also a good find, featuring steak and other game. It is open year-round from 5 pm to 10 pm daily.

Italian Fisherman (☎ 716-386-7000), on the lake, has two menus. Inside is a northern Italian fine dining area, with dinners in the $12 to $18 range. More casual and cheaper is the waterfront deck patio with a 'steak-on-the-lake' menu and an open grill; it serves sandwiches, chops, burgers and big salads, mostly in the $6 to $10 range. The restaurant is open from mid-April to mid-September daily from 11:30 am to 10 pm.

Jamestown

This town is the birthplace of comedian Lucille Ball. Check out the town's tribute to her at the **Lucy-Desi Museum** (☎ 716-484-7070), 212 Pine St, in the theater district. Next door is **Lucille Ball Little Theater of Jamestown**, the largest community theater in New York State, and **Reg Lenna Civic Center**, formerly the Palace Theater. The museum tells the personal story of Lucille Ball and Desi Arnez through audio- and video-taped interviews and clips from movies and TV. The museum is open daily mid-May to mid-October and weekends mid-October to mid-May, Monday through Saturday from 10 am to 5:30 pm and Sunday from 1 pm to 5 pm.

Jamestown is 18 miles south of Chautauqua Institution. From I-86 take exit 12 south to the center of town. At Third St turn left and then right onto Pine St. The museum is near the corner on the left. It is open from May to October Monday through Saturday from 10am to 5:30 pm, Sunday from 1 pm to 5 pm; from November to May, it is open Saturday from 10am to 5:30pm and Sunday from 1 pm to 5 pm.

ALLEGANY STATE PARK

About 25 miles east of Chautauqua along scenic Route 17/I-86 lies the 65,000 acre Allegany State Park (☎ 716-354-9121), with over 80 miles of hiking trails. The park is popular year-round, but is probably best known for its winter facilities, which include ice-fishing, snowmobiling and cross-country skiing. Summer activities range from swimming on two sandy beaches to horseback riding to biking and fishing. There is year-round camping. Both tent sites and winterized cabins are available. The cost for visiting the park is $6 a day per car.

Nearby is the **Seneca-Iroquois National Museum** (☎ 716-945-1738), on Broad St in the Allegheny Indian Reservation. The museum is open April to October Tuesday through Saturday from 10 am to 5 pm. Admission is $4/3/2 for adults/students/children. The word 'National' in the museum's name refers to the Iroquois confederacy, which included the Seneca nation.

New Jersey

Facts about New Jersey

It's easy to see why the Garden State is largely ignored and often mocked. It stands in the shadow of confident, popular and powerful New York City. Moreover, it's one of the few states in America without its own major media market – New Jersey's north is part of the New York City broadcast areas, and the south gets TV and radio from Philadelphia. For most Americans, New Jersey is merely a suburb of both cities. For foreign visitors, it's a crowded corridor of smelly oil refineries, shipping docks and dirty marshland along the New Jersey Turnpike leading into New York City from Newark airport.

This is the New Jersey of punch lines and snickering asides. But in recent years, the state government has made great and largely successful efforts to emphasize the area's varied pleasures – 127 miles of beaches, millions of acres of preserved parkland and historic sites inexorably tied to the nation's colonial history. Indeed, the tourism trade brings in $30 billion a year, largely from weekenders who seek the pleasures of the beaches or want to try their luck at the casinos in Atlantic City.

New Jersey is both the most densely populated and the most urbanized state in the US, with more than 1,000 people per sq mile. Yet this statistic is misleading, because about two-thirds of the population lives in northern New Jersey, within 30 miles of New York City. (Another large population nexus is in the Trenton-Camden area, opposite Philadelphia.) In fact, almost a quarter of the state's 7419-sq-mile land area is farmland, and another 40% is forest. There is also nearly 700 sq miles of water within the state's borders.

Just 15 miles directly west of the troubled city of Newark, there are pretty suburban towns such as Morristown and large mansion communities such as Bedminster, where the new rich (Hollywood stars such as Eddie Murphy) mix with the older class (Governor Christine Todd Whitman) on large tracts of verdant land. This horse country gives way to

State Trivia

Nickname: The Garden State
Bird: Eastern Goldfinch
Fish: Brook Trout
Animal: Horse
Dinosaur: *Hadrosaurus foulkii*
Insect: Honeybee
Tree: Red Oak
Flower: Common Meadow Violet
Shell: Knobbed Whelk
Dance: Square Dance
Colors: Buff and Jersey Blue
Demon: Jersey Devil

sparsely populated land as you head further west toward Pennsylvania. On the Jersey Shore – an area that begins at Atlantic Highlands, in the middle of the state, and runs south to its tip, at Cape May – the population is concentrated within 5 miles of the ocean, with suburbs and farmland becoming more prevalent as you travel west.

Those who explore New Jersey off the beaten track will be rewarded with a change of attitude about this much-maligned state.

INFORMATION
Tourist Offices

For information, you can call or write to the New Jersey Division of Travel & Tourism (☎ 800-537-7397). Phone lines are staffed from 8 am to 11 pm daily, and you can leave a recorded message. Alternatively, you can check out a calendar of state events and regional highlights on the Internet at www.state.nj.us/travel.

The regional visitors' associations are:

Atlantic City
☎ 609-965-6316
Cape May
☎ 609-465-7181
Gateway
☎ 201-915-3401, urban northern NJ

462

Shore Area
☎ 732-544-9300, ext 708

Skylands
☎ 800-847-4865, rural northern NJ

Southern Shore
☎ 609-399-2629

Tourist visitors' centers are at:

Atlantic City
(☎ 609-965-6316) Expressway Farley Plaza, on the Expressway just before the entrance to town

Deepwater
(☎ 609-299-5272) I-295 north, 2 miles north of the Delaware Memorial Bridge

Knowlton
(☎ 908-496-4994) I-80 east, 5 miles from Delaware Water Gap

Liberty State Park
(☎ 908-915-3400) exit 14B off the NJ Turnpike near Jersey City

Montvale
(☎ 201-391-5737/7951) exit 172 off the Garden State Pkwy

Ocean View
(☎ 609-624-0918) off the Garden State Pkwy, Seaville

Trenton
(☎ 609-695-0640) 115 W State St, Trenton

Accommodations

Camping The are many campgrounds in New Jersey, and a listing of state and privately run facilities is available from the Department of Environmental Protection's Division of Parks & Forestry (☎ 609-984-0370, 800-843-6420). Information on campgrounds is also found through the New Jersey chapter of the American Camping Association (☎ 609-852-0145) and the Cape May County Campground Association (☎ 800-441-2267). You can also contact the private Campground Owners Association (☎ 609-465-8444) for listings and advice.

Hotels & Motels The New Jersey Hotel & Motel Association (☎ 800-365-6965) has a statewide reservation service.

B&Bs The Bed & Breakfast Innkeepers Association of New Jersey can be reached ☎ 908-449-3535. Bed & Breakfast Adventures can be contacted at ☎ 800-992-2632.

Other services specializing in New Jersey are:

Amanda's B&B Reservation Service
(☎ 908-249-4944) 21 S Woodland Ave, East Brunswick, NJ 08816

Bed & Breakfast of Princeton
(☎ 609-924-3189, fax 609-921-6271)

New Jersey B&B Adventures
(☎ 609-522-4000) 103 Godwin Ave, suite 132, Midland Park, NJ 07432

Plain & Fancy B&B Reservation Service
(☎ 800-374-7829) 1905 Breckenridge Place, Toms River, NJ 08753

Taxes

New Jersey's sales tax is 6%, but clothes are not subject to the tariff, which is why many New Yorkers patronize outlet stores to avoid their state's 8.25% sales tax. There's a reduced 3% state sales tax in designated economic-development areas of downtown Trenton, Newark and Camden, as well as the Meadowlands, near Hackensack, where there are the massive IKEA housewares store and the factory outlets of the city of Secaucus.

Gasoline

New Jersey is one of just three states that are not allowed by law to have self-serve gas stations. Moreover, you won't pay a lot for the full-service experience; at many places in New Jersey, the price of a gallon of unleaded gasoline is often as low as $1.50. The downside: long lines at the service stations in the heat of summer. (A small price to pay if you're visiting from a European country, where petrol prices are five times higher!)

HISTORY
The Original Americans

New Jersey's original residents were a migratory group called the Lenni Lenape ('Original People'). The European colonists dubbed them the 'Delaware,' after the river where their communities were located. There were probably less than 20,000 Lenni Lenape living in New Jersey when European settlers first arrived in the mid-17th century. By 1758, the remaining Native

NEW JERSEY

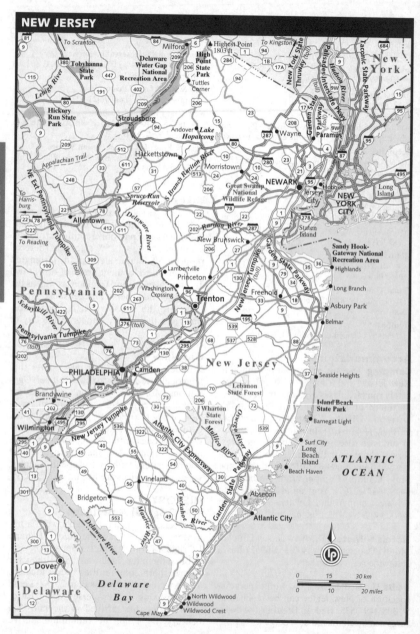

NEW JERSEY

Americans had been placed in the Brotherton reservation in Burlington County, one of the first reservations in the New World. In 1802, the Native Americans on the Brotherton reservation moved to New York State and then to Wisconsin 20 years later.

European Arrival & Colonialism

New Jersey's early colonial history is indistinguishable from New York's. New York Harbor and northern New Jersey were first explored by Giovanni da Verrazano, who anchored off Sandy Hook in 1524. In 1609, Henry Hudson arrived to examine and chart Raritan and Newark Bays and the rocky Palisades west of Manhattan Island. Cornelius Mey, for whom Cape May is somewhat inaccurately named, explored the Delaware River in 1614. Dutch settlers built a trading post at Bergen (now Jersey City) circa 1618 and another one at Camden in 1623. Native Americans also maintained trading posts along the Hudson at Hoboken.

Swedish and Finnish traders followed and established New Sweden along the Delaware River in 1638, but the Dutch of New Netherlands annexed the colony in 1655. In 1664, the English peacefully took over New Netherlands, which included much of New Jersey (see Facts about New York).

Charles II of England subsequently bequeathed New Amsterdam to his brother, the Duke of York, who in turn separated the territory south of New York between the Delaware and Hudson Rivers from his land and gave it to his friends Lord John Berkeley and Sir George Carteret. This new colony was named *Nova Caesarea*, or New Jersey, in honor of Carteret's use of the Isle of Jersey as a Royalist stronghold during the English Civil War.

To attract settlers, Berkeley and Carteret offered fairly generous terms for colonists, including some representation in a territorial assembly. At the same time, Richard Nicolls, the British governor of New York, began recognizing land titles in New Jersey, unaware of Berkeley's and Carteret's similar moves. As a result, land disputes in New Jersey continued throughout the Revolutionary War.

Within a few years, Berkeley sold his land to a group of Quakers. In 1676, these Quakers and Carteret divided New Jersey into East Jersey and West Jersey. East Jersey, Carteret's portion, was actually the land *north* of a line drawn southeast from about Delaware Water Gap to Little Egg Harbor on the coast. West Jersey (the *southern* portion) became the first Quaker settlement in America. In 1681, Carteret's widow sold East Jersey to another group of Quakers, led by William Penn.

The two Jerseys maintained freedom of religion, a liberal land policy and representative government, which attracted many settlers, who brought African slaves with them. In 1702, the Quaker-run regions were united under a royal governor when their respective proprietors surrendered rights to the crown of England. (Nonetheless, each part of New Jersey maintained its own capital – Burlington and Perth Amboy – from 1703 to 1775, and the assembly was forced to alternate between them.)

Today, Berkeley's and Carteret's pivotal roles in the creation of New Jersey's boundaries are almost totally forgotten. A once-grand hotel was named after the men in the seashore resort of Asbury Park, but it has long since closed, and little else remains to remind modern New Jerseyans of the two Englishmen.

War of Independence

During the Revolutionary War, New Jersey's residents were divided on the issue of separation from Britain. In spite of significant anti-British sentiment, loyalists were able to raise six battalions of men during the war. In 1774, a group of New Jersey residents, following the example of Bostonian rebels, dressed as Indians and burned a British tea ship in the Delaware River, an act dubbed the 'Greenwich Tea Party.' Once the war started, undecided residents were swayed to the rebel cause by the conduct of Britain's Hessian mercenaries, who pillaged the countryside.

Quite a few Revolutionary War battles were fought in New Jersey, and George Washington spent significant amounts of time in the state. He established the Continental Army's headquarters at Morristown during the winters of 1776–77 and 1779–80. The general led a group of soldiers across the Delaware River on a freezing Christmas day in 1776 to surprise the sleeping enemy. This event is marked by the town of Washington's Crossing, in the south of the state.

Because of its relatively small size, New Jersey fought aggressively for the political representation of the less-populated states at the Constitutional Convention of 1787. The New Jersey Plan called for a national legislature with a single house of equal representation for each state, regardless of population. This countered the Virginia Plan, which proposed proportional representation.

Under the so-called 'Great Compromise,' the US Senate, with equal representation for each state, was created, along with the proportional House of Representatives. New Jersey adopted the US Constitution on December 18, 1787, the third state to do so. Three years later, Trenton became the state's capital. New Jersey laws that were passed in 1790 and 1797 gave women the right to vote. But in 1807, women were disenfranchised by a law that was called 'highly necessary to the safety, quiet, good order and dignity of the State.'

Early Independence to Civil War

During the early independence years, New Jersey upgraded its transportation system, improving roads and canals to link the state to New York and Philadelphia. Its population grew from about 15,000 in 1700 to more than 185,000 by 1795. With the population explosion came increasing industrial success. Federalist Alexander Hamilton founded his Society for Useful Manufactures in 1791 and chose the Passaic River Falls as the site of the city of Paterson – the first planned manufacturing town in US history. (Hamilton, who went on to serve as George Washington's secretary of the treasury, was shot and killed by Aaron Burr in a famous duel fought in Weehawken Heights, NJ, in 1804.)

Many New Jersey Quakers were active in the Underground Railroad (which helped slaves flee the South) in the years before the Civil War, but the general population of the state was divided about supporting the Union. Those who sold goods to the South feared the loss of southern markets, though they made up for the loss by supplying the Union Army.

Industrialization & 20th Century

After the Civil War, the process of industrialization picked up, especially in the densely populated areas outside New York City. As its economy expanded, a reform movement grew to limit the power of corporations and to give employees better working conditions. One of the leaders of the reform movement was Democratic Governor Woodrow Wilson, the former president of Princeton University who later served as US president from 1913 to 1921. On the political side, New Jersey's large cities were controlled by Democratic 'machines,' which controlled public-works jobs and stifled opposition well into the 1960s, when the middle class moved to the suburbs, depriving these organizations of their base support.

Meanwhile, Thomas Edison was almost single-handedly moving the industrial northern part of the state into a research-oriented scientific development as he perfected the electric light, phonograph and motion-picture camera at his laboratories in Menlo Park, NJ. Thanks largely to his innovations, narrative motion pictures became possible, and Fort Lee was the world's first major film-production center until around 1915, when the industry began moving to the West Coast. During WWI and WWII, the state's industrial machine supplied chemicals, munitions and ships for the war effort.

For most of the mid-20th century, New Jersey's economy was split between the industrial urban north and the agricultural west and south. Newark was the factory powerhouse, producing clothing, machine tools and leatherwork. The main produce from the farmlands were dairy products, corn, tomatoes and cranberries cultivated in the boglands of the state's south. This economic split continues to this day – but the major difference is the incredible growth of

New Jersey's suburban belt, which dominates the middle and east coast of the state.

As the US experienced a boom in suburban population after WWII, New Jersey's northern cities suffered job and population losses similar to those in other urban areas in the northeastern states. The cities of Newark and Jersey City became repopulated by recent immigrants from Portugal, Cuba and India. By the mid-80s, Monmouth and Ocean Counties, lining the Jersey Shore on the Atlantic, were among the fastest-growing areas in the entire US. Even the formerly placid areas of Princeton and Morristown have experienced explosive population growth in recent years, and their roads have certainly suffered from overcrowding.

GEOGRAPHY

New Jersey is on the Atlantic seaboard and is bordered by the Hudson and Delaware Rivers. The state is actually a peninsula, since its only land border is shared with New York to the north. To the west, the Delaware River separates 100 miles of New Jersey from Pennsylvania and a few remaining miles from its southern neighbor of Delaware. Jersey's east coast is defined by the Hudson River and 127 miles of Atlantic Ocean beaches, which include a narrow strip of land – a peninsula, barely connected to the mainland, that leads to several islands – from Bay Head to Wildwood Crest. This odd land mass actually gives that part of the state both an Atlantic Ocean coast and an inlet coast.

New Jersey is one of the smallest states in the Union with regards to land area. The state is 166 by 65 miles at its greatest dimensions. Its highest point is 1803 feet, at High Point, in the Kittatinny Mountains, which run along the northwestern part of the state from the New York border into the Delaware Water Gap, a national recreational area (NRA) on the Pennsylvania border.

The ugly industrial zones near Newark and Hackensack are actually marshes called the Meadowlands. These marshes have long been abused by the dumping of toxic wastes and garbage.

The coastal plain covers the southern 60% of the state, from Perth Amboy on the northeastern coast to Trenton on the Delaware River. In the interior of the state are low-lying marshes and coastal bays. The southern third of the state is largely a spare tract of protected land with sandy soil. Nearly all the state is at or near sea level, with the exception of the mountainous areas of the Piedmont Plateau in the northern part of the state.

New Jersey's chief rivers are the Delaware, Hackensack, Raritan and Passaic. Water flows from the Appalachian Ridge and Valley to the Hudson and Delaware River systems. Mineral deposits found in New Jersey include zinc and iron ore, along with sand and gravel – the basic ingredients for construction projects.

CLIMATE

Although New Jersey faces the Atlantic on its eastern side, the ocean has only a minor effect on temperatures in the state – though the salt air leads to lower snowfall rates along the shoreline. Hurricanes from the south often lose their power as they make their way up the eastern seaboard, though the state can suffer severe damage every few years from an unexpectedly strong storm.

The main weather patterns are influenced by the winds coming off the mass of land to the west and by the winter Arctic blasts from Canada that often plunge the entire northeast into freezing temperatures. Generally, the northern Appalachian and Highland areas have the coldest winters, and the shore has the hottest summers. New Jersey gets 40 inches of precipitation in the south annually, with slightly increasing totals to the north (to over 50 inches).

Average temperatures in the state are 33°F in January, 51°F in April, 74°F in July and 55°F in October.

For a five-day projection of weather conditions on land and for a maritime forecast, call the National Weather Service Forecast Line (☎ 201-624-8118), which is updated every five hours.

NEW JERSEY

STATE PARKS & FORESTS

New Jersey is a transitional zone for plants and animals. Many northern species end their range in the state, and many southern ones begin here. The coastal plain is the most important area for the mixing of flora and fauna.

About 40% of New Jersey is forested, with oak, beech, birch and hickory in the northern part of the state, while the Pine Barrens, in the southern portion of the state, are dominated by pine and oak. The Pine Barrens also have over 30 species of orchid and plants such as pixie moss, bladderwort and ferns.

White-tailed deer are all over the state and pose a danger to drivers on backroads at night. In more mountainous areas, you can still find black bears, bobcats and coyotes. Much more common are smaller animals such as squirrels, raccoons, skunks and opossum.

Fresh and saltwater fish abound in the waters of New Jersey. The ocean offers striped bass, bluefish, weakfish and mackerel. The Delaware River is a fertile spot to fish for shad, walleye, small-mouth bass, catfish and other freshwater catches.

New Jersey is on the Atlantic flyway, and ducks, osprey and other migratory waterfowl – along with hawks and other raptors – are frequently seen. Common songbirds include orioles, bluebirds, cardinals and goldfinches.

Many of New Jersey's state parks are along the shoreline and offer watersport opportunities. The most prominent of these attractions include Lake Hopatcong, the state's largest lake, and the Gateway NRA, in Atlantic Highlands. Camping, canoeing and hiking can be found at the Delaware Water Gap NRA, off Route 80 in the northwestern region of the state, and the Pine Barrens, near Atlantic City, offer more than a million acres of protected wilderness. (See the Northern New Jersey chapter for more information on the Delaware Water Gap and Appalachian Trail.)

GOVERNMENT & POLITICS

New Jersey is governed by a bicameral legislature, which is composed of a 40-member state senate (with four-year terms) and an 80-member General Assembly (popularly elected to two-year terms). Under the local constitution, the governor is one of the most powerful state executives in the nation and serves a four-year term, after which he or she can be reelected once.

In presidential politics, New Jersey is considered a bellwether state for the last generations. Voters are not beholden to either of the two major parties and tend to back the ultimate winner; they supported Ronald Reagan in 1980 and 1984, George Bush in 1988, and Bill Clinton in 1992 and 1996. For statewide offices, New Jerseyans divide their choices fairly evenly between the Democratic and Republican Parties, with voter turnout at about 50% of the qualified population. Former New Jersey senator Bill Bradley, a popular and thoughtful Democratic politician, unsuccessfully sought his party's nomination for president in the 2000 race.

New Jersey has 15 electoral votes, a reflection of its congressional representation of two US senators and 13 US representatives. The current governor, Republican Christine Todd Whitman, was a political neophyte from northern New Jersey who first won fame running on an anti-tax platform for US senate in 1990, and she narrowly lost to incumbent Bill Bradley. Whitman opposed then-governor Jim Florio's controversial plan to increase taxes to better fund education in depressed areas of New Jersey and use the remainder to balance the state budget. Three years later, Whitman beat Florio, promising to roll back taxes 30% during her first term. She kept that promise in part by borrowing against the state-employee pension funds to balance the budget, a gambit that critics claimed will eventually lead to disaster after she leaves office. Nevertheless, Whitman was reelected in 1997, and the state, which recovered faster than the rest of the nation from the recession of the early 90s, has seemingly 'grown' its way out of fiscal danger.

Governor Whitman, a popular pro-choice Republican moderate, was the favorite to succeed retiring Democratic Senator Frank Lautenberg in 2000, but she bowed out of the race, complaining about the time she was spending raising money instead of attending to her governor's duties. Still, she is considered to have a bright future, perhaps as a vice-presidential candidate or even as a presidential runner in her own right.

ECONOMY
This state is home to a huge number of suburban residents who work in the areas surrounding Philadelphia and New York City. So it's not surprising that New Jersey's per capita income of around $20,000 is among the highest in the US. The state benefits from being located between two of the busiest container ports in the world – the Port of New York and New Jersey (the largest container port in the country) and the Delaware River Ports.

New Jersey had early industrial successes with leather making in Newark and Orange; glassmaking and ironworks began the era of heavy industrialization in the latter part of the 18th century. Today, a high proportion of New Jersey's labor force is engaged in high-tech industries and research, and several Japanese companies have set up shop along Route 3 in the northern part of the state. New Jersey is also a national leader in pharmaceutical research and development, with industry leaders Johnson & Johnson, Merck and Carter Wallace headquartered in the state.

There are currently just over four million people in New Jersey's labor force. The service sector employs 30%. Other major employment sectors are wholesale and retail (20%), trade (18%), manufacturing (17%) and government (14%).

Tourism is an important part of the state's economy, and several regions (including the Jersey Shore, Atlantic City and the Skylands area, in the northwest) cater largely to weekenders and summer visitors. Tourism currently brings some $30 billion to the state and is responsible for 300,000 jobs.

Only about 1% of New Jersey residents work in agriculture, though the state is renowned for its peaches, blueberries and tomatoes. New Jersey corn is known for being among the sweetest available in the northeast, and hundreds of cranberry bogs are found throughout the southern half of the state. Over 25% of farm income comes from greenhouses or plant nurseries growing flowers and trees, and a similar amount comes from poultry, livestock, milk and eggs.

POPULATION & PEOPLE
The first big wave of European immigrants in the post-colonial period came in the 1840s, when large groups of Irish came to the area to escape famine. They were followed by Germans, Italians and Poles, and most settled in the big cities along New York Harbor.

New Jersey's current population is eight million people, about 80% of whom are white. Blacks account for 13%. Latinos are the third-largest group, at about 7% of the population. There are statistically small but culturally significant communities (30,000 people or more) of Koreans, Indian Asians and Filipinos.

Almost 90% of state residents live in urban areas. Newark is New Jersey's largest city, with 275,000 people; followed by Jersey City, with 230,000. It seems likely that the population will show to be larger and more diverse once it is again measured in the 2000 census.

MEDIA
New Jersey, situated between the large markets of New York City and Philadelphia, does not have its own TV industry and is

Ringing Up Growth

One of the indices of New Jersey's healthy economy is the astounding explosion in the demand for telephone numbers in the state. Thanks to the many cell phones, faxes and second residential phones, the number of areas codes has doubled to six separate zones. The major cities covered are:

☎ 201   Jersey City
☎ 973   Newark
☎ 908   Flemington
☎ 732   Jersey Shore communities
☎ 856   Camden
☎ 609   Trenton, Atlantic City

NEW JERSEY

largely dominated in the north by New York City's radio stations. Cable and broadcast station WWOR/Channel 9 has its studios in Secaucus, and New York public TV station WNET is officially licensed out of Newark.

New Jersey's first weekly newspaper, the *New Jersey Gazette*, started in Burlington in 1777. Its first daily was the *Newark Daily Advertiser* in 1832. Today there are over 20 daily and 175 weekly newspapers in the

state. The leading paper is the *Newark Star-Ledger*, with regions dominated by the Bergen *Record*; *Asbury Park Press*, Central Jersey's largest newspaper; and the *Trentonian*, a tabloid based in the state capital.

ARTS
Music

Ever since Thomas Edison perfected the phonograph in 1878, New Jersey has played

The Boss: A New Jersey Icon

With the death of Frank Sinatra in 1998, the crown as New Jersey's most famous singer passed down a few generations to Bruce Springsteen.

The rocker has long been identified with the state – and specifically with its middle-class, suburban life – since the early 1970s. Born in Freehold on September 23, 1949, the man who became known as 'The Boss' tried to break into the New York City folk scene after graduating high school. His early forays were not successful, and he returned to the Jersey Shore to knock out a hardscrabble living as a lead singer and guitarist for forgotten bar bands with names like The Rouges and Dr Zoom and the Sonic Boom. Eventually, he joined up with a group of talented locals called the E Street Band (named after the Belmar road where one of the band members lived).

The group's big break came in 1972, when Columbia Records' talent spotter John Hammond, Sr, signed Springsteen. His rough voice and subject matter brought widespread comparisons with Bob Dylan, whom Hammond had earlier signed to the record label. Two early albums – *Greetings from Asbury Park* and *The Wild, the Innocent and the E Street Shuffle* – earned respectable reviews and generated moderate sales. But the 1975 release of *Born to Run*, with its hard-driving title track, made Springsteen a national figure and got him on the cover of *Newsweek* and *Time* on the same week.

The man called 'The Boss' became famous for his improvisational and marathon live shows throughout the 70s. By 1984, politicians from Ronald Reagan on down were trying to associate themselves with Springsteen's hit album *Born in the USA*, which sold 20 million copies. The song title and the singer's blue-collar image led many to assume, wrongly, that he was a right-winger. In fact, Springsteen is a staunch liberal with an ambivalent attitude toward fame. He has appeared at many charitable events and recorded two socially conscious albums – *Nebraska* (1982) and *The Ghost of Tom Joad* (1995), the latter inspired by the writings of John Steinbeck. He also won an Academy Award for the theme song for the 1993 film *Philadelphia*. In 1995, he made a symbolic appearance at a concert in honor of Frank Sinatra's 80th birthday.

In 1999, the year Springsteen turned 50, he reformed the E Street Band after a 10-year hiatus and hit the road again, playing before more than 1.5 million fans worldwide. He also proved that he was still New Jersey's favorite son, headlining a record 15 dates at the 20,000-seat Meadowlands Arena.

Once upon a time, a group of New Jersey legislators got the bright idea to try to designate 'Born to Run,' as the state song. It didn't take long for cooler heads to discover that a song calling the state 'a rat trap – a suicide rap' and advising kids to 'get out while they're young' wasn't exactly an ideal anthem. The embarrassed lawmakers – undoubtedly not rock fans – hastily named 'Born to Run' an 'unofficial' state song.

a big role in popular music. Frank Sinatra, the patron saint of all Jersey musicians, was born in Hoboken more than 80 years ago. Jazz great Count Basie hailed from Red Bank, and the 1500-seat theater in the town's Monmouth Arts Center is named in his honor. Soul singers Lauryn Hill, Brandy and Whitney Houston all hail from New Jersey, as does Paul Simon and Frankie Valli. The region also spawned rocker Jon Bon Jovi and the metal band Twisted Sister.

Most of these local artists have returned to play at the Garden State Arts center, an open-air venue in Telegraph State Park, at exit 116 on the Garden State Pkwy. It's also the site for ethnic festivals from May to October.

The New Jersey Symphony Orchestra (☎ 800-255-3476) is a well-regarded group based at the new Newark New Jersey Performing Arts Center. It plays a winter pops concert series and a full array of summertime events throughout the state. The New Jersey State Opera (☎ 201-623-5757) shares space with the orchestra.

New Jersey's major annual music event is the Waterloo Festival of the Arts, which takes place at Waterloo Village, in Stanhope, from June to August (☎ 609-520-8383) and features concerts by well-known jazz and rock bands, along with a program of classical concerts. The village is open most of the year for other cultural events.

Theater

Millburn's Paper Mill Playhouse is a nonprofit institution that is the official state theater of New Jersey. It offers a program of six plays and musicals each year. The McCarter Theater Center, in Princeton, has won a Broadway Tony Award for best regional theater in the US. It also hosts performances from internationally known dance companies and soloists. Foreign dance companies make visits to New Brunswick's State Theater, a restored 1921 vaudeville palace. It's also the performance site of the Crossroads Theater Company (the state's best-known black acting ensemble) and several other cultural institutions (see New Brunswick).

Visual Arts

It's hard to compete with New York City's array of visual arts, but the Newark Museum has nearly 70 galleries of ancient and modern art, as well as the country's largest collection of Tibetan crafts. Crafts shows take place throughout the state, notably in Margate, Allaire State Park, Cape May and Waterloo Village. The Antiques Show, which takes place each March at the Atlantic City Convention

Jersey Cool

For years, New Jersey has been dismissed as a suburban hell, populated with losers who weren't ready for the bright lights of New York. In the 1980s, comedian Billy Crystal portrayed a nerdy, annoying character from New Jersey whose constant refrain was 'I'm from Joisey – are you from Joisey? What exit?' This was a neat, if cruel, play on the fact that the state is crisscrossed by two major highways, and just about everyone who grew up there could answer such a question.

But after a generation of mockery, New Jersey is…well…almost cool. You could chalk it up to these postmodern times, but the state is getting a fair shake in popular culture. Plus, there's a lot of local talent about: singer Lauryn Hill hails from West Orange; and actors Tom Cruise, Kevin Spacey, Eddie Murphy, Jack Nicholson and Joe Pesci were born in the state. Independent film director Kevin Smith has found success with a trio of films he calls his 'Jersey Trilogy' – *Clerks*, *Mallrats* and *Chasing Amy* – as well as with his 1999 release of *Dogma*, which also took place largely in New Jersey.

In all, some 605 projects were filmed in the state in 1998, including 85 feature films. Recent films include *Copland*, *Happiness*, *Welcome to the Dollhouse* and the acclaimed Mafia TV series *The Sopranos*, which the *New York Times* called 'perhaps the single most important piece of popular culture of the last 25 years.' Ironically, most of these projects still portray the state as a middle-class suburban wasteland.

Hall, is the largest such event in the world. In Flemington, near Princeton, you can see glassmakers at work at the Flemington Cut Glass Company and view old kilns that were built when the town was dominated by the pottery industry.

RELIGION

Although New Jersey was the first Quaker settlement in America, today, 46% of New Jersey's citizens identify themselves as Roman Catholic, and there's a strong conservative Catholic presence in the suburbs. Other major religious groups include Baptists (10%), Methodists (7%) and Jews (4%). A few small towns in the south of the state are home to Orthodox Jewish sects. There are also small numbers of Moslems, Hindus and Buddhists concentrated in the northern cities.

Jersey Shore

The New Jersey coast stretches nearly 130 miles from Sandy Hook in the north to Cape May in the south. Thanks to its beaches and the casinos of Atlantic City it's the most-visited area of the state, accounting for a large portion of New Jersey's 200 million annual visitors. Jersey Shore, the area along the central part of the coast from Sandy Hook to Island Beach State Park, offers diverse activities that could include a visit to the dry Methodist village of Ocean Grove and the massive Six Flags Great Adventure theme park on the same day. The shore towns run from seedy to beautiful and their beaches and boardwalks range from crowded to deserted.

Resort towns like Avon, Spring Lake, Manasquan and Bay Head are quiet and appeal to middle-class families. Belmar, Point Pleasant Beach, Seaside Heights and Long Beach Island have a greater number of bars and attract a younger (and noisier) crowd. Ocean Grove is a historic village with architecture that dates back to the late 19th century and is a peaceful weekend getaway.

Fishing is a draw at Belmar, Point Pleasant and Island Beach State Park. Manasquan and Long Beach Island attract surfers and other watersports enthusiasts. Seaside boardwalks with rides or food vendors can be found in almost every shore town.

Towns are listed from north to south; the population figures given are deceptive since they only reflect the year-round population. During summer all towns have massive influxes of seasonal residents, who boost the populations 10 or 20 fold and create big traffic jams.

This chapter covers the northern part of the shore from Atlantic Highlands to Long Beach Island. For coverage of towns south of Long Beach, including Atlantic City and Cape May, see the Southern New Jersey chapter.

INFORMATION
The Shore Regional Tourist Board (☎ 732-899-6686) is in Point Pleasant Beach.

Highlights

- Monmouth Park, one of the nicest thoroughbred racetracks in the northeast
- The raucous bars, amusement piers and day-long fishing trips in Belmar, Point Pleasant and Seaside Heights
- Quirky square-mile Ocean Grove, a former Methodist camp and now a popular resort for young couples

Look for the *Coast Star*, a weekly local newspaper covering events from Long Branch to Avon, and *Sunny Day*, a free summer guide for beach information and advertisements. The central shore area's main newspaper is the daily *Asbury Park Press*.

ACCOMMODATIONS
In the high season, room rates will run from $35 for a motel to just over $125 a night for colonial inns and holiday weekends. Almost every oceanfront town in New Jersey shuts down for the season about two weeks after Labor Day. Many accommodations listed in this chapter essentially shut down outside summer, even to the extent of disconnecting their phones.

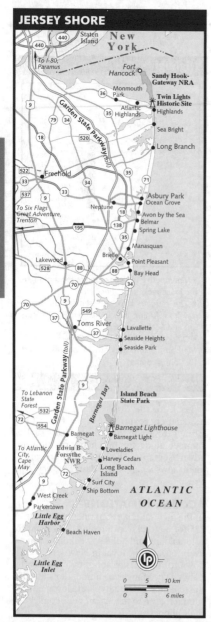

JERSEY SHORE

You can obtain hotel, camping and inn information by contacting the state tourism department at ☎ 800-VISIT NJ or 609-777-0885.

When booking a room, remember to ask if the hotel or inn provides air-con. Many simply have fans, and despite the proximity to the Atlantic Ocean, the shore can get uncomfortably muggy during August and September. On the flip side, make sure the shore motels offer heating if you're staying in the off-season.

GETTING THERE & AROUND
Bus & Train
Beaches from Long Branch to Bay Head are served by NJ Transit train service; points further south (such as Seaside Heights and Cape May which are covered in the Southern New Jersey chapter) are served by bus. See the Facts about New Jersey chapter for NJ Transit's phone numbers specific to the location of the caller.

NJ Transit's (☎ 973-762-5100 for out-of-state calls) North Jersey Coast rail line runs frequently from New York City (Penn Station), Hoboken and Newark to shore points (including Long Branch, Asbury Park, Belmar, Spring Lake, Manasquan, Point Pleasant and Bay Head). There are shuttle buses running from some stations to the beach, which is usually about a half mile away. Regular roundtrip tickets cost $13 to $14 to most shore towns from New York and $10 to $10.50 from Newark and from Hoboken.

The summer beach package includes a combination roundtrip train ticket and one-day beach pass to these points and costs $12 from Hoboken or Newark and $15 from New York.

Car & Motorcycle
If you're in a hurry, it's best to take the Garden State Pkwy, which runs from near New York City along the entire length of the shore a few miles inland from the beaches and towns. There are exits from the Garden State Pkwy for most shore points. To obtain recorded information on conditions along the Garden State Pkwy, call ☎ 908-727-5929.

If you have more time, driving along the coast or near to it on local roads can be pleasant, although Route 71, which runs along the shore points about 2 miles in from the ocean, gets crowded in summer. Be aware that local police are particularly aggressive about issuing speeding tickets, and, at night, pulling over drivers on suspicion of drunk driving.

SANDY HOOK

This beach is part of the Gateway National Recreation Area (NRA), which encompasses the estuary between northeast New Jersey and New York City, parts of Staten Island as well as the Rockaway Peninsula of Brooklyn. The Gateway NRA was established in 1972 as the first urban national park in the US.

On the New Jersey side Sandy Hook is exactly what it sounds like – a large permanent sandbar off the coast. The beach areas include marshes and dunes for hiking and bird-watching as well as a historic fort and lighthouse maintained by the federal government.

Sandy Hook's visitors' center (☎ 732-872-5970), about 2 miles past the toll plaza, is staffed by park rangers and has pamphlets, maps and some books. The address for Gateway NRA's headquarters (☎ 718-338-3338) is Bldg 69, Floyd Bennett Field, Brooklyn, NY 11234.

Admission is charged for the parking areas and costs $8 per car on weekdays and $10 on weekends from Memorial Day to Labor Day.

Lifesaving Museum

Inside the visitors' center there is a small exhibit on the US Lifesaving Service. The service began in 1848 on Sandy Hook at Spermaceti Cove and was formally established by the federal government in 1878. Several times during the summer a shipwreck rescue with original equipment is reenacted from the beach behind the visitors' center.

Admission to the museum is free, and visitors are advised to come during the week to avoid weekend crowds.

Hitting the Beaches

The Jersey Shore beaches are beautiful, although narrow, particularly the further north you go. The shore suffers from frequent battering by storm and erosion, which washes the sand out to sea or further south. In recent years the shore area has used generous federal funds to offset the damage done by winter storms and insure that the beaches, and by extension the revenues they bring in, do not disappear. Erosion control efforts include monitoring tides, planting sand grass and rebuilding seawalls – costly projects that many environmentalists think are ultimately fruitless. The cost of replenishing the damaged beach in Atlantic City alone has been at least $10 million in recent years.

Almost all towns impose a fee for use of the beaches. Day rates are about $5 to $8 per person, but rates go down if you pay by the week, month or season. (Seasonal passes cost around $40, with discounts for children and seniors.) Badges that can be pinned on your suit are sold at the beaches and in town halls, and are almost invariably checked by retirees guarding beach entrances. Access to the beaches is usually free before 9 am or after 5 pm, when lifeguards are not on duty.

Fort Hancock & Sandy Hook Museum

Because ships sailing into the New York Harbor pass close to Sandy Hook, the tip of the peninsula has been an important location for forts since the Revolutionary War. Various gun emplacements were built over the years, with the greatest emphasis from 1890 to 1904. The army designated the collection of emplacements Fort Hancock in 1895. The fort's original buildings went up in 1898 and 1899, and today there are more than 100 century-old brick buildings.

Sandy Hook Museum was originally built as a jail in 1899. Inside, the jail cells are still intact and there are also photographs and information on Sandy

Hook Lighthouse, the oldest lighthouse still operating in the US. The lighthouse is closed to the public. The museum is open during July and August from 1 to 5 pm weekdays, and from 10 am to 5 pm weekends. Admission is free.

Beaches

There are 7 miles of ocean beaches each with its own parking area. Area F is reserved exclusively for fishing. Windsurfing is best on Sandy Hook Bay opposite Area C. Once inside the NRA, there are clearly marked signs to the parking areas for beaches on the ocean as well as the bay side of the park.

Special Events

There are free summer concerts on the beach from late June through early August. The park schedules about a dozen concerts each summer in a wide variety of styles, including blues, jazz, country and swing.

Places to Stay & Eat

Park campsite information is available at ☎ 732-872-5970.

Fairbanks Motel & Marina (☎ 732-842-8450, 344 Ocean Ave) is in Sea Bright, the first town across the Highlands Bridge south of the Hook. It's open most of the year with high-season rates of $80.

Sea Gull's Nest, at Area D beach, has a bar and restaurant that serves seafood in season. *Mirasol* (☎ 732-741-7522) is a Portuguese restaurant next to the Fairbanks Motel.

Getting There & Away

There are no direct public transportation links to Sandy Hook. Seastreak (☎ 800-262-8743) offers up to 11 ferry departures from piers in Highlands and Atlantic Highlands to W 34th St in New York City. These commuter boats cost $15/$28 one way/roundtrip and take about 45 minutes each way, but *won't* get you to the park. For the final stretch of the journey call Sea Bright Shore Cab (☎ 732-345-9099).

By car take the Garden State Pkwy to exit 117 to Route 36 east toward Highland. The turnoffs from Route 36 for Sandy Hook

are clearly marked as you cross the Highlands Bridge.

HIGHLANDS

The Highlands area is typical of New Jersey shore towns. In the summer months, these towns along the Sandy Hook Bay (which constitutes the 'shoulder' of the state's landmass) are packed with cars on the roadways and patrons in the restaurants. In the colder months, the towns and beaches are windswept and rather desolate. The Atlantic Highlands Chamber of Commerce (☎ 732-872-8711), 17 First Ave in Atlantic Highlands, offers information for visitors.

Twin Lights Historic Site

The twin towers of this historic lighthouse (☎ 732-872-1814), also known as Navesink Light Station, were originally built in 1828, but previous lighthouses had stood on this site since 1756. The structure that stands today was built in 1862 after the original towers had fallen into disrepair. A storage gallery and lighthouse keeper's quarters were added at this time to connect the towers.

Navesink was once the testing ground for new navigational equipment and technology. It was the first lighthouse to be powered by kerosene (1883), which replaced whale oil; and 15 years later, the first to be powered by electricity. This was also the sight of the first wireless telegraph tower, which was set up by Guglielmo Marconi in 1899.

The south tower – a light of the 'first order' – indicated a landfall and was so bright it was visible from 22 miles at sea. The north tower – a light of the 'second order' – signaled the approach to the lower bay of New York Harbor. There are two towers here so mariners would not confuse this lighthouse with the one on Sandy Hook, only 5 miles away.

You can walk up the north tower for a fantastic view of the harbor and Sandy Hook. On the ground level there is a museum with exhibits on the lighthouse and lifesaving. The museum shop has one of the better collections of books on New Jersey.

The grounds are open daily from 9 am until sunset; admission is free.

To reach the lighthouse from Route 36 east, make a right 50 feet before the 'Sandy Hook Next Right' sign, which is just before the bridge to Sea Bright. You will be on Portland Rd; then take an immediate right onto Highland Ave. Go uphill, left onto Lighthouse Rd, then take the left fork onto Twin Light Terrace.

If you've just come across the bridge onto Route 36 west, take the exit marked 'Highlands Business Center.' Make a circle going under the bridge and then come up onto Portland Rd and continue as above.

Fishing

As with most shore fishing trips, you're going for bluefish, red hake and flounder. The boats stay pretty close to the shore and the shelf is high in the area. Schupp's Landing (☎ 732-872-1479), 12 Bay Ave, rents fishing boats; a fiberglass four-seater costs $55 per day and a wood three-seater costs $50. It also sells bait, tackle, ice and food. Schupp's is open April to November, weekdays from 5:30 am to 6 pm; opening time on weekends is 5 am. Boats must be returned by 5 pm.

Places to Stay & Eat

The most famous place in the Highlands is **Doris & Ed's** (☎ 732-872-1565, 348 Shore Drive). This is a shore institution but the eponymous owners are no longer there. The restaurant serves great clam chowder, fresh seafood and has a good wine list. Reservations are essential. Main dishes average $25 and even the children's menu is over $10 per plate. Surf and turf is $35. You cannot get into this place without wearing smart casual, but it has been named in *Gourmet* magazine as one of the state's top dining choices.

Conners Hotel (☎ 732-872-1500, 326 Shore Drive) is a 20-room hotel with its own pool on the bay. The rooms are small and clean. There is a restaurant (main dishes cost $15 to $20) and bar. Rates for singles/doubles are $42/47; the two rooms with kitchens cost $67/77. The hotel is open only from Memorial Day to Labor Day.

Moby's, at the very end of Bay Ave past Schupp's Landing, has fish ($6) and clam ($4.25) sandwiches, seafood platters ($8 to $9) and lobster (around $10). The food is take-out but some seating is available. *Bahr's* (☎ 732-872-1245, 2 Bay Ave) is across from Moby's. It has seafood at slightly higher prices. *Clam Hut* (☎ 732-872-0909) is on Atlantic St on the waterfront with similar food to Bahr's.

Getting There & Away

The Highlands area is served by Seastreak (☎ 800-262-8743), which runs ferries from Manhattan (Pier 11 and E 34th St); ferries dock in Highlands behind Conner's Hotel. There are scheduled commuter boats traveling in either direction Monday to Friday and extra boats during the summer. The one-way/roundtrip fare is $15/28.

There are two exits from Route 36 to Highlands. Coming east on Route 36 from Atlantic Highlands the exit leads north and intersects with the western end of Bay Ave, Highlands' main street. Coming west on Route 36 the exit takes you almost immediately to the eastern end of Bay Ave near Moby's restaurant.

MONMOUTH PARK

New Jersey's nicest racetrack, Monmouth Park (☎ 732-222-5100), is 2 miles inland from Long Branch on Route 36. Thoroughbreds have raced on this site in three different structures on and off since 1870. President Ulysses S Grant had a box at the first track. Monmouth is considered one of the best-run tracks in the northeast, and its picnic area is usually solidly booked throughout the summer; call ahead for picnic information. Monmouth Park is a far more pleasant place to visit than the two New York racetracks and the Meadowlands in North Jersey, and is easily accessible by train. If you want to spend a day with the horses, head here.

The racing season is from Memorial Day to Labor Day. There are 10 races a day on Tuesday, Wednesday and Friday to Sunday, with the first post time at 1 pm.

Admission is $2 for grandstand with a small charge for parking.

Getting There & Away

Academy (☎ 732-291-1300) and Monmouth (☎ 732-774-7780) bus lines run to the park from New York City and surrounding towns.

The NJ Transit *Pony Express* (☎ 800-772-2222) runs from Manhattan directly to the track with stops along the way. It takes about two hours from New York City and costs $16 roundtrip, including admission.

If driving take Route 36 west from Long Branch for 2 miles into Oceanport. Make a right at the large sign for 'Monmouth Park.'

Seastreak (☎ 800-262-8743) runs ferries to Highlands on Tuesday, Saturday, Sunday and holidays from Pier 11 in Manhattan and the Brooklyn Academy Pier at 58th St in Brooklyn. From the dock the ferry provides buses to the racetrack. The cost is $30 roundtrip and includes admission and a program.

LONG BRANCH

According to legend, Long Branch (population 28,658) was founded following a wrestling match held here in 1688 to settle a dispute between Native Americans and European settlers. The Europeans won and began building, and by the mid-19th century Long Branch was a major seaside town featuring gambling and wide beaches. Seven US presidents – including Ulysses S Grant, William McKinley and Woodrow Wilson – vacationed in the town.

When President James Garfield was shot on July 2, 1881, just four months into his term, he was brought to Long Branch to recover from his wounds. Although the summer White House issued bulletins assuring the nation of Garfield's recovery, he died two months after being wounded. Grant, Garfield, McKinley (himself a victim of an assassin's bullet) and Wilson (a former New Jersey governor) spent so much time in the town that the waterfront area is called 'Four Presidents Park.'

Gambling was stopped in the 1890s, and Long Branch became a middle-class resort. Throughout the 1940s and 1950s, people flocked to the beachfront clubs where having a cabana was a form of middle-class luxury. But in the past 20 years Long Branch

has become depressed, and the beach has severely eroded.

Part of the problem is that the tides along its 2-mile beach tend to be too rough for good swimming. Long Branch attracts surfers these days, and a recent beach improvement program has helped things recover (thousands of tons of sand were dumped on the strand to increase the bathing areas).

Places to Stay & Eat

The best place to stay is *Ocean Place Hilton Resort & Spa* (☎ 732-571-4000, fax 732-71-33145, 1 Ocean Blvd). It has large rooms with access to the beach (free passes for guests). Rooms start at $90 weekday and go up to $150 on weekends. *Fountains Motel* (☎ 732-222-7200, 160 Ocean Ave), at Morris Ave, has 116 efficiencies with TVs and phones for under $50.

The best dining spot is the beachfront *Ocean Crab Restaurant*, a short walk from the Hilton. Along the boardwalk there are hot dog and hamburger vendors, including *Max's*, which has been serving food to daytrippers since the 1930s. *Nunzio's (220 Westwood)*, near Morris Ave, serves submarine sandwiches.

Entertainment

Club Paradise (☎ 732-870-9292, 160 Ocean Ave), next to Fountains Motel, is a big disco with five bars. The crowd is young, and the bar is open year-round Thursday to Saturday from 9 pm to 2 am. *Cafe Bar* (☎ 732-222-9729) is on the small commercial boardwalk opposite Franklin Terrace. It has seven bars and pool tables and is open year-round daily from noon to 2 am.

Getting There & Away

NJ Transit trains and buses stop at the station on 3rd Ave between N Bath Ave and Morris Ave. The M27 bus runs between Long Branch and Asbury Park.

Long Branch is reached via exit 105 on the Garden State Pkwy.

ASBURY PARK

Asbury Park (population 16,800) was founded in 1871 and named after Francis Asbury, the man who established American Methodism. It's always been known as a dowdy resort for the middle class and was famous in the 1920s for its summer 'Baby Parade' of costumed kids. Cole Porter's 'At Long Last Love' puckishly played on its reputation with a single line: 'Is that Grenada I see, or only Asbury Park?'

Asbury Park had a minor resurgence in the 1970s, when Bruce Springsteen exploded on the national scene after making a name for himself at the local Stone Pony club. But in the '80s, Asbury Park let its amusement area fall into decline, and pinned hopes of becoming a full-service summer resort area of high-rise condos and beach clubs on a planned $500 million development. But the scheme never found a well-heeled backer, despite rampant rumors that various famous artists were interested in buying land for a theme park. Today an unfinished high-rise condo complex sits on Ocean Ave – a concrete monument to the town's failure to revive.

Meanwhile, all the town's amusement areas were closed, the famous carousel sold, and the old Convention Hall was condemned. Things hit rock bottom in January 1994, when the mayor of Asbury Park was arrested for purchasing cocaine in a bar across the street from city hall.

When even the Stone Pony was shuttered, there was little to recommend. Yet a serious effort is being made to turn over Cookman Ave (the main street that heads toward the boardwalk area) into a pedestrian mall. Small shops and artists are being welcomed into the city center. Part of the improvement comes from the resurgence of neighboring Ocean Grove, a summer resort favored by young families. Springsteen even headlined a homecoming concert in the decrepit convention hall, designed to raise money for the rehabilitation effort; Asbury Park certainly needs the help.

Things to See & Do

Asbury Park has a fair beach and a wide wooden boardwalk dotted with a few abandoned attractions and a dusty scale model of the development plan. Badges for the beach

(☎ 732-775-0900) cost $3 per day during the week and $4 on weekends; a season pass costs $20 for adults and $10 for seniors and children (ages 12 to 17).

On the southern end of the boardwalk separating Asbury Park from Ocean Grove, there is a casino where the carousel once stood. Now there are some dealers selling second-hand curios, and an antique auction on Saturday evenings during the summer around 6 pm.

Places to Stay & Eat

Most of the better B&Bs and restaurants are in neighboring Ocean Grove, and it is recommended that you stay there instead of in Asbury Park. One local choice, **Daisy's Place** (☎ 732-775-1238, 605 Sunset Ave), has four rooms and charges $45/60; it is open year-round.

Berkeley Carteret Hotel (☎ 732-776-6700, 1401 Ocean Ave), near the convention hall, is Asbury's only top-end facility, but it has opened and closed several times in the past. It's best to call ahead to find out whether it is still serving the public. At last check, there were 200 rooms available at $99 for a double and $150 for a suite.

Here are some (highly average) eateries, most of which come in at under $10 per person: **Caribbean** (☎ 732-774-3318, 1004 Main St) is a cheerful place with West Indian fare. **Castaways** (☎ 732-775-8566) offers a similar menu. Huge submarine sandwiches can be had at **Frank's Deli** (☎ 732-775-6682, 1406 Main St). **Posillipo** (☎ 732-774-5918, 715 2nd Ave) is one of the older restaurants in Asbury and is popular with locals for its large selection of Northern Italian dishes ($15 to $20 for a main course).

Getting There & Away

The NJ Transit train and bus station is at the Transportation Center on Cookman Ave and Main St, almost on the border of Asbury Park and Ocean Grove. NJ Transit local bus No M20 runs along the coast, stopping at many points between the Asbury Park and Point Pleasant Beach.

Asbury Park is off exit 100A or 100B from the Garden State Pkwy.

NEW JERSEY

OCEAN GROVE

For about a hundred years, Ocean Grove (population 8000) was run by a Methodist group that held summertime revival meetings in this square-mile community. Driving a car was not allowed on Sunday (unless it was the newspaper delivery truck), and crusty 'peace officers' strictly enforced the ban on Sabbath swimming. All that ended in 1979 when the Supreme Court ruled that the town charter was unconstitutional.

The town was founded in 1869 by the Ocean Grove Camp Meeting Association. According to its head, Dr William Osborn, it had the highest beach, the best grove of trees and no mosquitoes. The town touts itself as a 'Victorian experience' and there is indeed a lot of Victorian architecture (although not nearly so much as Cape May to the south). The contrast with decrepit Asbury Park, from which it is separated by narrow Wesley Lake, is striking. You can still see the cottage-backed tents lined up around the great auditorium in which the original founders used to stay during the summer.

Ocean Grove used to be populated by seniors, earning it the informally rude nickname 'Ocean Grave.' But the past few years have seen a real demographic shift as young couples have begun to buy up the decaying yet fixable and affordable Victorian properties. As a consequence, many more young people have been visiting, and the restaurants have become a bit better.

Orientation

Ocean Grove is laid out on a grid pattern, and you enter the town through one of several gates along Main St to the west. Gates are on Stockton, Broadway and Main Aves, which run east to west to Ocean Ave along the boardwalk and a half mile of coast. The most pleasant of the east-west streets running from the ocean is Pilgrim Pathway, which is actually two parallel streets separated by a narrow park.

Information

The tourist office (☎ 732-774-4736) is at 64 Main Ave in the offices of the *Times*, the local weekly newspaper. It's open during the summer only, Monday to Friday from 10 am to 4 pm. Off-season, contact the chamber of commerce (☎ 800-388-4768). During the summer a tourist information booth is set up near the great auditorium.

The post office is on Main Ave just south of Pilgrim Pathway. The New Jersey National Bank (☎ 732-988-3585), at the northwest corner of Main Ave and Pilgrim Pathway, changes foreign currency for a $10 fee; it's open Monday to Friday from 9 am to 2:30 pm, Saturday from 9 am to noon. The Mid-Atlantic National Bank at the northeast corner changes traveler's checks and has an ATM. It's open Monday to Friday from 9 am to 3 pm, Saturday from 9 am to noon.

There are two laundries, the Ocean Grove Launderette, at 53 Olin Ave, and the Main Avenue Launderette on Main Ave right near the intersection with Central.

The Great Auditorium

This 6500-seat wood auditorium stands in the center of town at the western end of Ocean Pathway. It was built to house the crowds that used to throng here (and still do in reduced numbers) to hear Sunday sermons by visiting ministers, and for occasional mainstream music concerts by touring troupes such as the Preservation Hall Jazz Band. Built in 1894 in just 92 days, the auditorium also played a role as the Hotel Stardust in the 1980 Woody Allen film *Stardust Memories*. Call ☎ 732-988-0645 for concert tickets.

Tent City

Visitors to Ocean Grove in the 19th century set up hundreds of tents around the great auditorium, and 114 of them are still clustered here. The uniform structures are actually tents at the front with small cabins at the back containing a kitchen and bathroom. The tents can be rented but there is a 15-year waiting list and they rent for $2500 to $3000 a season. The Camp Meeting Association maintains the site.

Centennial Cottage

This 1874 cottage at the corner of McClintock St and Central Ave was moved here from

Not exactly as beautiful as the real thing, Atlantic City, NJ

Cruisin' on the boardwalk, Atlantic City, NJ

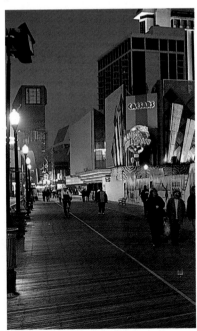

Nighttime boardwalk scene, Atlantic City, NJ

Typical Jersey shore home

You should have seen the one that got away - fishing in southern NJ.

Cookman Ave in 1969 and is filled with period furniture and artifacts. It's open Monday to Saturday from 11 am to 3 pm in July and August, and Saturday only in June and September; there's a $1 donation to enter.

Outdoor Activities

The half-mile beach and boardwalk (☎ 732-988-5533) are clean and well maintained. Sunset Water Sports (☎ 732-776-5293), in the Shark Island Yacht Club at 1601 Route 35 in neighboring Neptune, rents jet skis on the inlet.

Places to Stay

Since Ocean Grove was always a transient summer place, there is a disproportionate number of hotels and inns here. Most are family run with a real personal presence on-site. Most offer reductions for long stays and continental breakfast.

Ocean Park Inn (☎ 732-988-5283, in winter 201-842-5516, 38 Surf Ave) is an immaculate B&B. There's a common kitchen with a microwave; surfboards and chairs are available for beach use. The continental breakfast, included in the room rate, has a different home-baked item daily. Rates are $45 to $100.

Pine Tree Inn (☎ 732-775-3264, 10 Main Ave), half a block from the beach, is the quintessential Victorian B&B. The furniture is tasteful and antique. All rooms are clean and have sinks; some have private baths and porches. Bicycles are available for guests. Room rates are $60 to $120, with reductions in the off-season.

Sandpiper (☎ 732-774-6261, 19 Ocean Pathway) is one of the nicest and most reasonable places to stay in Ocean Grove. This seven-room guesthouse is a block and a half from the beach. Rooms in front of the house have a view of the beach across the grassy middle of Ocean Pathway. The doubles are large, and the house is immaculate. There are indoor and outdoor porches on the 2nd floor and one on the ground level. Jan and Bill Knight, who own the house, are friendly and full of advice but never intrusive. Singles/doubles cost $27/$55 nightly.

House by the Sea (☎ 732-775-2847, 14 Ocean Ave) is the nicest of the hotels facing the shore. There are excellent views from the porches, and the hotel is airy thanks to internal design. Single and double rates are the same and can be $50 to $100 depending on view and bath. Rates include continental breakfast.

Other choices, with rates from $35 to $110, include *Shawmont Hotel* (☎ 732-776-6985, 17 Ocean Ave), *Albatross Hotel* (☎ 732-775-2085, 34 Ocean Pathway) and *Chealsea Morning* (☎ 732-775-8847, 27 Webb Ave).

Places to Eat

The majority of the restaurants are on Main Ave between Central Ave and Pilgrim Pathway. Hotels dominate the oceanfront and it seems like eating on the beach is frowned upon.

Main Avenue Deli (☎ 732-502-0400, 54 Main Ave) sells pizza and Italian heroes. *Elizabeth's* (☎ 732-502-0306, 60½ Main Ave) has good lunches for about $7. *Ocean Grove Bakery* (☎ 732-774-8235, 55 Main Ave) specializes in morning baked goods and java. *Grove Café* (☎ 732-774-2444, 68 Main Ave) and *Raspberry Café* (☎ 732-988-0833, 60 Main Ave) are also good choices.

Getting There & Away

By train, take NJ Transit to Asbury Park and walk through the Ocean Grove gateways two blocks away.

Ocean Grove is reached via exit 100A on the Garden State Pkwy.

AVON BY THE SEA

Residents pronounce the name of this quiet, family oriented town (population 2165) as 'AH-von,' as if having their tonsils examined, and drop the precious 'by the Sea.'

The town's boardwalk is actually an asphalt walk – a sign of a storm that devastated many beach communities. Avon doesn't have the small arcades and amusement halls that you find in Belmar and Point Pleasant Beach. It's all quiet sun worship here.

Places to Stay & Eat

Sands of Avon (☎ 732-776-8386, 42 Sylvania Ave) charges under $50 for a room,

NEW JERSEY

including breakfast, and is open in the summer only.

The following hotels and inns charge $80 to $100 a night during the off-season, and more during the summer. ***Victoria Hotel*** (☎ 732-988-9798, 105 Woodland Ave) has 14 rooms and there is a shared refrigerator, microwave, barbecue, telephone and TV. Also worth trying is ***The Ocean Mist Inn*** (☎ 732-775-9625, 28 Woodland Ave).

Castlemara (☎ 732-776-8727, 800-821-2976, 22 Lakeside Ave) is at the northern end of town, half a block back from the shore, and faces a small lake. ***Summer House*** (☎ 732-775-3992, 101 Sylvania Ave) has rooms in pink, yellow and blue pastels and offers continental breakfast during the week and full breakfast on weekends.

Columns By The Sea (☎ 732-988-3213, 601 Ocean Ave), on the beach, is Avon's ritziest restaurant and is popular with families celebrating their children's high school graduation. Dinner costs about $25 per head.

Getting There & Away

The nearest NJ Transit train stations are at Bradley Beach to the north and Belmar to the south. The M20 bus stops at Main Ave and Sylvania Ave. Avon can be reached via exits 98 and 100A on the Garden State Pkwy.

BELMAR

Belmar (population 5900) is a gathering place for people in their 20s, but community officials have always been ambivalent about the town's partying image, and there are periodic moves to crack down on the local bars.

Belmar's northern stretch of beach is popular with gays, who gather at 2nd Ave near the border with Avon. But as yet, there are no overtly gay gathering places in town. There are gay bars in Asbury Park 2 miles to the north.

Belmar's local chamber of commerce (☎ 732-681-1176) offers information on events and activities.

Fishing

Mackerel, whiting, striped bass and tuna, depending on the season, are among the many types of fish caught in the surf and ocean around Belmar. The most common catch here is bluefish. Boats leave the busy Belmar Marina (☎ 732-681-6137) daily, with most trips offered from April to November. Departures are usually 7 am to 7:30 pm; the cost is generally $45 per person. Two of the best-known boats are the 100-foot *Golden Eagle* (☎ 732-681-6144) and the 80-foot *American Eagle* (☎ 732-681-6148). Captain Paul Hepler (☎ 732-928-4519) runs charters from the marina. Fisherman's Den tackle shop (☎ 732-681-6677) rents small motorboats for $30 per day and is open from 6 am.

Other Activities

Besides the beach, there's a small amusement area with a rooftop miniature golf course on Ocean Ave between 14th and 15th Aves. It's open until about 11 pm and costs $5 per person. The Skate Rental store (☎ 732-681-7767) in the Mayfair Hotel rents in-line skates and bicycles for $20 a day and boogie boards for $12 a day. Iron City Gym (☎ 732-681-8098), on Ocean Ave between 8th and 9th Aves, has day passes for $8; it is open year-round.

Places to Stay

Belmar's accommodations have improved in recent years, moving away from the rooming house reputation. Rates at the following hotels range from $90 to $120. ***Belmar Motor Lodge*** (☎ 732-681-6600, fax 681-6604) is on the marina at Route 35 and 10th Ave. ***Berkeley Hotel*** (☎ 732-681-9617, 107 12th Ave) is a casual place half a block from the beach with rooms starting at $75; it is open May to September.

Inn at the Shore (☎ 732-681-3762, 301 4th Ave) is three blocks from the beach on the northern end of town, away from the crowds. ***Carol's Guest House*** (☎ 732-681-4422, 201 11th Ave) is inexpensive and has basic rooms starting at $30.

Mayfair Hotel (☎ 732-681-2620, 1000 Ocean Ave) is open year-round.

Places to Eat

Fast food and fresh seafood are specialties in Belmar. There is a food court serving pizza, burgers and Chinese food at the corner of Ocean and 14th Aves, and a ***McDonald's*** on the beach opposite 13th Ave.

Havens & Hampton (☎ 732-681-1231), at 5th and Main Sts, is an austere dining room overlooking the Shark River. Fresh seafood dishes start at $12 and prices for lobster specials depend on the catch. ***Ollie Klein's*** (☎ 732-681-1177, 708 River Rd), on the south side of the Main St bridge, has a similar menu.

Circus Drive-In (☎ 732-449-2650), near Belmar on Route 35, is worth a trip if you have a car. This is an old-fashioned '50s-style drive-in where the waitstaff serves food to patrons sitting in their cars. It's open only in summer. ***Wingz Clam Bar***, on Ocean Ave between 16th and 17th Aves, serves chicken wings and clams. It is open till about 11 pm weekdays and 3 am weekends.

Entertainment

Belmar bars – and many other places along the shore – tend to require collared shirts, so you'll be turned away from the door for wearing a $100 Armani black T-shirt, but welcomed if wearing a $10 polo shirt. They also 'proof' just about everyone to ensure customers are of legal drinking age (21), so bring along ID. But Jersey Shore doormen are pretty shameless when it comes to bending

the rules for women. If you're ambulatory and female, it doesn't matter what your age is or how you're dressed. (Well, actually, the skimpier the better.)

Bar Anticipation (☎ 732-681-7422, 703 16th Ave) is a massive complex with live music and swimsuit competitions. 'Bar A,' as it is sometimes called, is Belmar's premier pickup place. ***D'Jais*** (☎ 732-681-5855), at the corner of Ocean and 18th Aves, is a large dance club open seven days a week from May to September; it shuts down around midnight. ***Reggie's***, on Ocean Ave between 11th and 12th Aves, attracts an older singles crowd; it is open from May to October with live music on weekends.

Getting There & Away

The local M20 bus stops at Main St (also known as F St) and 10th Ave. The train station is at 10th Ave and Belmar Plaza, between 9th and 10th Aves behind Belmar Mall, one block east of Route 35.

If driving take exit 98 on the Garden State Pkwy to Route 138 east.

SPRING LAKE

Spring Lake (population 5341) was developed as a 19th-century resort around the lake that gives the town its name. It is one of the wealthier shore communities and was once popular with 'lace-curtain' Irish families and known locally as the 'Irish Riviera.' Locals, who tend to hang out on the town's quiet and charming Main St, would prefer less tourism as the town is beginning to become a full-time home for New York City commuters.

Spring Lake used to have a number of huge oceanfront hotels that became too expensive to run by the 1970s. The last remaining resort, the Essex & Sussex Hotel, has been converted into a condominium complex. Immediately south of the 'E&S' was the equally huge Monmouth, which was torn down to make way for the tract of new beachfront housing that extends several blocks from the beach.

After storms destroyed Spring Lake's 2-mile boardwalk, town officials decided to

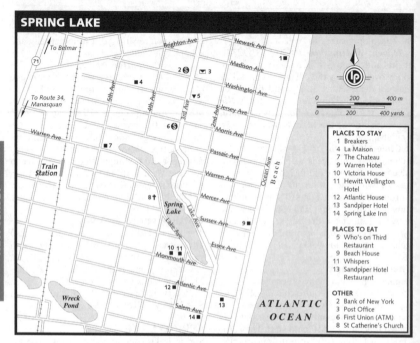

SPRING LAKE

To Belmar
71
To Route 34,
Manasquan

Brighton Ave
Newark Ave
Madison Ave
Washington Ave
Jersey Ave
Morris Ave
Passaic Ave
Warren Ave
Warren Ave
Mercer Ave
Sussex Ave
Essex Ave
Monmouth Ave
Atlantic Ave
Salem Ave

5th Ave
4th Ave
3rd Ave
2nd Ave

Train
Station

Spring
Lake

Lake Ave

Lake Ave

Ocean Ave

Beach

Wreck
Pond

ATLANTIC
OCEAN

0   200   400 m
0   200   400 yards

PLACES TO STAY
1   Breakers
4   La Maison
7   The Chateau
9   Warren Hotel
10 Victoria House
11 Hewitt Wellington Hotel
12 Atlantic House
13 Sandpiper Hotel
14 Spring Lake Inn

PLACES TO EAT
5   Who's on Third Restaurant
9   Beach House
11 Whispers
13 Sandpiper Hotel Restaurant

OTHER
2   Bank of New York
3   Post Office
6   First Union (ATM)
8   St Catherine's Church

replace it with a gray-colored material that looks like wood plank but is actually a composite of recycled plastic bags and wood-pallet chips. This springy surface lasts longer, and better yet, doesn't give you splinters.

Information
Maps and information are available from the chamber of commerce (☎ 732-449-0577), PO Box 694, Spring Lake, NJ 07762. The post office is at 1410 3rd Ave. The Bank of New York (☎ 732-449-0888), at 3rd and Washington Aves, exchanges foreign currency. First Union (☎ 732-449-5500), at 3rd and Morris Aves, has an ATM.

Outdoor Activities
The beach (☎ 732-449-8005) costs $3.50 daily and $43 for the season; passes for children (ages 11 and under) are free. On each end of the boardwalk are salt-water pools for resident use only.

Places to Stay
Spring Lake's hotels and B&Bs tend to be among the most expensive on the Jersey Shore, with daily rates over $125.

B&Bs The *Johnson House* (☎ *609-449-1860, 25 Tuttle Ave*) has rooms with private baths for $110 and shared baths for $70. There is also free parking.

A Victorian-era house, *Spring Lake Inn* (☎ *609-449-2010, 104 Salem Ave*) features an 80-foot wraparound porch. It's only open from July 4 to Labor Day, but is large, airy and clean. *Victoria House* (☎ *732-974-1882, 214 Monmouth Ave*) has 10 well-appointed rooms, with a two-night minimum in summer. *La Maison* (☎ *732-449-0969, 404 Jersey Ave*) is an eight-room B&B with rates around $160.

Hotels The following have rooms for $50 to $150, depending on the season: *Atlantic House* (☎ *732-449-8500, 305 2nd Ave*), which is open May to September; **Sandpiper Hotel** (☎ *732-449-6060, 7 Atlantic Ave*); **The Chateau** (☎ *732-974-2000, 500 Warren Ave*); and **Hewitt Wellington Hotel** (☎ *732-974-1212, fax 974-2338, 200 Monmouth Ave*), which overlooks the lake and is open April to October.

Breakers (☎ *732-449-7700, fax 449-0161, 1507 Ocean Ave*) is one of Spring Lake's most upscale establishments with rooms costing around $270. The large, white and brown chateau-style **Warren Hotel** (☎ *732-449-8800, fax 449-7216, 901 Ocean Ave*) is set half a block from the beach with standard rooms starting at $200 and off-season rates at almost half that amount.

Places to Eat

The **Beach House** (☎ *732-449-9646, 901 Ocean Ave*) serves cocktails on its beachfront porch. For lunch, burgers, sandwiches and pizzas cost about $10; dinner entrees cost $15. It's open May to October. **Who's on Third** (☎ *609-449-4233, 1300 3rd Ave*) is the best deli in town for a quick bite. **Whispers** (☎ *732-449-3330*), at the Hewitt Wellington Hotel, serves seafood dishes for about $25 per person. The restaurant in the **Sandpiper Hotel** (☎ *732-449-6060, 7 Atlantic Ave*) serves a large Sunday seafood brunch buffet.

Getting There & Away

The train station is at Railroad Plaza and Warren Ave, one block east of Route 71. Check out the elaborate weathervane on top of the old structure.

To get to Spring Lake, take exit 98 on the Garden State Pkwy, which will bring you to Route 138 west; follow that to Route 71 south.

MANASQUAN

Located about 65 miles from New York City to the north and Philadelphia to the southwest, Manasquan (population 5400) is one of the quietest towns on the Jersey Shore, with a rowdy beachfront area separated from the main town by a small canal. The beachfront and the surrounding blocks to the west are filled with two-story cottages that stand empty after Labor Day.

There are a few popular bars near the intersection of Main St and 1st Ave, and the jetty at the southern end of town is considered one of the best surfing areas in the state.

Manasquan has a very nice downtown area, with a movie theater that has been turned into an arts center. Unfortunately, its restored train station was destroyed by an electrical fire. Manasquan's town center is along Main St immediately west of Route 71, one block from the train station.

Information

The Manasquan Chamber of Commerce (☎ 732-223-8303) can provide information on opening hours for local businesses, but there is no formal visitors' center. There's an ATM a few doors away from the movie theater, and a post office in the parking lot immediately south of Main St.

On Route 71 between Manasquan and Point Pleasant Beach, and officially in the town of Brielle, is Escargot Books (☎ 732-528-5955), 503 Route 71, which features 20,000 used books.

Outdoor Activities

The beach (☎ 609-223-0544) costs $4 per day and $38 for the season ($16 for seniors). It has an asphalt pathway and is populated by teens. There are three small amusement areas on the beach and a few stands selling hats and T-shirts.

The Manasquan Inlet Beach, immediately north of the jetty marking the northern side of the Manasquan inlet, is rated highly by shore surfers. It's possible to get onto this beach along the jetty without a beach badge (though you are officially required to have one).

Places to Stay & Eat

O'Neill's Guesthouse (☎ *732-528-5666, 390 E Main St*), four blocks from the train station, is a renovated hotel with 20 guest rooms, most with private baths. A slightly noisy bar & grill is on the premises. **Cooper House** (☎ *732-223-1443, 324 E Main St*) is a more traditional B&B with rates in the $75

NEW JERSEY

range. **Squan Tavern** (☎ 732-223-3324, 15 Broad St), off Main St, has been serving pizzas and heroes to locals for 35 years. **Edgar's** (☎ 732-449-4422), on the corner of Sea Girt Ave and Route 71, is a bar that serves sandwich lunch specials for $8.95.

Entertainment

The **Osprey Hotel** (☎ 732-528-1800), at Main St and 1st Ave, is a local landmark with live music in its eight different bars Friday to Sunday ($8 cover). At other times the disc jockey plays rock, house and even techno music to the under 30 crowd. It's open Tuesday to Sunday from 5 pm to 2 am, April to late September.

Leggett's (☎ 732-223-3951), on 1st Ave, is a few doors south of the Osprey Hotel. It's a year-round, seven-days-a-week bar with no cover. The music is generally conservative rock and the patrons are usually 35 and under.

Getting There & Away

The train station is on E Main St and Colby Ave about 500 feet east of Route 71, and the bus stops at several points along Main St.

Take exit 98 off the Garden State Pkwy to Route 34, following signs to the Manasquan beach area (Route 71 north to Main St, turn east toward the shore).

POINT PLEASANT

Point Pleasant (population 5600) is the northernmost community on the Barnegat Peninsula, a narrow 22-mile barrier strip between the Atlantic and Barnegat Bay. European fishermen and farmers first settled along the bay in the early 19th century, and though some farms took in boarders who wanted to be near the shore, it wasn't until 1878 that lawyers from Trenton made the town of Point Pleasant into a resort. They created the Point Pleasant Land Company and bought 250 acres on the peninsula, naming it Point Pleasant City.

In 1875 the first bridge was built linking Brielle and Point Pleasant; the railroad and further development followed in 1880. Even today, the idea of private enterprise holds in

Point Pleasant, since the beach is dominated by two companies that have a hammerlock on beachfront business in town.

Information

The chamber of commerce (☎ 732-899-2424), 517-A Arnold Ave, has general information, and there's an ATM next door.

The post office is at 410 Arnold Ave, within sight of the train station. The Beach Laundromat is on Ocean Ave opposite the intersection with Homestead Ave. It's open from 7 am to 8 pm.

The streets near the boardwalk fill up with cars, so you may have to park a block or two away from the beach. There are parking lots on Arnold and Ocean Aves that charge $10 a day.

Jenkinson's Pavilion & Aquarium

Rebuilt after a devastating fire a few years back, Jenkinson's Pavilion (☎ 732-892-0844), on the boardwalk near the intersection with Arnold Ave, offers 50 amusement rides. Tickets are 50¢ each and rides cost from two to six tickets. It is open April to October (indoor arcades are open year-round).

The aquarium (☎ 732-899-1212) is open year-round and has seals, sharks, penguins and alligators. There is also a small pool with turtles, sea urchins and other shellfish. Admission is $7/4.50 for adults/children and seniors.

Beaches

The town's first boardwalk was built in 1885. Today the boardwalk has the usual collection of beach food – pizza, burgers, clams – plus a couple of huge bars stretching out over the water, and an amusement park with rides mostly for kids.

Point Pleasant has the strange distinction in this area of having two privately owned beaches along the its boardwalk. Both feature wide beaches and changing areas and can get very crowded on weekends.

Risden's Beach (☎ 732-892-8410) goes from the southern end of the boardwalk to a point just north of Trenton Ave. Risden's also provides two large bathhouses (☎ 732-892-9743, 892-9580) along its section of the beach. For $5 during the week (and $6 on weekends) you can get a beach pass, unlimited access to a small wooden cubicle and a shower. Be aware that the lockers tend to sell out early on weekends. It's open from about 9 am to 5 pm.

And there's also **Jenkinson's Beach** (☎ 732-892-3274), which runs from Trenton Ave north to the Manasquan River and includes an amusement park and a small aquarium. The beach costs $4/5 for weekdays/weekends and $1 for children (ages five to 11). Jenkinson's has two small bathhouses.

Fishing

The beaches here are long enough for good surf casting and the inlet has several marinas. Many party and charter boats are run out of the inlet north of the beach area. At Ken's Landing (☎ 732-892-9787, 899-5491), 30 Broadway, departure times and costs are posted. A half-day trip usually runs between $18 and $25. Some boats also run 90-minute night cruises along the shore for $8/5 for adults/children. Clark's Landing (☎ 732-223-6546) also has charter boats.

Scuba Diving

The ocean floor just off the coast of New Jersey is littered with sunken ships of war, commerce and transportation that were leaving or entering New York Harbor when ill fortune struck. One of the most popular shipwrecks around Point Pleasant is the *Mohawk*, a passenger line that sunk in 1935. Divers frequently recover artifacts, such as china and silverware, from the site. Blue Abyss Dive Center (☎ 732-714-0200), 69 Channel Drive, offers rentals and lessons; its website is www.blueabyss.com.

Places to Stay

Motels are predominantly on Broadway between Chicago and Boston Aves and on the southern end of Ocean Ave. There are also a few guesthouses. Most places are seasonal – and on the Jersey Shore that means an almost complete shut down on Labor Day.

The guesthouse *Kieffer's* (☎ 732-892-2292, 17 Arnold Ave) is half a block from the beach and has eight rooms with TVs. The rate is $70 during the week. Another guesthouse, *Century House* (☎ 732-899-8208, 18 Forman Ave), is half a block from the boardwalk and has a pool, porch, grill, refrigerators and parking. Rooms cost $50 to $75 depending on the time of year.

The places on Broadway are fairly noisy due to traffic. The motels all come with bland but fairly new furniture, air-con, TVs, parking and usually refrigerators. All rates are around $70 to $100 a night and assume double occupancy. Among the choices are *Atlantic Motel* (☎ 732-899-7711, fax 899-4342, 215 Broadway), *Mariner's Cove* (☎ 732-899-0060, 50 Broadway), *Surfside Motel* (☎ 732-899-1109, 101 Broadway) and *Point Beach Motel* (☎ 732-892-5100), at Ocean and Trenton Aves.

The motels on Arnold Ave tend to be quieter than those on Broadway. These include *Colonial Motel* (☎ 732-899-2394, 210 Arnold Ave) and *Bel-Aire* (☎ 732-892-2248, 202 Arnold Ave). The *White Sands/Ebb Tide* complex (☎ 732-899-3370, 1106 Ocean Ave) is an amalgamation of three hotels to create an oceanfront resort with 72 rooms and a 350-foot private beach. Rates are $100 to $150.

Places to Eat

The boardwalk has the usual pizza, burger and clam fast-food places and there are a few delis and breakfast places along Ocean Ave behind the boardwalk.

The nicest place to eat is *Jack Baker's Wharfside* (☎ 732-892-9100, 101 Channel Drive Point), with booths overlooking Manasquan inlet. It serves reasonably priced seafood for $15 and under with numerous lunch specials (reservations are recommended on summer weekends).

Spike's Fish Market & Restaurant (☎ 732-295-9400, 415 Broadway) also cooks what it sells. A large tin bucket of steamers (soft-shell clams) runs $12. Spike's is open year-round. *The Shrimp Box* (☎ 732-899-1637), at Ken's Landing marina on Broadway a few blocks west of Ocean Ave, has tables on Lake Louise, where the fishing boats have their slips. Seafood appetizers cost $5 to $6, and fish entrees cost $13 to $17.

NEW JERSEY

Entertainment

Martell's Tiki Bar (☎ 732-892-0131), on the boardwalk, is a beachfront bar-concert complex that serves food right on the sand in the summer. It's open most of the year, seven days a week, with folk and typical bar bands playing on Monday. The cover is generally $5 for seating inside the bar. This is the spot for seeing wet T-shirt contests, smoking fat cigars and picking up new friends.

Shopping

The Point Pleasant Antique Emporium (☎ 732-892-2222, 800-322-8002), at the corner of Bay and Trenton Aves, has 100 dealers under one roof. Most of the town's shops are on Arnold Ave to the west of the train station.

Getting There & Away

The train and bus station is at Route 35 north and Arnold Ave. The local M20 bus terminates here as well.

You can get to Point Pleasant by taking exit 98 on the Garden State Pkwy, then Route 34 south to the traffic circle leading to the town.

SIX FLAGS GREAT ADVENTURE & SAFARI THEME PARK

This theme park (☎ 908-928-1821) is in Jackson Township west of the Jersey Shore towns and features a 350-acre drive-through safari with 200 animals, most of them in natural environments. There are also more than 100 rides, with a few heart-stoppingly fast roller coasters and several 'Wild West' shows and attractions featuring famous cartoon and film characters.

Summer evenings often feature free concerts by aging or B-list entertainers (events line ☎ 732-928-1821). On summer weekends, Great Adventure has extremely long lines at its most popular rides, so it's important to go early or on a weekday.

The theme park is open from April to October from 10 am to midnight, and the safari park is open from 9 am to 4 pm. Admission is $30 for both the rides and the safari park; children pay $19. Adult season tickets cost $60, and family season tickets

cost around $200 (call ahead for prices, which often change and are subject to late-season specials). The park is off exit 7A on the NJ Turnpike or exit 98 to I-195 on the Garden State Pkwy.

BAY HEAD

The land that became the community of Bay Head (population 1226) was bought in 1876 by Princeton banker David Mount, who purchased it from a retired sea captain. A few years later Mount and two other investors created the Bay Head Land Company to develop the town.

Bay Head remains a proper and quiet community with private Cape Cod-style homes along the beach. Although there is public access to the ocean, there's no boardwalk and it's very peaceful even in the high season.

There's a very small permanent population along Route 35, but traveling here in the winter you'll see that the area is ghostly, save for a few bars and coffee shops.

Information

The post office is at 82 Bridge Ave, one block from the train terminus. Bay Head Book House, 89 Bridge Ave, has a small selection of books.

Beaches

The beach, just about the only activity here, was only opened to nonresidents after the state sued the town. It has clean white sand and very few people, so it's worth coming even if you're staying in another town. But the 'crown jewel of the Jersey Shore' tacitly discourages day-trippers by not providing areas for public parking. Beach passes are available from the Bay Head Association (☎ 732-892-4179) on the western end of Mount St (though the address is 532 Lake Ave).

Places to Stay & Eat

The *Bay Head Sands* (☎ 732-899-7016, 2 Twilight Rd) has clean rooms, some with private baths. Rates, including breakfast and beach badges, run up to $150 on weekends. *Bay Head Gables* (☎ 732-892-9844, 200

Main Ave) has air-con and private baths; some rooms have porches. ***Bentley Inn*** *(☎ 732-892-9589, 694 Main Ave)* is a casual place with rates around $90. ***Conover's Bay Head Inn*** *(☎ 732-892-4664, 646 Main Ave)* is famous for its antique-filled rooms and well-tended English-style garden. ***Kaptain's Haven*** *(☎ 732-892-4479, 548 Main Ave)* rents apartments and efficiencies for $300 to $550 a week.

Grenville Hotel & Restaurant *(☎ 732-892-3100, 345 Main Ave)* is a year-round Victorian hotel with 31 rooms and rates up to $200 on weekends. ***Bluff's Hotel & Restaurant*** *(☎ 732-892-1114, 575 East Ave)*, on the beach, has air-con rooms from $145 to $200 in season.

The hotels have decent restaurants. The ***Bentley Inn*** and ***Grenville Hotel*** have main dishes around $20 for dinner. ***Bluff's Restaurant*** *(575 East Ave)* is another casual choice with main dishes around $15 to $20.

Entertainment
Bluff's Bar *(☎ 732-892-1719)*, a windowless two-room structure under the Bluff's Hotel, has live music on Tuesday and Thursday; the younger crowd gathers in the whitewashed back room.

Getting There & Away
Bay Head is the terminus of NJ Transit's North Jersey Coast service. The station is at Osborne Ave and Twilight Rd two blocks west of Route 35.

From the north, take exit 98 from the Garden State Pkwy and take Route 34 to the junction with Route 35; you'll come to Bay Head after Point Pleasant Beach. If you're driving south and inland from the coast along Route 35, you'll drive right into Bay Head after Point Pleasant Beach.

From the south, you can take Garden State Pkwy exit 90 and drive 7 miles to the coast on Route 88. Bay Head is at the eastern end of the highway.

SEASIDE HEIGHTS
This town (population 2400) and its sister Seaside Park feature lots of motels, a mile-long boardwalk with two amusement piers,

several bars and a good white-sand beach, although it is not as wide as Point Pleasant's beach and drops off sharply into the surf. This is a major summer destination for people ages 21 and over because of its bars and clubs.

Information
Town information and special events can be obtained by calling ☎ 732-793-1510. The post office is at 55 Sumner Ave. The best place for parking is on Central Ave, which is immediately west of (and parallel to) Atlantic Blvd. Central Ave has a wide median where many people park and walk the few blocks to the beach to save time searching for an elusive parking space.

Most of the town's bars and restaurants are along Atlantic Blvd, called 'the Boulevard' by the locals even though there's more than one boulevard in town.

Outdoor Activities
Seaside Heights is full of activities from swimming and jet skiing at the beach to in-line skating and bicycling. There are also waterslides and waterfront amusement parks if the traditional beach activities grow tiresome.

The Parking Police

Many towns along the shore aren't satisfied generating revenue from beach passes, and they know that parking spaces are at a premium on weekends. So in places like Seaside Heights, there are parking meters set up on every available piece of open street. Most cost 25¢ per half hour, making it impossible to avoid expensive parking lots (which run about $15 a day). In summer, meters are constantly monitored by aggressive police officers. The shore towns also love slapping people with fines for public drinking and minor infractions against local speed limits.

It's all a very good argument for using public transportation whenever you can in this region.

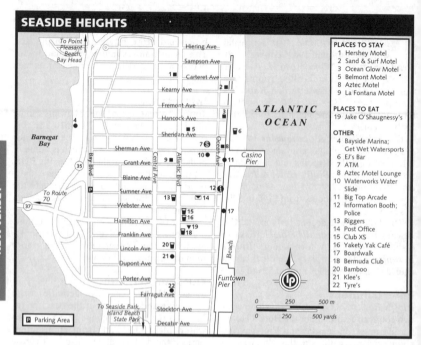

SEASIDE HEIGHTS

PLACES TO STAY
1 Hershey Motel
2 Sand & Surf Motel
3 Ocean Glow Motel
5 Belmont Motel
8 Aztec Motel
9 La Fontana Motel

PLACES TO EAT
19 Jake O'Shaugnessy's

OTHER
4 Bayside Marina;
  Get Wet Watersports
6 EJ's Bar
7 ATM
8 Aztec Motel Lounge
10 Waterworks Water
   Slide
11 Big Top Arcade
12 Information Booth;
   Police
13 Riggers
14 Post Office
15 Club XS
16 Yakety Yak Café
17 Boardwalk
18 Bermuda Club
20 Bamboo
21 Klee's
22 Tyre's

The **beach** (☎ 732-793-9100) is wide and access is free several days during the week. Other times, badges cost $3.50. The beach is famous for being unlocked at night and a good spot for partying; town officials are contemplating closing the beach at sunset to prevent public drinking. Get Wet Watersports (☎ 732-830-6424), at the Bayside Marina on Route 35 south just past the A&P, has jet skis for half-hour/hour rental at $35/60.

Funtown Pier (☎ 732-830-0191) is the southern pier and has a log flume ($4), go-carts ($4), a Ferris wheel and a number of kiddie rides. Tickets are 50¢ each and rides cost from two to six tickets each. **Casino Pier** (☎ 732-793-6488) is the northern (former fishing) pier, which is now packed with more rides than Funtown. The highlight is a carousel (☎ 732-830-4183) dating from about 1910, with carved animals from the 1890s and music provided by a 1923 Wurlitzer organ. Ticket costs for Casino Pier's

rides are the same as Funtown. The pier is open from April to September.

The biggest and best waterslide in town is **Waterworks** (☎ 732-793-6495) at Sherman and Ocean Aves. It costs $10 for two hours, but if you come at 9 am or 7 pm, you can get three hours. It is open from 9 am to 10 pm.

In-line skates can be rented at several places on the boardwalk and the Boulevard. The Big Top Arcade at 1020 Boardwalk has all-day rentals for $20. It's open daily from 10 am to 8 pm.

Bike shops are on the boardwalk and the Boulevard. Tyre's (☎ 732-830-2050), 1900 Atlantic Blvd at Farragut St, rents bikes for weekly rates of $50.

Places to Stay

Seaside Heights has a number of standard motels. Rates are high and are aggravated by the groups of young people willing to double (and triple) up in overpriced rooms near the ocean. During the peak season you'll be lucky to get something under $75 a night. It's vital to have a reservation during the summer, so call around to the following places for information before you get off the bus or point the car in the direction of Seaside.

Boardwalk area choices include the following: *Aztec Motel* (☎ 732-793-3000, *901 Boardwalk*), between Sherman and Sheridan Sts; *Sand & Surf Motel* (☎ 732-793-7311, *1201 Ocean Terrace*); *Ocean Glow Motel* (☎ 732-793-1300), at Hancock and Boardwalk; and *Island Beach Motor Lodge* (☎ 732-793-5400), at 24th and Central Aves in South Seaside Park, before the entrance to Island Beach State Park.

La Fontana Motel (☎ 908-793-0804, *135 Grant St*), at E Central Ave, has room rates around $100. *Belmont Motel* (☎ 732-793-8519, *120 Sheridan Ave*) has phones in its rooms. *Aquarius Arms Motel* (☎ 732-793-0011), at Kearney and Central Aves, charges $85 for a room. The huge *Hershey Motel* (☎ 732-793-5000, *1415 Atlantic Blvd*) has doubles around $90 in season.

In Seaside Park, there are motels south of the Funtown Pier on Ocean Ave. These places all have motel standards (with rates of $75 to $125) and are good choices because they're close to the beach rather than the crowded boardwalk. Offerings include the following: *Charlroy Motel* (☎ 732-793-0712, *1601 N Ocean Ave*); *Luna-Mar* (☎ 732-793-7955), at N Ocean Ave and L St; *Holiday Motel* (☎ 732-793-1488, *1505 N Ocean Ave*); *Sea Gull Motel* (☎ 732-793-0815, *1401 N Ocean Ave*); and *Seascape Motel* (☎ 732-793-8770, *1315 N Ocean Ave*). These motels shut down in September and re-open the week before Memorial Day.

Places to Eat
The boardwalk is full of fabulous fast-food stands, including vendors selling fresh-cut french fries and orange ice cream. *Kohr's* ice cream stands dot the boardwalk. *Bum Rogers Tavern* (☎ 732-830-2770), on Central Ave between 22nd and 23rd Aves, is a dark bar-restaurant that serves excellent Cajun garlic crabs. There are often two-for-one dinner specials during the week. *Jake*

Jersey Fries

The Jersey Shore offers its own proud variation of the french fry, freshly cut from whole potatoes. You can find them on the boardwalks in Seaside Heights and the Wildwoods. A special machine slices the potatoes in huge chunks, then brings them onto a conveyer belt that drops the slices into a fryer. For about $2, you'll get a huge cone of steaming Jersey fries, covered in sweet tomato catsup and salt, making it a cheap and filling (if not especially healthy) snack.

O'Shaughnessy's (☎ 732-830-6068), at Atlantic Blvd and Hamilton St, is a restaurant and bar with live music from Sunday to Wednesday.

Berkeley Seafood Restaurant (☎ 732-793-0400), at 24th and Central Aves, is a seafood market with an upstairs restaurant (you can bring in your own bottle of alcohol).

Entertainment
Most bars and clubs are on the Boulevard between Sumner and Dupont St, or on the boardwalk.

Rigger's (☎ 732-830-9600, *519 Atlantic Blvd*) is a year-round neighborhood bar, open from 7 am to 2 am daily. *Yakety Yak Café* (☎ 732-830-1999) and *Club XS* (☎ 732-830-3036) are next to each other at 406-408 Atlantic Blvd. The other large and popular nightspots nearby are *Bamboo* (☎ 732-830-3660), at Lincoln Ave and Atlantic Blvd, and *Bermuda Club* (☎ 732-793-7567, *302 Atlantic Blvd*), which offers potent cocktails and beer specials during the week.

EJ's (☎ 732-793-4622), at Sheridan Ave and the boardwalk, is open 364 days a year from 10 am to 2 am. The *Aztec Motel* (☎ 732-793-1010), at Sherman St and the boardwalk, has a lounge with local live music Friday to Sunday. *Klee's* (☎ 732-830-1996), at Dupont and Atlantic Blvd, has live music from Tuesday to Sunday during the summer and on weekends in the winter.

Getting There & Away

NJ Transit runs buses from New York City and Philadelphia to Seaside Heights (Bus Shore Service Route 137). The roundtrip ticket costs $20.

Seaside Heights is reached via exit 82 off the Garden State Pkwy. You exit from the parkway onto Route 37 east, which goes right into Seaside after 8 miles. You can also drive down the Barnegat Peninsula on Route 35 south from Point Pleasant and Bay Head.

ISLAND BEACH STATE PARK

This 3000-acre state park (☎ 908-793-0506) takes up the southern third of the Barnegat Peninsula and offers 5 miles of bike trails, 10 miles of beach, as well as a horseback riding trail. The preserve is a combination of shore and marsh that stretches about 9 miles from the end of Seaside Park to the inlet separating the peninsula from Long Beach Island. The land was bought in 1926 by Henry Phipps, a Pittsburgh steel millionaire, for development as a resort, but the stock market crash put a stop to the scheme. The tract of land remained untouched until the state bought it in 1953 and opened the park six years later, representing one of New Jersey's first efforts at preservation.

Because there is no public transportation to nearby Long Beach Island, you'll need a car to get to the state park – which is unfortunate because the traffic tends to be brutal in July and August.

Information

The park is divided into northern and southern natural areas and a recreational zone. Some 15,000 people use this park on summer weekends, so it is very busy. Parking costs $6/7 for in season weekday/weekend, $4 off-season. Bikers can get in for free, and parking is free on Tuesday. During the summer, the park charges an extra dollar to enter the southern natural area, and limits the number of cars to about 300 (which is the number of parking spaces). The park information center (☎ 732-793-0506) is at the parking lot and has details on walks and ser-

vices. The park is open year-round from 8 am to dusk.

Beaches

The sand is at its whitest and purest in the park, and it's a great place for swimming. The 1-mile strip of beach on the Atlantic is called the recreational zone and has lifeguards. There are beachside showers for rinsing sand off, but only rudimentary changing facilities in the bathrooms.

Fishing

The park has excellent surf fishing, particularly for bluefish and striped bass. In the summer you can haul in flounder, weakfish and kingfish. Surf fishers may remain in the park overnight, but they must be 'actively engaged in fishing activities' from midnight to 4 am. Those caught sleeping are kicked out.

A limited number of Mobile Sport Fishing Vehicle (MSFV) permits are issued for people who want to drive onto the beach at the southern end of the island and fish. Permits cost $25 for three days, $125 for the season. Fishing without a vehicle is free.

Bird-Watching

The park has several nature trails and an observation blind. Marsh bird species can be spotted from this well-marked blind, which is a 10-minute walk from the road in the southern zone. The blind is equipped with log seats, and overlooks an osprey nest on a pole nearby. Depending on the season, you'll also be able to see egrets, herons, ibises, ducks and other migratory birds.

Places to Stay & Eat

Camping is not allowed in the park so it is best visited as a day trip. In season there is a concession stand with mediocre food. You can cook freshly caught fish in the southern zone where fires are allowed.

LONG BEACH ISLAND

Long Beach Island is an 18-mile-long barrier island with a series of small towns. Barnegat Light is in the north, Surf City and Ship Bottom at the center, and Beach Haven stands almost at the southern tip. The island is connected to the mainland by a causeway at its halfway point – the town of Ship Bottom.

This is the place to head if you want to immerse yourself in New Jersey's wide array of oceanfront activities. While the things to see and do are spread out along the island's length, the main points of interests are at Barnegat Light and Beach Haven.

Strict zoning laws ban the construction of high-rises, but the entire land surface is crossed by streets and dotted with summer season motels and cottages. Vegetation is sparse, and during severe storms parts of the island are cut off from the mainland.

Orientation & Information

Long Beach Blvd is the main – and in some spots the only – street running from Barnegat Light to points further south; though Long Beach Blvd gives way to Bay Blvd as it approaches Beach Haven. Bay Blvd is often referred to by locals simply as 'the Boulevard.'

The chamber of commerce (☎ 609-494-7211) for Southern Ocean County and Long Beach Island is at 265 W 9th St in Ship Bottom. Route 72, the causeway from the mainland, puts you on 9th St and the chamber of commerce is two blocks in from the causeway. You can pick up information on lodging and activities there.

The *Beach Haven Times* is the weekly newspaper for the island. If you want information about entertainment, restaurants or discount coupons, pick up a copy of the free weeklies *Summer Times Islander* and *Beachcomber*, which are distributed in most stores.

Barnegat Lighthouse

The famous 'Old Barney' lighthouse (☎ 609-494-2016) sits at the northern tip of Long Beach Island on the 31-acre Barnegat Light State Park in the town of Barnegat Light.

Built in 1859, Old Barney was originally 900 feet from the shore and has been rescued several times from being undermined by erosion. The structure is made of internal and external circular walls 10 feet apart at the base and 18 inches apart at the

top. The outer wall is 4½ feet thick at the base, tapering to 1½ feet at the top. The original light itself could be seen for 30 miles. If you climb the tower's 217 steps, you'll get a fantastic view of the mainland, Long Beach and the Barnegat Peninsula.

The lighthouse is open daily from 10 am to 4:30 pm from Memorial Day to Labor Day, and on weekends in May, September and October. Admission is $1.

This is one of the most popular places to watch the sunset (even though the lighthouse is, of course, positioned to guide seafarers to the east). To get there by car, go north on Central Ave to the end of the street.

Barnegat Light Museum

This museum (☎ 609-494-2096), at the corner of 5th St and Long Beach Blvd in Barnegat Light, is in a late-19th-century one-room schoolhouse. Its displays are dedicated to the shipping industry of the 19th century and include whale vertebrae, a stingray tail, bottles and photos among other things. The Fresnel lens from the lighthouse is also on display here; it's 10 feet tall and has over 1000 thick glass prisms.

The museum is open daily during July and August from 2 to 5 pm and in June and September (weekends only) from 2 to 5 pm; admission is free.

Fantasy Island & Thundering Surf

Fantasy Island (☎ 609-492-4000), 320 W 7th St in Beach Haven, is an old Victorian-style amusement park that has children's rides and various clown shows during the day. Ride tokens cost 50¢ each, and rides require three to five tokens. It's open from Memorial Day to Labor Day, and the indoor arcade is open year-round.

Thundering Surf (☎ 609-492-0869) is a large waterslide next door to Fantasy Island with a half-hour/hourly charge of $6/8. If you come at 9 or 10 am or at 7 pm, you can get a full hour for $6.

Long Beach Island Foundation of the Arts & Sciences

The foundation (☎ 609-494-1241), 120 Long Beach Blvd in Loveladies, offers courses in ceramics, jewelry, basketry, Chinese calligraphy, silk painting and other arts. It also has exhibits, shows, lectures and special children's programs during the summer. The town of Loveladies is between Beach Haven and Barnegat Light.

Beaches

The beaches are wide at the northern end of the island in Barnegat Light, where reclamation has put about half a mile of sand and dune between houses that used to be beachfront. This is primarily the result of jetties built to protect Barnegat Lighthouse from being eroded into the bay. Elsewhere, beaches are a short walk from the end of the street to the water.

Beach Badges There are six separate entities issuing badges among the 21 communities on Long Beach Island. Seniors can use all of the island's beaches for free. Seasonal passes are generally cheaper if you buy them in May and, in some places, in early June. It's a bit confusing, so it's best to pick a single beach and stick with it.

Seasonal passes generally cost $10 if you buy before June 1, and jump to $15 to $20 after June 1. A weekly/weekend pass costs $5/4. Daily passes range from $3 to $5. The following contact numbers can give more definitive prices and reserve passes:

Barnegat Light	☎ 609-494-9196
Beach Haven	☎ 609-492-0111
Harvey Cedars	☎ 609-494-2843
Ship Bottom	☎ 609-494-2171
Surf City	☎ 609-494-3064

Long Beach Township (☎ 609-494-7606) sells a single badge good for all the communities not listed above. The drawback is that not all of the Long Beach Township communities are next to each other. Badges cost $3/7/12 for the day/week/season before June 15 and $3/7/15 after.

Water's Edge (☎ 609-494-4620) runs a bathhouse at 20th St and the ocean in Ship Bottom. Showers, bathrooms, lockers and a beach badge cost $4.75 for the day.

Sailing

Most sailing is done in the bay near Spray Beach. Todt Sailing Center (☎ 609-492-8550), at 25th and Atlantic Blvd, rents sailing equipment. All rates are per hour/two hours/additional hours. Sailboards cost $17/28/14, and two-person Sunfish cost $19/29/15.

Day boats come in three sizes: the 14-footer holds three and costs $32/52/27, the 15- to 17-footer holds five and costs $35/59/29 and the 19- to 20-footer holds seven and costs $45/75/38. Todt also has catamarans for rent. A 14-footer for two people costs $31/52/26, a 16-footer for three costs $38/66/33 and an 18-footer for four costs $48/86. Lessons are available in packages for $70 to $210, depending on the item. Todt's is open April to September from 9 am to 5 pm.

Scuba Diving

During WWI and WWII, German U-boats stalked the murky waters of Barnegat inlet, sinking oil tankers and almost crippling US shipping. Divers can view these sunken testaments of history as well as an 1890s passenger ship (known as the 'Spanish Wreck' because of the wealthy Cubans that drowned on board the ship). Triton Divers (☎ 609-494-5599), 819 Barnegat Ave located at the causeway in Ship Bottom, offers classes in dive certification. Plan on spending about $450 for a week's rental of equipment. Triton also runs trips for certified divers.

Fishing

With its many marinas and long, quiet stretches of unoccupied beach, Long Beach Island is a weekend fisherman's paradise. The inlet is popular with sailors and jet skiers, and the island itself is the departure point for many day-long ocean-bound fishing trips, in the hunt for a bucketful of flounder and bluefish.

Charter boats can be rented from the Barnegat Light Yacht Basin, at the end of 18th St and the bay in Barnegat Light, for about $45 to $100 per day for small boats. Among the boats available are:

Connie Claire	☎ 609-494-6787
Fleet King	☎ 609-693-3321
Frances	☎ 609-494-8956, 494-5090
Lady Caroline II	☎ 609-693-3181
Pirate King II	☎ 609-494-0823, 667-2762
Roc-Lo	☎ 609-275-9150, 494-4825
Searcher	☎ 609-494-2369
Sun Bird	☎ 609-494-0006, 215-257-6661

Half-day fishing trips and cruises to Atlantic City run on the *Black Whale II* (☎ 609-492-0333, 492-0202), which is docked at the Beach Haven Fishing Center at Center St and the bay in Beach Haven. The roundtrip to Atlantic City costs $30 and includes a roll of coins for the slot machines.

Other Activities

Ron Jon (☎ 609-494-8844), at 9th St and Central Ave in Ship Bottom, rents surfboards, wakeboards and kneeboards for $10/15/50 per half day/full day/week. Renting wetsuits costs $5/8/25 and boogie boards cost $3/5/18 for foam and $3/8/30 for slick. Ron Jon also rents umbrellas and chairs for $5 a day.

The Acme Surf Company (☎ 609-492-1024), at 13th St and Long Beach Blvd in Beach Haven, rents out body boards for $10/29, surfboards for $15/60 and wetsuits for $15/60 on a daily/weekly basis.

Briggs Bicycles (☎ 609-492-1143), at 8401 Long Beach Blvd in Brighton Beach, rents bicycles at about $40 per week. Island Skates (☎ 609-492-6522), at 13th St and Long Beach Blvd in Beach Haven, rents in-line skates by the day.

Faria's (☎ 800-332-7427) has a wide selection of items for rent, including beach equipment, bicycles, in-line skates, things for the home (fans, high chairs, TVs, tables) and sports equipment for volleyball, tennis and other beach sports. It has four locations: in Beach Haven, at the corner of Taylor and Bay Aves (☎ 609-492-0200) and at Center St (☎ 609-492-7484); in Ship Bottom, at the corner of 28th and Boulevard (☎ 609-494-7368); and in Surf City, at 5th and Boulevard (☎ 609-494-8616). All of Faria's stores are open Monday

to Friday 9 am to 6 pm and Saturday and Sunday 8 am to 6 pm. Body boards cost $9 a day, $22 a week.

Places to Stay

The liveliest town on Long Beach Island is Beach Haven, where there is the greatest concentration of B&Bs and nightlife. A quieter time can be found in the small community of Barnegat Light at the northern end of the island.

Camping There's no camping on Long Beach Island. The nearest mainland campgrounds are on Route 9 south of the intersection with Route 72, which takes you onto the island. If you don't mind commuting 10 miles, *Sea Pirate Campground* (☎ 609-296-7400, Route 9), in West Creek, has daily tent sites from $20. There's a pool and amenities needed for RVs. It is open from late April to late September. *Baker's Acres* (☎ 609-296-2664, 230 Willets Ave), in Parkertown, is a mile or so south of West Creek on Route 9.

B&Bs Almost all the B&Bs in Beach Haven are packed into an area six blocks long by one block wide within a block of the beach – from 3rd St in the north to Coral St in the south and between Atlantic and Beach Aves. Most are top-end B&Bs with a Victorian theme, and charge about $150 to $250 (depending on their proximity to the ocean). *Green Gables Inn & Restaurant* (☎ 609-492-3553, 212 Centre St) has nicely decorated rooms and an excellent restaurant. Rates include a buffet breakfast and the owners speak French and Italian. Weekday/weekend rates are $75 to $105. *Pierrot by-the-Sea* (☎ 609-492-4424, 101 Centre St) is right across from the beach with nine bedrooms and shared showers.

Hotels & Guesthouses There are hotels all over Long Beach Island. Rates begin at $45 and run as high as $175 daily for the top-end hotels. Expect to pay $60 to $80 for those listed below. Generally speaking, the cheaper places are outside Beach Haven and Barnegat Light, and you can find motels up and down Long Beach Blvd from Surf City to towns further south.

In Barnegat Light, *Ella's Motel* (☎ 609-494-3200), at 18th and Long Beach Blvd, is a traditional motel that's open year-round. The casual *Inlet of Breakers Hotel* (☎ 609-494-4848, 10 W 5th St), between Broadway and Central Ave, is an 11-room, red and white shingle house that dates to the 1890s and was originally known as 'the Social.' In its history, the house has served as a speakeasy and a brothel. *White Whale Motel* (☎ 609-494-3020, 20 W 7th St) has eight rooms, three efficiencies and a two-bedroom apartment; it's open April to October.

In Surf City, the *Surf City Hotel* (☎ 609-494-7281), at 8th St and Long Beach Blvd, has a bar and restaurant. *Sandpiper Motel* (☎ 609-494-6909), at 10th St and Long Beach Blvd, offers standard, clean rooms for $65. *Admiral Motel* (☎ 609-494-0410, 102 E 16th St) has moderate rooms and efficiencies but no phones in the rooms. *Sharp's Guest House* (☎ 609-494-6981, 1216 Long Beach Blvd), at 13th St, has four rooms with shared baths for $85.

In Beach Haven, *St Rita Hotel* (☎ 609-492-9192/1704, 127 Engleside Ave) is the last surviving old hotel in this town. It's open mid-April to October. *Engleside Inn* (☎ 609-492-1251, 30 Engleside Ave) has standard motel rooms right on the beach, an outdoor bar-restaurant and a small health club. It's open year-round. *Sea Shell Motel & Club* (☎ 609-492-4611, 10 S Atlantic Ave) is on the oceanfront. Standard room rates are $160. *Mussel Beach Club* (☎ 609-492-9644, in winter 492-6130, 310 S Atlantic Ave) has efficiency rooms for $125. *Garrison's Motel* (☎ 609-492-2266, 4804 S Long Beach Blvd) is a standard motel charging $80 on weekdays.

On the bay side of Beach Haven, *Lorry's Island End Motel* (☎ 609-492-6363, 23 Washington Ave) is at the south end of the island. The motel has nine rooms with TVs, full-size refrigerators and microwaves; its rates are inexpensive for this area (only cash is accepted).

Places to Eat

As you drive along Long Beach Blvd, you'll pass delis, a few pizza places and a lot of seafood restaurants. Most of the seafood places serve fresh but uninspiring fare for about $10.

The restaurants in Barnegat Light get very crowded at breakfast and dinner, and you may face an hour-long wait for a table.

In Beach Haven there are three highly regarded seafood restaurants all along the bay at the end of Dock St. *Morrison's* (☎ 609-492-5111), at 2nd St, specializes in broiled or fried seafood platters. Patrons flock here to eat buckets of fried shrimp, clams and chicken at tables overlooking the bay. *Boat House* (☎ 609-492-1066), at Dock St and West Ave, has a more adventurous menu including a $20 bouillabaisse. There's a sunny deck in back that opens at 5 pm daily for dinner. The most expensive place on the island is the Victorian *Green Gables Inn* (☎ 609-492-3553, 212 Centre St), which offers a different five-course, fixed-price dinner every day. Reservations are required for the meal, which will run about $50 per person.

Entertainment

Check the free *Summer Times Islander* and *Beachcomber* for listings of club appearances and concerts.

In Beach Haven, *Tuckers* (☎ 609-492-2300), on Engleside Ave and the bay, features pop music Friday, Saturday and Sunday year-round. Some of the hotels have bars that support the local nightlife. The bar in *Engleside Inn* (☎ 609-492-1251, 30 Engleside Ave) is popular, as is the nightclub and raw bar at *Sea Shell Motel* (☎ 609-492-4611, 10 S Atlantic Ave). *Buckalew's* (☎ 609-492-2252), at Bay Ave and Center St, is a late-night piano bar.

The Quarter Deck (☎ 609-494-3334, 351 W 9th St), in Ship Bottom, holds a Mr Long Beach Island contest.

Shopping

Bay Village and Schooner's Wharf are shopping complexes on opposite sides of 9th St in Beach Haven. These stores sell beachwear, overpriced gift items and food.

Historic Viking Village is a string of former fishermen's shacks renovated into shops at 19th St and the bay in Barnegat Light. Each shop is independently run and sells wood carvings, jewelry and gourmet food items. For things Victorian, tarry awhile at Cinnamon & Spice (☎ 609-494-5413), 7th St and Broadway in Barnegat Light.

The Kite Store (☎ 609-361-0014), at 3rd St and Long Beach Blvd in Surf City, sells kites and sponsors a once-a-week kite fly on the beach.

Getting There & Away

The island is reached via exit 63 off the Garden State Pkwy on Route 72 across the causeway.

Northern New Jersey

New Jersey's north is a study in contrasts – crowded urban cities paired with mountain ranges and farmlands that separate the state from Pennsylvania. Along the shore of the Hudson River, you can find the satellite cities of Hoboken and Jersey City, old industrial towns with large ethnic populations. The terrain then changes dramatically in the northeastern gateway to the Poconos and northern Pennsylvania. This rural respite from urban bustle is known as the Skylands region and includes the Great Swamp National Wildlife Refuge and the Delaware Water Gap National Recreation Area, ideal places for hiking, bird-watching and fishing. The Appalachian Trail, which runs from Georgia to Maine, cuts through this part of the state.

The cities – Newark, Jersey City and Hoboken – are all easily reached via the PATH trains from Manhattan. Short Line buses travel to selected suburban points, but a car is a must to explore most of northern New Jersey. The top half of the state is traversed by a well-traveled US interstate highway (I-80), which runs from the George Washington Bridge to Stroudsburg, PA (in the Poconos), and points west. The region is also cut through by I-78, which runs just west of Jersey City to Allentown, PA.

Rural New Jersey

Some 25 miles directly west of New York City, you'll find the rural Skylands region (taking I-80 west from the city brings you to the Delaware River in about 90 minutes). Located in the under-populated northwest portion of the state, it is New Jersey's most concentrated area of outdoor activity – there are hot-air balloon flights, outdoor festivals and several state parks, including the Great Swamp National Wildlife Refuge. Made up officially of Warren, Sussex, Hunterdon and Somerset

Highlights

- Hoboken's hip clubs and bars, as well as shrines and memorabilia dedicated to Frank Sinatra, the town's native son
- Hiking along the storied Appalachian Trail in the Skylands region
- Ellis Island – it's now officially New Jersey territory

counties, the hill-and-forest region is completely different in character from the urbanized industrial belt in the northeast, and it's best reached and toured by car. Hunterdon County, with its rich farmland, offers scenic drives along Routes 519 and 12 and is particularly beautiful in the autumn. There are many scenic drives through the Skylands area, especially Route 515, which winds its way through some rich, forested valleys.

The top half of the state is transversed by I-80 and I-78. Route 206 heads north-south off Route 78 or 80. Routes 15 or 23 take you into the countryside north of I-80.

The Skylands Regional Tourism Council (☎ 201-366-6889) in Denville offers maps, information on activities and lodging listings.

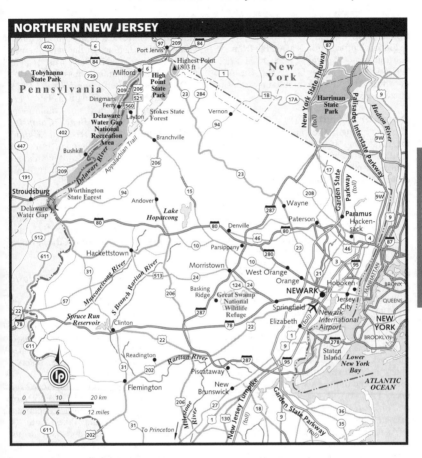

NORTHERN NEW JERSEY

NEW JERSEY

DELAWARE WATER GAP NATIONAL RECREATION AREA

The Delaware Water Gap National Recreation Area (NRA) is a park scattered across 37 miles along both sides of the Delaware River. It defines the border of northwestern New Jersey and Pennsylvania. The 'gap' is a chasm made by the river as it cuts though Kittatinny Ridge at the southern end of the park. The Appalachian Trail passes through this area (see the Appalachian National Scenic Trail section, later in this chapter). Because the Delaware Water Gap includes 200 miles of internal roads, you should have a car to explore.

The Delaware Water Gap NRA consists of not only federally protected lands but also many New Jersey and Pennsylvania parks. (For more information on Pennsylvania's portion of this area, see the Poconos section in the Northern Pennsylvania chapter.)

Information

Kittatinny Point Visitor Center (☎ 908-496-4458), off I-80 on the New Jersey side, is open daily 9 am to 5 pm from April to October. During July and August the center is open on Friday and Sunday until 7 pm;

October to March it's open weekends only from 9 am to 4:30 pm.

General information is available from the National Park Service (NPS; ☎ 717-772-0239), Delaware Water Gap NRA, Bushkill, PA 18324. The NPS also maintains a website at www.nps.gov/dewa.

Outdoor Activities

The best **hiking** in the park is along the Appalachian Trail. It traverses across the park for 25 miles (from the park's southern end, it continues north, and exits the park at its eastern boundary). Hikers on trips of at least two days are allowed to camp within 100 feet of the Appalachian Trail. There are also several other shorter trails throughout the park. The visitors' centers have trail maps.

At certain designated points, the Delaware River is safe for **swimming**. From mid-June to Labor Day there are beaches at Milford and Smithfield with lifeguards and bathhouses.

The Delaware River also offers opportunities for **canoeing** and **white-water rafting**. Park visitors' centers offer a list of outfitters. These include the following: Kittatinny Canoes (☎ 717-828-2338, 800-356-2852), at the park center in Dingmans Ferry; Pack Shack Adventures (☎ 717-424-8533), at the southern end of the park in Delaware Water Gap, PA; and River Beach Campsites (☎ 717-296-7421), at the northern end of the park in Milford, PA.

As for **fishing**, the lakes and ponds in the park support bass and pickerel, and the streams have rainbow, brook and brown trout. In the Delaware River it's possible to catch shad, smallmouth bass, walleye, eels and catfish. See the Fishing section in the Outdoor Activities chapter for information on obtaining a fishing license.

For those interested in **bird-watching**, the park is a good place to see hawks and turkey vultures, and it's also one of the few places in the East where bald eagles are found during the winter. The best time for eagle spotting is mid-morning or late afternoon in January and February.

Other popular outdoor pursuits include **hang gliding** and **rock climbing**.

Places to Stay

Camping There are many campgrounds within driving distance of the park; the visitors' centers and the NPS have a list of all facilities within a 40-mile radius of the park.

Dingmans Campground (☎ 717-828-2266) is in the park at Dingmans Ferry, PA. Other campgrounds in Pennsylvania along the river include *River Beach Campsites* (☎ 717-296-7241) and *Tri-State Canoe/Campground* (☎ 800-562-2663). For additional lodging options in Pennsylvania, see the Poconos section of the Northern Pennsylvania chapter.

In New Jersey, camps along the Delaware River include the following: *Cedar Ridge Campground* (☎ 201-293-3512), *Delaware River Campground* (☎ 908-475-4517) and *Worthington State Forest Campground* (☎ 908-841-9575).

Hostels The HI-AYH *Old Mine Rd Hostel* (☎ 973-948-6750), PO Box 172, Layton, NJ 07851, is in the park beside the Delaware River. There are 12 beds for $12 each. It has a kitchen, a common room and separate dormitories for men and women. Lockout time is 10 am to 5 pm. The hostel is open year-round, and you should make reservations for weekend stays.

From eastern New Jersey or New York City, take I-80 west to exit 34B. Go north on Route 15 for 18 miles, until it becomes Route 206 at Ross Corner. Take Route 206 north to Route 560 west, and then go just over 2 miles to Layton. Make a right at the Layton General Store and go for another 2 miles to Old Mine Rd. Make a sharp right on Old Mine Rd and go 2 miles more to the hostel.

From Milford, PA, take Route 209 south across the Milford Bridge into New Jersey. Take the first right turn onto Old Mine Rd and drive 4½ miles south to the hostel.

APPALACHIAN NATIONAL SCENIC TRAIL

The Appalachian Trail is an original Native American byway that weaves through the Appalachian Mountain range along the East Coast of the US. Stretching from Springer

Mountain, GA, all the way to Katahdin, ME, this 2160-mile trail could be called the first American highway.

Although the trail is officially a part of the NPS, it's comprised of some 60 different state parks and game lands. The trail is also maintained and cared for by thousands of enthusiastic volunteers. The following New Jersey state parks offer access to the trail, and all have camping facilities for about $10 per site.

High Point State Park

This state park, created from donated land in 1923, includes the 1803-foot High Point Peak, the highest elevation in New Jersey. There's also Lake Marcia, a spring-fed lake that is popular for swimming, and Dryden Kuser Natural Area, a 1500-acre swamp that's a native habitat for several endangered species such as Cooper's Hawk. In the winter, there's a cross-country ski center (☎ 973-702-1222).

High Point State Park (☎ 973-875-4800) is near the state's border with both New York and Pennsylvania – it's 7 miles north of Sussex, NJ, and 4 miles south of Port Jervis, NY. You can get there by using I-80 to Route 206 at Lake Hopatcong, then taking Route 521. The park is part of the Delaware Water Gap NRA.

Worthington State Forest

This 5878-acre forest (☎ 908-841-9575) was popular with Dutch fur traders who traveled along the Delaware River with their wares. The Old Mine Road, one of the oldest established roads in the state, follows the riverbed. The forest has a trail that circles a pond and offers views for hikers who reach the top of 1527-foot Mount Tammany. There are some 70 campsites and clean toilets, with fees of $10 per site.

You can get there by taking Route 80 west to the Millbrook-Flatbrookeville exit and turning right at the end of the ramp. The forest office is 3 miles down the road on the left.

Stokes State Forest

Stokes State Forest (☎ 973-948-3820) follows the Appalachian Trail along the crest of Sunrise Mountain. A pavilion at the summit of the mountain, built in the 1930s, is very popular with hikers during the fall-foliage season. Hikers also like the Evergreen Walk along the Tillman Ravine in the park. There are summer campsites, and in the winter there's ice fishing. The forest is reached by taking Route 206 to Branchville and following the signs.

GREAT SWAMP NATIONAL WILDLIFE REFUGE

The Great Swamp National Wildlife Refuge is a 7200-acre site with 10 miles of trails through a habitat that's home to more than 220 birds, along with populations of muskrat, fox and fish. Two boardwalks wind along marshland, hardwood ridges, cattail marsh and water, brush, pasture and cropland. The swamp also contains many large, old oak and beech trees, stands of mountain laurel and other plant species from both northern and southern botanical zones.

The creation of the Great Swamp began roughly 25,000 years ago when the Wisconsin glacier reached its furthest point south here. As the melting glacier withdrew northward, it left behind a barren landscape of sand and gravel ridges. These blocked the outlet of an ancient river basin, and when the water that had melted from the glacier flowed into the basin, a natural dam formed a giant lake, 30 miles long and 10 miles wide. The lake eventually drained away, leaving extensive marshes and swamps.

In 1708 the Delaware Indians deeded a 30,000-acre tract that included the Great Swamp to British settlers for a barrel of rum, 15 kettles, four pistols, four cutlasses, some other goods and £30. Settlements slowly began to appear in the area, using wood from the Great Swamp for construction. By 1844, farms were established on the uplands. They drained the marshlands, and hay became a major crop.

These small farms were uneconomical and eventually disappeared, and much of the uplands reverted to woods, the lower flatlands to swamp. An airport plan was scuttled in the early 1960s by local residents who wanted the land saved as a preserve. The

NEW JERSEY

ensuing establishment of the Great Swamp National Wildlife Refuge was one of first such conservation attempts in New Jersey.

Information

The Wildlife Observation Center, off Long Hill Rd, is particularly good for observation and photography. It has an unstaffed information booth, interpretive displays, rest rooms and two blinds for observing wildlife and trails.

The Great Swamp National Wildlife Refuge Headquarters (☎ 201-425-1222), off Pleasant Plains Rd, is open weekdays 8 am to 4:30 pm. Volunteer staff are on hand on Sunday during spring and fall.

The Outdoor Education Center (☎ 201-635-6629), on Southern Blvd, is a starting point for canoe and bird-watching trips.

Walking Trails

The trails are open daily from dawn to dusk. Early morning and late afternoon are the best times to observe wildlife. Waterproof footwear or old sneakers are recommended for most of the year. From May to September insect repellent is a good idea due to the threat of bites from numerous mosquitoes, ticks and deer flies.

Raptor Trust

This is a nonprofit organization (☎ 908-647-2353) dedicated to the preservation of birds of prey. It operates a rehabilitation center where hundreds of distressed wild birds are given medical care, diet and housing each year. Orphaned birds are raised using techniques that avoid creating dependence on humans. The trust's goal is to always return healthy, self-sufficient birds back to their natural environment.

There is an outdoor area where several hawks and owls are kept. This gives you a rare opportunity to see these amazing creatures at close range. It's open daily 8:30 am to 4:30 pm; admission is free, but donations are requested.

Places to Stay

Camping is the only type of accommodations in the *Great Swamp* (☎ 973-425-1222), but

the nearby **Olde Mill Inn** (☎ 908-221-1100, 225 Route 202), in Basking Ridge, is a renovated Colonial-style facility with rooms from $135. In Morristown, you can stay at the **Best Western Morristown Inn** (☎ 201-540-1700, 270 South St), at exit 31 off I-287, a standard roadside hotel with rooms around $100.

Getting There & Away

The Great Swamp is approximately one hour from both New York City and Philadelphia, providing there is little traffic leading out of either city. By car from New York, take I-80 west to I-287 south to exit 30A for Basking Ridge. Follow the signs along Maple Ave for the Great Swamp and Lord Stirling Rd. Signs lead you to the refuge headquarters (where you can pick up brochures) and the Wildlife Observation Center on Long Hill Rd, the site of two boardwalk trails and an information kiosk.

VERNON
Winter Activities

Located off Route 94, the Mountain Creek ski resort (☎ 973-827-3900) was once known as Vernon Valley Great Gorge. It was renamed after a $26 million investment. It's too early to tell exactly what changes will be made, but there are already some 50 trails over three mountains (open December to March annually). The vertical drop exceeds 1000 feet. There is a lodge, ski rental, ski school and restaurant. If there is not enough snow, the resort has the 'world's largest snowmaking system,' capable of producing 8 miles of 3-foot-deep snow overnight. All-day lift tickets (including access to lighted slopes at night) are about $50/35 for adults/children, with cheaper rates after 10 am. A 'learn-to-ski' day package is available for $50.

For information on special events, rates, lodging and restaurants within the resort, call ☎ 973-827-2222 or write to Mountain Creek at 200 Route 94, Vernon, NJ 07462; the resort's website is www.mountaincreek.com.

Summer Activities

The popular amusement area and water-sport center at Mountain Creek is open from April to Thanksgiving. It features some 75 attractions, such as spectacular water slides and a tidal wave pool, bumper cars, mini racers, bungee jumping, speedboats and a brewery.

Urban New Jersey

People, factories, highways and cities all compete for space in the northeastern part of the state. It is home to two-thirds of New Jersey's population, and is a center for industry and manufacturing. The landscape reflects this density and it is far from picturesque. But the monotony of concrete is broken by the diversity of the area's population, which is a rich mix of races and ethnicities. Close enough for a day trip from New York City, these old industrial cities offer breathtaking views of Manhattan's skyline, a variety of ethnic cuisines and historic sites dedicated to such notables as the old-crooner Frank Sinatra and the prolific inventor Thomas Edison.

HOBOKEN
Hoboken (population 33,400) is a New Jersey version of New York's Brooklyn

NEW JERSEY

HOBOKEN

PLACES TO EAT
1 Schnackenberg's Luncheonette
3 Helmer's
8 Ali Ba Ba's
9 Vito's Italian Deli
11 Café Louis
16 Leo's Grandevous Restaurant
22 City Hall Bakery
24 Piccolo's
28 Clam Broth House

BARS & CLUBS
4 Maxwell's
5 McMahon's Brownstone Ale House
6 Cafe Elysian
7 Excalibur
14 Louise & Jerry's
15 Bahama Mama's
17 Black Bear
18 Brass Rail
23 Scotland Yard
25 Bar None
27 Boo Boo Funkadelic Lounge
29 Shooters
31 Santa Fe Yacht Club
32 Widow McShane's
33 Texas/Arizona

OTHER
2 Baseball Plaque
10 Hoboken Books
12 United Decorating Co
13 Cheap Maggie
19 Hand Made
20 City Hall & Historical Museum
21 ATM
26 Platters' Records
30 Post Office
34 Erie Lackawanna Train Terminal
35 Ferry Terminal

Heights – a gentrified community of well-preserved brownstones and apartments within easy commuting distance of Manhattan. Socially, the town is pretty evenly split between long-time residents and young professionals who've moved in looking for cheap rent. On Friday night, the younger folks get a bit rowdy as they wind-down from the work week at local taverns' happy hours. Because Hoboken has a reputation as a weekend party town, the police have become rather aggressive about cracking down on drinking in public, so beware if you're out for a night of it in Hoboken.

The city has an important place in US popular culture. It's generally agreed that the first organized baseball game was played here on a plain overlooking Manhattan in 1846. There's a memorial at the corner of Washington and 11th Sts. 'The Chairman of the Board,' Frank Sinatra, was born in Hoboken in 1915 and got his start in local clubs; and the film classic *On the Waterfront* was shot on the city's docks in 1954.

Orientation & Information

Occupying little more than a square mile, the city is easily explored on foot, and a grid system makes getting around quite easy. Most of Hoboken's shops and restaurants are within a few blocks of the ornate old Erie Lackawanna Train Terminal, where the PATH trains stop, or along Washington St.

Parking in Hoboken can be a headache, especially at night and on weekends. With the parking police aggressively checking for offenders, you should consider paying for parking rather than risk getting a ticket.

The city has no tourist office, but you can pick up a copy of the free weekly *Hudson Current* at bars and shops all around town. It covers local arts and special events.

ATMs are found all along Washington St. The main post office is on River St between Newark and 1st Sts.

Hoboken Books (☎ 201-963-7781), 626 Washington St between 6th and 7th Aves, is a good bookstore.

Hoboken City Hall & Historical Museum

Built in 1881, city hall (☎ 201-420-2026), at 1st and Washington Sts, is a registered State and National Historic Landmark. Inside, the Hoboken Historical Museum has display cases of local history and mementos of Frank Sinatra. (His birthplace was torn down some years ago, so this museum is the main Frank shrine.) The museum is open Monday to Friday from 9 am to 4 pm.

Places to Eat

There is a growing array of cafes and fancier restaurants in Hoboken, especially on Washington St. The following are more colorful and/or traditional choices.

Vito's Italian Deli (☎ 201-792-4944, 806 Washington St), between 8th and 9th Sts, makes great submarine sandwiches. *City Hall Bakery* (☎ 201-659-3671, 95 Washington St), between Newark and 1st Sts, has the standard fare of cookies, cakes and coffee.

Schnackenberg's Luncheonette (☎ 201-659-9834, 1110 Washington St), between 11th and 12th Sts, is a wonderfully retro place from the 1940s, with prices from the '70s: most items cost less than $5, including burgers, sandwiches and milkshakes. It's open Monday to Saturday 7:30 am to 6 pm.

Piccolo's (☎ 201-653-0564, 92 Clinton St), between Newark and 1st Sts, has been serving delicious cheese steak sandwiches at this location since 1955.

Clam Broth House (☎ 201-659-6767, 38 Newark St), by the train station, was established in 1899 and it specializes in seafood dishes. It's decorated with photos of Frank Sinatra and other celebrities who've visited.

Helmer's (☎ 201-963-3333, 1036 Washington St), at 11th St, is a traditional German bar-restaurant from the 1930s. It's open from Monday to Thursday noon to 10 pm (11 pm on Friday and Saturday) and is closed Sunday. There are $7 lunch specials, with German specialties such as knockwurst sandwiches with sauerkraut.

Leo's Grandevous Restaurant (☎ 201-659-9467, 200 Grand St), at 2nd St, is another classic. In the neighborhood where Frank Sinatra grew up, it is decorated with pictures of the singer, and it still attracts Frank's old neighbors with its standard Italian dishes priced at $20 to $30.

Established in 1985, *Cafe Louis* (☎ 201-659-9542, 505 Washington St), between 5th and 6th Sts, has varying cuisines, such as Cajun or Spanish, with consistently good food in a pleasant room; prices are less than $20. It's serves Sunday brunch, and it's open daily 11 am to 3 pm.

Ali Ba Ba's (☎ 201-653-5319, 912 Washington St), between 9th and 10th Sts, serves Middle Eastern food, with main courses less than $20.

Entertainment

Hoboken has a lively music scene and even a few independent record labels. The indie group Yo La Tengo was launched here, and many big-name groups appear at Maxwell's, the city's most legendary club. At last count, Hoboken had 40 clubs and bars.

Most dance clubs stay open until 3 am on Friday and Saturday, and at least one club on Washington St seems to be rocking during the weekdays.

Bars Built in 1896, the *Cafe Elysian* (☎ 201-659-9110, 1001 Washington St), at 10th St, has a beautiful old bar that became a beauty parlor and an ice cream parlor to survive the Prohibition years. Some of the regulars – many of whom park their motorcycles out front – look like extras in the movie *On the Waterfront* (some of its scenes were filmed here).

An old Hoboken standby, *Louise & Jerry's* (☎ 201-656-9698, 329 Washington St), between 3rd and 4th Sts, is a classic basement-level hangout complete with a coin-operated pool table and happy hour specials. The *Black Bear* (☎ 201-656-5511, 205 Washington St) is a sports lounge and cigar bar for the Wall Street crowd.

McMahon's Brownstone Ale House (☎ 201-798-5650, 1034 Willow Ave) is a classic Irish pub with a Sunday buffet.

The bars across from the PATH station attract large crowds of young professional patrons. *Texas/Arizona* (☎ 201-420-0304, 76 River Rd), on the corner of Hudson Place,

and *Santa Fe Yacht Club* (☎ 201-420-8317, 44 Hudson Place) both serve Tex-Mex food at reasonable prices, and it can be washed down with a broad range of beers. Between them, the raucous *Widow McShane's* (☎ 201-659-9690), across from the PATH station, offers a more traditional pub setting. *Scotland Yard* (☎ 201-222-9273, 72 Hudson St) serves British expatriates Fullers, Bass and Double Diamond from the tap, and on Friday night you'll find people quaffing yards of ale.

Music The club *Maxwell's* (☎ 201-798-4064, 1039 Washington St), at 11th St, is the reason many visit the town. In the mid-1990s, Maxwell's was disastrously relaunched as a microbrewery, but regulars shunned the club and music loyalists took it over and restored the old ways. The bar's back room has been featuring acts since 1978, and visitors include REM, Sonic Youth and Nirvana. Bruce Springsteen filmed his 'Glory Days' video here (directed by city resident John Sayles). There's usually $12 cover charge for music, and the restaurant features pub fare.

The *Brass Rail* (☎ 201-659-7074, 135 Washington St) is a classic bar-restaurant serving French food, with live jazz Thursday, Friday and Saturday night.

Boo Boo Funkadelic Lounge (☎ 201-659-5527, 40-42 Newark St) has live bands Wednesday and Thursday and DJs playing house and funk on weekends. *Bar None* (☎ 201-420-1112, 84 Washington St) plays top 40 and offers 'beat-the-clock' drink specials Monday to Friday. Patrons, understandably, get pretty rowdy as the night goes on. *Bahama Mama's* (☎ 201-217-1642, 215 Washington St) has no cover before 10 pm and $1 margaritas until 11 pm on Friday.

Excalibur (☎ 201-795-1161, 1000 Jefferson St), between 9th and 10th St, has a largely gay clientele. *Shooters* (☎ 201-656-3889, 92 River St), at the corner of Newark St, goes more for the college crowd from Hoboken's Stevens Institute of Technology, with DJs spinning house and drum and bass.

NEW JERSEY

Frank Sinatra

Francis Albert Sinatra, Hoboken, New Jersey's most famous son was born of immigrant Italian parents on December 12, 1915.

In the 1930s he started his long career as an entertainer, singing in local venues around Hoboken. After winning an amateur talent competition he began singing on New Jersey radio, then later joined the Harry James and Tommy Dorsey bands, before going solo in 1942. While he was with Tommy Dorsey, he had several hit songs and appeared in his first movie. By this time he had become a highly publicized teenage idol and in his public appearances were met by legions of screaming female fans – long before Elvis or the Beatles.

His first musical film was *Higher and Higher* (1943), but the best-remembered ones from this period were *Anchors Aweigh* (1945) and *On the Town* (1949), both of which also starred Pittsburgh's Gene Kelly.

In the early 1950s his popularity waned, and his time in the entertainment industry seemed over after his vocal chords ruptured, sending him off the performance stage. But he successfully revived his career when he won an Oscar for best supporting actor in *From Here to Eternity* (1953). A non-musical role, it established Sinatra as a serious actor. He then went on to make a number of memorable films, some musicals, others dramas, including *High Society* (1956), with Grace Kelly and Bing Crosby, the spy thriller *The Manchurian Candidate* (1962) and *The Detective* (1968). Sinatra also broke ground by portraying a drug addict in the drama *The Man with the Golden Arm* (1955), the first major Hollywood film to realistically portray junkie life.

This success in films was matched by a revival in his music career. His albums of the late 1950s – recorded late at night, with an orchestra using Nelson Riddle's arrangements – were alternately moody *(In the Wee Small Hours)* or upbeat *(Sinatra's Swinging Session)* and introduced the idea of a 'concept' album. His singing had a new-found maturity and he garnered an international follow-

Shopping

Platters Records, 56 Newark St between Washington and Hudson, is an independent store renowned for its alternative collection, including both vinyl and rare collectors' 7-inch records – mostly from the past seven years. Hand Made (☎ 201-653-7276), 116 Washington St, is an eclectic gift store offering 'folk, funk and fine art.' United Decorating Co (☎ 201-659-1922), 421 Washington St, is a funky store with vintage postcards, novelties, collectibles, Americana and tacky gifts.

Cheap Maggie (☎ 201-795-3770), 314 Washington St, is a downbeat version of the Gap with inexpensive jeans and other casual clothing.

Getting There & Away

The PATH train from Manhattan stops at the Erie Lackawanna Train Terminal in Hoboken.

If you're travelling by car from Manhattan, take either the Holland or Lincoln Tunnels and follow the signs.

From the NJ Turnpike, take exit 14C (Holland Tunnel exit), go to the bottom of the ramp and take a left at the first light, bear right under the overpass onto Observer Hwy (with the town's main streets to your

Frank Sinatra

ing as a cabaret performer. He appeared regularly at Caesar's Palace in Las Vegas and made numerous TV specials. The album *Come Fly With Me* (1959) proved hugely popular and his recordings of such songs as 'That's Life' and 'My Way' have become classics. He had almost 100 hit singles during his long career.

Controversy always dogged Sinatra. His earlier marriages to Ava Gardner and Mia Farrow were turbulent, and there were constant stories about his Mafia connections. In the *Godfather*, the character of Johnny Fontaine, who approaches Don Corleone looking for a big movie role to boost his career, was widely assumed to be based on Sinatra. Those connections led to his inability to invest in the casinos that he helped popularize. When his home state of New Jersey opened casinos in Atlantic City, Sinatra was one of the first to embrace the woebegone resort community.

Sinatra was known for his arrogance and quick temper, but also for his generosity, and in 1971 he received the Jean Hersholt Humanitarian Award. He was a strong supporter of the Democratic party and sang at John F Kennedy's inauguration, but after being frozen-out by the Kennedys due to his reputed underworld connections, he became more conservative. In 1985 it was Republican President Ronald Reagan who awarded him the Medal of Honor, the US's highest civilian accolade, in recognition of his contribution to American life. It was an honor criticized as inappropriate by some columnists.

The last years of his life were spent in comfortable retirement in Beverly Hills. In 1994, Sinatra received a Legend Award at the Grammy Awards Show, in recognition of his contribution to music. On May 14, 1998, he died of a heart attack at Cedars-Sinai Hospital in Los Angeles.

Sinatra Shrines Frank Sinatra was born at 416 Monroe St. There's an empty lot there now, but a gold star marks the site. But 'The Voice' is remembered in different ways: city hall features memorabilia, shops along Washington St sell Frank T-shirts, and the singer's visage adorns just about every old bar and restaurant in town. The best Sinatra shrine is Leo's Grandevous Restaurant, 200 Grand St, followed by Piccolo's at 92 Clinton St, which plays Sinatra tunes constantly. (See Places to Eat for more information.)

A website set up by *The Star-Ledger* (www.nj.com/sinatra) keeps track of all Sinatra-related events in the old town.

left). Or take exit 16E (Lincoln Tunnel exit), bear right at the Hoboken exit and continue through the first light to the bottom of the ramp, turn right onto Park Ave, left onto 14th St. You'll find Washington St is three blocks later on the right.

If traveling by ferry, you can take New York Waterway Ferry (☎ 800-533-3779), which runs ferries between Hoboken (near the Erie Lackawanna Train Terminal) and the World Financial Center in Lower Manhattan. Ferries leave every 10 minutes during rush hour and every 20 minutes at off-peak times from 6:30 am to 11 pm (weekends on the half hour from 10 am to 10 pm). The trip takes eight minutes and costs $2 each way, with a monthly pass costing $75.

JERSEY CITY

The area that is now Jersey City (population 228,500) was established by the Dutch in 1630, and the port town eventually became a strategic transportation link between New York and cities to the west and south.

Today, most people, even many residents, would question whether Jersey City is worth a detour. It has earned dubious fame throughout the state for having an ineffective local government and a school system so bad that state officials seized control of the board of education. The city also has the dubious distinction of being the home of the terrorists who bombed New York City's World Trade Center in 1993.

Yet things are looking up as more families move into Jersey City and prompt change. It's the gateway to Liberty State Park and the Liberty Science Museum that overlook the Statue of Liberty from the west side of New York Harbor.

Manhattan Skyline Viewpoint

Located immediately outside the Exchange Place PATH station, the small **Grundy Park** offers a superb vantage point for views across the Hudson River to downtown Manhattan. It's a great place to watch the sunset or, if you're lucky, to see one of the remaining ocean liners gliding past the skyscrapers.

Facing Manhattan, to your right on the Jersey City side, stands the landmark **Colgate Clock** at 105 Hudson St. It's said to be the world's largest, with a dial 50 feet in diameter; the minute hand alone weighs 2200 pounds.

Liberty State Park

This 1200-acre park (π 201-915-3403) faces the Statue of Liberty and also offers spectacular views of Manhattan. Ferries depart here for Ellis and Liberty Islands and are always far less crowded than their counterparts operating from Battery Park (see the Manhattan section in the New York City chapter for information the Statue of Liberty and the islands). With its combination of views, access to the islands, two terrific museums, picnic area, paths for walking, jogging, cycling and horse riding, children's playground, boating, swimming, fishing and summer concerts, Liberty State Park is well worth a visit.

Entering the park, you drive along State Flag Row (with the flags arranged in order of induction into the union) and 1750 feet ahead of you stands the Statue of Liberty. Beyond, you can also see the Brooklyn Bridge, and to the right the bridge linking Staten Island to Brooklyn. Also check out the **Liberation Monument**. 'Dedicated to America's role of preserving freedom and rescuing the oppressed,' this statue features a US soldier carrying a WWII concentration camp survivor.

The visitors' center is open daily May to November from 6 am to 6 pm and during the winter from 8 am to 4 pm; it provides information on the park's facilities and special events.

To get to the park by car, take exit 14B off the NJ Turnpike feeder road. Connecting NJ Transit bus service is available from the Exchange Place PATH station for $1.25.

Statue of Liberty Tours Ferries (π 201-435-0499) depart Liberty State Park for the Statue of Liberty and Ellis Island every day except Christmas Day. The trip takes just 15 minutes and the cost is $7 for adults, $6 for seniors and $3 for children. The boats tend to be slightly less crowded than those leaving from Lower Manhattan, but the mobs on both islands mean you will not be able to take in both sites unless you depart well before noon.

Liberty Science Center Also in the state park is this spectacular modern museum (π 201-200-1000) that bills itself as a family learning center for science, technology and nature. It features permanent exhibitions, with three of the four floors dedicated to the theme of invention. There are interactive exhibits, theater shows and presentations throughout the museum. On the entrance floor you can learn how to see in 3-D through live demonstrations and a 3-D slide

New Jersey's Ownership

After several years of dispute with New York, a special adjudicator appointed by the US Supreme Court ruled in 1998 that Ellis Island was largely the territory of the state of New Jersey. This ruling mainly has to do with bragging rights for the famous tourist spot, but the winning state does get to collect tax revenues from the sale of items in the Ellis Island shop.

show. Alternating shows feature the 'Superstars of Science,' and you can participate in the action by transmitting sound through a laser beam and watching a million watts of electricity flow through a coil to create lightning bolts.

The museum's shop, Tools & Toys, sells science-related products, books and toys. The *Laser Lights Cafe* has terrific views across the Hudson to the Statue of Liberty and the Manhattan skyline, but you'll probably go mad from the noise of the school kids.

Schedules vary daily, so check if you are interested in any specific exhibits or presentations. Admission is $9.50 for adults, $7.50 for students and seniors and $6.50 for children ages 2 to 12. The science center is open daily April to September 9:30 am to 5:30 pm and during the winter Tuesday to Sunday noon to 5 pm.

Central Railroad of New Jersey Museum

This railroad museum, housed in a beautiful Victorian building, was the departure point for 20 trains and was the ferry slip to the immigration center on Ellis Island. The facility, in use from 1892 to 1954, handled tens of thousands of people daily, but it went into decline with the development of road transportation. Thirty years ago this whole park area was a wasteland with rotting docks and undeveloped marshlands. It is now a scenic 2-mile promenade with beautiful views on sunny days.

In 1964 the state park was established, and a cleanup was completed in time for the 1976 US Bicentennial, with more improvements made for the Statue of Liberty's centennial in 1986. At the now deserted platforms, some of the old train names, routes and schedules are still posted, and displays highlight the history of the terminal and the people who passed through. It's open daily 10 am to 5 pm.

NEWARK

With its rapidly growing international airport and a location across the Hudson River from New York City, Newark (population 314,000) is known by many tourists as the start or finish point for a visit to the Middle-Atlantic states.

Newark began as a small village established by Puritan settlers in 1666, but soon grew larger thanks to the colonial leather-making industry. Ironworks and other heavy industries came to Newark in the late 18th and early 19th centuries, and the city was a leading supplier for the Union Army during the Civil War. The development of commercial businesses followed the end of the war, with both the Prudential and Mutual Benefit insurance companies being founded in Newark.

Although it's New Jersey's largest city, Newark lost population and jobs during the lean years following WWII. Today, Newark is known to travelers mainly for its airport, with a huge new international terminal that puts overcrowded JFK in New York City to shame.

Though not a popular tourist destination, Newark does justify a quick day-trip from Manhattan if you're in the area for more than a week. The city is also home to a lively enclave of Portuguese immigrants and has one of the country's most beautiful museums.

Most of the city's attractions are centered around or within walking distance of Newark Penn Station, a busy terminal that is often confused with New York's Penn Station. The area east of the train station is called the **Ironbound District**, a vibrant, multi-ethnic community that was once surrounded by the major railroad lines. It has long been a home for European immigrants, and since the 1960s, it has been home to a large block of new arrivals from Portugal who have established their own restaurants, shops and fresh-food markets on and around Ferry St.

City officials know that Newark has a bad reputation, and all tourist sites tend to emphasize how safe or convenient it is to get around. Indeed, there are so many new signs for every conceivable tourist destination that it is nearly impossible to get lost here.

Information

There is no conventional tourist office in Newark, but a map and a guide to the city

NEW JERSEY

can be obtained by contacting the City Hall Public Information Office (☎ 973-733-8165), 920 Broad St, room 214, Newark, NJ 07102. The office is open weekdays 9 am to 5 pm and welcomes drop-ins.

The post office is on Franklin St, east of Broad St. There are ATMs on Ferry St in the Ironbound District.

New Jersey Performing Arts Center

This ambitious complex is the biggest addition to Newark in more than 30 years, and it's serious evidence of an effort to turn the town around. This $180 million, 12-acre complex opened in 1999 to become the new home of the New Jersey Symphony. There are two theaters, including the 2500-seat Prudential Hall, and a lawn area with room to accommodate 1500 people for an alfresco concert. Like many urban center cultural attractions, it may merely bring in suburbanites for events and do little for the surrounding neighborhood. But its location near the Ironbound District and next to Riverfront Stadium does seem like a cause for optimism that Newark's fortunes are improving.

There is also an acclaimed restaurant on site called *Theatre Square Grill* (☎ 973-642-1226) that serves meals before and after all events.

Newark Museum

Founded in 1909, the Newark Museum (☎ 973-596-6550), 49 Washington St, features permanent galleries with frequently changing exhibits. In 1989 the museum opened 60,000 sq feet of new exhibition space designed by the architect Michael Graves (who makes his home in Princeton). In all, the museum features some 60 galleries covering all aspects and eras. It's a first class – though it should be noted, not world class – cultural facility.

The museum is especially proud of its world-renowned **Tibetan Collection** featuring a Buddhist altar that was consecrated in 1990 by the Dalai Lama. There are also significant objects from Japan, Korea, China, India and other Himalayan areas. It is the largest and most comprehensive selection of Tibetan art in the US.

In addition to many other galleries, you'll find **American Painting & Sculpture** from the 18th to 20th centuries, and the **Decorative Arts** collection features glass, ceramics and textiles from the Renaissance to the present. There are also well known pieces of American silver, furniture and pottery, along with important objects from the Victorian era.

Permanent galleries feature selections from Africa, the Americas and the Pacific, ranging from the pre-Columbian era to the present. Temporary exhibitions highlight various aspects of these diverse cultures.

The **Classical Art** collection includes works representing life in early Mediterranean societies – Egyptian, Greek, Etruscan, Roman – along with a permanent exhibit of Coptic art. There is also the highly regarded Eugene Schaeffer Collection of Ancient Glass. The **Natural Science** collection includes a planetarium and a minizoo with more than a hundred animals housed in naturalistic habitats. In the museum's garden there is a 1794 schoolhouse, the Newark Fire Museum (dedicated to fire-fighting history and lore) and a collection of contemporary sculpture.

The Newark museum is open Wednesday to Sunday from noon to 5 pm, and admission is free. The museum is on Washington St at Central Ave in the University Heights section of downtown Newark. You can walk to the museum or take bus No 44 or No 72 from Penn Station. Parking is available; be sure to have your parking ticket validated at the museum's information desk.

Places to Stay

Newark's accommodations revolve around the needs of business travelers using the airport. There's really no need to stay here, unless you're looking for motel-style airport accommodations at a slight discount from New York City rates. *Days Inn-Newark Airport* (☎ 973-242-0900) and *Hampton Inn-Newark Airport* (☎ 908-355-0500) are both just outside the area of the airport and feature typical chain-motel amenities.

The only recommendable downtown hotel is the **Gateway Hilton** (☎ *973-622-5000, 800-345-6565*), on Raymond Blvd, directly across the street from the train station. Rooms begin at around $160 a night, with weekend discounts available. Unless you get a good weekend or discount rate, stay in New York City.

Places to Eat
The best places to dine are the Portuguese and Spanish eateries in the Ironbound District surrounding Penn Station. With the good value, authentic decor and swift, efficient service, you really feel like you have been transported to Lisbon. Lunchtime is where you'll get real bargains, when you can enjoy excellent specials for $5 to $10. In the evening, prices change to about $18 per person. Seafood and barbecued meat dishes dominate the menus. Portions are large and it's taken for granted that you'll leave with leftovers (although you can't do that at an all-you-can eat buffet).

Mediterranean Manor (☎ *973-465-1966, 255 Jefferson St*) features live Portuguese *fado* music. The oldest restaurant in the neighborhood, **Iberia Tavern & Restaurant** (☎ *973-344-7603, 82-84 Ferry St*) is spotlessly clean and has seats at the bar and tables. Across the street, its newer branch, **Iberian Peninsula Restaurant** (☎ *973-344-5611, 67-69 Ferry St*) features the same menu, plus barbecued dishes. **Spain** (☎ *973-344-0994, 419 Market St*) is a little more formal (waiters wear tuxedo jackets instead of just crisp white shirts).

You can have a hearty *riodizio de churrasco*, or all-you-can-eat Brazilian barbecue, for just $15 at **Brasilia Restaurant** (☎ *973-465-1227, 132 Ferry St*), between Madison and Monroe Sts.

If you just want a quick bite to eat or prefer to spend less, try **Picnic Barbecue** (☎ *973-589-4630, 232 Ferry St*), between Wilson Ave and Alyea St.

There are a couple of Portuguese bakeries serving up snacks like *bolo de arroz*, sweet rice pudding cakes, and floury round bread. The best known is **Coutinho's Bakery** (☎ *973-344-7384, 121 Ferry St*).

Spectator Sports
The spanking new Riverfront Stadium, a $30-million baseball stadium opened in 1999 as the home of the Newark Bears minor league team. Riverfront Stadium is right next to the New Jersey Performing Arts Center and just a few blocks away from Penn Station. Tickets, which at $6 and $8 are much cheaper than major league ducats, can be ordered ahead of time (☎ 973-483-6900), but you needn't order ahead – if there's a game, simply go to the box office.

Getting There & Away
For information on Newark International Airport, see the Getting There & Away section of the New York City chapter.

You should visit Newark via Amtrak, PATH or NJ Transit, because most of the city's attractions are centered around or within walking distance of Newark Penn Station (not to be confused with New York's Penn Station). The cheapest choice – the $1 PATH train – is also the most convenient. For a day trip from New York City, driving makes little sense, especially because Newark achieved notoriety in the 1990s as one of the worst places in the country for car theft.

HACKENSACK
Meadowlands Sports Complex
Opened in 1976, this 750-acre complex (☎ 201-935-8500) includes Giants Stadium, the Meadowlands Race Track and the Continental Airlines Arena.

Originally, the whole Meadowlands area was 30 sq miles of swamp and landfill, but it was drained in the 1970s for the new 76,000-seat home of the NFL Giants, who left Yankee Stadium for New Jersey. They were soon joined at Giants Stadium by the homeless (and hapless) New York Jets, who abandoned New York City's Shea Stadium without first cutting a deal for their own namesake place. The Meadowlands is also the area's outdoor rock concert venue, and virtually every major act on tour appears at either Giants Stadium or the Continental Airlines Arena.

NEW JERSEY

Continental Airlines Arena is home to the NBA New Jersey Nets, and the NHL New Jersey Devils – winners of the 1995 Stanley Cup. The Meadowlands Race Track has harness racing from late December to August and thoroughbred racing from Labor Day to early December.

The complex is accessed by Route 3 off the NJ Turnpike (Meadowlands exit) and by public transportation from the Port Authority Bus Terminal in New York City. The Nos 129 bus leaves the Port Authority Bus Terminal every half-hour weekdays 6 am to 3:30 pm; the fare is $1.90 each way. Additional buses leave Port Authority in New York City two hours before the starting time of events at the Meadowlands complex.

Secaucus Outlet Center

This collection of brand-name discount outlets (☎ 201-348-4780) is spread over three industrial park areas in the Meadowlands. The best strategy is to head for the Harmon Cove Outlet center, pick up a map and begin exploring its 55 shops and the dozens of surrounding outlet centers. You'll find, to name a few, Liz Claiborne and Calvin Klein clothing, Mikasa china, Church's Shoes, Door Store design center and the Passport International Food Hall. This is a place for shopaholics only, and it's best to have a car.

Traveling west out of New York from the Lincoln Tunnel, take Route 3 west to the Meadowlands Parkway. Follow the signs for the 'Outlet Center.'

THOMAS EDISON HISTORIC SITE

Sadly, few people today fully know the impact on modern society made by America's greatest inventor Thomas Alva Edison. His labs at Main St and Lakeside Ave in West Orange (☎ 201-736-0550) are open to the public as a national landmark.

Edison (1847-1931) perfected the electric light bulb, phonograph and movie camera, and had 1093 US patents issued to him, more than any other single person. This thoroughly ordinary man was not eccentric in any discernible way, although he was partial to afternoon naps on his workbenches at the lab. But he had a genius for applied science that literally changed the world – and at one time 7000 people worked for him at the lab and machine shop. Near his laboratory is a replica of the Black Maria, one of the first motion picture studios – it was built on a railway turnaround to catch the afternoon sun in the days before artificial floodlights. Also at the site is Glenmont, his 22-room mansion, which is now a museum.

It's open daily 9 am to 5 pm; tours of the labs begin at 9:30 am and continue to 3:30 pm. Admission is $2.

You can reach the Edison site by taking the NJ Turnpike out of New York to I-280 west (exit 15W). From I-280, take exit 10 at West Orange and make the first right onto Main St and follow the signs.

Near the Edison site in West Orange is the **Turtle Back Zoo** (☎ 201-731-5800), 560 Northfield Ave, a 16-acre park dedicated to endangered species that has a petting zoo and train ride perfect for small children.

Central New Jersey

The beltway between urban northern New Jersey and Pennsylvania is an odd combination of mid-sized cities and quiet rural towns. It was a crossroad of the War for Independence, and as such is studded with colonial history sites, including those in the state capital of Trenton.

FLEMINGTON

This pleasant town (population 4132) was once a major manufacturing area for pottery, but declined in the postwar period. Visitors now flock here for the town's inexpensive outlet stores. Information on Flemington and its attractions can be found at the Ramada Inn (☎ 908-806-8165) on Route 202.

The **Lindbergh Museum** (☎ 908-782-2610), 2 Einstein Ct, offers evidence and folklore on the 'trial of the century' – the kidnapping of the famed aviator's son and the subsequent execution of the man convicted of the crime, Bruno Richard Hauptman, who went to his death proclaiming his innocence. (Although the baby was kidnapped from the family home in Hopewell, NJ, near Princeton, the famous trial was held in Flemington at the Hunterdon County Court House in 1935.)

Nortlandz (☎ 908-782-4022), 495 Route 202, claims to be the home of the largest miniature railway in the world. This home of curios also has a 100-room dollhouse and a huge old theater pipe organ.

Flemington's **outlet stores** are a big draw for people who live in the Princeton area. Route 202 around the Flemington Circle offers shoppers several choices. The largest is Liberty Village (☎ 908-782-8550), 1 Church St, with 60 stores selling cut-rate crockery, clothing and athletic wear. Nearby are the Feed Mill Outlet Center (☎ 908-788-0386), next to Liberty Village, and the Dansk Factory Outlet (☎ 908-782-7077), on Flemington Circle.

Places to Stay

The *Ramada Inn* (☎ 908-782-7472), on Route 202, offers cheaper accommodations than

Highlights

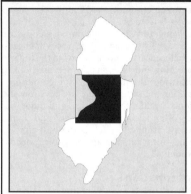

- The prototypical university town of Princeton, with its lush campus, historic homes and impressive art collection
- The state capital of Trenton, chock-full of colonial heritage
- New Brunswick, a university town that is also New Jersey's leading cultural center
- The revamped Camden waterfront, a diamond in a troubled city

some alternatives closer to Princeton. There are several B&Bs, including *Cabbage Rose* (☎ 908-788-0247, 162 Main St), which charges $85 to $135 per room, and *Jerica Hill* (☎ 908-782-8234, 96 Broad St), which charges $100 to $125 with a $25 additional guest charge.

Getting There & Away

Buses run from New York's Port Authority to Flemington several times a day, and directly to the outlets. The fare is about $15 roundtrip.

Flemington is about an hour by car from New York City. Take the NJ Turnpike out of New York City to Route 287 south, and at Somerville take Route 202 to Flemington.

NEW JERSEY

NEW JERSEY

PRINCETON

Princeton (population 13,016) is known throughout the world for its Ivy League college. In addition to the university's beautiful campus, the town has some lovely architecture, interesting historic sites and a nice selection of shops and restaurants along Nassau St.

Princeton is particularly sleepy on Monday, when many of the places of interest are closed, and you should avoid the town in late May and June, since hotels are booked solid months in advance for graduation. During the summer there are very few students around; there's peace and quiet, but it's often accompanied by hot and humid temperatures. The fall is the best time to visit – for what is a university town without students?

Information

The Princeton Convention & Visitors Bureau (☎ 609-683-1760), 20 Nassau St, offers maps and brochures for those planning a trip to Princeton, but it doesn't provide much help for those already in town; the phone line is almost never answered by a live person. Two other groups can assist you in town: the Historical Society of Princeton (☎ 609-921-6748) and, for university information, Orange Key Guide Service & Campus Information Office (☎ 609-258-6303) in MacLean House.

ATMs can be found along Nassau St; the post office is in the middle of Palmer Square. Micawber Books (☎ 609-921-8454), 112 Nassau St, is open Monday to Saturday from 9 am to 8 pm and Sunday from 11 am to 5 pm. The store often has readings by visiting authors and local writers.

Princeton Public Library (☎ 609-924-9529) is at 65 Witherspoon St and is open Monday to Thursday from 9 am to 9 pm, Friday and Saturday from 9 am to 5:30 pm and Sunday from 1 to 5:30 pm.

A map of literary Princeton, which immortalizes the homes and hangouts of local writers, can be bought for $10 at the town's bookstores. Profits benefit high school writing contests organized by the Humanities Council.

Historic Houses

Princeton has long been a haven for the wealthy, and the town is dotted with Colonial- and Federal-style homes. Several of these are open to the public or worth a mention because of their historic significance and links to the famous occupants.

Bainbridge House This Georgian-style house (☎ 609-921-6748), 158 Nassau St, was built in 1766 for local tanner Job Stockton, and was the birthplace of Commodore William Bainbridge, commander of the USS *Constitution*. Now the location of the Historical Society of Princeton, it offers a museum, library and shop where you can pick up free informational literature and self-guided walking tour maps plus various books and other souvenirs of Princeton. The house is open Tuesday to Sunday from noon to 4 pm; admission is free.

Morven This mansion (☎ 609-683-4495), 55 Stockton St, is a bright yellow estate built in 1750 for the Declaration of Independence signer Richard Stockton. It was later the residence of Robert Wood Johnson (founder of Johnson & Johnson), and from 1953 to 1981 served as the official residence of New Jersey governors. It's open Wednesday from 11 am to 2 pm or by appointment; admission is free.

Drumthwacket This historic home (☎ 609-683-0057), on Route 206, was built in 1835 by Charles Olden, a governor during the Civil War. It was donated to the state and became a designated residence for the New Jersey governor in 1981. The home is effectively a museum and working residence. The location of the governor's residence in tony Princeton is symbolic of the powerful, executive nature of the office vis-à-vis the less powerful legislature.

Free tours are offered of the public 1st-floor rooms on Wednesday from noon to 2 pm. Be sure to call ahead as these tours are not always operating. There is no admission fee but donations are welcomed.

Einstein's House Physicist Albert Einstein lived at 112 Mercer St, but the home is not

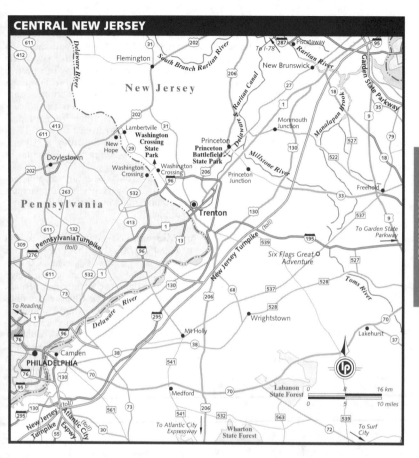

CENTRAL NEW JERSEY

open to the public. It is currently owned by a member of the Institute for Advanced Studies, where Einstein once taught. Einstein's study was in the back of the house on the 2nd floor and had views of pine and oak trees.

Thomas Clark House This house (☎ 609-921-0074), on the road into Princeton Battlefield State Park, was built in 1770 by Thomas Clarke, a Quaker farmer. During the Battle of Princeton, General Hugh Mercer received severe bayonet wounds and was brought to the house (along with other wounded soldiers from both sides) where he died nine days later. The house is furnished as it would have been at the time of the Revolutionary War. There are occasional period demonstrations of domestic chores such as cooking, textile production and other daily tasks.

The house is open Wednesday to Saturday from 10 am to noon and 1 to 4 pm, and Sunday from 1 to 4 pm; admission is free.

Princeton University

Princeton is one of the nation's oldest and most distinguished centers of learning and a frontline member of the so-called Ivy League. It was established in 1746 as the College of New Jersey and was originally located in Elizabeth and then Newark. The university campus that we know today was built in 1756 on 10 acres of donated land. It was largely a haven for wealthy Presbyterian families during the 18th and 19th centuries. Today Princeton is home to about 5000 undergraduates and some 2000 graduate students, the majority of whom pursue degrees in liberal arts or engineering.

The university's famous graduates include US presidents James Madison and Woodrow Wilson (who also served as the university's president), as well as actors James Stewart and Brooke Shields. The faculty is equally noteworthy and includes many famous writers and scientists. The exiled Albert Einstein spent the final years of his life here. Twenty-six Nobel prize winners – including Professor in the Humanities Toni Morrison, winner of the 1993 Nobel prize in literature – have made Princeton their academic home.

Free tours of the campus are offered by Orange Key (☎ 609-258-3603). Its office is in MacLean House, which is not well marked – it's the light-mustard colored

Ivy League Princeton University

building adjacent to the gate across from Palmer Square. This is a volunteer organization staffed by students and the tours include a history of the university along with some information for any prospective students about academic and social life on the campus. Reservations are not necessary but notification is appreciated. The office is open Monday to Saturday from 9 am to 5 pm and on Sunday from 1 to 5 pm. Tours operate Monday to Saturday at 10 and 11 am, 1:30 and 3:30 pm, and on Sunday at 1:30 and 3:30 pm.

A collection of 20th-century sculpture, including works by Henry Moore, Jacques Lipchitz and Picasso, is scattered throughout the campus.

Art Museum Located in McCormick Hall (☎ 609-452-3787) on the campus, this museum is well worth a visit. Exhibits include paintings and sculpture that range from ancient times to contemporary periods. Of special note are the Chinese paintings and bronzes, examples of pre-Columbian and African art and some modern art, including works by Pablo Picasso, Alexander Calder and Andy Warhol. The museum is open Tuesday to Saturday from 10 am to 5 pm and Sunday from 1 to 5 pm; admission is free. There is a free guided tour at 2 pm on Saturday.

Princeton Battlefield State Park

Located at 500 Mercer St about a mile southwest of downtown, Princeton Battlefield State Park commemorates the historic battle of Princeton. Fought on January 3, 1777, the encounter here with British troops was a decisive victory for George Washington and was one in a series battles that marked a turning point in the American Revolution.

This is one of the few battlefields of the Revolution to remain virtually unchanged. An illustrated plan stands next to the flagpole, and the graves of soldiers killed during the battle are to the north of the memorial columns. It's interesting to note that because Princeton was a Loyalist town, it

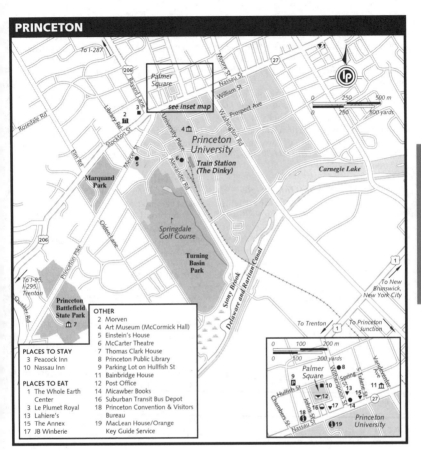

PRINCETON

OTHER
2   Morven
4   Art Museum (McCormick Hall)
5   Einstein's House
6   McCarter Theatre
7   Thomas Clark House
8   Princeton Public Library
9   Parking Lot on Hullfish St
11 Bainbridge House
12 Post Office
14 Micawber Books
16 Suburban Transit Bus Depot
18 Princeton Convention & Visitors
     Bureau
19 MacLean House/Orange
     Key Guide Service

PLACES TO STAY
3   Peacock Inn
10 Nassau Inn

PLACES TO EAT
1   The Whole Earth
     Center
3   Le Plumet Royal
13 Lahiere's
15 The Annex
17 JB Winberie

was looted after the battle by the victorious
rebel troops.

The park is open daily from dawn to dusk
and admission is free. Be sure to get a copy
of the free leaflet describing the battle from
Bainbridge House.

Outdoor Activities

Princeton Country Club (☎ 609-452-9382), 1
Wheeler Way off Route 1, has golf courses
open to the public. The cost for non-county
residents is around $24 on weekdays and
$28 on weekends.

Places to Stay

Budget There are few budget places in
Princeton. The motels along Route 1 are the
closest, making it awkward to stay inexpen-
sively overnight here without a car.

Mid-Range Bed & Breakfast of Princeton
(☎ 609-924-3189, fax 609-921-6271) is a clearinghouse for local establishments and has information on all of Princeton's inns and
B&Bs.

Heading south toward Princeton from
New York on Route 1 there are several motel

choices. The moderate **Red Roof** (☎ 908-821-8800, 208 New Rd), at Monmouth Junction off Route 1, has singles for $55. **Days Inn** (☎ 908-329-4555, 4191 Route 1) and **Ramada Inn** (☎ 609-452-2400, 4355 Route 1) both have daily rates of $100 to $125.

Driving along Route 1 north from Trenton is **McIntosh Inn of Princeton** (☎ 609-896-2544), near the Quaker Bridge Mall about 5 miles south of Princeton; its room rates start at $60. About a mile south of town on Route 1, **Best Western Palmer Inn** (☎ 609-452-2500) has rooms for $100.

Top End The **Nassau Inn** (☎ 609-921-7500), on Palmer Square, is a 1756 structure with modern extensions. Famous visitors to the inn have included Fidel Castro, Indira Ghandi and just about anyone who's ever received an honorary degree at the university. The 1775 **Peacock Inn** (☎ 609-924-1707, 20 Bayard Lane) has 17 rooms with rates starting at $100 (including bath and continental breakfast). The Peacock Inn has the comfortable feel of an informal wealthy home.

Hyatt Regency Princeton (☎ 609-987-2584, 102 Carnegie Center), off Route 1 north, has single/double rates at $180 for weekdays and under $100 for weekends. **Marriott Residence Inn** (☎ 908-389-8100), on Route 1 south, has weekday rates starting at $150.

Places to Eat
Budget **JB Winberie** (☎ 609-921-0700, 1 Palmer Square) is a restaurant and bar with entrees under $15, a daily happy hour and an all-you-can-eat Sunday brunch buffet. **Hoagie Haven** (☎ 609-921-7723, 242 Nassau St) is open daily from 9 am to 1 am and serves the student crowd large submarine sandwiches under $8.

The Annex (☎ 609-921-7555, 128 Nassau St) offers pub grub for under $10. No college town would be complete without a veggie place, and the best is **The Whole Earth Center** (☎ 609-924-7429, 360 Nassau St), which offers organic choices such as sandwich rolls ($5 to $8).

Top End **Lahiere's** (☎ 609-921-2798, 11 Witherspoon St) is probably the toniest place in town, with French-continental cuisine; it is closed on Sunday. Meals cost $30 per person.

Le Plumet Royal (☎ 609-924-1707, 20 Bayard Lane), at the Peacock Inn, has a special $30 menu with à la carte selections at about $40 per head. It is open daily for lunch and dinner and for Sunday brunch. Both Le Plumet Royal and Lahiere's require that men wear jackets at dinner service.

Entertainment
Check the *Princeton Weekly Bulletin* for the latest calendar of events.

Princeton University's **McCarter Theatre** (☎ 609-683-8000), on the campus, stages plays, musicals, concerts and various other events.

Spectator Sports
For information on the university sporting events, call ☎ 609-258-3545.

Getting There & Away
Suburban Transit buses (☎ 609-249-1100) leave from New York City's Port Authority to Princeton's Palmer Square.

NJ Transit and Amtrak offer several daily trains to Princeton Junction. Passengers must then cross over to a smaller train (known to locals as 'the dinky') to make the five-minute trip to Princeton itself. That train stops right next to the university campus.

By car from New York and northern New Jersey, take the NJ Turnpike to exit 9; follow Route 1 south to Princeton and take the Washington Rd exit (Route 571) to Nassau St. You can also take Route 1 all the way instead of the NJ Turnpike. From Philadelphia, take I-95 north to Route 1 north; from there follow the directions given above. You can also take Route 206 north from I-95 all the way to Princeton.

Getting Around
Princeton is small enough for you to walk around. However, if arriving via public transport, note that the only hotels within

walking distance are expensive; the rest are miles away on Route 1. Associated Taxi (☎ 609-924-1222) can help if you're in a hurry.

If you have a car, it's best to leave it at the lot on Hulfish St if you're in for a day trip. Don't park on the street with a meter – your car will be a magnet for a ticket.

TRENTON

Travelers often ignore New Jersey's state capital (population 88,675), and that's a pity, since it has a lot of colonial history. Its land plan was devised in the early part of the 18th century by William Trent, and residents called the place 'Trent's Town' – later shortened to the name used today. The Continental Congress met here briefly in 1784, but the town soon lost its status as the young republic's capital moved to New York City and then the District of Columbia. The town became the state capital in 1790.

Trenton gained a reputation for building, becoming one of the most important industrial towns in the United States during the 19th century. For example, the Roebling Wire Rope Company manufactured the suspension cables used on the Brooklyn Bridge and other engineering feats, and the Lenox China Company was established in 1889 to rival the fine work produced by older European manufacturers.

Trenton has had several periods of recession, though the city has always been anchored by the state government, which has a number of office buildings downtown. Interestingly enough, the governor's residence is in Princeton, a symbol of the division between the powerful executive branch and the weaker legislature – as well as the class divisions of these towns. (The Drumthwacket mansion in Princeton was designated the official governor's residence in 1981, but only one of the three officeholders since then has lived in the house full-time. Current governor Christine Todd Whitman uses it part-time.)

Trenton's sights can be enjoyed in half a day, making it a good stopover point between New York City and Philadelphia, or a place to visit while staying in Princeton;

there's no real need to stay overnight in Trenton. Most of the city's attractions in Trenton are along Broad St, which runs north-south through town, and State St, which crosses Broad St.

Information

The Trenton Convention & Visitors Bureau (☎ 609-777-1771) is at the corner of Lafayette and Barrack Sts. The Mercer County Chamber of Commerce (☎ 609-393-4143), 214 W State St, provides a map and brochure of historic sites.

New Jersey State Museum

Right next to the state house is the New Jersey State Museum (☎ 609-292-6308), 205 W State St, which has a decent collection of 19th- and 20th-century American art, dinosaur fossils, displays on Native American history and a collection of porcelain made in Trenton. It's worth a visit and there's no admission charge. Shows in the 200-seat planetarium cost $1.

The museum is open Tuesday to Saturday from 9 am to 4:45 pm and Sunday from noon to 5 pm.

State House

The New Jersey State House (☎ 609-633-2709) was built in 1792, and remodeled and expanded extensively after an 1885 fire to become the large building that lords over W State St in downtown Trenton. Free tours of the building, which has recently undergone a $43 million refurbishing, embark from the grand rotunda on Tuesday, Wednesday, Friday and Saturday, and are keyed to the schedules of the many school groups that visit. It's best to call ahead to get a schedule and secure a spot. The hour-long tour brings you to the senate and assembly chambers, senate majority conference rooms and the governor's reception area.

Trenton City Museum

Ellarsie, an 1850 Italianate villa once owned by businessman Henry McCall, is the site of the Trenton City Museum (☎ 609-989-3632). It's at Cadwalader Park, a mile west of the state house. The museum's 1st floor is a gallery space for local artists, and its 2nd floor houses artifacts of city history. It's open Tuesday to Saturday from 11 am to 3 pm and Sunday from 2 pm to 4 pm; admission is free.

Old Barracks Museum

This museum (☎ 609-396-1776), on Barrack St, is housed in former soldier barracks built around 1760 for the French and Indian War; these are the last such structures still standing in the US. The barracks also housed Hessian mercenaries fighting on the side of the British during the Revolutionary War. It was here on December 25, 1776 that Washington's troops attacked the unsuspecting Hessian soldiers and won an important battle that marked a turning point in the war. The museum is open Monday to Sunday from 10 am to 5 pm; admission is $2/1/50¢ for adults/seniors/children.

Special Events

The New Jersey State Fair is held in Garden State Park the first week in August; call ☎ 609-646-3340 for information. Trenton Heritage Days (☎ 609-393-8998) are held on the commons on the first weekend in June and feature local arts and crafts stands.

Places to Stay & Eat

Trenton isn't particularly dangerous, though it has some dicey neighborhoods away from the town center. The downtown area is quite dead at night, so you are better off booking accommodations around Princeton to the north or outside Trenton than in the city's center.

McIntosh Inn (☎ 609-896-3700), on Route 1 in Lawrenceville, is a reliable chain hotel with 116 rooms for $90 midweek. *Marriott* (☎ 609-452-7900), at Forrestal Village about 25 minutes north on Route 1, has a good weekend deal of $80 for a double. The hotel is next to one of the state's newest outlet malls.

A good B&B choice is *Inn to the Woods* (☎ 609-493-1974, 150 Glenwood Drive) in Washington Crossing. Room rates are around $125 a night.

Tattoni's, at the corner of Chestnut and Morris Aves, is a good budget choice for lunch. *Rossi's Bar & Grill* (☎ 609-394-9089, 501 Morris Ave) and *Marley's Ale House* (☎ 609-771-0100, 1400 Parkway Ave) are solid places for a burger and beer ($10).

Getting There & Away

NJ Transit trains run from New York's Penn Station to Trenton. Fares are $10/$14 one way/roundtrip. Amtrak (☎ 800-872-7245) also runs several lines that stop at Trenton en route to New York, Washington and Philadelphia. During peak hours, SEPTA (☎ 215-580-7852) offers service between Trenton and Philadelphia ($5 roundtrip).

By car, take the NJ Turnpike to Route 1, which runs directly into downtown Trenton.

AROUND TRENTON
Washington Crossing State Park

This park (☎ 609-737-0623), 8 miles north of Trenton in Titusville on Route 29, is where the general made his Christmas night trip from Pennsylvania in 1776 to surprise the sleeping Hessian soldiers and retake a British-held village. The move halted the Revolutionary Army's winter retreat and led to decisive victories in Trenton and Princeton. The crossing is reenacted every year on Christmas, and the park is a lovely spot for picnicking and biking during the summer. The visitors' center actually displays the oldest known American dog tag. The park is open year-round from 8 am to 8 pm daily.

In the park, **Ferry House** (☎ 609-737-2515) is the building where Washington and his officers planned the attack. It's been restored to resemble a farmhouse of the period.

Across the river in Pennsylvania, Washington Crossing Historic Park marks the spot from where Washington launched his attack (see the Around Philadelphia section in the Philadelphia chapter for more information).

About 5 miles north of the park is the charming town of **Lambertville**, a wonderful village full of antique shops and nice restaurants that stands in contrast to the more touristy New Hope, just across the Delaware River in Pennsylvania.

NEW BRUNSWICK

New Brunswick (population 41,442) is the home of Rutgers University (the state's prestigious public university) and is arguably New Jersey's most important cultural center.

The Middlesex County Chamber of Commerce (☎ 732-745-4489), 703 Jersey Ave, is the best single source for local cultural events.

Rutgers University

The state university (☎ 732-932-1766) has a handsome campus right in town that dates back to its founding in 1766 as a colonial-era college. Rutgers has a strong reputation for scientific studies and has a number of well-regarded professors. The campus features an arboretum (☎ 732-932-8451) and a geology museum.

Places to Stay & Eat

Econo Lodge (☎ 732-828-8000, 26 Route 1) and *Hyatt Regency* (☎ 732-873-1234, 2 Albany St) have rooms starting at $75, but both are completely booked at the beginning and end of each school year.

Harvest Moon Brewery (☎ 732-249-6666, 392 George St) is a microbrewery and pub; the beer is strong, burgers are decent and the place is popular with students. *Court Tavern* (☎ 732-545-7265, 124 Church St) is a dive bar with a full roster of singer-songwriters. Both places charge about $10 for sandwiches and burgers.

Entertainment

The New Brunswick Cultural Center (☎ 732-247-7200), at 11 Livingstone Ave, is the main information spot for what's happening in town.

There are several theaters in New Brunswick, and there isn't a week without a major concert, play or dance performance. Many of the venues are right next to each other on Livingstone Ave. Among the town's culture spots are the State Theatre (☎ 732-246-7469), 15 Livingstone Ave, which hosts major visiting performers; Crossroads Theater Company (☎ 732-249-5560), 7 Livingstone Ave, New Jersey's premier African-American company; and American Rep Ballet (☎ 732-246-1254), 80 Albany St.

Getting There & Away

Take the Garden State Pkwy to Route 18 north (New Brunswick exit). Take the George St-Rutgers University or New Street exit; most sites are along Albany St. The town can also be reached by taking the trains run from Philadelphia and New York City via NJ Transit or Amtrak. On Amtrak the fare from New York or Philadelphia is $25/40 one way/roundtrip. The trip takes about 45 minutes each way. NJ Transit trains take about one hour and the fare is about $5 cheaper.

CAMDEN

Located directly across the Delaware River from Philadelphia, Camden (population 87,492) is a very troubled city with a rich history. Its proximity to Philadelphia has been the main reason for its development as well as the source of its current problems with crime. Many rich industrialists built grand homes in Camden, and Walt Whitman lived in the city from 1884 until his death in 1892. The Campbell Soup Company was located in the town from 1869, when it began selling its famous soup. But the fabled factory closed in 1999 after years of watching its hometown decline.

Despite the state's efforts – which have included the construction of a new aquarium – to develop the waterfront near the Ben Franklin Bridge, Camden is still an outpost for Philadelphia drug dealers, and violent crime is a big problem. In July 1999 the state seized control of the city's finances in an attempt to stem years of corruption and mismanagement. But there's no need to shun the city entirely if you're on your way to or from Philadelphia. Camden's aquarium and waterfront park can easily be visited on a day trip.

Walt Whitman Landmarks

Two Camden landmarks are dedicated to America's famous poet. The **Walt Whitman Cultural Arts Center** is on the Camden campus of Rutgers University. A neoclassical library is at the corner of 2nd and Cooper Sts at Johnson Park Square. Established in 1916, the Whitman Center promotes dance events and poetry readings. Every May the center holds a series of events in honor of Whitman.

Walt Whitman House (☎ 856-964-5383), where the poet spent the final years of his life, is at 330 Mickle Blvd. Walt Whitman designed the tomb that is his final resting place. The house is open to visitors year-round Wednesday to Saturday from 10 am to noon and 1 to 4 pm. On Sunday it's is open from 1 to 4 pm.

Waterfront Park

The crown jewel of Camden's redevelopment effort is this park created in the mid-1990s. It consists of **Sony-Blockbuster Entertainment Center**, a multipurpose venue. In the summer, concerts are held in the outdoor amphitheater, which has a capacity of 25,000 people. In the colder weather the center hosts indoor concerts in its covered area of 2000 seats. The center is the best concert venue in the state. A new minor-league baseball park is also being built on site.

New Jersey State Aquarium

This massive facility (☎ 856-365-3300), built on a former ferry terminal, opened in 1990 as a sign of the state's commitment to the redevelopment of Camden. Dubbed the Ocean Base Atlantic Center, it features eight big displays, including a coral station of colorful Caribbean fish, a shark tank and an archway where you pass under schools of darting fish. The aquarium gets quite crowded on weekends.

The facility is open weekdays from 9:30 am to 4:30 pm and on weekends from 10 am to 5 pm; admission is $11.95/8.95/10.45 for adults/children/seniors, free for children under two years of age. The Riverpass, which includes entry to the aquarium and Independence Seaport Museum (see that section in the Philadelphia chapter) plus a return ferry trip to Philadelphia, costs $18.50/13.50/16 for adults/seniors/children.

Getting There & Away

Camden is on the NJ Turnpike just before the Ben Franklin Bridge. Greyhound (☎ 212-971-6300, 800-231-2222) has buses to Camden from New York City's Port Authority, but take Greyhound only if you have accommodations lined up in Philadelphia, which is accessible by ferry directly from the aquarium.

The Riverlink ferries (☎ 215-925-5465) depart on the hour from Philadelphia and on the half-hour from Camden. Regular roundtrip tickets cost $5/4/3 for adults/seniors/children. The ferry is closed January through March.

Southern New Jersey

The state's southern coastline is far less populated than the area covered in the Jersey Shore chapter, and the terrain is noticeably less developed, especially along the Atlantic City Expressway where pine trees dominate the sides of the road. The character of the shore towns also reflects a change, giving way to a lot of housing stock, including motels, bungalows, hotels and colonial inns – many of which clearly aren't designed for year-round living and often don't have heating systems. The area, which starts south of Long Beach Island, is dominated by the booming gambling town of Atlantic City, the noisy resorts of Wildwoods and the quaint, Victorian-era village of Cape May, home to the most pristine beach in the state.

PINE BARRENS

The Pine Barrens (also known locally as the Pinelands) makes up a huge part of the less populated southeast portion of New Jersey. Essentially, this is a region of one million acres of pine forest, containing several state parks that serve as havens for birders and other wildlife enthusiasts. One-third of the acreage is made up of wholly protected state lands; the remainder is privately owned and serves as a 'belt' surrounding towns along the shore. You can see the change in the terrain as you go along the Atlantic City Expressway or travel the southern part of the Garden State Pkwy to Cape May. The main attractions for visitors are Batsto Village and the Wharton State Forest. A good source for information is the Pine Barrens office at Wharton (☎ 609-561-0024); this office has information on seasonal activities, such as camping, horseback riding and hiking.

Wharton State Forest

This state forest (☎ 609-561-0024), near Hammonton, is made up of more than 100,000 acres of the Pinelands, making it the largest single forest site in the state park system. Although part of the forest includes Batsto Village, the main visitors' center is in

Atsion. In this part of the park you'll find a nature center, several picnic areas, freshwater fishing, swimming in Atsion Lake and hiking trails.

There are three camping areas in the park, and directions to each can be obtained from the visitors' center. Camping is $8 to $10 per site per night, or for large groups, about $1 per person. Campsites are open April to October, though the Godfrey Bridge campsite is open year-round.

You can get to the Atsion center by taking the Garden State Pkwy exit 52 and following signs to Hammonton, then traveling 8 miles north on Route 206 to the center's entrance.

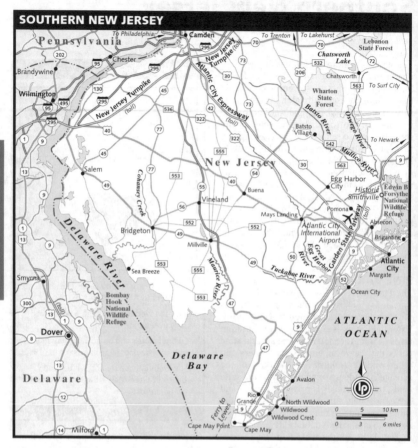

Historic Batsto Village

This well-restored 19th-century settlement (☎ 609-561-3262) is a former glass- and iron-making center that served as a major ammunition source for the Continental army during the American Revolution. Its name is derived from the Swedish word *batstu*, which means 'bathing place.' The grounds reflect life in the area at that time with guided tours of the Italianate Batsto Mansion and various outhouses. Sights include a charcoal kiln, ice and milk houses, woodhouse, carriage house, stable, threshing barn, piggery, blacksmith and wheel-

wright shops, general store, post office and church.

The village is open daily from 9 am to 4:30 pm. The mansion tour costs $2 and there is a parking fee on weekends and holidays from Memorial Day through Labor Day. To get here, take Route 542 off Route 9.

Edwin B Forsythe National Wildlife Refuge

This 40,000-acre wildlife refuge (☎ 609-652-1665) is one of New Jersey's main flyover points for migrating birds. There are short nature walks and an 8-mile wildlife drive, where, at various points in the season, you can spot more than 200 different species of birds, including sandpipers, egrets, several types of owls and snow geese. The park also includes a 6,000-acre unspoiled barrier beach area that serves as a resting place for migratory birds and is off-limits to birders.

The Forsythe refuge, along with several bird blinds in and around Cape May, has gained an international reputation as a birder's paradise. The visitors' entrance is open year-round from 8 am to 4 pm.

You can get to the refuge by taking the Garden State Pkwy to exit 48, and then driving south on Route 9 for 6 miles to Oceanville. There are signs for the refuge's entrance on the right-hand side of Route 9. After turning, follow Great Creek Rd east to the entrance and visitors' building.

Outdoor Activities

Bel Haven (☎ 609-965-2205), on Route 2 in Egg Harbor, rents canoes, kayaks, inner tubes and rafts for some terrific trips around the Pine Barrens. Trips can last from two hours to two days. Canoe rentals cost $29 to $38 with reductions for the second day. Rafting trips vary from 2½ hours to six hours; rates vary from $15 to $35, depending on the length of the trip and number of vessels. Small rafts carry three or four people, larger rafts four to six.

Places to Stay

Wharton State Forest (☎ 609-561-3262, 561-0024) has overnight cabin facilities; the cost is $30 per night for four. The facilities include kitchens, baths and showers.

ATLANTIC CITY

Since casino gambling came to Atlantic City (population 38,000) in 1977, the town has become the most popular tourist destination in the US, with 37 million annual visitors spending some $4 billion at its 13 casinos and restaurants. Proximity accounts for much of that popularity, since nearly one-third of the US population lives within 300 miles of Atlantic City (sometimes referred to as 'AC'). But the town is now getting gambling competition from the Foxwoods casino

in Connecticut, and state revenues from gaming are threatened by other gambling operations and big-money 'powerball' multi-state lotteries. Although the $4 billion in gaming revenues beats the amount dropped at the casino tables in Las Vegas ($3.2 million), the Nevada golden city earns additional money from non-gaming enterprises because of the substantial independent tourist trade it has developed.

While Atlantic City's casino industry has created 45,000 jobs and experienced record profits, little of this money has benefited the town itself. Homelessness and crime are still a big problem and the four-block stretch from the end of the Atlantic City Expressway to the beachfront casinos is still a depressing collection of empty lots, rough-looking bars and abandoned warehouses. The boardwalk itself is an odd collection of fortress-like casinos punctuated by the odd T-shirt shop and gyro stand. Since the self-contained casinos have their own restaurants, bars and nightclubs (the better to keep players entertained and spending in one place), there is no walking culture in the city.

The bottom line is that for non-gamblers, there is no reason to visit Atlantic City unless you're on your way to Cape May or Philadelphia. For one thing, casino security people do not look kindly upon those simply wandering through the gaming areas without any intention of playing – which is probably just as well, since watching other people spend their money on noisy $1 slot machines gets old very quickly. But if you want to gamble, you can't beat Atlantic City's selection of 700 blackjack tables and nearly 30,000 slot machines. If you visit, plan on trying your luck at something – even if you wish to spend only $10 or $15 – and remember that it's no sin to walk away if you're ahead of the game.

History

Established in 1793, the town that today is Atlantic City was the first settlement of Absecon Island, along with its neighboring municipalities of Ventnor, Margate and Longport. Some 50 years later, a group of businessmen, led by Dr Jonathan Pitney, decided to develop a bathing village and

NEW JERSEY

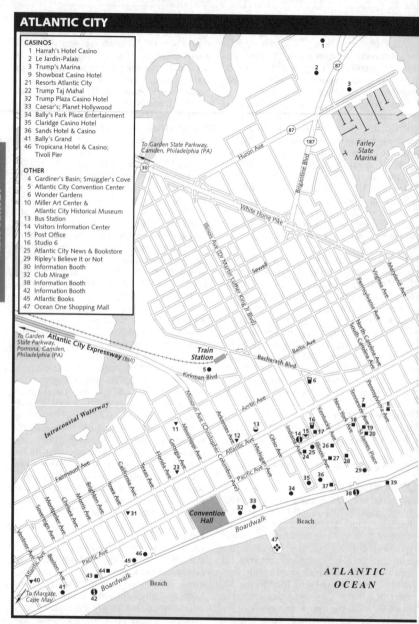

ATLANTIC CITY

CASINOS
1 Harrah's Hotel Casino
2 Le Jardin-Palais
3 Trump's Marina
9 Showboat Casino Hotel
21 Resorts Atlantic City
22 Trump Taj Mahal
32 Trump Plaza Casino Hotel
33 Caesar's; Planet Hollywood
34 Bally's Park Place Entertainment
35 Claridge Casino Hotel
36 Sands Hotel & Casino
41 Bally's Grand
46 Tropicana Hotel & Casino;
    Tivoli Pier

OTHER
4 Gardiner's Basin; Smuggler's Cove
5 Atlantic City Convention Center
6 Wonder Gardens
10 Miller Art Center &
    Atlantic City Historical Museum
13 Bus Station
14 Visitors Information Center
15 Post Office
16 Studio 6
25 Atlantic City News & Bookstore
29 Ripley's Believe It or Not
30 Information Booth
32 Club Mirage
38 Information Booth
42 Information Booth
45 Atlantic Books
47 Ocean One Shopping Mall

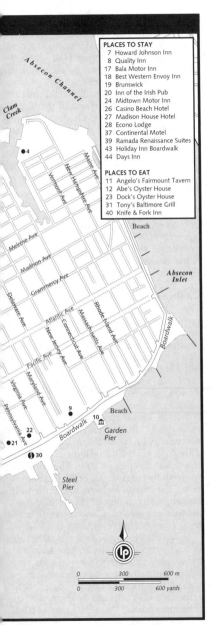

NEW JERSEY

health resort on the island. A charter was obtained to operate a railroad between booming Camden and the site, and by 1854 an engineer named Richard Osborne had designed and named Atlantic City, which was incorporated that year.

The city's proximity to large population centers and inexpensive rail transportation made it possible for thousands of city dwellers to escape the summer heat and enjoy the seaside.

Atlantic City's famous Boardwalk was the world's first; it was built in 1870 by local business owners who wanted to cut down on the sand being tracked into hotel lobbies by guests returning from the beach. A man named Alexander Boardman came up with the idea, and the long stretch of planks became known as 'Boardman's Walk' – later shortened to 'Boardwalk.'

The resort was a playground for the rich and famous in the 1920s, and also became a stop on the pre-Broadway theater circuit. In 1921 the first Miss America pageant was held here, scheduled for September as a way of extending the season beyond Labor Day. By the 1930s, Atlantic City's population totaled 66,000, and its nightclubs attracted the top talent of the day on the Steel Pier, which was dubbed 'the showplace of the nation.'

Decline set in after WWII, when jet travel and prosperity made it easier to travel to vacation spots in Florida, the Caribbean and Europe. Until the mid-1970s, Atlantic City suffered from severe economic problems with a drop in tourism, rampant drug use and crime. The 1964 Democratic Convention that nominated Lyndon B Johnson for the presidency highlighted the city's woes – there was such a shortage of support services for the delegates that it was obvious that Atlantic City could no longer handle such a major event.

After an intensive campaign to convince state voters, casino gambling was approved as a means of revitalizing the city, and the Resorts International casino opened in May 1978, attracting long lines at its slot machines and blackjack tables. By the '80s, gambling was a 24-hours-a-day affair, and a rail service was resumed connecting the town to Philadelphia.

Atlantic City still has a long way to go before it can market itself as a family resort. A bit belatedly, and with no small sense of shame, local officials have begun to push for non-gambling related attractions for the town. The New Jersey legislature has rewritten the casino law to try and ensure that more of the money made by the casinos is used in the city. The city is also taking a page out of Las Vegas' game plan by introducing amusements, rides and over-the-top architecture in its new facilities to divert the attentions of children.

Orientation

To get around, note that Atlantic City is on a grid with each block comprising 100 numbers. From the Boardwalk, the principal parallel northeast-southwest avenues are Pacific, Atlantic, Arctic and Baltic. The cross-streets perpendicular to the Boardwalk are mostly avenues named after states. What can be confusing is the fact that they are not in any logical order, that some states are not represented and that some state capitals make an appearance. As well, Missouri Ave was recently renamed Christopher Columbus Ave (Columbus Ave), and Illinois Ave was renamed Dr Martin Luther King Jr Blvd (MLK Blvd), and the old and new names are used interchangeably.

Information

The Visitors Information Center (☎ 609-344-8338) is at 1716 Pacific Ave (between Indiana Ave and MLK Blvd). Five information

An Official Superstition

In Atlantic City, luck is a lady assiduously courted by the town's 37 million annual visitors. As a consequence, many of the casinos don't have a 13th floor. Before the Mirage's Le Jardin-Palais resort opens in 2002, Atlantic City will have a total of 13 casinos, though some local literature puts the total at 12.

booths stand along the Boardwalk between the Taj Mahal to the north and the old Grand Casino hall to the south. There is also a desk inside the old Convention Hall providing many brochures for local hotels; it is open daily from 10 am to 7 pm.

The best of the free guides to the area are the monthly *AC Shoreline* and the weekly *Whoot* and *At the Shore*. Guides explaining the rules of all available games of chance are free at all casinos.

Unsurprisingly, you can find banks and ATMs near the gaming areas of all the casinos. Casinos also do foreign exchange and give advances against credit cards.

The main post office is on the corner of Pacific Ave and MLK Blvd, one block west of the beach. Atlantic City News & Bookstore (☎ 609-344-9444) is across from the post office, and is open 24 hours daily. Atlantic Books is on the Boardwalk between Brighton and Iowa Aves.

Casinos

The casinos are obviously Atlantic City's major attraction, and though high rollers seem to have a 'favorite,' the gaming areas tend to look alike (garish) and sound alike (loud and clangy). Most casinos are dedicated to gaming and – with the exception of the Taj Mahal – do not emphasize glitz and showmanship like their Las Vegas counterparts do.

But all should change when Las Vegas casino giant Mirage Resorts opens a brand new casino, Le Jardin-Palais, at the marina. This high-tech $1.2 billion complex is scheduled to open in 2002. The company successfully demanded that the state fund a new $330 million highway and cross-town tunnel project as part of the development, another example of vested interests benefiting from gaming revenues.

If you plan to spend a great deal of time in one particular casino, be sure to sign up for its player's card before you start gambling. The frequent-gambler cards offer a variety of perks, including reduced hotel rates, food discounts and beverage and entertainment deals. These are awarded based on a combination of how much you play and

how long you play. At the time of writing, the best frequent-gambler deals were being offered at Resorts casino.

If you're a complete novice gambler, you can ask for a free gaming guide that should explain the basics of the various games played in that casino. The best casino to visit if you're a beginner is Claridge's, which markets itself as the 'friendly' casino in Atlantic City. It's a bit smaller in scale, and there are quite a few low-stakes tables for blackjack and roulette. Claridge's has not kept up with the times, and has had financial problems of late.

It's worth taking the tour of the Taj Mahal; the tour meets at the concierge desk in the casino's lobby Monday to Friday at 2 pm. You'll be bombarded with facts about the casino business and Atlantic City, and the $5 tour fee is donated to local charities.

There is no strict dress code in Atlantic City's casinos; shorts and T-shirts can be worn at any time. *You must be at least 21 years old to gamble or be on the gambling floor.*

The following Atlantic City casino resorts are listed east to west along the Boardwalk:

Showboat Casino Hotel
(☎ 609-343-4000, 800-621-0200), Delaware Ave and Boardwalk; a riverboat-themed interior dominates the 700 rooms.

Trump Taj Mahal
(☎ 609-449-1000, 800-825-8786), 1000 Boardwalk; this extravagant property has nine 2-ton limestone elephants to welcome visitors and 70 bright minarets crowning the rooftops. The German-crystal chandeliers in the casino and lobby alone cost $15 million, and despite the garish nature of the interior, the room rates are similar to those found in more modest facilities. This is also the site of the Hard Rock Cafe.

Resorts Atlantic City
(☎ 609-340-6000, 800-438-7424), N Carolina Ave and Boardwalk; this 670-room Victorian hotel served as a hospital during WWII and was the center of what was known as 'Camp Boardwalk.'

Sands Hotel & Casino
(☎ 609-441-4000, 800-257-8580), Brighton Park and Indiana Ave; this black glass box was originally named the Brighton Hotel when it opened.

Claridge Casino Hotel
(☎ 609-340-3400, 800-257-8585), Indiana Ave and Boardwalk; Claridge's is one block west of the Boardwalk and accessible by a moving walkway that operates in one direction only – into the casino, not out. The casino has 500 rooms and a three-floor, claustrophobic gaming area that is popular with low-rolling senior citizens.

Bally's Park Place Entertainment
(☎ 609-340-2000, 800-225-5977), Park Place and Boardwalk; this 1200-room casino occupies the site of the 1860 Dennis Hotel, which is incorporated into the newer facility; it's the site of many heavyweight boxing matches.

Caesar's
(☎ 609-348-4411, 800-443-0104), Arkansas Ave and Boardwalk; this 1000-room hotel is also the site of Atlantic City's Planet Hollywood theme-restaurant

Trump Plaza Casino Hotel
(☎ 609-441-6700, 800-677-7378), Mississippi Ave and Boardwalk; this modern tower, next to the convention center, has 560 rooms and a Warner Bros Studio Store overlooking the Boardwalk.

Tropicana Hotel & Casino
(☎ 609-340-4000, 800-843-8767), Iowa Ave and Boardwalk; this is one of the biggest places (90,000-sq-foot casino and 1020 rooms) in town, with its own indoor theme park, Tivoli Pier.

Atlantic City Hilton
(☎ 609-340-7100), Boardwalk between Boston and Pacific Aves; this southernmost casino has over 500 rooms.

Trump Plaza
(☎ 609-441-6000, 800-677-7378), 2500 Boardwalk; this casino has little to recommend it save for the garish portrait of the owner above the escalators to the gaming area.

Le Jardin-Palais
This is the name of the new $1.2 billion complex at the marina slated to open in late 2002; the

resort will feature over 1000 rooms, a 25-story tower overlooking a 19th-century-style French garden and 170,000 sq feet of gaming space.

Trump Marina
(☎ 609-441-2000, 800-677-7378), Huron Ave and Brigantine Blvd; away from the Boardwalk, this facility offers a more relaxed setting, overlooks the Farley State Marina and has an art deco theme.

Harrah's Hotel Casino
(☎ 609-441-5000, 800-242-7724), Brigantine Blvd; this casino has 760 rooms in its two towers.

The Boardwalk

Atlantic City Historical Museum & Miller Art Center On the site of the restored Garden Pier, at Connecticut Ave, this complex (☎ 609-347-5839) opened in 1994 and provides a look at the city's colorful past. Visitors to the museum will be reminded that in its heyday, Atlantic City had a lot more going for it as a tourist attraction than it now does. Atlantic City was a place where such stars as Benny Goodman, Frank Sinatra and Duke Ellington headlined.

The arts center, which occupies the building on the north of the pier, has changing exhibits of regional and local art. It's open daily from 10 am to 4 pm.

Steel Pier This amusement pier, directly in front of the Taj Mahal casino, is a part of Donald Trump's empire and was the site of the famous high-diving horse that plunged into the Atlantic before crowds of spectators. Today it's just a collection of small amusement rides and candy stands.

Convention Hall The former site of the Miss America pageant was the largest auditorium in the world without interior roof posts or pillars when it opened in 1929. If there is not an event in progress, see if you can take a look at the superb interior of the main hall and the world's largest pipe organ. Every year, Miss America contestants line up for publicity shots amid the columns by the Convention Hall's entrance.

The hall has been refurbished as part of a $225 million project to restore the Columbus Ave approach to the Boardwalk.

Miss America

The oldest, most enduring beauty contest in America started as a small affair in 1921. Since then, it has survived changing tastes, feminism, a scandal involving nude pictures of one winner and a 30-year decline in the fortunes of the host city. The annual broadcast of the contest is now considered something of a quaint anachronism, even though winners tend to adopt a social issue to address during their year-long 'reign.'

During Miss America Pageant Week every September, three nights of preliminary competition take place before the Saturday-night televised finale (the show was first broadcast in 1954). In 1995, there was an attempt to get rid of the swimsuit competition; this notion was defeated by a TV viewers' vote, and in 1997 contestants were allowed to wear two-piece bathing suits for the first time. (Contestants are still chaperoned during the week's events.)

The Miss America Parade kicks off the week, when the 50 contestants, one representing each state, cruise along the Boardwalk in the back of convertibles. The day after Miss America is crowned, the winner appears on the beach to frolic in the surf, regardless of the weather. Call ☎ 609-347-7571 for a schedule of events.

Tivoli Pier This 2-acre family amusement center (☎ 609-340-4020) is inside the Tropicana Hotel & Casino, at Iowa Ave, and has Victorian-era rides and musical shows. Admission prices vary for rides and attractions. It is open all year.

Ripley's Believe It or Not This museum (☎ 609-347-2001) is based on the famous old comic strip about spooky coincidences and natural curiosities. It's a good place to take kids. Opening hours are 10 am to 8 pm daily; admission is $8.95 adults, $6.95 children.

Atlantic City Convention Center

This $300 million convention center (☎ 888-222-3838) opened above the train station in

1998 and houses a non-casino hotel with 12,000 rooms, shops, theaters and restaurants. The project, built by the same company responsible for New York's successful South Street Seaport complex and Baltimore's Inner Harbor, is now the site of the Miss America pageant.

Gardiner's Basin & Smuggler's Cove

The Atlantic City marina area is the city's new hot spot, as it is the site of the new Mirage casino and a serious housing development of luxury homes, all of which have two boat slips apiece. This inlet off the Absecon Channel was the transport site of illegal booze for the nightclubs during Prohibition, thus giving it the name Smuggler's Cove. The town is ready to cash in on this bit of colorful (and probably factually enhanced) history, and is building a new Ocean Life Center here. The marina's waterfront park is already host to many festivals and several good seafood restaurants. Call ☎ 609-348-2880 for information on current activities.

Outdoor Activities

Blue Heron Pines Golf Club (☎ 609-965-1800), a public course in nearby Pomona, can be reached by exit 14 eastbound on the Atlantic City Expressway.

Cycling is allowed along the Boardwalk from 6 to 10 am only. Bikes can be rented on the Boardwalk in front of the Taj Mahal, by the ramps leading up to the Boardwalk at Resorts casino and between the Sands and Claridge casinos at Indiana Ave. On weekends you can rent bikes at Ocean One (☎ 609-344-8008) on the Boardwalk. A valid ID or a deposit is required.

Special Events

In early March, the St Patrick's Day Parade is held along the Boardwalk. The Puerto Rican Day Parade is staged in July. Miss America Pageant Week occurs in September or October, and the Atlantic City Marathon is held in October. Call the visitors' information center (☎ 609-344-8338) for specific dates.

Places to Stay

Atlantic City offers a good reservations service (☎ 800-447-6667) with package deals and rooms at all price levels. The town's room rates vary considerably depending on the season. In the winter, it's possible to stay in a hotel such as Resorts for as little as $50 a night. In the summer the rates run much higher, and these prices continue to apply during the week of the Miss America festivities.

If you plan to gamble and want a good mid-range hotel, book a package deal through a casino hotel or travel agent. The AmeriRoom Reservations hotline (☎ 800-888-5825) specializes in these packages, which usually include meals, show tickets and complimentary chips.

Budget Shoestring travelers are not well-served in Atlantic City, since motels and bars a few blocks off the Boardwalk are known to be pickup spots for prostitutes.

The ***Inn of the Irish Pub*** (☎ *609-344-9063, 164 St James Place*) is right off the Boardwalk but on one of the city's gamiest blocks. Singles/doubles cost $25/60 with shared bath, and $90 with private facilities. Just next door is the ***Brunswick*** (☎ *609-344-8098*), which has similar rates.

Mid-Range The following motels charge about $25 to $30 during winter midweek, $50 to $80 winter weekends, $35 to $45 summer midweek, and $60 to $100 summer weekends. Holiday weekend rates range from $60 to $200.

Bala Motor Inn (☎ *609-348-3031*), MLK Blvd and Pacific Ave

Best Western Envoy Inn (☎ *609-344-7117*), Pacific and New York Aves

Casino Beach Hotel (☎ *609-348-4000, 154 Kentucky Ave*), between Boardwalk and Pacific Ave

Continental Motel (☎ *609-345-5141*), Boardwalk and MLK Blvd

Days Inn (☎ *609-344-6101*), Boardwalk and Morris Ave

Econo Lodge (☎ *609-344-9093, 800-323-6410, 117 S Kentucky Ave*), between Boardwalk and Pacific

NEW JERSEY

Holiday Inn Boardwalk (☎ *609-348-2200*), Boardwalk and Chelsea Ave

Howard Johnson Inn (☎ *609-344-4193*), Tennessee and Pacific Aves

Madison House Hotel (☎ *609-345-1400, 123 MLK Blvd*), near the Sands Casino

Midtown Motor Inn (☎ *609-348-3031*), Indiana and Pacific Aves

Ramada Renaissance Suites (☎ *609-344-1200*), Boardwalk and New York Ave

Quality Inn (☎ *609-345-7070*), S Carolina and Pacific Aves

Top End Atlantic City's casino hotels (see Casinos, earlier in this section) dominate the expensive choices. Rates run from $120 to $370 depending on the season and day of the week. (When booking, ask about what amenities are included in the rate.) In the winter, rates can be as low as $50 – the trick is to walk up to the reception desk and act uncertain about whether you plan to stay the night. You will most likely be offered a room at a deep discount, provided you look well-dressed enough to spend money in the casino.

One Way to Win in Atlantic City

If you're hungry, some of the best bargains can be found at the various buffet restaurants offered by the casinos to keep patrons inside. Wander around and you'll find all sorts of 'all-you-can-eat' bargains that cost $5.96 to $15. With names like the 'Epic Buffet,' 'Sultan's Feast' and special events like the '1950s experience,' these dining rooms offer plentiful choices and all vie for the title of best boardwalk bargain. (Repeat visitors will readily share tips on the best places to go.)

The resorts have some reasonable standing restaurants that offer waiter service and moderately priced fare. Some of the more popular choices include Caesar's **Boardwalk Café** and **Planet Hollywood**, the Tropicana's **Pasta Pavilion**, Bally's **Pickles** and the Taj Mahal's **New Delhi Deli**.

Places to Eat
Budget & Mid-Range *Tony's Baltimore Grill* (☎ *609-345-5766, 2800 Atlantic Ave*), at Iowa Ave, and *Angelo's Fairmount Tavern* (☎ *609-344-2439*), at Mississippi and Fairmount Aves, are two budget Italian restaurants with main dishes around $10.

The fare in the casinos' delis and pubs strays into the lower mid-range level, but there is nothing special to recommend.

Top End All casinos have high-end dining rooms with menus posted at the entrance. Most specialize in surf and turf items – huge steaks, big lobsters and pretty lousy wine.

If you'd like to experience a real over-the-top entertainment venue, try *The Bacchanal* at Caesar's casino (☎ *609-348-4411*). For $45 a person you'll get a seven-course meal, entertainment by 'Augustus' and enjoy wine poured into your mouth from pitchers held by 'wine wenches.' Of course, this place is popular for hen nights and bachelor parties.

The *Knife & Fork Inn* (☎ *609-344-1133*), at the junction of Atlantic and Pacific Aves near Albany Ave, has been an institution since 1927; it serves seafood and steaks for $45 and up, and is closed Sunday. This is a taste of the old Atlantic City.

Two of the town's top seafood restaurants are *Docks Oyster House* (☎ *609-345-0092, 2405 Atlantic Ave*) and *Abe's Oyster House* (☎ *609-344-7701*), at Atlantic and Arkansas Aves, with main dishes for around $30.

In Venice Park, away from all the casinos, stands *Old Waterway Inn* (☎ *609-347-1793, 1700 Riverside Drive*), which has a deck overlooking the water.

Entertainment
Each casino offers a full schedule of entertainment, ranging from ragtime and jazz bands in hotel lobbies to top-name entertainers in the casino auditoriums. Ticket prices range from $15 to $400, and the smaller lounges provide free entertainment.

Check the *Whoot* weekly and the monthly *AC Shorecast* for current concerts. The

Comedy Stop (☎ 609-340-4000), in the Tropicana Casino, is Atlantic City's top comedy club, and charges $12 for admission.

Wonder Gardens (☎ 609-347-1466), at Arctic and Kentucky Aves, is a reminder of the old days when this was a busy strip of jazz nightspots. *Studio 6* (☎ 609-348-3310), at Mt Vernon Ave between Pacific and Atlantic Aves, is a club with a mixed gay-straight crowd. *Club Mirage*, in front of Trump Plaza on the Boardwalk by Mississippi Ave, is a standard disco.

Spectator Sports
The Atlantic City Surf minor-league baseball team plays in the spanking new $15 million Sandcastle Stadium during the summer. Call ☎ 609-344-8873 for schedule details and tickets. The Atlantic City Seagulls basketball team plays in less exalted confines – the Atlantic City High School gym (☎ 609-466-7797). College basketball tournaments and various car shows take place at the Convention Hall (☎ 609-355-7155) during the winter.

Shopping
Gordon's Alley (☎ 609-344-5000) was New Jersey's first pedestrian shopping mall and has some 30 stores covering a two-block area between Atlantic, Pacific, Virginia and Pennsylvania Aves.

Ocean One, Atlantic City's major shopping center (☎ 609-347-8086), is on a pier shaped like an ocean liner, on the Boardwalk between Arkansas Ave and Missouri Ave (Columbus Ave). Nearby shopping complexes include the Shore Mall (☎ 609-484-9500) in Egg Harbor and the Lenox china outlet (☎ 609-965-8535).

Getting There & Away
Air Atlantic City International Airport (☎ 609-645-7895) is off Tilton Rd in Pomona. Spirit Airlines (☎ 800-772-7117) and US Airways Express (☎ 800-428-4322) connect the town with Cleveland, Detroit, Philadelphia and several Florida cities. It will cost about $75 (one way) to fly to Atlantic City from Philadelphia, and about $300 (roundtrip) from Florida cities.

The Royal Airport Shuttle (☎ 609-748-9777) and Sky Shuttle (☎ 800-825-3759) offer service to New York, Newark and Philadelphia airports several times a day.

Bus NJ Transit also runs buses from New York City to the depot on Arctic Ave between Michigan and Ohio Aves. For a better deal, check out the casino buses from New York and Philadelphia; tickets cost about $20 roundtrip but include food vouchers and quarters for the slots.

For transport from New York's Port Authority, contact Academy (☎ 800-442-7272) or Greyhound (☎ 800-231-2222). Academy's buses go directly to several casinos, and fares are $37.50 roundtrip, though casinos sponsor buses at lower fares. Gray Line (☎ 212-397-2620) operates from 900 8th Ave, between 53rd and 54th Sts.

If traveling from Philadelphia, contact Leisure (☎ 800-257-7510); roundtrip tickets are normally valid for just 72 hours. A roundtrip ticket will cost about $26.

The Philadelphia Airport Shuttle (☎ 610-521-1854, 800-774-8885) goes from the Philadelphia airport to Atlantic City for $25/45 one way/roundtrip. The shuttle runs four times a day. You can arrange for on-demand service, though it's only a good value if you have three or more people in your party.

Train NJ Transit runs trains from Philadelphia to Atlantic City; the trip takes about an hour and costs $9.

Car & Motorcycle Atlantic City is reached via exit 38 on the Garden State Pkwy. The Atlantic City Expressway runs directly from Philadelphia to Atlantic City.

Getting Around
Shuttle buses to downtown from the airport cost $8/15 one way/roundtrip. By taxi, it costs around $25 to get to/from the casinos and the airport, which is about 10 miles away.

The jitney buses operate 24 hours daily with stops on every corner throughout Atlantic City. Every sign has a color-coded number by each casino stop, telling you

NEW JERSEY

which jitney to take (the jitneys have a color-coded number on their hoods).

An Atlantic City tradition, the wicker rolling chairs are a sort of rickshaw that is pushed (rather than towed) along the Boardwalk. Rates are clearly posted inside each chair and a ride of up to five blocks costs about $5.

For a cheaper alternative to the rolling chairs, try the blue trams that run up and down the Boardwalk. It costs $2 one way, $5 for an all-day pass.

For a taxi, call Atlantic City Yellow Cabs (☎ 609-344-1221). Casinos also arrange cab service to Margate and Cape May.

AROUND ATLANTIC CITY
Historic Smithville

The town of Historic Smithville (☎ 609-652-7777) began with the Smithville Inn, which was built in 1787. It was originally just one room on a busy stagecoach route but soon expanded to six rooms. Abandoned by 1900, the inn was restored and reopened in 1952 as a restaurant. The success of the venture triggered the development of Historic Smithville, with buildings from the region's past brought here and restored. It's a worthy day trip from Atlantic City or a rest stop when passing through the area since there are several interesting shops, a colorful carousel, a miniature railway, and water amusements on a lake. *Smithville Inn* (☎ *609-652-0001*) has a restaurant and colonial-era bakery.

Historic Smithville is 12 miles north from Atlantic City on Route 9, or exit 48 on the Garden State Pkwy.

Renault Winery

This 130-year-old vineyard (☎ 609-965-2111), 72 N Bremen Ave in Egg Harbor City, claims to be the oldest continuously operating winery in the country. It offers a free guided tour, tastings and a museum with a priceless collection of champagne glasses and wine goblets, some dating back to the Middle Ages. At the end of each summer, the winery offers a lighthearted grape-stomping festival.

To get to the winery, take Route 30 west from Atlantic City for 16 miles to Bremen

Ave, turn right and continue for 2½ miles to the winery.

MARGATE

A pleasant town just 5 miles south of Atlantic City on Absecon Island, Margate (population 8431) is best known for its gaudy motels and famous landmark – Lucy the Elephant. It also has a great beach and several popular bars that draw a young crowd. The town of Margate itself doesn't offer much for the traveler, other than cheaper accommodations for visitors with cars who want to spend some time in the Atlantic City area.

Lucy the Elephant

This 65-foot folly (☎ 609-823-6473) was built in Margate near Atlantic City in 1881 to attract prospective buyers to the new summer homes built by a local real estate developer named James V Lafferty. The six-story elephant is constructed of nearly a million pieces of wood covered with a gray tin 'skin.' Lafferty sold Lucy in 1887 and she became a tourist attraction, a tavern, a summer home for an English physician and his family and a centerpiece for a hotel (although Lucy was never a hotel herself). Visitors who have enjoyed the view from the top of Lucy include Henry Ford and Woodrow Wilson.

After WWII, Lucy fell into neglect and was closed to the public in the 1960s. The quirky landmark was saved by a committee of concerned locals, who moved her to her current location and raised sufficient funds to restore her exterior. Now Lucy is sporting a new $60,000 howdah.

Lucy is open to the public in the summer daily from 10 am to 9 pm, and before Memorial Day and after Labor Day Saturday and Sunday from 10 am to 5 pm. Admission is $2/1 adults/children.

Places to Stay

A Margate alternative for Atlantic City visitors is *White Sands Motor Inn* (☎ *609-822-7141, fax 822-2650, 9010 Atlantic Ave*), just north of Lucy. Rates are $85/100 for singles/doubles.

Places to Eat

Several bar-restaurants are clustered near Lucy the Elephant, including *Ventura's Greenhouse* (☎ 609-822-0140), right in the elephant's shadow. The menu features appetizers and salads for about $10. *Red's Club* (☎ 609-822-1539), at Ventnor and Atlantic Ave, has live bands during the summer months. *Maloney's Tavern* (☎ 609-823-3546, 23 S Washington St) is a standard bar.

Omar's (☎ 609-822-6627), at Washington and Amherst Sts, serves inexpensive Mexican food. Right across the street are *Polo Bay* (☎ 609-487-9189) and *Maynard's* (☎ 609-822-8423), both of which are decent spots for a meal. Both are inexpensive, with main dishes running from $8 to $12.

Getting There & Away

Margate is reached by car via exit 36 on the Garden State Pkwy. Traveling from the west via the Atlantic City Expressway, take exit 2.

WILDWOODS

The Wildwoods (population 4500) are three towns – North Wildwood, Wildwood and Wildwood Crest – on the southernmost island off the mainland of New Jersey. The majority of the boardwalk and shops are in noisy Wildwood, which is a big hangout for local teens and a favorite for college students, mainly from Australia and Ireland, who spend the summers working at the amusement areas.

It's worth taking a drive out to Wildwood Crest, the southernmost town, during summer nights to look at the perfectly preserved 1950s motels with their garish neon signs. Even if you're not interested in joining the summer hoards of teenagers that stay in Wildwood, the local tourist office sponsors tours of the town's Eisenhowerera motels and diners during the high season. The tours are worth inquiring about if you're visiting nearby Cape May.

Information

The Wildwood Information Center (☎ 609-522-1407, 800-992-9732) is at the midpoint of the boardwalk at Schellenger Ave. It's open daily from 9 am to 10 pm in season, and from 9 am to 4 pm after Labor Day.

The post office is at 3311 Atlantic Ave between Wildwood and Oak Aves.

The city has set up parking meters with the clumsiest design you'll probably ever encounter. You have to lift a tiny metal hatch, maneuver a quarter into a hole, and spin a flimsy knob. Meters must be fed daily from 8 am to 3 pm; 25¢ gets you only 20 minutes, so head to a parking lot if you're here for the day.

George F Boyer Historical Museum

This museum (☎ 609-523-0277), at 3907 Pacific Ave in Wildwood, offers a good primer on local history and lore. It's wheelchair accessible and open daily in the high season from 11 am to 5pm.

Hereford Inlet Lighthouse

This lighthouse (☎ 609-522-4520), at 1st and Central Aves in North Wildwood, is one of several historic lighthouses in the state. It was constructed in 1874. The lighthouse, with a beacon visible for 13 miles, was maintained by a keeper until 1964, when an automated light was installed. It's open in summer Monday to Saturday from 9 am to 5 pm and Sunday from 11 am to 4 pm; admission is free.

Beaches

Because of the southern migration of sand, Wildwood's free beach is over a half-mile wide at some points and growing. The beach angles very softly into the sea, without a sharp drop as you find at some northern shore beaches, and the sand is fine and white.

The boardwalk is lined with cheap T-shirt and knick-knack shops, usually selling items for under $5. There are also amusement piers off the boardwalk. From north to south are Morey's Pier (☎ 609-522-5477), at 25th St, Mariner's Landing (☎ 609-729-0586) and Nickel's Midway Pier (☎ 609-522-9124), both of which are on Schellenger Ave. All three piers are open from April through the end of September and sell ride passes for $14.50. For $26 you can get access to two piers and the Raging Waters waterslide (for

NEW JERSEY

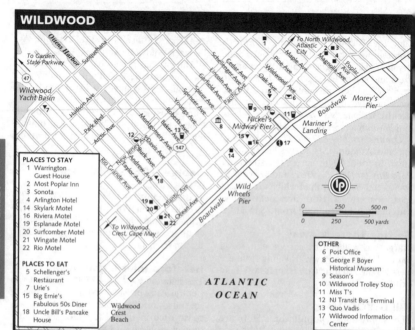

WILDWOOD

PLACES TO STAY
1 Warrington Guest House
2 Most Poplar Inn
3 Sonota
4 Arlington Hotel
14 Skylark Motel
16 Riviera Motel
19 Esplanade Motel
20 Surfcomber Motel
21 Wingate Motel
22 Rio Motel

PLACES TO EAT
5 Schellenger's Restaurant
7 Urie's
15 Big Ernie's Fabulous 50s Diner
18 Uncle Bill's Pancake House

OTHER
6 Post Office
8 George F Boyer Historical Museum
9 Season's
10 Wildwood Trolley Stop
11 Miss T's
12 NJ Transit Bus Terminal
13 Quo Vadis
17 Wildwood Information Center

two hours). A little further south is Wild Wheels Pier, which is a standard amusement area with rides for children.

Fishing

The inlet here makes it a great place to go crabbing. Crabbing cages can be rented at Canal Side Boat Rental (☎ 609-522-7676), at 18th and Delaware Aves in North Wildwood; they also rent kayaks. Also try Aqua Boat Rentals (☎ 609-522-5778), at 5th and New York Aves.

In Wildwood Crest there are boat rental places and party boats along the bay on Park Blvd between Columbine and Astor Rds. Try Starlight/Twilight Fishing (☎ 609-729-7776) at Blake's Dock, 6200 Park Blvd; and the boats at Captain Royles Dock (☎ 609-522-1395), 6100 Park Blvd.

Other Activities

You can go **parasailing** in Wildwood Crest; Atlantic Parasail (☎ 609-522-1869), at Two Mile Landing Crab House Restaurant & Marina on Ocean Drive near the Cape May Inlet Bridge, gets you up in the air for about 10 minutes, provided you know how to stand up on water skis first.

Jet skiing is popular in Wildwood. Ocean Watersafaris (☎ 609-522-3017), at the Wildwood Yacht Basin on Rio Grande Ave just before the inlet bridge, rents jet skis by the half hour/hour for $35/60.

You can go **whale-** and **dolphin-watching** through Captain Sinn's (☎ 609-522-3934), 6006 Park Blvd in North Wildwood. Boat trips operate all summer and into the autumn. The trip lasts about three hours and costs $10 per person, or $8 per person with a group rate.

Places to Stay

Your choices are cheap rooming houses, a few guesthouses, or one of the over 250 motels that can quickly fill up with teens looking for a good time.

Budget Within 5 miles of Wildwood is *North Wildwood Camping Resort* (☎ 609-465-4440, 527-L Shellbay Rd), in Cape May Courthouse just off exit 9 from the Garden State Pkwy. Sites cost up to $180 weekly. (See Places to Stay in the Cape May section for other campgrounds in the area.)

The cheapest guesthouses and hotels are generally in the quadrant bordered to the north and south by New Jersey and Atlantic Aves and to the east and west by Poplar and Pine Aves. Almost all close down after Labor Day.

Warrington Guest House (☎ 609-522-2340, 118 E Maple Ave) has 16 rooms with sinks, air-con and refrigerators for $50 a double. *Most Poplar Inn* (☎ 609-729-9238, 305 E Poplar Ave) has clean, basic rooms with refrigerators, TVs and shared baths for under $30, with weekly discounts. It is open year-round.

Arlington Hotel (☎ 609-522-2374, 325 E Magnolia Ave) is a five-story building with rates of $120 a week. Clean and basic furnishings can be found at *Sea Inn* (☎ 609-522-5731, 107 E Magnolia Ave); rooms have sinks and fans but baths are shared. Sea Inn charges $120 to $160, depending on the location of the room.

Mid-Range & Top End There are dozens of mid-range motels that line Ocean and Atlantic Aves in Wildwood and stretch into Wildwood Crest. Rates are essentially determined by proximity to the boardwalk; those closest are $175 to $190 a night and many people double up to cut the costs. Minimum rates are about $100 a night.

Sonota (☎ 609-729-0967, 2703 Atlantic Ave) is near the beach and has off-street parking. *Riviera Motel* (☎ 609-522-5353) is at Spicer and Ocean Aves. *Skylark Motel* (☎ 609-522-5082, 3917 Atlantic Ave), at Spencer Ave, is a basic motel with doubles for $80. *Esplanade Motel* (☎ 609-522-7890, fax 522-7204, 230 E Taylor Ave) has a pool for crowded beach days and laundry facilities.

Other decent motels include *Wingate Motel* (☎ 609-522-7412), at Atlantic and Rio Grande Aves; *Surfcomber Motel* (☎ 609-522-2267, 4800 Atlantic Ave), near Taylor Ave; and *Rio Motel* (☎ 609-522-1461, 4800 Ocean Ave), at the end of Rio Grande Ave, which has 115 rooms. All three offer rooms from $65 to $130.

Places to Eat

Expect to spend a lot of time eating fast food on the boardwalk.

Wildwood restaurants specialize in all-you-can-eat buffets and some cash in on the popularity of '50s diners. *Uncle Bill's Pancake House* (☎ 609-729-7557), at Pacific and Andrew, is a classic '50s-style pancake house; you can eat like a king for about $7 per person. *Big Ernie's Fabulous 50s Diner* (☎ 609-522-8288, 3801 Atlantic Ave), at Garfield, is open 24 hours daily and features old 45s, posters and hubcaps on the walls. Burgers, sandwiches and egg dishes cost about $10.

If you're looking to pig out on lobsters, head to *Schellenger's Restaurant* (☎ 609-522-0433, 3516 Atlantic Ave). You can eat seafood at market prices. Near the bridge to the mainland, *Urie's*, on the waterfront at the Wildwood Yacht Basin on Rio Grande Ave, is a steak house and a seafood restaurant in the $15 to $28 range.

There's a buffet at *Grand Smorgasbord* (☎ 609-522-6742), at 16th Ave and the boardwalk in North Wildwood, which serves huge breakfasts and dinners.

One mile south of Wildwood Crest, *Two Mile Landing Crab House Restaurant* (☎ 609-522-1341), on the pier off Ocean Drive, has seafood dishes for $12 to $25.

Entertainment

Look at copies of *Free Time* and *Shout*'s entertainment section to find out what's happening at the local clubs.

In Wildwood, *Quo Vadis* (☎ 609-522-4949, 4200 Pacific Ave) is a large dance club with colored disco lights and features wet T-shirt contests; it is open until 5 am. *Miss T's* (☎ 609-522-7771), at Oak Ave and the boardwalk, is open from noon to 5 am with a daily happy hour. *Season's* (☎ 609-522-4400, 222 E Schellenger) has pop and oldies and is open every day year-round. On Friday there's a free buffet during happy hour.

NEW JERSEY

Harrigan's (☎ 609-522-5071), 100 East Walnut Ave in North Wildwood, has live music shows.

Getting There & Away

The bus stop (☎ 609-522-2491) is at New Jersey Ave (between Davis and Burk). NJ Transit runs buses from New York City (two hours) and Philadelphia (90 minutes). From New York City the fare is $30/45.75 one way/roundtrip; from Philadelphia, $12.50/22.25.

Take exit 4 on the Garden State Pkwy to Rio Grande Ave, which runs east to the beachfront Ocean Drive in Wildwood. Exit 6 on the Garden State Pkwy leads to Route 147, which enters North Wildwood as Ocean Drive and then becomes New Jersey Ave.

Getting Around

The Sightseer Tram (☎ 609-522-6700) runs up and down the boardwalk from 10 am to 1 am during the summer. Catch it at one of the shelters that look like bus stops; the fare is $1.50. The Wildwood trolley (☎ 609-884-0450) runs back and forth on Ocean and Atlantic Aves, from Schellenger Ave in Wildwood to Jefferson Ave in Wildwood Crest, in the high season. It makes several stops along this route and costs $1.50.

CAPE MAY

Cape May (population 4700), which stands at the southern tip of New Jersey, is one of the oldest seashore resorts in the US. A quiet collection of more than 600 gingerbread Victorian homes, the entire town was designated a national historic landmark in 1976. In addition to its attractive architecture, accommodations and eating places, Cape May boasts a lovely beach, a famous lighthouse, crafts shops and bird-watching. It's the only place in New Jersey where you can watch the sun both rise and set over the water.

Cape May is divided into Cape May City, which has hotels, the main beach and a boardwalk, and Cape May Point State Park, which has the lighthouse, Sunset Beach and a bird refuge.

History

Cape May is named after Dutch sea captain Cornelius Mey, who claimed the land for Holland in 1621. By 1660, the region was in British hands, and became a whaling center in the 18th century. The town really flourished as a resort over the next 100 years and by 1853 the Mount Vernon Hotel, the world's largest vacation facility with a capacity for 3000 guests, opened in Cape May. (It burned down just three years later.) A massive fire wiped out most of the town center in 1878, and much of the Victorian architecture that exists today can be dated back to the rebuilding process in the late 19th century.

The town was in danger of becoming an overdeveloped, motel-ridden carbon copy of Wildwood following a hurricane in 1962. But several residents – including Bruce Minnix, who served as the town's mayor from 1972 to 1976 – successfully fought to have the area designated a national historic landmark.

Incidentally, Cape May is far enough south that it's below the Mason-Dixon line, the traditional demarcation between the northern and southern states.

Information

Comprehensive information on Cape May County attractions is available from the welcome center at milepost 11 on the Garden State Pkwy.

Cape May City's welcome center (☎ 609-884-9562) is at 405 Lafayette St. *This Week*, a publication of the Mid-Atlantic Center for the Arts, lists all activities in town. The post office is at 700 Washington St.

Emlen Physick Estate

This 18-room mansion (☎ 609-884-5404) 1048 Washington St, was built in 1879 and is now the home of the Mid-Atlantic Center for the Arts. You can book a tour for nearby Historic Cold Spring Village and buy Victorian and history books at the museum shop. Despite the age of the house, the facility is wheelchair accessible. It is open daily from 10 am to 5 pm; tours of the house are conducted hourly. Admission is $7/3.50 for adults/children.

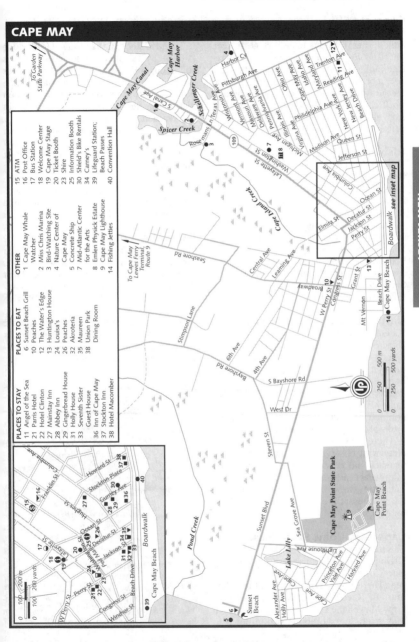

CAPE MAY

NEW JERSEY

PLACES TO STAY
11 Angel of the Sea
21 Parris Hotel
22 Hotel Clinton
27 Mainstay Inn
28 Abbey Inn
29 Gingerbread House
31 Holly House
33 Seventh Sister
   Guest House
36 Inn of Cape May
37 Stockton Inn
38 Hotel Macomber

PLACES TO EAT
6 Sunset Beach Grill
10 Peaches
12 The Water's Edge
13 Huntington House
24 Louisa's
26 Peaches
32 Akroteria
35 Maureen
38 Union Park
   Dining Room

OTHER
1 Cape May Whale
  Watcher
2 Miss Chris Marina
3 Bird-Watching Site
4 Nature Center of
  Cape May
5 Concrete Ship
7 Mid-Atlantic Center
  for the Arts
8 Emlen Physick Estate
9 Cape May Lighthouse
14 Fishing Jetties
15 ATM
16 Post Office
17 Bus Station
18 Welcome Center
19 Cape May Stage
20 Ticket Booth
23 Shire
25 Information Booth
30 Shield's Bike Rentals
34 Carney's
39 Lifeguard Station;
   Beach Passes
40 Convention Hall

Concrete Ship

Twelve experimental concrete ships were built during WWI due to a shortage of steel. The *Atlantis*, with a 5-inch concrete aggregate hull, was built in 1918, but eight years later it broke free in a storm and ran aground on the western side of Cape May Point. A small chunk of the hull still sits a few feet from shore on Sunset Beach at the end of Sunset Blvd.

Historic Cold Spring Village

This rural re-creation (☎ 609-898-2300), 720 Route 9, is one of those places where volunteers don colonial dress and reenact village life as it was. Admission is $5/4/3 for adults/seniors/children.

Historic Cold Spring Village is open from 10 am to 4:30 pm weekends from Memorial Day to mid-June. It's open daily at the same hours from June to mid-September. The exit for visitors traveling south on the Garden State Pkwy is 4A south; from Cape May follow signs from Route 109.

Nature Center of Cape May

Associated with the Audubon Society, this 18-acre site is the best place to get information on the different types of birds that pass through southern New Jersey. The information center (☎ 609-884-9590), 1600 Delaware Ave, is on the harbor and has an exhibition gallery. The center also maintains a birding hotline (☎ 609-861-0466) and offers guided bird walks through the area.

There is an open bird-watching site, complete with observation platforms over the marshes and beaches leading to the Cape May canal nearby. You can get to it by taking Lafayette Ave west out of town and turning left just before the Route 109 bridge (look for signs).

Cape May Point State Park

This state park (☎ 609-884-2736), 707 E Lake Drive just off Lighthouse Drive, is a resting place for millions of migratory birds each year. There is an observatory here that offers tours of Reed's Beach, 12 miles north of Cape May on the Delaware Bay, where each May migrating shorebirds swoop down to feed on the eggs laid by thousands of horseshoe crabs.

The 157-foot **Cape May Lighthouse** (☎ 609-884-2159) was built in 1859 and is still in operation; its light is visible 25 miles out to sea. It is also one of Cape May's prime bird-watching spots. The lighthouse is open daily during the summer months from 10 am to 5 pm; admission is $3.50.

The park is open from 9 am to 5 pm daily, and there is a hotline (☎ 609-884-2626) that offers information on the latest bird sightings.

To get to the park, drive west from Cape May on Sunset Blvd about 2 miles to Lighthouse Rd. Make a left and drive half a mile to the lighthouse, which is in the park.

Cape May County Park & Zoo

One of this area's nicest discoveries is Cape May County Park & Zoo (☎ 609-465-5271), a few miles north of town just off exit 11 of the Garden State Pkwy. The park is a beautifully maintained, 200-acre facility with some 250 different species of animals, many of which wander freely across a re-created African savanna and other natural habitats while humans observe the action from a discreet distance along the elevated board-

walk. There are also buildings where you can observe birds, reptiles and aquatic life from closer quarters.

The park, which is busy but not crowded even in summer, also offers nature and bike trails, a children's playground and a fishing pond. Best of all, access to the entire park is free, though they do encourage donations from visitors as they enter the parking lot. It is open from 10 am to 4:30 pm.

Beaches

The narrow Cape May Beach (☎ 609-884-9525) requires passes, which are sold at the lifeguard station on the boardwalk at the end of Grant St. At print time passes were $13/10/4 for a season/week/day, but a substantial price hike is looming. The Cape May Point Beach is free and accessible from the parking lot at Cape May Point State Park, near the lighthouse. Sunset Beach, at the end of Sunset Blvd, is also free.

Whale-Watching

Cape May Whale Watcher (☎ 609-884-5445), 2nd Ave and Wilson Drive, 'guarantees' the sighting of a marine mammal – if you don't see a whale or dolphin, you will get credit for another trip. There are three trips daily at 10 am, 1 and 6:30 pm. The charge is $24/12 for adults/children.

Fishing & Boating

There are popular fishing jetties at the end of Beach Drive. Offshore fishing often pulls in tuna and blue marlin in summers and varieties of shark year-round. Party Boats leave daily from the Miss Chris Marina (☎ 609-884-3939) at Third Ave and Wilson Drive.

The 80-foot wooden *Schooner Yankee* (☎ 609-884-1919) sails from the Ocean Highway dock at the foot of Two Mile Bridge near Cape May. Three-hour trips cost $23.50 and are available from May to September.

Bicycling

Bikes may be rented by the day at Shield's (☎ 609-884-1818), 11 Gurney near the beach. It's open daily from 7 am to 7 pm.

Organized Tours

The Mid-Atlantic Center for the Arts (☎ 609-884-5404, 800-275-4278), 1048 Washington St, offers a range of Cape May tours. You can buy tickets at the ticket booth on the western end of the Washington St pedestrian mall, just before Decatur St. Prices are around $5 for walking tours and $15 or under for special events.

The following is a list of available tours:

Cape May Historic Districts Walking Tour – held year-round

Champagne Brunch Tour – a walking tour followed by brunch at the Mad Batter; Easter to Thanksgiving

Gourmet Brunch Tour – a walking tour followed by a Southern breakfast at the Chalfonte Hotel; Easter to Thanksgiving

Ocean Walk – a walk along the beach to discuss ecology; Memorial Day to Labor Day

Mansions by Gaslight – a tour of the Emlen Physick House, the Abbey (1869), the Mainstay Inn (1872) and the Humphrey Hughes House (1901); Wednesdays during the summer

Trolley Tours – three different drives around the east end, the west end and beachfront; year-round. There are also children's trolley tours at the same price and moonlight trolley tours; June to September

Cape May by Boat – the boat leaves from Wildwood and circles Cape May; summer only

Cape May Candlelight House Tour – tour of local homes during the Christmas season

Special Events

In November the Cape May Jazz Festival (☎ 609-884-7277) presents talented jazz and classical performers. Victorian Sherlock Holmes Weekend also occurs in November.

Places to Stay

Cape May is packed with expensive B&Bs and inns, and you can't walk 50 feet in the center of town without passing one.

Budget *Holly Shores Holiday Trav-L-Park* (☎ 609-886-1234, 491 Route 9) has sites without/with hookups for $20/22. *Beachcomber Camping Resort* (☎ 609-886-6035, 800-233-0150, 462-G Seashore Rd) has campsites for $20. It is open from April to October.

Hotel Clinton (☎ 609-884-3993, off-season 516-799-8889, 202 Perry St), near Lafayette, is a seasonal choice. Next door is *Parris Hotel* (☎ 609-884-8015/6363, 204 Perry St), which has some rooms with private baths and TVs. Rates for these two places range from $90 to $125 per room.

Mid-Range Many of these places offer rooms for under $120 in the high season. *Holly House* (☎ 609-884-7365, 20 Jackson St) is an 1890 cottage run by a former mayor of Cape May. It's one of the so-called Seven Sisters – seven identical homes, five of which are along Jackson St. Holly House has six rooms, each with three windows and a shared bath.

Seventh Sister Guest House (☎ 609-884-2280, 10 Jackson St) is a few doors down from Holly House. The *Hotel Macomber* (☎ 609-884-3020, 727 Beach Drive), on the corner of Howard St, also has one of the best restaurants in Cape May (see Places to Eat). They are both handsome Victorian homes.

Top End The *Gingerbread House* (☎ 609-884-0211, 28 Gurney St) is a six-room B&B, with rates of $100 to $150. *Stockton Inn* (☎ 609-884-4036, 800-524-4283, 809 Beach Drive) is a motel and a 'manor house.' The motel has standard motel furnishings and a pool with rooms costing $100. The manor is a converted Victorian house with 10 rooms and three suites (all with private bath) and is slightly more expensive.

Inn of Cape May (☎ 800-257-0432), at the corner of Beach Drive and Ocean Ave, is a sprawling white wooden structure with lavender trim. Rooms come in a wide variety of sizes, and generally have high ceilings and white wicker furniture. In the low season rates are $65 to $100; in the high season, $140 to $200. *Mainstay Inn* (☎ 609-884-8690, 635 Columbia Ave) is a hotel built in 1872 as a men's gambling club. Rooms are furnished in opulent dark woods with large beds and all have private baths. Rates are $115 to $225 per room and an extra person is an additional $35. *Abbey Inn* (☎ 609-884-4506, 34 Gurney St), at the

Just a few of Cape May's 600 painted ladies

ANGUS OBORN

corner of Columbia Ave, is one of the more ostentatious places in town. It is packed with antique furniture, has high ceilings and offers a tour ($5) of the grounds and house. Rates, including breakfast, are $120 to $250.

Angel of the Sea (☎ 609-884-3369, 800-848-3369, 5-7 Trenton Ave) is renowned for its service. All rooms have baths and ceiling fans and access to wraparound porches. Weekday/weekend room rates, including breakfast, are $150/250.

Places to Eat

Budget *Akroteria*, on Beach Drive between Jackson and Perry Sts, is a collection of small fast-food shacks with fare for under $10. *Sunset Beach Grill* is at the end of Sunset Blvd on Sunset Beach overlooking the beached *Atlantis* and the ocean. It's the perfect place to order a sandwich and watch the waves.

Mid-Range *Louisa's* (☎ 609-884-5882, 104 Jackson St) is an excellent small restaurant serving dinner only; it's open Tuesday to Saturday from 5 pm. Prices for dishes are around $10. *Huntington House* (☎ 609-884-5868), on Grant and North Sts, has an all-you-can-eat buffet for $15.

Top End Cape May is known for fine and ambitious restaurants. *Union Park Dining Room* (☎ 609-884-8811, 727 Beach Drive) is at the Hotel Macomber. The menu features French fare with some Asian accents. The desserts are a house specialty. (Reservations are essential in summer; bring your own bottle of alcohol.) *The Water's Edge* (☎ 609-884-1717), at Beach Drive and Pittsburgh Ave, looks out on the Atlantic and serves seafood with something of a Mediterranean flavor, but also serves a good steak. Dinner, including wine, will cost about $35.

Maureen (☎ 609-884-3774), on Beach Drive and Decatur St, is a good place to splurge on seafood or steak (under $20).

Peaches is at two locations: (☎ 609-884-0202, 322 Carpenter's Lane) and (☎ 609-898-0100, 1 Sunset Blvd). This restaurant offers contemporary American dining at high prices; main dishes cost $15 to $25.

Entertainment

The *Cape May Stage* (☎ 609-884-1341) is an excellent regional theater with a March to December season of plays.

Carney's (☎ 609-884-4424, 401 Beach Drive), between Decatur and Jackson Sts, has two bars and a weird decor of wagon-wheel lights and carved fish as well as fake plants, beams and brick. It is, however, a popular and unpretentious place to drink and listen to music.

Shire (☎ 609-884-4700, 315 Washington St) has live music daily during the summer with a small cover charge.

Shopping

The pedestrian mall along Washington St is crammed with shops and tourists. There are also 11 antique stores all over town; the welcome center offers a map noting all of them.

Getting There & Away

Bus NJ Transit (☎ 201-762-5100, 800-772-2222) runs buses from New York City and Philadelphia. The bus station is next to the chamber of commerce building, near the corner of Lafayette and Elmira Sts.

Car & Motorcycle Cape May is at the southern extreme of the Garden State Pkwy, which leads right into town.

Boat A ferry runs daily between North Cape May and the Delaware coastal town of Lewes (pronounced 'Lewis'). The 17-mile trip across the Delaware Bay takes about 70 minutes and is a popular way for residents of Delaware and Maryland to visit the southern Jersey Shore. It also saves some time for New Jersey–based travelers who are heading south from Cape May for a visit to Washington, DC, and points south. If you're traveling to points further south see Lonely Planet's *Virginia & the Capital Region* as well as the forthcoming city guide, *Washington, DC*.

Ferries leave North Cape May between 6:20 am and 7:40 pm and Lewes between 8 am and 9:20 pm. There are at least five trips a day in winter with additional trips in

NEW JERSEY

summer. The one-way fare for vehicle and driver is $18; foot passengers, $4.50; children (ages six to 12), $2.25.

North Cape May's ferry terminal is on Route 9 west of the Garden State Pkwy. For additional details and directions call the Lewes terminal (☎ 302-645-6346) or the North Cape May terminal (☎ 609-886-9699). Call ☎ 800-643-3779 for recorded information and ☎ 800-717-7245 for reservations, which should be made a day in advance in the high season.

Pennsylvania

Facts about Pennsylvania

Pennsylvania's proud slogan, 'America Starts Here' (as seen on license plates and in tourist literature) alludes to the fact that the historical events before, during and after the American Revolution helped create and shape the USA. Today, Pennsylvania's wealth of historical sites and beautiful scenery are rightly a major draw for visitors.

Philadelphia – sometimes overlooked by visitors short on time and rushing between New York and Washington, DC – is enjoying a well-deserved renaissance due to its rich blend of history, architecture, cultural attractions, parks, shops and myriad eating and entertainment options. To the west of the city is Valley Forge National Historic Park, and to the south there is the picturesque Brandywine Valley. Northeast of Philadelphia it's a scenic trip through Bucks County to Washington Crossing Historic Park and New Hope.

Pennsylvania Dutch Country, only some 90 minutes' drive west of Philadelphia, is a major attraction because of its Amish community. Further west is Gettysburg, where visitors can follow the course of the bloodiest battle of the Civil War in the National Military Park. Other popular destinations are Hershey (home of the chocolate company) and York, where Harley-Davidson motorcycles are assembled.

In the southwest, the state's other big city, Pittsburgh, used to be called 'Smokey City' because extensive mining emitted coal dust into the air. Today, like Philadelphia, it is being reborn and is now a beautiful city well worth visiting. Southeast of Pittsburgh are the scenic Laurel Highlands – a center for white-water rafting and the place Frank Lloyd Wright built his architectural masterpieces Fallingwater and Kentuck Knob.

Northwest Pennsylvania saw the start of the US oil industry, the remains of which are still visible, a stark contrast to the natural beauty of the surrounding Allegheny National Forest. The forests of the north are particularly beautiful in the fall. The city of Erie gives Pennsylvania access to the Great Lakes and played an important part in the War of 1812. Route 6, also called the Grand Army of the Republic Hwy, offers a picturesque journey across the north of the state (and a nostalgic reminder of what it was like before the interstate highway system). The Pocono Mountains, in the northeast, form a resort region famous as a honeymoon destination, but also offer a wealth of outdoor activities.

State Trivia

Statehood: December 12, 1787
Area: 45,555 sq miles
Population: 12 million
Capital: Harrisburg
Nickname: The Keystone State
Motto: Virtue, Liberty and Independence
Animal: White-tailed deer
Dog: Great Dane
Bird: Ruffed grouse
Fish: Brook trout
Flower: Mountain laurel
Tree: Hemlock
Beautification & Conservation Plant: Penngift crownvetch
Insect: Firefly
Beverage: Milk
Fossil: *Phacops rana* (a trilobite)
Flagship: US Brig *Niagara*

INFORMATION
Tourist Offices

The main state authority is the Pennsylvania Center for Travel, Tourism & Film Staff (☎ 717-787-5453, fax 717-787-0687), 453 Forum Building, Harrisburg, PA 17120. For the latest information, visit its website at www.state.pa.us/visit. It oversees the state's regional, county and local tourist offices. For a copy of the free annual *Pennsylvania Visitors'*

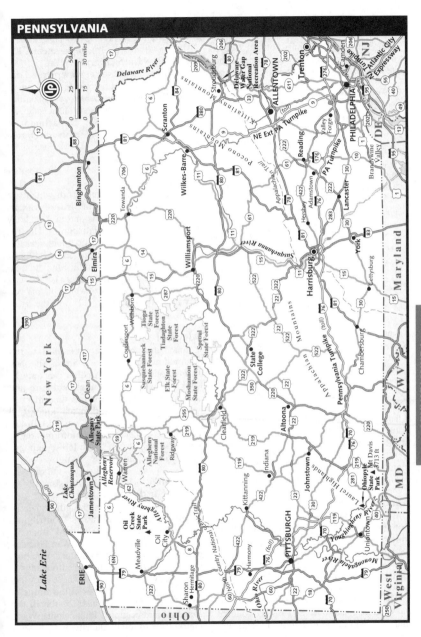

Guide, write to the above address or call
☎ 800-847-4872.

Pennsylvania has 13 tourist offices, known as Welcome Centers, at key locations on the state's highways. These are:

I-70 West – Warfordsburg, half a mile east of the Pennsylvania/Maryland border

I-70 East – Claysville, 5 miles west of the Pennsylvania/West Virginia border

I-78 West – Easton, 1 mile west of the Pennsylvania/New Jersey border

I-79 South – Edinboro, 1 mile south of the Edinboro exit

I-79 North – Kirby, 5 miles north of the Pennsylvania/West Virginia border

I-80 East – West Middlesex, half a mile east of the Pennsylvania/Ohio border

I-81 North – State Line, 1½ miles north of the Pennsylvania/Maryland border

I-81 South – Lenox, 4 miles south of exit 64 for Lenox

I-83 North – Shrewsbury, half a mile north of the Pennsylvania/Maryland border

I-84 – Matamoras, at exit 11

I-95 North – Linwood, half a mile north of the Pennsylvania/Delaware border

Neshaminy – on the Pennsylvania Turnpike mile marker 351, 7 miles west of the Pennsylvania/New Jersey border

Zelienople – eastbound on the Pennsylvania Turnpike at mile marker 21, 21 miles east of the Pennsylvania/Ohio border

All are open daily 7 am to 7 pm, and staff can book accommodations for you. If you need more information, contact the Welcome Center Division (☎ 717-787-4433), Department of Transportation, 1211 Transportation & Safety Building, Harrisburg, PA 17120.

Accommodations

The Private Campground Owners Association (☎ 610-767-5026, fax 610-767-5034, lowhill@fast.net), PO Box 5, New Tripoli, PA 18066, publishes the annual *Pennsylvania Campground Directory*. It lists almost 200 campgrounds in Pennsylvania. You can visit its website at www.pacamping.com.

The annual *Unique Lodging of Pennsylvania* directory lists over 200 B&Bs, country inns and farm accommodations in the state.

You can obtain a copy from the Pennsylvania Travel Council (☎ 717-232-8880, fax 717-232-2948, info@patravel.org), Department ULP-VG99, 902 N 2nd St, Harrisburg, PA 17102, or you can find its website at www.patravel.org.

You can also get a copy of the *Pennsylvania Farm Vacation Directory* by sending a stamped, self-addressed, business envelope to Farm Vacations, Department of Agriculture, 2301 N Cameron St, Harrisburg, PA 17110-9408. Its website is at www.pafarmstay.com.

Taxes

Except for clothing and food, which are exempt, the state sales tax is 6%, with an extra 1% in Philadelphia and in Allegheny County (which covers Pittsburgh). This tax does, however, apply to food bought in cafes and restaurants. Local municipalities may also charge their own additional tax. In Philadelphia, for example, there is a 7% city tax on accommodations, which means you pay a total surcharge of 14% on the listed price.

Alcohol

Pennsylvania has a network of state-run liquor stores, called Wine & Spirits Shoppes, throughout the state. Alcohol can only be sold at these package outlets and in restaurants and bars. Grocery stores, supermarkets and delis aren't allowed to sell liquor. Call the Pennsylvania Liquor Control Board (☎ 800-332-7522) for further information, or visit its website at www.lcb.state.pa.us/agency/index.htm.

HISTORY
War of Independence

Owing to its economic strength and large population, Pennsylvania contributed heavily in men, material and financial support to the Revolutionary War. Philadelphia was made the capital of the new nation, and British troops marched into Pennsylvania in September 1777, where they defeated Washington's forces at the Battle of Brandywine. On September 26, the British captured and occupied Philadelphia. Washington tried to retake the city on October 4, but failed and withdrew to Valley Forge, where his forces spent the harsh winter being retrained.

In the meantime, the capital was moved to York, where an American congress approved the Articles of Confederation, which was later to become the country's first constitution. Benjamin Franklin (see the boxed text 'Benjamin Franklin' in the Philadelphia chapter) helped negotiate an alliance with France, the news of which persuaded the British to withdraw to New York from Philadelphia in June 1778. Apart from some loyalist and Indian attacks on settlements, the main campaigns took place in other states for the rest of the war.

The Years after Independence

After the war, it was felt that the Articles of Confederation were no longer adequate to keep the newly independent states together, and in 1787, a federal constitutional convention was held in Philadelphia. On December 12, the Pennsylvania delegates, among whom were four signatories of the Declaration of Independence, ratified the new federal constitution. In 1790, Pennsylvania adopted a new state constitution. New York City had been made the nation's capital after the war, but Philadelphia became the capital again from 1790 to 1800, after which it moved finally to Washington, DC.

The postwar years saw Pennsylvania invest energy and money in internal development, including the construction of an extensive system of canals, turnpikes and, later, railroads. As a result, the population expanded westward and northward. Pennsylvania became the country's main supplier of coal, iron and timber, but agriculture was also important in areas such as Lancaster County. At the same time, Philadelphia and Pittsburgh developed rapidly as manufacturing centers.

Just as merchants and others had opposed excessive British taxation before the Revolutionary War, so some people opposed excessive US federal taxation after the war. During the Whiskey Rebellion of 1794, western Pennsylvania farmers rebelled against taxes on homemade whiskey, which they sold to offset the costs of transporting grain. To suppress the farmers, President George Washington had to call out an army larger than the one he commanded during the Revolutionary War. Five years later, residents of eastern Pennsylvania objected to being taxed based on the number of windows in their houses. This revolt was known as the Hot Water Rebellion, because homeowners threw hot water on assessors. Taxation issues subsided when Thomas Jefferson was elected president in 1800 and reduced taxes.

Slavery wasn't deeply entrenched in Pennsylvania, because the state's Quakers had always been opposed to it. The state's first antislavery society began meeting in 1775, and the legislature passed the Gradual Emancipation Act on March 1, 1780, which said that no child born in Pennsylvania after that date could be enslaved. By 1850, all black people living in the state were free. Many Pennsylvanians also opposed the slavery that existed in the other states. In the state's south, towns such as Gettysburg, Lancaster, York and Chambersburg, near the Maryland border (known as the Mason-Dixon Line, which separated northern 'free' states from southern 'slave' states), became main points on the Underground Railroad – a network of homes and people that helped shelter and guide the slaves during their escape to freedom in Canada.

This opposition to slavery led many into the ranks of the Republican party, which was to dominate state politics until well into the 20th century.

Civil War, Reconstruction & Industrialization

About 350,000 Pennsylvanians, including 8600 blacks, served in the Union army during the Civil War, second only in number to New York. The state's industries, agriculture and natural resources contributed vitally to the North's war effort. It was in Pennsylvania, along the Cumberland Valley, that Southern forces tried to invade the North. The biggest invasion – a force of 75,000 Confederates led by General Robert

PENNSYLVANIA

E Lee – was halted by Union forces under General Meade at the bloody three-day Battle of Gettysburg in July 1863. It caused more casualties than any other battle (and more American casualties than the whole of the Vietnam War) and was a turning point in the Civil War.

Although Pennsylvania's influence on national politics waned in the postwar years, its industrial production expanded enormously, and business magnates gained immense power. The discovery of oil in Titusville in 1859 spawned such giants as John D Rockefeller's Standard Oil Company. Henry Clay Frick bought up the state's coal reserves and he expanded the coke industry. Andrew Carnegie built his huge Carnegie Steel Company, which later became the main component of US Steel, the first billion-dollar corporation in the US.

The workforce for these expanding industries came from waves of European immigrants, and as industry grew in the second half of the 19th century, so did Pennsylvania's labor unions. Local iron molders formed a union in 1859 that eventually grew into the National Labor Union. Coal miners joined the Molly Maguires (a secret group that initially worked for miners of Irish descent) and later the United Mine Workers' Union. Railroad workers joined the Trainsmen's Union. The three largest nationwide organizations of workers were all founded in the state – the Knights of Labor (in 1869), the American Federation of Labor (in 1888) and the Congress of Industrial Organizations (in 1938).

Pittsburgh was the scene of several major labor strikes during this period: the Great Railroad Strike of 1877, the 1892 steel-industry strike at Homestead (a suburb of Pittsburgh) and a strike in the greater Pittsburgh region in 1919 that included the iron, steel and coal industries.

20th Century

During the two world wars, Pennsylvania again played a vital role in supplying materials for the war effort. In WWI, over 300,000 Pennsylvanian men served in the armed forces, and during WWII, official state histories claim, incredibly, that one out of every seven members of the US armed forces was a Pennsylvanian.

Although Pennsylvania's economy was boosted by the world wars, the massive production efforts lasted only a few years after the end of each conflict. Eventually, some of the state's natural resources, such as oil, became exhausted or more difficult and more expensive to extract; there was a decline in the demand for coal, the textile industry departed and there was strong out-of-state and international competition for iron and steel. In response, Pennsylvania moved from heavy industry to service industries, high technology and tourism. A number of corporate giants have made their headquarters in the state, and agriculture continues to be an important part of the economy.

Beginning in the 1930s, Republican dominance of state politics was gradually eroded by Democratic President Franklin D Roosevelt's New Deal (a response to the hopelessness of the Depression), as well as by the influence of organized labor and the urbanization of the state. Philadelphia and Pittsburgh became important Democratic centers. Since the 1930s, political control of the state has alternated regularly between the two parties. In 1986 and 1990, Democrat Robert Casey of Scranton was elected governor; in 1992, Democrats held majorities in both houses of the assembly. In 1994, Republican Tom Ridge was elected governor.

As was common in many US cities, Pennsylvania's major urban centers saw their downtown areas decline during the 1950s, '60s and early '70s, as automobiles increased people's mobility, and many middle-class people took to the suburbs, taking their money with them. Downtown areas were left to the poor, and there was little money to spend on the cities' infrastructure, education system or social services. Since the mid-1970s, however, a number of these downtown areas – initially in Pittsburgh and Philadelphia, but now also in places such as York – have undergone a significant revival.

GEOGRAPHY

Pennsylvania is roughly rectangular, occupying 44,820 sq miles; its share of Lake Erie measures another 735 sq miles. At its longest points, Pennsylvania stretches 310 miles west to east and 180 miles north to south. The Delaware River, in the east, separates the state from New Jersey and New York, while its western border abuts Ohio and West Virginia. To the north is New York state, and in the northwest is a 40-mile stretch of shoreline along Lake Erie; to the south are West Virginia, Maryland and Delaware. Its highest elevation is 3213 feet (on Mt Davis, in the southwest), and its lowest is sea level, on the Delaware River.

Seven geographical regions run diagonally across the state from southwest to northeast.

In the northwestern corner is a narrow strip of the Central Lowland called the Erie Lowland. It follows the Lake Erie shoreline and is excellent for grape growing. It's separated from the Appalachian Plateau (which, in Pennsylvania, is often referred to as the Allegheny Plateau) by an escarpment. The Appalachian Plateau is a large area of low mountains (including the Poconos and the Alleghenies) and deep but narrow valleys separated by smaller plateaus, and it occupies over half the state, including all of western and most of northern Pennsylvania. The horizontal rock layers make it easy to mine bituminous (soft) coal in the southwestern part of the plateau.

Another escarpment, the Allegheny Front, separates the Appalachian Plateau from the next region to the south and east, the Appalachian Ridge & Valley. This is a 50-mile-wide strip of low ridges separated by valleys that sweep and curve northeastward through central Pennsylvania. It includes the Blue, Tuscarora and Bald Eagle Mountains, as well as the Lebanon, Lehigh and Cumberland Valleys. Most of the nation's anthracite (hard) coal comes from here.

Two small regions divide part of the Appalachian Ridge & Valley from the Piedmont Plateau to the south. One, to the southwest, is the northern extension of the Blue Ridge Mountains known as South Mountain, which includes Gettysburg; the other, to the northeast, is the Reading Prong (part of the New England Upland), which juts out from the Delaware River. The Piedmont Plateau consists of fertile limestone lowlands along the southeastern segment of the state, on which lies the Pennsylvania Dutch region. Some of the richest soil in the country lies between the Allegheny River and Philadelphia.

Southeast of the Piedmont Plateau is a tiny strip of the Atlantic Coastal Plain that is now mostly covered by Philadelphia and parts of Bucks and Delaware Counties.

Pennsylvania has three major river systems – the Delaware in the east, the Susquehanna in the middle and the Ohio in the west. Pittsburgh sits at the juncture of the Allegheny, Monongahela and Ohio Rivers. Philadelphia is on the Delaware River (which is second only to the Mississippi in the amount of cargo it carries) and its tributary the Schuylkill River.

CLIMATE

Pennsylvania has a humid continental climate, but some small climatic variations occur within the state, mainly because of elevation. In the southeast around Philadelphia and Pennsylvania Dutch Country, in the area near Lake Erie and along the Ohio and Monongahela River Valleys, the frost-free (or growing) period is longest, around six months. On the Appalachian Plateau, the summers are shorter, and the winters more severe.

Pennsylvania generally gets between 32 and 40 inches of precipitation a year, but snowfall in the colder regions can be well over 60 inches a year. See the Philadelphia and Pittsburgh climate charts in the Facts about the Region chapter.

ECOLOGY & ENVIRONMENT

Pennsylvania has been mining and burning coal for a long time, and its use at one time led Pittsburgh to be given the nickname 'Smokey City.' The state government has imposed stringent environmental regulations on the production and use of coal. The federal government's Clean Air Act and

Clean Water Act also meant that mining companies and electrical utilities had to make their technologies less pollutive.

Southeast of Pittsburgh, the Youghiogheny River was once heavily polluted with waste from the coal mines that were worked beneath the river. It has recovered and now supports intense recreational activity and a flourishing fish population.

About 35% of the state's electricity is produced by nuclear power. Since the nuclear accident at Three Mile Island, near Harrisburg, in 1979, when one of the reactors partially melted (see the South-Central Pennsylvania chapter), the nuclear industry has improved its technology and safety procedures. Many people, however, remain unconvinced that nuclear power can ever be safe, and there is continuing opposition to its use.

One of the world's first environmentalists was Rachel Carson (1907–64) from the small town of Springdale, east of Pittsburgh. In her writing, she expressed the view that human beings were only one part of nature and were distinguished mainly by their power to alter it. Testifying before Congress in 1963, she called for policies to protect the environment and human health.

The Nature Conservancy's Pennsylvania Field Office (☎ 610-834-1323, fax 610-834-6533) is at Lee Park, 1100 East Hector St, suite 470, Conshohocken, PA 19428. The Western Pennsylvania Conservancy (☎ 412-288-2777), 209 4th Ave, Pittsburgh, PA 15222, is an independent organization that preserves natural lands in the west for public use. The two organizations are separate but cooperate on some projects.

STATE PARKS & FORESTS

Pennsylvania has 116 state parks (covering nearly 3750 sq miles) that offer a wide range of activities, from hiking, bicycling, swimming, boating, fishing and white-water rafting in the warmer months to downhill and cross-country skiing in winter. Many parks have visitor centers that, in addition to providing information, offer interpretive programs on nature and environmental issues. For more details, contact the Bureau of State Parks

Pennsylvania is a great place for outdoor pursuits.

(☎ 717-558-2710, 888-727-2757), PO Box 8551, Harrisburg, PA 17105-8551; or visit its website at www.dcnr.state.pa.us.

There are nearly 3240 sq miles of state forests, with over 4500 miles of trails for hiking, bicycling, horseback riding, cross-country skiing and snowmobiling. Within that area, there are 280 sq miles of natural and wilderness areas for wildlife viewing. Information and maps are available from the Bureau of Forestry (☎ 717-783-7941), PO Box 8552, Harrisburg, PA 17105-8552.

The more than 2000 sq miles of state game lands also have hiking and cycling trails. For information and maps contact the Pennsylvania Game Commission (☎ 717-783-7507), Department MS, 2001 Elmerton Ave, Harrisburg, PA 17110-9797; or visit its website at www.pgc.state.pa.us.

GOVERNMENT & POLITICS

Pennsylvania – like Kentucky, Massachusetts and Virginia – is officially designated a 'commonwealth,' which comes from 'common weal,' meaning the general well-being of the population. The term is used interchangeably with the word 'state'; there is no legal distinction between the two. Pennsylvania is governed by a bicameral legislature, or general assembly, consisting of a 50-member senate (elected every four years) and a 203-member house of representatives (elected every two years).

Since the 1950s, Democratic and Republican membership of the general assembly has been split fairly equally. The current state governor, Tom Ridge from Erie, is a moderate Republican. The governor serves a four-year term and may be elected to a maximum of two terms. The basic conservatism of the state is reflected in the Washington, DC, joke that Pennsylvania consists of Philadelphia and Pittsburgh, with Alabama in the middle.

The judiciary is headed by a supreme court comprising a chief justice and six associate justices, who are all elected for 10-year terms. At the local level, Pennsylvania is made up of 66 counties (run by a three-member board of commissioners) and the city-county of Philadelphia, which is administered by a mayor and council.

ECONOMY

Less than 2% of Pennsylvania's residents work in agriculture, but it's the state's chief industry. Over 30% of Pennsylvania is classified as farmland, of which about 70% is used for poultry and dairy farming. The state ranks fourth in the nation in chicken-egg production. Hay and corn (maize) are the main crops, but the most valuable, believe it or not, is button mushrooms. Pennsylvania leads the nation in the production of apples, peaches and cherries, but grapes and berries are also important, as are trees for the Christmas market.

After agriculture, tourism is the next big money-spinner, with foreign and domestic travelers spending more than $10 billion a year in the state.

Pennsylvania is second only to West Virginia in bituminous (soft) coal production, and it produces most of the anthracite (hard) coal in the US, of which it has large reserves. It's also a center for stone, lime-stone, slate, clay and sand. The petroleum industry had its peak year of production in 1891, but northwestern Pennsylvania still has oil (and natural gas), and the Quaker State Company is headquartered in Oil City, where the company's McClintock Well has been operating continuously since 1861.

Manufacturing has always been an important part of the state's economy. Pittsburgh leads the US in iron and steel production, and although the industry has declined relative to other sectors of the economy, it's still strong enough that demand outstrips production. Other leading manufactured products are food (including carbonated drinks, chocolate, meats, ice cream and pretzels), chemicals, building materials, industrial machinery, electronic equipment, precision instruments, paper and glass.

There are 6 million people in Pennsylvania's labor force. The service sector employs 23%. Other jobs are in wholesale and retail sales (21%), manufacturing (20%), trade (18%) and government (12%). The per capita income is around $14,000.

POPULATION & PEOPLE

Pennsylvania is the country's fifth-most populous state, with a little over 12 million people – more than half of whom live in and around Philadelphia or Pittsburgh. Most of Northern Pennsylvania is sparsely populated. The two largest ethnic groups are whites (88.5%) and African-Americans (9.2%). Native Americans number around 15,560. Some other ethnic groups in the state are Latinos (220,480, more than half of whom are Puerto Ricans), Chinese (29,470), East Indians (28,400), Koreans (27,500), Vietnamese (15,000), Filipinos (12,900) and Japanese (6770).

Prior to colonization, Native Indians occupying what is now Pennsylvania were the Leni-Lenape (or Delaware), Susquehannock, Shawnee and Iroquois.

William Penn's tolerant ideals attracted immigrants from Europe, as well as from other British colonies, in the early years. The first to come were English and Welsh Quakers. German Mennonites began arriving in 1683 and founded Germantown near

Philadelphia. Other German sects included the Amish, the Brethren, and the Moravians.

After the first quarter of the 18th century came Scotch and Scotch-Irish immigrants, as well as Germans from the larger Lutheran and Reform churches. Many Irish came in the mid-19th century following a series of famines in their homeland. The latter part of the 19th century saw the pattern of immigration switch to southern and eastern Europe, and the descendants of these people – Slavs, Italians, Poles – form the largest group of Pennsylvania's population. African-American immigration increased in the 20th century, and since the 1960s, the Latino and Asian populations have grown.

EDUCATION

Tinicum was the site of Pennsylvania's first school, which was established by Swedish settlers in the 1640s. William Penn's 1682 Frame of Government called for the education of all children in the colony, and attempts to do this were first made by religious groups. In 1689, Quakers founded the Friends' Public School in Philadelphia, Pennsylvania's first public school. The Free School Act of 1834 provided for free elementary education, and later laws expanded schooling to high schools.

There are now over 3200 public schools, and the largest number of religious schools are Catholic.

There are more than 270 institutions of tertiary education. Pennsylvania State University ('Penn State') is the commonwealth's university and has 21 campuses, the main one being in the town of State College, in central Pennsylvania. Other major tertiary institutions are the University of Pennsylvania ('Penn,' an Ivy League school and the country's first university), Drexel University and Temple University, all in Philadelphia; in Pittsburgh are the University of Pittsburgh and Carnegie-Mellon University. Rural Pennsylvania has many Catholic colleges.

PENNSYLVANIA

Philadelphia

Best known for its historical sites such as the Liberty Bell and Independence Hall – as well as for its cheese steaks and hoagies – Philly (population 1,498,970), as it's often called, is recognized as a major cultural center with world-class museums, performing arts centers and some stunning architecture. Fairmount Park, said to be the world's largest city park, and the tree-lined squares that help form the city's nucleus contrast beautifully with their urban surroundings. Philly's diverse culinary scene ranges from the traditional cheese steaks and Italian food to hundreds of terrific restaurants serving a variety of domestic and international cuisine at all budget levels. Along with the numerous bars, coffeehouses, concerts, galleries and shopping options, Philadelphia is no longer, as it was once cautioned, a place to leave before dark.

Philadelphia was once the butt of jokes by detractors, most memorably the film actor WC Fields, who said 'I'd rather be dead than live in Philadelphia.' (The famous comedian and Philly native requested his epitaph to be 'On the whole I'd rather be in Philadelphia.') The 1976 Bicentennial celebrations inspired the city to renovate its historical buildings and cultural institutions, and the city center has enjoyed a considerable renaissance. And this revitalization is gradually radiating out from the central core.

The city does have its share of crime, urban decay and homelessness, though these are mainly outside the downtown tourist area. The steady decline in the city's population since the 1950s is partly a response to these problems. However, Philadelphia has been ranked by the FBI as the safest of the nation's 12 largest metropolitan areas.

Around the Old City you'll see tourists riding in horse-drawn carriages, lining up to visit Independence Hall or the Liberty Bell, following tour guides around the sights or just resting their feet in the parks. Market St, east of City Hall, is where Philadelphians of every description do their shopping. West of

Highlights

- For anyone interested in the birth of the US, a trip to Independence Hall and the Liberty Bell is a must.

- Along Benjamin Franklin Pkwy there are some great museums culminating in the magnificent Philadelphia Museum of Art on the edge of Fairmount Park.

- City Hall is the country's largest municipal building and an architectural delight; it has great views of the city from the observation deck.

- The Civil War Library & Museum is a must for students of the war.

- The renowned Museum of Archaeology & Anthropology in University City contains archaeological treasures from around the world.

- Eating possibilities are extensive – from the street food carts, to the Italian and Reading Terminal markets, to fine dining at some of the country's best restaurants.

- The Barnes Foundation Gallery in Merion houses an impressive art collection.

- Numerous science museums and children-oriented centers offer lots of educational activities for the inquisitive visitor.

City Hall are the office workers, some of whom cluster in small groups outside their office buildings puffing on a much-needed cigarette. University City, in West Philadelphia, is where college campuses and students dominate.

So ignore the disparaging remarks you may sometimes hear – the 'biggest small town in America' is well worth a visit.

HISTORY

William Penn made Philadelphia his capital in 1682, naming it after the Greek for 'brotherly love.' A survivor of London's Great Fire of 1666, Penn oversaw the plans for the city that included a grid system with wide streets, not the narrow, winding maze that caused so much havoc in England's capital. This format was the inspiration for most American cities.

Philadelphia quickly grew to become the second largest city (after London) in the British Empire, before ceding that title to New York City. Opposition to British policy in the colonies became focused here, and colonial leaders met to plan their course of action. The end result was the Declaration of Independence, and in 1790 the city became the temporary capital of the new United States before Washington, DC, got the job in 1800. The US Constitution was drawn up and first read here in 1786. Often led by the amazingly talented Benjamin Franklin, Philadelphia became a center of exciting new developments in the world of arts and science.

Between 1793 and 1820 Philadelphia suffered five yellow fever epidemics, which killed thousands but led to the construction of the nation's first city water system.

Philadelphia's fortunes declined in the 1800s as New York City took over as the nation's cultural, commercial and industrial center. Philly never regained its initial status, despite the continuation of cultural and educational innovation, commerce and shipbuilding. In the mid-20th century, like many American cities, it suffered an exodus of middle-class people to the suburbs. In the 1970s, lavish celebrations for the nation's bicentennial inspired a massive cleanup and renovation campaign for a Philadelphia that had become notoriously neglected. That renovation and restoration continues today.

ORIENTATION

Philadelphia sits on the west bank of the Delaware River in southeastern Pennsylvania. Most of the central area lies between the Delaware River in the east and the Schuylkill River, a tributary, in the west.

Philadelphia is easy to get around. It's laid out in a grid and most of the major sights and accommodations are within walking distance or a short bus ride or drive from each other. East-west streets are given names. North-south streets are mostly numbered, except for Broad St, the main north-south street (and the equivalent of 14th St), and Front St (the equivalent of 1st St). Market St is the main east-west route and divides the city's center between north and south.

Neighborhoods

Most of your time will probably be spent in the Historic District and Center City, a total of 26 blocks east to west. This part of Philly is laid out around public squares, with City Hall more or less at the center in Penn (formerly Center) Square. The other squares, whose names have also been changed, are: Washington (formerly Southeast) Square, near Society Hill; Rittenhouse (Southwest) Square, west of Broad St; Franklin (Northeast) Square, near Independence Hall; and Logan (Northwest) Square (with Logan Circle in the center), at the southeast end of Benjamin Franklin Pkwy.

The other central areas of interest are University City (in West Philadelphia), Fairmount Park (northwest of downtown) and South Philadelphia.

Historic District This area includes Independence National Historic Park and Old City, with Front and 8th Sts marking its east-west borders, Vine St its northern and South St its southern border. Here you'll find major sights such as the Liberty Bell Pavilion, Independence Hall and Congress

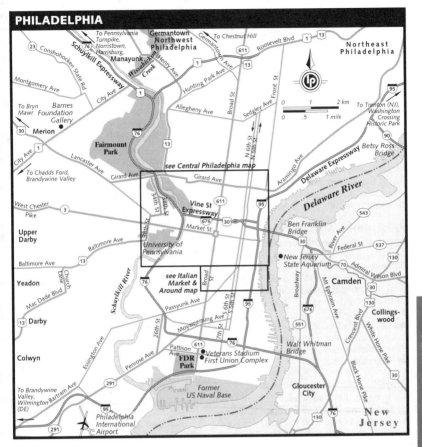

Hall. Also here are the quiet residential streets of Society Hill and the busy South St area.

Penn's Landing, beside the Delaware River, where William Penn's boat docked after arriving from England, has several attractions. Christopher Columbus Blvd (formerly Delaware Ave) on the waterfront alongside the Delaware River has a number of nightclubs, especially north of the Benjamin Franklin Bridge.

This area has two hostels, a B&B and some hotels, along with numerous eating and drinking places.

Center City This part of downtown, from west of the historic district to the Schuylkill River, consists of a mixture of commercial, business and residential neighborhoods. Among the places of interest are City Hall, Antique Row, Chinatown, Reading Terminal Market plus numerous hotels, restaurants and shops.

South Philadelphia Bordered by South St to the north and by the Delaware and Schuylkill Rivers to the east, south and west, South Philadelphia has been the destination of many of the city's waves of immigrants.

The colorful Italian Market is the main draw, along with the many popular restaurants, bars and food shops; a Vietnamese enclave has developed around S 8th St. In the far south are the Veterans and First Union Spectrum sports stadiums. (The major highlights of this area are covered in the South St & Around and Italian Market & Around sections.)

University City West over the Schuylkill River, this area is so called because it's home to the University of Pennsylvania and Drexel University. One of the main attractions is the Museum of Archaeology & Anthropology; also here are the main post office and Amtrak's 30th St Station.

Other Districts Well worth a visit if time permits are the genteel Northwest Philadelphia suburbs of Chestnut Hill, Manayunk and Germantown, which are 4 to 6 miles northwest of downtown; in Merion, you'll find the prestigious Barnes Foundation Gallery.

More central, Northern Liberties, north of Old City between Vine St and Gerard Ave, is the city's oldest neighborhood and where William Penn actually lived. These days, with a few exceptions, it's rundown and has little to see or do.

Maps

The maps in the *Philadelphia Official Visitors Guide* (available free from the Philadelphia Visitors Center in JFK Plaza) are good for most purposes but don't include some of the smaller streets. *Streetwise Philadelphia* is a laminated folding map of downtown and University City and also contains maps of the SEPTA rail and bus system. The Gousha Travel Publications map has details of Greater Philadelphia and includes a street index and a list of places of interest. If you'll be spending some time in and around Philadelphia, it might be worth getting the large-format street atlas *Greater Philadelphia*, by ADC The Map People, which includes Bucks, Chester, Montgomery and Delaware counties. AAA (see Travel Agencies, later in this chapter) provides maps to members.

INFORMATION
Tourist Offices

The Philadelphia Convention & Visitors Bureau (☎ 215-636-1666, 800-537-7676) produces the free *Philadelphia Official Visitors Guide* as well as various special-interest brochures. You can obtain these and other information from the Philadelphia Visitors Center in JFK Plaza at 16th St and JFK Blvd. It is open daily 9 am to 5 pm (Memorial Day to Labor Day to 6 pm). There is also a city visitor information desk in the lobby of the NPS Visitors Center in the Independence National Historic Park and in the baggage-claim area of Terminal A at Philadelphia International Airport, and there is a website (www.libertynet.org/phila-visitor).

Money

The basic banking hours in the city are Monday to Friday 9 am to 3 pm, though there are some variations with certain branches opening earlier and closing later, especially on Friday, and some opening on Saturday. Automatic teller machines (ATMs), known as money access centers (MACs), are readily available around the city and most accept Cirrus, MasterCard, Visa, Honor, Plus System, Express Cash and Discover.

Mellon PSFS Bank has foreign-exchange facilities at its downtown branches: 1417 Walnut St (☎ 215-561-1438) and at 1234 Market St (☎ 215-561-5800).

Thomas Cook (☎ 215-563-7348), 1800 JFK Blvd is open Monday to Friday 9 am to 5 pm. American Express (☎ 215-587-2300), 2 Penn Center Plaza at N 16th St and JFK Blvd, opposite the Philadelphia Visitors Center, also opens Monday to Friday 9 am to 5 pm.

Terminal A at Philadelphia International Airport has a foreign-exchange counter (open for most flight arrivals) in the 1st-floor baggage-claim area and another on the 2nd floor operated by Thomas Cook. Some hotels and restaurants (such as Dickens Inn, ☎ 215-928-9307, Head House Square, S 2nd St) also change money.

Post & Communications

The main post office (☎ 215-596-5577), 2970 Market St opposite Amtrak's 30th St Station in University City, is open 24 hours daily. It has photocopiers and an information desk; general delivery is at the window with the sign '24 Hour Box Caller.' The zip code is 19104.

A more central branch (☎ 215-592-9610) is in the federal building at 900 Market St at 9th St, open Monday to Friday 8:30 am to 6 pm, Saturday 9 am to 4 pm. In the Historic District, the B Free Franklin Post Office (☎ 215-592-1289), 316 Market St, is a working post office with postal workers sometimes dressed in period costume (but charging modern prices), open daily from 9 am to 5 pm.

Cyber Loft (☎ 215-564-4380, mostafa@cyberloft.com), 1525 Walnut Street, is a cybercafe offering access to the Internet for 15¢ a minute if you book for an hour. If you book for a week you pay $25 with 10 hours free and $2 per hour thereafter. You can visit its website at www.cyberloft.com. Another place to try is Access Caffe (☎ 215-988-1891), 1207 Race St; it also has a website (www.access-caffe.com).

The Free Library of Philadelphia (see Libraries, later in this section) has several rooms with computers where you can access the Internet. Ask at the information desk in the lobby. See also the Email & Internet Access section in the Facts for the Visitor chapter.

Internet Resources

There are a number of helpful websites on Philadelphia. A good place to start is the Philadelphia Convention & Visitors Bureau official website (www.libertynet.org/philavisitor). Two useful websites with lots of links to attractions, accommodations, dining, entertainment, transportation and news are www.philly.com and www.libertynet.com.

The free entertainment newspaper *Philadelphia Weekly* has an online version at www.phillyweekly.com as does *City Paper* at www.citypaper.com. Gays and lesbians can check out the virtual version of *Philadelphia Gay News* at www.epgn.com. For informa-

tion about what's happening in University City, go to www.gowest.org and for the University of Pennsylvania visit www.upenn.edu. See also the Internet Resources section in the Facts for the Visitor chapter.

Travel Agencies

HI-AYH Travel Center (☎ 215-925-6004), 624 S 3rd St near South St, sells discounted airline and Amtrak tickets, as well as Eurail passes. It is open weekdays noon to 6 pm, Saturday noon to 4 pm. Council Travel (☎ 215-382-0343, www.ciee.org), 3606A Chestnut St, University City, and STA Travel (☎ 215-568-7999), 1905 Walnut St (with a branch at International House, 3701 Chestnut St), offer competitive discount rates. American Express (see Money, earlier in this section) also provides travel services.

If you're traveling the region by car, AAA (☎ 215-864-5000), 2040 Market St, is a regular travel agency and specializes in auto-travel maps and services. It is open Monday to Friday 8 am to 6 pm. It also has a website at www.aaamidatlantic.com.

Also, check the free weekly *City Paper* or the classified ads in the Sunday edition of the *Philadelphia Inquirer*.

Bookstores

Borders (☎ 215-568-7400), 1727 Walnut St, near Rittenhouse Square, has a wide selection of titles on most subjects and a busy cafe upstairs; it also runs a regular program of author readings and children's events. It's open Monday to Friday 8 am to 10 pm, Saturday 9 am to 10 pm and Sunday 10 am to 7 pm. Nearby, Barnes & Noble (☎ 215-665-0716), 1805 Walnut St, also has a program of events and an upstairs cafe overlooking Rittenhouse Square. It is open Monday to Friday 8 am to 11 pm, Saturday 9 am to 11 pm, Sunday 10 am to 9 pm.

In University City, the large University of Pennsylvania Bookstore (☎ 215-898-7595), on the corner of Walnut and S 36th Sts, carries general titles, including travel guides and maps, as well as academic ones. It is open Monday to Saturday 8:30 am to 11 pm, Sunday 10 am to 6 pm.

The Book Trader (☎ 215-925-9909), located at S 5th and South Sts, is a large store that sells used books and also exchanges and sells records and CDs. Tower Books (☎ 215-925-9909), 425 South St, carries a wide variety of titles. Hibberd's Books (☎ 215-546-8811), 1310 Walnut St, also sells used books and has a knowledgeable staff.

Open daily, Giovanni's Room (☎ 215-923-2960), 345 S 12th St at Pine St, specializes in lesbian and gay titles and acts as a resource center for the gay and lesbian community.

Rand McNally Map & Travel Bookstore (☎ 215-563-1101), 1 Liberty Place at Market St, has a good selection of maps and travel guides as well as travel gear. Traveler's Emporium (☎ 215-546-2021), 210 S 17th St, is another store with a range of travel guides. Both carry Lonely Planet titles.

Libraries
The Free Library of Philadelphia (☎ 215-686-5322), Logan Square at 19th and Vine Sts, was the country's first lending library. It houses over 6 million books, magazines, newspapers, recordings and other materials plus computer databases and Internet access. Feature films, concerts, lectures and children's programs take place on Sunday afternoons. It is open Monday to Wednesday 9 am to 9 pm, Thursday and Friday 9 am to 6 pm, Saturday 9 am to 5 pm and Sunday 1 to 5 pm (closed Sunday June to August). It also sells used books (☎ 215-567-0527) at the rear of the building. Bus No 76 passes by. Visit the library's website for a preview (www.library.phila.gov).

Other libraries include Library Hall (in Independence National Historic Park), the Civil War Library & Museum and Rosenbach Museum & Library (in Center City), all of which are covered later in this chapter.

Laundry
Self-serve laundry facilities are available in hostels and budget hotels, while the more expensive hotels will do your laundry for you. Downtown, at U-Do-It Laundry (☎ 215-735-1255), 1513 Spruce St at S 15th St, open daily 7 am to 11 pm, you can do your own dry cleaning as well as laundry. In

South Philadelphia, Tenth St Cleaners (☎ 215-463-3100), 1141-43 S 10th St at Ellsworth St near the Italian Market, opens daily 7 am to 10 pm.

Medical Services
Philadelphia has many hospitals including the country's first, Pennsylvania Hospital (☎ 215-829-3000), 800 Spruce St at S 8th St, founded by Ben Franklin. Also in the city's center, the Thomas Jefferson University Hospital (☎ 215-955-6000) is at Walnut and S 11th Sts. In University City is the Hospital of the University of Pennsylvania (☎ 215-662-4000), 3400 Spruce St.

Call the Philadelphia County Medical Society (☎ 215-563-5343), 200 Spring Garden St, if you need a doctor to visit you.

Emergency
For police or fire and medical emergencies call ☎ 911. Other important emergency telephone numbers are:

Accidental Poisoning	☎ 215-386-2100
Dentist	☎ 215-925-6050
Lesbian & Gay Violence & Discrimination Hotline	☎ 215-772-2005
Suicide Prevention & Crisis Intervention Center	☎ 215-686-4420
Travelers' Aid Society	☎ 215-546-0571
Women Organized Against Rape (WOAR)	☎ 215-985-3333

Dangers & Annoyances
As in any major city, avoid the bad neighborhoods, especially West Philadelphia to the west of University City, and parts of North Philadelphia. Downtown, the area around Walnut and S 13th Sts gets a bit sleazy at night, particularly on weekends when you may see a few police around.

Stay alert, avoid the subway at night unless you're going to a sports event in South Philly with thousands of others. Watch your wallet and pocketbooks; don't wear expensive watches and jewelry; keep car doors locked when driving as well as when parked; and avoid quiet, poorly lit streets at night.

On Friday and Saturday nights, there's a lot of traffic going to and from and between the nightclubs on the waterfront along Christopher Columbus Blvd (Delaware Ave) north of the Benjamin Franklin Bridge. Pedestrians should be very careful. Also, the amount of traffic in and around South St makes driving there problematic. See also the Dangers & Annoyances section in the Facts for the Visitor chapter.

WALKING TOUR

Much of downtown Philadelphia is best explored on foot. The following suggested walking tour covers Independence National Historic Park and takes in sections of Old City and Center City – you can follow the tour on our Historic District & Waterfront map. Most sites have additional information under their own headings, later in this chapter.

Start at the **NPS Visitors Center**, on S 3rd St, where you can pick up information on the historic park. Outside the visitors' center is the **Bicentennial Bell**, donated to the US by Britain in 1976. As you turn left, on the other side of the road you'll see the Neoclassic **First Bank of the US** (1797), which served as the country's bank until 1811. Further south, at S 3rd and Walnut Sts, is the Greek Revival **Philadelphia Exchange** (1834), which was designed by William Strickland and is being fully restored. These two buildings aren't open to the public.

Turning right on Walnut St you come to a group of 18th-century Georgian buildings, the first of which is **Bishop White House**, home of Reverend William White, first Episcopal bishop of Pennsylvania from 1787 to 1836. At the other end is the headquarters of the **Pennsylvania Horticultural Society**. Continuing west, you'll see **Todd House**, on Walnut St near S 4th St, occupied 1791–93 by lawyer John Todd, before he died of yellow fever.

Turn left (south) on S 4th St then left into Willing's Alley to **St Joseph's Church** (1838). The church that pre-dated the current one was the first Roman Catholic church in the city.

Returning to S 4th St head north past **Carpenters' Hall** (1770), where the First Continental Congress met in 1744, to Chestnut St.

Turn left and cross over S 4th St to the Greek Revival **Second Bank of the US**, home of the National Portrait Gallery. Beside the bank but set further back is **Library Hall**, containing the library of the American Philosophical Society, on the site of the country's first subscription library (1789).

Crossing over S 5th St brings you to several of the most important historical buildings in Philadelphia. The first is **Old City Hall** (1791), which served as the US Supreme Court from 1791 to 1800. Behind it is **Philosophical Hall** (1789), owned by the American Philosophical Society. In the center, **Independence Hall** (1756), a World Heritage Site, is where the Declaration of Independence was adopted and the US Constitution drafted. Beside Independence Hall, at the corner of S 6th St is **Congress Hall**, where the US Congress met between 1790 and 1800 when Philadelphia was the nation's capital.

Independence Hall

CENTRAL PHILADELPHIA

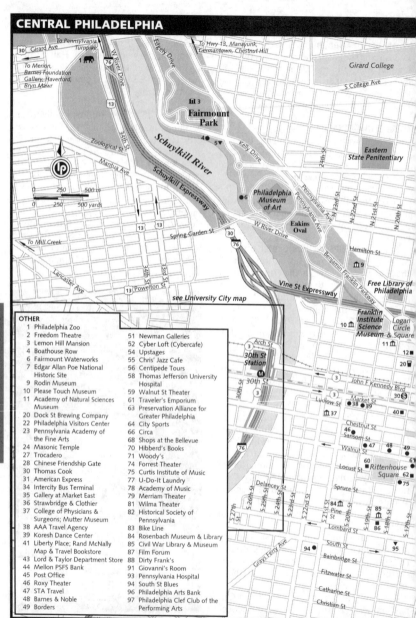

To Pennsylvania
Turnpike

Girard Ave

To Merion,
Barnes Foundation
Gallery; Haverford,
Bryn Mawr

To Hwy 13, Manayunk,
Germantown, Chestnut Hill

Girard College

S College Ave

Fairmount
Park

Eddely Drive

W River Drive

Schuylkill River

Kelly Drive

Eastern
State Penitentiary

Zoological St

Mantua Ave

34th St

Schuylkill Expressway

Philadelphia
Museum
of Art

Pennsylvania Ave

N 23rd St

N 22nd St

N 21st St

N 20th St

Eakins
Oval

To Mill Creek

13

13

W River Drive

Hamilton St

Spring Garden St

Lancaster Ave

34th St

33rd St

Powelton St

see University City map

Vine St Expressway

Benjamin Franklin Parkway

Free Library of
Philadelphia

Franklin
Institute
Science
Museum

Logan
Circle
& Square

OTHER

1 Philadelphia Zoo
2 Freedom Theatre
3 Lemon Hill Mansion
4 Boathouse Row
6 Fairmount Waterworks
7 Edgar Allan Poe National
  Historic Site
9 Rodin Museum
10 Please Touch Museum
11 Academy of Natural Sciences
   Museum
20 Dock St Brewing Company
22 Philadelphia Visitors Center
23 Pennsylvania Academy of
   the Fine Arts
24 Masonic Temple
27 Trocadero
28 Chinese Friendship Gate
30 Thomas Cook
31 American Express
34 Intercity Bus Terminal
35 Gallery at Market East
36 Strawbridge & Clothier
37 College of Physicians &
   Surgeons; Mutter Museum
38 AAA Travel Agency
39 Koresh Dance Center
41 Liberty Place; Rand McNally
   Map & Travel Bookstore
43 Lord & Taylor Department Store
44 Mellon PSFS Bank
45 Post Office
46 Roxy Theater
47 STA Travel
48 Barnes & Noble
49 Borders

51 Newman Galleries
52 Cyber Loft (Cybercafe!)
54 Upstages
55 Chris' Jazz Cafe
56 Centipede Tours
58 Thomas Jefferson University
   Hospital
59 Walnut St Theater
61 Traveler's Emporium
63 Preservation Alliance for
   Greater Philadelphia
64 City Sports
66 Circa
68 Shops at the Bellevue
70 Hibberd's Books
71 Woody's
74 Forrest Theater
77 U-Do-It Laundry
78 Academy of Music
79 Merriam Theater
81 Wilma Theater
82 Historical Society of
   Pennsylvania
83 Bike Line
84 Rosenbach Museum & Library
85 Civil War Library & Museum
87 Film Forum
88 Dirty Frank's
91 Giovanni's Room
93 Pennsylvania Hospital
94 South St Blues
96 Philadelphia Arts Bank
97 Philadelphia Clef Club of the
   Performing Arts

Arch St

30th St
Station

30th St

John F Kennedy Blvd

Market St

Ludlow St

Chestnut St

Sansom St

Walnut St

Rittenhouse
Square

Locust St

Spruce St

Pine
St

Delancey St

S 27th St

S 26th St

S 25th St

S 24th St

S 23rd St

S 22nd St

S 21st St

S 20th St

S 19th St

S 18th St

S 17th St

Lombard St

South St

Grays Ferry Ave

Bainbridge St

Fitzwater St

Catharine St

Christian St

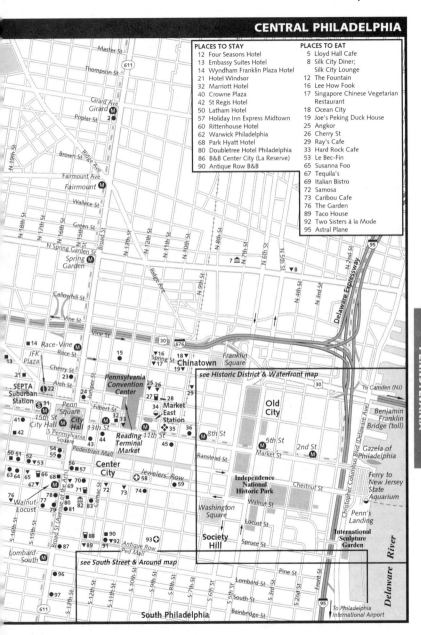

CENTRAL PHILADELPHIA

PLACES TO STAY
12 Four Seasons Hotel
13 Embassy Suites Hotel
14 Wyndham Franklin Plaza Hotel
21 Hotel Windsor
32 Marriott Hotel
40 Crowne Plaza
42 St Regis Hotel
50 Latham Hotel
57 Holiday Inn Express Midtown
60 Rittenhouse Hotel
62 Warwick Philadelphia
68 Park Hyatt Hotel
80 Doubletree Hotel Philadelphia
86 B&B Center City (La Reserve)
90 Antique Row B&B

PLACES TO EAT
5 Lloyd Hall Cafe
8 Silk City Diner;
   Silk City Lounge
12 The Fountain
16 Lee How Fook
17 Singapore Chinese Vegetarian
   Restaurant
18 Ocean City
19 Joe's Peking Duck House
25 Angkor
26 Cherry St
29 Ray's Cafe
33 Hard Rock Cafe
53 Le Bec-Fin
65 Susanna Foo
67 Tequila's
69 Italian Bistro
72 Samosa
73 Caribou Cafe
76 The Garden
89 Taco House
92 Two Sisters á la Mode
95 Astral Plane

PENNSYLVANIA

Save with a CityPass

CityPass is a discount ticket to six of the Philadelphia area's attractions. These are the Academy of Natural Sciences, Franklin Institute of Science Museum, Independence Seaport Museum, Philadelphia Museum of Art, Philadelphia Zoo and – across the Delaware River – the New Jersey State Aquarium & Camden Children's Garden. The pass represents a 50% discount on the normal admission and costs $27.50/20/23.75 for adults/children/seniors. It's good for nine days from the first day of use and is available for sale at the sights mentioned here.

Turn left (south) on S 6th St and walk to Walnut St. As you do so, on your left you pass **Independence Square**, where the Declaration of Independence was read publicly for the first time on July 8, 1776.

Turn right (west) on Walnut St. On the corner of S 6th St is the former **Curtis Publishing Company** building (now converted to apartments) where the celebrated artist Norman Rockwell delivered his paintings for the cover of the *Saturday Evening Post*. Opposite is **Washington Square**, one of the city's original squares. Continue along Walnut St to S 7th St, then make a turn to the right (north).

As you head toward Market St, you pass Sansom St or **Jewelers' Row**, the center of the local jewelry trade. North of Ranstead St is the **Balch Institute for Ethnic Studies** and opposite is **Atwater Kent Museum**, which documents the history of the city. At the corner of S 7th and Market Sts is **Declaration House**, also called Graff House, a reconstruction of the house where Thomas Jefferson wrote the Declaration of Independence.

Turning right (east) on Market St and crossing over 6th St brings you to the **Liberty Bell Pavilion**, housing the revered symbol of American independence. If you continue east along Market St past S 5th and S 4th Sts, you come to a group of 18th-century Geor-

gian buildings, among which is the **B Free Franklin Post Office**; behind them is **Franklin Court**, site of Ben Franklin's home and workplace.

Head back westward and turn right (north) on N 5th St to Arch St. On the corner is the **Free Quaker Meeting House** (1783); unlike other Quakers, the Free Quakers supported and fought in the Revolutionary War. On the other side of the street is **Christ Church Cemetery**, with the graves of Benjamin and Deborah Franklin. On the north side of Arch St is the **US Mint**. East along Arch St you come first to **Arch St Friends Meeting House** (1804) then **Betsy Ross House** (1740); Betsy Ross is believed to have made the first US flag.

Continue east to N 2nd St, turn left (north) then right (east) into **Elfreth's Alley**, a residential thoroughfare with houses dating from the 18th and early 19th centuries and Mantua Maker's Museum House. On N 2nd St just north of the alley is **Fireman's Hall** (1876), originally a firehouse but now a museum.

Back south over Arch St you come to **Christ Church** (1754), once used by many of the city's early dignitaries. Carry on south over Market and Chestnut Sts; just past the entrance to the parking lot is **Thomas Bond House**, former home of the co-founder of the Pennsylvania Hospital and now a B&B. A little further south at the corner of Walnut St is **City Tavern**, a reconstruction of the 1773 original, where you can try some of the kinds of food the people that you have learned about might have eaten.

HISTORIC DISTRICT & WATERFRONT
Independence National Historic Park

This park, combined with the rest of Old City, forms what has been dubbed 'America's most historic square mile.' The L-shaped park is administered by the NPS and covers 45 acres west of the Delaware River between Walnut and Arch Sts and 2nd and 6th Sts. Independence Hall and the Liberty Bell are on most visitors' lists of 'must-sees,' but other sights are well worth

HISTORIC DISTRICT & WATERFRONT

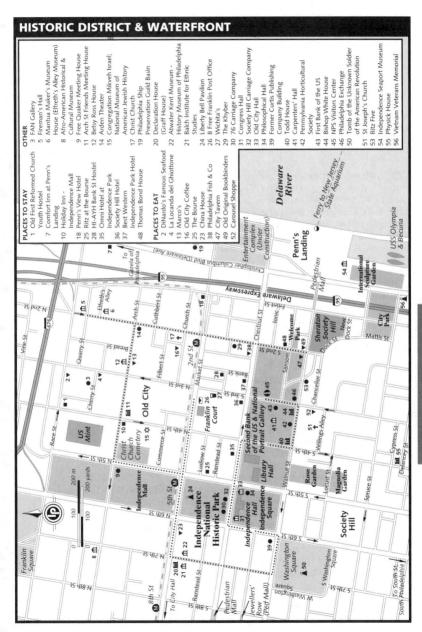

PLACES TO STAY
1 Old First Reformed Church Youth Hostel
7 Comfort Inn at Penn's Landing
10 Holiday Inn - Independence Mall
18 Penn's View Hotel
25 Ritz at the Bourse
28 HI-AYH Bank St Hostel
35 Omni Hotel at Independence Park
36 Society Hill Hotel
37 Best Western Independence Park Hotel
48 Thomas Bond House

PLACES TO EAT
2 DiNardo's Famous Seafood
13 La Locanda del Ghiottone
14 Marco's
16 Old City Coffee
23 China House
38 Philadelphia Fish & Co
47 City Tavern
49 Old Original Bookbinders
52 Carousel Shoppe

OTHER
3 FAN Gallery
5 Fireman's Hall
6 Mantua Maker's Museum House (Elfreth's Alley Museum)
8 Afro-American Historical & Cultural Museum
9 Free Quaker Meeting House
11 Arch St Friends Meeting House
12 Betsy Ross House
14 Arden Theater
15 Congregation Mikveh Israel; National Museum of American Jewish History
17 Christ Church
19 Philadelphia Ship Preservation Guild Basin
20 Declaration House (Graff House)
22 Atwater Kent Museum - History Museum of Philadelphia
21 Balch Institute for Ethnic Studies
24 Liberty Bell Pavilion
26 B Free Franklin Post Office
27 Wichita's
29 The Khyber
30 76 Carriage Company
31 Congress Hall
32 Society Hill Carriage Company
33 Old City Hall
34 Philosophical Hall
39 Former Curtis Publishing Company Building
40 Todd House
41 Carpenters' Hall
42 Pennsylvania Horticultural Society
43 First Bank of the US
44 Bishop White House
45 NPS Visitors Center
46 Philadelphia Exchange
50 Tomb of the Unknown Soldier of the American Revolution
51 St Joseph's Church
53 Ritz Five
54 Independence Seaport Museum
55 Physick House
56 Vietnam Veterans Memorial

PENNSYLVANIA

seeing too. Several sights lie outside the 'L,' in Old City and Center City.

Most places are open daily 9 am to 5 pm, but this can vary by an hour or so, while some hours are extended during the summer and some buildings close on Monday. Admission to the visitors' center and the park's buildings is free, as are the walking tours and other activities. Some buildings in the park aren't open to the public.

To get there take bus No 76 or the SEPTA subway line.

NPS Visitors' Center For an overview, the best place to start is the NPS Visitors' Center (☎ 215-597-8974), near the corner of S 3rd and Chestnut Sts; the staff can answer park questions and give you a map and brochures on attractions, free walking tours and events. A desk operated by the Philadelphia Convention & Visitors Bureau and its website (www.nps.gov/inde) also provide help with general city information.

In the upstairs theater are continuous free showings of the 28-minute film *Independence* (directed by John Huston) about the creation of the US. The visitors' center is open daily 9 am to 5 pm (July and August to 6 pm).

Carpenters' Hall Founded in 1724 to teach its members architectural skills, the Carpenter's Company, America's oldest trade guild, had much influence on Philadelphia's development; its members gave advice on building techniques and worked as architects on many projects. This Georgian building (☎ 215-925-0167), 320 Chestnut St, built in 1770 and still owned by the Carpenter's Company, was designed by Robert Smith (a master carpenter and a leading light of the group). It served as the site of the First Continental Congress in 1774. The exhibits are all carpentry-related and include a scale model of the building during its construction, early tools and some Windsor chairs used by Congress delegates. It is open Tuesday to Sunday 10 am to 4 pm.

Second Bank of the US Modeled after the Greek Parthenon, this 1824 marble-faced Greek Revival masterpiece was home to the world's most powerful financial institution until its charter was dissolved by President Andrew Jackson in 1836 – he didn't approve of the bank's conservative policies. The building then became the Philadelphia Customs House till 1935; it was restored in 1974.

The bank is now home to the **National Portrait Gallery**, with several pieces by Charles Willson Peale, America's top portraitist at the time of the American Revolution, whose subjects were among the most prominent men of the day. (See Painting in the Art section of the Facts about the Region chapter.) Other exhibits include a copy of the first edition of the Declaration of Independence (the original is in Washington, DC) and early prints of Philadelphia when it was the nation's capital. Entry is $2 for adults, free for children.

Library Hall Worth a visit to see a copy of the Declaration of Independence (handwritten by Thomas Jefferson), first editions of Darwin's *Origins of Species* and Lewis and Clark's field notes, this is the research library and offices of the American Philosophical Society. The site on which the library sits was originally home to the first subscription library in the US. The Library Company of Philadelphia, a forerunner of the Library of Congress, was later founded here in 1789, remaining until 1888 when the building was demolished. The present building, at 105 S 5th St, was constructed in 1959, and its facade is an exact reproduction of the original.

Independence Hall Independence Hall, on Chestnut St between S 5th and S 6th Sts, is a World Heritage Site. The birthplace of American government, it was built between 1732 and 1756 and started life as Pennsylvania State House, the colony's headquarters. At that time, it was on the outskirts of the city. The Second Continental Congress met here from 1775 to 1783. In the Assembly Room the delegates from the 13 colonies met to approve the Declaration of Independence (July 4, 1776) and the design of the

US flag (1777), the Articles of the Confederation were drafted (1781) and the Constitutional Convention produced the US Constitution (1787). The assassinated body of President Abraham Lincoln lay in state here on April 22, 1865.

One of the country's best examples of Georgian architecture, the hall's simple, understated lines show the Quaker influence of Philadelphia's early days. British troops used the furniture in the 1st floor's two rooms and the large central hallway for firewood when they occupied the city from 1777–78. What you see today are examples from the period. The **Supreme Court Chamber** is to your right as you enter. The Pennsylvania coat of arms, dating from 1785, hangs over the judge's chair. It replaced King George III's coat of arms, which was publicly burned outside in Independence Square after the Declaration of Independence was read in public for the first time.

The **Assembly Room**, across the hall, is where the events mentioned above took place, and you can see original fixtures, including the chair George Washington used during the Constitutional Convention. The 2nd floor features the **Governor's Council Chamber**, where royal governors conducted affairs of state; the **Long Gallery**, where American patriots were imprisoned by the British during the Revolution; and the **Committee of the Assembly's Chamber**, which has a display of weapons used during the war.

To see the building you need to join one of the free tours that run about every 15 minutes between 9 am and 3 pm from behind the hall in Independence Square. Lasting about 30 minutes, these tours can be crowded. Try to visit early or later in the day during the peak seasons – May through June and late September through October.

Congress Hall When Philadelphia was the nation's capital, this Federal-style west wing of Independence Hall, originally the Philadelphia County Courthouse, is where the US Congress met 1790–1800. Here, the Bill of Rights (the first 10 amendments) was added to the Constitution, the US Mint was established, George Washington was inaugurated for his second term and Vermont, Kentucky and Tennessee were admitted to the Union. Beautifully restored and still with some of its original furnishings, the hall is at S 6th and Chestnut Sts.

Old City Hall Built in 1791, Old City Hall, at S 5th and Chestnut Sts, was home to the US Supreme Court until 1800, while Philadelphia was the nation's capital. It became City Hall when the federal government moved to Washington, DC. In 1901, the local government moved over to Center Square. Today the hall contains exhibits on the early Supreme Court and the daily life of Philadelphia's late-18th-century citizens.

Philosophical Hall Behind Old City Hall is Philosophical Hall (☎ 215-440-3400), home of the American Philosophical Society, which was founded in 1743 by Benjamin Franklin and is the US's oldest learned society. Past members have included Thomas Jefferson, Marie Curie, Thomas Edison, Charles Darwin and Albert Einstein. The society is still active in many fields, including medicine, computers, literary studies and quantum physics. It isn't open to the public.

Independence Square This pleasant park, behind the Independence Hall complex, is where the Declaration of Independence was first read in public on July 8, 1776. Today, it makes a great spot to sit and relax and is an attractive shortcut between Walnut and Chestnut, S 5th and 6th Sts.

Liberty Bell Pavilion Philadelphia's top tourist attraction, the famous bell is housed in an unattractive glass-and-concrete pavilion on Market St (between S 5th and 6th Sts), but there are plans to replace the pavilion with a new, larger building.

Commissioned to commemorate the 50th anniversary of the Charter of Privileges (Pennsylvania's constitution enacted in 1701 by William Penn), this 2080-pound bronze bell was made in London's East End by the Whitechapel Bell Foundry. The

PENNSYLVANIA

The Liberty Bell – all it's cracked up to be

bell's inscription, from Leviticus 25:10, reads: 'Proclaim liberty through all the land, to all the inhabitants thereof.' The bell was secured in the belfry of the Pennsylvania State House (now Independence Hall) and tolled on important occasions, most notably the first public reading of the Declaration of Independence in Independence Square. The bell became badly cracked during the 19th century; despite initial repairs it eventually became unusable in 1846 after tolling for George Washington's birthday.

The bell only became famous after it was adopted by slavery abolitionists in the mid-19th century, who were inspired by its biblical inscription, which they took to symbolize liberty. In 1976 the bell was moved from Independence Hall for the country's Bicentennial celebrations as the large number of visitors couldn't be accommodated there. Visitors are admitted to the pavilion in groups, and a park ranger gives a rundown of its history. The bell is floodlit after dark, and when the pavilion is closed you can listen to a recorded commentary outside.

Franklin Court This complex, a tribute to Benjamin Franklin, is built on the site where he lived and worked. On Market St, he rented out a row of tenements that have been restored with exhibits illustrating some of his work. An archway leads to the courtyard where his house used to stand, now marked by a steel frame in the shape of the house. An **Underground Museum** displaying Franklin's various inventions reveals just how much this genius managed to achieve in a lifetime that spanned most of the 18th century. There's also a short biographical film and a phone bank where actors give voice to comments made about him by his contemporaries. The museum is open daily 9 am to 5 pm.

Franklin was the nation's first postmaster and **B Free Franklin Post Office** (☎ 215-592-1289), 316 Market St, is a working post office with period furniture. Upstairs the **US Postal Service Museum** illustrates US postal history, with exhibits including pony express pouches and originals of Franklin's *Pennsylvania Gazette*; it is open 9 am to 5 pm.

Inspired by the Great Fire of London, Franklin designed the fireproof structure next door at 318 Market St. His **printing office and bindery** at 320 Market St has working demonstrations of his equipment. At 322 Market St is a replica of an office of the *Aurora & General Advertiser*, a newspaper published by Franklin's grandson.

Christ Church This beautiful Episcopal church (☎ 215-922-1695), at Church and N 2nd Sts, was built in 1744. Its white steeple, added in 1754, dominated the city skyline in those early days. George Washington, Benjamin Franklin and Betsy Ross worshiped here, and the signers of the Declaration of Independence prayed here on July 5, 1776. It is open Monday to Saturday 9 am to 5 pm, Sunday 1 to 5 pm, and a donation is requested. Three blocks west on N 5th St is **Christ Church Cemetery**, containing the graves of some of the city's dignitaries. Although you can't enter you can easily see the grave of Benjamin and Deborah Franklin. There's a good view of

The Amazing Mr Franklin

A visit to Philadelphia should give you a deep appreciation for the talents and achievements of this remarkable man – a newspaperman, scientist, inventor, philosopher, politician and diplomat.

Born in Boston, the son of a soap maker, Franklin (1707–90) joined the workforce at the age of 12 as an apprentice at his brother's printshop. He moved to Philadelphia in 1723 and founded the *Pennsylvania Gazette*, which soon became the colonies' top newspaper. He became involved in local politics by helping to launch public works projects to pave, clean and light Philadelphia's streets. He founded America's first circulating library, the American Philosophical Society, and an academy that would later become the University of Pennsylvania. While still in his 20s, he invented flippers for swimming, and in 1743 he invented a heat-efficient stove to warm houses. In 1748, he retired from the newspaper business to study electricity. In a famous experiment, he verified the identity of electricity in lightning by using a kite and in the process invented the lightning rod.

By now a political leader in Pennsylvania, Franklin sailed to Britain in 1757 to represent the colony. He became an agent for several other colonies and the de facto ambassador for all 13. He had supported a united empire, but was disillusioned by the corrupt ways of the British political and aristocratic scene. He gradually became opposed to British taxes on the colonies, and when he returned to America in 1775 he caused a stir by declaring his support for independence.

Franklin worked with Thomas Jefferson to draft the Declaration of Independence, served in the Continental Congress, then sailed to France in 1776 to become ambassador to the court of Louis XVI. Dressed in simple Quaker clothes, he made quite an impression in his extravagant surroundings as a great speaker. His popularity helped him persuade the French king to stand by the 1778 Treaty of Alliance, saving the struggling American Revolution from certain bankruptcy. Franklin remained in France for five years, playing a pivotal role in the important European side of the struggle.

Returning to America in 1784, he was involved in the final draft of the US Constitution in 1787. Shortly before his death, at the age of 84, his final public act was to sign a memorial to Congress urging the abolition of slavery.

Among the other public enterprises Franklin either launched or helped to create were the first fire-fighting company in America, the first fire-insurance company, street lighting and paving, the reorganization of the town watch, a local militia, the post office and the country's first hospital.

PENNSYLVANIA

the cemetery from the windows on the 2nd floor of the US Mint.

Declaration House Thomas Jefferson drafted the Declaration of Independence in rented rooms on this site at Market and S 7th Sts. The 18th-century house was de-

molished in 1883 and reconstructed in 1975 for the Bicentennial. It's also known as Graff House after the original owner, Jacob Graff. There's an exhibition of Jefferson memorabilia, an eight-minute documentary film about him called *The Extraordinary Citizen* and replications of his two upstairs rooms with period furnishings including reproductions of the chair and desk he used to write the declaration. It is open daily 9 am to 1 pm.

Todd House Lawyer John Todd lived here from 1791 to 1793 before dying of yellow fever during an epidemic that hit the city. His widow, Dolley Payne Todd (1768–1849), later became Dolley Madison, wife of James Madison, the nation's fourth president. The Georgian redbrick house, at S 4th and Walnut Sts, is typical of a middle-class home in the late 18th century. You can only visit as part of one of the popular free park service tours. To be sure of a spot, get your ticket at the visitors' center early in the morning.

Bishop William White House This house, at 309 Walnut St, is the restored home of Reverend William White, first bishop of the Episcopal Diocese of Pennsylvania. Built in 1787, the house's eight levels reflect 18th-century, upper-class Philadelphia life and are furnished with period pieces. Again, to be sure of a space in the free park service tour, get your ticket early at the visitors' center.

Old St Joseph's Church This is the site of the city's first Roman Catholic church, built in 1733 when Catholic services were strictly banned in Britain and its empire. Nevertheless, William Penn tolerated all faiths in his colony though, as a precaution, the church was purposely hidden from view by an alley and courtyard. Its pastor dressed as a Quaker when traveling around the city. Irish and German craftsmen and domestic staff dominated the original congregation. The current church, built in 1839, is at 321 Willing's Alley. Check at the rectory (☎ 215-923-1733) daily between 10 am and 4 pm about visiting the church when services aren't being held.

Philadelphia Exchange Another beautiful piece of architecture, this Greek Revival building, at S 3rd and Walnut Sts, stands out from its Federal and Georgian brick neighbors with its semicircular Corinthian portico and lantern tower. It was designed in the

1830s by William Strickland, who was also responsible for the nearby Second Bank of the US. The country's first stock exchange opened here in 1834 and operated until the Civil War. The building is being fully restored and is closed to the public.

Old City
Along with Society Hill, Old City – the area within Walnut and Vine Sts and Front and 6th Sts – *was* Philadelphia in the city's early days. As the city developed, the neighborhood's proximity to the Delaware River inspired the construction of warehouses, factories, banks and stores. When the city's manufacturing center relocated further west, the neighborhood declined, and it wasn't until the gentrification of Society Hill in the 1970s that people started to look at Old City's dilapidated warehouses as suitable for conversion into apartments, galleries and other small businesses. The area has some great old buildings, especially Georgian ones, which have been revitalized, but a few remain rundown. Unfortunately, the Old City is now separated from the river by I-95 (Delaware Expressway), though footbridges over the expressway connect it with Penn's Landing.

Elfreth's Alley Believed to be America's oldest residential street, this picturesque alley connects N Front St with N 2nd St. However, the huge concrete wall at the western end of the alley blocking off I-95 detracts a little from its aesthetic impact. Along the alley, 33 privately owned houses date from 1728 to 1836. The small **Mantua Maker's Museum House** (☎ 215-574-0560), at No 126 and also called Elfreth's Alley Museum, has period furniture and changing exhibits. It is open daily 10 am to 4 pm, weekends only in January. Admission costs $2/1 for adults/children, which includes a guided tour.

Fireman's Hall North of Elfreth's Alley, this restored 1876 firehouse, 147 N 2nd St, is a museum (☎ 215-923-1438) that portrays the history of fire fighting in America with a terrific collection of fire-fighting memorabilia, graphics, photographs, film and restored early models of pumpers and rolling stock. The 1st floor deals with the early days, showing bucket brigades and the rise of an organized volunteer department led by Ben Franklin. It also houses several large fire trucks. The 2nd floor deals with the inception of the paid department, with models of early equipment and fire-fighting techniques. Brass name plaques list those who died in the line of duty.

Other exhibits include a fireboat wheelhouse and a re-creation of the typical living quarters of early professional firefighters. The museum is open Tuesday to Saturday 9 am to 5 pm. A donation is requested.

Betsy Ross House Some uncertainty surrounds Betsy Griscom Ross (1752–1836), an 18th-century upholsterer and seamstress. Although it's now known that she didn't design the American flag, she may or may not have sewn the first US flag for the early federal government. This is either the house where she lived or it's next to the site where her house once stood. Though sparsely furnished, inside the two-story house (☎ 215-627-5343), 239 Arch St, built in 1740 (but restored to how it appeared in early 1777), you can see Betsy's sewing machine and other tools. It is open Tuesday to Sunday from 9 am to 5 pm; a donation of $2/1 for adults/children is requested.

Arch St Meeting House Arch St Meeting House (☎ 215-627-2667), 320 Arch St at N 4th St, was built in 1804 on land donated by William Penn and is the country's largest Quaker meeting house. It's a good place to learn more about the Quakers, who still meet here twice a week. A receptionist answers questions and there's a small exhibit on Quakerism and a 14-minute slide show about William Penn. It is open Monday to Saturday 10 am to 4 pm and a $1 donation is requested.

US Mint The US Mint (☎ 215-408-0114), on Arch St opposite Christ Church Cemetery (of which there is a good view from the 2nd floor), is the world's largest mint, and the

fourth one built on this site (the current building dates from 1969). It makes coins (including over one million Lincoln pennies a day!) and medals, performs designing and engraving and processes mutilated coins. There are self-guided audiovisual tours, and you can watch the coinage operation from a long, glass-enclosed gallery. It is open July and August daily 9 am to 4:30 pm, May and June Monday to Saturday, September to April Monday to Friday. Admission is free.

Balch Institute for Ethnic Studies The institute (☎ 215-925-8090), 18 S 7th St, whose purpose is to promote greater understanding between different ethnic groups, has a small museum documenting Philadelphia's and other cities' immigrant experience. It also has changing exhibitions, workshops, film screenings and lectures. In the lobby, a computer tells you which city organizations cater to which ethnic group. The institute opens Monday to Saturday 10 am to 4 pm; entry is $3/1.50 for adults/children. Its website is at www.balchinstitute.org.

Atwater Kent Museum – History Museum of Philadelphia Over 300 years of the city's social history and local culture are represented at the museum (☎ 215-922-3031, www.philadelphiahistory.org), 15 S 7th St. Its collection of more than 75,000 artifacts – including military uniforms, dolls, model ships and radios – are used to depict ordinary daily life in Philadelphia's past. It acquired the Norman Rockwell Museum's exhibits when that museum closed, and there is a permanent exhibition of Rockwell's work here. The museum is open Wednesday to Monday 10 am to 5 pm. Admission costs $3/1.50/2 for adults/children/seniors, but it's free Sunday 10 am to noon.

Congregation Mikveh Israel Congregation Mikveh Israel (☎ 215-922-5446), 44 N 4th St, was founded in 1740 and is the oldest congregation in Philadelphia, the second oldest in the country. There are services Friday at 7:15 pm, Saturday at 8 or 9 am and 7 pm, and on Jewish holidays. Among the artifacts is a letter from George Washington to

PENNSYLVANIA

First Friday & Third Thursday

If you're in Philly between October and July, be sure to enjoy 'First Friday.' On the first Friday of each month, the 40-plus Old City galleries, showrooms and cooperatives stay open until 9 pm. Young artists, students and other onlookers hang out and enjoy the exhibits. Things get going around 5 pm. For details call ☎ 215-592-7752.

Similar events take place on the 'Third Thursday' of each month in University City. For information call ☎ 888-469-3787 or check the website (www.gowest.org).

the congregation, thanking them for their congratulations to him on his becoming president.

Next door, in the same building (and using the same entrance) is the **National Museum of American Jewish History** (☎ 215-923-3811), the country's only museum devoted to the role of Jews in American history. The American Jewish Experience is a permanent exhibition and there are other smaller changing exhibits. The museum is open Monday to Thursday 10 am to 5 pm, Friday 10 am to 3 pm, Sunday noon to 5 pm. Admission costs $3/2 for adults/children.

Afro-American Historical & Cultural Museum

The museum (☎ 215-574-0380), 701 Arch St at N 7th St, contains one of the country's best collections on black history and culture. It has exhibits on African heritage through slavery, emancipation, the civil rights movement and beyond. There's also a renowned gift shop selling craftwork. The museum is open Tuesday to Saturday 10 am to 5 pm, Sunday noon to 6 pm. Admission costs $6/4 for adults/children.

Society Hill

Society Hill is between S 6th and S Front Sts and Walnut and Lombard Sts, straddling Independence National Historic Park. This is a lovely residential neighborhood dominated by 18th- and 19th-century architecture and named after the Free Society of Traders, a group of businesspeople who settled here with their families in 1683 at the behest of William Penn. The area underwent major restoration during the 1960s and '70s. It's a pleasant place to stroll through, especially Delancey, American, Cypress and Philip Sts, narrow side streets lined with an attractive mix of colonial and contemporary homes, renovated warehouses converted into art galleries and high-end apartments.

Washington Square On the northwest edge of Society Hill, this square is one of those in William Penn's original city plan, and its shaded benches offer a peaceful respite from a day's sight-seeing. The **Tomb of the Unknown Soldier** is the country's only monument to the unknown American and British dead of the Revolutionary War. The square was once an upper-class residential district, and in the 19th century Philadelphia's publishing industry became concentrated in the surrounding offices. These days, there's a mix of apartments as well as various offices and small businesses.

Pennsylvania Horticultural Society The society's headquarters (☎ 215-625-8250), 325 Walnut St, offer a soothing escape from the streets. There's a 1st-floor exhibition of flower-related artwork and a beautiful 18th-century formal garden beside the building. It is open Monday to Friday 9 am to 5 pm and admission is free. In late February/early March the spectacular Philadelphia Flower Show (at the Pennsylvania Convention Center) is organized by the society.

Physick House Built in 1786 by Henry Hill, a wine importer, and home later to Dr Philip Syng Physick (known as the father of American surgery and whose patients included Andrew Jackson), this is the only freestanding, Federal-style mansion remaining in Society Hill. Restored in the 1960s, it's one of the few sites still displaying original Neoclassic furnishings. The house (☎ 215-925-7866), 321 S 4th St at Delancey St, opens Thursday to Saturday 11 am to 2 pm. Admission costs $3/2 for adults/children and includes a guided tour.

Benjamin Franklin Bridge

The world's largest suspension bridge (1.8 miles long) when it was completed in 1926 at a cost of $37 million, the 800,000 ton Benjamin Franklin Bridge crosses the Delaware River between Philly's Old City and Camden, NJ, with the waterfront piers below. The bridge dominates the skyline here, especially at night when it's beautifully lit – each cable is illuminated by computer in a domino-like effect to follow the trains as they cross.

Penn's Landing

This is the riverfront area between Vine and South Sts and separated from the city by I-95 (Delaware Expressway). Once Philadelphia's main commercial district, it fell into decline as shipping became concentrated at the southern end of the city. In the 1960s redevelopment of the area began, and the rotting piers were replaced by the current system of footbridges over I-95 from Chestnut and Walnut Sts. The Great Plaza amphitheater, built as part of that redevelopment, was a popular site for free concerts, festivals and ethnic celebrations, but is being replaced by a new, large, family entertainment complex presently under construction. For information call ☎ 215-922-2386 or check the website at www.pennslandingcorp.com.

Independence Seaport Museum The ground floor of this maritime museum (☎ 215-925-5439, www.libertynet.org/~seaport), 211 S Columbia Blvd, contains descriptions of Philadelphia's shipyard (which closed in 1995 after 200 years) with photos and audiotaped oral histories of people who worked there. There are also displays on underwater exploration, hunting, fishing, rowing on the Delaware and Schuylkill Rivers and models of ships.

Another section of the museum focuses on immigration. Before the growth of New York City, Philly was the country's main arrival point for immigrants and the busiest trading port. There's also the Workshop on the Water for boat-building artisans and for teaching would-be small-boat builders. Children enjoy the interactive devices like the one that uses a crane to simulate the unloading of a ship's cargo. Upstairs, the library contains over 12,000 books on maritime matters, plus manuscripts, photos and ships' plans.

The museum is open daily 10 am to 5 pm and admission costs $5/2.50/4 for adults/children/seniors, free for children under five. A combined ticket to see the museum and USS *Olympia* and USS *Becuna* is $7.50/3.50/6, free for children under five. Another combined ticket, the 'Riverpass,' which includes entry to the New Jersey State Aquarium (see later in this section) and a return ferry trip costs $18.50/13.50/16.

USS *Olympia* & *Becuna* The former naval cruiser and submarine now serve as floating museums (☎ 215-922-1898). The USS *Olympia*, one of America's first steel ships and one of the few survivors of the Spanish-American War, saw action at the Battle of Manila Bay, in 1898. The submarine USS *Becuna*, commissioned in 1944, served in WWII and the Korean and Vietnam Wars. Both are open May through October daily 10 am to 5 pm (Memorial Day to late September, weekends to 6 pm). Admission costs $5/2.50/4 for adults/children/seniors.

Vietnam Veterans Memorial Dedicated in 1987, this memorial honoring the 80,000 Philadelphians who served in the Vietnam War, including the 642 who died, is at Christopher Columbus Blvd and Spruce St. The black 'Missing in Action' flags fly alongside the Stars and Stripes.

Philadelphia Ship Preservation Guild Basin The *Gazela of Philadelphia*, a 177-foot, square-rigged tall ship built in 1883, operates as a training vessel and museum. When it's not out sailing you can visit it near the corner of Christopher Columbus Blvd and Market St. Opening hours vary according to sailing schedules: call ☎ 215-923-9030.

A donation is requested. The tug *Jupiter* also docks here.

New Jersey State Aquarium Across the Delaware River in Camden, NJ, is the region's largest aquarium (☎ 800-616-5297). For admission costs and opening hours, see the Camden section in the Central New Jersey chapter.

Taking the Riverlink ferry (☎ 215-925-5465) from Penn's Landing to the aquarium saves you the hassle of dealing with traffic, the Benjamin Franklin Bridge and parking. The ferry takes 10 minutes and offers a good view of Philly. Boats run every 30 minutes Monday to Friday 10 am to 5 pm, weekends 10 am to 9 pm. The roundtrip fare is $5/3/4.

SOUTH ST & AROUND

Usually compared to New York's Greenwich Village, South St (specifically the area between S 2nd to 10th Sts and stretching north to Pine St and south to Fitzwater St) is a concentrated neighborhood of funky, bohemian boutiques, eating and drinking places and music venues. It's a popular place for a night out on the town.

You should visit the area at least once at night and also during the day to see more of what's here. Try not to drive, though – the volume of commercial and other traffic and the lack of parking space plus the number of pedestrians make it pointless.

Head House Square

Between Pine and South Sts, this attractive square is named after the fire-engine houses, called 'head houses,' built in the early 19th century. With cupolas, alarm bells and a fire officers' social club upstairs, the head house at Second and Pine Sts escaped demolition and was restored. The shed between Lombard and Pine Sts was one of several built in 1745 for street trading; also restored, it's home to an open-air craft market on summer weekends.

Mother Bethel AME Church

Founded by two local freed slaves in 1787, this is the South St area's major historic building and is regarded as the birthplace of the African Methodist Episcopal (AME) Order. As a stop on the Underground Railroad, this church and its pastor, Richard Allen, hid hundreds of fugitive slaves prior to the Civil War.

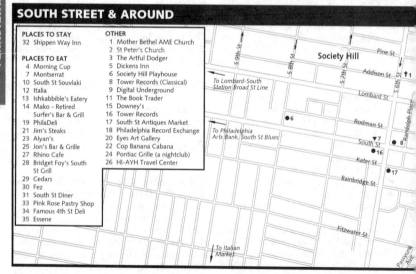

SOUTH STREET & AROUND

PLACES TO STAY
32 Shippen Way Inn

PLACES TO EAT
4 Morning Cup
7 Montserrat
10 South St Souvlaki
12 Italia
13 Ishkabbible's Eatery
14 Mako - Retired Surfer's Bar & Grill
19 PhilaDeli
21 Jim's Steaks
23 Alyan's
25 Jon's Bar & Grille
27 Rhino Cafe
28 Bridget Foy's South St Grill
29 Cedars
30 Fez
31 South St Diner
33 Pink Rose Pastry Shop
34 Famous 4th St Deli
35 Essene

OTHER
1 Mother Bethel AME Church
2 St Peter's Church
3 The Artful Dodger
5 Dickens Inn
6 Society Hill Playhouse
8 Tower Records (Classical)
9 Digital Underground
11 The Book Trader
15 Downey's
16 Tower Records
17 South St Antiques Market
18 Philadelphia Record Exchange
20 Eyes Art Gallery
22 Cop Banana Cabana
24 Pontiac Grille (a nightclub)
26 HI-AYH Travel Center

The present church (☎ 215-925-0616), 419 S 6th St, is the fourth one built on this site; it dates from 1890 and was restored in 1987. Most of the congregation now live in West Philadelphia, but still worship here. A small, free museum opens officially Tuesday to Saturday 10 am to 2 pm, but may not always be open at that time so it's best to call ahead.

St Peter's Church

Robert Smith, who also built Christ Church and Carpenters' Hall, built this beautiful church in 1758–64 (though people started using it in 1761) when Christ Church was unable to cater to the growing Anglican congregation. Apart from the mid-19th century steeple, the church (☎ 215-925-5968), at Pine and S 3rd Sts, looks much as it did when George Washington and his family worshiped here. Buried in the graveyard is the artist Charles Willson Peale. The church opens Saturday 11 am to 3 pm, Sunday 1 to 3 pm.

ITALIAN MARKET & AROUND

This area, which makes up part of South Philadelphia, has been settled by succeeding waves of immigrants, from the Dutch and Swedish settlers of the 17th century, through the Jewish and Italian arrivals in the 19th and early 20th centuries, to the black, Hispanic and Asian settlers of more recent years. The Italian Market is still largely Italian, but vendors and customers alike reflect this ethnic diversity. The area is served by SEPTA's Broad St Line and by bus Nos 2, 5, 17, 23, 47 and 50 from downtown.

The Italian Market, on S 9th St (between Christian St and Washington Ave) is the country's largest outdoor market. The stalls and specialty stores offer sights, sounds and smells rarely found in this age of supermarkets and gourmet stores. Closed on Sunday and Monday, the market's pace builds up during the week to the busiest days of Friday and Saturday. The market offers a wide selection of items at low prices, and locals regularly travel miles to shop here. Easter and Christmas are especially good times to visit.

As well as the street stalls and the many butchers on S 9th St, look out for D'Angelo Brothers, specializing in sausages and paté; Claudio's with its cheese and olive selection; Talluto's, a traditional Italian deli; and Fante's Cookware (see Places to Eat and Shopping, later in this chapter).

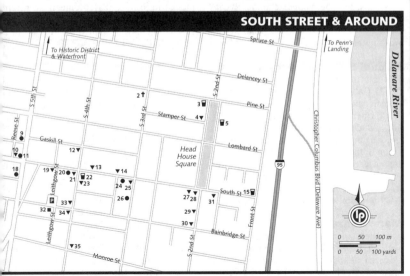

SOUTH STREET & AROUND

PENNSYLVANIA

ITALIAN MARKET & AROUND

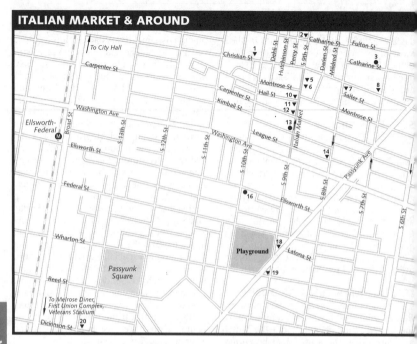

Nearby, the Vietnamese community has established shops and restaurants on and around S 8th St between Christian St and Washington Ave.

Samuel S Fleisher Art Memorial

This is a free art school (☎ 215-922-3456), 709-21 Catharine St, founded by a wealthy woolens manufacturer in 1898, now housed in a former church. Administered today by the Philadelphia Museum of Art, it has a good art museum open to the public. In addition to the regular exhibits, four highly regarded art shows are held here during the year. It also offers free art lessons. It is open weekdays 11 am to 5 pm and 6:30 to 9:30 pm. Admission is free.

Mario Lanza Museum

Local legend and international celebrity Mario Lanza (1921–59) was born Freddie Cocozza nearby at 634 Christian St. The museum (☎ 215-468-3623) is in the Settlement Music School, 416 Queen St, where the tenor singer and movie actor first studied singing. It's on the 3rd floor in a room dedicated to his talents and full of photos, stills from his films, posters and other memorabilia. Films of his performances are also shown. The museum opens Monday to Saturday 10 am to 3:30 pm (closed Saturday in July and August). Admission is free.

Gloria Dei (Olde Swedes') Church

Philadelphia's original settlers were Swedish Lutherans and this is the site of their first church, built in 1643. The original log structure was replaced in 1700 by the current brick version, which is the oldest church building in Philadelphia. The church (☎ 215-389-1513), 916 S Swanson St squeezed between I-95 and Christopher Columbus Blvd, is surrounded by a graveyard and several other 18th-century buildings. It's

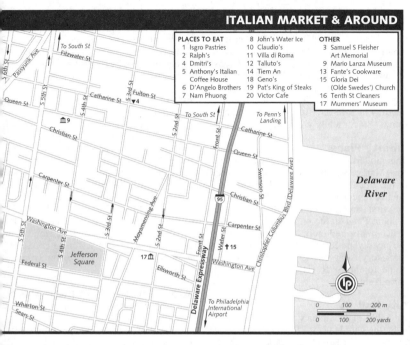

ITALIAN MARKET & AROUND

PLACES TO EAT
1 Isgro Pastries
2 Ralph's
4 Dmitri's
5 Anthony's Italian
  Coffee House
6 D'Angelo Brothers
7 Nam Phuong

8 John's Water Ice
10 Claudio's
11 Villa di Roma
12 Talluto's
14 Tiem An
18 Geno's
19 Pat's King of Steaks
20 Victor Cafe

OTHER
3 Samuel S Fleisher
  Art Memorial
9 Mario Lanza Museum
13 Fante's Cookware
15 Gloria Dei
  (Olde Swedes') Church
16 Tenth St Cleaners
17 Mummers' Museum

open daily April to October 9 am to 5 pm and by appointment at other times. A donation is requested.

Mummers' Museum

At this museum (☎ 215-336-3050), 100 S 2nd St at Washington Ave, learn about the historic tradition of Philadelphia's Mummers and their annual New Year's Day parade. A 'mummer' is one who disguises or masquerades. Exhibits include some of their extravagant costumes, photographs, a video of the most recent parade and a digital clock that counts down the days to the next January 1. If you're lucky you may even catch one of the string bands rehearsing. It's open Tuesday to Saturday 9:30 am to 5 pm, Sunday noon to 5 pm (but closed on Sunday in July and August). Weather permitting, May to September there are free outdoor string band concerts on Tuesday. Admission is $2.50/2 for adults/children.

CENTER CITY
Rittenhouse Square

The best known and most popular and prestigious of the city's squares laid out by William Penn is named after the local 18th-century astronomer, mathematician and clockmaker, David Rittenhouse. Surrounded by fancy apartment buildings, hotels and restaurants, the square features a fine collection of statues as well as a children's wading pool and wooden benches. It's popular with city workers and tourists alike, who come here in fine weather to rest under the shade of the trees, read, enjoy a sandwich or drink or feed the squirrels.

Mutter Museum

Housed in the College of Physicians & Surgeons (☎ 215-587-9919), 19 S 22nd St, this collection of pathological and anatomical specimens and medical artifacts was started in the late 19th century to educate medical students. It features a fascinating but often gruesome collection of exhibits, including the double liver shared by 19th-century Siamese twins Chang and Eng Bunker, the tumor removed from President Cleveland's cancerous jawbone and numerous skeletons of dwarves and unusually tall people. Another display features various items swallowed by patients. The museum is open Tuesday to Saturday 10 am to 4 pm; admission is $8/4 for adults/children.

Liberty Place

This modern art deco, 60-story complex at 1650 Market St, can be seen from most parts of the city. It's notable not only for its distinctive blue-glass facade, but also for being the first building built higher than the William Penn statue on City Hall. Its construction inspired more high-rises, changing the city skyline completely. The complex has a 58-story twin, at 2 Liberty Place, and is home to the St Regis Hotel, offices and various shops.

City Hall

Probably Philadelphia's architectural highlight, the City Hall (☎ 215-686-9074), at the intersection of Broad and Market Sts, is the country's largest municipal building. Completed in 1901, it took 30 years to build. The elaborately designed building was constructed without a steel framework so the 22-foot-thick granite walls at the base support the central tower. It was the city's tallest building until the completion of Liberty Place in 1987. The 548-foot-high City Hall is crowned by a 27-ton, 37-foot-high bronze statue of William Penn. Before Liberty Place, a 'gentlemen's agreement' had limited the height of Philadelphia's buildings to the hat on Penn's statue. Now City Hall no longer dominates the Philadelphia skyline.

City Hall opens Monday to Friday 9:30 am to 4:30 pm with free tours of the interior at 12:30 pm from room 121. You can also visit the observation deck of the tower for a magnificent view of the city from 40 floors up. From the northeast corner, take the elevator to the 7th floor, from where you follow a red line to a waiting area. Here you get your ticket and are escorted in another elevator to the deck. These trips are popular, but you can go to the waiting area and book a time. Note that 10 am to noon is usually reserved for school or other special groups. Entry is free.

Masonic Temple

This temple (☎ 215-988-1917), 1 N Broad St, is the headquarters of the Grand Lodge of Free & Accepted Masons of Pennsylvania. Some of the Founding Fathers, including George Washington, were members, and the temple library and museum contain letters and books from the period. The seven lodge halls are designed in different architectural styles: Corinthian, Egyptian, Gothic, Ionic, Norman, Oriental and Renaissance. Free 45-minute guided tours take place Monday to Friday at 10 and 11 am, 1, 2 and 3 pm, Saturday at 10 and 11 am. It's closed on Saturday in July and August.

Lord & Taylor Department Store

Formerly known as Sam Wanamaker, this graceful, landmark store (☎ 215-241-9000), on Market St between Juniper and S 13th Sts, was built between 1902 and 1910. The main shopping concourse, on the ground floor, features a large bronze eagle and a 30,000 pipe organ (reputedly the world's largest); you can enjoy free performances Monday to Saturday 11:15 am and 5:15 pm. The store opens Monday to Saturday 10 am to 7 pm (Wednesday to 8 pm), Sunday noon to 5 pm.

Pennsylvania Academy of the Fine Arts

The Pennsylvania Academy of the Fine Arts (PAFA; ☎ 215-972-7600), 118 N Broad St, was founded in 1805 and boasts a prestigious art school and museum, the nation's oldest. Its present home is a magnificent Victorian Gothic-style building designed by Frank Furness and built in 1876. Its collection of American paintings and sculpture includes the works of such noted early American painters as Charles Willson Peale (1741–1827), Gilbert Stuart (1755–1828) and Thomas Eakins (1844–1916). The museum

Mummers' Parade

Said to be the country's oldest continual folk festival, it isn't known for sure how the Mummers' Parade started. It may have originated from a Swedish and Finnish custom of celebrating a 'Second Christmas' with wandering minstrels, or from the English Mummery Play, a kind of burlesque with harlequins dressed in silk and satin. In German, Mummerkleid means 'fancy dress' and Mummenspiel means 'masquerade.' Philadelphia's first Mummers appeared in the 1700s parading in the Washington Ave area, and the bands grew in size until, in 1901, an official site, at Broad St from South Philadelphia to City Hall, was ordained for the parade.

Staged each New Year's Day, participants number over 25,000, mostly heterosexual men wearing sequins, feathers, makeup and outrageous costumes. Women dress up too, and they all strut their way along Broad St. They're accompanied by bands that are traditionally limited to accordions, saxophones, drums, violins, banjos, bass fiddles, glockenspiels and clarinets.

As with Mardi Gras, the extravagant costumes are the highlight of the show. The Mummers are members of clubs that represent different city neighborhoods. They spend all year (and a lot of money) designing and creating their costumes, not to mention practicing the music and choreographing their routines. Each year features different themes, such as fairy tales or Broadway shows.

The parade starts at 7 am and can last as long as 12 hours. Despite the low temperatures, there's always a large, enthusiastic and often hard-drinking turnout. If you miss the parade, you can catch the Mummers' bands performing at the Mummers' Museum and at other special performances. To catch them in all their glory, though, you really need to see them on New Year's Day.

The parade's theme song is 'Oh Dem Golden Slippers,' written by James Bland (1854–1911) in 1879. He was born of free African-American parents in Flushing, NY, and studied at Howard University. He worked for a while as a page in the House of Representatives and later became a successful minstrel in England where he gave a command performance for Queen Victoria. He wrote about 700 songs, including 'Carry me back to Old Virginny,' but was only credited with 37. Around the turn of the 20th century he settled in Philadelphia where he died in poverty.

opens Monday to Saturday 10 am to 5 pm, Sunday 11 am to 5 pm. Guided tours are available daily at 12:30 and 2 pm and are included in the admission fee of $5/3/4 for adults/children/seniors. Admission is free from 3 to 5 pm on Sunday. Visit its website for a preview (www.pafa.org).

Historical Society of Pennsylvania

The society was founded in 1824 and its museum (☎ 215-732-6201), 1300 Locust St, displays interesting exhibitions on Pennsylvanian and colonial history. It contains important historical documents including many of William Penn's political papers and letters. Other exhibits include George Washington's desk, the first draft of the Constitution and a painting of Ben Franklin by Charles Willson Peale, plus videos in the small theater.

The museum opens Tuesday and Thursday to Saturday 10 am to 4:45 pm, Wednesday 2 to 8:45 pm. Admission costs $5/2 for adults/children. Plan on spending about 1½ hours here, depending on your interest.

Reading Terminal Market

The large, indoor Reading Terminal Market (☎ 215-922-2317) started in 1893 by the Delaware River when the old markets spread along High St (renamed Market St in their honor) to here, under the Philadelphia & Reading Railroad's train shed. The farmers' market was renovated as part of the Convention Center development.

You'll find some of the city's best pretzels, hoagies and high-quality groceries here, though you won't find the bargains of the Italian Market in South Philly. It's a terrific place to come for breakfast, lunch or a snack with a choice of good-value, top-quality food stalls. Another attraction in their own right are the Amish families who have a section where they sell their produce Wednesday to Saturday. Most food stalls close by 3 pm (see Places to Eat for suggestions).

Pennsylvania Convention Center

A modern city landmark, the Pennsylvania Convention Center, 1101 Arch St, between N 11th and N 13th Sts, was built in 1993 at a cost of $522 million. It covers a huge area and incorporates the Reading Terminal's former train shed and head house, which now make up part of the main exhibition hall on the 2nd floor. The 1200-room Marriott Hotel is also part of the complex. The center is the site of several annual events and regular conferences. Tours of the convention center are by appointment and their availability and extent depends on how busy the center is with other activities. For details call Ella Evans (☎ 215-418-4735), the visitor services coordinator.

Chinatown

Philadelphia's eight-block Chinatown, between N 8th and N 11th Sts and Vine and Arch Sts, lacks the ambience of its New York and San Francisco counterparts. Nor does it have much in the way of landmarks or sights – except for the colorful **Chinese Friendship Gate**, at N 10th St (between Arch and Cherry Sts). It's a decorative arch, built in 1984 as a joint project between Philadelphia and its Chinese sister city, Tianjin. Nonetheless, the neighborhood does offer a good selection of Chinese, Vietnamese, Thai and vegetarian eating places, many of which are inexpensive.

Pennsylvania Hospital

Founded in 1751 by Benjamin Franklin and Dr Thomas Bond, Pennsylvania Hospital (☎ 215-829-7352), 800 Spruce St, was the country's first hospital. A booklet offering a self-guided walking tour is available from the information desk/welcome center in the ground floor lobby of the modern section of the hospital, and it maintains a website (www.pahosp.com).

Entry to the old part of the hospital is on 8th St. Here, the **Pine Building** has been in continuous use since 1755. Inside you'll find the **History of Nursing Museum, Historic Library of Pennsylvania Hospital** (containing important collections on the history of medicine) and North America's oldest surgical amphitheater for medical students. Outside, in front of the west wing of the Pine Building is the tranquil **Physic Garden**, where plants used in the 18th century as herbal remedies are grown.

Visiting hours are Monday to Friday 9 am to 5 pm. Admission is free.

Civil War Library & Museum

Highly recommended for Civil War buffs, the three-story building (☎ 215-735-8196), 1805 Pine St, contains one of the country's most comprehensive Civil War libraries and museums. The library houses over 12,000 volumes plus manuscripts and other archival material, while the museum boasts some unique artifacts, including items that belonged to Generals Grant, Sherman, Meade and Mulholland. A gallery of changing exhibitions deals with different aspects of the war. The library and museum open Tuesday to Saturday 11 am to 4:30 pm; admission costs $5/3/4 for adults/children/seniors.

Rosenbach Museum & Library

Housed in a superb 19th-century townhouse on one of the city's loveliest streets, this small museum (☎ 215-732-1600), 2010 Delancey St, contains a top collection of rare books and manuscripts. The original manuscript of James Joyce's *Ulysses* is on permanent display, as are the first four pages of Bram Stoker's *Dracula* and most of Joseph Conrad's manuscripts. Its collection also includes paintings by Canaletto and original illustrations by author Maurice Sendak. The museum and library open Tuesday to Sunday with 75-minute guided tours between 11 am and 4 pm (the last tour starts at 2:45 pm); it's closed in August. Admission costs $5/3 for adults/children. It maintains a website (www.rosenbach.org).

Edgar Allan Poe National Historic Site

Poe, America's noted 19th-century horror-story writer, wrote 'The Black Cat' among others while he lived in the modest brick house on this site in 1843–44. In the museum next door there's information and an audio-visual presentation on the man and his work. Operated by the NPS, the site (☎ 215-597-8780), 532 N 7th St, opens June to October daily 9 am to 5 pm, the rest of the year Wednesday to Sunday only. Admission is free. It's north of the city center, but bus No 47 runs past.

Eastern State Penitentiary

The penitentiary (☎ 215-236 3300), on Fairmount Ave between N 20th and N 22nd Sts, was once home to Al Capone. The Gothic Revival building dates from 1829 and ceased being a prison in 1971. Its grim exterior is matched by the neglected appearance of the surrounding streets. One-hour tours are available June to August, Wednesday to Sunday 10 am to 5 pm, and May, September and October, weekends only. Admission costs $7/3 for adults/children. Children under five aren't admitted. Starting in the Old Visitor's Room where you're issued a hard hat, you stroll through the decaying cell blocks, prison greenhouse and death row. For a preview, visit its website (www.easternstate.com). Take a bus to Benjamin Franklin Pkwy and walk north on N 22nd St.

BENJAMIN FRANKLIN PARKWAY

Benjamin Franklin Pkwy is the focus for a superb collection of museums and other landmarks. Designed by French architects Jacques Greber and Paul Cret, the 250-foot-wide parkway extends from JFK Plaza northwest through Logan Square to Eskins Oval in front of the Philadelphia Museum of Art. Here it splits to become Pennsylvania Ave, which in turn becomes Kelly and West River Drive; both continue along either side of the Schuylkill River. Built in 1924 and modeled on the Champs-Élysées in Paris, the parkway is a multilane thoroughfare lined with trees, flags from around the world,

statues and fountains. Philly's version, however, is dominated more by traffic than cafes and promenading pedestrians. The parkway is served by bus Nos 32, 38, 48 and 76 from downtown.

Academy of Natural Sciences Museum

The country's oldest natural history museum (☎ 215-299-1000), 1900 Benjamin Franklin Pkwy, was founded in 1812, though the building itself dates from 1868. It has a terrific permanent 'Discovering Dinosaurs' display on the 1st floor, complete with computer videos and reconstructed skeletons. The museum also features 'Outside In,' a hands-on nature center for kids on the 3rd floor, separate halls on Africa, Asia and North America and a section on butterflies.

PENNSYLVANIA

TONY WHEELER

View of the Benjamin Franklin Parkway

You can even go on a 'dig' for fossils in a simulated New Mexico field station. For a preview, visit the museum's website at www.acnatsci.org.

It's open Monday to Friday from 10 am to 4:30 pm, weekends and holidays from 10 am to 5 pm. Admission costs $8.50/7.50/7.75 for adults/children/seniors.

Please Touch Museum

Designed for children seven years of age and younger, the highly regarded Please Touch Museum (☎ 215-963-0667), 210 N 21st St, emphasizes learning through playing. Its interactive exhibits feature a mock TV studio with a working camera, a real SEPTA bus and a miniature supermarket. In the Sendak area children meet oversize creatures from books such as *Where the Wild Things Are* by Maurice Sendak. Outside is a science park, jointly administered with the Franklin Institute Science Museum. It's an interactive learning area where exhibits include a miniature golf course and a radar detector.

The museum opens July 1 to Labor Day daily 9 am to 6 pm, to 4:30 pm the rest of the year. Admission costs $6.95, adult or child; but on Sunday between 9 and 10 am, the normal entry rate is waived and visitors are asked to make a donation instead. Visit its website at www.libertynet.org/~pleastch.

Franklin Institute Science Museum

Founded in 1824, the world-class Franklin Institute Science Museum (☎ 215-448-1200), at N 20th St and Benjamin Franklin Pkwy, moved into this four-story, Greek Revival building in 1934. The museum pioneered the hands-on science concept so widespread nowadays.

In the **Science Center** you can walk through a 4-ton, two-story papier-mâché replica of a beating heart. Other working devices demonstrate various aspects of physics, and the train-related exhibits (including a ride on a steam train) are especially popular with children. You'll also find a giant pinball machine here. Downstairs, the **Fels Planetarium** has a computer-driven

look at the cosmos, plus laser shows and astronomy exhibits. Housed in a four-story dome, the **Tuttleman Omniverse Theater**, or Omni, features a 79-foot movie screen that surrounds the audience and uses an eight-track sound system.

The **Mandell Futures Center**, a 1991 addition to the museum, traces the development of computers, telecommunications and space travel into the near future, and examines environmental concerns.

The museum opens daily 9:30 to 5 pm. The Mandell Futures Center opens Sunday to Thursday 9:30 to 5 pm, Friday and Saturday to 9 pm. Admission to the museum and center costs $9.75/8.50 for adults/children. Entry to these two plus the Tuttleman Omniverse Theater *or* Fels Planetarium costs $12.75/10.50; to everything it's $14.75/12.50. For a preview, visit the museum's website at www.fi.edu.

Rodin Museum

A must-see for many, this noteworthy museum (☎ 215-763-8100), on Callowhill St near the corner of N 22nd St and Benjamin Franklin Pkwy, is home to the largest collection outside Paris of Auguste Rodin's sculptures. These include his famous *The Burghers of Calais* and *Gates of Hell* and a bronze cast replica of *The Thinker*. It is open Tuesday to Sunday 10 am to 5 pm and a donation is requested.

FAIRMOUNT PARK

Said to be the world's largest urban park, Fairmount Park (☎ 215-685-0000) covers nearly 14 sq miles – 10% of the city's land. The southern section, roughly the shape of South America, stretches some 4 miles northwest from the Philadelphia Museum of Art to the Falls Bridge, near the East Falls neighborhood. Most of the park is divided by the Schuylkill River into East and West Fairmount Park. Northwest from East Falls the park stretches along Wissahickon Creek (a tributary of the Schuylkill River) past Chestnut Hill.

The park is popular with city residents and is a great place for a picnic or a stroll (see the Activities section, later in this chapter, for additional suggestions). In summer there are free classical music concerts. It also has a fine group of authentic early-American houses, which are open to the public. Litter, in some parts of the park, is a real problem.

Bus Nos 38 and 76 take you to the Philadelphia Museum of Art and the zoo, and the PHLASH bus takes you to the museum. If you don't have transport, to see all the sights in Fairmount Park it's worth considering taking Philadelphia Trolley Works (see the Organized Tours section later in this chapter).

Philadelphia Museum of Art

The country's third largest art museum is home to over 300,000 paintings, sculptures, drawings, prints and decorative arts. Many of the major artists of the 19th and 20th centuries are represented in its collection of mostly Asian, European and US art. Architecturally, the museum consists of three Greek-style 'temples,' with fluted columns supporting a blue-tiled roof topped by bronze griffins.

In the Great Stair Hall, just past the 1st-floor entrance, stands the 1892 statue of the nude huntress *Diana* by Augustus St Gaudens; it was brought here from New

York in 1932 after being saved from the demolished Madison Square Garden.

Highlights include the 19th-century European & Impressionist Galleries, featuring the work of Brancusi, Degas, Renoir, Manet and Van Gogh. There are galleries for special exhibitions, and other permanent exhibition galleries include American Art, Early-20th-Century Art, Contemporary Art, Japanese & Chinese Art, Near Eastern & Asian Art, Medieval & European Art, Arms & Armor, European Art 1500–1700, English Period Rooms, European Art 1700–1850 and American Period Rooms. The museum also features complete buildings, including an Indian Hindu temple and a Japanese Buddhist temple from Nara.

The museum (☎ 215-763-8100) opens Tuesday and Thursday to Sunday 10 am to 5 pm, Wednesday to 8:45 pm. Normal admission costs $8/5/5 for adults/children/ seniors, but on Sunday before 1 pm it's free. Particularly worthwhile are Wednesday nights between 5 and 8:45 pm when there is live music, films, talks, guided tours, food and drink. Its website is at www .philamuseum.org.

Fairmount Waterworks

A National Historic Engineering Landmark, this beautiful Greek-style complex (☎ 215-685-0144) was built in 1815, and was designed to pump 4 million gallons of water daily from the Schuylkill River to a reservoir on the site now occupied by the Philadelphia Museum of Art. It was closed in 1909 due to pollution and at the time of writing was being fully restored.

Schuylkill River

Its name is Dutch for 'Hidden River,' and it stretches 100 miles from its source in Schuylkill County to the Delaware River in South Philadelphia. The Schuylkill River (pronounced 'SKOO-kill') was a major factor in the city's growth in the 18th and 19th centuries. Today, it provides Philadelphia with recreational benefits, particularly in Fairmount Park. Scullers are a familiar year-round sight, and people love to jog, cycle, skate or stroll along the riverside.

Rocky Was Here

The steps in front of the Philadelphia Museum of Art are the ones that Sylvester Stallone's character Rocky Balboa ascended in the original *Rocky* movie, for which Stallone won an Oscar for best screenplay. In the early 1980s, a bronze statue of the enduring character was erected outside the museum for the filming of *Rocky III*. Although it appeared again in *Rocky V*, it was eventually deemed inappropriate for permanent residency here and was moved to the front of what's now the First Union Spectrum Stadium. Even though the statue has long gone, you can still enjoy Rocky's terrific view of the city from the top of the steps looking back along Benjamin Franklin Pkwy toward City Hall.

PENNSYLVANIA

Boathouse Row

Another major Philly landmark, this is home to the 'Schuylkill Navy,' a collection of rowing clubs renowned for their distinctive Tudor-style Victorian buildings on the east bank of the Schuylkill River. These buildings, dating from the late 19th and early 20th centuries, are a lovely enough sight during the day, but after dark are illuminated to marvelous effect. Nearby is Lloyd Hall Cafe where you can have a drink or snack while watching all the activity.

Early American Houses

Fairmount Park encloses a number of fine early American houses. They're open Wednesday to Sunday 10 am to 4 pm though the hours sometimes vary, so call ahead. Admission costs $2.50/1.25 for adults/children per house.

The 19th-century, Federal-style **Lemon Hill Mansion** (☎ 215-232-4337), Poplar Drive, was owned by financier Robert Morris and is furnished with period artifacts. It is closed from mid-December to mid-February.

Described by John Adams as 'the most elegant seat in Pennsylvania,' Georgian-style **Mt Pleasant** (☎ 215-763-8100), Mt Pleasant Drive, was built in 1763–64 by a wealthy Scottish privateer and owned for a time by Benedict Arnold. Inside there's Chippendale furniture and other ornate woodwork.

Further north off Dauphin St, **Woodford** (☎ 215-229-6115), a Georgian mansion dating back to 1756, has a wonderful collection of Colonial furniture and decorative art. **Laurel Hill** (☎ 215-235-1776), on E Edgely Drive, built in the 1760s and once owned by Dr Philip Syng Physick, contains some fine Federal furnishings.

The largest house in the park, **Strawberry Mansion** (☎ 215-228-8364), Strawberry Mansion Drive, features a Federal-style main section built in the 1790s, while the Greek Revival wings were added on in the 1820s. The owner's son was a strawberry grower. Today, an antique toy exhibit, the mixture of Empire, Federal and Regency furniture and Tucker porcelain are the main attractions.

Japanese House & Gardens

A gift of the American-Japan Society of Tokyo, the authentic 17th-century-style upper-class Japanese house (☎ 215-763-8003), in West Fairmount Park, provides a peaceful retreat from the city bustle. Set in beautiful Japanese gardens beside a stream, it's open for guided or self-guided tours May to Labor Day, Tuesday to Sunday 10 am to 4 pm; weekends only Labor Day to October; closed November to April. Admission costs $2.50/2 for adults/children. You can also enjoy tea ceremonies and origami demonstrations here.

The house and gardens are part of the 22-acre **Horticultural Center** (☎ 215-685-0096), which you enter via Horticultural Drive off Belmont Ave and which opens daily 9 am to 5 pm.

Philadelphia Zoo

The 42-acre Philadelphia Zoo (☎ 215-243-1100), at Girard Ave and N 34th St in West Fairmount Park, is the country's oldest zoo, having opened in 1874. It houses over 1800 mammals, birds, reptiles and amphibians. Despite its age and Victorian touches, the zoo has been modernized and features natural habitats, not just cages, for many of its 'stars.' The primate house, destroyed by fire in 1995, was reopened in 1999 on the zoo's 125th anniversary. The zoo opens daily 9:30 am to 4:45 pm and admission costs $10.50/8 for adults/children. Set aside at least three hours. The zoo maintains a website (www.philadelphiazoo.org).

Scenic Drives

A great Philadelphia experience is to enjoy the views from the winding roads that run along the Schuylkill River. Kelly Drive, formerly E River Drive, is named after John B Kelly, father of Princess Grace. West River Drive runs along the opposite bank. Belmont Plateau off Belmont Mansion Drive in West Fairmount Park offers spectacular views of Philadelphia especially at night. From Center City, take the Schuylkill Expressway or the W River Drive to Montgomery Drive and make a right at Belmont Mansion Drive.

Take special care when driving: the roads have sharp curves and accidents occur when gawking drivers don't pay enough attention to the road.

UNIVERSITY CITY

The Philadelphia area is host to numerous colleges and a temporary home to over 30,000 students. University City, in West Philadelphia, is the area west of the Schuylkill River and south of Market St stretching to about 42nd St where college campuses and students dominate. The two largest tertiary institutions here are the University of Pennsylvania (known as Penn and considered an Ivy League school) and Drexel University.

For the visitor, University City's main attractions are the architecture of 30th St Station and Penn's campus, Penn's Museum of Archaeology & Anthropology and the Institute for Contemporary Art.

The area can be reached from downtown on the Market-Frankford and Subway-Surface lines, by the PHLASH bus or by bus Nos 21 and 42. The LUCY bus does a circuit of University City from 30th St Station.

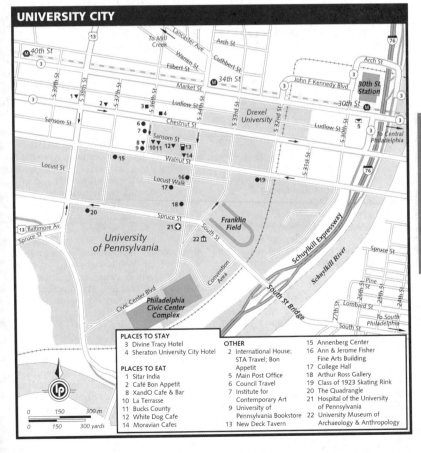

UNIVERSITY CITY

PENNSYLVANIA

PLACES TO STAY
3 Divine Tracy Hotel
4 Sheraton University City Hotel

PLACES TO EAT
1 Sitar India
2 Café Bon Appetit
8 XandO Cafe & Bar
10 La Terrasse
11 Bucks County
12 White Dog Cafe
14 Moravian Cafes

OTHER
2 International House;
   STA Travel; Bon
   Appetit
5 Main Post Office
6 Council Travel
7 Institute for
   Contemporary Art
9 University of
   Pennsylvania Bookstore
13 New Deck Tavern

15 Annenberg Center
16 Ann & Jerome Fisher
    Fine Arts Building
17 College Hall
18 Arthur Ross Gallery
19 Class of 1923 Skating Rink
20 The Quadrangle
21 Hospital of the University
    of Pennsylvania
22 University Museum of
    Archaeology & Anthropology

30th St Station

Worth a visit even if you're not catching a train, the Neoclassic station's main concourse is one of Philly's most romantic public spaces. The grand exterior, with its Corinthian columns, can be seen across the river from JFK Blvd and Market St Bridge and is beautifully floodlit at night. The station's south side is a pleasant place for a quick snack and is where people often just hang out, sometimes playing chess.

University of Pennsylvania

Founded in 1740 as a charity school by William Penn, it combined with Benjamin Franklin's Public Academy of Philadelphia in 1750. This academy became the nation's first university in 1779 and moved to this 260-acre campus from east of the river in the 1870s. It has several architectural highlights.

On Locust Walk between S 34th and S 36th Sts, **College Hall**, used for administration, was the first building and is a classic example of the 'collegiate Gothic' style. The **Ann & Jerome Fisher Fine Arts Building**, on S 34th St between Walnut and Spruce Sts and facing the College Green, is generally referred to as the Furness Building, as it was designed by renowned local architect Frank Furness. Also designed by Furness is the nearby **Arthur Ross Gallery** (☎ 215-898-4401), 220 S 34th St, a free art gallery with changing exhibitions (open Tuesday to Friday 10 am to 5 pm, weekends noon to 5 pm). **The Quadrangle**, on Spruce St between S 36th and S 38th Sts, dates from 1895 and features collegiate Gothic-style dorms.

Museum of Archaeology & Anthropology

This world-renowned museum (☎ 215-898-4000), 3260 South St, is a magical place with interesting permanent exhibits and a wide range of changing exhibitions. Its archaeological treasures hail from ancient Egypt, Mesopotamia, the Mayan peninsula, Asia, Greece, Rome, Africa, Polynesia and North America. Highlights include one of the world's largest crystal balls (a 55-pounder which may have belonged to the Empress

Dowager of China); samples of the oldest writing ever found, from Sumeria; bronzes from Benin in Nigeria; and a 12-ton granite Sphinx of Ramesses II, circa 1293–1185 BC, from Egypt.

The museum opens Memorial Day to Labor Day, Tuesday to Saturday 10 am to 4:30 pm (plus Sunday 1 to 5 pm the rest of the year). Admission costs $5/2.50 for adults/children. Visit its website (www.upenn.edu/museum) for additional information.

Institute for Contemporary Art

The Institute for Contemporary Art (ICA; ☎ 215-898-7108), 118 S 36th St, is Philadelphia's principal contemporary art museum. It has regularly changing exhibitions of up-and-coming artists, some of whom, like Andy Warhol, have gone on to receive national and international recognition. It is open Wednesday to Friday noon to 8 pm, weekends 11 am to 5 pm. Admission costs $3/2 for adults/children (free Sunday 11 am to 1 pm). The ICA maintains a website at www.upenn.edu/ica.

NORTHWEST PHILADELPHIA

In the 17th and 18th centuries, colonists established paper and textile mills, farms and country retreats in northwest Philadelphia. With the coming of the railroads, separate towns developed. Three of these, Manayunk, Germantown and Chestnut Hill, with their interesting historical sights and selection of shops and restaurants are especially noteworthy and worth a visit. They're easily accessible from downtown by car, bus or train. Nearby is the northern extension of Fairmount Park straddling Wissahickon Creek. West of these suburbs is Merion, home of the Barnes Foundation Gallery.

Manayunk

With its steep hills and Victorian row houses overlooking the Schuylkill River, Manayunk (from a Native American expression meaning 'where we go to drink') is the place to go to eat, shop – and drink. In this former textile-manufacturing neighborhood about 4 miles northwest of downtown you can spend a pleasant afternoon strolling gentrified **Main St** – a National Historic District with chic boutiques, art galleries, restaurants and bars – or walking along the former towpath beside the **Manayunk Canal**.

To get there, take the SEPTA Norristown R6 suburban train or bus Nos 27, 32 and 61. By car, from Fairmount Park follow Kelly Drive north into Manayunk.

Germantown

Established on land deeded by William Penn to 13 German-speaking families in 1683, Germantown, 6 miles northwest of downtown, first became a papermaking, printing and publishing center. In the 19th century, textile manufacturing spurred its growth. With the Depression in the 1930s it went into decline, and in the 1950s a number of its wealthier and middle-class residents moved to the suburbs. Areas of urban decay remain, but there are some superb restored Georgian, Victorian and early American mansions especially along and around **Germantown Ave**.

Start by visiting the **Germantown Historical Society** (☎ 215-844-0514), 5501 Germantown Ave, a museum where you can learn about Germantown's history and the location of its historic houses. Some architectural gems open to the public are the Victorian Gothic **Ebenezer Maxwell Mansion** (☎ 215-438-1861), 200 W Tulpehocken St, built in 1859; **Cliveden** (☎ 215-848-1777), 6401 Germantown Ave, a Palladian-style Georgian house dating from 1763; the 1750s Federal-style **Upsala** (☎ 215-842-1798), 6430 Germantown Ave; and the charming **Wyck** (☎ 215-848-1690), 6026 Germantown Ave, a Quaker home built in 1690. Many of Germantown's historic sights are closed December/January through March.

Take either the SEPTA Chestnut Hill East R7 suburban train and get off at Germantown, or the Chestnut Hill West R8 train and get off at Queen Lane, Chelten Ave or Tulpehocken St. Alternatively, catch bus No 23 north along 11th St. By car, head north along Broad St, turn left onto Pike St, then take a right onto Germantown Ave.

Chestnut Hill

Further north, Germantown Ave is also the main street of the residential suburb of Chestnut Hill, scenically positioned along the Wissahickon Valley and one of Philadelphia's most exclusive neighborhoods. The area was mostly farmland until the Pennsylvania Railroad connected it with downtown Philadelphia at the end of the 19th century. Along Germantown Ave and its cobblestoned side streets you'll find fashionable shops, cafes and restaurants.

The 92-acre **Morris Arboretum of the University of Pennsylvania** (☎ 215-247-5777, www.upenn.edu/morris), 100 Northwestern Ave, north of town, is a public park open daily. **Woodmere Art Museum** (☎ 215-247-0476), 9201 Germantown Ave, displays 19th- and 20th-century American and European art.

Take the SEPTA Chestnut Hill East R7 or Chestnut Hill West R8 suburban train or catch bus No 23 north along 11th St. By car, head north along Broad St, turn left onto Pike St then right onto Germantown Ave, which takes you through Germantown and Mt Airy to Chestnut Hill.

Barnes Foundation Gallery

The Barnes Foundation Gallery (☎ 610-667-0290 information only), 300 N Latches Lane, is in Merion about 6 miles northwest of downtown. It houses the world's largest private collection of impressionist, post-impressionist and early French modern paintings. It contains works by Cézanne (more than in all the galleries of France), Degas, Matisse, Manet, Monet, Modigliani, Picasso, Renoir, Rousseau, Seurat and van Gogh. As well as these, there is art and craftwork from around the world including antique furniture, ceramics, hand-wrought iron and Native American jewelry. The gallery also provides an educational program on the world's different artistic traditions. Unfortunately, the gallery is only open Friday and Saturday 9:30 to 5 pm, Sunday 12:30 to 5 pm and you must make a reservation (☎ 610-664-7917) at least 30 days in advance. Admission costs $5.

PENNSYLVANIA

The gallery is in a 13-acre property that is maintained as an **arboretum** and contains a wide diversity of plants. The arboretum school here teaches students botany, horticulture and landscaping.

Take SEPTA's R5 train to Merion or bus No 44 from downtown; if you're driving, follow the Schuylkill Expressway northwest then turn left at the City Ave turnoff. Follow City Ave then turn right onto Lancaster Rd; Latches Lane is the fourth turn on the left.

ACTIVITIES

The huge Fairmount Park is the city's main center for outdoor activities. With around 100 miles of jogging, cycling and bridle paths and the Schuylkill River and Wissahickon Creek within its borders, the park is very popular with city residents. For details of what's available in the park call Fairmount Park Information (☎ 215-685-0000). See also the Outdoor Activities chapter.

For walking, jogging and bicycling, a paved 8.2-mile loop from the Philadelphia Museum of Art heads along Kelly Drive on the east bank of the Schuylkill River to the Falls Bridge then returns to the museum via West River Drive. Further north, Forbidden Drive is a 5.5-mile traffic-free gravel path on the west bank of Wissahickon Creek with some spectacular scenery.

Rowing and canoeing are popular on the Schuylkill River. Fairmount Park also has 115 tennis courts free to the public and five outdoor swimming pools. Call Fairmount Park Information for details. There are six 18-hole public golf courses too; for information call ☎ 215-877-8813. Weekends tend to be fully booked.

In town, Bike Line (☎ 215-735-1503), 1234 Locust St at S 13th St, rents mountain bikes for $15/25 a day/weekend plus deposit. In Fairmount Park beside Boathouse Row, Park à la Carte (☎ 215-765-3123) rents bikes for $10/35 for an hour/day, and in-line skates for $7.50/25. It operates Thursday 4 to 8 pm, Friday 2 to 8 pm and weekends 9 am to 6 pm. You can also hire in-line skates from City Sports (☎ 215-985-5860), 1606 Walnut St, for $15 per day plus deposit.

In University City, the Class of 1923 Skating Rink (☎ 215-898-1923), Walnut St, opens for ice skating from mid-September to early April; entry is $4.50, rental $1.50. Alternatively, late November to March there's outdoor skating at the Blue Cross Riving Rink (☎ 215-925-7465), on Penn's Landing at Chestnut St and Columbus Blvd, for $6.

ORGANIZED TOURS

A variety of tours exist to help you explore the city. They can be booked directly with the operators, through your hotel reception, at the Philadelphia Visitors Center (see Tourist Offices in the Information section, earlier in this chapter) or with a travel agent.

Walking Tours

Free walking tours are offered by the park rangers at Independence National Historic Park; check with the NPS Visitors Center for the current schedule.

May to October, Centipede Tours (☎ 215-735-3123), 1315 Walnut St, has 90-minute walking tours of Society Hill every Friday and Saturday evening at 6:30 pm for $5/4 for adults/children. The tours leave from Welcome Park, on S 2nd St between Chestnut and Walnut Sts, and the guides dress in period costume.

The Preservation Alliance for Greater Philadelphia (☎ 215-546-1146), 1616 Walnut St, offers a range of guided theme tours that change monthly. Call for a schedule, or visit its website (www.libertynet.org/~historic). Tours cost $10 for members and $15 for nonmembers.

Trolley Bus & Carriage Tours

A good way to get a comfortable overview of the city is with Philadelphia Trolley Works (☎ 215-928-8687), 60 Laurel St, whose popular motorized 'trolley' buses give you a 90-minute tour of the city plus a 40-minute trip through Fairmount Park. You can get off and reboard as often as you like within one full loop. Trolleys leave daily about every 30 minutes. Stops include Independence Hall, the Philadelphia Museum of

Art and the zoo. The full tour costs $15/5 for adults/children, or for a tour of the city only $10/5. Visit the website for a preview (www.phillytour.com).

On Chestnut St at S 6th St near Independence Hall the 76 Carriage Company (☎ 215-923-8516) operates a fleet of horse-drawn carriages with a driver/commentator. A 20-minute tour of Independence National Historic Park costs $15 for four people; and each additional person costs $3 extra. Longer tours take in Society Hill and Old City. Society Hill Carriage Company (☎ 215-627-6128) has similar tours from Independence Hall.

Cruises

From Penn's Landing the *Spirit of Philadelphia* (☎ 215-923-1419) offers popular two-hour lunch ($26.90) and three-hour dinner ($44.75) cruises along the Delaware River. Its website is www.spiritcruises.com. The *Liberty Belle* (☎ 215-629-1131), a former Mississippi paddleboat, offers similar cruises and is a little cheaper. Its website is www.libertybelle.com.

For $10/6 (for adults/children), narrated 1½-hour boat rides are available three to four times daily on the *Holiday* (☎ 215-629-8687) from the waterfront two blocks north of the Benjamin Franklin Bridge. Good views of the river and city are also possible on the Riverlink ferry to the New Jersey State Aquarium.

SPECIAL EVENTS

Highlights of the Philadelphia calendar include:

January

Mummers Parade (☎ 215-636-3050) on January 1 is a New Year's Day parade along Broad St of 25,000 spectacularly dressed Mummers. (See the boxed text 'Mummers' Parade,' earlier.)

February

Black History Month (☎ 215-574-0380) has many special events, exhibitions, screenings and concerts at the Afro-American Historical & Cultural Museum and other venues.

February/March

Philadelphia Flower Show (☎ 215-988-8800), a spectacular weeklong, indoor flower show in the Convention Center, is the world's largest.

March/April

The Book & the Cook (☎ 215-686-3662) is a five-day festival bringing together cookbook authors, food critics, chefs and restaurateurs to prepare special meals in many city restaurants.

April

Philadelphia Antique Show (☎ 215-387-300) is the premier show of its kind in the country, at 103 Engineer's Armory, N 33rd St, West Philadelphia; it is held the first weekend of the month.

Penn Relays (☎ 215-898-6154) is one of the world's oldest, largest and best amateur athletic carnivals; it has been held for over 100 years on Franklin Field at the University of Pennsylvania in late April.

May

Philadelphia Festival of World Cinema (☎ 800-969-7392), a 10-day festival in early May, features some of the best international independent films.

July

Sunoco Welcome America (☎ 215-636-1666) is a series of Independence Day celebrations with parades, concerts and fireworks during the first week of the month.

August

Pennsylvania Dutch Festival (☎ 215-922-2317) lasts for three days in early August with buggy rides, bluegrass music and more centered on Reading Terminal Market.

Philadelphia Folk Festival (☎ 215-247-1300) is three days of international music held at Old Poole Farm in Schwenksville in late August.

September

Super Sunday (☎ 215-665-1050) is organized by the Academy of Natural Sciences on the second Sunday and aimed mainly at kids, with activities around town and a parade along Benjamin Franklin Pkwy.

October

Columbus Day Parade (☎ 215-636-1666) is held on the second Monday along S Broad St.

November

Philadelphia Marathon (☎ 215-683-2070) is on the second or third Sunday of the month in Fairmount Park.

Thanksgiving Day Parade (☎ 215-636-1666) is the country's oldest Thanksgiving parade with floats and bands along Market St and Benjamin Franklin Pkwy.

December

Christmas Tours of Historic Houses (☎ 215-7875449) features some of the historic houses in Fairmount Park and Germantown in mid-December.

PENNSYLVANIA

PLACES TO STAY

Philadelphia has a wide range of accommodations, but finding a bed may be difficult at times – booking your room in advance will make life easier. Try to avoid visiting Philadelphia during school graduation week in late May when many B&Bs and hotel rooms are booked months ahead by proud families and friends. The frequent events at the Pennsylvania Convention Center bring many visitors to the city and put pressure on availability. Hotels often offer attractively priced weekend packages so rooms may be hard to find then.

If you're driving, you may need to factor in the cost of parking the car overnight, though some hotels offer free parking; check when booking.

You may see some of the cheaper downtown hotels advertised around town (at the Greyhound bus station for example) offering 'cheap accommodations and friendly service' – these aren't recommended.

Places to Stay – Budget

Camping *Timberlane Campground* (☎ 609-423-6677, 117 Timber Lane, Clarksboro, NJ 08020), 15 miles southwest across the Delaware River, is the closest campground. It has full facilities, accepts pets, opens year-round (though only the hardiest campers would consider staying in the winter months) and has sites for $23, or $25 with hookup. From downtown, cross the Benjamin Franklin Bridge, take I-676 then I-76 south to I-295 south; at exit 18A, turn onto Cohawkin Rd for about 800 yards then turn right onto Friendship Rd; one block north turn right onto Timber Lane. Alternatively, from West Philadelphia follow I-76 to I-295 south and follow the directions as above.

Southwest of Philadelphia, *West Chester KOA* (☎ 610-486-0447, PO Box 920P, Unionville 19375) is 3 miles north of Unionville on Route 162 beside the Brandywine River. It has 110 sites and is closed November through March. Riverside tent sites are $22 to $31.

Hostels The HI-AYH *Bank St Hostel* (☎ 215-922-0222, 800-392-4678, 2 S Bank St)

is a terrific, clean, comfortable hostel in Old City. In separate men's and women's dormitories, a bed costs $16 to $19. It has a large, well-equipped kitchen and dining area with free tea and coffee, a pool table, washer-drier facilities and TV lounge. It's closed between 10 am and 4:30 pm, but you can drop off your bags during this time. There's a 12:30 am curfew Sunday to Thursday, 1 am on Friday and Saturday. It's a few minutes' walk from 2nd St Station (on the Market-Frankford subway line).

Also central, the renovated *Old First Reformed Church Youth Hostel* (☎ 215-922-9663/4566), at N 4th and Race Sts, only opens July to early September. It costs $15 for a foam bed on the floor and includes a small breakfast. It has shower and laundry facilities and an 11 pm curfew; check in between 4 and 10 pm.

The 48 bed HI-AYH *Chamounix Mansion Hostel* (☎ 215-878-3676, 800-379-0017, Chamounix Drive, West Fairmount Park) is in a 19th-century mansion in an attractive park setting, but a fair distance from downtown. Dorm beds are $11/14 for members/non-members; if the hostel isn't busy, a smaller dorm can be used as a private room for couples or families. There's a kitchen, snack and drink vending machines, TV lounge, tennis courts, free bikes and free parking. It's closed between 11 am and 4:30 pm with a midnight curfew. It's also closed December 15 to January 15. To avoid a wasted trip, especially July through September, call ahead. It's 30 minutes on bus No 38 from Market St to the corner of Ford and Cranston Rds in West Fairmount Park. From the stop sign walk 1 mile on Ford Rd then turn left onto Chamounix Drive and continue to the hostel at the end of the road. Women should not try this at night. You can also visit the hostel's website at www.libertynet.org/chmounix.

Hotels *Divine Tracy Hotel* (☎ 215-382-4310, 20 S 36th St, University City) is a Christian-run, clean, 100-room hotel that doesn't accept credit cards. It has singles at $28 to $30 with shared bathroom, $33 to $40 with private bathroom; doubles are $40/50 with shared/private bathroom. Some rooms are available for low weekly rates from $65/75 to $72/95 for singles with shared/private bathroom, $110/130 for doubles – but you'll need to book ahead. The hotel has strict rules: no smoking, no alcohol, no swearing, separate floors for men and women and a modest public dress code. There's no curfew; check in between 7 am and 11 pm.

Places to Stay – Mid-Range

B&Bs The city has some great central B&Bs offering superb value with friendly hosts, pleasant surroundings, lovely rooms and facilities and good breakfasts. Most B&Bs only have a few rooms, so try to book ahead, especially for weekends. Most cost from $40 to $125 and accept major credit cards or personal checks. Some reservation agencies offering a selection of accommodations in and around Philadelphia are:

B&B Center City
   (☎ 215-735-1137/0582, 800-354-8401) 1804 Pine St, Philadelphia, PA 19103

B&B Connections
   (☎ 610-687-3565, 800-448-3619) PO Box 21, Devon, PA 19333

B&B of Philadelphia
   (☎ 215-735-1917, 800-220-1917) 1530 Locust St, suite K, Philadelphia, PA 19102

Distressed Gentlewomen's Reservation Service
   (☎ 215-592-7802, fax 592-9692) 341 S 12th St – run by Barbara Pope at Antique Row B&B

Antique Row B&B (☎ *215-592-7802, fax 592-9692, 341 S 12th St*), off Pine St, is in a lovely, comfortable house. Prices range from $60 for a single with a shared bathroom to $100 for an apartment with bathroom and kitchen. There are discounts for longer stays. Most rooms have telephone (local calls are free) and all have cable TV. A good, substantial breakfast is served in the dining room/lounge. Barbara Pope is a friendly host; if she has no vacancies, she'll help you book rooms elsewhere.

La Reserve (☎ *215-735-1137/0582, 800-354-8401, 1804 Pine St*), in a beautiful, elegant 1868 townhouse, has five rooms from $65 to $95 with shared bathroom, and three suites with private bathroom for $110. Bill Buchanan (La Reserve's host and operator of the booking agency B&B Center City) can book rooms elsewhere if it's full. Breakfast is served in the large chandeliered dining room. Check-in time is between 3 and 7:30 pm, unless you arrange otherwise when making your room reservation.

The friendly *Shippen Way Inn* (☎ *215-627-7266, 416-418 Bainbridge St*), one block south of South St, is a lovely, restored circa 1750 B&B. Family owned and operated, it has nine rooms, each with private bath, phone and air-con. Prices range from $80 to $110 according to size and location. Breakfast features home-baked breads and fresh fruits.

Thomas Bond House (☎ *215-923-8523, 800-845-2663, 129 S 2nd St*) is a beautifully restored colonial house (1769) on the National Register of Historic Places. It has 12 period-furnished rooms, all with private bath. The rates vary, according to room size, from $95 to $175. A continental breakfast is served weekdays, a full breakfast weekends. Wine and cheese are served in the evening.

Hotels The following hotels are in the **Historic District**. Choosing to stay in this location puts you within a few minutes walk of 'America's most historic square mile.'

On the waterfront, *Comfort Inn at Penn's Landing* (☎ *215-627-7900, 800-228-5150, 100 N Christopher Columbus Blvd*), near the corner of Race St, has singles/doubles for $99/129, including continental breakfast, gym and free parking. In a beautiful old building, the intimate *Penn's View Hotel* (☎ *215-922-7600, 800-331-7634*), at Front and Market Sts, overlooks the Delaware River. A pity about the expressway out the front though. Some of the 27 rooms in this boutique property have fireplaces and Jacuzzis. Singles or doubles cost $145 to $185, including continental breakfast. It also has a renowned Italian restaurant and extensive wine bar.

Society Hill Hotel (☎ *215-925-1919, 301 Chestnut St*) has 12 rooms from $88 to $155 above a popular bar. The rooms are small and the breakfast (included in the price) is OK, but the cheerfully decorated rooms are quiet with fresh flowers and brass beds. The European atmosphere, friendly staff and location make this a good choice. The 364-room *Holiday Inn – Independence Mall* (☎ 215-923-8660, 800-843-2355, 400 Arch St) is a modern eight-story structure close to many sights and amenities. Room rates depend on how busy the hotel is and start from \$99/169.

Best Western Independence Park Hotel (☎ 215-922-4443, 800-624-2988, 235 Chestnut St) has 36 designer-decorated rooms in a 19th-century building. Singles or doubles with king-size beds cost \$125 to \$185; the price includes continental breakfast and afternoon tea.

The following hotels are in **Center City**. Just off Rittenhouse Square, the grand *Warwick Philadelphia* (☎ 215-735-6000, 1701 Locust St) features 200 spacious rooms furnished with old-world decor. Rooms cost from \$165/195, but ask about any special deals.

In a commercially and culturally active area, the modern, 25-story *Doubletree Hotel Philadelphia* (☎ 215-893-1600), at Broad and Locust Sts, has an ugly concrete-slab exterior but a plush interior. Facilities include an indoor swimming pool and health club. Rooms cost \$169 to \$189, but are cheaper on weekends.

Embassy Suites Hotel (☎ 215-561-1776, 800-362-2779, 1776 Benjamin Franklin Pkwy) is near the parkway museums and other local sights. Featuring 288 complete suites with living room, kitchen area, wet bar, microwave, coffeemaker and separate bedroom, each suite has a balcony with city views. Rates run from \$109 to \$204. *Hotel Windsor* (☎ 215-981-5678, fax 981-5630, 1700 Benjamin Franklin Pkwy) has spacious rooms from \$119 and a 24-hour fitness center. Rates include a continental breakfast. *Holiday Inn Express Midtown* (☎ 215-735-9300, 800-643-8696, 1305 Walnut St) is also near the Convention Center and business district with singles/doubles from \$120/130. The 23-story *Marriott Hotel* (☎ 215-625-

2900, fax 625-6000, 1201 Market St,) is part of the Convention Center complex; facilities include cable TV and an indoor pool. Singles/doubles start at \$190/210. Its website is at www.marriott.com.

Places to Stay – Top End

The following hotels are in the **Historic District**. A luxury property featuring a health club with pool, Jacuzzi and sauna, the *Omni Hotel at Independence Park* (☎ 215-925-0000, 800-843-6664, 401 Chestnut St) has 150 rooms and rates of \$249. The large *Sheraton Society Hill* (☎ 215-238-6000, 800-325-3535, 1 Dock St) has 365 rooms, a four-story atrium lobby, indoor pool and health club. Singles/doubles cost \$169/250.

The following hotels are in **Center City**. *Crowne Plaza* (☎ 215-561-7500, 1800 Market St) is within walking distance of the Convention Center, historic sights and stores. Its 445 rooms are often full. Its room rates change daily and range from \$169 to \$259. The intimate, European-style *Latham Hotel* (☎ 215-563-7474, 800-528-4261, 135 S 17th St) has 139 rooms, health club and pool, and is walking distance to shops and attractions. Singles/doubles cost \$199/219.

Wyndham Franklin Plaza Hotel (☎ 215-448-2000, 800-996-3426, 2 Franklin Plaza), at N 17th and Race Sts, is a massive complex offering health and sports facilities. It's a 15-minute walk from the Convention Center or the shops on Walnut and Chestnut Sts and is close to the parkway museums. Rates are \$185/218 to \$215/225.

Park Hyatt Hotel (☎ 215-790-2804, 800-233-1234), at S Broad and Walnut Sts, occupies the top seven floors of the Bellevue building, renowned for its French Renaissance facade. Reception is on the 19th floor. The beautifully refurbished, luxury, old-style rooms have good views and cost \$175 to \$295.

Philadelphia boasts three deluxe properties. *Rittenhouse Hotel* (☎ 215-546-9000, 800-635-1042, 210 Rittenhouse Square West) occupies the first nine floors of this attractive building. The rooms feature floor-to-ceiling windows with city or square views. Rates are \$310/330. The *St Regis Hotel* (☎ 215-563-

1600), at Chestnut and S 17th Sts, is part of the modern Liberty Place complex, but the interior has an elegant atmosphere of bygone days. Prices fluctuate but singles or doubles cost from $245 to $355. Possibly the city's best hotel, the *Four Seasons Hotel* (☎ *215-963-1500, 800-332-3442, 1 Logan Square)*, near the Philadelphia Museum of Art, opened in 1983, but with its beautiful reproduction Federal furnishings has the feel of a much older place. Room rates start at $300/340.

In the **University City** area, the slightly faded *Sheraton University City Hotel* (☎ *215-387-8000, 800-325-3535)*, at S 36th and Chestnut Sts, is near the universities and four blocks from the Civic Center. It has 375 rooms, a gym and outdoor pool. Singles/doubles cost $225/240, but prices vary and can often be up to 50% less.

PLACES TO EAT

Eating is a definite highlight of a visit to Philadelphia, which is famous for its cheese steak sandwiches, hoagies and pretzels. The city boasts some of the top restaurants in the country, but Philadelphia isn't only a winner in fine dining. Budget travelers can buy cheap food from one of the many street carts or from food courts in the shopping

centers, and there's terrific grocery shopping at South Philly's Italian Market and Center City's Reading Terminal Market. There are good restaurants where you spend about $15, and many more great places to eat for about $30.

Historic District & Around
Budget This is the heart of the tourist area so there aren't many budget places. *The Bourse*, on S 5th St, beside the Liberty Bell Pavilion, has a large, elegant food court with counters selling Italian, Greek and Chinese food, cheese steaks and more, all in the $3 to $6 range. *Carousel Shoppe*, on S 3rd St, near Walnut St, is a small luncheonette with a pretty storefront serving breakfast for $1.35, sandwiches for $2.25 to $3.25 and Hershey's ice cream.

China House (☎ *215-829-1521, 618 Market St)* is a small, basic Chinese restaurant serving food to eat in or to go. Beef dishes cost $7, poultry $6.75.

Old City Coffee (221 Church St), in Old City, is an attractive, quiet place to stop for good brewed coffee, cookies or a salad. In the South St area, the *Rhino Cafe (212 South St)* serves great coffee, hot or cold, while the *Morning Cup (422 S 2nd St)*, on Head House Square, is another good source.

The Hoagie, Cheese Steak & Pretzel

The hoagie got its name from the city's Hog Island Shipyard. The workers there used to call their lunchtime staple 'hoggies' before today's name stuck. Cheese steaks were also invented in Philadelphia, and several places claim to make the best, including archrivals Pat's King of Steaks and Geno's, near the Italian Market (see the Italian market section for details).

Soft pretzels are another specialty. Locals say that you should buy them from the Amish at Reading Terminal Market, they should be stuck together and rectangular or they're not the real thing, and you should eat them with mustard.

The Morning Cup transforms into a bar and bistro at night.

Mid-Range *Marco's* (☎ 215-592-8887, 232 Arch St), decorated with paintings and prints, is a tiny restaurant serving an eclectic range of reasonably priced specials. Try the Thai red curry for $14.75 or the paella for $14.25. The popular **La Locanda del Ghiottone** (30 N 3rd St) has a range of pastas for less than $10 and sidewalk tables; it's a good idea to book reservations for dinner.

Popular with families, *DiNardo's Famous Seafood* (☎ 215-925-5115, 312 Race St) is a branch of a Wilmington, DE, restaurant. Baltimore-style steamed crabs are the specialty, but the fish is also good. It's open Monday to Saturday for lunch and dinner (dinner only on Sunday). Main courses are between $13 and $20. Another good seafood place to try is *Philadelphia Fish & Co* (☎ 215-625-8605, 207 Chestnut St), which has soups starting at $3.95 and grilled shrimp for $17.95; it also serves meat dishes.

Top End *City Tavern* (☎ 215-413-1443, 138 S 2nd St), at Walnut St, is where Paul Revere arrived on horseback in 1774 with news of the British Parliament's closure of Boston Harbor. Today's building is a reconstruction of the original 1773 tavern popular with the political elite of the day. Presenting food that the Founding Fathers – and Mothers – would have eaten but 'adapted to modern tastes,' it's open daily. Hillary and Bill Clinton have eaten here. At lunchtime main dishes are $8 to $17; braised rabbit costs $9.95. Dinner mains are between $18 to $26; roast prime rib of beef with Yorkshire pudding costs $23.95. Reservations are recommended.

Old Original Bookbinders (☎ 215-925-7027, 125 Walnut St), at S 2nd opposite City Tavern, is a long-established Philadelphia landmark serving traditional seafood favorites like lobster and broiled fish. It's open for lunch and dinner Tuesday to Sunday. Lunch mains are $8 to $11, dinner mains $17 to $35; reservations are required.

South St & Around

Budget *South St Diner* (☎ 215-627-5258, 140 South St), near Head House Square, is a popular restaurant serving reasonable food 24 hours a day. Omelettes are $3.50, club sandwiches $5 to $6; it also does pastas for about $6.

Mako – Retired Surfer's Bar & Grill (☎ 215-625-3820, 301 South St), with its brightly painted exterior, serves two dozen mussels for $8.95 and chicken wings from $4.50. It has a second bar upstairs. The small *Ishkabbible's Eatery* (☎ 215-923-4337, 337 South St) opens for breakfast, lunch and dinner, serving savory, inexpensive dishes like chicken cheese steak ($4.50 to $6.25), burgers ($3.75 to $5.50) including a variety of veggie burgers, and cookies baked on the premises. Here since 1939, a top contender for Philadelphia's best cheese steak honor is *Jim's Steaks* (☎ 215-928-1911, 400 South St), where the city's specialty starts at $4.50.

South St Souvlaki (☎ 215-925-3026, 509 South St) is a terrific Greek taverna serving classic versions of gyros and souvlaki for $5.25, grilled fish and kebabs for $10.95. It has live Greek entertainment on Sunday nights.

PhilaDeli (☎ 215-923-1986, 410 South St) is good for diner food, especially its all-day breakfast, hoagie sandwiches ($4 to $7), veggie burgers ($4.95) and desserts.

The popular weekend brunch spot *Montserrat* (☎ 215-627-4224, 623 South St) is an established South St favorite for its varied menu offering items like French onion soup for $4.50, grilled hamburgers $5.95 and black bean quesadilla $6.95. Its bar also serves great cocktails.

The *Pink Rose Pastry Shop* (☎ 215-592-0565, 630 S 4th St), at Bainbridge St, is great for carrot cake, muffins, cookies and coffee. It's closed Monday. Established in 1923, the *Famous 4th St Deli* (☎ 215-922-3274), at S 4th and Bainbridge Sts, is a Jewish delicatessen serving classic pastrami sandwiches and bagels for $6.75 and delicious homemade cookies (85¢ each). It's open for breakfast and lunch. *Alyan's* (☎ 215-922-3553, 603 S 4th St) is an inexpensive Middle

Eastern restaurant serving great hummus for $3.50 and falafel platters for $7.50.

Essene (☎ 215-922-1146, 719 S 4th St) is a cafe at the rear of a health-food store, and serves organically grown produce for lunch and dinner. Tofu curry or paella cost $6.50.

Mid-Range *Italia (☎ 215-625-0777, 526 S 4th St)* is a simple, casual Italian restaurant offering inexpensive, well-prepared dishes. Pastas cost $9 to $11, pizzas $5 to $9.50. *Cedars (☎ 215-925-4950, 616 S 2nd St)* serves appetizing Lebanese favorites like falafel for $3.75 and grilled tuna for $14.95. Mediterranean food with a Moroccan flavor can be found nearby at *Fez*, where a chicken kebab costs $9.95.

On the site of the birthplace of Larry Fine, one of the legendary Three Stooges comedy trio, *Jon's Bar & Grille (☎ 215-592-1390, 606 S 3rd St)*, at South St, has a pleasant outside dining area and a generally good, eclectic menu. A Mexican chili burger is $6.95, spicy Italian sausage $8.95.

Bridget Foy's South St Grill (☎ 215-922-1813, 200 South St) is a popular bar and restaurant with an outdoor eating area where you can watch the crowds go by. Open daily for lunch and dinner, evening plates (like vegetarian jambalaya pasta) cost $12 to $20.

Center City

Budget There are large food courts on the 2nd floor of *1 Liberty Place* and on the lower level at *Gallery at Market East* on Market St.

Pine St's Antique Row is home to some good-value options. *Two Sisters à la Mode (☎ 215-574-0586, 1141 Pine St)* is a pleasant, popular bistro offering dishes like blueberry pancakes for $6.50 or quiche for $7.25; you can bring your own wine, and it only accepts cash. Further along, *Taco House (☎ 215-735-2240, 1218 Pine St)* is a tiny Mexican shop serving quesadillas for $4 and burritos starting at $3 to $4.30. *Samosa (☎ 215-545-7776, 1214 Walnut St)*, at Camac St, offers tasty vegetarian Indian dishes, with lunchtime buffets for only $4.95, dinner buffets $7.95. It's open daily for lunch and dinner.

In the Northern Liberties neighborhood just to the north of the historic district, *Silk City Diner (☎ 215-592-8838)*, at Spring Garden and N 5th St, is a great 1940s diner. With jukeboxes and tasty food, it's open 24 hours daily. A cheese steak or veggie burger is $4.75, omelette $4.25.

The colorful *Reading Terminal Market*, an indoor food market, is one of your best bets for either groceries or delicious good-value eateries. Take a wander around and check out the selections. The market opens Monday to Saturday from 8 am to 6 pm, although many food stalls start to close at 3 pm.

The Amish section opens Wednesday to Saturday only. *Fisher's Soft Pretzels & Ice Cream* serves ice cream from $1.40 and perhaps the city's best pretzels ($1.25).

Other popular choices include *Le Bus Bakery*, with great breads starting at $3 and pastries, muffins and other delights for $1.75; and *12th St Cantina*, with its homemade Mexican food, burritos for $3.75 and tacos for $2. Try *Ricky's Philly Steaks* for terrific cheese steaks at $4.60. *The Basic 4 Vegetarian Snack Bar*, serves vegetarian, natural foods and baked goods, including spinach pie for $3.70. *Bassett's Ice Cream*, extremely popular with the locals – despite, or because of, its ice cream's high butterfat content – has single cones for $2.10 and Italian water ice (crushed ice and fruit pulp).

There are many other good options, including Greek, Chinese, Japanese and Middle Eastern food stalls.

Mid-Range Open for lunch and dinner in one of Philly's nicest residential neighborhoods, *Astral Plane (☎ 215-546-6230, 1708 Lombard St)* features a varied menu in a casually decorated townhouse. At dinner, a Caesar salad is $6, salmon filet $17.

The *Hard Rock Cafe (☎ 215-238-1000, 1113-31 Market St)*, at 12th St, is hard to miss with its giant, red, revolving electric guitar above the entrance. Inside there's lots of the usual music memorabilia and burgers ($6.80 to $8.80). *Caribou Cafe (☎ 215-625-9535, 1126 Walnut St)* is a French-style cafe with marble-topped tables and serving great croissants and muffins for breakfast. Lunch

PENNSYLVANIA

and dinner feature bistro-style fare – with starters $6 to $9 and mains, like trout almondine, starting at $12 to $19.

The **Italian Bistro** (☎ *215-731-0700, 211 South Broad St*) is a casual eatery specializing in wood-fired pizzas for $8 to $10, but also offering an interesting seafood menu.

Chinatown has plenty of reasonably priced restaurants with some good choices for Vietnamese and vegetarian as well as Chinese food. The greatest concentration of restaurants is near the intersection of Race and N 10th Sts.

Open daily, the clean **Angkor** (☎ *215-923-2438, 121 N 11th St*), at Cherry St, is a combined Cambodian and Vietnamese restaurant. It serves fried spring rolls for $3.50, shredded pork and rice for $6.50. For vegetarian Chinese (certified kosher by the city's rabbis) **Cherry St** (☎ *215-923-3663, 1010 Cherry St*) has mock beef (made from wheat gluten) for $7.25 or vegetable tempura for $9.95. Most main dishes are $7 to $10, and it also does seafood. Another place serving kosher food is **Singapore Chinese Vegetarian Restaurant** (☎ *922-3288, 1029 Race St*), where tempura costs $8.95.

A good choice for Chinese nonvegetarian dishes is **Lee How Fook** (☎ *215-925-7266, 219 N 11th St*), which serves sea bass and lemon chicken. Mains are $5 to $13, and you can bring your own wine or beer. It's closed Monday. The hole-in-the-wall **Joe's Peking Duck House** (☎ *215-922-3277, 925 Race St*) serves hot-and-sour soup of mushrooms and bean curd ($2.50) and noodles with seafood ($7.95). **Ocean City** (☎ *215-829-0688, 234 N 9th St*) offers delicious braised duck for $13. Most mains are $8 to $15, and it is open daily.

Nothing special to look at, **Ray's Cafe** (☎ *215-922-5122, 141 N 9th St*) serves delicious Taiwanese food (mains $9 to $19) and an upscale gourmet coffee list. A lot of attention is paid to the coffee roasting, brewing process and presentation, using some of the world's finest beans. A cup costs $3.75 to $5.50 for most choices. It also has a selection of teas.

Top End **The Garden** (☎ *215-546-4455, 1617 Spruce St*) serves superb European cuisine in an 1870 townhouse originally built for the Philadelphia Musical Academy. Beautifully decorated, it's one of the city's top restaurants, and reservations are recommended. Dinner mains are $16 to $26. It's closed Sunday.

The elegant, good-value **Ciboulette** (☎ *215-790-1210*), upstairs in the Bellevue building at 200 S Broad St at Walnut St, features French Provincial cuisine. Main courses are $16 to $24; roasted cod is $20. Try to get a table with a Broad St view.

One of the city's best and most authentic Mexican restaurants is **Tequila's** (☎ *215-546-0181, 1511 Locust St*); expect to pay about $35 for a three-course meal.

Le Bec-Fin (☎ *215-567-1000, 1523 Walnut St*) is, for many, reason enough to travel miles to the city. Rated as one of the country's top restaurants, it serves classic French cuisine in a formal setting and has a prix fixe dinner menu for $118. The same food is served for a bit less in **Le Bar Lyonnais** downstairs. Book your table well in advance.

Earning almost as much praise, the Four Seasons Hotel's **The Fountain** (☎ *215-963-1500*) serves American-European cuisine, with mains $28 to $40. In addition, there's **Susanna Foo** (☎ *215-545-2666, 1512 Walnut*), a consistently top-rated, elegantly furnished restaurant serving Chinese specialties with New American inspiration. Dinner mains cost $18 to $30.

Italian Market & Around

Budget Visit the Italian Market, on S 9th St between Christian St and Washington Ave, and the area around it for the best prices for groceries, classic Philadelphia cheese steaks, traditional Italian restaurants and some Vietnamese newcomers.

If you're buying groceries try **D'Angelo Brothers** (*909 S 9th St*) for meat; **Claudio's** (*924-26 S 9th St*) for cheese, salami and other Italian goods; and **Talluto's**, at S 9th St near Carpenter St, for varieties of fresh pasta. Then there's **Isgro Pastries** (*1009 Christian St*), near the corner of 10th St, for cakes and pastries; it has been here since 1904.

Two of Philadelphia's most popular cheese steak places are open 24 hours daily at the intersection of S 9th St and Passyunk Ave: *Geno's* (☎ 215-389-1455) and *Pat's King of Steaks* (☎ 215-468-1564). At Geno's cheese steaks cost $4.75, an Italian hoagie $5.25. As well as cheese steaks, Pat serves hot dogs for $4.45.

Villa Di Roma (☎ 215-592-1295, 936 S 9th St) is plain looking but serves good pasta with dishes around $6 to $9. At Christian and S 7th Sts, tasty water ice – called lemonhead regardless of its flavor – can be found at *John's Water Ice*, which has been serving the neighborhood since 1945. A cup of either lemon, cherry, chocolate or pineapple starts at 75¢. It's closed Tuesday.

Tiem An (☎ 215-923-4390, 1030 S 8th St), at League St near Washington Ave, serves good Vietnamese food in plain surroundings. Spring rolls cost $1.20, bean curd casserole $7.95. For Vietnamese and Chinese, try *Nam Phuong* (☎ 215-629-4002), around the corner at 746 Christian St (at S 8th St) which has beef and rice soup for $2.95 and chicken with black bean sauce for $6.75. It also serves Chinese beer. Both open for lunch and dinner.

In South Philadelphia, *Anthony's Italian Coffee House* (903 S 9th St) is a small cafe serving good cakes and coffee. It has live music on weekends, small art exhibitions and poetry readings.

Mid-Range Established in 1900, *Ralph's* (☎ 215-627-6011, 760 S 9th St) is a decent Italian restaurant open for lunch and dinner. Ask for a table upstairs in the huge hall with traditional murals. Main courses like baked lasagna are in the $10 to $18 range.

Offering terrific value for the money, the popular, award-winning *Dmitri's* (☎ 215-625-0556, 795 S 3rd St), at Catharine St, serves a platter of feta cheese with olives for $6 and seafood fettucine for $13. It has only 25 tables and doesn't take reservations, so be prepared to wait. Bring your own wine.

A South Philly classic, *Victor Cafe* (☎ 215-468-3040, 1303 Dickinson St), near S 13th St, is renowned both for its Italian cuisine and its opera-singing waitstaff. They

are often students from the nearby Curtis School of Music or moonlighting professionals and regularly burst into song, performing operas and arias. Reservations are recommended. Mains are $13 to $20.

Even further south, *Melrose Diner* (☎ 215-467-6644, 1501 Snyder Ave) is a family-owned restaurant that's been serving American comfort food since 1935. According to some, it 'has its own culture' with vintage '70s interiors and a history of mob-boss clientele. It's a busy place with its own bakery (you can order cakes to take out) and it opens 24 hours daily. Grilled sandwiches cost $3.25, roast lamb $7 to $9.

University City

Budget This student area has several inexpensive options. One of the bargain delights of Philadelphia is the array of food carts lining the streets. Although there are some in Center City, the biggest concentration is in University City. Places where you'll find lots of them are on the corners of S 34th and Walnut Sts, S 32nd and Market Sts and along Market St between S 36th and S 34th Sts. Cheese steaks and hoagies are about $3, Chinese and Thai dishes $3 to $3.75.

The *food court* on the Market St side of 30th St Station offers a surprisingly good choice of eateries including Asian and Italian food. *Bain's Cheesesteak Deli* has cheese steaks starting at $3.60, while *Au Bon Pain*, part of the French cafe chain, has filled bagels and croissants for about $1.60.

Moravian Cafes, on Walnut St near the corner of S 34th St, is a collection of food stalls around a central eating area and gets very busy at lunchtime; options include pizza slices ($2.15) from Cosimo's Pizza and Chinese dishes ($5.50) from Oriental Gourmet.

Popular with students, *Café Bon Appetit* (☎ 215-222-5520, 3701 Chestnut St) is a large cafeteria in International House, offering snacks and meals; soup is $2.50, pasta $4.95. It is open from 11 am and is closed weekends.

If you'd like something spicy, *Sitar India* (☎ 215-662-0818, 60 S 38th St), near Chestnut

St, has an all-you-can-eat, daily buffet for $5.95 at lunchtime, $8.95 at dinner.

Bucks County (☎ 215-387-6722, 3430 Sansom St), in University City, has good coffee and pastries to get you started in the mornings. ***XandO Cafe & Bar***, on S 36th St next to the University of Pennsylvania Bookstore, is a large, modern, trendy two-story place with background music helping to create a relaxed, pleasant atmosphere. It has tables outside, and its 'xandwiches' start at $3.50. It has several other outlets around the city.

Mid-Range & Top End *White Dog Cafe* (☎ 215-386-9224, 3420 Sansom St), in addition to being a good restaurant with a pleasant bar, it is where owner Judy Wicks stages lectures and seminars on political and social issues. She has also published her own cookbook. The restaurant serves mostly organic New American cuisine – mains like salmon burger or tuna salad cost $8 to $12.50. It's open Monday to Saturday for lunch and dinner and has a popular Sunday brunch.

La Terrasse (☎ 215-386-5000, 2432 Sansom St) is a beautifully restored French bistro with mains from $9 to $17.50; pan-seared salmon is $16.50. It is open for lunch and dinner but is closed Sunday.

ENTERTAINMENT
Philadelphia has something for everyone. The Avenue of the Arts (Broad St south of City Hall) is Philly's premier cultural destination. South St is popular at night for drinking,

---

'Make It a Night'

To encourage people to stay downtown midweek, 'Make It a Night' promotes Wednesday evening with free metered parking after 5 pm (after 6:30 pm in restricted zones), free outdoor entertainment, reduced prices at cinemas, late hours in shops and museums and other special events. Call the 'Make It a Night' hotline at ☎ 215-592-8282 or check the local press.

---

eating, window shopping, listening to a band or people-watching. There are popular nightclubs on the waterfront along Christopher Columbus Blvd (Delaware Ave) north of the Benjamin Franklin Bridge – between midnight and 2 am on Friday and Saturday traffic jams are common. A new entertainment complex is being built at Penn's Landing.

For current events, check the 'Weekend' section of Friday's *Philadelphia Inquirer* and the *Philadelphia Daily News* and the free weeklies *City Paper* and *Philadelphia Weekly*. Also check Tower Records (open 9 am to midnight daily) on South St for the latest music and dance-club happenings.

You can buy tickets for most entertainment from Ticketmaster (☎ 215-336-2000), a computerized ticket service with locations around the city, or from Upstages (☎ 215-569-9786), 1412 Chestnut St in Center City, where you can buy full price tickets or half-price on the day of the performance.

Theater
Philadelphia has a rich and varied theater scene. Productions range from Broadway shows in the major theaters to experimental drama in student repertory and community theaters. Prices for tickets run from as little as $10 in the smaller neighborhood theaters to between $15 and $60 or more for bigger productions in one of the main venues downtown.

Walnut St Theater (☎ 215-574-3550, 825 Walnut St), at 9th St, established in 1809, and ***Merriam Theater*** (☎ 215-732-5446, 250 S Broad St), part of the Avenue of the Arts, stage mostly mainstream drama, dance and musical productions by local and touring companies. ***Forrest Theater*** (☎ 215-923-1515, 1114 Walnut St) usually puts on big Broadway musical hits.

Philadelphia Arts Bank (☎ 215-545-0590, 601 S Broad St), run by the University of the Arts, has a 230-seat theater with performances by local theater companies. The ***Arden Theater Company*** (☎ 215-922-8900, 40-50 Arch St), at N 2nd St, presents works by both established and first-time playwrights in an arts complex.

Wilma Theater (☎ 215-963-0345), in its new 300-seat home at Spruce and Broad Sts, provides good avant-garde drama and comedy. The *Society Hill Playhouse (☎ 215-923-0210, 507 S 8th St)*, near South St, features contemporary drama, comedy and musicals.

The *Annenberg Center (☎ 215-898-6791, 3680 Walnut St)*, in University City, has several theaters and hosts performances by national and international artists as well as local companies.

Freedom Theatre (☎ 215-765-2793, 1346 N Broad St) stages potent dramas drawing on the African-American experience.

Dance

If you're a ballet lover, the acclaimed Pennsylvania Ballet (☎ 215-551-7000, 1101 S Broad St), is a must-see. The company performs at the *Academy of Music* and *Merriam Theater* from September through June, including its traditional annual production of Tchaikovsky's *Nutcracker* over Christmas. A subsidiary of the company is Off-Center Ballet, which experiments with new works.

The Philadelphia Dance Company (☎ 215-387-8200, 9 Philadanco Way), also known as Philadanco, explores the black experience through modern dance and ballet at the *Annenberg Center* and other venues. The company at the small *Koresh Dance Center (☎ 215-751-0959, 104 S 20th St)* puts on a range of performances from ballet to jazz.

Cinema

Philadelphia has a large selection of cinemas showing mainstream movies. Downtown, try the four-screen *Sameric (☎ 215-567-0604, 1908 Chestnut St)*. *Ritz Five (☎ 215-925-7900, 214 Walnut St)*, in Society Hill, and *Ritz at the Bourse* (same phone number as Ritz Five), at S 4th and Ranstead Sts, show a mix of mainstream, limited-release and foreign films. Admission costs $7.50 at both.

The 'arthouses,' *Film Forum (☎ 215-732-7704, 509 S Broad St)*, at Lombard St, and *Roxy Theater (☎ 215-563-9088, 2021 Sansom St)* show classic cult US and foreign films. *International House (☎ 215-387-5125, 3701 Chestnut St)*, in University City, puts on first-run US films plus movies and documentaries from around the world; admission costs $6.50. Visit its website at www.libertynet .org/ihouse.

Classical Music & Opera

The world-class Philadelphia Orchestra performs September through May at the *Academy of Music (☎ 215-893-1999, S Broad St)*, at Locust St; tickets cost $12 to $80. It also does free evening concerts in a six-week summer season at the *Mann Music Center (☎ 215-567-0707, www.manncenter .org, George's Hill Drive)*, near N 52nd St and Parkside Ave, in Fairmount Park.

Still in Fairmount Park, you can listen to chamber music at *Laurel Hill Mansion (☎ 215-235-1776, E Edgely Drive)*. After each recital there's a 'collation' – concertgoers gather to drink fruit punch and eat cakes.

Concerto Soloists of Philadelphia performs a series of evening concerts of chamber music at the *Walnut St Theater (☎ 215-574-3550, 825 Walnut St)*. Many of the city's musicians receive their training at the *Curtis Institute of Music (☎ 215-893-5261, 1726 Locust St)* which has among its public offerings free student recitals during the academic year on Monday, Wednesday and Friday evenings.

November to April, the Opera Company of Philadelphia (☎ 215-928-2100, 510 Walnut St) puts on large-scale operas with international stars at the *Academy of Music*. The Pennsylvania Opera Theater (☎ 215-731-1212) is a company that performs in English at the *Merriam Theater (☎ 215-732-5446, 250 S Broad St)*. Another company, the Academy of Vocal Arts (☎ 215-735-1685), 1920 Spruce St, performs at various venues in and around Philadelphia.

Jazz, Blues & Gospel

Philadelphia has a strong jazz and blues tradition, its own sound and some terrific venues. The *Philadelphia Clef Club of the Performing Arts (☎ 215-893-9912)*, at S Broad and Fitzwater Sts, is part of the Avenue of the Arts. It's a nonprofit organization that promotes jazz by hosting public performances, keeping records of its history and training musicians.

Some of the best jazz is at the upmarket **Zanzibar Blue** (☎ 215-732-5200, 200 S Broad St) below the Bellevue building at Chestnut St. A dining room serves international cuisine, but you don't have to eat. There's a cover charge of $10 to $20.

The earthy **Ortlieb's Jazzhaus** (☎ 215-922-1035, 847 N 3rd St) is in an old brewery in a rundown neighborhood north of the Old City. Music usually begins at 9:30 pm but the Tuesday night jam session, when audience members show their stuff, gets going around 8:30 pm. There's no cover charge and parking is free. **Chris' Jazz Cafe** (☎ 215-568-3131, 1421 Sansom St) has live sessions upstairs every night with no cover charge.

South St Blues (☎ 215-546-9009, 2100 South St) is a small bar that's been around a long time serving up live blues nightly; weekend nights are probably the best time to go. **Warmdaddy's** (☎ 215-627-2500, 4 S Front St) is a refined, upscale blues-club-cum-restaurant serving Southern-style food with live music nightly Tuesday to Sunday.

You can enjoy free jazz at **Reading Terminal Market** on Friday noon to 2 pm. Jazz, blues and gospel programs are also organized by the Mill Creek Jazz & Cultural Society at the **The Loft at Milk Creek** (☎ 215-473-2880, Mill Creek Community Center, 4624 Lancaster Ave) in West Philadelphia.

Rock

The Khyber (☎ 215-238-5888, 56 S 2nd St) is a small venue popular with college students, where you can eat, drink and see unsigned bands for a cover charge of around $5. The **Pontiac Grille** (☎ 215-925-4053, 304 South St) is a club where live bands perform most nights (cover $5 to $10).

Bigger-name acts perform at the **Trocadero** (see Dance Clubs) with a $10 to $15 cover charge. There's something happening most nights at **Silk City Lounge** (☎ 215-592-8838), at Spring Garden and N 5th Sts next to Silk City Diner. It's a bar-lounge featuring live bands or DJs; there's no cover charge

during the week, but on weekend nights it's about $6.

In summer, the waterfront north of Benjamin Franklin Bridge is the center of Philadelphia nightlife with plenty of clubs providing music and drink. Some are seasonal, so call ahead. Aboard an old ferryboat, **KatManDu** (☎ 215-629-1101), at No 417, has classic rock in a Caribbean atmosphere and opens year-round. Further north, **Maui** (☎ 215-423-8116, Pier 53, 1143 N Christopher Columbus Blvd) is one of the biggest with alternative live music nightly and a huge dance floor. A water taxi takes people between the clubs.

Mann Music Center (☎ 215-567-0707, George's Hill Drive), near N 52nd St and Parkside Ave, Fairmount Park, is the city's top outdoor venue. Major acts perform there during the summer, while the biggest of them play **Veterans Stadium** (☎ 215-686-1776) or **First Union Spectrum Stadium** (☎ 215-336-3600), both in South Philadelphia.

On Friday and Saturday night at the **Fels Planetarium**, in the Franklin Institute Science Museum (☎ 215-448-1200), laser light shows feature the recorded music of rock bands like Pink Floyd as well as the latest alternative music.

Bars & Dance Clubs

Most of Philly's bars stay open till 2 am. In Old City, **Wichita's** (☎ 215-627-4825, 22 S 3rd St) is a trendy, cavernous bar and restaurant selling 60 microbrews ($3 per pint) on tap.

Towards South St in Head House Square are **The Artful Dodger** (☎ 215-922-7880, 400-402 S 2nd St) and the **Dickens Inn** (☎ 215-928-9397, 421 S 2nd St). Both pubs serve British-style food and imported ales. **Downey's** (☎ 215-625-9500, 526 Front St), at South St, is a beautiful Irish place with furnishings imported from the old country. It serves decent food and has a rooftop deck and balcony overlooking the Delaware River. Other options include **Cop Banana Cabana**, at S 4th and South Sts and **Mako-Retired Surfer's Bar & Grill** (☎ 215-625-3820, 301 South St).

On Antique Row, at Pine and S 13th Sts, *Dirty Frank's* (☎ *215-732-5010)* is a real dive, with boarded up windows and no sign (look for the plain gray door), but it's a local institution. It has cheap booze and an interesting mix of patrons, including writers and artists. For a crowded pub with plenty of atmosphere try *McGuinn's Old Ale House* which is in a narrow lane squeezed between Sansom and Chestnut Sts near the southeast corner of Penn Square and dates from 1860.

In University City, *New Deck Tavern* (☎ *215-386-4600, 3408 Sansom St),* just down from the White Dog Cafe, is a popular student hangout. Try also *KelliAnne's* (☎ *215-349-8400),* on Spruce St at 44th St, a dive bar attracting an interesting mix of students and locals.

Philly has several microbreweries. *Dock St Brewing Company* (☎ *215-496-0413, 2 Logan Square),* at N 18th and Cherry Sts, offers a contemporary setting and jazz or Latin American music on weekends. It closes Sunday. *Poor Henry's American St Brew Pub* (☎ *215-413-3500, 829 N American St),* is north of Spring Garden St between 2nd and 3rd Sts. It's part of the Ortlieb Brewery, which has been operating here since 1869.

In the trendy suburb of Manayunk, the *Manayunk Brewery & Restaurant* (☎ *482-8220, 420 Main St)* is another popular spot for a traditional brew.

For sophisticated clubbers there's *Circa* (☎ *215-545-6800, 1518 Walnut St),* which, as well as being a top restaurant, is possibly Center City's hottest nightspot. Thursday to Saturday night, after a fairly pricey meal, you can strut to '70s disco and other pop music. There's an $8 cover charge after 10 pm.

In Chinatown, *Trocadero* (☎ *215-923-7625, 1003 Arch St)* has dancing to the latest rock bands with admission from $6. *Shampoo* (☎ *215-922-7500, 417 N 8th St),* open Thursday to Saturday nights from 9 pm, has three dance floors with music ranging from alternative to retro.

Woody's (☎ *215-545-1893, 202 S 13th St)* is a popular gay bar and dance club.

SPECTATOR SPORTS

Philadelphia's professional and college sports teams enjoy an enthusiastic following. The two major venues, Veterans Stadium and the First Union Complex, are at the southern end of South Philadelphia on S Broad St. Tickets can be bought from Ticketmaster (☎ 215-336-2000). Admission to baseball and hockey games varies from $6 to $20, and to football and basketball games from $15 to $60.

The sports complex is easily reached by subway on the SEPTA Broad St Line to Pattison Ave station which is within walking distance, or by bus C along Broad St. By car take exit 14 off I-95 or the Broad St southbound exit off I-76.

With a 67,000 capacity, **Veterans Stadium**, 3501 S Broad St, is home to the Philadelphia Phillies National League baseball team, the Philadelphia Eagles of the National Football League and the Temple University Owls football team. The annual Army-Navy football game is played here, and major rock concerts are sometimes staged here, too. Tickets for the Phillies' games are difficult to get (fans are not just fair-weather friends), and the best seats for Eagles' games are taken by season-ticket holders. For schedules and information on the Phillies call ☎ 215-463-1000, for the Eagles call ☎ 215-463-5500.

The **First Union Complex** is made up of two stadiums: the First Union Center and the First Union Spectrum (formerly CoreStates Spectrum). The new 21,000-seat First Union Center is home to the NBA's Philadelphia 76ers (also called the 'Sixers') basketball team and the NHL's Philadelphia Flyers hockey team. Unless the home team has a chance of reaching the play-offs, you can usually buy a ticket on the day of the game. For schedules and information on the Sixers call ☎ 215-339-7600, for the Flyers call ☎ 215-465-4500.

The indoor, 17,500-seat First Union Spectrum stages other big sporting events, including the US Pro Indoor Tennis Championships, and rock music concerts.

In University City at Walnut and S 33rd Sts, **Franklin Field** is part of the University of

PENNSYLVANIA

Pennsylvania's sports facilities. It hosts the Penn Relays world-class amateur athletic meet each April as well as Penn's football games and other sporting events.

SHOPPING

Philadelphia's main shopping districts are along Market, Walnut and Chestnut Sts east of Broad St, but South St, Reading Terminal Market and Italian Market are also worth visiting. Check the 'Weekend' section of Friday's *Philadelphia Inquirer* for listings of antique fairs and art galleries.

Antique Row, along Pine St between S 9th and S 12th Sts, offers some wonderful items in its many antique stores. For fine Americana including furniture, quilts and folk art try Finkel & Daughter (☎ 215-627-7797) at No 927.

Walnut St in Center City has several commercial art galleries. Newman Galleries (☎ 215-563-1779, www.newmangalleries1865.com), 1625 Walnut St, is one of the oldest in Philadelphia, displaying works of local, national and European artists. Old City's galleries are concentrated on N 3rd St around Cherry and Race Sts. The FAN Gallery (☎ 215-922-5155), 311 Cherry St, has regular exhibitions of contemporary artists.

The main center for jewelry is Jewelers' Row, on and around Sansom St between S 7th and S 8th Sts, where you'll find dozens of craftspeople, wholesalers and retailers. Some substantial discounts are available on metal jewelry and precious stones.

The South St area has a variety of interesting shopping. For music, Tower Records has two stores: one branch (☎ 215-574-9888) is at No 610, while the other (☎ 215-925-0422) selling classical music is across the road at No 537; both are open till midnight. Philadelphia Record Exchange (☎ 215-925-7892), 608 S 5th St, is a long-established source of alternative rock with old 45s and LPs as well as CDs (it has another store nearby selling jazz). Digital Underground (☎ 215-925-5324), 526 S 5th St, specializes in new and used CDs, with an emphasis on independent artists. Both these stores open daily.

South St Antiques Market (☎ 215-592-0256), 615 S 6th St, in a former synagogue,

houses a selection of vintage clothing, jewelry, furniture and other items. It's open Wednesday to Thursday and Sunday from noon to 7 pm, Friday and Saturday noon to 8 pm. Eyes Art Gallery (☎ 215-925-0193), 402 South St, is a gift shop carrying a selection of exotic jewelry and handicrafts from third world sources. Head House Square has an interesting craft market on weekends that continues to 11 pm.

Philadelphia's two most notable department stores are Lord & Taylor (☎ 215-422-2000), on Market St between Juniper and S 13th Sts, and Strawbridge & Clothier (☎ 215-629-6000), on Market St between N 8th and N 9th Sts. Strawbridge & Clothier (usually shortened to Strawbridge's) is connected to the Gallery at Market East, a large shopping mall that also houses the JC Penney department store (☎ 215-238-9100), other shops and a good food court. Two other large shopping malls are the modern Shops at Liberty Place (☎ 215-851-9055), 2 Liberty Place, at S 16th and Market Sts, and the elegant Shops at The Bellevue (☎ 215-875-8350), at S Broad and Walnut Sts.

Family-run, nationally renowned Fante's Cookware (☎ 215-878-5557), 1006 S 9th St in

The Stetson

The Stetson hat, the 'Boss of the Plains,' was a unique hat with a high crown and wide brim. Though associated with cowboys, the hat that 'won the west' was made here in Philadelphia. John B Stetson began making hats in 1865 and by 1900 was the largest hatmaker in the world. At its height, his plant at 4th and Montgomery Sts in North Philadelphia covered 9 acres and employed 5000 workers. Stetson provided employees with a hospital and a savings and loan association to help them buy homes in the neighborhood. Eventually, the Depression and changing men's fashions crippled the company, and now all that remain of the city's connection with the Stetson hat are vacant lots.

the Italian Market, has operated since 1906 and sells everything for the cook from wooden spoons to copper utensils.

GETTING THERE & AWAY
Air
Philadelphia International Airport (☎ 215-937-6800, 800-745-4283, www.phl.org) is served by direct flights from Europe, the Caribbean and Canada, and offers connections to Asia, Africa and South America. Domestically, it has flights to over 100 destinations in the USA. (See also the introductory Getting There & Away and Getting Around chapters.)

The following airlines have offices in the Philadelphia area:

Air Jamaica
(☎ 800-523-5585) Philadelphia International Airport

Atlantic Air
(☎ 215-365-7270) Philadelphia International Airport

British Airways
(☎ 800-247-9297) Philadelphia International Airport

Continental Airlines
(☎ 215-492-4318) Philadelphia International Airport

Delta Air Lines
(☎ 800-325-1999) Philadelphia International Airport

Japan Airlines
(☎ 215-546-6350, 800-525-3663) 230 S Broad St

Korean Air
(☎ 800-525-4480) Philadelphia International Airport

Midway Airlines
(☎ 215-492-6222) Philadelphia International Airport

Spirit Airlines
(☎ 215-563-7799, 800-772-7117) 1845 Walnut St

US Airways
(☎ 800-428-4322) 123 S Broad St, (☎ 800-428-4322) 1 Penn Center

United Airlines
(☎ 800-241-6522) 1617 JFK Blvd

Other airlines that fly to Philadelphia are Midwest Express (☎ 800-452-2022), America West (☎ 800-235-9292) and Northwest Airlines (☎ 800-225-2525 domestic, 800-447-4747 international) and TWA (☎ 215-923-3710, 800-892-2746).

The airport has five terminals labeled A to E. All international flights arrive and depart at Terminal A except US Airways international departures, which leave from Terminal C. A new US Airways international terminal is planned. Terminals B and C are used by US Airways for domestic departures and arrivals, while Terminals D and E are used by other domestic carriers.

There's an information desk and an ATM (MAC) in every terminal, while Terminals A, B and C each have a currency-exchange office. Terminals A and C also have postal vending machines for domestic mail. Beside the ground-transportation desk in each baggage-claim area there's a bank of TV monitors listing the type of local transport available, airport contact number, destination and approximate cost. Car rental companies also have phones; you make a call and a shuttle bus will pick you up and take you to your car.

The roundtrip airfare to Pittsburgh starts at $158. One-way fares to New York City are $191 and Atlantic City $95.

Bus
The intercity bus terminal is at 1001 Filbert St at N 10th St. Greyhound (☎ 800-231-2222), Peter Pan Bus Lines (☎ 800-343-9999), Capitol Trailways (☎ 800-444-2877) and NJ Transit (☎ 215-569-3752, 800-228-8246) buses stop here. Left-luggage lockers cost $2 for up to six hours.

The return fare to New York City is $34 (2½ hours each way), to Atlantic City $15 (1½ hours) and to Washington, DC $30 (three hours). The one-way fare to San Francisco is $139 (27 ½ hours). There's no intercity bus to Jersey City, but you can catch one to Newark then take NJ Transit. See also the Getting There & Away chapter.

Train
Amtrak (☎ 800-872-7245) trains stop at 30th St Station on Market St beside the Schuylkill River in University City. Philadelphia is on Amtrak's Northeast Corridor route which runs between Richmond, VA,

and Boston, MA, via Washington, DC, and New York City; there are also trains west to Lancaster, Harrisburg, Altoona, Pittsburgh and Chicago and south to Florida. Amtrak maintains a website (www.amtrak.com).

The ticket office opens Monday to Friday 5:10 am to 10:30 pm, weekends 6:10 am to 10:30 pm. Baggage storage is available for $1.50 per item per day. There's a Travelers' Aid Society desk in case of emergency – call ☎ 215-546-0571 if no one's there.

To New York City (2½ hours) the one-way fare is $40, to Washington, DC (2¼ hours) it's $37. There are numerous fares to Pittsburgh depending on availability and the day, and time you travel – the one-way fare ranges from $42 to $80.

A cheaper but slightly longer way to get to New York City is to take the SEPTA R7 suburban train to Trenton ($6) in New Jersey. You can pick up this train from the SEPTA Suburban Station on John F Kennedy Blvd opposite the tourist office. There you connect with NJ Transit to Newark's Penn Station then continue on NJ Transit to New York City's Penn Station.

NJ Transit has a frequent rail service between Philadelphia and Atlantic City (about 1½ hours) for $6/12 one-way/roundtrip. For information on this service call ☎ 800-626-7433.

Subway

The Port Authority Transit Corporation (PATCO; ☎ 215-922-4600) has frequent Hi-Speedline subway trains to Camden, NJ, for 85¢. City stops are: 15th-16th St Station, 11th-12th St Station and 9th-10th St Station along Locust St, and 8th St Station at Market St. Then it's a scenic ride across the Benjamin Franklin Bridge to Camden.

Car & Motorcycle

Several highways lead through and around Philadelphia. From the north and south, I-95 (Delaware Expressway) follows the eastern edge of the city beside the Delaware River, with several exits for midtown.

I-276 (Pennsylvania Turnpike) runs east across the north of the city and over the river to connect with the New Jersey Turnpike.

From the west, I-76 (Pennsylvania Turnpike/Schuylkill Expressway) branches off the Pennsylvania Turnpike to follow the Schuylkill River to South Philadelphia and over the Walt Whitman Bridge into New Jersey south of Camden. Just north of downtown I-676 (Vine St Expressway) heads east over the Benjamin Franklin Bridge into Camden itself. If you're coming from the east, take I-295 or the New Jersey Turnpike, which connects to I-676 over the Benjamin Franklin Bridge into downtown.

Like any other big city, Philadelphia traffic 'enjoys' morning and evening peak hours. To avoid the worst of these, use I-676 (Vine St Expressway), which leads under the busier city streets to Old City.

Boat

The Riverlink ferry (☎ 215-925-5465) operates across the Delaware River from Penn's Landing to the New Jersey State Aquarium in Camden. (See the New Jersey State Aquarium section, earlier in this chapter, for fares and schedules.)

GETTING AROUND
To/From the Airport

Philadelphia International Airport (☎ 215-937-6800, 800-745-4283), 8 miles southwest of Center City, is easily accessed on SEPTA's (☎ 215-580-7800) R1 airport rail line, which operates daily every 30 minutes from 5:25 am to midnight and takes about 20 minutes. The R1 can be boarded at Market East, Suburban, 30th St or University City stations; the one-way fare is $5, but there's an additional $2 handling charge if you buy a ticket on the train.

Shuttle bus and limousine services also operate between the airport and the city. The cheaper ones cost only a few dollars more than the train and take you door to door. A shuttle to Center City costs about $7 to $10, to University City $8. A sedan costs $10 to $20. Some companies to try are Lady Liberty Airport Shuttle (☎ 215-222-8888), Airport Express (☎ 215-331-1130) and Airport One Limousine Service (☎ 215-535-4040).

Taxis to Center City cost a flat $20, and take about 20 to 25 minutes. To University City the fare is around $15 to $17.

Bus

The Southeastern Pennsylvania Transportation System (SEPTA; www.septa.org) provides comprehensive transportation service in the city and suburbs. SEPTA's information line (☎ 215-580-7800) operates daily from 6 am to midnight. The one-way fare on most routes is $1.60 for which you'll need the exact change or a token. If you're going to be doing a lot of traveling SEPTA's DayPass is a great value. It gives you a day's unlimited riding on all city transit vehicles plus a one-way trip on the R1 airport rail line. It costs $5 and is available at regional rail stations or SEPTA sales outlets. Transit maps can be bought at some stations for $7.

The bus No 76 route (punningly known as the 'Ben FrankLine') runs from Penn's Landing, through the Society Hill-South St area, along Market St to City Hall and the Benjamin Franklin Pkwy to the Philadelphia Museum of Art, Fairmount Park and the zoo. For only $1.60 you get to see many of the major sights; it leaves every 10 minutes Monday to Friday, every 20 minutes on weekends. Bus No 42 is another useful service that connects Old City with the Civic Center and University City in West Philadelphia.

Designed especially for visitors, PHLASH is a bus shuttle that does a loop through downtown from Spring Garden St in the north to South St, and from Christopher Columbus Blvd (Delaware Ave) in the east to the Philadelphia Museum of Art in the west. It operates daily 10 am to midnight. The normal one-way fare is $1.50, or you can ride all day for $3.

Another shuttle service, called LUCY, loops through the University City area from 30th St Station, Monday to Friday from 6:30 am to 8 pm. A single journey costs 50¢.

Trolley Bus

Motorized trolley buses are a pleasant way to visit many of the sights. See the Organized Tours section, earlier.

Train

Philadelphia's rail network is run by SEPTA (☎ 215-580-7800) and connects downtown with the suburbs and surrounding counties. Seven major routes are divided into six fare zones radiating from the city. One-way fares range from $3 to $5 during peak periods; off-peak fares are 50¢ to 75¢ cheaper. The main downtown stations are 30th St Station in University City, Penn Center Suburban Station at JFK Blvd and N 16th St, and Market East Station at Market and N 10th Sts beneath The Gallery shopping complex.

Useful routes are R7 to Germantown and Chestnut Hill East, R8 to Chestnut Hill West and R1 to the airport.

Subway

SEPTA operates three subway lines in Philadelphia. The Market-Frankford line runs east-west along Market St from 69th St in West Philadelphia to Front St from where it heads north to Frankford. The Broad St line runs north-south from Fern Rock in North Philadelphia to Pattison Ave in South Philadelphia near the Veterans and First Union Spectrum sports stadiums. The Subway-Surface line heads east-west along Market St from 13th St Station near City Hall to 33rd St, from where it forks to the northwest and southwest. A single journey costs $1.60.

The PATCO (☎ 215-922-4600) subway line to Camden, NJ, is a convenient, cheap way of getting across downtown (85¢).

Car & Motorcycle

Driving isn't recommended in central Philadelphia; parking is difficult and regulations are strictly enforced. Anyway, downtown distances are short enough to let you see most places on foot, and a bus or taxi can get you to places further out relatively easily. Park your car in a guarded lot and save it for trips out of the city or for evening trips. When booking a room with a hotel ask about its parking facilities.

If you want to cross downtown east-west, remember that the I-676 (Vine St Expressway) runs under the city streets and will save you a lot of time. Most downtown streets have alternate one-way traffic. The exceptions are Broad St, with three lanes in both directions, Vine St, Benjamin Franklin Pkwy and Market St between City Hall and Front St and west of 20th St (between 20th and 15th Sts, it's one-way eastbound). And Chestnut St is closed to traffic between 8th and 18th Sts.

Avoid South St on weekends and every evening as the traffic jams are notorious; also avoid Christopher Columbus Blvd (Delaware Ave) north of the Benjamin Franklin Bridge on weekend evenings.

Car Rental The main rental companies have desks at the airport (in addition to the offices listed below). Typical weekday rental rates for a compact car cost from $32 to $50 per day with unlimited mileage, but insurance, taxes and other charges can add around $20 a day to the cost. Weekend and weekly hire rates are cheaper. Some of the main rental companies in Philadelphia are:

Avis
(☎ 800-831-2847) 200 Arch St and 30th St Station

Budget
(☎ 215-492-9400) Corner of 21st and Market Sts

Dollar
(☎ 215-365-2700) Philadelphia International Airport

Enterprise
(☎ 800-736-8222) 510 N Front St and 1109 S Broad St, offers free pickup from hotel

Express
(☎ 215-259-0404) 4100 Presidential Blvd

Hertz
(☎ 800-654-3131) 31 S 19th St and 30th St Station

There are many other local and specialist rental companies, which are listed in the yellow pages under 'Automobile Renting'; some offer competitive rates compared to the national companies.

Taxi
Philadelphia's cabs are carefully regulated. Downtown and in University City you can hail a cab easily enough during the day especially at 30th St Station, other train stations and around the major hotels. At night and in the suburbs you're better off phoning for one.

Fares are $1.80 for the first one-sixth of a mile, then 30¢ for each subsequent one-sixth plus 20¢ for every minute of waiting time. The fare from University City to Penn's Landing is about $7. Some cabs accept credit cards.

Cab companies to try are:

Liberty Cab
(☎ 215-389-8000) 842 S 2nd St

United Cab Association
(☎ 215-625-2881) 500 N 2nd St

Yellow Cab
(☎ 215-225-6010) 1405 Pike St

Bicycle
Philadelphia isn't a bad place to get around by bicycle as it's reasonably flat, but there are few cycle lanes. Fairmount Park, however, has popular recreational cycling paths. See the Activities section, earlier, for more details and for information about bike rentals. If you'd like to bicycle outside the city, you can take your bike on off-peak SEPTA and PATCO trains with a valid permit, available from ticket offices.

Around Philadelphia

VALLEY FORGE NATIONAL HISTORIC PARK
This 5½-sq-mile park, 20 miles northwest of downtown Philadelphia at N Gulph Rd and Route 23, was the site of the Continental army's renowned winter encampment from December 19, 1777, to June 19, 1778, while the British occupied Philadelphia. Not a battlefield, the site is held as a symbol of bravery and endurance – 2000 of George Washington's 12,000 troops perished because of freezing temperatures, hunger and disease. Despite such losses, the army was reorganized and emerged to eventually defeat the British.

For a travel brochure on Valley Forge and Montgomery County, contact the Valley Forge Convention & Visitors Bureau (☎ 610-834-1550, 800-345-8112), 600 W Germantown

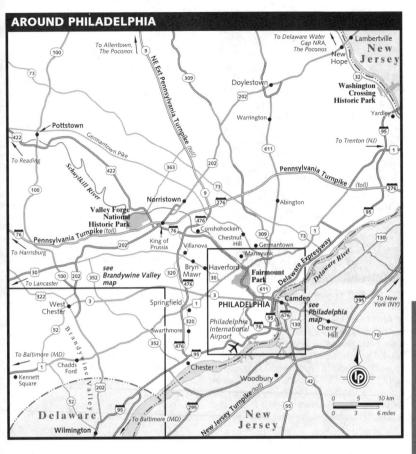

AROUND PHILADELPHIA

Pike, Plymouth Meeting, PA 19462; it also operates a 24-hour Funline (☎ 610-834-8844) with a recorded message that details upcoming special events.

The visitors' center (☎ 610-783-1077), open daily 9 am to 5 pm, contains exhibits and an information desk with maps and brochures highlighting the park's major points of interest and the area's other attractions. There's also a 15-minute film, *Valley Forge: A Winter Encampment*. Costumed reenactments of the Continental army's training procedures are staged occasionally during warmer weather. If you have a car, you can get a map from the visitors' center and take a 10-mile self-guided tour (tape $8, player $5) of the park. There are also organized bus tours every 30 minutes ($5.50/4.50 for adults/children) from the visitors' center.

The park opens daily 8:30 am to 5 pm, and admission to the site and visitors' center is free.

Things to See

Important sights include the **National Memorial Arch** to the soldiers who endured that winter and the **Monument to Patriots**

Yeah, I crossed a frozen river.

of African Descent, a bronze statue honoring the 5000 blacks who died in the war. Isaac Potts House, built in 1774, was used as Washington's headquarters and is furnished with period reproductions. It's open daily 9:30 am to 5 pm; the $2/free admission includes a short tour. The Valley Forge Historical Society Museum (☎ 610-783-0535), Route 23, houses items that belonged to George and Martha Washington, as well as other artifacts from the encampment. It's open Monday to Saturday 10 am to 5 pm, Sunday 1 to 5 pm. Admission costs $2/free for adults/children. The Washington Memorial Chapel built in 1903 is next door.

Getting There & Away

Weekdays only, from Philadelphia you can board SEPTA bus No 125 at the corner of N 16th St and JFK Blvd or at 30th St Station. The trip takes about 40 minutes and costs $6.

By car take I-76 (Schuylkill Expressway) west to exit 25, then follow Route 363 to N Gulph Rd and follow the signs. Following I-276 (Pennsylvania Turnpike) west across the north of the city, take exit 24 to Route 363.

WASHINGTON CROSSING HISTORIC PARK

This park (☎ 215-493-4076), PO Box 103, Washington Crossing, PA 18977, is in Bucks County, northeast of Philadelphia. It marks the site where George Washington's army crossed the Delaware River into New Jersey on Christmas night, 1776, to surprise and defeat an encampment of Hessian mercenaries of the British army at Trenton. It was a turning point in the war. A reenactment of the crossing takes place every Christmas.

The park is divided into two parts. The visitors' center, in the lower park, has a short film on the events (and an exhibition of paintings by New Hope painters). Nearby, next to the bridge, McConkey Ferry Inn is where Washington dined before the crossing. In the upper park, toward New Hope, the 110-foot Bowman's Hill Tower affords a great view of the Delaware Valley. Washington used the hill as a lookout. To the north of the tower is the Bowman's Hill Wildflower Preserve (☎ 215-493-4076) housing numerous species of plants native to Pennsylvania.

Across the river in New Jersey is the Washington Crossing State Park (see the Around Trenton section in the Central New Jersey chapter).

Admission to the grounds and visitors' center is free. A 45-minute tour of the historic buildings in the lower park and to Bowman's Hill Tower is $4/2/3.50 for adults/children/seniors. The park opens daily 9 am to sunset; the buildings open Tuesday to Saturday 9 am to 5 pm, Sunday noon to 5 pm.

About 7 miles north of the visitors' center, the historic town of New Hope is home to many artists and craftspeople, and has lots of crafts shops. North from here it's a scenic drive beside the Delaware River to the Delaware Water Gap NRA and the Poconos (see the Northern Pennsylvania chapter).

Getting There & Away

There's no public transportation to the park, but the SEPTA R3 train stops at Yardley

The Philadelphia Museum of Art is the third largest museum in the US.

Fountain, Logan Circle, Philadelphia, PA

Elfreth's Alley, Philadelphia, PA

They say the lights are bright on Broadway, Jim Thorpe, PA.

Frank Lloyd Wright's masterpiece, Fallingwater, in southwestern PA

about 5 miles south. By car, take I-95 north from Philadelphia to exit 31 and follow Route 32 north for 3 miles. At the junction with Route 532 turn right for the visitors' center, left for Bownan's Hill Tower and New Hope.

BRANDYWINE VALLEY

Straddling Delaware and Pennsylvania, the Brandywine Valley is about 25 miles south-west of Philadelphia and features a terrific collection of mansions, gardens, museums and art collections. Fifteen miles wide and 35 miles long, it's a patchwork of wooded and rolling countryside, historic villages, ancient farmhouses and chateau estates.

It was after defeat at the Battle of Brandywine Creek on September 11, 1777, that George Washington's army spent the following winter camped at Valley Forge. The valley is closely associated with the du Pont family, who came here after fleeing Napoleon's France, made money selling gunpowder to an expanding US and went on to develop chemical factories, textile mills and landscaped gardens. Howard Pyle and Andrew Wyeth are two artists also closely connected with the area.

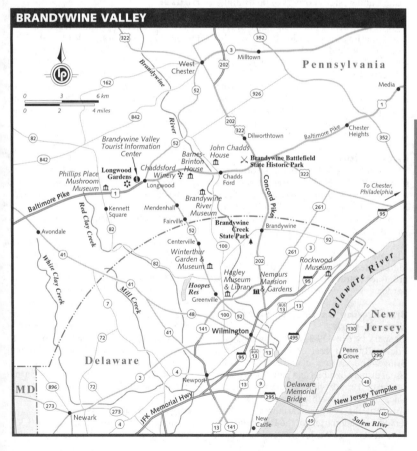

Most people's 'must-sees' include the Winterthur and Hagley estates; if time permits, you could also stop in at Nemours, Longwood Gardens, Rockwood and the Brandywine River Museum. The Brandywine's wealth of attractions is mostly in Delaware, while most country inns and restaurants are in Pennsylvania.

Christmas exhibitions and events at most Brandywine Valley museums run from Thanksgiving through New Year's Day.

Orientation

Route 52 and Route 202 form the general eastern and western borders of the Brandywine Valley, which is accessible from Wilmington, DE. From Philadelphia, Route 1 heads southwest to Chadds Ford, Brandywine Battlefield Park and Longwood Gardens. I-95 goes to Wilmington. Route 52 connects Route 1 and I-95.

There's no public transportation from Philadelphia to the area, but Greyhound and Amtrak have frequent daily departures to nearby Wilmington in Delaware. You'll need your own transport to get around.

Information

The Brandywine Valley Tourist Information Center (☎ 610-388-2900, 800-228-9933) is outside the gates of Longwood Gardens, Route 1, Kennett Square, PA. It is open April to September daily 10 am until 6 pm; October to March the center closes at 5 pm.

The Greater Wilmington Convention & Visitors Bureau (☎ 302-652-4088), 1300 Market St, Suite 504, Wilmington, DE 19801, promotes attractions on both sides of the border.

Brandywine Battlefield State Historic Park

The park (☎ 610-459-3342) lies on the north side of Route 1 east of the Chadds Ford Bridge. The visitors' center has an audio-visual display, exhibits and pamphlets on the Battle of Brandywine Creek, which took place on farms north of the park. You can also visit the restored farmhouses, which served as headquarters of the Revolutionary generals, George Washington and his French comrade the Marquis de Lafayette, who came close to losing their bid for American independence at Brandywine.

Revolutionary Times at Brandywine is a two-day reenactment of the Battle of Brandywine Creek in mid-September; there are crafts and food then, too.

The park opens Tuesday to Saturday 9 am to 5 pm, Sunday noon to 5 pm; admission to the park is free but to the buildings it's $3.50/1.50/2.50 for adults/children/seniors, including a guided tour.

John Chadds & Barns-Brinton Houses

A former home of a ferryman, farmer and tavern keeper, **John Chadds House** was built around 1725. The house (☎ 610-388-7376), Route 100, Chadds Ford, PA, opens May to September, Saturday and Sunday noon to 5 pm. Admission costs $3/1 for adults/children. You can park nearby at the Chadds Ford Historical Society lot. The society runs both John Chadds House and Barns-Brinton House.

Barns-Brinton House (☎ 610-388-7376), on Route 1 beside the Chadds Ford Winery, was originally built as a tavern in 1714 and has been restored to its original appearance. It's open May to September, Saturday and Sunday noon to 5 pm. Admission costs $3/1.

Chaddsford Winery

Operating from a renovated 18th-century barn, this boutique winery (☎ 610-388-6221) is on Route 1, 5 miles south of Route 202, Chadds Ford, PA. Producing small lots of varietal wines with grapes imported from the surrounding area, Chaddsford offers free guided and self-guided tours to see the grapes being crushed, fermented, barrel-aged and bottled. You're given a sample to taste when you first arrive, but a full tasting of around 10 wines costs $5. There are picnic tables around the barn. It is open daily noon to 6 pm.

From here a footpath leads to Barns-Brinton House.

Longwood Gardens

The superb 1050-acre gardens (☎ 610-388-1000), Route 1, Kennett Square, PA, were

The Battle of Brandywine Creek

The British army nearly ended the American Revolution when it attacked and overwhelmed the American forces at Brandywine Creek on September 11, 1777.

In August, George Washington learned that 13,000 British and 5000 Hessian mercenaries (from Hesse in Germany) under General William Howe had landed at the head of the Chesapeake Bay. They had been advancing slowly through Delaware, gathering intelligence and securing supply lines for an attack on Philadelphia, the new national capital.

In defense of Philadelphia, Washington moved 11,000 troops to the Wilmington area. Realizing that the Brandywine Valley presented a geographical obstacle to Howe, Washington and his French supporter, the Marquis de Lafayette, set up the bulk of their defenses along the high ground east of the creek at Chadds Ford, the most likely place for the British to cross. In addition, American troops covered two other fords on the Brandywine in hopes of forcing Howe to fight at Chadds Ford.

Howe anticipated Washington's plans and, using intelligence from local British sympathizers, on September 11 sent the bulk of his troops on a long march to the north around Washington's right flank under the cover of darkness and fog. Back at Chadds Ford, when the fog lifted, Howe's generals made a decoy attack and marched a few columns back and forth among the hills to give Washington's scouts the impression that the main British force was gathering at Chadds Ford for a charge. Preoccupied there, Washington didn't realize until mid-afternoon that Howe, with 11,000 redcoats, had nearly encircled his army. After brutal fighting, the remains of the American force escaped to Chester, PA. British troops suffered 600 dead and wounded; the Americans had 900 casualties and lost 400 men as prisoners of war.

Fifteen days later, Howe's troops marched into Philadelphia unopposed. Although Washington had been defeated, the battle helped persuade the French to make a formal alliance with the Americans, an alliance that would prove crucial to the final outcome of the Revolution. In the meantime, Washington was able to regroup (at Valley Forge) to fight again the following year. As he reported to Congress following the battle: 'Notwithstanding the misfortune of the day, I am happy to find the troops in good spirits; and I hope another time we shall compensate for the losses now sustained.'

established by Samuel du Pont at the beginning of the 20th century. The gardens have beautifully maintained grounds and several large heated conservatories. There are 11,000 different kinds of plants, roses and orchids in bloom year-round. In addition, there's an indoor children's garden with a maze, the historic Pierce du Pont House and one of the world's mightiest pipe organs. Nighttime displays of illuminated fountains (in summer), and festive lights at Christmas are breathtaking. The gardens also have many well-publicized seasonal events.

Opening hours are April to October daily 9 am to 6 pm, November to March daily 9 am to 5 pm. Admission costs $12/2 for adults/children, youths 16 to 20 years of age $6; on Tuesday adults are charged $8.

Phillips Place Mushroom Museum

This museum (☎ 610-388-6082) is half a mile south of Longwood Gardens on Route 1, Kennett Square, PA. It houses a unique collection of exhibits explaining the history, lore and mystique of mushrooms (mushroom farming is a local tradition and the state's main money-making crop), featuring films, slides and nutritional charts. It's open daily 10 am to 6 pm. Admission costs $1.25/50¢/75¢ for adults/children/seniors.

Brandywine River Museum

A renowned showcase of American art, this museum (☎ 610-388-2700) is famous for its collection of works by three generations of the Wyeth family. Housed in a 19th-century grist mill on Routes 1 and 100, Chadds Ford, PA, the galleries also feature other American artists including Howard Pyle, Maxfield Parrish, William Trost Richards and Horace Pippin, among hundreds of others. Seasonal events include an Antiques Show in May, and the Harvest Market & Christmas Shops from September through December. The museum opens daily 9:30 am to 4:30 pm. Admission costs $5; children, senior citizens and students $2.50.

Winterthur Garden & Museum (Delaware)

The Brandywine Valley's most famous attraction, Winterthur (☎ 302-888-4600, 800-448-3883) was the country estate of Henry Francis du Pont until he opened it to the public in 1951. When du Pont inherited the estate in 1927, he moved the best of his American furniture collection here, doubling the size of the existing house and converting it to a showplace for the world's most important collection of early American decorative arts. During the next 20 years, du Pont continued to increase his collection and the size of Winterthur.

The museum consists of two buildings, one with 175 period rooms and another with three exhibition galleries. There are over 89,000 objects made or used in America between 1640 and 1860, including furniture, textiles, paintings, prints, pewter, silver, ceramics, glass, needlework and brass. The museum is surrounded by 980 acres, of which 60 acres are beautifully planted with native and exotic plants.

Unless you join a special tour, you're free to stroll the galleries, explore the grounds or ride the year-round tram (space permitting) at your leisure. General admission costs $8/4 for adults/children, seniors and students $6. For an additional fee, excellent guided tours are available (reservations required). These are Introduction to Winterthur (add $5); Garden Walk, available seasonally (add $5); Decorative Arts Tours, one/two hours (add $9/13). Call ahead because the tours are popular and fill quickly.

Opening hours are Monday to Saturday 9 am to 5 pm; Sunday noon to 5 pm, with the garden open till dusk and the last tickets sold at 3:45 pm. It's closed New Year's Day, July 4, Thanksgiving, Christmas Day and December 26.

Winterthur is 6 miles northwest of Wilmington, DE, on Route 52, 10 minutes off I-95 via exit 7 (Delaware Ave, Route 52 north). If you're coming from Chadds Ford, PA, drive west 3 miles on Route 1 to Route 52 south; from Longwood Gardens, Route 52 south is 1 mile east on Route 1. Visit its website for a preview (www.udel.edu/winterthur).

Hagley Museum & Library (Delaware)

Beautifully situated on the banks of the Brandywine River, Hagley is another 'must-see.' This 240-acre outdoor museum on the site of the birthplace of the Du Pont company tells the story of the du Ponts as part of the broader history of America's Industrial Revolution. Du Pont started operations here as a gunpowder manufacturer in 1802.

A shuttle bus takes you from the visitors' center to the Eleutherian Mills and the 1803 residence of EI du Pont. You can also explore the ruins of the original mills and visit restored buildings with exhibits, models and live demonstrations.

Allow at least three to four hours for your visit. Hagley is a large site with great natural beauty and lots of things to see and do. It is open March to December daily 9:30 to 4:30 pm. Admission costs $9.75/3.50 for adults/children; admission for students and senior citizens costs $7.50.

The museum (☎ 302-658-2400) is on Route 141 north of Wilmington, DE. From I-95, take exit 7 to Route 52 north, to Route 100 north, to Route 141 north; or take exit 8 from I-95 (Route 202 north) to Route 141 south, and follow the signs to Hagley Museum. From Chadds Ford, PA, take Route 100 south to Route 141 north.

Nemours Mansion & Gardens (Delaware)

Nemours (☎ 302-651-6912), on Rockland Rd at Route 202 (in Wilmington), is the estate of Alfred I du Pont. It's named after the site of the family's ancestral home in north central France. Surrounded by 300 acres of gardens and natural woodlands, the Louis XVI-style chateau was built in 1909–10 and has 102 rooms. Today it contains fine examples of antique furniture, oriental rugs, tapestries and paintings dating back to the 15th century. Nemours' exhibits illustrate the du Ponts' lavish lifestyle, including vintage cars, a billiards room and bowling alley. The French gardens, stretching almost one-third of a mile along the main vista from the mansion, are generally considered to be among the finest of their kind in America.

Nemours has guided tours May to November Tuesday to Saturday at 9 and 11 am, 1 and 3 pm; Sunday 11 am, 1 and 3 pm. Admission costs $10 and visitors must be 12 or over. Tours take a minimum of two hours and include the mansion followed by a bus tour through the gardens. You need to arrive at reception (the building in the parking lot) a good 15 minutes before the start of the tour. Reservations are recommended; the office is open Monday to Friday 8:30 am to 4:30 pm.

Rockwood Museum (Delaware)

This 1851 Gothic country estate, built by the merchant-banker Joseph Shipley, stands on 72 of its original 300 acres. The museum consists of the porter's lodge, gardener's cottage, barn and sundry outbuildings. A collection of British, Continental and American decorative arts from the 17th to 19th centuries is exhibited in the manor house, while the grounds contain six acres of exotic foliage. The Rockwood Museum (☎ 302-761-4340, www.rockwood.org), 610 Shipley Rd, is south of I-95 in Wilmington. At the time of writing it was closed for restoration work. Call for opening times and entry fees.

Places to Stay

Accommodations in Wilmington, New Castle and Philadelphia are within easy reach of the Brandywine Valley. However, there are also options, a few very charming, that are closer. Route 202 (Concord Pike) has a larger selection of accommodations, with only one on Route 52 (Kennett Pike).

Most motels and hotels offer good value packages (especially on weekends) which include room and admission to Brandywine Valley museums. Most accommodations are in the middle price range.

On Route 202, the **Best Western Brandywine Valley Inn** (☎ 800-537-7772, 1807 Concord Pike) is at the junction of Routes 202 and 141 about 1½ miles north of exit 8 on I-95. Rooms cost from $77/97. In the same area the **Holiday Inn of Wilmington – North** (☎ 302-478-2222, 4000 Concord Pike) has rooms for $99. Further north, the **Doubletree Hotel** (☎ 302-478-6000, 4727 Concord Pike) has rooms ranging from $129 to $189. Just south of the Pennsylvania border at the junction of Route 92, the cheaper **Days Inn** (☎ 302-478-0300, 5209 Concord Pike) has rooms for $65.

In Pennsylvania there is a selection of country-style inns and B&Bs. The 1987-built **Brandywine River Hotel** (☎ 610-388-1200), at Route 1 and Route 100, Chadds Ford, has 40 rooms for $125, suites $169. This hotel is not a piece of antiquity, but it is nicely designed to blend in with the surroundings, and it has a colonial-style interior.

The luxurious, top-end **Fairville Inn** (☎ 610-388-5900, 506 Kennett Pike), Route 52 in Mendenhall, is a delightful establishment, run by Ole and Patricia Retlev. The main house was built in 1826, and there is a rear carriage house and barn. Seven of the 15 rooms have fireplaces and the entire place is beautifully decorated. Prices range from $135 to $195. A substantial continental breakfast and light but delicious afternoon tea are included. From Route 1 west of Chadds Ford, take Route 52 south to Mendenhall; Fairville is almost a mile past Mendenhall on the left side.

Places to Eat

At Greenville, DE, on Kennett Pike (Route 52) and convenient for many of the Brandywine attractions, there are a couple of nice places in the Powder Mill Square shopping complex. **Brew ha ha!** (☎ 302-658-6336) is an espresso cafe serving soup, sandwiches ($4 to $5) and salads along with coffee. **Cromwell's** (☎ 302-571-0561) is an upscale tavern serving pasta for $7 to $15, mains $15 to $18. It is open daily 11 to 1 am (Sunday 10 pm).

Buckley's Tavern (☎ 302-656-9776, 5812 Kennett Pike), Centerville, DE, is one of the region's most popular drinking spots. There's a small pub with a dining room and garden room at the back. Everyone from gentry to farmers are regulars here, and the place is usually packed. A small menu features good food with dishes ranging from $6.25 to $11. It is open daily.

Chadds Ford Inn (☎ 610-388-7361), at the junction of Routes 1 and 100, dates back to the 1700s. The house was built by Francis Chadsey, an English Quaker who had bought the land from William Penn's commissioner of land grants. In 1736, his eldest son turned the house into a tavern, which through the centuries has evolved into a popular restaurant, furnished with colonial antiques. The international cuisine served is up to date, though, with lunch mains $7 to $14, dinner mains $15.50 to $22; it's open daily. For home-style food, try **Hank's Place** a busy restaurant at Routes 1 and 100 in Chadds Ford; mushroom burgers with french fries cost $5.95.

Another popular historic restaurant is **Dilworthtown Inn** (☎ 610-399-1390, Old Wilmington Pike), at Brinton Bridge Rd, Dilworthtown, PA. Open daily for dinner, this wood, stone and brick structure with fireplaces and gas lamps dates back to 1758 and serves French cuisine. Starters are $7 to $12, mains $17.25 to $30. To find the inn, head north on Route 202 from the junction with Route 1. After a mile and a half, turn left at the second traffic light (a Getty service station is on the right). After about 200 yards you come to a stop sign; turn right and the restaurant is the building on your right.

Pennsylvania Dutch Country

Pennsylvania Dutch Country is home to a community of Amish (AH-mish), Mennonites and Brethren collectively known as 'plain people.' The Old Order Amish in particular, with their distinctive clothing, are a major draw for tourism – the area is one of the most visited in Pennsylvania. It must be odd for people whose forebears emigrated to the New World to escape the attention and persecution of others to find themselves the object of intense curiosity by camera-toting tourists. To maintain their privacy, some have moved to farm other, less developed parts of the state. It's actually more correct to say Pennsylvania German, since the use of 'Dutch' is a corruption of 'Deutsch,' meaning German; many of the early settlers came from German-speaking parts of Europe. Also, the Amish refer to anyone outside their community as 'English,' wherever they're from.

Most Pennsylvania Dutch live on carefully manicured farms, but because of the rising population, urbanization and other outside pressures, many also work in small-scale industries, producing quilts, furniture and crafts that are sold to tourists from outlets along the local highways. Others work in family-style restaurants, sell produce at farmers' markets or offer buggy rides to tourists. There *are* tourist traps, but you can escape some of the commercialism by staying on a farm or at one of the more remote tourist homes, or by visiting the back roads, where you'll see Amish people doing their daily farmwork. See the boxed text 'Amish, Mennonites & Brethren' for more information about the lifestyle and history of the 'plain people.'

The region is famous for its large meals. It's more correct to call the cuisine 'Pennsylvania Dutch food' rather than 'Amish food,' and it's served in a number of restaurants 'family style,' with diners often sitting together at long tables and eating as much as they please. Meals are standard, but huge and hearty, and they generally include

Highlights

- A guided visit to an Amish or Mennonite community or home
- A horse-and-buggy ride through Amish country
- The farmers' markets, where you can buy baked goods, jams, meat, fruit, vegetables and crafts
- Locally made pretzels
- Bird-watching at Hawk Mountain Sanctuary

three meats (usually chicken, beef and ham or sausage), applesauce, pepper cabbage (a variety of cabbage), candied sweet potatoes, corn, string beans, noodles and shoofly pie (the lack of a top crust on this gooey molasses concoction attracts flies, hence its name). Family-style meals are generally $13 to $15 for adults, and roughly half that price for children.

In addition, Pennsylvania Dutch Country is famous for its soft and hard pretzels. You can visit pretzel-making operations near Lancaster and in Lititz, and there are small hand-rolling shops everywhere. Lititz also has a chocolate factory (and museum). Another popular food item is Lebanon bologna, and there are smokehouses in Palmyra and Lebanon that you can visit. See also the boxed text 'Local Grub,' in the Facts for the Visitor chapter.

There are ample camping, motels, hotels and B&Bs in the area. An alternative to the usual accommodations is to stay on one of the many farmhouses in the area, which often rent rooms for around $40. The dairy farms and other farms that rent rooms welcome kids, and guests are generally welcome to milk the cows (although it's usually done by machine) and sometimes to feed the calves if they want to get close to nature. Some of these places are listed here, and the names of more are available from the visitors' centers.

Many roads in the area, especially Routes 30 and 340, are lined with craft shops. Popular items are quilts, wooden furniture, faceless dolls, hex signs (found on barns and quilts, they were originally used to ward off bad luck and evil, today they're merely decorative), tools and candles. The farmers' markets in Lancaster and Bird-in-Hand and near Reading are popular for their selection of pies, jams, meat, preserved vegetables and fresh fruit and vegetables. Many people visit Reading simply for the bargains available at its factory outlets, but there is an increasing number of factory outlets all over the region.

You shouldn't take photographs of the Amish; they prefer that no one makes what they consider graven images of them. Don't even ask whether they mind; they do, and will be uncomfortable about being approached.

ORIENTATION

The core of the Pennsylvania Dutch region is a string of towns, farms and sights spread out over an area of perhaps 20 miles by 15 miles. These lie to the east of Lancaster – the area's main city and more or less its western boundary. Lancaster has a popular farmers' market, a pretzel bakery and some historic sights, including the home of President Buchanan.

East of Lancaster, the road most traveled by tourists is Route 340 (Old Philadelphia Pike), along which are the towns of Bird-in-Hand and Intercourse. South of this, and also running east and west, is Route 30 (Lincoln Hwy), which has many dairy farms and farmhouses with rooms for rent. Route 896

(Hartman Bridge Rd) runs north and south between Routes 30 and 340, meeting Strasburg to the south at the junction with Route 741. To get off the beaten track, take any one of the side roads between Routes 30 and 340.

To the north of this core is the town of Lititz, home of the country's first commercial pretzel bakery, and to its northeast is Ephrata, where the Ephrata Cloister was the site of an 18th-century ascetic religious community called the Pietists.

Though really separate, Reading, to the northeast of the true Pennsylvania Dutch region, is usually discussed as part of it. Most visitors to Reading go there to shop for factory-outlet bargains, but the Daniel Boone Homestead to the east and the Hawk Mountain Sanctuary to the north are well worth visiting. The towns of Palmyra and Lebanon, west of Reading, are also included in the region.

GETTING THERE & AROUND

Pennsylvania Dutch Country is about a 90-minute drive west of Philadelphia on Route 30. If you're coming from further north, take I-76 (Pennsylvania Turnpike) to Route 222 south, which runs directly into Lancaster. Route 422 north, off I-76 near Valley Forge, will take you to Reading. You can reach Lancaster and Reading by plane, bus or train (see Getting There & Away under those cities), but to explore the region adequately, you'll need a car, motorcycle or bicycle.

Note: The Amish use their horses and buggies as a means of transportation, so if you're driving, at times you'll need to slow down considerably and travel at their pace for a while.

Organized Tours

Air Glick Aviation at Smoketown airport (☎ 717-394-6750), Airport Drive, a mile west of Bird-in-Hand, does a 15-minute flyover of Lancaster County for $30/45 (plus tax) for two/three passengers. Weather permitting, planes fly Monday to Saturday 9 am to 5 pm and Sunday 1 to 5 pm.

Bus Amish Country Tours (☎ 717-392-8622, 768-3600), PO Box 414, Bird-in-Hand, PA

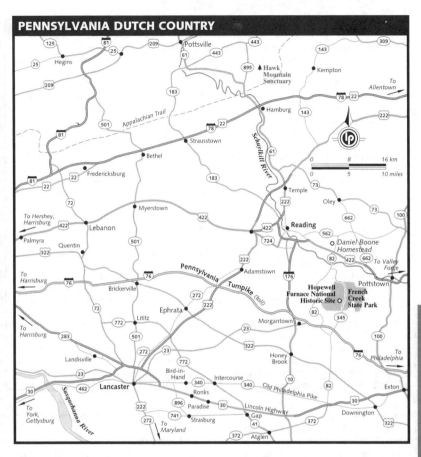

PENNSYLVANIA DUTCH COUNTRY

17505, is the largest bus-tour operator in the area. The company runs several narrated bus tours from the Plain 'N' Fancy Farm, on Route 340, midway between Bird-in-Hand and Intercourse. The 2¼-hour tour takes the back roads past farmlands and homes, visits an Amish dairy farm to sample ice cream and stops at Amish shops and at the Mt Hope Wine Gallery for a tasting. From April to October, it leaves twice daily Monday to Saturday and once on Sunday; in November, it leaves once daily; from December to March, there are tours on weekends only. It costs $18.95/10.95 adults/children.

Similar tours are run by the Pennsylvania Dutch Convention & Visitors Bureau (see Tourist Offices under Lancaster, later in this chapter).

Connective Tours (☎ 215-925-8687) offers day trips to the area from Philadelphia. You travel by train to Lancaster, and from there, a bus takes you on a guided tour of Amish country. Trips are available April to October, last 10 hours and cost $85.

Personal Guide Personal guides are a good way to see the region, because they direct you (they sit in your car while you

Amish, Mennonites & Brethren

The Old Order Amish are the most distinctive of the 'plain people' of Lancaster County, but the Amish are just one of three major groups – the Amish, the Mennonites and the Brethren – that are themselves further divided into various smaller churches and groups with differing beliefs.

The Amish, Mennonites and Brethren all trace their origins to 16th-century Switzerland. A religious sect calling itself the Brethren began in Zurich in 1525. They believed that a church should be made up of a group of individuals baptized as adults, because only adults can repent from sin and confess their faith in Christ before they are baptized. The name 'Anabaptist,' which means 'baptized again,' was applied to them by their opponents, and they were persecuted. Some Anabaptists became known as Mennonites after Menno Simons, a Dutchman who was formerly a Roman Catholic priest before becoming an early leader of the group. In 1693, a Swiss Mennonite bishop named Jacob Ammann split from the Anabaptists, and his followers eventually became known as the Amish. The first colony of Mennonites settled in 1683 in Germantown, now a suburb of Pennsylvania, and the first large groups of Amish arrived in Pennsylvania in the early decades of the 18th century.

The Amish, Mennonites and Brethren are unified on the issues of separation of church and state, a Bible-centered life, voluntary adult membership and a 'forgiving love' that translates into conscientious objection to military service or even lawsuits. Where they differ is in dress, use of technology, some Biblical interpretation and language (the Amish speak Pennsylvania Dutch at home, and the others speak English).

Most of Lancaster's Brethren and Mennonites are indistinguishable from the rest of the county's worldly folk in dress, although their clothing emphasizes modesty. The distinctive Old Order Amish and Old Order Mennonites dress similarly (but not quite the same) and have certain prohibitions on the use of technology. Then there are other groups of Mennonites, Brethren and even Amish – the Amish Mennonites or 'Beachy Amish' – who wear distinctive clothing but use 'worldly' items.

The Old Order Amish, who make up the bulk of the local community, are farmers who generally travel by horse and buggy, wear distinctive clothing and prohibit certain technology. Decisions about technology are made by Amish bishops based on whether the item in question is too

drive) to communities and homes away from the commercial areas.

The friendly Old Order Amish Tours (☎ 717-299-6535), 63 Eastbrook Rd, on Route 896 near Ronks, takes individuals or small groups on private tours of Amish farms and homes. You're not allowed to take photographs. The rate for a two-hour tour is $27 for two people; a three-hour tour costs an additional $15. If you choose the three-hour tour, you also have the option of having a specially prepared meal in an Amish home, which costs another $13 per person.

The Mennonite Information Center (☎ 717-299-0954), 2209 Millstream Rd, Lancaster, PA 17602, provides visitors with a personal guide at $26 for two hours. The center also provides other tourist informa-tion (see Tourist Offices under Information for Lancaster, later in this chapter).

LANCASTER

Lancaster (population 55,000) is a pleasant town 57 miles west of Philadelphia. Settled first by Swiss Mennonites around 1700, it was originally called Gibson's Pasture. Then, in the mid-18th century, it was renamed after the birthplace (in Lancashire, England) of Lancaster County's first commissioner, John Wright. Lancaster is noted for having been the capital of the US for a day (September 27, 1777) when Congress fled Philadelphia following George Washington's defeat at the Battle of Brandywine. They stopped here overnight before continuing to York, PA.

Prior to the Civil War, Lancaster was a staging post on the Underground Railroad,

Amish, Mennonites & Brethren

'worldly' and whether its use may result in the disintegration of the closely knit community. Any prohibitions are constantly under reinterpretation.

Men wear unlapelled dark suits, suspenders, solid-colored shirts, black socks and shoes and broad-brimmed straw hats. Women wear dresses of solid-colored fabric that cover their arms and go past their knees. These dresses are covered by a cape and apron. Women wear their hair in a bun on the back of the head. Single women wear black prayer coverings for church services and white after marriage. Single men wait to grow beards (but never mustaches) until after they are married.

While many Amish won't drive a car, they'll ride with friends or hire vehicles to take them somewhere, and bus travel is acceptable. This brings us to the wheel. Bicycles, which encourage young people to go far from their homes, aren't used. Rubber wheels are permitted on wagons, tricycles and scooters, but not on large farm equipment. The most obvious example is the tractor, which must have steel wheels. Tractors are permitted around the barn and to power machinery, but not in the fields. The tractor speeds up farming and eliminates the need for labor, which is considered beneficial.

Power is acceptable if it comes from batteries or some fuel generators; gas lanterns are fine. Phones are allowed outside homes but not inside.

Children attend one-room Amish schoolhouses until the eighth grade, where they are given the basics in reading, writing and arithmetic. They're exempt from the usual compulsory US school attendance to age 16. Any other education they receive is in the form of on-the-job training. In their late teens, Amish youngsters have a choice to stay or leave the community – about 85% choose to stay. The Amish speak Pennsylvania Dutch (a German dialect), High German at worship services and English. The community is divided into church districts of 150 to 200 people. They have no central church – the district members gather at a different home every second Sunday for a three-hour service of hymn singing (without music) and scripture reading.

Lancaster County has around 15,000 Amish, most of whom live east of the city of Lancaster. Owing to the shortage of farms, some move to other parts of Pennsylvania or interstate, and there are large communities of Amish in Ohio and Indiana.

and Thaddeus Stevens (1792-1868), a Republican politician and opponent of slavery, is buried here. James Buchanan (1791-1868), following his term as the 15th president of the US (1856-68), made his home in Lancaster.

Today, the town is known for its farmers' market, some historic buildings and its outlet stores.

Orientation

Penn Square, with its Soldiers & Sailors monument, is the town's central point. King St (between Water and Duke Sts) and Queen St (between Orange and Vine Sts) mark the main downtown commercial area. Queen St divides the city into east and west, Orange St divides it into north and south. A one-way system operates downtown: Route 222 runs north along Lime St and south along Prince St; Route 462 runs east along King St and west along Orange St; Route 23 runs east along Chestnut St and west along Walnut St.

Information

Tourist Offices The Pennsylvania Dutch Convention & Visitors Bureau (☎ 717-299-8901, 800-723-8824), 501 Greenfield Rd, Lancaster, PA 17601, is the tourist office for the region. It's on the northeast side of the city, off Route 30 west at the Greenfield Rd exit. It has a 15-minute audiovisual display about the region, *People, Places & Passions*, that gives a basic overview of what you can see in the area. Get a copy of the free *Pennsylvania Dutch Country/Lancaster County Map & Visitors Guide*; it contains discount coupons for attractions, accommodations and restaurants. The center is open Sunday to Thursday 8:30 am to 5 pm and Friday and Saturday to 6 pm; in July and August, it is open daily 8 am to 6 pm. Its official website is at www.padutchcountry.com.

The Mennonite Information Center (☎ 717-299-0954), 2209 Millstream Rd, Lancaster, PA 17602, has general tourist advice and is also a center for information about the Mennonites; it has a wide selection of books. It shows a 20-minute film, *Postcards from a Heritage of Faith*, which explains the beliefs of the Mennonites and the Amish, as well as the differences between them. Open Monday to Saturday 8 am to 5 pm, the information center is east of Lancaster, off Route 30.

Lancaster's downtown Visitors Information Center/Chamber of Commerce (☎ 717-397-3531), 100 S Queen St, on the corner of Vine St, is open weekdays 8:30 am to 4:50 pm, Saturday 9 am to 4 pm and Sunday 10 am to 3 pm.

Money Mellon Bank has several locations in Lancaster. The main branch is at 28 Penn Square.

Post The main post office, at W Chestnut and N Prince Sts, is open weekdays 7:30 am to 4:30 pm and Saturday 8 am to noon. Postal services are also available at the Rite Aid drugstore on the corner of Queen and Orange Sts.

Libraries Lancaster County Library (☎ 717-394-2651), 125 N Duke St, is open Monday to Thursday 9 am to 9 pm and Friday and Saturday to 5:30 pm.

Bookstores Two good used bookstores are near Central Market. Book Haven (☎ 717-393-0920), 146 N Prince St, is open weekdays 9 am to 5 pm (Wednesday to 9 pm) and Saturday 10 am to 4 pm. Chestnut St Books (☎ 717-393-3773), 11 W Chestnut St, has old and rare books, maps and prints and is open Tuesday to Saturday 10 am to 5 pm.

Travel Agencies Council Travel (☎ 717-392-8272) has an office at College Square, 931 Harrisburg Ave.

Central Market

Although it's a tourist attraction today, the Central Market (☎ 717-291-4723), 125 N Duke St, on the northwest corner of Penn Square, is worth a visit. It's one of the country's oldest publicly owned farmers' markets and has been operating since the early 18th century. The red-brick building housing the market dates from 1889, making this one of the oldest covered markets in the US. On sale is a good selection of fruit, vegetables, meat, baked goods and crafts. It's open year-round Tuesday and Friday 6 am to 4 pm and Saturday to 2 pm.

Heritage Center Museum

Near Central Market, the Heritage Center Museum (☎ 717-299-6440), 13 W King St, in the old city hall, contains 18th- and 19th-century paintings, pewter items, period furniture and other craft work and fine art done by local artisans and artists. It also has a series of changing exhibitions on the ground floor. The museum is open Tuesday to Saturday 10 am to 4 pm May to December; admission is free, but donations are accepted.

Wheatland

Wheatland (☎ 717-392-8721), 1120 Marietta Ave (Route 23), is an 1828 Federal mansion located about a mile northwest of downtown. It was once home to James Buchanan – America's only bachelor president. Surrounded by four acres of gardens, the restored mansion features Buchanan's furnishings, many of which were gifts from foreign heads of state. It is open daily 10 am to 4:15 pm from April through November; admission is $5.50/1.75 for adults/children; seniors pay $4.50, and students pay $3.50.

Landis Valley Museum

This 16-acre outdoor museum (☎ 717-569-0401), 2451 Kissel Hill Rd, about 2½ miles northeast of town, is composed of homes, workshops and stores dating from 1760 to the early 20th century. The buildings have been assembled in one place to re-create the Pennsylvania Dutch rural life and work of that period. You can see presentations of

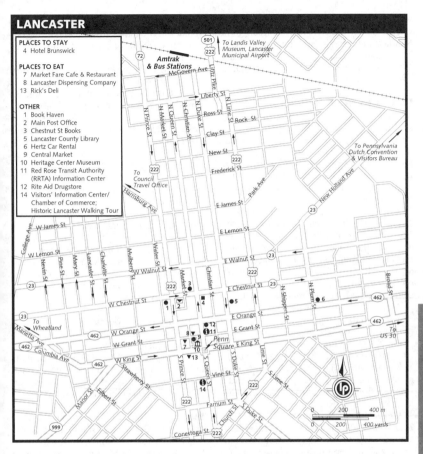

LANCASTER

PLACES TO STAY
4 Hotel Brunswick

PLACES TO EAT
7 Market Fare Cafe & Restaurant
8 Lancaster Dispensing Company
13 Rick's Deli

OTHER
1 Book Haven
2 Main Post Office
3 Chestnut St Books
5 Lancaster County Library
6 Hertz Car Rental
9 Central Market
10 Heritage Center Museum
11 Red Rose Transit Authority
    (RRTA) Information Center
12 Rite Aid Drugstore
14 Visitors' Information Center/
    Chamber of Commerce;
    Historic Lancaster Walking Tour

craft making, including blacksmithing, leather working, spinning, basket weaving, tin smithing, lace making and chair caning. The museum is open Monday to Saturday 9 am to 5 pm and Sunday noon to 5 pm from March to December; admission is $7/5 for adults/children, and seniors pay $6.

From downtown, take Lime St (Route 222) north to the exit for Route 272, turn right and follow Route 272 to the traffic lights just past the Quality Inn, turn left at the traffic light onto Kissel Hill Rd. The entrance to the museum is about 300 yards away, on the right.

Anderson Pretzel Bakery

This large pretzel bakery (☎ 717-299-2321), 2060 Old Philadelphia Pike, is 2 miles east of town on Route 340. You can tour the bakery along an overhead catwalk weekdays 8:30 am to 4 pm; admission is free. The factory store is open year-round weekdays 8:30 am to 5 pm; from April to December, it also is open Saturday 8:30 am to 3 pm.

Organized Tours

Historic Lancaster Walking Tour (☎ 717-392-1776), 100 S Queen St, in the downtown Visitors Information Center, does daily walking tours from April through October. On Monday, Wednesday, Thursday and Sunday, tours begin at 1 pm; on Tuesday, Friday and Saturday, they start at 10 am and 1 pm. A tour costs $7/4 for adults/children, and seniors pay $6.

Places to Stay

You can't stay in town cheaply, but if you go southeast on Route 462/30, there's a commercial strip with plenty of hotels and motels, and further out into Pennsylvania Dutch Country, there are campgrounds and farmhouses. (See Places to Stay under Intercourse, Bird-in-Hand and Strasburg, later in this chapter.)

There are two B&Bs in the Lancaster area. *O'Flaherty's Dingeldein House* (☎ 717-293-1723, 800-779-7765, 1105 E King St), on Route 462, is 2 miles east of town before the intersection with Route 30. It's small and comfortable and has five rooms – two with shared bath and three with private baths. The common areas have gas fireplaces, and there's parking in the back. Rooms with private baths cost $80/100 for a single/double. You can visit its website at www.800padutch.com/ofhouse .html. Nearby, *King's Cottage* (☎ 717-397-1017, 800-747-8717, 1049 E King St) is a large, airy place with a library, fireplace and afternoon tea. Its eight rooms have private baths, wooden floors, good carpet, big beds and antique furniture. Rates are $100 to $185.

Garden Spot Motel (☎ 717-394-4736, 2291 Route 30), 5 miles east of Lancaster, is a good value. It has 18 clean, well-lit rooms and a coffee shop on the premises. Singles/doubles cost $54/61 in the peak season. If you want to stay downtown, it'll have to be at the 225-room *Hotel Brunswick* (☎ 717-397-4801, 800-233-0182), at the corner of E Chestnut and N Queen Sts. The exterior is an unattractive mix of concrete and brick, and the standard rooms cost $119. It has free parking. For reservations, special deals and other information, visit the hotel's website at www.hotelbrunswick.com.

Places to Eat

In addition to fresh food from the *Central Market*, you can buy prepared Middle Eastern food from *Saife's* in the market; spinach or meat pies are $2, and the vegetarian kibbe (made of bulgur, potato, parsley and peas) is $1.85.

The *Market Fare Cafe & Restaurant* (☎ 717-299-7090), across from Central Market, offers light breakfasts and lunches upstairs; sandwiches cost around $3.65, and the chicken salad goes for $6.75. You can have a full lunch or dinner in the restaurant downstairs. *Rick's Deli* (☎ 717-299-7295, 50 W King St) serves salad specialties, such as the Marseille salad (tuna, pasta, olives, tomato and eggs) for $4.30; sandwiches cost $4 to $4.75, and hamburgers cost $3.45. It's closed Sunday.

Lancaster Dispensing Company (☎ 717-299-4602, 3335 N Market St) is a pub with a varied menu of sandwiches, seafood and pasta salads; it also has a good vegetarian- and Mexican-cuisine selection. Main dishes cost $5 to $7; fajitas cost $6.75. It's open Monday to Saturday 11 am to 2 am and Sunday 1 to 10 pm.

Getting There & Away

Air Lancaster municipal airport (☎ 717-569-1221) is 6 miles north of town on Route 501. US Airways (☎ 800-428-4322) has five daily flights to Philadelphia, up to seven to Pittsburgh and two to Reading. Standard round-trip fares to Philadelphia cost $250.

Bus Capitol Trailways (☎ 800-444-2877) operates from the Amtrak station on McGovern Ave. There are three buses daily to Philadelphia ($13.85, two hours) and to Pittsburgh ($36.40, five hours).

Train The Amtrak station (☎ 717-291-5080) is at 53 McGovern Ave, about a mile north of downtown. There are three one-way trains daily to both Philadelphia ($12, 80 minutes) and Pittsburgh ($76, five hours). Tickets on the train to Pittsburgh must be reserved.

Car & Motorcycle The quickest way to Lancaster from Philadelphia is via the Pennsylvania Turnpike (I-76); at exit 21 take Route 222 south into town. Northward, Route 222 leads to Reading; southeast of town it leads to Maryland. Another option from Philadelphia is to take Route 30 west, which passes through the heart of Pennsylvania Dutch Country. From Lancaster, Route 30 continues southwest to York and Gettysburg. Route 283 leads northwest from Lancaster to Harrisburg, and Route 501 heads north to I-78.

Getting Around

Red Rose Transit Authority (RRTA; ☎ 717-397-4246) is Lancaster County's bus service; it has an information center (open weekdays 8:15 am to 5:15 pm and Saturday 10 am to 2 pm) at 47 N Queen St, where you can also buy tickets. Lancaster County is divided into five fare zones, with the city of Lancaster as the central, or base, zone. One-way fares range from $1.10 to $2.30.

Cars can be rented from Hertz (☎ 717-396-0000), 625 E Orange St.

INTERCOURSE & AROUND

This small town along Route 340 (Old Philadelphia Pike), 8 miles east of Lancaster, was founded in 1754 and was originally called Cross Keys. No one knows for sure how it obtained its current name. The reason usually given is that the town stands at the intersection of the old King's Hwy (Route 340) and the old Newport Rd (Route 772). Another possible explanation is that the name evolved from a sign, which read 'Enter Course,' at the entrance to an old racing track on King's Hwy. Intercourse became the town's official name in 1814.

Harrison Ford's Pay Phone

In two scenes of the movie *Witness* (1986), Harrison Ford uses the pay telephone on the porch in front of WL Zimmerman & Sons grocery store, near the junction of Routes 772 and 340. When Harrison Ford's character, a police officer who's hiding in an Amish household, asks where to find the nearest phone, he is told Strasburg – it was thought to be too goofy to say it was in Intercourse!

Almost everything in Intercourse is along Route 340.

Information

The Amish Mennonite Information Center (☎ 717-768-0807), on Old Philadelphia Pike near the Kitchen Kettle Village shopping center, has tourist information, as well as information on the Amish and Mennonites. It's open Monday to Saturday 11 am to 4 pm (shorter hours from November to April).

People's Place

The People's Place (☎ 717-768-7171), 3513 Old Philadelphia Pike, is a cultural center that gives visitors a sensitive introduction to Amish and Mennonite life; it's very informative and has parts that are geared toward children. It shows *Who Are the Amish?* – a 30-minute film about Amish life from birth to death – for $4/2 adults/children. It also has the **20Q Museum**, with a display of questions and answers for adults and children about Amish and Mennonite life; there are also exhibits on clothing, buggies and religious practices. It also costs $4/2. You can see both for $7/3.50. You can purchase a video of *Hazel's People*, a film about the Mennonite community starring Geraldine Page. The bookstore here has a wide selection of books on Amish and Mennonite life.

The People's Place is open Monday to Saturday 9:30 am to 5 pm (to 8 pm in July and August).

Amish Experience Theater & Country Homestead

These are at the Plain 'N' Fancy Farm (☎ 717-768-8400) restaurant and shopping area on Route 340 between Intercourse and Bird-in-Hand. The theater shows the film *Jacob's Choice*, dealing with a young Amish man's dilemma – whether to stay and follow the traditional way of life or to enter the world of the 'English.' Opening hours from April to June are Monday to Saturday 9 am to 5 pm and Sunday 11 am to 6 pm; from July to October, hours are Monday to Saturday 9 am to 8 pm and Sunday 11 am to 6 pm; there are shorter

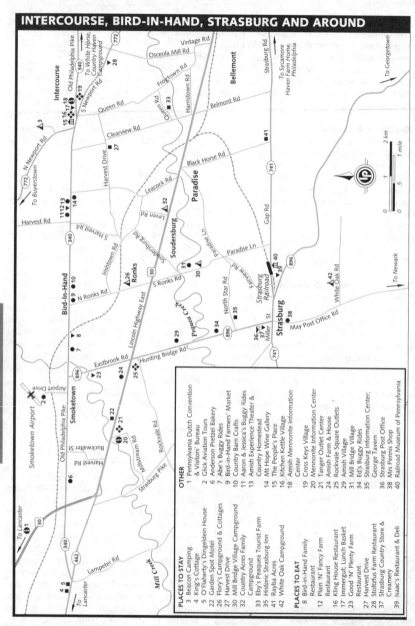

INTERCOURSE, BIRD-IN-HAND, STRASBURG AND AROUND

PENNSYLVANIA

PLACES TO STAY
3 Beacon Camping
4 King's Cottage
5 O'Flaherty's Dingeldein House
22 Garden Spot Motel
26 Flory's Campground & Cottages
27 Harvest Drive
30 Mill Bridge Village Campground
32 Country Acres Family Campground
33 Eby's Pequea Tourist Farm
35 Historic Strasburg Inn
41 Rayba Acres
42 White Oak Campground

PLACES TO EAT
8 Bird-in-Hand Family Restaurant
12 Plain 'N' Fancy Farm Restaurant
16 Kling House Restaurant
17 Immergut; Lunch Basket
23 Good 'N' Plenty Farm Restaurant
27 Harvest Drive
28 Stoltzfus Farm Restaurant
37 Strasburg Country Store & Creamery
39 Isaac's Restaurant & Deli

OTHER
1 Pennsylvania Dutch Convention & Visitors' Bureau
2 Glick Aviation Tours
6 Anderson Pretzel Bakery
7 Abe's Buggy Rides
9 Bird-in-Hand Farmers' Market
10 Country Barn Crafts
11 Aaron & Jessica's Buggy Rides
13 Amish Experience Theater & Country Homestead
14 Mt Hope Wine Gallery
15 The People's Place
16 Kitchen Kettle Village
18 Amish Mennonite Information Center
19 Cross Keys Village
20 Mennonite Information Center
21 Tanger Outlet Center
24 Amish Farm & House
25 Rockvale Square Outlets
29 Amish Village
31 Mill Bridge Village
34 Ed's Buggy Rides
35 Strasburg Information Center; George Tavern
36 Strasburg Post Office
38 Mrs Penn's Shop
40 Railroad Museum of Pennsylvania

business hours from November to March. Admission is $6.50/3.75 adults/children.

There are 40-minute tours of the nearby Amish Country Homestead, a replica of an Old Order Amish home. From April to June, the tours run Monday to Saturday 9:45 am to 4:15 pm and Sunday 10:45 am to 4:45 pm; from July to October, they run Monday to Saturday 9:45 am to 6:15 pm and Sunday 10:45 am to 4:45 pm. Entry is $5/3.25 adults/children. Combined entry to the theater and homestead is $10/6.50. On-site is Aaron & Jessica's Buggy Rides (☎ 717-768-8828).

Places to Stay

Beacon Camping (☎ 717-768-8775) is off Route 772 and half a mile northwest of Intercourse, on a hilltop overlooking the farmlands. It has 46 sites at $21 for two people, or $22.50 for sites with full hookup.

Country Haven Campground (☎ 717-354-7926, 354 Springville Rd) has 55 shaded sites on a tranquil hillside overlooking miles of farmland. It is priced at $24 and has full hookups. Take Route 340 east about 5 miles to White Horse and then Route 897 (Springville Rd) north 1½ miles to the campground. It's open all year.

Eby's Peaquea Tourist Farm (☎ 717-768-3615, 459A Queen Rd) is the closest farm home to Intercourse. It has doubles for $55 and efficiency apartments for $75. Rates include breakfast. From town, follow Queen Rd south off Route 772.

At ***Harvest Drive*** (☎ 717-768-7186, 800-233-0176, 3370 Harvest Drive), rooms have a TV, phone and private bath. The rate is $79 for one or two people during the peak season (mid-June through October). Take Route 340 west half a mile to Clearview Rd, then go south about three-quarters of a mile to Harvest Drive, then turn west.

Places to Eat

On the main street, ***Immergut*** (the name means 'always good' in German) sells soft and hand-rolled pretzels starting at 90¢. The ***Lunch Basket***, next to the Amish Mennonite Information Center, is a simple but popular sandwich-and-pizza shop ($2 to $3.50) that also does good ice cream. ***Kling House***

Restaurant (☎ 717-768-7300), in the Kitchen Kettle Village shopping area, serves breakfasts of egg, sausage and potato, or peach melba pancakes in raspberry syrup, for $4.95; sandwiches cost around $5. At lunch, main dishes, such as French beef stew, cost $5.50 to $7. Desserts here are also good. It is closed Sunday.

Stoltzfus Farm Restaurant (☎ 717-768-8156), one block southeast of Intercourse on Route 772, in a large barnlike building behind the Stoltzfus meat factory, is one of the least commercial (but it still gets a hefty share of visitors) of the family-style places. A set-price, family-style meal costs $13.20/6.50. It's open from May through October, Monday to Saturday 11:30 am to 8 pm; from April and November, it is only open on Saturday. The Stoltzfus Market next door sells meat and baked goods.

Plain 'N' Fancy Farm Restaurant (☎ 717-768-8281), between Intercourse and Bird-In-Hand, on Route 340, is open daily year-round. Set-price, family-style meals are $14.95/6.95. ***Harvest Drive*** (☎ 717-768-7186, 3370 Harvest Drive) offers a choice of family-style or menu meals. Family-style meals cost $14.95/6.55, and sandwiches cost $5 to $7.

Shopping

Intercourse is the epicenter of shopping for Pennsylvania Dutch goods. There are stores in town selling quilts, handmade wooden furniture, decoys (wooden ducks), pewter, fudge, brass, clothing and more. It's hard to choose one over another – look around.

Kitchen Kettle Village is a collection of shops at the west end of town. Bratton's Woodcraft (☎ 717-768-3214) in the 'village' sells wooden gifts and knickknacks. Nearby, Martin's Chair (☎ 717-768-0687) makes wooden furniture, including an array of differently styled chairs. A little further west, at the intersection of Routes 340 and 772, Cross Keys Village is a smaller shopping center. Across the road from Cross Keys, you can watch candle making downstairs at the Old Candle Barn (☎ 717-768-8926). For quilts, try Nancy's Corner of Quilts (☎ 717-768-8790), on the main street.

On Route 772, for several miles northwest of Intercourse, there are a number of places selling wooden furniture, quilts and secondhand wares.

Getting There & Away

RRTA bus No 13 from Duke St in Lancaster stops up to nine times daily Monday to Saturday on Route 772 (N Newport Rd) in Intercourse. By car from Lancaster, follow King St (Route 462) east out of the city, then take the left fork onto Route 340. If you're coming from Philadelphia, Route 772 connects Route 222 and Route 30 with Intercourse.

BIRD-IN-HAND & AROUND

Bird-in-Hand, a few miles east of Lancaster on Route 340, was named in 1734. The name may have been taken from the sign at the town's then-main hotel. Today, the small town has many stores and restaurants.

Bird-in-Hand Farmers' Market

The farmers' market (☎ 717-393-9674), on the main street (Route 340), has fewer 'gourmet' items than Lancaster's Central Market, but has more Amish homemade jams, pies, pretzels, fudge and other foods. The market is open year-round Friday and Saturday 8:30 am to 5:30 pm. From April through November, it is also open Wednesday, and from July through September, it is also open Thursday. Skip the gifts from the gift shop connected to the market; you're better off shopping in Intercourse. Also see Shopping, later in this section.

Amish Farm & House

This is a reconstruction of an Old Order Amish farm (☎ 717-394-6185), 2395 Route 30 East, with animals and buildings spread out over 25 acres. It's open daily 8:30 am to 5 pm (to 6 pm June to August); admission is $5.95/3.50 for adults/children, and seniors pay $5.50. The ticket gets you a guided tour of the house, with a description of the Amish culture and way of life. After the tour, you can wander around the farm by yourself. To get there from Bird-in-Hand, take Route 340 west to Route 896, then turn south to Route 30 and head west for just under a mile.

Horse & Buggy Rides

Abe's Buggy Rides (☎ 717-392-1794), on Route 340, half a mile west of Bird-in-Hand, does a 2-mile tour year-round Monday to Saturday for $10/5 for adults/children. Groups are taken throughout the day, from 8 am to dusk.

Places to Stay & Eat

Flory's Campground & Cottages (☎ 717-687-6670), on N Ronks Rd between Routes 30 and 340, a mile south of Bird-in-Hand, has 71 sites starting at $22. It also rents four rooms in a guesthouse for $59/64 for singles/doubles, and it is possible to rent bicycles. It's open year-round. *Country Acres Family Campground* (☎ 717-687-8014, 20 Leven Rd) has 60 sites at $18 to $21 (with water and electricity) each. From Bird-in-Hand, take N Ronks Rd south to Route 30, then go east to Leven Rd.

Good 'N' Plenty Farm Restaurant (☎ 717-394-7111), on Eastbrook Rd, Route 896, is a large family-style restaurant open Monday to Saturday 11:30 am to 8 pm. It is closed in December and January. The set-price meals are $14.40 ($6.85 for children aged four to 10). Take Route 340 west to Route 896, then head south to the restaurant.

Bird-in-Hand Family Restaurant, on Route 340, is a diner and restaurant offering all-you-can-eat buffets for lunch ($7.25) and dinner ($9.25). It is open Monday to Saturday 6 am to 9 pm.

Shopping

Country Barn Crafts (no phone), just east of Bird-in-Hand on Route 340, is an Amish-owned store operated in a converted tobacco barn on an Amish farm. It has a good selection of carpets, quilts, dolls, wall hangings, pillows and carvings – all of which are made locally. It's open Monday to Saturday 9 am to 5 pm.

Two discount factory-outlet malls are south of town on Route 30. Rockvale Square Outlets (☎ 717-293-9595) is at the intersection with Route 896. Tanger Outlet Center (☎ 717-392-7260) is on the corner of Millstream Rd, opposite the Mennonite Information Center.

Getting There & Away

RRTA bus No 13 from Duke St in Lancaster stops up to nine times a day Monday to Saturday in Bird-in-Hand. By car from Lancaster, follow King St (Route 462) east out of the city, then take the left fork onto Route 340. If you're coming from Philadelphia, Route 772 connects Route 222 and Route 30 with Route 340.

STRASBURG & AROUND

Strasburg, at the less visited southern end of Pennsylvania Dutch Country on Route 741, makes for a pleasant visit. It's the most picturesque and least commercialized of the regional towns and has some interesting attractions for train buffs.

The Strasburg Information Center (☎ 717-687-7922) is at the reception desk in the Historic Strasburg Inn, north of town, off Route 896. There's a post office near the intersection of Routes 896 and 741; it's open weekdays 8 am to 4:30 pm and Saturday 9 am to 1 pm.

Mill Bridge Village

The most elaborate of the replicas, Mill Bridge Village (☎ 717-687-8181), 2 miles south of Ronks on S Ronks Rd, is a re-created colonial 'village' that includes an Amish house, a school, a covered bridge, a blacksmith shop, a log cabin, a broom maker, a mill, a barnyard and a zoo. Often, there's someone working in each building who can tell you how that building functioned in the 18th century. Admission is $10/5, and seniors pay $8, which includes a buggy ride. If you camp here (see Places to Stay & Eat), you get free admission to the village.

Amish Village

This re-created Amish village (☎ 717-687-8511) is composed of about six major buildings, including an Old Order Amish house, a blacksmith shop and a schoolhouse. It is on Route 896, 2 miles north of Strasburg. Admission is $5.75/2, which includes a tour of an Amish home. The village is open daily 9 am to 5 pm (to 6 pm June to August).

Strasburg Railroad

From the Strasburg Railroad station (☎ 717-687-7522) on Route 741, a mile east of town, a steam train does a 45-minute, 9-mile, scenic roundtrip tour through the countryside to the village of Paradise. The train runs up to 10 times daily April through November (weekends only December through March). The regular fare is $8.25/4, and the open-air observation car is $9.25/5; an all-day ticket with unlimited travel costs a flat $16.50.

Railroad Museum of Pennsylvania

Opposite the Strasburg Railroad station is the huge Railroad Museum of Pennsylvania (☎ 717-687-8628). Spanning 150 years of Pennsylvania railroads since 1825, it features a collection of steam locomotives and railcars from different periods, as well as artifacts such as uniforms and engineers' tools. It's open Monday to Thursday 9 am to 5 pm, Friday and Saturday to 7 pm and Sunday 11 am to 5 pm (closed Monday from November to March). Admission is $6/4, and seniors pay $5.50.

Horse & Buggy Rides

Ed's Buggy Rides (☎ 717-687-0360), on Route 896, a mile north of Strasburg, provides leisurely 3-mile rides through the county. It's not Amish, but the buggy-ride experience is the same. A half-hour ride costs $7/3.50. Ed's also does sleigh rides in the winter.

Ghost Tours of Lancaster County (☎ 717-687-6687) takes you on a 75-minute candlelit walking tour of Strasburg's historic district. From April to November, tours leave daily at 8 pm from Mrs Penn's Shoppe (at the intersection of Routes 741 and 896) and cost $10/5.

Places to Stay & Eat

White Oak Campground (☎ 717-687-6207), on White Oak Rd, has 180 year-round sites in the woods or on the grass at $18 ($20 with power) for two adults and two children; each extra person is $2. Take May Post Office Rd south for about 1¼ miles, then turn east on White Oak Rd and go a quarter mile. *Mill Bridge Village Campground* (☎ 717-687-8181) has fishing, free buggy rides and free admission to Mill Bridge Village. Camping rates are $25 Friday and Saturday, or $20 during the rest of the week; power and water cost another $4.

Rayba Acres (☎ 717-687-6729, 183 Black Horse Rd), about 3 miles east of Strasburg, off Route 741, is a dairy farm that's been in the family for over 100 years. Rooms are available in the old and new houses. The old farmhouse has six large carpeted rooms with shared bathroom; the rates are $34 to $39 for two people, plus $5 for each additional person. The new house has motel-style units for $55.

Sycamore Haven Farm Home (☎ 717-442-4901, 35 S Kinzers Rd) is a working farm next to a large sycamore tree. Double rooms are $30 to $45, plus $5 for each additional person. Take Route 741 east for about 6 miles, then turn right on S Kinzers Rd. Go under the railroad bridge, and it's about 300 yards down, on the left.

Dating back to 1793, *Historic Strasburg Inn* (☎ 717-687-7691, 800-872-0201) is set in 58 peaceful acres off Route 896, north of town. It has a pool, restaurant and pub (the George Tavern), and rooms start at $119.

Isaac's Restaurant & Deli is part of a small shopping mall on Route 741, just east of Strasburg. Fitted out like an old railroad carriage, it mostly serves sandwiches and pizzas for $4.95 to $6.95. It has a good vegetarian selection. As a treat, try the homemade ice cream from the *Strasburg Country Store & Creamery*, in the center of town at the intersection of Routes 741 and 896.

Getting There & Away

Strasburg is at the intersection of Routes 741 and 896, about 3 miles south of Route 30. There's no public transportation from Lancaster, although RRTA bus No 14 stops several times daily at Rockvale Square, about 3 miles to the north, at the intersection of Routes 896 and 30.

LITITZ

A pretty town with many 18th- and 19th-century red-brick buildings, Lititz was

founded in 1756 by Moravians who had fled religious persecution in Europe. In 1861, Julius Sturgis established the first commercial pretzel bakery in the US in Lititz. At the **Sturgis Pretzel House** (☎ 717-626-4354, 800-227-9342), 419 E Main St, you can take a 20-minute tour of the bakery and make your own pretzels for $2. There are also a number of rooms full of all sorts of crafts. It's open Monday to Saturday 9:30 am to 4:30 pm from April to December; during January and February, it is open Saturday only 9:30 am to 4:40 pm.

West along Main St and around the corner is the **Wilbur Candy Americana Museum** (☎ 717-626-3249), 45 N Broad St. Though fairly small, it's probably more interesting for adults than Hershey's Chocolate World. A two-room display of old chocolate-making equipment, including molds for Easter eggs, is at the rear of the chocolate shop. The museum and shop are open Monday to Saturday 10 am to 5 pm. Admission is free.

RRTA bus No 10 from Lancaster stops up to 16 times daily Monday to Saturday in Lititz. Lititz is about 10 miles north of Lancaster on Route 501.

EPHRATA

Ephrata (EH-fra-ta, population 12,130) is on Route 322, approximately midway between Lancaster and Reading. The Chamber of Commerce Visitor Center (☎ 717-738-9010), 77 Park Ave, off Main St and in a quiet residential neighborhood, is open weekdays 9 am to 2 pm. The center's website is at www.Ephrata-area.org.

Ephrata is home to the **Ephrata Cloister** (☎ 717-733-6600), 632 W Main St. The town was founded in 1732 by Conrad Beissel, a Pietist (Pietism was a reform movement in the German Lutheran church in the 18th and 19th centuries). It was a communal society made up of religious celibates and ascetics of both sexes, as well as affiliated married householders; at its peak, it had about 300 people, and its last celibate member died in 1813. The word Ephrata means 'fruitful' or 'plentiful' in old Hebrew.

The striking collection of medieval-style buildings – tall, steep-roofed, wood-and-shingle structures – are in their original locations. The doors were made low to force most people to bend 'in humility.' Members of the community lived and worked under a rigorous schedule and only ate enough food to maintain their strength. Note the bed made of a 15-inch-wide plank, with a wooden block for a pillow.

Many books were printed at the cloister, including a translation of the Mennonites' *Martyrs Mirror*. Ephrata is also known for its *Frakturschriften* ('broken writing'), a script in which each letter is a combination of strokes, as well as for its beautiful a cappella singing. It's open Monday to Saturday 9 am to 5 pm and Sunday noon to 5 pm. Admission is $6/4 for adults/children; seniors pay $5.50 and families pay $17; a slide show and guided tour are included in the price of admission.

RRTA bus No 11 runs Monday to Saturday between Lancaster and Ephrata. By car, take Route 222 north from Lancaster or south from Reading to Route 322 west.

READING

Reading (RED-ding, population 78,400) straddles the Schuylkill River about 45 miles northwest of Philadelphia. The area was originally settled by the Leni-Lenape people, who fished the river. The Dutch set up a trading post there in 1663, and European settlers began arriving toward the end of that century. The town was laid out in the 1740s by the sons of William Penn (Thomas and Richard), and it was named after Penn's county seat in Berkshire, England. During the 19th century, it became an important manufacturing and industrial center – a position it maintains today.

Reading itself doesn't have the attractions of the rest of Pennsylvania Dutch Country, but there are a few sights outside town, including Daniel Boone's birthplace. Reading is more noted for its huge collection of factory-outlet stores, and it modestly promotes itself as 'the outlet capital of the world.' The town gets busy starting in mid-September – when visitors combine a trip to see Pennsylvania's fall colors with some early Christmas shopping – and it stays busy until after Christmas.

Orientation

Downtown Reading is on the east bank of the Schuylkill River. Business Route 422 east becomes Penn St, the main street in town, which leads west over the river to the suburbs of West Reading and Wyomissing, and to the factory outlets as well. Penn St divides the town into north and south. The north-south Business Route 222 becomes 5th St in town.

Information

The Reading & Berks Visitors Bureau (☎ 610-375-4085, 800-443-6610), 352 Penn St, has lots of information about the factory outlets, plus other attractions and amenities. It is open weekdays 9 am to 5 pm and Saturday 10 am to 2 pm, and its website is at www.readingberkspa.com. There's also a visitor center in VF Outlet Village. It mostly has information on the factory outlets, but it can help with other things; business hours are Monday to Saturday 9 am to 5 pm and Sunday 10 am to 5 pm.

The main post office, on N 5th St between Court and Washington Sts, is open weekdays 8 am to 5 pm and Saturday 8 am to 2 pm. The library, at Franklin and S 5th Sts, is open Monday to Wednesday 8:15 am to 9 pm, Thursday and Friday to 5:30 pm and Saturday 8:45 am to 5 pm.

Reading Pagoda

It's odd to see a Japanese pagoda in the middle of Pennsylvania, but there it is, red-and-gold, neon-lit at night and several stories high. Sitting on a hill in Mt Penn Forest Reservation, east of the town's center and with good views across Reading, the pagoda (☎ 610-372-0553) is open daily 11 am to 4:50 pm; admission is free. Take Duryea Drive up through the reserve to get there.

Places to Stay

Reading is busiest from mid-September till after Christmas, so it's best to book ahead.

READING

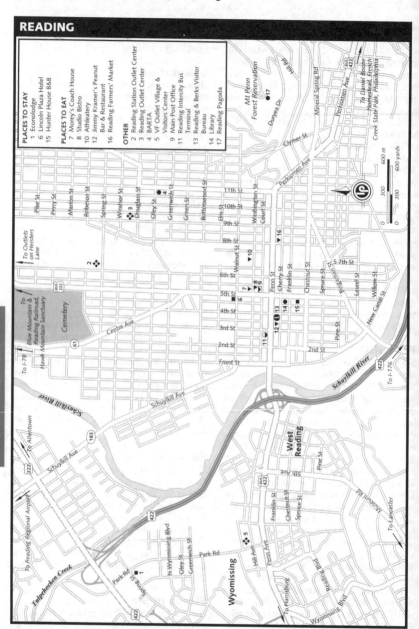

PLACES TO STAY
1 Econolodge
6 Lincoln Plaza Hotel
15 Hunter House B&B

PLACES TO EAT
7 Morey's Coach House
8 Studio Bistro
10 Athleatery
12 Jimmy Kramer's Peanut
    Bar & Restaurant
16 Reading Farmers' Market

OTHER
2 Reading Station Outlet Center
3 Reading Outlet Center
4 BARTA
5 VF Outlet Village &
   Visitors Center
9 Main Post Office
11 Reading Intercity Bus
    Terminal
13 Reading & Berks Visitor
    Bureau
14 Library
17 Reading Pagoda

During that time, room rates at the hotels and motels go up by as much as 40% to 50%.

The nearest private campground is ***Sill's Family Campground*** (☎ 610-484-4806), 10 miles southwest in Adamstown. It has 125 sites starting at $20, most with water and electricity hookups. It's open April through October. Take Route 222 south until you get to Route 272. Go southwest for a quarter of a mile, until you see the signs, and then go southeast on Bowmansville Rd to the campground. ***French Creek State Park*** (☎ 610-582-9680, 843 Park Rd), 14 miles southeast of Reading (see the Around Reading section), has forested campsites with showers and flushing toilets for $16.

You can get a list of B&Bs from the visitors' center. The central ***Hunter House B&B*** (☎ 610-374-6608, 118 S 5th St) is a delightful townhouse that was built in 1847; it has several comfortable rooms. Prices for singles/doubles with private baths start at $90/95.

In West Reading and Wyomissing, west of the river, most of the places are chain motels with standard, clean rooms and no surprises. The ***Econolodge*** (☎ 610-378-5105, 635 Spring St), at Park Rd, just off Route 422 in Wyomissing, has rooms starting at $45 for a single or double. Downtown, the 104-room ***Lincoln Plaza Hotel & Conference Center*** (☎ 610-372-3700), at 5th and Washington Sts, is the Reading's top hotel. It has its own restaurant and fitness center, and room rates start at $85.

Dutch Colony Inn & Suites (☎ 610-779-2345, 4635 Perkiomen Ave), on Business Route 422, is the closest motel on the east side of town (5 miles from the center). It has a restaurant (see Places to Eat, below), bar, laundry facilities, heated swimming pool, gym and rates starting at $68/78.

Places to Eat

If you're self-catering, the ***Reading Farmers' Market***, at Penn and S 8th Sts, is a good place to stock up, but it is only open Thursday and Friday 10 am to 6 pm and Saturday to 2 pm.

The factory outlets have food courts inside, and there are chain restaurants around them.

In town, the ***Athleatery*** restaurant, at the YMCA (☎ 610-375-4700, 631 Washington St), sells burgers for $2.50 and a pork-chop platter with sauerkraut, mashed potatoes and a roll for $4.50. It's open to members and nonmembers alike between 6:30 am and 3 pm.

The ***Studio Bistro*** (46 N 6th St), at Washington St, is (in spite of its name) a standard diner/restaurant, but the food is reasonable. It is open for breakfast and lunch but is closed Sunday. Eggs Benedict or a tuna melt with fries cost $4.50. Kosher deli sandwiches are also available.

Jimmy Kramer's Peanut Bar & Restaurant (☎ 610-376-8500, 332 Penn St) is named after the free peanuts everyone there gets. Just throw the shells on the floor. The place has good pub food; beef stew is $3.95, and a shrimp platter costs $8.95.

Morey's Coach House, in the same building as the Royal Bank of Pennsylvania on the corner of N 5th and Washington Sts, is a large, spacious restaurant. Its lunchtime specials are a good value: a cheese steak sandwich is $3.50, and a BLT with soup and a beverage is $5.

The ***Antique Airplane Restaurant*** (☎ 610-779-2345), in the Dutch Colony Inn & Suites (see Places to Stay, above), has a large airplane (a 1927 Monocoupe) that's been hanging from the restaurant's ceiling since 1967, as well as photos of pioneer aviators. The restaurant serves omelettes starting at $2.50 and pancakes starting at $2.25.

Shopping

The major factory outlets are in Wyomissing, west of town. They sell clothes (including designer labels and sportswear), crockery, cosmetics and other items. The largest is the VF Factory Outlet (☎ 610-378-0408), in the VF Outlet Village, at Park Rd and Hill Ave. Among the others spread around town are the following: Reading Outlet Center (☎ 610-373-5495), 801 N 9th St; Outlets on Hiesters Lane (☎ 610-921-8130), 755 Hiesters Lane; and Reading Station Outlets (☎ 610-478-7000), 951 N 6th St.

PENNSYLVANIA

Getting There & Away

Air Reading Regional Airport (☎ 610-372-4666) is 2 miles northwest, at 251 Bernville Rd (Route 183). US Airways (☎ 800-428-4322) has nine daily flights to Philadelphia, six to Pittsburgh and two to Lancaster. The one-way fare to Philadelphia is $125; to Lancaster from $25 one way; and to Pittsburgh $305 one way.

Bus The Reading Intercity Bus Terminal (☎ 610-374-3182), at N 3rd and Court Sts, is served by Bieber Tourways (☎ 610-683-7333) and Capitol Trailways (☎ 800-333-8444). Bieber Tourways' one-way fare to New York City is $19 (two hours). With Capitol Trailways, the one-way fare to Philadelphia is $9.35 (1¼ hours); to Pittsburgh, it's $49 (5¾ hours).

Car & Motorcycle From Philadelphia, take I-76 (Schuylkill Expressway) north to the Pennsylvania Turnpike, then head west to exit 22; take I-176 north to Route 422, and follow it west into downtown. From Harrisburg, you can either take I-76 (Pennsylvania Turnpike) east to exit 21, then Route 222 northeast, or you can take Route 322, then Route 422 east into Reading.

Getting Around

The Berks Area Reading Transportation Authority (BARTA; ☎ 610-921-0601), 1700 N 11th St, is the county bus line. Most fares around town are $1.10.

AROUND READING
Daniel Boone Homestead

The famous outdoorsman was born and raised till the age of 15 in a log house on the site of the present homestead (☎ 610-582-4900), 400 Daniel Boone Rd, Birdsboro (9 miles east of Reading). The reconstructed house includes the original foundation, portions of the 18th- and 19th-century building material, period German and English furnishings and a spring in the basement. Inside the visitors' center is a video of a fellow in old garb talking as though he knew Boone. Admission is $4/2 for adults/children; seniors pay $3.50, and families pay $10. The price of admission includes a guided tour. Around the homestead are 600 acres of land with hiking and biking trails. The house is open to visitors from Memorial Day to Labor Day; business hours are Tuesday to

> ### Daniel Boone
>
> Daniel Boone (1734 –1820) is one of America's most famous 'frontiersmen.' Boone owes much of his fame to John Filson, who added an appendix concerning 'The Adventures of Col Daniel Boone' to his book *The Discovery, Settlement, and Present State of Kentucke* [sic.] He was also the model for James Fenimore Cooper's *Leatherstocking* character and is even mentioned in Byron's *Don Juan*.
>
> Boone was born east of Reading, the sixth of 11 children, to a Quaker family. He had little schooling, although he did have some early experience as a farmer, weaver and blacksmith. When Daniel was 15, his family moved to northwestern North Carolina.
>
> The Boone family home in North Carolina was on the American frontier, and although Daniel married Rebecca Bryan and had 10 children, he spent much of his life on expeditions around the country. One of his earliest (a year before his marriage to Rebecca) was with British General Braddock in his expedition to Fort Duquesne (today's Pittsburgh) in 1755.
>
> Boone is famous for his travels in Kentucky and for fighting against Native Americans there, beginning in 1767. He built a wagon road through the Cumberland Mountains to Kentucky, which became known as the Cumberland Gap and was a major route west for settlers. He loved the 'dark and bloody ground' so much that he decided to build Boonesboro in Kentucky in 1774. From 1775 to 1783, Boone was a major force in expanding settlement in Kentucky and defending settlements from Native Americans. Boone himself was captured several times, but he always escaped.
>
> He was a good fighter and wilderness guide but a lousy businessman. In 1799, after losing his Kentucky lands, he went to Missouri and stayed there until his death, 21 years later.

Saturday from 9 am to 5 pm and Sunday from noon to 5 pm.

Take Route 422 east to the intersection with Route 82; continue straight through the traffic lights, and after the sign for the homestead, turn left onto Daniel Boone Rd. The entrance to the property is about a mile from the turn.

Hawk Mountain Sanctuary

The 2400-acre sanctuary (☎ 610-756-6961, 756-6000), Rural Route 2, Kempton, 25 miles north of Reading, was established in 1934 to protect migrating hawks from hunters. Today, it's a preserve for bald eagles, ospreys, peregrine falcons, hawks and other migrating birds, such as the swift and the swallow. Spring and fall bring thousands of birds to the sanctuary, and the best spot for viewing them is the 1521-foot-high North Lookout. A 4-mile walking trail connects the sanctuary with the Appalachian Trail. You can rent binoculars at the visitors' center, which is open daily December through August 9 am to 5 pm, and September through November from 8 am. Admission is $6/3 for adults/children; seniors pay $4. Bear in mind that the sanctuary gets busy on weekends. Take Route 61 north, then Rural Route 2 east.

French Creek State Park

The 11½-sq-mile French Creek State Park (☎ 610-582-9680), 843 Park Rd, Elverson, about 14 miles southeast of Reading, off Route 422, has over 32 miles of hiking trails. Fishing and canoeing are possible on Scotts Run and Hopewell Lakes. From Memorial Day to Labor Day, there's swimming daily 11 am to 7 pm in a pool beside Hopewell Lake. Wildlife in the park includes deer, squirrels and, in the spring and fall, many migratory birds. The park also has camping facilities (see Places to Stay under Reading, earlier). From Route 422, take Route 82 south, Route 724 east, then Route 345 south into the park.

Surrounded on three sides by the park is **Hopewell Furnace National Historic Site** (☎ 610-582-8773), 2 Mark Bird Lane, which is administered by the National Park Service (NPS). Restoration work continues on this early-19th-century village, which has a cold-blast iron-making furnace. There's an audio-visual presentation, and in summer, guides dressed in period costume demonstrate different village crafts. The site is open daily 9 am to 5 pm year-round, and entry is $4/free for adults/children.

LEBANON & AROUND

On the east side of Lebanon (population 24,800), Weaver's (☎ 717-274-6100), at 15th Ave and Weavertown Rd, is a competitor to the larger Seltzer's (see Palmyra, later) in the production of Lebanon bologna. There's no tour, but you can take a look at the smokehouses Monday to Saturday 9 am from to 4 pm.

If you head east on Route 422, you'll come to **Willow Spring Park** (☎ 717-866-5801), which has a small lake that is open for swimming from Memorial Day to Labor Day daily 10 am to 6 pm. It costs $5/3 for adults/children on weekends, or $3/2.50 weekdays. During the same period, there's also scuba diving daily 8 am to 6 pm for $14; during the rest of the year, diving is only possible on weekends and appointments are necessary. Scuba divers and their families can also camp here. Scuba Venture West (☎ 717-866-5535), opposite the entrance to Willow Springs, rents snorkeling and scuba-diving equipment, tests oxygen tanks and provides training. From Lebanon, head along Route 422 to the traffic lights 2 miles east of the junction with Route 501; turn

Hawk Mountain is a preserve for the bald eagle and other birds.

right at the lights onto Millardsville Rd, and the park is a quarter of a mile down, on the left.

Getting There & Away

Lebanon is on Route 422, 8 miles east of Palmyra and 87 miles west of Reading. Capitol Trailways stops at Great Vacations Travel Agency (☎ 717-272-0161, 273-1646), 201 Cumberland St (Route 442 west); the office is open Monday, Tuesday, Thursday and Friday 9 am to 5 pm, Wednesday 8 am to 5 pm and Saturday 9 am to 1 pm. Up to six buses leave daily for Harrisburg, and four for Reading; the one-way fare for each is $5.50.

Getting Around

The office of County of Lebanon Transit (COLT; ☎ 717-274-3664) is at 200 Willow St; the main bus stop is at Willow and N 7th Sts.

PALMYRA

Palmyra, about 2 miles east of Hershey on Route 422, is the home of Seltzer's (☎ 800-282-6336), 230 N College St. Seltzer's is the largest producer of Lebanon bologna in the USA. The US government officially classifies the bologna as 'semi-dry fermented sausage.' Whatever it's called, they make tons of it here.

According to the company, after the meat arrives, it is aged, cured, ground and smoked, then put through a metal detector and cut into appropriate sizes. It's not cooked so much as fermented – a combination of lowering the pH balance, salting and smoking.

There is a free tour of the small plant and the smokehouses weekdays 8:45 to 11:45 am and 12:30 to 3:15 pm. The sales outlet is open weekdays 7 am to 5 pm and Saturday 7 am to 1 pm. Seltzer's is signed off Main St (Route 422), but not too clearly – turn at the intersection that has Turkey Hill Minit Mart and Cinderella Shoppe on opposite corners.

Capitol Trailways buses stop at Lauck's Brothers store (☎ 717-838-9652), 30 E Main St.

South Central Pennsylvania

The terrain of south central Pennsylvania tends to be fairly flat and monotonous and consists mostly of farmland. The area's major river is the Susquehanna, which flows through Harrisburg (the state capital) south-eastward between Lancaster and York into Maryland and Chesapeake Bay. Gettysburg, with its Civil War battleground, is clearly the most interesting place to visit. The town of Hershey, too, is hard to resist, although for many, it may be something of a letdown unless they're young enough to enjoy the chocolate-world fantasy.

Other notable places are the Harley-Davidson factory in York and the Three Mile Island nuclear plant near Harrisburg.

GETTYSBURG

Gettysburg (population 8700) is around 55 miles southwest of Lancaster and 30 miles southwest of Harrisburg. As a conse-quence of its position at the junction of several roads and its proximity to the Mason-Dixon line, it became the site of the bloodiest battle in US history. The battle was a turning point in the Civil War and helped inspire Abraham Lincoln's Gettys-burg Address (see the boxed text 'Lincoln's Gettysburg Address').

It also helped inspire today's busy tourist industry, which capitalizes on both the battle and the war. In spite of the commercialism in the town, Gettysburg National Military Park is certainly worth visiting to see where the Union and Confederate armies con-fronted each other. In addition, the former home of President Dwight D Eisenhower is another nearby attraction. Most of the rest of the tourist attractions can be skipped, unless you have a particular interest in one of them. The town itself, with its many fine historic buildings, is small enough to walk around.

Orientation

The approximately 1½ sq miles of Gettys-burg are laid out around Lincoln Square.

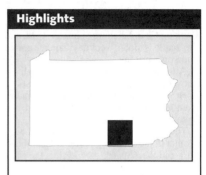

Highlights

- Gettysburg National Military Park, a must for those wanting to learn more about one of the defining events in US history

- The Harley-Davidson assembly plant and museum in York, high on any motorhead's list of places to visit

- For children, the sweet delights of Hersheypark and Chocolate World

Several large roads converge in the town. Route 30 (York and Chambersburg Sts in town) and Route 116 (Hanover, York and W Middle Sts) cross east to west. Route 97 enters from the south (Baltimore St) and leaves from the north as Route 34 (Carlisle St). Business Route 15 enters town as Stein-wehr Ave from the southwest and exits in the northeast as Harrisburg St. Finally, Route 134 enters from the south as Taney-town Rd and ends in town as Washington St.

Gettysburg National Military Park sur-rounds the town and still has homes and stores in it, as the area did at the time of the battle.

Information

The town tourist office is the Gettysburg Travel Council (☎ 717-334-6274), 35 Carlisle St. It's open 9 am to 5 pm daily, and the office maintains a website (www.gettysburg.com).

The national military park also has a visitor center (see the Gettysburg National Military Park section, below).

The main post office, 155 Buford Ave, is open 8 am to 4:30 pm weekdays and 9 am to noon on Saturday. The First Federal Savings Bank on Chambersburg St has an ATM, and the bank is open weekdays and 9 am to noon on Saturday.

Adams County Library, on High St between Baltimore and S Stratton Sts, is open 9 am to 8:30 pm Monday to Thursday, 9 am to 5 pm Friday and Saturday and 1 to 5 pm Sunday.

The Laundercenter is a self-serve Laundromat in the shopping center at Chambersburg and West Sts.

Walking Tour

Start at the Gettysburg Travel Council, 35 Carlisle St, one block north of Lincoln Square, and walk south toward the square. On the first day of battle, Union soldiers streamed into town from the north and west and crossed **Lincoln Square** as they retreated south toward Cemetery Hill. As they retreated, they stopped periodically to fire cannons north along the streets toward the pursuing Confederate troops.

Continue west (right) on Chambersburg St to **Christ Evangelical Lutheran Church** on your left. Here, a Union chaplain who was tending to the wounded inside was killed by advancing Confederate troops because he didn't identify himself as a man of the cloth when challenged by the Confederates.

Continue west, then go left (south) for one block on S Washington St to W Middle St, which, during the second and third days of the battle, was part of the Confederate line. Continue south for one block and turn left (east) onto W High St. Here, on the site of the **United Methodist Church** (built after the war), was an earlier church in which the wounded were treated. In front of the earlier church two trenches were dug in which the dead, wrapped in blankets and packed next to each other, were buried.

Nearby, Abraham Lincoln sat in a pew in the **United Presbyterian Church**, on the corner of Baltimore St, and the retired

President Eisenhower worshipped here as well. President Lincoln paraded south along Baltimore St on his way to give his famous address at the dedication of the Soldiers National Cemetery.

Turn north (left) on S Stratton St and go two blocks to the intersection with York St. Before turning west (left) on York St, look at the northeastern corner (at N Stratton St). There, after the battle, a dead, unidentified Union soldier was found holding a photo of his three children. The photo was reproduced in newspapers all over the country until his wife in upstate New York identified the man as Sergeant Amos Humiston.

Continue west on York St to Lincoln Square; note the **Wills House** (with the Lincoln Statue in front), where Lincoln completed the final draft of the Gettysburg Address.

Gettysburg National Military Park

Established February 11, 1895, the 8-sq-mile park encompasses almost the entire area of the three-day battle. The park, in essence, is a huge shrine that attracts thousands of visitors each year. The battlefield contains more than 1600 monuments, statues, cannons and plaques set up in dedication to the people who fought at Gettysburg. All were erected in good faith, but with so many, the effect is somewhat cluttered.

The Battle of Gettysburg is the most famous battle of the Civil War. Some war buffs spend their lives studying the battle or only one day of it, and each year there are regular reenacts of events relating to this pivotal event in US history. At Gettysburg, from July 1 to 3, 1863, the 75,000 men of Robert E Lee's Confederate army met the 97,000 men of Union General George G Meade. The battle was the result of a chance sighting of some of Meade's troops by a group of Confederate troops who were sent to get supplies.

The battle began on July 1, with Confederate troops attacking Union troops on McPherson Ridge, west of Gettysburg. The Union troops held their position until the

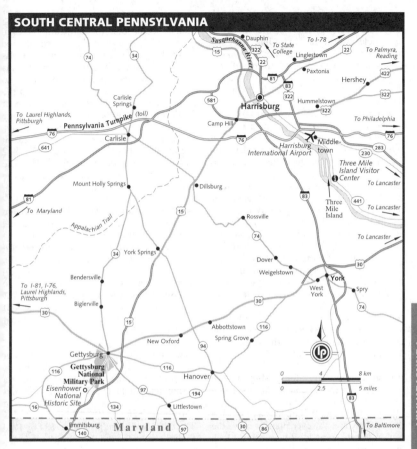

SOUTH CENTRAL PENNSYLVANIA

afternoon, when they were beaten back in a rout through town. Thousands were captured before they could regroup south of town on Cemetery Hill. The first day of battle ended with the Union troops, who had retreated, fortifying their positions while the bulk of Meade's army arrived to reinforce them.

By dawn of the second day the Confederate troops were laid out along an arc running through the middle of Gettysburg and along Seminary Hill. Facing them, a mile away to the east, was a smaller arc of Union troops on Cemetery Ridge. Lee ordered

attacks against both flanks of the Union line. Confederate James Longstreet's attack smashed through the Union left flank at a peach orchard south of town and overran the Union position on Little Round Top. On the other flank, though, RS Ewell's attack didn't succeed in dislodging the Union troops and, ultimately, Longstreet's success couldn't be exploited successfully by the Confederates.

On the third day, Lee's artillery bombarded Union positions on Cemetery Ridge and Cemetery Hill; the Union artillery responded. The sickening high point came when Confederate General George Pickett led a massive charge of 12,000 men across an open field toward the Union line at Cemetery Ridge. In less than an hour, 10,000 of Pickett's men were dead or wounded, and the expression 'Pickett's Charge' entered the lexicon as a brave but futile attempt to defeat an enemy.

After the battle, there were 51,000 dead, wounded and missing troops, and 5000 dead horses. Lee's invasion of the North had been stymied, and his army was exhausted. Union General Meade 'won' the battle, but was too cautious (or too afraid) to pursue the Confederate army. Although the war continued for two more years, the Confederacy never recovered from its losses at Gettysburg.

The dead were buried all over the battlefield in hastily dug graves, and some weren't buried at all until Pennsylvania Governor Andrew Curtin ordered that land be purchased for a cemetery. This became the Soldiers National Cemetery at Gettysburg, and on November 19, 1863, the cemetery was dedicated. Near the end of the dedication ceremony, Abraham Lincoln gave a two-minute speech that became known as the Gettysburg Address. (See the boxed text 'Lincoln's Gettysburg Address.')

Visitor Center The National Military Park Visitor Center (☎ 717-334-1124), less than a mile south of Lincoln Square, is in the park off Taneytown Rd. It is open 8 am to 5 pm daily. (There are, however, plans to move the center despite some local opposition.) Pick up the *Gettysburg Official Map & Guide*. It includes a self-guided driving tour (allow two to three hours) that follows a route that is marked by signposts (with a single large white star) that describe the battle action at important points.

Licensed battlefield guides charge $30 per carload (up to five people) for a two-hour tour. These tours are well worth it. The guides are available on a first-come, first-served basis, so you need to get to the visitor center early, except in the winter. There are also free guided walks with park rangers of the National Cemetery and High Water Mark Trail.

The visitor center also sells a large selection of books about the battle and the Civil War, and it houses the good, small, free **Gettysburg Museum of the Civil War**. Its exhibits include uniforms, guns, implements and other artifacts that are just enough to satisfy the moderately curious. Also in the visitor center is the **electric map**. Visitors sit in tiered seats looking down on a large diorama illuminated with colored lights, and a park ranger narrates the progress of the three-day battle. Admission is $3/2.50/2 for adults/seniors/children under 16. The museum and electric map are open the same hours as the visitor center.

Soldiers National Cemetery Across from the visitor center is the Soldiers National Cemetery at Gettysburg. It contains the graves of more than 7000 US servicemen, including 3582 Union soldiers killed in the Civil War (the remains of Confederate soldiers killed at Gettysburg were removed to the South). Nearly half of the Civil War burials here were of unknown soldiers. It was at the dedication of the cemetery that Lincoln gave his celebrated address.

Cyclorama Center The Cyclorama Center has a large 360° mural of Pickett's Charge. It's displayed around an auditorium, and in a 20-minute sound and light show, a guide describes the battle and illuminates different parts of the painting. Think of it as early TV. The cyclorama was finished in 1884 by Paul Philippoteaux (he did three other versions), who was already known for his cycloramas on the Battle of Waterloo and the Crucifixion of Jesus. The Cyclorama Center is open 9 am to 5 pm daily; admission is $3/2.50/2 for adults/seniors/children.

The Battlefield The most famous part of the battlefield is probably the portion of **Cemetery Ridge** against which Confederate General Pickett hurled his cavalry – known as Pickett's Charge – resulting in 80% casualties. The spot is less than half a mile south of the visitor center, and you can walk to it on the **High Water Mark Trail**. There are other longer hikes. The 1-mile **Big Round**

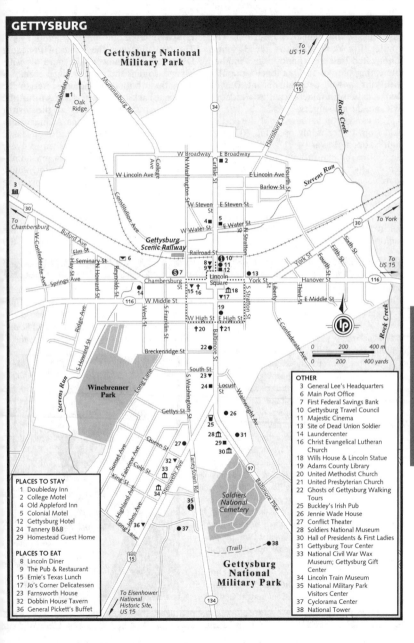

GETTYSBURG

Gettysburg National Military Park

To US 15

Oak Ridge

Doubleday Ave
Mummasburg Rd
Rock Creek

34

■1

College Ave

N Washington St

Carlisle St

Harrisburg St

W Broadway   E Broadway

■2

W Lincoln Ave   E Lincoln Ave

Barlow St

Fourth St

Stevens Run

To Chambersburg

Constitution Ave

W Steven St   E Steven St

W Water St   ■4   5   E Water St

Gettysburg Scenic Railway

Railroad St

☒6

W Seminary St

Elm St

Chambersburg St

30

Buford Ave

W Confederate Ave

Hay St   Reynolds Ave

Springs Ave

3
✦

14

116

30   To York

N Stratton St

S Stratton St

10
11
12

9☒
8☒

✿7

Lincoln Square

York St

13

Hanover St

Stevens Run

York St   Fourth St   Fifth St   Sixth St

Liberty St   Third St

To US 15

116

■18
▼17
19

E Middle St

W Middle St

E High St

✝20   ✝21

Breckenridge St

22●

South St

23▼

24●   Locust St

Winebrenner Park

West St

S Franklin St

Baltimore St

S Washington St

Gettys St

Long Lane

25

26●

28✿   ●31

27●   29■

30✿

32▼
33✿

34✿

97

Wainwright Ave

Queen St   Culp St

Sunset Ave   Fairview Ave

King St

Highland Ave   Johns Ave

35
ℹ

36▼   ●37

Long Lane

Taneytown Rd

Steinwehr Ave

Soldiers National Cemetery

●38   (Trail)

BUS
15

To Eisenhower National Historic Site, US 15

134

Gettysburg National Military Park

PENNSYLVANIA

0   200   400 m
0   200   400 yards

PLACES TO STAY
1 Doubleday Inn
2 College Motel
5 Old Appleford Inn
5 Colonial Motel
12 Gettysburg Hotel
24 Tannery B&B
29 Homestead Guest Home

PLACES TO EAT
8 Lincoln Diner
9 The Pub & Restaurant
15 Ernie's Texas Lunch
17 Jo's Corner Delicatessen
23 Farnsworth House
32 Dobbin House Tavern
36 General Pickett's Buffet

OTHER
3 General Lee's Headquarters
6 Main Post Office
7 First Federal Savings Bank
10 Gettysburg Travel Council
11 Majestic Cinema
13 Site of Dead Union Soldier
14 Laundercenter
16 Christ Evangelical Lutheran Church
18 Wills House & Lincoln Statue
19 Adams County Library
20 United Methodist Church
21 United Presbyterian Church
22 Ghosts of Gettysburg Walking Tours
25 Buckley's Irish Pub
26 Jennie Wade House
27 Conflict Theater
28 Soldiers National Museum
30 Hall of Presidents & First Ladies
31 Gettysburg Tour Center
33 National Civil War Wax Museum; Gettysburg Gift Center
34 Lincoln Train Museum
35 National Military Park Visitors Center
37 Cyclorama Center
38 National Tower

Top Loop Trail goes through a forest and past breastworks built by both troops. The 9-mile **Billy Yank Trail** and the 3½-mile **Johnny Reb Trail** are other options. Another interesting part of the battlefield, popular with kids as well as adults, is the **Devil's Den**, a mass of boulders used as a hideout by Confederate snipers.

You can get an aerial view of the battlefield from the privately operated 307-foot-high **National Tower** (☎ 717-334-6754), 999 Baltimore Pike, southeast of the visitor center. It's open 10 am to 4 pm daily in March; 9 am to 5:30 pm daily April through June and September through October; 9 am to 6:30 pm daily in July and August; and 10 am to 4 pm Friday to Sunday in November. Admission is $5.25/4.50/3.25 for adults/seniors/children.

Eisenhower National Historic Site

The farm that was the home of President Dwight D Eisenhower (Ike) and his wife, Mamie, adjoins the southwestern corner of the national park and is administered by the National Parks Service (NPS) as a historic site. You purchase tickets at the visitor center in Gettysburg National Military Park (see above), from where a shuttle bus takes you to the farm house. The bus leaves every 30 minutes between 9 am and 4 pm; admission to the house is $5.25/$2.25 for adults/children, and those younger than six have free entry.

General Lee's Headquarters

One of the few old homes open to the public, this house (☎ 717-334-3141), 401

Lincoln's Gettysburg Address

Four score and seven years ago our fathers brought forth on this continent, a new nation, conceived in Liberty, and dedicated to the proposition that all men are created equal. Now we are engaged in a great civil war, testing whether that nation, or any nation so conceived and so dedicated, can long endure. We are met on a great battlefield of war. We have come to dedicate a portion of that field, as a final resting place for those who here gave their lives that that nation might live. It is altogether

fitting and proper that we should do this. But, in a larger sense, we can not dedicate – we can not consecrate – we can not hallow – this ground. The brave men, living and dead, who struggled here, have consecrated it, far above our poor power to add or detract. The world will little note, nor long remember what we say here, but it can never forget what they did here. It is for us the living, rather, to be dedicated here to the unfinished work which they who fought here have thus far so nobly advanced. It is rather for us to be here dedicated to the great task remaining before us – that from these honored dead we take increased devotion – that we here highly resolve that these dead shall not have died in vain – that this nation, under God, shall have a new birth of freedom – and that government of the people, by the people, for the people, shall not perish from the earth.

– Abraham Lincoln,
November 19, 1863, at the dedication of
Soldiers National Cemetery at Gettysburg

Handmade quilts for sale

Antique car show, south central PA

Fort Pitt Bridge, spanning the Monongehela River, Pittsburgh, PA

Fall produce for sale in northern PA

George Washington's HQ, Valley Forge, PA

Local watering hole, Fort Necessity, PA

Buford Ave (Route 30), was Lee's headquarters during the battle on July 1, 1863, and it has a collection of memorabilia from the period. It is open 9 am to 9 pm daily mid-April to mid-October; 9 am to 5 pm mid-March to mid-April and mid-October through November; admission is $3/1 for adults/children.

Wills House

This house (☎ 717-334-8188), 12 Lincoln Square, in which Lincoln stayed prior to giving his Gettysburg Address, has some Lincoln artifacts in a room (the Lincoln Room Museum) on the 2nd floor. Contrary to popular belief, Lincoln didn't write his most famous speech on the back of an envelope while on the way to Gettysburg. He actually wrote a draft in Washington, then revised it here before delivering it at the National Cemetery on November 19, 1863. The house is open 9 am to 7:30 pm Monday to Thursday, 9 am to 8 pm Friday and Saturday; admission is $3.50/2 for adults/children.

The Conflict Theater

The Conflict Theater (☎ 717-334-8003), 213 Steinwehr Ave, shows a range of 50-minute audiovisual programs – narrated stories told against a backdrop of slides, photos and period music. Programs include: 'Gettysburg: A Study in Valor' (the story of the battle as told by a soldier), 'The War Within' (the story of the Civil War), 'O' How I dread Tomorrow' (the story of the civilians during the battle) and 'Adventure at Gettysburg' (aimed at children, it's a fictional story about a young boy who becomes involved in the battle).

From June to Labor Day the theater is open 10:30 am to 10 pm Monday and Thursday; 10:30 am to 9 pm Sunday, Tuesday and Wednesday; 10:30 am to 11 pm Friday and Saturday. March through May and early September through November it is open 10:30 am to 6 pm Sunday to Thursday, 7 pm on Friday and to 8 pm on Saturday. December to February it's open 11 am to 5 pm Monday to Saturday. Admission is $5/4 for adults/children.

Jennie Wade House

Twenty year old Jennie Wade, shot by a stray bullet while making bread in her house, was the only Gettysburg civilian killed in the battle. The house was hit by more than 200 bullets. Although many Gettysburg residents prefer not to discuss it, the Wade house (☎ 717-334-4100), on Baltimore Pike, is believed by locals to be haunted. Allegedly, there have been incidents of 'positive movement' of items in the cellar, including a swinging chain. It's open 9 am to 7 pm daily; admission is $5.75/3.50 for adults/children.

Gettysburg Scenic Railway

April through October, the Gettysburg Scenic Railway (☎ 717-334-6932), 106 N Washington St, runs a 1½-hour, 16-mile steam train ride through the battlefield to Biglerville; the roundtrip fare is $10/9/6 for adults/seniors/children.

Other Attractions

The **National Civil War Wax Museum** (☎ 717-334-6245), 297 Steinwehr Ave, is one of those tacky-tourist sights that's actually worth a visit, although it doesn't have any horror figures. Inside is the **Battleroom Auditorium**, a show of electronically controlled, life-sized mannequins re-enacting Pickett's Charge and the Gettysburg Address. It's open 9 am to 5 pm daily (to 9 pm mid-June to Labor Day), and admission is $4.50/2.50/1.50 for adults/youth/children.

The **Hall of Presidents & First Ladies** (☎ 717-334-5717, 800-447-8788), on Baltimore St near the main entrance to the National Cemetery, features portraits and wax sculptures of presidents and their first ladies. It's open 9 am to 5 pm daily in spring and fall and until 9 pm mid-June to Labor Day. Admission is $5.75/4.50/3.50 for adults/seniors/children.

The **Soldiers National Museum** (☎ 717-334-4890), on Baltimore St, houses a huge collection of uniforms, guns, detailed dioramas of Civil War scenes and other memorabilia. It's open 9 am to 5 pm daily (to 9 pm June to August), and admission is $5.75/3.50 for adults/children.

PENNSYLVANIA

The **Lincoln Train Museum** (☎ 717-334-6296), 200 Steinwehr Ave, has a simulated train ride with Lincoln onboard (as exciting as it sounds), plus toy trains and dioramas. It's open 9 am to 5 pm daily (to 9 pm mid-June to Labor Day), and admission is $5.75/3.50 for adults/children.

Organized Tours

Gettysburg Tour Center (☎ 717-334-6296), 778 Baltimore St, has two packages. Package Plan I does a 23-mile bus tour of the battlefield and visits the Hall of Presidents & First Ladies *or* Soldiers National Museum; and the Lincoln Train Museum *or* Gettysburg Battle Theater. It costs $33.95/20.95 for adults/children. Package Plan II does the battlefield, the National Tower, the National Wax Museum, Soldier's National Museum, the Lincoln Train Museum, Gettysburg Battle Theater, the Wills House, the Hall of Presidents & First Ladies and the Jennie Wade House for $47.95/29.75 for adults/children.

The Gettysburg Tour Center also offers two-hour tours of the battlefield for $14.95/10.50 for adults/children, and it sells an audio-tape tour ($12.95) that takes about two hours.

The Ghosts of Gettysburg Candlelight Walking Tours (☎ 717-337-0445), 271 Baltimore St, leads 1½-hour tours of two sites where ghostly happenings are said to occur. The cost is $6.50. Tours of Baltimore St depart at 8 and 9:45 pm daily; tours of Carlisle St depart at 9 pm daily. You need to book ahead.

Special Events

May

Gettysburg Spring Bluegrass Festival
The festival is two days of concerts, usually on the first weekend of the month (☎ 717-642-8749).

June/July

Gettysburg Civil War Heritage Days
This is a commemoration of the Battle of Gettysburg, with an encampment, concerts and battle re-enactments during the last weekend in June and first week in July (☎ 717-334-6274).

August

Gettysburg Fall Bluegrass Festival
The festival is four days of concerts held over the third weekend of the month (☎ 717-642-8749).

November

Anniversary of Lincoln's Gettysburg Address
This event on November 19, with memorial services at the National Cemetery, commemorates Lincoln's famous address (☎ 717-334-6274).

Places to Stay

There's a fair number of accommodations in Gettysburg and in the surrounding area, but it gets crowded in summer, especially on weekends and during the Gettysburg Civil War Heritage Days (see the Special Events section). The cheaper places are generally a few miles out of town; check Business Route 15 heading south or Route 34 heading north.

Camping Gettysburg has a number of large campgrounds within 3 or 4 miles of town; all have major facilities such as swimming pools, laundries, stores, propane gas and anything else you might need.

Artillery Ridge Camping Resort (☎ 717-334-1288, 610 Taneytown Rd), 3 miles south of Gettysburg on Route 134, has sites for $15.50 for two people, $21.50 with water and electricity; each extra person is an additional $4. It has bicycle rentals and a swimming pool and organizes horseback rides to the battlefield. One mile farther south, *Round Top Campground* (☎ 717-334-9565, 180 Knight Rd), off Taneytown Rd, has tent sites for $16.50, RV sites for $22.35. *Gettysburg Battlefield Camp* (☎ 717-337-3363), 3 miles southwest on Business Route 15 (Steinwehr Ave), has over 200 sites for RVs only. Rates start at $19.80 per site for two people, $25.80 with electricity and water.

The wooded *Drummer Boy Camping Resort* (☎ 800-293-2808, 1300 Hanover Rd) has sites for $20, or $24 with water and electricity. Rates are an extra $3 on Friday and Saturday nights, or $5 on public-holiday weekends. It's open April through October, organizes entertainment and activities on weekends and rents bicycles. From town take Route 116 east for 1½ miles (to just past the junction with Route 15), then turn left onto Hanover Rd.

Open April to November, *Gettysburg Campground* (☎ 717-334-3304, 2030 Fairfield Rd) has sites for $20.90 each, $25.90 with water and electricity. From town take Route 116 (which becomes Fairfield Rd) west for 3 miles. Three miles farther west is *Granite Hill Campground* (☎ 717-642-8749, *3340 Fairfield Rd*). It has sites for $22, $25 with water and electricity, and it's open year round.

Hostels HI-AYH *Pine Grove Furnace State Park Hostel* (☎ 717-486-7575, *tomha@epix.net, 1212 Pine Grove Rd*), a three-story mansion built in 1829, is in beautiful surroundings. It's on the Appalachian Trail, and there are biking and cross-country skiing trails nearby. Beds cost $14 and the hostel is open year round. It's about 20 miles northwest of Gettysburg: Take Route 34 north, then turn left at Twirly Top Ice Cream Parlor; the hostel is another 7 miles, and it's on the left side of the road.

Guesthouses A real bargain, the *Homestead Guest Home* (☎ 717-334-2037, *785 Baltimore St*) is in the building that was the former Soldiers' Orphans Homestead – it was built for the orphans of men killed at Gettysburg. It's a friendly place run by Mrs Mary Collins, who was raised in the house; she'll happily tell you about its history. Rooms, with shared bathroom, cost $30 to $35.

Motels & Hotels The period-style *Colonial Motel* (☎ 717-334-3126, *157 Carlisle St*) has singles/doubles for $68/82. Farther out of the town center, the clean *College Motel* (☎ 717-334-6731, *345 Carlisle St*) has a pool and 21 rooms at $76 each (mid-June to Labor Day; it's cheaper the rest of the year).

In a quiet location, the *Blue Sky Motel* (☎ 717-677-7736, *2585 Biglerville Rd*), on Route 34 heading north, is a small place with 16 rooms, a small picnic area and a heated pool. Rooms cost $49/54. From town, take Route 34 north for 4½ miles.

Built in 1797, the renovated *Gettysburg Hotel* (☎ 717-337-2000, 800-528-1234, *1 Lincoln Square*), in the center of town, has rooms for $95 to $175.

B&Bs & Inns The three-story *Tannery B&B* (☎ 717-334-2454, *449 Baltimore St*) is a large

Gothic house decorated with Civil War memorabilia. All rooms have private baths. Rates, including full breakfast, are $100/155.

The 1867 *Old Appleford Inn* (☎ 717-337-1711, 800-275-3373, *218 Carlisle St*) is a large, beautiful Victorian house that has 10 en suite rooms. The house is tastefully furnished, with high ceilings, a library, five wood-burning fireplaces, wooden floors and a large sunroom. Rooms (named after Union and Confederate generals) cost $80/105.

The *Doubleday Inn* (☎ 717-334-9119, *104 Doubleday Ave*), at Oak Ridge, near stop No 3 on the self-guided driving tour of the battlefield, is a large white house that overlooks a quiet part of the battlefield and Gettysburg College. There are nine rooms, five with private baths that have claw-footed tubs. On selected evenings a historian from the National Military Park Visitors Center comes to the house to speak and answer questions about the battle. Rooms are $89/99 with shared bath, $109/119 with private bath.

Places to Eat

Budget On Steinwehr Ave, opposite the entrance to the park, there is a conglomeration of fast-food places.

In town, the clean, bright *Jo's Corner Delicatessen* (☎ 717-334-7371, *48 Baltimore St*) is good for sandwiches (from $3), including hoagies (from $3.50). It's closed Sunday. *Ernie's Texas Lunch* (*58 Chambersburg St*) is a neighborhood place with booths and Formica-topped tables. It serves burgers and hot dogs from $1.40 and hoagies from $3.50. It's closed on Sunday. The *Lincoln Diner* (☎ 717-334-3900, *32 Carlisle St*), next to the railroad tracks, is a good diner that's popular for lunch and is open 24 hours a day. Hamburgers cost $2.35, salad $5.50 and roast beef $7.50; it also serves delicious baked desserts such as blueberry pie for $1.95.

Mid-Range & Top End If you like to gorge yourself, *General Pickett's Buffet* (☎ 717-334-7580, *571 Steinwehr Ave*), behind Gettysburg Battle Theater, has an all-you-can-eat lunch buffet for $6 and a dinner buffet for $10. A soup and salad buffet costs $3.95 at either lunch or dinner. Children under 10 and accompanied by an adult can eat for $2.

The Pub & Restaurant (☎ 717-334-7100), on the corner of Lincoln Square, is a popular eatery with large windows that afford good views of the square. You can also dine outside on the sidewalk. It serves pasta dishes for $10.50 to $17.50 and a variety of burgers and sandwiches for $6.95; it also offers a wide selection of beer and wine.

Dobbin House Tavern (☎ 717-334-2100, *89 Steinwehr Ave*) has two eating areas. On the ground floor, the *Springhouse Tavern* is an old inn with a bar built in the early 19th century by the great-great-great grandfather of the present owner. Caesar salad costs $5.25, and main dishes such as char-grilled chicken cost $9 to $16. Above Springhouse Tavern, the more formal *Alexander Dobbin Dining Rooms* are open 5:30 to 9:30 pm daily for dinner only. Main dishes, such as drunken scallops (that is, marinated in Chablis, then sautéed with bacon and herbs), range from $17 to $26.

Farnsworth House (☎ 717-334-8838, *farnhous@mail.cvn.net, 401 Baltimore St)* is a restaurant in an 1810 brick-and-wood home with most of the original walls, floors and rafters intact. The meals are served by staff dressed in period outfits, and the cuisine is early American. Open for lunch and dinner daily, most main dishes, such as baked fillet of flounder, cost $13 to $18.

Entertainment

The *Majestic Cinema* (☎ 717-334-2513), just north of Lincoln Square on Carlisle St, shows movies for $6.50 (matinees $4.50). For a beer, try the *Pub & Restaurant* on Lincoln Square, or *Buckley's Irish Pub (44 Steinwehr Ave)*.

Shopping

Gettysburg is full of shops selling Civil War trinkets, most of which appear comparable in quality and price, but you'll have to wade through a lot to find anything of quality. Innumerable items are emblazoned with the word 'Gettysburg' or some Blue (Union) or Gray (Confederate) icon. The Gettysburg Gift Center (☎ 717-334-6245), part of the Civil War Wax Museum at 297 Steinwehr Ave, is as good a place as any for trinkets. Other shops advertise antiques and you might find them worth a look.

Getting There & Away

Incredibly, for a major tourist destination, there's no public transportation to or around Gettysburg. By car, it's accessible on Route 30 from Philadelphia, Lancaster or York; on Route 15 from Harrisburg; and on Routes 15 and 97 from Maryland. From Philadelphia you can also take I-76 (Pennsylvania Turnpike) west to exit 17 and follow Route 15 south.

HARRISBURG

Harrisburg (population 52,375), the state capital, is a small, picturesque city on the shores of the Susquehanna River. Originally a ferryboat station known as Harris's Ferry, it was renamed Harrisburg in 1785 when John Harris, son of one of the first European settlers here, refused a state-government order to name it Louisburg in honor of France's Louis XVI. It became the state capital in 1812 and was incorporated as a city in 1860. It still retains a small-town feel, though, and it has managed to preserve many of its 18th- and 19th-century buildings, especially in the residential area near the town center and along Front St. It's not a heavily touristed place, and the nearby town of Hershey and the Three Mile Island nuclear power plant somewhat overshadow it.

Orientation & Information

Market St divides the city from north to south; 2nd St, between State and Market Sts, is a busy shopping area. The Harrisburg, Hershey & Carlisle Tourism & Convention Bureau (☎ 717-231-7788, 800-995-0969), 25 North Front St, is open 9 am to 5 pm weekdays, and it has a website (www.visithhc .com).

The main post office at 813 Market St, down past the bus and train station, is open 7 am to 6 pm weekdays, 8 am to 2 pm Saturday; a more central post office is in the Federal Building at Third and Walnut Sts.

Suds City, a Laundromat, is located at 227 N 2nd St.

State Capitol

Italian Renaissance in style, the impressive 651 room State Capitol (☎ 717-787-6810), on N 3rd St between North and Walnut Sts, has a 27-foot-high bronze dome that's modeled on St Peter's Basilica in Rome, as well as bronze doors, paintings, murals depicting Pennsylvania's history, sculptures and stained glass. The marble staircase and surrounding balconies are modeled on the Opera House in Paris. On the 4th floor there's a viewing area from which visitors can watch the action in the senate chamber. There are free guided tours every 30 minutes from 8:30 am to 4:30 pm (except at noon) weekdays, and 9 am to 4 pm (except at noon) weekends.

State Museum of Pennsylvania

This museum (☎ 717-787-4978), at N 3rd and North Sts, beside the State Capitol, houses many Civil War artifacts and the huge *Battle of Gettysburg* painting by Rothermel. Also on view are exhibits on archeology, geology and industry; a small planetarium operates on weekends, plus weekdays in summer. On the ground floor the original 1681 charter granting Pennsylvania to William Penn is exhibited. The museum is open 9 am to 5 pm Tuesday to Saturday, noon to 5 pm Sunday, and it is free.

Whitaker Center for Science & the Arts

The Whitaker Center (☎ 717-221-8201), 222 Market St, was still under construction at the time of research, but should be open by the time you read this. Its main attractions include an interactive science museum, a 600-seat theater and a 200-seat IMAX cinema.

City Island

City Island is an island park in the Susquehanna River. You can reach it from downtown on foot via the Walnut St footbridge,

or by car via the Market St Bridge. It has a bathing beach, nature trails and jogging tracks. Local baseball games are played here, too. From the island the *Pride of the Susquehanna* paddle steamer runs 45-minute cruises on the river four times daily Tuesday to Sunday for $4.95/3 for adults/children.

Places to Stay & Eat

There are few accommodations in the center of town. The only budget hotel is the *Alva Restaurant & Hotel* (☎ 717-238-7553, *19 S 4th St*), opposite the entrance to the Harrisburg Transportation Center. The rooms, which cost $35, are basic, and it should only be considered as a last resort.

Most accommodations are in motels north of town along N Front St, near I-81 and I-83. *Super 8 Motel* (☎ 717-233-5891, *4125 N Front St*), near the I-81 Front St exit, is the closest and has standard, clean rooms from $45/50. A more centrally located place is the upscale, refurbished *Ramada Inn on Market Square* (☎ 717-234-5021, *23 S 2nd St*), with full facilities and rooms from $69/79.

As for places to eat, the *Strawberry Square Shopping Center*, at N 3rd and Walnut Sts, has a food court on the upper level. *Esquire Deli*, on N 3rd St, opposite the Capitol, serves veggie burgers for $3.40 and roast beef sandwiches for $3.90. The preceding places are open 9 am to 5 pm Monday through Saturday. Nearby, the *Bangkok Wok*, at N 3rd and Liberty Sts, is a small Thai restaurant with most main dishes about $6.50, but it's open for lunch only.

There are several places along N 2nd St, including the popular *Zephyr Express* (☎ 717-257-1328, *400 N 2nd St*), which dishes up pasta for $5.75 and pizza for $4.75. It has good vegetarian selections and is open daily 11 am until late. *The Spot*, a popular diner at Walnut and N 2nd St, reputedly has the best hot dogs ($1.45) in town.

Getting There & Away

Air Harrisburg International Airport (☎ 717-948-3900) is in Middletown, north of the Susquehanna River, about 8 miles southeast of Harrisburg. United Airlines (☎ 800-241-6522, from outside the US ☎ 800-538-2929) has six flights daily to Philadelphia and Pittsburgh. Roundtrip fares to Philadelphia cost around $230.

Bus & Train The bus and train stations are in the Harrisburg Transportation Center, 411 Market St at S 4th St. The center has a cobbled forecourt, and its train section has an elegant, wood-paneled interior. There's an Amtrak train (☎ 800-872-7245) to Philadelphia ($17 one way, 55 minutes) and to Pittsburgh ($61 one way, 5¾ hours). Both trains run several times daily, and schedules are available on Amtrak's website (www.Amtrak.com). The Greyhound bus station (☎ 717-232-4251, 800-231-2222) is below the train station; Capitol Trailways (☎ 800-444-2877) and Fullington Trailways (☎ 800-942-8287 in Pennsylvania only) buses also stop here. Capitol has five buses daily to Philadelphia ($15 one way, 2½ hours).

Car & Motorcycle Harrisburg is at the intersection of a number of major highways. The east-west Pennsylvania Turnpike (I-76) passes through Harrisburg (the I-76 runs between Philadelphia and Pittsburgh). I-81 and I-83 pass through town and connect it with Maryland to the south; I-83 also connects with York, 25 miles to the south. Route 230 joins Harrisburg with Lancaster, which is about 43 miles to the southeast.

Getting Around

Capitol Area Transit (CAT; ☎ 717-238-8304), 901 N Cameron St, operates the city's buses. The CAT Transfer Center, in Market Square at Market St and S 2nd St, is the main downtown bus stop and has a customer-service kiosk (open 7 to 9 am and 10:30 am to 1 pm weekdays) where you can obtain route maps, schedules and bus passes. The one-way fare to any destination in town is $1.35. CAT also runs a free motorized trolley service between the State Capitol, Strawberry Square Shopping Center and the Midtown Market District.

THREE MILE ISLAND

Three Mile Island, in the Susquehanna River, off Route 441, about 10 miles south of Harrisburg, is America's most famous nuclear plant as a result of its partial meltdown in 1979. The plant consists of two units, named Unit 1 and Unit 2 (also known as TMI-1 and TMI-2). It cost about $1.1 billion to build, but today it would cost five times that much, making nuclear power (surprise!) vastly unprofitable. Unit 2, in which the accident occurred, is permanently shut down, but Unit 1, which was shut down after Unit 2's accident, was reactivated in 1985 and is expected to run until about 2014. The steam coming out of the tower is warm water vapor from the cooling process.

The Three Mile Island Visitor Center (☎ 717-948-8829) is outside the nuclear power plant on Route 441 and is open noon to 4:30 pm Monday to Thursday. The center has an exhibition that shows how the plant operates, and tours are available Tuesday to Friday, but you'll need to book (on the above phone number) at least two weeks in advance. Both the tour and admission to the visitor center are free. You can take photographs of the plant from the 2nd-floor observation deck in the visitor center, but not when you're touring the island.

There's no public transportation to Three Mile Island, though CAT bus No 7 from Harrisburg goes as far as Middletown, which is a couple of miles to the north. By road from Harrisburg take I-83 north, then I-283 south, Route 230 east and Route 441 south.

HERSHEY

Hershey (population 11,800), 12 miles east of Harrisburg, is the home of the Hershey chocolate empire. It is a rather ordinary, one-company town that nevertheless attracts millions of visitors with its amusement park and chocolate theme.

Milton S Hershey, a Mennonite, was born in 1857 in Derry Church, Pennsylvania. His career as a confectioner began at the age of 19 when he opened a candy store in Philadelphia, but success only came after he

Nuclear Accident at Three Mile Island

On March 28, 1979, the core of the Unit 2 nuclear reactor, which had only been operating for about three months, overheated and partially melted. In the process the plant released significant amounts of radioactive gases.

The essential problem was that a valve became stuck open and allowed water that normally cooled the core to flow out. Reactor operators failed to notice the stuck valve for over two hours (due to inadequate training). When the valve finally closed, operators noticed that water had been lost, and they added water to cool the reactor. This colder water caused many of the very hot fuel rods to shatter.

Pennsylvania's governor ordered pregnant women in the Harrisburg area to be evacuated, and many others left as well. Subsequent reports found that there were no 'significant' health effects caused by the meltdown.

The cleanup, which cost about $1 billion, included evaporating 2.3 million gallons of 'slightly radioactive' water into the atmosphere. During the 1980s, around 10,000 people were involved in the cleanup, and the last shipment of damaged fuel left Unit 2 on April 15, 1990.

It can be argued that the Three Mile Island accident was profoundly helpful to the US anti-nuclear movement. Afterwards, opponents had a clear-cut example of a near-disaster, and massive demonstrations against nuclear power followed in the 1980s. The industry has been under intense scrutiny since the accident, and no new nuclear plants have been planned, although those already under construction were completed.

The accident also provided a salutary lesson to the nuclear industry, which thereafter sought to improve training and safety procedures and to design more user-friendly operating equipment.

started the Lancaster Caramel Company 10 years later. Eventually, in 1903, with money from that enterprise, he bought some land back in Derry Church to build a chocolate factory, and the small town, whose name was later changed to Hershey, expanded around it.

Orientation & Information

In town, Route 422 becomes Chocolate Ave, the main thoroughfare (you know you've arrived when you see street lamps in the shape of a Hershey chocolate 'Kiss'). Most attractions are north of Chocolate Ave.

Visitor information (☎ 717-534-4900, 800-437-7439) is available inside the main entrance to Hershey's Chocolate World in Hersheypark; it has a list of accommodations. There is also a website (www.HersheyPA.com).

The post office, off Chocolate Ave West and behind the Goodyear store, is open 6:30 am to 4:30 pm weekdays, 9 am to noon Saturday.

There are several banks with ATMs lining Chocolate Ave.

Try to avoid visiting Hershey on the weekends, when it gets really busy – and be prepared to spend lots of money.

Hersheypark

Hersheypark is a 90-acre-landscaped amusement park that Milton Hershey originally established in 1906 as a recreation area for his workers. It now has over 50 rides. The admission price of $30.95/16.95 for adults/children entitles you to use all the rides, plus entry to nearby ZooAmerica. The opening hours are fairly complicated, but Hersheypark is open Memorial Day to Labor Day, 10 am to generally 10 pm weekdays (11 pm weekends); it's also open some weekends in May and September.

Visitors can't tour the actual chocolate factory due to health regulations, but there is a free tour through **Chocolate World** (☎ 717-534-4900). It's a mock factory where visitors sit in little plastic cars that move along a conveyor past exhibits telling the story of the making of chocolate. At the end you get a free chocolate sample – a Hershey's 'Kiss.' Young kids love it, but others might be disappointed by the tackiness. Naturally, you exit through a candy store selling Hershey products, and a food court. Chocolate World is open at 9 am daily year round; however, closing hours vary – May through September it closes mostly at 10 pm, at 5 pm the rest of the year.

ZooAmerica

ZooAmerica (☎ 717-534-3860) is an 11-acre wildlife park beside Hersheypark, featuring more than 200 native North American animals. It's open 10 am to 8 pm daily mid-June to August; 10 am to 5 pm daily September through mid-June. Entry to the zoo only is $5.75/5.25/4.50 for adults/seniors/children.

Hershey Museum

The small museum (☎ 717-534-3439), 170 W Hershey Park Drive, displays a collection of American Indian and Inuit art, Hershey chocolate-making machinery and a collection of Pennsylvania Dutch artifacts. There's also an exhibition on the life of Milton S Hershey. The admission price is a hefty $5/4.50/2.50 for adults/seniors/children. It's open daily 10 am to 6 pm Memorial Day to Labor Day (to 5 pm the rest of the year).

Hershey Gardens

The 23-acre botanical gardens (☎ 717-534-3492), on Hotel Rd, north off Hershey Park Drive, began life in 1937 as a rose garden and grew to include various other flowers, shrubs and specimen trees such as European beech and Japanese maple. There's also a butterfly house containing over 25 North American species. It's open 9 am to 6 pm daily mid-April through October. Admission is $5/4.50/2.50 for adults/seniors/children.

Hershey Trolleyworks

Departing from Chocolate World's main entrance, motorized trolley buses (☎ 717-533-3000) take you on a tour of Hershey with a narration sung by the conductor. Tours cost $6.75/5 for adults/children.

Places to Stay

Room rates are higher in the summer months when children are on vacation, and the hotels and motels can fill up quickly on weekends. The rates quoted below are for that period. Apart from the campground, there are no budget places in town; most mid-range places are along Chocolate Ave.

Campground *Hershey Highmeadow Camp* (☎ 717-566-0902) is fully equipped with showers, laundry, a grocery store and two swimming pools. A site for up to a family of four is $27.50, or $34.95 with full hookup. To get there follow Chocolate Ave west to the junction with Hershey Park Drive (Route 39), turn right for about 500 yards, then left onto Matlack Rd.

Motels & Hotels *Hershey Travel Motel* (☎ 717-533-7950, 905 E Chocolate Ave) has modest but clean rooms with cable TV and attached bathroom for $45/55. About 1½ miles south of Chocolate Ave, the *Cocoa Motel* (☎ 717-534-1243, 914 Cocoa Ave), at the intersection with Route 322, has fine rooms for $70 to $90.

The neat, two story *White Rose Motel* (☎ 717-533-9876, 1060 E Chocolate Ave) is surrounded by flowers and has rooms for $122. At the renovated, 52-room *Spinner's Inn* (☎ 717-533-9157, 845 E Chocolate Ave) facilities include a game room and heated pool; room rates are $89 to $150. The *Simmons Motel* (☎ 717-533-9177, 355 W Chocolate Ave) is close to most attractions and amenities and has rooms from $165 in several two-story houses.

Set on a 90-acre hilltop, the luxurious, Mediterranean-style *Hotel Hershey* (☎ 800-533-3131), on Hotel Rd, north of Hersheypark, is the premier place to stay in town. Facilities include indoor and outdoor pools, tennis courts, golf, horseback riding and croquet. Rates start at $289.

Places to Eat

Hershey's Chocolate World has a food court with the emphasis on sweets. Most of the town's eateries are along Chocolate Ave. For fast food, there's *Hardee's*, on W

Chocolate Ave. **Breads 'N' Cheeses Coffee House** (☎ *717-533-4546, 243 W Chocolate Ave*) has delicious pastries from 85¢ and slices of cake such as lemon torte for $1.95. It also sells a range of breads from $2, cheeses from around the world and more than 20 kinds of coffee. **Lucy's Cafe** (☎ *717-533-1045, 267 W Chocolate Ave*) is an Italian-style bar and restaurant serving pastas from $11 to $13, as well as steaks. It is only open for dinner and is closed on Sunday.

Catherine's Restaurant (☎ *717-533-9050, 845 E Chocolate Ave*), at Spinner's Inn, specializes in pasta, seafood and beef. Pasta main dishes are $10 to $17, others $13 to $27. It's open 5 to 10 pm Tuesday to Saturday for dinner only. At the top end, Hotel Hershey's **Circular Dining Room** (☎ *717-533-2171*), on Hotel Rd, is dominated by stained-glass windows and overlooks formal gardens. At lunch and dinner men must wear jackets and women must dress 'appropriately.' Starters, such as shrimp cocktail, cost $13, and main dishes such as roast chicken with leek and lemon range from $24 to $32.

Getting There & Away

Bus Capitol Trailways (☎ 800-444-2877) buses stop outside the Riteway pharmacy on W Chocolate Ave, west of Lucy's Cafe. You can buy tickets on the bus. There are two buses daily to Lancaster ($8.85 one way, 2½ hours) and two buses daily to Reading ($7.60 one way, 1½ hours).

Car & Motorcycle From Harrisburg follow Route 322 east, then Route 422 into town. From Philadelphia take I-76 (Pennsylvania Turnpike) to exit 20; take Route 72 north, then Route 322 west to Route 422. From Pittsburgh take I-76 east to exit 19, then Route 283 north and Route 322 east.

YORK

York (population 42,000), about 20 miles southeast of Harrisburg and 25 miles southwest of Lancaster, was Pennsylvania's first settlement west of the Susquehanna River. Established in 1741, it was the capital of the US between September 30, 1777 and June 27, 1778, when Congress fled Philadelphia following the British victory at the Battle of Brandywine. During that period, Congress met at the York County Colonial Courthouse where the Articles of Confederation, later to become the country's first constitution, were drafted and adopted.

Today, York is the home of the Harley-Davidson motorcycle final assembly plant (though the company is headquartered in Milwaukee, WI). In addition, the downtown area has some fine colonial and other historic buildings and is undergoing a revival.

Information

York's downtown visitor center (☎ 717-699-4430), 155 W Market St, is open 9:30 am to 4 pm daily. It also maintains a website (www.yorkonline.org). Near the Harley-Davidson assembly plant, there's another visitor center (☎ 717-843-6660), 1618 Toronita St, at the intersection of I-83 and Route 30; take exit 9E off I-83 and follow the signs. It's open 9 am to 5 pm daily.

The post office (☎ 717-848-2381), 200 S George St, is open 7:30 am to 5 pm weekdays, 8:30 am to noon Saturday.

The Mellon Bank, with an ATM, is located at N George and E Market Sts.

Harley-Davidson Company

Visitors with an interest in motorbikes come to York just to see Harley-Davidson (☎ 717-848-1177), 1425 Eden Rd, where America's legendary motorcycles are assembled. A guided tour starts with the **Rodney Gott Antique Motorcycle Museum**, which displays a bike from every production year from 1906 onwards. You then go into the

Harley Hogs

They say that the reason Harley-Davidsons are called 'hogs' is because years ago a young motorcycle racer used to parade around with a small pig on his gas tank after winning a race. Others followed his lead, and the 'hog' became inseparable from the motorcycle.

assembly plant to see workers making parts and building the motorcycles. In the entrance area you can see a good film about the history of the company, and there's a gift shop that sells all kinds of Harley-Davidson merchandise.

Free tours of the plant and museum are given at 9:30 and 10:30 am and 12:30 and 1:30 pm weekdays, and they last 1½ hours. Tours of just the museum take place at 10 and 11 am and 1 and 2 pm Saturday and last 30 minutes. Take exit 9E off I-83 onto Route 30 east; at the third set of traffic lights turn left onto Eden Rd.

York County Colonial Courthouse

The court house (☎ 717-845-2951), 205 W Market St, at N Pershing Ave, close to the visitor center, is a near-exact facsimile of the original building that Congress met in when York was the national capital. Inside, there's an audiovisual presentation, and copies of the Articles of Confederation and the Declaration of Independence are on display. You can only visit the court house on guided tours ($6/3 for adults/children). Tours are offered at 10 am, noon and 2 pm Monday to Saturday and 1 and 2:30 pm Sunday. Other historical buildings, including the Golden Plough Tavern and General Gates House, are included.

Getting There & Away

Bus York is not served by any bus companies anymore. The closest bus stations are in Lancaster or Harrisburg (for bus information, see the Getting There & Away sections for those towns).

Car & Motorcycle From Harrisburg travel south on I-83; from Gettysburg travel northeast on Route 30; and from Lancaster travel southwest on Route 30.

Southwestern Pennsylvania

Southwestern Pennsylvania is dominated by Pittsburgh – a city that was originally built on iron and steel but which has successfully reinvented itself since the decline of those industries. Many work-weary Pittsburghers head southeast for the Laurel Highlands, a popular outdoor playground that is especially noted for its white-water rafting in the Youghiogheny (YOCK-a-GAY-nee, generally just called 'the Yock') River. The highlands are also the location of Fallingwater, Frank Lloyd Wright's architectural masterpiece. The Johnstown area, northeast of the highlands, has been the site of a series of devastating floods, the most horrific of which occurred in 1889.

Around Pittsburgh are several state parks (Raccoon Creek to the west and Moraine and McConnell's Mill to the north) that are popular outdoor recreation areas. Also to the north is the small town of Harmony, the site of a 19th-century celibate commune.

PITTSBURGH

Pittsburgh (population 369,800) once had a reputation as the most polluted city in the US – the daytime air was so blackened by coal smoke that the town was called 'Smokey City.' Fortunately, those days are long gone. Pittsburgh has undergone a remarkable transformation and today is a diverse and attractive corporate, financial and educational center, as well as one of the US's most livable cities. It's also a city that offers much to visitors. The Andy Warhol Museum is reason enough for many people to make the trip, but outside the downtown glass and steel, there's the student district of Oakland and some picturesque old neighborhoods, such as Troy Hill in North Side and the area along E Carson St in South Side.

History

Pittsburgh's strategic location, at the point where the Monongahela and the Allegheny Rivers join the Ohio River, has made it a natural commercial and transportation

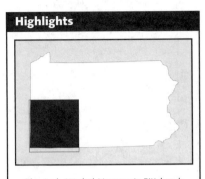

Highlights

- The Andy Warhol Museum in Pittsburgh – the largest art museum in the US that is dedicated to one person
- An incline-train ride up Mt Washington, to view Pittsburgh from above
- White-water rafting and canoeing on the Youghiogheny River in the Laurel Highlands
- Hiking the Laurel Highlands Trail
- Fallingwater – Frank Lloyd Wright's architectural masterpiece

center since the 18th century. During that period, the area became a flash point in French and British rivalry over the Ohio River Valley.

In 1753, before the start of the French & Indian War (1754–63), 22-year-old George Washington was sent to establish a British presence in the region. He chose the point near the tip of today's Golden Triangle, at the fork of the three rivers, to build a fortification. Some sources say the French claimed the spot and built Fort Duquesne *before* Washington built his fort, others say that the French took it from him. In any case, this ideal location allowed the French to control the upper Ohio River Valley. But after a few defeats (see the boxed text 'The Battle of Fort Necessity,' later in this chapter), the

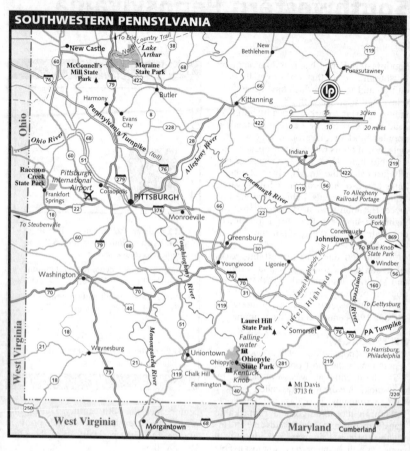

SOUTHWESTERN PENNSYLVANIA

British returned in 1758, ejected the French and built Fort Pitt, which was named after Prime Minister William Pitt the Elder. From this, Pittsburgh was named.

During the 19th century, Pittsburgh became famous for iron and steel production, as it helped fulfill the needs of the country's westward expansion. The Civil War gave its industries further stimulus, and by the end of the war, Pittsburgh was producing 50% of the country's iron and steel. Scottish-born immigrant Andrew Carnegie then modernized and expanded steel production, becoming the world's richest man in

the process. But the city's growth was not without conflict, and there were violent strikes at Homestead in 1892 and throughout greater Pittsburgh in 1919.

Despite a downturn during the Depression of the 1930s, the mass production of the automobile and the advent of WWII stimulated demand for steel once more. During the 1960s and '70s, the industry declined, but in the 1990s, Pittsburgh re-emerged as a high-technology, finance and service-oriented center. An urban-renewal program saw the downtown area transformed, but not without a price: many architecturally important

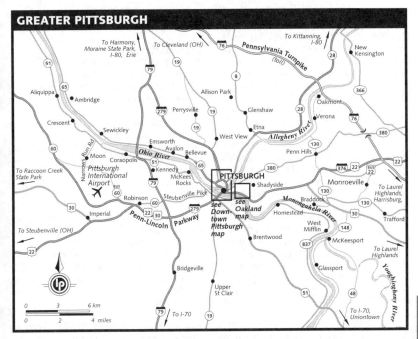

GREATER PITTSBURGH

buildings were razed to make way for glass skyscrapers. Fortunately, many (such as the Allegheny County Courthouse) remain, and some of Pittsburgh's traditional character can be seen in the older residential neighborhoods.

Although a strong blue-collar element remains, the shift in employment to the service and high-technology industries means there is now a large and growing white-collar workforce. The city's ethnic diversity is reflected in the different architectural flavors of its neighborhoods and is symbolized by the University of Pittsburgh Nationality Rooms. The North Side shows many touches of its German heritage, including Penn Brewery (originally called Eberhardt & Ober Brewery). On the South Side, Eastern European influences can be seen in the Ukrainian, Serbian and Lithuanian churches. Many Eastern European Jews settled in Squirrel Hill in the 1920s.

Bloomfield has a strong Italian heritage, while nearby Lawrenceville and Polish Hill have a mix of Irish, Italian and Polish communities. African-Americans have also settled in the city, but in terms of numbers, their presence isn't as evident as in Philadelphia. There are also people from the Middle East, most notably Lebanese and Syrians.

Orientation

Pittsburgh is a fairly confusing city to navigate because of its shape – downtown and Oakland form a triangle of land that is separated from the city's northern and southern parts by rivers. There's no consistent street pattern, although major thoroughfares in the city often run parallel to the rivers. To ease the confusion, there's a color-coded network of prominently displayed directional street signs called the Wayfinder System.

Fifth Ave and Liberty Ave are the major downtown streets.

The approach to Pittsburgh from the south is spectacular. You enter through Fort Pitt Tunnel then cross Fort Pitt Bridge into the heart of the Golden Triangle, the westernmost portion of the city center (basically 'downtown') bounded to the north by the Allegheny River, to the south by the Monongahela River and to the east by I-579 (Crosstown Blvd). The bus and train stations are in the northern corner of the triangle.

Slightly northeast of downtown and close to the Allegheny River is an area called The Strip, where wholesale and retail fresh-food stores, cheap restaurants and clubs line Smallman St and Penn Ave between 17th and 22nd Sts. It's also a good place to walk around and people-watch.

East of downtown is Oakland, Pittsburgh's university area, which is dominated by the University of Pittsburgh's Cathedral of Learning, Carnegie-Mellon University, The Carnegie complex and Schenley Park. It too has some good, cheap places to eat. Fifth Ave and Blvd of the Allies connect it with downtown.

The North Side, the part of town north of the Allegheny River, is home to the Andy Warhol Museum, Three Rivers Stadium, Carnegie Science Center, National Aviary in Pittsburgh and the small neighborhood of Troy Hill.

On the South Side, south of the Monongahela River, Mt Washington overlooks the Golden Triangle. You can drive up or take either of the two incline railways. At the bottom of the mountain, along the river beside Smithfield St Bridge, is Station Square, full of shops and restaurants. To the east is a residential neighborhood where the main drag, E Carson St, has an interesting collection of cafes, bars and shops.

Maps The tourist office has a free simple map of central Pittsburgh and Oakland that comes with its visitors' guide and shows the major landmarks. The *Pittsburgh Walking Map & Guide* is a map that covers the same areas in greater detail and includes lists of sights, restaurants, entertainment venues, etc. Rand McNally's *Pittsburgh Metro* is another useful map that includes the surrounding suburbs and has a street index.

Information

Tourist Offices The Greater Pittsburgh Convention & Visitors Bureau (☎ 412-281-7711, 800-366-0093) operates a number of visitors' centers around the city; you can visit the website at www.visitpittsburgh.com.

The downtown branch, on Liberty Ave in front of 4 Gateway Center, is open weekdays 9 am to 5 pm and weekends until 3 pm; it's closed on Sunday in January and February. The visitor center in Oakland, which is in a log cabin on Forbes Ave near the Cathedral of Learning, is open Monday 9 am to 4 pm and Tuesday to Sunday 10 am to 4 pm. In Station Square next to the Grand Concourse, the visitor center is open daily 9:30 am to 6:30 pm.

Finally, the bureau has a desk in each terminal of Pittsburgh's airport. The Landside visitors' center is open daily 8 am to 8 pm; the Airside one is open daily from 7:30 am to 6:30 pm.

Money Mellon Bank (☎ 412-234-5000), on Mellon Square, and PNC Bank (☎ 412-762-2510), at Fifth Ave and Wood St, have currency-exchange counters and ATMs. At the PPG Place shopping center, American Express (☎ 412-391-3202), 2 PPG Place, on Market Square, is open weekdays 9 am to 5 pm. At Pittsburgh's airport, there's also a Mutual of Omaha's Travelex Business Service Center (☎ 412-472-5151) offering currency exchange.

Post The main post office (☎ 412-642-4476), at Seventh Ave and Grant St, is open weekdays 7 am to 6 pm and Saturday 7 am to 2:30 pm. There's also a post office at 213 Shiloh St, at the top of the Monongahela Incline in Mt Washington (open weekdays 8:30 am to 5 pm and Saturday 8:30 am to noon), as well as another at the airport.

Email & Internet Access On the North Side, Riverhead Cyber Cafe (☎ 412-322-2223, ddinardo@riverhd.com), 607 East Ohio St, is open Monday, Thursday and Friday

The US Iron & Steel Industry

Pittsburgh has long been one of the main centers of the American iron and steel industries. Soon after they arrived in the 17th century, colonial settlers collected iron from bogs and then from mines. By the 18th century, American iron production had increased so much that Britain passed the 1750 Iron Act, which forbade the building of mills in the colony, but allowed pig iron (crude unfinished iron) to be sent to Britain for manufacturing.

With the expansion of US railroad industry, beginning in the 1830s, the demand for iron increased. A leading producer of iron for years, Pennsylvania also had huge deposits of anthracite coal, which, it was discovered in the mid-19th century, could be substituted for charcoal in the smelting of iron. The combination of Pennsylvania coal, Great Lakes iron ore and cheap water transportation ensured that the Midwest would be the center of the US iron industry.

The true boom came when an inexpensive way to manufacture steel – a hard metal formed by combining iron and carbon – was discovered. In 1856, Englishman Henry Bessemer created the Bessemer process for making steel, in which hot air is blasted through molten iron to burn out its impurities. By 1872, 2% of US pig iron was being converted to steel; 20 years later, it was up to 50%. By the 1920s, it was over 90%, with the US producing almost 25 million tons a year – more than any other country.

Huge new steel factories also created whole new labor conditions. Steel mills required thousands of workers and many more specialists than in iron production. Each worker had to be competent at an individual job, but at the same time was given less autonomy by management. Steelworkers were some of the first workers in the US to establish strong unions to battle management control of working conditions and hours.

In 1901, the US Steel Corporation, formed partly from Pittsburgh industrialist Andrew Carnegie's steel company, became the single largest industrial operation on earth. US annual steel production continued to grow until it peaked in 1969 at 141 million tons. By then, more efficient plants abroad with lower labor costs were out-competing the US steel plants. In 1975, US production was down to 89 million tons.

American steel subsequently rebounded and is now competitive. However, it is much less labor intensive these days, and the industry's relative position in the US economy has declined. The end of the Industrial Age coincided to some degree with the end of the massive US steel industry. Even the US Steel Corporation, wanting to distance itself from its origins, changed its name to USX.

8 am to 5 pm; on Tuesday and Wednesday, it's open 8 am to 8 pm, and on Saturday, 9 am to 2 pm. Internet access costs $5 an hour.

Internet Resources Pittsburgh has a number of helpful websites. A good place to start is the Greater Pittsburgh Convention & Visitors Bureau's official website (see Tourist Offices, earlier). Two sites with links to attractions, accommodations, dining, entertainment and transportation are www.realpittsburgh.com and www.pittsburgh.net. The free entertainment weekly *City Paper* has a website at www.pghcitypaper.com. For information about the University of Pittsburgh, go to www.pitt.edu.

Travel Agencies Council Travel (☎ 412-683-1881) has its office in Oakland at 118 Meyran Ave, Pittsburgh, PA 15123.

Bookstores A branch of B Dalton Bookseller (☎ 412-261-4680) is in Station Square, and Barnes & Noble (☎ 412-642-4324), 339 Sixth Ave, is open weekdays 7 am to 7 pm, Saturday 9 am to 7 pm and Sunday 11 am to 6 pm.

There are three good used bookstores close together in Oakland. The best of them is

DOWNTOWN PITTSBURGH

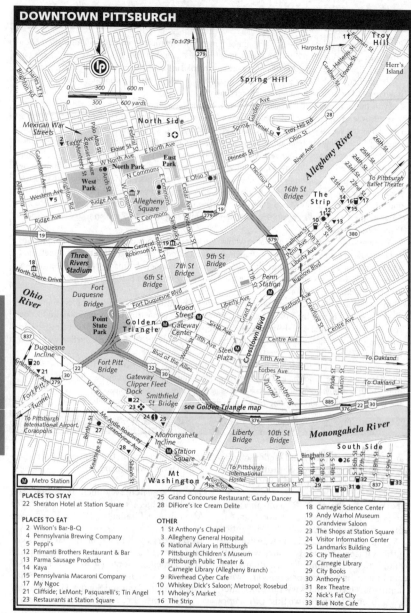

PLACES TO STAY
22 Sheraton Hotel at Station Square

PLACES TO EAT
2 Wilson's Bar-B-Q
4 Pennsylvania Brewing Company
5 Peppi's
12 Primanti Brothers Restaurant & Bar
13 Parma Sausage Products
14 Kaya
15 Pennsylvania Macaroni Company
17 My Ngoc
21 Cliffside; LeMont; Pasquarelli's; Tin Angel
23 Restaurants at Station Square

25 Grand Concourse Restaurant; Gandy Dancer
28 DiFiore's Ice Cream Delite

OTHER
1 St Anthony's Chapel
3 Allegheny General Hospital
6 National Aviary in Pittsburgh
7 Pittsburgh Children's Museum
8 Pittsburgh Public Theater &
   Carnegie Library (Allegheny Branch)
9 Riverhead Cyber Cafe
10 Whiskey Dick's Saloon; Metropol; Rosebud
11 Wholey's Market
16 The Strip

18 Carnegie Science Center
19 Andy Warhol Museum
20 Grandview Saloon
23 The Shops at Station Square
24 Visitor Information Center
25 Landmarks Building
26 City Theater
27 Carnegie Library
29 City Books
30 Anthony's
31 Rex Theatre
32 Nick's Fat City
33 Blue Note Cafe

Caliban Book Shop (☎ 412-681-9111), 410 S Craig St, run by John Schulman and Emily Hetzel. There are also two off S Craig St – the Bryn Mawr-Vassar Book Store (☎ 412-687-3433), 4612 Winthrop St, and Townsend Booksellers (☎ 412-682-8030), 4612 Henry St.

In South Side, another used bookstore is City Books (☎ 412-481-7555), 1111 E Carson St; it has a cafe upstairs.

Libraries Part of the Carnegie complex, the Carnegie Library (☎ 412-622-3116), 4400 Forbes Ave in Oakland, is one of the best in the US. It is open Monday to Wednesday and Friday 9 am to 9 pm, Thursday and Saturday 10 am to 5 pm and Sunday 1 to 5 pm (it's closed on Sunday during summer). It also has branches in Allegheny Square, on the North Side, and on Grandview Ave, in Mt Washington. You can visit its website at www.clpgh.org.

Medical Services Pittsburgh has many hospitals, including a number of teaching hospitals that offer routine patient care. Montefiore University Hospital (☎ 412-648-6000), 200 Lothrop St in Oakland, is part of the University of Pittsburgh Medical Center. The Allegheny General Hospital (☎ 412-359-3131) is at 320 E North Ave on the North Side. For women only there is the Magee-Women's Hospital (☎ 412-641-1000), 300 Halket St in Oakland.

For doctor referral in the Pittsburgh area, call ☎ 412-321-5810.

Emergency In the case of fire and medical emergencies, or for police, call ☎ 911. Other important emergency telephone numbers include the following:

Dentist
  ☎ 412-321-5810

Pittsburgh Council for International Visitors
  ☎ 412-624-7800

Pittsburgh Action Against Rape
  ☎ 412-765-2731

Travelers' Aid Society
  ☎ 412-281-5474

See also 'Hotlines & Crisis Numbers' in the yellow pages phone book.

Golden Triangle

Point State Park, the green park with the huge spouting fountain where the three rivers meet is a small oasis downtown and isn't as crowded as other city parks. In the park, **Fort Pitt Museum** (☎ 412-281-9284), 101 Commonwealth Place, relates Pittsburgh's early history with Native American artifacts, military artifacts and displays on the French-British conflict for control of the region. The museum is open Wednesday to Saturday 10 am to 4:30 pm and Sunday noon to 4:30 pm; admission is $4/2 for adults/children and $3.50 for seniors.

Nearby, the free sandstone-and-brick **Fort Pitt Blockhouse**, is the only portion left of the original Fort Pitt; entry is free, but there's little to see. It is open the same hours as the museum.

Built around a central courtyard, **Allegheny County Courthouse**, a magnificent 19th-century Romanesque-style courthouse (☎ 412-350-5410), on the corner of Forbes Ave and Grant St, was designed by architect Henry Hobson Richardson. Its interior resembles a medieval monastery. It is open weekdays 8:30 am to 4:30 pm, and entry is free. At lunchtime on Fridays during the summer, there are free concerts in the courtyard.

North Side

Andy Warhol Museum Andy Warhol (1928–87) was born and raised in Pittsburgh, although he achieved fame for his innovative and often challenging artwork in New York. This interesting museum (☎ 412-237-8300), 117 Sandusky St, on the North Side just over the 7th St Bridge, is administered by The Carnegie (see 'The Carnegie,' later in this section). You can visit the museum's website at www.warhol.org/warhol.

As well as depicting the story of his life, the museum's seven floors display Warhol's classic reproductions of Campbell's soup cans and celebrity portraits, along with lesser-known items, such as his time capsules, drawings, prints, sculptures and films. The business hours are Sunday and Wednesday 11 am to 6 pm and Thursday to Saturday 11 am to 8 pm. Admission is $7/4 for adults/

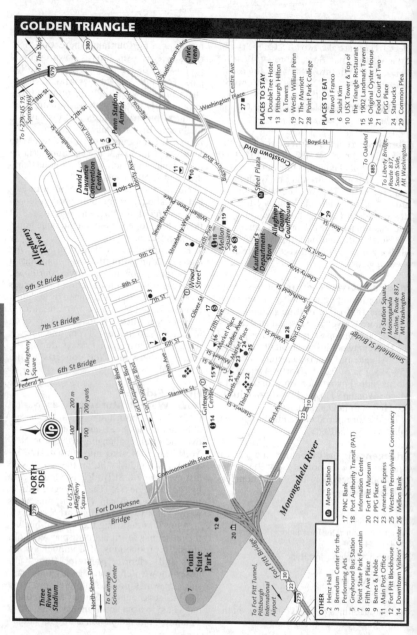

GOLDEN TRIANGLE

PLACES TO STAY
4   DoubleTree Hotel
13   Pittsburgh Hilton
     & Towers
19   Westin William Penn
27   The Marriott
28   Point Park College

PLACES TO EAT
1   Bravo! Franco
6   Sushi Kim
10   USX Tower & Top of
     the Triangle Restaurant
15   1902 Landmark Tavern
16   Original Oyster House
21   Food Court at Two
     PGG Place
24   Starbucks
29   Common Plea

OTHER
2   Heinz Hall
3   Benedum Center for the
     Performing Arts
5   Greyhound Bus Station
7   Point State Park Fountain
8   Fifth Ave Place
9   Barnes & Noble
11   Main Post Office
12   Fort Pitt Blockhouse
14   Downtown Visitors' Center

Ⓜ Metro Station

17   PNC Bank
18   Port Authority Transit (PAT)
     Information Center
20   Fort Pitt Museum
23   American Express
25   Western Pennsylvania Conservancy
26   Mellon Bank

children and $6 for seniors. Quite a few buses take you there, including bus Nos 13A, 13B and 13C.

For more on the artist's life, see the boxed text 'Andy Warhol' in the Facts about the Region chapter.

Carnegie Science Center The Carnegie Science Center (☎ 412-237-3400), 1 Allegheny Ave, at North Shore Drive near Three Rivers Stadium, is good for kids, but adults may find it less interesting. It has lots of hands-on exhibits, plus an aquarium, a simulated plane ride, the Henry Buhl Junior Planetarium, the Rangos Omnimax theater, laser shows and the USS *Requin* (a WWII submarine). You can visit its website at www.csc.clpgh.org.

The center is open Sunday to Friday 10 am to 5 pm (to 6 pm in summer) and Saturday 10 am to 9 pm. The Omnimax shows take place Friday and Saturday at 7, 8, 9 and 10 pm. Admission prices are quite complicated: to see the exhibits only costs $6.50/4.50 for adults/children and seniors, the Omnimax Theater only is $6.50/4.50 and admission to both is $10/6; for the exhibits and planetarium, it is $10/6; for the Omnimax, the exhibits and the planetarium, it is $12/8; for the submarine only, it is $4/2. To see the whole thing, it costs $14/8.50. Parking costs extra – there isn't any free parking around. You can get there on bus No 16A, 16D, 16U or 18E from downtown.

National Aviary in Pittsburgh The highly rated national aviary (☎ 412-323-7235), on Arch St west of Allegheny Square, is one of the few in the US where visitors are welcome to wander through simulated habitats while birds fly freely around (though some are caged). The more than 400 species from around the world include a pair of blue-winged kookaburras, rare Micronesian kingfishers and Mickey, the talking crow. The aviary is open daily 9 am to 5 pm (though admission ceases at 4:30 pm). Admission is $5/3.50 for adults/children and $4 for seniors. You can visit the website at www.aviary.org. Take bus No 16B, 16C, 16D or 16U.

Pittsburgh Children's Museum The three-story museum (☎ 412-322-5058) is at 10 Children's Way, in the Old Post Office Building in Allegheny Square. It has interactive exhibits (including a two-story climbing maze), puppets and live performances that emphasize the different cultures that make up Pittsburgh. It is open Saturday to Thursday 10 am to 5 pm and Friday 10 am to 8 pm. Admission is $4.50, or $3.50 for seniors; on Thursday, there's a flat admission price of $2.50. For a preview, visit the website at www.pittsburghkids.org. To get there take bus No 16B, 16C, 16D or 16U.

Mexican War Streets North of the national aviary, these are a series of streets off North Ave built after the Mexican War (1846–48); some of them are named after battles in the war. Buildings on these streets – especially Taylor Ave and Monterey, Resaca and Palo Alto Sts – are examples of attractively redone homes (mostly Greek Revival and Victorian). Bus Nos 16B and 16C pass by.

St Anthony's Chapel Off the main tourist route, this church (☎ 412-323-9504), 1704 Harpster St, above the city in Troy Hill, has over 5000 religious relics contained in elaborately carved and decorated reliquaries. The main attraction is one reliquary, in the left transept, that holds over 700 items, including (reputedly) a thorn from Jesus' crown of thorns, a splinter from his cross and a piece of stone from the Holy Sepulcher. The interior of the church is beautifully ornate, and the walls are dominated by a near-life-size depiction of the Stations of the Cross. Viewing hours are Tuesday, Thursday and Saturday 1 to 4 pm and Sunday 11 am to 4 pm.

To get there using public transportation, take bus No 6A up Troy Hill Rd to Lowrie St. By car, take North Ave to the second traffic light after I-279, which is Vinial St. Go right on Vinial St, then left on Troy Hill Rd; follow this road to the top of the hill and make a right on Lowrie St; turn left on Froman St and left again onto Harpster St.

South Side

Incline Railroads The Monongahela Incline
(☎ 412-442-2000) and Duquesne (doo-
KANE) Incline (☎ 412-381-1665) are two
single-car trains that run up and down the
steep Mt Washington. They're all that remain
of 15 incline railroads that opened up the
mountain to development in the 19th century
and allowed easier access to the city. These
are the original 19th-century cars, with hand-
carved cherry and maple interiors and
amber-glass transoms. The views of Pittsburgh from the top are great.

The fare is $1 each way, and the ride takes
two or three minutes. The inclines run
Monday to Saturday 5:30 am to 12:45 am; on
Sunday, the Duquesne Incline operates 7 am
to 12:45 am and the Monongahela Incline
runs 8:45 am to midnight.

For an interesting trip, go to Station
Square and walk across W Carson St to
the Monongahela Incline entrance. Ride
up the Monongahela Incline, walk west
along Grandview Ave/Mt Washington
Overlook to the Duquesne Incline. Then
ride down, walk over the footbridge and
back east to Station Square (the last part
of the walk is less interesting, as it's mostly
past parking lots).

Station Square Station Square (☎ 412-261-
9911) is a group of shops and restaurants in
a renovated former railroad warehouse
complex; it's off W Carson St at the base of
Mt Washington. The Landmarks Building, at
1 Station Square, is the former terminal of
the Pittsburgh & Lake Erie Railroad. The
complex's website is at www.stationsquare
.com.

The Station Square stop on the light-rail
and subway system is east of the complex
and south of the Smithfield St Bridge and
Carson St. Bus Nos 41A to 41E, 41G, 46A
to 46D, 46F to 46H, 46K, 51A, 51C and 53C
pass by.

Oakland & Around

Phipps Conservatory Phipps Conservatory (☎ 412-622-6914), on Curto Drive, is in
the 456-acre **Schenley Park** in Oakland.
Given to the city by Andrew Carnegie's

partner Andrew Phipps in 1893, the conservatory is an excellent collection of iron-and-
glass greenhouses connected by high, wide
passageways also made of iron and glass. It
contains tropical plants, orchids, bonsai and
giant topiary and is open Tuesday to Sunday
9 am to 5 pm. Normal admission is $5/2 for
adults/children and $3.50 for seniors, but this
goes up slightly for seasonal flower shows.
The conservatory's website is at www.phipps
.conservatory.org.

Bus No 84B runs nearby, and bus Nos
53F, 53H, 53K, 56U and 67H run through
the park.

The Carnegie The Carnegie (☎ 412-622-
3313), 4400 Forbes Ave in Oakland, is the
commonly abbreviated name for the building
complex containing the **Carnegie Museum of
Art**, the **Carnegie Museum of Natural History**,
the **Carnegie Library of Pittsburgh** and the
Carnegie Music Hall. The museum of natural
history has a great dinosaur collection, including a complete Tyrannosaurus rex skele-
ton; there are videos and lots of hands-on
displays for children. The museum of art has
an extensive display of Impressionist, post-
Impressionist and modern American and European art, as well as replicas of ancient
sculptures and friezes.

The Carnegie is open Tuesday to Saturday 10 am to 5 pm and Sunday 1 to 5 pm.
Admission to all museums is $6/4 for adults/
children and $5 for seniors. There are free
tours of the library Tuesday, Thursday and
Saturday at 11 am and 2 pm; meet at the
library entrance. You can visit the website at
www.clpgh.org.

To get there, take bus No 54C, 61A, 61B,
61C, 67A, 67C, 67E, 67F or 67J along
Forbes Ave.

Cathedral of Learning

Built in 1937, the Cathedral of Learning is
the name given to the imposing Gothic 42-
story, 535-foot University of Pittsburgh
building (☎ 412-624-6000) at Bigelow Blvd
and Fifth Ave. Inside, on the 1st floor, the
students' **Commons Room**, with its vaulted
ceilings supported by 50-foot columns, is
indeed like the interior of a cathedral.

Andrew Carnegie

Pittsburgh industrialist Andrew Carnegie (1835–1919) is one of the most interesting and certainly the best remembered of America's 19th-century industrial barons. He amassed a fortune by driving his steelworkers hard, often brutally, but when he retired, he gave much of his fortune away, claiming it was the duty of the wealthy to do so.

Growing up in impoverished surroundings in Dunfermline, Scotland, Carnegie emigrated to Pittsburgh at the age of 12 with his parents. While working as a telegrapher for the Pennsylvania Railroad, he caught the eye of Thomas Scott, one of the company's officials. Scott ensured that Carnegie was promoted (by the age of 24) to superintendent of the western division of the railroad. He lent Carnegie money and gave him financial advice, so that by his thirties, the young Scotsman was a wealthy investor.

Carnegie left the railroad to form the Keystone Bridge Company, and during the depression of the 1870s, he put all his assets and efforts into the emerging steel industry. He built plants, held down wages and reinvested profits in capital improvements. Soon, the Carnegie Steel Company was the dominant force in the industry. Carnegie believed firmly in 'vertical integration,' and his corporation owned everything from the raw materials to the final product. In 1901, he sold his Carnegie Steel Company to the US Steel Corporation for the then-astronomical price of $250 million.

Interestingly, Carnegie had mixed feelings about the rights of labor and the duties of capitalists. His most famous ideas on the subject were published in the 1889 essay 'The Gospel of Wealth.' Carnegie wrote that it was the duty of the wealthy to return 'their surplus wealth to the mass of their fellows in the forms best calculated to do the lasting good.' In his latter years, Carnegie lived up to his words, endowing an amazing number of libraries, cultural institutions, universities and other noble causes throughout the US.

Surrounding the Commons Room are the interesting **Nationality Classrooms**. Each of the mostly functioning 24 classrooms is designed and decorated in a particular ethnic style and historic period. The Irish one, for example, represents a 6th-century church oratory. Some, such as the Syria-Lebanon room (which was actually brought over from Damascus), can only be seen with guides.

You can enter the building and look at the rooms Monday to Saturday 9 am to 4:30 pm and Sunday 11 am to 4:30 pm. The guided 1½-hour tours are given daily for $2/50¢ for adults/children and $1.50 for seniors; the last tour is at 3 pm.

Take bus No 54C, 61A to 61C, 67A, 67C, 67E, 67F or 67J along Forbes Ave.

Frick Art & Historical Center This is a 6-acre complex (☎ 412-371-0600) at 7227 Reynolds St, in Point Breeze, east of Oakland. It includes Clayton, the former home of famous Pittsburgh industrialist and Carnegie partner Henry Clay Frick (see the boxed text 'Henry Clay Frick,' later in this chapter), the Frick Art Museum, the Carriage Museum, a greenhouse and a two-story children's playhouse. The center is open Tuesday to Saturday 10 am to 5:30 pm and Sunday noon to 6 pm. Admission is free.

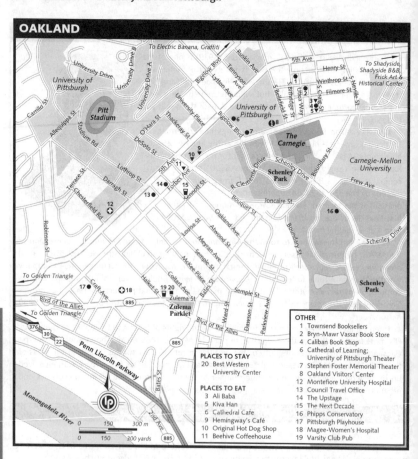

OAKLAND

Map labels:
- To Electric Banana, Graffiti
- University Drive
- University Drive B
- University Drive A
- University of Pittsburgh
- Pitt Stadium
- Carrillo St
- Allequippa St
- Stadium Rd
- O'Hara St
- Thackeray St
- University Place
- Bigelow Blvd
- Desoto St
- 5th Ave
- Lothrop St
- Terrace St
- Darragh St
- Chesterfield Rd
- Robinson St
- Forbes Ave
- Bennett St
- Ruskin Ave
- Tennyson Ave
- Lytton Ave
- 5th Ave
- Henry St
- Winthrop St
- Filmore St
- Neville St
- To Shadyside, Shadyside B&B, Frick Art & Historical Center
- University of Pittsburgh
- S Bithridge St
- Uhba Way
- S Craig St
- S Bellefield St
- The Carnegie
- Schenley Drive
- Boundary St
- Schenley Park
- Carnegie-Mellon University
- Frew Ave
- R Clement Drive
- Bouquet St
- Joncaire St
- Louisa St
- Oakland Ave
- Atwood St
- Meyran Ave
- Semple St
- McKee Place
- Bates St
- Collart Ave
- Halket St
- Café Ave
- Zulema St
- Zulema Parklet
- Blvd of the Allies
- To Golden Triangle
- Ward St
- Dawson St
- Parkview Ave
- Semple St
- Schenley Park
- Schenley Drive
- Boundary St
- Penn Lincoln Parkway
- Monongahela River
- 2nd Ave
- To Golden Triangle
- 376
- 30
- 22
- 885

Scale:
0   150   300 m
0   150   300 yards

OTHER
1 Townsend Booksellers
2 Bryn-Mawr Vassar Book Store
4 Caliban Book Shop
6 Cathedral of Learning;
   University of Pittsburgh Theater
7 Stephen Foster Memorial Theater
8 Oakland Visitors' Center
12 Montefiore University Hospital
13 Council Travel Office
14 The Upstage
15 The Next Decade
16 Phipps Conservatory
17 Pittsburgh Playhouse
18 Magee-Women's Hospital
19 Varsity Club Pub

PLACES TO STAY
20 Best Western
   University Center

PLACES TO EAT
3 Ali Baba
5 Kiva Han
6 Cathedral Café
9 Hemingway's Café
10 Original Hot Dog Shop
11 Beehive Coffeehouse

The **Frick Art Museum** displays Flemish, French and Italian paintings, including works by Peter Paul Rubens; there is also an exhibition of royal art from the Nigerian kingdom of Benin. Entry is free. There are also free tours of the museum on Wednesday, Saturday and Sunday at 2 pm.

Clayton (☎ 412-371-0606), completed in 1872 and then subsequently remodeled and expanded, was a modest residence for a 19th-century multimillionaire. Frick entertained Teddy Roosevelt here in 1902. It was expertly restored in 1990 to its original state (at a cost of $6 million) and contains the world's only player organ (it plays on command from music rolls, like a player piano). The house can only be seen by guided tour, which must be booked in advance. Tours are Wednesday to Saturday 10 am to 5:30 pm and Sunday noon to 6 pm; they cost $6.

To get there using public transportation, bus Nos 67A, 67C, 67E, 67F, 71C and 74A take you there from downtown. By car, take Parkway East (Route 376) to the Edgewood/Swissvale exit. At the exit ramp, follow the signs to Edgewood, then turn right on Braddock Ave. Go 1.3 miles and then turn left on Penn Ave. At the

Henry Clay Frick

Henry Clay Frick (1849–1919), Pittsburgh's second-best-known industrialist and the son of a modest farmer, achieved his aim of becoming a millionaire by the age of 30.

Despite only a few years of schooling, Frick was always good with numbers. While still in his teens, he began working for his maternal grandfather, who owned the Overholt Distillery, and by 19 was the firm's bookkeeper. At age 20, Frick saw the value of coal for the burgeoning US steel industry and bought as much land containing coal reserves (then at low prices because of the 1870s depression) as he could. Early in his career, he obtained a $10,000 bank loan to expand his coke ovens, which converted coal to useful fuel.

While on his wedding trip in 1881, Frick fortuitously met steel magnate Andrew Carnegie in New York City. Carnegie proposed a merger between his company and the Frick Coke Company. Frick accepted and became chairman of the Carnegie Steel Company. The union joined Carnegie's steel mills with the masses of coal they needed for fuel.

Although Frick and Carnegie were business partners and industrialists, they had different views on the responsibility of the wealthy and the rights of workers. Nothing symbolized their clash more than Frick's handling of a strike at Carnegie's Homestead steel plant. Carnegie wanted the union broken, but believed that Frick went too far in calling in hundreds of armed Pinkerton strikebreakers to attack them. For his brutality in breaking the strike, Frick was stabbed three times and shot twice by New York anarchist Alexander Berkman in 1892. Frick recovered, but in 1900, he and Carnegie parted ways.

Frick became head of the new US Steel Corporation, which arose from the sale of the Carnegie Steel Company. He soon resigned, with tens of millions of dollars in assets, and moved to New York City, where he built a home at 70th St and Fifth Ave. This is now the Frick Collection Museum, which houses much of the artwork he accumulated during his lifetime. More of the family's art collection can be seen at the Frick Art & Historical Center in Pittsburgh, the legacy of his daughter Helen.

second traffic light, turn left on S Homewood Ave. Go one block to Reynolds St, then take another left turn. The parking lot is on the left. From Oakland, take Fifth Ave to Penn Ave and make a right; go about eight blocks and then make a right on S Homewood Ave, and follow the directions as above.

Pittsburgh Zoo The 77-acre Pittsburgh Zoo (☎ 800-474-4966), 1 Hill Rd in Highland Park, northeast of downtown, has over 4000 animals in re-created habitats, including a number of endangered species, such as the white rhino and the silverback gorilla. From Memorial Day to Labor Day, it is open daily 10 am to 5 pm; during the rest of the year, it's open 9 am to 4 pm. Admission is $6/4 for adults/children; parking costs $2.50. You can visit the zoo's website at www.zoo.pgh.pa.us.

From downtown, take bus No 71A or 71B from Fifth Ave; by car, take Route 28 north to exit 5 over Highland Park Bridge, then follow the signs.

Organized Tours

Gray Line (☎ 412-741-2720, 761-7000) does a two-hour 'historic' trolley-bus tour of downtown, Mt Washington (with a ride on the Duquesne Incline) and the North Side that costs $18/9 for adults/children. A 'cultural neighborhood' tour of downtown and Oakland includes a visit to the Nationality Classrooms in the Cathedral of Learning; it costs $18/9. Gray Line also combines the historic tour with a river cruise on one of the boats of the Gateway Clipper Fleet for $26/13.

The Gateway Clipper Fleet (☎ 412-355-7980) operates a series of cruises from the dock next to the Sheraton Hotel in the

Station Square complex. A narrated 2¼-hour 'three rivers' cruise leaves Monday to Saturday at 11:30 am; its two-hour 'twilight fountain' cruise leaves Tuesday and Thursday at 7:30 pm. Both cost $8/5 for adults/children. There are many other special cruises combining dining, music and dancing.

For something a little different, Just Ducky Tours (☎ 412-402-3825) gives you a narrated one-hour tour of downtown and then along the rivers in one of its amphibian craft. Tours cost $13/9 for adults/children and $12 for seniors; they leave from Station Square.

Special Events

Following are some of the highlights of the Pittsburgh calendar:

May
Pittsburgh Folk Festival – in late May, the city celebrates its ethnic diversity in the IC Light Amphitheater, Station Square, with folk music, dancing, crafts and food (☎ 412-278-1276).

June
Three Rivers Arts Festival – this festival combines arts, crafts, food and performances for three weeks at Gateway Plaza and Point State Park (☎ 412-281-8723).

June to July
Three Rivers Shakespeare Festival – productions are performed at the Stephen Foster Memorial Theater in Oakland (☎ 412-624-0102).

July
South Side Summer Street Spectacular – the town's largest neighborhood festival, this takes place on E Carson St in mid-July (☎ 412-481-0651).

July to August
Pittsburgh Three Rivers Regatta – the world's largest inland regatta takes place at Point State Park (☎ 412-338-8765).

August
Shadyside Summer Arts Festival – this three-day festival of the visual and performing arts takes place in mid-August on Ellesworth Ave, Shadyside (☎ 412-681-2809).

September
A Fair in the Park – this arts-and-crafts show takes place in Shadyside during mid-September and is sponsored by the Craftsmen's Guild of Pittsburgh (☎ 412-431-6270).

Places to Stay

Pittsburgh suffers in general from not having a large number of places to stay, especially in the center, and what is available is usually expensive. Even if you can afford it, you may not be able to find a room in town on peak weekends, especially when the hotels offer cheaper weekend packages. Most mid-range places are northwest of town, near the airport, and require a car to be reached. In the center, budget choices are very limited.

For B&B information, check the website www.pittsburghbnb.com.

Places to Stay – Budget

Downtown, *Point Park College* (☎ 412-392-3824, 201 Wood St), at Blvd of the Allies, rents two-person dormitory rooms with separate baths for $15 per person from June to mid-August. Bring your own sheets and towels.

The nearest campground is in *Raccoon Creek State Park* (☎ 412-899-2200), 25 miles northwest of town. It has all the conveniences and 172 sites for $17 to $19; it is open year-round. Take Routes 22/30 west to Route 18 north, which passes through the park. The campground is about 2 miles north of Frankfort Springs.

The HI-AYH *Pittsburgh International Hostel* (☎ 412-431-1267, ayh@trfn.clpgh.org, 830 East Warrington Ave), at Arlington, across from the Gulf service station in South Side, is in a splendid building that was once a bank. Dorm beds cost $17/20 for members/nonmembers, and the hostel closes between 10 am and 5 pm. Take the 'T' light rail to South Hills, then bus 51A to the hostel.

Places to Stay – Mid-Range

The majority of the mid-range places are about 15 miles northwest of town in suburbs such as Crescent, Moon, Robinson, Kennedy and Coraopolis, clustered toward the Pittsburgh International Airport.

Beers School Rd toward Coraopolis is lined with independent and chain motels. Take Route 60 to exit 3, then follow Business Route 60 north a couple of miles to the Beers School Rd exit. The independent motels are sometimes cheaper and the chains sometimes nicer. The cheapest is **Glass Tower Motor Inn** (☎ 412-264-6101, 1457 Beers School Rd), with singles/doubles for $40/45; it also has a restaurant and bar. The **Pittsburgh Plaza Hotel** (☎ 412-264-7900, 1500 Beers School Rd) has rooms for $50, including a continental breakfast. **Hampton Inn Airport** (☎ 412-264-0020, 1420 Beers School Rd) is another that includes a free continental breakfast and is one of the more elegant of the chain motels; it has rooms for $70.

The Steubenville Pike also has a number of motels. To get there, take exit 16 from I-79. The **Econolodge** (☎ 412-922-6900, 4800 Steubenville Pike) provides large singles/ doubles for $46/54 with a continental breakfast thrown in.

If you want to be close to town, the **Best Western University Center** (☎ 412-683-6100, fax 682-6115, 3401 Blvd of the Allies), at Halket St in Oakland, has rooms for $75/85. There's a diner and pub next door.

Places to Stay – Top End

In Oakland, **Shadyside B&B** (☎ 412-683-6501, 5516 Maple Heights Court), off Fifth Ave between Graham and Ivy Sts, is a large Jacobean stone mansion with a library/ sitting room, a billiards room, and a balcony and kitchen. There are eight rooms, six with a private bath. Room rates are $100 to $135.

The **Marriott** (☎ 412-471-4000, 800-228-9290, fax 281-4797, 112 Washington Place), near the Civic Arena, is a renovated brick-and-glass tower with good views of the city. It has an indoor heated pool and health club. Rooms cost $89 to $179 single or double. The 700-room **Pittsburgh Hilton & Towers** (☎ 412-391-4600, 800-445-8667, fax 594-5161, 600 Commonwealth Place), at Gateway Center, has views across the Allegheny River, a health club and several restaurants. Room rates range from $89 to $179. In the Station Square complex, the **Sheraton Hotel at Station Square** (☎ 412-261-2000) has standard rooms for $139 to $159 during the week; rooms with views of the Golden Triangle cost extra, but on weekends, all rooms are discounted.

The **DoubleTree Hotel** (☎ 412-281-3700, 800-445-8667, fax 281-2652, 1000 Penn Ave) is connected by walkway to the David L Lawrence Convention Center next door. The rooms, which are decorated with prints by Pittsburgh artists, cost $169 (on weekend nights, $119).

Downtown, **Westin William Penn** (☎ 412-281-7100, 800-228-3000, fax 553-5239, 530 William Penn Place), in Mellon Square, is a renovated national historic landmark built by Henry Clay Frick in 1916. The plush bedrooms are decorated in French-provincial, Italian or American-colonial styles. The normal rates are $198 to $224, depending on the style of the room, but prices can drop considerably on weekends.

Places to Eat – Budget & Mid-Range

Golden Triangle Starbucks has a number of coffee houses around town, including one in Market Place that has sofas, background music and views of the square. The food court below street level at **Two PPG Place**, the smaller of the Gothic black-glass buildings on Market Square, has stalls selling burgers and Chinese, Greek and Italian dishes. The court is busy at lunchtime, and most meals are between $3.50 and $8. There's also a food court on the 2nd floor of the **Fifth Avenue Place** shopping center on Fifth Ave.

The **Original Oyster House** (☎ 412-566-7925, 20 Market Place), diagonally opposite the PPG food court, is a seafood restaurant with a long marble bar where you stand and eat raw shellfish at market prices. Large platters of fried fish, crab cutlets, shrimp and fries cost $5.95. The **1902 Landmark Tavern** (☎ 412-471-1902, 24 Market Place), is a modern lunch place with pressed-tin ceilings, wooden booths and a long bar. Prices are higher than the Oyster House, and the atmosphere is less casual. It sells a mixture of seafood and other dishes; oyster stew is $5.95, and pesto chicken costs $15.95.

Kaufmann's department store (☎ 412-232-2320), 400 Fifth Ave, contains a number of eateries, including the cafeteria-style **Tic Toc Restaurant** on the 1st floor. It has sandwiches for $3.75 to $6 and daily specials, such as soup with tuna salad, for $3.95.

Sushi Kim (☎ *412-281-9956, 1241 Penn Ave*), near 13th St and the train station, serves Korean and Japanese food and some of Pittsburgh's best sushi ($3.50 to $6). Large meat dishes, such as *bulgogi* (marinated beef), are grilled at your table and cost $6.95 at lunchtime. Evening meals are more pricey, and it has a special vegetarian menu. It is closed the first Sunday of each month.

The Strip If you're buying food to cook, try the deli *Pennsylvania Macaroni Company*, the *Parma Sausage Products* store or *Wholey's Market* for fish, cheese, fruit and vegetables, all on Penn Ave in The Strip just northeast of downtown. *The Strip* (☎ *412-471-1043, 2106 Penn Ave*), in The Strip, is brewery-restaurant offering music all night; it's open late on weekends.

The Strip also has a lot of dining choices. *My Ngoc*, on Penn Ave, serves Vietnamese, Thai and Chinese dishes for $5 to $9, while *Primanti Brothers Restaurant & Bar*, at Smallman and 18th Sts, dishes up Italian submarine sandwiches 24 hours daily: a jumbo fish with cheese costs $4.25.

Kaya (☎ *412-261-6565, 2000 Smallman St*), at 20th St, serves delicious Caribbean and Spanish food daily 11 am until late and has a wide selection of microbrew beers, cocktails, wines and spirits. Soup costs $3.50 to $4.50, and main dishes, such as Jamaican green curry, cost $7.25. It also does excellent vegetarian food.

North Side The basic *Wilson's Bar-B-Q* (☎ *412-322-7427, 700 N Taylor Ave*) has a few tables, an old counter and good barbecue. Smell the wood smoke and order from the simple menu: a 'whole slab of ribs' is $18.10, but there are plates that cost $7 to $10. It's closed weekends. The popular *Peppi's* (☎ *412-231-9009, 925–27 Western Ave*) serves good sandwiches for under $6; the interior decor consists of wooden floors and benches and a pressed-tin ceiling. You order at the counter, then wait for your number to be called.

The landmark *Pennsylvania Brewing Company* (☎ *412-237-9402*), at Troy Hill Rd

and Vinial St, is a redbrick, authentic German brewery and pub-restaurant. The owner is a descendant of Franz Daniel Pastorius, who founded Germantown in Philadelphia in 1683 and drank beer with William Penn at Penn's own brew house. Diners can view the spotless copper brewing tanks from the dining area. Bratwurst on a baguette is $4.75, salads are around $7.50 and hot meals (such as Wiener schnitzel) are around $8.25. The brewery makes 12 authentic naturally brewed German beers from $2.25. It's open Monday to Saturday 11 am to midnight.

South Side Station Square, at the foot of the Monongahela Incline, has a mix of food choices. Budget options include *Jimbo's Food & Drinks*, for sandwiches (from $3.50) and hot dogs (from $1.90), and *Coffee Express*, for coffee and pastries. Mid-range choices include the *Sesame Inn* (☎ *412-281-8282*), a Chinese restaurant serving wonton soup for $1.50, shrimp main dishes for $9.95 to $10.50 and good vegetarian dishes, such as Buddhist Delight (stir-fried vegetables), for $7.95. The *Cheese Cellar* (☎ *412-471-3355*) serves a mix of dishes; *bruschetta* (tomatoes and olive oil on toast) is $4.95, and Cajun chicken is $10.95.

At the top of the Monongahela Incline, you'll find *DiFiore's Ice Cream Delite* (☎ *412-381-4640, 120 Shiloh St*), selling burgers (starting at $1.35) and hoagies in half and whole sizes ($2.95 to $5.95), as well as ice cream.

Oakland As befitting a student neighborhood, Oakland is full of cheap places to eat, including fast-food outlets, most of them along Forbes Ave between Bouquet St and Meyran Ave. S Craig St between Forbes and Fifth Aves is another restaurant area.

The *Beehive Coffeehouse* (☎ *412-683-4483, 3807 Forbes Ave*) is in the lobby of the art-house movie theater and sells a variety of international coffees and teas, as well as cakes and pastries. It also has a vegetarian menu. You can take your drink into the theater, at the back of which are some tables and chairs. The busy *Kiva Han* (☎ *412-687-4844, 420 S Craig St*), at Forbes Ave, serves a variety of coffees, teas and organic foods. It's a good place to relax with a newspaper or a good book.

The *Cathedral Cafe*, on the floor below the Commons Room in the Cathedral of Learning, is a smart, inexpensive cafeteria selling things such as chicken sandwiches for a reasonable $2.40.

The *Original Hot Dog Shop* (☎ 412-687-8327, 3901 Forbes Ave), at Bouquet St, is known as 'The O' and has a U-shaped counter, two street entrances and tables. Not surprisingly, it sells hot dogs (starting at $2.40), but it also does spaghetti for $4, pizzas and fish with fries. The busy *Hemingway's Cafe* (☎ 412-621-4100, 3911 Forbes Ave) does Cajun chicken salad for $6.95 and turkey Rueben sandwiches for $5.95. It serves cocktails at the bar and has poetry readings.

Ali Baba (☎ 412-682-2829, 404 S Craig St) serves Middle Eastern food. Lunch prices are good, with hummus dishes starting at $2.95 and falafel for $3.95. At dinner most main dishes cost less than $10.

Places to Eat – Top End

Golden Triangle The *Common Plea* (☎ 412-281-5140, 308 Ross St), near the Allegheny Courthouse, has dark wooden walls and antique pictures. As much of its clientele is from the legal world, its menus are printed as summonses and feature a mix of seafood, beef and veal; main dishes cost $18 to $30.

Catering mainly to theatergoers visiting Heinz Hall, opposite, *Bravo! Franco* (☎ 412-642-6677, 613 Penn Ave), serves up fine Italian cuisine daily and has a small bar that is open until 2 am. Expect to pay around $30.

Top of the Triangle (☎ 412-471-4100, 600 Grant St), on the 62nd floor of the USX Tower, offers great views of the city while you dine. It specializes in steak and seafood and has an extensive wine list. Lunch entrees cost $7 to $15, but dinner main dishes are in the $19-to-$30 range. Its bar is open until 1 am.

South Side The Landmarks Building, at 1 Station Square, houses the *Grand Concourse Restaurant* (☎ 412-261-1717), part of which overlooks the river. Set in the magnificent main hall of the former railroad terminal, it specializes in seafood, such as baked Boston cod for $17 and lobster for $25.

A row of restaurants with great views of the Golden Triangle line Grandview Ave at the top of the Duquesne Incline; most serve Italian or American cuisine in the $15 to $40 range. The fully refurbished *LeMont* (☎ 412-431-3100, 1114 Grandview Ave) is the largest, with lots of limousines pulling up outside at dinnertime. Other good restaurants nearby include *Tin Angel* (☎ 412-381-1919), at No 1200; *Pasquarelli's* (☎ 412-431-1660), at No 1204, which specializes in North Italian food; and *Cliffside* (☎ 412-431-6996), at No 1208.

Entertainment

The free weeklies *City Paper* and *In Pittsburgh* have detailed listings of current events and schedules. You can also check the entertainment sections of the daily newspapers the *Pittsburgh Post-Gazette* and the *Pittsburgh Tribune-Review* or call the 24-hour Activities Hot Line (☎ 800-366-0093).

For tickets call Ticketmaster (☎ 412-323-1919) or TIX (☎ 412-281-2098).

Theater The *Pittsburgh Public Theater* (☎ 412-321-9800, 6 Allegheny Square), in the Allegheny branch of the Carnegie Library in North Side, puts on six productions a season (October through June), from contemporary musicals to classic dramas. Tickets are between $25 and $40. Downtown, the *Benedum Center for the Performing Arts* (☎ 412-456-6666, 719 Liberty Ave), with the entrance on 7th St, has many Broadway shows.

City Theater (☎ 412-431-4400, 57 S 13th St), in South Side, is noted for its innovative performances. In Oakland, there's the *University of Pittsburgh Theater* (☎ 412-624-0933), in the Cathedral of Learning, and the *Stephen Foster Memorial Theater* (☎ 412-648-7547, Forbes Ave), at Bigelow Blvd, home of the annual Three Rivers Shakespeare Festival (see Special Events, earlier in this chapter).

Music & Dance The Pittsburgh Symphony Orchestra plays October through May at the elaborately designed **Heinz Hall** (☎ 412-392-4900, 600 Penn Ave) and in summer at Point State Park. The **Benedum Center for the Performing Arts** (see Theater, immediately preceding) is the venue for performances by the Pittsburgh Dance Council, Pittsburgh Ballet Theater Company, Pittsburgh Opera and Civic Light Opera.

Cinema The **Beehive** (☎ 412-687-9428, 3807 Forbes Ave), in Oakland, is an art-house movie theater showing US and foreign cult and classic films. It has an excellent coffee shop. Also in Oakland, the **Pittsburgh Playhouse** (☎ 412-471-9700, 222 Craft Ave) puts on first-run alternative movies and hosts regular festivals. The **Rex Theatre** (☎ 412-381-2200, 1602 E Carson St), South Side, features mostly first-release movies, plus some classic and foreign films, for $6.50; before 6 pm, films cost only $4.

Live Music Oakland and South Side have a number of venues for rock music, R&B and jazz. In Oakland, **Electric Banana** (☎ 412-682-8296, 3887 Bigelow Blvd) offers the latest in contemporary alternative-rock music by mostly local musicians. The cover charge ranges from about $3 to $8. Open Wednesday to Saturday, the multistory **Graffiti** (☎ 412-682-4210, 4615 Baum Blvd) attracts top acts performing anything from hard rock to folk.

The **Next Decade** (☎ 412-687-6990, 223 Atwood St), at Sennett St in Oakland, is a popular student bar and has music by local and national bands nightly; the cover can be up to $6.

In South Side, E Carson St is the place to go. The art deco **Nick's Fat City** (☎ 412-481-6881, 1601 E Carson St) hosts local R&B and rock bands Tuesday to Sunday. **Anthony's** (☎ 412-431-8960), at No 1306, has music nightly with no cover charge. The **Blue Note Cafe** (☎ 412-431-7080), at E Carson and 19th Sts, serves up blues or jazz nightly with a cover charge of $2 to $3; it also has jazz sessions on weekend afternoons.

Dance Clubs In The Strip, the stark **Metropol** (☎ 412-261-4512, 1600 Smallman St), in a former warehouse, and the **Rosebud** (☎ 412-261-2221), at No 1650, have dancing to live bands. Music ranges from salsa to reggae. Alongside the Allegheny River, at the **Patio Deck** (☎ 412-281-3680) – one of several clubs in The Boardwalk entertainment complex at 1501 Smallman St – bands perform on a floating stage.

The **Upstage** (☎ 412-681-9777, 3609 Forbes Ave), in Oakland, has nightly dancing to alternative music; the cover is around $5.

Bars & Brewpubs **Whiskey Dick's Saloon** (☎ 412-471-9555), next to the Metropol on Smallman St in The Strip, is an inexpensive, down-to-earth but sometimes noisy bar. In Mt Washington, the **Grandview Saloon** (☎ 412-431-1400, 1212 Grandview Ave) is a trendy bar with loud music and outdoor balconies, where you can drink and dine with great views of the Golden Triangle.

Next to the Grand Concourse Restaurant, in the Landmarks Building at Station Square, is the elegant **Gandy Dancer** (☎ 412-261-1717), where the food is good and there's a piano player in the evenings.

In Oakland, the **Varsity Club Pub** (☎ 412-681-8756, 3401 Blvd of the Allies), next to the Best Western University Center hotel, is open until 2 am on Friday and Saturday night and to 1 am the rest of the week. See also **The Next Decade** under Live Music, earlier.

The **Pennsylvania Brewing Company** (☎ 412-237-9402) is at Troy Hill Rd and Vinial St in North Side (see Places to Eat, earlier). **The Strip** (☎ 412-471-1043, 2106 Penn Ave), in The Strip, is brewery-restaurant offering music until it closes; it's open late on weekends.

Spectator Sports

The **Three Rivers Stadium** (☎ 412-321-0650, 400 Stadium Circle) is by the river on the North Side. The Pittsburgh Pirates (☎ 412-323-1150) baseball team plays here April through October, while the Pittsburgh Steelers (☎ 412-323-1200) football team uses it August through December. The Pittsburgh Penguins (☎ 412-642-7367) play ice hockey at the *Civic Arena (☎ 412-642-2062, 300 Auditorium Place)*, at Washington Place and Center Ave east of downtown, October through April. All of them are national-league teams.

The Pittsburgh Marathon (☎ 412-647-7866) takes place in early May, and the finishing line is in Point State Park.

Shopping

Downtown, Kaufmann's (☎ 412-232-2320), 400 Fifth Ave, is a long-established department store. Two modern shopping centers are PPG Place (☎ 412-434-1900), in the black-glass Gothic tower at Market Square, and Fifth Avenue Place (☎ 412-456-7800), 120 Fifth Ave. In South Side, Station Square (☎ 412-261-9911), at W Carson St near Smithfield St Bridge, has more than 50 shops in the former railroad warehouse complex.

Getting There & Away

Air Pittsburgh International Airport (☎ 412-472-3500), 16 miles west of downtown, is the headquarters of US Airways (☎ 412-922-6407, 800-428-4322) and has direct connections to Europe, Canada and Japan, as well as all major centers in the US. US Airways has offices downtown at 4 Gateway Center and 525 Grant St.

Other airlines with city offices are:

British Airways
(☎ 800-247-9297) suite 2415, 1 Mellon Bank Center, 500 Grant St

Delta Air Lines
(☎ 412-456-2240, 800-221-1212) suite 2420, 1 Mellon Bank Center, 500 Grant St

United Airlines
(☎ 800-241-6522) Westin William Penn Hotel, Mellon Square

Other airlines that serve Pittsburgh include American Airlines (☎ 800-433-7300), Continental Airlines (☎ 800-525-0280) and Northwest Airlines (☎ 800-225-2525).

The airport has two terminals – Landside, where you check in and pick up baggage, and Airside, where the boarding gates are located; the terminals are con-

nected by the 'People Mover,' an underground rail shuttle. Nonpassengers can visit the Airside terminal, but must go through a security check.

Both terminals have a Pittsburgh Visitor Information Center (☎ 412-472-0868). The one in the Landside terminal is open daily 8 am to 8 pm, and the Airside one is open daily 7:30 am to 6:30 pm. Also in the Landside terminal you'll find a Travelers' Aid Society desk (☎ 412-472-3599), which answers questions about transportation and rents car seats for children; the Mutual of Omaha's Travelex Business Center (☎ 412-472-5151), which changes money and provides business services (there's also a cluster of ATMs nearby); a post office that is open weekdays 8:30 am to 4 pm; and car rental services. Both terminals have an information desk.

The following are some examples of standard economy fares: to New York's JFK airport, $149/258 one way/roundtrip; to Los Angeles, $918/1836. The roundtrip airfare to Philadelphia starts at $158.

Bus The Greyhound bus station (☎ 412-392-6513), at 11th St and Liberty Ave, is near the Amtrak station. It has luggage lockers ($4 per day) and a Travelers' Aid Society office (☎ 412-281-5474), which has information on local transportation. The one-way fare to Philadelphia is $37 (seven hours), and to New York City, it's $53 (10½ hours).

Train Amtrak (☎ 412-471-6172) operates from Penn Central station, 1100 Liberty Ave at Grant St. The original railroad station is a magnificent stone building with a domed forecourt and marble flooring in the huge hall now occupied by offices. The more prosaic modern Amtrak station is at the rear. There are daily trains to Philadelphia ($80 one way, eight hours), Harrisburg ($61, 5¾ hours) and New York City ($107, 10 hours); these fares are cheaper if you book in advance.

Car & Motorcycle Pittsburgh is amply served by the interstate system. I-79 passes through western Pittsburgh, connecting it

PENNSYLVANIA

with West Virginia to the south and Lake Erie to the north. From I-79, I-279 leads into town. I-76 (Pennsylvania Turnpike) passes through the north and east of Pittsburgh; from the east, take exit 6 onto I-376 into town; from the north, take I-79/279.

Getting Around
To/From the Airport The Airline Transportation Company (☎ 412-471-8900) runs buses every 30 minutes to/from downtown for $12/20 one way/roundtrip and to/from Oakland for $12.50/21. PAT bus No 28X (Airport Flyer) runs daily between Oakland and the airport via the Golden Triangle every 20 minutes or so. From Oakland, it costs $1.95 one way and takes 45 minutes.

A cab to downtown costs about $30, to Oakland about $35. To get to the airport by car from downtown, follow Route 60 (Airport Expressway) north to exit 6.

Bus & the 'T' The Port Authority of Allegheny County (☎ 412-442-2000) operates the city's local transport system. It has a downtown information center (☎ 412-255-1356), 534 Smithfield St, that is open Tuesday, Wednesday and Friday 7:30 am to 5 pm and Monday and Thursday to 6 pm. Find more information at www.nauticom.net/users/alcopa/services/portauth/.

Buses – known as PAT (which stands for Port Authority Transit) buses – are free within downtown's Golden Triangle until 7 pm, after which the one-way fare is 75¢.

The Port Authority of Allegheny County also runs a 22.5-mile light-rail system called the 'T' between downtown and Mt Washington/South Side. Three of the five downtown stations are underground – Gateway Center, Wood St and Steel Plaza; the other two are Penn Station and Station Square. The 'T' is free between Gateway Center, Wood St, Steel Plaza and Penn Station.

The city is divided into a several zones, and most sights and facilities are in the Downtown Zone and Zone 1. Most bus and T-fares around the city are $1.25; transfers cost 25¢.

Bus Nos 61A to 61C and 71A to 71D along Fifth Ave connect downtown with Oakland.

Taxi Although most taxis are carefully regulated, if you're arriving by bus or train, be aware that some taxis at the stations may be operating uninsured or are otherwise unsafe, especially if they're unmarked. Approved companies include Yellow Cab (☎ 412-665-8100), People's Cab (☎ 412-681-3131) and Eagle Taxis (☎ 412-763-4555). Rates are $1.80 for the first one-seventh of a mile and 20¢ for each additional one-seventh. A ride between downtown and Oakland costs about $7.

Car & Motorcycle The highways and roads are fairly confusing and crowded at approaches to the tunnels and on many bridges across the Allegheny and Monongahela Rivers. The approaches are not always marked, and when driving, you may find yourself suddenly on a bridge approach with no turnoff, then without warning, you're out of downtown and on the North or South Side.

The two main thoroughfares connecting the North and South Sides via downtown are I-279 and I-579. Penn Lincoln Parkway (I-376) runs east-west beside the Monongahela River. Most downtown streets have alternate one-way traffic systems, and parking can be difficult; a tourist map of the city, available from one of the visitors' centers, indicates public parking lots.

Some of the main car rental companies are:

Avis
  (☎ 412-472-5200, 800-331-1212)
  Pittsburgh International Airport
Budget
  (☎ 412-261-1628, 800-435-7751)
  700 Fifth Ave
Dollar
  (☎ 412-472-5100, 800-800-4000)
  Pittsburgh International Airport
Enterprise
  (☎ 412-505-5000)
  4489 Campbells Run Rd
Hertz
  (☎ 412-472-3346)
  Pittsburgh International Airport

A midweek daily rental with Enterprise for a compact car is $31.95 plus tax and insurance;

if you stay within Pennsylvania, West Virginia and Ohio, the mileage is free.

Bicycle Golden Triangle Bike Rentals (☎ 412-655-0835, goldentrianglebikes@yahoo.com), 416 Woodrift Lane, offers bike rentals for $5/20 per hour/day and two-hour bike tours along riverfront trails starting from Point State Park for $12.

AROUND PITTSBURGH
Raccoon Creek State Park
The 11.4-sq-mile Raccoon Creek State Park (☎ 412-899-2200), 25 miles west of town on Route 18, offers plenty of opportunities for outdoor recreation throughout the year. There's swimming and fishing in, and canoeing on, Raccoon Creek Lake. The park has six short walking trails and some 10 miles of horseback-riding trails. In winter, there's ice fishing, ice skating and, on designated trails and roads, cross-country skiing and snowmobiling.

Wildlife includes deer, rabbits and squirrels, and there are scores of bird species. In the southeast of the park is a 314-acre **wildflower reserve** with around 500 native species; these bloom from April to fall but are seen at their colorful best in the second week of May. The park allows camping mid-April to mid-December (see Pittsburgh's Places to Stay). Take Route 60 north from Pittsburgh to exit 9, then follow the signs.

Harmony
Harmony (population 1054), west of I-79 and about 25 miles north of Pittsburgh on Route 19, is a National Historic Landmark. It was the home of the Harmony Society, a communal group founded in 1804. Possessions were owned collectively, and within a few years, the Harmonists had planted thousands of acres of farms and orchards and had constructed over 100 buildings. In 1807, members made the self-extinguishing decision to adopt celibacy. In 1814, the Harmonists moved to Indiana, then Ohio, before dissolving in 1905. The village of Harmony was purchased by Abraham Zeigler, a Mennonite whose descendants still live here.

Several original buildings remain, including one that is now the **Harmony Museum** (☎ 412-452-7341), 218 Mercer St, where Harmonist and early Mennonite exhibits are displayed. It is open Tuesday to Sunday 1 to 4 pm, and admission is $3.50/1.50 for adults/children. From Pittsburgh, take I-79 north to exit 27, onto Route 19, which leads to the town of Zelienople; Harmony is signed from there.

Moraine State Park
About 10 miles north of Harmony, Moraine State Park (☎ 412-368-8811), east of I-79 and off Routes 8 and 442, is named after the moraine, fragments of rock left by receding glaciers after the last Ice Age. In the more recent past, it was heavily mined and drilled for coal and oil, but the area was so well restored that little evidence of those days remains.

The 5-sq-mile **Lake Arthur** is a 1960s recreation of a glacial lake that existed here thousands of years ago. It was produced by damming the tributaries of Muddy Creek and has formed a series of habitats that now support a wide variety of bird species. Sailing, windsurfing, canoeing and fishing are available, and you can go swimming at a couple of beaches. Along the northern shore is a paved 7-mile bike trail and there is a 6-mile loop trail specifically for mountain bikes; rentals are available on North Shore Drive.

There's no public camping, but there are some cabins to rent, and you can get a list of local private campgrounds from the park office just inside the southern entrance off Route 442.

McConnell's Mill State Park
Near Moraine State Park, west of I-79 off Route 422 and Route 19, the 4-sq-mile McConnell's Mill State Park (☎ 412-368-8091) got its name from the restored 19th-century grist mill that operated here beside Slippery Rock Creek until 1928. From Memorial Day to Labor Day, there are free guided tours of the mill daily 10 am to 6 pm.

The main attraction, however, is the 400-foot-deep **Slippery Rock Gorge**, carved by a receding glacier some 20,000 years ago. Experienced rock climbers hone their skills on **Breakneck Ridge**, while novice climbers practice on **Rim Road**, near the mill. Slippery Creek, which runs through the gorge, is popular for kayaking and white-water canoeing, but there are no rentals in the park. Trout fishing in the creek near Armstrong Bridge is also popular. There are several hiking trails, the longest of which is the scenic 6-mile **Slippery Rock Gorge Trail**.

Camping isn't permitted but the park office keeps a list of private campgrounds that are in the area.

LAUREL HIGHLANDS

The Laurel Highlands (regional population 857,000) is a beautiful, wooded, hilly region that runs, broadly speaking, from east of Uniontown, which is near the West Virginia/Maryland border, northeastward to near Johnstown, 56 miles almost due east of Pittsburgh. The most interesting areas of the highlands are in its lower section, particularly Ohiopyle State Park, with the Youghiogheny River running through it; Frank Lloyd Wright's Fallingwater and Kentuck Knob; Bear Run Nature Reserve; and a 30-mile scenic stretch along Route 40. Route 30 and I-70/76 (Pennsylvania Turnpike) cross the region east-west; north-south Route 381 crosses Route 30 and goes southwest to Route 40, traversing the heart of this region.

The Laurel Highlands Visitors Bureau (☎ 724-238-5661), in the town hall at 120 E Main St in Ligonier, is open weekdays 9 am to 5 pm; you can visit its website at www.laurelhighlands.org. The picturesque town of Ligonier is on Route 30 about 40 miles east of Pittsburgh.

You'll need your own transportation to fully explore the area.

Ohiopyle State Park

This scenic, 29½ sq mile park is bisected by the 1700-foot Youghiogheny River Gorge and surrounds the village of Ohiopyle (oh-HI-oh-pile), a center for white-water rafting and other activities. The park is crowded in summer, especially on week-ends; the best times to visit are May and September.

In the village, just off the main street near the river and bridge, is a Laurel Highlands visitors' center (☎ 724-329-1127), in a former railroad station. It is open May through October but isn't always staffed. The park office (☎ 724-329-8591, ohiopyle.sp@al.dcnr.state.pa.us) is about half a mile south of Ohiopyle, off Route 381.

Across the river and immediately east of Ohiopyle village is **Ferncliff Peninsula**, which is a 4-acre teardrop of land formed by a loop in the river. The area is covered with wildflowers in season.

White-Water Rafting Rafting trips are run on the Youghiogheny River in Pennsylvania and Maryland, as well as on nearby rivers in West Virginia. The Youghiogheny is generally divided into the 'Middle Yough' (9 miles of easy rapids, classes I and II), 'Lower Yough' (7 miles of moderate rapids, classes III and IV) and 'Upper Yough' (11 miles of moderate-to-challenging rapids, classes IV and V). The Middle and Lower Yough are in Ohiopyle State Park, and the Upper Yough is in Maryland.

On weekends, if you rent or bring your own gear, you have to get a launch permit for $2.50 per person from the park office; the allocation of permits is limited, so reserve in advance. You don't need a permit weekdays.

The offices of the rafting companies are in the village on or near the main street (Route 381). Rates are lower during the week and vary according to the season. Laurel Highlands River Tours (☎ 800-472-3846) does guided trips on the Middle Yough for $23 to $32 per person, the Lower Yough for $30 to $59 and the Upper Yough for $110 to $136. All trips include lunch. Other companies offering guided trips are Wilderness Voyageurs (☎ 800-272-4141), Mountain Streams (☎ 800-723-8669) and White Water Adventurers (☎ 800-992-7238).

Ohiopyle Trading Post (☎ 724-329-1450) and Youghiogheny Outfitters (☎ 800-967-2387) rent (but don't sell) tents and other outdoor gear.

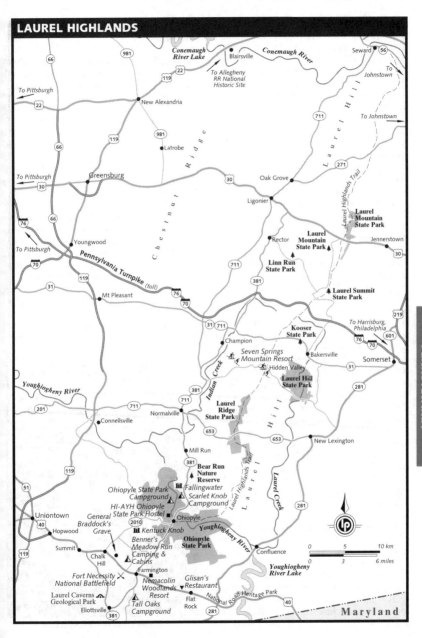

LAUREL HIGHLANDS

PENNSYLVANIA

Other Activities White-water **canoeing** and **kayaking**, for which the aforementioned companies offer courses, are also immensely popular on the river. A one-day clinic with Laurel Highland River Tours costs $70 to $80. Boat rental is $21 per person.

The park has a 28-mile **cycling** trail along the river, an off-road mountain-bike trail and more than 41 miles of **hiking** trails. The southern trailhead of the **Laurel Highlands Trail** (see that section, later) is on King Rd just north of the village. You can hike or drive to overlooks above the river at Baughman Rock, Tharp Knob and the Kentuck Scenic Overlook. Bicycle rental is available around the village; a mountain bike costs $3/12 per hour/day. In winter, there's **cross-country skiing** and 19 miles of trails for **snowmobiling**.

Places to Stay & Eat The *park campground* (☎ 724-329-8591) has 224 sites, with hot showers and toilets for $13 per site (add another $3 for Friday and Saturday nights). Most sites are available early April to December; some are open in winter, but access isn't guaranteed. The privately run *Scarlett Knob Campground* (☎ 724-329-5200), on a hillside adjoining the north of the park, has wooded sites for two people starting at $16.

The 25-bed HI-AYH *Ohiopyle State Park Hostel* (☎ 724-329-4476), north of the village by the river, is a large white house with a kitchen, dining room, living room, day lockers and showers. The hostel is open year-round (but is closed each day between 10 am and 5 pm), and rates are $10/12 for members/nonmembers; family rooms are available. Up past the visitors' center on the right is the *Ohiopyle Guest House* (☎ 800-472-3846) with four rooms for $70/74 for singles/doubles.

Falls Market Inn & Restaurant (☎ 724-329-4973, Main St), near the visitors' center, has basic singles/doubles upstairs for $35/50 (in peak periods) with laundry and shared bath. It's the only place in the village to buy groceries, and its small restaurant (open daily 7 am to 9 pm) has hoagies for $2.25 and other sandwiches starting at $1.70. *Fox's Pizza* (☎ 724-329-1111), in the Ohiopyle-Stewart Community Center, has pizzas beginning at $4.75.

Getting There & Away There's no public transportation to Ohiopyle, though there are buses from Pittsburgh to Uniontown, 20 miles to the west. Route 381 passes through the park, connecting with I-70/76 (Pennsylvania Turnpike) to the north and Route 40 to the south; Route 40 runs northwest to Uniontown and southeast into Maryland.

Fallingwater

Three miles north of Ohiopyle on Route 381, beside the Youghiogheny River, is Fallingwater (☎ 412-329-8501), which was designed by Frank Lloyd Wright. It's an impressive house made of concrete and sandstone quarried on the site, and constructed as a series of levels cantilevered over a stream leading to a waterfall. The house is in the Zen artistic tradition of a viewer being one with the artwork – more precisely here, the resident is one with the waterfall. The home was completed in 1939 as a weekend retreat for Edgar Kaufmann, heir to the Pittsburgh

Complete with running water

department-store fortune. Kaufmann donated it to the Western Pennsylvania Conservancy (see the Ecology & Environment section in the Facts about the Region chapter). Its furnishings and fittings are intact and displayed as Wright designed them.

Tours are given April to mid-November from Tuesday to Sunday 10 am to 4 pm. From mid-November to March, tours are on weekends, weather permitting. The 45-minute tour of the house costs $8/6 for adults/children. Alternatively, you can walk around the grounds, which open at 8:30 am, and view the house from the outside for $3. Children under nine years old can't go on a tour, but supervised care ($2 an hour) is available.

Kentuck Knob

Wright's other architectural masterpiece, Kentuck Knob (☎ 724-329-1901), is southwest of Ohiopyle off Route 2010. He designed the low-level house with honeycomb skylights, built into the side of a rolling hill 2000 feet above sea level, in 1953 (when he was 85 years old) for the Hagan family of Uniontown. Today, Lord and Lady Palumbo of London, UK, own the house. There are hour-long tours of the house Tuesday to Sunday 10 am to 4 pm; they cost $10 ($15 weekends). Children under 12 aren't permitted to tour the house.

Bear Run Nature Reserve

Half a mile north of Fallingwater, on the western slope of Laurel Ridge, the 8-sq-mile Bear Run Nature Reserve, Route 381, Mill Run, PA 15464, is administered by the Western Pennsylvania Conservancy (☎ 724-329-8501). The reserve provides a habitat for field mice, white-tailed deer, bobcats and black bears; more than 130 bird species have been observed here. This reserve also has 20 miles of hiking trails through oak and hemlock forests beside the Youghiogheny River Gorge, and there's cross-country skiing in winter. Rough camping is allowed in six camping areas, but you must bring your own water.

The nearest town for supplies and tent rentals is Ohiopyle.

Skiing

The ski season in the highlands runs roughly from mid-December to early April. There's cross-country skiing in state parks and forests and in Bear Run Nature Reserve (see that section, immediately preceding), and there are several resorts that also offer downhill skiing. Ski packages that include accommodations, rentals, lift tickets and skiing lessons are available at the resorts.

Seven miles east of Route 381, **Seven Springs Mountain Resort** (☎ 814-352-7777, 800-452-2223), Champion, PA 15622, has a vertical drop of 750 feet and lift fees from $32 to $40; for a snow report, call ☎ 800-523-7777.

Hidden Valley (☎ 814-443-2600, 800-443-7544), 4 Craighead Drive, Hidden Valley, PA 15502, south of I-70/76 (Pennsylvania Turnpike) on Route 31, has a vertical drop of 610 feet and lift fees for $25 to $40; they also offer rentals, instructors and child care. For a snow report, call ☎ 800-443-7544.

Laurel Highlands Trail

The 70-mile hiking trail runs northeast from Ohiopyle State Park through Laurel Ridge, Laurel Summit and Laurel Mountain State Parks to the Conemaugh River near Seward on Route 56, northwest of Johnstown. Some parts are rough, particularly in the south, but since most of the trail follows the ridge top, the going is generally easy to moderate. In winter, it's suitable for cross-country skiing and snowshoeing. There are eight camping areas with toilets and water; campsites must be booked in advance, and you're limited to one night's stay.

You can obtain a trail guide from the Sierra Club, Pennsylvania Chapter, PO Box 8241, Pittsburgh, PA 15217. For more information about the trail, contact Laurel Ridge State Park (☎ 724-455-3744), RD 3, PO Box 246, Rockwood, PA 15557.

Along Route 40

Route 40, which cuts through the southwest corner of Pennsylvania, was the first federal public-works project in the nation, and it helped open the Ohio River Valley to settlement by Europeans. Begun in 1811 in

Cumberland, Maryland, it pushed on to Wheeling, West Virginia, in 1818, then on to Vandalia, Illinois, in 1830. The National Road, as it was called, was the primary route from the East Coast to the western frontier until the 1850s. Today's Route 40 follows essentially the same direction and is called the **National Road Heritage Park** (☎ 724-430-1248). Its purpose is to preserve and promote the cultural, historic, natural and recreational resources along the road. There are a number of places to stay, but bring camping gear if you plan to sleep out.

Fort Necessity National Battlefield The battlefield (☎ 724-329-5512), 11 miles southeast of Uniontown, commemorates the battle that began the French & Indian War on July 3, 1754. It contains a replica of the original fort – actually just a one-room log building encircled by a low wooden palisade. The visitors' center has an audiovisual display on French-British rivalry in North America, George Washington and the Battle of Fort Necessity. Guides in period costume

give talks on local history at scheduled times (check with the visitors' center). The battlefield also encompasses the nearby, but unrelated **Mt Washington Tavern**, built in 1828 for travelers on the National Road, and the **grave of General Braddock** (a mile west on Route 40), whose body was moved to the roadside in 1804, though he was killed 50 years earlier.

The battlefield is open daily 8 am to sunset, and the visitors' center and Mt Washington Tavern are open 8:30 am to 6:30 pm (9 am to 5 pm October to May). Admission is $2/free for adults/children.

Laurel Caverns Geological Park Laurel Caverns Geological Park (☎ 724-438-3003, cavern@sgi.net), about 12 miles southeast of Uniontown off Route 381, contains Pennsylvania's largest cave, with 2.8 miles of passageways and a depth of 450 feet. You enter via the Norman E Cales Visitors Center. The inside temperature is a constant 52°F, so bring warm clothing no matter what the outside weather. There's a

The Battle of Fort Necessity

In late 1753, George Washington, then in the colonial army, was sent to present-day Pittsburgh on a diplomatic mission to persuade the French to leave the Ohio River Valley, but was unsuccessful. The following year, the British built a fort where the Allegheny and Monongahela Rivers meet to form the Ohio River (in today's Point State Park), but it was captured by the French, who named it Fort Duquesne.

As the British forces (mostly Virginians) retreated, they encountered a detachment of French troops, killing a number of them in the subsequent skirmish. The British commander was also killed, and Washington, at the age of 22, was made a colonel and was placed in charge of the expedition.

Washington and his troops withdrew to Great Meadows, which he described as a 'charming field for an encounter.' Anticipating French retaliation, he built a 'fort of necessity' and surrounded it with trenches. A combined French and Algonquian force of about 700 attacked Washington's 400 men on July 3, and following a day of fighting, Washington surrendered. After negotiations, he and his men were allowed to walk home, and the French burned the fort.

The battle marked the beginning of the French & Indian War. For more information on the war, see the boxed text 'French & Indian War' in the Adirondack Region chapter.

In 1755, Washington returned to the area as an aide to British General Edward Braddock. In a poorly planned attack, Braddock was killed near Fort Duquesne (and eventually interred next to Route 40), as were over 900 redcoats. The British continued to lose the war until William Pitt the Elder, the British prime minister, dedicated more of Britain's resources to it. By 1760, the British had gained virtual control of North America, a fact later ratified by the 1763 Treaty of Paris.

one-hour guided tour of the lighted, developed section, which takes a short foray into the undeveloped part; these run every 20 minutes. Self-guided explorations are possible, but you'll need to bring a flashlight. The caverns are open May through October daily 9 am to 5 pm; weekends only March, April and November from 9 am to 5 pm. Admission is $9/6 for adults/children and $8 for seniors.

Places to Stay – Camping The secluded *Tall Oaks Campground* (☎ 724-329-4777, *544 Camp Riamo Rd*), a mile south of Farmington on Route 381, has a pool and over 100 sites that are open year-round (though tent camping in winter is a bit rough) for $7.50 per person (no hookups). *Benner's Meadow Run Camping & Cabins* (☎ 724-329-4097, *Nelson Rd*), in Farmington, just 2½ miles north of Route 40, is a huge site with a laundry, playground, store and swimming pool. There are 250 sites for $19 each, plus $4 with full hookup. It's open from mid-April through mid-November and has a program of weekend activities.

Places to Stay – Hotels & Motels *Chalk Hill Motel* (☎ 724-438-4500), on Route 40 about 3 miles east of the junction with Route 381, is behind an outdoor museum of farm equipment, stoves and other items. The motel has small rooms with a double bed and TV and rates at $35/50 a single/double. The nearby *Lodge at Chalk Hill* (☎ 724-438-8880, 800-833-4283), set back from the road, has a few low wooden buildings with balconies overlooking a small lake. The comfortable rooms start at $63/75.

The *Nemacolin Woodlands Resort* (☎ 724-329-8555, 800-422-2736), on Route 40 just east of Farmington, is one of Pennsylvania's top places to stay. It has a choice of accommodations from an English Tudor-style lodge to a French-style chateau. The larger rooms have their own whirlpools, king-size beds and balconies. Rates are $235 to $2000. The resort has a large, well-equipped spa, polo field, ski slopes, two golf courses, a rose garden, nine eateries and a huge wine cellar.

Places to Eat In Chalk Hill, there's a *Subway* sandwich shop, with most subs under $5, and *Zeb's Pizza*, serving small pizzas from $2.25 and hoagies for $3 to $9. Occasional diners and neighborhood places line Route 40. One of the better ones is *Glisan's Restaurant* (☎ 724-329-4636), a mile west of Flat Rock, which has CD jukeboxes at the table. Large lunchtime specials of a roll, pork, sauerkraut and mashed potatoes cost $3.75.

JOHNSTOWN

Johnstown (population 28,100) is 70 miles east of Pittsburgh at the fork of the Little Conemaugh and Stoneycreek Rivers. It's named after Joseph Schantz, a Swiss Mennonite immigrant who changed his surname to Johns and founded the town at the start of the 19th century. The town has been flooded often, but the most devastating flood took place in 1889 – the worst flood in US history.

Information

The visitors' center (☎ 814-536-5107), 111 Market St at Washington St, is open weekdays 8:30 am to 4:30 pm and weekends 11 am to 3 pm; www.visitjohnstownpa.com is its website. The post office, on Franklin St, is open weekdays 8 am to 5 pm and Saturday 8 am to noon. Cambria County Library (☎ 814-536-5131), 238 Main St, is open Monday to Thursday 9 am to 9 pm and Friday to 5 pm.

Johnstown Flood Museum

The museum (☎ 814-539-1889), 304 Washington St, has flood debris, models and 3-D photographs of the damage done by the flood. In the theater on the 2nd floor, an excellent 30-minute documentary called *The Johnstown Flood* describes the cause of the 1889 flood and its aftermath. The building (originally a library) was rebuilt with money given by Andrew Carnegie after the flood, as it was caused a dam that burst at the private club he helped finance. The museum is open November to April daily 10 am to 5 pm; from May to October, it stays open until 7 pm on Friday and Saturday. Admission is $4/2.50 for adults/children and $3.25 for seniors.

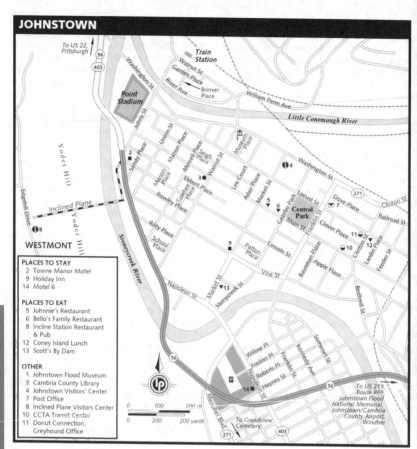

JOHNSTOWN

PLACES TO STAY
2 Towne Manor Motel
9 Holiday Inn
14 Motel 6

PLACES TO EAT
5 Johnnie's Restaurant
6 Bello's Family Restaurant
8 Incline Station Restaurant
   & Pub
12 Coney Island Lunch
13 Scott's By Dam

OTHER
1 Johnstown Flood Museum
3 Cambria County Library
4 Johnstown Visitors' Center
7 Post Office
8 Inclined Plane Visitors Center
10 CCTA Transit Center
11 Donut Connection,
    Greyhound Office

Inclined Plane

The Inclined Plane (☎ 814-536-1816) is a cable car that rises 900 feet up Yoder Hill at a 71.9% gradient from Johns St (Route 56) in central Johnstown to Edgehill Drive in Westmont, a leafy residential suburb. It was opened in 1891 to provide fast passage to higher ground and is the steepest on Earth according to *The Guinness Book of World Records*. The cable car has enough space for two automobiles. At the top is a visitors' center, where you can see the drum turning the cable, and a platform with views of Johnstown and the river valleys.

The Inclined Plane runs every 15 minutes and is open Monday to Thursday 6:30 am to 10 pm, Friday 6:30 am to midnight, Saturday 7:30 am to midnight and Sunday 9 am to 10 pm. The one-way/return fare for a foot passenger is $1.75/3; for a car and driver, it is a flat $5. More information can be obtained at www.inclinedplane.com.

Places to Stay

Camping The nearest campground is *Woodland Park* (☎ 814-472-9857, 220 Campground Rd), near Ebensburg, about 18 miles north of town. It has shaded tent sites for $12 and RV sites for $16; it is open mid-April to mid-October. Its website is www.paonline.com/jwv. Take Route 56 east to Route 219 north; then take Route 22 west for 3¾ miles to Campground Rd and follow it a mile north to the campground.

Hotels & Motels *Towne Manor Motel* (☎ *814-536-8771, 155 John St*) is actually better than its exterior appearance suggests. It has large rooms at $30/35, including continental breakfast and 24-hour coffee, but there are no bathroom towels. The *Holiday Inn* (☎ *814-535-7777, 800-446-4656, 250 Market St*) is the best place in town and has rooms for $79 to $109.

Motel 6 (☎ *814-536-1114, 430 Napoleon St*) is a modern motel that's part of a new shopping complex south of the Stoneycreek River. It has rooms for $50/56.

About 5 miles south of town, at the junction of Routes 56 and 219, is a commercial strip with motels and fast-food outlets.

Places to Eat
Johnstown doesn't have a great deal of choice. Main St has some chain restaurants. Also here is the Italian *Bello's Family Restaurant* (☎ *814-535-3722, 421 Main St*), which makes good pasta starting at $5.25 and hamburgers for $2.75. It's closed weekends. Nearby, *Johnnie's Restaurant*, probably the best of the cheapies, serves baked Virginia ham and veggies for $4.65 and antipasto salad for $3.50.

Coney Island Lunch (☎ *814-535-2885, 127 Clinton St*) must be one of the cheapest places in Pennsylvania to eat. It serves hot dogs ($1.10), hamburgers (from $1.10) and breakfast all day (eg omelette, toast and coffee for $1.25). A sign behind the counter says 'Please no Tips'!

Scott's By Dam (☎ *814-535-1676, 327 Market St*) is a reasonably priced, cozy restaurant/bar that is open for lunch and dinner. Soup costs $1.50, tacos are $3 and steak is $4.

With good views of Johnstown, the *Incline Station Restaurant & Pub*, in the Inclined Plane's visitors' center, has burgers and sandwiches at lunchtime for $3.95 and evening main dishes, such as filet mignon, in the $7.50 to $14 range.

Getting There & Away
Air Johnstown/Cambria County airport (☎ 814-536-0002), 479 Airport Rd, outside town, is served by US Airways. Take Route 56 east to Route 219 north, then take the first exit to the airport.

Bus Greyhound (☎ 814-536-4714) has a desk inside the Donut Connection cafe, 139 Clinton St, at Locust St. The desk is staffed weekdays 10:30 am to 3:30 pm; at other times, you can get tickets from the person behind the food counter. There are two buses daily to Harrisburg ($27, five hours), Philadelphia ($44, eight hours) and Pittsburgh ($13, four hours).

Train From the Amtrak station (☎ 814-535-3313), 47 Walnut St, at Johns St, there are two trains daily to Harrisburg ($45, three hours), Philadelphia ($77, 4¼ hours) and Pittsburgh ($20, 1½ hours). Cheaper fares are available if you book in advance.

Getting Around
Cambria Country Transit Authority (CCTA; ☎ 814-535-5526, ccta@ctcnet.net) provides the local bus service. Timetables are available from the 'Bus Stop' general store (open weekdays 7 am to 5 pm and Saturday 9 am to 2 pm) in the Transit Center, where local buses arrive and depart. Fares are $1 to $1.75.

AROUND JOHNSTOWN
Johnstown Flood National Memorial
A memorial (☎ 814-495-4643) about 10 miles northeast of Johnstown, is at the site of the former South Fork Dam, where the flood began. A short trail leads from the visitors' center to the site of what is left of the dam. The visitors' center has exhibits similar to the Johnstown Flood Museum and a gripping dramatized 35-minute black-and-white film entitled *Black Friday*. This tells the story of the flood using still photos and clips from fictional flood movies. The memorial and the center are open daily

from Memorial Day to Labor Day 9 am to 6 pm; during the rest of the year, they're open until 5 pm. Entry is $2/free for adults/children. See www.nps.gov/jofl for more information.

From Johnstown, take Route 56 east to Route 219 north and follow it to the St Michael/Sidman exit. Take Route 869 east for 1½ miles, then make a left onto Lake Rd at the sign for the memorial. Follow Lake Rd for 1½ miles to the visitors' center.

Windber Coal Heritage Center

The center (☎ 814-467-6680, 800-898-3636), 501 15th St, in Windber, is about 12 miles southeast of Johnstown off Route 56. It's a fascinating museum that documents the area's rich, labor-intensive coal industry

---

The Johnstown Flood

The Johnstown flood of May 31, 1889, killed more people than any other in US history. When the South Fork Dam (about 10 miles northeast of Johnstown up the Little Conemaugh River) broke, a wall of water roiling with debris was sent crashing into town.

The dam was originally built by the state with the intention of creating a water supply to support a canal system. However, by the time the dam was finished in 1853, the canals were obsolete. It was allowed to deteriorate for four years before being bought first by the Pennsylvania Railroad, then by a US congressman from Altoona, who removed the discharge pipes and sold them but did little maintenance. Every spring, people who lived along the river wondered if the dam would hold. The dam actually did break in 1862, but fortunately, the lake water was so low that minimal damage was caused. Then, in 1879, Benjamin Ruff bought the dam and built an exclusive club beside the 2-mile-wide lake.

Ruff enlisted wealthy Pittsburgh industrialists Andrew Carnegie, Henry Clay Frick and Andrew Mellon, among others, to finance the club. It was officially christened the South Fork Fishing & Hunting Club, but locals referred to it as the 'Bosses' Club.' Ruff recruited Edward Pearson, who wasn't an engineer, to rebuild the dam. Pearson refused engineering advice from Cambria Iron officials downstream, who were worried about the dam. He didn't replace the discharge pipes; he renovated the dam with hay, tree stumps and manure, installed only one spillway and, worst of all, lowered the height of the dam. To keep their fish from swimming downstream, club members had a screen installed over the spillway. The screen became clogged with debris.

In the week before May 31, heavy rains saturated the Johnstown area. On May 30, the lake waters rose an inch every 10 minutes. At 3:10 pm on the 31st, the dam broke, and the water swept 14 miles along the floodplain toward Johnstown. It took only 45 minutes for the lake to empty. On the way, the water smashed through several small towns, tore up train tracks and obliterated a 75-foot-high stone viaduct. A railroad engineer raced his train ahead of the flood with the whistle tied down to warn people.

Just under an hour after the dam broke, a 35-foot-high wall of water choked with debris roared into town at 40 mph. People tried to get out of the way, but parts of the town were already under 2 to 7 feet of water from the previous week's rain, and progress was difficult. The water eventually stopped at the seven-arched Pennsylvania Stone Bridge, below the junction of the rivers. Tons of debris – most of the town of Johnstown, trains, logs, machinery, animals and hundreds of people – jammed up against the bridge. Many people were trapped in rolls of barbed wire from the Gautier Wire Works in town.

The debris, covered in oil spilled from railroad tank cars, caught fire (possibly lit by coals from steam engines) and burned for two days, killing 80 people trapped against the bridge in the water.

The official death toll from the flood was 2209. Typhoid killed 40 more. Many of the victims were never identified, and hundreds disappeared never to be found.

and the everyday life of coal miners and their families from the late 19th to the early 20th century. Often dubbed 'underground farmers,' these miners looked for 'black gold.' The museum includes tools from former miners, videos and interactive displays.

It is open Wednesday to Saturday 10 am to 5 pm and Sunday noon to 5 pm from May to October; during the rest of the year, entry is by appointment only. Admission is $3.50/2.50 for adults/children.

Allegheny Railroad Portage

When the Allegheny Railroad Portage opened in 1834, it reduced traveling time between Pittsburgh and Philadelphia from three weeks to four days and helped open up the west. A major feat of engineering, the portage consisted of a series of inclined planes over the Allegheny Mountains. The 2.3-sq-mile national historic site (☎ 814-884-6150), about 25 miles northeast of Johnstown, off Route 22, provides interpretive programs and guided hikes. It is open daily from Memorial Day to Labor Day 9 am to 6 pm, and to 5 pm the rest of the year; entry is $2/free for adults/children.

Blue Knob State Park

This state park (☎ 814-276-3576) is around 20 miles east of Johnstown, on Route 869, east of Route 219. Within the park, you can go downhill skiing at **Blue Knob Ski Resort** (☎ 814-239-5111, 800-458-3403), on the north side of Blue Knob Mountain (3146 feet). Lift fees range from $22 to $39. For a snow report, call ☎ 800-822-3045 in Pennsylvania, or ☎ 800-458-3403 from outside the state; you can also visit www.blueknob.com for more information. This park itself has 8 miles of snowmobiling trails and, in summer, 17 miles of hiking trails, which are also suitable for mountain biking. A primitive campground near the top of the mountain is open mid-April to mid-October.

Northern Pennsylvania

More remote, more forested and less populated than the southern part of the state, northern Pennsylvania stretches along New York state's southern border, from Lake Erie in the west to the Delaware River in the east. In late September and early October, the fall colors of the leaves make the region particularly beautiful.

The Allegheny National Forest is a mighty presence in the west, and the area south of Erie is where the world's commercial oil industry began in the mid-19th century, especially around Oil City, Titusville and Oil Creek. Northern Pennsylvania is dotted with many state forests suitable for outdoor activities and also has its own 'Grand Canyon' – Pine Creek Gorge, near Wellsboro. In Scranton, to the east, lies more evidence of the state's industrial past. The scenic Pocono Mountains, to the south and east of Scranton, are immensely popular for outdoor recreational activities.

I-80 cuts east and west across the state, but farther north, Route 6, also called the Grand Army of the Republic Hwy, is much more scenic and connects with the many attractions of northern Pennsylvania.

ERIE & AROUND

The port town of Erie (population 109,000) lies on the southern shore of Lake Erie, about 127 miles north of Pittsburgh. It's named after the Eriez Indians, who were killed off by the Seneca Indians during the 17th century. The town was laid out in 1795 and played an important role in America's victory in the Battle of Lake Erie during the War of 1812 with Britain. Today, Erie is an important industrial and manufacturing center. North of town, the Presque Isle peninsula helps form a natural, sheltered harbor on the lake. Erie is the shallowest of the Great Lakes and is especially vulnerable to pollution, which by the 1970s had wiped out much of the lake's marine life. A combined community effort reversed this, and the fish population recovered.

Highlights

- Hiking and other outdoor activities in Allegheny National Forest and the Poconos
- The fall colors of the forests
- Pine Creek Gorge – Pennsylvania's 'Grand Canyon'
- Bird-watching in Presque Isle State Park, Erie

Orientation

Peach and State Sts are the main north-south streets. State St leads north to the lake's public dock at Dobbin's Landing. The area around Dobbin's Landing is being redeveloped and includes the Bicentennial Tower and Erie Maritime Museum. Route 5 splits in two as it runs east and west through Erie – as 6th St, it heads through downtown, while as 12th St, it skirts downtown's southern edge.

Information

The Erie Area Convention & Visitor Bureau (☎ 814-454-7191), 109 Boston Store Place, at State and W 7th Sts, is open weekdays 8:30 am to 5 pm; you can find its website at www.eriepa.com.

The main post office, in the Federal Building & US Courthouse (at State St and S Park Row), is open weekdays 9 am to 4 pm. There are a number of banks with ATMs along State St downtown.

Mid-City Laundry, at E 4th and State Sts, is open daily 7 am to 11 pm and charges $1.25 per wash.

Presque Isle State Park

Presque Isle (the name means 'almost an island' in French) is a peninsula one mile across at its widest point and 6½ miles long; it's attached to the mainland just west of Erie. The peninsula is actually getting longer – despite continual loss of sand from the main body (breakwaters have been put in place to slow this process down), there is growth at Gull Point, at the eastern end. The peninsula forms and protects Presque Isle Bay, considered to be one of the finest natural harbors on the Great Lakes. The park office (☎ 814-833-7424) is open weekdays 8 am to 4 pm.

Stull Interpretive Center (☎ 814-833-0351) has information on the habitats and wildlife in the park and is open daily 10 am to 5 pm. You can arrange to go on a free pontoon trip to the lagoons. The 5-sq-mile park contains six distinct ecological zones and around 600 plant species; it is also an important spot for migrating water and wading birds, as well as land birds (including hawks). Over 320 bird species have been recorded here, and many can be seen at **Gull Point Sanctuary**. The **Perry Monument**, near the Gull Point Sanctuary, commemorates Commodore Perry's victory in the Battle of Lake Erie, which took place on September 10, 1813.

The park has a 5.8-mile bike trail, 13 miles of hiking trails and guarded beaches that are great for swimming. Bikes can be rented at Sarah Coyne Plaza, just before the entrance to the park. Presque Isle Canoe & Boat Livery (☎ 814-838-3938) rents canoes for $7 an hour, or $20 for seven hours or more. It's open weekdays 10 am to 5 pm and weekends to 6 pm (hours are extended in the summer).

The strong winds on Presque Isle Bay make it ideal for windsurfing and sailing.

To get to the park, take I-79 or Routes 19 or 5 to 6th St, then head west to Peninsula Drive and turn north. The Presque Isle Express (☎ 814-452-6946) is a water taxi that runs daily across the bay from Dobbin's

---

The Battle of Lake Erie

In the War of 1812, the British gained command of the Great Lakes. Oliver Hazard Perry, a 27-year-old lieutenant, was sent to engage them. The natural bays and inlets on the south side of Presque Isle provided Perry with the raw materials and protection needed for building six of his fleet's ships, including the brigs *Lawrence* and *Niagara*. Many of the seamen in Perry's fleet were black. Ironically, the peninsula presented the final obstacle to the launch of the ships into Lake Erie. A sandbar at the entrance to the bay prevented them from moving through, but the problem was solved by floating the ships across the bar on empty tanks known as 'camels.'

Perry engaged the British fleet at Put-in-Bay, near present-day Sandusky, Ohio, on September 10, 1813. Both fleets had equal firepower, and two hours into the battle, Perry lost his flagship, *Lawrence*, and most of its crew. Transferring into *Niagara*, he sailed into the British fleet, and within an hour, the British flag was lowered in surrender. Perry then penned the immortal words: 'We have met the enemy and they are ours....' The victory opened US supply lines and ended the British threat to the Northwest.

Landing to the peninsula; it costs $3 one way and $5 roundtrip.

Dobbin's Landing

The large, modern **Erie Maritime Museum** (☎ 814-452-2744), 150 East Front St, hosts a number of exhibitions, including the War of 1812, the USS *Wolverine* (the US Navy's first iron-hulled ship), life aboard a wooden warship and the maritime history of northwestern Pennsylvania. There's also a video about the US Brig *Niagara*, Pennsylvania's official flagship. The current ship is a replica of the *Niagara*, which took part in the Battle of Lake Erie. When it's not away sailing, it docks behind the museum, where visitors can view it. The museum is open Monday to Saturday 9 am to 5 pm and Sunday noon to

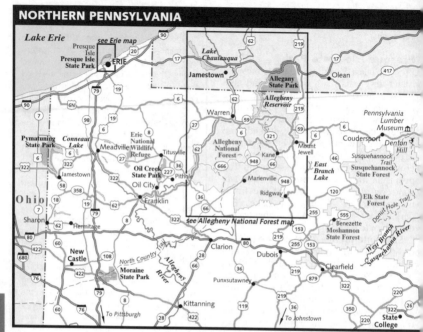

NORTHERN PENNSYLVANIA

5 pm. If the *Niagara* is out of port, admission is $4/2 for adults/children, or $3.50 for seniors. If the *Niagara* is in port, admission is $6/3, or $5 for seniors.

On the pier is the 187-foot **Bicentennial Tower** (☎ 814-455-6055), built in 1995 to commemorate Erie's 200th birthday. You can take an elevator to the top ($2/1 for adults/children, Tuesday free), from which there are great views of the bay and town, especially at sunset. At the bottom, you can buy food to feed the ducks and birds. In April, the tower is open daily 10 am to 6 pm; in May and from after Labor Day to the end of September, it's open 10 am to 8 pm; from June to Labor Day, it is open 9:30 am to 10 pm. You can also fish from the pier.

Discovery Square

Discovery Square comprises three museums, each with its own entry and business hours.

Housed in the 1839 Greek Revival-style Old Custom House, **Erie Art Museum** (☎ 814-459-5477), 411 State St, has temporary exhibitions, as well as permanent displays, of American, European and Asian paintings, drawings and sculptures. On permanent display is a scene depicting local people (looking rather like characters from the Muppets) in a former Erie diner. The museum is open Tuesday to Saturday 11 am to 5 pm and Sunday 1 to 5 pm. Admission is $2/50¢ for adults/children and $1 for seniors, but it's free on Wednesday.

Nearby, **Erie History Center** (☎ 814-454-1813), 419 State St, displays changing exhibitions and has an extensive library on local history, including many maps and photographs. A donation is requested, and it is open Tuesday to Saturday 9 am to 5 pm.

The **Experience Children's Museum** (☎ 814-453-3743), 420 French St, is a hands-on museum with all sorts of activities and displays aimed at making learning fun. It's open Wednesday to Saturday 10 am to 4 pm

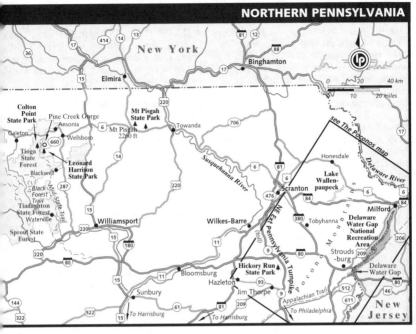

NORTHERN PENNSYLVANIA

(plus Tuesday in July and August) and Sunday 1 to 4 pm. Entry is a flat $3.50.

Wineries

The Lake Erie shoreline stretching from Pennsylvania into New York and Ohio is excellent for growing wine. The best place to visit in this region is about 12 miles east of Erie, where you'll find a number of vineyards clustered around the small town of **North East**. For more information, contact the North East Area Chamber of Commerce (☎ 814-725-4262), 21 South Lake St.

If you're especially interested in wine, you could continue driving east to New York state's Finger Lakes region, about a 2½-hour drive on Route 17. See the Finger Lakes Region chapter for more information.

Organized Tours

From Dobbin's Landing, the steamer *Lady Kate* (☎ 814-836-0201) provides a 14-mile,

90-minute narrated cruise of Lake Erie for $13/9 for adults/children. The ship operates four times daily from mid-June to Labor Day; from May to mid-June and from Labor Day to the end of October, it operates on weekends only. From November to the end of April, the operation is closed.

Places to Stay

Sara Coyne Campground (☎ 814-833-4560, 50 Peninsula Drive), just outside Presque Isle State Park, has a laundry, showers and tent sites for $15; RV sites cost $20. The sites are close together, but the beach is nearby.

Super 8 Downtown Inn (☎ 814-456-6251, 205 W 10th St), at Sassafras St, has a swimming pool and rooms for $45/50 for a single/double. Close by, the more upmarket *Avalon Hotel* (☎ 814-459-2220, 16 West 10th St) provides large, clean rooms for $69/79.

There are many motels west of town around Peninsula Drive (Route 832) near the intersections of Route 5 (West 12th St) and Alternative Route 5 (West 8th St/West Lake Rd) – but they tend to be a bit pricey because of their proximity to Presque Isle. *Lake Erie Lodge (☎ 814-833-9855, 1015 Peninsula Drive)* has a pool and singles/doubles for $73/84, which includes a continental breakfast. More motels can be found south of town on Peach St (Route 19).

Places to Eat

Chain restaurants and fast-food outlets line Peach St south of 26th St and around Peninsula Drive between the intersections of Route 5 and Alternative Route 5.

In town, the friendly *George's Restaurant (☎ 814-455-0860)*, near the intersection of State and 26th Sts, is a popular diner serving omelettes starting at $3.65 and French toast for $3.75. At Dobbin's Landing, there are two mid-range restaurants, *Smugglers' Inn (☎ 814-459-4273)* and *The Waterfront (☎ 814-459-0606)*, both serving seafood, pasta and steaks and both complete with views of Presque Isle Bay. Seafood main dishes cost $15 to $25, and the steaks cost $14 to $19.

Entertainment

Rum Runners, a bar at Dobbin's Landing about 200 yards east of Smugglers' Inn, looks out over Presque Isle Bay. *Sullivan's*, at French and E 3rd Sts, is an old Irish-style pub serving food and featuring music on the weekends.

Getting There & Away

Erie International Airport (☎ 814-833-4258) is southwest of town, at 4411 W 12th St. It's served by Northwest (☎ 814-833-3030), US Airways (☎ 814-838-3552) and Continental Express (☎ 814-835-3895).

Greyhound buses leave from the Transportation Center (☎ 814-864-5949), 5759 Peach St, about 3 miles south of downtown. It is open daily 8:30 am to 10:30 pm. There are four buses daily to Pittsburgh ($17 one way, 2¼ hours).

If you're driving from Pittsburgh, I-79 takes you directly to Erie. I-90 heads west to Ohio and east to New York along the lakeshore.

Getting Around

Erie Metro Transit Authority (EMTA; ☎ 814-459-4287), 127 E 14th St, operates the local bus service. The one-way fare is $1.10. Some routes don't operate on Sunday or holidays. For a taxi, call Erie Yellow Cab (☎ 814-455-4441), 1619 State St.

PYMATUNING STATE PARK

Pymatuning State Park (☎ 412-932-3141) is about 45 miles southwest of Erie and straddles the Ohio border. It's accessible on Routes 6 or 322 west of I-79. The park office is just inside the Jamestown entrance.

The park contains the 21½-sq-mile Pymatuning Reservoir – the largest artificial lake in the state – built to control the flow of the Beaver and Shenango Rivers and to protect the waters entering the Pymatuning Swamp. The land around the reservoir provides habitat for a wide variety of bird species, and in the fall, the **Pymatuning Wildlife Management Area** is home to 20,000 Canada geese. The visitors' center (☎ 814-683-5545) on **Ford Island**, in the park's north, has exhibits on local flora and fauna.

There are four protected swimming beaches (open Memorial Day to Labor Day); fishing is popular on the lake, and in winter, there's cross-country skiing. The park has three camping areas with a total of over 650 sites; each costs $11 or $13. Food and other supplies can be found in Jamestown or around Conneaut Lake.

ERIE NATIONAL WILDLIFE REFUGE

In spite of its name, this refuge begins about 40 miles southeast of Erie. It's made up of two parts: the 5206-acre **Sugar Lake** division lies between Titusville and Meadville, while the 3571-acre **Seneca** division is 10 miles to the north. The visitors' center (☎ 814-789-3585), 11296 Wood Duck Lane, Guys Mills, PA 16327, is in the Sugar Lake division, just off Route 198. It is open weekdays 8 am to 4:30 pm.

The refuge provides diverse habitats for wildlife. Migratory birds, such as Canada geese and wood duck, nest here, as do raptors such as the red-tailed hawk, bald

ERIE

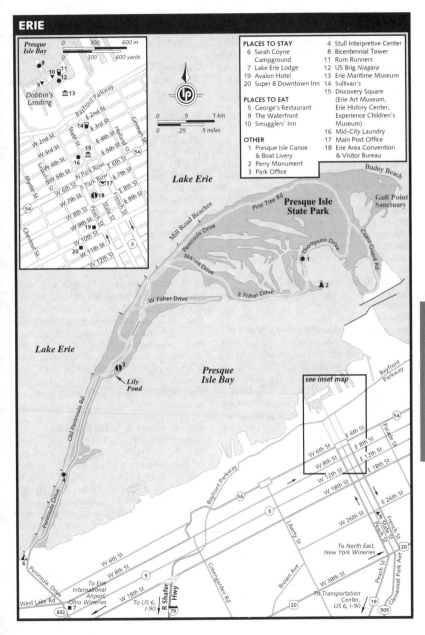

Presque Isle Bay

0   300   600 m
0   300   600 yards

Dobbin's Landing

PLACES TO STAY
6 Sarah Coyne Campground
7 Lake Erie Lodge
19 Avalon Hotel
20 Super 8 Downtown Inn

PLACES TO EAT
5 George's Restaurant
9 The Waterfront
10 Smugglers' Inn

OTHER
1 Presque Isle Canoe & Boat Livery
2 Perry Monument
3 Park Office

4 Stull Interpretive Center
8 Bicentennial Tower
11 Rum Runners
12 US Brig *Niagara*
13 Erie Maritime Museum
14 Sullivan's
15 Discovery Square (Erie Art Museum, Erie History Center, Experience Children's Museum)
16 Mid-City Laundry
17 Main Post Office
18 Erie Area Convention & Visitor Bureau

Lake Erie

Pine Tree Rd

Presque Isle State Park

Budny Beach

Gull Point Sanctuary

Mill Road Beaches

Peninsula Drive

Marina Drive

W Fisher Drive   E Fisher Drive

Thompson Drive

Coast Guard Rd

Lake Erie

Lily Pond

Presque Isle Bay

see inset map

Bayfront Parkway

Old Peninsula Rd

Peninsula Drive

Bayfront Parkway

W 6th St   E 6th St
W 8th St   E 8th St
             E 12th St
W 12th St
W 18th St   E 18th St
             E 26th St
W 26th St

Liberty St

Parade St

State St

French St

Peach St

To North East, New York Wineries

To Erie International Airport, Ohio Wineries

West Lake Rd

W 6th St
W 8th St

W 18th St

To US 6, I-90

R Shafer Hwy

Greengarden Rd

Brown Ave

W 38th St

To Transportation Center, US 6, I-90

Glenwood Park Ave

PENNSYLVANIA

eagle, osprey and kestrel. Of the 40-odd species of mammals, the most common are beaver, muskrat, white-tailed deer and woodchuck. There are several walking trails from which you can view the wildlife, and you can fish for bass, perch or trout in the lakes and rivers.

Access to Sugar Lake is via Routes 27, 173 and 198; access to Seneca is off Route 408.

TITUSVILLE

Titusville (population 6450), about 42 miles southeast of Erie on the banks of Oil Creek, was founded in 1796 and was named after Jonathan Titus, one of the early surveyors of the area. Lumber was the main industry until Edwin Drake drilled the world's first oil well. It's a small working town and is developing its tourism around oil history. It's worth a stop on the way through to see the world's first commercial oil well.

Drake Well Memorial Park

The memorial park (☎ 814-827-2797) commemorates the spot where oil was first drilled by Edwin Drake of the Seneca Oil Company in August 1859. Through artifacts, documents and photographs, the museum there examines the development of the oil industry and its social and economic impact. The museum also shows a 27-minute film (starring Vincent Price as Edwin Drake) about the construction of the well. In the park, there's a replica of the original derrick and steam-driven drill, as well as some old oil pumps and a couple of carriages.

The park is open Monday to Saturday 9 am to 5 pm and Sunday 10 am to 5 pm. Admission is $4/2 for adults/children; seniors pay $3.50, and families pay $10. To get there, take Route 8 southeast from Titusville for 1¼ miles, then go east on Bloss St to the park just past the bridge.

Places to Stay & Eat

Oil Creek Campground (☎ 814-827-1023) is just outside Oil Creek State Park and has large sites for two people at $15, or $19 with full hookup. The turnoff for the campground is 4 miles south of Titusville off Route 8; it's then another 1½ miles east

along Turkey Farm Rd. In town, there are fast-food places on Franklin St, Central Ave and W Main St.

Getting There & Away

Titusville is at the intersection of Routes 8 and 27, about 15 miles north of Oil City. It is about a 40-minute drive east of I-79 or about 40 minutes north of I-80.

OIL CITY & AROUND

The aptly named Oil City (population 12,000), straddling the Allegheny River and its tributary Oil Creek, was the center of the 19th-century oil industry in the region. Oil was shipped along the creek to Oil City, from where it was transported by steamboat or barge to Pittsburgh. Oil magnate John D Rockefeller raised his first million dollars here. (See the boxed text 'The Rockefeller Legacy' in the New York City chapter.)

The countryside is littered with remnants from that time, but the streams and much of the wilderness of the Allegheny foothills have been allowed to recover from the early industrial onslaught. Oil City, a fairly unattractive industrial town, is still involved in the refining of oil and the manufacture of related machinery. Oil City is also the headquarters of the Quaker State Corporation – one of the first companies to produce motor oil.

Orientation & Information

Seneca and Center Sts form the downtown core, which is bounded to the south by the Allegheny River and to the west and north by Oil Creek. South of the Allegheny River, over the State St Bridge, is another small commercial center. Route 8 becomes Seneca St (one way, southbound) and Elm St (one way, northbound) in town.

The visitors' center (☎ 814-676-1733), 7 Elm St, on the north side of the river and in an old railroad station, is run by the local historical society. From June to October, it is open weekdays 9 am to 5 pm; during the rest of the year, it is open weekdays 9 am to 4 pm. The post office, on Seneca St opposite the Venango Museum, is open weekdays 8:30 am to 1 pm and 2 to 4 pm.

With the exception of the Venango Museum, the things to see are outside Oil City proper.

The World's First Oil Well

When we think of oil, we usually think of the Middle East, Texas or the North Sea, but today's mammoth oil industry had its humble beginnings back in the mid-19th century in Titusville, Pennsylvania.

For thousands of years, Native Americans had petroleum in medicine and paint. They collected it from springs or along the tops of creeks, where it appeared naturally. In the 19th century, European Americans used it in its natural, foul-smelling state as a medicine, to grease wagon wheels and to burn for light. By the early 1850s, whale oil was becoming scarce, and people began refining petroleum into kerosene.

In 1859, the Seneca Oil Company was leasing a natural-oil spring in the Oil Creek Valley near Titusville; wanting to increase production, it sent Edwin Drake to accomplish the task. He first dug for oil, then he decided to drill, so he recruited William ('Uncle Billy') Smith, a salt-well driller from near Pittsburgh, to build the well.

Smith built a derrick, engine house and steam engine. Drilling began in June, but was unsuccessful until Drake hit on the idea of driving a cast-iron pipe down into the rock first, then drilling inside it. On August 26, the drill bit hit a cavity; the drilling material was pulled out and work was stopped for the day. The next morning, when Uncle Billy went to check the well, he found it full of oil. After a pump was attached, the well yielded 20 barrels a day – double that of any other production method at the time.

Oil speculators soon followed Drake, and many wells were dug in the area along Oil Creek at places such as Petroleum Center and Pithole. By 1862, the region was producing thousands of barrels of oil daily, driving the price of oil so low that Drake's well proved unprofitable and had to be shut down.

Venango Museum

Venango Museum (☎ 814-676-2007), 270 Seneca St, in a former post-office building, is a small museum with changing exhibits on the region, its people and the oil and other industries. The museum is open Tuesday to Saturday 10 am to 4 pm and Sunday 1 to 4 pm. Admission is $2/1 for adults/children.

McClintock Well

The McClintock Well, the oldest continuously operating oil well in the US (it has been pumping since August 1861) is an interesting piece of history, but not much to look at.

As you head north out of town on Route 8, turn left onto Waitz Rd at the derelict blue building marked 'bmi' just before the bridge. Walk about 80 yards west between two fences and continue across some railroad tracks; look to your right and you'll see the small well, which is quietly pumping oil into green Quaker State Corporation tanks.

Oil Creek & Titusville Railroad

This restored train runs along a 13½-mile scenic rail line through Oil Creek Valley from Perry St station in Titusville to Rynd Farm station, 4 miles north of Oil City just off Route 8. On the way, it stops at Drake Well Museum and at Petroleum Center in Oil Creek State Park (a flag stop only). The train operates a working postal service and runs mid-June to the end of October, Wednesday to Sunday. October is the busiest period because of the fall colors, so you need to book ahead. The fare on the 2½-hour journey is $10/6 for adults/children, and seniors pay $9. For more information, contact Oil Creek & Titusville Railroad (☎ 814-676-1733), 7 Elm St, Oil City, PA 16301; also, you can visit the website at http://octrr.clarion.edu.

Oil Creek State Park

Entry to the 11-sq-mile park is just north of Rynd Farm station, over the bridge. The park office (☎ 814-676-5915) is at Petroleum Center, an oil-industry hub during the 1860s boom, although today with the area's restored natural beauty, you wouldn't know it.

The park has over 52 miles of hiking trails, including the 32-mile **Oil Creek Hiking Trail**, which follows the Oil Creek Valley from Drakes Well in the north to Rynd Farm in the south. There's also a 9.5-mile paved **cycling trail**, and you can rent bikes form Oil Creek Outfitters (☎ 814-677-4684) in Petroleum Center for $5 for the first hour and $2.50 for each succeeding hour. The trails provide access to remote parts of the park that are good for **bird-watching**. The creek also offers conditions for beginner-level **canoeing**, but the season only runs from March to June. In winter, there's **cross-country skiing**.

Pithole

There isn't much left of Pithole – a ghost town off Route 227 and 6 miles east of Oil Creek State Park – just cellar holes on a hillside. The discovery of oil in January 1865 attracted many people, and the town was laid out the following May. By September, Pithole had 15,000 people, 57 hotels, a daily paper and the third-busiest post office in the state. When the oil ran out, so did the people. By the following year, the population had rapidly reduced to 2000, and in 1870, it was down to only 281. Since then, nature has reclaimed most of the land.

The visitors' center (☎ 814-827-2797) has a small exhibition on Pithole's history. It is open Wednesday noon to 5 pm and Thursday to Sunday 10 am to 5 pm; entry is $2.50/50¢ for adults/children; seniors pay $2, and families pay $5.50.

Crude Oil

Crude oil is found under the western slopes of the Appalachian Mountains in western Pennsylvania, southwestern New York, eastern Ohio and West Virginia. It's renowned for its paraffin base (from the Latin *para finum* – 'little affinity' – meaning it has little affinity for chemical change; ie, it is very stable). It also has high natural lubricity and viscosity and is relatively free of impurities such as sulfur, tar or asphalt.

Places to Stay

You can camp at *Oil Creek Campground*; see Titusville, earlier. In town, there are few accommodations. The *Holiday Inn* (☎ 814-677-1221, 1 Seneca St), with rooms overlooking the Allegheny River, offers rates of $74/79.

Places to Eat

There are fast-food places along Seneca St. The busy *Hoss's Steak & Sea House* (☎ 814-677-3002, 520 N Seneca St), north of the center, has a lunchtime all-you-can-eat soup-and-salad bar for $4.99.

The nicest place for a coffee and a snack is *Monarch Park Cafe*, south over the bridge and across from the library. It has a good choice of coffees, and its filled bagels are priced starting at $3.25. Around the corner, *Yuen's Chinese Restaurant* (☎ 814-677-0818, 11 E 1st St) is mostly a take-out place, but you can eat at the tables; it has reasonable chow mein for $5.50 and seafood for $5 to $9. *Kate's*, in the Holiday Inn, has a bar and serves salads for $5.50 and burgers with fries for $3.95.

Getting There & Away

Buses leave from outside McNerneny's store (☎ 814-677-1307), 245 Seneca St; you can purchase tickets inside. There's a daily bus to Pittsburgh ($30 one way, 5¼ hours) at 5:15 pm. Route 62 heads west to I-79; Route 8 runs south to I-80.

Getting Around

Venango Bus Public Transport (☎ 814-677-0818) operates the local bus service Monday to Saturday. Schedules are available from the visitors' center. Fares within Oil City and to the nearby towns of Franklin and Cranberry are $1.

HERMITAGE & SHARON

Near the Ohio border, Hermitage (population 15,300) and its neighbor town of Sharon (population 17,500) are home to a collection of 'world's largests.' There's no reason to stay here, but if you're in the area, it might be worth a quick look. Hermitage has no real center other than the ugly commercial

PENNSYLVANIA

strip along Route 62. However, Sharon, on the Shenango River, is much older, and there are some fine old red-brick buildings on State St, the main street downtown. To get there from I-80, take Route 18 north to Sharon; from I-79, Route 62 runs west to Hermitage and Sharon.

Information

The stylish Mercer County Visitors Center (☎ 800-637-2370), 50 N Water Ave, just off State St in downtown Sharon, is open weekdays 9 am to 5 pm and Saturday 9:30 am to 5 pm.

Things to See

In Hermitage is the **Avenue of 444 Flags**. It's the 'world's largest display of American flags,' and it lines the entrance road to Hillcrest Memorial Park. There's one flag for every day that the 52 US citizens from the US Embassy in Iran were held hostage in 1979–81, plus there are other American flags dedicated to people who served the community or country.

Next door, **Kraynak's Santa's Christmasland** (☎ 724-347-4511) is said to be the largest Christmas store in the world. True or not, it does have a huge collection of artificial trees, trains, stuffed animals, toys, candy and animated figures. It is open Monday to Saturday 9 am to 5 pm.

In Sharon, **Daffin's Candies** (☎ 724-342-2892), 496 E State St (Route 62), claims to be the 'world's largest candy store,' but it doesn't seem *that* large. At the back, in a small room called the Chocolate Kingdom, are some large chocolate animals on permanent display. Daffin's is open Monday to Saturday 9 am to 9 pm and Sunday 11 am to 5 pm. Also in Sharon, **Reyers** (☎ 724-981-2200) claims to be the 'world's largest shoe store.' The store is on W State St, and it has a factory outlet on E State St.

Places to Stay & Eat

Route 62 has many motels. In Hermitage, the ***Royal Motel*** (☎ *724-347-5546, 301 S Hermitage Rd)*, near the junction of Routes 18 and 62, has rooms with TV and phone for $58.

Punxsutawney Phil

Punxsutawney, a town about 90 miles northwest of Pittsburgh, on Route 36 near Route 119, is home to the famous 'weather forecaster' Punxsutawney Phil, a groundhog. Groundhog is another name for woodchuck, which is a type of marmot.

According to legend, if Phil casts a shadow on Groundhog Day (February 2), winter will last six more weeks. The elaborate ceremony takes place at Gobbler's Knob, a hill just outside town, but for most of the year Phil lives in the children's library in Mahoning East Civic Center in town. In June, there's also the Groundhog Festival, when Phil is given a 'magic potion' to ensure that he lives a long time. For information on the ceremony and festival, call

☎ 800-752-7445 or 814-938-7700, or visit www.punxsutawneyphil.com.

Punxsutawney Phil was made even more famous by the 1993 film *Groundhog Day*, starring Andie MacDowell and Bill Murray.

In Sharon, *Quaker Steak & Lube* (☎ 724-981-7221, 110 Connelly Blvd), by the river, is a former gas station converted into a restaurant that sells chicken wings in a variety of sauces, ranging from mild to atomic, starting at $4.99. It also operates the nearby *Hot Rod Cafe*, a bar and cafe selling similar food and displaying automobile and motorcycling memorabilia.

ALLEGHENY NATIONAL FOREST & AROUND

When the 797-sq-mile Allegheny National Forest (ANF) was first proclaimed by President Coolidge in 1923, people called it the 'Allegheny Brushpatch' because it had been stripped of most its timber in the late 19th and early 20th century. Thousands of acres of old-growth forests had been cut for the shipbuilding and construction industries, and much of the land was polluted by oil exploration and iron smelting. The local wildlife population, as a result, was drastically reduced.

In the Great Depression of the 1930s, thousands of men were given work planting trees and combating the effects of pollution. The timber has since grown back, and today, the ANF consists mostly of hardwoods such as hemlock, maple, white ash, yellow poplar and black cherry. Under the management of the US Forest Service (USFS), parts of the ANF continue to be harvested, and Allegheny black cherry is one of the most valuable woods in the world.

The ANF is once again full of wildlife, amongst which you'll find black bear, elk, deer, raccoon, fox, beaver, muskrat, turkey and grouse. Black bears aren't usually harmful unless you come between a mother and her cubs; generally, they can be scared off by yelling, waving and clapping. Don't bring food to your tent; bears have a keen sense of smell – keep it in a car or out of bear reach by hanging it from a line 10 feet above the ground between two trees.

The US Army Corps of Engineers administers a series of lakes and dams in the region as part of a system of flood-control projects in the Allegheny and upper Ohio River Valleys. The ANF also encompasses several state parks.

Orientation

The ANF, running along New York's southern border, sits on the rugged northwestern section of the Allegheny Plateau; the elevation of much of the area covered by the forest is between 1000 feet and 2300 feet.

The major landmark, the Allegheny Reservoir to the north, crosses the state border into New York. The southern end of the reservoir forks to form two bodies of water: to the east, Kinzua Bay stretches for 8 miles into the forest; to the west, the Allegheny River flows west, then south, marking the western boundary of the ANF. The Clarion River forms much of the forest's southern border.

Warren, west of the reservoir, is the main town in the region and is the best place to pick up supplies. There's a large supermarket in town, and if people want a taste of civilization after (or before) roughing it in the forest, it has some restaurants and motels.

Kane, southeast of Kinzua Bay, is a major town to the east. The other principal settlements are Ridgway, in the southeastern corner of the ANF; Marienville, which is south-central; and Tionesta, in the southwest. At the forest's center is the village of Sheffield.

Route 6 crosses the ANF from Warren through Sheffield then runs southeast to Kane. Route 62 follows the ANF's western border and the Allegheny River south of Route 6. Route 66 runs southwest from Kane to Marienville and onto Cook Forest State Park.

Information

In Warren, the USFS (☎ 814-723-5150), 222 Liberty St, is open weekdays 8 am to 4:30 pm. The friendly, helpful staff provide lots of information on activities and camping in the ANF; they sell topographical maps of the region too. The USFS has an office at Kinzua Point Information Center (☎ 814-726-1290), on Route 59 at the fork of the Allegheny Reservoir, 9 miles east of Warren. It's open Memorial Day to Labor Day,

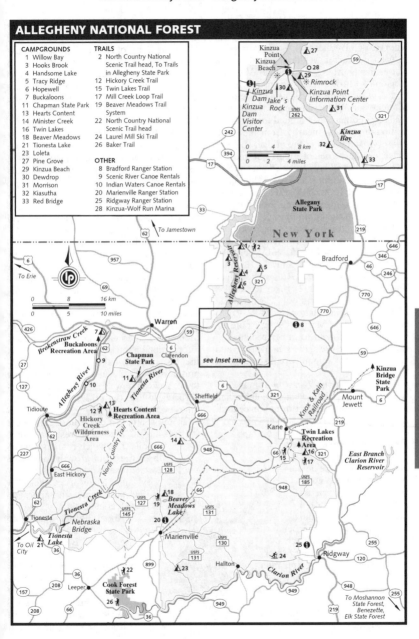

ALLEGHENY NATIONAL FOREST

CAMPGROUNDS
1 Willow Bay
3 Hooks Brook
4 Handsome Lake
5 Tracy Ridge
6 Hopewell
7 Buckaloons
11 Chapman State Park
13 Hearts Content
14 Minister Creek
16 Twin Lakes
18 Beaver Meadows
21 Tionesta Lake
23 Loleta
27 Pine Grove
29 Kinzua Beach
30 Dewdrop
31 Morrison
32 Kiasutha
33 Red Bridge

TRAILS
2 North Country National
  Scenic Trail head, To Trails
  in Allegheny State Park
12 Hickory Creek Trail
15 Twin Lakes Trail
17 Mill Creek Loop Trail
19 Beaver Meadows Trail
  System
22 North Country National
  Scenic Trail head
24 Laurel Mill Ski Trail
26 Baker Trail

OTHER
8 Bradford Ranger Station
9 Scenic River Canoe Rentals
10 Indian Waters Canoe Rentals
20 Marienville Ranger Station
25 Ridgway Ranger Station
28 Kinzua-Wolf Run Marina

PENNSYLVANIA

Sunday, Monday, Tuesday and Thursday 10 am to 5 pm, and Friday and Saturday to 6 pm (closed Wednesday).

Also in Warren is the regional tourist office, the Northern Alleghenies Vacation Region (☎ 814-726-1222), downstairs at 315 2nd Ave at Pennsylvania Ave. It is open Monday and Wednesday to Friday 9 am to 4:30 pm; at other times, limited tourist information is available nearby from the Kwik Fill service station near the bridge. The post office, on the corner of Liberty St and 3rd Ave, is open weekdays 9 am to 5 pm and Saturday 9 am to 2 pm. The O-So White Coin Laundry is at Thorne's Market Place; head east from downtown along Pennsylvania Ave, then turn right onto Market St.

The USFS also has three ranger stations where you can get information. Bradford Ranger Station (☎ 814-362-4613) is at the junction of Routes 321 and 59, 12 miles southwest of Bradford. Ridgway Ranger Station (☎ 814-776-6172) is on Route 948 about 2 miles north of town, while Marienville Ranger Station (☎ 814-927-6628) is 2 miles north of Marienville on Route 66. Camping is the main form of accommodations, but there are motels in Warren and Kane. If you're camping, bring some insect repellent.

Allegheny National Forest, by Tom Dwyer, is an overall guide to what's available and can be bought from the information centers, including the USFS office in Warren.

Parks & Nature Areas

The **Allegheny Reservoir** is an 18¾-sq-mile lake held back by the **Kinzua Dam** (built in 1966), which together form part of a project to control flooding in the Allegheny and Upper Ohio River Valleys. Much of the land that is now underwater was granted to Chief Cornplanter (son of a Seneca woman and a Dutchman) in 1791. His descendants were removed from the land and sent to live in New York in the 19th century.

Below the dam, the Kinzua Dam Visitor Center (☎ 814-726-0661), operated by the US Army Corps of Engineers, is open weekdays noon to 4 pm and weekends 10 am to 5 pm; October through March, it only is open weekends 10 am to 4 pm. There are great views from **Jake's Rock**, near the Kinzua Dam, and at **Rimrock**, across Kinzua Bay on Route 59.

The 13½-sq-mile **Hickory Creek** area, east of Tidioute, is a designated 'wilderness' and can be reached from the **Hearts Content Recreation Area**, which itself contains stands of old-growth hemlock and white-pine forest. The only other wilderness consists of seven islands on the Allegheny River between Buckaloons Recreation Area and Tionesta; they are collectively called the **Allegheny Islands Wilderness**.

The **Tionesta Lake** area is in the southwest corner of the ANF, about 15 miles northeast of Oil City. The natural lake, fed by the Allegheny River and Tionesta Creek, is surrounded by 2000 acres of old-growth forest. The visitors' center (☎ 814-755-3524) in Tionesta is open daily 10 am to 4 pm from Memorial Day to early December and has information on the lake and hiking trails. At the eastern end of the lake, near the Nebraska Bridge, is a usually submerged **ghost town**. You can only see it when the water is particularly low; the bridge itself is sometimes even underwater.

To the south, in **Cook Forest State Park** (☎ 814-744-8407), is the Forest Cathedral Natural Area, which contains one of the largest old-growth forests of white pine and hemlock in Pennsylvania. Many trees exceed 3 feet in diameter and approach 200 feet in height.

About 30 miles southeast of the ANF and east of the town of Benezette, off Route 555 (ask for directions in Ridgway), is **Elk State Forest** (☎ 814-834-3723). Here, roam over 300 wild wapiti (elk), which were introduced from the west (the eastern wapiti became extinct in the 19th century). The best time to see them is in the early morning or late afternoon.

Hiking & Backpacking

There are over 600 miles of hiking trails throughout the ANF, and you can camp along most of them (see Camping, later in this section). The USFS office in Warren and the ranger stations (see Information, earlier in this section) have trail maps, topographical maps and information on conditions. For guidebooks, check out *Fifty Hikes in Western Pennsylvania*, by Tom Thwaites.

The 86.8-mile section of the **North Country National Scenic Trail** is the longest in the ANF. To the south, it connects with Baker Trail in Cook Forest, and to the north to trails in Allegheny State Park in New York. The trail enters the ANF west of Marienville and runs north to the New York border. For a trail guide, contact the North Country Trail Association (☎ 616-454-5506, NCTAssoc@AOL.com), 49 Monroe Center, NW, suite 200B, Grand Rapids, MI 49503, or visit its website (www.northcountrytrail.org).

Other good trails include the 16.7-mile **Mill Creek Loop Trail**, just south of the Twin Lakes recreation area, near Kane; the 14.7-mile **Twin Lakes Trail**, between the Twin Lakes recreation area and the North Country National Scenic Trail; the **Beaver Meadows Trail System**, near the Beaver Meadows recreation area, which is north of Marienville (it's a 7.1-mile system of five interconnecting trails); and the 11.6-mile **Hickory Creek Trail**, which starts near Hearts Content campground and loops through the wilderness between Middle Hickory and East Hickory Creeks.

Canoeing

April through October, the reservoirs, lakes, rivers and creeks of the ANF offer opportunities for novice and experienced paddlers. There are plenty of boat-launching sites, campgrounds and outfitters renting canoes and equipment.

To give you an idea of cost, the Kinzua-Wolf Run Marina rents canoes for $6/22 per hour/day. Some outfitters offer two- to three-day guided trips on the Allegheny River that include camping. Outback Adventures offers two-day guided trips for $45 to $50, which includes canoe rental, paddles and life jackets. Outfitters include:

Allegheny Outfitters
   (☎ 814-723-1203), Market St Plaza, Warren

Eagle Rock Motel & Campground
   (☎ 814-755-4444), 633 Elm St, Tionesta

Indian Waters
   (☎ 814-484-3252), Route 62, south of Warren

Kinzua-Wolf Run Marina
   (☎ 814-726-1650), Route 59, 4 miles east of Kinzua Dam

Outback Adventures
   (☎ 814-589-7539), Old Hunter Station Rd, Tionesta

Scenic River
   (☎ 814-563-9795), Route 62, south of Warren

The **Allegheny Reservoir** has 91 miles of shoreline, and there are free boat ramps at the Kiasutha, Willow Bay and Dewdrop campgrounds, as well as at the Elijah Run and Roper Hollow launch sites. It's a pleasant 45-mile float on the calm **Allegheny River** south from Kinzua Dam at the reservoir to Tionesta, where the river curves westward, away from the forest. **Tionesta Creek** is a calm 45-mile run through scenic wilderness from Chapman State Park (5 miles south of Warren) to Tionesta Dam, near Tionesta. The water level from Sheffield to the dam is too low to paddle after mid-May or early June. The creek partially follows Route 6, then Route 666.

The **Clarion River** can be paddled for 60 miles from Ridgway to its confluence with the Allegheny River. The first 19 miles of the float (from Ridgway to Hallton) are faster water and have four rapid areas that the park service classifies as 'intermediate' until mid-May. The first rapid is 6 miles south of Ridgway, near a railroad trestle – beware of the underwater pipe beneath the trestle. The other rapids are at the 15-, 15.5- and 16-mile points. These three rapids are known as 'X,' 'Y' and 'Z.'

For 12 miles, **Brokenstraw Creek**, between Spring Creek (about 15 miles west of Warren) to the Allegheny River near Buckaloons campground, has some of the best fast-water canoeing. **Beaver Meadows Lake**, a small lake in the Beaver Meadows recreation area, just 5 miles southwest of Clarendon, is good for wildlife watching and has a campground and canoe launch.

Chapman State Park (☎ 814-723-5030), about 5 miles southwest of Clarendon, has a small lake where the Tionesta Creek begins and is good for flat-water paddling. Although the park is completely within the ANF, it isn't managed by the USFS; for information, contact the park office.

Cross-Country Skiing
The ANF has 54 miles of ski trails, with additional trails in nearby state parks and forests. **Laurel Mill Trail** (11.6 miles), starting about 2 miles west of Ridgway on Spring Creek Rd, is the longest within the national forest and offers easy to intermediate skiing. It's groomed when conditions allow it. Outside the ANF, the more challenging **Quehanna Trail**, southeast past Benezette in Moshannon State Forest (☎ 814-765-3741), is much longer at 73 miles.

Bird-Watching
The ANF provides a variety of habitats for birds, from the frequently seen red-winged blackbird to the less common bald eagle. Migrating raptors and waterfowl arrive in early March, and songbirds arrive in mid-April. A comprehensive checklist indicating the seasonal presence of bird types is available from the USFS. Some good viewing spots are along the Allegheny and Clarion Rivers, the North Country National Scenic Trail, the Allegheny Reservoir and Tionesta Lake.

Fishing
The ANF has some of the best fishing in the country's northeast, combining as it does the Allegheny Reservoir, many small lakes and the Allegheny River and its tributaries. Fish vary from walleye and muskellunge in the Kinzua Dam to brook and brown trout in the mountain streams. For information, check with the USFS office in Warren and the ranger stations; call the 24-hour fishing hotline (☎ 814-726-0164) for water condi-

tions. Licenses are available from campgrounds, bait shops and gas stations.

Places to Stay
Camping is allowed for a maximum of 14 continuous days on ANF land, including along hiking trails. There's no camping within 1500 feet of the Allegheny Reservoir, except in developed campgrounds.

The campgrounds are rated from grade 1 (where campgrounds are walk-in only, have no water or toilets and usually involve no fee) to grade 5 (where campgrounds are accessed by paved roads, have electricity, hot showers, interpretive programs and sites for RVs). Fees at most designated camping areas vary from $7 to $16, depending on facilities. You can make reservations through the National Recreation Reservation System (☎ 800-280-2267), which charges a reservation fee. If you're looking for a last-minute site, call Bradford Ranger Station (☎ 814-362-4613). Most of the higher-grade campgrounds are open mid-April to mid-December, while the lower-level ones are open all year.

Many of the designated maintained campgrounds are near the Allegheny Reservoir: *Tracy Ridge* and *Willow Bay*, close to the New York border, are accessible by car, but four others are only accessible by boat or on foot – *Hooks Brook*, *Handsome Lake*, *Hopewell* and *Pine Grove*. Near Kinzua Bay, on the southeastern fork of the reservoir that stretches toward Kane, there are developed campgrounds at *Kinzua Beach*, *Dewdrop*, *Kiasutha*, and *Red Bridge*, but *Morrison* is only accessible by boat or on foot.

Close to the Allegheny River, there are campgrounds at *Buckaloons* and *Hearts Content*. Other campgrounds are at *Twin Lakes*, south of Kane; *Beaver Meadows*, 5 miles north of Marienville; *Loleta*, 6 miles south of Marienville; *Minister Creek*, in the center of the forest off Route 666; *Chapman State Park* (☎ 814-723-0250), operated by the state; and *Tionesta Lake*, near the town of Tionesta.

There are also many privately operated campgrounds in the region. Contact the Northern Alleghenies Vacation Region tourist office in Warren (see Information, earlier in this section for details).

Getting There & Away

The nearest intercity buses stop at Oil City and Erie and at Jamestown, NY. You'll need your own wheels to get around.

Route 6 runs east of I-79 to Warren and through the ANF to Kane. From Erie, take Route 19 south to Route 6 east, or take I-90 north to Route 17 east to Jamestown, NY, where it hooks up with Route 60/62 south to Warren. Route 62 runs northeast, from Oil City along the Allegheny River and the western perimeter of the ANF to Warren, then on to New York state.

From Pittsburgh, take Route 28 north to I-80 at Brookville, where it meets Route 36, which runs northwest to Tionesta. Northeast off Route 36, Route 949 leads to Ridgway, while Route 899 heads north to Marienville.

ROUTE 6: ALLEGHENY NATIONAL FOREST TO SCRANTON

Route 6, otherwise known as the Grand Army of the Republic Hwy in honor of the Civil War fallen, is a designated National Recreational Trail. It traverses more than 400 miles across the north of the state through some of Pennsylvania's most beautiful scenery. With the fall colors of the forests, mid-September through October is a particularly good time to visit.

Kinzua Railroad Bridge

Just east of the ANF, the 301-foot-high Kinzua Railroad Bridge, in Kinzua Bridge State Park, stretches 2053 feet across the Kinzua Creek Valley. The second-highest railroad viaduct in the US and the fourth-highest in the world, it's fairly spectacular. You can walk across it when there are no trains scheduled. The Knox & Kane Railroad (☎ 814-927-6621) runs steam trains from Kane and Marienville across the bridge from June through October. The roundtrip fare from Marienville for adults/children is $22/14; from Kane, it's $16/9. To get to the bridge by road, follow Route 6 northeast of Kane until just past the town of Mt Jewett, then take the first road north (left) to the park.

Kinzua Railroad Bridge

From the mid-19th century, rapid industrial growth around Buffalo, NY, produced high demand for coal. The railroads carried the coal that fueled the fires of industry, heated homes and also powered the trains. But between Pennsylvania's coal and the awaiting industry to the north lay an obstacle – the Kinzua Valley.

The Kinzua Railroad Bridge was first built in 1882 to allow a branch of the Erie Railroad to ship coal north across the valley. Remarkably, it took a 40-man crew only 94 working days to complete what was at the time the world's highest viaduct and longest rail viaduct. Completely rebuilt in 1900 to carry heavier loads, it was in service till 1959.

Susquehannock Trail System

About 60 miles east of Kane, this 85-mile system heads south off Route 6. It's a series of old railroad grades and logging and fire trails that loop through the 412-sq-mile Susquehannock State Forest and connects with the 42-mile **Black Forest** and 100-mile **Donut Hole** trails farther south. A map and information are available from the office at the entrance (open daily 8 am to 4 pm) or from the state's District Forester (☎ 814-274-8474), PO Box 673, Coudersport, PA 16915.

Denton Hill Ski Area

In the northern tip of Susquehanna State Forest, about 7 miles east of Coudersport, on Route 6, is the Denton Hill downhill and cross-country skiing area (☎ 814-435-2115). It has night skiing and some of the steepest slopes in the northeast; ski rentals and lessons are available. Lift tickets cost $28.

Pennsylvania Lumber Museum

This museum (☎ 814-435-2652), opposite the entrance to the Denton Hill skiing area, shows the history of logging in the region and includes a restored logging camp and steam-powered sawmill, a nature trail and a picnic area. The visitors' center also has an information desk on the region. The museum is open from April to November daily 9 am to 5 pm, though the logging camp closes at 4:30 pm. Entry is $3.50/1.50 for adults/children.

Pine Creek Gorge

Frequently promoted as Pennsylvania's 'Grand Canyon,' this striking natural feature is a 47-mile-long valley that reaches a depth of 1450 feet at Waterville to the south near Williamsport. Off Route 6, you can reach the canyon south from Ansonia or by taking Route 660 west from Wellsboro.

Pine Creek Gorge passes through **Leonard Harrison State Park** and **Colton Point State Park**, both of which offer camping from early April to mid-October. There's white-water rafting and canoeing in spring on Pine Creek when the water is high enough, and the state parks also have short hiking and horseback-riding trails. Call ☎ 717-724-3061 for information.

From Ansonia, the 30-mile **West Rim Trail** roughly follows the creek south to meet the 190-mile **Mid-State Trail** just north of Blackwell.

Wellsboro

Ten miles east of Pine Creek, Wellsboro is the main town in the area and the seat of Tioga County. It's a picturesque place, with a tree-lined Main St lit at night by electric 'gaslights.' The Tioga County Visitors Bureau (☎ 717-724-0635), 114 Main St, is open weekdays 9 am to 4:30 pm. There are several places offering lodging. **Penn Wells Hotel & Lodge** (☎ 717-724-2111, 62 Main St) is an old-world hotel with rooms starting at $35/45, a bar and an elegant dining room serving filling breakfast specials for $5.95. **Wellsboro Diner**, at Main and Queen Sts, is fast and efficient and serves a breakfast of two eggs, home fries and toast for $3; bagels start at $1.25.

Mt Pisgah State Park

This state park (☎ 570-297-2734) is 45 miles to the east of Wellsboro and 2 miles north of Route 6 (the turnoff is in the village of West Burlington). It consists of 1302 acres along Mill Creek and at the foot of Mt Pisgah (2260 feet) and has a series of short hiking

trails, some of which become cross-country ski trails in winter. There's also canoeing and fishing on Stephen Foster Lake and swimming in a nearby pool. There are good views of the lake from a hilltop pavilion, where you can also have a picnic.

SCRANTON

First settled in 1771 and then known as Slocum Hollow, Scranton (population 82,000) is an industrial city in the Lackawanna Valley. It's named after Seldon Scranton, who created the Delaware, Lackawanna & Western (DL&W) railroad in 1853.

The city lies at the center of the anthracite coal-mining area that fueled northeastern Pennsylvania's iron and steel industries in the 19th century. Coal's heyday lasted till around 1950, when increasing road haulage and the introduction of diesel locomotives reduced demand for it. Since then, Scranton has successfully developed alternative industries, such as printing and electronics.

Information is available from the Northeast Pennsylvania Visitor Bureau (☎ 570-457-1320, pntvb@epix.net), 305 Linden St at Penn Ave, open weekdays 9 am to 5 pm; you can visit the bureau's website at www.visitnepa .org. The main post office, 235 N Washington Ave at Linden St, is open weekdays 7:30 am to 5:15 pm and Saturday 9 am to noon. There are several banks with ATMs along Washington Ave.

Not surprisingly, the town's main attractions relate to its industrial past.

Steamtown National Historic Site

The history of the railroads, both local and national, can be seen at the Steamtown National Historic Site (☎ 570-340-5204, 888-693-9391), 150 S Washington Ave, in the former DL&W rail yard; you can visit www.nps.gov/stea for more information. It's managed by the National Park Service (NPS). In the visitors' center, the museum has exhibits, audiotapes and videotapes of people who worked for the railroads and a film called *Steel & Steam* about the history of steam trains in Pennsylvania.

Scranton's Steamtown National Historic Site

TOM SMALLMAN

Outside is a working roundhouse (where steam trains were stored and repaired) and several operating steam locomotives. Hours are 9 am to 5 pm daily (to 6 pm July to Labor Day), and entry is $6/2 for adults/children (seniors pay $5). You can also take a two-hour steam train excursion on the former DL&W railroad between Scranton and Moscow for $10/5 (seniors pay $8). A combined ticket costs $15/6, or $13 for seniors.

Other Attractions

You can learn more about the fossil fuel and the life of the migrants who came to Scranton to mine it by visiting the **Pennsylvania Anthracite Heritage Museum** (☎ 570-963-4804). It is open Monday to Saturday 9 am to 5 pm and Sunday noon to 5 pm; admission is $3.50/2 for adults/children, or $3 for seniors. Next door, a walking tour led by ex-coal miners is available 300 feet down in the cool darkness of the former **Lackawanna Coal Mine** (☎ 800-238-7245). It is open April to November daily 10 am to 4:30 pm; tours cost $6/4.

Both are in the 200-acre McDade Park (☎ 570-963-6764), off Keyser Ave, west of town; take exit 57B off I-81 or exit 38 off I-476 (Pennsylvania Turnpike, Northeast Extension) and follow the signs.

Getting There & Away

Martz Trailways bus terminal (☎ 570-342-0146) is at 23 Lackawanna Ave, opposite the Steamtown Mall; Capitol Trailways (☎ 800-444-2877) and Greyhound (☎ 800-231-2222) buses also stop here. There are three daily buses to New York City ($26.45 one way, 2½ hours) and two to Philadelphia ($18 one way, three hours).

I-476 (Pennsylvania Turnpike, Northeast Extension) runs north directly to Scranton from Philadelphia. I-81 north and I-84 and Route 6 east connect the city with New York State and New Jersey.

WILLIAMSPORT

Williamsport (population 32,000) is in north-central Pennsylvania, on Route 15, about 16 miles north of I-80 along the western branch of the Susquehanna River. The town was first settled in the late 18th century. It became the main northern river port in the valleys of the Susquehanna and the center of a huge lumber industry that brought immense wealth to the region. This wealth produced quite a few millionaires, who toward the end of the 19th century built grand mansions along W 4th St near Campbell St, part of which today is known as Millionaires' Row.

For information, contact the Lycoming County Visitors Bureau (☎ 570-326-1971,

PENNSYLVANIA

800-358-9900), downtown at 454 Pine St, or visit www.williamsport.org/visitpa.

Little League baseball began in Williamsport in 1939, and annually, in the third week of August, young baseball teams from around the world compete in the **Little League World Series** (☎ 570-326-1921). About 50,000 people travel to Williamsport to watch the games. During the rest of the year, you can visit the **Little League Museum** (☎ 570-326-3607), on Route 15, about a mile south of town, which recounts the development of Little League baseball from its humble beginnings. The museum is open Memorial Day to Labor Day, Monday to Saturday 9 am to 7 pm and Sunday noon to 7 pm; the rest of the year, it's open Monday to Saturday 9 am to 5 pm and Sunday noon to 5 pm. Entry is $5/1.50 for adults/children; seniors pay $3.

Susquehanna Trailways (☎ 800-692-6314) has daily buses to Philadelphia and New York City. You can obtain more information from the website: www.susquehannabus.com.

THE POCONOS

Southeast of Scranton, and running northeast from Bucks County, are the Poconos, which contain 2400 sq miles of mountains, streams, waterfalls, lakes and an abundance of forests that are home to more than 100 varieties of trees and many rare species of plants and animals. The range of ecosystems found here and the need to preserve them led the Nature Conservancy to name the Poconos as one of the world's '40 Last Great Places.' The name 'Pocono' comes from 'pocohanne,' a Lenape word meaning 'stream between the mountains.' The mountain region contains one state forest and eight state parks.

A natural 'four-season' choice for nature, sports and outdoor enthusiasts, it's a touristy area, especially on weekends and in the fall, when visitors come to see the changing colors of the hardwood trees. Many people stay at the expensive resorts offering guided programs and a range of activities (as well as heart-shaped beds). However, the Poconos can be seen for a reasonably modest price if you do a little of your own research.

Orientation & Information

The Poconos occupy the northeast corner of Pennsylvania, bordering New York and New Jersey. I-80, I-84 and Route 6 head east and west through them, and Route 191 runs north and south through most of the length of the region. The northeastern extension of the Pennsylvania Turnpike, I-476 (Route 9), cuts through the southeastern corner.

Stroudsburg, at the intersection of several highways, including I-80, is the main commercial center for the Poconos. The Pocono Mountains Vacation Bureau (☎ 570-421-5791, pocomts@poconos.org), Box TG, 1004 Main St, Stroudsburg, PA 18360, operates nine information centers throughout the region. It is open weekdays 9 am to 5 pm. Call ☎ 800-722-6667 for brochures or call ☎ 570-424-6050 for current information; you can also visit the website at www.poconos.org. The *Poconos Vacation Guide* has a comprehensive listing of services.

If you come to see the fall colors, you can call the 24-hour Pocono Fall Foliage Hotline (☎ 570-421-5565) from mid-September to mid-November to find out where the best viewing is.

You can get online at the Hubb Cyber Cafe (☎ 570-476-8858), 611 Main St, in Stroudsburg, for $4.80 per hour; it has a website at www.hubbysystems.com.

Jim Thorpe

The small town of Jim Thorpe (population 5100), set in the hillside rising above the Lehigh River, is one of the prettiest in Pennsylvania, with many of its early buildings still intact. Originally settled in 1815 as Mauch Chunk ('Bear Mountain'), in 1954 it combined with the neighboring towns of Upper Mauch Chunk and East Mauch Chunk and changed its name to Jim Thorpe, in honor of the great Native American athlete (see the boxed text, 'Jim Thorpe – the Man').

The visitors' center information office (☎ 570-325-3673), in a former railroad station at Lehigh Ave and Broadway, is open weekdays 9 am to 4:30 pm, weekends 10 am to 5 pm.

On Race St is **Stone Row**, a collection of original row houses built in 1849 by Asa

THE POCONOS

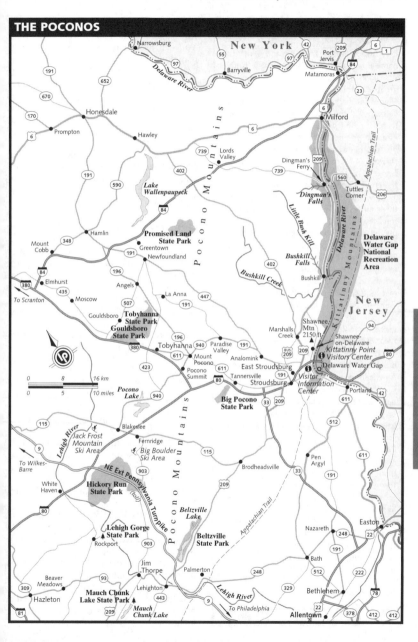

Jim Thorpe – the Man

Born in Oklahoma in 1888 and given the name Bright Path, Jim Thorpe was a Native American who became one of America's greatest athletes. At the 1912 Olympic Games in Stockholm, he won both the decathlon and the pentathlon, breaking many records in the process. Unfortunately, soon after, despite protesting that he didn't know he had been breaking any rules, he was stripped of his medals for having played professional baseball (for $60 a month) and thereby forfeited his amateur sporting status.

Between 1913 and 1919, he played on three major-league baseball teams, including the New York Giants, and from 1915, he played professional football. In 1920, he became the first president of the American Professional Football Association (later renamed the National Football League). When he gave up professional sport in the mid-1920s, he found it difficult to adjust and went to Hollywood, lured by promises of stardom, but the Depression arrived, and he was only able to find work as a laborer. Alcohol eventually got the better of him, and by 1951, he was penniless, having spent much of his money on his fellow Native Americans or having otherwise given it away.

After his death in 1953, his wife sought to have a memorial built in his honor. When neither his home state of Oklahoma, nor the town of Carlisle, PA, where he had gone to school, would help her, she approached the Pennsylvania communities of Mauch Chunk and East Mauch Chunk. She'd heard about them in the news, because their citizens were trying to save the towns by setting up a local economic development fund. The communities agreed to combine and change their name to Jim Thorpe in an effort to promote local tourism and to honor the man and his achievements.

Eventually, Jim Thorpe's Olympic records were restored, and his medals were given to his family. Today, his daughter, Grace, is campaigning to have him named the 'Greatest Athlete of the Century.'

Packer (1805–79), a wealthy industrialist who founded the Lehigh Valley Railroad. You can also visit his 20-room Italianate **mansion** (☎ 570-325-3229), open daily from late May through October from 11 am to 4:15 pm; the 45-minute guided tour costs $5/3 for adults/children. To get there, head up Packer Hill off Lehigh Ave. On Route 903, about half a mile east of town, is the **Jim Thorpe Memorial**, the athlete's final resting place.

Outdoor recreation is available at **Mauch Chunk Lake State Park** (☎ 570-325-3669), 3 miles southwest of town, and at **Beltzville State Park** (☎ 610-377-0045), about 7 miles east of town.

Delaware Water Gap NRA

Administered by the NPS, this is a 37-mile-long, 109-sq-mile national recreation area straddling the Delaware River. It's on the border with northwestern New Jersey (see also the Northern New Jersey chapter) and is full of opportunities to hike, mountain bike, ski, canoe, raft, sail, view wildlife and camp.

The visitors' center (☎ 570-476-0167) at Delaware Water Gap (take exit 53 off I-80) has information on Pennsylvania, as well as on the Poconos and the National Recreation Area (NRA). From June to September, it is open Monday to Thursday and Saturday 9:30 am to 5:30 pm, Friday to 6:30 pm and Sunday to 4:30 pm; from October to April, it is open weekends only, 9:30 am to 4:30 pm.

The main NPS visitors' center (☎ 570-588-2451), on River Rd, 1 mile from Route 209 in Bushkill, is open weekdays 8 am to 4:30 pm; you can visit the website at www.nps.gov/dewa. There is also a visitors' center at Dingman's Falls, at Kittatinny Point in New Jersey.

The 'gap' itself, at the southern end of the NRA, is a 1400-foot-high chasm formed by the Delaware River cutting its way through the Kittatinny Mountains. Promoted as 'Pennsylvania's Niagara Falls,' **Bushkill Falls**, north of Bushkill off Route 209, is a series of eight waterfalls, the largest of which drop 100 feet over siltstone and shale. Farther north, **Dingman's Falls**, off Route 739, is the highest in the state at 130 feet.

Hiking

Ranging in difficulty from novice to expert, the Poconos have more than 116 maintained hiking trails that can be used for overnight or day excursions. These trails include about 25 miles of the **Appalachian Trail** in the New Jersey section of the Delaware Water Gap NRA, which itself has more than 60 trails. Several state parks offer hiking and camping, including **Hickory Run State Park** (☎ 570-443-0400), near White Haven, which has 45 miles of trails. **Promised Land State Park** (☎ 570-676-3428), farther north near Greentown, has 29 miles of trails.

Mountain Biking

The Poconos have a variety of mountain-biking facilities, and many Pocono resorts offer bicycle riding (check in the *Poconos Vacation Guide*). Biking trails range from forest paths to canal towpaths and abandoned railroad beds. In **Lehigh Gorge State Park** (same telephone number as Hickory Run), near Jim Thorpe, bicyclists can traverse 25 miles of gentle grades along the western bank of the Lehigh River through the Lehigh Gorge. Nearby, the steep, 15-mile **Switchback Gravity Railroad Trail** is an abandoned railroad bed, which begins on Hill Rd in Jim Thorpe.

Bike rental is available in Jim Thorpe. Blue Mountain Sports (☎ 800-599-4421), at Race and Susquehanna Sts, rents bikes for $25 a day.

Skiing

The Pocono Mountains have a number of large ski areas. Camelback (☎ 570-629-1661, sales@skicamelback.com), PO Box 168, Tannersville, PA 18372, is in Big Pocono State Park, just south of I-80. It has 33 trails, a vertical drop of 800 feet and snowboarding facilities; for a snow report, call ☎ 800-233-8100.

North of Stroudsburg, Shawnee Mountain (☎ 570-421-7231), PO Box 339, Shawnee-on-Delaware, PA 18356, offers 23 trails and a vertical drop of 700 feet; for a snow report, call ☎ 800-233-4218.

Close to each other on either side of I-80 northeast of White Haven are Big Boulder Ski Area (☎ 570-722-0101) and Jack Frost Mountain Ski Area (☎ 570-443-8425). They share the same postal address: PO Box 707, Blakeslee, PA 18610. The vertical drop at Big Boulder is 475 feet; at Jack Frost, the drop is 600 feet. For a snow report on either, call ☎ 800-475-7669; for accommodations, call ☎ 800-468-2442.

Cross-country ski trails can be found in the resorts, and many hiking trails in state parks and forests become cross-country ski trails in winter.

Watersports

Mauch Chunk Lake and Lake Wallenpaupeck are two of the many lakes offering opportunities for **sailing** and **canoeing**. For the more adventurous, there's white-water canoeing and **rafting** on the Lehigh River through the Lehigh Gorge and on the Delaware River. A number of companies provide rentals and guided trips. Kittatinny Canoes (☎ 800-356-2852), at Dingman's Ferry, has guided canoeing and rafting trips for $21 to $28 per person. Pocono Whitewater Adventures (☎ 570-325-3656, 800-9448-39183), H-C2 Box 2245, Jim Thorpe, PA 18229, has guided day trips for $49; its website is at www.whitewaterrafting.com.

Adventure Sports (☎ 800-487-2628), PO Box 175, Marshalls Creek, PA 18335, rents rafts and canoes for $25 per person (minimum of two in a canoe, four in a raft). Lehigh Rafting Rentals (☎ 570-443-4441, 800-580-2847), PO Box 296, White Haven, PA 18661, rents canoes and rafts at similar rates; its website is at www.lehighrafting.com.

For information on fishing, see the Delaware Water Gap in the Northern New Jersey chapter.

Places to Stay

The Poconos offer luxury resorts (including the 'couples resorts,' with their heart-shaped pools and beds for honeymooners) and family resorts offering room-and-recreational packages, but there are also many regular hotels, motels, B&Bs, housekeeping cottages, small country inns, an HI-AYH hostel and campgrounds. The *Poconos Vacation Guide*, available from the Pocono Mountains Vacation Bureau (see Orientation & Information, earlier in this section) has a listing of accommodations, and you can reserve a room by calling ☎ 800-722-6667. Prices often rise on weekends and public holidays.

Camping You can backpack along the Appalachian Trail and in the Delaware Water Gap NRA; see Hiking in the Outdoor Activities chapter.

Several state parks offer camping. *Hickory Run State Park* (☎ 570-443-0400), south of the junction of I-80 and I-476/Route 9 (Pennsylvania Turnpike, Northeast Extension) and *Promised Land State Park* (☎ 570-676-3428), off I-84, have lots of campgrounds with toilets and showers, as well as more primitive sites. *Tobyhanna State Park* (☎ 570-894-8336), off Route 423, has 140 sites, but no flushing toilets or running water. Rates are $11 to $13.

There are also many private campgrounds. *Hemlock Campground* (☎ 570-894-4388), 362 Hemlock Drive, Tobyhanna, PA 18466, off Route 611, has full facilities and well-spaced sites starting at $17. The secluded, wooded *Mt Pocono Campground* (☎ 570-839-7573), PO Box 65, Mt Pocono, PA 18344, is off Route 196. It has a grocery store, hot showers and sites for $25, or $28 with electricity and water.

Hostels The HI-AYH *La Anna Hostel* (☎ 570-676-9076), RR 2, PO Box 1026, Cresco, PA 18326, is on La Anna Rd, which runs between Routes 191 and 423 north of the village of La Anna. It has a kitchen, wood stove and 40 beds for $12; private rooms are available. Open all year, the hostel is near the Tobyhanna and Promised Land State Parks.

B&Bs Jim Thorpe has some beautiful old B&Bs. *Cozy Corner* (☎ 570-325-2961, 504 North St) is in a Victorian house replete with antiques. It's open all year and has singles or doubles from $65/75 without/with private bathroom. *Rendon House* (☎ 570-325-5515, 80 Broadway), on the corner of Quarry St, is a beautiful, central B&B with rooms for $70.

Motels & Hotels In Jim Thorpe, the ornate, Victorian *Inn at Jim Thorpe* (☎ 570-325-2599), 24 Broadway, has a restaurant and bar and rooms from $70.

In Stroudsburg, *Days Inn* (☎ 570-424-1771, 100 Park Ave) has a small pool and singles/doubles from $58/69. To get there, take 7th St south off Main St. The *Best Western Pocono Inn* (☎ 570-421-2200, 700 Main St) has rooms for $85 single or double; for more information and reservations, visit www.bestwesternpocono.com. Business Route 209 south of town has more hotels.

Places to Eat

If you're self-catering, you can pick up supplies in Stroudsburg, Jim Thorpe, Hazleton or Lehighton.

In Jim Thorpe, *Chunkers*, on Broadway, is a small cafe that is open daily for lunch from 11 am; it serves turkey club sandwiches for $4.50. Open Wednesday to Sunday for lunch and dinner, the *Black Bread Cafe* (☎ 570-325-8957), 47 Race St, is adorned with paintings by local artists. It serves soup (starting at $1.95) and a wide range of sandwiches, including a BLT for $4.25; it also has vegetarian options, and dinner main dishes start at $14.95.

In Stroudsburg, the diner in the *Best Western Pocono Inn* (700 Main St) does standard food and is popular at breakfast time. A breakfast special or pancakes cost $3.25. It also has a restaurant serving evening meals. Nearby, *Marita's*, also on Main St, is a brightly decorated Mexican restaurant open for lunch and dinner; it serves quesadillas for $4 to $6. You can enjoy a cup of coffee while surfing the Internet at Hubby Cyber Cafe (see Orientation & Information, earlier in this section).

Getting There & Away

Bus Susquehanna Trailways (☎ 800-692-6314) operates part of the Greyhound network between Philadelphia and Scranton and stops in Jim Thorpe, Lehighton and Hazleton four times daily. The one-way fare from Philadelphia to Jim Thorpe is $15.40; the journey time is 2¼ hours.

Visit www.susquehannabus.com for more information. Martz Trailways (☎ 800-220-3133) stops in Mt Pocono and Stroudsburg three times daily on weekdays and has services to Philadelphia, New York, Scranton and Wilkes-Barre; the company's website is www.martztrailways.com.

Car & Motorcycle From Philadelphia, I-476 (Pennsylvania Turnpike, Northeast Extension) leads directly into the Poconos, as does I-80 from New Jersey and I-84 from New York. I-81 south from New York state (Binghamton) skirts Scranton to join I-380, which connects with both I-84 and I-80.

Acknowledgments

THANKS

Many thanks to the following readers (apologies if we have misspelled your name) who took the time to write to us about their experiences in New York, New Jersey and Pennsylvania:

Bob Jackson, Dale View, Flavie de Groot, Georg Jacobs, Helen Price, Hua Chee, Gianfranco Muntoni & Isabella Riva, Linda Corriveau, Mick Walsh, Peter F Ormand, Ray Wilkinson, Slav Cvitic, Stuart Neve.

LONELY PLANET

You already know that Lonely Planet produces more than this one guidebook, but you might not be aware of the other products we have on this region. Here is a selection of titles which you may want to check out as well:

USA
ISBN 0 86442 513 9
US$24.95 • UK£14.99

New England
ISBN 0 86442 570 8
US$ 19.95 • UK£ 12.99

Virginia & the Capital Region
ISBN 0 86442 769 7
US$21.99 • UK£13.99

New York City
ISBN 1 86450 180 4
US$16.99 • UK£10.99

New York Condensed
ISBN 1 86450 046 8
US$9.95 • UK£5.99

New York City map
ISBN 1 86450 010 7
US$5.95 • UK£3.99

Available wherever books are sold.

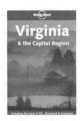

Index

Bold indicates maps.

Bold indicates maps.

O

P

Bold indicates maps.

Bold indicates maps.

Boxed Text

MAP LEGEND

BOUNDARIES

··—··—··—··—	International
···—··—··—··	Province
—···—···—···	County

HYDROGRAPHY

	Water
	Coastline
	Beach
	River, Waterfall
	Swamp, Spring

✪	**NATIONAL CAPITAL**
◉	**State, Provincial Capital**
●	**LARGE CITY**
●	**Medium City**
●	Small City
●	Town, Village
○	Point of Interest
■	Place to Stay
▲	Campground
⛁	RV Park
▼	Place to Eat
☗	Bar (Place to Drink)

ROUTES & TRANSPORT

	Freeway
	Toll Freeway
	Primary Road
	Secondary Road
	Tertiary Road
	Unpaved Road
	Pedestrian Mall
	Trail
	Walking Tour
	Ferry Route
++++	Railway, Train Station
—Ⓜ—	Mass Transit Line & Station

ROUTE SHIELDS

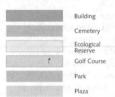

80	Interstate	7	State Highway
1	US Highway	539	Country Road

AREA FEATURES

	Building
	Cemetery
	Ecological Reserve
	Golf Course
	Park
	Plaza

MAP SYMBOLS

Symbol		Symbol	
✚	Airfield	▲	Monument
✈	Airport	☪	Mosque
🏦	Bank	▲	Mountain
◗	Baseball Diamond	🏛	Museum
✕	Battlefield	⌂	Observatory
⌿	Beach	←	One-Way Street
✦✦	Border Crossing	♣	Park
⚖	Buddhist Temple	🅿	Parking
☻	Bus Depot, Bus Stop	) (	Pass
⌂	Cave	⊓	Picnic Area
✝	Church	★	Police Station
◥	Dive Site	✉	Post Office
◗	Embassy	☒	Shipwreck
⤙	Footbridge	❖	Shopping Mall
⬐	Fish Hatchery	⚐	Skiing (Alpine)
✿	Garden	⚐	Skiing (Nordic)
⛽	Gas Station	⬛	Stately Home
✛	Hospital, Clinic	✡	Synagogue
❶	Information	⚐	Trailhead
🗼	Lighthouse	⚐	Winery
☀	Lookout	🐾	Zoo

Note: Not all symbols displayed above appear in this book.

LONELY PLANET OFFICES

Australia
Locked Bag 1, Footscray, Victoria 3011
☎ 03 8379 8000 fax 03 8379 8111
email talk2us@lonelyplanet.com.au

UK
10A Spring Place, London NW5 3BH
☎ 020 7428 4800 fax 020 7428 4828
email go@lonelyplanet.co.uk

USA
150 Linden Street, Oakland, California 94607
☎ 510 893 8555, TOLL FREE 800 275 8555
fax 510 893 8572
email info@lonelyplanet.com

France
1 rue du Dahomey, 75011 Paris
☎ 01 55 25 33 00 fax 01 55 25 33 01
email: bip@lonelyplanet.fr
www.lonelyplanet.fr

World Wide Web: www.lonelyplanet.com *or* AOL keyword: lp
Lonely Planet Images: lpi@lonelyplanet.com.au